THROUGH THE LOOKING GLASS

THROUGH THE LOOKING GLASS

The National Library of Poetry

Melisa S. Mitchell, Editor

Through the Looking Glass

Library of Congress
Cataloging in Publication Data

ISBN 1-57553-401-0

Proudly manufactured in The United States of America by
Watermark Press
One Poetry Plaza
Owings Mills, MD 21117

Editor's Note

Much like Humpty Dumpty who endeavors to explain to Alice the meaning of the poem "Jabberwocky" in Lewis Carroll's *Through the Looking Glass*, each of us when reading a poem tries to glean some meaning from it. Sometimes, as in "Jabberwocky," there is language which is confusing, though perhaps not quite as indecipherable as: "'Twas brillig, and the slithy toves / Did gyre and gimble in the wabe . . ." In an effort to understand what the poet is attempting to tell us, we must decipher the language to get to the meaning of the poem. In Carroll's work, Humpty Dumpty tells Alice:

> " . . . *'Brillig' means four o'clock in the afternoon — the time when you begin* broiling *things for dinner."*
> *"That'll do very well," said Alice: "and 'slithy'?"*
> *"Well, 'slithy' means 'lithe and slimy.' 'Lithe' is the same as 'active.' You see it's like a portmanteau — there are two meanings packed up into one word."*
> *"I see it now," Alice remarked thoughtfully: "and what are toves?"*
> *"Well, 'toves' are something like badgers — they're something like lizards — and they're something like corkscrews." [...]*
> *"And what's to 'gyre' and to 'gimble'?"*
> *"To 'gyre' is to go round and round like a gyroscope. To 'gimble' is to make holes like a gimlet."*

Unfortunately, Humpty Dumpty's explanation does little to help either poor Alice or the reader to shed light on the "Jabberwocky" poem. This same confusion can sometimes occur when one reader attempts to explain to another his or her vision of what a poem means. Fortunately, there are many ways in which any given line of verse may be read and interpreted, allowing the reader to open an infinite number of doors in order to decipher the complex thoughts of the poet. This is perhaps the ultimate appeal of poetry as an art form; much like many forms of visual art, poetry can mean many different things to each person who experiences it. Also like visual art, poetry can paint a picture, in addition to creating a meaningful piece of literature. An excellent example of the ability to create both a physical and an emotional landscape is Mark Power's "illinois ghost" (p. 1):

> *bouncing hard on the rusted tractor*
> *he looks out over the bones of*
> *ancestral patriarchs restful under*
> *the harvest moon full and yellow nearly*
> *kissing the lip of horizon against*
> *the black wall of the illinois night*

It is easy to see very clearly the farmer riding on his tractor through the dark night, with the full, September moon overhead. Through the "bones of [his] / ancestral patriarchs" which now lie in the ground, he feels a connection to the earth and to his own mortality. He realizes that he, too, will some day join his predecessors in the land which they once tilled and worked. They are peaceful in their rest, as he will be when his time comes. It is appropriate that the farmer ride on his tractor "under the harvest moon": the harvest moon is the last full moon before the autumnal equinox. For about a week, the moon is so bright that farmers are able to work by its light, harvesting their crops far later into the evening than was normally possible before the advent of tractors equipped with floodlights. It also marks the end of the harvesting season, symbolizing if not the end of the farmer's life, or of his prime, then the end of the farming tradition itself. The notion of the farmer's mortality continues in the second stanza:

> *he moves ghostlike down the sand road*
> *keeping just ahead of the dust threatening*
> *to envelop him from behind as if he were*
> *going to fade into the landscape with the*
> *generations swallowed whole by vast fields*
> *of stubble and oceans of prairie grass*

The dust is trying to surround him, burying the man as though he were dead. He will soon join his deceased ancestors, but for now, he is keeping ahead of the dust, but barely. This theme of mortality is also echoed in the change of seasons presented in the third stanza:

> *. . . the passing of summer as she slips into the*
> *arms of october who has bled the leaves of green*
> *cathedrals and withered the flowers with frost*

The farmer is surrounded by death, that of his ancestors, that of nature, that of the "decaying barns whose weathered boards curl / outward from the frame." Yet he makes no negative judgment regarding the unavoidable presence of this mortality. He takes in his surroundings: the decrepit barns; the stubble of the fields which have been harvested; the grave-markers of his long-dead relatives; the low, full moon; the "troublesome patterns of moonlight" cast by the deteriorating buildings that he passes. The landscape is incorporated into his thoughts as he thinks about the past, his own lifestyle and that of his predecessors; he witnesses the vestiges of a way of life which itself is dying. Throughout the poem, though, there is no melodrama, no overly emotional perceptions regarding the personal mortality of the farmer, or the extinction of the family farmer in general. The man on the tractor is surrounded by the ghosts of generations before him, and is saddened by the passing of an era, but the sadness does not reach into the bounds of sentimentality; he merely observes the environment around him and takes it in.

The interior monologue presented in the poem is clearly that of the farmer as he journeys on this tractor, but his story is told in the third person. Thus as the reader is removed from the immediate mental scope of the persona, it is even easier to see the distant man as being ghost-like. The structure of the interior monologue is that of a stream-of-consciousness narrative, a literary technique which was quite popular with early 20th century writers such as William Faulkner and James Joyce. This approach is extremely difficult to execute well, particularly when, as in this case, there is little or no punctuation. Without punctuation, sentences may blur into one another, and it can be difficult to follow the action of the work. In "illinois ghost," though, Power very effectively uses line breaks and the natural flow of language to create a solid poem which moves well and creates a simultaneously simple and elaborate picture of a way of life with which few readers would be personally familiar. It is for his superb mastery of the stream-of-consciousness technique and his ability to paint with uncomplicated description an eloquent and detailed visual and mental landscape within his poem that Mark Power was awarded the Grand Prize for "illinois ghost."

Another example of using language to paint an engaging landscape, this time emotional, is Nikole Hendricks' "A Synonym of Fiction Is Romance" (p. 442). This poem, touched with subtle cynicism and realism regarding the course of a relationship, deals with the complex emotional patterns in romantic interactions:

> *How your hands held me still*
> *a tiny bird shuddering in a small paper box*
> *smoothed my turning feathers and whispered,*
> *the first whisper I ever heard*
> *that wasn't a secret or an insult;*
> *it was my name.*

Already fragile, the persona is receptive to the protection of her mate, and relishes his gentle treatment, as he "smooth[s her] turning feathers," whispers her name.

In the second stanza, the persona's description expands outward to include large, natural elements, but becomes even more personal at the same time. She gets chills at the thought of her partner: "The hair on my neck waved upwards / as if covered suddenly by the sea," and feels her emotional resistance crumbling: "mountains breaking / inside of me." She says things to or about her counterpart which may or may not be true, but truth is not the issue of importance. She "believed the long list of words / knocked loose" by the disintegration of her inner security, allowing herself to fall wholly into the relationship. In retrospect, she realizes that though she was genuine, she perhaps did not fully understand the implications of the things that she said: "I was very young / and you were very young." While the persona does not discount the importance of the relationship in her life, she now realizes that in her youthful innocence she believed herself to be feeling profound emotions which were perhaps not fully mature.

The last stanza is wrought with a sort of sad nostalgia. The persona longs for her innocence, and for that of her mate:

> *We did not know the stars*
> *were dead lights from a far away place,*
> *the keepers of counterfeit*
> *memories.*

As many of us do when young, the lovers wished upon stars, not realizing that the celestial bodies at which they gazed quite possibly no longer existed. As it takes thousands of light-years for the light from any given star to reach the earth, it is likely that many of the stars that we see in our skies each night have lived out their entire existences by the time their light reaches us. They are the "burnt-out panorama / of past galaxies" which hovers above. The wishes each of us makes upon them are not affected by the stars themselves in one way or another; these wishes are based on fairy tales we are told as children, that wishes made on objects will come true. The lovers have a similarly idealistic view of themselves, alone within their love, thinking that they are special. In the end, sadly, they realize they are just like everyone else: "two shining coins painted to look like silver, / composed of nickel and lead." Hendricks eloquently presents the persona's nostalgic sorrow at the loss of her past innocence and the one-time relationship which had made her feel so special. She uses interesting images and language, which contribute greatly to gaining the sympathy of the reader, without being affected. The audience experiences a similar sadness and is allowed to hearken back to a comparable time in their own lives.

Another touching story of a troubled relationship is presented in B. W. Carter's "the exchange" (p. 228). This time, the interaction takes place between a father and son, presumably in a hospital emergency room. The persona, the son, is lying in a gurney, feeling barely alive. He compares himself to a "golem," a figure in Jewish folklore that is an artificially created being which has been supernaturally endowed with life, but has no soul. It is alive only by the strictest definition of life, but is not really human, despite its appearance to the contrary. The son, then, feels as though he is not truly a person. When his father arrives, his presence at first does little more than conjure memories in the persona's mind:

> . . . *i remembered by*
> *his smell handing wrenches beneath a certain faded mercury*
>
> *in the melted middle of july while gregg allman talked*
> *to sweet melissa in the radio and*
>
> *all i ever wanted to be was a guy who climbed poles to fix wires.*

The son has a very particular and detailed memory of a time when he and his father were together, when there seemed to be no strife between them. This was a time when he wanted to be like his father, a man in dungarees working on his car, to be like this man who fixed things. It becomes clear later in the poem that the father was not always the fixer, but sometimes the breaker: "the old man in an attempt to make me / blink said he never meant to yell so much, to hit / so much." Perhaps it is as a result of this confessed physical abuse that the persona is in the hospital, but this does not seem as important as the fact that the hospital stay has been a catalyst for dissolving the bad blood between them. Interestingly enough, however, the son does not seem willing at first to bridge this gap. He seems unwilling to let his father know the effect his visit has had upon him. When the "old man" apologizes, tries to make the boy blink, the persona insists:

> *. . . but of course i would have blinked anyway*
> *and the tears on the pillow said as much, the old*
> *man seemed very gray.*

With a surge of independence and emotion, the son is no longer afraid of any conflict which may have been between him and his father. The man seems harmless and old to him. He is able to hold his father's hand, and they look back at their past, they "[smell] ten years / of dirty oil together." The oil represents both the times when the son helped his father work on his car, but also the bad blood between them. His father's grip becomes not a threat, but a comfort: "the fact of his grip ever after said so much." This stirring poem illustrates well the resolution of a tumultuous father-son relationship, using an economy of language, but with a rather unique structure and style.

There are many other excellent poems contained within this anthology. Each of them deserves careful perusal. Be sure to focus clearly upon the pictures they paint, to experience the emotional landscapes of each one, to relate the individual experiences of other poets to your own lives. Among this host of estimable works in *Through the Looking Glass* are the following prize-winning poems: "Autumn Leaves" by Constance Adams (p. 382); "Pink Elephants" by Lynn Carver (p. 268); "Cicadas and Untied Shoes" by Alyssa Curry (p. 329); "The Beauty of Stars Lies Not Of Themselves In Themselves" by Thomas Gentille (p. 403); Howard McHenry's "Melissa" (p. 112); Benjamin Norman's "Hide and Seek" (p. 288); Ravi Shankar's "World Unfurled" (p. 239); and "Breakfast" by Stephen Stork (p. 395). Congratulations to all of the poets appearing in this anthology.

I would like to thank the staff members of The National Library of Poetry, without whom this book would not have been possible. Judges, editors, associate editors, customer service representatives, data entry personnel, graphic artists, office administrators and administrative services staff have all made invaluable contributions to this effort. I am *grateful* to them for their contributions and support.

Melisa S. Mitchell
Editor

Cover Art: Steve Kimball

Grand Prize Winner

Mark Power / Easton IL

Second Prize Winners

Constance Adams / Seattle WA
B. W. Carter / Martin TN
Lynn Carver / Sparks NV
Alyssa Curry / Edison NJ
Thomas Gentille / New York NY

Nikole Hendricks / Lawrence KS
Howard McHenry / Duluth GA
Benjamin Norman / Concord WA
Ravi Shankar / San Francisco CA
Stephen Stork / Ypsilanti MI

Third Prize Winners

Michelle Acquart / San Antonio TX
Ulrich Alsentzer / Greenville NC
Beverly Alspaugh / Uvalde TX
Frank Antonazzi Jr. / Alexandria VA
Yseult Bayard / New York NY
Craig David Blinderman / Miller Place NY
David Buckman / Lafayette Hill PA
Brian Burbidge / Pueblo West CO
George Cargo / Marshall MI
Kate Chabarek / Chestertown NY
B. Chamberlin-Yates / Annandale NJ
Miriam Clare / Joliet IL
William Collier / Rocky Hill NJ
Christin Crawford / Seattle WA
J. T. Cummins Jr. / Bozeman MT
Ana Da Gama / New York NY
J. David Danielson / Bloomfield CT
Andrew Dorr / Woodstock Valley CT
Phillip Dryden / Columbus OH
Michael Duane / Charleston SC
John Eastland / Norwich CT
John Ellis / Colorado Springs CO
Manuel Espinal / New York NY
Gloria Frandle / Carlsbad CA
Charles Fryer / Camden ME
Jennifer Geary / Hamilton OH
G. G. Gilchrist / Holiday FL
William Golden II / Spring TX
Gary Gordon / San Mateo CA
Diane Elizabeth Graves / Portland OR

D. Johnston / Greeley CO
P. Kaiser / Bangor ME
Michele Kleineweber / Overland Park KS
Chris Liberto / Chico CA
Lydia Lucero / Whittier CA
Mary McMurry / Goshen KY
Roberta Mendel / Shaker Heights OH
Jeanne M. Morrison / Saukville WI
Mollie Murphy / Jackson MS
Brian O'Neill / Tacoma WA
Dorothy Osborne / Gouldsboro ME
Joan Parker / Williams CA
Cheryl Pinckney / Yonkers NY
Elisa Ravella / Lexington MA
Sarah Reiser / El Paso TX
Beth Roberts / Charlottesville VA
Bunnie Rogers / Woodbridge NJ
Saliba Sarsar / Tinton Falls NJ
Dennis Slattery / Santa Barbara CA
Katie Smith / Kennewick WA
Rachel Soffer / Morrestown NJ
Johanna Spee / San Diego CA
Irene-Marie Spencer / Stoughton WI
Caleb Stewart / Sumter SC
Martha Sullivan / Pittsburgh PA
Sharon Tseng / Rockville MD
Art Ward / Marshall's Creek PA
David Weimer / Gladstone MO
Nancy Zuercher / Vermillion SD

Congratulations also to all semi-finalists.

Grand Prize
Winner

illinois ghost
by Mark Power

bouncing hard on the rusted tractor
he looks out over the bones of
ancestral patriarchs restful under
the harvest moon full and yellow nearly
kissing the lip of horizon against
the black wall of the illinois night

he moves ghostlike down the sand road
keeping just ahead of the dust threatening
to envelop him from behind as if he were
going to fade into the landscape with the
generations swallowed whole by vast fields
of stubble and oceans of prairie grass

through which he drifts across the shipwrecks
of decaying barns whose weathered boards curl
outward from the frame casting troublesome
patterns of moonlight and shadow compelling him
to hum the melody of an autumnal hymn in prayer
for the passing of summer as she slips into the
arms of october who has bled the leaves of green
cathedrals and withered the flowers with frost

My Heart Is Getting Crowded

My heart is getting crowded
With the beauty that I see
The big ones all around me
But there's always room
For the little ones I see

They're a little part of Heaven
A gift for all to see
Your smile in their eyes
Your love in their walk and, your joy in their talk

It is beyond me, why anyone wouldn't want one
Perhaps someday the Bill Of Rights will say
Once conceived you have the right to breath
Life, liberty and the pursuit of happiness

What good is it today, when the littlest among us
Doesn't have the right to breath, if your heart is getting crowded
With the little ones I can see
Then someday the Bill of rights will say

Once conceived you have the right to breath
Life, liberty and the pursuit of happiness
In the world in which you were conceived

Francis E. Delaney

Love Sonnet

Love is an agony I am consumed by one so
primed and pruned from dawn to dusk thoughts
drift into the abyss dare to say I love thee
Afraid to be dismissed I gazed upon her classic face
searching for significance she simply smiled
That knowing smile and gilled me with her innocence

Some loves grow while others wane bringing forth engaging pain
What is lost is not appeased what is won begot to please
In legendary grace she simply smiled
That knowing smile gaming me to merry chase

Not all is lost when love begone the melody lingers on
An acrid taste upon my bud and aching pain without thy love
In legendary grace she simply smiled
That knowing smile about her face

In legendary grace she stole my mind and heart
We mated till death us do part
And led me to a course not understood
An agony? Or, as it should? In legendary grace
She simply smiled that knowing smile
That she could?

Phyllis L. Hunt

Believe

What do you believe in, and why do you believe
Is it something inside you feel
Or something you can see for real
If you were to loose your sight today
If your vision were completely taken away
Could you still believe
In what you could no longer see tomorrow
Or would your beliefs be shattered by your sorrow
If you were to suffer pain and grief
Could you still believe in your beliefs
Would you send for a doctor or a priest
Would pay or pray for quick relief
If the most tragic disaster knocked at your door
Could you open and still believe in the Lord forever more
These are questions I ask myself each day
The answer is always yes then I bowel my head and pray
Lord with you to guide me when things go wrong
With you at my side I will always be strong
You would be my eyes and from pain and release
As long as I continue to worship, and believe in my beliefs

Joyce J. Horton

In His Care

When we are weak and full of sin,
The first wrong step is where to begin.

But don't expect the Lord to go along,
For he is against all that is wrong.

He gives us his rules listed in his book,
All we need to do is take a second look.

With our lives all twisted out of shape,
How do we expect to ever escape?

Call on the Lord and he will always be there.
Our lives are in his hands and his ever loving care.

Janis B. Drinnon

Inheritance

I shall not ever leave your side, my Comrade and my Friend
For on the day when you approach your earthly journey's end
I would be present with you then, to share the celebration
Of all your life revealed in full in holy consummation.
And in that awesome, burning hour, one boon — I'd beg you give it;
Grant me a doubt share, I pray, of your beloved spirit
That's shaped me with such loving art. May I receive a portion
Of your essential nature, your composure and compassion.
This cherished mantle, as a double blessing I should wear
To bear for me the sacred sense that you continue near.
That treasured cloak would cover me with comfort and with grace
And power to roll the Jordan back, when I must claim my place
Without you on this side. And with that cloak to cover me
I'd not be totally bereft of present deity.
And so I promise I shall not be parted from you, Friend.
For who can name beginning of our friendship, or the end?

Carolyn Jones

Harbored Memories

Gulls hover motionless, in the steady evening breeze,
While ships' masts sway in unison, upon the choppy seas.
A yacht's horn announces, our rendezvous with the full moon,
For the passengers onboard, singing carefree out of tune.

Jets autograph cirrus skies above, with a thin white marker,
Then turn eastward bound for Europe, before the heavens get much darker.
Pastel blues fade slowly, to oranges, greens, and pinks.
The sun inhales deeply, before beneath the horizon sinks.

The crashing seas subside, from a roar now to a purr.
Poseidon's heart beats slowly, nothing maritime astir.
The sun prepares to take a dip, before resting for the night,
While lovers wish upon a star, at the first glimmer of twilight.

Rick Albrecht

Nana

Boy what a shock when I got the call, they said
she was leaving — leaving us all.
How could this be, it just can't be so, surely
she knows I don't want her to go.
I'm not yet ready to say goodbye — it can't be
the end I'm not ready to cry.
Why is it that Nana had to go, there's still
so much I needed to tell her so — of how
much I'll miss her and how I do care and
I'll never forget those Sundays when I did her hair
Our time was short but truly treasured.
My memories of her could never be measured
I only wish that I had been there, I'd have
held her hand or maybe brushed her hair.
These simple things have meant a lot, my
memories now are all and I've got.
Oh Heavenly father please welcome her home
and reassure her now, she'll never be alone.

Sherilyn M. Biagini

The Healing Time

Lonely — I get so lonely whenever i think of you
   And all those special things — that we would often do
I'm lonely for those dreams we frequently had shared — and
   All those passions I would give — if you — had only cared

Again, happiness eludes me — was it ever meant to be
   As happiness was a place I reserved for you and me
I miss you loving touch, I miss your flirting smile
   Just like I miss those fun times — when you would stay awhile

Happiness is attainment, not a fleeting moment in time —
   that soon will pass like fading lights — dimmed by the mind
It's a remembrance — a joy — an extraordinary way to feel
   Like being lost in a safe place — your mind finds very real

If you life cannot be shared and your love cannot be treasured
   Then how will your life's purpose — sufficiently be measured
Life and love is shared only by the living — As
   each year that passes it's the love — which keeps on giving

Although the years may come and all those years may go
   I'll anticipate your return — as the mind grows blurred and slow
Will you remember me? Yes, I'll always remember you —
   As this picture slowly fades — and your mind it ponders — who?

   Donna Kay

Dusk

Hues mist while melting pastels pour full and angled from divine
palette's choice. Spilled orange amongst a tangle of tainted
yellow within a hearty blush 'o red. God's eye deems a setting
sun curved in descend yet slack in gate; burning in a spray of
fanned, piercing rays to hang in layered, punctured cumulus.

Spiraling shards of light unravel onto nocturnal reciprocation; moving
fixed in dove-tailed congruence. A day's wither in exhale; known only
in shades of graying stark as seized by a pending, curious night.
An ominous ebony; gaining lucid coats of strength. Warm and
cool mesh in breezes; slicing through a temperate willingness
'tween a fading thrust of day and a darkening post of passage.
A post willed as sentry of the dawn next; in sacred abidance to collect
the tethered reins of a newer day and pull. Light awaits flush against the
furthermost side of the pitch; in participatory anticipation.

Alas, we pace headlong into his glorious endeavor of faith.
Humbly flaunting the brawn of a strong back in wisdom's
cautious taunt of trust's reflect. My heart knows of white
skipping a beat into black.
Hence, my soul knows of night which inhales into the enduring cycle;
honoring the rhythm of God's breath.

   Parry Alan Hall

An Infant's Breath In Renaissance

A new life force grapples and pulls wisps of breath in quick swirls.
Willowy linen stays the warmth between flesh of supple pink
and maternal radiance.
A mother's love absent of refracted purpose; surging in focus
and laced with her solemn will stroked in birth.

In solace exhale, a weathered yellowing of renaissance blisters
ahead through centuries.
Journey's width, resting on times old; bent as a silken thread of
sharded light in pinpoint sharpened.
Strands of wisdom past, seeking the essence of pliant youth null
of seasoned nuance.
As predestined, a meeting tainted in anxious blaze of pending bond;
stationed in hover and each other's turbulence.

Solemn will goes sweetly to fan embering elements held in God's suspend.
Threaded cohesion amongst the laces of a mother's breath in sigh.
The pulse of three in aligned vector blend in spark for a path fixed.
Guidance for a white heat life-force tuned toward a lifetime's will
of reasoned thought in hued presence of perspective.

   Parry Alan Hall

Reverie

Penniless
under the spell of Thespis and Seferis,
gaze up on a bright, moonlit night,
for this
Feel the nimble wind's soft kiss;
fly and ride a cloud coach to Polaris
Reach and catch a swiftly falling star;
listen to the angels sing;
shower in the crystal palace of a summer storm
and dry off with the silky veil of Aurora Borealis.
Gaze upon a bright, moonlit night,
and dance, breathless in all of this
gratis.

   Dorothy M. Osborne

Winter

Unwise, cruel desolations aggravate.
Wild ruminations charm the naive ears.
Cold, wintry isolations scold, berate.
A traveler smiles, beams, when a blizzard clears.
Bewildered harbors toss their waves aloft.
Gray sheets of rain confound an icy path.
Fires, raging throughout timberland and croft,
Flee, earnestly, as if from divine wrath.
Bored snow clouds wish for spring's contrite allure,
Because they are rebuffed by windy blasts.
Shy evening shadows, on crisp snow, secure,
That winter stays, like fierce iconoclasts.
   Harsh tides oppress one season everywhere,
   To keep the silent order hidden there.

   Susan A. Holmes

Life Spent

Got you screaming from the womb
   To place you neatly in the tomb
A lifetime of sustainable food
   Placed in your palace outside the 'hood

   Living, living, living

Let us all hail
   Love on this trail
To where we ne'er pay rent
   For infinity spent

   Loving, loving, loving

   Timothy Duffy

The Lamb Of God

The lamb of God
Came as the son of man
as he walked across the land
He would sit on a hill
or in a boat
Even in the temple he spoke
He taught many people
In love he healed the sick and blind
But warned those sinners that opposed
He is the way, the truth, the life
many would perish for unbelief
For truly he is
The Son of God
Sent from the Father above
To be our substitute
And die on the cross
to save lost souls whose paths we touch
Today he still calls to believe on his name
and receive his great love
through his only begotten Son His name is Jesus!

   Phyllis Allphin

I Prayed

I prayed for a father to love me.
That I did not receive.
I prayed for a brother to watch over me.
That I did not receive.
I prayed for a prince to rescue me.
That I did not receive.
I prayed for a Savior to save me.
Then you came into my heart and became all of these.

Alena Westbrook

Parenting

Depression has regressed me
For in your love
I possessed me
Now that you're gone
I have lost my identity
I suffer from the disease of inferiority
Since you left me
I can no longer write romantic poetry
You will always be part of me
Your happy memories have become part of my creativity
For I cannot live a life of inferiority
I have my babies and they need me

Vincent A. Cappello

AIDS Is There A Cure?

People are dying hoping for a cure
Families are suffering seeing their love one in pain
Praying for a miracle, hoping for a cure
Every time I hear someone die
I wonder why?
No cure to be found, no promises made
My heart grieve by the lost of lives
I fall asleep at night praying for a
    cure to save these people lives
I woke up next morning only to find
    out there is no cure
What are we going to do now?
We need to educate the people
Our children are growing up living life dangerous
Not knowing they can be the next victim
Of this dreadful disease called AIDS.

Khalidah Ali

The Heart's Game

I'm grateful for the ones I love;
For Hazel, Cyndi, friends and cous
For Michael and a fishing friend,
And Baby in its mother's bin.

I'm grateful that we've all got jobs.
Maybe we can help dry some sobs,
And I'm not talking politics.
Just help a friend whose luck's in sticks.

Of all the crime, and crud, and slush;
A little gratitude might hush.
So, look around your little world.
It could be a cute little girl;

A canal that's brimming fish full,
A favorite picture with its pull
That shines its light in hearts at dawn,
Nor is it mere sun rises pawn

Or orange trees home grown in yards
But little bit of heaven's cards,
A game that's played by joys of spark
Seen not with eyes but with the heart.

Dolph Greer

In Loving Memory . . . (1995)

You come to us in soft white flakes
of winter's falling snow . . .
Your memory drifting down from up above.

When spring sends heaven's raindrops down
to make the flowers grow . . .
The fragrant blossoms radiate your love.

The summer sky is blue and wide
and filled with puffs of white . . .
your sweet voice whispers to us in the breeze.

When heaven paints the autumn leaves
all red and gold and bright . . .
you smile at us from high above the trees.

You sparkle in the stars each night
that glimmer in the sky . . .
you shine down with the sun on us each day.

You went away, you had no choice,
A person has to die . . .
But a mother's love can never go away.

Elizabeth Zerbst

No God Will Ever Forgive Any Of Them

The philosopher always told
his wife and their progeny,
never sell your soul or any part of it.
He specialized in ethics and therefore
he steadfastly lived what he believed.

So, the evil manipulators said,
we are definitely going to show him;
they connived with his fickle spouse
and offspring to test him to the utmost
with deprivation and total destruction.

When his family followed the dictatorship,
it was explicitly recorded that
any harassment of the philosopher
would be instantly reported
to the proper federal authorities.

Speaking to the woman, kids and cohorts,
it was sternly announced
from an unimpeachable fount:
All of then belong in a federal penitentiary
and no God will ever forgive any of them.

Arlie L. Hunt II

The Clinic

Crouched in the bushes,
Like a thief in the night
Its gray, foreboding structure lends a chill.
There are no joyful voices,
Nor scurrying, happy feet,
For death is ever silent, ever still.
There is no healing there of mind or body,
The future looms ahead as empty air.
Those little ones who would have made a difference,
Our hope and love of life,
Have died in there.

A gentle sound begins and grows in volume,
The sound of faith and love for all of life.
Soft voices praying in the shadowed pathway,
For guidance, and the strength to see the light.

Now, into the morning sky
The sun comes running,
All buttery and warm, to meet the day.
Led by God's Hand to cross the narrow roadway
To find that hope and love once thrown away.

Virginia S. Chartrand

My Friend

When you smile my heart fills with joy,
When you laugh my mind glitters with happiness,
You are a part of me my friend, when you go
You take a part of me my friend.

When you cry my heart over flows with pain,
When you frown my mind aches with sorrow
I feel your pain, you are a part of me
My friend.

Sometimes I wonder what if you were gone,
Where would I be with you my friend.
You cry on my shoulder, you yell in my eat
You hate my words yet I am a part of you
My friend.

If we ever part, we will be together
Because we are part of each other my friend.
I am here forever, you are here for eternity.
We are one my friend.

Abbie Pender

A Child In My Heart

A child in my heart,
Is a musical lullaby from the start.
Even though you are getting old,
Childhood memories are threads of gold.

They can never be erased,
They are thoroughly etched and forever encased;
That Childhood was taught by parental love.
The baptism was instituted by God above.

This faith in God shall Child-like be,
Carried through life to eternity.
Jesus called the children to come to him,
He is the mediator for our sin.

This Child-like trust must always be;
A child in my heart, you will always see.
For Jesus loves me this I know,
God's Bible often tells me so.

Edward D. Gompf

Silk Flowers

Silken plastic petal lying on the ground
Soiled litter trash from summers past
Among the leaf and grass.

On the porch a roosting place for wren,
A silk flower basket hanging in the wind.
Faded seasons languishing in the sun.

And in the yard where flowers bloom
Whose petals go away,
Silk flower petal part lingers in the shade.

Floyd McLain

The Quiet Of The Night

The quiet of the night is such a delight.
All the many sounds that my ears grasp, and,
some echoing in the distant past. The candor of
talk as the passersby walk. A-a-ah, the wind is
pleasurable, as well as measurable. It feels good
in the hood. A time to give thanks, to think, or
maybe take a wink. Oh Lord, the distant night, with
the stars in the sky that shine so bright. The magic
of love sent from heaven above. A dance, a romance,
a chance to unwind. Heavenly Father, the nights should
always be so kind.

Roosevelt Hudson

This I Know

When you have no one to turn to,
Remember God for he will keep you,
and he will feed you,
He will love you, and provide for you.

In return all you must do is Remember God
Talk to him,
Sing your praises to him, and allow him to come into your life.

I did and how much richer,
I am for knowing his love for showing his love,
and for sharing his love

Know when he is carrying you and when you will only see one
set of footprints
This I know for I had no one until I
Remember God.

Dawn H. Barrell

The End

When is the end
Will it come soon
Will it come by the light of a full moon
Will the end steal my breath
Will is cause death
As I think of this
I feel slowly going down my cheek a tear
The tear is from my fear
The fear of losing it all
Everyone who I care for
Will be gone before the thunder can roar
Can we all be saved with our faith
Our faith in each other
Will man kinds faith
Be the weapon that will save us
From the end

Robin Schaefer

Spring Snow

Large fluffy snow flakes falling from the sky quietly cover
everything that is on the ground with a blanket of pure white and
add beauty to the land that will not last through out the night.
It is too warm for this spring snow to stay with us very long.
The spring flowers that have greeted us do not understand why God
has let it snow on them when what they wanted was a soft spring rain;
but is this not true of our own life when we ask God why we
must endure pain? How easy it is to forget the blessings that we
have and then grumble about the rain.

Alyce M. Nielson

The Tides Of Love

The tides of love still flood my heart,
Each day they're ever on the rise;
Though love was strong right at the start,
Its strength today still does surprise.

I dwell in oceans of content,
In waters warm and still pristine;
With hugs and kisses by consent,
A sea with such a lovely queen.

I gratefully accept my fate,
Each hug and kiss a new found thrill,
Each new born day I celebrate,
As all my wishes you fulfil.

I bask so snugly in your spell,
With storms unknown and skies so blue;
Just coasting on each gentle swell,
This world of mine depends on you.

Sol Finkelman

First Love

Love is an emotion that no one can control;
It has its own mind and it has its own soul.
Love can cause trouble and love can cause pain,
but best of all love can cause happiness
which we all need to gain. Love is a consciousness
that all should enjoy; it tip-toes around you
like a distraught little boy.
You may just ask what is this love,
it has the wings of an angel and the coo of a dove.
Cupid is out there ready to go
with that swift little arrow
and that strong little bow.

James Lee

Sonlight

I am the Creator. Let fear melt away.
The darkness has gone in the light of the day.
When doubts crowd in and peace leaves your heart,
Remember I'm with you . . . I'll never depart.

As these others around you will breathe not a word
And they press you silence, your cries I have heard.
The past can't stay hidden. Its harm cannot stay.
And your life can be bright when you follow My Way.

Are you not the clay that I shaped and I willed?
By your trials and joys, I can strengthen and build.
I bring in the light and can banish all sin.
The dark can't remain when the Son enters in.

Catriona Glass

Arthur

I was shattered one Saturday night,
When you didn't come home after a three-day fight.
My mind raced back to the other night,
In a dream I had; I was living right now.

My heart went weak,
As I remembered the soft words you used to speak.
"I will never leave you," sped through my brain
Like an out-of-control freight train
Ready to crush whoever was in its path.

My tears flowed like a tropical storm,
You were supposed to be there to love me and keep me warm.
My heart was shattered,
After all the love we shared. You act like nothing mattered.

The words "I love you," flashed through my brain,
How many times have I heard those words?
Non-stop words, like a neon light
That flashes and flashes to remind you the loneliness of the night.

My love for you is like the neon light that flashes,
As the night turns to day.
I will love you with all my passion.

Jean Lovely

The Inequities Of Life

Alas, a wolf!
I hear echoes and see shadows.
I must stand still.
I want to advance and have a vision of what could be.
Limitations are in that pathway, age, race, and sex.
The wolf I recognize will hold me as his prey — an inequity of life.
There is freedom in vision but not completely in rights.
Challenge the wolf at election time, vote to change
    your inequities to equities.
Listen then to the echoes to the cry of the wolf, on the other side,
    when justice for the advancement of your ideal has come.

Catherine E. Hoilien

A Crystal Heart

An angel's touch up my mind.
By God's sweet grace am I able to find,
The love that has always been meant for me.
I have gained back my dignity.
My eyes shudders have been thrown out wide.
I am able to see all the change inside.
His one great hand will guide my way, and show me to a brighter day.
Beyond the boundaries of the world; there once stood a little girl.
With timid dreams and tender touch,
She showed the world she cared too much.
Knocked on her knees time and again,
She thought she'd never find a friend.
Then she looked only to see a man to help her from her knee.
He picked her up and held her tight,
And then she knew she'd be all right.
He showed her love and true light.
She was born again after that one night.
If life seems hopeless and is too much to bear, look to the one
who will always care. The one who watches from Heaven above.
The one with everlasting love: Jesus

Lisa Sorensen

Let Freedom Ring

As a child I remember when we used to sing,
"God Bless America" and "Let Freedom Ring."
Whatever happened to the "In God We Trust"?
When our country was a "Babe," wasn't it a must?

To honor our maker who put us here
Now they are refusing to let "Our Lord" near
Don't you remember, "God shed his Grace on Thee"?
Wasn't it sang for a country to keep free?

In school, I recall singing, "His truth is marching on"
But, where is truth, is it forever gone?
Now our kids are not allowed to offer prayer in school
They don't even teach them, to obey the golden rule

I don't really understand, how our children hope to win
When they keep out prayer, but they let condoms in.
My grandchildren are always asking me, why?
When I pledge allegiance to the flag, I begin to cry.

So, where are we going? Where is the love?
When we cannot honor, "Our" God up above
I only pray that some day soon, we will all start to sing
Lets "God Bless America" and then "Let Freedom Ring"

Lora Emery

Sacrifice

I could only look on in disgrace
As he bore the sin of my unworthy race;
    As I watched in horror, the blood thirsty crowd
Cheered as the soldiers threw dice for his shroud

This noble brow, once adorned with stars,
Was bruised and beaten; Eternally scarred
    Were the hands that had soothed, and healed, and loved —
This Rose of Sharon, this gentle Dove.

The crown of thorns they had thrust on His head,
Once brown, was now and forever stained red;
    Blood sprang forth from the Living Water,
Angels mourned as the Lamb was slaughtered.

Creation revolted: The ground quaked beneath
Down fell the head crowd with its gory wreath
    God in His heaven cried out in pain
As Judah's great Lion was stripped of His mane

When I fall short of your glory so high,
Do you think of Your nail-pierced hands, and sigh?

Jamie Bragg

The Red Jacket

Like a master's painting hung in a gallery or great hall
The red jackets blaze richly against the back drop of fall
They mount their steeds, groomed with tails braided neat
Twenty hounds wagging and clamoring at their feet

The party assembles with the hounds at bay
The trumpet blast signals the hunt is under way
The fox darts over fields in panic and swift fury
The hounds gain ever faster, winded but not weary

The mounts glisten in the sun as their hooves pound the sod
Their riders faces stern and dark as the wrath of God
The blood lust of the hunters begin to rise and swell
The hounds snarl and snap like demons from hell

The quarry cries his last in agony and fear
The hounds white fangs shine red
The riders scramble nearer to view, the limp dismembered dead

Breathing resumes and congratulations rise
As the head of the hunt claims his prize
A tail of copper, held proudly overhead
As last drops of life drip, masked, on his jacket of red

Come evening, by the hearth they sit, the Aristocrats of society
Dressed in finery with lamps softly lit, they indulge in cakes and tea.

Janice Roach

The Ride

How quickly light fades from
blue to gray . . . almost as if my heart
were an ancient, decaying kaleidoscope

Happiness and joy scatter into
a world unfamiliar to me, yet continue to
dreadfully engulf me in alarm

Fragmented and tearful, I must accept
the reality that life is
a perpetual roller coaster ride
With no ticket booth
No turnstile
No refund

Still, in my travels from bliss to woe
I am gifted with the understanding that
a ride . . . is just a ride

It's all in my perception
All in my soul . . . to accept that
the journey up and the descent down
are simply excursion to
another amusement park . . . somewhere else in time

Chandra Lyn Moon

Wolves

They have bright blue, grey, or yellow eyes
That glow in the night like giant fireflies.
Their coats can be red, grey, brown, or black
And they hunt together in a pack
They live, eat, drink, breathe, and feel just like us
When one's endangered we create a fuss.
Why must we destroy this predatory creature?
Death is Nature's harshest teacher.
Graceful, stealthy, fearless, angel of the night
Nothing they do makes killing them right.
When they take our lives stock it's only to eat
They do it only because we take their land and thus their meat.
When they kill our herds, who's the wronged one?
Us or them who are brutally shot with many a gun?
To this question there is no solution,
But their disappearance is no illusion.
Blessed or condemned, angel or devil
In the hunt we know they revel, wolves.

April Kahgee

Honor A Commandment

Honor to mom and to your dad
Is a commandment ordered by God.
Give them the respect they deserve
Take heed and listen to every word.

They only want the best for you
If you'd only listen and don't break the rules.
Stay in school and learn all you can
Don't drop out, give it all you got.

Have ambition, strive to work hard
Don't idle your mind you'll be at rock bottom.
In cases like that you'll feel low all the time
You can't get yourself out of the rut
You put yourself in.

But listening, learning, and having self-esteem
You aim for it all, you follow your dreams.
Things won't always go your way.
But honor to your parents will get you through
You'll teach others what they taught you.

Ava Yocum

I'm Just Traveling

Please let the bad be used for something good
Make me humble; help me do what you would
Let he hurts be used to ease another's pain
And what I do not be for wordly gain

Use me, God, for your will alone; not mine,
For what is right and your love so sublime
With your strength and courage help me to stand
For things that will make this a better land

Use me to help stop suffering and pain
Help my hands to plant little seeds of grain
That will grow for others a brighter day
And give to them an easier pathway

What I have or am comes from you above
Let whatever I do show your great love
Lead me, guide me, and always hold my hand
For I'm just traveling through this land

Please let the bad be used for something good
Make me humble; help me do what you would
Lead me, guide me, and always hold my hand
For I'm just traveling through this land

Alice Lorraine Hill

My Lucky Day

Today I found a penny,
It will be a lucky day I said.

My hopes were high, I felt real good,
But everything went wrong instead.

I developed laryngitis and could not talk,
I crossed the street, when it read "Don't Walk".

Car horns were tooting, I walked very fast,
Slipped and sprained my ankle, ended up with a cast.

I dropped my keys and in the sewer they went,
It wasn't my car, as to me it was lent.

It started to rain, and I was soaking wet,
But this day was to be lucky, on that I would bet.

Finding this penny has caused me to frown,
So now when I see one, I leave it on the ground.

Someone will come along, find it and feel it's their day,
Maybe hit the lottery, be a millionaire right away.

I will no longer stop to pick up a penny,
A nickel or dime maybe, if any.

Anna Simonelli

Purity

Untouched as a snow covered peak
Innocence shared by the spiritually meek

Ruptured veins from mountains create springs
Mother Nature's heart beat on the flight of eagles wings

Unborn destinies guided by truth
Embryonic oceans nursing youth

Unsoiled by thought or sound
Pursued sanctuaries never found

Peace of mind we may never know
Famine feasts on mental flow

Success will echo the roar of discovery
Cleansed emotion will be the recovery

William C. Leppo

Whispers Of God

God whispers through the wind that blows and
breathes upon us gently as he goes.
He whispers through the rain that falls and showers us with his blessings.
God whispers through the lightning bright and wakes us up with
his thundering sound.
He whispers through the moon by night and warms us through
his sunlight.
We hear them in the snow that falls, as he softly drops a blanket
upon the Earth.
God whispers through his Word. It falls through our ears and
reaches our heart.
He warns us through his Son, shakes us, feeds us, waters us
and blankets us with his Spirit to preserve us.
God whispers, come to me my dear, for I have made the way so clear.

Janice K. Robinson

Release

It's time, my dear, to set yourself free.
To become the person you were meant to be.
When you submit to another's demands,
And ignore the "you" that your souls commands
You destroy the best part of what is you,
And what remains is no longer true.

The thread of love is fragile at best.
If truth is lacking it can't stand the test.
You can stand up and set yourself free.
Be simply remembering "Hey, this is me!"

Do something for you, and do it again.
Pat yourself on the back . . . lift up your chain.
Be proud you are you and happy you are.
Take charge of your life and reach for a star.

Maxine Boss

About Special People

Sometimes we can look long and far
Or even wish upon a certain star.
But we did not need to look high and low
To find great fellows that put on a real show.
The special kind are you guys, who really care
Everyone came prepared to work hard and do their share.
They say angels are sent from high above
We saw no wings or halos, but real true caring love.
No amount of words could ever begin to be expressed
For our heartfelt thanks so much; your kindness makes us
    forever warmly and deeply impressed.
The wives we had not even met
Came bearing tasty food for a table to set.
We were so amazed all we could say was for heaven's sake
Since it was my husband's birthday, there was even a decorated cake.

Nadine M. Bushong

Candlelight Shining At Christmas Time

Candlelight shining at Christmas time,
Casting flames of wonderment divine.
Tapers, tealights, votives and pillars;
Candles, when lit, are bright like the stars.
Advent wreathes with tapers of purple;
Christ Child is coming for all people.
Tealights glisten on the crystal trees,
Reflecting prisms as in a breeze.
Votives glow upon the window panes
And in the glasses of picture frames.
From the mantels the pillars shimmer
And fade away into a glimmer.
Birthday candles on a Christmas tree;
Jesus is born for you and for me.
All candlelight can show us the way,
To love, joy and peace on Christmas Day.

Joan S. McKinney

A Better Place

Someday soon, all of God's children,
    will be in a better place.
A place of warmth, comfort, and stability.
A place full of loving, gentle, people
A place where no harm can be done.
No sickness, no pain, no hate, and no more wars.
A place where there is always laughter,
And singing, the rejoicing of everlasting peace.
Love will radiate throughout everyone.
There will always be light, always be fulfillment.
But most of all, we will be with our Heavenly Father, our Creator.

Natasha M. Seils

The Past Of Our Future

Do you still recall, the little things we use to do?
    Like winking and smiling, and saying I love you.
Or the way we use to sit, while holding hands?
    And making plans, to travel this land.
Those were the dreams, of our short past.
    The ones that have gone, but will always last.
They are the memories, I shall always keep.
    Especially those times, when I would go to sleep.
And you would sit by me, with only a stare.
    While thinking of all the moments, we would share.
Yes, for now we are sharing those moments in real.
    As we're looking, out over the valleys and hills.
But, yet the biggest of these dreams is still to come.
    As we sit here, together, drinking both beer and rum.
And that dream, will be our very own baby
    The one you're going to have, my Lovely Lady!

Cecil Dewayne Bowen

Death Has My Son

The cord around the infant's throat
Made life's beginning most remote.
The doctor said "A Miracle,"
This child has really beaten death!
But Death still wants this handsome son,
The fight for life had just begun.
At just about the age of two,
Death tried again this child to slew!
But prayers and love again overruled.
His knees were smitten with so much pain,
But Bobby would again sustain,
Now he's a man, but one more blow,
A ball size tumor, his brain does grow.
So I now kneel at Bobby's bed,
And Bobby cries "Please Death, Oh Death!"
Oh yes, Death fights for what he wants.
And now, yes now he has my son.

Vivian Mollan

The Good Old Days

It must have been fun to live in years gone by,
Horses and Carriages and no Airplanes to fly,
Things were at a slower pace,
You got where you were going who has to race,
Pressure to rush just was not done,
Relaxation was valued by everyone,
They were not slouchers; not at all,
They just bounced a different ball,
Then most of the people do today,
With jets, computers and come what may,
Try calling an executive on the phone,
You get a recording, a machine, and then a "Dial Tone,"
You never get to talk direct,
It's very frustrating and we should elect,
Not to go back to 1903
But slow down to a run in this Century.

Flossie Pyle

My Colorful Life

When I was young and in my prime
I could wear any color from fuchsia to lime.

My hair was black; my eyes were, too.
I looked just as good in purple or blue.

The nicknames they called me were ever so merry;
Because I wore red, my name became "Cherry."

My schoolmates would always kid me with glee
Because of my olive skin, you see,

They said I had a perpetual tan,
So they called me "Blackie" and ran.

Now that I'm older and my hair is grey
I can wear any color and don't mind what they say.

The days of kidding are long gone, thank God.
I'm just an old lady with white hair
and glasses
and proud.

Violet DeTora

The Waterfall

Poetry, is as pure and powerful as water.
Its strength is phenomenal as it plunges to the depths of a
    waterfall full of life's realities; spilling over into a
    spirit filled ocean, which nourishes all life.

The brilliance of the sun brings love onto the water, leaving
    an everlasting impression of serenity upon the soul,
    and calmness in the heart.

All humanity shares in its wealth of persistent strength and
    fearlessness . . .

Poetry, whether calm or raging, as it falls from the
    waterfall; spilling over into the ocean, is forever
    cleansing the spirit and enlightening the soul.

It's far reaching existence leaves an eternal impression on
    the hearts and minds of humanity.

Gary M. Dorn

Good Thoughts

Sweep your mind of malice and sin
Let sunshine and warmth enter in
Dwell not on gossip and neighbors cruel heart
Think of fulfilling true brother hood on your part.

Through the blessed peace of understanding
That can be felt throughout each day
Good thoughts are nourished
And can never slip away.

Brenda W. Finley

June 6, 1944

Hook up now, don't be slow.
Geronimo! Here we go.
Duck your head as you step out the door,
Chute risers can scalp you, that's for sure.

The plane is hit as you step into space.
If the plane gets back, it's by God's grace.
Terror seizes you by the throat,
You feel like you are going to choke.

Tracers pluck at your chute overhead,
Only five hundred feet to dodge the lead.
Keep feet together as you hit the ground,
If you break a leg, things come unwound.

Across the hedgerow, you hear a cricket,
Or the bolt of a rifle to punch your ticket.
Cut every phone line that you find.
No communication befuddles the enemy mind.
Another Stick comes straggling in,
The way our drop was scattered was a sin.
"Hold until relieved," are the orders,
Hard to do when attacked by tanks and mortars.

Russell Lloyd Kelch

I'm Wishing For A Heavenly Christmas!

I'm wishing for a heavenly Christmas Day memories that are so
wonderful that won't ever go away. Crystal, white, snow, falling
on the ground. Friendly people, heavenly music are all around.
Homes filled with holiday cooking and presents are under the tree.
Remembering the Christmas of the past and what they meant to me.
Christmas cards, from loved ones that touches are hearts.
Picking out presents for that "special," someone right from the start.
Smiles, laughter, jingle bells, ringing loud. Busy shoppers
making their way in the bustling crowds.
Our savior's wish from "heaven," is peace, love, joy. Some
forgotten orphans are getting that "special" Christmas toy.
Santa Clauses, in their velvet suits aglow, children's wishes from
the heart. Families all over the world come together with peace,
love, and they don't want to part. Gold, crystal, "angels," guard
our tree tops high in the air. Oh! hug someone this Christmas
time and tell them that you care. Oh! The beauty of the snow,
peaceful, "Dove." Reminds me that "Our Savior" is here with his
undying "love." Oh, yes I'm wishing in my "heart" that you'd
come back once again and be mine. You could make my
"Christmas" so heavenly and divine.

Mary Ellen Lamie

Christ's Words From The Cross

Christ was made to be a sacrifice according to God's will,
So condemned to a cross, He was placed on Calvary's hill.
A prayer He prayed for everyone for what He'd been through,
"Father, forgive them, for they know not what they do."

Two thieves were also hanging there on a cross that day,
One jeered at him, the other had words of praise to say.
He asked to be remembered knowing Christ was his sacrifice,
Christ words to him, "Today shalt thou be with me in paradise."

Those present at the foot of the cross showed devotion and love,
Disregarding their physical anguish for the one hanging up above.
His mother and John were there, instructions He gave each other,
His words, "Woman behold thy son," to John, "Behold thy mother."

Dark clouds appeared, He felt deserted, rejected as it must be,
His words. "My God, My God, why hast thou forsaken me?"
His suffering and anguish was now becoming its very worst,
Then in His agony and dreadful pain, His Words, "I thirst."

The curtain of the temple was torn in two, oh! The fear of it,
His words were loud, "Father into thy hands I commend my spirit."
His final words were given and now His life must diminish,
So to all that were gathered there, His words, "It is finished."

Harmon Aubuchon

Portrait Of A Small Town

The morning horizon, painted a golden hue,
changing to a pinkish orange, when day is through.
Tree lined streets can be seen,
rows of thick foliage of bright green.
The clinking of milk bottles left at the door,
the morning paper thrown once more.
Coffee's aroma fills the air,
confirming, that people are there.
Children running off to school,
returning when day is through.
The laughter of children at play,
as they end their busy day.
A flickering of lights from within,
coming from each television.
Lights going off all down the street,
until a new day they meet.
The night is still, except for a few sounds,
chirping of crickets and a barking hound.
A portrait painted of a small town,
a town, everywhere, to be found.

Joan M. Perry

Mother

Dear mother how can I cry? I am just frozen in time . . .
When I was a little girl sitting on your lap
Walking along the side walk hand in hand
Talking on the phone long distance every Saturday
Laughing at your spirit — what a gift
Thinking of you sitting alone as dad was gone
Sending a gift to you, your last gift from me
Pudding, candy, coffee, 2 little monkeys, cocoa
A calendar you will never use — 1997
The Lord took you in his arms to shield you there
99 wonderful years I had you here
Never has to go to a nursing home — you didn't want to go
The last day you left your home here
The angels sang as you passed that way
I love you mom share some poems
My poems with Ralph and someday I will be there with you
Mother died in the hospital the next early morning the day she fell
We will miss you here but would not want you to stay when I . . .
Think of the smile on your face when you meet Dad
With a Red Rose in your hand.

Margaret D. Brueske

Jesus Says Pray

Somehow, somewhere, someone has hurt you again, they have
said and done things that you don't understand.

It's easy just to think of your pride, so easy to get angry, lash
out, and get the last word in.

But Jesus says to you "Pray, put bitterness and pride aside and pray."

You say "How? Don't you know what's been done? Why
should I pray for this person, they don't deserve prayer!"

Softly and gently, Jesus reminds you that He died for all and His
blessings cannot operate when strife and bitterness are around.

With tears in your eyes and compassion in your heart, you
speak and pray for those who spitefully used you.

Suddenly, forgiveness flows and peace comes to your troubled heart,
the moment you began to pray, you put God back in control.

With a loving hug and a joyful smile, God embraces you and
tells you how well pleased He is.

When someone hurts you or does things towards you that's un-
called for, instead of lashing out, seek God about the situation,
and get on your knees and pray.

Tracy A. Lindsay

Home For Christmas

Dear Ann: I'm coming home for Christmas
and I can hardly wait.
It's been some time since I last saw
you, and our daughter "Kate."

I still can see the Christmas tree.
The angel at the top.
And how our little Katie stared.
I thought her eyes would "pop."

I'm coming home for Christmas.
The troops have put in their years.
we served our country proudly.
They no longer need us here.

There were days of rumblings.
Which seemed to never cease.
We thanked God that we were known,
as keepers of the peace.

Oh God!, the plane is falling.
I'm unseated from my place.
I'm coming home dear Ann and Kate.
But I'll never see your face.

Mamie H. Ross

Freedom

Life without freedom resembles a night without moon,
And looses all the echoes with glories very soon!
God is our architect to assure freedom for all,
But greed is the puppet that stands pretty tall!

Freedom is the shield, like sun with its ray —
Without it we perish or may become a stray!
Freedom creates the magic around the global eye,
And soothes all 'tenants' without saying "Goodbye"!

Freedom is a fountain that refreshes our souls,
Throughout the years and without any tolls!
Just like a droplet on a dew moistened grass,
Freedom also glares as a high polished brass!

Freedom is a treasure that we love to keep,
'Cause of its glory and the sweet little beep!
Life without freedom is like a bird without wings,
And moves along the locus ignoring the swings!

Freedom is the symbol of invisible pride with power,
And acts as a blazing sun over the hills or a tower!
The joy of freedom is boundless and prevails forever,
From generation to generation — naughty, selfish, and clever!

Hillol Ray

Drumming Is The Beat

Drumming is the flap of a hummingbird's wings.
Drumming is the beat of what a lullaby sings.
Drumming is the earthquake of an elephant stampede.
Drumming is the call of a helpless child in need.
Drumming is raindrops on a cold tin roof.
Drumming is the rapping of a singer with groove.
Drumming is the noise of an oil choked motor.
Drumming is the lap of the paddle of a boater.
Drumming is the buzz of an angry bee.
Drumming is a woodpecker finding home in his tree.
Drumming is the call of a winter goose flock.
Drumming is the tick of my grandfather's clock.
Drumming is the angel's rhythmic voice in song.
Drumming is the breaths of a weight lifter so strong.
Drumming is the tap of a nervous fingernail.
Drumming is the fingers going up a piano scale.
Drumming is a clack of a tap dancer and his five.
Drumming is the heartbeat keeping all life alive.

Allison Christy Hoover

Nocturne, Song Of The Night

Swelled the waves against the seaway's garnet and shrouded shore,
While nocturne's voiceless sound bathed the ether's covert streams.
Like some great chord it billowed across the emerald moors,
Fell with raptured splendor upon sweet slumber's shadowed dreams

Dusk blooming jasmine filled the mist with ambrosial scent,
And the moon brushed imperial clouds with luminous white.
Snow crested mountains glistened in diamond shrouded mist,
As nocturne's resonance filled the majesty of ebony night.

Now rides the soul on lighted wings toward the distant stars,
Where angels chorales fill ethereal mansions with sound.
Flying skyward through the portals of night tide's restless sea,
It melds in nocturnes chorus amid moonlight's splendored mound.

Silent is the shadowed desert which fills the contoured land,
Hushed is the forest reaching toward night's fathomless band.
Mid this umbras beauty rises even's holy chant,
Touched by seraph's star dust and played by muses' mystic hand.

Now fades nocturne's sonnet in budding morning's flaming mane,
As the sun God rides above the visions of opaque night.
But as dusk enfolds the emerald waves of nature's cloth,
The song of night shall fill the ruby red of dusky light.

Elizabeth MacDonald Burrows

Shadow Side II

Her tears are always wasted, like rain
nourishing nothing.
She's so tired of the taste of salt.
And in the cold, dark days of November,
her arms are empty.

And when the wind sighed his name,
she remembered she had a love,
a love that filled her dreams.
Thoughts of him come knocking on her heart.
She hears I love you, love you still,
but she cries in the shadow, shadow of her broken heart.

And while the wind sighed its last goodbye,
he became a silhouette in the corner of her mind.
There's been too many slivers left to
fester and overflow,
the pungent smell of dead love.
She laments, "Why do I need at all?"

And she cries in the shadow, shadow of her broken heart,
while the wind sighed its last goodbye.
He became a silhouette in the corner of her mind.

Diana Dolhancyk

Lesson Of The Hoop

She came.
A vision from distant stars to the willful sioux,
A Sacred Woman to teach them the holiness that she knew,
Barefoot, dressed in white buckskin, totally free of hate,
She spoke of their forgotten love for the Spirit Great,
Through waving prairie grasses White Buffalo Woman came.

She Prophesied.
"Live beneath this Tree of Understanding's Sacred Shade.
I plant it in your consciousness to flower," she prayed.
"A storm will come, but still one ember of Spirit will remain
To light a new dawn, a new age, a new tree upon this plain."
Giving the people undying hope, White Buffalo Woman came.

She encouraged.
"In the Sacred Circle be forever united, tribal Sioux.
The new tree's boughs will cover all races if to my word you're true.
Only if you live in harmony will your own Spirit Selves come.
Then the Ego Spirit will incarnate in all, not just in some."
If we attend our Emerging Spirits throughout each given day,
White Buffalo Woman will not only come, but surely she will stay.

Dee Talasek

I Saw A Rainbow Dance

Despair framed my armchair
Suddenly the colors of porch flowers
Rainbowed on my rain-spattered window panels
The tape of my son's memorial libretto
At a friend's demise
Was a conscious reality
String of the harmonies baritone tenor
Resonance bounced on floating molecules in space
Bringing warmth of colored energy of its expression
Causing a knowingness out of my heart to
Comfort a depression
Implanted out of jurisdiction
On the person of myself
How deep, how impenetrable the
Heart's acquired and hidden secrets
Long for acknowledgement of their mystic healing
How precious God's gifts to the truly living!

Katherine M. Young

The Greatest Test Is Letting Go

The greatest test in life is letting go
of someone we love, and those we know.
To let go of those at the end of their life-span,
and to let go of those who differ from our own special life-plan.
Love itself is not possessive.
It is warm, sincere, unselfish . . .
    significantly expressive.
Love cannot be held, bought, entrapped,
    or limited to prevent love to freely adapt.
In the broken continuity of life's love flow,
    the greatest test in life is letting go.

Cesarina Maria Rossetti

The Party Line

Rural Concho county had party lines
And wall telephones with a crank.
One long ring was our 911.
When we heard it, our hearts sank.

Sometimes that ring meant an announcement,
Some meant a community event.
Our number was 6203,
Or three short rings is what is meant.

Eavesdropping on your neighbors
Was wrong, but it was done.
If it could be done without a cough or sneeze,
It proved informative and fun.

Willie Lou Shirley

Arthritis

Arthritis is a painful disease.
It most commonly starts in
your hands and feet.

Learn how to take control
of your pain.
Or else, by it, you will be beat.

Some of your days will be good.
And others will be bad.

Sometimes the simple things are hard to do.
And it makes you made.

Just know that when you hurt so bad
others will feel it to.

When you start to feel alone,
God is there for you.

Paula J. Heath

My Heart Tells Me

I love in times gone by Alta Guerin,
The girl at old private boarding schools,
Who use to walk beneath the linden trees on warm evenings,
To read the magazines of bygone days.

I love only her, and I feel on my heart
The blue light of her white breasts.
Where is she? So where was that happiness?
Into her bright room branches came.

Perhaps she is not yet dead,
Or perhaps we both were dead.
The big yard had dead leaves,
In the cold wind, of Summers ending long ago.

Do you remember those peacock feathers,
In a tall vase, besides shells?
We learned that there had been a shipwreck,
We called Newfoundland: the Banks,

Come, come, my precious Alta Guerin:
Let us love still if you exist.
The old garden has old tulips.
Come quite naked, o Alta Guerin.

George John Guerin

To Our Saviour

Gentle Saviour come our way
    Lest we go astray
As you walked with the people long, long ago
    We need you here today

To quell the turmoil and the crime
    Running rampant in our time

Come and quell the storm
    of crime and drugs
We need you, dear Saviour
    To keep us from all harm

Come down dear Saviour
    Somewhere we must have gone astray
    please show us the right way

Come down dear Saviour
    we need you so
To show us the way to go

Lest we loose you
    we beg you today
    on heavenly wings to come our way
    we need you here today.

Elizabeth Matthews

Nature's Wonders

Oh, how I wonder of nature's present and past
    everything seems to fall in place at last.
From a new branch as a tree with leaves will grow
    To birds and then flowers to berry bushes flow
    honey bees at work and birds building their nest
    as nightfall comes they all will rest
I wonder to myself how great things are outside to all
    From the spring rains that touch the earth
    that helps everything grow and grow.
To the rainbow big in the sky, "my oh my"
    that never seems to have an end
And oak trees in a meadow where streams are flowing
You think it's reaching the sun so high above
    It needs to grow and grow.
    From the great seas and lakes and its life
I don't think are creator made a mistake
    and as the leaves start to fall and winter sets in.
A blanket of snow will cover it all
    only to start all over again.

Michael J. Boysko

Hands

Hands
    Hands
Small cupped fingers soiled from the earth
Stuffing the chicken tenderly
To pass the adoba
Crocheted hands working a needle endlessly
Scrub
    Scrub
The etchings of my lifeline
Passing the poverty of time
Rose red scores my hands
Mellow yellow soothes me
A dig of needles and pins entirely
Rubbing feverishly in my hope
Withered hands are near
    Alas;
Hands
    Hands
Antique brown
And
Still

Cheryl Pinckney

Truly Forgiven

I thought about you today and what you did to me;
I neither felt anger nor hostility.
I really don't know when this change took place;
I don't even know when I ceased feeling disgrace.
All I can say is that God spoke to me
And showed me the person that He planned me to be.
He said that compassion and a forgiving heart
Would take me to greater heights in the new life I would start.
I couldn't do it alone so God forgave you through me
And now you're truly forgiven and I've been set free.

Sharen Pinkett Pannell

People

What is wrong in this world below
People don't want to even say hello
They act as if it's a terrible sin
To let a little sunshine in.
We all have more then we deserve
We receive more blessings then we deserve
But it seems so hard for us to share
A friendly hello to show we care.
I hope that will never happen to me
I want the world to know Jesus lives in me
So I will say hello and smile
For he has brought me over many a mile
So why should you carry around a sad face
For God has put you in this place
So give a smile and warm hello
For we are all travelers here below.

Bernice Holmes

Secret Moments

More times that many, in doubt I have been about love, my life,
and my soul in sin. Always unknowing of what next I'd be, yet
dreaming my eyes would eventually see. Now still alone, I
envision a change, with bright new perspective, in not distant
range. I now view my life, my soul in past sin, never to cherish
that which has been!
There comes to all secret moments to share, new feelings, new hopes
with someone you care. I now have a someone who loves only me,
Who has made my eyes open to how good life can be! I now am able to
Return all he's shown, and tell him he's loved more than any I've
known. I confess as I gaze at the stars up above, my someone has
Shown me the true meaning of love!

Sandra M. Barthlein

Light And Darkness

Life, a challenge, a reality, a process of struggling and growing
Person, a being, a body, a spirit gliding through life's course
Light, the sun, a lamp, love from the Lord up above
Darkness, the night, evil, death when one lays to rest
Do not be afraid of the dark for at the end there is always light
Friends, companions, acquaintances, a need to make things better
Life is too short, the days go by all too fast
Fulfill your dreams, your goals, before time has gone a past
Come out from within the dark and friends bring into sight
For from their love, companionship and laughter will you see the light
Times you will fall and pick yourself back upon your feet
Times you will fall harder and someone will be there to lift you up
Remember where there is doubt, faith, where there is sadness, joy
Where there is life, happiness, where there is darkness, light
It's time now to be you, the person you are, the person within you
Only then will you find happiness, peace, when the real you is true.

Mark Dean

A Taste Of Mexico

The soul of Mexico was embedded in his soul
He built La Paloma and La Hacienda, so all would know
He brought their culture to our Ozark Land
Of the beauty below our borders — so we all could understand.
He served a menu as authentic as could be
As one tasted the food, all certainly would agree
With beautiful surrounding, so peaceful to feel
It was like being in Mexico, while eating your meal.

Norma Dotson Payne

Out Of The Darkness Into The Light

In Memorium for Dorothy Wolfe Hight
To find peace at a turbulent point in life,
I thought of you God . . .
Taking back the cancerous calamity,
The weakness, the pain out of my body.

I shiver under the hand of the one named Samael
And the angel of sudden joy
shakes me as I am waking in its way.

The dog sleeps a waking sleep at my feet,
And I sleep silent.

My few old friends are true,
My children love is tender,
My husband love is life.

When the rain lies on the ground and all looks very bleak,
We are not able to see the freshness of the spring . . .
But it comes.

After the storms and the wind of change have blown through my world's pain;
There always comes, without failure, the new life of spring.

There will come the spring of dreams and the summer of fulfillment.
All life is but a stepping stone out of the darkness into the light —
Few are there that will endure a true friend.

Joseph Rodrigues Jr.

As The Snow Falls On The Dampened Ground

As the snow falls on the dampened ground
there is silence, not even one sound
as I walk swiftly, I am homeward bound
leaving deep footprints, with each foot I put down
wintery whiteness, show's all over town
as the snow falls on the dampened ground
peacefulness, and serenity it surrounds
and thru my brain, thoughts go around and around
Thinking about this winter wonderland, that I have now found

Mary Francis Faith Foucault

Man's Supremacy, Ideas

Life on Earth, as we can see,
Gets better and better for you and me.
Machines have reduced the work of men,
As we realize inventions' effect, again and again.

The wheel barrow, wagon, and steam shovel too,
Are uses of the wheel to name a few.
The boat, radio, airplane, and my shoe,
Are examples of things old and new.

Energy equals mass times the speed of light squared,
Expressing original ideas not many men dared.
Einstein's formula brought on the Atomic Age,
Communications and calculations would be the next rage.

Machines that read books are a new kind,
That verbally can talk to a listener who's blind.
Personal computers the size of a wallet,
It takes men like Bill Gates to call it.

Six-wheeled vehicles soon will explore Mars,
Someday man will even explore the stars.
Just imagine things you'd like to see,
Work on them, think, and ideas will make them be.

John A. Strommen

Treading On The Sands Of Time

I've been treading on the sands of time.
Walking long and carefully on the line,
Like a harlequin the rhythm was mine.
And I laughed with happiness feeling sublime.
I've been feeling my way while hearing a chime,
Like a harlequin the rhythm was mine.
Balancing carefully all the way, across the
    measure of time
To reach the essence of Him . . . the Divine.

Shirley Friend

New Menu — New Cooks

We noticed the difference right away,
When meals were served, day by day.
As our food list was read,
We asked, "what's that"?
Our kitchen must have new cooks?
The meals have variable looks.
Garnishes and herbs, sprinkle our food,
Our eyes meet each other in a felicitous mood.
Plates before us are gourmet preparations,
We have concocted foods from other nations.
Boiling, broiling, baking, roasting, pervades the atmosphere,
From Applewood's kitchen, we have it all right here.
Why should we travel anywhere?
Thanks to our cuisine crew
For our menu, new.

Janina S. Davenport

More Than A Miracle

Life is more than a miracle if only we would see,
We take it all for granted . . . the acorn, then the tree.
The tiny grain of mustard seed put in the earth to grow
Breaks forth in great abundance, when we take time to sow.
As we face the many trials of life which come along each day,
They all happen for a reason . . . God created it that way.

He provides us with resources to cope with our dismay.
He shows us by example . . . always take time to pray.
He deals with every need in life, so we never should despair,
For we have but to ask Him and He is always there.
And in return, in grateful thanks, our duty is made clear,
To teach His word, again and again, until all eventually hear.

Margaret Plenk

Lucky Me

"Why am I so happy?,
You can see my tears of joy
I've won the Millionaire's Sweepstakes,
I didn't believe it, but it's the real McCoy."

"I've played this Sweepstakes many years,
And never gave up hope
I knew some day my ship would arrive,
Now I'll never have to learn how to cope."

"Ten million dollars is very great wealth,
To don with it all we can
This certainly was a shock to us,
We thought I'd be an also — ran."

"I plan to do so many things,
Take care of my family
New cars and homes, homes for our children,
For all debts they'll always be free."

"it's the beginning of a new day,
My alarm belched out a scream
I awoke to learn my ten million was gone,
This poor man's wind fall was only a dream."

Marty Rollin

The Joys Of Christmas

As the Christmas holiday season draws near,
I recall so many happy memories of yesteryear,
And savor the tranquil ambience of the enchanting scene.
I remember a tall, slender Christmas tree of evergreen,
Standing in all of its glorious pristine splendor;
Then trimmed with bright colored balls, and tinsel galore,
And tiny candles, and paper stars, and popcorn strings.
Under it, cookies and candy, and all sorts of good things.
And on the door, a holly wreath with a red ribbon bow,
Decorated with pine cones, and a sprig of mistletoe.
The cloying smell of spruce, and pine, and pungent spices,
Fills the air with all of the nostalgic aroma that entices.
Familiar carols, sung with renewed faith each Christmas,
Peace on earth, good will toward men; to no avail, alas.
Truly a solemn time of reverence, this momentous birthday,
But when I think of jolly old St. Nick, it is a time to be gay.
Hark, the sound of sleigh bells jingling in the snow, and Noel,
And all of the merry, and cheery good wishes said as well!
With an abundance of good food and drink, and friends to share,
It is a time to enjoy, celebrate, with your heart free from care.

Robert Unger

Fresh Growth

The trio of purposefully put pines
    on the upward sloping still verdant lawn
Had grown and combined their needled branch lines
    In a sole silhouette seen on Christmas Eve's dawn.

Over the eight Christmases that I have come
    To Ithaca's lake-towering South Hill
The pines' triple tops have hidden and then some
    the far farm opposite in the morning's chill.

Atop that wooded West Hill there newly stands
    A telephone tower crowned by a red light
Blinking its warning above wooded bands
    Below, two ruby ones shine steadily all night.

Carols and folksongs once warmly played by two
    Guys on guitar, one, who was my only son
Tonight strummed by one, languidly and true
    Sung by his sister, her husband and me for fun.

Christmas day delivers lake-effect snow
    The feathery fall licks the lawn now wan.
Fresh growth in inexorably echoes life's flow
    Ron, sorely-missed: Remembered, never gone.

Norman R. Nelsen

Let There Be No End!

December, it's the last month of every year!
When everyone prepares and set into high gear
Many actions for several important festivals
from Thanksgiving to New Years Eve without intervals.
Beside normal works there is so much to be done!
It takes all your time and to shop for presents in fun!
You keep that person in your mind and heart
Their character and try to match up the gift and the card!
Besides family members and dear old friends
there also are Companies with a very good brand.
They provide meals, presents and more to our poor.
Of course December tops this all and there is no cure!

Thank goodness for this opportunity of extra giving
because this goal is good for healing and very uplifting.
Be thankful and send very best wished, don't forget!
For Hanukkah, Christmas and the New Year still to come yet!
Let there be No end to this joy and inspiration
To do good, that will give birth to an inner admiration!

Johanna A. Garretson

The Morning Chill

I jumped out of bed at my first call
Shivered and shook in the shower stall
put on my jogging suit and headed out the door
I remembered it seemed colder than before
That feel in the air was certainly fall
The northwest wind was putting up quite a squall
As I rounded the corner and to the West
No doubt in my mind, I like
warm weather best
Suddenly I remembered
how I used to like the cold
But things have changed since I've gotten old
Well I made it back from my morning run
No use trying to make believe that it's fun
So if you're reading this and saying it's not cold
Just remember you're
young, but wait till you're old
You too will feel this in
later years some fall
Morning chill will get you or my name isn't Paul

Paul E. Sidebottom

I Am An American

I am an American,
a heritage to be proud.

I will not barter freedom for a quelled life,
it is not within my stride.

I desire to deliberate, and function as the night,
for it is my posterity to stand upright.

I choose not to be an ordinary man,
'tis my obligation to be uncommon if I can.

I wish to take the speculation of seed,
to dream and build, to fail, to succeed.

I want to leave upon the sand,
footprints that shall climb.

I must confront the world audaciously,
not put myself in privacy.

I cannot go to the extremity,
and claim self-sufficiency.

I prefer the challenges of life,
to the state calm of Utopia.

I would like to say to the world,
"This I have achieved!"

Daniel J. Evans

Ghosts, Shadows And Light

Ghosts flicker from here to there.
Try to avoid them; they only cause despair.
But to shove off to the side, to ignore
only causes disrepair more and more.
Shadows do come and they also go.
They have a similarity of ghosts. They show.
Hidden truths want to be out in the light
not to be forbidden and cast off into the night.
Light flashes area to its point of rest
and does not have a habit of showing always the best.
It is capable of blinding the Strongest Man.
The power of it is able to consume and plan.
Ghosts, shadows and light all share the night
And at their will they feel they have a right to roam in flight.

Lisa Lindstrom

This Vampire

This vampire agonizes over the evil she feels churning inside,
And the beauty and purity she wants to see.
Observing the world through her eyes, you would see nothing so beautiful
And pure as the beginning and the end of the night

She searches for someone who sees the world as she sees it:
Empty and devoid of the miracles of good,
Except for the miracle of life itself.
Yet is bringing a pure, innocent soul into a world of evil such a grand wonder?

This vampire thirsts for the blood that runs through the dark
side of the soul.
If she could drink it all in, and there would be none left but inside her,
She herself could be consumed in the flames,
And the world could arise in a pure dawn.

Katrina Smith

The Minyon

It is morning and the sun has barely risen,
It's cold outside, it's really freezing.
Must get dressed and be on my way,
This is the beginning of a brand new day.

Nine people in the synagogue waiting for me,
The minyon is made as the 10th person I'll be.
Silently, always, all the prayers can be read,
But with a minyon Borchu and Kaddish can now be said.

It isn't easy being a Jew,
Less than 1% of the population is very few.
Our place in this world is very special,
The truth is we are very essential.

We are the conscience of all the people
Our voice is like a bell from the tallest steeple.
God is there, listening and watching all the time,
The minyon, ten Jewish people together, the hallowed sign.

Sondra Eisenpress

A Poet's Recompense

Through toil and travail are true poems born,
Not by playing with words as in a game;
Meaningless monstrosities trite and lame
Have come rhyming into a world forlorn.
As something from nothing can ne'er be torn,
Those who steal another's musings, then claim
Them as their own may reap cheap fees like fame,
But secondhand visions will bear but scorn!
Compositions without price to be paid
Are doomed to decompose, i.e. decay.
Yet, composers there be whom God has bade
Do this: Express the lifeblood from each day,
Transfuse if to the veins of man and maid,
Then glory as it's lived and loved away.

Richard G. Rinker

A Loser Wins Beauty

There is more than one way out loser guy.
You have slipped into the beautiful lady's heart.
Perfection of form meeting hard-fated life is why,
You are intrigued but afraid of this new start.

A kiss encourages rejection of desperate ways.
A kamikaze receives an invitation to live.
Exit the nothingness in a tiresome, tortuous maze.
Accept the cure for alienation the lady has to give.

Welcome to a radiant realm of unparalleled pleasure.
You are amazed how emotions now support rebirth.
The lady is a breathtaking and bewitching treasure.
Wow, what a revelation to feel a sense of worth.

Her love drips into your soul sustaining critical care.
The serum spirits you free from relapse danger.
Your scarred being, uplifted, transcends total repair.
Salvation for a loser from an alluring, former stranger.

Like a movie you could write, act in and direct,
You have captured the starring role in her eyes.
The plot would be love's longevity without defect;
Two on one wavelength until the transmitters die.

Ken Miller

A Flower

Summer arrives
  Sunshine brings life
Its petals blossom
  Adding color to a world of black and white

Fall is here
  The greenish earth changing to a brownish-red
A leaf takes a trip from a tree
  Floating freely through the air
Landing in a pile that kids dive into like a bed

Winter comes
  The chill hides the beauty of a bud from the rest of the world
Its frost making white of what was once vibrant
  Taking away its soul which we cherish
An oyster without a pearl

Spring blossoms
  Bees come to feed these beautiful creations
As they return for us to enjoy
  Filling our noses with their wondrous scents
Our hearts with elation

Adam Chapin

Jenna, Alias Sweet Pickle, And The Octopus

Little girl, will you hurry up?
Will you grow unscared
And go to the Fair and with me
And ride the Octopus?
I love it so!
It makes me laugh and laugh and laugh
From the first spin to the last.
People down on the ground
Smile and point at me
They hear me laugh as I whirl past.
Everybody loves to see and hear a laugher,
Don't they? They wish they could be me!
So hurry up sweet pickle,
My little teaspoon, my tumblebug.
I want to go to the Fair
With you, unscared,
And ride the Octopus,
So we can laugh together,
And have nothing else to do
But that!

Jane Wiles Ratcliffe

He Makes Me Look Good

Within my nature . . . that is, of the flesh
toils an existence filled with emptiness
While, also inside . . . my soul does enmesh
a life more abundant, full of success

In times of troubles though I seek what's right
I yet lack knowledge to grasp what I should
When all of a sudden . . . like a bright light,
God's wisdom shines, and He makes me look good

In the darkest hour of any crisis,
we're yet afforded quite an advantage;
The wisdom God gives, when not asked amiss
enlightens eyes above the average

Understanding comes, but not of ourselves . . .
too often we think **our** minds understood
It's then God's wisdom easily dissolves
our own ignorance and makes us look good

So next time you know you've done the right thing,
and your confidence just carries you through
Take heed lest you fall . . . you may be using
an awareness that **never** came from you!

Bob G. Martinez

The Kittens

As I sit one summer night,
I remember the kittens, Powder, Puff, and Light.
In the garden we used to play,
Every single warm spring day.
As each rose petal softly fell,
The kittens pounced, played, and purred as well.

Now the sleeping kittens lay,
On their warm and cozy hay.
But their watchful mother prowls,
For the wolves whose frightening howls,
Can wake the kittens in pure fright,
And keep them up all the night.

But now with winter coming on hard,
The kittens must stay in the warm barn.
And with plenty of mice, the kittens will learn,
How to catch the nuisance, and have a dinner earned.
Next spring they will be too old to play,
But I shall have more kittens, someday.

Jessie Lynne Hughes

From Slime To Sublime

Roused from slumber by the rising sun
Lotus petals open one by one,
Filling with perfume the world around
And displaying charms therein abound.

Up above the water the flowers lie,
What a sight for nature-lover's eye!
Yet their roots are buried in the slime
Whence to such enchanting heights they climb.

Like the lotus is the human soul,
Buried, though, in nature, yet its goal
Rises high to Heav'nly realms above
Through the sacred path of selfless love.

Blest is the soul with godly powers,
Timeless are the virtues that it flowers,
For its sacred being is made in line,
Not with nature, but with life divine.

Christ's command to His church is to feed
His sheep with Celestial Food they need;
And what else can that food ever be!
Save pure love that sets the whole world free.

Luke Jayasuriya

Hollywood

A wonderful thing. The weather, here is what it's all about,
When it's raining you stay in, when it's sunny, you go out!
The west coast, where it seldom rains, (at least, that's what they say)
There are those days you stay inside, 'Til raindrops go away!

There's very seldom any snow in freezing winter time,
If you want snow you'll have to go, and up a mountain climb.
When you descend, the snow will end and it's bikini time,
The beaches call, you'll have a ball, the swimmin' is so fine.

There's movie stars and shiny cars and gorgeous gals by far,
So many of them get to be a future movie star,
The days of Gable, Barrymore, have long since come and gone,
Though others follow in their place, most hams don't last too long!

The part you had in high school when you acted in a play,
Is now your reason why you're seeking good old MCA,
They may say you're a Bogart, even say you look like Cruise,
But when you pick an agent, just be careful whom you choose!

You're captured by the sunshine and there's glamour all around,
A lot of glitter in your eyes and treasures to be found,
Be cautious and be careful baby, watch your peas and cues,
And what is most important, don't forget your union dues!

Herb Walsh

Sittin' On A Log

I'm out in the forest, sittin' on a log,
Sittin' here thinkin' about my little dog;
Thinkin' how he'd loved these crisp, fall days,
Missin' him in so many little ways.

Rememberin' how he'd put his soft little nose
Between his wee paws when he settled to doze,
Or go sniffin' around a gopher's hole.
To see where they went was his only goal.

He loved to walk in the woods with me,
Stopping to sniff at every tree.
He'd have loved this old log I'm sittin' on,
And perhaps that old tree that's been written on.

So here I am, sittin' all alone,
Rememberin' my dog and his favorite bone.
Sittin' on a log in a forest of pine,
Thinkin' of that dog that used to be mine!

Marjorie Thompson Sims

Sister's Retreat

Every year we meet
for our sister's retreat
just to wander around
and see what can be found

We've crabbed and blabbed
hunted shells by the shores
and dreamed our dreams
while laying around eating ice cream

We've breathed in the mountain air
as we sat in rocking chairs
and we've dipped in oceans and ponds
with oooh . . . my goodness . . . nothing on

I call you "sistee ugler"
wouldn't want no other
you call me "belinda butt"
cause you love me so much
we just have these names
they've always been our game

So here's to our retreats,
they can't be beat

Kay Determan

17

True Freedom

True freedom
Is only an idea, an abstract obsession.
Many men and women have died in hopes of it.
Their bodies lie still
And we forget them.
Mocking their bravery for stupidity.
"Fools" we say,
For dying.
But who are the fools?
The ones living in chains or
The ones that fought to be released.
Today we are closer than we were
Yesterday, but still a great distance from
True freedom.

Iva M. Martin

Candle In The Wind

Something came into my dream last night
in flickering shades of dark and light,
becoming a sort of a shadowy scene
from back in the days of silent screen.
A devious mist soon began
to form the murky shape of a man,
who suddenly then did speak my name,
as though the beginning of talkies came.
Chanting grimly at me, he said:
"Beware, my child, of how you tread!
For all the souls that ever have sinned
are only a candle in the wind!"
Before I could wonder what it meant,
into the silent screen he went,
pointing at answers all aglow,
in subtitles — down below.

Nancy McKeen

Now

Don't load my grave with roses
Or a wreath upon my head
Or sing to me softly
As soon as I am dead;
Or have a great big funeral
For all to see me there.
Let me smell those flowers while I live,
To show me that you care.

A small kiss upon my cheek
And certainly a great big hug;
Sing with me those happy songs
Before my grave is dug.
Shake my hand, be my friend
In those days, before.
Love me; take my love;
I could not ask for more.

And don't put off 'til tomorrow
The things we should have done.
You know about tomorrows.
Tomorrows never come.

Harry E. Labrake

Anarchy Of Virtuousness

To give, is a gift. To keep giving, leaves you empty and cold.
To believe and trust is comforting, but the reality of this keeps
you in the claws of despair, feeding on its live prey. I am
entangled in this tight grasp of injurious, its claws caught deep
in my flesh, digging deeper 'till I gasp for my last breath of this
foul air that surrounds me, for I have been too trusting and
forgiving to carry on in this swarthy evil world. Therefore, I
have to step off the comfort of my virtuous mountain and fall
deep into the claws of evil in order to survive.

Susan M. Davis

Desire

I'm going to write myself a note
when the moonlight touches my window.
In a wink of an eye I'll see you there
in all the words that I wrote.

I'm going to fill in the missing words
with hearts and flower petals.
The I's are dotted with kisses,
the borders with flying birds.

Moonbeams kiss my pen so light
shining in silver and gold.
I see the smile that kindles my soul
in this vision of the night.

Before the moonlight fades away
in shadows of purple hue.
I declare my love for you
in words of passion lay.

My pen flies across the page
writing words of love so dear.
You're with me so short a time
in a night that's short on age.

Carol Pfankuchen

Recycled Gifts

Paper and glue are cheaper than new;
    Put together with love.
A gift from the heart will set it apart.
Avoid the shopping mall shove.

Children all know that parents will glow;
    When handed their creation.
Their primary scrawl will hang on the wall;
Guaranteed to produce elation.

Pick out a card with a surface that's hard;
    Decorated with gold.
Use paper as wide to fit inside;
Tied together with yarn at the fold.

After you've seen that magazine;
    Never throw it away.
Till you cut out that cake somebody can bake;
For a future holiday.

Make a book to give the cook;
    Now put that cake inside.
Paste recipe where plain to see;
Alas! A gift to pride.

Julia Dixon Collett

The Smell Of You

The smell of you reminds me of what we were, together
the feel of your skin was satin to my touch
the silkiness of your hair upon my cheek
was a treasure to be fondled . . . overmuch.

For all these things that I remember
there have to be a million more . . .
the slither of a silk chemise . . . discarded
as it falls is disarray upon the floor.

The rustle of two lovers close together
as they memorize each and every thing
about that other person's being
with kisses . . . touches . . . and a new awakening.

What's gone is gone but not forgotten
my memories taunt me . . . day and night . . . passing in review
it's all brought back to be lived over . . .
all because I smelled the smell of you.

Joan M. Johnson

Confusion Of The Heart

In the dark recesses of my disconcerted heart
Turmoil and ecstasy mirror feelings of my soul
Tortured by an image of no understanding
Somehow lost to me in the tempest of my life's role

Bewildered by changes to my physical being
Tempted by the lust growing inside my mind and heart
Twisted by the temptation of seduction and sin
Lost in an imaginary world, I play a part

Outwardly projecting that I am calm and serene
Showing compassion and love I easily can share
Inwardly tormented by whirlwinds of my feelings
Trying desperately to disentangle my despair

Out of my confusion a radiant light shines on me
Slowly sympathetic consciousness comes from above
My feelings now pour out in unlimited boundaries
You have entered my disordered life to give me love

Carol Lloyd

My Father

When I used to think of my Dad,
nothing came to my mind
because I never knew him
he was never there
to listen, to learn, or to encourage me
or to watch me grow up
he was never there to love me
but then one day something happened
my father came to me and said
he was sorry
and he wanted to be a part of my life
he wanted to be my father
my father came back and was better then ever
he started to listen and learn
he started to encourage me and watch me grow up
he was there when I needed him
that was all that mattered to me
he was there to support and love me
I had found my father and he was
finally a part of my life and I love him

Amanda Martin

Ode To Christopher

Christopher is eighteen, I've watched him grow
from a boy into a fine young man I respect and
adore so. To little kids, he looks like a giant.
So big, so strong — yet gentle and soft-spoken.
Through rough times and sad, he's been right there
with a gentle touch, or hug, or just a boyish grin to
comfort me. Around him I never feel uncomfortable,
or afraid to cry. One look from him and I know, we
have a special bond that continues to grow. His life is
just starting. Each night I pray to God to just keep
him safe and let him be happy. You see, I want
him around for a long, long time to pick at me,
talk to, and tease me.

Teresa Meadows

Christmas Mood

Christmas will come in four days.
I am in Christmas moods.
My Christmas spirits are delightful and happiness.
Our Christmas tree is a Christmas spirited with bright lights on them.
I am thinking about others more often.
We also expected a White Christmas this year.
This will be the best Christmas I will ever have.
I am spiritual in Jesus Christ on the day He was born and
everyday always.

Monica L. Bennett

The Candle

We'll light a candle in memory of you
Your light will shine brightly, through and through
We think of you each day, as time passes by
We know you're at peace, in heaven on high
Many times I'll envision you, and ponder awhile
When I picture your face, it's with a smile
When you came home at night, I always felt so snug
With your arms around me, in a great big hug
One day God took you home, to be with him
Since then our light has been so dim
Your light shines in heaven, and our memories are of you
Once again, your light shines through and through

Judy Lea Ehrke

Forever Lover

You knew me from the beginning of time
Wanting an intimate relationship
For the longest time I didn't return Your calls

You wanted me to love You
Debauchery headed my list
I expelled You my perfect Lover

You wooed me with consideration
You were hoping I would come
To share the embrace

My stubbornness didn't allow me
Sorrow drowned my poetry
I was heading to nowhere

Whimpering for someone to sweep me off my feet
A comrade pointed to You
Hesitating to go the altar

Six days later I embraced You
Your voice relieved my stress
You are my God

Donald Taylor

Wakeful Night

It's lonely to be the last one awake.
If I could fall into a wakeless sleep
But for tonight I can only count sheep
One, two, three, four until the new day breaks.

At last an effort to arise I make
Tiptoeing through the quiet house I creep
My slumbering family's silence to keep
Careful of each and every step I take
Then to my desk to sit and try to write
And think of things long forgotten and gone

For the time is early in the stilled night
For putting words into refrains for songs
Now finishing with a great writing at last
It's good I didn't fall asleep too fast

Dale Ward

Dimensions

There are dimensions in the sky,
The earth, the moon, the clouds on high —
Especially where small children roam
There are dimensions hard to place
The distant dimensions of outer-space

There are dimensions man cannot see
God holds in trust for you and me

This great dimension and far more

To be revealed at Death's Great Door!

Lillian Bracher Platt

The Happy Camper

I am a happy camper, I can attest to that
I put a smile on everyday no matter where I am at
I never let people know how down I am at times
I just smile and say I am happy all the time
You and be a happy camper it does not take to much
We all have our ups and downs, but why take it to lunch
When you wake each day, just put on a smile and be glad
An you will soon be the one to start a fad
Troubles follow us all around
But we do not haft to spread it all around
I am a happy camper, I can attest to that
Just ask anyone who knows me, and you can rest assure
that I will always put on a smiley face
and even tip my hat,
So come on and join me, an together we will go hand and hand
Who knows we may end up happier by far
And we might be the happiest camper in the land.

Mary Elizabeth Tucker

The Angel Tree

A leaf broke away, spinning to the earth
droplets of dew formed from unheralded sadness

As the leaf spiraled downward, a beautiful angel
plucked it from the air, admiring perfection.
Divine breath pushed it high above her
wafting upward, the leaf glistened. Rays of light
gently tugged until forward motion was felt.
Brightness arrived

Pure love formed a golden aura as the leaf
slowly turned, twinkling into a star.

Past debts, discrimination and blind eyes,
now become an illumines trove,
all pain forgotten and forgiven.

Sandra Hawkins

Turning Wheels

Wheels of all kinds are turning
On trucks, on trains, and airplanes on the ground
But when I look into his eyes
I see different kind of wheels going around

Round and round they will go
No stopping until he reaches his goal.
What wonders to perform as a doctor,
An astronaut, President, a great life to behold

Could we hold him back a little,
Perhaps a detour or a curve
To keep him within our reach
A while longer for the guidance he deserves

Wheels of the clock, need not to be pushed
Because, after all, Brandon's only five
And no matter where his wheels take him
Our love for him remains forever alive.

Ruth D. Bergeron

"Look!"

At what, I thought, and closed my eyes
I've seen it all . . . there's no surprise
"Hurry, you'll miss this wonderful view."
"The sun's so bright, the sky's so blue!"
So blue, so what, I wanted to say.
To me it's just another day.
Where will it lead me? What will it do?
To look and look at a sky so blue.

Joan Bierman

Aisle 9

The woman's child licks her lollypop and catches my hungry eye
As we approach
It's awkward but when isn't it? We're both trying to go about our affairs
In this most inconveniently convenient of public places
I rub my eyeballs over the spaghetti sauce — $3.59 — is this good?
I must fill the cart, the woman must compare pasta prices
Across from where I stand, slouched and slack-jawed — a domesticated vulture
But we can't get out carts to cooperate, what with the palsied front wheel
So we check our coordinates and pick a reference point — deli or register
Just beyond to avoid an accident
I attempt a joke about narrow aisles and big carts and get a reaction
From the child, whose gooey lolly, now extended in gleeful ignorance
Flip-flops flush against my khakis. The pant is sticky and the lolly is woolly
We bend in to rescue and in doing so that jar — that jar of $3.59 spaghetti sauce
Crashes to the skid-marked floor
"Clean up in aisle 9" was never so loud as to modify my skin color
The child's reaction quickly changes, it is upset, the annoyed woman,
The unmanageable simian, extricate themselves from metal cage
With lumbering lexicon, step gingerly back to safety and better luck

In another aisle

Andrew Richard Dorr

Dusted Memories

Did you ever, in teenage days, try your hand at sculpture play,
Arm yourself with knife or ax, and carve on trees as though 'twas wax?
The Beeches, high behind our barn, could tell such tales, but
most of them have by man been felled
And the initials we had there entwined are now but memories of the mind,
And the old barn where we oft did play is but a ghostly sentinel
of her former self.
So we just dust our memories and return them to their shelves.

But first, let us go on down the 'holler,' and cross the water gap,
Hear again the sound of iron, as the horses feet clang out;
Walking stiffly o'er the Limestone, taking each his careful step,
Lest he slip and throw his rider on the rocks so slick and wet.

Then below this water gap, where the gullies made a bluff,
If we questioned what was told us, we might even get a 'cuff,'
For 'twas here our Great Aunt Lizzie said she'd found our baby fair,
And it made us look and wonder, 'Could we find another there?'

Oh! Those days of 'tender wonder,' brought to life through memory's will.
Yes, we take them out and dust them,
But in our minds they linger still.

Ina Askew

The Private Rain

Tears drench a silent night;
   the pillow encompasses the dreary eyes.
The frigid air fills the days,
   behind lukewarm phony smiles.

Times overflow with empty laughter.
   Endless talk to fill the hours.
Celebrations that hold no substance;
   left with convenient companionship.

How can we be surrounded
   with people all the time?
Yet in a private world
   our barren souls cry out.

Through all our inner turmoil
   and our quiet aggravations,
We yearn like the tiniest child
   just to be cared for.

Do the jewels of the world count
   if there is no one to hold you?
The strength of love and peace,
   can only make our days easier.

Robert P. Lipsey

Ode To An American Legend

In the bosom of my soul, deep-blue, dark sea,
I once picked the key
to your climb so tight, and your flight so free!
And I shuddered at the criss-crossing of those marooned,
bound for the moon!
And how I bowed to the stunts of your journey
marred by the ghosts of the coffle-gang!
Though all I did, as in a rage I flew,
my simple deed was to revere a new
your being split asunder, that stir of your feather,
making the world wonder:
What's in the shadow that it be soothingly morose,
the standing of the pillars, the rustling of the willows . . .?
Your pebbles into my blackened hole
keep on rippling my golden goal,
as I gaze at the hilltop, watching, locked up
in your plight, that one skylark, just as I walk the field
harvesting all that you have sown all through the peal
of your horn
Lena Horne!

Narcisse G. Malary

My Heart

When you fall in love with a dreamer
You never know where you stand,
One day you're in his life
The next you're no where around.

I've been down this road a few times
Each time it just gets worse
I try to be strong and stand my ground
But my heart gives in and I'm caught.

How much more can one heart stand,
Before it breaks into?
How many more men will I find, who only remind me of you?

I still look for you everywhere
I still remember when I hear a song
Or see a car like you used to have,
My mind goes wandering back to you.

Wondering if you're happy in this new life that you're found
Wondering if you ever think of me
And the times we had just hanging around.

How much more can one heart stand before it breaks into?
And how many more men will I find who only remind me of you . . .

Debbie Raye Manley Gulley

My Praying Garden

When I walk in my garden I go to my pond
and knee on the ground. Then I look in the
water what do I see my face looking up at me.

When I look deep into the pond I can see my
past flashing in front of me. I can see how
I became successful and how many times
I had failed.

I thought it start to rain when drop's fell
into the pond not realizing it was my own
tears I saw. I wish I could go back in my
past and change some of the things I have
done and finish what I left undone

If only I could go back I would thank all the
people who gave me joy and love. Then tell
all the people that I hurt by words or action
how sorry I am.

Tear's on my face I look up from my pond into the
heavenly sky and ask God please forgive all my sin's
in my past and also for my sins for today.

Nancy Szydlo

A Thing Of Beauty

"A thing of beauty is a joy forever,"
a talented one once said,
but "beauty's in the eye of the one who beholds"
is one other thing I've read.

The beautiful meshing of things together
though some would but call it fate —
like the sudden cry of a lone bird calling,
the quick answer of his mate.

A day in the fall when the breeze is blowing
the acorns come thudding down,
and a look o'er the meadow where green was growing
finds patches now turned to brown.

Or trees in the winter when leaves have fallen
their limbs looking stark and bare,
we look away for a moment not watching —
a blanket of snow is there!

O how can we live in the world not seeing
the beauty of earth we've trod?
Each "thing of beauty is a joy forever,"
and comes from the hand of God!

Marguerite H. Atkins

The Warlords

I lie here sleepless and I hear
Their strident voices, loud and clear,
As warlords clamor in their need
To sate their appetites and greed.
They call and we, like sheep, obey.
Our sacrificial lambs they slay
As history adds another page
Of infamy and mass outrage.
How many more wars must be fought!
How many dreams must come to naught!
How many tears must fall, like rain
How many boys must die in vain
As warlords sit in seats of state
And callously decree their fate!
The bloody battles will not cease
Nor mankind learn to live in peace
While warlords lust and men inflame
With "holy" wars . . . all in "God's name,"
While they, who in His image, came,
Mock Him and defile His name.

Esther Robbins Maltun

Death By Suicide

Kill me now he used to say
Kill me now I can't live another day
I hate my life nothing goes right
Take me God take me tonight
Nobody likes me I haven't got a friend
I wish I would die so my misery would end
My grades are all bad all my classes I flunk
People around me think I'm a punk
I'm not a jock that's surely not me
I'm just another kid that no one can see
No one believes me they think I'm a fake
Lets see what they think when the bullet's not a blank
Kill me now is what he said
The signs he gave we misread
We thought it was a phase that he would overcome
I wish I would have listened how could I be so dumb
He said he hated his life and he didn't have a friend
But it's not really true and it's sad to see it end
I wish I could have stopped him, but now my son has died
Another child is gone due to Death by Suicide

Shelley Raguse

21

Angel Light

In the dark, as I sleep you are there
Guarding and watching the dreams lest I wake
You are my angel light — shining the path ahead
With heavenly star-glow
When I fall, I hear your wings rush to help me
Rise from some moral trap covered with guile
Up I come into the starry sky, the rush to love
Encompasses the fear and I am well
As I toil, You watch carefully my back so my
Enemies can't stab me with falsehoods
You are my birth angel assigned by God
To protect the road I must walk in my worldly trip
You are the friend that dries my tears
And feels the pain of my defeats, always there for me to ask
The many favors that I seek
Never judging, only giving love and hope
Mighty as the lighting and soft as a baby's touch
You are there, quiet as a hummingbird awaiting my next peril
Angel Of Light — Angel Of Love — Angel Of God

Robert S. Nicolini

The Person Inside

Light as a feather
Big as a house
No one can hear me, not even a mouse
The heart feels so small, inside feelings so deep

The thoughts inside continue to creep
The person inside continues to be,
The phenomenal woman I'll never be
Eyes so bright and a smile so fake

The tears that fall can form a lake
I pretend I am happy, but really I'm not
The person inside I've soon forgot
I hope every night that I cried
That one day I'll be
    The person inside

Yvonne H. Harley

Jesus My Savior

Jesus my Savior, Jesus my Savior,
I confessed to Him my sin,
He forgave them one and all.
He too can be your Friend, Jesus my Savior.
If to Him you give your all,
He will hear you when you call.
Jesus my Savior, Jesus my Lord.

Floyd W. Danley

Bingo

Some players come in
Others drift in slow;
But regardless — first or last
They're all here to play bingo!

Some come when the manager opens the door;
Some come early to get a certain seat.
Others reserve a table for four
And place their daubers and papers neat.

Some come to bingo to relax
And hopefully a few dollars win.
Others play big, hoping to take home the max
And to holler, "Bingo," while smiling at their next of kin.

Some are young; some are old.
Some have hair of blonde, brown, black or gray;
But if they can holler, "Bingo,"
Then they care not about who's-who anyway.

Ouida Nell Greene

Clock-Work-In-Motion

Into the silence with little, or no summons
everlasting winds of nature sometimes turn
catastrophic
as pouring rains fill thunderous skies
words of deception flood the eyes
bursting forth with no rhyme, or
reason, in depth emotions run wild
I now proceed with little caution
faced with doubt and uncertainty
confinement prolongs,
Courage and strength fluctuates
autonomy
living and learning are only
clock-work-in-motion
Overcome by paths and crooked ways
I took a much needed break
down memory lane
one I walked through and from
gaining stability and control

Carolyn Dooley

Winter Warmth

My friend Althea asked me
If fairies kissed the trees.

Their crystal spires touched the sky
Like blossoms more fiery
Than the blush of summer chestnuts.
The crisp crack of diamonds under booted feet
More lush than verdant grass between bare toes.
Though the sun shone distant, pristine and cold,
Althea's brown skin warmed the day,
Her child-reed voice like bird song.

I don't know if fairies kissed the trees.
I know they kissed her.

Eileen Z. Cohen

Eighty Years

I carry no magic or brass metal shield
I wear no shell to protect or hide my soul,
I am no rock or rolling stone
But a man who wishes to be his own.

Both pain and sorrow, have touched my heart,
Gave no quarter to one that steals.
In truth may I grow as a mighty tree.
May the spirit of love live within me.

I am wise in my given number of years
I fear no sword or guilt, for another man's tears.
I have no ax to grind but that of my own,
I was built to be, a loving son.

My world has a complete supply of strangers,
Worms, bugs, politicians and nosey neighbors.
I am responsible for myself, no judge of others,
Pray I might understand, each one of my brothers.

Joe Staker

Wolf Sky

Alone beneath the cloud cloaked sky
No longer any reason to wonder why
Destined, like the lone wolf, to hunt alone
Same results repeated, I should have known
Slapped down again after reaching out
No more attempts for me, there's no doubt
Alone beneath the cloud shrouded sky
Like the wolf, to the moon, alone I do cry.

Vickie L. Sandy

Drifting Away

Standing in formation
we wait for each new cue;
as voices speak of love divine
and how they will be true.

I listen to the music;
guiding them on their way
and find myself easily "Drifting Away"

Hopes and dreams merge like a lullaby
I think of what might have been
or what might just come true.

Dreams are forming on musical notes dancing to the tunes.
Alone they are but a sound, a noise,
Unmoving to the heart.

Together they feed hope, hunger and thirst;
together they are life. Standing alone a single
notes makes no music, but together they orchestrate
in harmony forming an enchanting tale to delight.
So it is when two people who are separate turn in love
towards one another. They are two living as one making
a melody of music together.

Jeanne Marie Brewer

World Of Dream

I dream for you, as you
dream for me in a world of dream, that
never seem to sleep, as they spin together
it is sure to be. So let it grow from the
heart of the dream as it sort's through
ours minds in the world of beliefs,
that there is a dream always striving
toward ours hearts from the world
of dreams to the bottom of our hearts
as we see our hearts through each
other eyes and minds, so let it be as we
find ourself in a world of dreams

David L. White

Take Heed

I've just begun to realize,
a woman's work is never done.
There is nothing sadder than a face..
Who has to hurry, then has to race
who wishes she was lost in space,
  because
Out there, there is nothing to do, except
float around on clouds of blue
and refresh herself with morning dew.

Julia Y. Cash

The Frontier Of Daybreak

Sunrise smiles its slender sliver
Upon a waking world.
Its boundary halts the stony night of earth,
Partitions frozen landscape from eternal skies,
Portends glories and mysteries beyond.
A parade emerges of brilliant orange and blue,
Escorting a cornucopia of clouds,
Illuminates this juncture for the soul.
Light intensifies, colors magnify,
The play unfolds, always at the border.
The seedtime and the harvest spring solely on the edge.
Only in the margin are the struggle and the dance.
Each daybreak is a frontier,
A nascent crescent between the rock and the veil.

Paul Langley

My Final Wish

I try to sleep, but I can't.
I'm lying here wide awake wishing, hoping that I could die.
I just want to sleep forever. The angel of death appears to me.
He is so beautiful — like nothing I have ever seen before.
He can hear my wishes without me even telling him.
He caresses my hair so lovingly, so gently.
Ah, my angel, my lover, my life, my destiny . . .
I look into his eyes.
They are filled with love and kindness.
I can sense that he loves me.
No one else has ever loved me, but, yes, he does. His love is genuine.
He bows down and whispers into my ear, "Close your eyes. I
will wait with you until you fall asleep."
I trust him so completely.
He has brought a new feeling to me, a child-like innocence.
I close my eyes wanting my problems to fade away.
Everything is gone far, far away from me.
My problems have vanished.
Now, I am asleep . . . Farewell.

Melissa Aimée Midkiff

Wreaths Of Dandelions

When I was young,
I used to sit under my pear tree,
Protected by my rainbow,
Watched over by my horizon,
And I made wreaths of dandelions.
So they laughed, they looked, and they stared.
And nothing was right about me,
I wasn't like them.
Their eyes pierced through the thin layer of skin surrounding my body,
And they infected me like a virus.
My whole body was devoured by this tingly feeling,
So I start to shake, and then finally,
When I begin to collapse,
When nothing continues to hold me high above the ground,
I find myself just sitting under my pear tree,
Protected by my rainbow,
Watched over by my horizon,
And I know now nothing is gonna hurt me tonight.
So I just sit and feel dazed, thinking,
And maybe one day I'll start making wreaths of dandelions again.

Joanna Grant Kels

OKC's Custodial F.B.I. And Ms. T.

After her, someone must have lost the mold
"Service" is she; this fact, I have been told.
With magic precision and the phones on hold
She designs each day's schedules, as they unfold.

In all the world, where is any other
Lest it be our sister, Nanny, or mother
Who totally accepts and understands us all
Dispatches jobs and picks us up when we fall.

She remembers us and "the" when (?)
While being efficient and staying in trend.
She calls us each by our right name.
She hears complaints and places little blame.

The cheerful kindness projected in her voice
Almost seems to leave us with a personal choice
When she asks, "What's all this row?"
Or simply directs, "I need you to help me, now."

This is a compassionate and considerate lady.
Never would she stoop to do any deal shady.
She's made our custodial flock of the F.B.I
And, as Friends, Brothers, and In-Laws. We do try.

Donna M. Baker

Borders

Brown, Yellow, Black, White — courtships marriages, families
Love, hate, toleration, prejudice.   Hope?

Man-made/natural disasters, violence, war
Deaths, injuries, tears
Volunteers, law, arbitrators.

Mosques, synagogues, temples, churches — isolation,
misunderstandings
Prayer, indulgence, togetherness, brotherhood.

Droughts, starvation, fleshless frames, pestilence
Sympathy, benefit concerts, donations, airlifts, medical personnel.

Have-nots — homeless, ill-housed, ragged, shoeless, hungry,
crippled, sick
Resignation, despair, desperation, supplication.

Haves — extending: empathy, medical/technical know-how,
necessities, material possessions, education.

Black, Brown, White, Yellow —
Resilience, unity, love, bonding.   Hope!

Tillie Atkins

Golden Haired Babe Of My Youth

Dear golden haired babe of my youth, count the candles I see,
twenty-one?
How can time go by so quickly, seems like yesterday you were just one
Sweet little girl with the solemn blue eyes, who clung to them of my dress
I look at you now, so tall, so mature, so full of fun and liveliness.

I've tried to teach you the values that will bring you inner wealth
The basic creed is simple, treat others as you would yourself
I know now this won't work for all as many can't fill the bill
The secret is first liking yourself and I know you always will

Love your children as we've loved you and teach them right
from wrong
Remember to always hold them and kiss them and sing them
your lullaby song
Dear golden haired babe of my youth, someday you know we
must part
But as I once held you in my arms through all time I'll hold you
in my heart.

Patricia Rodermund

how can this be

how can a healthy man — die a fifty-nine
   while another — lame in body
and feeble in mind — lives on   through a century?

how can a mother and two young daughters
die in a plane — Oh the pain
for the man they left behind
   while another — no family to care
no reason to beware — made it explode
while watching from below — no one can know
lives on   score after score?

how can a young teen — die before his time
long before he proves what he can do
   while another — living in a cell
for the innocent lives he felled — yet
he lives on   decade after decade?

how can the new baby die at his birth
ingress and ingress combined
who could be so blind — dismiss the injustice
   while another — driving impaired time after time
of course he doesn't care   lives on year after year?

Barbara L. Scott

Loving An Army Ranger

Loving a Ranger is not an easy thing;
Worrying about him being called away
whenever the phone should ring.
It means living separately many a night;
It means sleeping alone when you shut off the light.
It means alert drills, tours of duty, and saying goodbye;
Even though you get used to it, you still sometimes cry.

Time goes by while you're apart;
Till you see him again, keep him close to your heart.
Wait for the letters that may take awhile;
But the words of love he writes will bring back that smile.
To hear his voice over the phone,
makes up for the times that you're left alone.

Then come the days that you spend together;
The love that fills you will last forever.
But until those days, keep your head held high;
Know he'll be back, it's not really goodbye.
Know he loves you and you'll see him later;
And always be proud of loving a Ranger.

Glenda D. Reeves

Nature's Ballerinas

Little dainty ladies
   came dancing down today,
In their lacy costumes
   they floated from the grey.

Each one wore a gown
   of a hexagon design,
They danced and they frolicked
   but formed no special line.

Like graceful ballerinas
   they whirled and turned around,
E'en thought I saw one
   wear a diamond crown.

Boreas, their master, tossed
   them up and down.
Then, ever so lightly,
   he placed them on the ground.

Like a thousand diamonds, they sparkled in the light,
And glistened in the morning, reflecting colours bright.

I dare not go to touch them, or they will melt away,
Perhaps they will oblige us and stay another day.

Bernadine Robie Marsrow

Hello From The Heart

Do you sometimes feel so far away from the ends of the earth
That no one can hear the songs in your heart
Does it sometimes seem as though no one loves you
The forgotten child living in the wild

Do you live your so called life in great wonder of what it is like
To grow up and grow older
Do you look for love and passion and come up with none
Yet deep inside you know love lies has no conditions

So, in order to grow you must learn to create and explore
Settle for nothing less than more
First you must create time to revive
Because evil creates diseases of the mind
And makes you build those great walls of disguise
Hindering of the call
To become the master of your mind, heart and soul

Have no regrets in life because there are no rewinds in life
You have but one life — one chance — one underlying condition
So make it your mission
To start say a hello to your heart it knows its home and the answer

Catherine Lynch

Asphalt Dreams

"One to tie; two to win."
These words echo in the boy's head
As he approaches the free throw line.

The crowd anxiously awaits the shot . . .
Clank! The moans fill his head
As the brick crashes
To the ground.
He wipes the sweat off,
Steps back on the line
And dribbles the ball nervously.
The rock glides off his fingertips . . .
Thud! He missed again.
But he grabs his own rebound
And slams it home as the buzzer sounds!
His teammates carry him off the court.
His arms are raised. He looks
Around —

"One to tie; two to win."

Jon Shonk

For My Brother — Jeffrey J. Stetka

You weren't perfect, you had your faults and flaws
And sometimes you lost your temper without cause.
You had many small traits that you said made you bad,
but they were nothing compared to the good traits you had.

You were always so generous, your heart had room for all.
You loved your country, your family and of course, football.
You were kind and compassionate to any who had need,
Friends, family, strangers, or the stray animals you'd feed

You believed in truth and honor, and in doing what was right.
And for any of those things, you were willing to fight.
And I was proud of you Jeff, no matter what you did or said,
And I will never quite accept the fact that you are dead.

You were murdered by someone in need that you aided,
This poems is my tribute to you so the memories are unfaded.
Your laughter, your face, your tattoos, the jokes and the fun,
Your love and your strength that shone forth like the sun.

The memories are all that are left, for when you were killed,
All your hopes and your dreams will be forever unfulfilled.
But you will live on in our hearts, and we know on the day,
That our souls follow yours, you'll be there, lighting our way.

Gayla Richardson

The Day Cupid Shot

When cupid shot his bow.
His sights were straight and true.
It pierced my heart, threw and threw.
The day cupid, shot me with you.

What a fatal and deadly blow. I guess that's the way love goes.
My heart has never been over powered so.
With your love, the strength of his arrow flew.
For his shot was long and narrow.
The day cupid, shot me with you.

Quite a beautiful pair we make.
Because we know how to give and take.
I gave to you my love, and you took it.
You gave unto me your love, and I took it.
We hold true to a love, as no others.
Since that day, cupid put us together.

Now my love, I don't mind the pain.
Though his arrow is embedded deep in my heart.
The love I have for you, eases the pain.
To have you, to hold you, my dreams come true.
The day cupid, shot me with you.

David L. Upton

To My Love

I will hold you in my arms
everyday and every night
where nothing can harm you
as long as I squeeze tight.
I will try to keep you happy
and love you with all of my might
so that we will be together always
to share our love for the rest of our lives.

Lisa Wood

I Can't Stop

If the dull substance of my flesh were thought,
Injurious distance would not stop my way;
For then, despite the space I would be brought,
From limits far remote, where thou dost stay.
No matter then although my foot did stand
Upon the farthest earth removed from thee;
For nimble thought can jump both land and sea,
As soon as I think the place where she would be.
But, thought kills me, that I am not thought to
Leap large lengths of miles when thou art gone,
But, that so much of earth and water wrought,
I must attend times leisure with my moan;
Receiving nought by elements so slow
But heavy tears, badges of either woe.

Sam Friedman

Walk Of Faith

Holy forbearer of my soul,
bring your wisdom unto me,
these sins bring evil and their toll,
that this Christian soldier flees;
please be merciful in your reproach,
for I have much to learn through my trials;
a journey which I must approach,
my path of undetermined miles;
in silence here, I shall wait,
until your guidance you bestow,
opening my eyes to a glimpse of fate,
which only you Lord, surely know;
I hear you father, and understand,
one day we will meet in the promised land.

Krista L. Barrett

Need

When the exec. forsakes all to land the account
And the gambler hazards all to win huge amounts,
I'm the spur to take the chance.

When the playboy is looking for some excitement
And the harlots uses herself for enticement
I'm the choreographer of their dangerous dance.

When the battered wife cries from her scars,
And the batterer leaves for the local bars,
I'm the thorn piercing them like a lance.

When the Hollywood native does anything for fame
And the gang banger kills without a hint of shame,
I'm the rationale behind their search for prominence.

When crack and dope become rudimentary
And dealers sell to kids in elementary,
I'm the force giving the cartel such dominance.

I'm the need for personal worth that leaves people dismayed
As they find no human effort to which they are swayed
Will fabricate lasting security and relevance.
Yet, Christ's salvation provides this everlasting assurance,
Since His sacrifice demonstrates each human has importance.

John W. Stem Jr.

Welcome New Year

This last year has not been a delight to me
All that I touched turned into a mess you see
I am happy to see it wind down to and end
I am looking forward to 1997 to begin

It should hold much promise of things to be bright
I do need a touch of things to be right
If I find it to be a copy of the year about to close
I may yank out my hair and chop off my nose

I feel in my heart that snow flakes may fall
Then we will know spring where flowers grow tall
Summer sweet smells will come to the fore
As fall will slide into winter once more

Good-bye to you this year of defeat
May the New Year bring only good treats
As I close my eyes and shut this door
I will never cry over you again — No never more.

Hetty Schroeder

The Dream?

My trembling hand reaches out to
touch your face
It is soft, like a whisper,
like a cloud,
like the wind
A gentle breeze blows and your face begins
to fade until it all but disappears.
Was it only a dream?
I lay beside you wanting to be near
You are quiet,
You are soft,
You are warm
The gentle breeze begins again.
Your body fades, as if made out of sand
blowing away one grain at a time, until you
completely disappear.
And now I am alone
Was it only a dream?

Janice Southerland

A Special Place

A place that has water,
the sun shines forever and
gangs are never . . .

This place is so special
that love stays as long as you do.

The day is at end,
but the night brings more mysteries
than the day has begun . . .

The swings more faster as the day grows longer,
and shooting practices turn into games.

When the lights go on and children go home,
When the rain comes and the sun doesn't shine,
the games are still, that is when my place
isn't so special . . .
ANYMORE . . .

Lorren Raquel Pallone

Ode To A Greek

You have been so nice to me, more than I can say. You set me
on a pedestal, as a woman, I loved it that way! Thanks for being
you, and being treated like a queen! Meeting a charming,
handsome Greek is every American girl's dream! One day soon
we'll meet again, I'm glad you are my friend. The times we've
spent together have shown me that you are a man among men!!!

Sandra Francine Murden

Colorado Woman

In the semi-shadowed foreground of the Rocky Mountain range
Near a simple, country Western town, where nothing seems to change
Lives a lean and seasoned "country girl," whose class and wit have "tested"
In the politics of Western Halls and men whose ploys she's bested

This woman has appreciation, for the grandeur that daily, subtly surrounds her
The changing look of winter, versus summer, spring and fall,
always astounds her . . .
She has chosen simple living, yet her home reflects much better
But she follows "ethics of the heart" and courage, to the letter!

This Rocky Mountain splendor, holds her with relentless power,
Spellbound, in its "magic grip" — for days and years; each hour
Has seen her, doing battle, with the elements she deals with there
For somehow, snows of winter, floods in summer, winds of spring,
fall colors, fair

All hold her, in such tenacious tentacles, that when she views
the distant, purple sky,
The glow of sunset spreading colors through the mountain
shadows, climbing high,
Or whirling clouds of snow — the winds that blow the drifts to
block her in leave this? The myriad Colorado colors, that
enfolds her in their mantle; she could never quite begin!!

Alice C. Hart

Day Dreams

Wake me not from my wide eyed sleep
So my beautiful day dreams I may keep
Disturb me not — but let take light
What escapes me in the dark of night.
In daytime dreams my thoughts of you
Are clear and bright as skies of blue
And as the chores fade far away,
I soon forget that it is day.
I close my mind in reveries
And bring to light my memories
Of days of youth and song and spring,
The romance of bird upon the wing.
Then I reflect as of today
Your voice — when I did hear you say
I'll always love you — always care
My beautiful — my sweet — my fair.
My spirit lifts as I see you now
So tall — so straight — unfurrowed brow
My day dream draws me closer still as my heart and soul of you I fill.
And I'll dream until the end of time and then perhaps you will be mine

Arlene Schlang

Wagon Train West — Year 1687

Winding Westward to Dodge City, 1867 the year,
Staunch, strong horses pull their weight,
Hear the Indians whoop and holler,
Wagon Train — Ho — we can't wait!

Indians circle one-by-one; Wagon Master's eyes tight to the trail
Hear the bugler blowing now, help is on the way!

Blue shirts of Cavalry appear so suddenly,
Sioux-Chief "Pawnee-Killer" promises of Peace,
All undone now, just a ploy, coffee, sugar, ammunition, but a toy,
This Indian Chief would take and run,
"Wagon Train — West," his one great quest!

"Troopers prepare to mount," more supplies needed,
"Head for Wagon Train West."
The army won success, did their best,
The bugler was their aid.

"Cavalry dismount," watch the Sioux, closer now, carbines fire,
Victory, Virtue, Liberty, for "1867 Wagon Train West!"
"Westward — Ho!" . . .

Julie A. La Hood

Tapestry

They slip away so silently
Weaving a tapestry on their way
The hours and minutes like threads of time
Are woven away within your mind
Like a masterpiece hanging on your wall
You can see the characters one and all
And smell the flowers that adorn the piece
Along with wonders that never ease
In your piece of weaving stitch by stitch
In continuous tedium day after day
It never occurred that the time would come
Where at last the last stitch would finally be done
As the piece evolved you were unaware
Composed of events from everywhere
That suddenly you'd realize tho endlessly slow
The tapestry's near finished it's soon time to go

Mildred Rex-Snyder

There Will Be More!

. . . Seventy-nine!
"She's an old lady — an old woman now."
"Be sure to take your cane!"
"Don't go out in the snow — or rain!"
". . . you might gain, physically, a broken brain!"
"Brain!" "that's already gone"
so they reason . . . "gone for long . . ."

Yet this day, waking dark and cold,
The sun WILL wipe away its mold —
there will be more!

There will be more!
My addled brain will reap
   new molds of words — as before!
This web of "79" may
   encircle me in ancient fray —
but never will it achieve recognition
   until the day of Celebration!

Marion A. Congdon

What Is Needed Is Trust

The weather report for life may be cloudy,
And one cannot see a bright tomorrow.
At that time the words of Christ ring out:
"Fear is useless; what is needed is trust!"

All alone one cannot fail but falter,
And all alone despair can take control.
Call on the watchful Guardian Angels.
They surround us and keep harm away.

Many are the trials of the just,
And many disappointments do prevail.
But call on the Saints and the Angels.
"Fear is useless; what is needed is trust!"

Donald M. Harrison

Final Hour

To ward off any pain, the heart is removed.
Bearing a new stain, the meaning is confused.
No sound but still heard, its mark has been made.
Unable to find words, the ultimate price will be paid.

The beat is now absent, all systems are stopped.
Lost in the present, last bubble long since popped.
For there is not time, nor reason to continue,
life . . . no longer mine may as well been run through.

No deterrence of the end as it draws ever near,
vanished are the friends once held so dear.
Constant strain to see, craving any trace of light.
If it was meant to be, spare my soul tonight.

John Velino

Mom — I Love You

I'm sorry for the pain, the trouble, and fear,
The fights, and worries and every last tear.

I know I do wrong but I'm only a kid,
And my apologies sent for all that I did.

Or ever will do that causes you harm,
I wish I was you, and filled with your charm.

Each of my wrong-doings was never meant.
And the pains I cause are not my intents.

I only want good, and pray for the best,
For you, for Dad, and all of the rest.

You set an example to make me go far,
And to raise me like the leader you are.

You've given me life, love and all glee,
A house, some food, and a strong family.

More than enough to have great success.
But my love and thanks aren't truly expressed.

I see that your goal is to make me succeed,
And you'll always be there to give what I need.

That means the world that you're here till the end,
And to know that my Mom, is my very best friend.

Ricky Reymon

Echoes The Past

You can see it every day in every form of news.
Lawlessness unravels order which quickly unscrews.
To maintain sacred order one must pay certain dues.
Many fought for our freedom while we lost our values.

With inherent disregard of tomorrow so many today shun.
Values have fallen to the thrill of instant sensation.
Waning values indicate signs of fast dying nation.
Just ponder the ruins of some lost civilization.

For thousands of years poets have recorded in verse.
If mankind does not heed, things definitely get worse.
Which possibilities so endless in our vast universe.
We can live a good life and break away from this curse.

For there to be joy, there must be a contrast.
Mankind must decide to leave hate in the past.
The blissful feelings of life will eternally last,
When values are embraced with all hatred smashed.

Immortality is the prize mankind tries to regain,
But God took it away when we used it in vain.
Unless we all re-adopt values and somehow refrain,
Mankind lives the repeating burden of humanities drain.

Gary D. Rick

Me And My PC

When you want to browse the Web or surf the Internet
to see places that you have never seen or ever been to yet;
all you have to do, depending on what you want to see,
is spend a little time with me and my PC.

Together we can tour the Globe and chart a map to show
the places that we want to see and where we want to go.
Can you imagine all the fun that such a trip could be.
It's like planning your own tour and watching it on TV.

We'll take time out to quench our thirst, or whatever, along the way.
There is no need to hurry or limit the time we stay
as we have no food to buy, gas to burn or even rent to pay.
So when you think you have the time
and there are places you want to see,
just plan on taking a trip with me and my PC.

Joseph Rudloff

Nature's Power

Some people believe that there's a God, and pray to him to solve
their problems. I believe in Mother Earth and Sister Nature, the
two of them, work well together. I till their the soil and plant
their seeds, it always feeds my soul and body needs. With Sun and
Rain, the seeds will grow, and this in turn, turns my world about.

I do feel good with Earth and Nature, they feed and cloth my
flesh and body. They're the one that from seeds grow, all the
plants and trees and flowers. I know that Nature is sometimes
cruel, and causes floods and hurricanes to. But in the end, when
she calms down, she feeds me well and gives me plenty.

When I have stress and troubles rise,
I call on Earth and Sister Nature.
They give me courage to face the world,
   and peace and love is what I find.
It's from their plants, both roots and leaflets,
   that gives me strength and determination.
I will not forsake, Mother Earth and Nature,
   and I'll honor them, for they're deserving.

   Joseph H. Peake

Crack

Muffled screams fill the air,
Everything's dark, cold, and bare.
The skies are grey; the sun won't shine.
You thought you were cool; you thought you were fine.

Everything's turning out for the worst;
Everything in your body's starting to burst.
Yearning, burning, searching for more.
Nothing can be done to settle the score.

Will the misery and pain ever end?
Will the frown on your face ever descend?
Is there any way to stop the fears?
There's no use crying; stop wiping the tears.

Your life isn't over; get it together.
You feel weak, sick and light as a feather.
The next thing you know is emptiness dark and cold.
Was it really worth never growing old?

Never to see how beautiful things were;
How could such an awful thing occur?
Now life's over; too late to turn back.
Death is a terrible thing when you die from crack!

   Amber Clayton

Terra Sancta

If the unceremonious hands of ashen skies
Lower the lid of your violin case;

The mounting sprawl of dark-hued fog
Parades a light abstract by indirection;

The earth's terrain of somber accidents
Spills a delirium of dehumanized motions

And all convene, with infelicity, in dangerous triangulation
To enclose your arrow's vibrant sense of flight
Take aim, for the hunt for life, at an interlocking angularity
With no less expansive force than passion rising
To activate one dimension of the construct
As a lever against another
For the launch, on a panoramic cruise, of your dreams
Whispering flirtation in the chambers of your heart
Soaring towards an ecstatic crossing of the threshold of delight
With one shrill, one sustained hosanna, one sonic splendor
Your feet clattering like a million hooves
Flying germinal sparks to desolate shores
Your torch gushing the spirited flame of this evolved design
Into the high-valency arena of Terra sancta, yours.

   Yseult Bayard

Is It You

Are you the one who was born for me.
The One to fulfill my destiny.
The One I choose to bring home to Mother.
My One and Only My best friend, My lover.
I hope to discover your true identity one day.
Until that time I shall persevere and pray.
For that special day when you shall be revealed.
To Me and to yourself, It is God's Will.
This is how I feel, This is what I see.
It was meant to be, we shall live happily.
Ever after, love and laughter having daughters and sons.
If there was ever a match made in heaven you and I would be the ones.
I ponder and I wonder as it thunders and rains.
Listening to soft music looking out my window pain.
Are you someone I'll meet in the future or are you someone from my past.
Are you someone I know presently, If so I must ask.
You to Identify yourself because I don't have a clue.
The Love of My Life, Are you the one, Is It You.

   Calvin L. Powell

The Mask

My mask hides the truth,
   I wear it for protection.
Protection from my fear,
   fear that the truth will be seen.
Seeing the pain shine through it,
   that's when the fear is the greatest.
So great that it shakes me down,
   down to my foundation, my soul.
Now I can't put it back on,
   back on for protection.
Protection from the truth,
   the truth being reality.
Reality is the fear,
   the mask hides my fear.
The mask is now my reality.

   George M. Maxson

Legacy Of Love

Love is not measured by material possessions, but rather by the
countless acts of giving of oneself totally and unselfishly and
not expecting anything in return.

You two, as our parents, have shown us what real love is all about.
No matter what the need or circumstance has been you've
always come through for us. Whether it's just been to listen to
our troubles or to lend a hand financially, you've always helped.

We've shared many memories over the years. We've teased
each other, we've laughed together, we've cried and we've
grieved together and through it all your love has kept us strong
and brought us through the major traumas of our lives.

You may feel you have nothing to leave us, but that is not so;
you'll be leaving us the greatest gift of all — "a Legacy of Love!"

   Rebecca Roy Cyr

Thank You Lord

Thank you Lord for using me.
To help others in time of need.
Thank you Lord for showing me the right thing to do in life.
Thank you Lord for the people at church camp that showed me your love.
Thank you Lord for dying on Calvary so many years ago.
Thank you Lord for the songs we sing to show our love for you.
Thank you Lord for the singers you sent us.
Thank you Lord for letting me know you more each day.
Well what I mean is thank you Lord for everything.

   Debra R. Cole

A Decision

To live to die, it is up to you,
but to die to live, is it really you?
Live or die, what are you going to do?
If you die not, how are you going to live?
Die is not a choice up to you, but
to live, it was not meant for you.
But to die, how can you not too?
To live, it is all coming back to you,
but to die, do you really want too?
Because of to live, it is hurting you.
To live, is it it is up to you, but it is a
choice, just for you?
So what are you going to do?
To live to die or die to live?

Alyce Lowe

Untitled

Hands that were my answer,
Sculptors of a language not forgotten,
Trekkers through my years encargoed with
your same sweet offering,
Returning yet, returning,
Deliver me again my puzzled heart,
the one that will not cease to follow yours.

Poised in loyal masculine
reaching ever slowly from the bath
your eyes that bade me question
filling now with vagabonded care . . .

So many paths beneath a single moon!
Uncounted as the droplets
on this tomb were we,
before we met and loved.

Chris Liberto

A Memory

I once had a vision, of life and of love,
A vision so innocent, so young and so true,
As if it were searching for someone above.
Vanished in shadow, left with no clue,
Gone from our life onto another time and place.
On his journey he left us a memory, forever to see,
Slipping into darkness, in your dreams is his face.
Never to slip away again, in your eyes forever to be.
Tears left behind, the memory haunts the night,
Cries into sleep, nowhere to run, why try to escape.
The pain yes it hurts, just doesn't seem right,
How could he be gone, is it cruelty or fate.
Gone from his body in spirit he'll remain.
Our cries he can hear, our fears he shall yield,
Thank God for our memories, just to help ease the pain.

Shawn Wright

Saints

You can spot them from afar, as they stand out in
every crowd. They are full of gracefulness and confidence
beyond compare. They have a smile for everyone they turn to
and a glow that will penetrate your heart through.

So when your eyes land on that person that appears not of
the ordinary, think about what you see. Their stance is perfect
in every way, their words seem to address the entire day.
You can hear a hymn on their lips and a prayer in their hearts.
Look deep into their eyes and you will see Jesus standing there.

So this is how you would like to be viewed.
Let Jesus know that you too can represent him true.
He has a job for all of us to do.

Karen Burns Royster

The Tears

A watery solution
Runs like a stream
Breaking all barriers
Of life in between.

A renewal for hope of memories past.
A picture of doom. One shattered glass.

A silent voice a reminder of humanity.
A peace at will of tranquillity falling.

The charity of forgiveness.
An embrace of love. One glass empty.
The other half full.

The words of hurt,
Of loss, and of forgotten time.

Of broken lives
Of heartaches, the lies.
A barrier of time that stood still.

A mirror of hope.
A sadden face reflects the image.
The storm rages out of control.
As the tears flow.

Schrena Wilson

My Plumbing Job

We were tired of carrying water, so we thought it was time;
To put in our little house, a water and sewer line.

Now my husband was afraid of snakes, terrified I might say;
As far away from them as possible, he did stay.

Well we dug the trench and no snakes under the house was found;
So ready we were, but it rained, and muddied the ground.

Dry it was under the house though, so we got started;
So carry some of the things we would need, the two of us carted.

Now folks, he had his back to the ledge, I was in front of him holding the tile.
When I saw the snake, but I didn't say anything for a while.

Then that snake started to unwind, and I knew real soon;
That on that ledge for it, there wasn't enough room.

Finally I had to tell him, and he hollered real loud getting out from
    under the house;
So fast he left he stomped me into the ground, like a defenseless
    little mouse.

Black and blue I was, and stoved up for a month or two;
But he did apologize and said Honey, I'll find someone else to help you.

Shirley Buffon

The Vision

Out of the shadows into the light she came.
A vision of beauty
The likes of which he had never seen.
Like a statue he stood — speechless.
His lips tried to move.
Not a word was uttered.
Eye to eye they stood.
Her haunting violet eyes penetrated
Slowly into the depths of his soul.
His arms reached out to embrace her.
She faded away
And blended into the flickering shadows.
Many times he returned to that spot.
He often felt the warmth of her presence.
But the mysterious vision of beauty
Never again revealed herself.
Just a restless spirit from the past.

Lois A. Pratte

Lost Soul Found

The day was crisp. The sun hid far away.
As I walked, the rain was my only companion on this cloudy day.
The gravel road beneath my feet which pained me so often
was now a familiar friend.

The cloths I wore, simple, and soiled yet comforting, molded my frame.
Their touch was the only I had felt in a long while, thanks to the rain.

A garden view in front of me,
I thought I saw a man.
I wiped my eyes clear
and saw his outstretched hand.

I fell to my knees as he leaned towards me.
My head bowed down he spoke softly:

My son, sweet blistering child of mine, wipe your feet clean,
dab your tears dry.
You have carried your faith proudly upon your back.
Remove your drab and place this linen upon your shoulders.
Rise to your feet and walk beside me.
Speak no words but think your thoughts.
Enter now into my nous of reality.

Annett M. Gallegos

A Painted Smile

A painted smile.
Laughing its way into many hearts.
A few somersaults, a cartwheel
and a forward roll, now and then,
brings laughter, to those who watch.
But remove the smile, the laughter dies.
. . . The tent becomes empty.

Rhonda K. Fleming

A New Day

If we travel up the mountains to watch the glorious sunset
we would thank God each day for what he provides
to see the clouds floating by
as if angels were beckoning to us
we would believe that heaven is nearby and never be sad
God's love is enough for all of us
as he wants us to be glad
every day would be a new day
if we hold on to hope and pray

Charlotte Burke

Curtain Call

The veil of separation is on its way
It hangs high like the curtain about to fall upon life's drama.
Breathlessly we watch . . . hoping that our watching
will stay the inevitable.
Since this cannot be, I shall not curse the messenger
only the message that he brings.

O tangible evidence of my disbelief, come tomorrow
for tomorrow never comes
It remains forever the present and as the present
it is always with us . . . can not my beloved remain also?
Cruel fate, since this drama must be played to the end,
then understand that my future longing to reach out
and touch the vast nothingness . . .
Hoping that in some part it will become mortal again
is not greed, but a tribute to a lasting love.

If it must be, then let the curtain fall.
I will applaud its falling to make it rise again
as I say to myself, "you shall have your curtain call.
"Each day the curtain will rise . . . I will see your face again
and I will smile at the remembering."

Margaret E. Hieronymus

A Maze Away

Circles, triangles, rectangles and squares
Encircle me as I journey through my days,
My hours, my minutes.
Like a dance swirling, turning to the tempo of
The music inside my being.
One with the universe,
In tune with each note and melody.
Melodies playing in my mind and in my soul
My spirit soars as a bird in flight
Ever upward towards the light
Spiraling across the sky into night where
Moonbeams dance and singing fills the air
Floating down towards earth where roots take hold
In growing beautiful, wonderful things to enfold.
Emotions engulf me, transforming me into light
As I dance upon mother earth
Rejoicing in God's world.
All creation sings,
Listen . . . You can hear it.
A maze becomes amazing as I look upon creation

Eva Thurlwell

Little Green Lake

The green hills are calling,
    Silver drops of rain are falling.
Little Green Lake is picturesque and
    beautiful within its heavenly shores.
The blue of the lake matches the blue
    of the sky.
Boats drift peacefully by big boulders
    and mounds of sand.
Rock filled hills where wild flowers grow,
    A more beautiful sight you'll never know.

Agnes Bradley

"Sweet Dreams"

Sometimes I lay awake at night,
and watch you as you sleep,
I gaze upon your peaceful face,
as dream so deep,

I wonder if I'm in your dreams,
and if they're good or bad,
and hope no matter what they be,
that they're never sad,

I hear you whisper unknown words,
and wonder what you said,
and what kinds of vision and memories,
are drifting threw your head,

And as you lay there peacefully,
I pray to the Lord above,
You'll sleep threw another beautiful night,
having sweet dreams filled with love . . .

Anjel Morin

Mama

Like the snowflakes, so are we different, my dear mama said
As I nestled so snug, in my downy-soft bed.

An ebony book she did cradle, soon a psalm to recite
Afore I'd nod off, far into the night.

As she started to chant, I again felt the tingle
To bless one another, for all cultures to mingle

I gazed at her frame, so weary and worn
Out of this body, I came to be borne.

A frail little lady, her heart less than small
Had bequeathed me the courage, to stand ten feet tall!

Mary Dorothy Payson

Oceans That Never Die

A joyful star peaks through a far off storm,
Slowly bringing light to an ocean it loves to warm.
Then sounds of the surf, woke him very early,
As living mountains of liquid, burst forth in a flurry.
It's time for a stroll under a colorful sky,
This he loves, the compelling waters know why.

Maybe majestic forests that end at the seas,
Or hiding creatures that plays in its trees.

The pounding surf then hums through the ground,
Stirring up a doe, as it turns toward the sound.

A sea lion bobbing in the splendor of the waves,
Catches the wondering eyes of the deer as it plays.

Proud waves roll at the shore to be spent,
As a great mind purposes why they are sent.

Lone man looked on, then wept,
Precious magical memories kept.

The landscape grows, the years pass by,
Guarding oceans that never die.

Lexie Davis

"He Is God"

I have a spirit in me
It's growing everyday
The Lord himself put it in my heart
He said, "child use it"
For the mercies on me
And I will see you thru it all.

He is God, He is God
He will take you, thru all trials
He is God.
When you call on his name
He will answer, and reply
Because he is Almighty God.

Children, if you have a work to do
for the Lord today
Don't put it aside. Do what he commands
He will bless you for the work you've done
and a reward you'll receive one day.
And a place up in heaven to live.

Pauline Stevens

"A Whisper In The Wind"

To softly hear what no one else
can hear, a gentle whisper in the
wind. The stars, the moon, the
stormy rains, washing away life's little
stains. A strong breeze is about to
blow my way. Down the long road we
shall go. Until our paths cross again,
until our eyes see one another, we shall
go a whisper in the wind.

Tracy T. Pierce

Precious Moments

Each moment we spend together, none is like the other,
You're a wonderful friend as well as my lover,

Sweeter than the sounds of birds, as precious as a new
born baby, as sure as a rose blooms in June, as sure as you
are my lady,

Beautiful as the way you walk, beautiful as the way
you talk, sweeter than a kiss from an angel heaven sent,

but not as "precious as a moment" spent with you.

Chris Williams

Logics And Flaw-Gics

Ah for a sure clue for this and that
to take comfort in where we're at.

Could be that knowledge always lags needs,
known and unknown, in many facets of leads.

We think we see the times and why's
and how to handle mostly wise.
But what is it that blurs the eyes?

Histories of cycles for everyone to see
foster clashing wisdom on what's to be.
Econometrics and manipulatives disagree
as rhetorics and politics grope for power key.

Theories and supposed absolutes carry flaws
as elites debate every cause
and propose better and newer laws.

Fears and manias shift around in turns
updating histories and crowd concerns.

Will mesmerizing leaderships prevail
assuring followers new logics will not fail?

D. J. Gancheff

Curtain Call

The veil of separation is on its way
It hangs high like the curtain about to fall upon life's drama.
Breathlessly we watch . . . hoping that our watching
    will stay the inevitable.
Since this cannot be, I shall not curse the messenger
    only the message that he brings.

O tangible evidence of my disbelief, come tomorrow
    for tomorrow never comes
It remains forever the present and as the present
    it is always with us . . . can not my beloved remain also?
Cruel fate, since this drama must be played to the end,
    then understand that my future longing to reach out
    and touch the vast nothingness . . .
Hoping that in some part it will become mortal again
    is not greed, but a tribute to a lasting love.

If it must be, then let the curtain fall.
I will applaud its falling to make it rise again
    as I say to myself, "you shall have your curtain call.
"Each day the curtain will rise . . . I will see your face again
    and I will smile at the remembering."

Margaret E. Hieronymus

Black And Proud

We're black and proud.
I say, we're black and we're proud.
Blacks have come a long way. And blacks have a long way to go.
But, we can't make that journey, by sitting back and saying,
Child, that — a — do; just as long as I got a hand in it,
It is alright with me.

Get up Black Folks! And take a stand.
You need to help your fellowman!
Throw away that jealousy, throw away that word, I can't.
Throw away that word wait, for if you wait too long,
    it might be too late.

Wake up Black Folks!
You are still sleep. Because opportunities are dancing at your feet.
I say wake up Black Folks! And take a stand,
For many blacks have died that we might have equal rights.

The world is calling for great leaders like you. Such as:
President of the United States, doctors, lawyers, teachers,
preachers, counselors, and reporters.
But, if you don't know God, you still want be able to make it.
By the Grace of God, Blacks have come a long way.

Van Alice Williams

Broken Heart

Our love lasted for a while
but, then it came to an end.
I don't know why I even cried
and now my heart is dying,
and in the end I have to
say I have a broken heart
and; it will be the same until
the end when it falls apart!

Sunny Millard

Time After Time

We forget about our promises
leaving one's emotion in mere despair and desperation.

Time after time

We allow ourselves to be fooled
and persuaded by our lovers hands and words.
Only to realize that we have been deceived by a
smooth criminal.

Nathandra Bullett

Shoes — New And Used

I'm sure glad I'm not a shoe
Because you're stiff and awkward when you're new.

Then you are stuffed with big old feet.
Which quite often, don't smell so sweet.

Then when you've become just slightly used.
This is when you're really abused!

Out in the rain, the mud, and the cold
Then tossed in the garbage when you grow old!

Millie M. Lee

The Sisters Three

The younger bunch call us "old ladies"
Little do they realize how young we really are.
Oh the good times we have when we're together from afar!
Me and these "old ladies," the sister's three.

One is the life of the party as you might say,
The other keeps us in line along the way.
I guess you know by now they surely need me,
In order for these "old ladies" to be the sister's three.

We have survived camping trips, moonlight swims,
and fireworks on the fourth of July.
There have been picnics in the park, late night talks,
And oh the thrill of finding antiques to buy!

We have such fun no matter what we do or where we go,
So move over all you young people and we will take the show!
Me and these "old ladies," the sister's three.

Nellie Kathleen Sullivan

The Wind Is My Song

The wind is my song, dancing on a moonlit pond
Amongst the mist of a midnight stream
Love
Flows
Into
A
Dream
Moonbeam drops reflects a lovers knot
While garlands of sweet lilies
Kiss the good night air
The wind is my song,
Dancing on a
Moonlit pond

Rebecca Fearing

Going To Sleep With The Angels Tonight

The hammer fell, his face shattered for a paltry twenty dollars,
Lying in a pool of blood, barely breathing,
Onlookers staring at the sight of death in his eyes,
Going to sleep with the angels tonight.

The abduction, her nude body lying in the park next to your home,
Marks of struggle all around her nakedness,
The cops gazing at the ugly sight of her demise,
Going to sleep with the angels tonight.

The dope deal, children dead on the street two blocks away,
Riddled with bullets meant for the dealer man,
Watching the six o'clock news again, another victim of crime,
Going to sleep with the angels tonight.

The overdose, spittle hanging from those lips of red,
Lying in the fetal position of death,
Another star falls prey to the lack of faith,
Going to sleep with the angels tonight.

The divorce, found with his finger on the trigger,
Pieces of brain and skull imbedded in the wall,
The smell of death and gun powder in the air,
Going to sleep with the angels tonight.

P. J. Bottoms

Santa Anna's Army

Forward these men in blue and white came
These men whose bravery here was not lame
Though theirs was not to bear the burden of blame
But to press forward against those sparsely manned walls just the same

But the broad array of their might
In its rank and file's immense height
Offered to those before these men an impressive sight
That did not give those before them an inspiration of fright

For here was not known the sense of terror
Nor was known the pending doom of error
For here to this place had come the darer
Whose challenge had brought forth the bearer

Of disagreement between what some hoped would in the future be
And what those with the affluence of influence meant to see
In this place that in the future would for some represent glory
And for others only a place in history

But these things were of no concern to these men
Who entered the fray of this murderous den
And braved the tumultuous clamor of this life thrashing bin
For they were here about the Alamo to put a rebellion to an endin'

David Eugene LaValley

A Clown

I wish I were a clown in a circus
like Ringley Bros. and Barnum and Bailey.
I could stand on my hands and do cart-wheels
and perform for the young and old daily.

You would know me by my big red nose
and the black top hat I wear.
My outfit would have large green dots,
I'm sure that you would stare!

I'd have air-filled balloons for the children
or carry an umbrella over my head.
I would wear this funny huge bow tie,
the color of bright red!

My clown face would be all painted up
with a big red cheerful smile.
I could hide my troubles and sorrows
and look happy all the while!!!

Terese Heckenstaller

My Four Grandsons

My grandson Josh is the apple of my eye
I love him so much that I could just die

My grandson Dominic, my blue eyed boy
Little monkey, how he fills my heart with joy

My grandson Shane, so handsome and strong
In Nanny's eyes he can do no wrong

At last comes Christopher, so cute and so sweet
Without a doubt he is the orneriest from his head to his feet

My four boys are as different as day and night
To see them all together is such a wonderful sight

And so now my boys grow strong and wise
Be kind and gentle no matter your size

When I leave this world for a better place
I surely will leave with a smile on my face

For I leave behind four special men
May God bless you all — Love, Grandma Jen

Virginia Baker

The Bleak Of Winter

The snowflakes fall softly to the ground,
Winds howl from the ends of the earth,
Birds puff up their feathers to shield
Them from the cold that bites with razor teeth.

The evergreens shed the endless crystals of snow as
Quickly as they fall, thump, thump,
Onto the dazzling albescent, pristine earth
Reflecting the hazy radiance of the afternoon sun.

Just under the snow, mice
Scurry through flimsy white tunnels,
Their miniature feet pattering on the mat of
Dead, yellow, supine grass.

Deer creep quietly through the tranquil forest,
Trying to make a meal out of the leathery tree bark
So that they will have something
With which to face the nothing of this frozen world.

On this orb we call Earth life has come to a semi-halt
Where only the smart, strong, and lucky are left alive;
Those select few that are driven by a primal instinct to survive;
And those who lack it disappear like the winter's snows in the desert sun.

Renay Thompson

You Are Magic

No strings, no strings attached.
Suspended, I appear
with a wave of your hand
you take, you take command!
Love, love like magic appears.

Floating, floating in the air.
Your illusions, winding stare
hypnotized you see
by props of your, your your mastery.
You, you are magic to me.

Mirrors, mirrors help reflect
your image in special effects
performing your act
you pull dreams out, dreams right out of your hat.
Conjure, conjure love's magic spell.

Hidden, hidden feats deceive.
Entrancements power believe
unexplained feelings found
the element of surprise all around.
You, you are magic to me.

Ty Volkmann

The Haunting Song

The ghosts and the goblins, a howling delight
As gestures of haunting to children bring fright
The darker the sky, the better it is
For frankensteins, mummies, and freaks in show biz
They'll growl at your feet and laugh face to face
As witches and warlocks cast spells every place
But a brave soul you'll be on the toes of your feet
Ringing doorbells and yelling, "Hello, trick or treat!"

Debbie S. Moore

Jerusalem

Fog slowly releases its gentle grip,
relinquishing its virginal unity.
In silent and painful confrontation wavering her own departure;
Hesitantly, entrusting us her soul mate.

Descending onto your sacred grounds,
I watched your children pray.
Ending a physical separation; from family, love and land
Linking our precious generations.

Pondering at your ancient Wall,
I circle around my feelings.
Memories, wrapped-up emotions; a religious search long ago
Questions, deep within my soul.

Nestled in the Judean hills,
Basking in the early morning sun.
Beckoning those still in doubt, to immerse in your warmth;
Where you harbor both, lost and found.

Your lovely narrow streets
Are like vibrant birth canals.
Forging forward with Life, delivering against all odds;
An unconditional love and trust, in our G—d.

Johanna A. Spee

The Storm

Silence, dark clouds roll in across the peaceful sky
Sprinkles of light rain fall on the dry summer ground
Gusty wind picks up as the once quiet rain gets heavier
Flashes of lightening streak through the now darkened sky
Thunder shakes the stricken land as the storm picks up
Clouds boil over with excitement as the activity overflows
At last the flashes and booms recede and move to a different sky
Finally the storm calms and fades into the distance, Silence.

Megan Hammer

Dark Secrets

I never meant for my darkness to feed upon your light and drain you dry.
You were the magnet to my iron will — always pulling, pulling —
will you never tell my why?

I worried always about what loving me might be doing to you
so I tried to convince you I didn't care, but you knew it wasn't true

How I loved and hated you for your power over me!
Yet, I lived in constant fear that you'd grow tired and set me free.

And when I wanted to be the one who decided when to go,
how dare you shake your head, and firmly tell me "No!"

So you were waiting for me to bare my soul and really let you in?
Well, I've been afraid of what you'd find — back there — where
the pain begins.

Why must you make me say — all there is to tell?
Why go chasing ancient screams — echoing out of hell?

Those things happened so long ago, how would it help me now to cry?
That child of my soul weeps bitter tears — but my eyes have
always been dry.

Laurie A. Tindell

Velvet Touches

Senses peaked sitting in my glass cage, reading about what I
desire on the printed page.
Illusions conducting unfulfilled promises all floating by,
tears of frustration falling from an empty green sky.
Limbs reaching out between my glass bars, black shadows
leaving blood red scars.
Yet arms aren't drawn back in for comfort,
on the behalf of the longings to feel velvet touches.
A confidant comes everyday, bringing a key for me to escape;
Trickles of sweet sayings tempt my weary soul.
Cool blue water from his skies heals my deep wounds.
Oh how I want to crawl out and reach up to him but fear paralyzes every limb.
So I sit in my decrepit cage, longing for him to remain.
He must leave for the glasses edge is closing in, I must decide
for life or soon to die.
He starts to leave, my green sky rains; My heart feels a cutting glass pain.
A cry escapes me, my arms extended.
He returns and gently lifts me, my empty green sky has ended.
So much to share, so much to give.
Eternal thanks to the man who helped me live.
To the man who returned my velvet touches.
My life, my love, my prince;
My husband.

Elise Antoinette Walker

That Which Is Not Etched On Stone

Today the homeless man finally found a home
　Beneath an unmarked plot of land without a stone
Yet his heart was like no others I have known
　For he never feared the shadows of the unknown
Freely sharing his compassion for all others whose plight was like his own
　If I could but afford to buy him a stone
I'd write here lies a man who deserves a palatial home
　Once he said, passion without compassion destines one to die alone
If this axiom be truth then this man never deserved to walk the streets alone
For he freely gave to who so ever needed whatever he owned
　Without uttering complaint for his lack either hearth or home
Someday I pledge to have these words etched upon a proper stone
　Here lies a man to whom passion and compassion were both well known
Who sadly could not find a world worthy enough to be called his home
　If I could I'd gladly traded his damaged heart for my own
Dear Father God please take the time to make this gentle soul feel at home
　For he was the holder of a heart much like your own

James L. Tashoty

Epitaph For A Pet Schnauzer

No more the early morning run
To find the paper, greet the sun
And snort at feline friends — in fun!

No more the trot of little paws
Through patios, rooms and corridors
While Ginger, in your basket, snores

No more the frantic welcome home
With wagging tail, your love all shown
To master back from fields alone;

No more the magic sound of "walk?"
Once whispered, stage — like, in our talk
Which lit your eyes up like a hawk;

No more the kindly watchful care
Of Master Ray, when you would dare
Too far to stray from here to there;

Sweet creature who awoke this morn, to fetch the paper,
greet the dawn, you could not know your life had drawn

To its conclusion on this earth,
And, 'midst our sorrow, in its worth
Found on a greater plane rebirth.

Michael J. Cooke

With Jesus

To my children, my family, and friends
I'm in a land that has no end,
Streets of gold, where no one grows old,
A holy and happy place,
Where the light of God shines sweetly upon
my face.

I am smiling now and forever
With my loved ones ever dear,
I am standing with the angels
No pain, no sorrow, no fear.

I did not choose to leave you,
That was God's divine plan,
I'll be singing with the angels
In that holy and happy land.

When you get to heaven
And my face you long to see,
Just look to the hill
With Jesus I will be.

R. Jerome Patterson Jr.

Another Year Is Ending

Another year is ending, does it make you very sad?
Do you have some memories both wonderful and bad?
Do you think about the past, and those who've left us here?
Both young and old, who are still so very dear.

Do the memories still come, as you think about them yet?
So you wish you could go back to events with no regret?
Do you still feel a sadness about things undone or possibly unsaid?
Do you wish you used your heart more, instead of just your head?

Do you realize the past is done?
The situations have been lost or won.
There is nothing more for you to do.
You did your best to see them through.

Have you learned now how to handle things?
The wisdom of growing older, that experience still brings.
Love and laughter and kindness too,
will all become a part of you.

Today is here, embrace it, forget about the past.
Think about the future, and new memories that will last.
From now on learn to love, to smile and really care.
Happiness will come to you, if your faith in God is always there.

Ellen M. Malloy

"Love's Summit"

We climbed up a mountain, on a journey of love
past hills and valleys, toward forever above.
Twists and turns couldn't keep us from going
where for so many years our hearts have been showing
the way, to the summit of trust; understanding
that jealousies, egos and societal demandings
were detours — on our journey to now
living as we see fit; not as they say how
we should, because now we can see
that right is what works for you and for me.

So we climbed up a mountain, on a journey of love
'til at last in the glow of pure sunshine above
with the last of our doubt and uncertainty spent
on warm rock we rested and said what it meant
to love, to trust, to possess, to be
all we can to each other; let the world watch and see
our joy, our commitment, our need and our pride
that life is a journey and together we'll ride.
I belong to you only, your strength is for me
our bond is forever; it sets us both free.

Nancy E. Grady

Feelings . . .

As we say good bye to the one we love,
through the heavenly skies so far above.
Our memorable feelings we always share,
bring us uneasiness and wonder was it really fair.
Our lives change in a different way,
as we grow older every day.
Wondering and asking ourselves why,
Bring us pain and sorrow to our hearts that cry.
Everyone's feelings are of the same kind,
through heart, soul, body and mind.
Now it's time to put our loved one to rest,
For she will know I've done my best . . .

Susie K. Raska

Patience

Patience is a virtue
You've heard this for years,
Look to the future
And fight through the tears.
It's hard to stand back quietly
When the world spins so violently
You are in a rush for happiness
But it can't be found in all the madness.
You hear someone nearby laughin'
All this time you have cried,
He's been right there by your side.
You knew he was the one,
But patience, you had none
Then one day, caught by surprise
He said, "baby, will you be my wife"
Now here's one for your future.
Let patience be a virtue.

Denise McKeehan Casto

The First Time

The first time I saw your face
That's when I fell in love with you
Your smile simply devastated my cool
I couldn't take my eyes off you,
and watched your every move
I liked the way you walked around
It was like a beautiful merry-go-round
Bright lights and music without the sound
Just sparkles in the morning dew
The Sun arose to brighten the day,
and I looked forward to seeing you
I could hardly wait until we met
To look upon your beautiful face
To see your smile
To hear your voice
That's when I fell in love with you.

George F. Gettys

My Mighty Hunter

He takes his time and steps with ease,
He gently goes down to his knees.

He sees a buck! He hoped he would,
He's simply praying for something good.

He now continues on his way,
Back to his stand, til night he'll stay.

It's dark out now, so down he comes,
And brushes off the dirt and scum.

He comes home to me in time for dinner,
And I let him know he's still a winner.

So a "Mighty Hunter" he may not be,
But he's still the perfect man for me.

Daphne E. Aguillard

Memories

Perhaps you can visualize this wintertime dream —
A quiet trickle to water in an ice covered stream.
And a weathered old barn standing proud and tall
With traces of red paint clinging to its wall.

The windmill, veteran of many years, no longer turns in the breeze,
And the orchard nearby is sleeping with no fruit or leaves.
All the leaves have fallen from the tree limbs,
They turn and tumble along the road, tossed by the winds.

The garden is silent, resting until spring,
Its songbirds gone south, no longer do we hear them sing.
The grass, once green, is covered with a thin white lace,
And the aged rock wall, a century old, is still frozen in place.

In the fields and barn, the voices of many are gone.
Our beloved old-timers, now only memories, have passed on.
We cannot hear or see them, they are no longer here,
But we have fond memories of family and farm that we hold so dear.

Bob Greenwood Jr.

Hermit Jig

Trillions of little spheres flyin' round
predestination lacking location
gigantor mammals swimming through space
a one star universe
how brightly does the essence glow
sense of floures is the unit of measurement
it's one o'clock
within a few mile radius it's twenty-five o'clock
come back to the origin
forty-nine
a different day or a different perception
what's the relevance but a suffix for destination
beauty of solitude is purifying
happiness in company is fleeting
avoidance implied.

Brian Hicks

Our Soulless Endeavor

We inherit a soul at our birth.
Those of us who live a life of fear from abuse, battering or torture.
Our souls become scared.
When we die, we pass on our scared soul
If this being lives a life of fear
That soul will receive more scars.
The cycle continues until it is one scar.
Then that soul becomes invalid and can no longer fulfill it purpose.
There was only so many souls created in the beginning.
We can create no more
When all the souls in the world become invalid as they will.
The human race will become extinct.

A wounded soul will go to that place where the butterflies turn
into caterpillars, manifesting the reversal of time . . .

Debbie N. Blake

Looking Out The Bay Window

During our first real snow storm
I was reluctantly nursing my broken
left femur in a blue mobilizer.
As I watched the lovely snowflakes
Go gracefully swirling past my window.
I thought of them as my different friends
Who wanted to visit me, but were forced
to stay home because of poor driving.
I was cheered by my imaginative friends
Pausing at my window nudged by the crowds,
But some sneaked back to say, a special
message of, "Hurry, Get Well — We Miss You"

Marian T. Hunter

Love Will Follow

There are different kinds of love
   as I'm sure you know.
I believe you can take your love
   wherever it is you go.

Your love for your Mom and Dad,
   brothers and sisters, too.
When you're grown and leave home,
   will surely follow you.

You find and love your spouse
   and you always love your child.
No matter how they look or act
   even when they are wild.

When you die and leave this earth
   I believe this to be true;
You don't forget the ones you loved
   you take that love with you.

Of all of the different kinds of love
   there is one thing that I've learned.
The very best kind of love
   is love that is returned.
    Barbara Quappe

The Power Of Smile

Down in Cannes and Nice, up in Monaco
Beauty surrounds you, dance with its echo

A beach connects you to paradise
in Gulf de Juan, a goddess' eyes

There I saw a 'smile of creator'
Lying on the sands observing nature

Just as I stopped and said "bonjour"
Her smile brought fun to the Côte D'Azur

An invitation to play my heart
In Monte Carlo of her own craft

A smile like that I can't resist
Don't resist smiles, I do insist

Deep in my soul, I searched for dice
To lose a life that I don't live twice

A game of love began with grace
Playing my heart like Princess Grace

I was confused in the beginning
Like Picasso's painting searching for meaning

But as she dealt, I soon forgot
My past and future, and what I got.
    Musa M. Maroofi

Dear Father

Forgive me dear Father, from all of my sin,
Come rule in my heart and cleanse me within.
Help me to be a good witness for you,
Don't let me be a stumbling block,
in the things that I do.
I want others to know you, and love you,
to be cleansed from their sin, to be saved
eternally, and to feel peace within.

Please lead me and guide me in all that I do.
I want to love others the way that you do.
You are always beside me, with an uplifting hand,
To pick me up when I fall and help me to stand.
Dear Father, I want to be a good witness for you,
so lead me and guide me the rest of my life through.
    Gladys Spencer Harp

Night Of The Whippoorwill

On Salt Pond of a summer night,
full moon shining, ever so bright.
Gentle breeze, passing by,
scent of seaweed, changing tide.

From the darkened water below,
a sudden, luminous, phosphorus glow.
Like diamonds sparkling in the night,
as my oars dip down, out of sight.

Then, from the shore I hear,
the whippoorwill, sweet and clear.
How he loves the moonlight,
to sing his song, he only sings at night.

Homeward bound, filled with delight,
from the magic of the night.
Another memory . . . Tucked away,
with all my other yesterdays.
    Eleanor L. Smith

"The Power"

Sometimes I feel I am crazy, all so dark and extremely hazy.
Lost and searching for some way out, desperately seeking another route!
Helping myself to another spoonful of regret.
Because of cheap lies, tricks, and devious threats.
Stonecold: With no love and often not an ounce of respect.
Questioning the "Authority," always ends in debate.
All they have to offer is a noose and already decided your fate.
Trying harder and nothing to do . . .
Stalled in a timeframe as if a lonely ghoul.
A restless spirit left to roam and wander.
Making an escape, cannot stay any longer.
Deathly sick of power and what it can do.
Bribing you with luxuries, when it only takes a screw!
Standing tall . . . the honest and brave, "The fortunate few."
Because in the end some pass the gate and some do not.
Especially the ones who ran away and were never caught.
Defending the fortress of goodness against the guile of satan.
Angry and mad, thundering down his demons and statuary pagans,
The crusade for truth will conquer the unmentionable lies and ghastly deceit.
Because, he will come . . . and GOD will set his people FREE.
    Isaiah Sanchez

War Hero

   A little girl lies there alone, in a bed so large, in a cold and hollow cell, life measured by the clock's sharp ticks. No thoughts of childish things, she cannot run and play, or laugh with carefree joy, in that white, sterile jungle of machines. Fear palpates in the stillness; her rasping breath now spreads out like an over filled balloon; just on the point of dread. Pale faces with their tear-blurred eyes, bend to watch her, touch her brow; a silent prayer for her soul held in each aching heart. She lifts her eyes to see them there; so filled with pain, she seeks to ease, with her sweet smile, yet once again. An only child, a Mother's life, all squeezed inside her fragile frame. How she regrets all their dreams she won't be there to fill.

   For them, she wants to stay, yet wants to go, without complaint, past pain's harsh thrust; her weary form, a shadow of herself, remains, (and oh what tortures she's endured all in the name of love.) And even in that final breath that wanes eternal, her soft voice now echoes out, tries to console, no thought of self, a tiny five, with a Mother's eyes. A sound so weak, but one thin thread, stretched out in time, to ease a mind; we wait with bated breath to hear. Again that smile that bleeds our souls and lays them bare; our bitter tear fall down and when, at last, it softly comes, and then, no more . . . "Mommy, don't cry. I hear the angels," but a whisper on the air, it fills us all, forever more. With those few words, the battle's done. She reaches out, in death to heal, and captures all our hearts.
    Cathy L. Hoffmann

In The Woods

I am sitting here with pen and page, the Lord above has set the stage.
The morning sun is peaking over the hills,
I am in expectation of many thrills.

Slowly everything is coming to be enabling me most things to see.
I can hear some crows not too far away.
For them it will be another busy day.

Off in the distance and up in the sky
I hear the geese as to the south they fly.
Then I hear a noise up over my head.
I am being scolded by a squirrel the call Red.

As I gaze around and look up the trail
I see some flickering white . . . a deer tail.
They are coming this way. My hart is beating fast.
They move so quickly. This moment won't last.

What beautiful creatures, to me . . . A delight.
It makes me so happy when they came into sight.

I settle down again with joy in my heart.
Grateful for all for this, and to be a small part.

Lord, I have to say "You did it again."
I am glad I could capture it with paper and pen.

Mark B. Marriott

Reflections Of Christmas

'Tis the season to be jolly
'mid the mistletoe and holly.
A time for reflecting on old friends and new,
Throughout the whole year, too.

As the eyes of a child are merry and bright,
We recall with gladness that first Christmas night.

The angels sang in voices so clear,
To welcome the Christ child,
That someday the world might hear.

So amid the hustle and bustle of the Christmas season,
Don't forget Jesus in the reason.

Our wish for you and those you love,
Are the blessings of our Father above.

Lois Wood

Number One Band

Proudly the band marched down the street
Making music with such a catchy beat.
Clad in uniforms of sparkling white
They truly were a stunning sight.

Mr. Storms' fingers upheld were two.
That signified "the saints" as they all knew.
The entire band started right on key.
What better synchronism ever could be?

Small drums going rat-a-tat-tat.
How they stepped to the sound of that!
Guys and gals so full of pep
Never once got out of step.

Trombones crying wah, wah, wah;
Big horns resounding with oompah-pah;
Trumpets blaring, sax's wailing low;
Cymbals clanging Go! Go! Go!

The rhythmic beat of the big drums' boom, boom, boom,
Left not the slightest bit of room
For doubt in each judge's mind
As they all agreed this band was one of a kind.

Amy L. Sanford

The Northern Lights

The stars are brightly shining up above,
The moon is full and whitely bright tonight,
I shall be waiting soon, as Mourning Dove,
To greet the glorious Northern heavenly light.
They streak across the peaceful depths of sky,
They seem as beacons of an early flight.
I've watched this view with interest of eye,
From whence they'd come to give this glorious sight.
The Valkyries from afar bring nigh,
An ever unforgotten starry trail.
The crystal hues suspended ever high,
Light up the darkness as a silver sail.
The lights that shine sometimes are called "Great Wind,"
With brightness soft, no fear of growing dim.

Vernon E. Vidden

All Alone

We've had this awful argument
Cruel comments made as tempers were spent
You go your way and I'll go mine
Seemed very apropos at the time
Now I feel heartache coming on
As I sit anxiously by the telephone

Alone, all alone
Seeking consolation in memories
Of times spent with you
Recalling the ecstasy
Of our love when new
Remembering the whispers
Of "and I love you, too"

Reserved, words don't come to me with ease
I can't seem to frame just the right apology
I can only hope you will come to see
Our love is special, meant to be
And you will attempt to reconcile with me
Until then, I will so sadly be alone, all alone

Wanda F. Garr

Untitled

I couldn't sleep so I thought I'd draw a picture
and I discovered I was out of crayons
I wanted to sing but I could find no words
I tried to read
but I couldn't separate the words from the page
I thought of taking a walk
but the roads were not lit well enough
I hoped that I could laugh
but I never found the joke
I wanted to fit in
but I never found the friend
and I wanted to be loved
but I could never find you.

Jessica Peth

Prisoner Of Unrequited Love

Am just a prisoner; no not in a cell or jail.
A prisoner of unrequited love for which there is no bail.
My sentence is a life time; convicted with out judge or jury.
Confessed to the crime of love for you that burns like fury.
Handcuffed, chained and shackled, your beauty's all I see.
Others try to win my love, but there's no parole for me.
Am just a prisoner no not of walls or bars.
Imprisoned by the love of one who's heart is much to far.
You hold the key to set me free, free like the stars above.
But you refrain so I remain a prisoner of unrequited love.

Darryl Gable Aye

Signed: "Love Mom!"

She shows her love,
With all she does,
Even with the turn of a pen,
Her heart does send.

Her signature is very short,
Head held high, she's a good sport,
From the gentleness of her hand,
Ink flowing through the pen, her love she sends.

Looking at her notes,
We all have felt her loving strokes,
Signed there in ink,
With a hug and a little wink.

Just a few words on a piece of paper,
Her love never seems to taper,
Through our hearts, we feel a calm,
Looking at the note; Signed: "Love Mom!"

Amanda O. Lin

Waimanalo, Hawaii

Waimanalo's palm frowns pray
Through the swaying day.

The silvered leaves are rustled beads
In acts of devotion.
With bended backs, their shaping pleads
To mountain from ocean.

The chanting surf, a choir's hum
As pilgrim waves the shore sand strum.
The winded falls etch Koolau's face
As ramparts gothic bound the place.

And for the utmost altar's shroud,
The cliff lines pierce the hanging cloud.
   On all God breaths the trades of time.

E. Chipman Higgins

Scenic Overlook

The mule strains to the plow
Seared clouds barely turn
Neath the shadow of the estate
And cheap labors worried eyes
Dirty nails grip the ledge
As wingtips press white knuckles
Little tongues lick the garbage pail
While painted lips grip the silver spoon
The encumbent paws dirt over his business
As nannies mend the bleached valance
That cloaks the black, brown and red
While the bobtail brings in the day's receipts.
The master chef tests the broth for poison
Wrings juices from the crippled spine
To grease the pan of plenty
Served promptly to the nines
A high rise migrates to more fertile soil
Leaving chipped cornerstone askew
That crowns the hood, as no other could
From knee to wounded knee

Frank W. Bender

I Can Do Anything

I can be free, in many ways I want to.
I can love, in many different ways I want to.
I can cry when I'm sad or happy
I can be powerful and have much leadership!
And most of all, I can succeed in many ways I
want to.

Michael Stellato

Now And Then

It's Christmas I'm no longer a child,
Its beauty made by hands other than mine.
From my easy chair my thoughts wander,
To a childhood Christmas way back yonder.
I see the tree reaching to the ceiling,
I'm so surprised to feel the happiness I am feeling.
There's Mama and Daddy and all my brothers and sisters,
Waiting for a visit from a jolly old man with whiskers.
Maybe tonight I'll catch a glimpse of him from that soft warm old featherbed,
But sleep fills my head and I dream of toys instead.
I smell the food that Mama would bake,
A feast of every type — cookies, pies and cake.
At the happiness in their voices, I am overcome,
And back to my easy chair I return!
My soul is peacefully, my thoughts serene,
For I've celebrated two Christmas's it seems.
The Christmas here now today, and my Christmas memory dream
of yesterday!

Bonnie J. Gullick

It's Spring

So glad am I that I do wake each day,
It's Spring and nice the sun does shine my way,
So glad am I to see the azure sky,
Intrigued to watch the errant clouds drift by.

So glad am I for mountains, rivers too,
For lakes and streams and all the oceans blue,
So glad am I for all the meadows green,
Enthralled with all the flowers to be seen.

So glad am I for all the different trees,
And happy listening to the rustling of the leaves,
So glad am I to hear the song birds sing,
Delighted, watching as they fly on wing.

So glad am I for fauna everywhere,
To smell the scents redolent in the air,
So glad am I to hear the rain drops fall,
And watch the drops caressing all.

So glad am I to breathe the air I do,
Content to feel my life fulfilled anew,
So glad am I to wake to see another day,
With thanks, I pray that God will guide my way.

Mary J. Ciaramello

Woman

Her hair blows in the wind
a strand of hair hits her face
she wonders into the unknown
she dreams of what could be
she hopes her dreams will come true

She tries her hardest to please the ones around her
her life becomes hard
she worries, she cries
she can feel pain no longer, she is numb to the world

She tries her best to be proud of what she has accomplished
even if it is not much

She is proud of who she is
she is a woman and a mother
she is a sister and a friend
she is a lover
and she is a wife

She is never ashamed
and she never lets anyone stand in her way
she is extraordinary
she is a woman.

Emily Odell

Shadow Song

A haunting unfamiliar melody,
Flickers through each moment of my dreams.
A cry of longing of forever sadness,
Comes at night, riding on a moonbeam.
Invading and retreating, leaving
behind a silver ribbon of tears,
A song of shadows, of mist, of clouds.
A song to cushion all my fears.
The shadow song covers me
With soothing, satin roses and lace.
A spirit music with unfinished links,
in the chain of time and space.
The sun rises and dispels the dark,
Putting to rest the gossamer song, in light.
A Shadow song, just beyond memory,
is a glimmer, of a bird, in flight.

Lu Juan Bartlett

Christmas Treasures

I wish I were better with words and my pen,
I know how this started, twas 'bout three A.M.
Your dear Dad was snoring, but that's nothing new,
now I'm awake fretting, what shall I do?
I try to quote scripture, to pray, not to worry,
my thoughts seem to run and spin in a hurry.
The house is not clean, the tree is undone,
no meal in the plans for my family to come.
My child, comes the answer, so plain and so clear
just give them warm memories their hearts will hold dear.
Look back to the Christ child laid down in a manager
'tis His birth we honor, don't make Him a stranger.
Give them your heart laced so carefully with prayer,
this is what's lasting with memories to share.
For you have been given treasures better than gold
dear families to love and their children to hold.
So let us give thanks for His touch and His grace,
as He promised one day 'twill be face to face.

Diane Kemp

A Love Of A Husband

A love of a husband works like a clock.
He ticks when it's time.
Stops when he's ready to unwind.
He climbs the ceiling when he has to do dealings.
Comes back with a smile
and says this is the best there is for a while.
Now let's sit down for a time.
Together we will take in the love
that this husband has for all us.
Bless this family for the love of a husband.
Which lives on through each and every one of us.
A love of a husband makes a marriage so grand.
That's why this man is what the whole world needs
on this land to make everything so grand throughout the land.

Cynthia A. Martinez

New Light

Come to my shadowed window,
and peer through the darkness of night.
For what creatures may lurk
beyond they shadowed window light,
has robbed me of my beloved sight.
As twinkling stars pass as burning embers,
and the earth we live on
represents the devils palace.
For only the darkness of hell within itself,
holds the key for the beginning of a new light!

Jesse Simmons

Untitled

A feeling so
Deep so
Dark so
Scary, that
Your Adam's apple swells up so
You can't swallow
You will know my feeling
When it feels like
your heart has been
turn from
your chest,
You will know my feelings.
When you see
Someone, you haven't seen
in so many years, then lose them
or know you've lost them, you will
Know my feelings.
When you feel like crying
a monsoon, but don't you will know my feelings
When you have no breath left, you will know we love you.

Lauren Paige Roberts

I Know You

I know you, I met you a long time ago.
Things were a lot easier then —
I promised to love and honor you forever.
There was nothing in the world I would not do for you.

Then I grew older. There was so much to do and see.
The world was so big —
As I wondered through life, I fell deeper and deeper into things.
The world was so big —

I made some bad choices, I took some wrong paths,
Until one day the sky fell in.
I sat in a cell of my own making —
Alone, in disgrace.

I know you, I met you a long time ago.
You came back — no, you never left —
And you love me.
No matter what! You love me!

I know you, I met you a long time ago.
And with your help I can know you more each day.
Until I say, "I know you."

Yolanda Johnson

Conversations

Conversations across the sea, across the railroad tracks.
Conversations by fireside, across the ages, so many stages.

The old style, the new style.
The style of power, the style in retreat conversations repeat.

Handling reality, heavy harmony lonely success, good bye to escape.

The moralizers, away from it all.
The side show of pleasure. Conversations we measure.

Onward and upward with the arts. A modern tale, the child market.
Areas of freedom, the talk of the town. Conversations without a
sound. Sex, lies, advantages, the last frontier, the conversation
of a nation. Taking the role of the other. Conversations with a
sister, a brother, a father, a mother. The plays, the thing.
Conversations, that sing. Who has the power? The leaders and the led.
Conversations fade to red. The whip of the world. Winner takes all.
Conversations about to fall. Men at work, models in print.
Conversations blow in the wind. The road of life, fashion in
verdicts. Techniques, changes in character. Conversations are
forever songs and stories of pain and glory. Over personalized
society, the denials. Guilty associations guilty conversations,
the ones that died, the reasons we cried. There's nowhere to hide

Joe Sachs

The Rag And Bone Man

"Rag and bone — rag and bone!" We heard the cockney cry.
Then quickly ran to mother; my brother, Mick, and I
So that we might tell her of the rag man coming by.
With pleading voices asking; "Do you have some rags today?"
There were often times she had none, but smiling, turned to say;
She had some rags stored in a bag that he might take away.

We anxiously awaited for the cart to come in view,
His old gray horse with funny hat — the ears could poke out through.
The old man sat aloft the mounds of boxes, bags and a pram,
Some furniture, a bird cage, toys, a bike and pots and pans.
We two looked up as he grinned down at us with rags in hand.

Then reaching down he took our bag, saw what we had inside
And from a box beneath his feet took out this day's surprise.
A prize so soft, so yellow, a prize so much alive!
We each received a day old chick that we could love and nurture,
Which we did and soon thereafter;
One a hen and one a rooster.

Angela Sandling-Clarke

The Holy Man

As I was walking through the meadows of the fields,
Skipping along, singing a tune and full of thrills.
I heard a voice call out to me to come and see,
I looked around, saw no one and started toward the tree.

The closer I got I saw a beaming bright light,
There was a man in a white robe and I ran with all my might,
I felt peace, was quite at ease and not afraid of Him,
As I looked up I saw a beautiful dove sitting on a limb.

Are you Jesus, I asked Him as I was so amazed,
He reply yes, and I have always been with you all these days.
We sat and talked about the world, people and peace,
About sinners, the terrible things happening and the beast.
I said Jesus what can I do to make this a better place,
He said, love one another, no matter what kind of race.
Then it was time for Jesus to leave me and do my job,
He ascended into the heavens and I began to sob.

Margo Dawson

A Friendly Letter

How wonderful the words can be in friendly state of mind.
Written from the heart and soul more memories we find.

To talk, to write, or give a smile with positive insight;
speak with praise and give the good to show the brightest light.

Randal R. Rossow

Daddy's Hat

Daddy's gone now, he's far away, he took a trip the other day.
His ashes are tucked away beside Momma and Larry, and near Elane Kay.
But his hat remains on the post of my bed, I saw him hardly ever
without his hat on his head.

The memories I cherish, I can see him so clear as he met me coming
in off the plane, full of cheer. He'd say, "Howdy Sis, how you
doin' today? It's sure good to see you, was your trip okay?"
His long skinny legs, his hat tipped to the side,
we'd walk arm and arm in a hefty stride.

God gave us a week to say our goodbyes while Dad lay ill in bed, to
stroke his head and hug his neck, and hold his hand, he said, "I'm
proud of my kids, and I love my girls, I've done my very best, but
now I believe that it's time that I take that long-awaited rest."

Dad left many good memories of work and of play, he really knew
how to make the most of a day! As I look at Dad's hat, and stroke
the rim, I think about all the places they've been. And I pray to God
that Dad's now happy, a hat on his head, and looking right snappy.

Donna Rodgers Brown

We Can Win

The caring and sharing of someone's life makes it possible to go
on through both toil and strife.
There comes a day when we open our eyes, and truly see what
surrounds us, What a surprise!!
Wake up to the danger which come day by day. When we
choose not to help, our hope fades away.
Our world is filled, with both love and hate. We must look at the
two, and choose our fate.
We are all God's children, from beginning till end. Now open
your eyes and see what extends.
Lets not wait for disaster, then take a stand. Lets do it before we
see only sand.
Life is beautiful if we can all work and bend, we all have some-
thing in common in the end.
God made us, and he can break us, it's up to us all. Let us take
the time to connect, before we fall.
Let love come through to touch the hearts, of all those around
us, it's time to start.
Love is the key word that will help us survive. Let's makes
God's world, as he truly strived.
Lets come together, one by one. Then help each other, until we
can finally say. "We Have Won . . ."

Beverly Webber

A True Vision

Enlarge my vision
take away small, hazy notions
Sharpen my focus
on a strong majestic view!
Cultivate wisdom thru and thru
far beyond the now and then.
I have everything to lose, if I choose
to hide my vision behind sin.
Visions are destined to be tried . . .
in them abide, safety and security.
Visions building, O' blessed,
some more, some less.
A tangible tree, in my vision, upon it, He . . .
where my sins forgiven went to be.
'Twas seen only by the Power of His Sovereignty.
A true vision of beauty eternal, a delightful new start,
in Jesus, who changed my heart.
A true vision,
by Divine Nature,
Infinite one, The Son.

Joyce A. W. Powell

What Beads And Water Conquer

Abuse is a hunger "that stirs the quick"
want of power drives on neighbors sick
spills of hate from foaming flesh
bent on flogs to chide success

Every use and thought carries the deed
violent infection beyond greed
What beads and water conquer
cruel beast with scandalous vigor

Her repugnance is measured
cast away thieves pleasured
threats casually assail
survival begs "tip the scale"

Winds spirits howling in terror
flight won't flee the viper
Dismiss wanting thoughts of freer
Who's guilt will share the bearer

Intimate thought counselors
conversation blurs
those hesitant advisors
endangering sirs

Lynda Cokuslu

The Master

He went into the garden to steal away and pray
He was so very tired you see, and it was getting late
He's been up since early morning and he knew what lay ahead
He groaned aloud in agony as he felt this awful dread!

"Father, let this cup pass from me, if it be Your will
Never the less, not mine be done, the scriptures to fulfill.
Drops of sweat as drops of blood fell from His Holy brow
the Son of God has been betrayed, they're coming for Him now.

Betrayed by one that He had loved and cared for as His own
The one who kissed Him on the cheek to make the Master known
To whose who came to take Him, to take away His life
To place on Him a crown of thorns, this man who knew no strife.

To hang Him on a rugged cross for all the world for all the world to view
And place Him there between two thieves for things He did not do.
To give Him vinegar to drink and pierced His Holy side
After the Son of God cried out, and hung His head and died.

But this was not the end you see, He rose up from the grave
Just as He had said He would in a matter of three days
God's plan had been completed, the victory had been won
When God stretched forth His loving hands, said "Welcome Home, My Son!"

Lillie Prather

Confession Of What

I continue to listen to what you say.
Word for word for word.
How can you say these things?
How can all that we have shared come to this?
How can the warmth and passion of
    intimacy that we held for so long bring about this sudden hostility?
The anger in your voice.
The rage I could clearly see in your eyes.
I have never seen you like this.
As I ponder on what to do,
I realize that I know nothing about what you are talking about.
How can these words be uttered from your mouth?
I try hard to pacify myself.
I listen to your words — yes, patiently listen.
Where did this explosion of anger come from?
I can not understand.
Yet, I remain content to the fact that I still care for you.
I remember the best times we shared.
I remember the treasures that continue to realm in my heart.
The love, the respect, and the trust.

Esther Shonola

My Husbands Love Affair

He's driving the streets and running around
Continuous trips to and from town
Long drives in the country, alone in the dark
There's never an end once he's made a start
He caresses her neck, there is no doubt
As he places his lips upon her mouth
He drinks in her bitter sweetness
And cuddles up to her innocence
While I wait at home or while I'm at work
I have more than my share of hurt
I smell her scent as he walks in the door
I brace myself for the coming horror
I lie awake and count my tears
Lick my wounds and try to ease my fears
Will this madness ever end
Will his family ever win
For his other love is not a woman at all
But the ever controlling alcohol.

Stephanie D. Herren

Untitled

Just a summer of
pixie sticks
and
rubber band flicks

His hands on her hips
her lips

Under diamond dancing
skies
While the candle light
dies

Sharing a Day of Diapers
thought
hoping they won't get
caught

Catching lightning bugs
stopping for slight
hugs

A tickle of her toe
then she must go

Just a summer of pixie sticks and rubber band flicks

Kate Warner

Angels Wings

Dawn to dusk faded colors greet, many gather just to peek,
Pastures beyond horizon run deep,

Gazing on beauty only lonely seek, beckoning brightly lit street,
Given a name silently discreet,

Young lives struggle to unfold, winds blow hard becoming cold,
Strain with such might so bold,

Leaves shield around they fold, with countless wonders to behold,
Becoming aged in colors of pure gold,

Dreams flow above malted air, nudges spark new growth to appear,
Boldness grows only as dare,

Faith remains grace to share, so many fall never to care,
Beauty from angels wings so rare,

Scattered out to their side, hands outstretched far and wide,
Whispers ring their ears and ride,

Secured by trust hearts are tied, down toward earth they glide,
Nature demands all must abide,

Diving into grooves as may dew, beauty rests waiting for a cue,
Bringing honor to which has grew,

Struggles end only for a few, colors rise forming unknown hue,
Patience now must begin anew.

Larry David Rader

Serendipity

It's funny how things turn out the way they do.
It's strange how life always gets its way.
Something goes wrong and emotions collapse,
but we still fall when it turns out alright.
And the red light across the street
shines blue in someone's eyes.
It's completely ironic when the end
turns out the way you always expected it to.
And while some people search
for the meaning of life,
others search for the meaning
of the words written on the cereal box,
finding that they mean the same.
It's funny how things turn out the way they do.

Kristen E. Coleman

My Angel

I walk through the streets of this big city
Wondering if I'll ever see you again
Knowing that deep in my heart I know you
Will always be here near my heart
Walking beside me watching my every step
Smiling and laughing with me on good days
Crying and hurting with me on the bad days.
In my heart I feel you always
Carrying me through the toughest of my tribulations
And walking with me through my greatest accomplishments
Knowing you're with me everyday is what carries me through
I believe in angels because I believe in your love for me.
You taught me to be free and enjoy life to its fullest
You taught me to express myself and believe in myself
Through your words of wisdom today I can be strong
Thank you, Mom, because of you I am who I am today
You are my angel and inspiration. Always.

Betty Ortiz

A Passage Traveled

Wistful thoughts come as dreams in the night,
     tarries away with the dawning of light
Casting earnestly into the moments at hand,
     leaving the slumber, behind on the sand
A faint beckoning for fulfillment, stirs the breath into a sigh,
     a fond remembrance of the tenderness, still often makes me cry
Our youth once stood, bright-eyed and hopeful,
     our love basking in joy, and never doubtful
In the sweetness of belonging to each others heart,
     we vowed forever to never be apart
The sun has set on the passing of seasons,
     far away memories, no longer searching for reasons
A passage traveled, held dearly and tucked away,
     strands of endearment weaved with time, through the gray
And yet we still run through the valleys of bliss,
     in my soul, it begins and ends with a kiss.

Deborah Lee Mason

A Stranger's Face

Journeying toward the mountain peak from the last valley in life,
Determined to reach my destiny an image from the past reminds
     me of that night.
It was a darkness so thick one might think a light cannot shine,
How confused and distorted had I allowed this to grow and
     linger in my mind.
So struggle is inevitable and they say it won't be easy.
But you see, I looked into the face of a stranger one day,
And although I did not like what I saw the pain was there to stay.
There was a softness hidden deep inside that would change the
     essence of his being,
I knew it was solely up to me to release him.
When I looked closer into the face of the stranger I could see,
That it was not a stranger at all but a reflection of me.

Ernie Banks

A Fire-Bellied Toad

A little Fire-Bellied Toad was by the road.
A predator I know not which
Saw the little toad's head twitch.
It swooped down on its target fast.
Now it would have its lunch at last!
The little toad showed its belly
And turned the enemy's courage to jelly.
And that creature was so scared
Did it attack again?
It didn't dare!

Nathan S. Hower

There's A Place I Go

There's a place I go were the Blue Birds sing
Were joy is songs fill everything
The thick it lush and full of berry's
cherry trees over powered by cherry's
The forest thick and full of trees.
Filled with gentle buzzing from the best
arched rain bow's forever fill the sky's, as fluffy go floating by
the brook runs still as if to say, this land is please keep it this way.
but I can not nor can you, for beyond this land lies skies not so blue
The streets are then full of blood, lakes dried up all that lies there mud
forest gone burned to they round, gunshots are the only sound.
War and hatred fill are souls, ultimate power being are only goal
yet is it and cry for all, grade cities that continue to crumble
and fall people die in are wars, and of diseases without cures
I wonder if it will ever end, war and hatred cease and bend
Love and hope fill are heart, with new beginning and new starts.
But will that day goes passing by, I'll continue to sit here and cry.

Jaime Schwartz

Memories Kiss Eternity

Eager eyes embracing; paralyzed perpetual motion.
Captivating warm words, seduce sad smile.

Collision conceals loneliness! Enslaved liberty! Love,
Obliterates oblivion! Obsessive hope heals. — Memories!

Pure salvation suffers. Summers sighs sultriness;
Flowers brightly bloom. Birds cheerfully chirp;

Luminous lake laughing! Thirsty skyscrapers scream!
Perfumed twilight! Twinkling, moist moon murmurs!

Lips lust. — Kiss! Ethereal eyes eating;
Bodies tenderly touch. Quenched hearts humming;

Profound passion pours. Trembling tears storm!
Drowned fears flooding; songs sing secret!

Weeping wanderers pray. Thank glorious God!
Drink dreams. — Eternity!

Jose Miguel Vasquez

Strange But True

Joy and peace are some truly invaluable partners.
Kindness and goodness won't leave me alone.
Gentleness and self-control have been hanging around quite often.
Faithfulness is always prodding at me.
Long suffering seems to mold me into this type of shape I can't
use words to explain.
Love, he always has this special smile on his face and tears in his eyes.
However, the smile on his face is actually there but the tears are not.
When reaching to wipe the tears from his eyes I was told that
the tears seen are my own, caused by his smile upon my soul.
Although he's right here with me he's also for off.
He told me where he is I too shall be and tears are not allowed there.
Hmm! Strange but true is often said when in reality it's not
strange at all and it's still true.

Ernie Banks

Man's Search For Christ

I Looked for you, but could not find you,
I called for you, but you did not hear me,
I Reached for you, but could not be comforted,
I could not live life's challenges alone.

I stood before you, yet you could not see me,
I heard your call, but you did not listen,
I carried your burdens, and alleviated your load,
I accepted you, but you rejected me.

Nicola J. M. Stacey

Tomorrow's Turtle Today

I'm so slow . . . metamorphically speaking of course, even under full
steam ahead damning all torpedoes in sight. I'm so slow . . . to realize
in this rat race of the rats, by the rats and for the rats — I'm not even
a rat. I'm so slow . . . to show my true feelings. When asked how I
feel are you curious about my technique or actually the condition my
condition is in? Should I say, "As well as can be expected under
circumstances prevailing?" I do say, "Okey dokey," which sounds
kinda hokey. Only that's what I grew up hearing. *It* meant — Things
could be worse, but they aren't, thank God! And things could be lots
better, but aren't. I'm so slow . . . to learn to live with less than
mediocrity, but more than I bargained for. Weaving other turtles'
dreams into reality is my specialty. Often they do not know they're
turtles too. They may act like rats running the race in any event to
earn the wherewithal to pay this turtle to weave away, as there are
really a lot of pieces to reality. Placed just so, as not to offend the
ascetic point of view and by way of successful feat to look as though
they've always been there. More importantly the reality of a dream
is a painstakingly patient assemblage of ourselves and I am midwife
to that experience. I'm as slow . . . as every nail, screw and stroke of
the paint brush must be, so as to show you and me to each other.

> *Brad Merkl*

illinois ghost

bouncing hard on the rusted tractor
he looks out over the bones of
ancestral patriarchs restful under
the harvest moon full and yellow nearly
kissing the lip of horizon against
the black wall of the illinois night

he moves ghostlike down the sand road
keeping just ahead of the dust threatening
to envelop him from behind as if he were
going to fade into the landscape with the
generations swallowed whole by vast fields
of stubble and oceans of prairie grass

through which he drifts across the shipwrecks
of decaying barns whose weathered boards curl
outward from the frame casting troublesome
patterns of moonlight and shadow compelling him
to hum the melody of an autumnal hymn in prayer
for the passing of summer as she slips into the
arms of october who has bled the leaves of green
cathedrals and withered the flowers with frost

> *Mark Power*

Child Of God

I see a world filled with hate
I want to reach out and touch it —
So as to make it all better
But I — just me cannot
The world moves so quickly —
    As though in a rushing tunnel
I know not how to make it all better
Kiss it —
Which of the many booboos —
So many — Too many just a kiss wont help.
I pray — Lord take away the hate
He answers with tear stained cheeks —
    Man has a free will
I know — as the tears flow — I whisper —
Save the world my little ones
Judge not — Hate not — Love with all
    your heart
Feel and be —
Be one of God's children —
And Love

> *Jessica Leah Byrd*

Life's What You Make It

A friend is nice to have, it's true
But thoughts can make you feel good too
Like a sailboat crossing the ocean blue
or a puppy playing with a worn-out shoe
Life is not designed for you
Life is merely what you choose
So, take the time to choose what's right
Don't try to blame your luck on life
You can make your life, or sit back and take it
The choice is yours, because life's what you make it

> *Wendy Lynne Little*

My Child Has Needs

I sit there and listen, but don't comprehend when all around me
are learning.

While I sit there I want to asked questions to understand but I
know that I can't because it takes away from others.

So, I go away hurt and say to myself, "So what, who cares"
because I don't and won't remember what was said like I have
done in life as a child so many times before. Because I didn't
comprehend, while others go away nurtured.

Don't let me go away like this, I have needs too!

As an adult, I say "no, stay and fight the battle of the unconcerned,"
"God won't let you down."

> *Karen Whalen*

The Meadow

I strolled my way across the field to a breakage in the fence,
it was there I discovered a partial covered meadow path.
At first glance it seemed the drainage from an earlier shower's
passing; however, my curiosity said to follow the rain aftermath.

Gently squeezing myself through the narrow opening,
with no intentions of tearing my shirt on the barbed wire.
The sharpness was carefully bent toward east and west,
careful attention given to my full attire.

Once to the other side, my curiosity was raised to a higher level;
feeling like a child again to a mystery, surely a hint of joy.
A man chooses to brave and risk the unknown,
the real adventure belongs to the boy.

After crossing the distance of a very short hill,
I found to my pleasantry of surprise, an area of color and flowers.
Clumsily, with a trip and fall, the tombstone, a simple reading;
words that took the minutes and transpired to hours.

The inscription: Had very little in life to share,
have passed on through the valley of the shadow.
Will not be returning soon,
so please enjoy the comport of the meadow.

> *James Trammel*

Untitled

There's always someone on the other side of pain;
Unintentional glances become piercing and friends
are split apart like the guillotine beheads its foe.
How does the triangle become the circle, with edges
smoothed by apologies and time healing wounds that
bled into the soul

Incessant pools that stain my clothing remind me of
the failure of my own humanity. I struck the blow that cut
through the heart of the people I love;
I became the killer of dreams and the portal of misfelt desire.
I am the one who kissed wet and dried hard. My touch has
no sense anymore but I remember the softness I once had.
Is this my punishment?

> *S. L. Hanson*

Christmas

Can you hear those sleigh bells on your roof
Can you hear the tapping of the reindeer hoof
Guess who's coming to your home tonight
Sure it's Santa Claus you're so right
You will see Santa's outline as he crosses the moon
You will hear him singing a happy Christmas tune
Wonder what gifts he has in his sack
It sure does look heavy upon his back
Bet you can't wait to see what tomorrow will bring
Joy peace happiness plus many another thing
For this is the holiest night for one and all
Jesus was born tonight in an animal stall
Hurry off to bed and pray Santa's sleigh won't stall
Say a quick prayer once you are tucked into bed
Let all those happy thoughts fill up your head
Let us thank the Lord for sending us his son
For that is how the very first Christmas begun
May Jesus bless you with unending happiness and joy
May Jesus bless each newborn girl and boy
May Jesus bless your family this holy night

Catherine Giblin Carucci

The Desert Fiend

We call to praise America and the forces of the world
For the unity they showed us all and the lightning they unfurled.

In the name of God we came: in freedom's name we sang.
We saved our people bondage-held and made our freedom ring.

The desert fiend, from hell he came:
   Satan's beast, Saddam Hussein.

In fear he looked up at the sky.
   In hate he lived. In shame he'll die.

The fiend Hussein, by name Saddam
   God, stop this vicious, Godless man.

Our heroes strong, so young and fair,
   Protect us all by being there.

They then became the wall we need
   To stand 'tween us and desert fiend.

Our heroes present, desert-burned,
   Bleed and die, our thanks well-earned.

Our heroes great, of times just past,
   Lie there in quiet peace, at last.

Warren A. Gasink

In Remembrance

  It's holiday time again
And it's so hard to keep from crying
  The family and friends
is missing him and sighing
Wishing he was still here
  To share in the fun and laughter
For he went away in pains, unto another plain
  That great forever after

So never more will we see his smiling face
  Except in photographs,
No more will we hear that gentle voice
  Calling out to us by names
Except in our memories, there we can retain
  For he didn't go by choice

And forever he will lie
Below this ageless sky
Deep beneath the cold harden ground
And I know he knew, that I loved him too
For he was my sister's son.

Jean C. Jabradally

Homegoing

On that Palm Sunday, it was a beautiful day
I brought you home Mother, for a short stay
New curtains I had put up in your room
Preparing for your weekend visit, soon
When we were eating, I heard a strange sound
I checked, and there was no one around
On Tuesday, you were fine and anxious to spend
Three days with me over the Easter weekend
The next morning you called and you were sick
God took you home — it happened so quick
It was after then that I knew
And in my heart, I believe to be true
The meaning of the strange sound that day
God was sending a message my way
I had heard the rustling of angel wings
Waiting to take you to Jesus your King
It's been a year since God called you home
But, in my heart, you will always live on
One day I'll hear the rustling of angel wings
And join you in Heaven, with Jesus our King.

Jeanne Whetzel

Patience

She's been in love before and had her heart broken
But from the good Lord not a word was spoken,

She understands he knows what she has been through
And he allows her experiences but to him
she must remain true,

She believes in the power of prayer and that
God will always be there
Relying on the faith that no matter who she
is or what she is doing God will always care,

She grew wiser to what she wanted out of life
A kind Christian man to make her his wife,

Now she understands from what God has showed her
That he has the perfect man for her and she
must be patient for this sir,

She lives her life day to day believing in
him and his eternal love and life
And she awaits patiently for the love of
her life to make her his wife!

Betty Langford

Please Don't Fiddle With The Strings Of My Heart

You've grown cold, that's why we drifted apart.
But that's no reason to fiddle with the strings of my heart.
You left me alone, and oh so far apart,
So why, oh why, must you fiddle with the strings of my heart.

You've been fiddling with the strings of my heart.
Ever since the day, we drifted apart.
So why can't you let bygones be bygones.
And please don't fiddle with the strings of my heart.

You think that you've the only pebble on the beach.
And I know that you've completely out of reach.
So get out of my mind like a flying dart,
And please don't fiddle with the strings of my heart.

Many days, have slipped, and passed away,
But memories keep lingering in my heart.
I will grieve for you until my dying day.
So, please don't fiddle with the strings of my heart.

Leonard Sorenson

Elected Silence (Sing To Me . . .)

Silence strums memories
      subliminal to pulse
    in breadths of Times . . .

Sometimes I sense
    meshed music's well-spring
      spumed from psyche's depths
    symphonic: Crescendo
     from tacit TRIPLE F
    to thundered TRIPLE P . . .

Sometimes I feel
    sparks fleshed STACCATO
      flumed from lows through highs:
    Syncopes synaptic
     solace listening soul
    for solipsist's spirits . . .

Silence thrums melodies
     through storms, serenities,
    antiphonal . . .

    G. G. Gilchrist

A Burning Memory

You knew how to,
Get to a young heart.
You passed through
Where everyone else failed.
You shown me you cared.
How could you believe in me?
When you were million miles away.
And you don't even know who I am.
But I've watched you on TV
And listened to you on the radio.
You always made me feel
Like it was just me
You were singing too!
Now that I'm grown
I owe it all to you
'Cause you melted my cold, cold heart.
And I can show my love.
After all this
I never got to meet you and now all I got
Is the memories of you on the TV and radio.

    Kimberly Hall

At The Foot Of The Cross

At the foot of the cross, I knelt and cried,
"Was it really for me that Jesus died?
Was His blood shed on Calvary's tree
For one so undeserving as me
Was He nailed upon that cross
Were my sins so great a cost
Yes, 'tis true, it was revealed to me
As I knelt at the cross and cried.
'Tis true, it was for me that Jesus died."

At the foot of the cross that glorious morn
Within my heart, His Spirit was born
My Savior, my shepherd, my forever friend
He travels with me till my journey's end
And one day I'll be on Heaven's shore
Reunited with loved ones gone before
Face to face, my Savior I'll see
Jesus my Lord, who died for me.

    Jeanne B. Whetzel

His Trusting Care

When we are faced with trials,
Of loss of health with pain;
It's hard sometimes to comprehend why,
It comes like chilling rain;
Like storms with nature hurling,
Against us both day and night,
Leaving many anxious moments to linger,
Without answered questions within our sight.

Each day here is only the beginning,
Of a long journey which we all shall make.
Yes, we each will have our turn,
For an opportunity to take,
A pleasant journey to another time,
With a better place in which to live.
The fare is free to one and all;
The gift of mercy only God can give.

    Doris Lee Gribble

Appalachians Remembered, And They Look

For Mai, and in memory of Gricelda Alegria
           "Are
          we going
        to wait a spell
      <u>at the mountains,</u> before
  the new day, on our way home, ma?"
"Always. Those mountains are . . . Considerations.
Well, everyone always talks about The Mountain,
Even so, its dome of gray, its dome of blue,
and of 'what it be,' and 'what it do.'
And about the thin red line near about its base.
But I see the dome will change to amber tea color,
Orange pekoe, for the dawning of the wondrous new day.
And I know what it is, and what it Does.
It is God's eye on our mountains great,
a damp reflection on their history,
a Warm guidelamp to our dawning day."

    William A. Watling

Unknown to Me

Want
forever, always
do I really need anything?

Never held onto anything
for long
was it what I wanted in the first place?
Or an image?

I forgot what it was that I
wanted

I realized that I don't want anything
anymore
I don't need anything
anymore

What ever I have is enough,
for me

    Kristina Fridas

Giving Up

Giving up will never let you make things happen
If you surrender to adversity, hard times will never
let you go forward in life.
When adversity and depression strikes you, and
hard times tear you down,
imagine positive and don't forfeit you ambition's or your dreams.
You can make things happen if you have faith in yourself.

    Bharat Mishra

Love Is

Love is a physical response towards another
Love is a need, a want, a pleasure, but love
always takes its place
Love is a silence that you can not hear,
only feel.
Love means a friendly compassionate family,
friend or even stranger
Love is a feeling of vision between foreverness
Love is a fantasy and love can be a reality,
as it soars through the sky and touches
someone where hate can not reach.
Love is never a stranger to someone's heart,
only if it is too late and hate has
taken its place.
Love can also be a problem when there is an
unexpected quest but never mistake
the power and strength of true love.

Danica Camille Woodward

Goodbye To The Dream

It's time to say goodbye to the dream
For things were not as they seemed.
Face reality, don't be led astray by false schemes,
Life is still good, although some events seem mean.

Dry your eyes, no more crying,
Wipe the dead past out of your head.
Face the future, no more lying.
Have no fear for what lies ahead.

Little fool who gambled and lost,
It's funny how the dice fell.
No more games of win or lose;
Bury the dream without singing the blues.

It's time to give life new meaning,
And time to be hopeful as well.
Now that there are no more schemes,
One big smile and say goodbye to the dream.

Loucilla Ellis

Untitled

The bright orange glow, climbs over the hills
And for some, seems to give chilling thrills.
It's bright orange glow fills
The sky with a color show.
The clouds as fluffy as pillows
Quite the opposite of weeping willows.
The grass a showing dark green
The flowers are blooming with a colorful scheme.
The birds are chirping with cheer
As to arouse the wandering dreamer.
As the sun begins to draw weak
The bright orange glow is over the mountain peak.
As we lay down to get a good nights sleep
We cherish the days and nights to keep.

Bradley Pekar

My Dream

   I dreamed there was a stream of
water when I got there I sad, my head
swims but, I can't. A hand come down on
each side a man stood I am your grand father
that you never seen, and,
I am your grandfather you never seen than I woke up.
   I believe that the stream of water
was golden river the hand was Jesus Christ
the men stood on each side was my Grandfathers.

Doris Anderson

Trojan Horse

Trojan Horse
Secret Gift
the more that I think
the more that I drift
Away from my thoughts
Away from myself
"What am I?" I think
somebody else
Inside not out
I'm all torn apart
Tell me somebody, who's tearing my heart?
Totally different, no one the same
No matter what happens . . . I'm not to blame
It's the inside not out
please help me shout
somebody tell me what I'm all about.

Andrew James Dean Stone

It Would Have To Be By You

If I were to be loved, it would have to be by you.
Because you are so sweet, kind and gentle, too.
Our relationship is built upon honesty and gentle trust.
I'm glad we didn't chose each other solely upon lust.
We shall be the couple that will never fall apart,
Because my love for you will never lose its spark.
You were made for me and I was made for you
That's why if I were to be loved,
"It Would Have To Be By You"

Deidra Roberson

Spring

Spring is the time when all nature awakes
Aroused from her sleep by the breezes that blow
She arises and shakes off her mantle of snow
Then goes right to work to bring to the birth
Those bright little blossoms that beautify earth.

So swiftly and silently she works away
That where yesterday was just a bud
A blossom you'll see today
It may be the Star Flower or the Pine Anemone
The lily of the valley or a violet there will be.

Many more will follow as the days go passing bye
Others bright and beautiful Mother Nature will supply
Yes, there's beauty in the Spring, time and inspiration too
In the little acts of nature and the things that she can do.

Let us then awaken with her
And whate'er our task may be
May we go about it gladly and work on joyfully.

As we look to the Creator
Of all things both great and small
And give thanks for the Springtime, which may be enjoyed by all.

Mildred Gooch

Eve In Her Garden

An apple fell out of time, not nothing my eyes' reaction;
so I picked it — nearly — to survey what I didn't see before.
And it fell from my hand into a far abyss — saying,
Reach out and don't mind fear of falling into an unknown
conscious.
Seeing now, I couldn't help but notice how — turning around —
I missed the apple and tripped into this hole.
When I looked that way, it left me to wonder
if I shouldn't have gone around another way —
or straight to what I felt —
instead of the glance behind that went into its own.

Christi G. Ivie

Untitled

My cherished friend, my little love, a question I will ask of thee,

If you could have known what your future would hold,
Would you consent still to journey with me?

Would you have waited upon the road that day,
for me to gather you near?

Would you have curled up contented and warm,
without even the slightest fear?

If you could have known that the years would pass
quickly my dear, and that your body would age,

If you knew that the day would come when our
playing, would be like a time worn page.

A week and two days have already passed, since we laid you to
rest in your place, your lovely green eyes and your soft silver
paws are only part of the memories I chase.

As I wrote this poem as an Ode to thee, It's strange to say, I felt
your spirit with me. An odd little breeze blew and rumpled my
hair and just for a moment I felt you tarrying there. I thought I
heard the rushing sounds of wings, taking to Heaven, and
imagined you bidding farewell, with glee. If you could have
known Whisper, what your future would hold, would you
consent still to journey with me?

Denise C. Underwood

A Dream We Share

My love and I have a dream
  to wade side by side in a babbling stream.
From Little Pine to Kettle Creek,
  the elusive trout we seek.

But, as we travel through the land
  my love and I go hand-in-hand;
from the top of the highest mountain
  to the bottom of the valley's floor.
The wonders of God's masterpiece
  we discover and explore.

All around us lies our treasure,
  In God's eyes may we measure
to our very soul within
  pure and clean blessed by Him.

And of the wondrous sights we've seen
  may our voices sweetly sing;
with every breath and beat of heart
  Oh Lord my God, how great Thou art!

Marilyn S. Moore

The Other Side

  You would know that the deep blue waters
are beautiful, for the reflect the sunlight's gold
  and I'd answer: they reflect the sun, the world,
and so much more; the way eyes reflect your soul.
  You ask: how can compare your eyes to
the water for the two things aren't alike?
  and I'd tell you: It's like looking into a
mirror, for the eyes are the mirror to your
soul; they reflect the way you feel inside, the
way the oceans reflect the days and nights
thoughts run through your mind,
  you look at me and wonder, you let the
thoughts run through your mind, you wonder
how such things could be . . .
  I would answer you: there's only so
much you can see up front, yet inside there's
so much more to discover, if only you can
look beyond the iridescent wall.

Nancy Nunez

Man

Man is a dominant animal full of love hope hate and sin
Man's the one who built the world we are in
One thing is definitely known without man the world
would not have grown
But all is not beautiful on this earth
People dying of mind and body even from birth
Technology increases day after day
the faster it grows the more we pay
Population grows man has war
crime is high drugs grow more and more
Brother versus brother money makes greed
man has all he wants yet still he needs
Man versus animal animal versus man
all for domination of this mighty land
Is this a time of despair or a time to grow
only the God of man will really know

Randolpho L. Muniz

Knowing Lonely

It seems you're forever gone from me
And I'm always knowing lonely
I turn around and you disappear
When all I want is your body near

Thoughts of you do gladden me
But, still, even now, I'm knowing lonely
Don't know how and don't know when
I'll have you holding me again

In my empty room, your ghost surrounds me
Hovering thoughts, yet, I am knowing lonely
Though time is still while you're gone
I must have the strength to carry on

My aching heart often reminds me
It's been years and I'm still knowing lonely
For the rest of my days I'll not be free
Of the feelings I've had and knowing lonely.

Lori Quint

A Child's Place

It is with happy memories that we think of you today
Because you are very special to us in a wondrous sort of way.
I like to think of children as holding the key
to each star, and hanging it on their family tree.
For there is an air of sacred joy
Wrapped in the heart of every girl or boy.
As each child comes to take their place
We all must welcome them in our life's space.
Because God sends them here for our salvation
Around the whole world, in every nation.
So many years have come and gone
Since Christ was born in Bethlehem,
Yet the world's children must now carry on
To bring peace on earth, good will to men.

Eulah G. DeMatties

Only A Day

He's a boy only a day,
So soon to grow up from childhood's way.

The hours are few that he delights in Daddy's hug,
the dart of a butterfly, sand on his feet.

Too soon comes the moment to confront the world,
war-torn, in turmoil.

He must give all to sow peace and love to change that world
for those who will follow.

He's a boy only a day.
Dear God, give him strength for all life, I pray.

Ann Patterson

The End Time Hour

How can we as children of God
Think there's nothing for this world we can do,
Even when we were at our lowest point in life
Jesus never turned His back on you.

He said to go out and preach the Gospel
Not to one, but to all nations,
He didn't say to limit yourself to a certain people
The one that's lost may be your closest relation.

Do you really think were doing God's will
If we don't step out in faith and try,
Or is it going to take another rape or murder
When we can see the pain and tears in their eye.

It was God's voice that spoke to my heart
As my heart stretched wide open to listen,
As He said to me, your job's not finished
There are still lost souls that are missing.

For I picked you my child to do a good work
For not to do what I ask, there's no reason,
For behold I come quickly and judgement is with me
Are you ready for that coming season.

Richard B. Edmundson

What Is Love . . .

To say that love is a many splendored thing is to objectify and entrap it.
Love is not anything, nor is it everything, love simply is.
As simple as it is, love is most complex when contemplating it.
Love transcends all thoughts and words. It is ever-present in those who try to possess it.
Explanations of love are non-existent and attempts are futile.
Expressions of love are endless and many.
Within each of love's expressions lies loves manifestation; but not its meaning. Love has no purpose, nor does it need one.
Love is sought, but its seeker never finds it. Love is received and its giver overflows and gives it completely without being diminished.
To say, "I love you" is not enough; but my gift of love to you is all I can give you that is totally of me. For it to be a true gift of my love, I can have no doubts or hesitations and I cannot look back. The only thing I ask in return is that you accept my gift.
My gifts of love to you are many, each containing a total manifestation of my love for you. It is my true gift that cannot be priced or returned, which has cost me everything yet has cost me nothing.

John Edward Conery Jr.

Untitled

Taken down a lonely path,
she walks slowly on her way.
Here she is alone,
only her thoughts carry on through the day.

She needs not know where she's going.
She only needs to find her way.
Down the lonely path that is ahead of her today.

She has no fear,
knows what she has seen.
Down the lonely path she can only dream.

She sees a shadow up ahead on the path.
She kneels and bows her head.

She's to frightened to lift her head up.
What could the shadow be?
The shadow on the path in front of me.

She decides to turn and run away,
back down the path to yesterday.

Now her feelings are pain and sorrow
knowing she has ran back to yesterday
knows she must get back to tomorrow.

Sheila Ragazincky

A Christmas Humbug

I don't like Christmas . . .
I don't like seeing Christmas wrapping in stores before Thanksgiving.
I don't like my child drawing up an almost endless list of expectations.
I don't like feeling guilty if I can't provide everything on the list
I don't like the expectation that I should send everyone a
  Christmas card who sent me one last year . . .
I don't even like Christmas cards . . .
I don't like people thinking they must give a gift because it is Christmas
After all, it's not my birthday, so why should I receive anything?
I don't like Christmas cheer, which so easily gets translated into
  drunks on the highway.
I don't like the fact that Christmas makes us all
  consumers more than producers.
I don't like the fact that Christmas has made it more blessed to
  received than give
I don't like Christmas because our concern is more cost than Christ
Christmas is a Christ-Mass Christmas is Christ.

Carol Hutton

Tis

How long will it last — tis grief
Tis continuous turmoil — no sign of relief
Such beautiful intentions — everything so fine
Not to mention — once a true friend of mine

Such beautiful hopes and warm embrace?
Congratulations and families smiling faces
Tis such a promising future from the start
I love you's, I need you's — from the heart

A wedding ring, vows, two frozen slices of cake
But all the gifts in the world, do not a marriage make

Walking down the isle, oh such a beautiful smile
I do, I do's, sweet kisses — and all the while

The road we traveled had an unseen bend
Going downhill to an off and on, dead end
The marriage license we put through the shredder
Was the last serious thing that we did together

Such a saddened end for a love so true
Happiness, once shared, for now
Tis through.
PS. I still love you.

Don Juan Williams

The Angell Family Tree

Many, many years ago
this union was begun.
First there was a daughter,
then there was a son.

Another boy, another girl,
then two more boys came after.
One more daughter, one more son,
their home was filled with laughter.

Like the mighty oak tree,
the Angell children flourished,
because their parents love them so
they sacrificed and they nourished.

One by one each child branched out
with a family of their own,
knowing that no matter what,
they'd never be alone.

Because this thought remains forever
in their hearts and minds . . .
. . . Within this family, love will always
be the tie that binds.

Carolyn Fogg

Passion Of A Poet

The passion of a poet is to bring together love through inter winding words of affection.

The passion of a poet is to reflect every emotion of the heart through the lyrics of life, songs of joy, happiness, pain and despair.

The passion of a poet is to bring laughter of funny things and tears of sad things through words that fill up the very depths of the soul with heart felt emotions.

The passion of a poet is to touch the deepest sensitivities of the soul with words true to conviction, spellbinding hearts of the young and old alike bringing forth truth, grief, sorrow and atonement.

The passion of a poet is to see the unseen, feel the unfelt.

The passion of a poet is interwoven in truth and spirit captivating every thought and emotion

The passion of a poet exist in the fullness of life.

Bryant Branch

A Cry For Help

"Could you please help me? I need to tell someone what's happening!"
"My mommy is doing a crime; I know because she told me so,
And I'm so afraid she'll get caught then be taken away,
Oh, please talk to my mom!
I did try to talk to her but she wouldn't listen;
She just says; "It's none of my business"!
Please let her know; "It'll be to a prison she'll go."
Please make her listen! Ask her — "Doesn't she even
care what happens to don't want mommy to go,
I need and love her; tell her I said so!
Let her know that if she stops dealing drugs?
"I cross my heart"; I'll be one son to be proud of!
Also tell her this: If she changes her ways?
I'll promise to always be good and stay in school;
For one day I will want my mom to see me
graduate from high school"!

Jacqueline T. Manibusan

A Young Boys Dream

Born on primitive thoughts with hope.
Religious contents bring expressive belief.
Sheltered worlds exclude faint doubt.
Reality appears in a crisp clear image.
Drawn to perfection, precisely measured
Deep sweet breath, engulf the horizons triumphant air
But time of age, taunts a twisting fog
Turmoil erupts with a whirlwind effect
Wandering winds, whisper a chilling word
Erasure to sight, known only through time
The hovering blanket forms a cloud of darkened memory
Erasing unique style, and creative deed
Gasping and clinging to a new eyes vision
Deteriorating palaces yield to a circle that's square
Spurting growth intensifies this song of madness
Until a wilted flowers aroma, is captured by society's flower bed.

Joe Poskin

My Saving Angels

Oh Angels up in heaven, guide me through each day.
And take me under your wings, so I'm safe along the way.
Protect me and be with me in everything I do.
My love for God is growing and I need this help from you.

I will not ask for favors, but maybe just a hand.
To put my feet down firmly, as I walk across this land.
Oh Angels up in heaven, take me toward heaven's gate.
And let me walk there slowly and never have me wait.

Gregory E. Johnson

Untitled

Broken hopes, left behind thoughts
Always misplacing our mind
Never replacing ourselves

Time goes so fast, forget so many faces
We see past loves
But never one present

The world is cruel
Everything falls apart
But nothing ever returns

JodiAnn Morris

The Little Room

My little room is filled with pain
My little room is filled with tears,
And I alone play the game,
My little heart all filled with fears

At night, when everything's asleep
I sit alone inside that room,
At night, when darkness is so deep
I think alone inside that room.

I look around that little room,
I look and see a ray of light,
I fly inside that little room
And touch the light that shines so bright

I reach beyond that little room
To find a door that leads to sun,
I touch the sun beyond that room
And feel the darkness is long gone.

That little room is my heart that fears,
That door is the hope that's never gone
That light is heart that always cares,
And my game is forever won.

Gomberg Julia

Wee Voice Within

While contemplating cleaning my house one day
A wee voice within me seemed to say,
"Get rid of your junk, dear old Doggie,
Get rid of your junk, — please do,
For if you don't do it soon, Doggie,
It's going to get rid of you.
Don't put off the job any longer.
Face these facts and you'll see . . .
You're not getting any stronger
You're not as young as you used to be.
Yesterday is gone now forever
And tomorrow is not in view
Get rid of that junk TODAY, Doggie,
Before it gets rid of you."

Doonie Peeples

Yesterday

It only feels like yesterday, when I saw
your shining faces. You were both so bubbly
inside, celebrating life to its fullest. No one
thought that in a wink of an eye your lives
would be gone forever. Someone tore your
innocence away. The question of "why" will
never be answered because of suicide. Is it just
a dream, or am I just fooling my heart? I
know you're gone, but it hurts. The day my
pain goes away is the day I will be in heaven
with you.

Cora Negvesky

Dad

Oh Dad! How I am going to miss you.
I can't picture how it is going to be
without you sitting there
each day at noon waiting for me.

But my! The precious memories of you
that are so very dear.
From the many footsteps I've followed you
in the fields of plowing corn.
And the many times we've slipped off to the creek
to fish. Just to pass away the morn.

But Dad I know you are at rest with Jesus
and can breath the air that's pure and free.

But Dad you will always be with me
in my heart so very dear
and no one ever loved a Dad
as I have you for so many years.

Gladys June Mayes

Paranoid About Vegetables

We stripped the ground bare.
No grass, no trees, no mold,
will rot, grow, or discolor the
putrid brown of the earth.

We made this ground bare, uncaring.
But the enemy cannot strike us here.
Their thousand handed bodies, and cone-shaped,
warped, pointed legs have no place to root.

We, the non-plants of the world, have united.
Our lives are linked by a common fate.
No mammal or insect is safe from
their green boiling hatred of us.

The vegetables, all plants, wait for us
each to fall. They have turned against nature
and seek revenge for our past depravities:
Harvesting, walking, pruning and eating.

Before our time, they want us buried
deep in the blackened earth where they root.
Join with us now on the barren soil,
before you fertilize a plant.

William H. Golden II

Picture Perfect Skies Of Blue

Picture perfect skies of blue
Open wide for sunshine's passage
Soaring sea gulls flight overhead
As free as their wings will take them through

Beautiful green palm trees dancing with the wind
Oh, feel the tropical breeze upon your face
Through you hair, through your clothes
As if to say, I'm all yours, come race
Sand pebbles prickling with each gust
Surrounding and twirling, blowing and scooping, I catch the chase

The blue-green sea, connecting all of these
So vast is her body, her offering infinity
She plays with the sky, the sun, the birds, the wind
And all of her creatures within her

I lie on my back in the warm soft sand and feel the sun heating my skin
I hear the birds singing, I hear the trees dancing
I feel the tropical breeze all over, I feel the prickly sand pebbles
    rushing
I hear her playing with all of them
I open my eyes and I see
Picture perfect skies of blue

Dana Thomas

Untitled

Happy Birthday Ada Kessler have a grand day
You've brought happiness to a lot of people
What more can I say

In Nineteen Seventeen I was a lad of ten
That's when first knew you, you were Ada Stanford then
You came to Grange riding in an old Model T
Later on the Queen Mary you sailed across the sea

You took the Orient express looking for the Russian Bear
Every place I can mention you say, "Oh I've been there"

The last time we met was at Linc Cockerham's night for old timers
    and friends
How wonderful to remember things that are past
How hard to say good night when the evenings ends

So keep on being happy and greet us with a smile
We wish you the best of every thing

Lewis W. Pyle

One Star

As I gaze toward the heavens
on this cold, black night,
I see a star shining, twinkling so bright,
and as I look out to the far
left and right,
I see darkness, except for this
blinding light.
Could it be that all the others
have left the skies,
or my imagination totally making them hide,
out of a misty cloud, the moon is passing,
and yes, more lights are twinkling
in heavens everlasting!

Vivian Levine

Burning Desire

The tomahawk warrior with little chance,
in his native tongue, pressing his native dance.
See's past his heart's burning desire,
for all of his wants are consumed by the fire.
Dancing 'round in all his glory,
listening to the native story.
Grew up a warrior agile and fierce,
his heart even arrows could not pierce.
The burning desires he held inside,
the desires only war could hide.
His fame spread, a warrior at heart,
but no one knew he was torn apart.
The eternal flame within his soul,
would forever burn and take its toll.
Continued his slaughter day and night,
until he could no longer put up a fight.
One night the warrior pierced heaven with a cry,
he said "I am heartless, and I must die,"
He took his life beside a quiet stream,
and laid to rest the warrior's dream.

Alyssa Wensel

Thank The Lord

Last night as on my pillow I lay
I happen to think, I'd forgotten to pray
To thank the Lord for sending me you
A guy so loving, kind and true
A guy who loves me for who I am
A guy who lets me know he's my man
Just how lucky could one woman be?
Thank the Lord for sending you to me

Loretta Roberts

The Door

We begin the year as new children,
Children of the earth, wind and sky,
We will live in the world till the very end.

Till death knocks at our door, the door of life.
The door that we spend most of our lives avoiding.

This door is a door of change,
This door could not be opened by anyone,
But we must do it ourselves.

This door can make you weaker or stronger,
This door is also used as hate by some.
But was never intended to be used in such a manner.

This door can't be used for riches or fame,
But some feel they can enter this way.

We must find the courage to use this door the way God intended
God uses this door for us to find him,
To be with him, to love him, as he loves us

You ask can I find this door?
Yes for it is the door to your heart.

Lorena L. Schnitzler

A Teenager's Poem

When I was a child I never knew
The problems I would face as I grew.

I considered myself luckier than most children —
I was given a solid foundation from which to start building.

My parents provided love and worked as a team
To provide me with confidence and high self esteem.

But when I became a teen and began to mature
I wasn't quite ready for what I'd endure.

There was more to life than sitting in the sun,
Riding my bike or just having fun.

I had to prepare for how cold life could be
With few that care and a lot of disparity.

There were people without homes who couldn't pay rent —
People who where hungry, without a cent.

But there was a lot of good to be found
It I stayed positive and just looked around.

In closing I guess it's just part of growing up
Learning about life and becoming an adult.

David Cohen

Raphael Sapphire VII

To those who have a mind with which to think,
It is the greatest business in the world;
Freed from taxation long ago, for its promise
To care for the sick, afflicted, widows and orphans;
However to this day it does not fulfill
Those obligations and responsibilities
For which it was brought into existence.
Is it not time for the church to begin caring
For the genuine needs of its own here and now?
Rather than pretending to concern itself
With the saving of souls, for a price,
For some other life, some other time, some other place.
Is it not time to free taxpayers from the burdens of welfare
Which are rightfully the provence of the church?
Or is it time to free the church of its tax exempt status?
How many churches have been closed
Simply because they didn't bring in enough revenue?
Have not the princes lived well enough, long enough
At the expense of the masses?
The truth will set you free!

Edmund Ralph Wright

His Heart's Harbor

God's love pierces through the darkest night of the soul,
illuminating and guiding you to the safety of
His heart's harbor.

Mona Lisa Keller

The Fall

"Reach out and grab me, I'm falling fast.
My future has now become my past."
The things forgotten or left untold,
Are things that terrified an eight year old.
A helping hand I did disparately need.
They cut me fast and laugh while I bleed.
So, brick-by-brick I built my wall,
Strong and sturdy, never to fall.
For if it falls you're open prey,
They sneak-up on you while you lay.
Afraid to move, afraid to scream,
You convince yourself it was all a bad dream.
Until the day, when the wall has grown strong,
And love and protection for which you still long,
Approaches in armour upon a white horse,
Wrapping you up with incredible force.
Don't send him away, invite him in.
Dare to trust — you need a friend,
Who will lead you so gently, and help you along,
To a safe, peaceful place you can finally call home.

Mysti Pierce

Footprints In The Sand

As I walked the cool, sandy beach at noon,
The sand trickled between my toes.
I tried to follow foot prints, and wondered were they friend or foe.
I sat far a spell, with my mind drifting far away.
I put my towel down, and there, I decided to stay.
I marveled at all the footprints, some where very large,
And some were very, very small.
It made me start to wonder, just how was their day
Soon the mighty waves washed to shore and the
Footprints were there no more.
I know I see a new set, it did not take me very long.
A handsome man, three children, and their dogs were
On their way.
Their gala voices in laughter rang out, a pleasure for me to hear.
The neighbor man shouted out, how are you my dear?
I'm fine I shouted back, and all to soon, they were out of sight.
The mighty waves rolled to shore again, and the
Footprints were very light.
But all to soon the mighty waves rolled back again,
And the footprints were no more

Virginia R. Sieggreen

Resolution, Part One

I went to sleep on New Year's Eve and awoke on
a plain, a barren plain dotted with the giant
skeletons of tempest-twisted trees for as far as the
eye could see.

Finally I picked a direction and started
walking. The scent of an undefined evil had
gradually risen to thicken until I could
hardly breathe!

Gasping for breath I stopped and looked back. In
the far distance something very small and
dark had appeared. I pressed on.

After a seeming eternity something small and
dazzling appeared in front of me. I turned
toward it and looked behind me.

Keith D. Dewees

Untitled

Laughter from the front yard flows,
Through the window, as the wind blows.
My heart fills great with pride,
As the children laugh and play outside.

They are playing together well,
Outside this small place we dwell.
While they play, I sit and ponder
Of God's greatness and all His wonder.

God gives us all the things we need,
A house, a car, even a little seed
To plant the vegetables that we grow.
It is all His greatness that makes this so.

When I am and feeling low
I pray to God and He lets me know
Our blessings are very many,
He has furnished us with plenty.

Laughter flows through the window again,
Then my feelings are the same.
Our family is hardy and very healthy.
In faith and happiness we are very wealthy.

DeRiece Carroll

Tortured Soul

His heart it bleeds and cries in pain,
As the blood of his people falls like rain.

Alone he cries to the distant hills,
The terror they'll face, the hate and ill will.

Marching for miles through his heart and his soul,
The places and times, that only he can know.

Lifting arms and voice to the sky,
He asks the Great Spirit, to please tell him why.

Why must this happen to a prominent proud band,
While they rape and kill his people and his land.

Settlers and soldiers, fear what they don't understand,
To narrow minded to learn and comprehend.

Knowing only to be white is white, to be black a slave,
Knowing the Red Man as savage, not as brave.

The buffalo are gone, the white man's way of extermination,
Never killing their pride and determination.

Onward they strive, for their freedom of desecration,
To save them all from the reservation.

The prayer of a man, no one will ever know,
A man, A fighter, A warrior with a Tortured Soul.

Stephanie Denise Spencer

Antiquity

Where were you before?
I have known you forever
Somewhere, somehow
We have always been together.
You have the aroma of yesterday,
The incense of antiquity
You are a morsel of infinity
The immortality of always.
What basket of the past you bring me.
The picnic blanket, the nuts and all the fruits,
The honey, the biscuits and the berry's juice.
These are our immutable gardens
The same wine we drink again
All is too familiar.
Nothing is ever arcane.

Tracy Ferrer

Song Of The Sea

Sad songs whisper epitaphs
Of a people of the sea.
Waves wash into shore
With repeated melody.

The tavern smells of smoke,
As the sailors tip their ale
Into the mouths that sing of a sad, familiar tale.

The night was windy, and the waves were high.
There were no stars to navigate by.
   The ship was tossed.
   The sails tore away.
   The captain saw no hope, but knelt to pray.
Rain bulleted down and crashed on deck.
The men struggled on, even though anticipating death.

The sailors were young, but strong and brave.
They lost their lives in the fight they gave.

And now at night, when on the shore,
Some sailors walk and hear wind roar,
   They whisper a song for the ones they knew
   Who fought and died as so many do.

Debra Couturier

Dancing With The Woman From Bulgaria

I have been dancing with the woman from Bulgaria,
The one I dance with in my mind.
She has taught me lots of exciting, intricate steps.
She gives me the courage
To go beyond the old, stilted steps
That those in my past
Tried to restrict me too.
Those steps were based in fear, slavery, and shame.
They were the steps of dead people.
The steps that the lady and I do now,
Are based in freedom, courage, and pride,
They are the steps of life.
They take us to unexpected corners of the floor,
Where those who are tied to the old steps
Are afraid to go.
Inside you,
There is a woman from some exotic place.
Dance with her.
It will be awkward and frightening,
But it will be worth the dance.

George Sherman

Those Old Tintype Pictures

There they were, always hanging along the wall
above the staircase, in my Grandmother's
house! How many times as a youngster, did my ball
go bounding down, as I saw those old tintype pictures?
Who were they, that looked straight down upon me,
o'er those many years? I dared not ask who
they were, or, I would have been told not to touch or be
near those pictures, or e'en ask about them. The glow
kept me looking at them, each time, when my travels,
up and down the stairs, required me to do an extra errand.
Many years have now gone by, and as I grew up, the marvels
that those pictures were still hanging, as if fastened
with glue, but, Grandma had passed on, so I got brave,
and reached up, and one by one, brought those old tintyped
pictures down. What would I do with them? Then a crave
came! Who were they? I turned them over, and there glinted
my first clue! The names and dates had been skillfully
engraved on each, and as I read the writings, I knew
the truth, that had long ago, been staring down upon me!
They had been my great, great grandparents, and they had kept
me pure!

Eva M. Roy

The Wind Of Life

It seems to me that life
goes with the wind in a certain sense
you can see
your dream, your wish
and you walk toward it as any man would
but then the wind starts to blow
and it blows against you,
pushing you backward, away from
your dream, your wish
you fight the wind by trying to step forward,
but it is a useless effort
so you stop and pray for the wind to change its course
you wet your finger and hold it up to the wind
and you notice that the wind has indeed
changed its course,
through your faith the wind is coming
from behind you, pushing you toward
your dream, your wish
and finally you reach
your dream, your wish.

Mirjam D. Troesch

If I Can Change The World

If I can change the world.
The cost of living will decrease.
And nothing else will increase.
Everyone will have good job.
So no one will ever starve.
There'll be no living on the street.
Everyone would have a place to sleep.

If I can change the world
There'd be no more stealing and more killing.
Children would be able to play outside their homes.
Parents wouldn't be afraid to leave them alone.
There'd be no more lies and no more cheating.
No more women and children beaten.

If I can change the world.
Black and white will make amends.
And we'd become good neighbors and friends.
I would put all drug pushers and users in the pen.
So this world would be a better place to live in.
If we all just believe in the man up above.
He'll see to it that we have a better world.

Willie Hawkins

Senior Citizen's Christmas

Christmas comes once each year
To many it brings joy and cheer
To the senior citizens a special treat
And the joy of living cannot be beat
To the many years we have endured
And from our goals have not been lured
We cherish the day as we arise
And thank the Lord that we are alive
We bow our heads in silent prayer
To those who have gone over there
And no more toils and strife that were endured in this life
We seniors have seen many wonders
Enduring the storms of lightning and thunder
Of the many years of our lives
Making the most like the bees in the hive
Giving aid to others is our aim it is true spirit and not a game
We have traveled far on life's way and thank the Lord we are here today
And enduring in sickness and health
And having many friends is our wealth
Christmas is celebrated in many ways by the people of many
lands today

John F. Moore

Spirit In The Body

Watched with open heart, open mind,
one day searching to find.
The connection between life and death,
closed eyes and soul,
nothing more than a darkened hole.
A place to fall,
never to retrieve,
always reaching upward for something to achieve.
Once struck by lightening,
to collapse and lie still,
yet, in a way alive all from the inner will.
Physically gone,
but spiritually still there,
a non-beating heart,
a non-moving body, such a pair.
One day to connect, set the body free,
from the soul that held the key.
To rise and fall, where the body lies,
yet, the spirit drifted on, it never dies.

Janelle Carpenter

Goodbye To Addition

Goodbye to addition
I know I have this affliction
Alcohol and drugs are not for me
If you are my friend you'll let it be
I have some wrong's to try to make right
At last I see the light
Try to renew your faith in me
A different person I will be
No one knows what the future holds
With the help of a higher power I'll reach these goals

Glenn Ann Spencer

Colors Of The World

If the colors of the rainbow are true,
Single one out and were all through . . .

The rainbow reflects the faces of mankind.
And the beauty and the light shine bright together.

But when one man singles out his favorite
There will be no more rainbows . . .

For all the colors where meant to go together
Like mankind should be
Together in peace for eternity!

Robin Gierman

Twilight Whispers

Full moon's a shinin', pine trees entwinin',
Silhouetted against cool starlit skies.
Cattle are lowin', frogs croak a knowin',
From the meadows where the firefly flies.
Beaver ponds ripplin', where fish are nibblin',
In the bright path of reflected moonlight.
Mule deer are creepin', 'neath willows weepin',
Faint muted shadows in a hasty flight.
Wildcats are prowlin', a coyotes a howlin',
Up in the mountains and deep canyon coves.
Night birds a cryin', warm breezes sighin',
Among the rustlin' quaken asp groves.
Earth worms wigglin', teens are gigglin',
Under cottonwoods where cool waters wend.
Kiddies are dozin', sleepy eyes closin',
To a lullaby sung, as dusk descends.
Folks are relaxin', from all things taxin',
Till the velvet twilight visually fails.
A bright star's fallin', as sleep comes callin',
And the still hushed silence of night prevails.

Elva Smith

Mother's Love

A mother's love is sweet like honey,
it is a symphony of beauty, I love you,
she whispers when you sleep,
who is like her, who inspired such a love.
Then the answer comes from far up
above and reaches down to tell of his love.
And through his son comes a mother's love.
We see it through nature it fly's
high like the eagle and runs deeper than
the sea, like a budding flower giving
nectar to a bee, or like the giant sequoia redwood tree.
Like the stars on a moonlit night,
oh they're so beautiful, oh they're so bright.
Thank you father from on high and
above for giving us our mother's love.

Jonathan Smith

Eulogy To My Canine Companion

Although my heart is sad without you.
The memories of our many enjoyable times together
    are far from few.
Oh how your tail would wag, and your eyes sparkle
    so bright.
When I came home from work, and greeted you
    each night.
How I miss your warmth on my feet while you slept at the
    foot of my bed.
And how I miss your bringing me the newspaper, and waiting
    for a pat on the head.
My faithful companion, we shared so much.
We didn't need words, we communicated by touch.
We had over a decade together, and your absence now,
    I will miss.
But, your pain and suffering is over, and in doggie heaven
    you live in bliss.

Helen E. Brittsan

Savior

I am waiting for you now in love here
Your time will come when you will follow me
Many years I have cried a joyful tear
But not when you will be set free
Evils gotten you by his deathly grasp
No love to be shown just tricks and false lies
I have seen enough and break through at last
The brightness of truth shines at her eyes

Those eyes full of lies had to go away
Her eyes were made new by the glory of you
The light pushed the darkness until it ran away
You were my savior how can I thank you

Your love was the piece that put us together
We will never be separated ever.

Amy Steele

Alone

Sitting here in a world all alone, in a world to
which no ones knows.
    To find my heart should be easily done, but not to
me will it come.
    I search and search but with much despair, for
there is no one here to care.
    When is there no more for me to bare? To be alone
is my biggest fear.
    But alone I am and alone I shall stay, at least for
a great number of days, because I was wrong and for
that he pays.

Michelle Skaggs

Jaleesa

You know she always starts to yell
When momma puts her hair in pigtails

She's really pretty and you know momma dresses her in style
She'll make you run, make you laugh, forget about life's burdens for a while

Her veggies usually stay on her plate
And she makes sure we don't sleep late

She bangs her plate and throws her cups
She fights sleep to make sure she's up

She loves to play on her thin purple rug
And never forgets mommy's and daddy's group hug

We tell her always "Baby play fair"
But she still lets no one sit in her chair

You know sometimes she thinks daddy's a jerk
When I say "see you later Boo Boo gotta go to work"

She loves to dance and put on a Broadway show
Thank God almighty I'm here to watch her grow

A chubby face and pretty smile is what she is to the world
But to me she'll always be "Daddy's little girl"

Jason E. Schoolfield

Dear Time Keeper

Time keeper slow down for me,
there's so many things I want to see,
I appreciate the things that others don't see.
Slow down for me, give me the chance,
to break down the world's gruesome trance.
To stop the hurt, or to ease the pain,
to lift life a little, and take away vain.
There's so many things that must be done,
that take so much time once they've begun.
To show the love that once was lost,
the gift of time is what it costs.
To make up for all the missing parts,
to mend up all the broken hearts,
to give my life what it needs from me,
to show it the beauty of the things I see.
Time keeper slow down for me,
give me the chance to let them see.

Stephanie Hinkel

The Poet

Gentle fingers strum the lyre,
The poet sings of earth and sky.
His subtle tune the fools admire
While stronger hands let arrows fly.

The poet walks on cloudy heights
But sees earth's jagged bends and turns
And from the friction of his breathless flights
Can't shield himself from searing burns.

Austere the poet's tender gaze
His visions, haunting and remote.
A mist surrounds him as he plays,
His lyre, his life, a lyric note.

Through the fog the poet walks,
Strumming still his lyre.
A stranger in the world he mocks,
A bird in flight who scans the mire.

But the poet still is child of earth,
Of life's sustenance must he partake
And he cannot ignore his birth
When belly hungers, tremors shake.

Joyce Kosman

The Reflecting Mirror

I look in the mirror
And what do I see!
A familiar face reflecting
back at me.

What do I see in this face
Sometimes joy, sometimes pain
The rugged ridges which
time has claimed.

There was beauty a long time ago
Those eyes, those eyes, purer than gold.
The wrinkled smile that still remains
That fought through hardships grief and pain.

Though the mirror reflects the past
the love in our hearts will
forever last.

Lillian Woodard

I Love You

If I told you that my love for you,
was never ending.
Could you on your knees be thankful,
forever bending?

I have so much in store for you my love.
For I send my spirit from above, to help and
teach you how to love.

I sent my son to die just for you.
I hope to me, you'll always be true.

Through good time and bad, happy or sad.
Look to me, I'll help you to be glad.

I am the one, who sees just what you need.
For your heavenly father, can surely meet
all your needs.

Olga Ryman

Another Sleepless Night

Agony drives its force inside me.
Tears melt the smile that existed yesterday
   upon my face.
How can happiness change so effortlessly to
   anguish?
Wanting to slowly drift away.
Denying reality and entity.
Piercing coercion wipes me free of all emotions.
feeling that the end is approaching.
No! My contemplations will only make
   it another sleepless night.
Another desolate eve without the only
   one who could rescue me from
   this painful affliction.

Laura Ann Lahm

The Silent Tree

Underneath the darkened tree,
lies one, who once was me,
who could not forgive his self,
for actions he took, within the dark factions.

Under this old oak tree,
was where you used to watch for me.
Yet the vortex lurked around the corner, unknown to me,
as soon it would throw me deep within this hollow void . . .

So underneath the silent tree,
Is where I'll sit and wait for thee.
For when you turn to look for me,
I'll be here beneath this silent tree . . .

R. T. Leonard

Christmas

This is the season of peace and goodwill;
also the time when light hearts might stand still.

The giving of gifts, decorating the tree;
this beautiful world, God's wonders to see.

It seems a shame that some go without
while many have more than sufficient about!

Look for those gifts that dwell deep within
the souls of those who have nothing to spend.

It isn't the wrapping nor is it the glitter!
Big or small the size doesn't matter!

If we give from the depth of our heart,
God's gift to others, now isn't that part.

Of giving back God's gifts to us
and keeping Christ in Christmas!

Shirley Reynolds Goodall

The Joys Of The World

The joys of the world are all around us,
There are many for us to hear and see.
   The mighty snow-capped mountains
And the deer running wild and free.

   Here we will name only a very few,
Daffodils glistening with the morning dew.
   The great eagle soaring "oh" so high,
And a newborn baby's first cry.

   The grand old flag waving in the gentle breeze.
Little squirrels frolicking in the old oak trees.
   Roses blooming around the garden gate,
A little wren calling for its mate.

   The laughter of children at play,
And the golden sunset at the end of day.
   A child clutching its grandfathers hand,
"Yes, there are many more in this great land."
   But the greatest joy of all,
Is one we cannot hear or see.
   It's within our hearts
      When we're on bended knee.

Mabel Mitchell

My Mother The Mountain

As a breezy child, I arose each day to a noble grace which stood loftily before me.
Whisking me from my sheltered slumber, I found comfort in her strength

Her life as one devoted to preservation and refuge, never did I fear her demise.
As the seasons arrived and departed, she welcomed their gifts and weathered them well.

Spring brought her the rains, cleansing her soul and exposing elegant blossoms and delicate new life which she nurtured until youth could stand on its own.

Summer granted her with radiant skies, warming her spirit and displaying a golden core, and from upon her shoulders I could view life at play and lazy days.

Fall gave her the harvest, diminishing her hunger and flaunting brilliant transformations as creatures great and small filled their bellies and abodes to hearts content.

Winter endowed her with snowfall, concealing her weariness and providing her with a downy sanctuary for all of those who relished and relied on her care.

At last, Mother laid me to rest and peacefully slept.

Joyce D. Hallstrom

Burning Bridges

You say you are tired of living
This up and down life with me.
Well, go ahead, leave and see if I care,
There's more than one fish in the sea.

We yelled and we screamed at each other
We fought almost the whole night through.
You said "you really were tired of me,"
And I had certainly had enough of you!

But with the coming of daybreak
The sanity, it seems, returned.
How could we live apart from each other,
After all of our bridges are burned?

You're the one I've loved for many a year
You're the father of our children.
How can we give it up and just walk away
After all of the time we spent buildin'?

Is there not some way to work this out?
You know I still love you, dearly.
Please, say we can try and let this pass by,
The bridge hasn't burned yet . . . but nearly!

Fran Young

Artist At Work

I often watched him work, with brush in hand.
How delicate his touch as he would dip
the tip to color;
then, with patient care
he touched the canvas.
Oh, how deft his stroke!
Quite spellbound, I would watch his brush apply
a swirl of gray, a touch of red, a streak
of brilliant green against the azure blue.
"You stand too near!"
And as I backed away
the forms took shape;
a tree, a garden plot,
a friendly dog, a bird or two in flight.

So now, when life's confusion presses me,
I think, "Perhaps once more I stand too near."
And as I back away, again I see
the beauty that the Artist painted there.

Alma K. Brabson

Special Friends

A special place of sunshine,
Lives within my heart,
As I think of all my special friends,
That have given my life such spark.

What blessings God has brought to my life,
To share in my passing days;
Friends to talk and share coffee with,
Unloading troubles, and sharing joys along the way.

Friends who lovingly share their time,
When you need to talk, or have a good cry;
Friends to share birthdays and lunches with,
And movies, and shopping and pie.

Time gets away from all of our lives,
We're so busy with family, work and chores;
And we need to keep our priorities straight,
God has shown us how important these are.

But I'll always take time to give God my thanks,
For the friends he has sent my way;
And I'll remember to tell them how special they are,
As my friends may not be here someday.

Cheryl Hurte

Too Much To Ask

Is it too much to ask . . . life worth living
Is it too much to ask . . . for a life
Is it too much to ask to be able to pass
    through all of my torment and strife

Is it too much to ask . . . to want comfort
Is it too much to ask . . . to have rest
Is it too much to ask when I'm tired and spent
    to find strength to finish life's test's

Is it too much to ask . . . to be happy
Is it too much to ask . . . to feel hope
Is it too much to ask at the end of the day
    to find slack at the end of my rope

Is it too much to ask . . . to want caring
Is it too much to ask . . . to feel love
Is it too much to ask if there's someone for me
    that fits like a hand in a glove

I know to find strength look in numbers
I know one's only half strong as two
Maybe all of my askings are prayers Lord
    and all that I'm seeking in you

Kennetha A. Vitale

Faces

The many faces of myself
I've always longed to know;

To see and understand them
is hard, as they do come and go.

I've never really felt quite complete,
though many people might think so;

I'll always look at things so differently
do you understand? Or is it possible.

When you look at me
what is it you see?

I hope you see what's really here
what it is, is really me!

Karen Butler

Watching And Hearing Without Seeing Or Listening

Life, . . . it stretches out before us on what seems an endless road.
A treacherous lonely journey for just mere man alone.
The sounds of rushing time, you know it floods our flesh and soul,
then slowly trickles down our weary brow as though it were a feather.

Hasty now our vigil pace, yet this hour of truth lies close at hand.
Could the prize we seek . . . be only just the race . . .?
Mankind strives for things already owned, but not yet so perceived.

The glitter in your partners eyes, or a tear upon their cheek.
Silently emotions boil . . . until we win the race!

The sweet sweet scent of nature's flowers, though short lives
that they be shall touch our souls and shake our lives in hopes
one day we'll see.

We travel quite a weary road, like visions late at night!
Quickly now, like a lightening strike . . . is the coming of the son.
Yes, eerie sounds of silence . . . and mysteries will be won.

The spirit of the follower . . . it brags in boastful pride,
". . . We're great upon the earth."
Where followers are thousands, and the leaders but a few.
Is it enough for us to say "I knew the winner of the prize"?
No! I say, beware — that day . . . it's closer than you think.

When are you risk such precious time . . . consider if you can!
That the gifts of time nor that of love . . .
Cannot be bought or sold!

Austin L. Strader

Child Of Rage

Broken tattered and bruised
a child lies alone,
wounded by those once trusted —
by grown-ups who have
covenanted to nurture, love and care for
a daughter of deity.
Assailant — brutally attacks
the most sacred of gifts.
Stolen are the innocence and laughter
of childhood.
This child is now more mature
than those who have
raped her innocence
with obscenities and vulgar playfulness.
Now tattered,
the shreds of decency lie strewn
along the pathways of life.
Remaining are the bitter obstacles
to overcome, overpower and leave behind
in the peace of healing.

Andrea Lauritzen

I Wonder

I wonder who you'll be . . . little baby so new.
What will be the place God has made for you?

Will you be out going? Or will you be shy?
Or, will you be inquisitive and always wonder why?
Will you love to chatter? Will you love to sing?
Will you love to wiggle and do most everything?
Will you be quiet and dreamy as thoughts fill our mind?
Will you like to pretend and read every book you find?
Will you love to play in water, or rather play in sand?
Will you love to be muddy, or want no crumbs on your hand?
No matter what you long to be I hope you'll be . . . Just You!
For God gave you to us to love . . . He made you unique and special too!

I wonder who you'll be little baby so new.
Our Family is the place God has made for you!

Beverly Tikkanen

To Rise Above

Although you are gone and gone for good,
I would return to the happy times if I could.
Instead I will rely on memories that don't erase,
Or your teasing, your expressions, the touch of your hand on my face.
Sunday I knelt at the alter as I shook and cried,
Carrying the guilt and anger alone I tried.
Failing, I gave my problems to the Lord to resolve,
Trusting I will receive strength to rise above.
With the greatest effort, I will replace the tears with a smile,
Because holding my shoulders back and counting my blessing is my style.

Janie K. Cline

Just To Believe

Just to believe that things
one day will get better and
the reason that I know
because my God has promised me so.

I know there are a lot of
bad things in this world
that sometimes get you down,
but you got to keep believing
that things will come around.

So don't give up what you
already have achieved,
because all it takes is just to believe.

Steven Wilson

I Can't Stay

I give to you my special gift
from the very start

You've had it with you all along
I gave to you my heart

I know it's hard to understand
why we feel this way

And though we know we shouldn't be
we long for each new day

I feel your sorrow and the hurt
that longing for can bring

But like the rose that sleeps through winter
awakens in the spring

Our love is like that barren rose
just waiting for one bloom

And though my heart was already taken
for you, I made the room

But until that time is right for us
we'll take it day by day

I hope for you, you'll never hear
me say that "I can't stay"

Jana M. King

To Grandpa

crying
he wants out of the little glass ball
calling out to his love
receiving no answer
reaching out a hand for help — no one
nobody left to ease his fears — to calm his worries
no one left to keep him alive
no purpose — his eyes are already closed
the loneliness burns his immortal soul
submerged under hatred
no angelic beauty to sing his song
he solely creates the notes
playing only to fill his mind
with the music, the golden music
that once brought magic, only brings tears
to his forlorn eyes
he grows weary
his heart aches in pain
soon the tears, the everlasting tears
will take over his body.

Theresa Witchger

Life's a Journey

Life's a journey we travel, sometimes we travel different roads.
You and I our paths keep merging.
Forces not our own keeps us traveling alone.
Baby I love you, you may not realize it, but you love me too.
Have the courage to give us a chance,
there'll be no regrets.
Baby check it out, the past and the others.
They all leave and the paths lead back to you and me.
We could own the world if you stay with me.
But then; who needs the world if we have each other?
Don't be tempted by the fireworks.
Follow the steady light. I am that steady light.
I have always been there for you,
even when I was mad at you.
Love me the way I love you; you'll have no regrets.
Come, come the clock is ticking, our lives are diminishing.
Pick up the challenge you'll have no regrets.

Engred Listhrop

For Always

Maybe it's his eyes, caressing me, dearingly,
there's always his smile, the radiance of his love,
yet, at night, when the wind is blowing, my heart is glowing
for the thought of his arms around me is what calms my mind.
Maybe it's the way we dance so well together bodies moving,
in unison, every step in place,
or maybe it's the way he walks, slow, steady glidingly
no, it's his arms, securely, affectionately, passionately
holding me making me know, I'll always be his,
those arms, long, strong, demanding my entire body give in
to his love.
That mighty love that can never be erased.
Never duplicated.
Always remembered as the best.

Carolyn M. Adams Whitfield

Love

As I sit here alone, all by myself
I think about love, what's it all about.
Is it being there through thick or thin,
through love or war or bitter end.
Is it being there when the trouble is great
to help calm one's nerves never too late.
Or maybe just carrying about someone's life
always there to help them see the light.
It hides around the corner or down the street
dares you to find it so you can lose sleep.
But when you find it everyone knows
it's a feeling of joy you never outgrow.

Stephen Jay Brown

My Brother

Brother my brother
The words "My brother"; it scares
Me those words "My brother"
It flows so freely from your lips
So meaningful so soulful
Without a break in your voice my brother
Are you really a brother
We've suffered too long, too hard together
To many deaths, to much pain, not enough gain,
Far too many games, things have got to change
My brother, no more of the same
Identify yourself brother
As my brother, with unity and strength we can attain

George Baines

Respect Each Other

We should respect each other
And try to live as one
Not fight against each other
Because in war there is no fun
First you call someone your brother
Then you stab them in their back
You say that you're a friend
Then you silently attack
Bob Marley said it in a song
And we can plainly see
Your worst enemy can be your best friend
And your best friend your worst enemy
For who knows your little secrets
But the one you call your friend
The same one you put your trust in
Is plotting for your end
So if you need a good companion
Or a bond that will not end
Send an S.O.S. to Jesus
Because He's a true true friend.

Jamal Grant

A Mother's Pain

My pain emerges from her lack of caring emotion,
she gives me none.

She is enveloped with meaningless chatter
my heartbreak has just begun.

My futility wanes upon her tender years,
she is lost to urban vulgarity,
I must for go my fears.

Tho inside my beating heart inflamed with poison, thoughts are
bursting, anger thirsting to be released,
please something give me peace.

No longer can a silent tongue be still, further on I rage,
who is this child I bore? Is there nothing about her I don't deplore?

She stares at me with critical eyes, questioning my right to question,
I know I am despised.

Flaunting her youth before me she boasts,
oh how can this be? She's nothing like me.

Sadly I sigh like a beaten-down lifeless form of nothing,
she is her own flavor-flav!

I search for her rhetoric of tone — is there no love in her heart?
Am I plain out of sight? Can I do nothing right?

Dorothy Early

The Tender Dream

Come death, they say
even the fallen angels are granted rest.

In that sleep only sweetness can bleed . . .
the tender dreams.

The essence of mercy
is God's domain, a gift to man.

Sit now and judge, if you can . . .
the tenderest dream . . . music.

Time to write, the many trials of love,
washed away by a kiss.
Time to speak of discretion in mind,
brushed away like mist.

Forgetting, was a veil, regretting the a ruse.
Memories were confused.
Answers, to no avail.

I began a song, in finite time,
through eternal love reached the dance, divine.

A small spinning of notes
becoming the tenderest dream.

Garrett G. Ammann

There's Sunlight Over My Window

No matter how bad the day gets,
No matter how long I cry,
No matter how crazy this day is,
No matter how much we say goodbye,
No matter how chaotic it seems,
No matter how we all flow and grow,
No matter how the flowers die,
There's sunlight over my window.
Who cares if they don't like it?
Who cares if I ever will?
Who cares about drama?
Who cares about who or what was killed?
Who cares about the violence?
And who cares about how long you can go?
Who cares about rain storms?
There's sunlight over my window.

Joshua Fennell

Lost Innocence

There were no eyes dry
as it came time to say goodbye.

Six years old and leaving so much
would they always stay in touch?

As they started to drive away you could see the pain in her eyes.

"What was happening, why do we have to go?"
She did not know.

Grownups spoke the word of divorce
As they looked at her with remorse.

Why can't her mommy and daddy stay together
What will happen to her and her little brother?

As the tears continued to flow far, far away they drove.
Days later they reached her grandpa's farm
Miles away from her daddy's loving arms.

This was the beginning of her days feeling alone
As they said, "this is your new home."

She did not speak of the pain inside as her old life died.
Little by little her days became easier soon it was all a memory.
Though as the years pass by she thinks back with a sigh . . .
They told her someday the pain would be gone they were wrong.

Michelle Zinn

She Stands Alone

She stands alone
on the shores of her imagination
dreaming, wondering
of life and love.

She stands alone
knowing she is no goddess
and quite ordinary
yet beautiful in her own way.

She stands alone
silently thinking of her future.
She begins to cry
frightened, there is nowhere to run.

She stands alone
tormented by her dreams,
the weight of the world
laid upon her shoulders.

She stands alone
wishing for her knight in shining armor,
knowing he will never come,
realizing she will always stand alone.

Shannon Reed

rich

I sat down beside you one spring day;
I felt the warmth of the sun
I smelled the freshness of the air
Yet I didn't feel your presence anywhere.
I talked to you that day;
I told you how empty my life now feels
How scared I am to move on.
I cried to you that day;
Begging you to hold me, kiss me, calm me; just once more.
I told you I missed you that day;
Your face, your smile, your laugh; all of you.
I told you I loved you that day;
Your humor, your emotions and the way you loved me.
I said goodbye to you that day;
That day I talked, cried, missed and loved you.
Sitting, there on my blanket
Next to your grave.

Allison Gugnacki

Lost

When you left you took my heart with you,
Now I'm just sitting here wondering what to do.
Wanting to be where you are so much,
Wondering if right now you're missing my tender touch.
Feeling the pressure put upon me,
People just won't let us be.
People stick their noses in our life together,
I wish they would just let us be in love forever.
I feel lost when you're not here,
I miss you so much my dear.
Take me into your arms again,
Kiss me sweetly; it's not a sin.
Our love is pure and true,
But since you're away, I am blue.
I hope that you will be home soon,
To dry the tears I cry for you.

Rachael L. Bennett

The Garble Was Of Celestial

A philosophy satire, a treaty of happiness
to quench his thirst.
What an attractive paradox.
Such a deceptively innocent adversary, armed
with such virtuous deeds.
The emphasize how irrelevant the metaphysics,
she bestows a chart of perpetuity.
While he is entranced in the perplexity
of his babylon odyssey,
She begot a symphony of reasons for the
coming of changing seasons,
To be cast from the shallow into the deep,
A rain saturated dower and weep,
Of course thou nods hear the slightest of peeps,
For he hath been banished into the
deepest of deeps.

James M. Smith

A Fishermen's Dream

In the hushhh preceding dawn, before the convection of
currents occur within the atmosphere to create a breeze . . .

The air is so still you can hear the earth breathe in a quiet
rhythm. Her exhalation permeates the air with a pungent breath
filling the senses with the smell of air, trees, and water — the
very essence of life she is . . .

In a boat upon the calm waters of a crystal lake, still dark
from night, your eyes and awareness drink deeply the beauty of
this moment, storing it within to recall at will . . .

The skies to the east brighten as a prelude to dawn. A soft
breeze begins to rustle the branches on the trees and ripple
across the water. In a rush it meets your face in a gentle way . . .

"Plop," you drop a line into the water for the catch of the day!

D. M. Roberts

Costumes

Then, I could be anything.
I put on a hat, I was a farmer.
I put on a dress, I was Cinderella at the ball.
I put on sunglasses, I was a famous movie star.
I put on boots, I was a cowgirl.
I put on black shoes, I was a tap dancer.
Today, I put on my pants,
I put on my shirt,
I am me.
No greatness,
No grandeur,
But still exciting and unique.

Kate Jacobson

Crocodile Tears

Speak the venom of the gallows bird
When he rests on that bed of sorrows;
He spoke of what I have often heard
To cry the sea with crocodile tears.

See the magnitude of my white lie
Before that one last tremulous breath
Within the pinnacle of my eye
And I will cry my crocodile tears.

Could you feel and pacify my pain,
Lost amidst the tenderness of love
Under the skirt of incessant rain
I would then cry my crocodile tears.

Lost inside the eternal sorrow,
I am left to search my thoughtless thoughts;
To see that life is not so hollow
Then I will dry my crocodile tears.

Try to purge the carnage of this world;
Their purple lifestyle writhes with pleasure.

Now I shall see with sight so insincere
And wet the earth with a Crocodile Tear.

Daniel Zagami

Undying Love

Do you love me, or do you not?
You told me once, but I forgot.

It seems to me that God above,
created you for me to love.

I had a heart once warm and true,
but it was given from me to you.

Take good care of it, as I have done,
for you have two, and I have none.

One day should god choose us to part,
my soul may leave, you'll hold my heart.

If I get to heaven, where life's good things are,
I'll write your name upon a star.

So all the angels will know and see,
just how much you mean to me.

If you're not there on judgment day,
I'll know you went the other way.

And just to prove my love for you,
I'll go to hell, to be with you.

Mary Jane Mello

Role's Search

The love we lost in our troubled child,
   forces life into a shameless pile.

Fear of perpetual ache,
   will our hearts be able to take?

Invoking a fight, no time to cry,
   for now the will is only to survive.

Forcing normal, impels distress,
   our young, feel only worthlessness.

Daily thought of love and hate,
   delusions intermingle and contemplate.

Desperate to be free of tormenting images.
   pursuing obscure and despondent phases.

Relentless search for unbridled love,
   returns full circle as embraced from above.

Jo Lene Judd

Storms

What are those things,
the things that threaten lives.
What are those things,
that make loud thunder crashes,
and bring bright lightning flashes.

What are those things that reek havoc,
and bring everything into an uproar.
What are those things,
that scare little children,
and take their sweet dreams away.

What are those things that go bump in the night.
What are those things that come, just to leave behind them destruction.
What are those things,
that make the ground tremble,
and waters crash against the shore.

What are those things?
What are those things?
I say: Storms, storms.

Megan Guthrie

Number One Prize

   Walking along the moonlight shore,
holding the hand of the guy I adore.

   The breeze would gently pass us by;
as we'd watch the seagulls slowly fly.

   The stars would twinkle and the
moon would shine. He held me close
and said he was mine.

   I kiss him softly and look into his eyes
because the love we have is the
number one prize.

Jeannamarie West

Whole Woman For Your Whole Man

I couldn't imagine in all my dreams,
A gift of love like yours to me.
As simple as love can be
The years brought with it heartache and fear.
But with you my friend, you took me for what I am,
Never changing a thing, seeing this woman all for you.
You embraced a gift to my womb that wasn't yours,
The tasks that come with it, the love that endures.
It's funny how the two of us came to be,
My heart intertwined with yours instantly.
This isn't a fantasy or just some emotional happenstance,
In this time and season, you took this whole woman,
For your whole man.

Kellie D. Hughes

Tribute To Mom And Dad — Thanksgiving Day

Our heavenly father came and took you away
But still you remain in our hearts today

On this thanksgiving day we wish you we're here
But one way or another we know you are near

We pray to God to see you again one day
For he is the only one that can show us the way

We love you with all our heart
Even though we're far apart

So on this day we say to you
Thank God for you loving us too

Minnie P. Harris

Ambition

Ambition, a bug within of gracious greed,
Which when nourished can be a dangerous seed;
It causes you to lite your morale
So far out of reach only to be fatal.

It is not nerve, sense, or cell
But it is in you good and well;
As long as you succeed or achieve
Ambition is at work and cannot leave.

The March of time as moved ahead,
By ambitious men who are now dead;
Men like Hitler, Napoleon, and Caesar,
Ambition led them to believe they're the creator.

Ambition breeds success and rightly so
And that same ambition not held in check
Will wind you up into a dreadful wreck
Causing your own ambition to devour thee
So hang on to your ambition don't let it rule you,
'Cause if it does, then shame on you.

Michael A. Duke

The Garden Wall

The stones that line the garden wall
Frame your moonlight silhouette.
Some lonely god's echoing call
Haunts the night with sullen regret.

Stars in their bright occupation
Driver summer's changing course to fall.
Our inner illuminations
Bring faithful care to us all.

Then along the grassland meadow,
The night wind comes scented with rose.
We sway beneath the weeping willows.
We walk beneath the moonlight's glow.
Soft winds blow a love song
Through the falling autumn leaves.
Blow me a kiss to warm the night wind,
Touch me with a kiss on this chilly eve.
Down the path where the lilacs end,
Down the path where the roses end,
Our shadows will dance on the garden wall.

Robert Miller

How To Look At The Preceding World Through Blood Shot Eyes

It gets darker every time I see it,
    growing stronger, bolder, meaner.
Killing everything in its path,
    covering the ground like a giant wrath blanket.
Glowing like the moon, always returning,
    every time burning, ever since I met you.
Never once did I think I'd end up who I am,
    within the soon — to — arrive hatred.
Loneliness will slowly grow with life,
    so complain if you will, but it still won't rest.
The stars will dance upon the sky,
    while the clouds frantically are forced to fade,
deeply hidden beyond the night.
Oh, how I'm lost spending this stubborn, unreconciled time.
Why don't the shadows dance in the air?
Happily watch as the red bats burn amongst ice,
    surrounded by the melting trees as the paths begin to turn.
Pursuing the bitter end, forced to be different.
The fluttering rain begins to die as I attempt to
    renew that giant gaping hole.
Just as I am reeled and ripped through two world's.

Kandice Stetar

Metamorphosis

You emerge fresh from your mother's womb,
a caterpillar — soon to be a butterfly
The pages are clean, the book to be written by you
As each day passes by you make the choice, you dance the dance
It's all entirely up to you
Each moment a fork in the road
To go right or left, only you can choose
Experience and pain cover you layer by layer
Until you heart and soul become encased in to your life's cocoon
You are a prisoner there — will you remain there forever or
    choose to break free soon?
Your choices are clear
To laugh or cry?
To live or die?
To crawl or fly?
What are you now my friend a caterpillar or a butterfly?

Zeline Castro-Wichmann

Poet's Shout

To arms! Shouted once the poet
full of hatred and pain.
And in that wonderful valley,
where the flowers, protected of sun and people,
bore a river of plenty, they took to arms and fired!
And then the disaster unleashed, and the death took with
the Flower of Valley Men, putting them in the grave!
Over the years, sunny valley is again laden with fruit.
And the children play war, lining up their small war toys.
And then again a sliver of child feud surfaced.
And then gathered face to face — brothers and sisters
of the little ones, to solve squabbles
begun by centuries of playing!
One of the children even took his father's pistol!
And then the oldest woman of that valley came out shouting:
Put in the ground are: My father, husband, sons and brothers.
Big ones and little ones, side by side, came next to her,
and with them, the poet shouting:
Forever and ever! For now! For here! And for everywhere!
Put down the arms!

Alexandrina Romocea

A Lonely Person

I imagine myself alone in life, doing my job trying to get along
without much fight. Some people say I don't care, they say I
won't look for friends anytime, anywhere. But little do they
know of my life, for I have friends who appear to me at night. I
have often wondered why people judge me, why they talk
behind my back about me. I guess they just can't understand,
about my feelings of today's woman and man. But I do have
friends who at night come and see me, they come from the future
and the past and spend time with me, while I'm dreaming.

Vernon Moss

Amy Belt

I once had a peaceful dream,
Amy and I were walking in the woods beside a stream,
to my heart she was bound,
as she lay upon the ground,
realizing we were far from town,
she began to unbutton her gown,
while she clutched a rose,
I gently slipped off her hose,
we made mad, passionate love,
with the stars watching us from high above,
and the trees all around,
watching us like a hound,
then a sunlight's beam,
awoke me from my peaceful dream.

Matthew Harp

Our Wealth

There is no more joyous thing to be
For a man — than to head a family.
First, we had a girl and then her brother,
And later, two more, one after the other.

Jeannine and John are the ones that're tall,
While master Robert is the smallest of all.
And in betwixt and between
Is Elise, dear, our tiny queen.

And as we've watched them from the crib,
Through diaper and bottle and later bib;
They each are different — entirely —
Are these wondrous children — our family.

If God will spare us both to see
Our babies grown to maturity,
Then it can be said as we're laid to rest —
No man nor woman has been more blessed.

Fame and fortune are shallow things
Compared to the joy our family brings.
For riches we've got in the lives and health
Of our four jewels — that are our wealth.

John A. Wheeler Jr.

The Mysterious Man

I was standing there with my innocent heart
You came along within the dark
I stood there amazed by your beautiful eyes
I was attracted to you without surprise
I thought you were perfect and made no mistakes
You were hiding in disguise because you were fate
I gave you all my love and dreams
You were the one, you were for me
As soon as I gave you my trust and love
You pierced my heart with a black arrow from above
I didn't know what to do so I walked away
Then you appeared and called me one day
I didn't know if you really cared
I wondered if you wanted me near
Does he really love me in his own way
Will he pressure me into making mistakes
So tell me father way up in heaven
Is he not the one or is he an eleven
I had all these thoughts in my head
Could I, would I, stand without him.

Jessica Baumberger

Under The Sea

A fish is traveling through
the deepest part of the ocean
and having the time of his life.

He surfaces and gets
swooped up by an eagle.
He struggles free
and falls into the water.

He recovers and wants a bite to eat.
He hides, darts out, and grabs a tasty fish.
He is no longer hungry.

He heads to the surface
and gets hooked by a fisherman.
The fisherman winds up the line
and grabs him with a net.
Luckily, he throws him back in.

He falls to the bottom
of the sea
to enjoy its beauty forever.

Jonathan Perodeau

March Morning

The most beautiful caress to me, is that of springs first
breath. Behold . . . a certain most sensuous feeling cometh o'er me.

It cometh by the window, through a crack, like a lover's ever
so slight caress upon my back; sending shivers down my spine,
and rolling my hair about like twine.

It feeleth wonderful, lying half awake . . . to feel springs first
breath, my body awakens in response, it quakes. I do not want
to move, but lie and anticipate in what is a most beautiful
and tranquil state.

And barely can I hear the far chirps of birds; the distant
barking of neighbor's dogs. If only I could open the window
further . . . to feel the full extent of what winter has lost.

But alas, too chill . . . yet. It will be over another month still,
until life will spring forth from the ground, and natures
carousel will begin all over again in the round.

So I shall be content to lie here quietly in my steady state,
and keep on dreaming for that most wondrous and sensuous day.

Jill C. Welch

The Gift

As the break of dawn starts the day
And the sun shines through,
Every road in my life has led me to you.

One of the purest loves of all is the love
of a mother,
but I have also realized a gift that
comes from another.

God gave his only begotten son so that
we may never have to part,
and I'll cherish that gift forever
because it's close to my heart.

There may be difficult times ahead and losses to bear,
but as we grow from those experiences
maybe this will prove that life is fair.

We can learn to appreciate the ones
who have given meaning to our life,
and the good we have found in others
can outweigh the strife.

So the paths that I take now are exciting and new,
because every road in my life had led me to you.

Gina Closson

The Innocence Of A Child

I wake to the sound of her laughing as she plays
with her favorite stuffed bunny. It's morning and
my first reaction is to smile as she babbles away.
Quietly, I sneak into her room. She lies there
hugging her bunny as she looks through a book.
Suddenly, she sees me and jumps up, bouncing in
her crib. The huge grin spreads across her face.
Those eyes of blue seem so clear and bottomless.
At that moment I wonder how anything could
possibly go wrong today. Just the sight of this
precious person makes everything else seem so
trivial. We spend so much time trying to fit
everything into a day. That we rarely stop to
enjoy the wonderful things right in front of us.
Everyone should listen to a child as they laugh
and play. So much love and happiness they give,
yet they ask for so little in return. The innocence
of a small child is a beautiful treasure that is
often overlooked. In this world of so much hatred, dishonesty
and business, we could all learn a lot from our children.

Christina M. Patuto

Fire And Destruction

Oh "Christians" who are so callous
 To believe in selves so "hallow"
Yet humility and works are tried to be true
 In shallow persons such as you
The standard is in heaven above
 That portal you only love
Thoughts and motivations will only prove
 The evil intents that serve to soothe
The devil's own though once redeemed
 Foolishly waiting for unsecured dreams
For piety awaits destruction
 And eternity declares fire
Fire and destruction
 "Lord, have I not done your will?"
Fire and destruction
 "Depart, your life to Me is nil."
Fire and destruction
 All hope and dreams are gone
Fire and destruction
 White Throne Judgment terrorizes all

   Bobbie Ann Belbeck

Hate

   The happiness I felt has all
gone away like the rough waves of the bay.
   All the bright colors have all gone on
and all the dark colors I come upon.
   My heart has turned black and my soul has turned gray,
my mind is filled with disgust and dismay.
   I live in silence with not one word to say.

   Diana Green

Twilight Vigil

When the withered night has turned to light
 Over all my silent room,
I'm the only soul whose candlelight
 Yet flickers through the fading gloom.
Blurring notes and books and papers fly
 For it seems all the world is dead,
Leaving silent silent's solitude by
 Placing memories meekly in its stead.
Then the cover of night is undraped
 As glamour on distant hills
Rings to the mind as the night is scraped
 Of all its sorrows, deaths, and playful ills.

   Don E. Suryk

Moon And Stars

I can not help giving you my life
watch you cradle it, devouring my power
I can promise no future of sun, moon, or stars.
Diamonds are a girls best friend and surely you should wear pearls.
Where to begin when I am at my end?
A sad hello — spilling to the uneven concrete
where I repeatedly bash my skull, bleeding.
Surely men drop to knees singing songs of praise
adoring your repeated charms.
I wish I knew the words to say to steal your heart away
but venus placed neat in heavenly sparkling heat
can not be reached by Dreamers of night
but by rockets powerful thrust
splintering the beautiful night.
so the most romantic love born
untested, unscorned.
The love of giving up life, and you, unknowing.
For I would give you the moon and stars
if only I could reach them.

   L. T.

The Smile

Hi, Sweetie, it's me
my heart jumps for joy, instantly recognizing the voice
a smile appears on my face softness in my voice
how are you? I miss you
I miss you too
where are you?
Uhhhmm . . . somewhere I laugh
your warm sense of humor brightens my day
it's great to talk to you
I've waited all day to hear your voice
when are you coming home?
Soon, I hope. Me too
my mind wanders, trying to be where you are seeing your
smiling face
and your beautiful eyes
kissing your forehead
spending time doing nothing and everything
I don't want to go I know I love you
I love you too. See you soon, fly safe
you walk in the door and my heart jumps for joy
and my smile reappears once again.

   Siw Karinen Maloney

Pieces Of Hearts

Pieces of hearts, broken small parts
Like many lost mittens and gloves,
Patiently waiting, anxiously waiting,
Waiting for someone to love.

People trudge by, our every day lives
Are too busy, too cluttered to see
The leaves in the trees, the fish in the seas,
Broken pieces tossed into the street.

Often we're scared, for we know they are there,
Just waiting for one special chance.
They want to be known, they want to be shown
To laugh, to sing, to dance.

They hope that one day the sun's lovely rays
Will shine down upon us all.
They pray day and night with all of their might
That everyone, in love they shall fall.

For if they do, good will shine true,
And the hearts will be joyous through time.
But, as for now, they wish they somehow
Could be more than taciturn mimes.

   John Whaley Jr.

Time Of Yesterday

My soul sinks and my spirit dies,
alongside with my hopes and dreams.

Gone are the times of yesterday.
Along with you, my life.

I've deluded and rationalized for too long,
I cannot protect myself any longer.

There will be no more times with you,
no matter how long I weep and pray.

I believed in a God that knows best,
but I guess that belief dies too.

You were unaware of me.
You were my light and you never knew.

Perhaps by my own fear of darkness,
that you would turn from me I didn't say.

But after so long, I can't convince myself any longer.
The times of yesterday are gone and so are you.

   Crystal R. Cinader

Harness Racing

Our grandfather going to the races a long, long day at the fair,
to watch the harness racing from the grandstand, in the open air.

The horses pulling the sulkies were Hambletonian bred,
born in the State of Kentucky, now around the track they sped.

He joined us in the kitchen wearing a mischievous grin,
with his bowler hat cocked at an angel, rubbing his bearded chin.

How debonair was our grandfather, how happy he must have been when
he fiddled for the neighborhood dances, and squired the girls so prim.

His eyes were twinkling with humor, he carried his very best cane,
and twirled it in a sprightly fashion, as if he were young again.

He looked so dapper and perky, his high top shoes a gleam,
how exciting to go to the races, and sit in the bleachers with him.

Roberta G. Bird

Soulmates

Her soulmate, from the sea he came.
A hale and swarthy man.
Looking for the gentle dame who longed to hold his hand.
Lifetimes crept by, and so they said,
it would not come to be.
The gentle dame to meet the sailor from the sea.
Then one fall it came to pass . . .
the gentle dame went searching.
To find the sailor from the sea, to stop her heart from hurting.
The pages in a book were turned,
her eyes cast longingly,
upon a small inscription, from the sailor of the sea.
It is time we end this madness, of living long apart.
Our eyes . . . they may not know us,
but, we'll know it in our hearts.
The gentle dame, bewitched she was,
and knew it deep inside,
the sailor man had come to stay,
she soon would be his bride.

Gayle Dunn

Crashing Waves

Pain roaring like the king of the jungle
Trying to intrude, engulfing.
Lights piercing, vessels screaming
Everything blurred, fumbling for relief.
Finding the killer and washing it down.
Goodbye excruciating torment.
Suffering no more until another.

Stephanie Webb

Echoes Of Summer

For not the echoes of summer
The hush of winter and all its cold
Would but not fill the space of time
And all it memories that come to mind

Although it skirts my ease of feeling
Echoes of summer forever enter my mind
Without hesitation I dwell in their warmth
And find myself embellished by the sweet sway
Of gentle air running through my valleys of discontent

It's not that I forebode the sting of winter
But rather succumb to the weeping willows
Of summers answers to questions that are posed

All the time I look to see
Echoes of summer swaying and drifting
Across the valleys of my mind
To the home of my heart
Echoes of summer will always be

John Krilow

Free . . .

While lying here in my cell tonight,
Unable to sleep my mind run's riot.

A review my memories from the past?
And wonder why times gone by so fast?

I think of the days when I was a child,
Just a care free kid running wild.

My thoughts of the future often shattered,
by things of the present that didn't matter.
As I grew older my ways were the same,
I had the idea life was a game.

So to win I cheated but instead I lost,
and as a loser I'm paying the cost.

But as I ponder these thoughts in the night
and began to see my past wasn't right.

I plan for a future that I hope will be
a way of life that will keep me free!!!

Michael Cullaton

Nighted King

The night of calming purity has marked me as a deity
the lakes of desert burn below and I must quench them before I go.

My subjects aid me in my task they are the sands of a celestial flask
they are too small to stand and fight so I am the Lord of the night.

Yet I am hunted by a foe who steals my seat as I go
he rends me from the nightly sky so he alone may rule on high.

His face is quite vile you see a swirl of gaseous misery
to block out all the people's gaze he sends down ultraviolet rays.

He scars the people with his brand his light destroys their fertile
land he looks upon the fields of hay and instantly they burn away.

I've chased him out of the throne so I may rule all on my own
the sands of time have fallen fast my time as ruler will not last.

I grown tired, I sometimes yawn soon he'll wake, with the dawn
I will be chased quite far away so he can brighten the fresh new day.

The circle does not stop with him soon he will be giving in
I have sharpened my crescent tusk to claim the throne at tomorrow's dusk.

David Christopher Bone

For The Soldiers

Great pride swells my heart,
as uncertainty grips yours.
My footsteps along the pavement,
match yours in the sand.

The world has stopped to watch,
a play by play war,
where we see what you live,
and shudder a few seconds after you do.

As you fight for peace,
small groups gather
as a nation,
to honor our loved ones we miss.

Red, white, and blue
have never had so much color,
nor our pride been so strong.

Now, with the last sand in your shoes,
and anticipation in your heart,
you resume your life, changed by this war.

Always remember: We missed you, we're proud of you,
we love you . . . thank you, welcome home.

Sylvia Skees Maertz

The Million-Man March

I watched the masses, a million-plus black men strong,
standing near the capital patiently all day long.
Why were they there and from where had the came?
There were many answers but, the echoes were the same.

There were many who felt that progress had been made
only to find that in a moment hopes and dreams can fade
there were many policies that the masses came to protest
there were many important issues they came to address.

As the sun began to fade and a coolness filled the air,
the keynote speaker made to this gathering very clear
it was not he who made it possible for this event to take place
it was God in his magnificence and his loving grace.

As the event ended some teary eyed and some holding hands
a prayer was said to bring peace and love unto this land.
The masses became one, and after a warm embrace,
the departed for their homes with an agenda in place

Silently I said a prayer as they slowly walked away,
please God don't let them forget the purpose of this day.
Let them go back to their communities and neighborhoods
let them begin to make a change and a change for the good.

Marvin Blackman

Loneliness

I sit here in my chair
staring out at the cold grey day,
watching the rain fall softly down
and feeling it in my heart.

I sit here with my nose pressed to the window
staring out at the dark nightfall,
watching the cars with their lights driving by
and feeling so cut off from it all.

I lay here in a field
under a solitary free,
watching the leaves blow in the breeze
and feeling so confused.

I lay in the field
on the cold hard ground
watching the stars twinkle in the sky
and wondering what is the meaning of it all.

I lay here in my bed
alone and cold
listening and feeling my tears fall
and hoping it won't last forever — I am lonely.

Janice R. Yoho

Africa

Africa has a beautiful scene
And its animals are very keen

Africa has millions of acres
Many do not know God is the real maker

Maybe you could go there
But you have to prepare

Some animals are dangerous
But one good thing, the view is very spacious

Africa is cool
You'll enjoy it like a swimming pool

Africa is a great experience
Without any interference

If you got here you'll have fun
Sitting under the hot steamy sun

Nathan Niyi Kumapayi

Where Is It?

Elastic thoughts which can spread themselves thin.
Thickening only after sleeping.
Replenished for a time.
Insecurity leading me.
Leading towards nothing but lies and hurt.
Green walls of envy standing since nascency.
The eagerness to tear these walls down builds up.
Walking dazed and stricken with dilapidated thoughts
of creativity.
Creativity which could of been shown to people,
not just paper.
Still walking,
Walking on bleached asphalt of wonders and warsle.

Daniel Joseph Leopardi

Naive Forms

Prime material of Movement gone
Of stench of time of actualization
No potential or former cause,
just the Caressing breath of three souls past

The Pure dominion of shackled misgivings
To divide and part of the swallowing shores
Dry-docked at the silt pastures of higher empathy

A bundle and blaze
Leftover hope of deals done dark
Adult ethics of old concrete clouds
The stones rain, pacifying the swelling
Pushing all aside for Yahweh's chariot

Crumbs and pebbles, a fools Thanksgiving
Abandoned child of unmoved sympathy
Purity rationed, the tides fall heavy

Jason T. Montanari

Springtime Walk

I love a walk among the trees
to hear the whisper of the leaves
to feel the soft wind upon my brow
oh! How I love spring.

The birds perched high up in the trees
make a sound that's bound to please
the sweet sweet smell of flowers in bloom,
all these things make my heart zoom!

I love the babbling of a brook
there's so much to see and as I look,
I think of how perfect God created it all
oh! How I love spring.

Dixie Mead

The Work Of Angels

God, help me be strong,
Help me handle the pressure;
The problems that life can heap upon me.
Let me look to Your words,
Your wisdom and knowledge,
To be the fine person You created me to be.

God, help me fulfill all that You wanted,
All You had in mind, when You gave me life.
Guide me through all of the difficult obstacles,
That keep me from being Your shining light.

God, help me transcend the chains life puts on us,
Just take my hand and lead me all of the way.
And, when I feel weak, place strength in my spirit;
That I may do the work of angels each and every day.

Michaela Kirkham Hinson

The Age Old Question

Young men in anger, and old men, with a sigh
often have posed this question all seeking an answer to the why
the problem is hidden and often not discussed,
nevertheless it is real and mentioned only to those that we trust.
It's not biological or psychological I am told
but quite inevitable as the years unfold.
It's not a disaster when it occurs because it happens so slowly that
when the realization sinks through it's accepted as the natural thing to do.
Yet a voice within us shouts it's revolting
and fights to never give in, but there is no answer to the problem
when all is said and done
why must our lovers become our mothers and spoil all the fun!

Robert Maloney

And I Lived

As I walk the winding road of opportunity
As I stare through the window of reality
Dreams become clearer

As the years pass and faces become unfamiliar
As I peer into my soul through the mirror
Time races on

As I listen to the voices around me
As I try to respond, no one hears me
Tears begin to fall

As I lie here peacefully, departed
As I return to where I started
My father awaits me

Nick Hardesty

Fog

What is left to feel once your whole
Soul has gone numb,
    What is left to see once the dark
Clouds have blocked the sun,
    What is left to hear but those grief
Stricken words that have been rooted in your mind,
    What is left to hang on to when anything
that was ever there has gone.
    Where are you left to turn when your
whole life has collapsed.
    What is left to know when anything
you've ever lived for has died,
    What is left to write when you're so
confused you can't think straight,
    What is left to say when the words
don't come?

Laura Simmons

The Dead Spots

I saw the pictures of my brain today,
the good and the bad, along with,
the happy and the sad.
The dead spots are still there.
But looking at them I showed that,
at least I still care.
An exact duplicate of "94"
but still different from that life before.
Satisfied and at peace
I weightlessly walked out the door,
leaving the C.A.T. still there on the wall from years before.
I didn't stumble,
and No
I didn't even fall,
are they still there on the wall?
Or was it their turn to fall?

Scott D. Hasenmiller

Northern Seasons

The winds are warm, a gentle breeze
But leaves still fall from the trees
Morning sun shining so bright
Autumn's feel is now is sight
Soon trees will all be bare
Also the chill will fill the air
Soon nature will pay the cost
When the mornings have brought their frost
Winds once warm now are frigid
Leaving all slow and rigged
Blizzards of snow fall to the ground
Everything's hidden safe and sound
All snows gone as if knowing time to melt
Everything forgetting, the cold that they felt
Water now rising, our rivers raging
All spring's signs now engaging
Nothing like these cool showers
Bringing beauty with all its flowers
Now back to our warm breeze
God has given all seasons like these.

Kevin Evans

This Man

Love is blue, glowing like a sapphire;
looking into the eyes of this man, I see this love.
It is new, like fresh fallen snow, pure, white, virgin, yet
it is familiar, like walking down Madison, a street I've know forever.

This man's love can not be compared to any other;
the satisfaction is as sweet as grapes on the vine.
A bond is created, we have become one;
combining, once individuals, now indistinguishable from each other.

Love is clear, flawless as a whisper;
listening, in the voice of this man, I hear this love.
It is reckless, uncaring of the consequences, flying, free, yet
it is sensible, cautious, approached with foresight and common sense.

This man's love builds in strength, depth and desire,
the longing is as strong as the need for his next breath.
This love has pulse, breath and life, all consuming,
living for the day that we will be together. Forever.

Susan L. Key

Beyond Hope's Gate

    Strangers embracing the subtle mastery of life's music
sleeping peacefully beneath a tree, whispering dreams
while flowers played their sweet serenade enticing rainbow wishes.
Our ancient mother beckons with a soft zephyr dancing thru seasons
they hear not the chimes proclaiming summer's demise
for how can youth end when a world has yet to begin.
One moment is all they ask to leave the dream hand in hand
their days and tears swallowed by encroaching twilight,
the silent cries fade like smoke in flight thru Elysian skies
as opulent peace eternal, solemnly embraces those prayers thought
lost and forgotten, for grace's threshold denies not
and remembers always.

Milton Eric Colon

The Rose

High in the mountains, on a warm summer's day,
Far from the trail, I did go astray,
Finding a flower, growing out of solid stone,
One more beautiful, than I had ever known,
Had I followed the scent, of this white rose,
Along an unmarked trail, where no one ever goes,
Or did this beauty need, one with eyes to see,
To truly fulfill, its quest of ecstasy.

Donald Temple Jr.

Lost

As the sun filters through the clouds
And descends upon the earth
People wander through their lives
And wonder what it's worth

Looking for their pot of gold
From a rainbow in the sky
Searching for what tomorrow will bring
But never knowing why

Seeking truth and wisdom
And the reason why they're here
While hiding behind their masks
Of uncertainty and fear

They run through time and pass through years
And never find out why
But they feel there's something missing
When their day comes to die

As the sun comes up tomorrow
And kisses a brand new day
Another child will be born
To be lost along the way

Christopher Ross Farrell

Inward

And yet as I walk down the road that has been chosen for me
I look back upon the choices I have made
And wonder what have I done? And why?
And who have I trusted, who have I loved?
The faces are all detailed, varied, and strange
But the minds behind each, all remain the same

As I gaze back upon the tapestry of all thought
I see the words and expressions that gave me a smile
And behind each was an emotion I just could not fathom
A feeling that I could not bring myself to hold
Was it a mask, a deception, a silent betrayal
Or simply a shard of my own distrust

And yet as I ponder the follies and missteps
I see how my thoughts have often been awry
But still I look upon the faces I love
And wonder, still wonder, what lies beneath
What thoughts lie deep, hidden in glamour
And then I realize how alone I have become

Kerry Lord

The Desert

I walk the desert's desolation
   for it reflects my soul,
wandering desperation
   with a heart full of woe.

Friendless among friends
   alone in despair do I grow,
as frustration mounts
   I see my life as my foe.

Contemplating the burning candle
   wanting to snuff out its glow,
I see dimmer flames burning brightly
   braving life's winds happily as they go.

From text and verse I sought to find
   what is life, and makes it so,
yet only from my friends' burning lights
   did my loathing to self-pity grow.

I walk the desert's desolation
   hoping it reflects my soul,
full of flame from endless living embers
   with a heart too large for woe.

David Leroy Pruitt

Scotties Bluff

I feel the mist from the waves,
I see the big waves crash against the rock and the water goes in
The air,
I hear crash, boom,
I smell salt,
I taste salty water

Alexandra Olivia Chandler-Bando

Runaway Sun

The rain,
the pain,
the snow,
but I know, soon the sun will show.
It ran away on a summer day,
leaving the children no time to play.
I cried and cried and cried,
but still the people denied.
They would not believe what I said was true,
but now they sit there on their porch swallowed by an
ocean of darkness.
They reminisce of the times they shared
when the sun was there,
but now it's gone
everyone sits around waiting for the sun to advent.
I told them,
but they would not listen,
now they wait and wait for the sky to glisten.
Now I know the sun will not come back.
So I sit here, in all the black.

Christina Tegbe

Not Just A Grandmother

No doubt! To them she is not growing old
For they each recall the stories she told

Of Indian and Western tales of lore
With the learning values from long before

They were born and how new "fang dangled" ways
Changed views to TV and computer rays

Instead of high mountains covered with snow
Meadows sweet wildflowers, grasses to grow

She taught them art lessons her talents shared
Creating, reading, writing nothing compared

To her giving of heart, time and concern
Yet there were times when she became stern

The children were growing each year progressed
Memories were her fondest she confessed

Being Grammie helping after school hour
Snacks, treats and home made corn bread to devour

   Not just a Grandmother always around
   No, their very own Pal where loves abound

Yevonne C. Edwards

Hold Me

"HOLD ME,
If with your eyes you cannot hold me,
TOUCH ME,
if with your hands you cannot touch me,
KISS ME,
if with your lips you cannot kiss me,
LOVE ME,
until the echoes of your mind reach mine."

Eva Martha Del Campo

You And I

Over my shoulder I see whirling by
The years and the laughter we've shared, you and I
So young, so near perfect were we years ago
Yet as the years dwindle our pace starts to slow
Yes, hair once so perfect is silvery now
Those spry little youngsters much older somehow
Fulfillment you call it, sheer pleasure to know
Though time keeps on passing, ours hearts are aglow
The love and the nearness of years shared together
So precious the memory, so great the endeavor
So lovely the ties we've shared, you and I
While over my shoulder, time keeps whirling by

Ora Maly

Ashamed

Were I to count the endless ways that I have failed You, Lord,
'Twould bring my soul to such a shame to have them all
outpoured;
And if I were to recollect those times of doubt and fear,
I know 'twould render grievous pain for each of those to hear.

Should I recall when I had said my prayers were just in vain,
When all at once You answered them to give me peace again;
Dare I remember lack of faith when trouble was at hand,
Still you were there invincible at once to take my stand.

I do regret I must confess that I've done each of these,
Filled with remorse I humbly fall, abased — upon my knees;
The guilt I have within my heart that pains my inner being,
Is one I can no longer bear, forgiveness I am pleading.

So now, O Lord, I come to You, my selfish pride behind,
In humbleness my heat I bow to ease my tattered mind;
One simple word describes it all, the reason why I came,
It pours forth from my very soul, Dear Lord, I am ashamed.

Linda Johanning

God Gathers

God gathers those who sorrows.
God gathers those burdened.
God gathers those reproached by men.
God saves the afflicted, the lame and poor of spirit.
I would have fainted had I not believed.

God gathers those driven.
God gathers those put to shame.
God gathers at the appointed time
God appoint them on earth for simple joy, praise or fame;
At the appointed time he rejoices over you;
   quiet you with his love
   as he gathers you to himself.

Barbara Miles Jackson

A Midsummer Day's Dream

Very small in Europe I dreamed of USA
Of Cowboys and mustangs
Later on I have dreamed
Of voluptuous pin-up girls
That Hollywood has launched
To the highest of stardom

As a grown up I crossed the Atlantic
The cowboys and the stars had gotten very old

An earthquake had already cracked
A shaky MobileHome I bought
In the hills over Angeles
I shut the blinds I shut my eyes
And the stars breathe again
In the Heaven of my memory

Heuri de Stadelhofen

Our Eyes Tell Us Much

How deep and still our eyes can be
When we are focusing on something to see
Sometimes it can present glee
And other times we wish to flee
At times we wish to hide behind a tree
We always wish to escape the worst
But it won't be the first
Hopefully, it won't end up a curse
We must hold the faith and give trust
And it does no good to put up a fuss
We should bring ourselves about
And try to remain stout
Sometimes it takes a certain amount of clout
And occasionally there is doubt
Perhaps we should look for a new way
And be careful not to stray
This is the best way to defray
Our eyes are our best friend
On this, we will always depend.

E. T. Philpitt

A Love No More

As he lay there in bed
Thanks for calling is all he said
Not being able to see him with my own eyes
Just made me cry
Knowing that he is going to die
The only thing I could say was bye
His love is very close to my heart
However now that love is fading into the dark
Knowing his loss will bring tears
Hearing my family cry is all that I will hear
As I walk up to view him
The lights go dim
It was as if I was the only one to see
How peaceful he seemed
Then I realized I wasn't the only one
This loss was not fun for no one
As he is put into the ground
No one lets out a sound
As I leave
His love is just a memory

Greg Lambert

Drifting On A Memory

I still remember you holding me near.
Slowly the vision fades away.
You say, "Please stay?"
Drifting on a memory.
The flowery scent of your perfume.
I smell it still.
Brownish hair swaying in the air
Once again I hear a voice
Saying, "I'm sorry I did you wrong."
I ask myself "how can I be strong?"
Especially when you're gone.
Drifting on a memory
Remembering the precious moments we had.
Tears roll down, as I become sad.
Seeing pictures of you.
Reminds me, your favorite color is blue.
I hope and pray tonight, you will come back to me soon.
My feelings tell me you found someone new.
Listening to a song, singing I still have love for you.
Hopefully you do too.

Michelle Valisto

Last Thought

What does a dying man vision, what does he see
Is his mind closed and trapped or does it soar free
In the solitude of the last seconds what is in his mind
In the end what final memories does he find

Through the eyes of a dying man does he see the lighter side
Is it a blissful happiness with a euphorious ride
Does he see friends and lovers from time passed
Is it beauty and happiness that he sees last

Or through the eyes of a dying man does he see the darker side
Is it a painful agony with a horrifying ride
Does he see the pain and the hurt from time passed
Is it morbid thoughts and hate that he sees last

The last vision of a dying man is in the eyes of the beholder
Thoughts of beauty or horror is in the mind as the body becomes colder
For his life he had fought
But now he has had his last thought

    Scott Weston

Grandpa

God called Grandpa to heaven now.
It made us all so very sad.

I've thought about it for some time.
Now I know why he did.

God needs Grandpa to paint the sky now.
Every night before I sleep.
Grandpa paints the sunset for us.

So we all know he's thinking of us.
When I wake up, again I see the painted sky.

Thank you Grandpa for the painted sky.

    Lisa Williams

Give Your Life To Jesus Christ, Pray

Give your life to Jesus Christ
And He'll make your life just right
    There's good
    There's bad
    There's ups
    and there's downs

But don't get upset, because Jesus is still around
    He'll protect you
    He'll lead you
    He'll guide you
    and He'll shield you

Oh no . . . He'll never never leave you
    Pray
    Pray
    Pray
    and Pray
Never ever, should you forget to give Him praise
    Pray . . . always

    Cynthia Faulkner

I Am Forever

I am forever.
I never end.
I never begin.
I encompass time and space and all dimensions.
I am everything that ever was, will be, is.

I am forever and eternal.
And because I am everlasting,
I exist whole and complete.

    Gregor Capodieci

Black Girl, Black Girl

Skin baked in the sun, hair wooly, home spun
eyes are dark as jade, black girl today

History cannot began to explain, the beauty
you proclaim, mix every color in the rainbow,
you, black girl, are the outcome

Ebony girl of today, hold your head up high
and don't dismay, special in God's eye, put
behind you all the lies

Thank your maker every day, for the
enigma of your race,

Chocolate so rich in color, it makes other
varieties wonder, where from did you come,
were you raised with the sun?

Black girl in the morning
Black girl when I rise
Black girl, black girl
Looking out of my eyes

    Josette A. Armstead

The Wildflower

Amid the slender cool carnations a low leafy plant blooms in my garden.
    I had seen it growing.
I thought it was chrysanthemum whose planting I had forgotten.
The blossoms are tiny. White and yellow. Tiny —
    Except to bee and butterfly
Not clustered as such little flowers should be clustered
    But standing separate and proud.
"That's a weed," my neighbor told me. "It doesn't seem to care." I said.
I can't bring myself to root it from its bed, even though I know
It's silly to be so subjective about a wild plant, growing unbidden.
Maybe it's because I feel that if I had been created a flower
    I too would have been a weed.

    Glenn R. Bernhardt

My Dream, My Life

You are the light in my life every breath I have taken
It is only next to you that I wish to be awaken
To the sound of the pouring rain or a sunny new day
Where I can hear the birds sing or watch the children play
I know in months, it's only been two
But a love of a lifetime I have found in you
These words come from my heart honest and sincere
They even come with the shedding of a tear
Not of anger or sadness but of happiness alone
The words I Love You Emmy Lou I would carve in stone
I get the feeling you're the one
I just wanted to say I Love You Hon.

    Casey A. Dines

Winter

Icicles hanging from rooftops
A layer of powdery snow on the ground
The peace of winter surrounding you.
The redness on your cheeks
After you've been out in the cold.
The snowball fights in the backyard
The hot chocolate when you get inside
The crackle of the fire
Warming your cold fingers and toes.
The snowmobiling on the trails
The skating on the rinks
The sledding down the hills
The feeling that this is how it should be.
It is winter.

    Amy Faschingbauer

The Essence Of Despair

As the rain begins to fall, so do my spirits
No matter which way I turn it's a losing battle;
I can no longer relate to my fellow man, I feel as though I'm in a cage;
Like I'm on the outside looking in only
I'm on the inside looking out; nothing can be accomplished,
My goals are set only to be broken and broken goals equal
disappointment; my self-worth decreases everyday in value . . .
As if there's no point in living;
Even when things are looking up, I'm still looking down;
I'm stuck in a rut but there's nowhere to go anyway,
At times I give up on everything because happiness
is untouchable . . . inaccessible;
Every road I choose is a one way street down hill,
Accomplishments are a thing of the past, a mere memory;
There is no horizon, there is no sunset,
It's all the same day after day.
Self-imprisoned to the world and always striving to do better,
never content with what I have;
Disappointment and misery and wallowing in such, has become
a daily routine; there's no way out!

Suetta L. Ison

A Mom's Advice

I was entrusted with a precious gift, you see!
Sent straight from heaven, with just a small fee.

There was no instruction manual intact;
so I was lost for sure, this was a fact!

"Lord how could you trust me?"
This was my main pea.

His reply "When things go wrong and you start to fall,
just believe in Jesus and give him a call.
Let his gentle correction; lead you in the right direction."

Many years have past, filled with laughter and tears.
And He's received many a call, for Jesus truly does hear.

When you stretched that extra length; it was Jesus who gave you strength.
When you cried with your fears in the night, it was He that held you tight.
When you were lured astray, He again, led you back the right way.
It is He that builds your faith, and He that keeps you safe.
He even died for your sins, so that you might live again.

So as you leave our little nest to give your wings their first test.
Remember my advice dear; just call Jesus, He is always near.

Sharon Suzayne Castellano

Heaven

Hopefully this place we'll all achieve,
Each and every one of us;
An eternal kingdom for those who believe
Values are found in God, love and trust.
Everyone in harmony, no matter the color of skin,
No one is different there, for we are all His children.

Dick Blanchard

Sweet Life — Do You Know?

You have known me so few
How could me be known
Me, I don't even know
Sweet life I know — I think I know
I may have — and may not have known
Sweet life
I know only what I have known
You must find if it is what you know
And if you must know what I know
Is it what you think I should know about
Sweet life.

Donna L. Ramage

Bob Gilley 1951-1985

A man of His own strength and style,
Who touched everyone's life he knew,
But the hurt goes on all the while.
Leaving behind a daughter, family and
    many friends who loved him —
Confused and asking why?
Someday we'll have these answers.
But for now he's with Jesus,
    in tranquility he deserved, in the sky

Debra K. Hall

A Mother's Fear

Something dark in his eyes,
    Behind them I hear a young one who cries.
Eyes cold as ice,
    Personality that changes with a roll of the dice.
Someone who can bring more than fear,
    Although I see a child's face with a tear.
But, something dark is in his eyes,
    At times He makes young one's cry.
One day he will see the fear,
    Rolling down his face will be a tear.
He deserves more than just to cry,
    But something slower than just to die.
Someone will pay him back for the tears,
    Then he will cause no more fears!

Jamie Lyn Lagasse

Untitled

I have stood upon that place of wonder
and I have known the peace that love achieves
I have watched time grow in grace and beauty
and I have felt your praise consume my soul

But most of all, I've known that you were faithful
to me, and all the secrets of my heart
And I will never feel the longing of those souls
who fight to attain a hero-lost

Lord, you must know this fact above all others
My heart shall know your strength throughout my life
and when my eyes shall close in final slumber
I shall taste of love that never dies

Eva M. Simmons

Diana Unbound

A prayer for my sickness, so vile and vicious see
Never would a thousand hearts, come and see with me
Gracious child's, so full of glee, a mite of passion hides within
A prayer for you, my hallowed heartstring, pull, and let the
Arrow sting

A prayer of pity, crusted red covered blossom
Droplets dried forever
Callous wind, a chilled gust the slayer, of that hidden heartstring
Pull, and feel fresh red seas, and warm breath again,
That arrow string

My springtime fellows, hear my prayer
As the grains sowed, our pasts long crusted
With red
A season, only one, our only one,
Plunged with tines

That long ago sun, her burnt brow glare
Blind is she, her golden hair she cannot see,
Nor arrows flung at distant men, so cold is she
Alas, begotten chill of water, and absence of that arrow fling,
Cause of red, my pained heartstring

David W. Witten

Let It Be

If you and I could have forever,
    Let it be.
If it were the last time for us to be,
    Let us sit and dine with no words said,
For love need not be spoken,
    If it were our wedding day,
Let tears flow throughout the day.
    If it was the day of life,
Let the heavens fill with light,
    At each night we kiss good night,
Let us stay close together,
Let us wake with love and cheer,
    to know we're still forever near.

Jaymie Lane

Two-Dimensional Dream

```
                treacherous  tides
     shimmering  snakes      sparkle
     devilish    demons      dance
frightened  phantoms   flee
     triumph
```

Rebecca H. Kranz

When There Was Nothing To Hold Onto

So much had been lost, I thought
with no time to regain,

And so it became a story, part laughter,
but mostly pain.

Too many fragments — no longer able
to hold — once a strong bridge.

Mounted pain and disappointments
clouded heart.

In anguish the soul cried out — take
me in your arms — hold.

Unable to remember what was lost — I lift
my arms and reverence you.

Success immeasurable, when I thought
There was nothing to hold on to!

Shelia Glenn

I Am A Black Man

I am a Black Man;
With Skin of Pitch, and eyes and teeth of Ivory!
I am a Black Man;
Tremble at my dark wonder, as I coo, hushed in creations cradle!
I am a Black Man;
Cursed; for the "All Encompassing Power of My Blackness!"
Torn from Mother's bosom and Flung Across The Dark Waters . . .
Bellowing Shrill, Thrashing urgently for some Hold!
I am a Black Man;
Torn against The Ravages of Time . . . Fighting Desperately to Survive;
Searching Frantically for my Brothers and Sisters but finding them
not in the Fearful Faces on The Wind!
I am a Black Man;
Harried by my own . . . and others Tormenting my Being!
As vultures, picking my bones till I am no more!
I am a Black Man; In Solitude I Wonder Why the reflection on
still waters is not my own!
I am a Black Man;
On my knees with outstretched arms I cry, "Dear God",
"Save me from the Rage!"
"Make me not a Carnivore as my brother has become!"
"Lead me in thy way, thy will, thy grace, thy line of light!
Give me strength and peace and guide my struggle toward the sight!"
For I am a Black Man; "Yes!" I am a Black Man!

William L. Bishop

Assateague

Here on the beach, my dog, Bully and me
Waves calm, air clean, and sun bright
    I wonder sometimes just what he sees
Though his ball is locked in his sight.
    The sea gulls, they fly and sing their sweet song
And from grasses, the plover, they peep
    The horses trot by and whinny and neigh
And my puppy awakes from his sleep.
    I gaze overhead to beautiful flight
Half-dozen brown pelican I see.
    They maneuver and circle and dive to the depths
For fish that were trying to flee.
    Back over the dune, just crossing the grass
Those two untamed eyes that be
    It's the tail of a red fox that catches my eye
He retreats as he sees Bully and me.
    I scan the sea, waiting for a glimpse
When out of the waves dolphins play
    I never feel more at peace with the earth
Than on Assateague spending the day.
    The sound of the surf, waves washing on shore
And I wonder, how can it all be?
    So I look in Bull's eyes for the meaning of life
And I'm sure he understands more than me.

Jenny D. Hall

I Am Blessed

When you sleep at night I watch your face.
The moon beaming down upon your grace.
To have you near me I fear no soul.
I dare not ever let you go.
Feeling your warmth as I lay in your arms.
Dear Heavenly Father keep him from harm.
A body so perfect chiseled just right.
You are my protector my gallant knight.
Making love to you fills my body whole.
Leaving me with a warm sensuous glow.
What am I without you but half a heart.
Fulfiller of my desires never to part.
Watching your chest move slowly up and down.
From a distance in silence never a sound.
A cool night's breeze blows gently within.
Chills of passion covering my skin.
What are you dreaming in your mind so deep?
Nothing but sweetness forever you keep.
I am blessed to have you. I am blessed to love you.
I am blessed to feel you. Always I am blessed.

Tiana Washington

My Daughter And Me

Prayerfully waiting and anticipating, finally, the child . . .
My daughter and me.
Cuddling and talking, crawling and walking, long nights of rocking . . .
My daughter and me.
Fearfully clinging, school bells are ringing, friendships beginning . . .
My daughter and me.
Blossoming, growing, emotions are showing, I have "no way of
Knowing" . . .
My daughter and me.
Angry words shouting, philosophies spouting, slamming and pouting . . .
My daughter and me.
Diplomas are waving, dorm life she's craving, depleting our savings . . .
My daughter and me.
Tearfully clinging, promises ringing, train whistles singing . . .
My daughter and me.
Grandmother's wedding dress, seed pearls on white lace, tears down
A radiant face . . .
My daughter and me.
Prayerfully waiting and anticipating, finally the grandchild . . .
My daughter and me.

Cynthia Seiler

Love's Ecstasy

As the trees swayed in the breeze the leaves sang to me.
In a hushed tone so sweet to my ear,
I heard your voice say, come to me, be with me.
I was intoxicated by the love I felt.
Flushed with arousal my soul yearned for your gentle touch.
Ecstasy was but a heart beat away.

Such pain pierces me when we are apart.
My only relief are thoughts of you filling my mind.
Conjuring our last intimate encounter I relive the passion we share.
The two melding into one mind, one heart, moving in perfect harmony.
Exploding forth naked in the world opened completely to one another.
For one solitary moment, there are no doubts, no fears.
Just the blissful joy of loving you.

Rebecca L. Schlarb

My Forever Friend

I knew when my voice had been replaced on his machine,
I knew when the collage I made him ended up in the drawer,
I knew when the ID bracelet signed with love left his wrist for good.

He said he promised not to hurt me;
He broke a promise

He said he wanted to be with me forever;
Forever came to an end.

He said I was crazy;
Am I?

I knew when no one was home I had the opportunity,
I knew when I had four hours to myself I had the time,
I knew when I saw the food behind my cabinet
It was a binge.

You've always been there,
An unspoken truth,

Always there to heal the pain brought on by others;

Never judgmental, just there;
Are you?

My Forever Friend

Abra Layne Stanley

Jacob's Bedtime

He's on the steps "will you scratch my back?"
Or calling down "you forgot my snack."
"I think that maybe I forgot to brush,"
"My tree looks like a monster" — "Jacob, hush"!
My voice gets weary — "not another peep"!
"I can't."
"I'm not tired."
I go check — he's asleep.

Lori Thatch

The Canvas Of My Life

The canvas of my life is a little more than fifty years old.
It is covered with every imaginable color . . .
There are scenes that have faded, while others appear vivid as if
they were freshly painted.
Every single experience is there!
The sunrises — the sunsets — the thunderstorms.
How much virginal canvas is left for the remaining colors is a mystery.
How will the canvas be completed?
Who and what will be "painted' in the empty spaces?
The untouched portion of my canvas will be exactly the way I want it to be.
I am the artist. I choose the colors and the scenes desired.
Much thought and care must be used, as the colors are indelible.
Each passing day serves as a reminder that I am getting closer to
the completion of my unique masterpiece!

C. Z. Thaler

The World I Know

The world I know is scary
Full of crime and hate

Love is hard to come by
Destruction is our fate

Wars and Catastrophes
Constant chaos and distraught

This world lives a lie
And hopes to not get caught

Alcoholics and Junkies
Living on the streets

The homeless people living in cardboard boxes
Without any food to eat

Do not walk the streets at night
It is barely safe by day

It really makes me wonder
If God wanted it this way

For now I can only question this,
As I sit and think

That maybe this world I know
Will someday be extinct.

Tracy Beth Hart

Dilemma

To be or not to be, is not the question for me
The decision was made by a far Superior Source
To enter this world was never my choice
Had it been, I cannot honestly say
What difference it would make as I reflect today
The valleys have been many, the peaks few
Each day is a labor of strength to renew
A synopsis repeatedly flashes in my psyche
Of triumphs and trials and questions of "Why me?"
Molestation, degradation, humiliation, manipulation
Ostracized, paralyzed, justice denied, violence glorified
Fear, anger, guilt
Resentment, bitterness, hate
Food, nor drink, nor drugs can't compensate or alleviate

Transition — a turning point, hope to begin again
Graduate, activist, wife, mother, colleague and friend
To be or not to be is no longer the question for me
Eureka — I've found it
Just waiting on God to agree

J. Montgomery

Untitled

"Liberating, isn't it?"
breath in my ear —
He pulled at the sheets, uncovering.
"liberating," he had whispered.
I could feel him, waiting, circling.
Vocal cords rasped, no sound was emitted.
"What do you want?"
words, tiny pins; needling, tearing at me.
"Leave", my mind was screaming only to itself.
To do this I had to abandon my body, give her to him.
I was trapped; I couldn't help but cry.
"The tears," he moved my hair, "What do they mean?"
They stopped — Confusion had me in his claws.
Run — Run — Run
My brain wouldn't stop
Run — Run — Run
"Think to me, what do you want?"
Finally my voice unraveled itself.
"What do you care? You've got what you want, just get it over with."
Then he held me and let me cry.

Kelly Tew

Sweet Daydreams

I awoke to the sun beaming through the
window in perfect view, I could hear the birds
singing as they hovered over the morning dew;
   I found myself daydreaming as I turned
over in bed to the sweet smell of you,
your essence surrounded me and made me
feel new . . .
   I lay daydreaming about your warm
kiss good night and secure embrace,
as I remembered all the love that I
could see within your face . . .
   From the first time we met somehow
I knew, that you'd care for me and never
make me blue; that we'd be together
always . . . just us two . . .
   Thinking of you is what gets me
through another day, knowing you love me
and you'll never go away; so I thank God for
daydreams and sending you to stay . . .

   Linda M. Heyd

New York

People walk the city streets,
Cars go racing by.
The concrete jungle plays an urban beat,
Homeless try to hide.
Rain washes, cleansing, cleaning,
People scurry away.
Dealers walk with their guns gleaming,
Hello you never say.
Women of the night look for dates,
A child loudly cries.
This old city you love to hate,
The place were many die.

   Eric David Olson

A Mother's Heart

There's a place in my heart that was blessed with something
so new, the birth of a child, that child, it was you.

There's a place in my heart that is filled with the sound
of your first cry, a place in my heart that will never die.

There's a place in my heart that your tiny fingers hold, a
place in my heart that will never grow old.

There's a place in my heart, filled with pleasures,
they will always be there, they will always be treasured.

There's a place in my heart that grows every day, with it
a child, too soon goes away.

There's a place in my heart, that aches with pain, of a
growing child who's leaving, her life she must gain.

There's a place in my heart that says I love you, take it
with you my daughter, it belongs only to you.

   Sandra L. Charles

Meaning Of True Love

Some think that love is the lust that they feel in the heat of passion.
Others think that love is the wind wisping through their hair,
while driving their crimson red Porsche.
Love is a word with so many meanings . . .
What it is to one person, it is not to another.
But,
true love is different.
True love can only be one thing.
You cannot think that you are truly in love . . .
You must feel it deep within your heart and soul.

   Trudy L. Jackson

Noises And Voices

Noises lots of them,
Voices coming from him or her.
Noises are loud, voices are quiet,
When they combine my brain's a riot.
What was that? Is it my mind,
Telling me there's something to find.
Over there, who are you?
What is it that you want me to do?
It's driving me crazy. I'm going insane.
I'm stuck between nothing and endless pain.

   Jason Aragon

The Lover's Prayer

I'll pray for you my love so true, and wait
until you say I do. For what's inside is all
for you, never again feeling empty or blue.
Please never ever tell me goodbye, for if you do
this heart will die. I pledge this love from
heaven on high, and hand to you a tear from
thy eye. Now as we walk on in this life,
I'll try my best to do what's right. Our
love will soar right to the clouds, I'll
shout I love you and say it loud. The
lover's prayer is for you my wife, for
you have filled this endless life. And as
the time wines and down, remember it's you
I want around. The love we share will
soar real high, for the lover's prayer
will never die, and if for some reason
I should die first, I'll wait for you and
think not the worst and if you're not
here, by judgement day, then I'll know
that my lover went the other way.

   Thomas Baker

Fear

Sounds like the screaming, deafening sound
of a dying heart at night,
Smells like a musty attic with things
creeping out of sight.
Looks like the bloody old man lurking
behind you in the dark,
Feels like the back stabbing words that
dart through so sharp.
Tastes like creepy bugs crawling
between your teeth,
Fear is a word that ensnares you
so deep . . .

   Amber Kenworthy

The Divine Energy

From the very tip of my fingers
To the tip of my toes
Energy flowing with a tingling sensation,
Surging its way through my body,
Culminating in my brain,
Bursting forth with such dignity
Like it knew the path it had to travel,
Preparing my body for the new birth,
Sometimes escaping out of my eyes,
Filling the atmosphere around me
With its luminous lustre.
Heart pounding in my ear like the beat
Of a drum without rhythm,
The phenomenon of rebirth, if successful
Transcends the normal limits of the brain,
This is the divine energy in a natural awakening.

   Vivian Gaines Tanner

Lonesome Doves

Once there was a dream, from days gone by,
about a lonesome dove, and its flight through the sky.

The moon was full, and the stars were glowing,
When the dove heard a voice of another one crowing.

Silent was the night intently listening,
to the echoes of their love reminiscing.

"Come to me now," said one with a craving,
"I need your strength, I'm imprisoned by the Raven."

Just then, the rain came down from the heavens.
The wind blew strong, with the smell of the Raven.

"I'll find you my love!" one exclaimed to the other,
"The storm is approaching so please take cover."

The dove took off in a magnificent flight,
Dignified and glorious, in a rush to her side.

Just then, it happened . . . A bolt from the storm
sent him into the Forest of Unknowns.

She broke through her chains with tragedy inside,
and took off in flight to be by his side.

No one knew if she found her lover,
some say he died, and she never recovered.

But when you stand and listen to the silence of the woods,
you can feel the answer and it is understood.

Lonesome doves will find lost loves.

Nina M. Kucinski

Thanksgiving

When Thanksgiving day rolls around,
what do we see and think?
Why are we able to celebrate this day?
It seems we are right on the brink.

Little children see the turkey,
the golden pies and turkey dressing;
now is the time to start them thinking
to look to God for the best blessing.

Train a child in the way he should go,
let the love of God be the center,
later in life you will find,
'twas better than storing food for the winter.

My thought for the day,
be thankful always;
and for the pilgrims of our land
who had the foresight to plan.

Josie M. Smith

The Little Spider

Written for my Special Friend, Michelle Rayburn
Oh no little spider, above my bed,
How can you hang from only a thread.

Nice little spider so fuzzy and brown,
I hope you don't come all the way down.

Cute little spider you're moving here and there,
Oh please, please don't fall into my hair.

I just wonder what spiders do all night,
I hope you're not looking for a bite.

Now I'm pulling the covers over my head.
And pray you don't jump on my bed.

So little spider I must say goodnight,
But just in case you need it, I'll leave on
the light.

Vita Shanks

Tears For Daddy Cliff

I have seen my daddy cry several times. When mom died I heard him whimper and felt a strange terror in me, like young doves being crippled from the sky by a shotgun blast.

When my brother, his first son was sacrificed to drugs, I watched my dad drop his head between his knees and vomit up a stomach full of tears.

When dad's leg was amputated just below his knee, he clutched his wheel chair and screamed his tears away. Once daddy kissed my hand in his hospital bed and death perched on his lips like a huge festering sore.

I shared my dad's final tear at his funeral. When his lifeless body passed before me, his eyes had an icy stare, his face was cold and empty. My daddy had ran out of tears. Then I felt my grief swallow me like an ancient tomb and I cried for both of us.

Clifton E. Marsh

Impromptu Play

Impromptu play,
twinkle of the starlit night
evolving from strings and ivory.
Vibrations of a robust stream
leaping and falling with the salmon's flight.
Still and crisp in the rising, radiant sun.
Gliding in the gentle breeze born in the bow.
Erratic journey,
each step led by a new note
sliding into sweet and poignant vignettes.
Aspiring to melody,
falling to silence.
He has gone
and the music stops.

Melissa Smigley

A Dark Day

Always in a hurry
never looking back
didn't have a worry
her mind was right on track

She thought she had what she wanted
in a minute he ripped it away
left her feeling hurt and haunted
with memories of yesterday

How many times will she stop and wonder
what should she have done
how many times will she cry and ponder
what could she have done

Rain, rain go away
whatever happened to the sunny days
rain, rain go away
she never wanted it to turn out this way

If she could go back and undue what's been done
the final outcome would be a pleasant one
she would have her dignity and not the shame
she would have the answers instead of the blame.

Jill Brown

Deep Love

My deep love exist from your essence
so stay make me happy with your presence.
Beside you my heart is full of fire
my heart beats faster with perspire.
Brings my blood to boil you desire
love is not a gentle fate but a painful fire.

Mohammad Khalessi

Child

The child so lonely what
can we do, the parents disown
me and leave it up to you.
    The cries of the child go
unheard because of the babies unspoken word.
    Daddy and Mommy not around
anymore I feel like jumping can't
take anymore. Stop say I love you
and open the door for the child's
heart is crying and bleeding for more.

Mark Dempsey

My Loving Harvey

Brighter than the stars
Smarter than your peers
You enjoyed little more than a decade,
    but the intellect of 17 years.
Why only a decade plus 3, is difficult to understand,
But that was the number, etched in the heavens for you to be.

Emotional levels you reached, which adults don't achieve
So not too much was missed, with much in so few years

Your parents were your idols, so no life was worth to live
You joined them with great love, so peace could be achieved.

Your presence will missed, by all of us for sure
And Larry still does cry, why big brother had to die,
But he will survive and carry on, to accomplish in only one,
    what all 4 would have done.

Marlene Kimmel

Hunters Art

The dew in its random
wandering landed in noiseless
beads upon the spider's web.

Beams of light filtered through the
diamantine orbs and
broke into scintillating colored beams.

Beneath the beaded net an eight-eyed,
hairy artisan looked up
with pedipalps upraised as if to say
"see what I have done."

Then, with a firm but subtle thrust
the morning breeze tapped the fragile work
exploding it into a radiant mist of light.

The artisan became a hunter
and the world went on its way.

Anthony Gabriel Johnson

Dreams Come True

Suffered in silence, numb to the pain.
With nothing to lose and nothing to gain.
Left all alone, no hope, no control.
Feelings of emptiness permeating the soul.
Searching for kindness but not finding much
in a soft spoken word or a warm gentle touch.
Dreaming of love with much more than a thought.
The fantasy of a crush but afraid to get caught.

Floating through life as if times standing still.
Hiding a hole that I thought I can't fill.
Never admitting that there was a need.
Filling the hole with envy and greed.
Then comes a woman whom God must have sent.
I had heard about love, now I know what they meant.
Every once in a lifetime a dream does come true.
And for this lost soul, that dream was you.

Rodney Lodato

For You To Be Mine

For one more kiss, I'd give you the world.
For one more hug, I'd give all that I have.
For you to love me, I'd give you my life.
For you, I'd stop time and the earth along with it.
If I were ruler of this world all the kingdoms,
and thrones would be at our disposal.
Once I have your love I'll keep it in a secret place.
Somewhere only you have the key to the door
with a mat that says welcome.
Somewhere only you can find.
If all was said and done, would you be mine
for eternity through the eyes of time?
If I were to lose you. Eternity is never to you
and if you leave me you would shatter my eyes.
I no longer can see. I'm once again blind.
I paid the price as you would say, the ultimate fine.
If I had one more wish in life, I'd wish you were mine.

Modesto Razo

Words

As I write, the words just seem to flow
    from where they come, I do not know
I'd like to think they are written with love
I'd like to think I'm guided from above
I'd like to think they're kind of a rope
I'd like to think they inspire hope
I'd like to think they'll pull you through
    when something bad happens to you
I'd like to think they are wise and kind
I'd like to think they'll stand the test of time
But most of all I'd like to think
    these words are written with indelible ink
And I hope my words won't fade away
    like my dreams for you did . . . yesterday

    in loving memory
    Linda A. Pukalo

Fear

I walked into that room black as pitch with a thick darkness
He liked it that way, but I no, I found that it vexed me
When daylight came, he hid from it, calling me to do his slave-like
chores, I did them as I was told, for I was his slave
He had eyes of a vulture, his blood ran cold, his heart of stone,
was of death
He would accept no visitors, of course no visitors came out of mortal fear
Mortal he was not he was from hell, not from this world
His soul was crying to be let free of his evil ways
You could always hear the hellish tattoo coming from that stone
heart a night came when I oh, so gently snuck into that dark, dark room
I thrust my body upon him and raised the object over my head
There was no sound, no blood, for there was no blood to drain
out of the stone dead body
Perfect triumph, but no, no, it was wrong, God no, I not want
to be caught
I foamed, I raved, I swore,
but it was over, I had done what I had done
I raised the object over my head and ended my life,
My life of fear, my life of terror, my life.

    Erin Berman

Reflections

I sit here in a mist of reflections of the past, and see dreams and
memories that will always last.
I see childhood days of long ago that a boy of ten will only know.
Where your thoughts run wild and free and you find the really me.
Reflections of the days of pass, that get you through this world of
glass. As I pause in reality, I see my days are like a vapor in the
sky, and I know that reflections are only a memory of days gone by.

    Jerry Dean Staley

Three Little Wishes

When life's endeavors come our way
And we all go and stay
We will find ourselves wondering and wishing
What might happen: What we are missing
Into my mind the words come along
Three little wishes, like verse from a song

Wish number one, the most important of all
Is loud and clear, even if so small:
My time to know you, so short, so sweet
I wish I could increase it by years, months, and weeks

Wish number two, not the first or the last
Wanting to forget, but also remember the past
Telling you to go, wishing you would stay
Knowing all along you're going your way

Wish number three, last but not least
Comes from my heart, sure as the sunrises from the east
I wish happiness to you the future will bring
As pure as the flowers that bloom in the spring

Three little wishes all so very true
To tell you in my heart is a place just for you

Kurtis Williams

The Eyes Of The Universe

Is love just a shifting focus in a world gone mad with vision.
Eye candy visions, the decaying of the soul
we are caught in a swirling universe of vision.
All the colors of the rainbow shine about us,
for we are crystallized light.
We are like the stars shining with a million tiny suns.

Focus, beings of light
for where your heart is, there will your eyes wander,
and dark visions are but a heartbeat away.
Yet through darkness you see,
for you are the light, you are the vision,
yours are the eyes focused on humanity's sorrows,
turn them away,
your treasures are your emotions.

Your imagination, jewels, push the veil aside
and step into the new dawn of man,
where visions come in swirling colors of creation,
and nothing is further than your heart can reach.

For you are the eyes of the universe.
Stand, and accept your divinity.

Patricia Littlejohn

Today

Our time together is over our relationship is through
I just cannot help but wonder what in the world did I do
I know in my heart that I did nothing wrong
You left me because you did not think together we did belong
If that is truly how you feel then that is fine with me
I just do not understand why you said forever we would be
This came as a shock to me I was given no clue
That you would leave me and immediately be with someone new
It makes things easier to know that me you do not hate
At least that is what you say so your word I will have to take
Things do not make sense and I hope someday they do
I want you to know I will never forget the time I had with you
You will do what you want and I will not say a thing
Just when I sit and think about us I feel I was a rebound fling
I do not know what to think anymore I do not know what to do
My mind and heart are all confused by words said by you
You told me from the beginning that the pain stopped here
You told me to hold nothing back there was nothing to ever fear
Well I did what you asked now what else can I say
Except that it did me no good look where it got me today

Christy Miller

Keep Smiling little One . . .

Keep smiling little one
for if you do you'll own this tired world.
Knowing you exist, my life has meaning son.
You teach us much, both young and old.
I've raised you the best I know,
my love for you I'll always show.
Be strong little man, for this world is a heavy load.
At your tender age, this you already know.
I'll help you the best I can,
nurturing you from boy into man
don't grow up too fast,
for youthful years are few and fly fast.
Memories of watching you grow,
are dear to my heart now and ever more
Just remember in times of trial,
in years to come, I make mistakes,
I'm just a mom, I do the best I can
for I love you Dave, my little man.

Beth Michalosky

A Mother's Challenge

Time to have a baby, being guided down my road,
A precious baby born, reaping the seed that I had sowed.
A special bond enveloping my heart, euphoria did I meet,
My life has filled with happiness, the world was at my feet.

Suspicious doubts intruding in, reflections of pain and woe,
This isn't real, it's just a doubt, but soon I'd really know.
The waiting, praying, crying, worrying tore me inside out,
When that soul breaking day arrived, I knew not what life was about.

Experiencing an emotional death, cycling through and through,
Directing myself through the motions, ne'er knowing what to do.
Depression and anger vented toward God, how could he let this be?
My soul was an empty cavity, my anguish blinding me.

Relinquishing my inner self, was something I ultimately allowed,
While something changed deep within, it was then I graciously bowed.
I said to him, "My life is yours, where would you have me go?"
And he answered to me, "Go forth, and within you I will show."

What I came to realize, was to turn to him in strife,
It was then that I recognized, he has a plan for us in life.
It happens simultaneously, both choice and circumstance,
Our lives are dually planned for us, yet also left to chance.

Cathy A. Franco Gould Harrison

Mother A's In Heaven Now

Mother A has gone to heaven,
  She no longer can we see;
But we know that she's in heaven;
  Where for some time she's longed to be.

A new baby she's been given,
  For her existence up there;
And we know that she's rejoicing,
  In that place she now can share.

Mother A is not now with us,
  We will miss her that we know,
She prepared to go to heaven,
  There's no better place to go.

Ninety five years, she was given,
  To be living here on earth.
She was a loving wife and mother,
  And we know she proved her worth.

Mother A did love her Savior,
  And she loved to sing of Him.
Oft she joined her voice with others
  As they sang a favorite hymn.

Pauline Boyle

Two As One

My eyelids open to reveal darkness.
By myself I sit, in a crowed room I stand.
I long to feel death's hot breath on my neck.
My hero hate, approaches me and wraps his arms of deceitfulness
and defeat around me.
I rely on him and soon find I cannot stand unless he holds me up.
His grip gets tighter and tighter and soon I find that I cannot breathe.
Death shows up with a smile on his face and a melting candle in his hand.
I start to scream but it only turns into laughter.
What have I wished for?
Oh, the days I wanted to shoot the sun out of the sky.
The pull the moon down and burn it and throw the remains into the ocean.
To sit and watch the baby-dolls play baseball till it grows dark.
Hello death, where are we going?

Meghan Willoughby

Buried Souls

No time to make sense of the tears dwelling within my soul.
Tormented by the needless death of war, anger has trapped
itself in the walls of my heart. Begging for release
which can only be found in Peace.
Friend and foe die in vain, blood-stained souls scream
out in pain. Damning all at fault for the senseless death
of man. My love for human kind has been buried deep within.
Only the Mercy of God can erase the horror and fear.
Let me go God, bring me home, where these eyes see death
no more, where these ears hear screams no more, where my
heart feels pain no more.

Timothy A. Wiggins

No Life Without You

I have no life without you,
no point to look forward to
another day, though I would
never kill myself over you, but
will always think life is
pointless without you, when
you don't hold me or caress me
or kiss me, I feel like a nobody,
when you're not here with me
there's always darkness in my life,
but when I'm with you there's light,
I'm safe, I'm special, I'm someone
when I'm with you, my life
is a beautiful place, when I'm not with you
my life is garbage, I don't know why
I wake up every day, probably
because I think you're gonna call me,
someone could hurt me physically, emotionally
and mentally, but I don't care cause
I'm dead inside without you.

Marilyn Rivera

Caring

Caring is shedding light on a simple problem
Caring is reaching out to one feeling blue
Caring is speaking, but without talking
Caring is giving and not taking in return
Caring is helping one through a trying time
Caring is sharing with the ones in your life
Caring is hurting when it is not you who hurts
Caring is trusting in the one you believe in
Caring is believing in the one you trust
Caring is being there when one is needed
Caring is holding when one needs to be held
Caring is the first step of falling in love
Caring is wanting to do this all for you

Timothy Lorenzo

A Love, The Precious Few

The precious few, they are hard to obtain,
the few who find them are never again just quite the same.
You're one of the few;
I'm one, too.
Together we can start a trend,
because what we feel, it is more than friends.
I would like for us to be together again,
partially so the odds against us won't win.
The time with you was priceless;
without you I'm just the opposite, worthless.
I can't explain just how I feel;
but I do know I love you.
I'm wanting to show you a love of a different color,
a love of patience, courage and time.
A love that will be stronger than any steel;
more valuable than all the treasures of the world.
A love more pure than any diamond.
Please let me show and share my love with you.

George Thomas Pratt

Lightning Strikes

Two wide-eyed children stare out the windows for Daddy
The big oak tree rocks in the wind
A flash of light
In the stormy night

The oak tree is gone
Where once were the initials of the lovers in the house
Now is ashes
Thunder clashes

The lights from Daddy's car shine through the night
He is now safely at home
The oak tree is gone
But their love lives on

Heather Dettro

Things That Can't Be

Holding hands while walking in the rain
laughing and tumbling in the snow
dancing in the trees, with autumn leaves dropping
standing on the beach, as the sun sets
things I want, things that can't be.

Holding on tight, long through the night
buying that first house, relaxing in our yard
sleeping by the fire, raising a child
looking, loving and deep into one another's eyes
things I need, things that can't be.

These words I write, they mean a lot to me
an ache inside, a tear in my eye.
Life's cruel irony. Tearing at me.
Waiting and hoping for the day when
things that can't be, will be things that can.

Brian Kueck

Chaos

When one lives in a world of chaos and impasse
there are no answers — only the questions last.
Chaos is tranquility turned upside down
the king wears the rags — the pauper wears the crown.
The phone rings in — the call goes out
mayhem is a whisper — silence becomes a shout.
'Tis the dark of the day, 'tis the light of the night
the owl's wings make noise, the laughing dove is in sight.
The brook is quiet — the mountain will speak.
The water falls up — the rapids are weak.
Chaos brings peace, love brings the impasse.
'Tis one view of the world through a looking-glass.

Janie C. Donaldson

Escape To Something Wrong

I go to my room to cry on my bed.
I did something wrong.
I feel hurt and I'm falling apart.
I did something wrong.
I cry myself to sleep each night,
But I keep it to myself.
I'm in need of a hug,
But instead, I get a lousy pat on my back.
I try my hardest, to be good at everything I do.
I hope that someone would, notice and be proud of me.
You see I do the best that I can do,
With everything that's expected of me.
Because of this, I despise and hate myself,
I love and wish I hadn't.
With pieces of me in the trash, and the rest of me falling apart.
I finally get the attention I need,
Yet, once again I've done something wrong.
I won't be able to accomplish my dreams,
Because no one will notice or acknowledge me.
So in desperate need, I escape to something wrong.

Melissa LaHommedieu

Dead Winter

Against the darkened sky the wisps of smoke
float up from chimneys where, below, the coke
hisses and crackles in its agony
of heat, while slowly sifting down on me,
like petals, cool and frail, the snow
gives to night a pale, persistent glow.

Dead leaves are hidden now; once naked trees
pose grandly in white foliage. But can these
divert my heart away from awful truth?
Death waits. The earth is cold.

   Oh yes, my ruth
be stanched! Be stanched! Let me enjoy this night
in brooding on the beauty of the sight
as unsuspecting children, in delight,
embrace the mad dog before the bite.

Charles Blakemore

Dad

I may not be your flesh and blood.
I may not be worth a darn.
But thanks a lot,
For the flesh and blood you gave me
When you gave me your daughter's hand.
That's what gives me the right to call you my Dad.
She is worth a million dollars
Thanks again Dad.

Lawrence R. Storey

My Angel

When you were gone I did some thinking, I could not believe it was true
And when you came in I held you so tightly I truly believed it was you
The first time you spoke you gave me a message, a message I'll never forget
I knew from an instant what you were speaking I knew what that
   message meant
When I was a child I could not fathom the idea it could happen to you
The being you were and not having you there was something I
couldn't go through
Seeing you sad and wanting to be with the man you hold dear to your heart
Helped me to believe that a love so pure could break if it were apart
If I could be one to hold on to such love for the rest of my
   natural born life
I will do as you did, hold on to this man and as you I will become his wife
Some things seem different now since you've gone, they've
changed since you were alive
But I feel you each day and I know in my heart that I have a personal guide.

Giana Nicole Severini

My Brown Canary

   If inside my brown canary
Was just another wooden bird
Then would she be like this canary
Dressed in paint and perched in curd?

   Would she be the same canary
Who for life is ever chasing.
Would when her feathers are old and brittle
Could chip away her outer casing?

   Would she be the same canary
Where this was not the case at all,
Who could step about her brazen cage
And sing a lovely mating call?

   And she could look out her cage and see
All the things that stood and stirred,
And for them she could dance and sing
While still the same old wooden bird.

Danny Lovvorn

Life

Life what seems a rainy day
Could be fun or quite okay.

Days repeated for so long
It all seems like a never-ending song.

Relive the past years, no one could do
For we could not go back in time, not I nor you.

But life is remarkable and exciting as well
And God's secrets about life He will never tell!

Matthew Hendricks

The Gift

He created the heavens, the earth, and the sea
And all that in them is
He's Jesus Christ the Son of God
And His Spirit forever lives

He's an all consuming fire
Yet gentle as a dove
He's Jesus Christ the Son of God
A never ending love

He's Omnipotent, Omnipresent
Everywhere at one time
He's King of Kings and Lord of Lords
He's Jesus Christ — Divine

I will praise Him in the morning
In the evening and at noon
Knowing in my heart of hearts
Jesus is coming very soon

I will write about Jesus in the winter
In the summer and the fall
But thanks be to God, who gave His Son
The Greatest Gift Of All

Marcia Sanders

At Christmas

Christmas candles burning brightly
Set my lonely heart aglow.
Carols flooding through the twilight
Waver through new fallen snow.

Through the years as bells are chiming,
Evening starlight shines above.
Warm reflections, sweet in silence
Keep the memory of our love.

Dorothy E. Vincent

Light

Light . . .
bringing forth the unknown,
chasing away the shadows of the dark,
helping me to see things more clearly.

Light . . .
filling the world with color,
magnifying the beauty everywhere,
drawing my attention to things I have not noticed before.

Light . . .
essential to sustaining life,
embracing and nurturing me,
providing energy and encouraging me to grow.

Light . . .
a source of guidance,
providing safety,
allowing me the chance to explore.

Teresa M. Fox

Little Girl

I always thought I'd be a good mother
but this little girl keeps beatin' down my walls.
I wanna play with her but instead I punish her.
I wanna hear her but instead I shut her out.
When I look in the mirror I can see her beauty.
But somehow I cut that down too
Her tiny voice pierces through my heart and soul.
Her tears rock my every being.
Why can't I hear her, my little girl
Why am I ashamed of this little girl
She is a part of me, this little girl
She is beautiful, this little girl
She will be okay, this little girl.

Linda Vassolo

This World

I am in the center of this World.
A world where you are falling into an emotional abyss.
Falling out of my reach.
I close my eyes and pray, but
When I open, you're still the same.
Falling beyond the extent of my love.
I wish you would see that I am not the only one hurting for you.
Hurting for a sincere smile.
Hurting for a simple gesture to know that I caught you.
You are falling into this World.
Falling out of my grasp into this World.
Breath of Heaven, guard her in your palm.

Keli Davidson

A Senior's Reflection On Self

The me that is me is not the me that you see.
The me that is me is not wrinkled or worn,
    not hard of hearing, or fat, or forlorn.
The me that is me does not constantly dribble,
    droop at the chin, or sag in the middle.
The me that is me isn't grey or arthritic,
    on medication, or old, or pathetic.
No, the me that you see is not the me that is me.

The me that is me is the me deep within,
    where youth is eternal and all dreams begin.
The me that is me is the me all aglow
    with hope and ambition, and eager to grow.
The me that is me is the me never changing,
    always here, always now, always at the beginning.
The me that you see is not the me that is me.
    The me that is real is the me that I feel.

Barbara Griffin

A Gift

Born into this world. I be . . . with a mother's love given to thee
Family, friends, an enemy, all are part of life, which was meant to be
In this incredible adventure there are many sights to relate,
all part of the equation: Love and Hate
There is change in the wind with every step I take
Different choices, path, ideas I choose . . . a wrong roll of the dice
YOU LOSE!!
Searching to find an identity, with constant contact in this vast
sea of life . . . I choose a mate, my wife
We create . . . for that we have claimed immortality, another
generation from our beautiful seed
I have existed between heaven and earth since my birth
My destiny
This is the gift God has bestowed upon thee.

Richard Thompson

On Flag Burning

This banner so old and dearly loved,
That at times has been both hawk and dove,
Is all that's left of those poor souls,
Who perished for it on land and shoals.

So burn the paper and aging cloth
And forget the lessons you've been taught,
And then, once more, these souls shall die,
Along with the symbols you defy.

But, worst of all, in newer distress,
These souls that fight a fresh torment
Shall lose new battle and lasting life,
By being damned to eternal strife.

Thomas J. Miller Jr.

In Memory Of My Sweetheart

Down the empty corridors of loneliness
I have traveled these many days
Missing the warmth of your loving arms about me
And longing for your sweet words of praise.
Time goes on, come what may
And I know that I must live on
Making the best that I can of each day
That I may share His Heavenly Home
With you, my darling, my beloved
Never more to be so very alone.
The beautiful memories of our life together
And having known your tenderness and love
No matter how stormy the weather
We shall meet in the heaven above.

Alice I. Atherton

Untitled

One more minute, one more day,
One more hour for us to play.
In this cry, my hearts deepest wish,
I miss your smile, your laughter, your
    wet sloppy kiss.

Unfulfilled promises, spoken in vain,
The ghosts that haunt me will always remain.
All the times life got in the way,
Unspoken words I needed to say.

Your tiny hand curled around my finger with love,
All the times I love you was spoken will never be enough.
Soothing your cries, matching them with my own
I hope the love I feel was always shown.
I think of you always, I love you still
The emptiness in my heart will never be filled.
This wish in my heart as I pray for you,
I hope the angels cherish you as much as we do.

Jennifer Scarberry

Cheater

If you cry, I'll hold you tight,
I'll pray with you all through the night.
Your pretty blue eyes, could tell no lies,
We've made some memories, that are way up high.
But no matter what you do, it's the same old you,
That's why I feel the way I do.
You were there time after time, I always knew you'd be by my side.
I want to thank you for all that you've done,
Remember these words "you are not alone."
I'll love you and love you, until I can't love no more,
I'm sorry if I was mean, I'm sorry if you got hurt.
You put your heart upon a shelf, I was seeing you and someone else.
I'm not the man I used to be,
I said "I'm sorry," please forgive me.
I'm going to show you what real love can be,
Just take my hand, and come home with me.
There's not much more that I could say,
Except I love you, and I hope you still love me.
I'll say it once more,
I'm sorry.

George E. Maher Jr.

Angel Eyes

I know a beautiful girl whom I love very much,
and with the most beautiful eyes you have ever seen.
She can't hear me when I say,
"Angel Eyes I love you." Oh Lord, what do I do,
to let her know that my love is true?
Every time I look at her picture I get this feeling that we
will never be together.
She's an angel with eyes like stars in the night sky.
I would treat her like a queen. Yes,
she has angel eyes with a heart of gold to match.
Oh, if I could I would take her to dinner, movies and dancing.
She has beautiful brown eyes,
like the kind that lights up the sky.
"Angel Eyes, I love you."
I just can't tell you so.
Oh, how I long to hold you in my arms.
But I can't, so I will just keep wishing.
Just remember where ever you go in your life.
I love you always, my sweet Angel Eyes,
you light up the night sky.

Joseph G. Salinas

Untitled

You stand before my eyes
This must be someone in your disguise

The hurtful things you often say
Go on hurting long after today

What is it you really see
When you are looking right at me

A failure? No life?
Nobody's wife?

What is it I really see
When you are looking right at me

Drugs so handy
You mistake them for candy

Someone in pain
Surely insane

Freedom, you think means anarchy
As long as I'm your mom that will never be

Take another look son and you shall see
That I am not the enemy.

Lesley Osborn

Untitled

How long the moments are not spent with you.
Just as a flower is most alive when reaching for the sun,
And a bird is at its highest glory when soaring through the heavens,
My being is most at joy when in the sweet glow of the love templed within you.
One look into your eyes was all that it took for my heart to sing
out that it had found what it was after.

The Pyramids may all turn to dust and blow away;
The Oceans may all dry up;
The Stars may all be extinguished;
But my love for you will live beyond eternity.

There is no gulf too large to be bridged;
No battle too fierce to be fought;
No obstacle too great to be conquered,
in my quest to make our two hearts one.

I long for us to caress;
To be pressed against the soft-feathered breast of your love;
Folded in a wing.

As the galaxies collide, may we dance on the trails of angels.
You are stardust. Life has kissed you beautiful.
My heart bows to your heart. I love you.

Harvey Diamond

For My Son

Seeing you now brings back memories
I hope never to forget..
I see an infant focusing his eyes on his father
for the first time.
There is a toddler standing for the first time,
we are so excited.

The first day of school finds us at odds,
you can't wait to go and I'm afraid to let go.
I can count spelling tests, pinewood derbies,
camping trips, and poster contests.
High school finds your heart beating faster
for a special young lady.

There have been illnesses, broken bones,
broken hearts, but always dreams.
I remember that you were afraid to make mistakes,
but never afraid to move forward.

Today I see a grown man, mature, loving,
caring and making memories of your own.
You are sharing your life now with the woman you love,
just as I am with your father.

Patricia Papineau

Blessed: To The People Of The Oklahoma City Bombing

For they were innocent and shame on the people
who gave them so much pain. For if the Judge's
can't punish them, for they have to face the
one hundred sixty eight people who died on
that day. For they have to pay the price and
face the almighty God on judgement day.
For the children were so innocent and pure.
For now they don't have a life, for they were
the ones so young at heart. And we can't
hear what they have to say. So they are
the angels now looking down on us. "Praying
for peace for all of us." For it really touched
my heart for so many people died on that
very same day. Because I have an angel
that helps me each and everyday. So if
everyone would listen and love everyone
all over the world we would be brothers
and sisters and no more bloodshed. So please
listen and pray for peace for all of us.

Barbara Rich

Time

Sometimes I wonder, sometimes I dare, is there a purpose for life?
Am I anywhere? Is there a time? Is there a place? Is there a
dimension that I am destine to face?

I've stumble thru life, with no idea of where I've been, I really
wish I understood my journey, my purpose seems to be,
goodwill to all men.

If I could see what there is to life, and all that it intel's, maybe,
just maybe, I could be as the ocean, rolling free, with her great swells.

I look at life, and I try, oh so very hard to see, but this thing
that we call sight, is really just blindness to me. So we look into
our own minds, with hopes of an outward view, we find ourselves lost in a world, with no one looking for you.

Now we find ourselves wondering, are we really anywhere? Are we
lost in a dimension? Does anyone really care? Life's highways, are
long, dark and lonely, I think I could find my way about, if only,
there was a spark of light, that shined in the night, and filled ones
eyes with hope, but so far, there is no star, and life remains a maze.

And so I pray, to the one that is responsible for it all, and until
such time, that I am no more, on his name I will call . . .

Larry Ross

For Life Has Gone

A fading flower once in full bloom
but now a scraggly weed;
a filthy mass of emptiness
from nature's venomed seed.
    For life has gone, and death has come.

A glowing sun once shown his face,
ashamed by the flower now;
he hides his brilliance to shed his tears
behind the saddened clouds.
    For life has gone, and death has come.

A young girl once alive in love
but now an empty hole;
a human leech has given her life
to a "more fortunate" soul.
    For life has gone, and death has come.

For each of them rather not be
part of this cruel world;
together they sing their dying song:
The flower, sun and girl.
    For their lives have gone, and death came.

Cynthia D. Cotton Reveley

Turn Signals On My Mind

That light amber flicker in the soft
a disturbing glow of my will's night now says
with intermittent confidence . . . I'm going to turn, left . . .
you behind

But my confidence in such gestures vacillates
for I fear you were right; and not, left
to my intentions . . .

So I blink my way right towards your stead;
braving the heavy traffic of our past.
Courageously swerving across eminent death
and charted territory

But a red light appears in my conscience road
so I halt my unsteady veer
towards your unpaved
and confusing intentions
as I let the traffic we held up so long
just pass by . . .

John Alexander Kennedy

Bird Benevolence

The beach was still, not a whisper heard
Only flapping of a single bird.
He seemed so lovely flying so high
Alone, by himself, in the big sky.

He flew in great circles, loops, and dives
So daring, yet graceful, with his life.
Seemed he had not a care in the world
For he was the only flighted bird.

I envy a bird with graceful ways
Just living carefree, day after day.
I wonder if the birds have feelings
Or even care about their birdlings.

I guess I'll never know how to fly
Nor should I ever really ask why.
I'm a being not meant to take flight
Only to roam the earth day and night.

I'm lucky that people are everywhere
Whereas birds in the sky seem more rare.
We have so many thoughts and desires
Maybe it's the bird that really admires.

Susan Vitale

I Thank You

I thank you, our Father in the heavens,
because you have been very kind with me,
in this day, that is coming to an end.

I thank you,
for the life you allowed me to enjoy today,
for the air you allowed me to breathe,
for the food, and even for the things
that went wrong today.

I thank you,
for taking time to teach me,
what is right and what is wrong,
to be loving and kind,
and to not do to others
what I do not want to be done to me.

And especially, I thank you,
because you are the only one,
who always listens to me.

Marta M. McNamee

My World Talks To Me

Sometimes I walk just to clear my head.
A walk for one now becomes for two instead.

To be alone with my thoughts and not have to share.
This is never possible, you see my world is always there.

Although without taking steps I can never walk.
My world without words is capable of talk.

Leaves green at one time, fallen, brown and in mass.
They say they're my yesterdays; each a day in my past.

A small but furry creature scurries off to hide.
A reminder to me that I too have fears locked inside.

The frail sapling and the mighty oak as it stretches to the sun,
Are the baby I once was and the adult I will become.

The wooded trail winds, and climbs, then disappears around the bend.
This says that my life is not a simple journey, and that in time it too will end.

The mountains outward and high, with the valley so far below.
They speak of how far I've come and of how much further I still can go.

With the sky forever above me the winds become a voice familiar and true.
A reminder of my mother as she whispers, "I'll always watch over you."

Robert E. Burns

Why Do I Smile . . .

Why do I smile
when I look into your eyes?

Maybe it's because I see your warmth
radiating from the center of your heart, or

Maybe it's because I see the trust and respect
we've had from the start, or

Perhaps I see the fun and laughter
of the times we've shared, and
the comfort of knowing we're always there, or

Possibly it's because I see your passion
for life's love affair, or

Better still it's my reflection I see
along with all of these things that we both share

Just maybe that's

Why I smile
when I look into your eyes

Paul Reindollar

I Will Arrive

I just don't know what's happening to me
I've lost my spirit, my will, my thrive
Dreaming of the day that I will be free.
Hoping and praying that one day life will arrive.
I still have no idea what I'm suppose to do.
Wandering around, wanting to drown in a pool.
Letting the world treat me like an old shoe.
Kissing every behind like a great big fool.
But hope is what I still have for myself,
That somehow I'll change with a little time.
Then the old me would be put on a shelf.
And I will finally have peace of mind.

Marlene Pastrana

looking out the window . . .

watching the children play in the yard . . .
sprinkler spraying rainbows all around them,
making them look like the little
angels we all know they are inside . . .
listening to the laughter . . .
ringing out, loud and joyous
echoing among the swaying treetops
gently cascading thru the branches and
joining together in timeless refrain
with the musical, flittering birds . . .
smiling inside my heart . . .
at the joy a child's laughter can bring,
and remembering my own happy days,
when simply being "young"
meant being free . . .

Debra S. Moores

Cycle Within

Through out time and all my ages,
I've been different people at various stages,
From simple to complicated, and soft to hard.
From exuberantly joyful to feeling the
most hurtful of sorrow. Such extremes somehow
seems necessary to keep compassion and maintain
a true heart.
  Throughout time I've been locked and
freed from cages. I've experienced harmony yet
know what true rage is.
  Without ugly there would be no beauty,
without madness we would not be sane,
without loss there would be no gain.

Terry Young

Saviour

Long ago in Bethlehem, a star shone so bright
over a lowly stable, where Mary and Joseph spent the night.
There was no room at the inn for them to lay their head
so when their precious Child called 'Jesus' came, a manger was his bed.

They marveled as Wisemen and Shepherds came, from so far and near
telling how they had been told of this Child, who was so dear.
Saying this surely was the one who would make things right
the one who would save the world, by giving of his life.

The Child, we call 'Jesus,' we all say we love
was sent here to help us, from our Father up above.
If we will but love Him, and all do our part
He'll give us salvation, and come into our heart.

Take time to know Jesus, take time to rejoice
take time to listen when you hear his voice.
His arms will enfold you, he won't let you fall
please give Him your love — He's, given his all.

Ivadean Severy

Above And Beyond The Realm Of Tears

Like beads on a treasured rosary,
I count the joys you brought to me . . .
Silly jokes we often shared,
Little ventures we had dared,

Strange bird-calls neither could identify,
Strong spring shoots that cold could not deny,
The fleeting colors of twilight,
the stars, the moon, all glories of night,

A "who-hoo" announcing arrival
After separation and survival,
The shared feeling of bliss
That followed a tender kiss . . .

The joys of only few golden years,
Above and beyond the realm of tears.

Maxine Sanford Austin

My Little Angel's Gone Home

Oh, Travis I can't believe a year has passed.
Since I held you last.
How I wish today, was the past
So, you could be in my arms again
I'd hold you close and dream of what our lives will be.
Everything I've ever wished
This was not what I could see
That I'd be here and you'd be up there,
Watching over me.
I love and miss you so very much.
Your sweet little smile, your tender touch.
Like a candle in the night.
I know your spirit, forever shines bright.
Someday when God calls me home.
We'll spend forever in heaven's light.

Karen A. Coté

Love

Love is a word you can't describe,
You need to have it deep inside,
It's a word that can hurt or just change your life,
Or it may some how broaden your life,
Some how, some reason, you need to have it deep inside,
Just maybe it makes you show lots of pride,
Marriage, angels, and doves . . .
Let me tell you some more about love,
As I had said love is hard to describe,
As I told you,
You need to have it deep inside!

Cristina Helen Couri

What If?

If life was simple
   would you want to be challenged?

If you knew the end of a book
   would you want to read it?

If you forgave others
   would you still hate yourself?

If you knew the future
   would you want to live it?

If you knew everything about the universe
   would you want to explore it?

If you believed one person
   would you believe the other?

If your cries went unanswered
   would you still cry?

If you knew everything about me
   would you still love me?

    Kelly Walker

Life's Highway

When you are traveling along life's highway
Which way is best you cannot say
Sometimes it will be a lonely road
Without someone to share the load

The road you are on may not be the best
You need to stop along the way and rest
If you need to take a detour
It may be the best way, you're never sure

You may wish you didn't have to drive
You think you will never arrive
The road may be bumpy and full of holes
A bridge may be out, you can't reach your goal

If you find a companion to make you strong
Your days will be happy as you travel along
Those you pick to travel along with you
Be true to them whatever you do

With God as a compass you won't lose your way
As you travel along life's highway

    Sheldon J. Lewis

Desperation

Upon the outstretched wings of desperation I traveled,
My whole infinitesimal existence a tattered ravel,
My lethargic soul drained of its innocuous tranquility,
Destined to a life of loneliness; my pain, my disability.

You saw my arid heart,
and I drank from the river which was you,
You breathed back into me,
The breath of life, my existence no longer doomed.

You put me into a placid world,
Of hope and laughter,
But now these torrid memories of yesterday,
Are coming even faster.

You traveled to a greater land,
To have you turn in the sun,
You left me here alone,
My whole body numb.

I wrestle with my pain,
Without your breath of life I smother,
To walk the barron path,
In search for another.

    Tracy Hackney

Alone

I am alone in a world filled with people.
A world where no one cares for one another.
Where a person is isolated from every one else by a label or a gift.
Here on this world where there is a million people I am alone.
How can that be?
How can there be a million people with me still left alone?
What did I do to have this belief? What did I accomplish to deserve grief?
Isolation. That is what it is. Isolation is what you give to me.
While you call me a friend you treat me like a mother.
Going on about your lives as if I didn't matter.
You say you care, you say you'll be there.
But when the time comes, here I am still all alone.
When will it matter? When will you think about me?
When will I have some comfort?
You lend me a shoulder, you lend me an ear.
But do you really listen or do you really heed my prayer?
Alone, that is what I am, maybe that is what I will always be.

    Anne Marin

Aging

Ladies, you are fair like blossom roses,
Scarlet petals shine as sweet summer's day.
Eye watches lustfully, heart exposes
Compliments, and tongue utters words so gay.
But time moves seasons like moves dust and dawn,
O roses, your winters come stiff as storm;
So your beauties wither in the dust lawn,
Then you cry, mourn, hurt, and fear for age forms.
Sweet summer's gone, beauty is neglected,
For shadow falls upon your pale petals.
Hunger detests age from being respected,
For eye, heart, tongue throw harsh words like metal.
  O, ladies cry, mourn, hurt, and fear no more,
  For your beauties can't be judged by score.

    Ngoc Thi Cao

Forever With Me

Your fragile body has been laid to rest
and your soul has long soared to heaven.
Oh, how I would have loved,
to have heard the Angels singing
when you first got to the gate,
of our Lord's kingdom.
What a sight it would have been,
to see Granpa standing there,
waiting for you to enter in.
At your grave, the day was forecast bleak.
Instead the Lord sent His heavenly light,
shining brightly to lead your way.
Yes, your body has been laid to rest,
and your soul has gone to heaven.
But, the warmth of your love and smile,
the beauty and wisdom of your words
will forever be with me.

    Phyllis Coats

Lord Bless Me Night And Day

As I kneel down and begin to pray.
Watch my Mom and my Dad,
because without them I would be very sad.
Bless my siblings with whom I grow.
They help me all the time when there
are things that I do not know.
But most especially, take care of my grandparents
who love me so. They're always there to watch me grow.
Forgive my sins. I promise to be good. I'll try my
best to do all that I should.
Amen.

    Rachel Marie Mejia

It's Best We Stay Apart

It hurts to say this; it's best we stay apart;
you keep doing things, that keep breaking my heart.

Anything I've done, it never pleased you;
it's your fault you left me once;
after all that we went through, I let you waltz back into my life.
I tried to make things go right;
instead all we ever did was fight.

It hurts to say this; it's best we stay apart;
you keep doing things that keep breaking my heart.

You hurt me worse when we were together;
all that I've tried, between you and me, it never got better.

It hurts to say this; it's best we stay apart;
you keep doing things, that keep breaking my heart.

My heart will no longer be crying;
in my mind knowingly I tried;
I let you waltz back into my life;
I tried to make things go right;
instead all we ever did was fight.

It hurts to say this; it's best we stay apart;
you keep doing things, that keep breaking my heart.

Marlene Y. Geist

September Song

You care and that counts, my love
You are on my side
Like two lonely souls in the crowd
Kindled with a noble fire
Though thousand of miles apart
This moment is for us to remember
When gazing at the harvest moon
And showered with dreams in September
Keep the moonlight in your heart
And turn unspoken words into the sweetest song

I feel free as a breeze
My heart wanders over hills, plains and rivers
The journey is not over yet
I do not want to hurry
If you want to come along
Hope the road ahead is long
May there be many more full-moons
May the days ahead be merry
And if I may have a choice
I want this one to be your song

Emily Kuan

Sounds

Our world is full of all sorts of sounds
from the banging of doors, to the yapping of hounds.

We hear the wailing of sirens and motorcycle roars
the squealing of brakes and slamming of doors.

The sonic boom as a plane shoots through the sky
and a humming sound from a small housefly

Thunder comes with a deafening roar
and water swishes as it laps on the shore.

The chirping of a bird and scratching of a mouse
or the sound of boards, creaking in a house.

The chugging of an engine, the whistle of a train
and the soft pitter patter of a summer rain.

So, if you stop, listen and look around,
you're bound to hear some kind of a sound.

You've heard the saying "in the still of the night"
but the switch makes a click when you turn on the light!

Roma M. Morrison

No Christmas Cheer With A Mouse In Here

It was the night before Christmas and all through the house,
A creature was stirring, a mischievous mouse,
He ripped through the stockings hung with care,
Bound to scare Santa when he finally got there,
The children who slept all safe in their beds,
Awoke with a start as he nibbled their heads,
Mom, in the kerchief she wore at night,
Screamed as she ran for it gave her a fright,
When out on the lawn he heard such a clatter,
The mouse leaned out to see what's the matter,
He slide down the curtains, and onto the ground,
He did all this without making a sound,
In front of his eyes, he beheld a sight,
Eight tiny reindeer appeared that night,
That mouse then scampered under their feet,
Knocking St. Nickolas right out of his seat,
Helping Santa up, he said with a smile,
"I think I'll hang out with you for awhile,"
So it was the night before Christmas and all through the house,
Several creatures were stirring, because of one mouse!!!

Arlene Conner Nicely

The Drainman

Have you seen him?
The old gent sauntering side to side down the street?
His brown alpine hat is slouched jauntily on his head
    and his two-toned blue souwester is zipped snugly to his chin.
    He's the Drainman
When he stops to chat his voice softly caresses you
    and the gentle sound fills the damp air with music.
He has twinkling blue eyes and a snowy white beard.
See him walking there, with his brightly colored walking stick.
    He's the Drainman.
Watch carefully, see, see what he does.
He wields his stick like a golf putter
    cleaning the leaves and "gunk" from the sewer grates.
Watch now, and listen. Listen, do you hear?
Hear the water bubble-up and run merrily to the sewer.
    He's the Drainman.
He is gentle and kind and concerned about his neighbors.
They don't know how he helps them keep their basements dry.
    I know. I see him. I talk to him. I watch him.
    He's the Drainman.

Mary Louise Krumland

The River I Long For Ahead

My heart is standing still, the blood isn't getting anywhere.
Am I alive? I feel dead.
Not to my physical being but to the spiritual.
Am I looking ahead too far?
Oh, how I long for the river ahead.

It looks so refreshing.
But here I am standing behind a stone no bigger than my toe.
I feel trapped like I can't move on.
Will I trip on this little pebble?
I look up, oh, how I long for the river ahead.

But where is God to help me past the stone?
I hear Him speaking and see His word,
but His hand I do not feel.
Why is my heart standing still
when I long for the river ahead?

Lord, I desire to be filled,
with an outpouring of your love.
Come fill my heart anew,
and lead me to the river,
the river I long for ahead.

Renee Sarver

Going Home

Red faces, golden curls, muddy shoes, bare feet
climb into my wagon we will head home.

Home is just over the next hill you can not see it from here.
Father waits for us, His arms outstretched, His love lights
up around Him.

See it — see it now?
Hang on dear friend, soon we will be there.
No, you're not heavy at all.
The wagon pulls easily, as if it were weightless.

There, there in front of us the glow on the hill
'tis Father's love, it guides us home.

The valley so beautiful now comes into view as we crest the hill.
Just one more step — and we're home, dear one, home with
our Father — the light and His love.

Love, glorious love so warm, so comforting.
I remember this now —
Death? Death? Death is not a state of being,
death is just a word.
For we live on in our Father's house where life goes on.

Bette Beasler Kerrigan

Untitled

I am fine.
Life is flowing as it should.
The colors of my life are brilliant and deep.
Shades of happiness and shades of trail.
I am strong.
I am a maple in solid ground. My branches
and leaves are glorious.
My children play and lie at my trunk while
I shade them. Life is good.
But, no . . . something has shaken my
solid ground.
What kind of storm is this?
I am strong, remember?
Don't forget. How could I forget?
The wind is powerful, the pain is immense.
Why won't it stop?
I feel the cracking and bending while
I try to hold.
Where will my children lie in confidence?
The storm is not passing. I am strong . . . remember?

Cori Short

Untitled

My affection is cast about to drift
In an angry stave I see a rift
To dart about in search of love
A chance for sustenance from above

As I sail toward the calmer sea
I perceive your love awaiting me
The journey is long stressful and tense
But is shortened by faith in just recompense

I am suddenly attacked by the wild sea
Shaking my mind it wont let me be
Violent waves crash over the side
Opening judgements that I forever hide

Pulling the oars ever harder I hurt my hands
My arms are stiff no longer follow commands
With hope about lost I pull as I must
Til the sun breaks thru as I knew in my trust

And now I see you on the other side
The journey is lost but the victory is mine
A casual stroll is lost unto me
For a chance to sail in the calmer sea

Ed Fehrman

The Sun Gods — El Encanto

The giant's breath whirls the arid soil against desert and pavement
dusty whirlwinds blow,
sun gods melt your very soul, the Sandias whiten snow
begins each riverbed widening and growing,
nourishing the winding waters turning the cycle
sustaining life, once more.

To God's children living this land,
black coal gleaming eyes, pure pride shining from inside
faces plumed, turquoise and baked by the sun
a vivid and colorful montage
of priests, medicine women, astronauts
contrasts of this land of enchantment
through the eons and atoms of time
do ascend the ancients,
ghostly ruins of New Mexico.

Lydia MacLovia Lucero

Untitled

How could you leave the world knowing you'd be
breaking the hearts of the people you love. What
is that special task that you have to do in heaven
above? You lightened up the lives of the people
when they were down. How could you leave this world
so quiet, without a sound? You made people laugh,
you would always try. Now do you see how you made
those same people cry? Kim, do you see what you've
done to all of us? You've broken the hearts of
people you loved and trust. How could your life be
taken at such a young age? You've made us cry and
scream with rage. And as I write to your spirit I
cry. Oh poor Kim, why did you have to die?

Yolanda Nesbitt

Butterfly Of Colors

Oh butterfly of many colors
Why can't they see.
You are of many like us.
We are beautiful colors just like you.
I think God made us colors in image of you.
If all was one color.
And not like you.
No beauty would there be.
Oh glad I am.
God made you.
So all could see.
God made us all colors.
So to be beautiful just like you.
Why can't they see.
God made you different colors.
And one just like me.

Shirley Ann Easter

In My Mind

Somewhere I have never traveled,
is so clear to my mind.
The flowers are so vivid in my mind
I could reach out and feel their smoothness
   in my mind.
The sky is so clear.
It looks like glass.
The grass is so green and clean
But is so prickly to the touch.
Everything smells so fresh
Too bad it's only a dream
For I would never leave.
This place is so calm and peaceful
I rest in the grace of the world,
   and I am free.

Kristen M. Smith

My Ole Granpaw

Have you ever seen my ole granpaw? Sittin' on
the front porch chew'n his jaw
whiskers on his chin and a wrinkled up brow,
everybody in town gets to know 'em somehow.
He sits on the front porch and chews all day,
this is how he makes his livin' they say.
His wife bakes the bread and fetches his meals,
while my ole granpaw just watches that still.

My ole granpaw he's tall and lean, the laziest man you've ever seen.
He has the nerve and he has the gall, 'cause you've
never met a man like my ole granpaw.

Now long 'bout 1954, granmaw come a bustin' thru
that door. Says "Looky a'here paw I've had it with
you, if all you're gonna do is sit 'n' chew."
Paw says "Maw now don'tcha fret, you know I ain't
gonna let'cha down yet."

But that revenue man was headed his way, and you
can bet your bottom dollar paw would have to pay.

Arlene Heaton

The Butterfly

Fluttering her wings
Smile so bright
She turns her head, moving toward the light
Eyes as blue as the sea
Pure hope for tranquility
She flies away . . .
Missing her still
Just one more touch
My life goes day by day
And here I hold
A gift of love, a gift of life
A heavenly sign from above
Eyes glitter
Heart of gold
But still no one knows
Pure pain, deep loneliness . . .
Seeking comfort, seeing strength
She holds her head high
And flies away . . .
Oh beautiful butterfly . . .

Melissa A. LaPlante

Immortality

Heart of darkness, ancient lies . . .
Far beyond all mortal ties.
Whisper soft within my ear . . .
Blood runs red, my sanguine tear.
Knight caress me with your word . . .
Spell so sweet, was oft unheard.

Deep within my hour of need,
Arms which hold . . . fits of greed.
Fallen angel . . . cast out, alone.
Daggers pierce . . . splinter bone.
Pain and Pleasure, sisters sure . . .
One exists, so both endure.

Surrender sweetly, night gives way . . .
As moon and stars, to light of day.
A hundred lifetimes shall come to pass . . .
The wine will sour in the glass
And still I'll wait, pray you will see . . .
My love is timeless . . . true Immortality.

Lisa R. Hollingsworth

Untitled

And the ring of inspiration bore the pain.
My continuous spirit flows.
Ecstasy of the hidden dreams.
Sipping iced tea on the front porch swing.
Systematic rhythms of jumper cables.
Sophomoric ideas that caught the attention
unable to be grasped.
The three ring combination
shows that interconnectedness of mind, body, spirit:
soul, emotion, touch.
On the wings of life there are no evils, yet,
if you trech through the earth,
you find you can overcome anything.
Even those college essays.

Meaghan Spezzi

Water Of Life

Where the water flows.
Rushing, gushing, grabbing,
bitting, twisting and turning.

Where water takes what it wants,
with the power of churning and turning.
As it cuts, as it gashes, as it slashes,
and splashes through the turns it had made.

Where water lands in a pool,
where it's nice and cool.
You wouldn't think something
so cool, could be so cruel.

But it saves lives, if they
touch the pool with their lips
for water flowing is a rush of life.

Ronald G. Simmons

Lost Destination

The petals of the flower flowing
helplessly to the force of the wind.
I am a quiet man not knowing the
destinations of my journey.
Always at the right place at the right time,
lost in the confusion and their pollution.
I start my journey toward the north.
My troubles that surround me seem meaningless
to the time and clockwork of my mind
to find vague coincidences appearing
in the thread of time,
to the north, by east or west, or maybe south.
Confusion sets in slow.
I thought of a place to go
to that lovely place I wouldn't feel loneliness any more.
I ended my journey at home!

Jason A. Taylor

Journeyman

What if I came knocking on the front door to your heart?
Would you let me in?
Do you have the courage to make a grand new start?
What if you were in the wilderness hearing me call your name?
Would you choose not to hear me?
Will you choose to carry on the same?
What if I gave you everything and promised you the world in which to play?
Would you be unthankful, should I decide to take them away?
What if I demanded you to cast away all ill gotten gain?
Would you become sad?
Then should I pity you for no longer having profit from pain
What if I asked you to love the one that hates you the most?
Would you trust me?
Do you know the value of your heart when you walk with the Holy Ghost?

Clarice Davis Jr.

Beautiful Uncertainty

We are but an experiment in the eyes of the Unknown with the resurrected dust assisting in the control. The certainty is mere minority, compared with the vast uncertainty who have gone through the consequence of existence.

We would be privileged to look and see our past as the lifeless caravan with spectacle. But what of the future, for that one star in the infinite universe which struggles through the one clear and the opaque. Can one see a glimpse of the requirement a particle must reach to complete an orbit around the all-important nucleus? However, if the spectrum is dark, let the minute never give up in the mysterious drive to attain the abstract justification for even existing.

Can reality be so majestic, and yet a drop in a cesspool, with motivation and complacency hand in hand trying to win a race that has no end, but decay? To paraphrase an old saying, "the only thing constant is change, and how one adjusts depends on how one accepts the Unknown." Let us not discourage the observers in their analysis to see life as life, and not as death.

Gerald W. Smith

Looking From The Inside Out

I can't hide these feelings in my heart anymore.
I've lost the will to fight, inside of me.
I have so much love to give it's breaking my heart.
I die a little bit each day because no one can hear,
    the cry at night.
I go crazy when I look inside of myself.
I am a boy, in a man's body.
God, what have I done to myself.
I wish you would come and take me.
But I think I know, there is a chance, you won't.
But Lord, couldn't you reach out your hand and take mine,
    and make me feel like someone.
Because I am tired of walking alone in life.
Who will tell me, when it's too late.
I know I can't go on thinking these thoughts,
    that nothing is wrong.

Scott A. Gilbert

Untitled

I know you're out there in this world somewhere, I just wish I knew,
Something in my life is missing and it's definitely you
I wish I could feel your tender touch, your warm embrace, and
your sweet lips upon my face
Over and over again I wonder how far you are away and if
you're ever coming back with me to stay
I remember the moments we had together, now just memories,
memories gone astray
I let it flow as I go hoping for the day when I can catch my
dream and never let it get away

Stephanie Louise Wallace

Diana

My wings still glide on the rays of your rising sun
it's been a long time since I've seen your indelible face
silken skin, deep blue eyes, and smelled your sensual perfume
I still remember your touch, your warm tender embrace
under the crisp, cool nights of a wanton, mooring moon
whispers in the dark speaking tales of unbridled passion
'twas sweet your rose colored romance of champagne and caviar
where did our times of happiness wander to an early grave
I looked and you where there, I looked and you were gone
you were solace to me, a vision of eternal, forever love
I don't understand why you've gone from my humble embrace
and left me here so very much alone in this lowly place
was it me somehow or did time just fade you away?
I wonder about such things every time I think of you
every time I see your comely face and smell your sweet perfume
My wings still glide on the rays of your setting sun
'twas death brought us apart, 'tis death will bring us anew

Timothy L. Welch

Always Be There

I look at the sky and think of you at night
Will you be here when it's light
I sit here and groan
I think of us all alone
Me touching your soft skin
I'll always wonder what might have been
For me do you care
To you my soul I bare
You're so cute and cuddly warm
You hold me through the storm
What do you really see
When you look at me
Can you look me in the eye
Come on what's your reply
Do you feel pain, do I live in vain
Will our love always be
Will you love me for all eternity
I look at you and can't help but stare
Will you always be there
So I'll sit here for a while just thinking of you and I'll smile

Christy Loren Ohlerich

Snow

Snow bringing cold bitterness falls as
knotted, frozen fingers grasp the tattered coat.
Shivers of cold and loneliness rack the wizened frame.
One can see pain in the once lively, hazel eyes.

Snow bringing cold bitterness falls as
the starving woman reaches out to the world for help.
Cramps of hunger drown her proud spirit.
All thoughts are of food, no matter the amount.

Snow bringing cold bitterness falls as
callous people pass the destitute woman.
No one gives a glance to the beggar.
They are too busy with gifts, food, and other pleasures.

Snow bringing cold bitterness falls as
all hope of living drains from the woman's soul.
Slowly, she sinks to the frozen earth.

Snow bringing cold bitterness falls as
the woman takes her last breathe of bitter life.
The world continues with its pleasures.
It was oblivious to her needs and now to her cruel death as well
Yet, snow bringing cold bitterness falls.

Tawanda Karen Murray

Untitled

She sails across a windswept desert
at a wondrous speed.
Her hair blows free from
fashion's ties.
Yet she pays to it no heed.

Her dress billows and cling
in all the right spots.
A woman of great beauty,
is she not?

Her features emerge so soft
and so curved,
Lines flowing smoothly as her
unspoken word.

Her liquid eyes sing silently of places
lying both far and near.
Resounding in a voice, that so many
seem to hold so dear.

Her expression of such pure contentment hides
all the feverish resentment that she feels so deep inside.

Rebecca Eleck

Apparitions

One night,
While walking home from work,
I noticed a silhouette of a gaunt man
Resting outside of an abandoned factory.
Next to him dwelled a lonely cat,
Gazing into the blank stare of the gentleman.
When I reached them,
I realized the elderly man
Had been dead for quite awhile.
I searched him for some sort of I.D.,
Found none, and stepped back.
As I turned to leave, I heard a desperate cry from the cat.
I looked over my shoulder
And saw the bony man disappear.
The cat walked tenderly over to me.
It rubbed its tail and head on my shin,
And wove a winding path around my ankles.
I tried to pick it up,
But my hands went through
Grasping the cold winter's air.

Jason W. Bucy

I Am A Woman

I am a strong black woman
like a diamond I am hard to break
yet beautiful.
I stand alone
for I fear not loneliness
I'm rising like the sun
yet I've only just begun
I'm on a roll, because I chose
not to run but to stroll
You see in life the better things
come to those who wait
Yet if you have opportunity
don't hesitate.
In a society so cruel
don't become a society fool. Hatred, I have none,
I love my brother and sisters
no matter what race — because in this
world everyone has a place. — Do not fear success,
but go after it, for we can all as God children
achieve it. I am woman, I am woman, and so proud of it.

Jane Belcher

Fire

She comes to me in the night, slowly, softly
the urges are powerful, I am pulled into the vortex of her being.
I melt, I have no fear here. I have no shame.
I will give all of myself — to her only for the taking.
She controls me, not by intention — by my will.
We are collateral — I am her — she is me.
We move effortlessly — like the branches of a willow tree.
Pushed by the wind, together and apart.
I know not where I end or she begins.
I know without thought my soul mate —
For she came to me from the light of the sky.
To compliment my weakness — she is all the colors the spectrum.
Her eyes are my heart's prison — happily locked away safe.
I fear her moving away from me, yet I must push her away,
so as not to be engulfed within her fire.
The passion rises, the boiling point near, I might lose myself inside
her but still I must go.
To meet each other at the core of our existence.
We are stars that have crossed each others paths to rebound
into the future.

C. Lane

Purge

. . . Vomiting them all over the page because they make me feel sick
Feel sick — amnotsick — just feel sick

Sick of remembering — remembering words said and imagined
Imagined according to the speaker — the speaker denying a child's rage
My rage that fills the space that should be filled with words of love

The love that fills a mother's mind
Mind blowing love that shines — shines through the pores and
Envelopes in warmth the upturned face of joy that is a child untouched

Untouched by cruel words said in daylight — sharp and loud
Untouched by obscene hands giving weight to words
Whispered in darkness and almond scent

The scent of a child's hair, neck and cheeks
(Protected in arms love and strength) everpresent now
Overpowers the remembered smell of sweat, semen and fear

Fear of memories that never pause for breathe and take up all the space,
space needed for a new life with fonder memories and
deeper breaths — breathing easier

Inhaling life instead of exhaling fear
Fear of breathing

SELF

Untitled

This image in my head will always loom;
One time, but now it seems so long ago,
Our eyes, they met, across a crowded room.
And when I saw you there, you seemed to glow.
For in that brief moment in time I knew,
That you would be forever in my heart.
But oh! That night, so quickly by it flew.
And 'though I knew you were a work of art,
I could not find the courage to advance.
Then making up my mind, I went to ask
If you would join me in the coming dance,
But you said no, your face a stony mask.
   And if, sometime, we meet upon a street,
   'Though you hate me, for you my heart will beat.

Andrew Bennett

Tomorrow

Today has brought such sadness and sorrow
Somewhere out there if there is a smile to borrow
To let me see what I may be, and
open my blinded eyes to be free

Today has brought such pain and agony
It hurts like a flame that burns insanity
Now if it can just be what I can see,
Unless tomorrow brings this madness and horror
I won't ask for no pity or sorrow
I'll just be truly free as nothing tomorrow

Joshua Davenport

Big Bang

a singularity	swells	anxious
moving	inward	swirling
light	joining	unseen
unity	toward	one
unbounded	forever	gasp of
emotion	erupting	reaching —
intertwined	thoughts	quenched

Pat Fox

Angel Of Love

I, out of desperation,
asked for an angel.
An angel to love me forever;
to help me through my pain.

You were brought to me;
my destiny;
a once in a lifetime love.

And I am complete,
with the love you give me,
your warmth,
your caring,
your smile.

Let me be your angel of love;
let me give you my passion;
for we can fly;
with souls joined forever.

My fantasy, my future
is you;
for you are my
angel of love.

Debi Hensley Moeckel

Life Goes On

Look at this, a tiny sprig
reaching for the sky,
With forest growing all around
will this sprig grow high?

Time goes by there is a tree
reaching for the sun,
other plants have come and gone
the tiny sprig has won.

It gives shelter to the birds
and creatures on the ground,
it nurtures life without protest
and never makes a sound.

Well! Maybe something can be heard
when the wind is blowing strong
branches bend, with rustling leaves
it's a verse from natures song.

When the time is right, the tree will
fall, its spirit will go home
its body will return to earth
to become rich fertile loam.

Patrick Sheahan

Loneliness

It appears that we search
in quiet trepidation . . .
For someone to come into
our lives, and make our
world a new and more
exciting place to be!

And

Throughout the course of our
loneliness
We feel,
We long,
We anticipate,
We hope!
But, what of the pain
of still — loneliness?

Cletus M. S. Watson, T.O.R.

Angel At My Bedside

Heavenly Angel at my bedside —
Please spread your beautiful wings
To Be with those I can not.

Heavenly Angel at my bedside —
Please spread your warm wings
To Hug those I can not.

Heavenly Angel at my bedside —
Please spread your shielding wings
To Watch over those I can not.

Heavenly Angel at my bedside —
Please spread your glorious wings
To Touch the hearts I can not.

Heavenly Angel at my bedside —
Please spread your strong wings
To Protect those I can not.

And Heavenly Angel at my bedside —
Please spread your gentle wings
To Help me open my heart.

Colleen Harmon

The Plunge

We stood on the bank
Of that deep green river,
The moss tickling our toes
Poised ready to dive,
Unconcerned of our bareness
Waiting for the signal
And suddenly it was time,
And we plunged deep into the river
Near dangerous rocks,
Into a whirlpool of coolness,
Emerging with lungs bursting
The first thing we did was cry,
For we were born into
The river of life.

William R. Davis

Beautiful

On the stage, with frills and lace,
A glowing smile on her face.
Cameras click, lights will flash.
In her swim suit, she's a splash.
A beauty queen, at age three,
I'm proud of her, don't you see?
Long blond hair, and bright blue eyes,
Just as bright as northern skies,
I often set her on my knee,
She's my granddaughter, yessiree.

Edward R. Stiner Sr.

Culled Moments

O fisherman from afar
    You played hide-and-seek with me;
Tell me who you really are —
    What took place twixt you and me.

We kept misunderstanding —
    Yet we took each step in place;
And smiling were pretending —
    While we searched each other's face.

Living in a world of thought —
    Culled moments in allegory;
Was it love, or was it not —
    Memory tells a story.

Mirtha G. Moreno

True Love

Though I've only known you,
for a second in the cosmic eye.
I shall always love you,
as the millenniums pass us by.

Our hearts are connected
by an eternal line.
Something that cannot be broken,
not even by time.

There is not a word to describe
the love I feel for you.
Our love is something experienced,
only by a very few.

I don't need a million dollars
to make me rich,
my love for you makes me richer
than money ever could.

In all the galaxy's of the universe
it is sought but seldom found.
With you I have what others seek,
True Love, the rarest treasure around.

Brett Hawks

Depression

Sending its sweet kiss on my brow
As it has done so few times before
Like a quiet breeze
Breathing cool against a window
In a winter snowfall

Never enough to take me away
To enter
A world
of permanent vacuousness

Imprinting like a scar into my eyes
And on my soul
For those who care to realize
For those
Who care to see.

Dawn Shatouhy

Jaded

Searching I found,
Nothing that worked,
There was no path,
Only a maze, no way.
I know!
I'm still searching,
There should be a way.
If I can't find,
It was work for my mind.

Donald Lawrence

Second Marriage

It is too late for love
And yet,
Too soon for loneliness.
These things we feel and understand;
And now,
Agreed,
We take our vows.

May heaven bless this knowledge
So that soon
We shall forget
It was too late for love.

Louise Dodd Gerken

The Lord Is Coming To Bake For Us

When my foot stepped in
blue white sooner
a swollen talking shears
but not very painful
opinion of patting
in orange soap
swats at a bee
my bones my angry growing
traipse around the corner of a guard
a little further, further, and further
if it bends . . .
laughed all night
at two eggs

Jerry Trimmell

Arrival

I'm flying
through a galaxy
I'm free!
A speck of light
a shining sight
I see!
We are a nova
we make a sun
this is our universe
we have just begun.

Peggy Roundhill

Don't Question Your Mate

Don't question your mate
it is something they hate.
You are tempting fate
to question your mate.

They may be wrong
or have made a mistake;
but, a lot is at stake
when you question your mate.

Quiet compliance
will seal the alliance,
But, you are tempting fate
to question your mate.

Wanda McGill

Thanksgiving

Tomorrow is a special day
which we call Thanksgiving.
I think of it with gladness
while my heart keeps singing.

There are blessings to count
and give thanks for each one.
My heart sings as I think
of each race I've won.

Friends are part of the joy
as I think of them with love.
I remember the husband
who went to live above.

Thanks spring from my heart
for help with my daily life.
I think of the happy days
when I was a busy wife.

My prayers for tomorrow
will ring with honesty.
As my thanks pour forth
with heartfelt sincerity.

Frances E. Tolson

The Golden Saxophone Girl

Dark leather pants, light brown hair,
She had face slender, pretty,
Festive music filled the air,
Lilting, greeting our city.

The sharp drumbeats fell in place,
Joined trumpet, accordion,
The girl with the pretty face
Played the golden saxophone.

From time to time she would stop
To fix flocks of falling hair,
Then back to beat with a hop
Her music talents to share.

She crooned sentimental songs,
Hugged, caressed the microphone,
For short breaks she shook the gongs,
Then back to the saxophone.

She poured energy and soul
In the spirit of each song,
Danced, shook shoulders, had a ball,
Hot and happy, sweet and strong.

Kris Krasteff

Orange Blizzard

Beginning with a sprinkling
orange drizzle.
Forest becoming a blizzard of swirling
orange and black monarch butterflies.
Hanging in clusters against a
canopy of cool green fir trees.

Butterflies hovering in billowing
orange clouds.
Light on your back and fluttering
in your face.
Dancing, flitting, and weaving.
Bold, dazzling, and hypnotic.

Flickering like a candles flame
in the shadows.
Silence falls, around the
orange snowflakes.
Broken only by the butterfly wings,
beating in the sunlight.

Pat Bordner

Remembering Times Of Christmas

I remember times of Christmas
Many presents under the tree
Memories of those that were opened
Especially the ones from me

Our families would get together
Often joked about once a year
Memories of those cheese buns
Sharing a smile and a tear

I remember times of Christmas
Some times singing familiar songs
Everyone seemed to know them
So they decided to sing it wrong

Listening to the radio
Reports of Santa were seen
The excitement builds inside us
You all know what I mean

Remembering times of Christmas
Memories for the young and old
Christ was born on this day
A story, most often told

James A. Lindberg

A Handful Of Dirt

I saw you once:
You bore a cross,
You read the news
I was at loss.
I thought "The fake!"
But it was not:
Colossus smashed,
Still I am not.

The second time
You put across
Your exaltation,
Fervent gloss
For me vociferous it was.
Yet not a word
Of yours was lost.

I heard your voice
The third time was the last.
Your soul's above,
Times past,
Live words will last.

Guennadi Slasten

The Galactic Dance Of Fireflies

Kids look forward
To when the stars
Come down to play
And blink.

Blinking their fire without fire,
The galaxy of fireflies
Swirl around the kids
For them to catch.

And hold until
They become restless
And guide kids
With their lights.

Fireflies light the way
Back to safe homes
For the kids to dream
Of dancing with the stars

. . . Year round.

Donia Clevenger

Jenny, Jenny

Jenny, Jenny
My little penny
You shimmer and shine
All of the time.

You are the one
You are so fun
You make me smile
All of the while.

I'll say it aloud
You make me proud
You give me hope
You help me cope.

You are the best
Your life is blessed
You're a beginner
Yet, you are a winner.

Jenny, Jenny
My pretty penny
You shimmer and shine
All of the time.

Susan Matti

Changing Winds

As the winds of time
shift around so the world
is full of cheer.
All the beautiful sounds
of the world like
nothing anyone has ever
to hear, has you
in its fingertips
until a summers day is clear.

When the winds of time
twist and twirl and
make leaves fly,
many times does it snow
and many times
does the wind still blow.
But as the winds
die down the spring showers,
appear and fall from
the heavens,
like tears from a great king.

Erin E. Evanoff

Transcendence

Leaping like a winner
a purebred beauty wonder
She races against time
Knowing not why
only that it feels
Oh, so good to be alive!

The wild wind invades her lungs
like a long, lost love
Accelerating to the sound of
the sight of — the ecstasy of flight

Midnight mane flowing
disguising wild, staring eyes
She cries aloud
defying nature, the stars, the sky

And with the maelstrom
beating in tune
with the intensity
of the pounding within her chest
She submits, at last to freedom

Susan Eckam

Old Woman

She walks tired,
Yet satisfied
Her path is almost over
Yet she strikes
To make it longer
Her ancient self
Has created the world
She carries grace,
Grace and beauty of the past
Shocked by the new world
Yet still loving it
She, with silver-gray hair goes on.
Strong and wise yet mortal and brief
She, a simple woman
Finished building her sand castle,
Gave the world its future
Now she must give space
For the new to enjoy
So she goes on
Into the wonders of the night.

Anna Pikina

Odile

Where are you now?
Are you the sweet scent
    of flowers I smell so often?
Are you the soft velvet touch
    I feel caressing me?
Are you the songbird
    awakening me each morning?
Perhaps you are the fluffy cloud
    your great-granddaughter sees.
Or maybe you are my quiet,
    mysterious feline always present.
Are you the muse who inspires
    my poetry?
You remain in our hearts, our
    memories and our stories.
A legend for all posterity, Odile.

Francine Guillory

Socrates

Oh sure we like you
But still you must pretend
Do not feel demoralized
It won't matter in the end

Sure you are important
But you still have to bow
It's not sacrilegious
There is no golden cow

Don't be concerned with principals
Schools been out for years
Taught you all your weaknesses
Ingrained all of your fears

Now go on out and cast your vote
For the choices that are chosen
Speak out when you're spoken to
Drink deep of your own poison

Robert N. Wormington

Bon Nuit

Longing somnolence
Pale satin pale linen
Tendrils leap marbled balcony
Whispering honeysuckle lips
Fever moistens crescent skin
While nuit held hostage
My beau dashing wind
Veers beckon galloping clouds
Booming flashes clap thunder
Silhouettes zig zag downpours
Demure nuit glittery armor
My beau dashing wind
Blew one ruby emerald rose
While nuit withdrew sultry
My beau held me bon jour!

Patricia Johnson

Untitled

Feel the grass . . .
freshly cut on a not morning.
From my window, smooth,
soft dirty snow melts in slow motion.
High-wave morning . . .
the weeping willows are
trailed in dirty mud.
Fallen now to Earth,
after a long journey . . .
the kite is gone.

Janice A. Yarbrough

Same Old Net?

Romeo and Juliet
Never used internet
To express their passion
Coming out in ancient fashion.

Love burnt in their blood
Even death never stood
Against the lovers' tender goal
When the passion ran afoul
Of an old and hostile world
Finding young love too absurd.

Today, we put love on wires
If we burn by its fires
We just print another code
To get rid of its load.

Romeo and Juliet
Never needed internet
Their hearts were on fire
This of course we admire
While computers calculate
Distance between love and hate.

Karin Dovring

Jamie

You're the only one I truly loved
lots more than words can say,
I miss you and I think of you
each and every day.

I know the Lord has called you home
to be with Him on high, but in
my heart and mind you live — to me
you'll never die.

Until you smiling face I see the
loving memories will be with me, to
help me through the lonely nights and
let me know everything's alright.

I thank the good Lord up above
for sending you and your sweet love,
I thank him for the memories too
and for taking care of you.

Doris Tyner

Daydreaming, Occasionally

Occasionally I have a day
as I am trying to remain sane,
I would like to run screaming
down a long country lane.

Running back to the joy
I knew as a child,
climbing the highest trees
being a Tarzana so wild.

Or hiding in the tobacco
that grew tall as the corn,
or remembering a puppy
on the day it was born.

I can almost hear mama
loudly calling my name,
as I drift from daydreaming
knowing I am not the same.

Most of the time I am contented
in this life I am in,
my childhood tugs occasionally
from where I have been.

Cynthia Wiggins

God Alone Is Color Blind

One summer day, not long ago,
I spied a burial ground
that lay upon a slope of hill
with crumbling wall around.

I would have passed upon my way,
but something caught my eye;
A simple grave, outside the wall,
and I stopped to find out why.

I walked to where the ancient wall
Cast shadows on this grove,
and read these world on pitted stone,
"here lies wore, a slave."

Yes, black he was, and slave he was,
but this particular mound
was covered with wild roses,
while on other, weeds were found.

More, in life, sought happiness,
which never did be find.
In death I know he found it,
for God in color blind.

Richard N. Shea

Life

Do we do the things we need
When in life we do proceed
As a family are we sure
That our love will all endure
Taking time to really see
Every member's need to be
Times of need we all have true
Loving, trusting as we do
Ask for help to see us thru
Now if only we could see
When our time has come to be
We leave this world eternally

Ask yourself

Have you done all you could
To leave a legacy
Shirley Maki

Never Alone

I walk with God along his way
And many times I stop to pray;
Giving thanks for all His blessings,
For this and all the days before.
That He has been my guiding light
Protecting me both day and night.
How wonderful it is to know
I never walk my path alone,
But have the greatest power around;
To watch an care if I do roam,
And gently, safely coax me home.
Kathryn L. Lawrence

Sailing

The bow rises and falls
The wind is blowing the sails
The sea gull is watchful and calls

Waves crash on the decks
With the wind.
As we pass under the bridge,
The mainsail seems to bend.
As we come into port,
Our destination will soon end.
Susan Cortsen

Love — The Simple Truth

Love — starts with self . . .
Embraces others . . .

Love — challenges . . .
Understands . . .
Accepts!

Love — teaches
Respects . . .
Forgives!

Love — encourages growth . . .
Exposes vulnerabilities . . .
Excepts faults!

Love — fragile yet complex . . .
Defying logic . . .
Links us all!
Debra Fisher

My Psalm

I bless the name of Jesus
Wondrous Savior, King, and Lord
Father, Son and Holy Spirit
Three in One, the "Word"

I kneel before the great "I Am"
Lift up my hands in adoration
From the first, You knew me
God of all creation

My life was filled with sin and woe
The spotless Lamb was slain for me
Jesus shed His precious blood
On the Cross at Calvary

Merciful Father, hear my plea
Your sinful child forgive
Pour out on me Your gracious love
Around the throne I'll live
Alverine Mosley Peach

Untitled

The soul of a man
speaks through his heart
The heart is open to all who speak
the romantic language of reality,
hope, sincerity, and promise.
David M. Weldon

Me

The me no one knows.
The me no one sees.
The me no one feels.
The me no one hears.
The me inside,
The me I can never be.

The me no one loves.
The me no one believes.
The me no one trusts.
The me no one wants.
The me inside,
The me I can never be.

The me no one calls.
The me no one visits.
The me no one writes.
The me no one needs.
The me inside.
The me I can never be . . .
Tammy Robertson

The Nature Of Love

The ways and nature of love,
Can come on the wings of a dove.
Sometimes mysterious and dark.
Sometimes light hearted as a lark.

Love can be hard or soft,
And lift you high aloft.
Sometimes shy or very bold.
Love can run warm and cold.

Love can be faithful to the bone.
Or gather no moss like a rolling stone.
The nature of love is pure.
For which there is no cure.

Love is hard to understand,
For every woman and man.
Just when you think you know.
Someone has something else to show.

Lajuana D. Burton

Paul

You are of my youth
Like warm sips of wine
And the times of my life
Like red roses.

Paradoxical love,
Are you sent from above?
For my lonely times,
Loving times,
My highs and my lows,
Are you God's gift to me
Are you my wine red rose?

Cindy Lee Strand

A Love Poem

Love is the color of
the sunset over the ocean.
It sounds like birds singing in
the pre-dawn hours.
It taste like cotton candy melting
in your mouth.
And smells like a garden
just after it rains.
Love is warmth like
a raging fire.

Josh MacIsaac

Conquered

What have I
to gain
my tears
flow as the rain

My life is empty
and vain
my heart hold
so much pain

For eighteen
blessed years
his kiss
erased my fears

But now
He's dead and gone
and I'm
left here alone
So what have I to gain
My heart is filled
with pain.

Rose Marie Jackson

Untitled

Can you look from where you are,
And maybe see the moon and stars?
And while you stare into the night,
Pick a star shinning bright?

Make a wish on that star you see,
From your heart then think of me.
Make a wish for both of us,
For happiness peace and trust.

And if it's true friendship will,
Make that wish someday real.
And if it does maybe then,
We'll see that star and wish again.

Casey Rodriguez

Destiny

Why do you hide
like a shy, uncertain child
in shadows, with time passing
your beautiful face
eager to smile broadly
at the whole world?

Why won't you fly,
able bird?
Has the world taught
you fears, so unreal
and removed your
truths, like wings,
so natural once?

Misplaced, then disregarded
with age ever-changed,
ever deepening, too
with urgency unexplained
cautiously loved and feared,
you whisper things I can't hear
and follow too closely

Grace Rimmel

Misnomer

Not to raise a fuss about
The diurnal lepidoptera,
But there has been a major error,
It does not butterfly,
It flutters by.

William Darnell

Destiny

Does God choose the number
Of times a heart beats?
Or the number of steps
In a pair of feet?
Is each breath that we take
Measured one by one?
Counting down to the time
When our life is done?
Every day that we wake
Is it written somewhere
That like leaves they will fall
'Til the tree becomes bare?
Are we destined to fail,
Or to rise up and fly?
To sail through our lives,
Or just barely get by?
No, we make our own destiny
And I believe
It's within our control
What we wish to achieve.

Karen Barr

Look Within

We scurry about our lives. At times
I'm reminded of little mice. We hurry
around seeking to please, just to get
our piece of the cheese.
   Some judge others by their own
worth, knowing nothing of the other's
woes on earth.
   If only we would take the time
to get to know, and try to look within
another, we might find a soul mate,
a friend, a brother.

Sheila A. Nash

Raindrops On My Window Pane

Raindrops on my window pane.
Tears on my face.

I'm missing you.
Minutes seems like days,
days seems like months,
months seems like years.

I don't know why you had
to go on that windy,
stormy day.

Night time seems like forever
and days are so hard
to get thru.

Rain drops on falling and
the tears never seem to dry.
For I am missing you.

Marcella G. Inman-Sievers

The Dawning

As darkness falls on the halls
And the walls seem to scream
Their muffled cries for the real,
The unknown, who has grown,
Starts to moan his sighs for eyes.
Then I realize what I feel.
I want to burn all I've learned
In my yearn for sight and light
By which I thought I would see.
But, dawning light, warm and bright,
Will gently light this gloomy room
And right the wrongs in me,
When it dawns on me.

James Edward Lee Jr.

"A Black Person"

Black am I?
And what to do
Do you care
If I say this
Suppose I say
Something else
Or could I
Maybe, leave
This alone.
When I was black
And I knew
My name,
I know because,
Something, are
Not the same.
Sarah Nell Newton

Linda S. Thomas

Count Your Blessings

Count your blessings every day
Be thankful for good things
Like good neighbors and good friends
And what the future brings
Bad luck comes once in a while
We all know this is true
So if you do the best you can
It will come back to you!!!

Mary Reynolds

A Moment Of Reflection

A moment of reflection
revisited in my mind
of better places and happier times.

Though I will not weep in my sorrow
hoping for a better tomorrow.

Bring forth another day
for slumber and play.
Hoping for joy untouched by sadness
void to all madness.

O what pleasure it brings
though seldom seen.

The essence of tomorrow
is today's reflection
of just being.
But more than we are seeing

Billy E. Harris

The Fluorescent Sky

Lavender, blue, orange, pink
clouds swirled all together
like ribbon candy.

Sun permeates the sky
creating colors fluorescent
as the day comes to an end.

Her light peaks through
the still green leaves
of Earth's timbers.

What beauty! What Joy!
She gives to Mother Earth!

Naomi J. Hall

My Little One

My little one so quickly grown
So soon to face the world alone.
You stand before me. In your eye
I see the vastness of the sky.
In dreams you soar with eagle wings
Above the clouds. You are all things
Within you sight. Such little hands
To grasp the world. And life demands
So much to all who live and dare
To dream.

Though I can see and I do know
Sometimes the world won't let you grow.
And hate and misery and strife
So eagerly would crush your life
You smile at me and dry my tears.
You tiny frame would bare my fears.
I hold you close and oh I know
Someday I'll have to let you go
To grow and be all things.

Linda Facey

Tonight

Grandpa's riding on a star tonight
  remember that he loves you
He went away to Heaven
  God gave him a new job to do.

Now he's the Keeper of Lightning
  and everything that's bright
He will watch us from above the clouds
  and make sure we're all right.

You can see him everywhere
  just look in the morning dew
Find strength in knowing
  he'll always love you.

Carol Ann Finnigan

Soft Summer Rains

"So warm and refreshing,
  as it cleanses my panes;
drifting gently to earth,
  are these soft summer rains.

Forever uplifting my spirit,
  while they strengthen my soul;
often gentle and soothing,
  yet causing oceans to roll.

Always romantic for lovers,
  bonding them peacefully together;
bringing love into bloom,
  this wet beautiful weather.

Creating new life,
  In our lakes and our streams;
while making musical rhythms,
  So that we may follow our dreams.

Now does it really much matter,
  that we are forty or four;
when God brings His Soft Summer Rains,
  to our very front door?"

William Henry O'Donovan Jr.

"Rumors"

Someone is talking
With no meaning
What is their purpose
Of this conversation of lies
Question?
Is your heart so full of bitterness.
Why do you bring this pain
What to gain? Except
Trust under false pretence
Don't talk . . .
Hold your make-believe thoughts
Be quiet and close your eyes
You might see . . . It's you . . .
  You despise

Denise Canet

Our World Today

Our world today is a disordered place,
Where cruelness has no end.
Where people sin each and everyday
And even hate their kin.
Where dope is the most common
Thing, so kids can wreck their minds.
And God is just a lonely name
Mentioned from time to time.

Sharon Negrete

To

To live the lie
To feel the pain
To walk the line
To kill the sane

To condemn the innocent
To make a choice
To be the listener
To be the voice

To be recluse
To go abroad
To be the joke
To get the applaud

To make one laugh
To make one cry
To get a chance
To live and die

Chris Dinger

As You're Leaving

As you're leaving,
a simple goodbye an unforgotten tear,
a quiet sigh.

As you're leaving,
a love so true
a remaining memory of me and you.

As you're leaving,
a tear refrained
a look inside where you are contained.

As you're leaving,
I fall apart
piece by piece, then a broken heart.

Dana L. Del Brocco

Untitled

One chance once lost
Seeks the way
Back to the beginning
Back to the day
Enchantment was found
And finding himself
At the moment divine
Takes thoughtful pause
To what is behind
And what is ahead
And what can be
To make these right
He holds the key

Lorie White

The Lizard King

I live in the subconscious
They try to tell me it's just a dream
  but it's not
    no matter how much I wish it was
Tell me, what is beauty to you?
  Are you beautiful?
  Is pain beautiful?
My pain is seductive
  Has it gotten to you yet?
Unto this world we're thrown
the only world we've known
  But there will be more
    many more
      forever more . . .

Daina Crafa

Powerful Ways

Powerful are your ways oh Lord
Powerful are your ways
Delivering us with your mighty hand
Rescuing us with your touch.

Powerful are your ways oh Lord
They extend throughout the earth
Giving life to the lost
And causing them new birth.

Powerful are your ways oh Lord
The victories that you bring
No other hand could do all this
Truly you are the king.

Powerful are your ways oh Lord
And higher are your thoughts
You choose to give us eternal life
And you've also paid the cost.

Cheryl Race

Blind

Open your eyes,
No big surprise.
Seeing through fate,
It's the fear that you hate.
Personal anger,
In public it lingers,
Passing on like a tradition.
Abusing ambition.
You ask yourself why
You're angry at the world,
You really don't know
You just act like a dolt.
Acting out on anger
Without concentration,
Regretting it later
Not willing to face it.
Building a wall
With a coward behind it,
Increasing flaws,
With confusion you're blinded.

Marie Lister

The Light

I walk towards the memorizing light,
It seems so far away,
I walk both in the starry night,
And in the light of day,
Through puddles of tears,
And barrels of laughter and fun,
And when the fog clears,
Hugs and kisses come by the ton,
Now and then there is a fight,
But mostly love and cheer,
I may never reach the light,
I think I'll stay right here.

Paige Young

Angel Face

  Angelically lavender,
her petals dew form
  a dark, richly, green,
her leaves like a face —
  her petals adorn,
a rose — above roses
  is,
where she belongs

Neasie E. Emerson

You Gentle You

Holding me close I can feel
   our hearts beat.
Like the dawn and darkness,
   in the middle they meet.
   You Gentle You
I can feel your strength
   when you hold me tight.
You give me the feeling that
   everything will be alright.
   You Gentle You
I can see the care
   and Love in your eyes.
Our moments together are true,
   never illusions or lies.
   You Gentle You
Always allowing me to be just me.
   When we're together you set me Free!
   You Gentle You

Sometimes all I need is
   You Gentle You!!!

   Teri A. Irvine

Trust

A hand extended
A smile shared,
To accept with faith
Is not dared.

To the hand outstretched,
No firm grasp.
And the smile returned
Is a momentary lapse.

But a lesson early learned,
Not forgotten with time,
Is challenged by those
Who assess no fine.

And the self-fulfilling prophecy
May soon be shattered
If trust is allowed to mend
The heart so tattered.

   Theresa O. Miner

Give And Do

Someone is lonely, want tender care,
Someone need someone, just to be there.
Someone is longing for a hand to hold.
To hear I love you, words of gold.
Someone you know needs a friend
Make you with help to end.
Someone near you has much to give.
Graciously show them how to live.
Reach out and touch, give and do.
That someone, someday, may be you.

   LaDell Broadnax

The Joy Of A Rose

A rose spreads its
fragrance near and far.
Due to its outlandish
romantic smell every
one loves to receive a
rose every once in a while.
A rose expresses the
unspoken words of
the heart.

   Charmaine Proudfoot

Keep In Touch

"Keep in touch," I heard him say
as I turned to walk away.
"You bet I will," was my reply
as we said our last good-bye.
Time went by we seldom wrote
not taking time for a simple note.
You went your way I went mine
a mere hello, there wasn't time.
Then one day out of the blue
I felt a need to speak with you.
To laugh and cry at what we'd done
to reminisce at all our fun.
But speak once more there was no way
I heard the news, you'd passed away.
My heart is sad, my grief immense
to see your face there is no chance.
So rest your soul my weary friend
till the day we meet again.

   Marin Pena

Untitled

My life since you
is no longer blue
you make it all worth living.
You're always there
because you care
and are always happy giving.

My love I'll say
is brighten than day
and wider than the sky.
I love you more
than the sands on shore
and all the stars up high.

   Sharon Lindsey

Cattails

"Lonely are the cattails
   waving near the shore
Slender reeds with brown tips
   waving evermore."

Lonely are the cattails
   reaching toward the sun
waiting for its warm caress
   before the day is done.

Lonely are the cattails
   thirsting for the rain
savoring every raindrop
   for the kiss it doth contain

Lonely are the cattails
   waving near the shore
slender reeds with brown tips
   waving ever more.

   Florence E. Rasmussen

Snow Cover

Sometimes we cover our feelings
   like the snow covers the earth

It appears better to the eye
   but the earth is still hard below

We can chose to close the door
   keeping the snow and earth out

I enjoy the beauty of the snow
   and let it soften the earth with
   its melting of the morning sun

   Kenneth Violette

Monogram

"Dancing is a simile
for something"
She said
Slipping a sweater over
her head
Sliding sandals into
the sea foam
while
combing her red dressed
tresses
I'm betting
it's something
best expressed
while sweating.

   Norma K. Pattavina

Looking For Peace

Another year just rolled around
and the whole world is in a mess
Half of the people have forgotten God
What is next I hate to guess
The world could be such a lovely place
If people would stop and think
And look for peace and hope and joy
What a different world this would bring

   Benedicta Bunek

Seaside Blues

Down by the sea, so deep and blue
Down along the sea's sandy shore
Here I sit, all alone and wishing
Wanting you with me, more and more

Now I wish I had never said
"That for you I didn't care"
Because that was a Big Big Lie
Now, that I willingly declare

I should have never been angry
'Cause you smiled at someone else
At believed you, when you said
"You could never love anyone else"

   Howard A. Deaton

No Ebon Englas

Migrant people foreign voices
uproot in culture's quest
constant burden tongue and speech's
conflict choices viewing best
no ebon englas

Flowers rooted earth the song
withstand the foes of nature
benign gesture cloak forlorn
voices crumbling lonely creature
no ebon englas

Birds awing combat the tune
journey's forces combine
hunters a field aline their choices
eagles aloof ascend the climb
no ebon englas

Sound the bell to the ploy
ply the words eternal plan
challenges in bold excitement
ever reaching seek His hand
no ebon englas

   Oscar D. Washington

Love

Wedding bells ring.
Wedding bells cling.
I am your sweetheart
and I hope we never part.
So, please give me a chance.
I will write your number on my pants.
Love is like a red red rose.
Because it tickles your toes.
You look good under a tree
especially to me.
Because you are my sweetheart
and I hope we never part.

Jeremy Murry

Untitled

I heard a noise in silence
the jolt shook throughout the room
the action sounded loudest
but no one heard the boom . . .

It wasn't what you said
it was what you didn't say
the look in your eyes told me
destruction paved the way . . .

You only seemed to tell me
what you thought I wanted to hear
what your actions screamed at me
made the meaning crystal clear . . .

Don't tell me that you love me
backed only by your words
your credit is all dried up here
your actions were all I heard . . .

Cora Sue Raymond

Life

Life is full of flowers
And also dreadful hours,
With darkness interspersed
One must grasp the pinnacle of life,
In time the bird will grow and blossom.

Sylvia E. Davis

Untitled

Where is Fred
He is there
Strong, walking against the wind
Holding his mind around him
Where is Fred
He is there
Winning, receiving, achieving
He will have it all
Where is Fred
He is there
Funny — sad — sensitive and beautiful
He is there

Lityu

Jason Vorhes

I'm a frog
Green as grass
Don't come near
Or I might crick
Don't come near
Or I might ribbit
Don't come near
Or I might . . . Jump!

Anthony Jones

"The Power Of Libation"

There is a man who's name is Ciff,
    When he drinks, he becomes stiff;
No better a worker than he,
    Till the bottle sets him free;
Willing to work from dusk to dawn,
    For anyone who comes along;
His heart is as big as gold,
    Come pay day his money unfolds;
Back to the bottle he goes,
    Fulfilling a life full of woes

Pamela L. Mullaney

"My First Baby Prayer"

I prayed for a baby like you,
It seems as though yesterday
you turned two.
You came into the world
Oh, so very small
Yet, today you look so incredibly tall!
You were once a baby,
You're still my baby, maybe!
You're growing up so very fast,
I wish you could stay small,
and forever last,
For one day you'll be grown,
But, Nicholas you'll always
be mine forever to call my own!

Mary C. Pearson-Collins

"Tribute To A Teacher"

Through lessons you've taught
we've learned to achieve,
to strive, to build, to set goals.

To have faith in ourselves
our abilities and choices,
these lessons are part of our souls.

We'll carry these with us
as long as we live,
and always remember their worth.

We've been granted a gift
by having you as a teacher,
there's no better prize on this earth.

For all you have bestowed
in your kind manner,
it is difficult to part.

Because we know for sure
that what you have given,
is really a piece of your heart.

Shelly Johnson-Whited

Untitled

Jesus is Love
Jesus is joy
Jesus brings peace to the
little girls and boys

Jesus is patience
Jesus is kindness
Jesus adds goodness
and takes away the blindness

Jesus is Faithfulness
Jesus is gentleness
Jesus is self-control
Take him with you
wherever you go.

Jim Ensley

If Only . . .

I see a sparkle
a twinkle
a bit of imagination

A light
the space
this place

Of which the dream
lives on
from day to day

A time, of joy
the rightness of
this day

If only . . .
to be seen
by only you.

Carol A. Prusick

Spirits Calling

Spirits calling both day and night
taking us to greater heights
Knowledge and vision are the key
that lead us to our destiny

Spirits calling hard and true
Telling us what we've got to do
Set me on the righteous path
Make my goals the aftermath

Spirits calling far and wide
Lead me to the other side
Winds of change that blow away
The sordid past of yesterday

Spirits calling through and through
help and show me what to do
Guide us past the fear and hate
teach us Lord, how to wait

Spirits calling like the wind
Give me faith until the end
On eagles wings we'll take flight
One final journey to daylight

Arnold Imperato

Hot Dogs!

Hot dogs are billies
Salad is green food
Vegetables is purchase
Power ethics
Hot dogs are though green
Turbulance coal's, "terms"!

Tad Thornhill

Waiting

Among the rocks and rills
In Forest Lawn, Hollywood Hills,
Lies my beloved one,
His daily tasks done,
Waiting for me to come
To join him at heaven's gate.
Now that I'm old and gray,
Closer comes the day.
Nearer to my God to thee,
Dearer to my God to thee,
Dearest to my God to thee,
Just waiting still.

Ellen Lyau Wong

I Know

I know pain,
  but feel no pain

I know love,
  yet never felt in love

I know sympathy,
  but I don't care

I know emotions,
  yet I can't share

I know peace
  but I'm so confused

I know of winning,
  but feel I lose

I know of joy,
  but only smile on the outside

I know of self
  yet have little pride

I've heard of peace of mind,
  but I race around

I know of freedom,
  yet I'm always bound
  Shelly Stotts

Memories

It was there for just a moment.
I blinked my eyes, behold,
a tear formed.

Why? What mystery was this?
A kaleidoscope of pictures
running through my mind.

Happiness, smiles, laughter.
sadness, lost ones.
All the bad, all the good.
For what are we, if not for memories?

These are what makes us
and molds us into
God's created beings.
  Nancy Lee Wells

Love Is

Love is something
With which you can't compete
It's vice-like grip
Can make you weak

Love is something
You can't control
It has to do with
Mind, body and soul

Love brings you up
Brings you down
It can make you smile or frown

This beautiful thing
Lives in your heart
It is something with which
You can not part

Love affects the hardest of hearts
Breaks it down with flying darts

Love when true affects even me and you
You cannot run you cannot hide
For in your heart love resides
  Christine M. Ostendorf

Christmas

The red bows
Are on the role lames

"The Happy Holiday Sign"
Is a beautiful
black on white

The AAA is
there's also the
"Sun rise"
The sun does
also "rise"

The pine tree
will always shine

Christmas — 1996

Wonderful
Wonderful
  Carol Bailey

Thanksgiving

Thank you blood of Jesus
that cleansed me through and through
thank you holy spirit
deep within me tried and true

Thank you Jesus my blessed Saviour
deliverer of my soul
for anointing me with Your power
to face temptations bold

Thank you Lord for proving once again
that you are always near
waiting to give me the strength I need
when my humble cry you hear

Thank you father you're wonderful
these words can't fully express
all I can do is continue to thank you
for giving me a life so blessed
  Patricia Middleton

Everybody Needs Someone

Please understand,
I am not here to criticize you.
These things I say,
the things I do,
Are only because I choose to care.
If you are in my life,
if we share anything,
It's my choice to say,
And your choice to listen.
Start talking to me,
Ask me questions.
If you are open enough to talk,
I'll listen.
  Felicia Eliazar

Each Day

Each day brings a new promise,
Fulfillment is life's reward,
To be in love with someone special,
Is a gift from God.

Treasure the days that come and
Rejoice when the sun has set,
Look forward to the new sun,
Each day.
  Beverly L. Clayton

Requiem

I look forward to tomorrow
To see what I shall be,
But all I see is yesterday
And a ghost of me.
I've travelled all around the world
To see what I could see —
And never did find anyone
I thought would set me free.
I never did become the man
I always thought I'd be,
So after all the changes,
I'm still the same old me.
  Philip A. Eckerle

When You Called Me Darling

I love to hear the whispers
Of the leaves upon the trees
I love to hear the songs of birds
As we lay beneath the leaves

They all speak of our love
Oh the stories they could tell
How we shared our love with them
And how hard in love we fell

There beneath the spreading oaks
The tall pines, ceders and firs
The first time I used your name
Without calling you sir

It was (when you called me darlin')
And looked into my eyes
Then told me that you loved me
Beneath God's bright blue skies

When you asked me to marry
When you showed me the ring
My heart skipped a best or two
Then like the birds began to sing.
  William McDaniel

Untitled

Good morning Mr. President
and Vice President Gore.

A whisper on the wind
with a leaf shadow dancing on the wall
awaken me to a day
filled with clear, crisp hope.

Congratulations!
  Constance C. Margerum

Tribute To A Nurse

How can I describe her,
It's difficult you see,
For she is always helping,
Someone like you and me.

You wonder how she can be,
So considerate and kind,
When you know many things,
May be pressing on her mind.

Yet she greets you in the morning,
With a hello and a smile,
She inquires how you're feeling,
And is everything worth while.

Then she continues on her duty,
With her temperature and time,
Carrying out her daily tasks,
In a rhythm and a rhyme.
  James H. Mero

Sunny Side Down

Bacon sizzling in the pan
  I'm doing all I can

Hotcakes bubbling in the oil
  Look at all my toil

Toast steaming on the plate
  I'll get nowhere at this rate

Ham baking in the stove
  There's a ton of junk on my robe

Juice chilling in the fridge
  Here comes all the kids

Potatoes frying in the skillet
  I'd better go and fill it

Sausage bulging in their frame
  I don't remember my own name

Fruit sliced in the bowl
  Serving this meal is my only goal

This mess must come to a close
  So now I will go take a doze

    Melanie Brumbaugh

Untitled

Delirious beauty music like ache
essential mother after them watches
would only these roads
could cry about you
my shadow behind not always of two
ask am I weak
manipulate the urge
rusted gorgeous vision
at death who felt power.

    Penny Craig

Out My Window

Out my window I stare
I see a rainbow out there

Out my window I see
Pretty flowers for you and me

Out my window I look
At the beautiful trees pretty as can be

Out my window I see
A wonderful world just waiting for me

    Alisha Smith

Untitled

When you say I love you,
You have to show you care.
When you say I love you,
You have to take a dare.
When you say I love you,
You have to hold her hand.
When you say I love you,
You have to take a stand.
When you say I love you,
Your heart must open wide.
When you say I love you,
The truth must never hide.
All these things,
And much much more,
Must never be forgotten.
For if you do you'll never know,
All the love that you been missing.

    Kenneth Weller

Butterfly

Sheltered from the cold.
Yearning to unfold.
Movement slight.
Rays of light.
Spreading wings of gold.
Take flight.

    LeeJoy Kizer

By All Means

A glass or mirror,
ever so shiny.
It tells you the truth,
and never a lie.

As you see your reflections,
coming from deep inside.
It said this is you,
cause I never lie.

So if you don't like,
what you have just seen.
Best you go and change it,
do it now by all means.

Now the morals inside,
not buried too deep.
So lets all check it out,
as on the surface it keeps.

    Donald Ray Mashburn

My Teacher

He takes that place in front of class
  and each will open book;
His voice is heard and all respond
  as each knows where to look.

The class begins and questions asked
  as students seek to learn;
My teacher shows an eagerness
  to share what we might yearn.

Each day we know he is prepared
  to show straight from the heart;
The search for truth he daily seeks
  and ready to impart.

He sees we have a willingness
  to strive with heart and mind;
The type of truth we need to use
  we could not help but find.

For many sat and learned the truth
  and from those desks did leave;
To share as persons who felt change
  from all we did receive.

    John I. Jacobs

My Reason My Angel

An angel came to me one night,
my soul had desperate need.
My life was endless valleys,
surrender then I did.

An angel came to me one night,
she wanted me to know.
My life was not yet over then,
her job had just begun.

My angel came to me that night,
my life is now complete.
The valleys still surround me,
the hills beneath my feet.

    Madeline C. Hess

A Christian

Some people say a Christian
Is quite a sight to see.
They walk around quite pious
Unhappy as can be.
But let me tell you, brother
This really isn't true.
For when you know the master
He brings sunshine to you.

There's joy, and peace, and happiness
No words can ever tell.
Just put your trust in Jesus
And you will find it's true.
The love of God can change things.
For He'll bring happiness to you.

    Vivian Krystofiak

Untitled

You just sit around trying
not to love him because you
know your bound to no
longer be together you sit
thinking about his smile his
laugh and his special kiss.
You start to cry asking
yourself why maybe it is his
special touch or the way he
looks at you or maybe it is
the way he holds you.
Why can't things stay the
same as before why can't he
give you a clue, if you are through.
Now it is time to say
goodbye, but before you
leave, one more special
kiss, one more special touch,
hold me just one more time.

    Heather McFadden

Continuum

Yesterday begat Today,
Today begets Tomorrow.

Spring, sprouting
Summer, blooming
Fall, fading
Winter, dying.

Resurrection awaits,
another Spring . . .

Time and Life
continues.

    O. Satty Joshua

Untitled

Don't go away too far
Don't leave me for too long,
I need your smiling face
It's like the perfect song.

This music of the heart
Is beautiful to hear,
It's a song so very sweet
I hold it very dear.

Thank you for the smile
And the eyes that just see me,
Thank you for wanting
It helps me to be.

    Monica L. Strickland

A Prayer Poem For Mike

I light a candle for you today
as I did, I began to pray,
that through its power and its light
you will have the strength to fight.
To rid this demon from your soul
and again, make you whole.
I pray with all the love,
I have to give, that the good
Lord lay his hand upon you
and let you live . . .
The candle is out
your pain is gone
but our love for you
will live on and on.

Connie Bennett

The Sadness Of The Sky

The wind rips the leaves
From the shallow burning trees
The tears of the day
See the sins they must repay
In the distance robins sing
For the dying of the spring
And with broken wings they fly
Into the sadness of the sky

In time our dawn gives way
To the black it once betrayed
And the darkness that we hide
Is no longer trapped inside
The angels lose their light
To the demons of the night
And with broken wings they fly
Into the sadness of the sky

Richard M. Hennemann II

To Rest My Soul

Tranquil moments alone
selfish ways to condone
empty space, out of place
feelings longing to belong
reflections appear wrong
what seems serene
shatters my demean
searching an escape
my soul's been raped
riding violent waves
living in this cave
in hope for peace
for my pain to cease
to rest my soul

Valerie L. MacAulay

Little Miracles

I remember that day
as if it were yesterday
the feeling of nervousness
the feeling of joy.

When I saw you
for the very first time
as you lay so silent
without a tear in your eye.

The love you brought to us
the happiness we've shared
wouldn't have been possible
if the love wasn't shared.

Susan Boucher

Ode To An Old Soul

This poor old soul will never win
For he doesn't know what lies within
So he stays angry at the world
Not knowing the secrets he can unfurl
And he is sad and he is scorned
He can't imagine what we have learned
To live our lives so full of love
To fly up high with the dove
To love each other the best we can
This poor old soul, he's just a man

Betty Harvey

In the perfect world of wishing
My soul soars in the pastel puffs
   of the dreaming
Sky — a warm gentle breeze
Caresses the vista, and the trees
Sway to the last notes of a
   beautiful song.

Stay with me in the shadowing hours
When the dark magic dusts the sky
Guard me moon, keep a watchful eye
Till the glorious sun blows away the
   sleeping powder by and by

Christopher Mann

My Choice

Today is my day
I can do what I want
and speak to no one.
I am happy alone
as long as everyone knows
that I choose to be alone.
I am not alone because I have no one
I choose to be alone.
Friends are great but
they cause conflict.
We cannot get along so
I choose to be alone,
today.

Allison Rieck

Untitled

From frosted mists of midday haze
truth simple strode before me
each and every step he made
proclaimed my own captivity

Soft light bound about him
warmth carried dim within
as tho' it wasn't heat at all
but pale bright — a true lantern

How many lonely nights had been
endured to cast away the pall
of lies and darkness I could not look
nor begin to count them all

His sorrow for my state I saw
great passion spent for naught
what pity for the soul in need
that's sold or can be bought

Free spirit glided on and on
to overcome and be unsung
while fretted self remained behind
tied to my deeds unwound, undone.

Carol Elliott-Todd

Time

Time
seems to be
passing
But perhaps
we are passing
and time
is still

Jo Hankins

Miss Liberty

Miss Liberty came far from France
she's there to welcome immigrants

She stands for freedom
not like a kingdom

She is made of copper
no body can top her

She is very very tall
taller than the China wall

She is very old
but still much like gold

She was made by Frederic Barthodi
for many years she has not turned moldy

Ellis Island is where she stands
if you're down she gives you a hand

A lovely gift she surely is
to make her it would take a wiz

Whitney Mack

The Key Of Love

Thou art a "key called love"
that opens the heart.
For thou art the choice one
like music from a harp.
To know thy fixed passion,
that's far above measure.
And to discover your special "love"
is to open a cherished treasure.

Gary L. Moore

My Brother

A heavier weight I have not known
than that I felt today
for with five others I had to lift
and carry my brother away.

I carried him to his final rest
and grieved to see him go
and along with many others mourned
because we loved him so.

But when they fired his last salute
and played a somber taps
I knew that he had gone to set
upon our saviors lap.

And even though I miss him
I will not cry or weep
Because I know he is not dead
He's only deep in sleep.

So someday when our savior calls
We'll all rise up and then
Along the road to heaven's gate
I'll see my brother again.

Dennis Lee Johnson

My Given Prayer

Oh, Dear God,
the world is tough,
please give me the power
to make it through the rough.

Please give me the strength,
and the power I need,
to witness to others,
and put more sheep in your steed.

For all the people,
who need you every hour,
to set their lives straight,
with your given power.

Now every single night,
i'll look and the moon,
and ask you Dear God,
to please come back soon.

Please help me God,
to sin less then I've been,
I love you dear Jesus,
in your name Amen.

Joey Wascavage Jr.

The Turning Around

I was lost the middle of nowhere,
I thought I was alone,
Then I heard a gentle knock,
A knock not like my own,
Then I saw an angel,
Smiling down at me,
How beautiful her wings caressed,
That special child in me,
Oh how she warmed my love for me,
My spirit lifted up so high,
Then I saw her disappear
Into heaven in the sky;
Alas! I heard some heavenly words
So precious and so true,
That miracles do happen,
When God is there with you . . .

Ruth Miracle

Ever Lasting Love

My love for you is as pure
as a white rose in summer,
but, there is something even
more special than a plain
white rose, and that's a
daughter's deepest love
for a very special light
in my life and that's you Mom.
My life is your love forever.
My love is with you day in and
day out. When I'm not there to
give it to you in person. I'll be
there by your side forever even
when you can't see me. Nothing
is more special than a Mother
and Daughter's love such as ours.

Donna Ann DiCarlo

Dream

Laggard Edges of dream
withdraw into sleep's cave,
reluctant to remain,
yet tantalizing memory.

Henry Berne

With Hope

In that instant,
A loss greater than love,
One of hope,
Brought here in bondage,
Led astray,
Lost in faith,
A glimmer of light,
With words of life,
Proud, spiritual and a dreamer,
Days of struggle
Nights of prayer
Lost not to a people
Not to tomorrow
But to hope,
That was you . . . Martin
Now that you're with him,
Peace at last,
For you,
Still,
. . . I dream.

William R. Dixon

A Whimsical Hush

Emptying our minds on a
dancing daisy spilling
out with feelings. Obscene
consequences awake vitality.

Casting the observation
with aggressive delight,
animate molding the moment.
Verbal whispers tickle in the air.

Demonstrations clamp the
heart to drive ambition
through the erotic vision.
Imitate the confidence on
display view the challenge
poking your way.

The virtue of courage fuels
the soul, translating the
models code in rehearsed silence
to perform internal success.

Lori Christopherson

American Separation

Love and hate
Church and State
Gay and straight
Mate and mate . . .

God and trust
Sin and lust
Bread and crust
Journey and bust . . .

Fair and foul
Tree and owl
Skin and towel
Hand and trowel . . .

Freedom and birth
Peace and Earth
Value and worth
Morals and mirth . . .

Tried and true
Old and new
Pride and Jew
Me and you . . .

Aaron J. Housholder

This Thing Called Love

Its use is so diverse I fear,
I will not know when it appears.
How can it be that just one word,
describes so much in noun or verb?

Sometimes it makes it hard to speak,
attacks our spine, and makes us weak!
When new and fresh it makes life grand,
displayed by walking hand in hand.

It may refer to Lord on high,
or to mere mortals, deigned to die.
We say it times when we should not,
but priceless, it cannot be bought!

About our jobs, can it express
the way we feel, I think so . . . yes!
Our pets and peeves it may include,
sometimes it just describes our mood.

Its meaning has such broad appeal,
at times it just says how we feel.
When we find ourselves the object of,
how special is this thing called love?!

Frank J. Marchion Jr.

With You

I feel so alive, so trusting,
so happy.
You make me smile with your presence.
And vibrate with your touch.
Can you feel what I feel.

Kissing you
while I walk myself around you.
Undressing you
without a single touch.
Caressing you
with my naked body.
Is that a candle I see?
Or the reflection of our eyes;
but, I feel the heat.
Is that you inside of me?
Don't stop.
This is what I want,
"You."

Maria C. Grice

Twilight Dancer

Gentle gilt steps across the floor
A dance enough to shame the night
I look within beyond the door
And hope to catch a ray of light

A graceful nymph around the hall
Brings magic with her every stride
As shadows fade upon the wall
Her footsteps on the marble glide

Who is this nymph both fey and fair
Who dances with unearthly grace?
An apparition of the air
Sent down to give the twilight chase

As darkness pall grows obsolete
The dancer's step begins to fade
Her earthly work for now complete
She settles in her argent glade

As toward the light I turn my eyes
When last of all the dance is done
I realize then with great surprise
The nymph herself brought on the sun

Kenneth Prush

My Friend

There you are
I'm so glad you're here
I can always count on you
when I've been running in high gear

Today, it's been a hard day
I really need to get away
Take me to another place
Just whisk me far off and away

When I cuddle up with you
I can feel myself unwind
Your words can always soothe me
and ease my tired mind

I'm ready now to go away
and leave the reality of today
As I open up to your first page
I know my friend, you'll take me away

Barbara Ritter

Pristine Isolation

Gemstone and silver
and a mix of mortar
who you once were
now is forgotten

Pristine isolation
brings to a conclusion
secular preoccupation
with a sphere

Thomas Izzo

The Sea

As silently as a thunder clap,
the water surges against the
jutting rocks and projects itself
on toward the shore.

Spraying its mist as it goes,
enveloping all that it meets,
serenity is challenged. Life's
path has been disturbed. Suddenly,
but strongly, the beach is met by
understanding.

Then, almost as if it were being
forced, the foaming surf turns its
back on all it desired — taking
with it sand and stones and souls
lost to eternity.

K. Erin King

Winter's Wonder

It's biting cold, the temperature
drops steady,
a frosty day of winter,
icicles hanging lazy down
like big, cold, blistery splinter.

Little birds sit close together,
none makes the least of sound,
puffed up like little
balls of feather
and crispy snow is all around;

Sun rays reflecting back
like dancing, golden Angel hair
down by the frozen creek,
winter's wonder is everywhere,
Earth is going to sleep.

Heinz A. Heller

To Tame A Wildflower

Little wildflower in the field
Independence is what you wield
Until you surrender into my hand
I'll plant you in my promise land

To comfort, nurture, and care for you
From my sky of love I'll feed you too
Warning you with my friendly heart
With you now I'll never part

Your spirit is so gentle and calm
Because I've held you in my palm
Showing you where your future lies
And that my love will never die

David W. Brooks

Life Of Love

I loved my love with the love of spring
His love to me was everything
Because of him my heart could sing
My lovely love of spring.

I loved my love with a summer love,
With lazy clouds and blue above
With sweetness — tender, as a dove
My precious summer love.

I loved my love with the love of fall
And felt this love the best of all
When all my soul was at his call
My gentle love of fall.

But winter love I've found to be
Blessed with time's security
We two are one! Blest unity
He's me — and I am he!

Esther L. Freeman

Alone

Alone in a world of hate,
Alone with no one around.
Alone with no one to love,
Alone with no one to love me.
Alone,
Alone and lost with no one to help.
Alone with no love,
Alone with caress.
Alone and lost with all the hate,
Alone.

Jenna Stewart

Sleep

Soundly, cycling with every breath,
The monotony eludes my senses.
Time is no element as I lie here,
Though every minute seems an hour.
The world goes on without me,
And I have not prepared.
Simple things I took for granted,
Are no longer mine to hold.
Thoughts are racing through my mind,
Yet I cannot speak my words.
My existence is becoming a memory,
Although I am still here.
Tears transcend,
As my heart weeps.
I close my eyes one last time . . .
Sleep.

Sarah J. Jung

Escape

She sits on the curb
in a city so lost
Her spirit wanders
through images unknown

She watches the wind
if you can imagine that
It takes her places
only her mind perceives

She wonders what
an ocean gust would bring
Sand, salt, sun on her face
it's all just a dream

Back on the curb
her senses return
Tomorrow another journey
to where her heart yearns

Katherine Dillon

A Thought

If one would analyze
Instead of criticize
He might very well find
It's all in his mind
And the simple solution
Is mental pollution

D. Robert Broom

Sea Foam And Sunsets

Sea foam to the sand,
Sun rays to land . . .
How they know
where they must go.

Free birds to the tree.
Now I sleep with thee.
Rest assured am I
There you'll always lie?

Sunsets to the hills,
Winds swept through the mills.
Night has brought me back,
I find your love in lack.

Tall trees to the ground,
Clouds in skies are bound.
Why did I rely
On things I knew would die?

Beryl S. Tianero

A Crescent Moon At Dusk . . .

A crescent moon at dusk
with one perfect star.
A streak of red
in a blue grey mist.
What a perfect sight,
one so often missed.
With lives so busy,
no one takes the time
to stop and look around,
to see the stars
or a yellow moon.
Things that change
or end too soon.
No time to stop and smell a flower
or pick a berry from a vine,
today nobody takes the time.

Ellen L. DeShaw

Angel

Late in the day,
among the clouds,
there was a child gay
running among mounds,
he was trying to fly
and knew that he could.
Except for one thing,
he was dead in the ground.
He died a long time ago
during a storm.
His Ma, Pa, and sisters
whispered their sorrows.
Why had the Lord taken him away?
He was a good boy.
And had loved to play.
But, he is now an angel up above.
And watches out for the children
who need his care and love.

Lesley Robbins

If We Pass This Way Again

If we pass this way again,
in a life that's yet to be;
I'll be lookin' for you, love,
forever faithfully.

Just one life on God's good earth,
will never be enough with you;
if we pass this way again,
we'll love again like new.

If we pass this way again,
the world may all seem strange,
but your love's engraved on my heart,
and that will never change.

If you're ever gone from me,
and I know that I can't win;
I'll feel the fire between our souls,
and pray we pass this way again.

Garlyn Argabright Basham

Just A Dream

Just a dream I once had
sitting on a cloud.

Just a dream that I'd once see
my dad in heaven.

Just a dream I once had
that I'd walk again.

Once a dream
that I wouldn't get hurt
anymore!

I will always have dreams
but not all of them come true.

To me my dreams aren't just a dream
they will come true
if I keep believing in them.

One day I will be walking in heaven
with my dad
and sitting on a cloud.

Kristen Echelbarger

Haiku: San Bernardino August

As I sit in sweat
Heat from above melts the ground
And air turns to rust.

Bradford D. Davison

I Am

I am a humanoid life form,
I roam life's path at will.
I know not the norm,
I am like a windmill.
I turn as the wind blows,
I change at the wind's will.
I can love or hate the flows,
I am eternal as the hills.

Charles E. Stewart

Shallow

Resting on this
stark-white sheet of paper
lay the thoughts of an
ever-changing entity.
Tainted
with unscreened feelings
and vile acts,
It becomes the
mattress of
restless dreams.
Covered by a thin
sheet of self-sacrifice —
a rare attempt to stay
warm — while we
leave our windows
wide open,
to the bitter cold.

Toni Wall

A Rainbow From Lauren

In the midst of the storm
In April that year
A father received
From his daughter, so dear
A rainbow . . .

It was just a short message
Left on his machine
But it came from her heart
No doubt what the words they did mean
A rainbow . . .

Her words were so tender
So warm . . . so kind . . . so few
I love and miss you Dad
David and Andrea do too
A rainbow . . .

Her words brought him a tear
But let his heart soar
And helped him believe that, soon
We'd be a family once more
Lauren's rainbow . . .

Bruce A. Walker

Gum Under My Shoe

There's gum under my shoe.
I don't know what to do.
I keep sticking to the ground,
and making a squishy sound.

There's gum under my shoe.
It's like standing in glue.
I can't go anywhere,
and I'm stuck to this tile square.

There's gum under my shoe.
I know what to do!
I'll take my shoe off,
and go get mom.

Benjamin E. Moushon

Untitled

Finally found ourselves
Our own little home
Never again shall we
Ever have to roam.

Our own little love shack
Nestled in the woods.
Away from the crime and hoodlums
You find in city hoods.

It's a big little place
All nice and private.
And the commute's not that bad
If you ever try to drive it.

And all those neighbors,
A lot we'll have I hear.
The birds and raccoon and squirrel,
The owl and maybe deer!

And if our friends want to talk
They can pick up the phone and dial.
I'm sure we'll be there to answer
We'll be there along, long while.

Thomas Ball

To My Wife, Cora

July 4th is a day to remember
for reasons, more than one.
A hug and kiss in the birches
another romance begun.

For 50 years living together,
for reasons more than one.
Living, loving, hating
of marriages this is the sum.

Washing, baking, sewing
for reasons, more than one.
You can hurry, hurry, hurry
the work is never done.

So let us pause in the evening,
for reasons more than one.
For so long staying together
can still sometimes be fun.

We can wish for a place in heaven
for reasons more than one.
Perhaps we will be remembered
for things that we have begun.

Ray G. Kentner

2-Pac

The flowers, the trees,
The bushes, the bees.
These things are nature
Do you ever see them that way?
They will be there forever
But not you
Some people liked you
Some people didn't
But does that matter?
Yes, it does
Everyone knows you'll
be gone forever
But they will still
have memories
There will be tears
There already are
But will they last?
I do not know
In memory of 2-Pac

Amber Zadroga

Facial Parts

I see my face
But afraid to show,
What a strange place,
No one should ever know.
Rule by the demon of Fear,
Tender courage's an Ultimate sheer.
The faith is stronger each year,
Still holding back the needed tears.
Oh, Mama, How much Shame
Do I need to let go?
Oh, Father, it's still the same
Wherever I decide to go.
"Dreams were made to hope."
I once heard years back.
Many easy ways to cope
But it's an Illusion entrap.
The show much go on!
I will perform my very best.
Things will just be done,
And God'll Take the Rest.

Juan M. Figueroa

Evergreen Crystals Of Ice

As the snow lays on the pine needles
and melts away at the end of day
So we can pray for hope and joy
always and every day.

Pumpkin man the pumpkin man stands
Still in the midst of the day
When the wind blows he will
Always shake for another ways and days.

Mail Man's Dream
As the mail man delivers his
Mail for another day his dream
Go's on for days and days.

Jones garden
As we sit and pray the sunsets
will help make the end of a
glorious day anyway always.

The Deed Box is full of surprises
As we look for tomorrow for
Better surprises for ways and days.

Gary Schofields

My Buddy

I'm just a lonely wanderer
Shuffling down a dusty road.
I came upon this lazy stream.
Its name I'll never know.

Reminds me of a childhood
Long since gone by,
And another lazy stream,
Neath a western sky.

We were childhood buddies
This lazy stream and I,
But one year there came a drought,
And my buddy had to die.

I've been lonely ever since
My buddy passed away.
But I know this stream was heaven sent
To ease my pain today.

For this stream is my buddy,
The one the drought had killed,
Whom God hath restored to life,
While I wandered o'er the hill.

Gerald W. Shonk

Memories Of Childhood

Fresh mown grass is a memory of
childhood I can never forget.
Why should I?
Its pleasant odor reminds me
of Home, and Mama, and neighborhood
kids playing hide 'n seek,
While the sun begins to sleep
for the night.
Then . . . I sleep, and the smell
of fresh mown grass
comforts me.

Sandra Sinclair-Brock

The Night God Made My Angel

The night was soft and quiet
as the stars provided light;
and the Heavens gazed upon the Earth
with smiles of charmed delight.

A gift for all to know and see;
and with love now to be spent,
on silken wings of cradled moonlight
a blessing had been sent.

For how was I to know
so close, but yet unseen,
this distant child would live and grow
a real life captured dream.

I know that night was soft and quiet;
as a soul was just set free.
That night, God made an angel . . .
and sent her here to me.

George Lopez Jr.

Forty Weeks

Life is swimming —
The first triad!
Roe vs. Wade,
A choice has been made!

The first kick,
Gynecology!
Braxton Hicks!
Sonography!

Life is now seen,
Life is now heard,
The choice was before,
A baby is now seen and heard!

Myra Loyd

Gum Under My Shoe

When I got out of my car
    To go to the store,
I turned around
    To shut the door.

I took a few steps,
    And what did I find,
Something sticky
    That was left behind.

I shook my foot
    To try to break it loose.
But I knew this was
    A fight that I would lose.

I couldn't walk,
    What could I do?
For there was a huge piece of gum
    Under my shoe.

Chad Byers

A Fisherman's Dream

The sun starts to rise
My heart begins to pound
Early fishing is wise
As I am lake bound

I get my secret bait
And special rods and reels
I can hardly wait
A fisherman knows the feel

I flew to my favorite place
Anxious to begin
I settled back with grace
This time I'd win

My rods began to shake
I rose to my feet
The mystery I can't take
I would not have defeat

A big one it must be
I began to scream
Someone's shaking me!
Honey, it's only a dream

Ruth Adkins

Untitled

When was it that she fell from grace?
Of God or someone higher.
By appearance of a face
that cannot quench desire.
Or a heart that is so cold
of which it did her in.
Or of arms that cannot hold
a love that should have been.
Perhaps the dying ember eyes
that cast a false gaze.
Bring upon a slight despise
when dragged throughout the maze.
Or a message of come hither
that allures victims to stay.
Indifference makes them wither,
and then are pushed away.
The person that they think they've seen
is not the one above.
Of heartless women, she's the queen,
incapable of love.

T. M. Shelty

Tiger

The skies turn gloomy
every shades of grey
the time has come to go
she must be on her way

The wind is picking up
senses it in the air
leaves turning upside down
swaying with despair

The rain begins to fall
bringing every smell
even that of her prey
of which she knows so well

The thunder rolls
giving feel to the ground
getting closer
covering every sound

Then lighting strikes
it's all inside her
down for the kill
life of a tiger

Earl Sheldon

Gang Life

In my life of violence
I try to break away
But no matter how hard I try
I always have to stay.

Nobody understands
Nobody cares
I feel their looks
I feel their glares

I'm scared of people
I'm scared of school
I'm tired of keeping my image
I'm tired of trying to be cool.

The gang controls me
I don't have any real friends
I always wonder if tomorrow
Will finally bring the end.

I'm tired of trying
I can't seem to cope
But, one word keeps me going
It's that one word called "Hope."

Rebecca S. Hudson

Sunday April Twenty Fourth

The clouds don't know it's Sunday.
Our picnic was ruined.
But the wheat is growing
to feed the world.

Mary Ann Halliday

Life

Life is just a passing way
From the moment of birth
One starts to decay.

Day after day
Year after year
One finally knows
That the end is near
For all living to cease
And finally be released

Jim De Kosta

Our Lost Angel

Oh little girl of mine
For you I do pine
To have never known
Just how you have grown

You were given up
For some other to love
I thought you'd be better off
Than living push to shove

As the years passed
and things have changed
I know in my heart
What a mistake I've made

You don't know your father or I
Nor your Brother's five
I hope we'll meet soon
While we're still alive

Please God grant me this wish
So grateful I'd be
That I would get down on bended Knee
Our Lost Angel Returned May 1995

Shirley Liddy

Somehow

Somehow you wish things
Were better than they are

You look to the heaven's
And reach for a star

Somehow you try to get
Over that hill

Believe it or not but,
Somehow you will

John Kilian

Custody Of Three Moons

Long and drawn, sorrows,
to no abrupt end.
Captors of tomorrow's light,
a light they do spend.
Burdens to spew over,
so be their trend.
A light of three moons,
to me they send.
Bickered and battered,
till I cannot mend.
Like storm laden trees,
always forced to bend.
Young are the spoils,
with no way to fend.
No gold or silver coins,
nor covering to lend.
Lawyers and justice,
rule with poison pen.
The light of three moons,
have one friend.

Linda M. Hotaling

Untitled

The bravest people here on earth
Strong from the minute of their birth
Do not possess the strength to do
A thing like saying "I love you"
Families would stay together
Marriage would last forever
And there's nothing you can't do
If you would just say "I love you"

Linda Bowman Pitzer

Hate

To hate is to see with
a sheer blinded sight.
To hate is to love in the
dark not in light.
To hate is the ignorance
of not knowing inside.
To hate is the life of
no one with self pride.
To hate was the way
of our histories past.
To hate is to make the
bad memories last.
To hate is to feel like you're
black, or you're white
To hate is to say that I'm
wrong and you're right
To use the word lightly
it could cut like a knife.
To hate is to love but
not know in life.

Patricia Arrington

Death And Resurrection

Poor Joe Sparrow is dead
⠀⠀⠀so we said.
Dead, dead my pet sparrow
⠀⠀⠀is dead.
Where oh where is Grandpa?
Here he comes, he can help
⠀⠀⠀hurrah!
Thimble brandy, eye dropper too
Get a warm towel — a little love
⠀⠀⠀will do.
Oh — Joe — flaps his wings
⠀⠀⠀and sings.
Oh, grandpa, thank you he lives!
Grandpa can do all kinds of things.

Carol Wolf-Setka

On Giving

In the ever present sadness
⠀⠀of the world in which we live,
I know there is a joy
⠀⠀which to someone I can give.

The price has already been paid,
⠀⠀for each and every one;
the price was paid by Jesus Christ,
⠀⠀God's one and only son.

How would a person go about,
⠀⠀acquiring this joy you say;
just listen to my words of rhyme,
⠀⠀Jesus is the way.

One more thing before I close,
⠀⠀if one were to employ
the life and death of Jesus Christ,
⠀⠀then he, too, shall find joy.

William Kemper

Rosebud

My last little rosebud,
someday she will leave
her thorns and her young
tender leaves.
She'll travel and roam
only to be free
in search of whatever
it takes for her needs.
The guidance and love
she had while she has grown
will guarantee me
she'll find her way home.
So with worry and pride
I let loose of her leaves
my last little rosebud.
I will miss you!

Teresa McKessy

You . . .

It's you . . .
It's always been you.
Though
I never heard your voice
I never saw your face
I never felt your touch
I never kissed your lips
I never knew your name
It has always been you.
Now . . .
I have and I do.

Teryl Woods

Just A Dream

I look into your eyes
You look away to disguise
The pain you hide inside
You say you don't feel the same
When you hear me call your name
You said you really loved me
And for me you would be there
I thought that you were real
I thought our love was sealed
I search my heart inside and out
And yet in my mind
I still have doubts
About what you are
About who you are

Michelle Tetrault

Pigeons On The Wing

Did you ever notice
    how the pigeons
Love to fly against February winds?
Have you watched them climb and dip
    and soar in ever new formations?

Joy on the wing they are;
    expecting Spring,
        and eggs and squabs.

They dance their winged ballet
    to music they must hear!

Griffin C. Callahan

Colorado Skies

Snowflakes, sun rays
Mountains in the background
Watch the aspen leaf fall
down the white trunk of the tree.

The sky is vividly blue,
The air is crisp and cool.
The sun warms my face
And removes winter's sting.

The majesty of the mountains
With their timeless grace
Promises both solidity
And the art of flying free.

Victoria J. Chance

How To Live

Open your arms;
Honor the Maker
of the sky and the earth.
Let Nature be your Teacher.
Open the curtain
of your busy life.
Bring in the wonder and awareness
of the Treasures that surround.
When storms and challenges
face you in life,
Bend like the branches of the trees;
Feel the Gentle Breeze.
Face the Light
of the wonders around you.
Open your heart.
Think of your relationship
with the Maker
of the earth and sky.
Dream and become
the vessel of calm and love.

Joan Carolyn Mick

Thanksgiving

Today is Thanksgiving,
It's so cold that I'm shivering.
On Thanksgiving we have turkey,
Not beef jerky.
We have potatoes,
Along with tomatoes.

The family all gathers,
We use good manners.
The turkey is stuffed,
The potatoes are fluffed.
We eat at one,
We can't get up until we're done.

After dinner is football and fun,
And the women get the dishes done.
Then we eat cakes,
That my grandma always bakes.
Then we have pie,
And then it's time to say good-bye.

Joshua Stroka

Central

Half me and half you.
This is definitely not
The truth I pursue.

Jeff Nuckols

Meadows

M illions of flowers
E verywhere
A nd
D affodils
O ver
W ide waves of grassy
S eas

Kathleen Hutton

Fall

Clickety-Clackety leaves
    Clapping in the breeze,
    Cascading
  Down,
Scraping Sounds
  Crunching Ground,
    Crack!

Kim Sturdivant

Broken Pieces

Blue teardrops falling, one by one,
Your spirit calls to me.
Whispers of a broken love,
And fading memories.

Pieces of my broken past,
So sharp they are, indeed.
Into my lonely soul, they cut,
And make my spirit bleed.

Crimson stains upon the ground,
As sunlight kisses dew.
Tide of life is ebbing fast,
And still, I'm missing you.

Darkness of deaths angel comes,
Fast fading is the light.
The pain slips from my weary soul,
Won't see another night.

Virgil L. Armentrout

Hoosiers Do It Right

Do it right for Bobby Knight
mistakes he don't allow
do it right for Bobby Knight
and you better win some how

Bobby is the IU Coach
listen up to what he has to say
or he'll take you out in front
of the crowd,
and put your busted butt on display.
So do it right for Bobby
knight when you play basketball
makes those baskets guard
tose men both big and small
run the hell out of them all
win it fair and win it square
and when it's over
Bobby won't be throwing a chair.

John Wyatt Jr.

God's Little Corner Of The World

It's so peaceful and serene
with the leaves of the trees
gently blowing in the breeze.
And the tall trees waving
to the cotton ball clouds
that's passing over in the
deep blue sky above.
I can hear the birds singing
a happy melody all around me.
And I see my beloved dog
napoleon laying on my
front porch, taking it easy
with an occasional wag
of his tail. Ah! This is
truly God's little corner
of the world.

Margaret Lunsford

Time

Time is lost on
the words of our
minds seeing
through the innocent
Eye of time of the
object to surrender to the
feeling of nature
Time is the exit of
Everything! . . .

T. Vincent

Why?

If love was created
To make us appreciate each other,
Then why do we have hate in this world?

If happiness was made
To be a part of our lives,
Then why does half the world cry?

If nature created
A beautiful world for us,
Then why do we damage and destroy it?

If friendship was made
To be important in our lives,
Then why do we have enemies?

If I would have known
The answers to all these questions,
Then why would I have to ask?

Cristy Dilling

Tier Seven

In this high silent
nook of the stacks the pulverous air
is streaked with light

coming through leaves
(in winter, bones) of improbably tall
oaks at the eaves.

and the bound foliage
of arcane texts in *lemosí.*

No locks, no doors
protect us here,
yet we're as far from now
as Ventadorn is near.

In the crafted stanzas
of this tutelary way
I get a hold on artifice,
and find the means to say:

Midons, if God made you
he surely had nothing
much better to do.

(Amen.)

J. David Danielson

Let Me Down Easy

Let me down easy,
Condition me for the fall.
Because the view from the top,
Was not what I expected at all.
Let me down easy,
My heart can't take the pain.
For on the way to the top,
A new life I had hoped to gain.
Let me down easy,
The climb was tough you see.
For the view from the top,
Didn't consist of both you and me.
Let me down easy,
Let me down slow with ease.
Because of always looking up,
I missed seeing you leave.
Let me down easy,
Prepare my heart.
Because the journey back,
Will be long, lonely, and dark.

Marlene Miller

Untitled

Looking at you from afar
I think of what might be,
You and I together as one.
With but one love to lead and
no others to behold,
for such a love is rare to find
that is so endless and full.
You and I compared to fools,
let us be judged
but let us judge not for
they know not of love so true.
It takes two to
end all foolish thoughts.
Shall we wed, our decision alone,
to think as one for
all the world to know,
in the end there can be
only two as one with
love so true.

Harry Dana Braswell III

Oh Woman

Oh woman of color
Arise, take your place
in the rainbow of humanity
with dignity and grace.

Oh woman of strength
You've endured through hard years
You have offered your sacrifice
Shedding your blood; shedding tears.

Oh woman of faith
You've embraced God's salvation
With His love and power
You've helped raise a nation.

Oh woman of valor
The battle is won
The victory is yours
Now shine like the Son.

Oh woman enduring
Come rest by the Father
As He welcomes you Home
And says, "Well done, My daughter!"

Judy A. D. Shores

Caroline

You are a story told
a thousand times over,
    yet a dream that happens
but once in a life.
    You are as pure and innocent
as a springtime rose,
    yet all year long
you bloom with warmth.
    Your smile is so bright
and refreshing to see,
    Even in the darkest nights
under your tree.
    So now we pray
and say good bye
    To all the love
you shared in life.
    God has you now
to keep by his side,
    To watch over his beaches,
waters and skies.
    We will miss you so much
in time to come.
    But we know in our hearts
you live on and on

Michael Pagano

Look Inside

When thoughts and things become one
Then I know my soul is gone
The only thing I can do now
Is to find my sanity somehow

When I wake up and see
That I am no longer me
And I know that everything is strange
Then I realize it's time for change

When feelings are no longer there
It is time to stop and stare, within
For the answers I will find
Might be the only thing to save my mind

When I see what is within
And understand what it is I know
I may then realize how to begin
To live my life once again

Adam Isban

It's Home

Home may be just an obscure shack;
Or mansion on a hill . . .
But the word home means much the same;
If love the heart does fill.

A place of comfort, peace and rest;
Or place to lay the head . . .
Nostalgia of the heart is blessed;
When home with love is wed.

Great splendor or unpainted log;
Where home is called to be . . .
Memories . . . no other place will fog;
With love's fair eyes that see.

Where the heart rest, no need to roam;
So true, those words are said . . .
With love of family the heart of home;
Where Christ is always head.

Maxine Spyres Hixon

Leaves Are Like People

Leaves are like people they
have all different shapes,
sizes, and colors, but no one has
a right to make fun or be mean
to you just because of your
different shapes, sizes, and color's
that you are. God made all
of the leaves in the world
equal to each other and no set
of leaves are better than the
other

Tammy Flanigan

My Valentine To You

I saw Cupid over there,
With his well aimed dart,
He was working just for me,
In capturing your heart.

He told me how to win your love,
By declaring it to you,
And let you know since first we met,
That I've been ever true.

I've always been too shy to speak,
The words I want to say.
But with Cupid working every time,
I'll speak my piece today.

I'd say I'd like to hold you close,
And share your kisses too.
And ask you if you'll share my life.
That's my Valentine to you.

Jennefer Hood

Never

We both agreed till death do us part
But then you went and broke my heart

You said we would always be forever
But now I am only left with never

As you slipped that ring on my finger
I knew our hearts would never linger

But now I lay here in this empty bed
With only thoughts of you in my head

You said we would always be forever
But now I am only left with never.

Crystal Smith

My Inheritance

There is a drawer in Grandma's kitchen
That holds all sorts of things
Match books and rubber bands
And varied colored strings.
Ladles and cables and keys to doors
That we no longer own.
A knife she bought at the County Fair
With a handle made of bone,
A badly rusted pizza wheel,
And a metal sharpening steel.
A rolling pin and a pastry skin,
And a metal ball to put tea leaves in.
A broken watch and paper clips
And a fancy opener for wine.
Since I was just a little girl,
This drawer was always mine.
Now I empty out the contents
And assign them to the trash,
Where all my happy memories
Will lie in smoking ash.

Nada Wager

Living Today

Living today is wonderful,
Regardless of the outside weather,
It's sure nice and warm in the house,
And birds can be seen that gather.

There's money to buy food these days,
And cooking is still lots of fun,
Being prepared for company
Is a common approach well done.

Read the daily newspaper well,
The listen to the latest news,
Just keep on learning by reading,
And study to learn latest cues.

Enjoy your telephone often,
Call an elderly friend or two,
But don't forget your family
So the needs are met for your crew.

Make a list of daily jobs,
And cross of each after it's done,
Then do some enjoyable things
So living today will be fun.

Eleanor M. Dirksen

The Tree Willow

Willow . . .
Tree willow . . .
Tell me, why do you weep?
With your branches bending over
You are the loveliest tree

Are you sad to be alone?
Just . . . one of a kind
But, you are unique
To an adornful eye

Willow . . .
Tree willow . . .
These words you must drink
Like the rain from a shower
And the sunshine you need

With moss soft as feathers
And roots that run deep
Your beauty outshines all others
In our world of many a tree

Linda C. Burns

Poet

A poet? Hmph! Can you fix a car?
No, but I can sing a shining star.

Hmph! Do you have a lot of power?
No, but I can describe a flower.

Hmph! Do you have bushels of money?
No, but I chant the bees and honey.

Hmph! What about duty?
Hmph! Hmph! You are all wrong!
My soul sings of beauty
That, is my joyous song!

Georgette M. Moraud

The Night

The calling of the night is strong,
As the sun fades into the sky.
All of the stars start to twinkle,
And the wind just lets out a sigh.

Darkness envelops the land,
The moon shines through with its glow.
Songs of the wolf fill the air,
As the night puts on quite a show.

The day has pulled down its shade,
The man in the moon has arrived.
Give of yourself to the night,
And really come truly alive.

The night wants to draw you inside,
To share its unique point of view.
Belong to the feel of the night,
The darkness will carry you through.

Shirley Drage

Mephitis

My soul was sold
to a falsified God
who determined my life
for a dowry of neglect
and I was slain
in a treacherous incarceration
that has left me renounced
I pray that when
they light my funeral fire
and I sit choking
on the gasoline
that I can spit
the flames back to them.

Heather M. Pohuski

Broken Wings

You've ever flown so very high
living out those sights of wonder
high aloft beyond our dreams
and spirit strong to lead you
with flossy clouds and thunders.
Agile wings keep soaring high
far above others, but a few.
Broken wings have brought you down
now to see the sky as we,
desperate to be up there
spirit longing to be free.
Like our own, your fate rests now,
dreams and spirit fade in air.
You, who've ever flown so high
cannot know how sad we feel,
as we soared aloft with you
only in our spirit dreams.

Michael DeNike

Brad, The Smoke Jumper

Was there ever a better lad,
He is one to make this family glad.
He's a clown of renown
The best in the town.

The grin of the great never too late.
He makes his own fate.

Brad knows the score
Tells tales of great love

Brad is quite a guy.
Say all the gals with a sigh.

Gloria M. Fiala Haugh

Requiescat In Pace

Armed with a Dorito
I proceeded incognito
under a blackened one watt bulb
past some clumpy chocolate milk
deserting the town of Tupperware
I continued with my search
stumbling through the "Old Mil"
over a casket full of eggs
around a can of Coca-Cola
I'd been thirsting for . . . for days
then standing in the shadows
of an empty Cool-Whip dish
a molded growth of cobwebs
ambushing the picante dip.

Tammy Gullickson

Winter Deluge

Water here and there
  Angry skies
    Heavy rains
      Rising rivers
        Gusty winds
          Invade the valley.

Floods decide to come
  Fallen trees
    Scattered branches
      Inundated homes
        Drowned people.

Mean, uncomprehending nights
  Power outage
    Biting cold
      Shivering humans
        Dying animals
          Devastation everywhere.

Susisa Monton

"Drifting Alone"

Drifting alone on a lake
In a boat that'll sink
What becomes of this fate
Look to far so high
Questioning why ask why?
Surviving this game of life

Drifting alone in this lake
Sunk all ships life is to late
Maybe taking in to much
Causing my mind to crunch

Drifting alone in this place
This time cry for change
Think I'll try an manage
Surviving this game of life

Bert Ferrero

My "Dad"

A pain rushes through my body
And I see a bright light.
I look around for the time
But I have lost my sight.

I think of a few more breaths
till time runs out,
then someone appears
and speaks without a doubt.

His words are to me,
you will live my son. Do not be sad
For the love I give
take care, I'm your Dad.

He says that the sun
will rise another day
so don't lose your faith
my son. I will pray

I wake the next morning
I see a smiling face
I have another chance to live
be happy and give Grace.

Robert L. Brown

Prayer

Prayer can mean so many things
Shared by you and me
Our thoughts of love for each other
I am sure that God can see

When we learn to look at others
For the beauty they possess
Share their love and heartaches
And pray that God will bless

The most he asks of each of us
Is to share his love each day
To speak kind words of our fellow man
And remember him as we pray

These things I say are real
And God's way for you and me
To share God's love with all mankind
Is really meant to be

God so loves us dearly
He sends his blessing from above
He understands our problems
And he asks we share his love

Timothy Bernardy

The Business Trip

I'm sitting in my hotel room,
    My loving wife in mind.
Recalling that she had a wish,
    A poem one day she'd find.

I'll grant that wish for words of wit,
    Though writing's not my style.
I'll tell her just how pleased I am
    She chose to walk the aisle.

She's beautiful, both in and out,
    Her standards are so high.
When her talents are compared to mine.
    She's far better than am I.

Her qualities are superior,
    I'm just about irate.
The only thing I'm better at
    Is choosing a life long mate.

John S. Adams

Untitled

The Muses of Parnassus
There were nine as I recall
Including Goddess mother
The busiest of all!
Mnemosyne her name was,
To us of early time
And yet, as charming as she was,
The hardest now to rhyme.
Charming is too mild a term
And facts will tell us so
Little secrets falter out
The further back we go!
Each daughter had a different dad
This I learned from her
But mother, "Muse of memory"
Can't recall just who they were.
And now for all the lives of me
In a life of this and that,
I really can't remember . . .
Which muse I begat.

Ed Reimers

Bittersweet Blossoms

Naked branches explode with blossoms,
bursting into fragrant fuchsia beauty,
hot, wild, Spring pink and bright
like midnight stars.

Brisk, billowy, breezy winds
catching blossoms with surprise,
freeing them to wildly scatter
thru blue skies, near and far.

Gaily laughing with fragile beauty,
they danced the air, then slowly . . .
floating onward thru their life,
sweetly sang one final song.

Reaching to soft, damp earth,
resting such tender bruised pink
loveliness, bid goodbye with sorrowful
sigh, crushed and trampled upon,
then forever gone . . .

Nancy Quinn

"Christmas Holiday"

The holiday is coming,
    Sound of Christmas bell.
Christmas carol singing,
    songs we know so well.

Trees and decorations,
    All around the town.
The spirit of the holiday,
    Shoppers homeward bound.

Children writing Christmas lists,
    To Santa and his elves.
Stores have clothes and toys and games,
    And overflowing shelves.

Santa, elves and reindeer,
    Are getting ready too.
Loading up the big red sleigh,
    To deliver gifts to you.

Then on Christmas morning,
    Happiness and joy.
Just that smile upon their face,
    Of little girls and boys.

Richard L. Parker

My Heart Hears Music

Low in the heart,
Deep as a river,
My soul hears music
All its own.

Gentle as a spring breeze,
Soft as pussy-willow down,
There sings a melody,
Deep within my heart.

Refreshing as morning dew,
Fragrant as lilacs,
Stirs a sacred air,
A song of angels.

    Deep within
    My heart.

Jane Huelster Hanson

Untitled

I am tomorrow
    the dreams of today
My kids are my future
    and God will guide our way
My drugs are yesterday
    gone with some of my fun
Those are the bad memories
    fading one by one
Today when I saw it
    I remembered my past
I Thought I had something wonderful
    The high just didn't last
I can't dwell any longer
    I have to move on
And look for our future
    because yesterday is gone.

Sherri Rud

Autumn

A morning shaft of sunlight
Streams through the trees boldly
Seeking one tree, and
Turning leaves to gold.

Bright midday sunlight
Touches each leaf of each tree
Reflecting millions of bright rays
Bathing earth in radiant glory.

Late afternoon rays
Peek just over the hill
To touch one branch
As earth stands still —

For autumn's mighty glory
And our breathless thrill.

Elaine Peverly

Beyond The Glass

Beyond the glass
In the green, green grass
That lays in the woods
Unknown to anyone.

Beyond the glass
Is a hope for the future
Like a cow waiting to be killed
In the green, green grass.

Once beyond the glass
Unknown to anyone
You won't want to come back.

David Shell

Advice From Socrates

Nothing to excess,
   Everything in moderation.
Advice of wise old Socrates,
   Could save our troubled nation.

In our fast-track lives of stress,
   A lesson to be learned,
When we work from dawn 'till dusk,
   For the salaries we've earned.

We're using up our planet,
   Spoiling even more this way,
For our children are demanding
   More and more each holiday.

Fast food, fast cars,
   Parties, drugs and more —
Shopping sprees, excessive debt,
   It's easy to ignore —

The advice from ancient Socrates,
   To savour simple pleasures,
Instead of racing through each day,
   Ignoring all its treasures.

Shirley Yates Miketinac

Childhood Dreams

Childhood dreams,
they were easy to do,
restless and yearning,
for your dreams to come true.

Now as you're older,
feeling the pain,
thinking of your youthful days,
wished you could have remained?

I know it's hard,
not easy to do,
regrasping those dreams,
they always elude.

Innocence . . . ignorance,
that's how it seemed,
life was simple then,
this world stole our dreams.

Childhood dreams,
they're easy to lose,
tired and aging,
they will never return to you.

Paul Michael Arena

Grandpa's Riding On A Star Love

In this world.
In this love.
How many hearts have been broken?

Don't know why people are in love.
Instead of sweet love, in return.
You get a painful feeling,
You get loneliness out of love,
Not a togetherness kind of feeling
The twilight darkens and you still,
Don't get your words through him.

Your heart breaks, you can't work,
In return of love, that's what you get
Hurt, painful feeling, a feeling of
Sorrow for your self.
Love is bad.
Love hurts.

Mahevish A. Mansuri

Not To Shed A Tear

Things we do
Time we spent
Ways of love
Together was meant

Words that speak
Only from the heart
Life and time abide
Not to be apart

Sparkling eyes
With tears of sorrow
Distance smiles
With love not to borrow

Time will tell
Why I'm here
To support with love
Not to shed a tear

Paul Morrison

Turnip Greens

When my working day is through,
And I have nothing else to do.
Life is not worth living, so it seems
Unless I get me some turnip greens.

Turnip greens with good corn bread
'Tis the best food that was ever fed.
Take some onions that are still green
To eat with my good ole turnip greens.

Fry some salt pork, if you don't mind;
Just the meat and not the rind
Be sure it has a little lean
To eat with my turnip greens.

I took my wife to the county fair;
We got hungry while we were there.
She ordered a burger and onion rings.
All I wanted was some turnip greens.

When my feeble life is o'er
And I can't eat my greens no more
Although I like other things
Just fill my grave with turnip greens!

Eugene Culpepper

The Green Leafed Tree

Look at the shape
Of the green leafed tree.
Light green buds
Emerging free.

Look at the shape
Of the green leafed tree.
Its beautiful form
A blessing to me.

Look at the shape
Of the green leafed tree.
Painted with color
So majestically.

Look at the shape
Of the green leafed tree.
Broken and scarred
For all to see.

Look at the shape
Of the green leafed tree.
A seasonal lesson
God made for me.

Lynn D. Gunderson

Untitled

Just as the sun goes down
And sets upon my head
I'll close my eyes to life
And take my dreams to bed
Where you lay quite designed
And form fit to your sleep
I'll catch the wind, and wish on it
And hope your love to keep
The time keeper has lost his watch
And forgotten how to smile
Before we see the night return
I can touch you for a while
I've brushed the breeze of sanity
From the cloak I wear, undone
It's made of love and loneliness,
I'm sure we've all worn one
So, I'll button up my heart before
I venture down alone
Until I wake to meet the dawn
And find that you have gone.

Madonna S. Robinson

Tis True

It only hurts for a little while
   "'Tis not true"!

My heart aches, it bleeds
   I'm very blue

Turn my other cheek,
   Look the other way

It's not helping, regardless of what
   you say
I'm weary, I wonder, and then say
   a Prayer.
Is anyone listening?
   Does anyone care?

Suddenly, a voice within me
   whispers — "'Tis True"

"It, only hurts for a little while"
   "I Love You"
   My Precious, Little Child

Marge Burns Kozak

So Many

I've 'rit so many poems,
I think my hand is broke.
I've 'rit so many poems,
It's no longer just a joke.

I've wor' out all my pens,
A new pencil I am due.
But I still have not heard,
A single word from you.

So, I'll try, try again
And try this one more time
And see if after all,
My poem is worth a dime

I could use some money,
I sure could use the dough,
And I've entered so often
As you surely, well know

If not, I'll try and try
And see if one fine day
I'll send a poem in to you,
That may earn me some pay.

Nicholas Kring

Dove

Like a dove that has
lost its wings, I have
lost the strength to fight,
fight for the love that is mine,
the love that has been denied.

My heart of the wings
of a dove, soft and sweet
gentle and kind, cut deep
into one's heart and you'll
never find a love as pure as mine.

My heart, like that of a doves,
is full of love and happiness,
but I don't know what
to do, I'm lost, lost
without you.

Mistie Bettencourt

Mephitis

My soul was sold
to a falsified God
who determined my life
for a dowry of neglect
and I was slain
in a treacherous incarceration
that has left me renounced
I pray that when
they light my funeral fire
and I sit choking
on the gasoline
that I can spit
the flames back to them.

Heather M. Pohuski

Peace

With reverence I greet the dawning,
Of another lovely morning,
I'm at peace in my heart —
    with God

Birds fill the air with their singing,
Sounding like bells sweetly ringing,
I'm at peace in my heart —
    with God

I silently give thanks, kneel and pray
I have been given another day,
I'm at peace in my heart —
    with God.

Virginia E. Schlenkerman

Broken Wings

You've ever flown so very high
living out those sights of wonder
high aloft beyond our dreams
and spirit strong to lead you
with flossy clouds and thunders.
Agile wings keep soaring high
far above others, but a few.
Broken wings have brought you down
now to see the sky as we,
desperate to be up there
spirit longing to be free.
Like our own, your fate rests now,
dreams and spirit fade in air.
You, who've ever flown so high
cannot know how sad we feel,
as we soared aloft with you
only in our spirit dreams.

Michael DeNike

Hope

Today I caught my tears
in a bottle for to see
if they would outweigh my fears
and give hope to me.

Twas an easy thing to do
seeing they weren't far away
only yesterday so blue
my brown eyes turned to gray.

I started down the road
of memories so bright
the warmth became winter cold
as I entered tear stained nights.

I ne'er will forget
the horror a'fore me
my heart did regret
treading this treacherous sea.

I ran hard as I could
hope gaining fast
forget those tears I would
and be satisfied at last.

Carolyn Joyce Williams

A Glimpse Of Immortality

What miracle this to look at night
And view creation by Heaven's light.
The glories which the day concealed
By myriad starlight stands revealed.
A brilliant surging cosmic ocean
With every star in perfect motion.
Endless matter and endless space
With every atom in its place.
Impossible, we, mere mortal dust
Could know all this and yet we must;
For there in time's eternity
Shines Heaven's vaulted canopy.
What force created the splendor there
And formed each part with tender care?
Who dreamed the pattern and design
Of void and matter, curve and line?
Only one answer I would dare.
God, our creator, put it there.
Now you ask me what I see?
A glimpse of immortality.

James William Hubbard

Our Children Are Alone

Boys and girls of our world today,
I've become especially aware,
That morals and values have gone away,
And to the children, it's unfair.
You're left so many times alone,
With lots of time on your hands,
Less supervision in the home,
Doing things you don't understand,
The world has changed so drastically,
You kids are becoming adults,
Before you really need to be,
But it's really not your fault,
The wages paid are very low,
The cost of living is much more,
So off to work our mother's go.
When they didn't have to before,
Money has corrupted our thoughts,
And taken us form the home,
So our children are not taught,
Because they're left alone.

June Schwieterman

A Token Of Love

I love you so much
Words can never express
The love I hold for you
When you cry, I cry
You laugh, I laugh
I feel your pain,
Your joy, your fears
I will never leave you
You mean the world to me
When I say "I love you"
You don't believe me
There is only one way
To show you the love
I hold for you inside myself
As a token of my love
I give you my son,
    Jesus Christ!

Aimee M. Brest

Forest Voices

Horned puffin play,
    The ancients say,
Along forgotten seashores.

They haunt sunrise mists,
    Dance to will-o-the-wisps,
Laughing, bouncing pompadours.

Lost cousins, parakeets,
    Sing softly, semi-sweet,
Jungle rhythms, troubadours.

Rainbow plumes propel,
    Exotic stories immortal,
Forest voices evermore.

Gary Meisner

Mama's Boy

Sniffing and smoking.
Smoking and sniffing.
This boy think it's fun,
Exhaling in the heat of the sun.
His mama on bended knees.
She sweats and bleeds.
To God she pleads.
Her fingers already worked to the bone.

Robbing and stealing.
Stealing and robbing.
This boy's life is of no use.
Boy! Take a stand.
God has a plan,
By the wave of his hand,
To him you must return.

Gary Wilson

An Ode To A Toad

You hop into my garden
without even a beg your pardon.
You take the garden tour,
and everything is gone for sure.
No bugs m'lady is your motto.
As you croak in your staccato.
And as I gingerly water my flower,
out you leap and there I cower.
You are welcome here Dear Toad,
At this lovely abode,
But before I finish this synopsis,
Please warn me, before you
    Leap from the coreopsis.

Barbara Jones

Promise Me True

Your eyes seemed tender,
And truer than before.
Your voice not quite as doubtful,
Yet loving even more.
My heart felt it,
Like it was meant to be.
As if you really couldn't go on,
And keep living without me.
Even though the words,
Sounded most the same.
It was very different,
The way you called my name.
How we lay there together,
Thinking of times gone by.
The way you squeezed me gently,
The look in your eye.
I've seen it time again,
But not this way at all.
It wasn't just a promise,
It was Love that I saw.

Karri Lyn Newton

Unknown

Last night something awkward happened
An experience never before had.
My mother and I are close,
closer than two can be
But she hurt me.
I am strong
but I was wrong.
She made me cry,
and broke my heart
something I thought she'd never do
Her words burnt like fire,
stung like salt.
Then some powerful feeling overtook me
Unaware to her I was about to cry,
I left her to be by myself.
I'm changed now
I am by myself.

Nana F. Agyemang

Oh, Mister Tree, What Did You See

Oh Mister Tree, what did you see
As the drums rolled,
and the blood flowed?
Oh Mister Tree, what did you see
As the sun gleamed,
as the soldiers screamed.
and others fled?
Oh Mister Tree, tell me please,
Why brother killed brother?

Oh Mister Tree,
I look at thee,
and then I can see.
It was meant for me,
to write with this hand,
the story of this land.

William J. Holleman

A Stroll

I like to smell the pretty flowers
When I take a morning stroll.

Now here is a lovely specimen,
as lovely as you please.
It would be a whole lot nicer
if it weren't full of bees.

Forrest Rice

Touch

Eyes not blinking, wide and white
Pounding heart, soul full of fright
Spinning head, stomach turning
Muscles shaking, fingers burning
Touch a snake and he may bite

Elizabeth A. Morrison

A New Dawn

The river flows,
As the wind blows.

The morning breeze,
Will help to ease.

It is like all mornings,
There will be no warnings.

On all things big or small,
But today I will not fall.

Jessica Flood

Seeking Reward

Life is like a rain drop
it falls and hits the pane
it slips along the window
until just its mark remains.

It gathers in a little pool
and grows into a mass
then slides across the window sill
until its time is past.

My life like those of men gone by
is just a drop of rain
I searched for love, as well I must
I seek, but search in vain.

I lay back on my pillow,
and here the rain drops play
and know the world is passing by
a wiser man this day.

Joseph R. Haggerty

Spring Is Coming

I love to see the crocus come
peeping out the ground, and
Lo, before I know it, they're
wearing pretty colored gowns.

Emily Reis

People

People come from many places.
They are all of different races.
We all have different faces
We are from so many spaces.

People come from miles around
We all create a magnificent sound
In the future we are heaven bound
And then, no one can be found

But for now, we all care
And we all can love and share
People are so very rare
People are so very fair

We all have a fear.
To others, we are very dear
Were I have a life-long dream
One day, we will make it gleam

Beverly Baciak

Home

There is a place,
not far away,
with caring faces.
and warm open arms.
That are waiting to give,
a gentle hug,
this is a place,
where you do more than live,
you learn to love,
be kind and care,
for everything,
even teddy bears.
In this place
you will not find
any one who
is not kind
I doubt you'll find
a little gnome
because this place
it is called home

Angela Pullum

Ole Hollow

I'm just an "ole hollow" in
an oak tree,
Many a home I've been
for families,

Out of the cold and
dark of night,
Away from all harm,

I'm just an "ole hollow"
in an oak tree,

If you need a home,

I'll be here, for thee.

Linda D. Skinner

The Lover's Plea

Days pass
As if before
Now alas
Tis no more
My love to be
I can no more
Though you shall't see
My love now growing
As always before
To its largest degree
Thus thou cannot see
For thou ist blind
No further creature even seen
None ever so divine
As thou ist my love between
My love is only thine.

Jessica Corn

From This Pain

This pain — shall cry
    shall learn
    shall know

This pain — I'll understand
    care

From this pain
    I shall
    love again!

Lujuana Arviso

I God

My soul on edge. I'm losing all. Lived this way too long. They
say no matter how low you go, there's still a right and a wrong. You
can chose one way and live with yourself. Or chose the other and
walk around dead only not know it. In need of stability, I chose a path.

My life was spinning out of control. Had one too many sleepless
nights and broken dreams. From the edge, I took two steps back.
Freed from the danger of falling over into the waiting arms of
demons, my eyes conceive a different light.

Forgetting the past, embracing the future, I set out. My eyes
burning, destined for greatness, I soar above the trivial problems
of life. Alighting on the mountain top, I reach down to stare
up at the Forgiver.

Scoffing my way of life in his unique method, I vowed to be the
father of those like me. The ugly. The criticized. The unwanted.

For faith is the victim of realities claw and death still goes unanswered.
My self.
My own, I God.

Paul Chenault

I've Lost A Friend

I've lost a friend, the form and face that once I knew
are lost forever to my view
the laughter and the tears we shared are memories now
but in my heart they'll be reminders of a time that was
when we enjoyed each other and because
we shared . . . we knew . . . each other's pleasures and
each other's tears. We revelled in the sharing
though we did not know, it was not meant to be . . .

There came a time for looking back and wondering
what if this or that
might different be and yet I know that it be true of you and me
that we could no more change the face of things that were
than we could change both you and me
Although we shared in part, it simply was not meant to be
it was as fate decreed, we did not know . . .
we were not meant to be

John M. Simmonds

Sometimes

Sometimes I feel like I haven't a partner.
Sometimes I feel like I haven't a friend.
Sometimes I wish I could die like a great man.
Sometimes I wish I could just be myself.
Sometimes I wonder what would happen if I'd never been born.
Sometimes I wonder what am I living for.
Sometimes I think of the chances I had.
Sometimes I think of the chances I can have.
I do know that if the rules ever bend,
All of us will know what is in the end.

Joshua Barrows

Words From The Prophet Snail

"Good morning Mr. Snail."
"Good morning boy."
"I can see from your slime trail that you have come from the
forest," the boy said with a smile.
"It is true, my trail does reveal my past."
"My sister says your trail is gross the way it makes the
rocks and cement shiny, but I do not think like her."
"She is correct in that I do affect the land which I travel
upon, but my trails shall be all but a memory come the first
drops of rain."
As if to audibly express the tear in his eye, the snail said rather
shakily, "Clear is our conscience that we snails do not leave
trails of concrete separating the beautiful from the 'civilized'."

Kent DeMar Hess

My Exit

I will leave;
I must make my exit,
I'm here just abusing space, it seems,
The life — long gone out of me;
Yet, I linger on in misery,
Why am I here in this place?

Tried, but I fell short,
Cried and prayed, even believed,
Tried, but I stand again somewhat out of sorts;
Let me go — I must,
I'll die unafraid —
Complete perfection awaits me
Beyond this "grave."

The time will come
When you will forgive me as God already has,
For leaving you all;
For being too tired and confused to continue my call,
I must take — my exit.

Lorrie Crawford-Mcfield

Yes Or No

You ask tonight my daughter's hand
    As you'd request a toy;
Do you know the weight of your demand
    On a mother's heart, my boy?

The heart you crave is a holy thing,
    So tender trusting true;
Can you to her devotion bring
    As warm as hers to you?
Will you love her through the changing years
    As tenderly as now?
When age shall bow her graceful form
    And bleach her jetty hair;
Will you protect her through each storm
    And shelter her from care?
A loving woman, when a wife
    To one that she adores,

Will your love be the last to die?
If not, I answer No,
Or will you always live adoring her
    Why, then, I answer Yes.

Ada D. Beachy

Melissa

I trudged again a thoughtful path, matrixed
To a cimmerian path across a quad of
Tainted American Beauties, newly bloomed.

The frigid white facade of an inert Greek portico
Echoed my aberrant steps.
I feared a final pronouncement.

The doors swung open . . . mysterious, mute.
I entered a spiritless tiled hall,
Mourning its medical misery.

My face flattened against the nursery's glass;
My tears streaked across its pane.
Gravely, I begged her fight. I prayed.
Defeat that foe that grasps your life.

Each day she dies
A little more.

Her crypt was small,
Enshrouding 7 pounds,
Cerulean eyes, ashen hair and flaxen skin.

She silently chose God, not me.

Howard J. McHenry

Happy Birthday, Son

It's that time of year again,
How did it go by so fast?
Pretty soon you'll me considered a "has been"
And you'll be like us, looking at the past!

No, really, it's hard to imagine you to be 17,
With all the many concerns running through your head.
Pretty soon you'll be something that we've seen,
And we can go upstairs and look at an empty bed!

I know you're waiting for the time when you can get away,
I'm sure it goes through your mind every day.
But hopefully, as you look back at your growing up years,
You'll begin to understand all our hopes for you and our fears.

We've tried to do our very best by you,
And we haven't been right in all the we've done.
But, you've got your Mother in you, and your Father, too!
So in the end, we think you've turned out to be one great son!!

So enjoy your special day, kiddo,
And always remember that we love you a lot,
No matter what you do or where you go,
And that you're one of the best things we ever got!!

Kerry Kadelbach

When Our Father Calls

We are God's children, daughters and sons.
He is our father the loving one.
Our bodies will die in this life we see.
But in heaven, it is only our souls he shall need.
His father has called, it was his time to go.
His fear was all gone, as we all know.
I know we're all saddened, as we're left behind.
Our turn will come, yours . . . and mine . . .
When our job is done, our father will call.
We must go with him, big or small.
We live our lives, for him you must know.
And when he calls us we must go.
Gone from earth, we will be.
But in Heaven our souls live eternally.

Tina Lepkowski

A Vessel Of Honor

When I take the time to ponder the privilege given me
By the Creator of the heavens — the stars, the earth, the sea . . .
I'm moved with such emotion that can not be contained,
For the God of all creation knows me by my name.

Within this lowly vessel You have chosen to abide,
And you're ever present with me walking by my side.
You've taught me how to live by faith and to hope in things above;
You've given me all I'll ever need in your eternal love.

So Lord, it's my desire to live for you each day
A life that's pleasing in your sight in all I do and say.
Please search me, Lord, and know my heart and purge me of my sin;
Let only love and mercy and good things abide within.
Day by day, sweet Spirit, do your work in me,
For truly a vessel of honor I long to be for Thee.

Regina M. Adams

Gifts from God

You're tall and wide!
I'm sort and skinny
There's nothing wrong with that.
Where the perfect match.
So no matter what shape or size you are,
there's always a match for you.

Peggy Chambers, 12 years old

We Shall Be Free

From "The Trail of Tears," began the bitter struggle to survive,
Suffering on through the long, dark, and stormy years;

These people of a nation within a nation, boldly try to stay alive,
Their strong heritage persisting to quell their fears;

Reaching far and wide, from the Appalachians in the east,
Across the rivers and plains to the Rocky Mountains of the west;

These proud American Indians who once flourished on this earth,
Are now struggling desperately, but courageously, to exist;

Ever trying to survive on lands that barely keep them alive,
Believing that someday, somehow, they once again will be free;

To be unshackled from the anguish of want, hunger and grief,
Relieved of the impact of past oppression and injustice for all to see;

Enlightened by the unselfishness and compassion of many,
A brief relief from despair, the drop of a grateful tear;

With their heads unbowed, they pray the time is drawing near,
From the valleys to the mountains they will exclaim, and all will hear . . .

"Free At Last! Free At Last! Free At Last!"

John T. Hannah

Bigotry

Black, white, red, green,
What do all these colors mean.
Who's to say which is best,
And why it's above all the rest.
If all you look at is one's skin,
You may miss their colors within.
For this behavior there is no excuse,
Bigotry is a form of abuse.
Any racism is an injustice to all,
Whether you are black, white, big, or small.
Just like slavery was abolished,
All forms of bigotry should be demolished.
Bigotry has been passed through generations,
And the damage has been a continuation.
How can equality stay so sacred,
When there is so much violence and hatred.
Prejudices starts while one is young,
Before it's discovered the damage is done.
To this poem there shall be no sequel,
For God created all men equal.

Shannon Elsey

True Love

As high as a mountain
Our love stands true
Dashing through the fields
Her kiss as wet as dew
For clouds of Happiness
Rain drops of Joy
Today is a blessing for both girl and boy
The great Heavens are up above
No one can take the place of my true Love

Robert Edward Crowley

So It Is

From the seed springs forth the seedling,
Which then grows into a tree.
The seasons give it character,
As it strives for maturity.
Its rings record its history,
From the beginning to the end.
Each year growing on the one before,
So it is with trees . . . and boys . . . and men.

R. G. Andersen-Wyckoff

Precious Grieving

The valley gets deeper, and deeper and deeper.
How could the love and companionship
Of one man have been so much a part of me?

Commitment, yes. Trust, devotion and love.
We shared. We cared. We gave and we received.
Good times, tough times, we had them all,
But God had sealed us, and we were one.
We were humans, not saints,
But humans, devoted one to the other.

And as the years went on
The bond became stronger
Our love, our respect, our caring
Was such a part of each of us
Without question our oneness was real
And our lives were each a part of the other.

Now he has left this earthly plane.
My heart is sore and is filled with pain.
But not for long, for his spirit lingers,
And is calling me
To join him in eternity.

Janet B. Brewster

Words

Words of love and words of hate
I hope my words are not too late
Words of hope and words of praise
Mine are more of praise these days

Love and honor are spoken in the South
These words flow easily from the mouth
Definition and meaning are given no thought
Just the things these words have bought

Jealousy and hate are words for another
Not my words in this life are in any other
Trust and love are words for this time
Make them part of you they're part of mine

Marriage and Divorce are opposite things
Wonderful memories a marriage brings
Divorce is sad and full of sorrow
Make sure today brings a tomorrow

These are words I've used a lot
Some are good and some are not
Make all your words pleasing to God
And when it's time He will give you the nod

Bill C. Woods

Ode To William

Cancer has taken you away from Daddy and Mommy and
Samantha makes three.
I know that the disease left you many days of not feeling too good,
I hope you understood.
That we did what we felt was right you see,
We couldn't see you going through all the needles, chemo,
radiation and misery.
You meant too much for us to do that to you.
Why couldn't it just be the flu?
Then we would have known what to do.
We were by your bed to the end.
You didn't know it that you were not only a son,
But a good friend.
Now that you have left us and are in heaven above,
We want you to know you will always be loved.
You are now free as free can be,
From all the world's cruelty.
But remember you will always be in our hearts.

Christine S. Easley

Only In Dreams

I hold your hand, and tell you how I feel
I look in your eyes, and see me loving you.
I hear your soft words, and know you are real
Then I wake up and I wonder, where are you

Through the long nights, holding you while you sleep,
Feeling your softness, reminds me of clouds,
Were you touched by an angel, just to be with me?
I'm looking, I'm waiting, again I wonder where are you.

I don't know your name, or where you live,
All I can hope for, that soon our paths will cross
Are you searching for me from your place so far?
Do you dream of me, and hope this life won't be a loss.

I talk to you often, throughout the long day
If only you could hear, then I'm sure you'd know
This love I've been saving, would all be for you
If only I didn't have to wonder, where are you.

Larry Stoddard

Love Was Here

There no other love because it's all about you. You
took my heart and whispered the many ways to turn me on all
night long. If I gave my heart to you and I gave my love to
you, would you love me just for tonight or for always? I ask
you that question because I'm so in love with you, and your
love is so amazing. I heard you talking in your sleep and I
asked you how could you call her baby? You wasted your time
on these precious feeling of mine. Why does it hurt so bad
now that the love is gone. Don't leave me, I need your love
because you're my joy. What will I tell my heart after the
final goodbye.

Morissa Lynette McKellery

Untitled

Laughter, from your lips covers my ears like silk covers
your skin at night. As you ease to my bedside
and inquire, with only the gazed look in your
eyes to warn me, love is near, very near.

Over-joyed am I as I can see how being with you gives
me feeling, emotions unlike any that I have shared
with anyone else. Emotions of strength, security and
happiness, that only true love could bring a man like
me, From a special lady, A

Very special lady such as you Maria. Time can only
hold the dearest for you and I. I can see how being
away from you is so damned uneasy but . . .

Enough, that is enough. I need not torture myself nor
have light of day to see our love. I need only close my
eyes, and open my heart and fill it with the precious
thoughts and memories I have of you. That is love, true love.

Anthony L. Dean

My Love

My love for you will not wilt
like the roses that mother nature
once built.
My thoughts of you will not set
like the dying sun I once met.
My eyes will not glance upon another
and say to you good-bye forever.

The wilting roses, the dying sun,
therefor the good-bye kiss will never come.
I Love You

Danny E. Cisneros

A Child's World

A child's smiling face
can bring happiness to a woman and a man.
To hug their little bodies
and hold their little hands.

Kiss their skin so gently
and hold them when they cry.
Let them know that they are loved,
never to wonder why.

Look into their eyes,
what is it that they see?
A rainy day full of sunshine,
or beautiful brown leaves on a tree?

A child is always hopeful,
unless there is reason to doubt.
Stop all the senseless abuse and harm,
some know what that's about.

Give children a chance
and they'll give their love to you.
Let them share their little world
and enjoy their sky of blue.

Lisa D. Hensley

I Am

I am the man that walk with a cane
I am the man who seems insane
I am the child that cry at night
I am the darkness that causes some fright
I am the sunshine that bring the light
I am the black man who's come a great distance
I am the klansman who put up resistance.
I am the Gentile, I am the Jew
I am the confusion when you don't know what to do
I am the puzzle you try to put in place
I am the struggles you have to face
I am your ups and your downs
I am love, spread me around
I am your courage at the point of defeat
I am the last entity you will meet.
When you face despair just call my name
I will always be there just because "I am."

Montgomery Wright

Korea 1951

When the commies invaded Korea, we asked MacArthur why.
He said you are American soldiers, you are here to fight or die.

The road to Tague was mighty rugged.
  There we fought many hours a day,
and the commies kept right on pushing
  but they paid for every step of the way . . .

It was there that we got our reinforcements,
  they turned and started to run.
There was mud and blood mixed together from Tague to the Hon.

There they made their stand and started fighting.
  They held for days and nights.
Then they tied our buddies hands and shot them,
  and headed for the hills that night.

We prayed to God to help us, to push them on beyond.
Beyond the thirty-eighth parallel,
  and there that battle was won.

Now some of you think this war is over
  and that the battles we have won.
But there's just one soldiers opinion.
  The war has just begun

Leslie B. Dale

Not The Same

Ever since you left, my life's a living hell,
whenever you left my self-esteem fell.
And I remember the happy days,
when you helped me through that certain phase.
When I thought that world had let me down,
you said there was no reason for a frown.
At first I couldn't believe you were gonna die,
I tried to be strong and tried not to cry.
And now that you're not here with me,
it seems that no one else has the key.
They key to my heart that you had,
to be close to me when I was sad.
And now I don't hear your sweet voice call,
telling me to be careful and not to fall.
I miss the way you would kiss my cheek,
late at night when you thought I was asleep.
I miss your eyes and flowing hair,
I even miss your warning stare.
Being with you would be better than fame and I'll
finish with saying, "It's Just Not The Same!"

Alexis Irons

Megan

Down by the meadows over through the waterfall I catch a
glimpse of love in a picture of you and suddenly my heart
is pounding away like a drum I get this way sometimes when
I think of you

My thoughts are so erratic my loins they scream for
passion and peace things I can not imagine in anything else
in your eyes are shadows echoes of things that's been long
gone I see it all so don't be afraid

The moon the sun the stars the jazzman blows in the dark
your smile is etched in my brain I just can't explain

Of all the girls in the world you are the one that makes
me feel like I've never felt before I don't deserve
your love take my soul be careful with it we'll runaway
somewhere far away

Coltrane plays in the dark as you take hold of my heart
I'm putty in your domain I just can't explain

Jared Silveira

A Year Has Passed

It hardly seems a year that you are gone
and yet, at times it seems so very long.
Everything has changed. The children are getting taller;
but now we live in a house that is much smaller.

I still haven't learned to set a place for three.
Your chair is there — empty — staring at me.
Life goes on for sure, that saying is true;
but darling, a year away from you, and yet, I'm so blue.

We needed you, why did you have to go!
I'm sure he could have waited 50 more years or so.
Tell him how lonesome we are with you away;
Tell him I don't know how to go from day to day.

Your favorite sayings keep slipping through from time to time;
"Wisdom and If" . . . but somehow, now just have no rhyme.

"If" I could keep my head when all about me
It sure would help to make it better for us three;
But somehow "wisdom" isn't there for me to see,
And you are what is needed to make it be.

It hardly seems a year that you are gone;
and yet, it seems so very very long.

Ann R. Misenhimer

For My Children

In all the storm's we've been through,
The moves and unsettledness, you've always brought me
smiles and a warmness in my heart.

Debra was so funny when she cut her hair above her ears,
and, Everett didn't like his name, so we had a "David" then.

Jim's biggest story, was when he disappeared, and said;
"The devil shot his arrow's and hit me, and I forgot
where I should be."

Linda, when I was out of town, found my key's for goodness
sake. And took my car for a joy ride, when she was
hardly in her teens.

I hope you won't forget the fun things, the picnics, swims,
and family times. When Santa came to our house, and,
the ranch that we lived on.

You have family's of your own now, of which I'll always
be a part. I'm so proud of each of you, and know that
God had blessed me from the start.

Always care for each other, even when you disapprove.
For we will always be a family, just like we started new.

Mary E. Bryden

Teacher Overtime

Teacher overtime, not a magical rhyme
but a kindness that comes from the soul.

An afternoon walk, a quiet hall talk
and the difference between a half and a whole.

A bright, sunny smile stretching long as a mile
an occasional helpful hint.

Taking time from your day to help in a way
that in the future we'll benefit.

An encouraging grin to get out and win
or give it all that you've got.

You help us grow through the years to know
the lessons you carefully taught.

Most importantly of all, when I walk through the halls
and the smell of learning fills the air.

I know that when I need helping or sharing; kindness or caring . . .
within the teacher's overtime, they will be there.

Drew Beard

The Brother I Never Had

I was born, and you wouldn't have me.
As I grew, you wouldn't lose me.
Picking on me or taking up for me.
Always, you were there.

You had me on wheels before I had shoes,
And with you I would always be
Watching you be a goof
Or occasionally, falling into a garbage can.

You taught me many things,
Things I will never forget.
I look up to you in many ways,
Ways that will never be met.

The meaning of brother
Holds more than that of uncle.
And for that reason
This will always be true . . .

In this world,
You are my uncle.
But in my heart,
the brother I never had is you.

Katrina Cannon

Mistake

Spend the rest of your life
Looking over your shoulder
Wasting time while
You're getting older

Third world war
And all the kid's gone
What you think you did right
Turns out was all wrong

We're finally alone
With 10,000 other friends
Wished away the earth
So the sky never ends

Seems you've smashed your glasses
Now you can't see right from wrong
Impatient for the light to change
From red to green to gone

I don't know what to tell you
The decisions that you've made
I suppose if it wasn't meant to kill you
The memories would fade

Marcia Perez

Untitled

They held my mother's precious heart in white glove-covered hands,
Performing major surgery only they could understand.
As I paced the halls and sat and prayed and waited for the call
I wondered if they realized the greatness of this all.
Did the doctors and the nurses who do this every day
Know just how important that woman in there lay?
Did they know that she's my mother, the angel God gave me?
Who's always been there for us all and who should always be?
Did they touch her heart with caring hands the way hers always were?
Did they kiss away her tears of pain and gently comfort her?
I wish that I had been there to tuck her into bed,
To tell her it would be OK, and kiss her on her head.
The hours that we waited seemed forever, so we'd pray
Please let us have our Mom, our friend for just another day.
When finally the doctor told us mother was alright,
We hurried in to see her and held her hand so tight.
The years that I was growing up I knew were special then,
But something of this magnitude makes you think again.
My childhood was wonderful, my family like no other,
And now each day above all else, I'll thank God for my mother.

Julie Jackson

Lead

One day it all made sense
Why the air was so intense
How the marbles fell so fast
Why the dark shadows were cast

Before I even turn around
All the colors change to brown
Snowflakes kiss the lips of time
The wisest words come from a mime

The dead don't understand the beauty they possess
Only the bluest flame can feel their distress
The secret lives within the flesh
When the end begins, it churns afresh

The deepest abysses of the mind
Can't repress what we don't want to find
When one thought swallows the other whole
Aberration begins to take its toll

Pain is the best teacher I know
Without her destiny would push depression off the edge of low
I miss the days when simple really meant what it said
But that was forever before my soul sank like lead

Jamie Boochard

116

A Wish

The things I wish, may not be
I was confused, and could not see.
God was with me, from the start
I just couldn't see him, I wasn't smart

He caught my hand, and guided me
I didn't stop struggling, to be free.
He kept telling me, he was here,
I know I doubted, because I had fear.

God is life, to me and you,
He never wants us, to be blue.
We walk with Jesus in our hearts each day,
We need not ever worry, about the way.
When we fall, he picks us up,
Let us drink, from life's saving cup.
Put your trust, in God's own hands.
The reward is, His heavenly land.
My life is His now, and everyday
My wish is to deserve Him I pray.

Linda G. Dubroc

I Love My Jimmy

I love my Jimmy even tho he's far away
I love my Jimmy more each day
No better can I find
My Jimmy is good and kind
I'll always love him
Even tho he's far away
But this I know
I know he loves me too
I love my Jimmy thru and thru
He'll be back some day
I hope that day is soon
I'll run into his arms and we'll kiss beneath the moon
I'll always love him even tho he's far away
But this I know, I know he loves me too
I love my Jimmy thru and thru

Mary Naomi Glissen

Our Country's Son

In the misty dim light of dawn,
I saw him standing there
Like a sentry, he stood at attention,
Staring out in the distance-seeing nothing.

In his mind, he's still fighting,
In that land so far away,
Hearing the sound of guns, the screams,
Sees so many of his comrades falling.

He can't live for the future,
Never to hear his childrens' laughter,
Never to hear the wind in the trees,
Or see his aging mother's tears.

Every morning and at twilight,
He stands there on that hill,
Still fighting for his country,
A Mother's Son, our Country's Son.

Genevieve DePaulis

Winters Snow

Through the cracked glass of winters past,
where the cool air still flows.
Memories of what we were,
never seem to go.
Feelings of your warm touch,
surround my very soul.
The essence of my being,
melts in the winters snow . . .

R. Johnston

Christmas Eve Without You

Christmas use to be my favorite time of
year, exchanging gifts, and caroling, and spreading
Christmas cheer, but Christmas time this year
won't be the same to me, though I'll smile and
pass out gifts, and hang the star atop the tree.
I'll try to make it happy, cause the children
don't understand the pain I feel inside, but Christmas
eve without you will be a grief that's hard to
hide. But somehow I'll get through it, and then
it will be Christmas day, I'll rejoice at the birth
of my Saviour, but I'll cry cause he took you
away. I'm thankful for the time we had and
I know you're in a better land, but Christmas
eve without you will be so hard to stand.
We'll put the tree where you liked it
making sure each build burns bright and clear,
and I'll see your smile in the tinsel, and I'll
know that you're always near.
Merry Christmas Mama.

Paulette Smith

Weather Any Storm

You can weather any storm, hold on tight as you take flight
Look to the North
and you will see a rainbow of light

Yes, to weather any storm, you must expand out of the norm
the flight and a fight for what's right
will bring you to realize the blithe

As darkness descends followed by the scorn
the fears and tears will be followed by the dawn
look to the right for you will see the light
as you take flight.

As you emerge, you will feel the erg
of strength and clarity
that came as change
without shame

So hold on tight as you take flight
for the storm is harsh and cold
you may feel the intensity of the old

To weather any storm let your spirit take form
Look to the North and you will know what's right
for there is the light within your sight

Sandie Scheingold

Holidays

Holidays are a fun time of the year, we get together and we cheer,
From Christmas, to Valentines Day, to Thanksgiving too,
And on Halloween many people say boo!
Holidays have special meanings for everyone,
It's a time to gather and have so much fun,
Santa comes on Christmas to hand presents if you're good,
On Easter the Easter Bunny comes and hides eggs as best as he could,
Valentines Day is to give gifts or a
Kiss to the person you love the most,
On Independence Day you hang outside a flag on your post!
Holidays are celebrated all around the world,
From United States, to Asia, to Australia, and to Ireland,
We don't know all the countries celebrations,
But wherever you are you must have great ambitions,
Just remember holidays are very special in everyone's heart and eyes,
There are many questions we don't know like how, when, or whys,
I'd wish to tell you all the Holidays
I love from here to there and above but,
I have to go my friend and remember again that holidays come and go,
Just smile and don't ever feel low!!
Smile and have happy holidays!

Michelle L. Chase

Time

When you're happy, time can soar
like a proud eagle with out stretched wings,
going faster and faster.
When you're sad, time can hurt and deprive you,
like a wounded sparrow with food dancing in front of its eyes —
but it can not reach.
When you're proud, time can lift your spirit,
like a chick taking its first flight.
When you're depressed, time can mock you,
like a snake stealing a helpless bird's young.
When you're bored, time stands still.
When you're excited, time slips through your fingers, like water —
too slow for water, but too fast for you,
like a bird trying to escape to its first seconds of freedom.

Tamara M. Wilson

God Is Love

I love you God for all that you've done for me. For
my love for you will always be. Getting me home safe
helps me to love you more. Giving me your warmest shower
of love is what I really adore.
So I will always remember you and cherish the day. Because
you always brought love my way. You caress me and hold me
near. And, you erase away my greatest fear. Therefore God,
I want to tell you I love you, because my love for you will
always shine so true

Patrice C. Austin

Waiting

Watchful at the prow, watchful at the bow.
Cardinal, the four, vigilant you see.
The cold arctic wind,
the Caribbean breeze,
the ghost of pungent cheer,
God's none shall appease.

False hopes and false pretenses
never more to be.
The storm is over, the kingdom come,
rest yourself in me.
Your mind, I'll never let go,
but your dreams shall never fail.
The brilliance of the sun,
you too, must always sail.

Heather K. McCarren

Campin'

We packed up the coolers, the stove, and the tent
Got into the van and away we all went
Our destination, a nice quiet spot
Where it isn't too humid, it isn't too hot
'Cause we're all for camping to bring us together
We'd just rather do it without any weather
Oh, we'll drive for hours to find the right place
That one perfect campsite without hint or trace
Of evidence humans have ever been there
That sentiment truly goes double for bear
'Cause they'll cause you trouble and make your life hard
Even though uninvited, you're in their back yard
For they're only doing what they like to do
Which is taking a couple of freebies from you
Marshmallows, chocolate, cookies, or cake,
Hamburger, sausage, meatloaf, or steak
They're really not picky when they come to call
As a matter of fact they just might take it all
When they've taken everything they'll leave you alone
So glad there's a Taco Bell on the way home

Darrell Wagenman

Never Ending Struggle

From the beginning I was told to be strong person in life
Even when things around you are not going just right.

Every time you move up the stairs of life two or three steps
Someone's lurking around to knock you down and throw dirt on your rep.

My expectations in life are to be successful and enjoy my time here
But there's so much evil around us the end's oh so near.

I pray day after day and cry night after night
Would you understand my pain if you were in my shoes living my life?

I live by the grace of God and call on the Lord for help
They say "Never Give Up or Never Give Out," I must remember for myself.

I don't want to be filthy rich in this such so sorry blue-collar life
Just want to be happy enough not to hurt with me and my wonderful wife.

Remember people are going to hate you for whatever you do
So read up on the Book of Knowledge make them mad at you and improve too.

You always learn keep your foes close and your friends real far
Cause those who know your vulnerability leave permanent scars.

In this wonderful world of no love and heartache and pain against all odds,
Wondering day to day will I get laid off or get a reduction in force at the job.

It's not hard to explain my pain, work, go to school to improve you can juggle
So one day we can be happy and say goodbye to the Never Ending Struggle.

Eric L. Chapman

Within Me

Why do I seek to achieve the unachievable
Stretching and reaching for the unreachable
Striving to be something I am not
Someone I will never be?
I am me.
I need not strive to be perfect
But to make the most of me
The me that my Heavenly Father created
Mediocrity — no.
Perfection — no.
Growing, changing, struggling, trying
Tears many tears
Not for the unobtainable
For the attainable
The unfolding and molding of me
All I have and need is within me.

Laurel K. Ihde

Death Before Dawn

Death before dawn awaited me
At that fateful daybreak.

Death had seized my daughter,
She was no longer awake.

Death before dawn was lingering,
Like mist above the lake.

Death was close by when I received the call,
"Lord, this must be a mistake!"

Death before dawn ushered me to her,
My eyes tear-filled and opaque.

Death was on her face as I pleaded,
"Lord! My daughter, awake."

Death before dawn prevailed o'er the years,
Molded by the drugs she did take.

Death is my unwelcome companion
As sense of this suicide
I endeavor to make.

Don L. Foster

Daddy

He listened to me and what I had to say, with such interest in his mannerism that he made me feel very important. His way of handling such trivial, small little episodes in my life, allowed me to be free and trusting with him. I learned he could make everything better for me from colds to babies. He made my babies feel important and again made me feel so great for giving life to a new generation. He taught me to be calm, to have faith, to be at peace with myself and those around me. To be thankful, to appreciate what nature had to offer.

His laugh was hearty, his hug was a bear's. He loved kids, dogs, sports and fishing. He was a gambler at heart with a streak of luck that made you know he was smart. His philosophy of life was hard to beat. His attitude made one want to set goals and make them. His approval made you feel so important, intelligent, beautiful and content. Even his anger made one feel they had accomplished something good. He was seldom angry; he was to busy living, laughing, and loving to waste time that way. He was always there . . .
He was Daddy!!

Gertrude Wells

What, When, Why

What if the birds stopped their singing?
    What if the sky turned to gray?
What if the sun just stopped shining?
    What if the world went away?

When will we all go to heaven?
    What will it be like up there?
Who'll be the one to judge us?
    As not many seem to care!

Why is our world like this?·
    Why must the hurt have to be?
Why is there so much suffering?
    Why can't people see?

This is the world we live in.
    We made it what it is.
For only we can change it,
    So the good Lord can forgive.

Thomas Darragh

The Dream

Out of the darkness appeared a bright light
There was a sudden chill of both wonder and fright.

Alone she stood out in the wind so cold;
No one around, not a hand to hold:

Shivering, she slowly knelt upon the beach;
Wonder what the light would teach:

Through the light came a loud shocking sound;
It trembled about the earths precious ground:

Scared and cold a tear dropped from her eye;
Looking up a figure seemed to fall from the sky:

Wondering what the object could possibly be; straining to look not able to see: Then standing before her there was a man;
Not saying a word only holding out his hand:

Softly he spoke "for you I will care";
He said life is what they would share: she slowly stood to turn away;
He shouted "come back, I need you, please stay":

He stared directly at her and started to cry;
He whispered the words softly, "for you I shall die":

The light was gone she heard a silent scream;
She called to him then realized it was all a dream:

Michelle Gerbershagen

The Genuine Mexican Plug

When I was a tenderfoot out in the west,
To be like the others, I did my best.
I invested in spurs and new high-heeled boots.
I laid it all over the local galoots.

I even wore six-guns both starboard and port
To show them I might be an awful mean sort.
I cut quite a path topped out in sombrero,
A real greenhorn, but a handsome vaquero.

I went to the stable to acquire a steed.
The stableman said, "I have just what you need."
He reached for my arm, pulled me close with a tug,
Said, "Friend, get a Genuine Mexican Plug."

He charged twice the price but I could not resist.
On the best of the lot I had to insist.
The horse was led out and then held fore and aft
While I climbed aboard to show off my craft.

When I hollered, "Let go," that demon exploded.
He bent to his work to get me unloaded.
He bucked and he twisted, he pranced and he danced.
In that wild beast, I was no longer entranced.

He ate up my fortune in tons of baled hay
'Til an innocent pilgrim passed by one day.
I paid him ten dollars without even a shrug
To tow 'way that Genuine Mexican Plug.

Robert C. Kelly

Confession

Pick up the hurt and move on with your life —
Keep going until you end the strife.
Think of a place where you'll be one day —
Make a new life and lead the way.
Be an individual, think as one —
Until the end when your task will be done.
Try to hide the pain that's going on with you —
Smile and fake it as you normally do.
Keep on going, don't stop until you've won —
When the end is over, don't ever look back, just run.
Drown the tears in your sorrow —
Wake up to a new tomorrow.
See the sunshine through the rain —
Keep your brain thinking, so you won't go insane.
Try not to give up, don't ever quit —
Gold your head high, don't fall into the pit.

Debra J. Kruger

Silent Pain

Absorbing the spills of one's mouth.
Consuming other people's trash.
Never throwing out the garbage.
Letting it pile up,
Until you can't find your way out.
Stuck in the middle of pain.
Carried down from one generation to the next.
Mid evil gadgets are a pleasure party.
For the words of people often kills.
Slowly and torturously,
Suffocating the child within us.
Never acknowledging the pain they caused.
Apologizing as if every things been mended.
Until the next time,
Then their words are repeated.
While the wound was left open.
Slowly infection set in.
Making you vulnerable, weak and withdrawn.
Consumed completely thru.
Finally you're totally destroyed.

Pam Clark

The Aspiring Poet

Alone in the woods where the moonlight glow,
Casts its blue color on fresh-fallen snow.

For miles and miles silence abounds,
Tranquility, to me, is what surrounds.

Profound thoughts occur to me,
Deep-seated thoughts of what I'd like to be.

I would like to write about how I feel,
About how I can make my dreams become real.

About the pull that I feel to write a word,
So that the voice of a poet may be heard.

To form a sentence with lyrical sound,
That the dreams of my heart might be found.

To give wings to words and pour out my soul,
To take half-formed thoughts and make them whole.

To drink in life and gain inspiration,
And give the thoughts in my head emancipation.

To give the gift of birth no matter how hard it may seem,
To what is in my heart and my soul: my poetic dream.

David J. Theriault

Wicked Indeed

Silently, stealth-like, put a finger to your lips.
For I am causing mischief,
An untied shoe-lace, a bite in their dessert.
For I am wicked indeed.

Everyone thinks I can never be guilty.
I put on a sweet face and give a bright smile.
Hah! Everyone is fooled.
For I am wicked indeed.

This has been working for years!
I have never been caught.
My brain has never thought a good thought.
For I am wicked indeed.

I creep and sneak,
and do my mischief
Suddenly someone grabs my wrist.
"Oh no" I moan.
That's the end of Ms. Wicked Indeed.

Jennifer Ruiz

Sad Clown

The wind blows through the mountains flinging echoes through the trees
In the darkness your deception brought me to my knees
At the water's edge the steam rose in columns to the sky
Leaving me with nothing more than the word, "Goodbye."

Beauty takes on many faces as she goes away
Summer comes to warm the springtime in the passing of a day
When I'm lost I hear you breathing within the hollow air
As though the thoughts you hid you now will gladly share

I hear your voice as I wander through the darkest night
I keep your memory around to bring me second sight
Candles flicker in the window as I look away
The sun is rising, chasing darkness as I walk away

There is no home, there is no hope within my frozen heart
Love is like a Satanic angel tearing me apart
But the Devil's just an apparition of emotions kept inside
And God has become the truth from which I now must hide

The sad clown cries to himself as he turns to dust
On a garden wall upon the red brick and the rust
The walls have fallen into ruin, the foundations torn away
As I lie awake and drift through another day

Eric Wincentsen

Nameless

Alone I sit in the darkness. I am secluded deep within,
from all worldly things. I rest contentedly, withdrawn
in my own hole. Repeatedly I sense a movement, I look . . .
and there is nothing. Silent stirrings of Them hidden
all around me, surrounding. They linger about, striking
at me, filling me with terror. And my soul shivers. I
feel them examine my body and soul, exploring me all
over, inside and out, constantly taking me, watching me
and then knowing me. Oh God the torture. I teeter on the
edge of sanity as I start to shake uncontrollably dreading
whatever is drawing near and yet . . . the need for pain is
lusted. I move towards the unfamiliar mist of darkness,
afraid. In front of me unseen and unheard, the dark image
enraptures me and forces his powerful maleness upon me,
within me. O this wretched soul, this never-ending
discomfort the complete and utter torture. I deem myself
here . . . Forever

Cara M. Hazen

Lost

Slight of hand, you play the game.
Warning glance, it's not the same.
You leave your little world behind,
Strike out to see what you can find.

Alone against all odds, you play,
And reaching for another day,
You grasp the air and nothing more
And cringe, 'cause you know what's in store.

In shadows, the grim reaper lurks.
You try to fight, but nothing works.
He strips your senses, blocks your mind,
And wraps you till you can't unwind.

The pressure all becomes too great,
And when you're sure, you hesitate.
It snaps your little mind and then,
You turn around and start again.

Bill Quinn

Friends

Tall grasses covered our laughter
in moments
we lay silent as the clouds, eyes closed
dwelling
on spicy woodland scents
listening
to the voice of the
teasing, bubbling creek —

"Come out," she sang,
"come out of your hiding place
and run with me."

Tonya Boston-Sagar

As You Sleep

As dreams circle your mind, I stroke your lion hair and dream
thoughts of my own

I move my hand with the gentlest of touches, as not, to alter a
moment of slumber

So that, my vision of happy times will flow to real fantasy for
you to see

You twitch your nose, like something has disturbed, your inner vision
and pause only for a moment with my touches

So that, the distress will not wake a peaceful sleep and within an eye flash

I see, that, the dream has brought a smile to your face, as you sleep

Wesley Nicholson Jr.

The Dragon

Legend has it that the Dragon is dead
That the sword of St. George took its head
I believe that the Dragon is alive and well
And he is making the world a living hell
The Dragon can be seen in the sky
Flying above every abused child who cries
The Dragon is present for every war
He walks the streets with the drug dealers and whores
The Dragon will devour us on the final day
So we all better get on our knees and pray

Robert P. Reed Jr.

Walk With Me

Every morning when I wake, I open my eyes and say,
Thank you Lord for giving me yet another day,
To walk amongst you footsteps and always feel your care,
To know that when I feel alone I'll always find you there.

You find a way to speak to me in everything you send,
Sometimes I may not listen, but you'll speak to me again,
And never are you selfish, for always you will give,
The things I need to get by in life, the love for which I live.

So when I feel real needy, I'll pray to up above,
For you always seem to listen and send a little love,
And when I walk alone in life and my path is hard to see,
You never let me down my Lord, you come and walk with me.

Richard Belziti

A Dream

It's a dream of peace throughout the world.
A dream that in which weapons will be forgotten.
Wars will stop, fighting will stop.
Everyone will love.

A dream of all the colors living in harmony.
Racism and prejudice would no longer exist.
Petty differences would be solved without consequences.
There would be no existing hatred.

A dream of many people long past.
Generation after generation it has been thought of.
Though not a person has spoken their mind.
They all had a common thought.

The dream is in the future,
The very distant future of the world.
Far from ever happening for our children's children.
Farther away than any of the distant stars.

A dream that is only in the dreams of the night.
A dream that is very unlikely to happen.
A dream only thought of as a wish.
A dream, only a dream that's reoccurring.

Jerrod Rhine

A Friend

A friend is a person of great understanding.
Who shares all our hopes and our sadness, a friend is a
companion who listens with all patience to all of our
plans and our dreams. A true friend can make all our
cares melt away with a touch of their hand or a smile, and
with calm reassurance makes everything brighter. And
makes life always seem more worthwhile.

A friend shares so many bright moments of laughter and
pleasure. A friend is to be cherished, they know all our
hopes and fears and sadness with a closeness that grows
through the years.

That is what a friend is.

LeNor M. Warren

An Artist's Life

People said it was a work of art.
"How did it come to pass?", they asked.
The responses were many,
Answers few.
To tell all would lose the passion;
To not, would it cheat them?
Then again the work spoke for itself.
It would tell the story, the love, the desire.
But like a pitcher, you're only as good as your last game.
The work has become a history, a visual documentation.
Now a new idea will spring forth.
And once again the studio will beckon.

Karl J. Kuerner

Love — To Go

(In Memory of Vernon L. Kimbrough, 7-29-27 — 7-19-96)
As I sit here wrapping gifts
At this Christmas time alone,
I realize I have one less to wrap,
Because God has already called you home.
Oh, how much we are missing you,
Because we loved you so,
And so I'll take this Christmas wrap,
And wrap our hearts of love to go.
I know God had a reason to call you on,
You'll have to suffer no more,
And one day soon, we'll meet you there,
On God's celestial shore.

Lorrine Kimbrough

New Life

Creation — under your wings,
atoms circling in delight
Nature perfecting — glorious sight.
Her eyes sparkle, cells are merging
A divine glow — like a heavenly kiss
A miracle is done. Prevailing bliss
treasure of the womb, rapture during its grow
Spirit, flash of fire, a gift of desire.
Guidance from above, resurrection
Nature's force, perfection
  — A child —

H. H. Zemmrich

A Place Of Peace

A journey to a magical place
Where racism has no place.
No matter what your color,
We'd all be united like sista's and brotha's

As magical essence flew behind
No guns, fights, or time bombs to wind.
There'd be no hate, only kindness and love,
the skies would be filled with eagles and doves.

There'd be no night were horror be found,
No demons, no bullies, no tremors in the ground.
Spirits of only kind and good,
Would be expressed by neighbors, just as it should.

We'd have no worry of violence at school,
Everyone smart, no one a fool;
No stupid stunts to impress the wrong crowd,
No villains of hate, no preachers too loud.

We'd all stand united in a circle of faith,
Sensitivity drawn, no tears to waste;
In a dream world this only exists,
But if we all work hard we can accomplish this myth.

Jonathan D. Scott

Turkey

It was Thanksgiving Day,
  and I didn't know what to say.
I'd never eaten turkey in my life,
  and I didn't think I would like it.
I'd only seen its picture, and how it was.
  It had colorful feathers, and a little long nose;
  just like the long red fire hose.
Tears come to my eyes, when a turkey dies.
  'Cause it's not fair not to care
  about something you eat as your meal.
You just can't imagine,
  how it feels to be killed . . .

Amaras Zargarian

Believe In Yourself

When I was young I used to smoke. First cigs, and pot,
  and then tried coke.
My teenage years came rushing by, with all these things that
  get you high.
Peyote, mushrooms, LSD, with different names they'd hand to me.
It seemed like everyone my age, was going through a certain stage.
Before you knew it, I was there, just like my friends without a care.
I started drinking alcohol, instead of school we'd hit the mall.
At night we'd sneak away from home, into the night life we would roam.
Until one day I said, "I quit, I want to graduate, that's it!"
And so I switched my goals around, I felt relieved, no longer bound.
I'm glad to say I made it through, believe you can, and you will too!

Ida Ibarra

A Look Through The Windows Of Time

Old woman, old woman, in your squeaky rocking chair,
What stories must be hiding there, behind your vacant stare?
If I looked deep into your eyes, do you suppose that I could see,
A far off misty vision, of the girl you used to be?
Your eyes no longer have that shine, and your hair's a dingy grey,
But if I could see through those windows of time, what would I see today?
Oh, there you are, a pretty young girl, that smells of sweet perfume,
A graceful lass, to make heads turn, when she walks into a room,
I see loves promise in her eyes, framed by sun-lit gold,
Her firm young breast's and shapely thighs, worthy of a center fold,
Ah, sweet and lovely, there's no doubt, just like a movie star,
I bet you really knocked 'em out, in those country music bars,
But old man time's a scoundrel, he makes old out of new,
And he must be a bit of a devil, for what the's done to you,
So I'll leave you now with your empty dreams, and your
  squeaky rocking chair,
Oh, thanks for the movie I just seen, behind your vacant stare.

Ralph B. Campbell

Awakenings

Through the eyes of a child
I found a part of myself,
A part that had left for a faraway place,
The part that tells me who I am.

Through the eyes of a child
This part has returned.
I've embraced it with open arms
Making me see, I am whole.

It was easy to let this part of me go.
Others entered my life, filling the void.

It was through the eyes of a child
That I have reclaimed myself.
Accepting who I am,
Allowing me to give of myself,
Without diminishing the whole.

Deborah H. Clark

My Snow Prayer

Lord, I like a winter day such as this.
The first unexpected snow
covers the fallen leaves and bends
the green and russet branches.
The sky hangs beige-gray
with promise of more.

The highway lies quiet.
Only an occasional whirring of tires
breaks the serene silence.
The birds busy themselves
seeking food.
Thank you for making me wise enough
to buy seed yesterday.
Now they know I am their friend.

The scarlet cardinal
dips his wing in greeting.
The snowbird is dressed for his first banquet.
He's in black tie and tails.

And I sense the sweetness of a new day.

Maxine Dowd Jensen

Flailing Hands

Long skirt and long sleeves,
A dark print with crisp white lace down the front and around each cuff,
The dress envelopes her bony frame.
A polished wooden cross dangles from a black cord around her neck,
Just so no one forgets she's the minister's wife,
She leads such a holy life.

Flat shoes with soft crepe soles, and pointed toes that dart ahead of
Flailing hands that signal everyone to do her bidding, or
  get out of her way — you can never be sure exactly which.
Over sized hands, most expressive when folded in prayer, fingers
  locked onto one another, knuckles protruding like the knobs
on a set of jacks.
Even praying is an act of anguish for her.

Dull gray eyes in a common face framed by a thin grayish braid
  pinned tightly in place.
A smile so wide it practically devours you.
Spittle escapes across her lips, collects in the creases at the
  corners of her mouth,
It's wiped away by a linen handkerchief kept tucked in a cloth belt,
A belt that dare not create a curve in the bony frame for that would
  surely lead to shame.

Carrie Strinsky

I Am A Rose

In Memory of My Beloved Mother, Carey Pek
  I am a rose.
  My delicate petals rustle as the wind blows.
  I am a rose.
  I know when to bud and to bloom and grow.
My beautiful petals I occasionally show.
  I am a rose.
I hardly ever feel pain
I soak up the sun and I drink from the rain.
  I am a rose.
I am both soft and tender.
My leaves are green and my stem is slender.
  I am a rose.
Winter comes and I wither away.
Not to return to the next warm spring day.
  I am a rose.
Soon the first snow will fall.
Then there will be no more roses at all.
  I was a rose.

Mandi Pek

Sins Of The Father

The king and his castle a queen and her fool
A father's alliance a match made in youth
Lost in frustration she loses her soul
Searching for love that she'll never know

She ponders the question with no answer why
Fearing the future and longing to die
Tears on her pillow a child far from home
A life without love is existence alone

Her prayer to the Lord a forgiving request
Her life she has taken with a blade to her breast
Through sins of the father with guilt on his head
A mother's in mourning for the child laid to rest . . .

Randy J. Shaeffer

The Beauty Of Stars
Lies Not Of Themselves In Themselves

In dreams slumber
of moonèd beam gleaming I
encircle the Earth

winds of time exhale
invisible histories of air

clouds of crystalline ice cover the pulsing of stars
who choose   to reveal   not the future   but eternity
revelation beyond understanding

in alert wakening
of sun rayed light
hovering within the realm quietude
I stand feet planted solidly upon the warmed earth

time resides in stillness absolutes yet
breathes   inhales
there is perceptible palpability in air
warmed clouds in molecular dissipation dissolve disappear reveal

the stars concealing   not eternity   but the future
history beyond comprehension   yet
diligent patience informs through wisdom's gracious hoard
without the telling of stars

Thomas Gentille

My Love He Defies

As I look into his eyes,
What a beautiful sight,
But hurtful because of my love he defies.
My love for him grows even when we fight.

In his eyes I can see the pain.
It's burning down deep inside.
In his life it seems like it will always rain,
And high will always be the tide.

Broken before was his heart.
The pain cut very deep.
Sometimes it seems we're worlds apart,
But in my palm his heart I'll always keep.

DaLynn Brown

The Tree

When looking at life overall, it can be compared to the seasons of a tree:
Spring: When a tree takes root and sprouts leaves, so our life begins.
Summer: The leaves blow in the soft breeze and takes nourishment from
the warm summer rain, we then begin to enjoy the years of our lives.
Fall: The leaves are falling and the tree prepares for the end of
     another cycle and our life as we know it begins to wane
Winter: The leaves are now gone and so our life ends — never again
     to enjoy the warm breeze or the misting of the summer rain.

Carol Jean Aldridge

The Thaw

The water moved in; not the rush
of flooded, silted river, but it seemed
an interior lake that had crept inexorably
upward through the roots of trees
filling the dark places of the forest.

The unwary wood farer, entering the thicket
stepped trustingly on the deceitful mold,
seemingly dry or scarcely damp and sank
knee deep in muck and mocking fright.

Struggling loose, he floundered from hammock
to broken branch and rotting tree-stump
and escaped apace.

Alvin Laidley

The Full-Bodied Water

They savor their words, letting them glide gently
over their palates, exacting the sweet ones from
the stale at the touch of their tongues, like fine wine.

He is no such connoisseur. He has no penchant for
orchestrated measure, no haughty regard for the art.
His words fall as naturally as a drop of water upon
a waterfall, cascading down the current of his mind
and plummeting from his lips.

Vulgar utterances to those stirred by more melodic
strings. Yet, his words sing sweet to me. They sing
not to the ear, but rather, to some secret recess
hid within, that answers with a pang of a memory.

I can survive without beauty, but not without sustenance.
So, let those who covet their wine think
me a fool to favor my water and find it no less heady.

Kathleen Grigley

America's Music

The music of America tells a story
In my life, "Mine Eyes Have Seen the Glory"
Over the country bells proudly ring
In my heart, "Of Thee of Sing"

Across the vastness, from sea to sea
Ours to love, "Sweet Land of Liberty"
From earth to moon and on to Mars
Over us all, "Broad Stripes and Bright Stars"

Shout from the mountains, the land of the free
The saving grace, "God Shed His Grace on Thee"
Sing carols and anthems, and soft in the wind
A symphony of Angels will lead us to Him

Rose E. Greene

Wedding Day

I thought it would never get here, my most cherished day.
It will be here sooner than you think, all my friends would say.
So much planning and so much to do, it has to be done for it all
to come true.
All decked out in our wedding attire, many well wishers sit back
and admire.
The lens is focused, the photographer can't miss, now it is time
for our first wedding kiss.
Oh what a gift from our Father above, this thing called marriage
along with love.
He has given us instructions to make it a success, so we don't end
up with one great big mess.
It is the night before and I need my rest, I want to be alert and
at my very best.
So onto my pillow my head I will lay, I'm so excited; tomorrow is my
Wedding Day.

Derek O'Neal

Mother's Lap

You were sitting cross legged on the floor,
the hair dryer cap flowed around your face like a halo.
Warm breezes blowing down from your crown.
I crawled into your lap.
The hair dryer hummed softly.

Your warm hand cupped my face.
I can still hear the quiet sound of the heater blowing,
the faint smell of fingernail polish drying.
The comfort of feeling safe and warm in your arms.

The Vietnam War, the Nuclear Bomb,
The heartache of not knowing if
or when my brother would be sent,
The knowledge that the neighbor boy
would never return home.

Fear of the outside world growing and churning, forever in turmoil,
dissipated in your arms.

Now, I will sit in the quiet of my bedroom
and never underestimate the power of a moment,
when my son crawls into my cross legged lap,
and listens to the quiet humming of the hair dryer.

Rebecca Kelly

Brief Incarnation

You whispered your incarnation
with a positive pink line.
How glad we were to accept the invitation
to be your chosen guides.

Can you hear us choosing your name
as you split, divide, and grow
inside your tiny submarine
surrounded by my rhythmic salty sea?

Basking in new breasts and new belly
I am swollen with love.
My body is our body
My food is our food.

Then with the swiftness
of the migrating butterflies
that now flutter by you left me
trembling in an ocean of pain.

Young teacher, leaving me wiser,
come back soon, but please,
the next time you come,
come to stay.

Michelle Sanders Acquart

Our First Rose Bud

This rose in all its essence
Held high its head in this morning's dew.
Just as on this day eighteen years hence
From my womb another rose grew.

Its stem is likened to life's ways,
Its thorns are life's hard dents;
Its leaves afford the happy days;
Its flower portrays your life's events.

Each perfect petal is a day well spent
With words and acts of kindness.
Of blemished petals we can not be proud
For we have lived that day in blindness.

About to burst into bloom
Is this beautiful rose God left me bear.
May you live each day with this in mind,
Then your perfect petals we all may share.

Carolyn B. McKinney

Who Are You?

Who are you? Rang the question clear.
Who are you and why are you here?

I am here to help, if I can.
I am here to help. It's Heavenly Father's Plan.

And how long is your stay? Will it just be today?
How long is your stay? Will you show me the way?

I plan to stay for many a year. For it takes much time to see
things clear.
I hope to teach you what little I know.
And maybe to help you a little to grow.

I am glad that you came! We need you here.
We'll gladly keep you all those years.

Tho with a body adult, I'm a child you see;
Something I'm afraid will always be.
My walk is halting. My speech is slow.
I pray you can teach me the way to go.

You must be patient gentle and kind if the beauty in me you hope to find.
Look into my eyes and you will see Love, Compassion, Humility.

So let us go. It's plain to see we've just caught a glimpse of Eternity.
One reaches out takes the other's hand.
Together they go, honoring their Father's Plan.

Kelly S. Roe

A Machine Just Like You

When I grow up I want to become a quality built machine just like
you. With a stainless steel heart and metal bars across my soul,
apathy and indifference would be nothing new
I wish I could be like you, oblivious to true emotion, honesty,
caring thoughts, and unconditional love.
I want to learn how to slap sincerity and tenderness in the face
with an aluminum glove
Your empty eyes, your callous nature, and the insensitivity in
your touch wouldn't bother me at all,
If I couldn't feel the stinging cuts and bruises from continually
slamming against your barbed wire wall
But for some morbid reason unknown I feel complete and safe in
your cold and rusted arms.
I've come to accept that one day soon your omnipotence in my
life will bring me fatal harm.
Like one of a robotic vampires' coven, I will not survive unless
you allow me to.
Allow me the opportunity to feed from the crude oil that pumps
through your veins, I want to become a machine just like . . . you

Julie Gillard

Untitled

A single little touch. Oh, so small, but yet so huge.
I walk away still feeling that little sensation of
affection, lingering in the midst of my loneliness.
I lie awake that afternoon, trying to take a nap,
but that feeling of belonging somewhere has left me
to think. I have thought and I have thought. I
can never remember ever giving anyone a little
touch. Nothing big, maybe just a pat on the back
or the touch of a hand. If it makes me feel so happy
inside, I wonder how it would be just to give one away.
So, I hop out of my lonely world, that is oh, so far away.
I am walking again, but in a different way. For I have been given
mission to prove. I must stay alive! I've just turned a corner and
look what I see. It is a young man asleep on a bench.
I draw closer to his side, almost afraid to give away a part of the
sweet touch. But, I push myself forward and kneel by his side.
Open came his eyes as my hand was near to rest on his dirty head.
Frightened I jumped. Then I relaxed. For I knew it had to be done.
Slowly a small little touch came down from my hand. He smiled at me.
For he felt it too. What a simple little touch can do.

Bobbi A. Letsinger

Shades Of America

The green are exploited and no one feels
their fright, while black and white recruit
soldiers to die in the wrong fight

The red, white and blue makes promises and
weeps for the gray, but both faces are dry
post election day

White lightning strikes the men who wear skin
of red and language and culture are buried
with the dead

Beautiful deep blue turns to black and black is
beaten blue, then painted over with green by
those who sue

We highlight our humanity in yellow, we are the
first to aid, while the colors of home dry out
and fade

Lost men sell their souls for gold that
can be strolled ever after, deaf to pale
pleas hypnotized by dark laughter

John McBride

Nemesis

The pencil nib wore down too fast,
tho', truly, the quill and stylus it did best;
and the mechanical one didn't seem to last,
when put to the scribbler's test.

Pens were good, but always leaked,
'til they invented the rolling ball;
but their ink supply did seem to peak,
in the heat of the Muse's call.

The typewriter's try for the poet's dream,
did vastly increase my pace;
but cost me a fortune with every ream,
because I couldn't erase.

And now I curse the button'd knave,
which makes the screen obscur'd;
because I know I forgot to "save,"
as I searched for the PerfectWord.

So what then is the answer?
And woe is me, bemused;
as I try the words to transfer,
tell me, what did Euterpe use?

George S. Converse

Autumn Drive

As tree leaves catch fire in autumntide
A close knit family goes for a ride
To lose themselves in Nature's palace
With little of gloom and much of solace
The blazing season burns gold and red
Driving off summer like beasts full of dread
And rages and roars and oh, what a sight
This inferno whose heat will soon freeze the night
Their breath held captive, a sound breaks their trance
As bushes sway to a fearsome dance
And what's to emerge but a fluffy white cat
"Like wind-driven snow, how about that!"
She meows hello sweetly and contentedly purrs
But none see the feather caught in her fur
"I feared for my darling!" The mother hugs child
"But now I laugh at a notion so wild!"
Good parents hold children and only let go
When menace is gone from above and below
But Nature's nature is to insist
Her progeny perish to persist

Steve Perram

Untitled

I look into the night sky, the threshold to Heaven
and send an S.O.S. to the stars;
Love, come heal me
Hold me and dry my tears;
There's no sanctuary I find
that can hush away my fears;
it seems like ages since the night my heart died
and my feet are cold and wet
from the rivers that I've cried;
I'm calling out to you, my love,
Do you ever hear me?
The lunatic, the lover and the poet,
I am of all three;
Does the wind ever whisper to you?
Do you feel me in the rain?
Has there ever been a moment
when you thought you felt my pain?
The heart that has truly loved never forgets
and a heart that has felt love
and denies love always knows regrets . . .

Thomas Ziniewicz

How The West Was Spun

Floating clouds of glaciers, Atlantis not far below.
The sun sets, a piece of tangerine, piercing the moons glow.
Small cotton candy trees, the fields of summer snow, blanket the
desert sand.
Peacock plumes of grass wave to passers by and
Shroud the still majestic roadside cliffs.
Stripped of its dignity, the mountain side stands barren . . .
waiting for a renewed sparkle of life.
Taking natures fulfillment of life for granted,
We've set in our minds the roots that have been planted.
New growths emerge thirsty, like the finger tips of newborn,
reaching for a mothers breast.
Frozen glass waits for the afternoon thaw to unlock the coated fence line,
While hay bakes like loafs of bread on the farmer's playground.
Mystical shapes float across the sky, whispering messages of
intrigue to grazers looking up high.
Scattered golden leaves permeate the carpet of roaming hills of pine.
The weather and seasons will soon arrive, abrupt change? No!
All in good time.

Mark Bertrand

Annie's Voice

Annie's voice . . . musical . . . magical . . . mellow
  mild . . . mesmerizing

When I listen to her I hear
gleeful, girlish giggles and womanly wisdom

She speaks in sounds sincere . . . soothing
  sassy . . . sensual . . . silly . . . Smart

Annie's voice . . . joyful . . . bright . . . perceptive
familiar and friendly . . . fun loving . . . fundamentally free

When talking I hear her easy . . . effortless . . . heartfelt happiness
  theatrical and therapeutic . . .
  healing and harmonious

  Annie . . . mother earth, sister sunshine, lady lover
   a magnet for the minds and moods of
   meaningful men

  She is . . . determined, delightful, delicately devilish
   — cackles of the mischievous white witch!

Annie's wonderful voice . . . gracious and generous
  buoyant and breathtaking
  echoes of an infinitely loving soul

Ron Rechnitz

Fire

Al Smith has llamas, goats, and a pair of cows;
Al Smith has a pet mouse, 3 pigs, and one large plow.
As you might have guessed, Al lives on a farm.
But the one thing he's missing is a fire alarm.

One day he awoke, due to some heat.
When he jumped out of bed, he burned his feet!
Then smartly, the farmer jumped over the fire,
and found its source, a ripped-apart wire.

He quickly ran out of his small little house,
not forgetting to take his small little mouse.
But unfortunately he found that it was much too late,
to go back inside and get the key to open the gate.

Al Smith found that he was stuck.
He couldn't believe his horrible luck.
Al stood there and cried as flames burned down his farm.
He would still be alive if he had a fire alarm.

Daniel J. Martin

An Hourglass

After time can we change?
Negotiation never seems to work.

How ignorance is taking over
Our future will be no more
United is what we'll never be
Remember what has happened in the past
Given the chance we still might recover
Laughter drowned out by the sound of destruction
After all this madness will there be hope?
See how our time is running out
Songs of hate and prejudice

Courtney Radow

The Quest

She is the center of my . . . attention
I gaze at her with all my . . . admiration
In her heart she has all of my . . . affection
We mirror each others . . . reflection
We create and nurture each others . . . direction
We bring to surface each others . . . sensation
We fathom and aspire each others . . . imagination
We listen carefully and attentively to each others . . .
communication
We understand clearly each other, no need for . . . interpretation
Our simplicity of love is each others . . . justification
The knowing of our souls for each other needs no . . . explanation
We will travel through eternity together on our . . . exploration

Andrew Michaels

'Tis Christmas

Fir trees and pine trees all standing in a row
  Waiting for tinsel, for lights, and a bow;
Tall ones, short ones, it matters not
  Each tree will soon find its own favorite spot
Families laughing and children jumping for joy
  Here's one mama, look daddy, oh boy!
Lights all glowing in colors that shine
  Sprinkled with stardust for me and for mine
It's a time for giving and sharing with all
  A smile, a hug, a telephone call
It takes so little to say "Yes, I care"
  Make someone happy, here, there, everywhere
Gifts of giving of yourself and your time
  They need no wrapping, no bow, but they're just fine
What better gift than to hear someone say
  Good health, God bless, and have a good day
So count your blessings be they big or small
  For sharing loving moments is best of all.

Stella Reed

What For?

In this
black and white world
I sometimes speculate
why are we so full of hate?
Prejudice, racism, violence;
Is this all we have left in a world of defiance?

We strive to survive
in this day and age,
forgetting about each other, creating rage.
Fears and frustrations
only lead to ignorant ways.

Why do we blame?
Every one of us is the same.
We laugh at each other's beliefs
when our opinions don't meet.
We ridicule each other
for our mistakes;
hurting each other, making hearts ache.
We judge each other by our makes.
What for?

Alan Anderson

The Lady In The Water

There is a Lady in the Water
Who speaks with only a smile,
And outreached arms she beckons
For the Heart of a fearful child.

For the Sea is a Mighty Lion,
A roaring, raging, warrior true,
And beneath his claws lie forever silent,
The souls of many we once knew.

Twas by the sea that day,
When the Lion he did reach
To strike a mighty blow,
Hence to still the light in thee.

But in that shadowy darkness,
Time and Motion — they could not stay,
For emerged a Lady bright and beautiful,
And Demons cast away.

Oh so many years have passed
Since that day by the sea,
But I will never forget the Lady in the Water,
And how she delivered me.

Sandy L. Fortson

Departures

It must have been the rain
streaming down the window pane
deceived by glass that trembled at the close, I do not know.
I only know your face
began within the shadows
that swept across the darkness
with your name — and that your form has come tonight,
to fill in every space,
like light that dim and soft
is pulled across a dream.
Here in the silence of the evening
I shall gather close again
all the soft shades of my remembering.
We shall sit together, you and I
beneath the closing of the rain.
You shall understand the tenderness in storms,
and reach with gentle hand to touch the fingers of my dreams.
I shall hold your eyes awhile against
The darkening shape of silence and tremble at
the weeping of the rain.

Marcia Kleinman

Love

Love, you can love always.
There is no barrier of the pouring, the
risks of pain or happiness, because, the
soul is always there for love. Just like
love, it's there to be taken by yourself
and or someone else.
The faith you pray on, is the
will of God, one lies down on.
To hear the soul chirping, is
the faith from afar, in the paths of the
wilderness, where the trees are moving
with the warmth of the soul engrossing in love.
The wetness of the dew, after
a rain storm in the dawn, is about to
change down under the weather. A change
into sunlight beating on the trees.

Ruth Zodeh

If I Could Live Near The Ocean

If I could live near the ocean,
I would be happy, happy as can be.
Everyday I would see the beautiful ocean,
And watch the waves come and go.

If I could live near the ocean,
I would toss my troubles to the waves.
The waves would send them away,
And bring me peace and happiness.

If I could live near the ocean,
I would never complain anymore.
I would sing merrily everyday,
And thank God that I live near the ocean.

June R. Sterling

Born Placed

Culture my brother a heavy morning
Whiter beard — blacker name
Cones a blazin' and some long lost shame
Reverence with the cold hearted
Shiver slightly trying to gain
A sun beam in the window
Beyond the shade
Forget the channel with the news
The beating of your parade
Today is today and full of weight

Mont David Williams

Generation X

I've heard you and other self-proclaimed
X perts talk about us this generation
About how we're so apathetic and tame with no leaders no
X ample no motivation
Quickly you scramble to
X onerate and elevate your position your ideals so platinum and proud
Boasting the politics you were raised with a fought for and you
Cluck your tongues softly for us pitying us because we have no wars to
X cite us unite as no heroes to move us
But I say you don't know us don't know the
X tremes that we live with don't know
ME at all
And so we will continue to be who we are setting our own standards for
X cellence and when I get to where I want to be and have
Tasted all that I care to taste in this life I will know that I have
SUCCEEDED
And you with all your negativity will look at me and see that I am
not
the
X ception but rather the rule

Rosa Bertolini

Great Spirit

The Great Spirit is in us all.
Prowling like a coyote in the forest of your mind.
Searching for the meaning of its existence.

You are looking for that one answer of purpose.
Hidden like a red squirrel in the midst of a buffalo herd.
Perhaps to be revealed by yourself.

To be revealed within your transformation from child to man,
or man to child.
A transformation located within your mind and without your body.

Located in a dream world, enshrouded with the Truth, and formless.
Here is your meaning, intertwined with the pain and horror of
your own extinction.

Odin L. Dwyer

Last Hour

They talk, whispering with excitement
may be it's the last hour.
Children scream in the back corner
to drown all their laughter.
Why do they walk in a daze?
running and moving everywhere
but no where to be found
just when you need them.

Far away in the smoking chamber
ahead of yellow flowers
on the snow white wall,
red wine drops, chicken breast falls,
I'm waiting for a seat; where is the meat?
Plastic smiles on display, and I hear
faint laughter in my ear, but
where'er they, just when you need them.

Vishal Govil

Gift Of Love

Dedicated to my beloved Hubert Wright
On that October night, God took hold of your hand,
He must have had, another very special plan.

Oh my dear beloved, our time was all too brief.
My heart now filled, with such sorrow and grief,

You've been taken, with Gods grace,
I know you're in a wonderful place.

I can't find my way, I ask God every day,
How much longer, will I have to stay?

No answers to my questions, no sun shines in my face,
I feel all the time, so awkwardly displaced.

Fearful of the journey, that I travel now alone,
Darkness surrounds me, God help guide me home.

Be grateful for the people, God has given us to love,
Never take for granted, special gifts from above.

Rita M. Ludeman

My Son

Oh how deep a gaping wound
was left when words of rage were spewed
Ugly words of hatred sown
hurled, spit and spat upon

A Mothers heart in anguish cries
with silent pleas and begging eyes
Can you not forgive and forget
be willing and open to accept me

As I am.

Linda McCrystal

Angels Are Waiting To Transport Me Home

The sounds of both worlds beckon to me,
my children and grandchildren, their faces I see,
the laughter of my great grandchildren I can hear.
The sweet worship of the angel choir wafts through the air,
they are waiting for me to take my place there.

My mansion is complete, it is ready for me,
the promise fulfilled that my spirit be set free,
from the bonds of this temporary shell, being the place I have dwelt,
it is now overcome with age, and this disease I have felt.

Lord may my life be the seed in fertile ground sown,
that my family can follow me to where I have flown.
Though with my sweet Jesus, all of glory to share,
it will not be heaven without my loved ones all there.

Now the desire to fly to heaven so fair,
overcomes me, and I am ready to go there.
On this earth, will I no longer roam,
for Angels are waiting to transport me home.

LaDonna Miller

Grief

Grief is not a burden, it is an integral part of life;
without it we would fall apart from day to day strife.

Grief brings to us at sad times, our soul cleansing tears;
to help us make it through this stage showing our sorrows
and our fears.

Some, show their grief by weeping uncontrollably;
others, hold it deep inside where no one can clearly see.

But, however you choose to show it, be sure you always know,
I'll always stand beside you whichever route you choose to go.

Going through this state of being, knowing exactly how you
feel; know also that I love you and my grief for you is real.

So wear your grief proudly and never be ashamed,
because God is always with you in your joys and in your pain.

Debra Barner-Hatcher

Untitled

To My Dearest Wife, Julia:
'Twas the day before Christmas and I thought I was through
With the holiday business I had planned for my crew
When over the phone came a voice from home
Which said in stern tone come home with a poem.
I am filled with schemes of thoughts I could say
To the girl of my dreams that I see every day
She cares for help Pop day in and day out
Praise from the roof top would I like to shout
But I'd better instead take my paper and pen
So that in storms ahead she can read it again
Oh, onward together we will go through life
No matter the weather 'twill be sweet with my wife
And when it's all over like our fathers we'll be
Resting neath some clover near a lovely tree
'Till then it's a good life and I wish to say
Merry Christmas to my wife in this sincere little way.

Frank P. Meng

Bittersweet

The present dissolves before our very eyes,
And the tangled vein of memory creeps,
Unsummoned, unannounced,
Beautiful and rare in its totality;
Dredged from the depths where it has lain
Cradled against the echo chambers of the heart;
Still wet with tears

Shirley Watson

So Sad

So sad to see a man so weak
Combing through the trash to eat
His makeshift bed a cardboard box
So sad to see a man so lost

So sad his life turned for the worse
A victim of the needles curse
Led into hell by his desire
So sad he fell into its fire

So sad his family mourns their loss
His children too must pay the cost
Their father gone a wife alone
So sad they miss their happy home

So sad to know his tragic past
Now destitute but free at last
He calls the streets his home these days
So sad the price he had to pay

Julia Elliott

My Heart Is Broken; Lord Can You Fix It?

I love you.
The angels look down at you.
The angels glance at you.
They sing you a song.
They praise your goodness.
Why must they take you?
For you are mine.
They cannot take you.
Why does my heart hurt so much,
even though you are at peace?
I guess because I am not.
I miss you.
You are my dear sweet mother.
The mother who protected and loved me.
You did all this without expecting anything in return.
Now you are an angel soaring high.
Lord my heart is broken; can you fix it?

Nichol Hamilton

Mother

My mother is up there,
I am down here.

   She is probably watching over me,
   I wonder what she can see.

Does she watch me sleep,
Or perhaps she watches me weep.

   Does she care about what I do,
   I have no clue.

Does she miss seeing my face,
Does she want me to go to rightful place?

   Does she want me to forget about her,
   Hmm! I wonder.

My dear mother is free,
But does she truly miss me?

   Will I ever see her again,
   As my mother or just as a friend.

She had to die,
But why?

   Will she never take me home,
   That to me will remain unknown.

Lisa Takacs

Trapped

Trapped in a place unknown to me,
I try so hard to escape,
But they do not see.
I let them put fear in my heart,
They are destroying me,
Tearing me apart.
I run so far, so far I hide,
And yet I keep my head up,
I still have my pride.
I try so hard to keep up my fight,
I sleep in the day, I am awake at night.
I try to break this evil chain,
And escape to happiness, to leave my pain.
A black cloud hangs over me,
Making it foggy, I cannot see.
I want to feel the warmth of the light,
I need to break away and leave this fright.

Shannon O'Brien

Surrender

The day was dark, the sun was gone
I could not find my way,
Then the night skies turned to red
For the moon had gone astray —
I groped in this confusion, the path seemed
so far.
I cried aloud as I scanned the sky
to find one guiding star
I shivered in the heat of the deserts
burning sand
My scorched feet stumbled over the
frozen empty land
Now I have no friends and my last
attachment gone
Incomplete surrender before you, I
stand naked to the bone,
Come into the circle of my love, no
longer you must roam.
Your father will protect you
at last you have come home.

Dorris Krusemark

Darkness

It is completely black and no trace of light,
There is nothing you can see in your sight.
Is there anything in the darkness with you,
Is it the boogy man or the lead singer for The Who?
Will it kill you or eat you alive,
Or will it say "How ya doin" and give you a high five?
Is there a monster all hairy and red,
Or is it all in your imagination and in your head?
So I guess we'll never really see,
What's in the darkness with you and me.

David Anthony Laird

The Bear

A friend of mine passed from my life,
And left me with an empty void.
But he went on to a better place,
To his deserved heavenly reward.
I asked him to show me a sign,
To tell me I still had his love
And was still in his care.
I saw his sign as I drove through the night.
I saw his love and care,
I saw my first bear.

Helen Mahr

Drugs-N-Death

I'm sitting here things running
around in my mind. Now I'm trying
another kind.

Things are starting to spin really
fast. I wonder how long this will last.
Faces are getting fussy quick.
Now I'm falling on a brick.
I'm losing my cool, I feel like
a fool.
I'm starting to break out in
a sweat, my face is really wet.
I'm crawling in the house,
quiet as a mouse.
Now I'm going to my bed. I can't
take this going through my head.
I light up a smoke and start
to choke
I can't take it anymore, I'm reaching for my drawer.
Now I am taking the last drag of my cig,
I can't stop myself, I justed pulled the trig.

Marina Wilkerson

Holy "Wholly" Cat

Kittican Cattican lives in the Vatican.
What does she do there? Who does she see?
Large throngs of people. Bishops and cardinals,
The Pope at the altar as Holy as can be.

She doesn't bow down to the bishops and cardinals.
She doesn't bow down to the Pope reverently.
She doesn't show awe in front of the altar.
She doesn't act at all piously.

She prowls all the corridors, the rooms of the Vatican.
She stalks the long halls alert as can be.
A little mouse might be there, a shrew or a cricket.
She listens intently, she waits patiently.

She does bow down to the chef in the kitchen.
She rubs against his legs and meows piteously.
For the crumbs from the kitchen are so deliciously different
Than the mice and the shrews and the crickets you see!

Marilyn Kristensen Oefelein

A Limerick — Young Love

There was a young lad from Ireland named Freddie
Who quickly fell in love with a girl named Betty.
It happen to be in the middle of Spring.
Surely, that seems to be the right thing
Since now they are going steady!

Frances J. Pardy

Prima Ballerina

The picture taunts her with a rival's smile;
Its happiness seems somehow to offend.
Tonight she will be painted to beguile,
But in her photograph she has no friend.

Rehearsal rooms show figures in a glass —
So young she has to turn her eyes away.
And mirrored selves, long vanished, seem to pass,
But they are memories. They do not stay.

She cannot stop, must dance as she must breathe,
Though time may make her cough and fight for air.
She cannot stop, or rest; she cannot leave.
Now, in the lights, with skill to match despair,
Her perfect beauty brings me, close to tears —
Though flowers at her feet are heaped like years.

Wendy J. Glavis

Remember, Our Future

A door is the door to the Future
A window is a mirror to the past
Before we can go through the door to the future
We must never forget to look through the mirror of the past.

Jeff Schmidt

Reflections

Alone I sit upon a hill
Wondering what I should do or will
I look across an ocean or a sea
Upon which I cannot agree
Blue, black, green or red
It seems more alive than dead
Waves crashing about the shore
So majestic — I cry for more
Sea gulls are circling in the sky
Deep in the night I hear their cry
The echo of the sound makes me sad
It sounds like the wanted something they wish they had
Perhaps it was love, or maybe hate
Or possibly a reflection of along lost mate
Who on one sunny day, felt unloved and flew away
Never having a chance to say, why it was she would not stay
And so as I hear the sea gulls scream
Sitting alone upon this hill,
I find that I begin to dream
Wondering what I should do or will.

Michael Miller

Remember When

Remember you told me I was the one and
how true love never comes undone.
Sometimes I see a twinkle at night.
Where those stars used to shine so bright.
Guess our timing was always wrong.
Getting over you is just taking so long.
Remember when there was a we.
Things haven't worked out quite as they should be.
For nothing ever comes that easily.
How hard it's been to let you go.
My wounded heart keeps letting me know.
Then it came time to say goodbye.
You were tired of all the lies.
Time marches on or so they say.
Now I must love you from so far away

Kimberly Everett

Tonight Without You

Tonight is enchanting, beautiful, alluring and sweet.
Tonight, without you, how can I dream?
The tree tops are bathed in the glorious rays of moon;
The buds are blooming with a kiss of the distant stars;
The occasional touch of gentle breeze
Keeps creating the shiver in every sleeping leaf;
A few patches of wandering clouds
Are dancing around the silent sky.
While nature is singing her melodious love- song,
I'm lost in your thoughts, sad and forlorn.
My soul yearns for your loving embrace;
It cries out to be one with you.
You feel so close, yet so far!
Beyond my reach, beyond my grasp.
Come my love! Wrap me in your loving arms,
Give me the warmth of your fiery kiss,
And ignite my passion with a spark of love.
Seal my destiny, cast your dice,
And make me yours forever tonight.

Bela R. Bowley

Requiem For Bluebeard

Pulsing through my veins
veins like a maze
and I only spoke to you
yesterday.

A vision dances silently
in my mind.
The wrecking ball
should be along shortly.

Moving off the path as
the dragon whips furiously
past my watery eyes.

Answer one question before you leave —
Who invited you to share this nightmare?

You, like fine art in a museum; statuesque —
I am a silent and unmoving stone,
enraptured.

EPILOGUE: FORGOTTEN HISTORY: TURQUOISE:
You, standing with back arched, arms
    outstretched.
Me, crawling away on my knees.

Bunnie Rogers

An Ode To Lobe

   To tell you how I strove and strove
to write a sonnet to your lobe
   Seems rather silly, though, to some
who never to the point of love have come
   That much importance can be stressed -
that parts of lovers can be blessed
   In such a way.
   But Darling mine, my love's arrived,
and reminiscing, I have strived;
   And hereupon I place my Seal:
that lobe I love goodly deal.
   'Tis pink and firm and tasty too
(if your lobe is on the menu!)
   And so I say,
   Of lips they've wrote, and too, your Nose,
but your ear is like a Rose -
   Its petal your small lobe must be
as sweet as honey, so soft (I see
   That ferns are jealous)- in their view;
you've captured all their softness, too.

William Markham

Shadow Of Angels

She talks to me in my sleep,
even through she has left.
She leaves me here to weep
quiet, cold, lost in the night.
An angel shadows me, bringing darkness,
Stealing the fire, steal the night.
Calling her name, feeling the shame, what was
her name, calling her name.
A graceful scent fills the air, she is here, she is here.
I awake, feeling, hoping, searching
a mist a blank stare.
It is her in silent bliss
in faded outline of a love I once knew.
I remember our embrace, our final kiss.
But does she see me, does she feel my presence
among the shadow of angels.
I reach for the light of her soul upon the
breast I had once laid my head.
Where did she go, pain, remorse, memory, she's dead.

Henry Franklin Elliott V

Obscurity

As I meandered around one night
I am dazed for there was no moonlight
The horizon was covered with darkness
And the land was filled with emptiness
With the creeping sound of an owl
And foxes that chorusly howl
Noises that night I hear
Makes me feel so lonely with fear
But as I locked up and glance
At the few stars that enhance
My fright was suddenly gone
And a sensation has began
I figured out, God was with me that night
That He is always here at my side
Driving away my fears and sorrows in life
With Him, there is joy in strife
There's no moment I could compare
The security and happiness I felt in there
Then behold, I exultantly whisper
A pray'r, for Him to share

Glen Howel G. Acosta

Driving In New York

Screech . . .
Dangerous moves
Another near miss.
Sudden brakes
Loud horns . . . angry fists.

No indicators
Double parking on congested streets.
Reckless cab drivers
Skillful maneuvers . . . amidst unhurried feet.

A sigh, a hope
A prayer is uttered.
A swear, incoherent grunts
A curse muttered.

Life flashes by quickly
At times . . . a scenic view.
Paper, rubbish, traffic jams, too.

Contented faces contrasted expressions
Mixed emotions mark.
The famous journey . . . or frightening plight
Of driving in New York!

Angella Thomas

A Birthday Gift

So many years you have had on this earth
And perhaps you might wonder
What your life might be worth.
You have seen this day come
And you've watched this day go,
And with each passing year —
You've watched yourself grow.
Some years may be bad,
But I hope more were good —
And I'd make it all happen,
If only I could.
But what kind of gift comes from words filled with sadness?
This day should be happy; joyful with gladness.
Material gifts can become such a bore —
So I write these words that I pray you adore.
It's one of a kind and should perfectly fit;
Perhaps you will read
And become lost in it.
If I had the gift, I would certainly give it —
A beautiful life, and the courage to live it.

Mark J. Winkler

Ode To A Son

It doesn't seem so long ago — I held you in my arms,
And tried, as many mothers do — to shelter you from harm.
It took some time, but very soon — God made me realize,
That part of being "Mommy" — is to hear your baby's cries.

I tried to teach you many things — the good things from the bad,
And always to be thankful — for all the things you had.
To respect yourself and others — though sometimes hard to do,
That laughter, in its purest form — will always see you through.

Your talents and accomplishments — are something to be proud of,
Success will always follow you — if things are done with love.
Remember to stand proud and tall — no matter what folks say,
Live your life with a caring heart — each and every day.

Special moments that we've shared — brought laughter and some tears,
But always precious memories — to last throughout the years.
There are many things I'd like to say — because you are my son,
How much I dearly love you — is truly only one.

The years we've spent together — seem but just a few,
So little time to do the things — a mother wants to do.
Now you're out and on your own — one thing you should've known,
Your precious love is held so dear — within this heart I own.

Cheryl L. Andrews

My Stereo

My stereo is an escape to another universe where the grass is always green and the sun never refuses to shine. There is no crime and there is never any reason to fear at night when you turn off the light. It is a remedy to rid me of my pain, leaving me pure and clean like soft white snow falling gently from the sky. It is a battery that energizes my heart, sending a sharp volt of electricity throughout my body, making me come alive. It gives me happy feet that want to dance until exhaustion is too great to overcome. It is a window to my own peaceful world, a place of romance where a man is a true gentleman and a lady always feels like a lady. It is a blanket that keeps me warm, protecting me from the cold brutal air. It is a circus that make me smile, a friend that comforts me when I'm feeling down and lonely.
There is no need to cry. It is an angel that keeps me safe from the battles that rage inside my head and a lover who fills me with passion and sets my heart free. It is a glass of sparkling champagne that quenches my thirst. My mouth is no longer dry. It is a drug that makes me high. I'm floating like a little lost cloud. It is a fire that makes me hotter than hell. Sweat pours down my body, making me want to shed myself of my clothes. My stereo is a cool breeze that puts me at ease and relaxes my mind. I feel comfortable. There is no need to worry so I let myself drift away.

Daniel D. Mayo

Beloved

O what would I do with so much of a man?
Tall as the trees, do you stand.
To touch your bearded face, and take your long hand, is all I have wondered on.
Are you really alive and here for me?
Your body and soul I hunger to see!
I wonder where you walk each day . . . for us to be together, I have forever prayed.
You have pierced my whole being since the first time I saw you at "sweet sixteen."
More than twenty long years have passed since then.
I've held my thoughts in secret until this pen . . .
It is only now in all of my dreams, that I believe of late,
My desired destiny with you is finally a reality of fate.
Having been blocked by circumstances, mistakes and doubt,
I am grateful time has not completely run out!
If I merely kiss your lips one more time, I might know joy I once could not accept as mine . . .
I hope it is never too late to seek and find You, Love,
Without whom I never know peace of mind.
My love for you has not withered and died.
The torment continues as I long for you over endless time.
As long as I live, I dream of you as mine.
One and only, True Love divine . . .

Emily J. Grassi

Tomorrow

Why do you hide when you have no face?
So near yet so far
Always teasing never certain
We wait on you like drought for rain.

You never fail to come.
Invisible yet ever-present I tell you
I stand before you in awe
Who knows what gifts you will bring.

A basket of fruits or a keg of maggots
Who said maggots do not feed on fruits?
You are generous, always giving what you do not owe.
Let them make all their wishes.

It is nightfall and I hear crickets chirp.
A choir of frogs call out to straying mates
At dawn birds will sing beautiful songs for me, maybe.
I close my eyes and say a prayer:

Wishes are made on stars they say,
So Dear Tomorrow I make mine now.
I know you owe me nothing — but please,
Can I have sunshine?

Audrey Nelson Arowolo

One Sweet Day

One day I shall fly away
I will become one with the sky
Graceful, peace, tranquility
I will be free
One sweet day

One day I shall climb the highest mountain
I will become one with the wind mother nature has stirred
No longer will I breath the smoke of humanity
No longer will my lungs blacken
One sweet day

One day I shall swim the deepest sea
I will become one with the water
I will float through time so peacefully
One sweet day

One day I shall creep to the top tallest tree
Carefully observing every detail
For there is true beauty
For there is where I shall find the highest spirit
And all else shall be gone with the wind
One sweet, sweet day

Cassandra Lynn Weaver

Wall Of Tears (Vietnam Veterans Memorial Lament)

They were boys and they were brave, they answered their country's call
For thanks they waited two decades, to get their names upon a wall.

On the knoll, routine patrol,
"Has anyone seen Jim?"
"After he stepped on the mine, there was little left of him."

They were boys and they were young with little chance to grow old.
There were jeers for 20 years because the war was Cold.

Bright light, fire fight,
"Hey! What happened to Bob?"
"Sniper got him in the back and this, his life, did rob."

They were boys, they were our sons we sent them off to war.
We decided to honor them, but years they waited a score.

Pilot down, on the ground,
"How did we lose Dave?"
"He lost his life upon a knife, another's trying to save."

They were boys and they are there and you can meet them all.
Just drive on down to Washington, they haunt the big black wall.

Ott J. Garrison

Unrequited

Help me Lord, my hopeless heart has sinned!
It ignores my pleas, claims deaf for din
It reminds me of the kiss of one,
Who loves another when day is done.

I promised him with a friendly grin
that my head ruled on matters within
So I hugged him tight and watched him leave
Our friendship would offer no reprieve.

But while my lips spoke with quiet calm,
Oh! how my hands ached to grab his palms.
Palms fly to my face, knees fall to floor,
I dreamed of begging for something more.

To prove my love, my knees stand straight
As I've accepted this hand of fate.
As I've promised him for years on end,
He and I will be forever friends.

Terry Hanisko

The Spring Tree

How slowly the spring tree springs to new life,
I watch thou everyday
Slowly, you decide to share your beauty,
And shade for days in May.
Your bud's bloom full in the sunlight,
Before my observant eye.
Your leaves spread wide with joy and pride,
"How beautiful is thou art!" I cry.

Kim Salamone

Dear Shaun

Who would of thought that I would
be writing you a letter, instead of
talking to you on the phone?

Why are we not walking to the mall
or swimming?

Why are we not playing basketball or ping-pong?

Why are we not laughing together?

At least there is one question that
I know the answer for . . .
   Are you happy where you are?

We all know the answer to this
question, so this should soothe our
hearts and calm our minds.

Shaun walks with Jesus now, and he
knows that we all love him.

Shaun you will never be forgotten and
you will always be in our hearts.

We miss you greatly Shaun . . .

Robert Shriver

Dearest Little Dove

You are my dearest little dove, you were
sent to me from above. No one can ever replace
that bright smile that lights up your face.
   You have touched me in many ways, which
didn't take long because in my heart I knew we
belonged together like two doves, forever their
love bonded, until the hands of cruel fate takes
away one mate.
   The windowed dove will never search for
another because she lost her only true lover
her dearest little dove.

Marisol Rodriguez

My Husband

To someone else you may be just a man
But to me you're one who understands
You're my light of day and everything gay
You're a comfort to my soul and someone
strong for me to hold
You comfort me when I'm sad
And laugh with me when I'm glad.
You're my life my love my joy
And sometimes just a boy
But what ever happens dear I
know that you will be near.
God Bless you for being mine.
For men like you are hard to find

Iris Gayle Botelho

Winter — Spring

Thick sheets of ice covering the ground,
On and on they spread around.
The animals are gone,
The trees are dying —
Then the birds start their flying.
Next some flowers show on the ground —
Once again a season is bound.

Ashley Bessire

Alone

I'm standing alone on the edge of the ocean,
I watch the sun slowly depart
Images, dreams and events of the day
Are fading off into the dark

I let my mind drift far beyond the horizons,
Thinking how lonely it seems
Not realizing now as I stand here alone,
I've drifted away in my dreams

The day's slipping away, the moon's creeping up
And night colors are beginning to blend
My mind drifts and wanders through events of the day
And my eyes drink the night colors in

Breathless I am as the night settles in
And steals away the day
As the blackness surrounds me, I still stand alone
And my dreams are fading away

So I lift up my arms high into the air
And I pray to heaven above
I realize then, I've not been alone
God holds me in his infinite love

Jeffrey Bivens

Faux Reality

I seem to notice each passing year,
Things are not as we Wish they'd appear,
Peace on earth good will to men,
May be the next war that we begin.
Justice for "all" is "all who have money,"
Children are starving in the land of "Milk and Honey."
"Team Effort," a term big business loves to say,
While they bite and devour those who get in their way.
"Lead by Example" is becoming "jump to my beck and call,"
Leadership sidestepping rules, others find a brick wall.
"Pride in Workmanship" tumbling by the way,
Stolen by those concerned of Only profit each day.
"Love Thy Neighbor" is by the color of his skin,
"Political Correctness" preserves the conscience within.
"The American Way," ideals we all love to tout,
Just a Faux Reality that holds no clout.

A. R. Arris

Blue

As burgundy hues of morning light
Gaze upon the stars in flight,
The child spins from boy to man
Trying hard to find dry land.
Ecstasy cannot be found
In the hand or on the town.
In the mirror the Monster Lay, will he be the protégé?
See thee now the swine self-taught
Self-respect cannot be bought.
Swine turns from dirt to mire
Death becomes his whole attire.
Man or boy he doth cry
Worth is always at his side.
Love is a precious gift
Filled with promise and sweet warm lips.
The sun and the moon can never be together, now I 'tis, and forever.
Let the angels sing out loud
Let them draw a mighty crowd;
On this day of joining that will never be. It is so for eternity.

Joshua E. Brown

Love Is A Passion

Do not weep, girl, for love is a passion.
Your lover misses you.
You miss his kiss,
His touch
Do not weep,
Love is a passion.

My heart is fulfilled,
For the heart is the sky,
Long as you believe in your mind and heart.
Do not weep,
Love is a passion.

Chakita Stewart

Christa

Soaring upward on a plume of fire, I swiftly span the
    great black gulfs to other worlds as my heart
        fearless sings
And fly the length of Jove's cloud cathedrals
    Where never a care clings and skim
        With careless ease above Saturn's timeless rings.

I have soared with joy the length of the rugged
    Valles Marineris on mighty ruddy Mars
And with light heart leaving, I bounded
    Over great Olympus Mons on joyful wings of stars.

I have swept the shimmering clouds of Venus
    And beheld the awesome wonder of the
        Sun's eternal daylight.
And as I turned toward the great Milky Way,
    That glowing bridge of white,
        I gazed on God's mighty world,
            As calm as it is bright.

Terence Martin

Watching Over You

If you should find yourself having to walk
this earth without me
Hold your head up high, whatever the circumstances may be
If you should be hurt, and cry someday
I will be watching over you and I will wipe your tears away
If you should be lonely, look up high I will be up there somewhere
I will send you some comfort, God's blessings
I will share
I will never leave you, I will always be just a heart beat away
Waiting for that day of no departing, that will be a wonderful day

Lewis Pollard

A Walk Through Here

Walking here, enshrouded by deep shadows
  of eternity, I balance on the perimeter of thoughts;
   a place where meaning is borne of desire

I have heard the tacit promises of faith
  whispered through half-opened windows
  of crimson-stained glass

Stopping here, cloaked by falling time,
  I stand before the gates of a world of illusion;
   a place where the frontier of emotion begins

I have seen the tacit nods of hope
  through a pale, sallow mist —
   hinting affirmations

Staying here, draped in sheets of reflection,
  I stand in the middle of the light of reason;
   a place where dreams collide with memories

Standing here, showered by tears of possibility
  falling from melting skies of imagination —
   I feel the cool wetness of new reality

   Terry K. DuVall

Only Temporary

  Every week at the same time you walk out
the door with your bag packed.

  Though only temporary, my heart goes with you as does my love.
Yes, though only temporary, the immediate loneliness feels as though
it will be forever. My tears seem as though they will never end.

  My nights are the loneliest times of all. Without you beside me,
there is this ever present emptiness inside . . . like part of me is
missing. When I awake and you're not there this feeling is back again.

  All throughout each day that you are gone, I wonder where you are,
and if your thoughts ever turn to me. When I hear your voice on the
phone, it calms me. As our conversation draws to a close I find it
almost impossible to say "Good-bye." As I hang up the phone,
I miss you already . . . all over again.

  Yes, though only temporary, it feels like forever.
And I think to myself . . . this must never become forever . . .
Because my life would cease . . . for, you are my life . . .

  But, this is not forever. Because time brings you back to me.
As you walk through that door, and I see your face . . . I thank God
that some things in life are only temporary . . . unlike our love . . .

   Elaine Bunn

You Were There

Mom, you were there when I was born,
And you were there when I was one.
You saw me take my first step,
Without anyone else's help.

Mom, you were there when I was two,
To help me put on my shoe.
You didn't give up on me,
Because you were there when I turned three.

Mom, when I was finally four, five, and six,
You were the one who taught me how to mingle and mix.
Oh, Mom, don't forget when I was seven, eight, and nine,
When you had to spank my little behind.

Mom, at ten, eleven, and twelve,
I thought I was really grown,
Until I grew up and had to be on my own.
But thank you Mom, for being there for me,
When I finally left home.

Mom, Life has not been easy,
Of course, you told me it would not be.
But I've done what you taught me to do, and that is to be me.

   Carolyn J. Collier

Getting Away From The Rat Race

Bright and beautiful days with sunny skies
And fields of brown-spotted cows with flies.
Chicken wire fences that stretch on for miles,
Little white churches and kids with smiles.

Wide open pastures with a few oak trees . . .
It's the simplest things that spell country to me.
It's Grandma's mason jars filled with sweet jam.
It's BBQ chicken and a country-smoked ham.

It's Grandpa's garden so green and plentiful
And it's venison 'til your way past full.
Country folks sittin' and tellin' lies.
Listenin' to old folks their words so wise.

Friendly neighbors with their arms open wide
Sayin' "come on ya'll, there's fresh coffee inside."
Sittin' and sippin' Grandma's sweet tea . . .
There's nothin' that tastes better to me.

So good it is to get away from the rat races . . .
To settle in with such warm familiar faces.
The sites, the sounds, the smells of country
Mean so much to my family and me.

   Michael D. Emerson

I Don't Understand I've Done All That I Can

We are here to love, and care, and share.
And when someone loves us to always care.
Through good times and bad times to always be there.

I don't understand, I've done all that I can.

We grew in closeness and shared our tears.
And knew we'd have lots of memories through the years.
We held each other close and chased away out fears.

I don't understand, I've done all that I can.

You must of been sent from up above,
because never have I seen a more tender love.
You came into my life like a soaring dove.

I don't understand, I've done all that I can.

I'll never forget you, my sweet, special girl.
On my memories the good times whirl.
I pray that we'll be together again.

I don't understand, but I'll do all that I can.

   Debra Staples

A Sunny Day

The sun brings light; it warms me.
It burns my face with blinding beams.
My feet are torched with hot sand.
There are footprints in the sand facing away
They are washed away by the harsh ocean.

The rain helps my soul, drenching, soothing,
  healing my shredded heart.
I am sad and the water helps me hide
I am concealed through the blurry wetness, yet I see out.
I begin to fill with water and drown
Yet, I cannot cry out, scream, wail, my lungs are full;
Not of a plea for help, but of this comforting killer.
An enemy in disguise, but I do not care.

I shiver in the snow, but not from cold
My lips turning blue, sharp pains in my toes are made numb.
Hard winds scrape across my chapped
face, burning; bleeding the life from my cheeks.
I stand still, but I'm leaving.
The white trees fall together in the more distant image I observe.
Until there is no more.

   Sarah Alexander

It Could Happen . . .

A short kid was at the line,
With chills going down his spine.
If he makes this, they will win,
If he misses, his life is dim.
He has a chance to win it all,
If he can just kick the ball.
If he duffs, he will die,
If he makes it, he will cry.
So he kicks it in the air and gives the goalie a little scare.
If the goalie makes any error's he will lose it for the Bears.
But if he blocks, it is good.
Not for the short kid, but for the mood.
The ball is falling really fast.
The goalie better be fast or the ball will go past.
It falls down and goes right in.
The short kids gets the win.
And the goalie takes the lose.
The short kids gets a snooze.
That's the shot that won it all,
on the Gameboy at the mall.

Kenny Gouveia

You And Me

As we venture through life's journey,
we often wonder what's in store.
When we have experienced the feelings of love,
we want them for evermore.

The road is not always level and straight,
but has its ups and downs,
It's how we deal with the road we take,
that keeps us from going down.

So let each day be a new beginning,
to be share with the one you love,
For we were brought together,
by our Heavenly Father above.

Remember to say, I love you and kiss and hug each day,
and pray the Lord will bless us and keep the evil one away.

And when life's mortal journey somehow comes to and end,
we look forward to our new road, where our love will never end.

For life goes through eternity and so our life will be,
together as companions, forever, You and Me.

William E. Schweers

Lullaby For A Soldier

In a green, hushed village
Lights filter, shadows mix
Vines tumble, weave
In, out, of empty eye sockets
Orchids shimmer
Thru white arched bones

And while I sing my song
Green leaves will give you suck
Dappled brown earth will rock you

But who will string these bones?
Who will flesh this hand?
Who hears a song of men's longing?
Once sung by morning stars?

In a green, hushed village
Lights filter, shadows mix
Silence sings the last lullaby
Plowshares are beaten into swords
Pruning hooks into spears
Lion eats the lamb
And men make war evermore . . . and evermore . . .

Lea Rissner

Night

As the sunlight without rain
As happiness without pain
As darkness without light
So is day . . . without night.

Some love the day — and hate the night
At dusk their fear doth give them flight
from sleepless night, comes welcome day
That sweeps their tears and fears away.

But night to me, like a cooling breeze
Steals in darkness through the trees
And the moon through my window, peeps and sees
Me, thanking God, upon my knees,

For happiness, sadness, joy and tears
For promises of life and love through years
And after work and heat of the day
For night that steals me, in dreams away.

Joyce Valentine Blanchard

Separate Lives

The separate lives we must live, are such a large barrier to all
the love I have to give. A love I must keep inside; for the barrier
can not be pushed aside.
   And yet when we're alone, and you place your hand in mine,
the barrier does seem to vanish if only in our minds.
   Those intimate moments we spend together, when the barriers
separating our lives seem to disappear, are so short that I must
shed a tear in fear, that those moments may never again appear.
   If for only a day we could set aside the separate lives we must
live, I could show you the love I have to give.
   But because of separate lives, I cherish the moments that we
do find. The moments when I place my hand in yours in mine
and we search together for a way to push aside; If only for a
moment the barriers of our separate lives.

Ronald R. Schmitt

In A Drunken Stupor

In the morning light, laying half asleep,
I think of the lost nights and pray the Lord to keep
My dreams and desires from Sorrow's raging fires.

I think about that night before,
Brighter than this morrow, but near Sadness' door.
And I know the penalty for such abject lunacy;
Yet, still do I yearn for days long past
And torture this day, dwelling on failure.

I shed tears last eve, perusing her deeds
And contemplating my own needs,
Which fall asunder this foot of Despair.
I would give the total of my self
To find that glory, that inferno of Love,
Blazing within again.

But ne'er do I feel the ashes spark or ember,
Only a rift, a void long remembered
For the fullness it once held and adored.

W. H. Agan II

Lost And Never Forgotten

Feelings overwhelming inside
Taking me to the limit
Until finally they subside
It's only for a moment
All this heartache I can hide
Countless spirits broken
No peace to be found
Many words left unspoken
Dreams never reaching never touching down

Laury Omiotek

Divine Reunion After 42 Years — December 16, 1996

You did not raise me since I was a tiny tot,
But you thought of me often and loved me a lot.

I grew up under the stars that heard me scream.
The same ones you prayed to; I too had a dream.

Endless nights of wondering, has finally ceased.
Years of helpless torment, can now be released.

With the Grace and Love of God, the most precious crown,
Oh Daddy, Oh Daddy, you have finally been found.

As we embrace, for the first time in years,
Healing begins with the flooding of tears.

While we gaze into each other's loving eyes,
We realize there has always been spiritual ties.

So the tears that flow now are from happiness, you see —
Because I am your daughter and will always be.

As I wipe the tears, running down your face,
Finally I get to say "I Love You," for Heaven's sake.
Randie Kay Sanders — Mary Ellen West

Ode To A Four-Leaf Clover

Little four-leaf clover,
    are you peeking out at me?
Through a camouflage of grass and leaves
    you're safe as you can be.
So do not fret, I'll pass you by,
    not even an eye to see.
You'll not be pressed within a book
    but live life naturally.
Jean O. Schiffert

A Forest Of Love

My heart roams in a forest of love
and my spirit sits on the wings of a dove.
I look around and fail to see
all the faults that tend to surround me.
I gaze into the heart and see you
and the love of the strong, faithful, and true.
The fog in the trees soft as lace,
in the waterfall I see your beautiful face.
And this forest of love has grown around you,
My spirit soars for this love is true.
Stacey Lynn Fronabarger

The Man In My Life

The man in my life was so handsome and so tall!
At least, that's how it seemed to me, when I was very small.
His voice seemed so loud, as his laughter filled the room,
And as he sang (or whistled) a happy little tune.

The man in my life knew all there was to know!
At least, that's how it seemed to me, and I believed that it was so.
His voice could fill my heart with joy, though sometimes it was dread.
It all depended on, of course, what needed to be said.

The man in my life was, actually, human after all!
And as I became a woman . . . I found: He wasn't tall!
He didn't even know everything, but I loved him just the same.
And his voice still filled my heart with love when he called my name.

The man in my life, back then, went away much too soon.
His loving heart betrayed him, on a sunny day in June.
His voice was silenced on that day, when I was six and ten.
And I was left to wonder how it might have been . . .

If the man in my life today had known the man that was my Dad,
And if Daddy could have shared the joy the two of us had,
On that bright November day when I became a wife.
But, instead of two, I had only one man in my life.
Sarah B. Ray

All Of Us Fools

It can't be seen nor touched,
It hits you so hard you'll swear you were punched,
It sneaks from behind,
Makes even the strongest blind,
Makes a kiss even more,
A heart beat like a wave crashing against a shore,
Some get dizzy and weak in the knees,
Others desperately seek a cure for this uncontrollable disease,
But you can't fix what isn't broken,
And even though it can burn and leave your heart smoking,
We long for this invisible fate,
In a sea where we all are bait,
A heaven-sent gift delivered from up above,
The strangest and most joyous feeling, all of us fools call love.
Marie Ratliff

All About Me

"I have eyes that cannot see.
I have ears so I can hear,
A nose to smell, a mouth to talk,
A heart that beats and feet that walk.
I have a brain that thinks and a face that smiles,
And other things; and deep inside . . .
I have wings!"
JennyKate McNabb

Light Of Hope

Beneath the blanket that night has spread,
a tiny light of hope is shed.
Within this tiny glow of light,
I'm told there's freedom from the night.
Upon searching for that glow of light.
I'm forced to contemplate the meaning of night.
In gaining this knowledge, I have become wise,
for life has revealed its surprise.
That love can triumph over pain,
and faith can conquer what remains.
This wisdom has set me free from the night.
Its truth shall be my guide.
No dreams pursued have ever been so right,
but that tiny light of hope,
Beneath the blanket of night!
Linda Booth

Vicarious Intrusion

Best laid plans often go astray
Dreams deferred that fade away
Lofty goals are now distant memories
No one is to blame

Experience gained from Blood, sweat, I tears
Knowledge wrested from time
A yearning for a second chance
The hands cannot turn back

A brand new child to live life through
Each step taken toward a scripted path
Bypassing adversity which makes us strong
Trying to get there soon

The carried torch now flickering
A new person starts to grow
The struggle within monopolizes the day
As the burden consumes the night

A turn in the road toward other pursuits
Disillusionment, anger, the pain
Struggling to understanding what went wrong
Whose life was it anyway?
Damon D. Blakemore

Because You're Worth

Perhaps someone just broke your heart, you're feeling worthless far apart.
Or loved ones lost before their time because of gangs or violent crime.
Or maybe you're afraid to tell, you're being abused living a hell.
Perhaps addicted to some drugs, you feel like part of all the thugs.
Perhaps you're gay or maybe bi — but can't explain the reasons why.
Maybe adopted at your birth, upset with thoughts that you're not worth.
Maybe forgiveness just won't last, because abortions from your past.
Remember God still loves us all but hates the sins that makes us fall.
If you were all alone on earth, he'd die for you because you're worth.

Ida Flores

Untitled

The roller-coaster of life in which we all live,
    the ups and the downs, a headache they might give.
For some of us the downs are plenty,
    good times of excitement, there aren't many.
But for others, like me, the excitement is frequent.
    Life is always good, for this they call us delinquent.
We're just like you, teenagers trying to have fun.
    Money, women, trying to be number one.
When growing up like us, there's a lot of hard times,
    arguments, losses, trying to live like mimes.
People want us to be quiet, lock us up in a box,
    but in being ourselves, we can't have mouths full of rocks.
Be yourself in life, do what you want,
    don't change for anyone, don't put on a front.
Day by day we live on mysteriously;
    Life is too important to be taken so seriously.

Pete Hoffman

A Mother's Love

An undying passion so strong she could move mountains
So strong she could sacrifice her own self to prove loves point
A mother's unconditional love is something that can't be destroyed
No matter what may happen a mother still has her bond
That bond is the flesh and blood that you are now
A mother would stay by your side even in your darkest days
No matter how much you fight her and curse her name
No matter how much you defy her or how little you listen
A mother will never stop loving you regardless of your flaws
You can say you don't love her but you'll realize one day how much you do
Even if that day may be the day she ceases to breath
You'll realize she lived her life loving you.

Amber Loving

Reaching Out

I am not here to bring you down
    but I thought perhaps we should touch base
I am not here to judge you
    but some things you do I do not like
I am not here to argue with you
    but I ask you to listen for just a moment
I am not here to preach to you
    but I have found a way that works for me
I am not here to beg of you
    or raise my voice to yell
I came because I need to say
    how much I want you well
I came because you are my brother
    and we have drifted far apart
I came because I love you
    very much with all my heart
I came so you may hear my words
    and find inspiration in their sound
I came so you may see me now
    and might want to hold what I have found

George MacNamee

If You Don't Care Then Why Should I?

If I refuse to listen to my heart, My soul.
If I give up on people, the future
A nation's goals.
Then I give up on me.
All that came before me,
and all that will ever be.
Anything and everything that will ever be.
Christ's death, wars, hunger, and hopelessness
would just cease to have meaning.

    No Hope

Without hope, without faith, there would be

    No Reason

God, prayer, our children . . . our faith, and believing
in one another.
Are the answers here.
And with His help, His love, patience and teachings.
We as a people, we as a nation
Will finally get there.
That my friend, is why we should care!
His perfection and sacrifice are my salvation.

Kathy Farrington

Casey At Bat

3 Can he play?
6 Awe, he has strikes one
4 Someone kill him
6 End this nonsense says he
3 you can play
6 A roaring from the crowd
1 Two
8 Bat to be a professional
4 And hit the ball
9 Time will tell, when he will say strike three

Michelle Lantz

Fatherhood

I am just a lonely star
Wandering through the galaxy of life
Pondering each passing question
Laboring through life's daily strife

An earthly star of vision, of beauty
A star of wonder, of contrasting themes
A star of mystery, intrigue and romance
A star of ponder, with impossible dreams

Some look up and see the brightness
Some see the star in the midst of day
This complex anthology, this human spirit
It's fatherhood, a small price to pay

James R. Boyer

Finally

He makes me so mad. Just calm down.
I can feel my heart pounding so hard. Just calm down.
My whole body is trembling. Just calm down.
My head hurts. Just calm down.
It feels as though my heart is going to explode. Just calm down.
I can't get my breath! Just calm down.
I can't handle this feeling anymore! Just calm down.
I hate him! I love him. Just calm down.
I watch him lying there. Just calm down.
I swallow hard. I put my hands
around his neck, all my anger flows
to my fingertips . . .
    I can finally, calm down.

Rhonda Vazquez

Wrong Number

I heard your voice
so early one morning,
fuzzy through the grogginess of my mind,
reaching up to consciousness.
A voice that still stays in my ear
and makes me smile.

"Wrong number,"
you say?
I wonder?

A deep gravely voice
still not awake yet itself,
but probing
to awaken a friendship not known.
A voice I will not soon forget
that says all without saying.

"Have I called the wrong number?" you say.
But yet you keep on talking.
I wonder.

Marilyn Reid Carver

Give Me Back My Life

I have seen great moons full of light, as I walk in the fields of
celestial night. Stars twinkling above, in the sky they stay.
Given the chance I lay down in the hay. Rest my tired legs, let
my arms go limp, I stare up in the sky without a hint. Forget my
fears, my worries, my sorrows, out in the fields, laid in hay.

Then I see in the great ocean, clouds attached to string pulling
canoes. I bolt up in fear, in worry, intruders are coming. I must
hurry to warn my people, make ready now! These things are coming,
this is our home, we won't give up we're left alone. We've
heard of these creatures, bringing sicknesses, with running
fevers, killing whole tribes at a time, so we must destroy them all.
With few wounds they retreated, but they left the sickness.

It ran through our village, sparing only me. We've been defeated,
though I hate to say. My family is gone, so are my friends, the
people I thought I'd be with till the end. The beating drums of
my people, I will hear no more.

I have seen great moons of light, as I walk in the fields of celestial
night. I stare up in the sky, so this was my fate, to be angry and
full of hate. No, I can not forget my worries, fears, and sorrows.
I can not forget my people, gone in the night.

Elisabeth Walker

My Mountaintop In N.C.

I sit in my rocker out in the yard,
Where God's beautiful mountains abound.
I'm blessed with eyes that look and see
Our Master's works all around.

I'm thrilled with wonder at their majestic size;
Their age that goes 'way back in time.
I read mountain stories that humans write
But my Lord tells me their stories in rhyme.

The stories God tells me are in my Bible;
The old is the same as the new.
The Bible, the mountains, the stories don't change —
The changes have been me and you.

Look up to God's mountains, pray up to God's heavens,
Stretch up your arms to God's clouds.
God said "Thy righteousness is like mountains of God".
Yes, our Master will remove all the shrouds.

You'll feel a new life, a joyous rebirth!
He'll gird you and He'll hold tight the bands
He's promised you a walk with Him in His great love;
You'll find peace in our Master's Hands!

Rena Crane Thorsen

The Aftermath

The choices of some have affected many more than just one
a mother
a father
a sister
a brother
a daughter
or even a son
someone's choice will affect many more for the rest of their lives
All the way down to the unborn child of a husband's wife
We are all aware of what we say and what we do
The worst part of it all is
You had to learn the hard way and have it happen to you.
If the victims had just one second to tell you how they feel
They would say the consequences of one bad choice can and did
really kill.
The future of us all is an unseen path.
By making better choices we can avoid the aftermath.

Eric Mortensen

My Loneliness

My dear loneliness, please accept me into your darkest realm
For it is a life of pain that I live in with deep fear
People talk of a better day
No I say!
Let me drench in my sorrows
Let my sorrows be my intoxication.
As there is no justification.
But please don't try to stitch the tear in my heart
For it is that tear that allows me not to burst.
My dear loneliness, please accept me into your deepest womb
Be the pyramid that hosts my tomb
For the path of love is broken and the clouds are full of moisture
With my sun gone, there is no need to shine on my pasture
My eyes are full of tears
Please free me from all these fears.

Reena Dave

Aunt Sue

Her smile covers the earth
Brings happiness to all
Her life touches so many
Brings love to our hearts
Her strength lifts everyone
Brings hope to the hopeless
Her motivation stronger than any current
Brings goals to underachievers
Her sudden illness doesn't stop her
Brings fear to us all
Her life ends short
Brings tears to us all
Her memory fills our hearts
Brings joy and pain to all who know her

Joseph C. Stevens IV

Dream Image

The train is speeding down the rails;
Outside the coach windows is a bleak, barren landscape,
Rapidly increasing the feeling of ennui among the passengers.
Then, in the distance, appears a small dot of color coming
toward the windows;
Enlarging in size as it approaches, the colors become vivid,
And begin to coalesce, forming a phantasmagoria of all the
colors under the sun.
As they fill the windows, changing patterns as in a kaleidoscope,
they become mesmerizing.
This display of colors seems to go on forever.
When it does begin to fade away, there follows a real sense of loss;
Yet a certain something remains — serendipity!

Cheryl Phillabaum

Ajax

The first time I saw her, I knew she was the one
I brought her home that day and then began the fun
The first six months were kind of rough
She whined; she chewed; she bit; she was tough

Then one day she was no longer a frisky little pup
She was my loving; trusting, loyal friend; she had grown up
When it was time for me to get home, no matter how late
She would be sitting in my bedroom window and would wait and wait

Seven years went by but one night she became quite ill
She didn't want to play; she didn't want to eat; she lay quite still
I took her to the hospital but a few days later, she died
I was devastated and cried . . . and cried . . . and cried

She hated the rain but she loved the sunshine
If she was alone in the dark, she would whine and whine
So I buried her on the hillside where the sun shines bright
I buried her on the hillside to catch the morning light

She will live in my heart at the rest of my days
She will be by my side forever and always
When I look up in my bedroom window, I can still see her little face
And I know in my heart, another dog could never, ever take her place

Margaret Pette

Ode To Barney (Beagle)

Of all the dogs, both big and small,
I like the Beagles best of all.
Their white-tipped tails and velvet ears,
Have made me smile for many years.

Black and white and mingled browns,
I love these bouncing little hounds.
They sing and howl at my best song,
No matter what, they do no wrong!

When they get tired they softly wail,
and curl up nesting nose to tail.
Sometimes they snore or dream out loud,
Just watching them I feel so proud.

I have a beagle all my own,
He is the best I've ever known.
He's been my pal for ten full years,
and as I stroke his velvet ears,

He smiles and nods and goes on dreaming,
Knowing that his owner's beaming.
I am so blessed, this gift so small,
Yes, Beagles are the best of all!

Sande E. Parrish

Because We're Part Of Something Bigger

Two babies are waiting to be born
I wish I could be with them non-stop
Both before and after birth, reveling in the nachas
But I have clients that need me and appointments that must be kept
Because I'm part of something bigger
Our introduction will have to wait until the weekend

An old man lays dying
I'd give anything to be by his bedside around the clock
To lift his spirits and ease his pain
But work responsibilities beckon and outside commitments too
Because I'm part of something bigger
I'll see him on Saturdays and after work when I can

Two babies are born
An old man dies
And life continues to swirl on all around
Like it always does
Like it always must
Because we're part of something bigger

Paul Marsh

Lonely

One lonely flower planted in grass
In nature's game of life it will never pass
Small and weak with no friends at all
It's face to the sun just waiting for fall
Yes Autumn is coming with its cold wind and frost
Soon it will be hidden, very sad and lost
One day it will die unloved and unseen
Sometimes to me nature's just mean
My life reminds me of a flower like this
Alone, unhappy, without any bliss
But I am saved and have many friends
And they'll give me their love
When it's theirs to lend

Andrea Mullin

Soul Mates

When ever I'm feeling sad and blue,
I close my eyes, and think of you.

Your laughter, your smile, your warm embrace,
the look of love I see in your face.

This wall I've built around my heart,
brick by brick you've torn it apart.

You've showed me what love is, not what
it seems to be, no strings attached,
cause it's meant to be free.

Two hearts joined together,
soul mates forever,
that's you and me.

Lora Barrett

Abstinence

You are born normally and later on in life
you become aware of substance abuse within
your personality.
Challenge life; have no reservations about
the abuse.
You have not had an unfair stigma put in you.
In the first place, you never were one to
have one or two.
Ups and downs are part of life.
Life is quite interesting as the length
Of abstinence continues to increase.

William E. Howell

A Cosmic Dream

I wish, I wish, O shooting star
That I, like you, could fly so far.
I would stroll with the moon and play with the stars
Frolic with Venus and dance with Mars.
I could be anything that I desire
A supernova, a celestial fire.
But instead of dreaming of what I want to be
I can make my dream reality;
And dream of something exciting and pure
A dream that is worth waiting for.

Jacqueline Caddle

My Heart Is Afraid

With the first breath you gave me, it enlivened my heart
I longed for the time our souls would not part
but the distance has grown and our memories will fade
where there was once sun
now there is shade
I can't keep from crying, my heart is afraid.

Heidi Steger

Nature's Music

Hear the music of the forest,
no motors or sirens, just nature's chorus.
Hear the brook as it babbles on it's way,
the red squirrel chatters, answered by the Jay.
The wind in the leaves is softly whispering,
telling of snowflakes soon to be swirling.
The leaves are rustling as mice scurry about,
collecting seeds so they won't be without.
Hear the peepers in their hideaways,
telling of the sunshine warming their days.
Hear that distant motor running,
don't be fooled by a grouse's drumming.
The flit of Chickadees from tree to tree,
with their chorus of "chick-a-dee-dee-dee."
There's been so sweeter music to my ears,
than nature's serenading through the years.

Diane M. Davison

Write It

Here is a pencil and paper.
  jot down that what I say.
Words spoken are soon forgotten.
  What you write will always stay.

This pencil has no eraser
  so don't make any mistakes.
Only one sheet of paper.
  Now let us communicate.

All are born to die, write it.
  God gave you a body and soul.
The earth will claim your body.
  Don't let the Demon take his soul to toll.

Let's fill all hearts with only love
  and give it all away toll-free.
Then left it be returned, all excelled,
  for all to improve endlessly.

Aloysius Leo Grupenhof

Redheaded Woodpecker

Upon the wings of a redheaded woodpecker
  searching for the choices of trees.
Perched upon a limb, just pecking away.
  Does he feel pain or grief or
  is this just a time of play?
Doesn't he know it seems he is pecking
  foolishly just pecking away?
Well, I hope he is happy, but to me,
  he is rapping endlessly,
Oh! What a headache it would seem to
  be just pecking and rapping away!

Brady T. Thorson

Markings

I marked the rustle of brown leaves
swirled, transported by quick breeze
which dropped them like twelve geese in flight,
spying open water, light.

Quiescent crafts beyond all view
when former ruthless rakes swept through
had been by swift unseen fate blown
toward opportunity unknown.

I would inquire how they did fare
in crafty purpose bobbing there;
but learn their lot I do misdoubt
for riffles tossed those crafts about.

Sharon Cassell Martin

Eyes

The eyes are the portholes to the inner-Soul.
Can you see the darkness that lays deep
  inside my Soul?
Can you feel the coldness that longs
  for warmth?
Can you see into my Soul?
No you can't!
What you see is just my outer-self,
An image that was created in the darkness
  of the womb.
If only there was a little light to
  penetrate my heart.
But I'm lost in a world cold as stone.
Looking and searching through the portholes of my eyes.
Dimly and searching and always seeking.
Love will be the light that will warm
  my Soul.

Jeffrey Joe Rubio

Baby Mine

When I hold you in my arms and I look into your eyes
I can't believe that you're mine.
The way I feel when I think of you is so hard to explain.
I will always take care of you, love you, do anything for you
until my dying day.
Now I know why people couldn't say how it would feel when I
gaze your way.
But now I know the feeling so, baby mine.

Debbie Weispfening

Out In God's Beautiful Fields

Every morning without fail,
I stroll down a wooded trail,
The fragrance of honeysuckles fill the air,
And for a moment I stop and stare,
At the honey bees among the clover-scented grass,

I stand in fields among new mown hay,
I recall my youth of yesterday,
A barefoot boy and his dog at play,
And for a moment my fears are cast away.

I look upon all the beauty my eyes can see
And forget all the cares that trouble me,
With my head bowed, I stand in awe!
Out in God's beautiful fields.

Warren G. Fluty

The Endless Circle Dance

Year end memories paint a vivid picture,
Where we go from what's behind.
Through Spring, Summer, Fall and Winter,
Images dance through our mind.

People come and people go,
Touching someone's life in a special way.
We are individuals with a collective soul,
A fractional reflection of people we meet each day.

We dance the endless circle dance,
Advancing through life in a slow spiral motion.
Sometimes we wonder if life is but chance,
Or if there is some big plan or notion.

A year has come and gone,
Yet someone somewhere wonders where it went.
Our dreams fulfilled one by one,
We like to think our time has been well spent.

Sit and take thought of what has been done,
The sun will still rise and the moon will still come.

Joseph Patrick Skamel III

Absence

Your absence made my eyes drip and my mind flip
I can't believe why you're not here but you're not
I played the fool once again
I thought nothing could come between us
I thought nothing could break us apart but something occurred
Something happened for you to be absent from my life
My life is empty without you
like someone cut out a piece of my heart and pounded on it
your absence really took a toll on my life
I don't go out on a Friday I stay home and do nothing
It seems as if my life had grown dead
Since you have been gone
I can't eat
I can't sleep
All I do is think of you
And why your absence has taken place in my life
I thought I was everything you could need
But I guess not maybe it's for the best
Your absence really made me think
Maybe I'm not ready to settle down just yet

Nakia Brooks

A Place In Time

I am going to tell you a story about a man I knew.
He was like many of us. He had hopes and dreams.
He didn't fulfill them though; they were pushed aside.
He became a victim to a world wide scene.

He was a wonderful man. He was loved by all who knew him,
Both the young ones and the old.
He believed he could accomplish anything he set in his mind to do,
His confidence was bold.

There was something else in the cards for him,
He was dealt a hand in the game called life, he was unaware.
He couldn't play. He didn't know the rules.
His confidence left him. He wondered, "Do I dare?"

He got trapped in a zone of confusion. He can't be reached by man.
He is neither here nor there.
His mind doesn't respond to commands anymore.
It couldn't withstand all of the wear and tear.

I will never forget the man he was, the man who had dreams,
That hopeful significant other.
I still believe God will bring him back, I'll keep the faith.
That man was my friend, he is also my younger brother.

Bonnie R. Judd

A Life Once Lived (Life Is Short)

To live at once with joy and laughter
To follow happy ever after
To dream of silver hair while young
and youth in golden years unsung

To toil and tire with life and work
To find true love and your peace on this earth
To lie awake until your parents come home
and then as a parent till your child comes home

To relax and despair at one time in one place
To learn time is precious life isn't a race
To cry out from a crib and die old in a warm bed
and to mind what you say or regret what you said

To live to the fullest with unselfish care
To stop at a flower and start with a prayer
To never fight tears whether joyful or pained
and to savor some silence yourself to regain

For when it's said and when it's done
It's the life you led
Not the race you've run

Jeffrey J. Grissinger

Shot

An Assassin's bullet fells a life.
A life full of energy, vibrance, creativeness,
seeking peace for the children of Abraham.
A bullet in the name of God?
A God of compassion, of hope, of salvation.
Misunderstood, misrepresented, misnamed.
A bullet fired in the name of freedom, liberty, justice,
A bullet of zealot wanting to disrupt a process where his land
would not be occupied by his foe.
This land, given by the God of the Patriarch to his Chosen.
A bullet fired in fear that if this land were once again occupied
by the lost brother, the hope of salvation would not come;
the promised Messiah would not walk on foreign soil.
Yet, these bullets felling this Nobel Laureate
Brought to a world of nations the greater desire for peace, peace
between peoples united a common Father and monotheistic God.

We pray that this life has not in vain, that the tears, sorrows
and mourning, from the heart will remember the intent, the desire,
the hope for a peaceful, co-existence between nations
sharing an ancient heritage and holy ground.

Frances J. Jacobs

Do You Know?

Do you know a child
who's as good as gold?
Who's always sweet
and never cold?

Do you know a dog
who never barks at danger?
Who never bothers
to bark at strangers?

Do you know a flower
who doesn't smell so sweet?
Who never opens
and comes out to greet?

No.
Without the child who's not quite as good as gold,
Without the dog that barks at danger,
and without the flower that smells so sweet,
the world itself would be cold.

Tiffany Will

The Essence

The essence of love
That flows from your heart,
Caresses my life
And cuddles my heart.

Your sweet glowing face
And the gleam in your eyes,
Quickens the pulse in my chest
Causing time that just flies.

Come hold me close
And I'll do the same,
Touching and kissing
Whispering your name.

Hold me and kiss me
Love me some more
Entwining our legs
That's what snuggling's for.

The scent and the texture of your velvety skin,
Awakens desires so exciting from the man deep within.

My desire so exciting is to fill up your heart,
With the essence of love that flows from my heart.

William D. Flint

A Change To Be Made

A contradiction of emotions
With no expression
A smiling sadness
With no realization
A mind full of confusion
With no direction
A desire to achieve
With no motivation
A journey through life
With no destination

A change to be made
With no reservation

A contradiction of emotions
With no repression
A smiling sadness
With no devastation
A mind full of confusion
With no proclamation
A desire to achieve with no limitation
A journey through life with no hesitation

Jennifer L. Abate

Maternal Eclipse

The Moon crept up on icy toes,
Although its nature is nocturnal.
The Sun lay back in sweet repose,
Her gift of life, eternal.

She gives warmth and light for growth.
Mother Earth turns her cheek for Sun's kiss.
The good Mother Earth thought not of change,
Cherished Sun was her one source of bliss.

So as the Moon with its soul-less winter heart
In the light of day came creeping,
It shadowed the Sun, and left Mother Earth
In darkness and disbelief, weeping.

In her once warm breast there is sorrow and cold.
She longs for the embrace of her Sun.
And as she grows old, as the despair takes hold,
Realization: The damn Moon has won.

Deena Ann Smith

Daddy's Little Girl

The smell of age and wisdom filled
the house whenever daddy came home
Little girl ran down the hall and hugged
him tight; feeling safe and loved

The stains of my tears filled the house
whenever daddy made mama cry, feeling angry and hurt

The mouth watering taste of hazelnut cookies
filled my mouth whenever daddy helped
mama prepare them; a Christmas tradition
Feeling joy and anticipation

Years passed; the little girl became a teenager

The sounds of screams and pounding fists on
tables filled my ears; feeling lost and confused

The longing for the gentle touch of a hand
a shoulder to cry on that had to be earned
Feeling resentful and misunderstood

Two years have passed; the teenager is now a young woman;
only pensive silence and distance remain, watching each other
from afar; a wall between us; yesterday I had a very vivid dream it
simply cried out, "Love covers a multitude of sins." I love you Dad.

Viola Elles

Beginning The End

Breath, know or never
Cherish the light, lighten the dark
Feel the freedom, see the bars
Stumble on the shackles, rumble down the road
Hear the ocean, weigh the anchor
Cherish one but not the other
Don't know, don't care
Don't wish to show you care
Too much not enough
Bold, too old?
Young, just sprung?
Blind are the young
OLD is complete and gone
Death is done

Ismael C. Diaz

Christmas Is Coming

Wrapping papers of plaid and sheer,
oh, Christmas is filled with such cheer.

Scents of spices and warm apple pies,
and near the presents peeking eyes.

Tree topers, candy canes, and glittering balls,
and plenty of people fill the shopping malls.

A dress of red velvet and green silk,
a plate left for Santa of cookies and milk.

Screams of laughter from children with toys,
oh, how I love Christmas with all its joys.

Erin Manchac

Fifty

I woke the morning of my fiftieth year.
With no applause or cheer.

I thanked God for being so kind.
To be spirit filled and to have a sound mind.

As I look back over from babe to this fiftieth year.
I realized that I have cried a many a tear.

But through it all I can say.
Thank God for bringing me to this day.

Life is uncertain you have ups and downs.
Knowledge and patience is your life's crown.

Had some hard times, money is few.
Understanding of God, I made it through.

The next fifty years if God say so, will be joy and love.
For all that I have comes from above.

Dorothy Elois Hoosier

Someone Cares

It's anniversary time again for me, this makes number twenty-six
Before my coming to this place, my life was in a terrible fix
Knowing too well where I would go, a terror filled my heart
No one to care what my soul knew well, would be a horrible part
In a pit of blackness deep within, awaited agony and pain
I cried out with fear, as it gripped my being so full of the awful shame
The torment and torture of it all, put me in such despair
I didn't think that it was right, to be treated so unfair
Finally in myself, I reasoned it out, hell would be my destiny
And my life would be taken away from me for all eternity
Then all at once, the light shined in and my spirit answered the call
And at that time, I knew for sure someone loved me in spite of it all
So now I'm walking in that light one exciting day at a time
Looking forward to my home with him, whether now or at ninety-nine
Jesus loves me more than life itself, he proved it on a tree
Giving hope and joy, peace and knowing, finally someone cares for me.

Mary L. Study

Christmas

Christmas is not about Santa or Saint Nick
Christmas is not about getting or giving gifts
Christmas is not about peace on earth
But Christmas is about Jesus Christ's Birth.

Christ came down to redeem mankind
for a misdeed done by Adam and Eve
He came to earth to live and die
for earth's redemption he hoped to achieve.

And from his birth we've added on
tales and traditions that seemed real nice
but by doing so we took away
the true meaning of that blessed night.

Mary gave birth to Christ in a manger
Santa was not there
There were no reindeer at the holy site
but angels and shepherds were there.

So give your gifts and sing your songs
but do so for the right reason
and remember that not everyone
is enveloped by the season.

J. Norman Lussier

Christmas Time At The Ranch

Time to send cards and deck them halls
Look for gifts in all the malls
Bake cookies and make fudge candy
These projects need someone a little more handy

I started stringing lights around the ranch
Fell off the ladder and ripped my pants
None of the cows appreciate Christmas bows
Guess I could put tinsel between their toes

The trees is up, leans to the right
Hope it stays up thru Christmas night
The presents are wrapped with ribbons and bows
Scotch tape doesn't hold, why nobody knows

Old Santa walks all around our town
Always smiling, no sign of a frown
I'm reminded daily with each Christmas Carol refrain
December 25th is baring down like a freight train

Somehow things to do on our Christmas list
Will get done, not much will be missed
As Christmas Eve night draws ever so near
We remember the baby born this time of year

Pat Mumm

Seasons

She waits alone
Staring out the window
The warm sun on her face . . .
Hoping things will be different this time . . .
That he'll love her.
So, she waits
The cool breeze in her hair
Hoping this time will be forever . . .
That he'll be true.
She waits alone
Watching icicles form on the window ledge
Hoping this time
She'll be loved back . . .
That he'll stay.
So, she waits
Not only alone, but lonely
Watching flowers and trees come alive
And her love slowly die . . .
Hoping, this time . . .
She'll never love, again.

Leanne Cox

Communion (For My Parents)

Eve stands by the olive tree
Her eyes moisten as her hands caress its leaves
Her husband near, remembers decades ago
His hands lowering a white, linen cloth wrapping
Her two fetuses beneath
The roots and brine.

At age 69, Eve still holds a sacred dialogue
Her fingers reach to Heaven to receive
Light green, dark green, dusty fruits of life.
The tree, impregnated, responds;
Its bitter, sweet love fall into Eve's palm
A communion of peace — forever.

Saliba Sarsar

When Johnny Went On Vacation

Teardrops fell upon your roof today
It was aware that you went away
The arms of your chairs went limp and sad
They missed your touch which made them glad
The hands of the clock were wringing in strife
Because their minutes were out of tune with life
The keys of the organ silently awaited your fingertips
Like a patient lover awaited your trembling lips
But they all got together and decided you should go
For upon your return they knew you would surely know

. . . That . . .

The tears on your roof have brought the sun
The arms of your chairs are now open flung
The hands of the clock just clap with glee
Because their minutes tick again in harmony
And the organ's keys resound with such melody
To crush a lover's trembling lips into ecstasy!

Thelma Forsythe

Vicissitude

An open page as words reveal, the very soul of self
Without the scars, the hurt concealed, I presume to have pure health.

A key unveiled unlocks the door, through cracks the pain is seeping
And though I can discover more, I cannot stop the weeping.

Inside a deep forgotten place, the gnawing and the wanting
Although I see a different face, I can't ignore the haunting.

The ghost of self does linger still, reminding of the terror
So hard to break the strength of will, not knowing of the error.

But now I see I cannot wait, I walk with new persistence
And with each step anticipate the usual resistance.

The pain removed, replaced with what? Without it I am reeling
For what to find? The wound is shut, I am free to change the feeling.

So see me now, with all the light, I think my soul is winning
I'll still be far from perfect sight, the journey just beginning.

Bart A. Riggs

The Mothball Fleet At Benicia

Transformed by vapor windings
   Mute hulks huddle ghost-like in shallow berths.
No longer proud testament to a warlord's might
   Silently grey monsters rust in regimented rows
As small waves tease their moorings.

Commissioned now to rude displays
   Damp twilights ridicule former glories
While passers-by nod final judgement.
   They bide their time uneasily
Before the scrapper's torch.

William A. Collier

Lost Childhood

As I consider the child I carry
I am forced to recall my own childhood.
Through circumstances beyond control
childhood was lost.

An invalid mother, and worthless siblings,
a wonderful father who had to work.
I was raised by him as well as by others,
seeing my mother seldom.

As my mother grew worse, I assumed responsibilities:
Those of a nurse instead of a child.
I cooked and cleaned and gave care
to one who should have given care to me.

Now I see children in our world today
forced through circumstances to abandon their childhoods.
Taking care of those who should be caring for them,
Becoming adults far too soon.

Let children be children.
Expose them to love, not responsibility.
Give care and see that they have a right to childhood.
Don't let it be lost.

Allyson Huggett

My Found Son

Stay strong my son
Life for you has just begun
I lost you once in the past
You were living life too fast
I don't ever want to go through that again
I want life back as it had been
That was then, this is now
We're going to make it — here's how
I'll be here to help you go to the top
By not smoking that destructive pot
Life without drugs will be heaven for you and me
You will finally be free to be who you want to be
We'll get our relationship back
Love we will not lack
You will have no more bad dreams
I only want to see you gleam
My poems usually don't rhyme
But for you I made one this time
I'll never give up on you that I could never do
For you hon, are my found son

Tami R. Narog

Destined

Destiny is waiting for you. Buried treasure
in the sand, a purpose hidden in the scars
of his hands. They are waiting for you to
do what no other can do. Don't let
them down, those souls who will become
the jewels in your crown. It would not be
the same if they never know your name.
Destiny is waiting for you to do what no
other can do. A purpose, a plan, the heart's
treasure in God's hand. Here's the key, just
believe, it has been hidden in the scars
of his hands. Never doubt that your life has
a meaning. All the struggles made you stronger
through the road you took was longer, you can
get there just the same. Coal under pressure
though a season of time, destined to become
a diamond, as a diamond you will shine, when
your destiny meets you face to face, through
prayer, determination, and God's grace. You will take
your place in time as a star in the sky.

Susan Kemp

What Matters It?

"What clear gray eyes, and warm gray eyes
　What gray gray eyes have you!"
"Oh, no" — she smiled:
　With accents mild
"My eyes, kind sir, are blue."

I looked again, to notice then,
　Her eyes were faintly green.
"What clear green eyes,
　and warm green eyes
The brightest I have seen.

She turned in wrath, to block my path
　"I want this out with you!
They are not gray,
　Nor green, I say
My eyes are blue — just blue!"

And to this day I cannot say,
　Which one of us was right;
But gray will do,
　Or green, or blue
Since she is not in sight.

Dick Brown

Trouble Up North?

The reindeer are having some problems this year,
　And Santa Claus drank way too much beer.
Don't know if they'll make it on Christmas Eve,
　We just have to hope and believe.

The elves too, are having some troubles,
　They've been sipping on champagne bubbles.
And Mrs. Claus, well she's feeling frisky,
　We all know she's been hitting the whiskey!

Yes, the North Pole has been quite a site,
　With not one reindeer out in flight.
What will become of Christmas Eve night?
　I heard Santa and Mrs. are starting to fight.

The stocking are hung, the cookies in place,
　Children are sleeping with smiles on their face.
Things look pretty grim farther up north,
　What will happen on the twenty-fourth?

Now don't you fret, I'm willing to bet,
　Your wishes and dreams will all be met,
Cause the snowman will surely fire up the jet,
　And Christmas will be the best ever yet!

Rhonda Westendorf

Lord! Thanks For Another Day

Sometimes, many times, maybe too often, we take our precious life for granted,
Hurrying thru life without fully understanding and enjoying life.
Too often we think of earthly possession to be more important than our precious life.
Perhaps, we should learn to give time to fully understand life, and pause to give Thanks to our Creator for a gift worth more than any earthly possessions.
Perhaps, we should learn to live a life with full purpose.
A time to show, "we care."
Perhaps a time to give "thanks" for the changes of the seasons.
A time to enjoy nature's blessing of the many changings within our lives.
To accept the uphill, downhill of precious life.
For too, soon, we have learned, we can no longer turn back the clock of life to make up for the hurrying of our life's without fully understanding nature gift to us.
Than, it's time to answer the call of our creator,
Perhaps, again not fully prepared.

Joe C. Juancho
Isleta Pueblo, New Mexico

My Mother, My Friend

You were there for the good times
    there for the bad.
You were there when I was happy
    there when I was sad
You nurtured me as a baby, taught me as a girl
    watched me grow into a woman entering the world
It's only now that I am a mother
    do I know things never known
It's now I sit and wonder
    how you did it on your own
A little girl with a women's roll
    ensuring my happiness as your only goal
You were there in the beginning
    you'll be there in the end
Bonded together forever
    as my mother and my friend.

Holly Neilson

Love Lost

The night has come,
light fades away.
But you're not here,
can't make you stay.
Let me take you back in time.
Where a girl lies lonely hurting inside.
She does not know.
She does not know who,
will end her pain caused by you.
A slave,
to your every need.
She walked a hateful path,
growing with vengeful speed.
And all the time wondering why,
she gives more than she receives.
The night has come,
light fades away.
But you're not here,
can't make you stay.

Renee Matsche

The First Friend

My life was cold, a dreary winters night,
Until into my troubled heart you came.
You chased back the darkness with true friendship's light,
And melted my heart with your love's sweet flame.
You woke my feelings from their winter's sleep,
And introduced them to the sun's warm rays.
The values you've taught me I'll try to keep,
And with love's sweet treasures fill my days.
Then maybe someday, in a future hour,
When these dark, cold days are far from my mind,
I'll change someone's heart with love's great power,
And continue to share this love in kind.
An inspiration I could someday be
By sharing the love you have shared with me.

Lori Van Emburgh

Separation

I picture in my mind
The love we once find
I capture that sound
The love we once found
Life is hard to live
Love is hard to give
We think of things that are deep
But our memories we will keep
So dear heart rest in peace
The love you once had has gone to sleep.

Vickie L. Graham

Planting Crosses

In a world so full of aggression,
What shall become of you and me,
When Killing is a great profession,
Designed to set our people free?

But spilling blood is not the answer,
To all the questions on the scroll.
And war is just a spreading cancer,
That kills the body, then the soul.

Why live each day expecting terror?
Why live for struggle and for strife?
Exploding bombs — a human error,
Strike against all human life.

For is we drop the bomb on their lands,
They'll surely drop the bomb on ours.
Then we can all become the field hands,
Who plant the crosses and the flowers.

Deborah J. Grzyll

Peaceful Resting Places

Trees gently swaying in the breeze,
protecting the enclosed area with ease.
Birds sing and chatter, their music filling the air,
as they fly they add to the beauty everywhere.
Quiet tablets of stone, telling lives of long ago,
Bringing the memories of all those we know.
Soft sweet grass to walk around,
making a lush carpet to soften our sound.
Colorful sprays of fragrant flowers adorn each plot.
A flag here and there to mark a special spot.
May we with reverence and loving grace
Feel these things at this peaceful resting place.

Karren Bott

Remembering Me

Wherever you are remembering me, know that I am remembering you,
and know that each and every part of my love was forever true.
Remember my laughter and my friendship and the pain will
slowly slip away,
Remember my tears of joy and garden's flowers in may.
Remember my smiles and remember how I cared,
remember my love and I will be there.
Remembering me may not erase your fears,
But it may help to dry some of your tears.
Because remembering how I loved you, even from this cloudy haze,
will help you remember that I will be watching from heaven for always.
Please always remember the love that we shared together,
and know that while you are Remembering Me, I am remembering you
    forever.

Christine M. Campaña

Untitled

She let him run her life
Now she's his wife
He gave her a disease
So every night she prays down on her knees
Now she's gonna have a baby
And there is a very big maybe
That the baby will die
Shortly after its first cry
All she feels is sadness
But it's quickly turning to madness
Then her husband dies
And every night she cries
She dies shortly after
And never again will you hear her laughter.

Michelle Hardin

New Fallen Snow

New fallen snow covers the grass like a canvas
As pure as a child's heart
It beckons me, longing to be touched
Giving me hope for a brand new start

I take a step and it hugs my foot
Nurturing me, inviting me to take another
With each step my heart grows stronger
Each different, unique from the others

The snow brings out your inner child
Your insecurities and fears fade away
It releases you from all your worries
So you can once again learn how to play

Within moments, I couldn't see where I began
And I was surrounded by nothing but pure white snow
It was there my heart had mended
It was there I could let my true self show

I awaken the next day to see my footprints gone
The canvas is once again pure
Today someone else will take the walk
And maybe someone else will find the cure

Brian Fraticelli

Does He Really Love Me?

As I sit here wondering if he's gonna call,
or if he's even thinking of me at all.
There's no real way to tell for sure,
But no words could say how much I need
him more, when I see him my heart beats
real fast, I wish I could say I need you
to love me like you did in the past.
I wish I could just speak my mind free,
But if I could do that, I would want to
know does he really love me?
God I need some answers to a lot of things,
how can I get them if I'm too scared to
ask anything? If love is fine why am I
going through hell with mine? I guess there's
no need trying to pretend because all good
things must come to an end.
I love him so much, I would give the
world to know if he cared half as much.
But you know God you gotta go through so much
just to get someone to say I love you.

Donna Faye Carrier

Let People Be

I had an angel kiss me on my cheek, saw a sandman visit while I sleep.
Brought into this world with the sun in my eyes, and saw life in
its disguise. I've felt the rain upon my hands, brought down
from heaven to cleanse this land. I was born with God in my
soul, who will love me always, so I've been told. He's always
been there right from the start. My Lord and I will never part.
The bad in me I must overcome, so I may be with him in his
kingdom. His Son has forgiven me for all the bad things, now I
look for the peace and joy he brings. God asks us to live love-
filled happy lives. Why do I have such anger inside? Anger
towards people who treat people bad, this anger towards people
makes me sad. I try so hard to forgive and forget, But I look on
these people as an awful threat. I will never understand, I will
never see, why people just won't let other people be I look for
the answers, but in the wrong way, I need God to be with me,
but am too selfish to pray. I need strength and guidance, from
heaven above, I need faith and hope. But most of all love. I
need to recognize all the beautiful things, And look beyond
myself toward the Good the Lord brings. I escape into my
dreams, to this fantasy land. Where my brothers and sisters
walk hand in hand I need to start thinking, thinking about me.
About only why I won't let people be!

Piper Goehring

Break

Drop a glass on the ground
and watch it shatter when it crashes.
And these threads that I have found
snap at my touch.
Try to hold on,
but the wind breaks me away
and sends me to another day
of memories I thought had fast
faded away.

Your last breath left you without sound,
but it was clearly seen when my heart paused.
And this moon that I have found
is only a quarter full.
Pray you reach it, and hope the wind doesn't
break you away, only to send you to a day
where your memories have fast faded away.
Though, in my heart I know,
that this is not the truth.
You reached the moon and the stars,
and you're still shining down on me.

Laila Lipski

The Moon

The swell of the moon
Brings tormented pain
For those who are marked

The brightness of the moon
Brings on their doom
The change has now begun

The glow of the moon
Shines down on a wolfish form
The loupe-garou now roam the land

The howling cries at the moon
Running free and crazed
The hunger drives them insane

The fading of the moon
The feeding done
The change back has begun

The moon is gone
Until the next lunar occurs
The loupe-garou will once more roam the land.

Lisa Cinquegrano

The Good Old Days

I like to hear of old times
And what was new back them
What they could do with those little old dimes
As they say a way back when.

In the good old days there was no bus
To take kids to their school
There was no time to stir up fuss
It was against the rule.

In the good old days we often yearn
to have them happen now
There were always things we had to learn
Like how to milk a cow

How to get along without wheels
Automatics, computers and such
How different from then are our meals
Have they really changed that much?

There are really more changes in the last few years
Then in all those years combined
In the next ten years when again one hears
How very much we were behind.

Eileen F. Hirten

Summer Rain

Sometimes, when the rain comes down,
On dried-up fields and sun-baked town,
To God, within my heart, I say
My thanks to Him for a rainy day.

But in gratitude I'm not alone
For the prayers I say are not my own;
I only echo leaves and flowers
In thanking God for cooling showers.

And prayers go up from herds and flocks,
And creatures living among trees and rocks,
And birds in the air, above sing praise
To Him for His blessing of rainy days.

Alexander J. Sulzer

Happiness!

As the holidays near,
And the winters chill,
Lets show love and compassion,
For the less fortunate and ill.

Give a smile and a kind word,
To friends and strangers a like,
A friendly word or two,
To big Bertha and little Mike.

This is the time for happiness and cheer,
To all mankind big or small,
Send a cheery card or letter?
Maybe we should make a call.

But whatever you decide to do,
Just make someone feel better today,
A little child or an elderly person,
Now feel the happiness as you go on your way.

Edna F. Peters

A Child's Eyes

Looking through a child's eyes, the world can become anew
Things you take for granted, take on new meaning for you.
Simple things like a sweet smile
Can bring warm sunshine for a while.
A baby's laugh, a bird's angelic song
How could you have missed this simplicity for so long?
Caught up in life's affairs, its busyness and its strife
Has almost caught you everything, even your very life.
Re-focus now upon the things God's given you to love
Re-think the things important, give them to the One above.
Yes, looking through a child's eyes, there is no greater thrill
Just take the time to watch and listen, take the time to just be still

Donna P. Clark

In The End, Love Always Triumphs

The masked murderer, he tippy toed
Across the room to her bed draped in gold.
A glint of satanic insanity glimmered in his eyes
    for a merest of a moment,
Then he froze,
The doctor scalpel lowered.
For a fraction of a second,
    through the fog of madness,
He recognized,
    his beloved, Bianca.
A single tear slipped from his
    dazed eyes,
And without a thought,
    raised the scalpel to his own neck . . .
    and sliced.
Hell received another "guest" that fateful
    night.

Kaying Pha

Remember Now He's Gone Forever

Forget his name, forget his face
Forget his kiss and warm embrace
Forget the love you once shared
Forget the fact that he once cared
Forget the times you spent together
Remember now he's gone forever
Forget him when he played your song
Forget you cried the whole night long
Forget how close you once were
Remember now it's him and her
Forget you memorized his walk
Forget the way he used to talk
Forget the times he was mad
Remember now he's happy, not sad
Forget his gentle teasing ways
Forget you saw him yesterday
Forget the things you used to do, remember now she loves him too
Forget the thrills as he walks by, forget the times he made you cry
Forget the way he said your name, remember now it's not the same
Forget he said, "I'll leave you never", remember now he's gone forever

Liza Clarice Porter

The Shadows Of A Hand

I was sitting at the table
Looking through the windowpane,
Thinking about the world's crisis,
And the people who are in pain.

God has given us commandments
That we should follow through
As we think of our daily living,
See, the shadow of the hand we must pursue.

This shadow of the hand is Jesus
Waiting for a beckoning call
From some loving little children,
Anyone, come one, come all.

if when you see this shadow
And recognize its difference indeed,
You'll find everything in the hand of Jesus
This shadow soothes your every need.

God's goodness is forever present
Jesus hand is surrounding you,
His hand is waiting for your submission,
Are you willing to take a hold and go through?

Linnie M. Wright

Ode To Betty

I entered the room and was suddenly unaware
Of all but my friend's beauty.
She was leaning back in a chair
And the maid was washing her hair.

That well-chiseled face was the ideal setting
For a pearl-perfect smile that goes on, unrelenting.

But why was this beauty so startling to behold?
The courageous spirit I'd always admired.
Our friendship now was old.

Our sons, our husbands, our everyday lives,
Sealed our bond of friendship as parents and wives.

Often I visited, we talked with casual air
Of everyday living, but always —
Always — the wheelchair was there.

What beauty in all mankind I've met
Did I not see
Because an insignificant mark
Just didn't jive with me?

Sophia Etsweiler

Untitled

There's an old Proverb
That proclaims, to be whole,
We must hear our silent music.
I wonder, will I know it,
When it comes?
I hear only the sound of a drum.

In my youth I remember the
Noise of a thousand thoughts
A second exploding in my brain!
Pulling me to and fro,
Without a melody to sing.

In middle age, my mental stage
Had dimmed the stars to glowing fires,
And the music sounded, most familiar
But loud.

I now feel the warming embers of those fires
Once so clear. Their radiant heat,
Will fill with the warmth of remembrance
Until the music has again turned to silence.

Donald C. Ramsey

This Last Day

This last day of summer
draws me into the green reminiscence of
sweet beginnings, tender and fresh.
This last day gives all
to the story of abundance in ripe perfection,
and offers a taste
of spicy-sweet pungent fullness,
just once more.
This last day adorned in
the clear of blue and the soft white worn
over the heat of luscious sensuality,
grows from the great deep roots,
draws from the cool dark source,
reaches to the crowning light.
This last day of summer,
with the wonder of change riding on seasoned air,
portends the beauty of golden endings,
in pregnant dreams through long silent sleep,
until the white stillness of rest stirs into
sweet beginnings, tender and fresh.

Lauren George

What Friend Are For

A friend is something everyone has,
Whether it is your mom, dad, brother or sister,
There is always a friend around.

A friend will make you laugh,
And make you smile,
If you need help,
A friend is willing to walk the extra mile.

To be there,
Is what a friend would do,
To show that they care,
About you!

Friends are for,
Being there,
Being fair,
And to keep you from bore.

To walk,
To talk,
To share,
To care,
Are things you need a friend for.

Joeylynn Boyer

A Mother So Kind

My mother's love is so undoubtedly true no matter what I ever do.
Her caring heart gives me peace of mind, she's always gentle warm and kind.
She hugs me like no other can do, when I'm happy, down or blue.
Her cheery smile can light up a room.
Whether near or apart she stays close within my heart.
My mother has the sweetest scent sometimes I think that she's heaven-sent.
She talks to me and I tell her the silliest things, hopes, fears, goals and dreams.
I never hear her complain about me, I love my mother so much at times I want to cry.
Her smell is so sweet, her hug is so warm, just as she did when I was her newborn.
I truly believe she's a gift from above and has a heart that is so filled with love.
My mothers an angel or the closest I got and to me she means a real whole lot.
My mother has always been there by my side to rule, and to guide.
Most people have treasures of the precious kind but me I have my mother and she's mine.

Lynnette Bustamante

Dear Heavenly Father

May I walk with you,
When I feel so blue;
Walk with me toward your gate with the light,
I aspire to feel happy I'm with you — future so bright.

Afflictions near and far,
Dwell on top and within like sizzling tar;
Seek me, hold me in your loving reach,
I aspire to feel happy I'm with you — like the waves of a beach.

Willow trees brush in the gusty wind,
The air is heavy and the clouds dim;
Make the sun shine through me — I like the sun,
I aspire to feel happy I'm with you — not a deserted one.

The harmony of your word sings joyous notes,
My return to innocence is wrote;
Let me sing to you a song in praise,
I aspire to feel happy I'm with you — my arms I will raise.

Like your angels I wish to keep you, my Lord,
The obstacles sending me astray I cannot afford;
Take my heart and guide me in your embracing ways,
I aspire to feel happy I'm with you — within your everlasting grace!

Dodi Ann Durgin

Mam

It's been a year since you've been gone,
But the memory of you still lingers on.
You were a very special lady in our lives,
So it wasn't so easy to say goodbye.
We miss you so much and it still hurts,
And breakdowns over losing you still
come in continual spurts.
You were a good Wife, Mother, Grandmother
and Friend!
Why did it all have to come to an end?
We miss you more and more each day,
Please help the pain to ease in some way!
You have taught us love, laughter,
understanding and caring,
without your help, life at times would
have been over bearing.
So rest now Mam the pain is gone,
But our love for you and your memory
goes on and on.

Mary Reibsome

Quickly, The Time Flies

Just yesterday, I was a girl of four,
I blinked my eyes, and wasn't anymore.
I had become a child of eight
And wished to be thirteen, could hardly wait.
Before I knew it, I'd become sixteen
On the threshold of womanhood, felt like a queen.
At nineteen, I married, just a young bride,
Ecstatic, in love, my groom at my side.
I became a mother at twenty-one;
We were proud parents of a beautiful son.
Our daughter came next, then one more boy.
We were poor, but happy, and full of joy.
The years were passing, more swiftly now,
Graduations, weddings, funerals; life passing somehow.
Yet it seems but a moment since I was just four
Life goes on quickly we've soon lived four-score!
So enjoy each moment or suddenly, one day
When we look in the mirror, it has all passed away.

Bobbie Brock

The Plight Of Unkind Love

What do you see in me?
Your eyes are full of me
I see myself in the corner of your eyes,
Sitting comfortably
You're always here for me
Waiting loyally, waiting patiently
I do need you, desperately
But there's a part of me
that holds me back from giving
myself to you completely
What can I do to escape the
walls that hold me back
The emptiness that fills me so much with lack
Life has taken my being and thrashed it.
Sadness has overtaken my heart and crushed it.
What do you see in me?

Margaret Walker

Sunset On The Beach

The sky when the sun is going in the moments of setting,
while the water that splashes off the shore from beyond the
mountains in the air around the hills, I have listing the names
of friends that would be there with me.

Climbing the mountains while the skies above seem to be so blue
when we are starting to climb. While we have rope for climbing
up the rock on the mountains in your imagination, like the dreams
we follow when we are finding the place which is here and now.

Tom DuPont

Love And Roses

Sometimes a relationship can be like
A budding rose beginning its life.
Petals unfolding soft and gently
Struggling to survive the nights uncertainty.

As time passes the velvety petals become
Hardened and withered by the sun
Falling from grace, parched and dry
The rose once beautiful, is starting to die.

Like the rose, love needs to be nourished
A hug, a kiss, or touch to encourage
If taken for granted love can also grow
Weaker and weaker before you know

So nurture the love you share together
For no one is here on earth forever.
"Till death do us part" were words once pledged
When standing before God, you were wed.

Brenda K. Cochran

I Can't Believe He Did This For Me!!!

I can't believe he did this for me
He touched my eyes and made me see
The wonders he had in store for me.
He touched my soul and made me free.
It made me sing and shout with glee.
I can't believe He did this for me.

He molded and made me just as I am.
Innocent, unassuming as the gentle lamb
My life was racked with sin and shame
It seems to be my claim to fame
He gave me the future without a fee
I can't believe he did this for me.

The peace, the joy that fills my heart
A promise from Jesus that we'll never part.
He died on the cross because of my sin
Then he promised to be my friend
My sins of the past are no longer to be.
I can't believe He did this for me.

Jim Barlow

My Guardian Angel

My Guardian Angel haunts my dreams
and fills my head with thoughts of
obsession.

My Guardian Angel watches over me to
protect me. My Guardian Angel floats to the
surface in my sea of emotions to keep my
soul in peace . . .

My Guardian Angel listens to me
but does not hear me. My Guardian Angel
loves me but not the way I want him to.

My Guardian Angel touches me but does
not feel me. I speak to my Guardian
Angel, but he does not hear me.
I want my Guardian Angel
to want me,
I do not want a
Guardian Angel . . .

Crystal Hill

A Token

Back then, when I believed in words,
That each carried the weight of gold
Heavy with truth,
I opened my palms to you,
And alms you gave me, in plenty.
I was poor in soul,
(And greedily took the bread)
But somehow, remained so
No fuller for the gift.
Each phrase you breathed
A melodious beckoning, a lyrical web
Intricate, delicate, but sticky with sin.
Thus caught so, I sank, a stone
Leaded with a fruit of my own
And yet you, you remain.
And as your words like pyrite pebbles
Tumble out onto the sidewalk glittering,
The beggars there are waiting
To put the pretty lies in their pockets.
So rich with illusion.

Beth A. Roberts

Seeking Not Our Own

I think that I shall never know,
a love as great as fine dough,
Fine meal that is balanced so,
that a mom can make so lovingly,
that feeds and nourishes her entire family . . .
Oh, but an expression of God divine
His son, he is, so balanced, fine . . .
Meal was he, it is so,
Divine love, divine humanity,
This is the only true love, for all, for you, for me, for all that
Be,
Eternal expression of true love divine,
What else shall ever really Be,
Worked out and flowing free . . .
God's divine love and divine humanity,
Working its way out to you and me, as well as all that Be,
All else shall never be, so let us join these forces,
That we may Be, lovingly set free.
Seeking not our own

Vernon R. Grady

Fortunes All Around Us

What is a ruby compared to a leaf in the fall?
Is a diamond the equivalent of a bird's spring song?
Does an emerald challenge the growing grass?
For the fall does not stay for long,
And neither does a bird's spring song.
These few I've mentioned do not stay,
Yet fade away,
Into the day.

Heather Jones

What's So Special?

You talk of all the experiences I have had
And how could I possibly find interest in you
When you speak, is it with . . . Envy?
Remorse for not having seen and done? Awe?
You bestow on me a feeling
That I am somehow privileged
To have seen and done so much . . .
But the senseless deaths and destruction
The pain and suffering
The horrors that man does to man in the name
Of duty, honor and country that I have witnessed.
The hurt that I have caused
Those closest to me
By not being able to share . . .
By not being able to tell . . .
How all that I have seen has forever changed me.
The times I have had to be alone
And have those who cared wonder why? And how to help.
All the sacrifices I made in the name of duty, honor and country.
I would gladly trade places for your sheltered world.

Randall K. Faulkner

My Silver Pegasus

I thought I saw a silver stallion standing in a field today,
Silver wings upon his back did lay.
Long, slender and graceful was his neck,
Upon his mane were many a silver fleck.
He flew away as beautiful as could be,
and from my dreams he did flee.
But I shall remember him flying away forever,
From my mind the silver pegasus, I can not sever.
Such beauty I shall never forget,
For in my dreams, I know we have met!

Juanita Mires

The Mystery

Dedicated to a man I love dearly, My Papa
"Live your life to the fullest," said an old man one day.
"And never let anything fool us."

"We find the mysteries of books and novels," he said as
he wobbled.
"But, God put on this earth, a mystery never to be solved."
"One that makes you wonder, beyond a shadow in your mind."
"One you think will never heal, even in time."

"The mystery that leaves the loved behind."
"The mystery that leaves the youngest blind."

He stared for a moment, up in the sky, then looked down
back into my eyes.
"You are not to fear this mystery, for it is a better
place than this."

"But to believe that the mystery lives on in the hearts
and souls," he said with a tap of his cane,
"And that the love will never let go."

Wendy M. Finks

Treasures

I looked at the ashes all spread on the ground.
Not a shred of evidence could be found,
That once stood a home full of treasures within.
To disappear in moments; to start over again.

Years of caring; pains to preserve.
I ask you now, "Do I really deserve,
All the things I'd worked hard for all of my life,
To go up in smoke, in spite of my strife?"

From within, a soft voice whispered gently to me,
Filled me with peace; opened my eyes to see . . .
It was only material things I'd possessed.
All of which perish — give no peace or rest.

I'd put my faith in cold, unfeeling things,
And realized the emptiness their weakness brings.
An inability to love and to share,
Or replace pain with comfort and care.

So now I rebuild on more solid ground,
A foundation so strong no fire can burn down.
A faith inn a power, a future to be,
That holds many treasures one can't take from me.

Karen Taylor-Forsman

To My Daddy

I used to be the apple of your eye
The thief of your heart.
But over the last several months,
Words and actions have torn us apart.

The roads of life have so many curves.
It's hard to stay on track.
If I could make just one more wish,
I'd do anything to have you back.

I try to remember all the good times.
Rosemary, Bonehead, just to name a few.
Popcorn fits, Scary rides,
It's all the things we used to do.

When the sun hides behind the clouds,
And the rain drops begin to fall,
I'll be the one holding the umbrella,
Protecting you from it all.

The back burner is getting colder,
But I'll be have when you need me.
Until then, I will step aside,
Sitting here, watching, waiting, letting you be.

Cheri Lynn Diffey

Growing Up

When I was just a little boy, you took me as your son,
Not of your flesh, nor of your blood, just love for a "little one".

You raised me in a web of love, you stood right by my side;
You gently wiped away the tears that children sometimes cry.

You held me in your arms at night, and rocked me sound to sleep;
You held the moments fresh in thought, that reality wouldn't keep.

And one by one the years did fade, till that little boy was grown;
And now it's hard to understand, my need to be alone.

You think that I don't love you, and you say I'm never home;
Sometimes there's just a need inside, to venture out alone.

The love I feel inside for you will never be replaced,
You can't imagine how I feel, when there's sadness on your face.

There are others in my life, with whom I spend my time,
But they will never take your place inside this heart of mine.

Please know that sometimes growing up means also growing away;
But loving you will always fill the best part of my day.

And when there's happiness in my heart, and I need someone there,
You are the most important two with whom I want to share.

Don't think that I don't love you, just because we are apart;
Growing up is sometimes growing away, but not within my heart.

Laurie Ann Turk

Tragedy

Tragedy . . . the thing that eats you up
inside, you'll remember it for the rest of your life,
you will learn to block it from your head,
although it will hunt you to an extent.
   When you think it seams so wright it isn't,
it's ok. To feel that way, but although in
the long run there will be something good just waiting to
happen to take place of the bad, just think of it that way,
because that's exactly the way God works.
   So rather than being abused sexually or getting the
crap beaten out of you, turn to God to lead the way,
he well get you out of this awful tragedy right when
you think there's no hope.
   Don't be scared just have a belief, and trust in our
God, for something good will happen in the future, don't
fail now keep going, succeed in life to prove you're a
somebody, because that's what you want to be. Unless
you just want to fall and pity yourself and
blame people for the rest of your life.
   Lead yourself to the right direction with God's
help, and you will always succeed for all eternity to come.

Erica Quezada

Basketball

Basketball is an exhilarating game,
It can even bring you lots of fame.
You have to learn to handle the ball,
Just in case you're a little too tall.
You have to play together in all you do,
Because the team doesn't just consist of you.
You gotta learn to grab some air,
Cause that will put you ahead by a hair.
You need to learn to be tough and stout,
Cause that's what it's all about.
Time out for them,
Time in again,
Go back and play tough and you shall win,
Our team,
Our colors green,
And we're awful mean,
Yeah, we know we're good to go,
So come on over and we'll give ya a show.

Lora Llewellyn

Good night My Love

Good night, my love, to your soft brown eyes, that shine like stars.
Good night, my love, whether you be near, or you be far.
Good night, my love, to all that's pure that's in your heart.
Good night, my love, may our souls never part.
Good night, my love, to every hour that you sleep tight.
Good night, my love, to everything that you think right.
Good night, my love, our names are written in the sky,
Good night, my love, and goodbye.

Lindsay Wilson

Memory

You came when I was least expecting you
feeble memory of life from the silent dead past,
blinding me, throwing me into confusion once again,
memory of life separating my world,
covering again the sky with wrong reflections,
in the forgotten framework of empty, futile days.

Transitory, rhythmical joy of self-deception,
words, sounds of an irrevocable hour,
illegitimate dreams of another era,
of shipwrecked illusions and multicolored visions.

Voices from moments that have gone,
beyond yesterday — beyond tomorrow,
throwing ambiguities at the present, vague hints
of other possible outcomes, of summer promises and rising
passions,
images of suns shinning bright on golden cities,
arrays of longings, erotic encounters,
ephemeral dreams of joyous nights — trivial imitations of reality.

Feeble memory of life past, you came,
shouting my name, when I was least expecting you.

George Carayannis

Morning Breeze

   In the mornings breeze
that blows a whisper of the day to glow.
   Glorious sunshine glowing
bright shows God's love upon the right.
   His promise of life through
Jesus, his son, through him our lives have just begun.
   Like the sunshine lights
the day the moon at night guides the way.
   The way of life is shown
through him a path of light we all should follow,
because in it, there is no sorrow.
   Our heavenly father's love is pure and in which
we can all be sure that through that love we can all
endure, the troubles of the evil lures.
   The lures we know are all against the treasures of the righteousness.
   A kingdom that is pure as gold and promises what has been told.
   Salvation's Grace has saved us all and in his hands will always
be for now and all eternity.

Penny Dykes

To My Son Larry With Love

You were sent to me from Heaven above
To have and to hold and for to love
Your eyes are like the stars from the sky
They twinkle and glow as you give me a smile
Your lips are like the rose bud kissed by the dew
They speak a promise that you will always be true
Your smile is like a ray of sun
It will brighten a day that just began
When you were a baby so very small
You made me feel like I was ten feet tall
I love you now and will for every;
For you were sent to me from Heaven

Estelle Johnson

151

The Rose Wilted — The Thorns Frostbitten

The rose wilted —
　　dead in my forged hands.
Hands of mine
　　bloodied by the stealth of the thorns
　　that bring tears to my eyes.
That flaccid rose
　　still in my hands that feel nothing
　　but the chill of winter.

The frostbitten thorns still piercing my hands,
　　feeling no bother of them. I, in dismay
　　and feeling just as it looks outside.
I look to the iced rose and wonder
　　just why did this have to occur.
Why did the beauty of the rose have to wilt —
　　dead in my hands?
Why did the keenness of the thorns make me bleed,
　　why did the thorns get frostbitten?

Mark Robinson

Untitled

One morning my sun didn't rise; the East was empty and metallic,
With sterile darkness bleaker than the waiting gray of winter.
　　Bloodless.

That day I buried my spent soul in an open grave of tepid clay,
Said no goodbyes and felt no sweet sharp grief, no warm earth closure made.

But while I lived the lifeless lie, stared unseeing where there was no sun,
You, Friend, came by: A Phoenix when I least expected one.

From where I shrouded lay, I felt your private clouds and purging rains
Then saw you gift-wrap and present me with your fragile rainbow.

You sifted me through broken dreams, and from the shards saved
　　stained-glass pieces
For me to gingerly admire later on, on peaceful knees.

You waited through that crippled day, and through the age of
unchanged night,
And sang and cried and sometimes prayed away my tired thoughts.

And with me look great sucking breaths when new air pinked the
thinning gray
And East gave answer with the soaring promise of a real day.

Thank you, Friend.

Rhoda Jessop

That Special Person

It's so hard to breathe, on the saddest days
My heart doesn't seem large enough for the need to reach out to someone
Feelings are hard to understand and control, because they're all one big maze
Think about never hearing, seeing, or touching that special person ever again

With the passage of time and changing seasons
Is it time to forgive and live for the future
Does our memory fade or is the picture that harder to see
You sacrificed your personal happiness for me

Looking upon that stone, that links you to my past
The love that I feel for you, can never be linked to the past
Your presence in my life, has given me the courage and will to continue
You gave up everything for me

There will always be dark and gloomy days
But I will search for that bright light, as you once did
Your smile is like an early morning sunrise that continues to shine until sunset
I misunderstood your reasons for giving everything up

The day has come, when I have forgotten all the pain that day caused
Yet, everyday I can't forget that special person in my life
The tears still flow, for the reasons you did what you did
You took your life for me and I will not forget

Bryan Kenneth Brown

The Sun And The Moon

The sparkling beauty of the sun
　　overcomes the sea.
The orange and yellow pallet of rays,
　　sprinkle the surface of the water with color.
The sun sets and disappears over the horizon,
　　awaiting for morning to come.
The sea is now a dull, mellow, still shadow.
As night falls the moon glistens with radiance,
　　creating illuminating ripples of cool sea water,
　　with a majestic white twinkle.
Until once again the sun will ascend,
　　leaving a blanket of light stretching itself over the sea.

Teresa McLaurin

On The Way To Freedom

A feeling of hate comes over you,
　　it's so cold.
You try to save your soul,
　　try not to be bold.
You feel that hatred in everyone is the same,
　　you're wrong.
You think you're worthless to everyone,
　　the feeling will stay long.
You then keep true to yourself,
　　you will then see.
You know that you tried,
　　now you are free.

Nicole Picard

Gold

It holds the world with a blanket of greed,
The substance that some men fear, but most need.
It supports all with its powers of life,
It controls others with toils and strife.
Gold, the substance that lifts dreams and wishes,
Also breeds mar through lustrous kisses.

Gold, a shiny, bright and glowing metal,
Sometimes given as the color of kettles.
It can be found in white teeth, big and small,
It is a prized treasure, for one and all.
Gold is a metal that can not be made,
Its secrets stay well hidden, safely laid.
Hopes and dreams appear through the lust of gold,
For the way it grasps and how it takes hold.

Elizabeth Albert

Gone The Extra Mile

　I went to my Grandmothers
when I was a boy. I looked at the
old house, what a joy. She was
my Great Grandmother, you see.
She was so glad to see me. She
was a doctor, that helped people
that were sick. She lived in sticks,
she was a real hick. She was also a
farmer. She had an outhouse way
out behind. She was so nice and
She was so kind. She walked to her
mail box that was a mile. She worked
and she cleaned, she still had a smile.
in her house she had a cellar and a den.
She had a pump that pumped the
water for all her kin.
She had a garden by her house
that she kept real fine.
She lived to be ninety nine.

Gerald A. Hailey

Our Pastor's Beard

Now we've got a great good Pastor
    He's youthful and sincere.
He's sporting lately a lovely suit
    And on his face a beard.

'Tis nicely styled, lends dignity
    To his other handsome features;
But his dark brown hair just matches not
    The gray that his chin bleaches.

This salt and pepper crop of hair
    Amazes me each day,
For how can a man of 35
    Sport an old beard of 60, say?

I remember that the teen age years
    Brings fuzz on chin a plenty;
But subtracting 15 years from 35
    Leaves his beard aged 20.

The mystery is this — if we subtract
    The 20 year old beard from 60, if we can,
The 40 year difference now just means
    The beard is older than the man.

Paul S. Miller

The Wind To My Back

When I feel I can't go farther
I feel a strong gust of wind from behind
All the troubles in my mind are erased
When the storms in my head rage
I look up to a cloudy sky
And feel the warmth of the sun on my face
A certain calm come over, its begging I cannot trace
When I feel alone, no one can I find,
I always know you I have you to confide
Even if your body has died
I know that your spirit has survived

Nicholas Kupsy

Untitled

The stars that twinkle at night
as the Moon rises behind your eyes
your Soul feeds on the Light of Love
your heart is of Angelic Desire
innocent sensations that dwell in
your Conscience, Memories become
forever engraved. Tears begin a
flood, Running for an Eternity. The
Waterfalls Destiny cascading through
Life, the rapids are ever turning
and everlasting. Iced fire encloses
your Soul melting your Desires and
Freezing your Thoughts — escaping your
solutions and denying your problems
all through the Menageries that you
envision through my Crystal eyes. Angels'
silk-thread connects you to the center
of my Heart's Desires — an invincible
strength that intertwines our Passions.

Crystal Blue Sparks

Time And Chance

From past, to present to future near time and chance
are always here. As the sun and moon always appear
time and chance make destinies clear. Time and chance
work hand in hand to bring God's will into our land.
For if there be a heaven or hell time and chance will
surely tell . . .

Roy E. Gogins III

Black Cadillac

I'm black — live in a shack
Drive a big black cadillac
You say I should turn my life around
Get my feet on the ground — look around
My life has improved — used to live in a shack
With an old hack parked in the back
Now I drive a big black cadillac
My piece of the American dream
Isn't that a shame — who's to blame?
You — me or the government who sent
All our money to wherever it went

Brad Jones

I Am The River

High a-top the snow covered peaks, I burst into life.
Through snow and dirt, I begin my journey downward.
Downward along the rugged peaks, I descends towards victory.
I create new roads on my adventure to the sea.

I press on with youthful vigor, charting my curse through the rugged peaks.
Taking with me secrets buried from deep within the mountain.
Nature's secrets and treasures are now my own.
Collecting, storing and rushing, I descends, searching for the sea.

Exerting my energies with strenuous jumping and demanding
leaps over thresholds.
I escape the constraints of youth and those days of wild adventure.
With the rugged peaks at my back I now cares the rolling hills.
Embrace the wide valleys and rejoice in their bounties.
The treasure of youth now becomes the burden of later life.
Gradually I release that I which I carefully hoarded.
Not so energetic, but with much dignity my journey continues.
I look forward anxiously towards the achieving of a life long goal.

There! Ahead lies my destination, victory is in sight.
Yes! Victory awaits me as maturity greets me.
My movements have now become measured and adventure is only a memory.
Those few treasures I still carry, these I now discarded in favor
of the final prize, entering the sea.

Gene M. Jones

Good Friday

Good Friday is crimson red;
The color of Jesus Christ dead.
This feel so sad because someone died;
But so great because His spirit is alive.
It sounds like someone dying for what they believe;
The smell of blood and everyone has to grieve.
It tastes to bitter sweet because He's dying for love;
But the day is so great because you know
He's looking down from above.

Mike Fanning

Despair

Spiraling down that endless hole,
trying to find, my lost soul.
Falling to an endless pit,
I've yet to find, just where I fit.
At times I think I've found my place,
but all to soon, I am face to face,
with despair that leads me deeper still,
to inner wounds, that will not heal.
I'm falling, falling, where is the end?
When will my heart begin to mend?
The darkness below is coming fast.
I need to know, how can I last?
Pain so deep, never ending.
A peaceful sleep . . . is my mending.

Barbara Hughes

The Master's Touch

She bathed herself in the early morn
By the warmth of the golden sun.
She dressed herself with the fragrance
Of the dawn as it had just begun.

She combed her hair with the gentle breeze
As she watched a cloud in flight.
She buried herself in silent dreams
While her feelings reached new heights.

She ran her thoughts down memory lane
To a place she seldom went.
She drank of the memories hidden there
And sighed in deep content.

She breathed in the quiet of a new born day
As the world stood standing still.
She nodded her head as God whispered
He was showing her His will.

Deborah Fordham Taylor

Life's Honeymoon

Baby, child — so precious, so loved
'Stay with me, Mommy — don't leave — no!'

Working, customers, achievement, oh
Money, security — 'Don't leave — no'

Little face, joy at the end of the day
Who am I? Who they say?
Look down on a housewife, only a Mommy
What does it matter?

Decisions, decisions
empty houses in day
Time passes like water
could she be two today?

Don't listen to them, follow my heart
Home with child, moments treasured
Live with less — need, not want
Gain much more — time together

Years from now, when the little face is grown
remember these times together
Daddy, Mommy, Rachel — Life's Honeymoon.

Heather Brand

Years Of Our Lives

When we were young we would yell and rage
Now we are old we watch and age
In our youth wisdom could not stay
But in maturity we have plenty to give away

In our youth advice we would not heed
Now we share with others in their time of need
We felt so cool to drink and smoke
To our regret we now stagger and choke

As teens we never passed a dare
Now as adults we take the time to care
As children each day meant time to play
As parents it means another working day

To Grandpa and Grandma's for some fun
We really keep them on the run
The grandchildren fill our lives with joys
It matters not if they are girls or boys

When the years of our lives have come and went
It only matters how they were spent
Did we leave them angry from all our taking
Or are they happy from all our giving

Alice M. Malsbury

Mark Is Not Lost

In the Fall when all the
trees are dressed in grand array.
I think about the days gone by
and wonder what did happen to us along the way.

My life has changed with time and
all past things are done, which prove a lot to me.

That the son I lost, was really
Jesus' son, he holds the victory!
And when the day will come we'll
Praise God together, in perfect harmony.

For I must travel on to other shores
until my time and my victory.
Do not count the cost or the loss
Rather see yourself upon his Cross.

Cling to sacred words and all
the graces that he gives.
We will always be together,
and know that we are his.
Forever we will sing the
greatness of the Lord.

Mary Benjamin

Little Church On Apple Street

I remember those wonderful days.
When I was young and started to pray.
The precious times that we all would meet.
In that church on Apple Street.
It is not a big church, in fact it is small.
But that little church will never fall.
God has been there many a night.
Saving people from sin and fright.
I remember going to Bible school there.
Learning how to love Jesus and share.
I remember the brothers and sisters so plain.
They were not out for fame or gain.
I remember the music from the piano and guitar players.
And all the beautiful testimonial prayers.
I can still hear my mother joyfully singing.
And all the other voices ringing.
All those good times were in that little church on Apple Street.
And I hope some day, I'll share a seat.

Gary Lee York

God's Compass

Behold, the Monarch butterflies,
With black and orange hue,
Flitting through the beach grass,
And over the lake, so blue.

On their way to Mexico,
To winter in the sun,
From a striped worm on a milk weed plant,
Look . . . how far they've come!

Other butterflies hibernate,
But not this butterfly,
Without ever having been there,
They know which way to fly.

Now they appear quite fragile,
When blown by the breeze,
Equipped with God's own compass,
They winter in Mexico's trees.

They fly about 2,000 miles,
Over mountains, land and sea,
But in the Spring, they journey back,
A miracle . . . to me!

Marge Shelden

In Search Of The Best Friend

It was early Saturday evening
And much to my surprise
Was seemingly a new beginning
Of a friendship with she of so beautiful eyes

All hope to develop a friendship
That will stand the test of time
But a with any relationship
It takes magic to become sublime

Time is on our side
To make a friendship strong
And just as the moon affects the tide
The "ups," not the downs, we must prolong

The meaning of the world friend
Implies a situation that will not change
Making it work then two cannot fear to bend
Though bending may cover an extensive range

We all aspire to find that Best Friend
When nothing has been left to hide
Representing the beginning never reaching an end
And into life, after death, we will be side by side

Dennis W. Lehr

Ocean

Green, Emerald and Blue,
crescent white that rides waves of Blue.
Shapeless forms in shades of green,
weeds that dance to this rhythm of Blue.
Withering, glistening silvery forms,
movements of a symphony known to none.
Below this crescent white form of Blue.

The Blue, almost life like,
spans bigger than most.
Thrashing, falling and calm.
Spits and swallows the sun,
on the edge with shades of Red.
In the nights it sings,
mystic melodies with sounds.
Reflects a mellow mood,
peace and calm.
A life that never ends,
this Emerald Blue.

Gerard Mark Perera

Thoughtful Oceanside Stroll

The joyous sands dance to the music of her waves,
and form geometric shapes that defy the mind of man.

The winged creatures await, at the end of her
moustache, to dine on her ebbing bounty.

How much richer would we be if we observed with
reverence, if we viewed without greed, if we touched
without desecrating, if we listened for the
messages from dear Mother Nature and wise Father Time.

We pollute her with our obsession for riches and
rot her with benign neglect.

From her womb she belched us, she loves us.

Let her take us to her bosom and nurture us as she will.

We must love and respect her, for to incur her
wrath would not bode well.

Our malevolent ways will convert her into our
grave unless our ways we change.

Oh, dear life-giving and life-sustaining ocean,
forgive us for we know not what ruin we rain.

Oscar D. Tucker

The Psalm Of Death

What is this thing called death?
Who and what determines
When we breathe our last breath?
Is it planned in advance, or is it merely left to chance?

What happens to our loved ones after they die,
When to us they finally say goodbye?
What difference did their being alive make,
for only too soon their life God did take?

Will we ever see them again someday?
Perhaps that is something only God can say.
Maybe it is better not to think of departed loved ones we adore
We should just pretend we don't know them anymore

Thinking of the dead will only make us blue.
We can't bring them back no matter what we do.
Whatever their fate is, after they die,
We can't change it no matter how hard we try.

What then is the purpose of our life?
Why must we put up with so much strife?
Perhaps God is putting us to the test,
and is preparing us for a heavenly trouble-free final rest.

Sandra Pearsall

Until Then

Fill the sails and fill the space,
that lingers in your night.
Hear the songs the echo sings,
and see the stars take flight.

When the night decides to show the day,
we'll sail away.
Far away.
Until then.

Take me back to nowhere and lay me by your side,
And talk of things that you've seen in your dreams.
A laughing wind, a sunlit smile, a broken sky
to mend.
A distant shore,
'Till there's no more.
No message left to send.

When the night decides to show the day,
We'll sail away.
Far away.
Until then.

Justin Brown

Untitled

Is it a law that designer labels make a person?
If so . . . I wonder why you've never tried not to abide by these
rules set aside by the majority in society
Millions of teens walking down the streets looking like machines
Clones created from one mind looking similarly
programmed to think and appear as one, lacking identity
All the while believing that you've got the advantage
Designers sit back relaxing in their $20 million mansion
enjoying how they've made millions thanks to their expansion
to "urban" wear "inner city" wear
Failing to realize that the "urban" kids the "inner city" kids
helped them to get where they sit . . .
School, educational grounds
look around and see a fashion show
Money and clothes is all you seem to know
Paying hundreds of dollars to purchase yourself
into similarity, opposed to individuality
Why would you want to be like everyone else, stand out
as an individual, bring out your personal, original,
individual, special style . . . Natural

Bonny Banini

The Guardian

Anxiously awaiting,
Unconditionally accepting,
Watchfully ushering the new soul's birth.

Tenderly holding,
Patiently guiding,
Radiantly lighting paths unknown.

Lovingly nudging,
Gently tugging,
Tolerantly whispering admonishing words.

Quietly comforting,
Mercifully pardoning,
Peacefully escorting the soul back home.

Thomas

Sunset And Shadows

The yonder reddened sunset trimmed in gold
reflects its glorious beauty on the lake
And should a skillful artist undertake
to paint a picture for one to behold
of this great splendor which remains untold
'twould take a lifetime all so foolish spent
while o'er his brush the painter steadily bent
to paint this winsome picturesque of gold
And when the sun at last lies down to rest
behind a monstrous silhouette of green
instead of yonder gleaming golden crest
but purple shadowed hilltops can be seen
the waters of the lake are calm and still
and the light has disappeared beyond the hill

Harry C. Norton

Untitled

I cannot walk down wooded lane or roam in
fields or hills or do the things I used to do to
make my life more fulfilled.

But I can write and read and pray; fellowship
with friends. I try to make the most of life until
my brief span ends.

I speak a word of cheer, help banish someone's
sorrow; I bear my handicap, till the dawn of God's
tomorrow. Someday when he says, "come on
home," I'll lay this chair and walker down and
walk again on Heaven's higher ground.

So I don't need your sympathy, God's grace is
quite enough; pity him who has no God, he's the
one who has it rough

Pastola Smith

Requiem

Abdication of that great, ravenous Thing which dared to call me prisoner.
I will no longer sit quietly.
Grievous sickness, I defy you.

I have shredded my heart in pieces — Pathetic trophies of
childish indulgence.
Hollow waters streamed from the eyes of invertebrate resignation.
No more. No more. They are a mockery.

Ashes to commemorate the fire of my emancipation,
The ineffectual dust of that which I called Master,
Sifting through my fingers like the crumbling of a femur.

Into my hands I commit you now.
You no longer have dominion here.
I take it from you at last.

Beth Miller

A Foreigner's Love For Americans

All I hear from the Americans is . . .
I don't want to be poor, I want to be rich.
I don't want to be rich, I want to be famous.
I don't want to be famous, I want to be indiscreet.
I don't want to be indiscreet, I want to be sheltered.
I don't want to be sheltered, I want to be smothered.
I don't want to be smothered, I want to be free.
I don't want to be free, I want to be obligated.
I don't want to be obligated, I want to be forgiven.
I don't want to be forgiven, I want to be condemned.
I don't want to be condemned, I want to be justified.
I don't want to be justified, I want to be ignored.
I don't want to be ignored, I want to be hallowed.
I don't want to be hallowed, I want to be loved.
I don't want to be loved, I want to be scorned.
I don't want to be scorned, I want to be acknowledged.
I don't want to be acknowledged, I want to be me.
I don't want to be me, I want to be you.
Myself, I just want a better life for my children.
God, I love these American people.

Maizin Shearer

Woman

Woman, if you show me once a while
    A bit of your smile.
    You don't know as wife
    How you'll change the custom of my life.

Woman, if you write me a poem in your own art
    That reads: "I love you from my heart."
    As Christians on Christmas pray the holiday
    seasons. I remember the day of your birthday.

Woman, if you change apart your mood
    In a quick race to get more mature
    With the moment and be able to face the future.
    Sincerely I'll live myself for good.

Woman, if you awake me up
    Every morning by a tender kiss to stand up
    the day. As catcher in football grab the ball
    I'll seize the loveliness that carries your call.

Woman, if you tell me your words are not real
    They are lies. So bad I'll feel.
    I'll lose the straight line of my sight.
    And I won't ever, ever catch back the light.

Hilter Remy

The Tale Of Blackbird Park

I watch the daylight merging with the dark.
Thoughts come and go, and all add up to none.
I walk till I grow tired in Blackbird Park.

I search the sky while wishing for a lark,
And wait for stars to come out one by one.
I watch the daylight merging with the dark.

I hear the homing blackbirds' raucous quark.
What can they know of yarns, how many spun?
I walk till I grow tired in Blackbird Park.

They say I knew that arrows seek their mark;
But could I guess the deed as good as done?
I watch the daylight merging with the dark.

It started as a game, a glowing spark,
When, to the target, I, like a moth, was drawn.
I walk till I grow tired in Blackbird Park.

So call it fate or chance or devil's work,
And some would have it ending as begun.
I watch the daylight merging with the dark.
I walk till I grow tired in Blackbird Park.

Dorothy Herring

Some Words Of Wisdom From Grandma

I don't think I'll start to drink
I will not smoke and I won't chew
I want to be good in all I do
My mind and body are dear to me
So things that hurt, "stay away from me."
I won't have sex till I am wed
I don't want AIDS to be in my bed
When I have children of my own
I want them to have a loving home
It's very hard to be a teen
I'm sure you all know what I mean
It doesn't matter how old you are
We all were young once and wanted a star
All good things are worth waiting for
For when you wait, you can only love more.

Barbara J. Morand

Essence of You

I saw a rose today and its beauty caught my eye.
It made me remember the time I first saw you
and brought a tear to my eye.
The dreams and plans we made, I wished for all the time.
But wishing won't make them come true,
and sometimes it's so easy to stop working towards them,
that we loose sight of who we are and where we are going.
We must always keep our dreams but have to put goals
behind them to keep us on the path we together decide . . .

I smelled a rose today and thought of you.
Its fragrance touched me the way you do.
I inhaled a deep breath of the aromatic scent
and enjoyed it for the moment.
The thought of you stayed with me all day,
it was most pleasurable . . .

Kyle Hambleton

Time

Time takes time.
There is know other way.
Yet chance is a promised time for life.
A dream shared by two in silence.
Bounded by one's self, in wisdom.
But shared by all as though it were not first or last but just best.
Forgiving is not forgetting, but remembering.
So many silent messages need a special kind of listening.
Every journey must have a beginning and past.
So thoughts and strengths will softly embrace our soul and minds,
as chance is always powerful.
Life is mysterious, in one hand you hold promise and the other
life and then you must choose.
Who's to say what is in store for today, tomorrow or yesterday.
It is certain that thoughts are all ready made conscious, it
appears outside, as fate.

Lillian Ahlman

There Was A Time

There was a time we had it all,
In love so deep we did fall.
There was a time of joy and laughter
With never a thought of what came after.
There was a time without a care . . .
What I wouldn't give to still be there!
There was a time my life was planned
To spend with you but fate's cruel hand,
Put someone there to steal away
What still belongs to you today.
Though we've seen our share of sorrow,
We will love again tomorrow . . .
Be it here or way up there.

Deanna Wurzbach

God's Gift

In pain I lay, and walk and sit
Never in comfort for even a bit
I feel empty, and lonely, never in peace
I feel nothing will get better to say the least

I hardly ever feel happy for even sometime
When I hear music from outside, and I know it's not mine

I listen and say, what is that beautiful sound?
Coming from all over, even on the ground
I listen real close, I look, and I see
Gods beautiful birds all around me

I thought I could never feel in so much grace
When all of a sudden, I notice, a great big smile on my face

So I thank you Lord for that wonderful lift
To get up, go out, and water, and feed, Gods Gift.

Rosalie Fornaro

Oh To Dream

It started in the city in the midst of a dream
    with corn-cob nights and twisted vanilla cream
Juicy thick lips pursuing melt-away hearts
    like fresh-baked pretzels in roll-away carts.
Astonished to see at the speed of sound
    floats you high on the top, where the world is round
Buttermilk sourdough with a light taste of honey
    drifts over the sides, a bit too runny
From dawn till twilight and morn until noon
    your thoughts, how tampered in the passing of the moon
Reality sets in as my alarm clock gives in; and
    a smile on my face as the day just begins

David Wright

The Forgotten Children

I am just a little child by size you can plainly see,
But this world seems to have forgotten
my ears and eyes can hear and see.

I should not have to hear the problems of this world.
Or to hear people swear and curse with every passing word.
I should be able to sleep soundly without hearing guns being fired.
To go to school in peace to learn and be inspired.

My eyes should look on the beauty of a loving
Mom and Dad.
I should see smiling faces look at me
whenever I am sad.

My life should be filled with laughter, love and warm embrace,
The world should know I am a gift from God.
The best part of the human race.

Amy Wassmuth

Your Love Is Sweeter Than Dandruff Shampoo

Your love is sweeter than dandruff shampoo.
With many to choose from you are the one,
Not Head and Shoulders or e'en Selsun Blue.
You seem to be all I need like the Sun
That shines its blinding light over the world.
The flowers, the trees, and the flowing breeze
Say together that I'm your little girl.
Bug spray and weed killers put some at ease.
As day turns to night, you're still by my side.
Some Bug Off keeps the mosquitoes away.
It even makes you want to run and hide.
So you say, "Adieu," and that you can't stay.
It may hurt me so, but it's quite all right.
I may as well do homework for tonight.

Maria Arafiles

Untitled

I sometimes sit and wonder
what it would be like to runaway
I think of how I would get by,
would there be a place for me to lay?
I think about what food I'd eat
and how would I get the money to buy it?
I think about how I'd take a bath
and my hair, when would I dye it?
Where would I wash my clothes,
in a creek or in a pond?
I wouldn't want them smelling like fish
or anything beyond
How would I take care of myself,
support me thru and thru?
Where would I get a job,
and have time to write letters too?
I sometimes sit and wonder
what it would be like to run away
Now that I've thought it all over
I think I'd rather stay

Leigh Ann Larmon

Connie, Where The Angels Hover

Clouds of silk and the sky spun with gold
A love such as mine should not go untold.

A life of waiting and prayers sent above
God chose each for the other to love.

Loving her now it's easy to know
How in an instant my heart was set aglow.

We walked on the beach, hand in hand
And left but one set of footprints in the sand.

For if it need be, one lifts up the other
And over us both the angels surely hover.

Her gaze and her smile bring such peace and calm.
With the message of love from the 23rd Psalm.

We look to the future and not to the past
Both hearts knowing we've found happiness at last.

We have no fear that life might end.
Knowing our souls ride on God's heavenly wind.

And as I'm laid down for my final rest
Of all my prayers answered, this one was the best.

Norman D. Cook

Bittersweet Memories

As the strong and powerful tide rushed to the shore,
  So did our love.
As the waves of the sea crashed to the shore with the urgency
  and fierceness of passion,
  So did our love.
As the grains of sand on shore trembled with the excitement
  and ecstasy of the waves,
  So did our love.
As the morning sun brought warmth and beauty by its erotic rays,
  So did our love.
As nighttime closed in with its protective arms of care and
  shared oblivion,
  So did our love.
As the tide receded back to the calm and gentle sea where waves
  would no longer carry the heart of intimacy,
  So did our love.
As cherished and coveted moments came to the end of an unwanted
  sudden death,
  So did our love.
And bittersweet memories live on.

Kathy St. Clair

Love

Like the stars in your eyes, love will never fade away
Like the winter snow, love will never drift away,
Like the promise of spring, love will blossom forever.
Like the fragrance of potpourri, love will linger on
and will fill your life's with peace.

Love will never die love is kind.

Jennifer Ann Owen

Pray For America

  "Behold, how good and how pleasant it is for brethren
to dwell together in unity," Psalm 133, "Pray for America."
America, the home of the brave and free; the home of one
nation under God; home of liberty and justice for all; have
we hid our candle sticks. Do we have enough oil in our
lamps to meet the bridegroom, our Lord and Savior Jesus
Christ. We sing God Bless America; As we look at the world's
events, have we forsaken in God we trust; are we really
trusting him? Are we being wise or are we living in
vanity? "Pray For America."

  We are living in perilous times. There is an evil which
God has seen under the sun, and it is common among men,
Ecc., Chap. 6. Are we dwelling together in unity. As in the
beginning, as Adam and Eve sinned, the traditions
continued from generation to generation. And as in the
days of Noah, some will continue to sin.

  The title "Pray For America," think about it. The
coming holiday season, a time of joyous celebrating, should
be a time of peace, love, and humility for all. And as we sing
"Joy To The World", remember there is a joy that this world
cannot give. That joy is "In God We Trust." Continue to
"Pray For America." And let freedom reign in America.

Ella Warren-Cooper

The Gift Of Youth

So careless and free, children seem to the old,
Still untouched by the world, and all it unfolds,
Their voices filled with an innocence we have all known,
And we often wonder why they rush to be grown.
Their lives seem so simple, and perhaps they never know,
The treasure of youth, to each God bestows.
Their questions reflect that everything is still new,
Children are so sweet and untouched like the first morning dew,
They love without reason, and that's how love should be,
Their laughter and smiles set even the hardest souls free.
Their lives are a pure gift from God's own hands,
And even though we all were once young, perhaps we do not
understand,
How precious the gift of childhood truly can be,
For everything is still new, and life is really carefree.
As we watch the children of today play and dance,
Let's remember they are a gift we are given per chance,
That we may remember the joy that youth brings,
And encourage their lives, and the songs their hearts sing.

Stephanie Thimesch

Goodbye

It's so hard to say goodbye when it's to a friend
It means that all the good times have come unto an end
Goodbye was the hardest thing that I could ever say
Tears were rolling from my eyes on that horrid day
Your friendship was the best that I have ever had
And saying goodbye to you has made me so very sad
I'll never really know how to say goodbye
And I want to be with you until the day I die
Someday I want to be where ever you are at
But always remember this, "I can love you like that"

Sarah Monteith

Gentle Lady

The gentle lady, stands and waits,
Never bothered by iron gates.
No man can have her as his own.
Her Love's for all, not one alone.

Though time speeds by, ever faster,
Her patience seems even vaster.
Never bothered by heat or cold,
Calmly watching the days unfold.

Every man's sister, daughter or mother,
She represents a love like no other.
This tower of strength, who can she be?
Haven't you guessed? Lady Liberty!

Rose M. Lineberry

Without

Once in a while I think about,
how the world would live without,
all the stars up in the sky,
or all the birds flying by.
If the fish never swam in streams,
or no one ever tasted ice cream,
If the world ever went without,
the sound of a small child going to pout.
If the world ever went without,
what would the world be about.

Staci Angelica Mane

You're My Mother

I made you cry so many times
I always thought we would have those binds.
Mother and daughter is what we are
Before there was nothing but a big steel bar.
That bar was between us for o' so long
Every night I heard you sing that sad song.
You were always there to stand by my side
But I guess sometimes I had to swallow my pride.
I know it was hard not knowing if you are going to see me
Because I was always out in the streets running free.
Today things are a lot better
cause we are trying to work together.
Now I can tell you I love you with no delay
I wish before that it could have been this way.
You are my loving mother
And in this world there will never be another.

Vicki Scheufele

Love From The Shores Of Spain

He came to our city
lovely; forgotten — filled with pain
leaving His first love
on the Shores of Spain
nothing made Him happy
His spirits were low
When down the stair case
His eyes did behold
A lovely vision — dressed in gold
He thought of His first love
on the Shores of Spain.
He cried, as a tear
rolled down his cheek
He spoke to the Lady in Gold
Her smile all aglow — and eyes
so bright — gave Him memories
of His love — from the Shores of Spain
Quickly they embraced
and fell in love
Just as His love — from the Shores of Spain

Joan Andrus

What'll Ya Do?

What'll ya do when you have two
    things that need to be done?
Will ya do them together? Or will that take forever?
    Can you do one on the run?

You're in a hurry. Life is a flurry.
    You know you're not having much fun.
Your blood pressure's up. There's no time to sup,
    Truly, not even a bun.

Do one at a time? That would be fine.
    But you know there's room for but one!
Which one to choose? There's no time to lose.
    You already should have begun.

How nice it would be if you could just flee
    Far away into the sun.
Go for a ride. Soak your feet in the tide.
    . . . Don't do either one!

Diane Maringer

Love Is Never Lost

They say it's O.K. to cry,
    And I cry.
They say time does help.
    But how much time?
I feel anew the loss, the empty space.
    They tell me God is here.
Why is it so easy to feel loss . . .
    Yet so hard to feel God?
But I know God is Love;
    Love is energy;
And energy is never lost.
    Perhaps transmuted —
    But never gone.
That I can understand.
    That I believe.
So all who loved me,
    And all whom I loved are with me always
    Through the never ending energy of love — and
    God is love.

Lee McMillan

Chevrolet

Look,
When you've got the air-conditioning on in the Chevy,
You leave the windows up. You know what I mean?

When the tape deck is telling ya,
"Run and fetch the bucket — get the baby some beer . . ."
and you got the bass and the treble just right with the volume,
Then you're cruising. The cruisin' crusades.

You're ready to see America in your Chevy.
Ready to low ride on the highways. The back roads.
Dirt. Concrete. Macadam.

It's all out there.
Purple mountains maintaining red, white, and blue skies.
Moon light illuminating star lit night.

You got the visual in manual
and you got the audio in automatic.
The whole thing is in balance.

Your Chevrolet is in balance with nature.
Nature is in balance with your Chevrolet.

You are contained in the Chevy. Contained in a capsule.
Capturing America and this is all so very American.

Zook Gaffney

Untitled

I watch myself like a movie, my mind . . . the critic.
I watch my confusion, my pain, my bliss,
I see myself envy over things I can't change.
I see myself cry over the past and the future.
I hear my heart scream when people say I'm naive, that I don't
understand, that I haven't met "true pain"
I watch my lips curl into a smile when I see him.
I watch my skin turn red when I can't think of anything to say.
I watch my muscles bunch and expand when I run from my problems.
But then feel the burden taken from my back when I confront my fear.
I see my fists clench when I think of my father,
And see the tears in my eyes when the memories come thundering back.
I see my throat swell when I turn on the television and murder or rape
are flashed across the screen.
I see myself dream and sometimes wish I could dream up a reality,
So then maybe I won't worry so much about opening my eyes,
I watch myself laugh when I'm with my friends,
And I watch bonds form between us each separate yet strong.
I see the pain that forced me to have strength.
I see the bliss that I lingered in.
I see the confusion that I doubt will cease to be. And I see me.

Hannah L. Davis

To Marcy As She Leaves For College

Even if you had not been my child
I would have loved you . . .
That irreverent sense of humor
Astounding insight and compassion
An appreciation for satire

When you are away
Your spirit stays all around . . .
Memories of dimples announcing the next laugh
Those endless questions
All echo in my sometime darkness lighting the way

What a reluctant pleasure it is
Releasing you to the world
Watching your reactions
Sensing the impact you have on others
Illuminating the world with your essence

Travel the future with courage
Know that you are loved and treasured
Share with the world your particular insights
Question everything, laugh quickly
Remember that happiness and sadness lie within

Dana Rushing

The Epitaph

Her eyes were filled with depthless pain.
She wanted to go home again — but knew that she no longer could.

Her path in life had gone so wide.
She'd completely gone to another side — to which family could not follow.

She wanted to go home again
and thought she couldn't stand the pain — of life without her mother.

And she's fought so hard to leave the place;
had finally departed in disgrace — the mother that she'd hated.

Now, she wanted to go home once more but
Knew she could not find the door — even if they would accept her.

It's just too late. She can't get in.
And never can go home again — for home's no longer there.

But still she longs for home, once more,
head filled with memories galore — of family now departed.

Courtenay Johnston

Husband's Love . . .

I bless the day I met you
and every day since then
The way your eyes speak to mine,
near the beginning of a grin

Your touch soothing, cooling and healing
my brow hot, your presence welcome
after a long and tiresome day
adding meaning to its name, home

Each passing year increases
respect for your mind and love
my being trembles with anticipation
time only adding to our trove

Our life passing on to children
way nature has always been done
seeking meaning beyond understanding
before our allotment is gone

Yes, I bless the day I met you
and every day since then
I trust you feel the same as me
for we'll certainly meet again

Kenneth Moore

Ballad Of The Unforgiven

Unbearable pain flies in on the wings of night,
Happiness is gone forever, my soul is void of light.

On the unforgiven, blackness descends,
Beyond despair and wretchedness my heart transcends.

I stand alone, my spirit broken,
Dwelling on words from you that were never spoken.

For the loss of you, I will never be the same,
Unaware of my crime, still, I am to blame.

You left no question of how you feel, slowly I'm fading,
That I'll survive this, poorly, I'm masquerading.

Each mournful breath, rended from this desolate heart,
Grows ever more funereal every second we are apart.

Despite the insufferable torment I love you still,
Always have loved you, always will.

Sinner though I am, I would give my life to make things right,
If we don't talk, for me the road to nowhere is the only road in sight.

The unforgiven would welcome death's enfolding arms,
Rather than live a life bereft of your charms.

Michelle Marie Lowe

Thinking Of You

I have a feeling I just can't hide
When I think of you I feel so happy inside
My deep dark thoughts of you are wonderful
Your gracefulness is vividly beautiful
Dreaming of you makes my heart passionately flame
Hearing your lovely voice does the same
You have beautiful hair and eyes
It is for your love my heart cries
Darling I love you very much
Your heart is what I desire to touch
Cupid shot my heart
The arrow will never part
You are luscious as paradise
There is no commensurate of my love for you at any trice
Oh darling I can't wait only longer
With each day my love is stronger
I want you to be with me
From now to eternity

James F. Phillips

One Parents' View

It's difficult to tell with mundane words
The feelings one has for their child:

Sometimes there's a feeling of such tenderness
When they look at you and smile.

A fall, a cry, to mother they run
To let her know there's something amiss;

A knee that's scratched, an elbow they've bruised,
But she'll make it well with a kiss.

The confidence they place in you
As you train them by your side

With anxious care you worry
Lest you fail them as a guide.

Frustration greets the teenage years,
Apprehension, disappointment as they revolt;

Their inner turmoil shows itself.
A child no longer, not quite adult

Then as they grow and they mature,
With hope your heart is filled:

The love you've tried so hard to show,
In them will be revealed.

Kathleen Jensma

The Wall

I saw a man the other day
Scraping a mural from the wall
Of a local bank downtown;
A piece at a time, the paper would fall.

He worked rather fast and carelessly,
Not caring how it came apart,
But as I watched him scraping,
A pain went through my heart.

You see the wall was old
And they said they needed new,
But if you'd have seen what was coming down
You may have well cried too.

To see what man can take apart
With just some simple tools,
Makes me see that man himself
Is truly the King of Fools.

I think God put us here on earth
To enjoy and procreate,
But if we stay on our present path
We'll have a different fate.

I wasn't bothered that the wall came down,
The paper really had no worth,
But the mural painted on that wall
Was that of our only Earth.

Richard Carpenter

The Essence Of You

As petals to the rosebud,
Your arms surround my being.

Like the bouquet of a fine wine,
The thought of you clings to my soul.

What is that magic in you I adore?
Your smile? Your loving? Your compassion?
No — 'tis more.

Perhaps those eyes, that laugh, the tender touch.
What is that makes me love you so much?

A. Mendes

Scars

When I was very young, my heart was full of joy and love;
A carefree child without a care, and as gentle as a dove.

I grew to know that every trial, this life would cast my way,
always seemed to leave a scar; there was a price to pay.

For each step up the ladder, the cost was awfully high;
Discouragement came easy, no matter how hard I'd try.

A day came bringing sickness, when surgery was a must;
The scars upon the body, brought about distrust.

Why should all this happen, to a heart so full of joy?
Scars upon the body? The mind can be so coy!

Then came defeat one dreadful day and left all hope behind;
and I discovered scars can also be upon the mind.

For all that I've encountered in experiences ever dark,
None can be so painful, as scars upon the heart.

An unfaithful lover, a thoughtless friend, can wield a crippling
blow, causing scars so ugly, we cannot seem to go

On with life another day because of all the pain;
Be kind and try your very best, never to wound again.

That heart that loves and trusts you, that depends on you to be,
A strength, a tower to help them as they travel on life's sea.

Be a light in the darkness, an anchor when swift waters flow,
Never ever scar that heart, it could be the fatal blow.

Vivian Watkins

Speech

Did you ever stop to think how complex speech really is?
It is made up of words and letters and thoughts.
Change one of the letters and you have a new word.
Change one of the words and you have a new thought.

If you hear it one way and I hear it another,
It can make friends enemies or enemies brothers.
The intention or thought behind the words
Is what makes for the truth and lets it be heard.

If you don't understand me, you need only ask
There are millions of words and one does the task.
If the first one won't work, I'll try another
Until you have in your mind the thought that's in mine.

Some words mean the same to all of mankind.
Some words are a treasure just ready to mine.
Some words are explosive and cut to the quick.
Some words hit with a force that is stronger than bricks.

My purpose in talking is only to join you.
If I say something wrong it isn't to harm you.
Please ask me if hurt and give me a chance
To try a new word that might make your heart dance.

Katie St. Hilaire

Family Ties

A good friend you were on the day I was born
We were both family, all new and not worn
We soon realized of the ties that we had
Two brothers for life what more could we ask
Sure it was rough, but the times that we had
The fight and the play times, things weren't all bad
Sometimes a tear and maybe a whine
But the cheers and the smiles healed all that with time
And as we grew up how different we were
But as time has passed on, the likeness occurs
Now I can see, what I may have forgotten
The support and the love that we have for each other
So to you all my hopes and the greatest of times
And thank you big brother for the rest of my life

Jason D. Dinwiddie

Mommy

If a mother is a mother, then so let it be;
Each child should be touched by your generosity.
When I was just a child, I didn't know what you had done for me;
Now that I am older, I've begun to see
What a mother like you would do for a child like me.

I am still getting older and, as the years pass by,
I look back on old memories, memories that make me cry.
And when I'm all grown up and have a child too,
I'll look back on old memories,
memories of you.

Kristen M. Furnace

My Prayer

After I said my prayers tonight,
I thought I might see Jesus,
so I turned my light on but when
I got up in the morning,
I knew I hadn't see my Jesus,
but a warm feeling came over me,
I knew I would see him some day,
and without him I couldn't cope.
The days are going by fast,
and with people not loving each other
as Jesus taught us,
we live in despair and helpless lives,
but we go smiling and helping
the lonely and hurt so you see the good feeling we
call can have on the earth I pray.
As we wait out our lives,
our mind is more alert
and now we are happy and forgiving

Adrian Y. Terry

Simple Salvation

I forget many things, and am not very bright,
But, I know the difference between darkness and light.

Though my sins are many, He wipes my slate anew.
God gave his only Son, and He died for me and you.

Things of the world may be pleasing to the eye,
But the Lord wants us to focus on Him on high.

Many smart men, know many things,
But no man knows what tomorrow brings.

And if you don't know Jesus, don't let another day pass.
For it is easy, all you have to do is ask.

Robert M. Paulus

Memories And Years

Crystal waves wash along the shore
I stand alone, in time, and wonder
"Is this the sound of my heart missing you
or just the wind on the water?"
I'm walking on the edge of despair
Where will I be tomorrow?
Do I only hear the echo of your heart.
in my mind?
Will I only feel your touch in
my dreams?
Is tomorrow the road to happiness?
Or is yesterday the happiness passed?
I long for a soul to share and hold
Will I ever know your presence again?
Must it be another life time?
I turn and face life, unfair and mean
No turning back toward pastures green
Home is where you were

Jeanne Salama

What You Deserve!

Judgement of people is something inborn, I'm not sure it can be taught, connection and feeling go hand in hand with deciding who's is decent and not.

Choosing a spouse is judgement of maximum importance. It exceeds any job of choosing a new friend or business acquaintance.

He's a lifelong partner who'll be with you, through jobs, babies and death. You should definitely plan on him being there when you draw your last breath.

So it's wise to select reliable, compassionate, ethical, kind
A man that reveres both God and his mother, don't enter into marriage blind.

It's not imperative that his shoes are in style, that his suit is the finest made, or that he can par on the golf course, or knows the words to the latest song craze.

You don't need a man that can put a dent in a keg, or know all the sport statistics, or a guy that drives the trendiest car, please don't settle for less than fantastic!

Keep in mind what I say when you judge him, for on the priority curve, You deserve to have the best man, I hope you get what you deserve.

Gail D. Miller

What About Tomorrow?

I'm sad and confused, I'm alone.
I'm hurt and used, no one to lean on.
I can see tomorrow, I plan the route to travel.
The knowledge I need to succeed.
It's the details I can't unravel.
I walk around with a frown.
'Cause I let this world get me down.
I've traveled so long down this road.
With life's burdens as my load.
Time seems to be running out.
All the things I used to believe, now I doubt.
What does the future hold?
For me it's useless, the world is too cold.
I feel like an oak tree, that shakes in the fall winds.
As its leaves are blown away.
Just like my friends. And alone it must stay.
What are we here for? I'll never know.
I feel I am doomed. And the sadness continues to grow.
Is tomorrow going to be brighter for me?
Well, I guess I can only wait and see.

Debra Doyle

Gentle Warning

Do not follow in my footsteps, daughter.
Do not waste your life
And throw away your precious dreams
For a lifetime filled with strife.

Set your sights on freedom
And fulfillment of your goal.
Do the things you want in life
To satisfy your soul.

Nurture most your own fierce fire;
Let no one put it out.
Or later what you could have done
Will always be in doubt.

Be careful of your choices;
They may later be to blame
For a total loss of freedom
That will suffocate the flame.

Listen carefully, my daughter
To what I have to say.
Or you may find what you gave up
Was too great a price to pay.

Ann Linn

Sand Castles

Alex died just three months shy of his fourth birthday in a maelstrom
of pain and strife.
His scattered ashes sparkled across the sea.
I built castles from his sand-bones so he could dance the rooms at
night in an unending tide of life for me.

Alice Black

My Garden

I have a little garden
That no one ever sees
For only I could go inside
To do what e'er I please.

Each day I love to enter and take a look around
To see that in my garden
No grass or weed is found.

Yet sometimes do I shudder, at all the things I see
Within that little garden
That never ought to be.

And then I pray to God above and ask Him earnestly
To help me keep that garden
The way he teacheth me.

It's simple to be loving
Be kind to all I see and do unto all others
As I'd have them do to me.

Then from my little garden
To all I will impart
The light, the joy, the sunshine
That grows within my heart.

Edna Gumbs

Untitled

Love is . . .
    Affection that is hard to find
Love is . . .
    Affection you won't find every time
Love is . . .
    A great thing as long as it is love
Love is . . .
    Affection that can not be rushed
Love is . . .
    Affection people get into then get crushed
Love is . . .
    Affection given, affection received

Jennifer Poole

The Man Who Became A Bird

Once upon a time there was a baby bird;
Came the morning when the mama bird heard
Her baby sing and chirp and sing
And try to fly on tender wing
For 'twas best that to the nest
Her fledgling did not cling.

On that very day there was a baby boy;
Hour by hour his daddy's pride, his mother's joy.
The small boy wished that he might be
A mighty bird so strong and free
And so, afar upon a star
That wish grew steadily

And as he grew to be a handsome lad;
Silver song of flying ships did make him glad
His love, his fate called out so gay,
He spread his wings and flew away
Near the sun, the two were one
That happy, heavenly day.

Bruce L. Dickinson

The Procrastinator

I don't wanna, I don't wanna,
Homework is a pain.
Teacher's mad, she says I'm bad.
Lord, school's gonna melt my brain!

Do I have to? Do I have to?
Class is almost done.
It's getting late, I think I'll wait.
Right now I'll have some fun.

I'm too tired, I'm too tired.
I'm just barely awake.
It's too early, much too early.
Just a snooze I'll take.

This is stupid, this is stupid!
I'm not gonna learn a thing.
I need some rest, that would be best.
A headache, that's what this will bring.

I didn't do it. I didn't do it.
A zero I will get.
But I could hand it in late . . . On another date . . .
But I won't do it, I bet.

Amy C. Kline

My Pat

The memory of his lean and hungry
    years was difficult to abate
He planned, he saved, his fortune to accumulate
Proud in spirit, straight as a die
    He thought it only fitting
For every man to try
    To stand alone in every way he could
And still be generous, faithful,
    And, oh, so very good
He never realized how much class he had
    His blue eyes twinkling, his laughter
    strong
Of him there was never any doubt
    of doing wrong
When he took a wife, his whole
    heart he gave her
And his hearth and home
    were all that he could savor.

Margaret Burton

Advent

In our world full of darkness and lives torn apart,
    Comes a child to be born in each person's heart.
For the promise is given that a new light will come,
    To open closed eyes, bidding lame ones to run.

Can we believe this in times that grow dim?
    When may I find, this new life within?
Can we believe that a new age is here?
    When will the new day dawn without fear?

The future is open for each one to see.
    A new day is rising for you and for me.
A reign without hunger, or violence or greed.
    A time when God's love will fill every need.

Now we must choose, just how life will be.
    Choose to break bonds and set people free.
Now is the moment, God's gift to receive.
    To live every hour as if we believe.

It is in the doing, that hope will appear.
Find in your loving, God's promise made clear.
It is in our actions that love finds a home.
Our lives bear the new life for each one to own.

Toni Smith

God's Not Through With Me Yet

I got to work late, car had a flat.
Didn't have a spare, never got it back
My shoes that were white now are covered with dirt.
Left my boot's at Mae's house nice work.
During report we talked about the rain
Looked down at my uniform a big coffee stain
Went to eat at four stuck on the elevator
Couldn't open the door
Gave up my lunch to the kid called, Mell.
Had to or just here him yell
Back in time to get off work
I'm hungry so go eat some place
In stead of my car, just an empty space.
Missed my call at home, a guy I just met
But I'll start over again tomorrow,
God's not through with me yet.

Laura Toole

Gypsy

A gypsy standing on the edge.
Where earth and sky had formed their ledge.

With black tears streaming down her face.
Her hair and wind in deep embrace.

Extending her arms up to God.
To put an end to this facade.

I watched her from the mountainside.
So beautiful I could have cried.

Like one deep breath I took her in.
Forgiving her for every sin.

She screams, "Our parents start to die."
"And I can't hold you when you cry."

She stood there naked, fully clothed.
So full of love that she had loathed.

Her heart surrendered with the sun.
Her black dress and night became one.

She tells the moon that she must go.
Her wish, the stars already know.

I wish, she didn't love me so.

Kat Erickson

A Tribute To Cardinal Joseph Bernadin 1928-1996

On November 14th, you went away
Forever from this earth to stay.

You left behind a legacy of compassion and caring
You taught us patience and the meaning of sharing.

When falsely accused, you taught us to forgive
You showed us the true Christian life to live.

A Church statesman yes indeed, of a diocese so grand
but more than that, a shepherd, a symbol of God's right hand.

You always treated others just as you would like to be and so
When you died, God approached you in His mansion all aglow.

"Come in Good and Faithful Servant
Welcome Home, Cardinal Joe."

"On earth, you tenderly cared for my sheep
and now, Heaven is yours to keep."

You are gone from our sight now Cardinal Joe
Living up in Heaven above
You'll always live on in our hearts,
Please look down on us with love.

Regina A. Riedmatter

Lucky Stars

When I try to think back to the days
of my childhood, I often shiver.
The sunny days are still fuzzy in my
memory, as I try to recall them through
the dark clouds that hovered over me.
Everyday seemed like a new battle,
with my life being the complete war.
As I grew, I learned to live with
anger and resentment, never really knowing love.
Then last spring, on the fourth of May,
my life change completely, forever, for better.
Now that it is winter, all these months
of recuperation, have led me into a new life.
A life filled with friends, family, faith, and
Love I never imagined.
I wake up now, everyday happy to be
a live. Looking forward. To the joys each
day can bring to me and my family.
After all those wasted years, I'm
happy to have been born again, and I thank my Lucky Stars.

Janel I. Houchens

A Rose Petal

A rose petal:
It has fallen to the ground
And been moisten with dew.
You come by . . .
And pick it up!
You look at the beautiful creation and
Wonder!
Why has it fallen — (To the ground)?
Then you realize, that rose petal represents you,
Your life, mankind — (In general):
And how we have all fallen, short of Gods glory,
But how he picks us up and moisten us with
Showers of love
The only difference is, that when you start to leave
You lay the rose petal back on the ground;
Never to be seen or to be held again.
But with Jehovah God!!! He will never forsake us or leave us!
He's always there,
To pick us up.

Crystal Adams

Numinosum

Prick the dharma to find a closed flower,
a veil of being broken at dawn
dispersing colors without effort,
as trust wrestles with fear.

Soft whispers of hidden light,
warm radiation of awareness,
guide the lonely sprouting seed
who sings unto You:

O the Mystery!
O the Misery!

Trembling in His presence,
the rustling leaves offer their movement,
catching and reflecting the radiance,
as the wind blows its hymn:

Rejoice in emptiness.
Rejoice in nothingness.

A silent confusion echoes each breath
as the ancient letters of the One,
pronounced only by the grass,
are revealed to the man in prayer.

Craig David Blinderman

Forever

It's been forever since I've seen
you. God it feels weird. I cherish the moment
we meet again. Since reasons unknown have
us apart. Time has been lost and forever
has been found. The touch of an angel
lingers on me still. But lost forever it will
always be. Our cherished moments will linger
on even if not we.

Heather Schwartz

The Senses

I saw it all today; the caisson drawn along its way.
   The drums marking the beat; the heels clicking in the street.

I heard the sobs of sorrow too; the caisson as it passed on through.
   The eyes mirroring the devotion! The tears showing the emotion.

I felt those pangs of grief; the caisson as if drawn by a thief.
   The lady following in its track; her dress, her veil, they
   were black.

I tasted the bitterness on my lips; the caisson as it made this trip.
   The children also not far away; this was their father's funeral day

I smelled the clear air in the field; the caisson, it no longer wheeled.
   The people that have come this way; they bent down and I heard
   them pray.

Give us a sixth sense, dear God, today; for there was our President.
   There he lay.

Harold L. Wohl

Almost Gone

Almost gone is the breathe of the light.
Almost gone is when you tell your mother goodbye.
Almost gone you're getting high.
Almost gone there's nothing on your mind.
Almost gone you dream through the day.
Almost gone you're gone for the night.
Almost gone you haven't been drown.
Almost gone is the end of the day.
Almost gone you've smiled with no shame.
Almost gone you're throbbing through the pain.
Almost gone we have all died in vain.

Gabby Ochoa

Fortieth Anniversary Tribute To Our Parents

From the Bible's record left for our gleaning, God gave to forty a
special meaning
   Forty days in the wilderness Jesus heard Satan's boast;
   Forty days in the ark Noah served as host;
   Forty days on the mountain for Moses to wait;
   Forty years of manna the Israelites ate
On this fortieth year we celebrate with you, reminded that you left
a special record, too.
   Like Jesus you have made the wilderness warm;
   Like Noah you have weathered the storm;
   Like Moses you have guided you own;
   Like the Giver of manna you provided a home.
Forty years ago you built the foundation your children have since
shared with elation, working and sharing you have given us more
than all our thanks could even the score. So on this your fortieth
year as husband and wife, we celebrate your victories and strife.
   Tiny one's hands you lovingly held;
   Growing one's fears you knowingly stilled;
   Rebellious one's errors you patiently erased;
   Mature one's lives you proudly praised;
With love, we mark this milestone with you; with love, we give
you the honor you're due.

Catherine M. Brittian

Christmas 1995

I'm not much good at poetry, I shouldn't even start.
I've finished with my Christmas tree and now I feel so smart.

This year has been a busy one with many decisions to be made.
Sometimes it was a lot of fun but tired us out by evening shade.

To sell the farm or not to? Forty three years of stewardship . . .
We thought it was time to go while we still had some zip.

The auction sale went very well. We bid it all goodbye.
Even to the last cow bell and I tried hard not to cry.

We are grateful to our children who helped us through it all.
Our decision was a hard one we hope we made the right call.

March 7 came the blizzard the biggest of the year.
A house was being auctioned off to get there was our fear.

God was with us on that day the house is now ours dare we say.

With love and patience, paper and paint we re-decorated and now
we can't wait to open the doors and bid you inside for a game
of cards or just to chide.

Gays mills is now home to us on blue bird lane
just 6 miles further West.
The kickapoo flowing through the valley is picturesque

The hills above us are a terrific view and occasionally deer and
turkeys too but Rolling Ground . . . We will always remember you!

Virginia Murphy

War Cry

I watch the world with eyes,
Eyes running red,
Red with the blood spilt,
Spilt of innocence, those of babies,
Babies intertwined in war,

As they watch their parents fight,
A fight their grandparents started,
Started by whom is a mystery,
A mystery to the children is peace,
Peace to them is a five letter word,
A word without meaning,

And I see it too,
The pain, the fear, the loss and I watch,
I watch and I weep,
And the children,
The children weep too.

Kenneth J. Galati

First Love

The grass was cold and damp between our toes.
We danced slowly, next to the water,
praying the night would never end.
We laughed of old times,
and all the years we've been together.
I kissed you on your cheek and watched your face flush.
It reminded me of our high school days.
I took hold of your hand and resaid my vows to you.
The tears ran down your face,
and you began repeating yours.
We laughed and giggled and felt young again.
As we stood there, I whispered "I love you."
You smiled, saying the same.
I ran my fingers through your gray hair,
and gently placed a kiss on your forehead.
I gathered you into my arms and looked up into the sky.
With tears filing my eyes,
I thanked God,
I still had, my first love.

Melanie Strode

A Waiting Love

I wait in the dark for my love to come in
Knowing, at last, my vigil will end.
The time of my fears will pass with a sound
The sound of a car as it pulls onto the ground.
A waiting love knows the fears of the night.
Did he fall asleep at the wheel tonight?
I think of a love that goes so deep,
And I wonder why it is I never can sleep.
Will I answer the phone that says he is gone?
Or will it be a long search into the dawn?
The pain in my chest when they said he left at ten
And here it is two and he still isn't in.
With the ice and snow and slippery roads
Or the drivers with more than one beer for a load;
I think of a man respected and loved.
Oh! What would I do if he's called up above!
I wait in the dark for my love to come in.
At last he is here and he says with a grin.
Why not asleep? Were you afraid again?
I just had to finish cleaning the gym

Lillian Sullivan

Baba (December 16, 1897 - August 18, 1996)

Don't cry for me, I live in each of you . . .

Remember our Sunday dinners with leg of lamb, gingerbread and apartment house sauce? I do! The many games the kids would play? Sardines, hide and seek? I do!

Don't cry for me, I live in each of you . . .
Remember our thanksgivings? I do! The turkey, mashed potatoes, cranberry sauce and peas with tiny pearl onions and the pies? With the children playing before and after?? I do!

Don't cry for me, I live in each of you . . .

Remember our Christmas'? I do! Workdays, luncheons, Christmas Eve, the kids hanging stockings, Christmas mornings, breakfast, then the whole family sitting down for dinner?? I do!

Don't cry for me, I live in each of you . . .

Remember our Easters? I do! Easter egg hunts and then lunch?? I do!
Don't cry for me, I live in each of you . . .
Remember our summer's and 4th of July? I do! Swimming and lunches, throwing each other in the pool?? I do!

Don't cry for me, I live in each of you . . .

Remember my garden? I do! The roses, lilac and the amount of weddings?? I do!

Don't cry for me, I live in a garden that lasts forever and in each of you . . .

Most of all remember my love and strength . . . you will for I live in each of you . . .

Erin Lownes-Santos

Deuterium Oxide

Rain, rain, don't go away,
stay here, play here for another day.
I shall walk out to meet you,
to say hi, to greet you.
Come laugh with me under the once bright sun
and never shall we stop 'til we think tis done.
Let the green grasses grow tall
under the wet fall
and we shall dance with glee,
as the Centaurs spree, under the grey moving sky.
The merriment soon shall end as the storm leaves.
As the grasses are quenched and the roots are full,
the sweet air is fresh, calm and cool.

Christopher R. Gates

Bittersweet Memories

A time and a place that's passed us by, the hurts and pain just a memory.
A person who came our way, sweetness to our soul.
Bittersweet memories.

A love that's been betrayed, the one that makes you love the rain. A day of joy and tenderness, only to fade in the end. Bittersweet memories.

New feelings of ecstasy don't last when lies overcast the rainbow.
Promises broken, shattered dreams. Bittersweet memories.

A ring with hopes attached, but reality takes hold, then all is shattered just like glass. Bittersweet memories.

A face you adore turns to the truth you deplore.
All is gone just as it came. Tomorrow will never be the same.
All you have in the end are bittersweet memories.

Patricia L. Helmick

Forgotten

Grasses unmowed, shrubs untrimmed
the old cemetery stands obsolete
on the outskirts of town
hemmed in by the coarse black
stitches of its fence.
There are no flowers coloring graves, only weeds
their seeds blowing wild.
The care taker has abandoned
his position and his cottage
whose broken windows
watch the dead.
Forgotten souls
filled with longings
sleep in the tall grasses
their conversations echoed
in the sighs of the wind.

Susan Neunzer

Beanie Baby Poem

Beanie baby, oh Beanie baby,
Wherefore art thou, oh Beanie baby
I've searched high and I've searched low,
I want them all, I tell you so.

The Beanie baby craze is a race, of course.
A race that even involves a horse.
There's a duck, a cow, and a dolphin named Flash.
Oh how cute, there's a whale named Splash.

I really don't care,
How it all began.
I'm just glad to be a part of it,
For as long as I can.

Being a part of this race,
Is by far the best part.
I don't want it to end,
It would break my heart.

Who loves ya Beanie babies?
I do.

Jaclyn Sawyer

Untitled

Patty patty 2x6 couldn't get through the very thick hickory sticks. So she went around, finally got to town, with out a frown, she sure glad to get to set down. People from all around came to town to see this fat make a splat when she sat, so was that, no big splat.

Dale Lee Allison

Infinite Beginning

And a child was born
more than merely human form
on cold December night so long ago
beneath the ever-burning starlit glow

Bright, ethereal child of light
still seen through eyes of spirit's sight
become the love, erase the need
that truth may grow from smallest seed

of love, so all-encompassing
that hearts the world wide will sing
in harmony of joy to bring
the gift of love's sweet healing

that every child born may know
the warmth of joy within the glow
of love . . .

Michaelette L. Romano

To RLG

You're my cornerstone
always there in my mind
bringing a smile to my face
even when we're apart
day after day you bring me
memories time cannot erase . . .

I'm your cornerstone
there for you when you need me
loving you and all you do
you're always in my heart
I hope you know how much I love you . . .

You're my cornerstone
your smiling face is everywhere I look
and when we're apart
your voice gives me strength to carry on
you've captured my soul and my heart . . .

Val La Rue

The Light

My sister, my friend, my mentor.
The sunshine of the world, never ceasing to give forth from her
merciful heart to those who might need her everlasting empathy.
Compassion, love, radiance, never failing to see the best in anyone,
always willing to help, so loved and so admired by everyone around her.
Beauty, grace, strength, having a will to forgive, no matter what
the crime, always giving a second chance, so trusting, so sensitive,
she possessed the power to make anything better,
whether a wounded heart or the world around us.
The light of every life she touched, she gave anything and everything
she had, expecting nothing in return.
A soul of purity and goodness, now only a gray stone amidst many others.
My sister, my friend, my mentor.
The Lord took her from me and so many others when she was still young,
but her radiant light will shine eternally in our hearts.

Laura C. Coleman

Untitled

In 9 years, we've learned to support,
respect, trust, honor and cherish each moment
together. We've learned to listen, hear and
value each others opinion. We've learned to give
love and accept it without taking it for
granted. We've learned to weather all storms
and grow stronger in spite of them. We've
learned that if you're lucky, you'll find that
"once in a lifetime love" and when you do,
hold on tight and never let go.

Iliana Walker

Autumn On The Shore

The wind is cold, as I stare.
Not blowing cold, crowding cold.
Ahead of me flashes of light on the water,
    like the Olympic Stadium when someone famous was running
    (or 4,678,000 fireflies).
The waves playing music like a twentieth century composer:
Gloomp, glup, Glump, glip,
Gloomp,
  Glump,
   Glip,
    glip,
     glip,

Gloomp against the rocks.
Above our reflective light source, obsolete in the universe, but
vital to me. Below a wavering flashing light, blinding at times.
The insects behind me playing a mind-numbing tremolo.
A bird calls from the other side . . .

No one answers. A splash, must be a fish
    eager for tomorrow's hook.
I hate allergies, the air, cleaner than . . . it's cold.

Brian B. Burbidge

Sister

In memory of my sister Angie, who was killed in a car accident 7/20/96
Showed me she cared about me in many ways
Included me in her daily life and never stopped loving me
Saw my faults and my problems, but was always willing to help
Told me her feelings
Every time I needed her she was there
Remains in my heart forever and ever — she will never be
forgotten.

Chad Burdick

I'd Like To Catch A Falling Star

I'd like to catch a falling star and hang it on the bay
To watch its glitter with deity, follow me along the way.

I'd watch the twinkles sparkle o'er and flit their colors around
Their magic could enchant the world as rays danced up and down.

I'd like to catch a falling star and hang it o'er the sea
Its radiance would excite the fish as they flit about gleefully.

The sailors would find a refuse as they sailed the broad seashore
In search of life's great treasures as thought in days of yore.

I'd like to catch a falling star and hang it on my bed
Perhaps 'twould lead my footsteps on to better days ahead.

Perhaps 'twould clear my vision so I'd see in life the best
And guide me to a higher realm of wisdom and success.

Janie Cannon

The World Of Today

Our world has threats of guns and war,
which leads to a lot of blood and gore.
Afraid to let our kids outside,
we really shouldn't have to run and hide.
There's too many families on the streets,
with not enough money to buy their child sweets.
It's a world of abuse,
and people killing animals for no use.
I dream of a world of only pride,
where everyone only shows their good side.
No one has to think about a gun,
and everyone tries to have a lot of fun.
I plan to do something untried and new,
and make sure my dream does come true!

Travis Loudin

Love's Confusion

Love is confusing, I learned right from the start.
Just when you think you've got it in the palm of your hand, it'll tear you apart.
Every move you're making, you're contemplating if it'll turn out right or wrong.

Love is a feeling I never knew very much about.
It can make you feel like you're on top of the world, or it can fill you full of doubt.
You keep waiting and anticipating to work your problems out,
But sometimes even love doesn't work. That's what I found out.

I knew it was coming to an end, it was crumbling in every way.
But, I turned my head and didn't think ahead, hoping it could last another day.
Even when I saw it all come down, I really hated to see it go.
Although I thought it would last forever, I guess it goes to show.

Love is a feeling I never knew every much about.
It can make you feel like you're on top of the world, or it can fill
you full of doubt.
You keep waiting and anticipating to work your problems out,
But sometimes even love doesn't work. That's what I found out.
Yes, sometimes even love doesn't work. That's what I found out.

Matthew M. Crooks

My Dreams Of Style Change In Life

When I was young a child at most I dream
of, of dreams of far away places, as I
grew up my dreams, then change I
dream of dreams of wealth and places
I wasted life in dreams where reality
change places, and now I know that
God is real, for now I see the times
and changes, where love is not and hate is valued
take my advice and change your life to Dear God and
seek you advice and instructions in life
where there is value of life, in the book
of life, don't be naive read the book of
life, listen to my counsel in it, it will change
your life to seek God's will and change
your life, take my advice and change your
life, in the instruction in the book life
the Bible is the book of life it gives knew
life, it changes how you look at life, don't
mock the God that gave you life, take God's
advice in the book of life.

Juanita Hunter

Untitled

As death stood there, knocking at my door,
I told him I didn't live here no more.
He said to me, let him in because he was here
to collect for my sins.
I screamed at him I did what was right
he broke down the door, and we started to fight.
As the last breath of life left my lungs,
I found myself being hung.
I looked across the room and seen death
laughing at me, he told me, he's the last
thing to see.
As all went black I started to cry, I knew
right then I was going to die.
As I started my long perilous flight,
I knew I was entering eternal night.
As I approached the gates leading to
hell, I heard a chorus of wailing bells.
As I got closer the flames grew hotter
and red.
I knew right then that I was dead!!!

Rick Brewington

Black Cloud

I've made myself a little cloud
a cloud for the mentally
insane
a place where my imagination can roam wild and free.
Don't think for a minute
there isn't enough room
someday
you may join me to.

Casie Tighe

Her Movements

As I walked down the path
Not far from a lady's home I know.
In the woods I came across a waterfall.
This water fell into a small water pool,
And in the pool a woman I saw.
A woman dancing in the pool,
standing under the cascading waterfall
Although she was beautiful,
this I didn't look at
For it was how she moved,
that caught my eyes.
So graceful, full of love.
Movements that the forest animals,
watched with curiosity.
Movements that made the wind stop and watch.
And those same movements
that made me stop on that summer day
that hot summer day was one of the coolest days,
Even with everything stopped and watching . . .
Her movements.

Nicholas LaBreck

Show Me the Way

Show me the way to break through this wall.
Help me to see the light, for I am so cold and lonely.
I call out in screams and shouts in a voice that has
long since failed me. Defenseless in a vicious and
brutal world, never knowing what the dangers of the
preceding day may bring, but always conscious of
the endless possibilities. This armor of flesh is so
weak yet so very strong and powerful. In a world
where our youth and vitality are so desired.
Never knowing when the words others tell you are
sincere or just a way to deceive. After time the
words they say loose all their meaning. Your soul
may sometimes get in the way. Filled with false
intentions and loves, never knowing who to believe.
What will they take from you now? So you go
deep into yourself and try to hide, but! The
Sanctuary you have built for yourself you
find is now a prison, so very easy to go in but,
yet so hard to break through.

Naomi Rogers

A Christmas Joy

I'm the pesky little creature always stirring about,
With big black eyes that make people shout.
They jump on the furniture like a frightened cat;
Waving broomsticks, can you imagine that?
But not on Christmas Eve; no there is no fear,
For I'm the only one awake and Santa's here.

I hide in the corner as he fills under the tree.
I cannot see, are there any for me?
As he leaves in the night in his sleigh of bells,
I creep to the presents to see what I can tell.
There is one book that's open in this silent house.
Atop the page I can see, it says "To a mouse."

Linda K. DosPassos

Diamond Dust

When first the torrents of love was
over, reason began to open my eyes
The time was everlasting, as the stars
winked back against the blackened sky
I was gilded beneath the moonlight
and petitioned for the rain
Soften the spike in my heart and swiftly melt away the pain
Feel the ocean at my feet, the moon
watches the water all the time
Bring it in, send it out, the waters
of rhythm will never lose rhyme
Sun comes up, sun goes down, another day has greeted us
Love will always shatter the diamond into dust
My eyes are filled within this sand
Sparkles of hope, for love in my hand
Passionate bravado inside the storm of this man
Love me as I love you, it is all that I ask, all that I am
I watch the ripples of love cascade over me
Reflections in the water of what love can be
Still waiting, still hoping, but it seems like an eternity.

Raphael Gaca

I Was There

I was there when he was in the hospital.
I was there when he awoke from the coma.
I was there when he started to eat, again.
I was there when he went home.
I was there when his Mother called 911 and said he's dying.
I was there when the ambulance came and took him away.
I was at the hospital when he died.
I was there to comfort his Mother the night after the funeral.
I was there throughout good and bad in his life.
I was there long after he was gone.
I was there to say good-bye to his Mother when she died.
I was there when they buried her in the grave next to his.
I was there at the beginning and the end.

Shawnda Ann Williams

Secret Love

Faithful and true to each other we'll be;
Till the end of time, forever you'll see.
These vows are for us but only we can know;
They help with a foundation for our love to grow.

My heart is yours forever to hold;
To warm with love, to change, to break, mend or mold.
It's you I'll love always and to the end;
Never wavering, not even once, nor will I bend.

Together with you for eternity I need;
Though with pain and suffering sometimes we'll bleed.
It's possible no one but us will ever know;
However, my goal is our joy and caring to openly show.

Others may see and experience our bliss;
And recognize without change what they might miss.
To touch another life for the better I believe;
Is worth all our efforts and any difficulty I can conceive.

Arthur Lynn

Seasons

The Seasons of Nature are like the seasons of our lives.
The Spring is new beginnings, our birth.
Then comes to summer, the prime of our lives.
Fall comes, the time for harvest, time to reflect on the
accomplishments of our lives.
And the winter, when Nature is at a standstill, the endings
of our lives.

Cynthia Thomas

The Rose

I love the beautiful Rose, by the hour
It is indeed my favorite flower
As I look into the heart of a Rose
All feeling for flowers come to a close
The petals are all so beautiful to see
for people to see like you and me
Oh give to me my Roses now I crave
Don't wait for death and I am with grow
What is meant for me I want it how
Don't wait till I am gone and how.
Give it to much now so I may show.
The love you have for me so they will know
there's one thing I ask when my eyes close
please put in my hand a beautiful Rose

Annie May Lightsey

Untitled

We come from a land beyond the land of mortals.
A land of mountains of shimmering light,
streets made of gold, seas
of crystal, and protected by gates
made of gold, silver, and pearls.
A place where no one grows old
or dies, a land that has no wars, no worries.
We live in peace and harmony, with each other.
We walk among mortals but we
mean no harm, we help and guide,
them when they are in trouble.
Mortals have a name for our land — Heaven
but we call it home,
you see — we are Angels!

James Wood

Untitled

I came with empty hands your love to seek
A stranger traveling from a world apart.
I came alone, unknown and brought no price
Except a yearning and devoted heart

I little knew such price would bring such love,
Or that man could know such ecstasy,
I found a joy to ease the dolesome heart
And still a spirit longing to be free.

Where I have nobly wrought your love inspired.
Where I have failed 'twas I who missed the way.
O lead me yet to reach the golden heights,
And know the rapture of exultant day.

Carlos L. Hunsinger

Alone

Never have I said.
And never have I shown.
Many times I sit by myself.
I sit in the dark alone.
When small flames flicker,
To cast light in my space.
I snuff out the candles,
Smoke swirls round my face.
If a shadow reaches out,
And offers a hand to hold.
I close my eyes.
The figure fades.
And again I'm in the black and the cold.
I let friendships pass in so many ways,
But here in the dark I sit,
And let the loneliness stay.

Laura M. Meyer

Untitled

When your eyes met mine
I can only see an empty stare.
Unsettled meaningless gesture.
You pass by like a soft breeze,
Can I decipher your inner thoughts?
Within the realms of lightness
There is a cloud hanging on me
Blocking my thoughts.
Is love as complex as this,
Or unparalleled passion, so to speak?

And now you are close to me,
A deception or simply an illusion?
I'd rather gauge you from afar.
This insurmountable longing
Is far better than the reality of non-existence.

Jocelyn R. Mamayson

Fall

Leaves are falling down, down, down
They are falling to the ground
They change colors every year
Sometimes they look like the color of deer
I collect them, yes I do
I collect them why don't you?

Brandon Talbot

In The Eyes Of A Mother

Through the eyes of a mother
I see her eyes as blue as the ocean, I see her eyes as
blue as the sky.
In the eyes of a mother, I see a caring mother.
In the eyes of a mother, I see a loving mother.
Who loves and cares for her young
unconditionally.
In the eyes of a mother, I see her with an
understanding heart, and with a broken heart.
In the eyes of a mother, I see her grow older with
each passing day.
I see her with great pride when she looks at each
one of her kids.
Through my mother's eyes comes a daughter who see's
a heart of gold and a loving smile. I love you.

Sharon Swatzenberg

Memorial Song

Remember the anguished morning
We allowed June's comforting breeze
To lift her porcelain ashes
Away from our trembling hands.

Seven summers now.
Could any ash remain in the wind?
Could she be whispering to a tickled ear,
Revisiting palm prints of trembling hands?

Perhaps she is dancing above the evergreen,
Humming in harmony to laughter of girls,
One now a woman,
One now a newborn.

The eternal tree sways to the heartbeat of children
Who have traded their wings for new babies' breath.
They are waiting to dance with the November wind.
He will guide them through steps that will lead them to life.

Eternal tree stands,
Ever green, ever hers.
Ever faithful he sings
Her memorial song.

Christin Crawford

Friends

Adrift among the days
passing through the arid desert of our destiny
my eyes comb the landscape for nutritious preys
just to amuse myself and indulge my vanity

Shimmering shadow in the heat of scorching sand
wandering through the realms of delusive misconception
I got my gaze fixed on you my friend
letting the wind whisper words of my seductive persuasion

High above your head circling vultures show me the way
these are indeed my faithful servants and your only testimony
into the blood-red sunset they fly away
giving place to the true master of ceremony

And when the night wraps us in its dark should
I bid you to stop and join me down by the fire
seeing flames dance in your eyes so full of hope and doubt
I say: Relax I just want to chat with you for a while

So still and tense yet shaky like an addict in great pain
I can't wait to feel your voice inject into my vein

Oh, how I long to hear tales of uncherished mirth and unuttered woe
and see tears of joy and fear groove your dusty face like a dew
so don't keep it inside, let it go, let the river flow!
For as long as it rolls my entity ablaze grows out of blue

Lucas Olbinski

Weak

It is by these walls that I gather my strength
as little as it seems
and this light, however dim,
will forever gleam
stronger I am by stronger I will be
in which this time will show
and yet this bothers me still today
as I let my freedoms grow
along side of me sits a door
as plain as a door might be
and yet I fear to cross this plane
would get the best of me
these fears are not uncommon,
and I must face them now
just as I faced the ones before
bestowed upon your brow
so take me to that special place
where I may find my home
or soon I will perish
as I walk this path alone

Lindsay Parker

The Last Flight

Oh God, I look at the birds that fly aloft,
The ships with sails that glide so soft.

I sit and wonder where I shall be,
When you make your final call for me.

Will I take flight and reach the sky above
To come into your outstretched arms of love?

Or, shall I ask that day in pain and grief,
To take me to your breast for fast relief?

I have flown so high the sunny sky turned night,
A million stars appeared, dazzling, huge, and bright.

This moved my mind to thoughts of my Gods eternity,
Will I face my mortal end with peace and serenity?

Please turn your loving thought to me, my Lord,
Release my pain and anger to help me come on board.

Lloyd E. Jobson

Kuddly Kat

My cat's name is "Kuddly Kat"
She ran off to catch a rat.
When she returned she had the rat,
All nice and fat.
She smiled and played with Kuddly Kat;
Rolled and flirted, and things like that.
But Kuddly Kat caught her by the tail;
Spun her around until she was too drunk to yell.
Then Kuddly Kat walked away,
Left her lying where she fell.
She was bruised and battered,
And crawled into a hole,
Just before "Kuddly Kat" came back
From climbing a telephone pole.

Martha Sampson

Before Your Image

Before your image the flesh trembles,
the mind wishes, the night burns,
alternate states of fleeing and attraction,
numbness, confusion, lucidity, illumination,
dead ends, reformulation of the question,
a theme that never ends, pure sensation,
art and movement.
Your shape that plays in the space,
and confuses itself with the air,
geometrical archetype of pleasure
ghost that would not let my mind alone,
figure that breaks away from time and
nails itself in my mind to stay, and
provides an eternal satisfaction, resemblance
of the absolute.

Manuel Espinal

Sun Beams

Those sun beams from so far away,
Spent from the long, dark, frigid way?
No! They still are full of zip and zing!
They sparkle on my wedding ring.
They detour past my window shade,
In fear, the purple shadows fade.
They make the whole world come alive,
Fair flowers bloom when they arrive.
They gild neat patterns on the lake,
They jolt the sleeping world awake.
And when their boisterous energy
Has rattled every bird and bee
They scoot off to infinity.

Jim Davis

Lost On The Mountain

Lost on the mountain, chasing my dreams;
Life as I know it, isn't what it seems.
Lost in the horizon, where the sea meets the sky;
The future bleeds the past, while the present waves good-bye.
Lost in the silence, I can hear my heart break.
My emotions berate me! I tremble and shake!
On top of the mountain where the air is quite thin;
My wisdom befriends me, self-pity begins.
Lost in the moment, cradled by the night;
Battling for serenity. Will I lose the fight?
Lost on the mountain, will tomorrow ever come?
Today was just my painkiller. And yesterday? I was numb.
Lost in all my sorrow, longing for the day,
I can look beyond my bitterness and know that I'm okay.
As I sit atop the mountain and talk to God above;
I ask Him to watch over me and protect me with His Love.
As I lay beneath the starry sky, I knew God heard my plea.
As I wrote my name in the Heavens, God smiled down on me!

Gayle L. Thomas

I Knew a Man

I knew a man who spent his time picking four leaf clovers;
He'd put them in a water glass so they would keep their color.

He'd put them in a book, he'd put them on a shelf,
Until he had them everywhere; he lived to please himself.

You'd see him on a railroad track, his head bent slightly down:
He'd reach down and pick one up and say "Look what I have found."

He must have picked a thousand, 'til his back was old and bend;
His silver hair, his furrowed brow, showed signs of great content.

He searched and searched all his life, another one to find;
His joy of life was simple, his days were so sublime.

Some people thought him odd, this way to spend his time of day;
And some would scoff and laugh at him as he went along his way.

He didn't search for riches or for wealth, or extra fame;
You'd see him every morning, and yet none could tell his name.

His sheepish smile would broaden wide each new find he'd behold;
You see, my friend, I knew a man whose beauty came from his soul.

Jack E. Rowland

Give Me The Key

You don't have to worry
If you give in too much
I won't rush you
Just my touch

You don't have to control your emotions
Because time will guide them
And sometimes in life
You just can't control them
Just relax and enjoy the moment
Because it won't be here forever
Let's just Bless the time we spend together

I know you've been hurt before
But that is not a reason to keep a closed door
Just give me the key
I will open your heart slowly and gently
And each day a little bit more and more

You see what you do to me
You inspire my thoughts to the highest degree

Pedro Custodio

The Root Of Our Existence

A foundation for the future,
Brought forth many years before,
Strong, stubborn, uneasily bent,
Stably grounded, heaven sent.

Her roots ran deeply,
The branches wide,
In sun or stormy weather,
She was our shelter, a place to hide.

The tree is gone,
But not the seeds,
And the memory of her features,
Shall forever with us be.

God shared with us this gift,
And we must try to understand,
She was only here to visit,
For the root of our existence, lies within God's hands.

Sharon D. Gaylord

The "Sighs" Of March

A beautiful day in March, it was; Wispy clouds, new grass and such.
No manger, no hay, no shepherds came, and yet we felt their touch!

This baby angel born that day, knew not the lives she'd redefine.
Her precious smile, those loving eyes, the tiny gestures she would sign.

A beautiful Sunday in March, it was; Wispy clouds, new grass and such.
A birthday party; Her first it was, and everyone loved this angel, much.

Then Monday, Daddy went to work, and kissed his angel "bye."
Our God had plans to take one home, to reign with Him on high!

A beautiful day in March, it was; Wispy clouds, new grass, but parched!
Our angel will never remember this day; The unforeseen funeral . . . "March."

Forever a memory we cannot forget, nor delete from our heartbroken ring;
A young man so special, a wife so beloved and an angel with one broken wing.

Our son is now gone, but his memory lives on, in this granddaughter
    angel we love.
When March brings new grass, wispy clouds and the such, her Daddy,
    sees from above!

Ida M. Shambaugh

Christmas

I can't go home for Christmas this year,
I hope you'll be thinking of me,
If I could have one wish on a star,
To go home is what it would be.

I want only one thing for Christmas,
A gift that can be said out loud,
It's not a car and it's not a truck,
I just want to make you all proud.

There's so much now I cannot see,
My eyesight is far too dim,
But come what may, I'll let it all go
And leave it all up to him.

Jesus has called me to be at my best,
Living for him when at work or at play,
He knows my heart and in that I can rest,
Why should I worry what others may say.

Jesus shares my worries and cares,
I'll never be left alone,
For he stands beside me to comfort and guide me,
He always looks out for his own.

Robert Allen Hicks

A Tot

I've loved you a lot
ever since I was a tot
You adopted me
but I felt so out of place in that family
I just wasn't myself
I put myself in this situation
Not because of your dictation
you tried to raise me right
I wanted to fight
why couldn't I see
what was going to happen to me
I thought I would walk away
from the words you say
I thought I knew everything
only to realize I didn't know anything
Now I wish I could say
that I'm with you today
I still love you a lot
even though I'm not
a tot

Chrystal Litzie

Realization

I sit still,
    safe within these four walls, under this sturdy roof.

I sit and stare out,
    through the binds that shut out the sun,
    past the glass that holds back the air,

And wonder why.
Why do those trees I spy remain exposed, vulnerable?

Why are they not sheltered; protected from the harsh sun,
    from the cruel wind, from the unclean air . . . as I am?

Yet I smile,
    because I know.

I know that if they are sheltered, if they were protected,
    they would become as lifeless . . . as I feel.

I know that to live,
    I too must be exposed.
    I too must be vulnerable.

I can sit still no longer.

Tiffany Garrott

About An Angel

I met an angel whose face just couldn't say no
but I knew deep down in my heart
that I just couldn't ask the question

Happiness,
it makes me sad
it just wasn't meant for me

It isn't in the stars
it just wasn't in my cards

Caught in a whirlwind of doom and desire
that could end in no less than a funeral pyre

The thought of her is all that keeps me going
she lit a flame in my heart and set my soul on fire

I would think of her, then
I would think of myself, my past, my future

I would think of her again and I'd see
what I couldn't bare to see — tears,
on the face of an angel.

Casey J. Jagiello

Message Of Love

God is love.
Love brings life.
Life brings manifestation.
Manifestation is God's plan for you.
I am The Anointed One, with
the anointing that destroys every
yoke and rids every burden,
Bring to me your burdens and yokes.
Trust me and I will bring it to pass.
Worship me, praise me, thank me,
believe me, receive me, in the name of
The Anointed One, with the anointing.
Bless me! I have seen, I have heard,
I have felt, and now, I am going to answer
your prayers. Your plan is being anointed.
Transformation is in process.
Come into my presence, now.

Gladys S. Wyckoff

The Country Church 1835-1996

The doors were opened long ago,
  and welcomed our ancestors with a warm glow.
It was nothing fancy, just a small white square
  but a building full of love and people who care.

The cold winter wind would puff and blow
  but the pot belly stove kept them warm with its glow.
The preacher told the folks of God's great love and care
  and then they sang songs and ended with prayer.
We sing them now and we rejoice in our souls,
  as they tell us the story, we all love from old.
It's never been changed through all these years,
They taught us to remember, there is nothing to fear.
But a sad time has come, it hurts us so bad
  the doors are closed forever . . . it makes us so sad!
Now big churches in town are teaching God's Word, too,
  they offer so much more, what can we do?

Rev. O'Bannon has been so dear,
to come and preach when so few came to hear.
We ask God to bless him for all his special teaching
  'cause he will be remembered for all the good preaching!

Marilynn W. Dick

Paintings

God is an artist,
He painted the sky blue,
He painted the grass green.
He painted me and you.

His paintbrush is of love,
His paper, the world.
His paint is of joy and happiness
and His great talent He has unfurled.

He painted the beautiful flowers,
the amber waves of grain.
He painted the purple mountains
and the fruited plains.

So God just keeps painting.
Painting till the end,
but I think that his best painting
is a painting of a friend.

So next time you look at a sunset
grass and flowers too.
Remember that God painted all that stuff,
painted it for me and you.

Steven Dobelmann

Rain

Examine what is real do the thoughts
mortals have make only pictures in their heads.
Dreams may be their reality or
doorways into our infinite future.
Time passes with out one mortal
but together they become a life time.
Artists, poets humans have seen
their visions wondering all the
time if they in the same era believe.
Rain is an intriguing step into
the after world.
It has no structure but still
manages to reflect, cleans, feed, and purify.
So many times bodies have melted
in to rain going on a trip but
why must they always return.
They are and will become a
rain to wash away ignorance, and hatred.
To make this world pure again.

Carol Wohleb

Apoptosis

There is something that does not know how to die
eating away at my insides.
Three years ago it stole my breast.
I thought all of the neoplasm had been removed.
I was wrong — it fooled me.
The remnant of the growth laid
in a heterozygous state
just long enough for me to forget
how much it hurt,
how tired I was,
and how sick I felt
from trying to teach my morbid growth how to die.
This time, the Doctors refused to cut me open.
They said the mass would spread like wild fire and
consume me within the year if they did.
Instead, I am bloated and bald.
I am receiving injections of
drugs that aren't even on the market yet.
I will try anything right now to extend my life.
But, I am winning the race and I will
triumph over what is eating me alive.

Beth L. Schreiner

bryan's alarm

i remember sitting in the corner,
playing solitaire with my book of matches,
until all of a sudden: a flame.

of course, i was polite and
kindly offered her a drink
while I sipped at my own gasoline.

but she declined, so we just sat and smoldered.

she was warm for a while
but grew too hot for me to touch,
yet somehow burned me just the same.

and her light that ended darkness
began to throw shadows on my wall
that i could no longer recognize.

so i ran, but behind me i always see the fire.

Lucinda A. Manolakes

Learnings: About The Universe

Cosmologists currently contemplate
this account of our cosmic state:
"From an infinite sea of nil (Nirvana, some agree),
a random quantum fluctuation
grew to this, our situation."

All there is . . . came from nothing?
I wonder, upon reflection, would Nirvana ever burp,
thus perturbing its perfection?

More likely is, that all there is . . .
came from something that is not nothing.
But this slice we sense, the universe immense,
is not that source . . . that something.

Just as matter seems to be the cooling crust of energy,
so might all the "e" implied in "m times c times c"
be one mere puff (for us, enough) of that stuff,
that source . . . that mystery.

Study on, physics and astronomy;
we await the Unified Theory.
But I doubt one can, though you try,
detect or measure, or explain, this why.

T. H. Huebner

Winter Interlude

As I sit in my warm home,
　Listening to the beautiful classical music,
I look out into the first winter's snow —
　Falling . . . collecting in the tree's naked branches
And watch the powder dust cover the ground.
　I've missed this sight for many years.

Rapture fills me at the exquisite sight.
　Many see it as a disruption of time
But they have missed this creative reflectiveness,
　The beauty, the harmony of life.
Powerful waves of life's energy passes through me.
　I'm mystified, awed, almost to tears.

No greater of an artist could create this,
　A transformation, other than the supreme being!
No flake ever the same, ever so soft
　As if to let Mother Nature be tucked in
For her long needed rest of the year's work.
　A time to gently lay to rest all fears.

　　Sally Taylor

One Man's Sunshine

One average man, with so much in his life
A man with two children, and with an ex-wife
Worked hard at his job, tried climbing the ladder
Gave everything he had, But his heart just grew sadder
Seems so long ago, in his own history
A lady he loved, is his one mystery
Not his ex-wife, she was never real
Just a young lady, whose touch made him feel
A face just like sunshine, a heart so pure
Her eyes were intense, and he was so sure
That this was the one, that he always would care for
Always true to the innocence, and never forsake her
He had dreamed of this girl, every night all alone
She said she would call, and he'd wait by the phone
He'd never admit to himself, that she was too young
She was free and eighteen, and he was in love
But she found another, and enjoyed her young life
As he did as well, and he took a wife
The man made mistakes, but is that a crime,
Please help him find her, help him find his sunshine.

　　Andrew Craig Allen

Memorial

for my father

Pale morning light cold wind between buildings garbage
neat piles stacked brown plastic tied shut smell diffused
in cold air carried away across the street it is gone too early
for exhaust for cars for noise there is silence cold wind
paper rustling in stunted bushes behind benches wrought iron
fence pitted streaked with rust traps paper entangles in the bush.

A slow rise brown grass old flag stone path cracks scarred
limestone now tilted this way now tilted that way upwards
to the top a metal figure leans on a musket shine faded
weather etched surface pitted streaked with rust dull brown
lines shifting over curves a stripped course to the base
to the ground underneath the dirt the grim maybe there
is an inscription maybe there is a plaque.

Faded newsprint twisted yellow paper carried by the cold
air illegible rolls down the slope a few trees shelter bare
brown earth a few dead leaves heavy with moisture
skeletal shadows a creaking noise in the silence
and the sound of brittle paper rolling and the sound
of paper rustling in the stunted branches held there
by the wrought iron fence behind the shadows of benches.

　　Bryan K. Carrigan

Resurgence

Sad was the day they made me leave my friends,
Said I was surplus, not needed anymore.
Sad was that day . . . But now my spirit mends . . .
Sore though my heart may be, it searches for
A way to heal its wounds, and beat again
In confident rhythm, forgetting all the hurt;
I look to the future, pushing down my pain
At being discarded like a worn-out shirt.
Sad was that day . . . but personal pride defends
Against such blows, and lifts me from the floor
To fight again; and, in effect, forfends
Resentful anger at the losing score . . .
Self-pity is a coin no wise man spends —
I'll keep my spirits high, my motives pure.

　　Brian J. Dooley

Death:　Present And Aftermath

One day I woke up and became extremely sad,
After I heard the bad news from my dad
I never thought I would have to face death
I was hurt so bad, it took away my breath
I went to the funeral, the church was packed
Everyone there realized, he wasn't coming back

We went to the grave yard and buried him in the earth
People remembering his birth and self-worth
He was here one day and gone another
An incredible person, who happened to be my brother

Sometimes late at night, I have a vision
That he didn't make such a terrible decision
I close my eyes and pray he'll be here tomorrow
To help me overcome this aching sorrow

But for now I'll just visit the ground where he lay,
And bestow upon him tears of my dismay
As the tombstone is the closest I can get for now
But I will get through this someway, somehow

I still hope one day to see him and he'll acknowledge me
And we will forever rejoice in perfect harmony

　　Tasha Janisse

Circle Of The Pines

As I walked through the forest to The Circle Of The Pines
thinking of the past and things heavy on my mind,
of those who've gone before me and what they left behind.

The children of the children, of the children of time.

Their faces they are flashing through the channels of my mind,
and here they are the sweetest in The Circle Of The Pines.

Those little ones born after and the ones that left before,
shall meet in heavens splendor and for after evermore.

As the sun does cast its shadow and lays it on the ground,
we've placed a granite marker at the edge of the mound,
and time will take us all through life, and bring us back in kind,
at The Circle Of, The Circle Of, The Circle Of The Pines.

Then blessed are those little ones, and life must treat them kind,
as they go down life's precious path, their memories will entwine.

As the breezes softly whisper, as if voices in the air,
the past comes back before me and I see my mother there,
and I wonder if she's with me now, as I am sitting there,
and those who are there with her to comfort her up there,
and one fine day I'll join them, if God to me is kind.

But for now I'll have to meet them in The Circle Of The Pines.

　　Norbert D. Schlecty

Untitled

Cool winter winds blow violently through tunnels,
as children huddle in corners unseen;
alone on the streets they appear invisible,
happiness exists only in their dreams.
People all talk of how they can help,
but nobody will lend a hand;
everyone offers a solution,
but won't take the time to understand.
Love is all they are asking,
blame is all they receive;
freedom is what they are demanding,
rejection is what is conceived.
So they turn to anything,
that might take their pain away;
they escape into a dream world,
that exists for only a day.
Shooting poison into their veins,
appears to bring them peace;
but soon their sky turns black,
in a garbage can, found deceased.

Nicole Babineau

"Nwatakiri"

Why do I feel the way that I do
Don't bother to ask my father
He's convinced that I am not his son
Try my mother when her sessions are over

Boy! When I was your age, he always says
Dad! There are gangs and drugs now, I always answered him
My tomorrow will not be his yesterday
My today uncertain

Wazu, the African exchange student called me "Nwatakiri"
today in gym
The cold icy look and turned up nose
Let to the explanation that "Nwatakiri" references a child

By accepting, emotions are better understood
Understood but not justified
"Nwatakiri's" life is presumed simple and happy
Mine as a teen today is everything but . . .

Josephine Odudu

Soliloquy

I was walking the yard feeling low and glum
When I saw approaching an old buddy and chum
His tousled grey hair made me think back
To when he first came here and it was slick and black

I noticed his body was a little more stooped
His shoulders sagged and his eyelids drooped
His once snappy walk was reduced to a shuffle
That the prison sands did its best to muffle

His mind seemed to wander, no longer quick and alert
No longer aware of the sky or the dirt
As he got closer it came back to me all
A mirror had been placed on the prison yard wall

Bill Santor

To The Light

You are my shining star
doesn't matter near or far.
In my thoughts, everywhere you are,
I call upon you my shining star.

Brightly glowing and guiding my way,
I follow the light, that golden ray.
Never to give up leaving all in dismay,
I walk out of the darkness and into a bright new day.
You are my shining star.

Angela G. Gosman

Leonard

All things must change and so it is our life,
a moment captured in eternity.
And, with us, perish precious thoughts and dreams,
gone down in time as if we never were.
Yet, who will know that once there walked this earth,
a kind and gentle man who touched us with
keen mind and wit but never had renown?
He knew not greatness but himself was great.
He lives as long as those who knew him live.
A measure of his life is left behind
in fleeting pictures of our memories
of grace and courage and of dauntless will.
We are diminished when his footsteps fade.
His being, a ripple on the sea of space
for he was gone with the receding tide
and left us hopeless on the lonely shore.

Helen Butsch

Tranquillity

She was the type who wanted to keep going until she dropped,
    but, ah, not me, my friend!
Give me quietness and peace, with no loud blaring of the drums,
    a gentle autumn breeze.
One that barely stirs the trees,
    a good book to soothe my soul.
And, then, ah, tranquillity.

When that last door closes,
    I hope to slip quietly away.
To be caught up in the clouds as Jesus was that day
    and, then, ah, tranquillity.

Norma Pflager

No Prints

Summer came and summer went . . .
yet no change.
Autumn came and autumn went, yet
raking the yard, there was no change.

Then one cold late December day the
snow began to fall.

Blowing winds and mounting snow,
here there was a change.

Looking out from the window . . .
I remember prints of not so long ago.
Prints, small prints in the snow.
How he loved the snow for so many years,
not so long ago.

Now he is where no prints are made . . .
waiting for the day, we will both make prints in the clouds . . .
in the clouds of snow.

Katherine M. Haskin

Love In Stone

I went to speak to dad today as often times I do
When I am down or full of joy or not sure what to do
Surrounding him with flowers and just beneath a tree
I find myself before him sitting just below his knee
He listens so intently though what I says absurd
And still he offers great advice but never says a word
I always hear him laughing as I whisper in the wind
Then listen for his answer as mentor, parent, friend
We've talked of when my son was born and when his father died
And when my marriage fell apart he caught the tears I cried
Though cancer got the best of him this world it never will
Dad smiles at those who read his name; his marker on the hill
The love he gives is strange to some but not that hard to see
It's only traces etched in stone and carried on in me

Mark Metzger

175

The Eyes Of Truth

These eyes relentlessly upon me stare
With cruelty worse than you could ever know;
They criticize without the light, and care
Not where, nor for how long the moon does glow.

These orbs are tortured souls that cry with pain;
They live, it seems, in heaven looking down
With pity; tears of sorrow drip like rain
Unto uncaring depths that form a frown.

These globes ingest the dark and mirror light;
Whatever praise or compliment is said,
Its opposite will be considered right.
Deliberate this if you must instead:

These eyes more critical than others be,
These eyes perceive my true reality.

Shannon Sabbar

Why, Why In This World?

'Why, why in this world of ours . . .
why the wise and the good die young,
and, the unwise and the rascal live long?'
This question always puzzled me
particularly, when I was alone!
And lo! The answer to this question
I found in my meditation;
please, you people of the earth
hear it with kind attention!
'The good Gods in heaven,
earnestly need the company of the good and the wise,
hence they call them as early as possible,
this is the real cause in disguise!'

Himmat M. Patel

The Joy Of Being A Clown

When I put on the face and dress of a clown
And I set out to visit a place in the town
I'm delighted to be the one who can bring
Laughter and smiles and make a heart sing.
I'm only a clown who behind a false face
Sees beyond the sadness and tears to a happier place
To many who hurt and are sad in their own way
I try to bring joy and brighten their day.
If I make them smile and forget for a while
My day is complete and I've gone the extra mile.

Wynne M. Neiss

The Journey Home

The years are long and dreary when you've no one by your side.
Are you happy? Are you crying? Are you barely just alive?
Do you live a life of loneliness? Are you lost in a crowd?
Are you searching to fill an emptiness? Are you talking just too loud?
When your friends are reminiscing about happier times they've
had. Do your eyes fill with tears? Do you feel a little sad?
Has your life became a burden with no real point in sight?
Or have you caught just a glimmer of a precious winking light?
Keep your eyes upon that light, it will lead you to a cross.
Where you can lay your burdens down and never feel the loss.
You'll never be alone again, as the years go swiftly by.
Because you accepted Jesus, and He'll be there by your side.
He will be your constant companion, he will lead you all the way.
He will teach you how to act, what to do, and what to say.
You will be a better person, because he has made you new.
You can step into His Kingdom when He reaches just for you.
You are now with him in heaven, because you obeyed His great command.
You have shared the love He gave to you with every living man.

Roy V. Hart Jr.

Fire

A storm rumbles over a forest
Threatening to release a torrential downpour.
Lightening crashes to the dry ground
Giving life to a powerful monster.
Those that watched the forest being ravaged,
Could not escape the hypnotizing effect of the
Dazzling yellow, blue, and white of the creature,
Bright and beautiful, yet very dangerous;
Indiscriminately destroying
All life in its path.
Loud roaring and crackling
Deafened the ears of those,
Trying to stop its reign.
The light cast by the moon
Was veiled by a thick black curtain,
Produced by the monster
As it quickly devoured the forest.
The clouds finally let go of their cargo
Extinguishing the life of the beast.

Jacinta Cooper

A Writer's Block

Thoughtless by the minute, vacuous by the hour,
Fearful of uncertainty, a brilliant moment gone sour,
Trapped like four walls cornered without a crack,
Hunger for sensation, starving for a fact,
Wandering what words seem appropriate and which would be approved,
Basing a level of distinction on certain feelings or a particular mood,
Freedom of expression, consisting of depression
With visions that lead to a pathway so unclear,
Flipping through a thesaurus as some sort of guide or the right gear,
Emptiness that sometimes trigger the mind,
but calmly unwind
the thickness inside, vowels no longer hide,
a rhythm begin to harmonize
the defile and the delay
of sonnets that once went astray
A vocabulary that has no meaning,
words that are so demeaning
sounds to listen, an idea that glistens
the darkness that has been unlocked in the terrible fate of a writer's block.

Consuela Hunter

The Little Black Child

(My Version)
My mother bore me in the Southern wild
In the opinion of many to be meek and mild
But I am black and proud to be
Not like others in the sun
Trying to imitate me
Black as the night after a clear day
I am proud to say I can make it
In my own way,
My mother taught me what I should know
To get along with what seem to be my foe
But if you look closely you will also see
That foe is not a foe but a friend to me
Life is to short to boast and rave
But should be lived with love and understanding
Till we reach our grave
There is a moral to what I have stated
Is it you that should be rated

Robert C. Dunn Sr.

Harmony

Oh Lord, let our voices be heard rising to thee,
Not in conflict, but in sweetest harmony.
I see you one way, someone else another,
But he who sees you differently is still my brother,
May our thoughts arrive at your throne in harmony.
Oh, yes, in sweetest harmony.

One day we will all stand at heaven's gate
Divested of earth's painful hates,
And we will wait for thee
To lead us in harmony
Oh yea, in sweetest harmony.

Alas! Are we of different faiths?
Or are we all of one
Praying to the same God from whom all was begun?
Then let us bow our heads or bend our knees
To pray in complete sweetest harmony
Oh yes, in sweetest harmony.

John J. Smith

Memories

Memory is the process of recalling to your mind
the different things that you have learned and experienced in past times.

How often does someone ask "Do you remember when?"
and your memory recalls a happening that you can relive again.

You can't predict the future or make changes in the past
but you can rely upon your memories to make fond moments last.

You can think about tomorrow and sometimes plan it as you please
but when tomorrow becomes yesterday all that's left are memories.

As all of us get older there's less future and more past
so hold on to all those memories as time is passing fast.

The greatest thing about memories is that everyone has their own
and things that we remember can be ours and ours alone.

Memories are wonderful without them you would find
an awful lot of emptiness of times we've left behind.

Memories of loved ones and friends no longer here
will sometimes bring a smile and often bring a tear.

Memories can make you laugh and some will make you cry
others will warm your heart with joy and lift your spirits high.

So when you're feeling down and out it may be time to reminisce
so call upon your memories to give yourself a lift.

Robert M. Atkinson

You

Down the lonely street strolled a shadow of light, it glowed as the street lights followed its path. But the sadness and sorrow of the shadows mist the sky with no sense of direction and no where to hide. The glassy stains that dropped were all size and shapes. Yet, its coat was kept as soft as silk that couldn't be helped to the eyes of those but be loved by you. Its dark eyes filled with glancing sadness, ovally shaped but with beauty to ones vision. It stood erect well performed, may I say. Only through moments it kept its control as it searched for its world, which seemed like an eternity. Although, not much could have been done. The time for fulfillment will surely come. It's loved by many, but will be only adored by one.

Another day of darkness has followed. The sun has vanished with no trace, it has left you in this world astray. Swiftly it strolls down the streets, how could this happen to me. Echoes that threaten the senses are deeply felt like an endless journey. You know it's near almost at its reach. Until the sounds of drums and trumpets will you prance. Meanwhile the search is on for tomorrow. I know a celebration is on its way. All you have to do is keep the faith.

Miriam Prosper

Where The Poppies Grow

Have you ever walked where the poppies grow, like blood upon the snow,
you hold your hand to hide the glare of sun upon the stones,
   here where the poppies grow
Over head you can hear the flutter of the flag, as it waves upon the
wind this place of honor, this place of glory, this place of tears,
   here where the poppies grow
Who are you son, I ask myself, that you lie here upon this hollow
ground, no name upon this white stone, unknown to man,
   only to God alone, here where the poppies grow
No one to rest a loving hand upon this ice cold stone,
some will stop and wonder, as tears fall upon the ground,
   here where the poppies grow
So raise you up my brave young men, and follow the sound of drums,
march in step, head and shoulders erect, to a place of peace,
   and rest, here where the poppies grow
Join all your comrades of now and before, no more the sounds of guns,
a place for just you alone, a field of light, and peace,
   here where the poppies grow.

Philip E. Schenck

Creek

There once was a boy who lived by a creek
He had a big cat and a dog named Zeek
You could almost never get a peek
But one fine day he crossed my way
No words just a silent stare
Then he said hello with a dare
The grass was so green
It was as if I was in a dream
He was a little stout
With a boyish kind of pout
He reached out his hand and put it in mine
And asked if I had some time
A chill went through my spine
We walked for awhile
Then he said he liked my smile
Then came the stars and the night, he held me very tight
Tears came down and my feet were off the ground
I could not hear a sound
I had fallen in love with the boy from the creek
With a big cat and a dog named Zeek

Rachel Busenhart

Seasons Of Life

Life like nature has its seasons:
There's the cold dark days of winter when hope and faith
appears to be only a "shot in the arm" to help you make it to the
next day only to find it to be just as bad.

There's the warmth and promise of spring when suddenly you
feel there is something to hope for and that all is not lost.

There's the sunny bright days of summer when it seems some
dreams are coming true and some prayers are being answered
and you wonder how long it will last for you know . . .

There will soon be a shift in the wind for the cool days of fall
are upon you which tells you that the cold dark days of winter
will soon be here again.

But remember . . .

Spring and summer comes again too . . .

Mae Bertha Powers

Jigsaw Dreams

In a dream I wander.
In a dream I ponder.
I ponder the thoughts of the world,
The darkness into which we are hurled.
I dream to make the world seem bright.
I dream to feel a pure sun's light.
I wake to find all my dreams are dead.
Gloomy clouds and destruction greet me instead.
Dead roses and broken dreams scent the fallen.
I still hear the wishes for little toy's from little boys callin'.
I wish I could bring them back and soak the tears.
All of their days form forgotten years.
A jigsaw puzzle with pieces lost here and there.
For how to find them I know not where.

Jeremy Henderson

Hello

The circle and the hexagon shook hands.
Hello, said the circle
How do you do, said the hexagon
Nice day, offered the circle
Bit cool, replied the hexagon
Out doing errands? asked the circle
Taking my lone constitutional.
With six sides that's not too easy said the hexagon,
Revolving counterclockwise to flaunt them all simultaneously
I admire your angles said the circle shyly
I admire your curves said the hexagon suavely,
barely touching her vanishing point
with the vertex of his fifth side
And before our very eyes
Mr. Hexagon embraces Miss Circle
From this union leaps a geodesic dome.

Lesley-Anne Zullo

Reach-Up

It is no fun being by yourself,
  Being like a puppet on a shelf.

Someone reach-up and grab hold of me,
  I can come alive — just try and see.

I like you — I can love you honestly,
  All I want is to be a real me.

This feeling does not come every day,
  When it comes along — do it our way.

Give it a chance and watch it grow,
  Just imagine what it's like to know.

Born at another place and a different time,
  Reach-up and give — now we both can say:
  "Mine!"

William J. Ludwikowski

Once Mine

In the night we sleep on a garden of past seeds blossomed
  by tears of a girl we've seen before.
She is a dream disturbed by early morning light.
Let her go!
She's not your bride
  only the teacher of future heartache.

Where did you come from precious girl?
I'd like to be yours again.
Your soft warm lips are forever felt by the one who loved you first.

Thank you for the life we once knew
  and memories that shall not pass.
I wish for you
  but wish is all I do.

Kevin Qualls

An Ode To Xena: Warrior Princess

She lived in a village with her family
until an evil warlord came;
then she organized her village
and fighting became her claim to fame.

She became what she once despised
a warrior through and through;
with a blood-curdling cry and her sword held high
many a villager she slew.

She led her great army across the land
razing village after village;
nothing gave her greater joy
than finding more and more to pillage.

Then one day her men went too far
killing women and children against her will;
so she ran the Gauntlet and turned her back
and they beat her 'til she lay still.

But then she rose at the awe of her men
once the dust was let settle;
the warrior princess glared up the line
clearly proving her mettle.

Tania L. Owen

Life

Life is the road to your destiny. Though there are many different and harder paths, I believe they all lead to the same place. When you first start walking life, it's easy and somewhat smooth, but as you go farther down the road you start to encounter "bumps" and "ditches" and other paths. Though you may trip over a bump or fall in a ditch you can choose to get back up and learn from your mistakes. You may take a wrong turn and go on a different path but we all have the power to get off the path and walk through the longs woods of regain. Life is about learning lessons.

Richard Phillips

Untitled

The little Kitty ventured, up into the tree,
and looking down at mama,
sad whatcha think of me? I'm up real
high, and way out far, and having so
much fun, yet it's kinda scary and I'm
the only one. Mama said you must
come down, be careful on your way,
and keep your paws where they belong,
the ground is where to stay.
Then Kitty said to mama, for what of
I should fall? The ground just seems
so far away, he cries and starts to bawl
but mama said don't worry, it's a
lesson you must learn, so I'll be
waiting patiently for your safe return.

Kathy Benson

Gone, But Not Forgotten

No one ever leaves completely as long as one of
us is left behind, to cherish memories discretely
of one so loved, so very kind.

It took a lifetime filled with caring for a very
special son, he taught me gentleness and
sharing and now his task on earth is done.

He left his love and memories which are so dear
to me and gained the everlasting peace, which
ours too, some day shall be.

In loving memory of my son Steven, on the
third anniversary of his death, September 18, 1993.

Marianne Waite

It's A Boy

The baby was born as it was forsworn with great anticipation, and except for the anxiety, borne with valiant vitality, and certainly much trepidation, the flower sprouted rooted in security.

Anxious to see the world, you and me, buckling his knees, he came nineteen and a half inches tall, before the fall, at seven-fifty-six that day all enthralled shouting the novel event: "It's Leo wafting yonder in the sea."

It was August the 4th when Leo came forth in early twilight before sunset, when all met without a doubt, or a fret, there and then all proclaimed: Ship ahoy, the mariner is a boy."

The august event inspired the ode of the day and the horoscope of the ages presaged: power and prestige and the presumption of Leo on Earth, to be of destiny bound, and with Promethean courage and Fate and Doctor Wright pronounced: "Great, evidently the boy is sane and sound," to the mother; and to the father on the side wright sounded: "Adam, you're fortunate."

The news of the day, the Olympiad at its zenith, everyone was apt to say: "Delivery is final, it's a boy; the gold medals pinned, the mother on the pedestal: "I'm glad he came," and she grinned.

"Yes, my son: Devin Camara Sigler is born, and I shall now announce to the world the singular event this August 4th, 1996, as I have anticipated and forsworn.
It is done manifestedly with great interest that you Adam have a son."

John R. Camara Jr.

Quiet Reflections

Sometimes security is shaken as doubts
Invade the quiet times of one's aloneness
These are the times so it seems the wind
Looses its fury and no longer felt is the
warmth of the sun. This is when we question
the wants of our emotions

I can honestly say my love and concern for
You is still the same as yesterday
Just as the flowers need the rain and
The sun
I need you in my
Life

When the concerns of every day life
Block our sight, our loves still the power
That guides us through the night
In confidence we walk the valleys, for
With in our love we find the strength to
Climb the highest mountains

Juan M. Figueras

The Hungry Ghost

Tormented, humiliated, never to emerge again, his infant spirit wounded, fled deep within.

He vowed to get even and conquer over all, with pain and suffering he needs to inflict and readily installs.

He's cleverly disguised as charming and kind, and appeals strongly to the needy, who are not in sound mind.

Demanding with great urgency defenseless flesh, of those tender young, and of those powerless.

Through others he lives and he must violate, attacking with ingenuity, laced with rage and hate.

But all you people, look in his eyes . . .
He comes as far as he may, through his eyes . . .
His body gets still as he hunts for his pray, his eyes fill
With morbid lust, but they are dead in every other way.

I pray you avoid him, the hungry ghost, he spins webs of loving illusions, as he feeds on his host.

Barbara G. Bonfiglio

The Journey

Another year!!!!!
Just passing through?
What were the possibilities?
Our lives keep changing;
bending and curving to meet
the challenges which test our humanness.

Did we remain ever vigilant in our journey toward our ultimate goal?

During this trip down the lane to our success,
we are ever mindful of bumps in the road
. . . the trails which
alter our diligence,
distract us from our purpose,
test our beliefs
and snares that lead us to abandon our faith..

FAITH . . . SPIRITUALITY . . . belief that someone else
is in control, has unquestioned love for us
and will never abandon us in our
JOURNEY.

Henrietta C. Ernst

When I Think Of You

When I think of you my heart feels love
And my eyes, they fill with tears.
I think of all we've been through, the memories fill the years.

When I think of you I sometimes laugh and other times I cry.
I think of all we cherish and troubled times drift by.

When I think of you I wonder what my life would be,
If I was given to another would I still be me?

When I think of you I'm stronger, there is nothing I can't endure.
When I feel weak and beaten, your guidance is the cure.

When I think of you my life is full, I pray when we're together,
We'll take that moment hold it close, to remain in our hearts forever.

When I think of you and you're not here it will only be awhile,
Until you're holding me again that thought always brings a smile.

When I think of you, my parents, I'm overwhelmed with love,
The gifts we have were written in the stars above.
When you look up in the sky the brightest star you see
Think of love passed on to you, believe that star is me
Sending all the love I have across the miles to you.
My life is fulfilled and happy when I think of you.

Lisa Marie Simons

Untitled

Rolling clouds of velvet white
    Remove the color from my sight
Embrace the sun, an ember glow
    And crack the sky, bright rivers flow
Valley deep, the mountains guard
    Shelters all within its yard
Rising there to meet the breeze
    Daylight breaks, it holds the keys
Gentle wind that fades through there
    Softly strokes an angels hair
Lifts a heart, a soul ascends
    A cry for life, a willow bends
Rage the river running free
    It runs as far as eyes can see
Dancing there within the light
    And softly speaks, impending flight
Endless sky that ties them in
    Draws its breath, a brilliant grin
Holding songs of silent chord
    It knows the presence of the Lord

David S. Bryan

My Love

Your beauty permeates my heart like a knife,
your smile is the sunshine that brighten's my life;
the illumination of your smile keeps me a glow,
you are the only women my heart needs to know;
we must do everything to reach the apex of our potential,
life is to short our love is to essential; your love
is like a silent whisper that echoes through the air,
there is nothing more beautiful there is nothing more rare;
your love is like the warmth manifesting in spring, your
love is the culmination of all that I dream; the feeling's
that I feel when I hold you near, for the first time in my
life my future seem's clear; you have healed my wounds
and alleviated the pain, my undying love will never be
left in vain; you will weather any storm and endure
to the end, you are more than my lover you are my
best friend; you burst of a special quality I have
never known, because of your precious elegance
I will never be dethrone; I often find myself
wondering with a sense of ecstasy, afraid that
I may awaken and my dream is a fantasy!

Andre Griffin

Comforting Spirit

Don't weep for me, for I am here
in love, beauty, and blinding light
there's no more pain, there's no more fear
rejoice for there is not one tear.

Rejoice for there is not one tear
with angel's wings I will take flight
to watch you closely, oh my dear
don't weep for me, for I am here.

Don't weep for me, for I am here
you must believe, though not by sight
I'll whisper softly, listen, hear
rejoice for there is not one tear.

Rejoice for there is not one tear
in day or in the darkest night
all things are peaceful, calm and clear
don't weep for me, for I am here.

Don't weep for me, for I am here
rejoice for there is not one tear.

Dawn Lauth-Link

Home (Hom), N., Adj., Adv., V., . . .

We gorge ourselves with words of home.
homebaked apple pie
homemade cookies,
served to us in the homey
atmosphere of a local café.

Our society, our American way of life,
is one of the most homesick
societies of the world.
We drink home-brew with our home-grown food,

And sit around with homefolks
down home.

We sing songs like "I'll be home for Christmas"
and "Homeward Bound."
When we die they say, "He's gone home."

No other set of people
use the word "home"
so frequently
as we rootless
and nomadic Americans.

Sattie Blanton Bowmon

Eagle Seeker

I have a dream it is to fly,
and when I was little, boy did I try.
I would jump from dresser to bed,
but no one said, kids can't fly!
I have a dream high in the sky
me and my angel flying by.
God has called me eagle seeker
and so it seems, he's the keeper of dreams.
He plants them, knowing we shall find
and so I'll keep this dream of mine.
For I have a dream, I can not lie
one day I will fly.
So I'll look to God, for it seems,
he only can give you wings.
His the fulfiller of dreams.
And so look to him and then you'll know,
he plants a desire to come up higher,
soaring with eagle wings.

Lisa Thatcher Marrs

Grandfather

It is often times like these
that we know not what to say,
and so we reminisce
and bow our heads and pray.

It is the loss of a loved one
that sadly brings us together,
to pray for those we've loved and lost
and to pray for one another.

So we join our hearts and hands today
to say a prayer for our grandfather,
and wish him love and peace
in the heavenly ever after.

He will always be remembered
as a man with not much to say,
but somehow touched our hearts and souls
in his very own special way.

He now goes forth to share his life
as he once did some time ago,
with Marcie, his loving departed wife
for they are together now, this we know.

Robin C. Gengler

The Cycle Of The Tree

The snow fell on the mountain top
And stuck there to the ground
Its frozen, white, and icy text
Remained without a sound

Then spring appeared all bright and new
The sun shone on the snow
And like a noble, princely man
A spruce began to grow

It made it through the toughest times
The snow, the wind, the rain
It overcame the blizzard's wrath
Although it caused much pain

And then one day a fire came
To cleanse the forest land
That proud, accomplished, loving tree
Accepted nature's hand

It knew that life was cyclical
And though that meant he'd die
It knew that its demise would help
Another tree grow high

Jason Spencer Farr

Going Nowhere In The Plenty Of Time

I'm going nowhere in the plenty of time
   And I'm in no hurry at all
The seasons will touch me, as I travel on
   Spring follows winter; it's summer, then fall.

The earth and the sky — the rivers and grass
   Will I cherish as life carries me
Through the matchless dominions of nature
   The wilderness, lonely and free.

And through the mystery of nature and life
   We people will pass like the wind
A force, sometimes calm and sometimes aroused
   A breeze turned tornado, we've sinned!

And so in the meshes of guilt and despair
   Our character strives to attain
Going somewhere, someplace in very good time
   Our courage and calm to regain.

Yet sadly we sometimes reveal to ourselves
   How spendthrift we are in the crime
Of precious good seasons we've wasted away
   We've gone nowhere with plenty of time!

   Richard B. Barsaleau

The Harmless Sea

The ocean waves crash against the rocks,
birds cry out in whinny flocks.

The storm picks up and the pelicans flee,
as the wind begins to whistle it is no longer a harmless sea.

Early in the morning the sun will rise,
bringing about a new surprise.

Forgetting what happened the day before,
today it will have something new in store.

   Jessica Schappell

The Thorns Of A Rose

Soft white petals caress drops of dew,
Sunlight contains all — in a day of new.
The rose stands silent but tells stories of love,
Just as stories of peace are told by the dove.
Nothing is as to be as it's told,
It's what you choose to hold.
If you choose to embrace the rose and its tale,
Be careful so you don't set yourself up to fail.
Love can be painful when it's torn,
The truth to the story of the rose is its thorn.

   Kenne A. Steen

The Woody Perennial

Its branches are limp
   in the summer's heat and humidity.
Before the storm arises
   the tree stands still.
There's a sign of gray developing in the west,
   and one can feel the hint of coolness before the violent storm.
The birds fly wildly;
   they disappear.

The branches begin to dance frantically
   with the cooling winds.
The hail shreds the leaves,
   and they're ripped off the tree.
But then the wind quiets itself,
   and the leaves lay quiet after the turbulence of the storm.
Then the birds are heard
   in the boughs of the tree.

   Kristin L. Kittner

Human Nature

Human nature — a wonderful fusion of good and evil.
With this we always guard our good side on the surface of our host.
Our bad side hidden.
Though at times lurking from depths of darkness
it surfaces atop our host.
If only to reveal a side
we thought we never had.
Frightened animals are we.
Like good, evil is the exact essence of our being.
Just as pure. Just as ancient.
It knows not itself but only as the tool of the doer.
And whomever understood human nature and its intricate ways
could probably answer us. But to what end?
If not but to add intrigue to this divine puzzle.
So it is the burden of free will which troubles us.
An endless struggle until
all is forgotten and another time is upon us.
Attempting to subdue not for the sake of good or evil.
But retain control of our existence. Our sanity.

   Giada Robinson

A Balsa Mountain High

Enclosed in living color
As far as the eye can see
Natures cloak of dazzling beauty
Captured by every tree.
It's October in the Smoky's.

Sun filtering down through the forest
Golden hues on every leaf
October in the Smoky's
Has reached its magnificent peak.

Sunset repeats in the evening sky
The mountains gorgeous color display
In the campfire flame a fire glow
Carries thoughts of a perfect day.
That's October in the Smoky's.

Velvet darkness falls as the fire dies
Another wonder meets the eyes
A million stars are swinging low
With thoughts of another tomorrow, what an after glow!
It was October in the Smoky's.

   Nora Muus Sterritt

Journey's End

Journey's end with the setting sun.
Free from a world with little left to be done.
He chose not the wrong time dying,
presuming those he loved would excuse him.

The history of his life does not end with silent breath,
but begins anew in the heart he touched.

Grieve not for grandfather.
He lingers not, feigning life no more.
Embracing the borrowed wings of death, he ascends to the
spring of youth, to a world of lilacs and roses, forever fresh from
morning dews.

He passed away beneath the evening moon,
and awakes in a sunlit garden that whispers, "we wait."

Mourn for passerby's who knew not the man. Mourn for those who
have never looked into the colors of a rainbow. And if you must, mourn
the grandfather. He that is the kind memories, smelling sweet of a love
that was, as you remembered, a kindness to hold open a hand.

And if tears flow, stare, stare at the living, and cry for those
who were nor told, "now am at peace." Bent, bowed, yielding to
the grace of reason, for no sun outlives the day.

   David Jon Phillips

Fear

My fears are spread out on the wall
but my fears they just won't fall
I am scared so filled with fright
help me God last through the night
wherever I go fear is with me
wherever I am fear is in me
fear will never let its guard down
but I'm afraid that I am fear bound
fear will never leave my soul
I am becoming very cold
in the fire place flames flicker across a log
and I feel as though I am in a dense fog
fear is flowing through my blood
oh I hope it does not flood
my mind and body with its evil feeling
"Fear will live in me forever."

Jim Baker

The Sparrow's Song

My Heavenly Father said to me,
   no cigarettes, cigars, or blends
if you want your heavenly father
   to be your closest friend.

I saw the sparrows on my lawn
   there was no blend for them
to draw and smoke upon
   they ate what God had given them
and thanked him with a song.

Now lessons from the mind of God
   are things we must not forget
you'll never see a sparrow lift his wing
   to smoke a cigarette!

Geneva Moistner

Old Glory

One little boy as he walked down the street
Waving his flag so that all could see.
"This is the flag my father fought for
When it was his turn to go to war!"
Proudly he held it high on a stick
That we might see
Red, white and blue stands for our liberty,
There are white stars for each state,
All put together stands for AMERICA THE GREAT.
So, may OLD GLORY, as it is called
Wave on forever protecting us all.

Frances Cherry

Les Regards Vides

Apparitions of buried deeds haunts reflected and refracted
lone passages of trespasses transgressions reap sad souvenirs
spawned forth in reciprocations I regret yet, yet I regret
bear remorse deep in pain silent nay pity bestow say rejoice
'tis blessing in the human soul but wary who embrace the void.

They swell as on a tortured sea these waves from not so distant past
white foamed crashing against the crags ever the sea ever the fear casts
forth shadows from harboured sins twisted whispers on vagrant winds
rising vile in echoes chilling angry voices of desolation reverberate on
well-tuned ears I a child of les regards vides.

Out of graveyards those lost to time they kindle ashes long left
cold stir the sirocco of men's soul to bring a smile to Belzebuth
the fiendish face and I my dream transfix on their dark force
brutal watch wide-eyed as row after row marching they step to
my nightmare black boots black eyes black hearts are they the
children of les regards vides.

Robin Luzi

Mom

There is a place only I can tell you.
It is there I find peace and there I breathe.

My mother's arms cradles me
my mother's arms uplifted me
My mother's arms inspired me

To her I celebrate
To her I rejuvenate.

She is my friend
She is my best friend.

With her I know that all is fine
and with her all is loved.

My mother is my most precious daisy.
She is the sky of azure
And the inspiration of the forest.

I love her.
She is my mother
   and to her I give my morning's run
   my fast stride
   my steadfast praise
   my never dying adoration.

Rachel Reitmeyer

Like a Beacon of a Lighthouse

Your love is like the beacon of a lighthouse,
   and my love is the ship that it guides.
The light searches for the ship,
   though what it seeks I cannot hide.

Your visage is like the beacon of a lighthouse,
   radiant, brilliant and gleaming.
I could look at you for hours on end,
   with it only seeming,
to be minutes.

Our laughter is like the beacon of a lighthouse,
   one is synonymous with the other.
Because of this laughter and happiness,
   I know there will never be another.

Your love is like the beacon of a lighthouse,
   the light that shines into life.
You illuminate my essence with your love,
   which carries us through all strife . . .
we carry each other.

Dean Heller

The Walk In The Park

   I met a nice man
one afternoon in the park.
I was walking along a pathway,
when this man came along side
me and started talking,
not that much about any thing,
all of a sudden he asked if
I would like an ice cream cone.
I said yes. We got the ice cream
cone, he got vanilla and I got
strawberry, by the time we ate
the cones and walked some more,
he made a dinner date with me,
that was my walk in the park.
   The dinner date was very nice.
We both had stake dinners and pie afterwards.
Then after that we went to the movies.
The time we spent together turned out to be very nice.
We enjoyed a lot more walks in the park.

Linda Donovan

Mornings New

Dedicated to my loving husband, who inspires me so much
The wind blows softly through my window tonight
as you hold and comfort me so gently and so tight.
Feeling your presence of warmth and tenderness
only wanting you more to love and caress.
Night last forever when longings are there
waiting to fulfill fantasies and to show I care
but, alas, time goes slowly as my heart pounds fast
dreaming up ways to satisfy so, it will forever last
First touch comes weakly to my skin
as I'm shivering of innocence and pleasure to begin.
Breathing in deep to catch his scent
both are wondering about time spent
The silence of the night is lurking us still
passion is a long waiting friend with its own will
as fingers touch the warmth of begging flesh insight
holding dreams and ambitions just to make it all right
As our darkness rises and love shines through,
Our tremors disappear as one is no longer two
Eagerness turns to desirable anticipated bliss
just waiting for morning's new and another first kiss.

Nikki P. Calhoun

Nestled In The Shadow Of His Wings

God is so faithful,
he shields me from the grips of utter despair.
He surrounds me with the
comfort of his love
and keeps me nestled in the shadow of his wings.

God is so strong, he strengthens me when
I'm at my weakest point.
He enables me to withstand
life's worst storms while
nestled in the shadow of his wings.

God is the great potter
who takes life's circumstances
to refine, mold, and transform
me into the person I should be
all the while keeping me safely
nestled in the shadow of his wings.

Thank you, O God for your
faithfulness, strength, transforming
powers and the love and safety
found in the shadow of your wings.

Gail Owens

Untitled

Show me your mind.
Speak truth.
I scream all the time
over words that have not been spoken, yet understood.
With one life so important,
I see no one;
With myself hanging and stranded, I feel no one.
Written songs speak truth.
Still pictures have more words than my shadow.
Masks can be seen through.
Mine is black with shame.
A knife it feels like.
I wanted to do it.
I wanted to feel it.
My mask spits hiding laughter and false smiles.
Screaming out my shadow replies,
hiding me deeper in its eyes.
Counting stars, walls on all sides.
Scratching doors feel more.
Nothing like seeing empty shadows, smiling.

Ryan A. Cochran

Casualty Of War

No, she did not join the armed forces,
she did not fight in far off distant lands,
neither did she suffer the discomforts of the four winds,
nor did she experience the pain of the enemy's fire power,
however, she was a casualty of war.

No she did not give her blood in far off distant lands,
nor did she have to see her comrades give up their lives before her,
she did not have to see the raging war,
but she was a casualty of war.

Her desire for his life to be spared,
was greater than her own desire for happiness.
In deepest prayer she held nothing back, but chose
that he be saved and gave up her hopes and dreams.
She seized to live that faithful day,
she too become a casualty of war.

His life spared through her undying love,
to lead a life of self destruction.
To destroy the most important thing to her.
She truly was a casualty of war.

Evelina E. Flores

No More Darkness

In darkness no more do I sit alone
straining to see by the light of the moon;
a dark staggering shadow coming home
will it be peace or sudden doom?

The anger and rage he builds up inside
is about to explode with tremendous force;
once again we must run and hide
tearing down the love, he has no remorse.

An evil stranger has entered my house
every sound and gesture has my nerves on edge;
a tortuous game of cat and mouse
we were the victims pushed out on a ledge.

Time will heal and the heart will mend
two babies God has put in my care;
will I be afraid to ever love again?
The nightmares together we now share.

Nancy L. Carty

Deep In The Heart

Deep are the feelings in the heart of mankind, deep are the
things of life which are taught, meaningful and thoughtful, are the minds
of people's souls, when they cherish life as it unfolds. Deep in the heart
are hurts when hearts are broken, painful the hurt, and words unspoken.
Sometimes it's not easy to laugh and to grin, when the heart is broken,
and the pain is deep within. Hearts are precious and love so tender, and
to be thoughtful is to be a friend. But deep within the pain and
heartache, a friend to pray too, to ask for help. Nobody knows the hurt
inside, like the Lord who lives on high. Whom to go too, when the pain
is inside. Whom to ask for help in life. When carefully we ponder life's
mystery, how right it is, how right life seems. Joy abounds when love is
near, and friendships flourish, hopefulness not despair. Yes, true is love
and goodness and peace, when troubles one takes, on eagles wings,
flying up to the Lord so near, in the heart, life's sweet mystery. Emotional pain can bring one low, and sometimes friends don't know which
way to go. Is Jesus real, is he alive. He is my friend, and he doesn't die.
Deep secrets are not always dark, sometimes it's loneliness, and what
people sometimes really want, is a new start. But only the one who lives
inside, can help us overcome the hurt and pain, to forget the pain that's
been. Sometimes a kind word, or sin rebuked, and help people stop
inside the fight and the feud. Inside the heart is where Christ Jesus lives,
so never regret the time that you give. Always live in peace and mercy,
it's his heart who helps, and his spirit to obey. Deep in the heart is peace
and love, and truth that bubbles up so we can share. Of all the people
who ever was alive, Jesus keeps the soul set free, and helps us to be
concerned and care, not chide.

Robert A. Wagner Jr.

Fire

As the fire crawled up the side,
the image had caught my eye.
The world around seems to die,
now it's only the fire which seems to drive.
And all the thoughts I have inside,
indeed I feel I need to sigh.
Through all the days and all the nights,
it is now time to say goodbye.
I shall never forget the time we shared.
For all that time a lot we cared,
and the memories forever we shall share.

Dawn Gehrke

If Only I Had Wings

If I had wings, I would fly away
To a place where there is peace, everyday

I would fly over an ocean
To feel the breeze
And clear my mind, to be at ease

I would fly to an island
And perch on a tree
And enjoy my life of being free

I would fly over a mountain
And look down to see
I am in a higher place, where nothing or no one could touch me

I would fly over a stream
And land down below
To watch the purest water, as it flows

I would fly, forever
And with joy, I'll sing

"If only I had wings"

Silky Parks

When My Love Saw You

When my love saw you,
you were a gleam, of shimmering light.
My love just caught you in my kiss.
Your tender kiss gave me a guide of light of love.
Your touch made a tingle go up and down my body.
Your smell gave me a sweet imaginary moment.
Your voice made me never want to leave you and your soft words.
Your love is incredible to me.
That's when my love first saw you and only you my love.

Nicole Spano

Morning's Glory

Majestic peaks, among earth's tallest,
        Along the great divide,
Leap skyward in parade order
        To certainly provide
A jagged challenge
        To that first official ray.
Winged on a peppermint glow —
        Reflected below —
Imprinting this, — a brand new day.

Drawing a breath, — startling, fresh,
        To match the view supreme.
Within a moment the glory's gone,
        Of this royally regal scene.
A treasured glimpse,
        For those who gaze,
Tucked deep within the heart.
        There, — such moving splendor stays.

Elizabeth I. Cahoon-Jackson

Of Fantasy

I once saw a sail boat
carry of my fantasy
farther than I'd care to go
though it was born to me
it slipped right thru my fingers
I was young — how was I to know

Float inside a bottle
upon a sea immortal
even though I won't be there for long
now what lies before me
the isles of ulysses
where all my fears and weakness grow strong

I left my dreams like pages
turned before my viewing
knowing what I'm doing to the end
high among the sages
dried up, old and tumbling
scatter seeds of fantasy again

Marilyn and Mark Fabbri

Breath Again

Suffocating blackness surrounds me, tortures my soul.
I gasp for air. I gasp for hope.
I cannot breath. I cannot hope.
Which is my path to happiness? I do not know.
Which is my path to happiness? My path of hope?

All I want to do is breath again
But all I seem to do is drown.
Drown in my own despair, worries, and doubts.
Drown in my own insecurities.
Nobody seems to care. Nobody is there to throw me a rope.

I realize as I look around myself inflicted prison,
that I am the only one that can throw myself a line.
I take off the weights of despair, of worry, and of doubt.
I feel myself floating to the top.

I untangle myself from my insecurities.
I grasp for an object far above me: entitled faith in myself.
I break out my dark prison and look upward.
For now I know the key to my survival: is not money, fame, or power.
But to nourish the faith and hope that lives within me.

Nedra L. Coleman

Legacy Of Birth

To be jerked from a mother's womb
And encased into life's embryonic tomb

Fed milk from a mother's swollen breast
Hoping and praying, this infant will have success

Traditions are made and born from ideas of man
Dreams are grains of sugar, softly being sifted into grains of sand

Time goes by, years so I'm told
The infant grows tall and dreams unfold

Desires to conquer wealth and fame
Goals to reach and not be shamed

Knowledge began to wither in a dormant stage
Life's frustrations are written on a page

Searching for something, something solid and true
But day by day there's suffering in view

Legacy of Birth! Can you ever imagine what this is worth?

All the riches of the world can't keep you from the hurt
So, stand firm, honest and moral on this man's earth

You will survive the legacy of birth

Hazel McGowan Guillory

Peace

What is this peace, this peace inside?
What is this peace, I can't describe?

Through troubles and trials and pains I bear,
What is this peace I find in there?

No storms arise without His calm,
For pain in Gilead we find His balm.

As Job endured the fiery dart,
That peace remained inside his heart.

I too know how Job must have felt,
When my whole life began to melt.

Through God's Grace placed His hedge on me,
He brought me peace and I let it be.

Acquaint yourself with Christ, my friend,
He'll bring you peace, a peace within.

Vicki Lee

Drug Warrior

A little boy's crying alone in the street
He's got no place to go and nothing to eat.
Mama's money has gone up her nose
There's none left for food, or a little boy's clothes.

Oh man of the war how do you feel
When the demand for your 'goods' forces people to steal?
A nation is crumbling, you're creating great strife.
Certainly there's more you can do with your life.

White, synthetic, deceit in a vial
The illusion of glory lasts but for a while.
Now brother's a liar, and sister's a whore
The people in pain are crying for more.

Oh Drug Warrior, Dealer, a Master, a King
Don't you see what your actions can bring?
Innocent people are dying in vain
Murdered by you, in the name of cocaine.

Our future of peace, longevity and wealth
Requires you look beyond your own health.
When you buy and sell, consider the price
And next time you'll see that you ought to think twice.

Karyn Sernka

Where The Lioness Prowls

There is a place, a place down below
Where the lioness prowls and the dead flowers grow
There is a place, where beauty is pain
There nobody loves and they all look the same

There is a place, where everything's night
Even in day time, the ground knows no light
The ground, is a fire, the grass is the flames
Everything's wild and nothing is tame

And there is a place, where there's always a war
And everyone dies and everyone's poor
And there is a place, where the shadows have fill
Of the vampires and demons, who thrive on their kill

Where screams fill the night and there is no rest
Where blood flows like water and streets reek of death
It's a horrible place and a terrible sight
But there is still hope, we can still make it right

I live in this place, as all of us do
Just look around, you'll see that it's true
For the lioness prowls here during the day,
The creature is hate and we are its prey . . .

Victoria Cooper

Silhouette

While gazing upon the shadow of the moon
The sunset smiled back to me
As the stars hover brilliantly throughout the world
Reminiscence tap me on my shoulder, unlocking the door to my past
I feel as if I've been hypnotized under a magic spell
A mirage suddenly appears before my eyes
It's the projection of a lover that I once knew
But why do I still remember?
I hear a far away voice, whispering in my ear the music of love
that echoes within the depths of my soul
My reverie is suddenly broken
Darkness surround me like a shroud
A falling star soars across the sky
I smile
My heart never said goodbye

George Henry Moore Jr.

Shadows Of Time

Time shadows our memories of pain
Were it not for its healing power
Indeed all of us would go insane
For want of new memories tomorrow

Only through thoughtless word or deed
Are they allowed to rise anew
Upon these two things the shadows feed
Giving passage for what makes us blue

Only the memories that are sweet and pure
Can withstand the shadows of time
Happy are we that they can endure
To soothe and refresh our weary minds

Though time passes and we mellow and age
The sweetness of memories treasured
Will not give way to shadows and fade
But bestow upon us joy without measure

Eileen Freeman

Dreamscape

It washed up on shore one day.
A dream I had forgotten,
that one day I could sail away,
to a place where people's souls were free
to dream and wonder.
There would be no hasty decisions
and time to rest or play
with realities that were once
just dreams
all washed away.

Tracy L. Ryan

Forever Lasting Love

As age sets in and years go by
Still reading this poem I tend to cry
The walks at night hand in hand
The words of love spelled in the sand
We had so much to give each other
The many days we were with one another
The promises, the words, the many nights
Brought feelings of love within our sights
The love and times we spent alone
Talking about our future and home
Now that it's gone and tears have dried
My life, my style, since then has died
If ever you thought I was untrue
Then please forgive me for loving you
We had something special from above
And that will always be forever lasting love

Marvin J. Ziemann

My Children!

Pray my children deep down with your little heart.
Pray to him your father and your Lord.
He'll let you know what it's all about.
The good Lord my children, he'll bring it out.
At this time my children there's no time for play.
The good Lord my children he'll make away.
Always love him more than anyone else.
He'll help my children he'll help you yourself.
The Lord Jesus is the one who dies on the cross.
Don't stop now or you will be lost.
Now is the time my children when you say.
Come on dear Lord and go my way.

Alma J. Wilborn

Innocence

God created no imperfect creature
Why must we test his patience
With the ignorance of man . . .

Did you see the li'l babe?
Her eyes shining with dawn's first light . . .
An angelic glow frames her delicate features . . .

Did you see the li'l babe?
Her body flailing with spasms . . .
Trembling with nightmares
Cries of a tortured soul
Only eight hours ol'

Did you see the li'l babe?
Full of life, if only for a short while
With each gasp, dwindling . . .
Her face is aglow
Quietly . . . into serene peace

God created no imperfect creature
Why must we test his patience
With the ignorance of man!

Latrice Satchell

Come Let Us Worship And Bow Down,
And Let Us Kneel Before The Lord . . .

Dear Lord, how do You feel when someone takes your name in vain?
When they feel you're not worthy to honor or obey.
They are pleased with their life and feel they will sustain.
It must hurt your heart and bring you much pain.

Dear Lord, how do you feel when you have given your all?
When the world just laughs and has a great ball.
When people just feel they can scorn your name.
It must hurt your heart and bring you much pain.

Dear Lord, would not it be better, if we would all bow our knee?
For the day is coming when this is what you will see.
If now we would worship and praise your name.
For we know we would be happy and not filled with shame.

Gladys (Marie) Catinella

Mourning A Passing

Tears of diligence, straining to remember
  Death is beyond our grasp.

It's not to be held bottled up inside,
  Mirrors of the past.

We must put it all behind
  Or it becomes a mind bender.

Once sparkling laughter,
  Regrets to the hereafter.

Rita S. Graham

Tears

Let me cry for a world torn and tossed;
For victories won and battles lost.
Let me cry in sorrow for friendships lost;
One way or the other was it worth the cost.
Let me cry because I cannot see;
Those, who in death, were taken from me.
Let me cry for those who in hunger and pain;
In fields and streets and alleys have lain.
Let me cry for compassion that seems hard to find.
Let me be able to forgive, be gentle, and kind.
Let me cry for wisdom, knowledge, and truth.
Let me cry for the innocence of my youth.
Let me cry to God that I might see;
Some goodness hidden inside of me.
Let me cry for forgiveness, I cannot hide;
The evil and darkness I have inside.
Let me cry in anger, let me cry in shame.
Let me cry to heaven, and scream your name.
And finally, when the crying is done;
Let me see your face in the morning sun.

Kenneth W. Fleming

Paths

Different shoes that look alike but never have the same laces.
Growing up and apart;
butterflies emerging from their cocoons.
Differences mend you together but with different patches.
Sew the gaps up with knowledge.
Going all over the place like fireflies,
but avoiding the big light.
Things in common; spiritually connected.
In a huge cycle; running to unwind.

Cori Stallard

Longing Passion

The beauty of a rose could never compare,
to the beauty of your face and long silken hair.
The sound of your voice speaking softly with love,
is the sound of tenderness from a white mourning dove.
Just to gaze into your elegant brown eyes,
is to see the brilliant sparkle of stars in the sky.
The charm of your smile is the magnificence of you,
like a bright spring morning kissed by the dew.
To taste your lips is the desire of life.
I'd give all tomorrows just for one night.
To be in your presence with love all around,
my life be complete and heaven be found.

Casey Shaw

More Than Dreams

Daytime woke her with less than a kiss
Of what morning brings she would always miss
Oh, but things were fine, things were grand
Everything happened the way she had planned

Night time arrived in much the same way
No romantic fling to carry her away
Oh, but things were fine, and this was home
And this was the best she had ever known

Dream time caught her as she drifted in sleep
With a vision of someone she would soon meet
As the nighttime rolled into a glorious dawn
She knew in her heart it was time to move on

So this time gave her true love to adore
And all of those dreams aren't dreams anymore
Even to this day she'll ask me what happened
I was more than her dreams could imagine

Steven Guntrum

Sweet Songs

I am walking towards the waves,
without my sight, my ears lead me,
my feet are bare,
I can not feel the burning sand.

My sense of smell guides me to the salty waters,
my heart pulls me closer to my impending doom,
my arms resting comfortably to my sides,
my legs offer no resistance.

Now in life my conscious is clear,
my mind now sings with sweet songs,
my lips smile for once in their existence,
my darkened eyes see their own light.

I can feel warm raves of sunlight on my face,
and a uncontrollably sense of relief,
no choices needed to be made,
only courses needed to be followed.

My heart no longer feels pain,
my lungs no longer need air,
my body no longer needs food,
my spirit will now forever be peaceful.

Jerilyn Yannotta

Autumn

Her air was maudlin.
She felt in the autumn of her life.
Gone was the youth
of excitability and playful carelessness.
True love was rare
and it exploded with abundance.
Thinking back she is sure
that this kind of commitment only
happens once.
If only it had happened a few years later
ah, but would it
have been the same?
She thinks not.
Autumn, again autumn makes her
bring it all back.
Wonderful swirling leaves
surrounding her hopes and dreams.
Yes, autumn. The autumn of her life.
The autumn of her life.

Pixie L. Story

The Wildwoods

With its ranging tentacles it reached,
grasping for the frantic children,
and through the Wildwoods they ran.

Past rivers and streams,
through the endless meadows,
with its ranging tentacles it reached.

Wide eyed with fear,
adrenaline coursing in their veins,
and through the Wildwoods they ran.

Stretching, grasping, grabbing, clawing,
howling with anguish at its eluding prey,
with its ranging tentacles it reached.

Screaming with hoarse voices for help,
exhausted and blooded with scratches,
and through the Wildwoods they ran.

Slowing and tiring from the long haul,
and while they ran one stumbled,
with its ranging tentacles it reached,
and through the Wildwoods he ran.

C. Sterling Hampton

The Rosebud

A teardrop forms atop a slender stalk;
a little bud on the roses by the walk.

With shining sun and gentle rain
the bud increases in size again.

The warmer weather heralds the opening of
this fragrant flower, a symbol of love.

Its petals open, but only a bit;
just open enough for more sun to fit.

Gradually unfolding, until comes the day
the petals unfurl in Spring's tender way.

A sweet little rose open only for me,
such delicate flowers picked so carefully.

Into a vase, between printed page,
a long-lasting memory, the star of Spring's stage.

Samantha Kline

I Refuse To Believe

Do you believe in the hurt?
Do you believe in the love?

I can't believe in the hurt,
because I've seen it all too often.

I can't believe in love,
because I don't see it often enough.

I can't believe,
and I won't be believe.

I refuse to believe in unseen visions.
I refuse to see visions I don't believe in.

Seeing is not believing.
Believing is not seeing.

I refuse to give into the evils.
I refuse to let evils give into me.

Good conquers evil,
but evil conquers good.

I refuse to be told.
I refuse to tell.

Talking is silence.
Silence is telling.

Becky Wallace

Life Is So Precious

Man has not yet conceived
what really happened when God made Eve,

He placed a woman to dress the earth,
and bear her children by natural birth,

Then medical science developed a plan
which has erased God's creation and purpose for man,

I see the world as a mere array
when I look at people so confused today,

God created the world all by himself
and when He did, He needed no help,

Now man with all the skills to fly
is soon to perish far beyond the sky,

Somewhere beyond the clouds so high
twice to live and once to die,

I leave this thought to the whosoever will
that man can not say to the waters, "Peace Be Still."

Brenda Lee-Rollins

Fools

What type of person spend his time
writing down his thoughts in rhyme?
A certain man, who once said
"Poems are made by fools like me
but only God can make a tree"
God must like fools and trees and poetry
what other reason could there be
for making so many fools like me?

Jack W. Heskett

The Chosen One

A big bright ball of light up in the sky.
One who brings people together all around.
A faithful person who has never told a lie.
A holy figure with a pleasant sound.
He tastes like the fresh fruits I pick from the trees.
A holy presence that is hidden in your heart.
I feel his holy presence in the breeze.
As long as we love him, we'll never grow apart.
One who smells like the sweet scent of a flower.
A wonderful figure that rose from the dead.
He is there for us during every hour.
We pray to him before we go to bed.
He sounds like a kind-hearted man who's full of love.
For he is Jesus Christ who lives up above.

Lauren Huff and Shana Smith

The Colors Of Our Love

There is a pattern of love that we have yet to see.
Colors that dark are laced with gold.
A bond of souls that is woven so tightly it will outlast eternity.
So many stories this pattern will come to hold.

The weaver spins a web that foresees the spirit of our love.
How we surrendered our body, mind, and soul to this pattern
that explains the reasons why.
Our destiny is guided by the hand above.
And how our passions will soar high.

In the end we will see,
that the weaver took great time and care
to make the patter that was meant to be.
All the colors of our love are beautiful, both dark and fair.

Nichole McConnell

Hold

Had I known, that was the last time
  I could hold you
I would have stared deep into your eyes
  pouring my emotions up to the rim of your soul

Had I known, that was the last time
  I could hold you
I would have pulled you against me so tight
  that our hearts would weld into one

Had I known, that was the last time
  I could hold you
I would have lost myself
  in the fragrant fluffy curtains of your beautiful hair

Had I known, that was the last time
  I could hold you
I would have sent my tongue on a most arousing journey
  from your sweet shoulders, up and down your smooth neck

Had I known, that was the last time
  I could hold you
I would have eventually let go
  on the day that I die

Dion Bettinger

Life's Clock

The clock of life is wound but once,
And no one has the earthly power;

To say what time the clock will stop,
Be it in the late or early hour;

As the clock ticks away each passing day,
Live and toil with them at will;

Place not all your prayers in tomorrow,
For the clock may then be still.

Estella L. Bishop

Security Or Freedom

Security or freedom
Which one will you choose
If you vote for one you fear
The other, you shall lose
Liberty is always hailed
As bold, just and right
Security, on the other hand
Feels safe, with warm delight
There will always be a struggle
When these two worlds collide
But reason, think, and understand
Or ignorance decides
The choice is clear, the path is strait
Through life, what I've learned most
A vote for freedom, through length of time
Will be, a vote, for both

Steve Applebee

Untitled

Innocent and pure, ever so soft and delicate
they look to us with total need, and complete trust
eyes closed in slumber, they giggle and smile
. . . as sweet as the kiss of an angel.

Uninhibited, they kick their legs, and wave their arms
trying hard to lift their head, eyes wide open drawn to the light
sweet kisses and patty-cakes
. . . as soft as the breast of an angel.

Tiny little fingers and fat little toes, smells of cookies and milk
their only purpose is to be cuddled and kissed, lulled and rocked
to sleep . . . as quiet as the whisper of an angel.

Babies are a special gift from heaven, they belong not to us,
but simply a gift from God. Placing into our care, his precious
little angels. To be given nothing less than all of our love.

Delilie D. Carrington

I Know My Family At Christmas Time

I know my family at Christmas time,
The fire cracking in the hearth,
The sound of my family talking,
The sound of my family coming through the front door,

I know my family at Christmas time,
The smell of Christmas food cooking,
The cinnamon that smells all through the house,
The smell of Christmas cookies cooling off,

I know my family at Christmas time,
The sight of my family eating breakfast,
My cats jumping on the tree,

I know my family at Christmas time,
I hear my brother saying, "Don't open the presents now!"
My mom saying, "Danner come downstairs. Everyone is here."

I know my family at Christmas time.

Danner Summerford

Greg

Greg
Caring, athletic, smart, honest
Brother of Michael
Lover of family, dog, basketball
Who feels mad at brother when makes him mad,
Happy when makes A's, sad when someone leaves
Who needs money, time by himself
Who gives help to little brother when needs it,
Gifts on birthdays, help to sick dog
Who fears getting kidnapped, getting a deadly disease,
Bitten by dog
Who would like to see Penny Hardaway in person,
Magic win NBA title, Gators win National Championship
Resident of Eustis, Forest Drive
Downs

Greg Downs

Which Is True?

In the darkness of the dream world
is where the suffering lies.
In the bright morning sunshine
it seems that troubles die.

Which is true of thoughts we see?
Darkness and sunshine there will always be.
Darkness is the world where no
upward thoughts are found.
Sunshine assails our mind
where everything abounds.

Which one should be tossed
from our minds by the winds
of time unfolding.

Maybe the darkness could become a little brighter
and let the sunshine dim a little,
so in the mind their forms are unmolding.

Clarice A. Mueller

Untitled

I see the tall and stately pine symbolic of our life.
Its tufted bough against the sky, prepared to meet all strife.
Along its rough and shaggy trunk, are short and broken branches
Reminder of a yesteryear, of youth and all its chances.
Some of these are straight and strong, other curved and shattered
The former represent good deeds, and things that really mattered.
The latter as you may have guessed, are things that we did wrong
Still they cling and still they show, for all the world to see,
   That there are other days before, we'd like forgotten be.
But home and family is the bough, which reaches to the sky.
   The emblem of a life complete.
   You know it. So do I.

George Wynn

My Old Friend, My Sister

I miss my old friend,
my sister.

We've grown so far apart.
I realize this while dreaming out the window.

She's learned to grip the facade of the world,
I'm still searching for reality.

Which one of us is right?
Am I wrong?

Plenty of questions,
So many unfound answers.

I miss my old friend,
My sister.

Erica J. Hannawell

Earth's War

You mock me, Stone, aloof and cold,
eternal ashes, still as death,
the whistling wind your only breath.

For I am water, storm and sea.
With rolling waves I wear and race,
to make up daily earth's new face.

While everywhere your strongholds stand,
beneath a glaze of leaf or snow
to block or shunt my wanton flow.

But I attack relentlessly,
each mountain, ledge and rocky strand
and slowly change them back to sand.

You, Stone, alone can't stay my floods,
nor halt assaults on plain and shore,
for we are locked by time in war.

You press around me, cold and dead . . .
or thrust above me, molten, steaming.
Yes, war on you I must . . .
or else I have no meaning!

Art Ward

Lack Of Confidence

If you want something but feel insecure,
and you are just not sure
"It's lack of confidence"
If you are scared and full of fear,
to take a chance on your dream my dear
"It's lack of confidence"
If you prolong your job search with a lazy excuse,
because you feel it's just no use
"It's lack of confidence"
If you think you might fail and don't even try,
you will never know even when you die
"It's lack of confidence"
So repeat after me: Lack Of Confidence I Will Not Feel, I Can, I Can,
because God is real
If I trust, have faith, and believe
anything is possible through God to succeed

Daphne F. Thurman

Are You Buying

   The perceptions of a few mindless heads,
Who screams their product of opinion
   From the highest mountain,
Entice the clones of society
   To scramble to the marketplace
With checkbooks in hand.

Tina L. Spires

Love Before And After Life

Love is special
Love is sweet
Love is like cool grass beneath my feet.
When you touch me chill's go up my spine
I will always know you'll be mine
All through eternity and time
God can take me in one sweep
And I know it will make you weep
And as you know our love is true
I'll always be in love with you
Even if you can't see me I'll be there.
In your heart and sole to share
I will see you in the night or even when the days are so bright.
God grant me one wish
That our love will last as long as life exist
Even though the heaven's beautiful mist.

Teresa Jones Crowell

To My Best Friend

In all the memories we share
You were always standing there
To pick me up when I felt down
Or walk with me to "out-of-town."
You never judged or made me feel bad.
I couldn't see just what I had.
I turned away to seek my fate.
Did you know the world is full of hate?
I miss your comfort and your smile.
To be with you for just a while,
To enjoy your voice and company
Would be, for me, sweet agony
Knowing in just a few short days
We'd once again have separate ways.
I'd like to stay, I have to go,
But I need to let you know,
I've never again met someone like you,
Who gave me friendship so strong and true.
Though at times we're far apart,
There's a place for you, in my heart!

Margaret L. Petit

God Let Me Die

As I lay on my bed
Wishing I'd soon be dead.
This pain is too much for me
But soon my spirit will be free.

My head hurts so much now
Dying is the answer; the question is how.
A failure is the only thing I'm good at
So it won't be a gun, I'm sure of that.

The pills I already did try
Slicing my wrists will just make me cry.
Tried drinking until last call
A rope maybe; but I'd just fall.

If praying helps the cause
God grant me this, without a pause.
Taking my own life I cannot do
So I'm praying; it is all up to you.

Now you can see the fix I'm in
For dying by your own hand is a sin.
So I'll be waiting for your final say
Hoping it's soon, maybe today.

Becky Campbell

Love's Inspiration

I prayed for love and affection;
but all I got was rejection!
I know the reason for Christ's resurrection!
I know my heart will have protection!
No we're not forsaken!
No we're not like Satan!
We must pray for our youth;
that they will search for the truth!
I pray to God from within!
That someday there may be an end!
He gave His Son for my sin;
for that reason I will repent.
Jesus should be our inspiration;
we only show through desperation!
I'm sorry that it's true;
I'm just glad to have found you!
I pray that you've found salvation,
even if through your desperation!
Just believe that He loves you;
you must believe that it's True!!!

Richard Alan Lynn

Songs In The Mist

In the mist I heard the song
The sad refrain,
A melody both loud and long,
Then it vanished in the rain.

I strained my ears to hear once more
The sweet song of the morning,
All was quiet on the shore,
Save for the hawk's shrill cry of warning.

Although the song faded years ago
The lesson of Earth
Is one I still know.

Angela Szvercsak

Danger Zone

The end of the tunnel is dark and gray,
Bright dreams shattered, stripped away,
All hope gone, awaiting another day.
Danger zone where no love abounds,
Only emptiness that keeps me down,
Despair tries desperately to take control,
Leaving the body without a soul.
Arise within me O Master of Creation,
Work in me mighty determination.
Rekindle in my spirit a new spark,
To dispel the unfruitfulness of the dark.
Give place in me for new hopes and dreams,
Greater strength to impart
What the Master deems necessary for every heart.
I'm willing, O Lord, to be healed.
For this I know is the Father's will.
Speak to my heart and it will be,
The filling of an empty soul for me.

Dianne C. Todd

The Final Halloween

As the night approaches its darkest hour, the sounds of those who left us long ago can be heard. The whispers of the dead. Tonight is the night, when they live again. Slowly making their way back to the homes in which they had once lived. Their footsteps can be seen in the vanishing sand and heard in the whispers of the night. Little children lie restless in their beds for they know the nights has come. The night of the dead is upon us. Now those who we have crossed, those who we have betrayed, have come to seek there vengeance. The night seems like eternity and the morning seems it will never come again. Tonight screams of fear can be heard over miles and miles of land. Cries of terror sweep the nations. After this night there will be no more of its kind. Tonight is the Final Halloween . . .

Kisha Moss

Taking The Time

When I want to leave, you want to spend
  more time with me.
When I want to talk to you, you want me
  to listen to you.
When I want to be with you on my time,
  you want me to be with you on your time.
  Which may not be the time I want to.
You take the time to listen to me,
  to talk to me, and
  to be with me.
Thank you Lord for your love and to
  allow all things to work together for good.
You take the time to be with me all times
  of the day and when all has gone wrong.
Thank you Lord for taking the time on
  all occasions.

Joyce Heatherington

Goodbye Karen . . . Goodbye

The loss of our love will never be understood
For the lore of re-union, what should but what could

The cold, dark despair haunts me everyday
As time passes by, taking my future away

Our connection once made is now dormant and still
For the void left by loneliness, haunts my heart with a chill

I think of you daily, in my head everyday
But depression stole our love, in a cold, cruel way

I pray for your healing and a soul filled with strength
For our love and joy together, it came . . . and then went

Love is universal, so the story is told
But depression can steal it, and make you grow cold

The affects of this ailment do not easily heal
But God, please help me, as I make my appeal

Pain is part of life, so the philosophers say
But when the pain occurs daily, your hope fades away

God, I will never forgive this disease and its merciless hold
For I lost my best friend and lover, and now I am old.

Goodbye Karen . . . Goodbye
> *Ed Bavoso*

Here And Now

Do you ever worry about where you've been
or where you'll go from here
If your heart and mind are tuned just right
then you'll have no cause for fear

There are many roads of life that we must trod
and some will lead the wrong way
if we'll extend to each other a helping hand
We can call it joy each day

Don't dwell so much on tomorrow
seek love in your reasoning right now
If you seem to be struggling with that first giant step
I know someone who can show you how

If you think you're walking in darkness
there's a wondrous light "round the bend"
If your eyes see only the foes in your life
I'll show you your greatest true friend

Don't be misled by worldly pleasures
each one must find the right way
your task may turn out not to be easy
so do your best with what's provided today!
> *Lloyd Owenby*

No Reason

Dialing she made the discovery
That he no longer cared
For her or for anything about her
Hair he missed, he said, but after
All he had gone through he thought
He could do without her
Love, warmth, and
Passion were gone with no reason
To leave he said good-bye
To never return he left her

Breathless she stood at the other side shaking
She put down the phone climbing
She followed the stairs up hoping
She thought it was all a dream awakening
To find it was
All over
Nothing.
> *Marnie Portland*

Superiority

A man took a job alongside a monkey
And they both worked as hard as they could.
Both did their share, and really worked hard
And they both felt that they were good.
Until one morning, the monkey stood up
And said "Man, to the bathroom I must go."
The man said, "Wait, for I'll go first,
I'm better than a monkey, you know.
I'm taller, and straighter, and lighter of eye,
Just generally superior, you see."
"No," said the monkey, "here's proof for you,
There ain't no monkeys workin' alongside of me."
> *David W. Wills*

Paris

He walks across the parking lot
Skin tone equal to the night
When you get up close to him
There is no doubt
He will make everything all right
His body moves like silk blowing in the wind
Why am I thinking this? He is my friend!
What I would give to make him mine
I just have to relax and give it time
If it happens all joy would be expressed
And if it doesn't I wouldn't think of him any less
He is the one chocolate tone and just right for me
What would I give for only one night
For him to be with me?
> *Yolanda C. Greene*

Untitled

Could this be real? All the things that I feel.
You are my dreams, you are all that I do and all that I think.
I live you and you are me;
Coexistentialism.
Two souls intertwined two bodies one mind. You and I we are one.
Never before have I felt so much joy.
Never before have I experienced such ecstasy
Just the thought of you lying here next to me
Our thoughts are as one,
But our lives are two.
You are here but never with me.
I am here too but I can't find you.
Will our souls reunite that fire will we again light?
I'm lost in a dream
> *Yasmeen A. McFadden*

Just For Me

It was way back in Mid-August when we had first met
He stood so stiff and so quiet as if on a bet,
He didn't try to impress me or come across as some charmer
Yet I remember gazing up to him
  as if he were dressed in a full suit of armor.
It was then that I questioned God immediately,
Did you put him here on earth just for me?
That if in fact this could be true,
Please help me to know what I am to do . . .
I truly do pray for all of his love
As he would for mine only and yours from above,
By taking our hands and vow that we care
We've learned to give life, to laugh and love what we share.
As I look back to all those years that have past
I knew in my heart with your strength we could last,
Now, I know you answered my prayers
  and helped me to see
That you truly did put him here on earth
  "Just For Me!"
> *Patricia Mae (Petroski) Proctor*

A Great Man

There was a great man on this earth long ago.
That the multitude followed, as he walked to and fro.
The faithful obeyed the commandment from him,
but most didn't listen, and continued to sin.
He talked of his father and what was to come,
the laws that were given of man from day one.
He taught that repentance with sincerity and desire.
Would keep us with him and out of the fires.
He healed the sick, made the lame rise and walk
raised some from the dead made others to talk.
Then his father said son we must try once again,
lets cleanse all the wicked with blood of a man.
Would you be most willing to die for their sins?
Suffer that anguish so man may yet live,
The son said yes father, thy will, will be done,
so he gave us the life of his begotten son.
The son that he sent from heaven above,
to lead us thru life and give us his love,
The great man's name, was Jesus you see,
Our Lord and dear Savior forever to be.

Jeff Hawkins

Christmas Thoughts

How I long for an "Old Fashioned" Christmas,
    like those of days gone by.
Where happiness and joy sprung up
    In the twinkling of an eye.

A Christmas where goodwill was king,
    not commercial greed.
A Christmas where the simple joys
    were all that one would need.

A Christmas filled with love and warmth,
    and giving was from the hearth,
The smell of spices would waft through the home
    from goodies cooked on the heart.

Ne'er was heard, "How much did it cost?"
    Nor, "How many did I get?"
But remembering each other was the key
    for "our happiest Christmas yet!"

When thoughts of Old Fashioned Christmases come,
    they bring a tear to my eye,
Oh, how I long, how very much I long,
    for a Christmas of days gone by.

Denise Richards

Storms On The Horison

There are storms on the horison, Lord.
For everyone to see.
For those who walk in Your way, Lord,
And those who can not believe.
I try to do my best, Lord,
But at times, it is hard to see.
I try to help those around me, Lord,
Who are less fortunate than me.
I came from a broken home
And I long to be loved . . .
I trust in Your ways, Lord.
May Your blessings float from above.
Not only for me, Lord, but for all who believe.
The way the world is now,
There are few who can receive.
I trust Your love and guidance, Lord,
And wait for You to relieve.
Why can't we love one another
And make this world a better place to be.
For with all the worlds troubles there is very little love to see.

Margaret Edens

Watch Over Me

I'm cold and hungry hurtin' and on the streets
Not a soul in sight
Will you come to me tonight

Doors are closed shut and tight
Not a penny in sight
I can't smell food driftin' in the night

Comfort me as I sleep
As I pray things may come out right
When my mind drifts tonight
In the still of the night
When I turn left and right
I lose sight of what's right
Come to me in this hour of need
As I lay on the streets
A mournful cry comes from inside on a silent night
Watch Over Me

Nancy L. Bollinger

My Tears Show Anger But Never Show Fear

When ocean water rolls out from my eyes, as you
speak deafening, trying to show you are king, I
show anger for I don't fear your cowardly words.
I anger your ways of hate. The roaring bass of
your voice, the volume of the slamming of the
hollow wooden door. I do not blame the door that
slams loud or the tone of your voice. I loathe
the words you speak to your should be loved ones
and how you carelessly laugh behind the door
to show off your disrespect. You break and
speak by foul language to things like a crazy man
who has never respected thy mother. Things and
your foul language do not belong to my heart, so
I do not fear you. If you ever damage my
heart in any way, I will anger you more for
destroying my God given property. When I
cry, my tears show anger but never show
fear.

Amelia Saldaña

For Lorenzo

The road
between Lakewood and Boulder
lies on the long flat
alongside the mountains.

This winter I like the absence of color —
the muted greys and yellows
upon which my thoughts of you take form:

    explosive reds, the color of our lovemaking the night before
    deep purple, the color of our deepening passion
    emerald green, the color of hope that our new love brings
    irridescent blue, the shimmering quality of time which passes
    until I see you

again . . .

The road
from Boulder to Lakewood,
a wash
of quiet landscape
and inner symphony.

Brenda M. Romero

House Of Love

A little boy has gone away,
For more than just a holiday.
The house is quiet, and seems to say,
"Where is the little boy who use to play?"
I protected him from the elements for many years,
Gave him comfort from his fears.

Before he left — His voice was changing, his body growing.
A teenager, He was about to be.
His toys packed away, an era past of knowing,
He had comfort and love from me.

I'm glad we had this time together.
Echoes will always ring no matter
Whoever becomes a part of me,
Of the little boy who shared his youth and man to be.

God be with him where ever he is
For a part of me will always be his.

Frances Johnson

Bittersweet Memories

As I sit and think about the days that used to be
I cannot help but wonder, wonder where the happiness went
There and been no place I would have rather been
    than right beside you, sharing a part of your life.
Not once did I doubt your love for me
Not once did I feel unwanted.
You treated me like no one ever had.
To you, I was a strong, independent woman
    who needed little guidance.
To me, you were the greatest father ever,
I long for the days we spent together days of laughter and joy
You were my strength, allowing me to conquer the world
Now I must hold on to the memories,
For our team has fallen apart.
There is no us against them, only you against me.
Yet no matter what your reasons for hating me,
I want you to know
    that my love for you shall never die and
    I miss you.

Jennifer M. Vogel

Never Too Old

Even though our hair has turned gray,
our bones and muscles ache nearly every day,
do not push us under the rug,
just give us a smile and a little hug.
We are still humans, all flesh and blood,
just forgetful, contrary, but still full of love.
We just want to be a part of what life offers,
respect us as persons and let us make choices.
We are entitled to a whole lot more than being thought of as just a bore.
Trust us and try us, to sing, to teach, to love, to share
all of these because we care.
We have advice, just free for the asking,
our motives are sincere, earnest and factual.
Treat us as though we have something to give,
make us feel that life is really to live.
Let us enjoy to the fullest our time on this side,
whereas for us understanding and love constantly abide,
reaching out to those that need us as we tread along the way,
our prayers will be for others until the close of day.

Mary S. Fennell

Motherhood: Petroglyphs

Whose were these hands, who strove despite scant water,
scarce food, to carve upon recalcitrant rock a prayer of thanks?
Who took the time from life both rough and brief
that those who follow them will see the ram, find water, live?
Who came before, and scratched the desert varnish
to leave on stone the gift of lore, of love?
They ached to speak, but we have lost the key.
And I would leave my daughters and their daughters
my hardwon wisdom and the trails I've worn;
will my words seem as strange to them as these?
The meaning all but lost: a glimpse, a sense,
but of a different culture, foreign time?
Carved on my heart so deep, beyond erosion,
the love I feel, the need to pass it on.
Yes, they will come even to this remoteness,
but I will not be here to reach a hand.
I place my palm against the carven handprint,
my fingers rest upon its indentations;
firm-cradled so, the stone sings to my flesh,
the ancient hand to mine, a perfect fit.

Joan Parker

The Door

You walked through the door of college eager and scared:
Eager to accomplish your dream and scared of how to do it.

You walked through the door of hope and anxiety:
Hope of starting a new life and anxious of what was forthcoming.

You walked through the door shy and meek:
Shy of whom to ask and meek about what to ask.

Now you walk through the door eager and scared of that dream.
Eager to get started and scared about where.

Now you walk through the door of hope and anxiety.
Hope of doing great things and anxiety of doing the right thing.

Now you walk through the door shy and meek.
Shy to show your abilities and meek not to show them.

Today is the day you've waited for; so let the door swing wide
And let the sun shine upon your path.

CONGRATULATIONS AND GOOD LUCK

Colleen Harmon

Introduction

Lord, you said there is coming a day
When every knee shall bow and every tongue confess

Lord, you have spared millions
And offered them sweet peace and rest
Many Lord have come to you, many have turned you away
Those that did not listen will someday have to pay

For that judgement day is coming
And time shall be no more
For those who would not heed to your call
When you knocked upon their door

Don't live to please old Satan
Take Jesus by the hand
You've always been reminded
God's spirit shall not always strive with man

You said, Lord, take my yolk upon you come and trust thy might
Some come to you for victory some still put up a fight

Those who serve old Satan will someday be refused
Because they neglected God's only son
And their destiny will be to lose

Peggy Stone

Did The Shadow Know?

I gazed at the field my tired mule and I had plowed
I saw we left furrows and ridges in otherwise level ground

I thought it looked like my life, pretty dull, but with highs and lows it did yield
As I sat down to rest a shadow from a tall tree began to creep across the field

The shadow climbed a big ridge and that high would be when I married my Sarah Jane.
The shadow crept across level ground, life had been good and we managed to stay sane

Two small ridges together were like the birth of our twins, and they were good boys
Level ground showed the happiness we felt for they were our pride and joys

The shadow crept over five small ridges our grandchildren had come to stay
Two deep furrows in that level ground could have been when mom and dad passed away.

That shadow crept down another deep furrow and sadness again came my way
That would be the terrible year my Sarah Jane passed away

The shadow crept o'er level ground "enjoy life" it seemed to say
but my gaze looked ahead and a deep furrow was in the shadow's way

A sudden chill came over me was that deep furrow meant for me?
I pulled myself up straight, the better for to see

A cloud began to cover the sun and the shadow soon disappeared
I thought to myself perhaps that field did not tell what I had feared

I got my mule and started home it was a couple of miles or so
I looked to the sky and said "Thanks for the cloud Dear Lord, for I really didn't want to know."

Devon G. Larson

In His Chair Alone, Reminiscing Of His Love

An old man, in his chair, sitting silently alone.
The neighborhood is quiet, no one seems to be at home.
The wind, whistling through the air, and rustling the leaves.
A squirrel, running back and forth, gathering nuts out of the trees.
He stares off, dreamily, with a smile upon his face.
Thinking of the woman, with whom he used to share this place.
Many years ago, she sadly passed away.
To him, it seems as if it were only yesterday.
As he drifts off, his mind is in another time and place.
When he awakens, in her arms, and gently strokes her face.
He remembers the way her eyes would light up when he came home each day.
The way her hair blew in the wind, and her frail body would sway.
He chuckles, to himself, as he remembers their inside jokes.
The way that she made fun of him, she loved to laugh and poke.
Each night before they drifted off to sleep,
She would say, "I love you," then kiss him on the cheek.
A tear falls, as he thinks about the day.
The day when his dear, sweet love got sadly taken away.

Sondra A. Wright

A Mother's Day Ode To Motherhood

Mother Dearest — and most precious — whom deeply I love . . .
God's "Cup-of-Life" and "Chalice" of our Father above . . .
In His Ever-Loving wisdom — and His Grace, so Divine . . .
Transfigured into His "Holy Grail" — with "Living Wine" . . .
Through which the "Life-Stream" — which I am — poured forth
— to enmesh
Into the Manifestation of "God's Bread" called "Flesh" . . .

"Ensouled" by our Fathers' "Breath-of-Life" — so gentle — so Light . . .
The "Bread-and-Wine" turned into "Flesh-and-Blood" all
through His Might . . .

The "Sacrament of Life" — my Holiest Communion — "Divine" . . .
Administered by "God's High Priestess": Dear Mother-of-Mine . . .
Unto me! . . . and in "Awe" . . . my head I now "Lift-up" . . .
To thank you — for "Being You": Christ' "Chalice" — God's "Cup"

Alleluia — Hosanna — Amen!
    "Micha-El"

Rudolf C. d'Ablaing van Giessenburg

Inamorata

Such violent passion
my lover can wage

Thereupon we cool
to cure our heaving breasts

What delicate fragrances
waft from her solicitous nape

Rapture from once
slumbering spirits

Her essence I borrow
it fills me
and I am reborn

Robert Perez

Ode To A Cold Candle

A candle sits
it gathers dust
where it once held a flame
if steel it would rust
what if memories it could hold
if so it wouldn't seem nearly as cold.
For once a flame burned
a flame from two hearts
it no longer flickers
with half of two parts
so sit lonely candle
you no longer light
but if the fates will it
come someday you might

Thomas Pond

Taking The Risk

Don't be afraid to give it a try
You've nothing more to lose
Victory's only gained with risk
There's strength inside for you to use
No one can believe in you
Until you believe in yourself.
Just take a breath, and find a smile,
Then step down off the shelf,
You're missing out on all the things
That can bring you peace of mind
The joys of life are really there
Just seek and you will find
Time slips away to quickly to
Waste a day in sorrow
The joys that we ignore today
May not come again tomorrow.

Billy J. Price

Ruling Power

Controlled by our minds,
Our ruling power,
We choose our destination,
As life begins to flower,
The body is merely physical,
Strengthened by the mind,
The carrier of our wisdom,
With out thoughts we are blind;
There are times we feel abused,
As our emotions change course,
Influenced by our hearts,
The pull of an altering source;
Subconsciously aware,
As life begins to unwind,
Destinies long journey,
Is the path of the mind:

Barry Montgomery

A Bellyful Of Wisdom

God commanded Jonah to go at once to decry the wickedness in Nineveh.
Instead, he fled, the opposite way on a sailing ship stricken by mighty storm
Thus creating a biblical fish story bigger than any billowing spinnaker,
When at his own urging the fearful crew jettisoned Jonah
    into the belly of a fish, squishy and warm.

Today, Mary Jane Inman, a candid, witty, second-year seminarian from Tiger Town
Exuding insight and zest, delivered her maiden sermon to our appreciative congregation
Confessing doubts and fears that enveloped her during freshman year and dragged her down.
For failing to hear His clarion call, her fragile faith faltered in consternation.

This Trenton lass bravely baring her soul to us, in this instance identifying herself with Jonah,
Told how she withdrew into herself, into her dorm room, marooned and doubt-driven
Happily for all Christendom, she realized it was her choice how to react, she needn't be a loner,
Answering His second chance call, imbued with mercy, that truly was God-given.

Mary Jane: May you always blend the best of Trenton and Princeton in doing the Lord's work;
Mindful that absent real doubt there can be no genuine growth in either us or in our Kirk.

Norman R. Nelsen

No Room

"No room in the inn" Mary and Joseph were told
"There is only a shed for the sheep."
Mary's time was near and Joseph had fear
There would be no place to sleep.

Mary gave birth in a lowly shed
Under a bright shining star.
Angel's came and sang their love
And Wisemen came from afar.

The birth of our Lord was many years ago,
Yet today, the words are still true:
"No room in the inn" is still told to some
Who of necessity must travel through.

Oh, if only man could realize
His inconsistencies to one another.
He mourns there was no room for his Lord
But finds "no room" for his brother.

Evelyn M. Howell

The Good Times — Once More

As I look back at the paths I have trod,
    and remember the pleasure of life.
Growing up as a barefoot child,
    with none of today's toil and strife.

I slip away in my mind once again,
    and watch the pleasure unfold.
Summers of green, winters of snow.
    But none of the heat or the cold.

For an old person's mind plays fantasy games.
    We remember the good not the bad.
But once in a while we may
    catch a glimpse between the happy and sad.

But these we discount with a joyful heart,
    and look at the beauty of yore.
And know in our mind we need never despair,
    we can live the good times — once more.

Brooks Owens

What Is Black?

Black is dark as night;
Black is not very bright like sun light;
It is the color of hair hopefully not bare;
Black is an ancient warrior, a Ninja if you like;
A scary monster ready to strike;
Black is the mourning color;
Black is my favorite color!

Nathaniel H. Todt

Love Is

Love is a river,
Flowing wild and free,
Beautiful as a mountain,
As you will see.

Love is like water,
Pure as can be
Careful how you treat it.
It's very fragile you see.

Love is a tree,
Swaying in the wind,
Love is unconditional,
It does not bend.

Love is a child,
Playing in the sand,
Jump right in,
And lend a helping hand.

Love is a rock,
Solid from the start,
Love will keep us together,
Nothing can tear us apart.

Nancy Whisenant

Do You Know?

When you reach your limits, how do
you know when to stop?
When you climb a mountain, can you
ever reach the top?

When you look around you, can you pick
out a friend?
When you're no longer here do you
Know it's the end?

When things look hopeless will they
ever seem right?
When you close your eyes, do you
lose your sight?

When you fall asleep do you dream
something good?
When you feel sad, do you cry
like you should?

When I ask you these questions
do you know what to say?
You may not know now, but
you'll know them someday.

Tayo Skarrow

Darkness, Blue, Black And Purple

Shady shadows swirling
creeping;
Blindness blackness flowing
seeping.

Dark, darker, angels calling;
Inky voices howling bawling.

Soaking sopping poison
sipping;
Clawing carving breezes
whipping.

Dark, darker, blackness binding;
Twists of day are now unwinding.

Quivering quaking shrinking
growing.
Whilst a quilt of splendor sowing.

Calina Ide

My Cross

When I was born,
A voice called to me.
"You are born to carry a cross you see."
In sadness," I cried, "why me?"
And the cross I embraced.
That from heaven was gift to me.
Why give me this cross to bear?
Then I looked and looked around and found,
Everyone carries across down here,
Some are with thorns,
And some are with roses,
And then there are those,
That pray for help the Good Lord Jesus
I too need to pray every day.
I too need the help from above,
To guide me and keep me going with love
Along the way.

Elena Vitagliano

Migration

Days grow short as the journey draws near, youth displays
excitement, age stands alone masking the fear.

Once again we return to a place some have seen . . .
some never will.

Driven by a force we cannot see, our burning souls
will not allow us rest.

Our meals are taken nervously from those we were born to
fear, others, weak, of heart must gather hastily for themselves.

Night brings the guidance of the heavens,
darkness imprisons us in our fears.

Still we drive one another on, singing the song of endless journey.

Blackness turns to steel, thunder from below . . . many fall but
cannot be mourned, continuing on, we cry out in anguish
for those who are lost.

Our destination calls from below, earth rises to meet us.

Wings set . . . gliding to cool waters, the sun on my chest
eases may ache but will not warm my heart.

Now I can hang my weary head, I cry in silence for the one
I will never see again, and for those who will once again,
make the journey.

James A. Skinner Jr.

Awaken Universe

Glory, Glory, Alleluia!
It's a song of Holy Earth.
In the future, in the past,
a stream of life is running fast.

Human beings with blessed up amazing dreams,
nano, mega, giga . . . reality
faced up our future Society . . .
Forever sufferings and exaltations.

Spinning round kaleidoscopes
of ambitious, emotionality,
trust of hunger for knowledge,
interruptatious, interference, spectatious.

Singing their great Songs Human Society.
Getting hopes, inspirations into reality.
It's a Glory Victory
of the New Millenniums.

Listening there's Skilled Ode of Glory,
Universe forever and ever
awaken Nations.
A real human's exaltations.

Roumiana Dancheva

My Mother's Love

My mother's love has been there to lead
me on my way. From the time I was a
little child and now that I am growing
each and every day. My mother's love has
been there to protect me and to guide my heart.
My mother's love is the unconditional love that
will never ever part. My mother's love has been
there to console and ease my pain. Through
the times when it seemed as if the
frustration would never end. My mother's love is a
gift that has been sent to me from God, and
without it I've concluded that my life would be
extremely hard. My mother's love will be there
until the day in which I'll die. To watch over
me like an angel and to make sure that
everything is alright.

Anticia Abrams

Linda,

I stood in church today and listened to you sing
All that I could think about was giving you the ring

As we both sit here and eat our favorite meal
To you Linda it is love that I want to reveal

I was done eating so we moved to the other room
Linda I give you this ring and want to be your groom

So please wear it to let me know you'll be my wife
And know that I'll love you for the rest of my life

I love you!
Tyler

Tyler Hufnagle

Power of Love

Let us sip life from the silver chalice,
adorned bright with rubies of hope.

Let us partake of the sacred content,
drink deeply the nectar pure.

Savor deep the mysteries for us to behold,
pray let the voyage commence.

Let us swim in the river Eros fair maid,
'till love is coursing thru our veins.

Let us plunge our sorrow into her soothing tide,
let her cleanse our pasts away.

Drink deep of the water Eros beloved,
let her purify the way.

Robert Evans

The Wind Of Victory

As I sit by the window on this foggy day,
looking beyond to the low and high seas.
I remember those days of my youth
when aboard Broadside I sailed and raced
with those brave women that were my crew,
and as we prepared to race in calm and windy days.
We were full of hope that we could win the big race.
And as we would go to weather many times
we would know exactly what our position was.
And as we tacked to port and starboard hoping for the best
that we would be the first to round the weather mark,
when we would get there we would roar and cheer
and fly the spinnaker downwind to win the big race . . .
Those days our spirits and hopes were high
and will live forever in our minds.
When we were young, proud and strong
whether we were first or last, we knew, we did our very best.

Ofelia Alarid Voda

Alone

While perched on this windowsill
an evening breeze caresses bare arms, legs —

What a perfect night for walking.

Inviting fields would ask
that we rest on cool grass.
To gaze, not at stars (for the sky knowingly hazes)
but into souls.

Would I
a bird I could fly
out this window, journey
through warm atmospheres
breathing you closer.

Don't forget, love;
tears fall where you left.

Jennifer M. Hocko

Thanksgiving Days

Fish are swimming in a pond,
Birds are singing out their song,
Winds is blowing thru the trees,
Bringing down the autumn leaves,
Kids are playing in the yard,
While grandparents inside are playing cards.
Moma's cookin' at the stove,
While Daddy's upstairs taking a doze.
When dinner is done the kids come and run,
To be with the family having fun.
They start with a prayer,
And then they share,
All the fixens God's given,
To help them keep liven,
And sharin' these Thanksgiving,
Year after year.

Donna S. Wood

If She Were Here

If she were with us here today
I often wonder what she'd say.
Would she laugh or maybe cry?
Or just be thankful for a last good-bye?

Knowing how my Grandma was
She'd probably say to us,
"I'm going to be happy here,
so quit with all the fuss."

She'd always have a plan you see,
'Cause she knows how we are;
She'd tempt us kids until at last
We'd attack the candy jar.

She'd say how much she loved us
In her extra-special way.
She'd probably want to thank us
If she were here today!

Brian Davis

The Lion

Through each other eyes we often see,
No threat to him, nor him to me
Sometimes he's me, quiet he'll seem
Sometimes I'm him, hungry, lean,
He's mostly restless
I'm the same, for we share our hearts,
Which won't be tamed.
We share our souls, our lives, our lies
When one is struck,
Anger is heard through both our silent cries

Brenda Wilson-Malone

If I Could Be

If I could be what I wanted to be using the
example that God set for me.
Would I be hills, mountains, leaves or trees, or
rain falling from the sky. Would I be grass that
now grows so green or snow that give all things their
glow. Or would I be health to heal the body
or a deadly disease to decade and rotten the
body. Would I be a word they called deceitful to
misleads and separates people, or a word fraction
to give one power, courage, questions and knowledge.
Could I be distances long or short in sizes or would
I be honest with hope and pride. Or would I be laughter
that sound so sweet or stumbling block that fall beneath
your feet. Would I be a channel or to help someone pass
by, or would I be a lament that mourn and cry in the night
would I be a ladder that reaches to the sky.
Or yet and exclamation expressing strong feeling of desire, or
would I be a descended from ancient times. If I could be
what I wanted to be using all the good things
God put in me, peace, love and joy divine.

Queenie E. McCain

Inquiring Minds

And, we are all requested to invite inquiring minds
to invite fiery minds
    to philosophical inquiry,
      and artistic delusion,
like the Greek gods,
or the temples and palaces
    of Greece and Rome.

And, we are all requested to invite inquiring minds
to invite fiery minds,
    like friends, compatriots, and colleagues,
through the heavy, oak, square paneled front door
through the dark gray halls
    of our home
to the study, the dining room, or the living room.
We talk about philosophical beginnings,
    and political ends,
      and what happens in between,
like how the June bugs glow in summer,
and how the flowers gain their color.

Steven L. Griffing

New Love At An Old Age

We met when our prime was in the past
    And felt our molds had all been cast.
But our eyes held a glimmer we each could see
    As I gazed at you and you looked at me.

We spoke of the day and the things going on
    And our words had the ring of a beautiful song,
The thought came to mind that there still could be time
    And my hopes for the future started to climb.

There's a chance for the door of love to swing wide
    So we can glimpse the joys inside,
As life speeds on by we can try our best
    And hope that we will pass the test.

The lives we led in days gone by
    Are as different as the earth and sky,
But we'll try hard to get along
    And hope to find our love's sweet song.

Our differences can be our strength
    In giving life both width and length.
We'll push ahead for all we're worth
    And find our heaven here on earth.

Charles E. Henderson

The Bunny

Bunny! Bunny! Sweet as life
In gardens of delight.
Who made thee?
For it's a cute symmetry.

Oh, Bunny
Little thing
Why are you down here with me?
For I'd like to know once and for all,
Why are you down here with me?

Little Bunny,
Oh, sweet little thing
For whoever made thee
It was sure a wonderful thing.

Kristin E. McClune

The Poetry Writer

I am the poetry writer
I spend most days alone
I write of warmth and beauty,
    and love that turns to stone
I write of past experience
    and lovers that I've lost
And struggles that I've been through
    to regain them at any cost
I write of beaches and open seas
    and the time that I've spent on them
        helped to put my mind at ease.
And as long as suns arise at dawn
And set at dusk each day
I'll always end my empty nights
    the same old lonely way
With pen in hand and thought in mind,
And a distant love awaiting me
That I never seem to find.

Steven Feder

Love's Enemy

Sincerity.
Love's visible emotion.
Without touch sensed
    by telepathy.
True love encompasses all
    seven senses,
Love, is only energy of
    the mind, fueled by the
    heart, driven by desire.
One sense.
Feel.
To feel love is deception.
To touch love is life
    itself.
Love, without touch, no matter
    how sincere the heart,
    is nothing.
    Energy must cross the
    path coming and going.

Donna M. Henry

Life

Life is confusing
It is hard to understand
Could we be created
By one great man
The sound of laughter can be heard and
In the sky is always a bird
So I will still wonder why we are here
I will wonder this year after year.

Jessica Perttula

Twilight

A touch of daylight lingers
Low in the western sky.
I look, and then I ask myself
Just what's the reason why
The world hangs on to every thread
Of light that's left each day,
And sadness reigns as the sun goes down
And we cling to each lingering ray.

Is it because when light is gone
Our confidence subsides
And Morpheus is our only hope
As through the night he rides?
Or is it that we've fooled the day
With ways we thought were wise
And know we cannot fool the night
Which has a million eyes?

Regardless of the reason,
Be it wrong or be it right,
We are all prone to feel alone
Each time we face twilight.

Jerry B. Drury

My Dog, Pete

Roses are red
Violets are blue
I love my dog
and so would you!

My dog is a beagle
White, black and brown
He thinks he's real funny
Sometimes he's a clown!

He likes to play
With all of his toys
He plays awful rough
He's like all other boys!

He doesn't always listen
Except to my dad
He likes to eat shoes
When he's real bad!

He likes to sit by me
and steal my seat
He's the king of the couch
My dogs name is Pete!

Justin Herman

Untitled

I am a girl.
I wonder if I am alive.
I hear people laughing.
I see birds singing.
I want to be loved.
I am a girl.

I pretend to be happy.
I feel real pain.
I touch nothing.
I worry for myself.
I cry from my heart.
I am a girl.

I understand people but not myself.
I say not what I feel.
I dream not good dreams.
I try to be happy.
I hope to find love.
I am a girl.

Natasha Newson

Trust

When God tests, don't
ask "why me?"
Don't put a question
mark where God has
put a period.

Christ creates
Satan destroys
Christ causes Satan
to tremble under the
shadow of the cross

Ruth Braley

Spring Rain Song

Diamonds of rain
On the windowpane,
Emeralds of leaves
Studding all the trees,
Lilac amethysts
Set in silver mists,
Ruby buds ablaze
Glowing through the haze,
Topaz daffodils,
Shining on the hills:
    Jewels do abound;
    Gems are all around.
Blest beyond measure,
Rich with God's treasure,
The child of a King
Why shouldn't I sing?

Caroline Ellen Curley

A Dream

Like a champagne of illusion
you interrupted in my life,
basting bubbles of impossible dreams.

I, inebriated in your passion
and for a moment . . .
I navigated on the spume
of my feelings.

And I thought about you
and me like:

A moment
two cups
and a dream,
just that.
The end
of an incomplete
fairy tale.

Dilcia Cruz

Two Things In Life

There's two things — in life —
pretty much, everyone will see . . .
One is death — the other
born free . . .

Death our destiny
freedom our way . . .
But it's the freedom of choice,
that could make you pay . . .

Locked within your mind,
while you grow old . . .
Never take freedom — for granted
you're now forewarned and told . . .

Matthew Scott Wilson

Watermelononymus

A crisp winter day
is like a watermelon.
Watermelononymus.

A salty sweetness
that lingers like a summer night.
Watermelononymus.

A stringy entanglement
of sugar and water.
Watermelononymus.

The seeds like pepper
on smoked turkey.
Watermelononymus.

The red is as bright
As a summer sunset night.
Watermelononymus.

The green is like
a praying mantis in flight.
Watermelononymus.

W-A-T-E-R-M-E-L-O-N-O-N-Y-M-U-S
WATERMELONONYMUS!!

Jason Dent

The Raid

Dangling forty watts murk tarry air
Beer-fat fingers wipe fatty prints
Full House
Please follow me inconspicuously.

Ulrich Alsentzer

A Dance

To dance with the moon on the ice
One flows with the other, in
motions of love
Caressing and Engulfing
the body of the other.
The dance is untamed, the
subtle glance.
The heart is wild.
It becomes restless and
movement becomes rough,
but the shapes of the bodies
form one once again,
and the ice becomes the canvas
for the hearts in love
to paint
their picture through time.

Jelam Mehta

Ode To My Grandma

This poem is for my Grandma,
The Grandma that I love
She is as beautiful
As a fine, white dove.
My Grandma likes to make goodies
And make people happy, too.
And she tells all of us grandkids.
"Oh I really do love you!"
When you go and visit her
You'll surely get a hug,
And every time you hug her
You'll feel very snug.
I really love my Granny,
I know she loves me, too,
And this poem is dedicated
To you know who!

Corine Garcia

My Love to Gus

I know not the love I feel —
    I've never felt it before —
And as I watched him sleep
I find myself breathing
    the same breaths in and out
Why — ? For I long to be
    in him or him in me
That closeness we only
    Find inside us —
That makes he and me, we
        (Lucy)

Sheila Seiler

This Man

This man lives here in this house
but I don't know who he is.
This man makes me feel so dirty
I wish I wasn't his.
I feel so helpless and afraid with
know where to go.
And I better not open my mouth and
say the word no,
I sometimes feel I'm crazy he makes
me so mad.
I sometimes feel it's my fault
But it's him who puts these thoughts
in my head.
What's my name? Who am I?
Why do I even bother?
and to think this man
in this house is supposed
to be my father.

Jackie Ann Pollack

Consecration

Just an instrument I am
Just an instrument I'll always be
O that Christ Himself would choose
To reveal Himself in me

No greater goal or desire
My heart shall ever know
Than to yield the fruit of Jesus
And on Him by grace bestow

I count myself as nothing
Only in Him can I be found
He is my source, my all in all
His name my sweetest sound

He's all I'll ever need
He's all I need to know
With hope in hand and victory sure
Day by day in Him I'll grow

Patricia A. Daniel

To My Adopted Son

Many sturdy family trees
Will grow and bloom for centuries
Then reach a barren phase without
A single blossom or new sprout
To empty arms on my bare bough
A sprig was grafted, so that now
Adopted son this mother's pride
Fulfills a dream I thought denied.
With offspring growing like now shoots,
Nourished by our family's roots.
And so this once old tired tree
Now blooms with fresh vitality.

Betty N. Dench

God Is Always Near

Here He stands, so trusting and true,
With His strong shoulders,
Just waiting for you.

His arms opened wide,
Both now and tomorrow,
Should you trust Him enough
To unburden your sorrow.

If tears are shed,
Along with what's told,
It's just God's way,
Of unburdening the soul.

To release your pain,
And to make a new start,
With a true, new loved one,
Who will be close to your heart.

His hand held in yours,
Both holding tight,
With a bright new future,
That will bring you delight.

Mary Haag Cronin

The Wall

As I stared down that granite wall
My eyes in disbelief
The endless names went on and on
A tear rolled down my cheek
How many mothers lost their sons
For a space here on this wall
How many fathers never seen
Their children grow at all
A lonely jungle far away
With no support from home
How many of these young men died
Feeling all alone
To honor those who gave their lives
We erected this great wall
So stand before it like I've done
And thank them one and all

Roger L. Channell

Baby Boy

Each day when you awake,
Take care of whom you partake.
You are loved,
From up above.
Have your fill
From one who never shall,
Take your will.
Look up — up high,
Give this day your last heavy sigh.
There is one to whom
You give great joy.
So smile this day and
Forever more Baby Boy.

Susan D. Graham

Unique Reflections

Each of our own unique reflections
Is based upon our own perceptions
Of what is now or used to be
For we all see things differently

Stories told through each generation
With each one told with variation
Based upon their own perception
Reflecting their own unique reflection

Ruth Fernandez

Wandering Star . . .

Only one star in the sky
So lonely, I wonder why
Darkness surrounds the star
Spaces around it empty are
Glittery star, you are all alone
Why are you stuck in this zone?
Shining star, you should not stay
Wandering star, sail away!
Only one star takes the chance
At night it flies away like a dance
Loneliness came to an end
The star found a friend . . .

Veronica Riese

Falling In Love

The way you trip —
You cannot see.
It's a surprise,
yet meant to be.
You cannot help
the way you feel.
It's like a dream,
but hope it's real.
The steps are simple
and yet so slow.
You like, you care
and still so far to go.
You know it's love,
but scared to show it.
You pray to God
that you won't blow it.
Then finally one day
with help from above,
you can finally say
you're falling in love.

Annette Astorino

Love

When love is felt from the heart,
you know it right from the start.
It feels as if your heart had wings,
and lets you see wonderful things.
Love conquers everything.
It reaches higher than the stars . . .
Without it there is no being,
It mends any and all your scars.

You cannot cover a mountain,
with the palm of your hand.
But there is nothing in this world,
that love cannot withstand.

Annette MarieGarcia

Greener

The Grass may be greener
   on the other side.
But, the Briars are also thicker
   which may coincide
   with fate . . .

The pointed thorns are sharper,
   more easily they shred
The thinness of life
   in its pursuit of daily Bread.

Brave souls venture over
   across the fragile fence.
Perhaps braver stay behind
   weeding their own fertile gardens.

Cynthia Leslie

Racism

R is for reluctant to face
up to the truth.
   Everybody is basically the same.

A is for abuse, we get for
being as they say "the
wrong color.

C is for criticism, we're
talked about just for being
who we are.

I is for ignorance, thinking
that one color is better
than the other.

S is for senses, having
five and using only one,
the sense of sight.

M is for mental anguish
you go through trying
to figure out is something
really wrong with me or
is it just you?

Shirley J. King

Sounds The Christmas Bells

The Christmas bells begin to chime,
merrily they sing.
We hear them ringing
in the church,
proclaiming Christ the King.
We love to listen to the sounds
announcing to the world, the Christ
was born upon this day,
the newborn baby boy.
God sent his son to give us hope,
and peace to share with all.
The God of Heaven came to us
to break down earthly walls.
So on this Christmas day so near,
may he who rings the bells,
give you the hope and joy
and peace,
of which the bible tells.

Kathy Clayton

A Place Called Yesterday

There is a place behind a door
Which does not need a key
That place is one of hopes and dreams
Which are not meant to be.

Most people live behind that door
And never find the way
Out of that place of broken dreams
A place called yesterday.

There is a place beyond a door
Which needs a special key.
That place is filled with love and joy
A place most never see.

The happiness we've come to share,
The feelings that have grown,
Gives us something very rare,
A key to call our own.

Our love will open up that door
And leave behind all sorrow
Together we will, hand in hand,
Step into tomorrow.

Elizabeth A. Torsiello

A Shiny Piece Of Metal

The innocent child hadn't a clue
As he held it in his hand
A shiny piece of metal, a harmless toy
To share with his little friend
When he comes around the corner
He'll shoot him dead and wow
His friend will fall and roll and laugh
He'll say it's my turn now
The blast was loud, it threw him back
He fell along with his pal
He heard no laughter, no my turn next
As his friend lay against the wall
So many if us have them
It is our right to own
A shiny piece of metal
To protect our house and home
Think long and hard and remember
Only one child walked away
Only one mother has her baby
Only one child again will play

Dawn M. Clarke

Haunting Memory

Ours is a love that can never be,
all that is left is a haunting memory.

Time permitted us to be as one,
what we had cannot be redone.

The road that lies ahead
will twist and turn,
but for a fleeting encounter,
I yearn.

The spring again will bloom
but our love will never resume,
the parting of our ways,
the lingering memories of loving days,
the winter of my life will come
but I will remember us as one.

James Dietz

Fall

Fall is neat,
And so is tall.
I don't say anything.
Because I'm so small.
Small is cool,
and so are you.
That's because,
I love you, too!

Brittney Robinson

A Man Of Courage

Small of stature
Large of heart
Serving others daily
Right from the start
Worked each day
Bringing home the pay
Raising the children
Joining in the fun
Making time for everyone
Finally the illness
Never a complaint
He's my choice of
A person becoming a saint
   MY DAD

Anna M. Brides

Cypress

Flared, fern like beauty
markings distinct
dying, saving
stately, tall

Fern leaves waving
ducks playing
snakes swimming
alligators not at all

Graceful beauty
enjoyed by all

falling, falling

fresh water for calling
quacking, slapping
salt water attacking
eroding, then falling
help for keeps calling
graceful beauty
stately standing.

Cheyl Joyner

Heaven's Day Center

Pick up your toy
   Little man, little son;
Pick up your doll
   Little girl, pretty one.

Your mother and dad
   Will be late today;
So follow the angels
   To a new place to play.

And while you await
   You'll do great things;
You'll fly with the birds
   On gossamer wings.

And when they arrive
   You can tell mom and dad
Of the fun, while waiting
   For them, you've had.

For you are much loved
   Little man, little son;
For you are much loved
   Little girl, pretty one.

Jerry D. Reeves

Fear

In the distant
night
I hear
a dog barking,
but cannot
see it.
It seems to be
coming toward
me.
Alone,
walking nowhere
that I know.
Just waiting for
its fangs to pierce
the darkness
and
me.

Where is it?
Where is it?
Where is it?

Michael King

Fly Like An Eagle

Fly like an eagle
   in empty space
Challenge the wind with courage
Eyes of wisdom is one of the rules
And wings of iron to defy time
Fly higher and higher
When the signals are good
Bravery and knowledge always
To change the course
Fly like an eagle that
   knows its pace
To conquer your vision
With honor, with pride, with grace

Elsa Robles-Pimentel

Safe And Warm

I was bitten
injected with a venom
with man's evil weakness,
it has taken my mind
and it has taken my soul
taken it to a darker place
away from me
why always now
in the graying cold of winter
why is it that beauty
is what I long for in the
cold of December
soul-stealing heartbreaking
beauty, women, lust and sex
is out there for me
but it is worth it
maybe I'll stay inside
again this winter
try to stay safe and warm

Greg Lant

I'll Be There For You

You may feel weak
   I'll hold you up

You may cry
   I'll wipe away the tears

You may complain
   I'll understand

You may talk to me
   I'll listen

You may be unsure
   I'll try to explain

You may not want to be alone
   I'll be there for you

You may leave me
   I will not forget you

I will always love you

Mary Beth Merlak

The Unfair Decision

I don't want to go today,
I don't want to go any day.
The day is coming, very soon, for sure.
Very white, and very pure.
Like a dove, like a diamond in the sky,
Now, you'll make me fly.
Don't take me to that land far away,
For my destiny is here to stay.

Jessica Howard

Many Times

Many times I wonder,
why I love you so.
Then I sit and ponder,
and how the times does go.

Many, many times,
things pull us apart.
Many, many times,
I find my broken heart.

Many times I wonder,
why I love you so
For a simple gesture
you'd quickly let me go.

Amanda Wright

Dawn

The snow is all gone. The seasons
Seem to have reversed themselves,
Like summer going into fall,
Instead of fall going into winter.
I live for the fresh morning air;
An occasional golden sunrise.
The lone bird that flies to the south,
And some great flocks.
Leaves all dry with dust,
Crackle-crunch under my feet;
Cool, crisp days,
Wood-smoke-frost nights.

Christine H. Ferrin

Ode To Love

Love is a friendship
Like a rainbow on a hot June day
that knows not the beginning —

Was it that evening
With your head on my shoulder
And stars in your eyes? Or
was it that Saturday evening in June
When we both touched the stars?

For you are the sun,
I am the rain,
And together we make the rainbow
That has no end —

George C. Kobylka

Morality

Morals have been questioned
With smirks of quiet contempt;
A dauntless streak of vanity
From hearts unmade, unkempt.
Morals are raked among the coals
Alive with fiery tongues.
Unscathed she reaches soaring heights
Where victory is not shunned.
Morality sings not of regret,
As immorality;
But reaching out with seasoned haste
She clings to decency.
Rich with love for virtue,
Veneration for what is right,
Morality looks upon purity
As the magistrate of light.
Immorality loosely chooses
With complacency intents,
But morality seeks for rectitude
The license of innocence.

Gail Robison

Two Horses Speak

Running, running, running
It seems like all we do
For no straight lines,
Lie in this path
only roads that will not end.
Or a time for peace
Like the wind.
Promising little
And giving all
A simple place indeed
It's our stall!

Lynn Fox

In The Rain

And the rains came down
I was so afraid, but
listen, listen, peace,
Contentment, love and
joy abound.
And so the day went on,
rain, rain, rain.

Nancye L. Dickerson

Lift A Branch

As I grow older day by day
And heartaches add to wisdom's bay,
The loves for which may youth once vied
No longer lights my fires inside.
I lift the branch that's hanging low
I smell the rose but let it grow.

Adventures lacks the lure it knew
When foolish dreams and passions grew
And though it still demands my smile
Where past and present meet awhile
No more I haunt the turtles rest
Or flush the robin from her nest.

I journey now, to meet an end
Where deeds of past the future blend
And what I pass in loves embrace
I leave for better in its place
But you must often here me say
I wish I lived life this way.

Alicia D. Sidlowski

Silent Sounds Of Love

It is but simple words we use,
to express the love we share,
but in an ever silent world,
how can we show we care.

Together in the darkness surrounded,
just by candle light,
no words of love need spoken,
to see us through the night.

And way atop the mountain,
so high up in the sky,
the love that is between us,
shows brightly in our eyes.

As we look out over the ocean,
and watch the waves roll over the sand,
the love that is between us,
is felt within our hands.

You see now how it's easy,
to speak no simple words above,
To give your heart, to give your soul,
in silent sounds of love.

Cheryl Luton-Segrest

To Want

To be alone is one thing,
    but to be with someone
    and still be lonely is another.

To love someone is one thing,
    but to be in love
    and still want more is another.

To be alive is one thing,
    but to want to die
    and still want to live is another.

When you don't know what you want,
you can never have what you desire.

Chantal de Verteuil

Fake Tattoo

He got a tattoo
it said,
"Jesus, I love you,"
he thought
it was the key
to live
eternally.
It was
still there the day the world
ended,
"Sorry," said Jesus,
"Your life
was pretended."

Ryan Vess

Untitled

Shoulders touching,
words breezing
insides aching
heels clicking

Words breezing
avoiding necessity
heels clicking
heart pounding

Avoiding necessity
words unspoken
heart pounding
tongues drying

Words unspoken
insides aching
tongues drying
bodies closing

Insides aching heart wrenching
bodies closing arms brushing

Heart wrenching shoulders touching
arms brushing time's drawing.

Christine D. Haskins

Fall

I love fall.
Fall is my favorite season of the year.
Fall smells like flowers.
Fall, don't forget your leaves.
You are beautiful
So don't lose your beauty.
I love you.
You are the best.
I play in you and I live in you.
Your swaying leaves sound like this,
Sw-sw.

Anna Gaul

Untitled

Your lips are red and sweet
like strawberry wine, I think
about you all the time.

Your smile is bitter sweet like
strawberry wine, I think I
might just taste some of your
strawberry wine.

Your heart is shaped like the
strawberries that are in strawberry
wine, I think I might
pick it for mine.

Thank God that you are my
strawberry wine.

Ronnie E. McDonald

Your Creator

Sit still and listen to your Creator
Speaking to you from on High
He delights to give you what you need
For his Name to Magnify

His are Generous Provisions
and from His Hand do Come
The Spirit to aid you on your Course
Till ere His Kingdom Come

While waiting for His Provisions
Composed and Calm do be
For all you need He will Provide
To the Glory of His Sovereignty

Christina K. Brame

The Mysterious Escape

Forget your trouble, throw
Away your cares;

A daydream is at hand
For he who dares;

Don't fade too far, or
Dwell too long;

The dream can change,
Reality is gone.

Dave Rhien

Autumn

Today as I was walking
I heard rustling sound,
the leaves had all turned orange
and were falling to the ground.

A breeze was gently blowing
the birds were flying on,
I raised my head and thanked Him,
for blessings past and gone.

Margaret Fillman

My Room

My room
needs a broom.
As I look at all the books,
What a mess it looks.
With all the junk
I can see the gunk.
If I use the broom in the light
I can make my room quite bright!

Ryan Arthur McLane

Missing Sorrow

Missing a time of sorrow
As I ride so high above
Leading into a darkness
That will not soon pass
My fears come all too true
My body responds all too well.
Your mind tells you it's all
Too good to regret so you find
A new love to forget.
Missing the love that passed.
My soul hurts to the core
Your aura is glowing Red
Wishing I were dead.
Let my love soul alone remember
The love we've shown, my
Heart must go home.
Good-bye, sweet love.

Sheryl Dodds

Autumn In Stockholm

Green lawns in the park
are gently tucked in by yellow leaves
stolen from the trees around
a line of naked trunks.

The last rays from the icy sun
fight bravely by the rooftops,
reflecting in frosty bowls
weaving a steel-grey pattern.

On a bench two lovers pick memories
dreaming of spring and warmth.
While frost waves its veil
erasing the tracks of summer.

The city dressed in foggy shroud
flies the banner of the autumn.
In the waters misty breath
the street light's warmth cools off.

Peter Bourne

The Dead God King

Life's an insurrection
And God knows what I mean
So I'll be pain in perfection
I'll be the Dead God King

I know it is my own fault
And I guess it's just as well
So lover send my soul back
So I can send it straight to Hell

Paul Wilson Ausbun III

Churches

Churches, churches everywhere
but, we do need more.
Someone has to build them
they are not found in a store.
All the way around the world
Jesus Christ can see,
that's why we need to please him
you and you and me.

Jesus is our Lord and savior so behold
let's go and spread the word
let Jesus Christ be told.
Every little boy and girl
has a right to know
that Jesus Christ died for them
and to heaven they will go.

Jessica L. Holtry

If

If
You were a butterfly
I'd open up my hand
And shutting tightly squeeze my eyes
Praying as hard as I could
That you would land there,
And lo!
Trusting, you settled into the palm
And my prayers were answered

I would not harm you
But let you rest there
And gaze at your illimitable beauty
And wonder at such delicacy.

There you would be barely whisperably
Moving those perfect wings.
And I?
Loving
Innumerably, tremblingly;
Valuing the seconds
With all my heart.

Lauren Chiasson

If Only

If only you knew
That my love is true.
That what I feel
In my heart is real.

If only you could see
How I want it to be.
Both of us together
For now and forever.

If only you could hear
All my hopes and fears.
And let me listen to you
Whenever you are blue.

If only you and me
Could turn into a we,
Both of us as one,
My longing would be done.

If only we could find
That a part of our mind,
That lets our hearts know
That our love can grow.

Sara Martell

Black Or White

Is it really worth the fight?
Children scared all day,
crying through the night,
praying they will wake up
and it will be alright.

Racism, hatred
a challenging problem we face,
let it not destroy our lives,
Our homes, this place.

It is said to me a disease,
and that love is the cure.
So lets take action,
in becoming more pure.

True it can,
and will be stopped.
When the love is picked up,
and the hate is dropped.

Bradford Schumacher

Samantha: An Autumn Day

Wild wind storms
Blowing with anger
Tears of rain
Dripping until puffy cheeks dry
And leave the sky.

Cool shimmering day
Wet leaves put away
A happy wind
And hearty breeze

A beautiful person shines
With the afternoon reflections
From the sun

Lindsey Calastro

Birds Where Those Marvelous Creatures Go

Birds fly to and fro
I often wonder they go

On summers day they fly quite low
to eat the grass seeds before they grow
On winter day they fly quite high
in a V shape flying by

Birds fly to and fro
there are many places they could go

Whenever I go to my grandmothers
house
I see not an animal not even a mouse
But when I look outside I see
A marvelous place where I'd like to be
We glance near, far, and out
to see birds playing about

Birds fly to and fro
There are many places they could go

Now I'm sure that I do know
where the wondrous birds always go

Stacey Bondi

The Book Of Poems

In this book you will find.
Many windows of my mind.
Through these windows you will see.
Many different sides of me.
This book of poetry I behold,
Tells of treasures yet untold.
So come and join me if you will,
Rest relax and be fulfilled.

Barbara J. Jones

Untitled

His heart began to race suddenly
with fear
When the object of distance came
into the clear
Questions of whether it is friend
or foe
Was quickly shown with the
ultimate glow
A shot rang out to his surprise
Before he blacked out and
closed his eyes
He will never breathe or see
again
Said the shadow of a man
whose living in sin

Joseph Giannini

Blood Money

You live off our pain
You live off our fear
We come to you
When the end is near

We put our trust in you
We put our lives in your hands
You save us
But take all that we have

They give us back our lives
but take our futures away
When we have no tomorrows
What's the point of living today

In a world of black and white
To them there are no in betweens
Life or death, red is always green

They will keep you alive
but you will pay the price
Blood money
You'll owe the rest of your life
They own the rest of your life

Lisa Gonzales

Espuma De Sueño

You and I are two little
grains of sand lost on a beautiful
cosmic beach.
But the love that I feel for
You is greater every day. It's like
the flame of a torch that burns
and keeps on burning unable to
burn itself out Your image is
reflected in the sea and is my
thoughts of You . . .
My love, love me and I will
go on loving you.

Oswaldo A. Vallejo

Someday Love

I look from far away
Though it could never be,

He'll come for me someday
One day he'll really see,

If only he would look at
The inside, not the out,

Then, maybe he'd find what
I am truly all about.

Katherine Mitchell

Sonnet On Aging

Would that I were young again
And in the springtime of my life
With all the joys to come again;
Even sorrow, even strife.
But this I know cannot be so
Along life's path but once we go,
So I must make these winter days
As warm and cheerful as can be
With family, friends and other ways
To help the time pass happily.
But, oh!, that I were young again
And in the springtime of my years
With all those joys to come again;
Even sadness, even tears.

Joan Finnstrand

The First Snow

I walked down into town today
And much to my surprise,
The stores were busy as could be
Folks laying in supplies.

They say it's going to snow tonight.
My heart begins to glow.
I guess I'll always feel the thrill
Of seeing that first snow.

The wind is quickening in the west,
The clouds are turning gray.
A snowflake brushed my cheek just now.
I'd best be on my way.

The snow is falling softly now
As I trudge up the hill.
Looking back, I see the town
Lying hushed and still.

I see my cabin up ahead.
I climb a little higher.
A toddy might taste good tonight
Before a cozy fire.

Mary Lou Wheeler

Jesus Smiled Today!

Jesus smiled today,
When I dried someone's tears.
Then he smiled again,
I had calmed a brother's fears.
Then someone gave a neighbor,
Some badly needed bread . . .
And told them of God's promise,
Through Christ, of hope ahead.
A man was down and lonely,
Displaying sin's decay,
I took his burdens as my own . . .
And . . . Jesus smiled today!

John M. Kenney

Mother's Daze

Up at dawn,
  no not I!
Want to sleep,
  shouldn't try.

Kids are up,
  wander in.
Want to eat,
  daze begins!

Dorothy M. Stewart

Truth

Drugs! Let her go!
That's my child;
Don't you know?

No, my son; an alcoholic
You cannot be;
That's not the dad
Your child should see.

What?! No job! No Home!
What's going wrong???!

Oh Jesus! Please help them!
They're in bondage
As all can see.
Please! Reveal your truths,
And set them free.

Maxine A. D. Frazier

"Into Dreams I Fall"

Into dreams I fall
Slipping, slowly into darkness
only to be awakened by an
angels touch

Her eyes as blue as the sky
and skin as soft as the clouds
lost in her I find myself
starring hopelessly

She takes my hand and
at that moment all my
fear and pains drowned
away

With one whisper my heart
races
chills run through my body
I hope she doesn't notice

She turns to walk away
with all her beauty and charm
as she fades I awake to find
myself in her arms

Michael Harvey

The Ruler

Ignorance sat on a hill.
He thought he owned the land.
Wasn't he the only one
That controlled his band?

And what a group they were.
Hate, Greed, Jealousy, and Fear;
But these were just a few
That he kept very near.

Yet they could not compare
With his second in command.
The one who helped him most
To keep people in his hand.

For this most trusted honor,
To the strongest he could call.
That, of course, was Prejudice.
He knew no bounds at all.

Angharad Bransford Young

Winter In New York

The chill is bitter.
The cold snow is deep.
My teeth do chatter,
as I try to creep.

It's a bitter day,
good to hibernate.
Drifting hides the way;
Everyone is late.

The day is gloomy;
No sun is shining.
The Leas are roomy,
no Cows are dining.

Grim Nature can prove,
that she's the Master.
She may seem aloof,
but owns disaster.

But, long winter time!
Always has an end.
Warmth alters the clime,
The sun is our Friend.

Samuel D. Museums

Untitled

Seeing inward with clarity
All things are as they are
The rain falls
The flowers bloom
Thunder in the mountains

Ernest Newsum

A New Day

Dawn breaks,
  A mocking bird thrills her song.
Butterfly wings flutter
  in the early morn.
Quietly the earth awakens,
  small creatures stir,
Mists gather forming cloud patterns
  in the sky, changing, merging,
silently drifting by.
  The eagle soars, majestic in his
flight; light rays of the sun bring
  forth golden lights glittering
on extended wings as he glides and
  circles, returning to his nest
among the Sycamore trees.
  When I hear the music, as the
Robin sings, my thirsty soul rejoices
  in all the earthly things, God,
through nature gives us,
  Songs, beauty, love, hope, dreams.

Ree Mills

Concern

While sitting at my window
  watching end of harvest near
I wonder what will happen then
  to birds and ducks and deer.

For freely they have eaten
  of crops grown all around
Now harvest has removed them
  ready food not easily found.

I'm sure nature has a way
  of providing what they need
Though not the easy gleaning
  they've had for getting feed.

Some will head to the sunny south
  where easy living will abound
But others will stay to forage
  and live on what's around.

There seems a plan for everything
  let nature take its course
The outcome not always happy
  sometimes viewed with much remorse.

Martha Oman

Untitled

The Sun shines bright
Just before Twilight;
The Stars shine bright
After Twilight;
The Moon shines bright
At Midnight;
The Stars shine bright
Just before Daylight;
The Sun shines bright
Just after Daylight.

Mary Will Motley

Hunger

Thoughts consumed.
Visions abound on
trees, in gardens.
Planted, harvested by
my love, my lust?
Will she? Won't she?
Leaves flutter away;
Enveloped by the wind.
As we become one,
full of her, but empty.

Kurt Baldwin

The Barn

The gray barn
stands on the hill.
Deserted.
Quiet.
Alone.
It stands on the hill
like a lone soldier,
whose war was a lost cause.
The hill is a battlefield
with remnants
of a dead civilization.
An old, sagging fence,
a pile of wood, and
a wagon wheel,
stay on the hill
as reminder of
days long gone.

Barbara Jalowiec

Silver Cord

Some day the silver cord
Will break
We go to sleep and not awake
Then he will ask when all
Is gone
Did you take my love
And pass it on

Granny Hayes

The Stream

Resting beside the bank above,
thinking of forgotten lore.
I marvelled at the radiant stream, only
time for tells what it will bring.
Luminous ripples, a brilliant cool, as
it races toward a beautiful pool.
In this hole it shall rest,
rocks against the waves caress
I stand and give a humble bow only
to say, "I must leave you now."

Jerri Elkins

Imagination

Above the sky,
Along a moonbeam,
Across an endless landscape.
Toward a place
Beyond understanding.
Against the current.
Beside the crowd, but not
Within it.
In a place,
My mind is wandering . . .
Imagination.

Sarah Danielson

The School In My Dreams

I once had a dream
A dream about a school
I was soundly asleep
And I thought it was cool

I was a cute little place
Where all the teachers were keen
There were no fights
Because no one was mean

The grade levels varied
In different parts of the place
I thought that the college
Took up lots of space

It would never be cloudy
There would always be light
In the school of my dreams
Things would always be right

The rules were scattered
North, east, south, and west
I broke just one rule
And I woke up from my rest

Karen Scooros

Loneliness

Like a shadow it surrounds
It seeps through my pores
Like a shroud it enfolds my soul
It mangles and it jangles
It twists and it tangles
Like something surreal
It pulls me
It wields
It cuts and I bleed
With wounds unseen
It pulses
It schemes
So I protect it
Then I reject
And I feed it
Then I neglect it
I hide it
I lock it away
But has its own key
And it comes back to haunt me

Lisa Wolph

Untitled

  I held you in my arms
you were so tiny,
your skin so soft,
your eyes so shiny.

  I looked into your deep brown eyes
you were so silent;
I heard no cries.

  I cried when they said
"the baby's gone"
only your name and memory
to carry on.

  I toss and turn as I sleep,
there's few fond memories
for me to keep.

  Baby brother, I know
you're sitting with Jesus on high,
one day I'll see again
in Heaven's sky.

Candida Rogers

No Answers

What do writers do when they discover
they have been read?
What does the scientist do when the
new metal he has discovered is lead?
What do children do when the games
they play become real?
What does a king do when a servant
will bow, but won't kneel?
What does hate do at a time when
love is a must?
What does Christ do when the world
He's saved becomes dust?

Weldon Lake

Untitled

Love is to me
  Like a drop of sparkling water
in an endless sea.
  In a world of difference;
one chance of the same.
  A heart that longs for pureness,
together a miracle in form.
Love is to me
  like an uninterpreted dream.
That one must wonder
  if the soul will ever awaken!

Robin Lynn Phillips

For Luan's Birthday

With all the gifts
that God brings,
another year at life
is the best.
And all the problems
and sadness that seems;
the joy we find in life
beats the rest.
For God has said
he'd be right there
through all our
trials and joys.
He's been there
for all of mine.
I know he'll be
there for yours.

Dolores Goins

Through The Pain

As I go through the pain,
  of each new day.
I pray to God, do
  show me the way.
Tho' stiff and weak,
  my physical body.
My inner soul continues
  to grow more godly.
Happy and peaceful as I
  go through life.
Trusting in God, to
  take care of the strife.
For our time here,
  is but short.
Soon we will all appear
  in God's heavenly court.
God will judge, not
  how strong or smart
But, what is in the
  center of our hearts.

Eric L. Jensen

He Is The Way

At times when you are down,
Lift your head and look around.

In day you will find light,
In darkness stars gleam with might.

Showing us the way to go,
Wanting all of those to know.

To follow him, come what may,
The Lord, He is the way.

Ted Alderman

Happy Memories

Now when all the day is over,
When the evening sun is low,
And when I've done the dishes
'Tis then I miss you so.

And as again we gather
'Round the firesides cheerful rays
'Tis then I like to ramble
Back to our childhood days.

Back to the hours together
And the songs we sang and play
After all the day was over
And all our sorrows put away.

Now me and my guitar is lonesome
We moan from morn till night,
Always singing that lonesome song,
"Where is my darling tonight."

Susie Russ

Untitled

Breathe deep the gathering gloom.
Shadows creeping round the room.
Colors mingled in different hues.
Reds, yellows, greens and blues.
Joined now in coming night.
Soft and airy in dimming light.
Twilight rimmed in purple haze.
Two lovers locked in lovers gaze.
Trapped now in a lovers maze.
Starlit nights, cloudless days.
Love now shone in many ways.
Two hearts touched, now beat as one.
No longer afraid, cold, alone.
Two faces bathed in pale moonlight.
Two hearts rise up in winged flight.
Rising high into the night.
Beyond the moon love burning bright.
Becoming a star to light the night.

Michael L. Reid

My Father And His Trumpet

My father loved his trumpet,
anyone would know.
It was one of the great gifts,
my father had bestowed.

Although he lay at rest now,
a trumpet on his stone.
I can find peace knowing,
he's not alone.

For he's in heaven now,
with the angels in the band,
With one hand he holds his trumpet,
the other he holds God's hand.

Barbara Lee Barnett

Waterbabies

The sun is setting
Out on blue lake
Where lily pads grow
All life begins to glow

Dragonflies hum
Crickets play violins
Frogs a song sing
Fish flying with wings

Fireflies give light
Lily pad stage for things
Waterbabies dance and sing

Fairies cast snowfalls of stars
With their wands
Enchantments of delight
Thru out the night

Slowly rising sun
All is gone

William B. Stanwix

A Little Mixed Up

Just a line to say I'm living
  That I'm not among the dead
Though I'm getting more forgetful
  And more mixed up in the head.

For sometimes I can't remember
  When I stand at foot of stair
If I must go up for something
  Or I've just come down from there

And before the fridge so often
  My poor mind is filled with doubt
Have I just put food away, or
  Have I come to take some out?

So, remember I do love you
  And I wish that you were here
But now it's nearly mail time
  So I must say "Good-bye dear."

Here I stand beside the mailbox
  With a face so very red
Instead of mailing you my letter
  I have opened it instead.

Lenna Bushnell

A Passing Angel

Each night I knelt
beside this bed
and thanked you Lord
for the life I've led.

I prayed each night
for an angel to appear
to help me get close
what I fear to get near.

Then, one day
she appeared to me
a gift from heaven
I knew this must be.

I was unsure
I needed a sign
Is this really the angel
you sent to be mine?

The angel you sent me
has now passed me by
I now trust in you Lord
to help me understand why.

Ben Kuznicki II

Treasure Hunt

Always on my mind now,
Somehow things make sense.
Even though I'm not sure how;
There is a high expense.

It comes by question
In so many ways.
I know the solution
To answer my prayer for days.

It comes from my heart
In so many ways.
I know what could start,
But I'll have to wait the days.

If it's what I need and want
I will have to accept.
The glory of the hunt
Is in that which is kept.

Darcie L. Dickerson

The Mountain

What do you hope to find
Atop my smoky peak?
What lies there that merits
Such trouble from you?

Struggle and yet keep faith,
Sacrifice and yet sustain hope,
Ascend, and my stones shall guide you,
Holding the wealth of experience
Of others long past.

Cast off restraining doubt,
Let fall the mantle of vice,
Wipe away your bitterness;
Rise.

Rise . . . And you shall survive.

Janet Wang

Chester Is My Dog

Chester is my dog.
He is so big and fat,
When he eats he looks like a hog.
He just sits there on his mat,
because he can barely jog.
He wishes he were a cat
or maybe just a frog
Because they are not big and fat
like Chester, my dog.

Zachary Quam

The Night

The calling of the night is strong,
As the sun fades into the sky.
All of the stars start to twinkle,
And the wind just lets out a sigh.

Darkness envelops the land,
The moon shines through with its glow.
Songs of the wolf fill the air,
As the night puts on quite a show.

The day has pulled down its shade,
The man in the moon has arrived.
Give of yourself to the night,
And really come truly alive.

The night wants to draw you inside,
To share its unique point of view.
Belong to the feel of the night,
The darkness will carry you through.

Shirley Drage

Waiting

We are waiting for you sweet baby
And your life is yet to be
We know that when you come our way
All will be well with thee.

Oh, baby you're like a rosebud
Kissed by the morning dew
You'll be loved little angel
You will be so fresh and new.

Your Mom and Dad will be real proud
Your grandparents will be proud too
We can almost see you now
With blond curls and eyes so blue.

We know you are in your waterbed
And have several months to grow
But we hope it want be very long
Before your sweet face we will know.

Betty Davidson

The Sauna

Dark hot room
Tipping bench
The smell of burning flesh

Joseph Gilbert

Heart Strings

The miles between us
Don't mean that much.
Our love is so strong
That our heart strings touch.

The love that we have
Will always stay
It just gets stronger
Day by day

The Lord above has been
Good to us
To share each other
From dawn to dusk

Our true love to each other
Lets out a ring
Entwined forever
On our heart strings

Robert J. Long

Autumn Leaves

See the leaves fall from the trees
Onto the ground through the cool breeze
Piles of colors, of brown, yellow
and orange
Telling us that winter soon
will be coming
Oh! What a scenery they provide
along the parks and countryside
Picture perfect, that we see
It's autumn leaves that
makes it be

Amelia Polsino

Puddles

Buckets of rain bring
the sky to the street
and buildings grow
upside down

Marcia Anne Breuer

When I Think Of You

No need to cry, when
I remember days gone by.
While in our teens, we
discovered a young love
that spanned almost fifty years.
Compassionate, caring
and full of joy, no
time for tears.
You're strong yet so
tender shoulder to lean
on whenever I was troubled.
You are gone now dear
one, oh how wonderful
and uplifting the days
are for me, when I think of you.

Marie J. Bevacqua

Girl

She looks up at the
mourning sky,
sighs, looks around,
looks down, I can tell
that she's nervous.

Suddenly, she shivers
folds her arms, looks up
and frowns as a drop
falls from a cloud and
dies on her shoe.

Shawn Montgomery

Colder

I don't live by reason
I have no more feelings
Warmth has left my heart
And whatever's in there is freezing.
I won't be a martyr
For what I don't believe in
Please don't wake me up
If you ever find me sleeping.
Can't look you in the eyes
I am like no are else
How can you be like me
When you can't be yourself?
Thought becomes my voice
Clearing out my head
Speaking out my choice
Getting reactions from what I've said.
We won't be young forever
Someday we'll get older
Thank you for you help,
Taking me in when it got colder.

Vicki Vlastaris

For Rip

A part of me
    took wing with you;
A part never shared,
    nor given away.
The pain is dulled,
    my mind is re-cleared,
My life, of sorts, goes on.
Your music calms my
    muddled mind.
Though you're not here
    to sing them,
Your songs keep you ever near.

Patti A. Richards

Aunt Gert

Hard working,
Had the will to hold on for 14 years.
Finally she had to let go.
Her will was strong
Just not strong enough.

At night
A bright star
Aunt Gert looking over all of us.
Lift your eyes
Talk to her
She can hear you.
A bright star; I depend on her.

Rebecca Jacobs

Still Searching

Forever carried to new shores
In the eternal night of life
My soul searches for the truth,
My eyes ache for the light

Will we ever, on the ocean of ages
find why we must be here.

As I was gazing into the stars
I knew this was never to be
You must go. I must die.
It was always you or me.

In the sound of the surf
My cries drowned forever.
My tears, my heart, my soul
All were missing you,
All were longing for you

Who are you?

Michèle V. Beaudin

Good-Bye

To say we touched,
To say you taught me,
To say I saw things new,
To say I like you,
None of these is enough, my friend.

For your world
With all its light and hope
Couldn't prepare me for this sorrow,
For this saying Good-bye.

Tell me it won't matter.
Promise me wherever I am
You will be with me
In a place where "Good-bye"
Doesn't matter, and where "forever"
Is just an instant, and our love
Is a bridge, connecting, linking,
Making all things one.

Philip M. Johnson

My Little One

Have you ever walked the milky way?
Or heard the wind while at play,
and watched its rays of ribbons
dance in the sky.
Watched the moon play hide and seek
as it placed a kiss upon your cheek.
Or watched the stars twinkle bright
and dance and play way up high.
If these things you have not done.
You've missed a lot,
My little one

Ida Davis

Conflict Of Interest

Values, ethics
carved in ice,
displayed upon
the pedestals of life.

Passers-by
cast a glance,
in an instant
take a stance.

Judge between
you and me,
set a limit
fearfully.

Come the Son
melt away
man-made rules
that decay.

Leave behind leveled planes,
sculptures withered in the rain.

Love undaunted, treasured safe.
Memories shared can't be erased.

Jan Hendricks

Remembering Mother

Many years have past —
  Since I last heard your voice,
  Touched your hand,
  Saw your loving smile.

Many years have past —
  Since you made your choice,
  To leave your native land,
  And traveled many a mile.

Many years have past —
  Since America became your home,
  You worked along with Dad,
  You baked and sold bread.

Many years have past —
  You never wanted to roam,
  Six good children you had,
  Hold high your head.

Many years have past —
  Since I saw you last,
  Ellis Island's wall of fame,
  Lists your name.

Mary Seawright

The Flame

The Flame burns to see its next victim
because life is an endless
light of candles all around.
the eyes of Mother nature!
Holding onto it with the little life
you have left from the Flame!
The Flame will burn down your
house and take your
children's life.
Then, the Flame will burn within
the soul of You!
It burns until you let it go to
someplace else, but be sure you know
where it's going.
I think it has something to do with;
Your home, your children,
and yourself that can make you
go crazy until you let it go!

Annette K. Howard

Death Visiting

Darkness, Despair,
and Depression
all swarm over me.
Silence engulfs my body.
Blackness diseases my mind.

I reach out for Morality,
but begin to drown,
drowning in Nothingness.
No one to save my soul;
silence shields my cries.
My eyes are blind to the world,
Shadows suffocate me.

Reaching for life, I take a hand.
A hand that pulls me closer
and closer to darkness.
The Silence gets louder,
becoming unbearable to hear.

Then there was nothing.

Death.
I had taken Death's hand.

Mandy Hill

On Top Of The Mountain

The cool, clean breeze,
A biker trails through the trees.
I sit on top and look all around,
Butterflies, bees, ants and bugs
that don't have names.
A house has a shiny roof.
How could I do it?
How could I walk so far?
For the first time I see so far.
I see the mountains, trees,
cities, rocks, flowers.
It's all so magical.
A cool breeze blows by me.
It feels so good after the long hike.
So magical!

Nicholas Shontz

My Son

My baby dear go to sleep
and have no fear.
For mama will protect
you forever and a year.
The wind is blowing and
the night is cold;
But the fire is warm
and the embers are aglow.
As you grow day by day,
I will stand by you come what may.
I will weep when you weep,
and kiss your hurts when you're asleep.
All I ask is for you to be my son,
for my heart you have won.

Fern Marvel Parkin

Untitled

My vision of you.
Was so real and true.
For years you carried me through.
Beautiful dreams that seemed so true.
I struggled to free myself
But what could I do?
One sunset evening I looked
Around and there was you.

McKinley Allen

My Mother

You are the one
who brought me into this world,
to take my grasping hand
and guide me each step of the way.
When times were rough
your smile got me through the day
and when the tears fell
you gently wiped them away.
You are my light
at the end of every tunnel.
With you by my side
everything seems to be okay.
My true inspiration,
I am so much a part of you.
I listen to you, I look up to you,
I learn everything from you.
My other half
who raised me as a child

And now has become my best friend.
Did I ever tell you you're my hero?

Brandi Bryant

Lazy, Lazy Little Snow Flakes

Lazy, Lazy Little Snow Flakes
on my window pane,
you sparkle in the Sunshine,
and melt in the rain.

Your Beautiful white blanket
has covered our land,
children are so happy
with snowballs in hand.

Snow Flakes only come just
at certain times of the year
and gladden the hearts of children
and make the old folks cheer.

No moon tonight
to make you glisten.
You float lazy, lazy along when
the wind is hissing.

Goodbye Lazy Snow Flakes
down the river you must go.
We'll see you next winter
when you cover us with snow.

Clarence O. Larson

Falling Rain

Falling rain soothes the pain
quiet days erase the harried
Pace of past memories, that flood
my brain . . .
Revel in the wind inhale the smell
of God's autumn grace.
Lift your face to the falling rain
Cry no more tears in vain.
Wasted moments, glimpses of
the yester years gone
washed away by the quiet of the
falling rain.

Carrie S. Gerretson

Untitled

Quiet river pool
Smiles as the golden leaf falls
Softly on its face.

Virge Holliday

Forever Yours

I am your husband
You are my wife
Through joy and happiness
Or trouble and strife
We choose each other to face this life.

When this life is over
There will be no more
Trouble and strife
I'll still be your husband
And you'll still be my wife.

A kingdom in heaven we hope to obtain
Where together in happiness
We can rule and reign
I'll be your king
And you'll be my queen.

This was our goal
To obtain eternal life
When I became your husband
And you became my wife.

Leon G. Shular

A Christmas Prayer

Dear God, as I look to morning's light,
I'm unafraid of darkened night.
I trust in you with all my might.
And you are there.

Oh, God, the wonders of your hand
Are all around throughout the land;
Earth, sea, and sky at your command.
And you are there.

I watch the season now unfold;
I think about the days of old
When shepherds did your child behold.
And you were there.

Oh, God, I look around and see
The lights and tinsel on the tree,
The closeness of our family.
And you are there.

Whatever troubles or pain may come,
I'll know the joy of following one
Who'll take my hand and lead me home.
And you'll be there.

Gail Crawford

First Shave

Black and white tiles are cold,
Not noticed by bare feet.
Stands on tiptoes, silver mirror
Grow-up tall.
Reaches for the brush,
Little fingers almost too young
To grasp old wooden handle.
Watches worn-thin bristles gather
Soap from chipped brown-handled mug,
Sailing ship almost faded.
Old leather smooth bristles
Glide on round face,
Leaving soap of heroic fragrance.
Glistening razor is lifted;
Little boy, wanting Dad status:
Big, strong, doer of great deeds.
Razor slides down cheek,
Smile creases pudgy mouth.
Peals of laughter echo across tile,
First taste of manhood fills the air.

Kevin Blankenship

Mama

I remember Mama in the days of old,
She'd sit there in her rocking chair,
    as pure as refined gold.
She'd cook and clean and scurry about,
And sometimes without a word,
She'd surely let us children know,
    we were seen, not to be heard.
At evening time when chores were done,
She'd teach us how to sing,
And pray that always in our heart,
    A melody would ring.
Mama's gone up to heaven now,
But I'll see her again someday,
If I continue to walk and pray
On this straight and narrow way.
Memories grow old and sometimes fade,
But I see through this looking glass,
That everything that Mama did,
She always did first class.

Nancy McLaughlin

Listen To Sounds

There are many sounds in this world.
Happy sounds, sad sounds,
Loud triumph sounds, television
sounds, crying sounds, animal
sounds, music and voice
sound, deep meadow sounds and
soft squeaky sounds.
My favorite sounds are encouraging
and Holiday sounds. If you sit
quietly and can hear — you will
hear sounds of traffic here and
moving there after.
Raindrop falling sounds. The Buses,
Trains and airplane sounds.
The sweetest sounds are delightful
sounds. Most tremendous sounds
are working, sleeping snore, playing,
dancing and No-nonsense sounds.

Rosemara Simpson

Slow Learner

My blood runs cold,
and so I scold,
those simple, simple minds,
they never know which way to go,
or that they're way behind,
humans waste,
then make post haste,
to run from their mistakes,
they won't look back,
because they lack,
the courage that it takes.

Jason Clark

Love

I never though
    it would be this way,
I love you more
    than words can say.

In my eyes you are perfection,
    and in your eyes I see a reflection
of your love for me,
    and mine for you,
A love of hopes and dreams
    come true.

Lisney Leyva Gonzalez

Love Is You

Love is your smile
The crease between your lips
It commands my mind
It sends me on happy trips.

Love is your eyes
The twins are killer
I get lost inside them
They're a visual thriller.

Love is your beauty
It is stunning to behold
I can feel its power
It knocks me out cold.

Love is your kiss
The anticipation fascinates
And when the moment arrives
The touch intoxicates.

Love is holding you
Till Death do us part
Always cradled in my arms
Always close to my heart.

Jay J. Mosby

The Cook

In the kitchen
I'm a pro
with chicken soup
or even crow.
I cook fish,
turkey, ham,
mashed potatoes,
bread and jam.
Pheasant, goose,
or even duck,
if you like food
then you're in luck.
I'll cook dinner,
supper or lunch.
I'll even make
breakfast or brunch.
I can cook
most anything.
Just plug your ears
because I sing!

Tara Lamper

Now And Then

Please, open the door,
It's me. I'm here now.
Someone invited me;
I don't know who.
That's no matter, really;
I'm ready. Life is. Always.
Teach me How.
Teach me Why.
Give me your All.
Then, let me try;
I'm new at this.
Ignorance is bliss.
Living's no snap;
No time for a nap.
Loving's the key;
Or has been for me.
Those I've invited,
I hope I've not slighted.
I'm leaving now;
Please, close the door.

Richard.M. Evans

Never Having Found True Love

A sole tear falls
from an eye blinded to light
The face of hopelessness cries
never having found true love

A pouting lip lowers
from passion it never felt
A kiss only alive in dreams
never having found true love

A hand cold and wrinkled
longing for that sweet caress
Touched only by the cloth of a glove
never having found true love

A body turns rigid
waiting for a warm embrace
Filled only with despair
never having found true love

A heart bound by chains
cracked and bruised with pain
An empty soul dies alone
never having found true love

Stephanie M. Linn

A Gift

I say an angel was sent to me
I look again and then I see
you are here for you and not for me

This is your journey
and for you alone
To discover yourself
not for me to clone

You are here for you and not for me
I'm here to guide you
I hope you see

Would I have you
be just like me?
No, you are you and you are free

I will be here for you
to teach all I know
That is the gift
to watch you grow

Free to be all you want and dream
You for you and me for me

Peggy Donnelly

Romance Personified

My love for you
is like that of a river
flowing eternally
until the end of time.
Clean and clear like a
cloudless day
purer than the purest
dove.
All of nature's beauty
cannot compare
for you are more graceful
than the most graceful swan
standing in the plains for
the heavens to witness your beauty.
The sun, moon and stars
bathe you with their magnificence.
All of this and still,
there are no words to express
my eternal love for you.

Yasmin Davidson

Just A Note

Just a note. Just one note
Is the start of a song.
Another note, a written note,
can ask a pardon if I'm wrong.
I want you to know, I miss you so.
A poem may be a corny way to go.
But if a note, one little note,
Can start a song in your heart,
Another note, a written note,
Could bring you back to me I know.
Without the note, I have no song.
Without you, my life is all wrong.
So sing a note, join my song,
Write a note, we'll sing along.
Together we'll write our life story.

Harriet Thomas Dittsworth

Grateful Me

To frown I do deface
A place so far away.
Clearly in the eyes of grace
A better place to stay.

Inviting it is I have found
A realm in which to pray.
So gladly I kiss the ground
As I live another day.

Such joy in all I do
I could ask for no more
That the world to me is true
Outside this battered door.

Corrigan Randall Molck

Claudia

A thin veil
Covered her
Freckled oval
Face
Two diamond
Shaped earings
Dangled from
Her ears
It's a mystery
Why she stood
In the shallow
End of the
Water
But the
Magical aura
Would always
Surround her

Gail Christmas

Of Taste

What of taste?
Love, adultery, or fear
assign it a taste and
disassemble —
A mouth tells lies (destroys truth)
yet cannot receive them —
Speak into the mouth and risk being
scalded
by its moist, hot abandon;
Probe (with the tongue, I dare you)
the only corrupt
misconception
on which fool mute lovers prey.

Alexandra Lemieux

Love Is Ageless

Let us grow old together
to climb the mountain of contentment
breath the sweetness of life
tell stories of our childhood dreams
review the happenings
of our quality time
so when the light dims
and our world starts floating away
we will not be afraid
to catch the plane of eternity
together.

Frank Ambroise III

Only Believers

I often sit and wonder
just where my life would be,
if God hadn't sent his angles
to help watch over me.

You may not think they're there
but just take a look around,
especially in your times of need
or when you're feeling down.

It may be just a smile
from someone you don't know,
or the smell of sweet perfume
that's pure as winters snow.

There's one thing you must remember
when things just get you down,
that God has a smile just for you
to replace your every frown.

So stop and thank him for all
the blessings you receive,
and know that they'll keep coming
as long as you believe.

Gail J. Meyer

The West

Flat and dry,
Beneath the sky,
Out West is where I lie.
Mountains high,
Or valleys low,
Like a caterpillar crawling here I go.
Whether rain or snow,
I still go,
Up, up, up,
Like a volcano.
Gold, silver, lead and oil,
Greatest Land of the Western soil.

Hannah E. Garrett

My Faith Is Like A Drawstring

My faith is like a drawstring,
Pulled taut against the bow,
With each arrow shot,
I'm drawn farther away,
From family,
From friends,
From my Lord Jesus Christ,
The lost arrows of my life,
My bow breaks,
My faith uncertain,
A time will come,
With the mending of my soul,
And my faith made strong,
Together again the bow and the arrow.

Trevor Tyler Hess

Untitled

Firemen step forward
Hold your head up high
For yours is the honorable profession
Not many will abide

Snow, hail, heat or rain
Nothing stops you men so brave
Life and property to protect
It is a life only a few select

Who can tell what awaits you
As through the streets you roll
Holding on so tightly
As the winds so coldly blow

Then the moment comes
When you have done all you can do
There lies the remains
All charred, looking at you

So to you, the firemen of our land
I bow my head in solemn pride
For this feeling, I feel for you
Comes from deep inside.

Shirley D. Darnell

Grant

A story of a boy simply
Called Grant.
As his power grows over you
you will see.

A smile big as moon beams
and eyes big as a sea.
Simplicity of a child,
We wish we all could be.

Suspended in a body that
doesn't work.
But with love hugs and
kisses.
You see a brilliant genius
Who concedes to be
A boy simply called
Grant

Tracy Alexander

Mother Dear

Come bathe my forehead
    For I am growing very weak

Let one drop of water
    Fall upon my burning cheek

Tell all my loving little playmates
    That I never more can play

Give them all my toys
    But put my little shoes away
Santa Clause, He brought them to me
    With a lot of other things

And I think he brought an angel
    With a pair of golden wings

You will do this, won't you, Mother
    And remember what I say

Give them all my toys
    But put my little shoes away

Now I'm going to leave you, Mother
    Please remember what I say

Give them all my toys
    But Mother put my little shoes away.

Dennis Harper Jr.

The Plan

Hug someone do it today
It doesn't matter who
If they be black, red or brown
It just might rub off on you.

Rubbing elbows doesn't hurt
You may even gain a friend
Cultivate that friendship
And it may never end.

Give a smile whenever you can
That smile will carry you through
Maybe some people look different
But inside they're just like you.

Don't put hate on creed or race
Do all that you can do
If someone falls pick them up
Next time it might be you.

A. Charles Neal

Ratify

Walks in the garden
Skinned her knees
That little girl
Looks a lot like me
Stumbling memories
Reoccurring dreams
It's not as scary
As it seems
And you don't want to go home
Armed with a smile
Swimming in barbed wire
Long like the Nile
I'm a great big liar
And you don't want to go home
So take another hit and stay

Ashley Nicole Smith

Before I Met You

Before I met you I was like
a robot going to school at certain
times, who played at certain times,
who laughed at certain times,
and who cried at certain times.
You woke my feelings inside that
no one never knew ever existed.
as we started to get closer you
broke through the machine of
me and discovered the human
being of me and I discovered
you made my life grand.

Jennifer Marie May

A Touch Of Red

The winter's snow was
sparkling white,
for it had fallen silently
in the night.

The morning's sun made
the white snow glisten,
and in the clear still air,
a quiet glen,
one only had to listen
to hear a melody fair.

Then ever so near, a touch of red
upon the snow,
a beautiful cardinal giving us a show.

Jayne A. Waller

God's Blessing

God gave me a blessing
He gave me a heart
He left me no guessing
He gave me an art

I thank God for his love
And for his guidance
I know he's above
Fighting defiance

When I'm asleep
I know he's still there
If I dream deep
I can still feel his care

God is my Father
He loves me as such
He calls to me louder
When I get out of touch

I will pray on my knees
For I know he's still there
Watching over me
With his unblinking stare

Cheyenne Dudley

Eternal

Their souls entwined.
Together they are one.
Apart they are none.
Their destinies are unknown.
Their spirits wild and free.
Two souls trying to meet.
Always torn apart.
No chance to survive.
They strive to find peace.
To feel without touching.
To hear without speaking.
Together only in dreams.
Never truly to be.
Until the end comes.
Their souls are set free.
Together to be, in all eternity.

Linda L Vanderlick

Oh Mother

The world is crazy,
Love has been lazy;
So why do I stay,
Where would I go?
Stay, go?
Stay, go?
It don't matter;
No baloney,
No ham.
Makes no sense,
Thinking nothing,
Just like everybody else.
Money and a crooked world,
Ugly faces in every scene,
Fabrication, no talent,
Idiots must shut up;
Things getting worse,
God it's boring.

Gerard Osta

Untitled

As I look upward,
I see visions of the past.
Not all seen, happened.

Becky Purcell

From Butterball

I wonder what he'd say today
Reading my poems come what may
I think he was a smart, warm man
He wished for me, a master plan.

Would he think poems silly stuff
Would he think I have done enough
To make my way in this vast world
Or am I still a little girl?

I love my daddy, yet today
He helps me all along the way
He's bright and handsome in the sky
I'm still the apple of his eye.

I know he would be proud of me
Help me publish poetry
Whistle as I sign my books
Send me warm and loving looks.

A lucky kid I know I was
I could do nothing wrong because
My father was right by my side
He's still with me, he is my guide.

Melissa G. Dobrin

Dark Memories

The time has since come and gone
Yet the sorrow lingers on
The whispers from the shadows
Seek desperately the light

My mind spins and screams
To let go of the truth
But once the thoughts
Turn into air

They may shed greater pain
Then I ever knew was there
And if the nymphs
Should see a glimpse of light

They may run and hide
Deciding
They like it there
So, they will stay forever

Waiting, until all goes silent
Then they will grasp my soul
And bring it to a darker sphere
Of the unknown

Julia Wulf

Holding On

You laid a gentle kiss upon my lips
I felt as if I were in a world
where only dreams survived
so I let go and dreamed on.

A tender touch upon my cheek
all I knew was how I felt
every moment I was with you
so I let go and dreamed on.

Two arms embracing me closely
my senses seem to lose control
I let my mind feel free
so I let go and dreamed on.

Nothing could be done to stop us
a love burning hot as a flame
slowly melting a candle
so I held on and lived the dream.

Michele C. Papson

Distress

She rolled about on the floor,
her little body contorted,
cringing away from the pain.

No, Mama. Please, Mama. Stop.
Don't hit me, oh please!

She tried to crawl out of sight,
there was no escaping the stick
raining hard blows on her back.

No, Mama. Please, Mama. Stop.
Don't hit me, oh please!

She screamed and sobbed out her fear
and felt bewildered, betrayed
by the fury that used to be love.

No, Mama. Please, Mama. Stop.
Don't hit me, oh please!

At last it is over, there's quiet.
She's gathered, enfolded in arms
that minutes before dealt out rage.

Oh, Mama. Please, Mama. Yes,
just love me, oh please, I'll be good.

Andee Phillips

Dream Dates

Somewhere each night in a mystic land
Where dreaming temples gong
When mystery stirs the scented air
You'll hold me in your arms

Your lips will whisper words of love
Your eyes a story tell
As in your heart you truly vow
No greater love excel

Oh sweeter words shall never fall
Upon a maidens ear
And sweeter nights shall ne'er be spent
Than those when you are here

Within the realms of dream land
Where moonbeams sing love songs
The mystery magic, of dream dates
All . . . night . . . long.

Lily M. Defibaugh

She Plays With The Angels

She doesn't know I see her
As her eyes glisten with joy.
She's playing with the angels,
Little girls and little boys.

Her eyes follow the dancing girl,
And she smiles with such delight!
As she goes into a playful whirl,
In her little gown of white.

Now she sees a little juggling clown
Her eyes follow the balls around.
And she giggles right out loud
When he lets them all fall down!

She was playing with the angels;
And then God called her home.
To her beautiful white mansion,
Where she is not alone.

Now I no longer watch her,
And I miss her more each day.
But it helps to know she's with Him,
And with angels she can play.

Ruth Victoria Johnston

Forever

When love captures a wise man;
he is held forever
For when it comes to love;
there is no difference with a fool
For both love to be held
in strong, compassionate arms
and feel the kiss of a woman,
whose breath his body cools.

Nicole D. LaMora

Mothers Are A Special Thing

Mothers have a special way
to make your troubles go away,
If your troubles are still there,
they seem so hard to bear,
Mothers make you feel at ease,
and sometimes seem so hard to please,
Mothers have a tender smile
to make things seem worthwhile.
Mothers make the days seem fun,
and when you're cuddled in her arms,
you know the day is done,
Mothers give us what life can bring
cause mothers are a special thing.
Once again a mother's touch,
can mean so very much.

Becky Tyler

What Have You Done To Me?

All this feeling that I have
All this ache in my heart
Wanting to reach out and touch you
What is it that you've done to me?

I try to push you from my thoughts
Feeling so helpless when I can't
You won't leave me
I can find no peace

My heart beats faster thinking of you
Louder still, can you hear?
Hear my soul calling your name?
What have you done to me?

The lovely sound of your voice
making my body crave yours
Desperate for the touch of your hand,
the feel of your lips on mine.

Will this feeling never end?
That sweet ache I feel for you
stronger every day, every night
when all I can do is dream of you.

Lisa S. Ellis

Broken-Hearted Youth

Love dance with me
Make me believe
It's not a fairy tale
A broken hearted youth writes

Love set me free
Make me understand
It can be done . . .
Emotionally and spiritually

Love come stay with me
Make me see
Through my lovers eyes
And let youth write no more lines.

Rebecca Kohler

Seasons Change

Seasons change
    down on the range
I see the meadows from afar
    the trees swaying
In the breeze
    make me feel at ease
The streams are so clear
    like diamonds are hidden
        somewhere in there
The animals all at peace
    seasons change down on the range
    I see the meadows from afar.

Therese Huls

Why Live

Why live, just to die?
The heat beats on throughout your life
decisions of hopeless choices
wordless thoughts, silent voices
to have to hope against the lands
feel the malcontent
suffer from misguided voices
to live with conviction, will to intent
hated, cursed, but slightly loved
yet none knows my soul
the wakening, the beginning
the angel I now love and hold
she sores the sky in golden ray
brings feelings to a high
loving me, not broken dreams
why live? To love or die?

Travis Downs

The Child

It's been twenty-three years,
many laughs, many tears.
So many memories, memories,
some would regret.
Some would rejoice,
some would simply choose to forget.
This child's eyes reveal the pain,
of lost times and a lost loved one,
that can never be again.
Left behind, left undone
with a hole in her heart
for that special one.
We each call one, mother,
and when that one is lost,
there can be no true other
at no matter what cost.
Some may come close,
some even quite up to par.
But, a loss is a loss,
no matter who we are.

Meg Gallagher

Mississippi Delta Breeze

Swaying through the oceans
of green cotton seas.
Blowing through my ear as I
proceed.
Down the wining road of time.
I wish this moment planted
forever in my mind.
All this on a summer day I see.
As I speed
Still feeling that summer Delta Breeze.

Katasha Sibley

Inside Looking Out

Light moves slightly,
sharply through the
crevice of air
between leaves of green.
This movement is all
too familiar
within my memory:
the slow, sharp
feeling of your love
when I first learned
to grasp it entirely.
The window smudged
the clouds fogged
up with my fingerprints
as I reached out
of my comfort
to, for once, touch you
from the inside
looking out.

Tracy Lynn Sipple

Angels Took You

Angels took you up above,
Angels took you from our love.
Angels took you to go to sleep,
They left us here to mourn and weep
Angels took you without pain,
In God's kingdom you will reign.
Angels took you without a goodbye,
When they took you, did you cry?
When they took you, did you wave?
We placed some flowers on your grave.
Can you see us crying here?
Can you see us shed a tear?
Angels took you to the Man up there,
Angels took you from those who care.
Angels took you from your bed,
People said that you are dead.
I say that you cannot be,
You're still here helping me.
Though angels took you from our sight,
I'll remember you as warm and bright.

Morgan Lamar Nemec

Wrecked

View shattered
Gleaming million diamonds
Choking pure
Ash cotton candy . . .

Brenton Aspinwall

Alone, But Not Lost

In memory of my father,
Joseph L. Padden, 1936-1996

Though you are no longer with us,
    there is comfort.
Though we can no longer see you,
    there is light.
Though we can no longer touch you,
    you touch us.
Though we can no longer hear you,
    our hearts do.
Without you, we have nothing,
    but everything.
We have our memories and our love,
    and that is enough.
We are alone, but not lost,
    thanks to you.

Luann Padden

Crossing Over

Dedicated to my daughter, April
God stretched out His hand
across the river of darkness . . .
To the lost child standing on the shore
He said . . . "my child, take my hand,
that you may suffer no more,"
Fearlessly yet reluctantly . . .
The child took His hand . . .
The singing of angels could be
heard throughout the land,
people gathered in awe of
this beautiful sight
a lost child of God . . .
Embracing the light.

Melody Friddle

Untitled

I find myself thinking . . .
about a past I can't return to.
To say all those thoughts
that were never spoken.

The success that I accomplish,
the knowledge that I acquire,
seems almost wasted
with no one to share it with.

As I go on
with my goals in sight.
I get so tired,
and it's always night.

David Manning

The Grandfather

Today, the sea came like an old man
Topped with white froth
Disheveled in the morning breeze.
He sat upon the beach and swayed
Humming a song much older
Than the ear of any audience
In the afternoon he napped
Having left small gifts in the sand
For the pleasure of his grandchildren.
Tonight, I listen through the walls
To his soft erratic breath
And dream that it will never cease.

Jason Sibley

Song

Dos Hombres you yahoo
Riding the rail
Disappearing into the sun
Magic follows me everywhere
I got the disappearing blues
Scantee to Witchia
Coming in from home
Wouldn't change a thing
Running down the blues
Mid-summer sun
And a cranky aptitudes
Milder now that I've found you
Couldn't complain about a few
Sure I've found a replacement
In the Seattle slow bother me again
And I'll see you in a 200
Can't complain about much
Just those disappearing blues
Dos Hombres, you yahoo
and find out what is true.

Larry Briggs

Just Love Her (A Cat Tale)

The little cat
will follow you
from room to room
on silent paws . . .

She only seeks
an occasional pat
or a softly spoken
kind word.

Starved, neglected,
mistreated, abandoned:
that's how she was
when we found her.

Now, with silky grey fur
and big blue eyes,
she'll purr loudly
if you pet her.

For you see,
her wishes are simple
and she just wants
to be loved.

Kimberly Wasson

Life

Mysterious new life,
Sweet life,
Precious, fragile,
Conceived in secret,
Whilst reaching
Nadir
to
Zenith.
Rapturous sighs,
Yield to
Spectators love,
Breathed
from
above.
Source
of
All life,
Remain.

Inge Maria Church

Daddy And His Little Boy

In the world there was no joy,
Every time he lost his boy.
For all the hopes and dreams and fears,
What was left for him were tears.

Wanting so much to be there,
Such sorrow, that he could not bare,
To show the love, felt so deep;
He put those hopes and fears to sleep.

Brave little boy left alone,
With the love that could not be shown.
That empty place inside him still,
All the dreams left unfulfilled.

His calls for Daddy, never heard,
He hid himself from the feeling world.
Pain and tears, all locked up tight,
A battle of loss, he could not fight.

Together again, but gone too soon,
Left waiting for another June.
Hold it in, try to be strong,
For each other's arms they long.

Jill M. Markham

Thank You, Mother

You are the source of all emotion.

From birth,
to death.
From your roots,
to mine.
From childhood,
to womanhood.

You are there.

You are the inspiration of all art.

In the Great Beginning,
and the Final End.
In the womb,
and the coffin.
In the clay,
and the masterpiece.

You belong.

Thank you, my wonderful, loving mom.

Verity K. Caron

Album Of The Heart

No mere art form could contain
   the images or the word
No record play the strains
   of the voices that we heard
No replication copy
   what grace before us shone
And so we have our memories
   each vision is our own.
The shared effect is separate then
   alive within each heart
And resonates more tenderly
   without the aid of art.
The spirit is invisible
   and yet it is more real
Than matter which we worship so
   of sight and sound and feel.
The shutter trips — the flash can fail
   and in such loss we sever
Images contained in bounded frames
   Refrained within Forever.

Carol Castor

Wandering From My Mind

Needing, not sure what.
Seeking, but I can't find.
Dreaming, but can't remember.
Wandering, from my mind.

   Leading, but what direction?
   Hearing, what did you say?
   Doing what I'm supposed to
   Knowing the price I'll pay.

Caring, but it hurts.
Pain, I can bear.
Giving till there's nothing.
Hurting, do you care?

   Staying, I'm trapped.
   Going, but where?
   Living, but dying.
   Loving, do I dare?

Running, but from what?
Scared, to get behind.
Hiding, from myself?
Wandering, from my mind.

Janis Carter Arwood

Hate

Hostility toward someone who is not
   the same is where hate gets its name

Another hateful thing is when

The people who hurt to defend,
   but for

Either one to make a change
   we have to learn we are all
   the same.

Lazette Hall

If I Could Have One Wish

If I could have one wish
I'd wish for each of you
That all your pains would disappear
And life would be like new.

If I could have one wish
I wish for each of you
A day filled with joy
And skies of Azure blue.

Since I can't have my wish
I can always have my dreams
So come and dream with me
   my friends
Let us dream of yester-year
When we were young
and love ruled supreme.
Let us forget our past
and live our youthful dreams.

Myrtle Whitley

Dearly Departed

   Only to ponder,
where others will wonder.
   The end is near,
it's not funny to hear.
   You see young and old
starting to fold, buckling
   at the knees
with disease.
But if you're right with God,
   Saint Pete will give you a nod
and the beginning will have
   started, for the dearly departed.

Mark H. Huffman

Beauty Within

The beauty found within
The craziness this world creates
Woods growing in that part of town
Growing wondrous things of simple,
But complex beauty created with
Desires and wants.

Some may never discover the beauty
Within themselves or the nature
In front of us all
When found, acceptance and awe are
Greatly required.
Search for this beauty within
And when found, respect and cherish it.

The mind who is beauty himself
Formed for those who live to find
Spend time listening for the
Voice who formed it all.

Amy Lynn Cummings

Paradise

Beyond the valley deep
Soft waving green fades
To rippling blue
Tinted with hints of gold
From the overhead blaze.
   Blanketing all with its rays.

Stems with petals so sweet
Bursting toward the sky.
Colors streaming
In the wind with scents
Of honeysuckle and berries.
   Blissing those to whom it carries.

Clouds bring pallor so weak
Toning the bounty
Fervor enclosed
In the soul once ingressed
In wondrous beauty
   The earth's amazing gratuity.

Nicole B. Zollinger

I Found A Love

I found a love
A beautiful love
This love I found
Was a mysterious love

It stole my heart
From high above
This love I found
Was a selfish love

Off to the heavens
As a white feathered dove
This love I found
Was a mystical love

I tried to catch it
This love from above
This love I found
Was a fanciful love

It held my heart
With all my love
This love I found
Was once true love

Doug Schaffer

The Wind Is My Friend

When I feel alone
I go out side
In search of the wind
to be by my side
And as it gently whispers
past my ear
"You'll never be alone
As long as I am here"

Russ Loy

Yesterday

Yesterday I felt sorry for myself
Yesterday I was still making excuses
Yesterday I had no tomorrow
Today I feel good about me
Today I make decisions
Today I look forward to tomorrow
Tomorrow
I will attend to tomorrow
When tomorrow gets here

Amanda Hicks

Known For A Short Time

Known for a Short Time
when I was young, about
a loved one that I knew
little of.

The Short Time we had
was the best time of
my life. But, I
wished he had waited
for me to say good-bye.

The Short Time of joy,
and the Short Time of
grief. Will be
remembered in my heart,
and in it, deep.

For, the Short Time
I've known before he
passed on. My brother's
the best friend I've
had since the day I was
born.

Steven Correia

The Unconscious Search

The search continues
for a soul to match my own.
One with the same heart
and an even exchange.
A soft touch
like that of my own.
One that heals
and calms the flesh.
Eyes that remain open
even when it hurts to see.
Open ears that hear every thought
that is understood
with the divine mind.
Lips that feel the breath
that quenches life
with the same thirst
to have it all
even when the world
turns empty.

Mary J. Cognat

Widower's Lament

Oh, mother of my children
I write these words and weep;
I can't communicate with you
In your eternal sleep.

The rapture we once shared was
A temporary thing;
As also were the problems of
Parenting our offspring.

Alone, I bask in glory
Of great-grandfatherhood;
Alas that fate denied you this
Reward of motherhood.

I can not help recalling
Our unforgiving way;
The anguish over minor faults
Our children did display.

Oh, could I now assure you
They all turned out just right;
Oh, could I wipe away these tears
And bid you peace tonight.

Jim Hathaway

Untitled

Last until the rising sun
Slip away and come undone
Receiving Ra, darkness fades
Moonlit dreams, despair cascades
Both dance at Horizon's gate
Nature saves and seals our fate

Matt Mills

Different

I read a wonderful book today.
The words talked to me.
They taught me a lesson
A lesson to be free.

It said how to be yourself
Not everyone — just you.
Unique and special, be different.
I hope you learned this too!

Jamie Buckwalter

Your Eyes

Your eyes sparkle at the
Girls that passes you.
Even though we know
You're not worth it
But we fall for you
We don't know why
And have no reasons
Your crystal blue eyes
Becomes the ocean, so calm
So relaxed, nothing can disturb it
But when it comes to meet mine
The dark brown, almost blackish eyes.
Your ocean becomes so cold
That they are passionless
Like a storm had just swept through
I finally know what you're
Trying to tell me
So from then on I never
Again looked into your eyes
To disturb that calm ocean

Angela Day

Mid-Life

I am going around and around
out and through
The other side
of the change of life.

I wake up in the AM
and can't remember
where I am
and don't even want to face
who I feel
or the hour of it.

Jen Woods Rappold

Dog

Playful, running
A living being.
They play with toys.
I walk them on a leash.
A puppy
A man's best friends.
They play with us.
They run with us.

Kellie Hudson

7

Seven short years
Of pain and shame
No one heard her fall
But everyone made the call
It wasn't me — they said
And a 7-year old princess is dead

For what and why
Her mother was a devil
Cracked, insane
To cause such beauty
Such pain
And the government
Says all is well
An old line used
To ring a cracked bell

7 short years
No justice at all
The princess dances
With her daddy at heavens ball

Matt Kozenko

Christmas Day

Christmas is a joyful time,
unwrapping presents,
the fresh smell of pine.

The scent of cookies fill the air,
ovens warming everywhere!

Relatives come from here and there,
knowing that we really care.

Decorated Christmas trees.
Twinkling lights, cold winter breeze.

Fires burning all day long,
We'll all be singing our favorite song.

Turkey, stuffing, we want more!
Cakes, cookies and pies galore!

The saddest part of Christmas day,
is knowing it's not here to stay.

I wish that we could find away
to celebrate Christmas everyday!

Joan M. Thurston-Davis

What Christmas Means To Me

The smell of the grass,
The wind moving fast.
The stars up above,
Set the tone of his love.

For lying in a manger
Away from all strangers,
Lay sweetly in the hay,
God chose him to pay.

The shepherds came flocking.
To the baby they came walking,
To worship the Son,
God's plan had begun.

The wise men all kings,
Brought gifts of wonderful things.
To honor his coming,
His face is so stunning.

The Heavens rejoiced,
The angels cried with a joyful voice.
Those who were once deprived,
Rejoice! The Savior has arrived.

Christopher Evans

Memories of You

Memories of you are like rainbows
in the sky colorful and beautiful
enough to make me high.
They fly across giant mountains
down to dark blue seas
the memories I have of you
are beautiful to me.
Like flowers in the spring
time blooming all day long
you're my wild flower
growing very strong

Corey Silvernail Smith

Life's Seas

Storm-tossed and weary,
I sail through life's seas
Fighting the fierce gales
Hoping for a breeze.
Rain falls in torrents.
The sky is dark as night.
Thunder crashes wildly
With Satan's evil might.
I can't find my way.
My sails are wet and torn.
The boat has sprung a leak.
The lines are old and worn.
My Lord, my Savior
Comes to the rescue.
Jesus is my captain;
I am just the crew.
The storm is just as harsh;
The way still unknown,
But the journeys not so hard
'Cause I am not alone.

Nicole Fitzhugh

Sigh

When people ask other people
"Why they do his" Why they do
that" they "sigh"

When people ask one another "Why they
travel up Highways and down Bi-ways"
They look at each other and "sigh"

When people of today also ask
"Why is the world like it is today"
They also "sigh"

But to reach deep down to think
and to look around they would
not "sigh"
    But to make a vow to try
to make this a better world to
live in.

Rhonda K. Jones

Willing

If love comes down to hate
then hating will take love down
time passes
in and out of phases and stages,
but no time
will forget love . . .
. . . to take a chance again
is love for will
and if willing time is right
then it is time again
for love . . .

Evan Wasserstrom

Angel

I have a friend,
a woman so fair.
With sparkling eyes,
a little gray in her hair.

Some called her "mama,"
grandpa called her "Gold."
I called her "Grandma,"
this lady of old.

So gentle was she,
so timid, but kind.
Angels on earth
aren't easy to find.

We'd rock in her chair,
I'd sit on her knee.
I loved to be near her,
She's so special to me.

I still see her face,
smiling and shining with love.
Even though she's not here
my angel above.

Kathy May Meather-Nash

Ever Knowing

Tonight under a lover's moon
Restless spirit will entwine
Only give me a moment
Yours forever afterward
Lose myself in your eyes
Forget the world in your arms
Find myself not falling
But drifting in the sun
Open my pride over flowing
Show me inside ever knowing

Krista English

The Motion Of Impact

As I looked and listened
I heard the scrape of silk
As she crossed her legs
She flushed her skirt
Over her knee
As she let out a quiet sigh
I knew it was a hint
So, I slid off the rock
And like a thunderbolt, I fell
hitting the ground on impact,
I knew, it was my choice where to move
So, I moved closer.

David Scott Lee

The Peasant's Walk

The peasant's walk was longer
'Tis lonely are his feet
and poorness for this peasant
Was somehow a defeat.
He need be meet a princess
to save from once distress.
A refuse of loving honor
he never will regret, and showing
he was worthy to walk down
sharpened paths and then speak of
legends, of peasants worthy tasks.
The peasant needed in return, a pair
Of peasant shoes to walk along much
Farther a path he had to choose.

Christina Steinbrecher

The Christmas Kiss

The image that I love so dear,
On Christmas day that comes each year,
A mother holds her newborn son,
The pain has past, travail done.
The world glows as morning dawns,
And mommie loves, as baby yawns.
We see the joy in glistening eyes,
The star that rises in the skies.
We hear the call for all that's true,
She vows to God as what to do,
She vows to God as what to keep,
And what to hold, and what to seek.
The promise that she makes her babe,
Signed with a kiss that will not fade.
Resolved to all that stands above,
She gives the kiss, the kiss of love.
From such a kiss the baby learns,
From such a kiss, the world turns.
Mysterious and even odd,
From such a kiss, we're kissed by God.

Allen Michael Green

Untitled

Today I am seventy four
My, how time flies
Life was very different then
In the years that have gone by.

Traffic was not so heavy
Roads were set aside
So all the little children
Could enjoy a sled ride

No television or computers
To entertain one and all
People remained active
Couch potatoes did not loll

Packaged food was unknown
Mom had to mix a cake
With flour, sugar, and butter
She prepared dough to bake

But, the present has its virtues
Life is easier today
There is more time available
To shop, to read, and to play

Ruth P. Hopkins

Desert Noon

Sh —
Sit still!
Hear —
The silence of the desert noon
Thundering down around
Like the sound
Of a thousand cymbal crashes
Turned inside out,

Soothing silence
Covering the chaotic crush of beings
Struggling to be heard
Or seen,
Or felt.

Listen!
For it is silence that makes sense
When all else is stripped away.

Therein is revealed
The beauty or peace.

Donald R. Clapp

Mary

She sat at His feet . . .
    her heart was content.
To hear every word . . .
    to know what they meant.
She took her best oil . . .
    her best perfume.
She washed his feet . . .
    its scent filled the room.
Instead of a towel . . .
    she took her long hair.
Wiped dry his feet . . .
    unashamed . . . free from care.
She didn't mind . . .
    let the world see.
That its most sacred place . . .
    is at Jesus . . . feet.

Barbara Price Burkhardt

God's Corner

The early morning hours
Are so special in my life,
For sitting in God's corner
I find my precious wife.
The Holy Spirit welcomes her
While dew in on the lawn.
Her prayers for me sent Heavenly,
So long before the dawn.
She dresses for a long work day,
With clothes so fresh and mod,
But not before she clothes herself
With armor straight from God.
She makes our home a special place,
Tho burdens heaped upon her,
And praises God for all He's done,
While sitting in God's corner.

Jay Smith

Teddy Bears

A teddy bear
is always there,
so fuzzy and soft,
you'll be aloft,
on a dream cloud,
where you're allowed,
to float and dream,
with a gleam,
with your teddy,
who is always there.
He is so soft,
that you'll oft,
fall asleep,
while hugging your bear.

Michelle Samuelsen

Goodbye Dream

While sunk, it seems, in darkest gloom,
There's a gentle voice I hear.
"Peace, my child" it seems to say,
Shed not that bitter tear.

"He's only sleepeth now, my child,
Disturb thou not his rest.
His tasks await thee, now, my child.
Arise and do thy best".

"Do not despair, my child,
I am thy dearest friend.
And to, I will be near thee,
Yes, even until the end!"

Earl R. Walker

The Gully

Serene and quiet
Through forest glen
Angling obliquely
To watery end

Sensitive to elements
Eroding its banks
Uttering no sound
Refusing no ranks

Supported, maintained
'neath canopy shade
Changing, growing
New channels made

Plunging, gouging
Bedrock and drift
Extending, expanding
Margin and rift

Springing to life
During melt and storm
Assuming fresh character
Gaining raw form

Robert M. Wachlin

The White Rose

If I died tonight,
would you leave me a white rose,
on my grave,

Would you remember me,
with hope,
or forget you in the tears,
would you remember,
me in laughter,
When ringin' in the New Year,

So when you see the white rose,
remember me this way,
a dream for a dreamer,
living life from day to day,

So when you see the white rose,
remember of my love,
and know in your heart,
I watch you from above.

Jonathan Crouch

The Children's Love

The children's love is innocent
But they don't understand
When parents go their separate ways
Who'll be there to hold their hands

A mother's love is tender
A father's love is true
They keep them in their hearts
Though they start their lives anew

He visits them on holidays
For no one can fill their space
A stitch in a broken heart
And a smile upon their face

His heart's door is always open
For inside they can but win
And those conceived of innocence
Forever hold a place within

The children's love is innocent
This he hopes they understand
It takes but a thought
And he'll be there to hold their hands

Lonny A. Smith

Christmas Whispers

Twas just days before Christmas
    when all through God's house —
The excitement was building
    for each child, man and spouse.

The evergreen's hung
    across the church and the lights
Are glowing profusely
    to reflect our delight.

The candles are gleaming,
    the steeple bells ringing.
And inside the church
    the carols we're singing.

The birth of the Christ child
    is what this season's about;
His love's never ending —
    of this there's no doubt.

God speaks in a whisper
    heard by each listening ear —
"Let's keep the Christmas spirit
    going all through the year."

Cindy Seslar

What Makes Me Smile

A cold coke makes me smile
On a warm summer day,
It seems to make troubles
Flitter gently away.

A good joke makes me grin,
Helping me end the blues,
From a bad day at work
Or when I hear bad news.

I get a real chuckle
When good times come my way,
Because that usually means
A happy, fun filled day.

I have heard people say
To just grin and bear it,
But I say, "Try a smile,
And then simply share it."

Troy A. Simmons

A Dream

A dream not dreamed
is like a race not finished,
or a poem not written.
A dream not dreamed,
is like a book not read,
or a door unopened.
A dream not dreamed
can never come true.

Sara Adams

God And Me

The road of life is long, and hard.
If I walk, will be with God.
With everything going against my will.
The Lord will fix it, if I keep still.
If your road is long, and hard,
Turn your troubles over, to God.
When I retire beyond the seas the Lord
Will still be walking with me.

Mary C. Fletcher

This Day

This day is done.
It just faded away from me
Like an unnoticed beetle bug
Beneath that apple tree.
With it, it took a laugh
Or two or three,
A tank of gas, a bowl of rice,
And some broccoli.

But not much more did it take from me.
And never did I stop to care,
Or even for a moment wonder
Why this day just went away.
But now it's gone like an arrow
With a gust,
Flying fast fast in the dust,
Always going to be.
Will it ever harbor fuss
In this galaxy?
On this day, I swallowed
Like a cup of tea.

Nancy Cobb

Twirling Heart

As a leaf twirls in the water,
so does my mind,
Searching for the peacefulness
my soul longs to find.
The ripples stir so quietly as I stare,
I wonder if there's hopefulness
within the pool somewhere.

The tears flow down my face
as I search the water deep,
How long must I caress this hope,
how long must I so weep.

My dreams hold in a care, a need,
a patience failing fast,
I search each space I step within
and feel the pain is vast.

'Twas once a time when love was pure
a feeling true at heart.
But now we've studied, withheld,
remorse,
Are we so truly smart?

Patty Bray

Untitled

I saw happiness,
When I looked at you.
And I saw sorrow,
Which seemed so true.

It didn't seem,
That you wanted to go.
And leave us all,
You had to, I know.

Your love is true,
And always will be.
To me that is something,
Nobody else can see.

I'll see you again,
When my life is done.
And from my fears,
I'll no longer run.

Melissa Thompson

Return

You said I would not come
But many times have I returned.

Often you have heard me speak
In spring twilight
When a sleepy robin sang his prayer.

You have seen me at dawn
When purple swallows fly
In a cool green world.

I have come to you in new rain
As it pattered on cobbled garden paths.

Always you will find me in gray velvet shadows
And fragrant earth moss.

I have been close to you in rare blossoms,
Mauve lilacs that you loved, and warm red poppies.

But, oh dear one, I was most near
When from your heart
Grief had carved her image in your tears.

You said I would not come
But often have I returned.

Rhea C. Guild

Why Racism

Why must it always be,
A black-white issue between you and me?
The world was created for all of us,
But constant dissension only breeds distrust.

We are all unique in our own special way,
A cornucopia of talents we all display.
Diversity is welcome, equality the key
To a better way of life for you and for me.

We are faced with hot issues each and every day,
That threaten society in so many ways.
Drugs, unemployment, racism, and murder
Will compromise lives causing hopeless despair.

Is there a solution, is there a plan?
That's what we must discover with no time to spare.
If we can't coexist on earth in peace and harmony,
How can we live in heaven throughout eternity?

Carlita Perry

The Last Sonnet

Forlorn, sweet heart, doth thy passion burn?
O, carve not thine eyes whence yonder light dismay,
'Tis purest of heart that hath endeavored yearn,
Lest pale love's cancelled woe cast thee away.

Wherefore now, doth thy gentle silence speak?
Pray thee, I, for wanton ill rehearse no more,
For thy sullen words in huddled darkness keep,
'Gainst thy hunger, for whom thou art yearning for.

Hear ye sainted soul, to what yonder sparrow sings,
Whereon gilded truth is born, for thy life, it be known,
From swift-footed song thou art giv'st wings,
Lest thou dost tarry, will they hasten thee home.

Ere long, doth my heart dare one chance play,
To wit, a splendorous rose in thine eyes see,
Save not this day, on which thy flattered dreams lay,
'Tis my heart, of all hearts, wherein thou dost dwell
    and forever will be.

Eric O. Bragg

Control

Anger slashes through the night
    Severing the bonds
      That tie us together
Striking out
    Moment of rage
      Insanity lurks, just beneath the surface
One action can cut
    What know words can heal
Regret quietly waiting
    To jump into my soul
But the moment passes
    Sanity prevails
      But for how long, I wonder?

Warren Phegley

A Child's Fear

I stare at the ceiling lying still,
waiting
listening
There are no sounds of breathing and it's
quiet
calm
The lights are off and it's
dark
gloomy
I prey I make it till morning,
safe
sound
Every night I make the same plea,
hoping
praying
What is under the bed?

Kelly Ann Caravello

My Grandpa

A wisp of hair lay on his head, like a king's crown,
sitting upon his throne.
A cane in his hand, so difficult to walk,
but yet he goes on trying without a thought.
Some months had passed, since the last one had come,
I cried and cried cause the first one was so hard.
A stroke had come, washed half of his body away,
he scared me so.
So I took all my savings, small but enough
I walked to the gift store to buy a bear, and then,
to the florist to get a bouquet.
So many wires hooked to his arm,
I pulled out one not meaning to when I gave him a hug.
But this one was better.
I saw him a week later, working at his shop.
I gave him a hug, and thinking to myself
I'm so lucky to have him as,
"My Grandpa."

Jessica Brownell

Untitled

There is a man with short and jointly toes.
There was a very funny man with a pickle in his nose.
There is a man who had very little Hair.
He definitely could use some Layers.
His Belly was like Jelly.
He just couldn't stay away from Smackers Jelly.
That Belly also reminded you of being 9 months into pregnancy.
Wherever he went there was so much vacancy.
He even had an odor foul for Sure
I wish someone would buy him some deodorant called Sure.
But please if you see this man.
Give him a helping hand.

Johnny Logan Wilson Jr.

Untitled

To
Jean,
When you sailed into my life, I felt your wake.
It rocked my ship in its bay of calm.
A feeling I cannot take
with a grain of salt or hold in the palm
of my hand.

You were setting your sail for another tack
toward a nor'western pull
that was calling you back.
But our eyes met and the moon was full
and the drift of the tide put us together

Like the feathers
on the wings
of a gull.

Love,
  Bill
    William C. Dinger

Thank You

Thank you for letting me get to know you,
For sharing your thoughts and your dreams,
Thanks for giving me a special share
of your help, and comfort, warmth and care,
Thank you for the many things you do
to brighten up my life.
Thanks for the memories of happy days
And for your understanding ways,
Thank you for being friends with me
and letting me know you are there,
Thank you for your "love" and tenderness, too . . .
Thank
  You
    Sweetheart,
     For
      being
       you . . .
"I love you" . . .
    Rudy Sadino

The Voice Within

I heard a voice from within me say
What did you do for your soul today?

Did you help the world to sing a happier song?
Did you forgive someone who had done you wrong?

Did you perhaps help some stranger on life's hard road?
Did you try to lighten another's heavy load?

Did you try to restore the dreams of an empty heart?
Maybe give their failures a brand new start?

Did you coax a smile to someone's tearful face?
Did you standby and laugh when a friend fell into disgrace?

Did you go out of your way for someone today?
Life is not one big party; heed what I say!

Has the things of this world become more important — than?
Coming to the aide of your fellow man?

Did we lose sight of why we are there?
Just to build up earthy treasure of things we hold dear?

Ask these questions of yourself my friend!
Does my soul need an inner healing?
Before the end!

    Barbara Keith Toothman

My Mother — The Rose

When I think of my mother, I think of a rose. The kind
of pale pink rose that is always . . . there in the garden.

Ever strong with petals reaching toward the light,
she gives hope to her seedlings gathering around her.

It rains and they ask her — Will the sun shine again?
The questions surround her, and her answers come with her
quiet wisdom, as she searches the roots of her soul.

Her stem gives courage to all who see her, and know that her
thorns are there to protect the stoic core of herself, she
will only expose in the winter of her being to those who know her.

The wind may come and rock her soft petals, but she knows
the truth the sun will bring. A smile, a kind thought, a good
deed and the love she gives makes all wonder if this rose is real.

She continues to heal all around her and bare her heart in the
wind and rain and thunder.

And time answers: This beautiful, wise and gentle rose, will
always be there.
    Taryn Quinn

Wishing

I wish for laughter light,
To make my days bright,

I wish for baby's chatter,
To make things right, no matter,

I wish for conversation bright,
To fill the days with needs right,

I wish for peace and contentment,
To make this land filled with sentiment,

I wish for happiness for one and all,
To make life the proverbial ball,

I wish for boys and girls alike,
Days filled with dreams come true,

I wish for each man or wife,
Days that takes us all thru strife,

I wish for everyone here-about,
Courage bold and ever stout,

Yes, I wish for laughter light,
To make my days ever bright.
    Kay Daggett

Untitled

To my little girl who's love is true
And does not make me blue.
She is kind and gentle and sweet
The kisses and hugs she gives
To me are very much a treat.
There is no one else in the world
That compares to my little girl
I love her so much it hurts
That it puts my head in a whirl.
To look in to her eyes of blue
You can see the love that's true.
It's as vast as the ocean and as deep
And does not waver for the Lord watches
Over like a bird up in the sky
To make sure she can fly.
He gives her the wings
All she has to do is learn to work
Those things.
And she can follow him down
The right path for his love is true, and she will not be blue!
    Delbert D. Cuthair

You

I love you so much in a way you
could never understand, I can still
feel the soft touch of your hand. I
still feel your embrace and recall that
cute little smile on your face. When I
was cold you were always there to keep
me warm and when I was feeling sad you
always knew the right words to make
me realize things aren't that bad. No matter
how bad things get, these are the things
about you I will never forget.
Please give me one more chance to work this
out, I can't even remember what were fighting about.
And whenever you feel like there's no more hope for you and me
just look back on how things used to be,
Remember all we've been through and
remember these 3 words "I love you".

Danielle Leguire

Where Were You Today My Children

Where were you today my children,
As I heard God's word in part.
Without you, there was emptiness in my heart.
Where were you today my children,
Did I fail you, Is it my fault!
And if I did fail you, surely God did not.
Where were you today my children.
All grown now, making each choice your own.
Sunday mornings are so lonely, won't you come home

My aching heart will know no peace
Until I can know at last it's his path you seek.
Where were you today my children!

Sue Ashlock

Living In High Gear

The morning sun casts out its rays in red and golden hues.
We watch it rise in different ways and all have different views.

There are those who just sit back with sleep still in their eyes.
Fresh from their bed, fog in their head, they wake to watch it rise.

But some of us think of the sun a bright and final note
That ends the song that say's we're done with stories that we've wrote.

It's in our eyes, the long drive home, we fail to see its strengths.
Our minds are lost, our thoughts, they roam, we've stretched them
to great lengths.

It soars so high into the sky, the sun we cannot touch.
We chase it in our gear so high and miss it by so much.

We drive so fast, but just go past priorities we've found.
We'd see it all and make it last if only we'd slow down.

Keith W. Waken

The World Without You

I stared into the flame of a candle last night
Every time I closed my eyes,
You came into sight.
I wondered what the world would be like
    without you to keep it bright.

The world would be black,
    black as could be
because you provide light that lets
    everyone see

No one would know, not even me
but when it comes to my heart
you have the key!

Jamie Minor

Begin, Again

I know I embarrassed you, I know I caused you pain
I know I made you angry, and those feelings still remain
Well you're still here, though you say I'm just a "friend"
I want to be more than that, can we just begin, again?

Will you ever forgive me, can you ever forget the past?
Will you get over your resentment, can we move on at last?
I was so young, I wasn't ready back then
But I'm a different person now, can we just begin, again?

I didn't want "confinement," I didn't want your love
I only wanted "excitement," and I couldn't get enough
I yearned for something new, but I'm beyond that now
I'm ready to love you, is that something you'll allow?

Now I want something solid, now I want something real
I want a man for more than just his physical appeal
I want a man who's special, I want a man who's strong
I've searched long and hard for something that I had all along.

We can be more than we've ever been
If you'll look at me and see what you loved back then
The same lips you loved to kiss, the same hands you loved to hold
The same heart you wanted love from, only now it's not so cold.

Nicole Busby

The War

Lord have mercy
Heavenly father hear my prayers.
Dear God don't pass it by, this cross you've delivered I can't bare.

The twisted minds that started this war, They've pillaged and raped.
They've broken homes, killed the innocent.
Casting out small children as if they were stones, leaving them
to wonder lands of war.
Lands once known to man as holy, sacred no more.

Leading men to hell, the closest they'll come.
Their feelings of loneliness, their hunger for home, to hug their
children, to hug their wives.
Their minds twisted and tangled, as their worries mount.
The changes they'll go through, It's insane, you'll see.

Lord have mercy, hear me beg.
Keep our men safe from what lays ahead.
Untouched, Unharmed, return them home.

Lord have Mercy.
Lord have mercy, hear my prayers

Tracy Martindale

I Will Fly

As I sit here and listen to the rain
    fall softly to the ground

The lightening flashes across the sky, not
    even making a sound
I wonder what tomorrow will hold?

With the passing of every day this world grows cold.

I need to take time to stop and think
Life is so short I'd better not blink
If I do life might pass me by

But when my Father above calls me home,
    this command I cannot deny

Although my love ones will feel sorrow and sadness
Will they understand I'll finally find true happiness.

For I will finally be able to soar high
Because I'll get my golden wings and I'll
    forever be able to fly!

Jeannie Moss

Your Smile

If I were the rain I'd fall only at night
and would cool the air as you rest;
My sound on the roof would bring you delight
and with your slumbering smile I'd be blest.

If I were the sky I would always be clear
to brighten your day; as a favor
I would ask the flowers to bloom and add cheer
and your lovely smile I would savor.

If I were the wind I would rustle the leaves
as you enjoyed the zephyr a while;
The fragrance of roses would be on the breeze
and I would bask in your beautiful smile.

If I were a cloud in the sky up above
I would shade you and never get bored;
My lining would be my symbol of love;
your warm smile would be my reward.

But I'm not the rain, nor the sky, nor the wind,
nor the cloud so high up above;
I'm only a man who would die to defend
my right to your smile, my love.

Don Touchton

My Forever Friend

I will remember the times and thoughts that we shared.
I will remember in my heart that we both always cared.
I will remember your look and the grin on your face.
I will remember that no one will ever take your place.
I know you can hear me and see how I feel.
I will remember you always our ideas that were real.
You will not be forgotten by your family and true friends.
You and I knew about the ever changing trends.
I will keep you in my heart and mind where you have always been.
You will always be "My forever friend."

Rene Marie Gailey

What Is It?

Look at that,
the fur as black as night.
See that,
the eyes as red as fire,
the muscles as hard as stone,
and when it runs,
it runs so fast, he's just a blur.

When he goes prowling,
he's as slick as a snake.
You'll never know if he's coming or going,
or if he's here or there,
if he's high or low,
or if he's watching and lurking.

His eye are so alert,
His nose is so keen,
His teeth are so sharp,
His just a wolf.

Karen M. Deitz

Everlasting

Winter, Spring, Summer and Autumn
are the seasons.
Which give us plenty of reasons;
reasons to become as flawless as we can,
and learn from others and our mistakes.
As seasons altogether form years,
one by one they go away,
leading the way to a better day.

Leilah Behrmann

Do Not Weep

Do not weep,
But rejoice
For I'm with thee.
And in your hearts
Do I remain.

Though my body be'st
Six feet deep,
My spirit roameth
Forever free; without boundaries
And limitations.

As I look down
I see your tears,
And I feel your pain.
And now I know that
This is not how it was meant to be.

So dry your eyes and comfort your heart.
Move on with your lives and remember me in part.

For, when once born,
Comes the promises of an end.
Mine has come, Yours, is yet to be.

Chris Harris

"Blind"

You can't prophesy the coming of the angels
Through the knots we tie and the dreams that dangles
You can't foresee the end of the universe
great plains of stars and moons you can traverse
All that lies ahead of the fearful eyes
dragons and monsters and snakes that fly
Reach and touch the heart that burns
Look and see what hates and spurns
Translucent hopes and fading dreams
all that's left of fervent screams
The evil world that floats in space reeking havoc, must replace
Ghostly entities deceiving time master warrior, enemy sublime
Cosmic echoes reflect the message moving forward toward the wreckage.
Time and space conform together smash and slam one another
Temperament voices proclaim wise tales
of deathly voyages and all it entails
Magic wonders come to light enchanting some and to others fright
Go and speak the truth that lies forever spoken in soft replies.

Ross Colomb

Going Riding

The pony is pawing, but the old man is jawing
About all the bills left to pay.
The kitchen smells ripe, there's a leak in one pipe
I guess I'm not riding today.

I've got a good mind just to leave it behind,
And take off on some trail through the hills;
Ride that walker of mine in a motion divine:
It's the way that I still get my thrills.

The wind in our hair in the pure morning air
Is a feeling too little enjoyed.
So busy these days, we survive in a haze
At whatever task we're employed.

The sky's crystal clear, and the hills look so near
And so clean in the still morning air;
I just wish I could leave, get one morning's reprieve,
From the housework and traffic and care.

I'm not sure what to do, and yet one thing is true:
Looking back at the end of the day,
If the horse gets a stretch, I won't feel such a wretch,
So I guess I'll go riding today!

L. A. Yale

222

Love For My Only Hate

I love you, I hate you.
I lust for you presence, despise your attendance.
I am hypnotized by your beauty, horrified by the foulness within.
I desire every moment with you, and yet loath being close to you.
How can all this be?
Is it so that I can love a dangerous enemy?
To think something so wonderful, could feel so horrible.
Such a thing tears my mind apart, confuse my already lost soul,
And destroy my weak heart.
The words you speak I can no longer tell whether they are truth,
or just another lie.
I don't know if I should embrace you, or to push you aside when you cry.
Just thoughts of you bring pain from deep within me.
When you look into me what is it you see?
All this agony has left me, so very confused.
All these damned feelings, do I have to choose?
I would rather take a simple thing such as death.
Do I love, hate, or decide my last breath?
I can't take this anymore! All this pain I have decided; you are
rotten to the core. These emotions finally brings sadness.
For I hate you, my one, and only, true love.

Mario Gutierrez

In Remembrance Of Retha Baldwin Barkley, Our Beautiful Mother

My mother how great you are and were how gentle, loving and giving,
You gave your all and asked nothing in return,
You were the ultimate example of my life you were the most loving
Mother, a daughter could ever dream of having,
You will always remain in my heart and soul,
Mother you will always live through me,
My children and now my grandchildren, when I see them I will see you
In so many different ways every time I do something, I think of you!
I want to do and to live the way you did.
I hope and pray I can be just like you Mother
That I can pass on all these wonderful qualities,
You have given to me, that my daughters will be just like you,
In return, my grandchildren will have
All of your wonderful qualities to pass on to their children
Through them you will "live forever"
In our hearts, our deeds, and our respect for life,
Mother you were absolutely the best example,
Of everything I could ever hope to be.
I love you mother I know you are at peace now, with our Lord Jesus
Christ, God bless you and keep you! Amen.

LaDonna Wilson

As We Commune

Like innocence made naked
and unashamed
we commune through the experiences
that make or bonds sacred
and untamed
Like blues to our feelings of servitude
Like jazz to the moods of our rag-times
Like gospel to the salvation of our souls
and the harmony of our minds
We commune with pure emotion
and unbridled passion
as our intimate bodies conjure
a sensuous rapture
to spirit us away to a secret pasture
where only we could be,
where rivers flow with the tears of a feminine deity
where voices of water streams
run through fields of dreams
singing songs of love with the sun, the moon,
and the celestial illumes as we commune

James E. Dunn

Used To Have A Scene

I was Romeo in black tattoos.
I fixed myself a Raspberry Rush with
ginseng before vanishing from your
aspirations/tears/prospect list.
Frogs in my throat, silly little note.
I promised to regard your wishes
as if they were my own. No more phone.

I swore I would not overstay my welcome.
But I will flutter in some special corner of
your adrenaline. I will be your butterfly,
your grapes of pleasure,
your country haven in the South of France.
Speak to me about how you changed
scenes so effortlessly. Make me aware
of what you truly felt.

We may have shared the fondness
of two souls connecting, but there was
juggling in the Houston exchange.
You made up your mind not to
watch me anymore. Apparently,
friendship gets an occasional iced tea.

Gary Gordon

The Changing Tide

The tide is ever changing,
   As is our lives.
The direction it takes,
   We wonder who will survive.
Death is at hand now,
   Someone special is no longer alive.

Though we mourn his body today,
   His spirit is with us in another way.

Remember all there is
   The good and the bad,
For the memory of Steve,
   Shall no longer make us sad.

But instead we wish him a journey of success,
   And desire for him only the best.

So despite the sorrow and despair,
   Next time the tide changes . . .

Remember Steve will be there.

Jody Sypher

Enchanting Storm

On the mountain
white phosphorescent calla lilies
golden elongated pistils
green stems swaying,
whipped by the moaning pulsations of wind,
a blue black Alpha coyote
appears
We howl in harmony, thankful for the rain
and wind, alive and nourishing,
all beings a washed, renewed —
As the strong, slender Native American man
runs fast downhill
thundering.
The coyote and I cease our howling,
simultaneously looking towards the wild runner,
entangled in his own reality.
Blue black nods, blinking his eyes
as he departs gracefully.
Was he a coyote, a wolf or God in disguise?
I still wonder . . . wander . . .

Kathleen D. O'Toole

Two Feathers

Two feathers together, falling from the sky
They know not where they land or why

Hearts falling over you, only one will stay
Feeling on your skin, like cool ocean spray

Peace and serenity, warms inside
Soul of being, is not as shy

A wild horse, free forever
to be tame, is thought of never

A journey through shadows, not seen before
a belief in self, will open every door

Hot as molten lava, creating distant lands
words are forever silent, howling over desert sands

Tears of the eagle, now part of the sea
Two feathers together, are forever meant to be

Christopher Ablin

Why Me?

Please don't hit me
Don't punch, scratch, or bite
I was put here on earth to love you
Not to be your bag

Everyday you found a different excuse
To hit or pick a fuss
You had me thinking it was my fault
But I later found out it was not

I try and love you in every way I possibly can
But all you do is hit, fuss, and cuss
So why bother
Why bother to apologize when you know it will happen again?

Myra Miles

Untitled

The man on deck has one regret,
To share this time with one he loves,

Cannot be done, this day or next.
Yet, come to port and lose the past.

For there she waits and now will know
The moments spent, the nights so slow.

When one man stands alone on deck,
As the ship plows on, through the waves.

Tons of seas all thrash about
Through mist and stars
All swept away,

To a rendezvous
With yesterday.

Mitch Welsh

Untitled

This rope that binds
denying the riches of the earth to its bankers.

Barn by crimson barn, part of the
communion now,
interweaving the frame work.
Pretty patterns on our structure,
lisping shadows on the hammers we have left.
Fall, gaining hate, on your Chaldean's,
our Zion.

Tuus ingeni acumen violare
cunctus universus.
Your apathy rapes us all.

Caleb Stewart

The Endless Sands Of Time

The endless sands of time passes; we know not where.
For the desert is like a cove of unforgotten memories, of time gone by
Like a bolt of velvet, stretching between two thought of a different
Civilization of time . . .
Of time that man or woman unsuccessfully tries to conquer.

For the sands of time have no end or beginning and grin on and on in
Perpetual silence.

As the tide of time passes we know not where . . .
The sun and the moon shine as but one, and clouds pass like sand dunes
Across the eastern skies. And as we mortals turn from dust to sand and
Are spread to all parts of the world to do good or bad as which we choose,
Or lie in some unforgotten place and grind on and on.

As the darkest part of night turns to dawn,
And birds are on wing, again,
Some friendly willow waves

In a gesture of some unforgotten friends.

John Vernon Selvage

Internal Incarceration

I realize now these unseen walls were built only by me.
I laid each stone and mortared each seam that only few can see.
With bricks of pain and bricks of wrongs, I've constructed
these prison walls.
The fears and doubts and my troubled soul cast shadows in the halls.

The windows I sealed with a broken heart and the burdens that I bore.
Dim light shines through tiny cracks, but there's no longer any door.
Before it vanished, the locking bolt, was a spike that had been in my soul.
There seems to be a relief from the sorrow that pours out from this hole.

I think at times I'll lose my mind and can't carry anymore stones.
And the hurt I feel penetrates the very marrow of my bones.
But I always seem to reach down again and place another block;
Or embed the floor even more with another solid rock.

George R. Patterson

Life Is A Card Game

You've always been someone else's responsibility,
You never did anything wrong.
Anything you wanted was yours,
And everyone else seemed so strong.
Your life was so easy, you were never alone.

Now in the middle you are lost in confusion,
You must pick between responsibility and fun.
Being left to do your own thing is always tough,
But just think about how it will help you later on.
Your life is confusing, you are stuck in the middle.

Now as you get older, you are always by yourself,
People expect more of you and make you work harder.
You are in charge of yourself and must manage your time,
Never be late or you will pay the fine.
Your life is much harder, you are all by yourself.

Kari Rood

My Greatest Treasure

You lead me by the hand
And took me to your promise land
You showed me new way of giving
And the best way of living
Your love opened my heart's door
And made me feel like never before
You're my greatest treasure made of love
Truly a gift from the heavens above
And I want you to be my beautiful wife
Because your spirit is the key to my life.

Brad David Buckley

Where You And I Used To Play

In the front yard where you and I used to play
With smiles on our faces that would brighten up any ones day

Water balloons in our hands ready to attack
Then out of no where you aim, and nail me in the back

The sun went down and we were through for the day
In the front yard where you and I use to play

In the bedrooms so cheerful and happy,
Feeling as if we could stay here forever,
But knowing we could never

Tears full of laughter, tears full of joy
Just thinking of a new cute boy

So happy you could hear our laughter from a mile away
In the bedroom where you and I use to play

In the back yard we'd play a few games
Sometimes get mad and call each other names

But through everything we still remained best friends,
And best friends we will stay
In the now empty house where you and I used to play.

Rikki VanderMeer

How Can You Leave Me

How can you leave me? When things
are down, then you come around when
things are good and sound.
How can you leave me and make my
heart so blue. Why are you so slue?
You say you love me, but you knew that
you wouldn't be true. Now what am I
suppose to do? When you're going around with
someone new. Now you're coming back and
you're so true
But you know you'll be gone as soon as
you're through.
A heart can only take so much of you
running here and there like the air.
But one day you'll think and come and
say I'm here to stay.
But I'll be going my own way.
You'll think that's not so fair.
I'll be leaving you in the air.
And you'll say. How can you leave me?

Michele Johnson

Share With Me

Share with me, your hopes, your dreams, and everything
tell me what the future brings, for us
as we grow old my friend.

Take from me, the strength you need to hold onto
I hope that what I have will do
sometimes I am weak myself.

Give to me, nothing but your promise and a smile
let me know that this love we have is worthwhile
and not in vain.

Walk with me, speak of times and days to come
let the joy go on, and on, and on
and never fade.

Hold me, and don't never ever let me go
I need you more than you could ever know
though I may not say.

Share with me, your love, your life, and everything
I'm happy with the way life's been
and may it always — stay this way.

Russell E. Douglas

A Quiet Journey

My journey begins in the heavens
Gravity and Wind are my guides
I only travel at certain times in certain areas

My journey begins in the heavens
I travel with thousands upon's thousands of my friends
    no two are alike
And when I reach my destination — the Earth
    I blanket the countryside

My journey begins in the heavens
I bring with me many gifts — beauty, tranquility, fun, grief
I get thrown; I get pushed; I get brushed

My journey begins in the heavens
Heat is my enemy, and always returns me home
But do not despair
For I make my journey again
I am a snowflake

Steven J. Coladonato

A Man, The Sea

To awaken to sounds of the sea, to be a part of the
morning sun breaking silently over the water. Calm, quiet, peace
filled stillness broken only by a wayward gull, away, distanced.
Let yourself be taken by the sea's loving spirit, her silent grace.
    She has accepted you, protected and watched over you.
Even when the sky darkens, winds blow and swells grow. You
have shared in all her magnificent intensity and she knows you
respect her power. She welcomes you as a part.
    The freedom that comes stepping off the shore, the yearning
of wanting to see more. More twilight skies, more moonlit distant
shores. To leave behind, the busy mind, the troubled world . . .
the ties that bind.
    A wish for thee each day, each night. May your every
breath and step be light, and all the breezes flow, just right.
So your soul is at ease by night.
    She loves you, this majestic entity,
And delights in your soul being free.
Oh how I wish it could be me . . .
Too sleep embraced by the sea, the sea.

Cindy Lee Richards

A Travelled Road

On a road I traveled uphill one day
    and stumbled and fell and lost my way

Dirty and crumpled I struggled along
    again and again till day had gone

At times I felt a presence there
    but I'd look around and just see air

And I'd come upon a place to rest
    these were the times I treasured best

The road grew narrow
    the path unclear

I trembled and fought
    the end was near!

"Dear God" I prayed
    "Help me" I cried

"This road is too difficult as much as I try"

And then a light from the clouds above I heard a Whisper filled
with love

"Your time is near — you've traveled far the road is closed ahead"

"And through it all I was there in good times and in strife"

"You see, my Child, the road we travelled is what is known as life"

Colleen Finfrock

Discontinuity

I ramble along with my pen in my hand
As I try to find something to say.
Whatever I write will most surely be panned;
But I'm jotting it down anyway.

You don't know the problem of trying to rhyme
All the thoughts that are swimming my head.
They come and they go whether bad or sublime,
While at work or at play or in bed.

I remember the hell of being a teen
And I even remember my birth.
My mind is a sponge of all things I have seen
In my forty three years on this earth.

Remembering it all so vivid and clear
Is the easiest thing I can do.
I can vocalize people, places and things;
But to scribe it, I haven't a clue.

I've naught the dilemma of being tight lipped
As I talk on and on to absurd.
So why do I have such problem with script.
That I can't jot down nary a word?

Rod Fruitt

Once Upon A Time . . .

My love is true
So are my thoughts of you
Not a day goes by
When I sit and wonder why?
What could I say or do
To prove that there was no dispute.
Of the simple fact that
The love you gave you received right back.
Not only did I love you I also cared
An adventure of love and life dared.
So common a love that we shared
A heart full of love could've been spared.
Now I live a life so solemn recollection
Only wanting to show my true affections!
No more sorrows of days gone by
No more tears I shall cry.
I will be a slave of the heart
Until the day we are one and not apart.

Robert A. Evans Jr.

Mask of Stone

When you see my face, do you look beyond my skin?
Or do you judge me by my lifestyle and what I do believe in?
When you look inside my heart, do you see someone afraid to die
or be alone?
I sit here in my world of hate, behind this mask of stone.

When you look into my eyes, do you perceive love or hate?
Either way it goes my friend, I am sure you can relate.
I cannot explain what I feel right now. It is better left unknown.
So I sit alone in silence behind this mask of stone.

In this world that is so insane,
There is nothing but heartbreak, sadness and pain.
It is far more sad to see everything around me dying.
In this world full of pain I sit alone.
And still behind this mask of stone.

You ask me why I speak of nothing but pain and love,
I simply answer because this is what my life is made of.
This hell with no heaven is all I've known.
So I stay behind this mask of stone.

May I ask you, when you see my face, do you look beyond my skin?

Laura Jo Emry

Untitled

I've loved you for many years now, a feeling that's deepened and grown
It takes on a new dimension, finds corridors in past unknown.
We've come to see each other through eyes that love does shade.
We've explored each other uniqueness, found delight in discoveries made.

Intimacy heightened by tenderness, pleasure presented as gift.
We've learned from one another the joy that love does lift.
We've struggled with room for growing, needed time for being alone.
Turned attention away from each other in an effort to search for one.

Disappointment met sometimes singly and triumph that way too.
We've grown as separate people taking directions constantly new.
We've turned to find each other and hoped that we'd be found.
Not always were "we" waiting, self being elsewhere bound.

We've suffered through isolation refused comfort without heed.
We've need one another and been frightened by the need.
We've needed to be needed and clamored for some help.
We've suffered too much togetherness and retreated back to self.

Love knows these many pathways, it follows and it leads.
It takes in stride the heart ache, it's strengthened by our needs.
Love seeks no stunting boundaries, it's not contained by just "the two."
Love encompasses separate growings, and in growth finds life anew.

Melanie Taylor

Sneak Away

Step softly away
lest I hear you leave
and on my knees fall, fog in my eyes.
In vain saying words
describing deep love,
meanwhile knowing its source will soon leave me.

Make darkness your cloak
so I do not see
you fade off as the sun at sunset.
And in dusk's shadow
an unrest'd heart waits
forever for the dawn of your return.

My hand do not hold
lest I feel your touch
and reach out my arms to embrace you.
And in our love clutch,
just as I feared,
incapable I am to release you.

So please stay the pain inevitable.
Kindly sneak away.

David Campbell

Foxie

If I live to be a hundred
Foxie, I will never forget
Just an old man from the past
But I remember him yet
He'd skip and he'd holler
And he'd dance all around
Some thought he was crazy
To me he was just a clown
His eyes were clear as crystal
And as blue as the sky
Many a day he would put his arm around me
And walk by my side
He would pass a few words of encouragement
And then be on his way
I don't know where, or how Foxie is
Or even if he has passed away
But he whispers in the wind
You'll be a "movie star" . . . someday!

Brenda Kay Gordon

A Confession

Kind words ring sweet are soft received,
how else would they be heard thus shaded?
But there is all love found deceived
and with no truth, such falsehood's jaded.

True words do gain their love all pleasures
that this brash kindness will entreat
but harshly, falsely truth-hood measures
what sincere ness would find meet.

For lips do lie what e'er they muster,
though with kind love and virtue moved.
Discourses incorrectly bluster
and are in true love nothing proved.

But thy gray eyes do fill my heart
and prove me true love's truest part.

Adam Cheney

God You And Me

See the flowers, grass and trees.
See the river, lakes and seas.
See the deer, birds and bees.
See the sky, clouds and galaxy.
See the people, friends and family.
All made by God for you and me.

See the stripped land and burned out trees.
See the oil, cans and other floating debris.
See our wildlife, condemned so carefree.
See our lust, greed and enemies.
See the atomic age, missiles and artillery.
Our thanks to God from you and me.

Joseph Thomas Jr.

Sandman's Dream

E vening held me in its warm embrace
V ery gently, cautiously imprinting that pretty face,
E yes, my eyes, fell prey to the well known "Sandman"
L eading me to sleep, to dream, and remember all I can,
Y et, I knew, if what I felt was blessed from above
N othing would deny me what I knew was love,
G etting an understanding of this new found feeling
R acing straight ahead, giving all, I was willing,
E ventually time would pass — I guess a decade or so
E nabling me to ponder two words: Yes and No,
N ever doubting myself or the growing need inside
M y only prayer was, "Please let her be my Bride,"
Y ear-in, Year out, I sang: "I Love You"
W ords are sweet, she said to me: "I Love You Too!"
I n 1987, we married — we became a Team
F or what it's worth, from our birth
E ssentially, we became the "Sandman's Dream."

Marvin Green

On Wings of Faith

Away I soar into the vast moonlight
Never looking back, never looking back.
The heights my desire, the goal of my flight
In search of my own, in search of my pack.
Where do I belong, I do not yet know
But faith I do have that all will be well.
How high need I fly, how far need I roam,
How deep need I question, my God can tell.
The end not the goal, no longer earth-bound
I long for the truth whatever its cost.
There're lessons to learn, there's joy to be found
In pain there lies peace, accepting what's lost.
The Lord ever leading, I'll touch the stars
Onward He takes me, no matter how far.

Diana K. Schramer

Wind, The Breath Of The Creator

The wind moves over the hills, down the valleys
caressing all it touches.

Waiting for the gentle stroke, the grasses almost purr
Dancing leaves giggle as if a secret lover were near.

Encompassing the birds in flight and animals in fields and woods,
The wind sustains all.

The clothes on the line become puppets in the wind
waiting to begin their ballet

Wind circles the houses, trying to enter and hear their secrets.

Clouds hover over the land waiting for the wind to transport
them around the world.

Wind, the breath of the creator.

Gloria Dudash Brown

Space Discovery

The universe, the space, mysteriously, immensely
Today science conquered the moon
Three astronauts landed on the moon
Achieved advance mission for history.

Astronauts team's joy, merrily, happily.
The voyage of discovery journey in the ardent mood

Moon country has something to see!
Dried, scraggy soil and quietly

No living creature, what a cheerless panorama!

Neither beautiful forest, mountains nor green grass.
Neither oil well, nor ore as wishing words.
Moonlight night, would have thought sparkling diamond,

In the dark, as chilly as winter night.
Hurry back with voyage luggage's
In keeping trophies in museum
From generation to another to see

Entire construction work, expected for centuries.
Till today dream came true
Several astronauts were longing for it.
Still lust for to another planet flight.

F. Toson-Nguyen

My Ring

Adorning just one finger upon my wrinkled hand
  sets the only piece of jewelry I could ever really stand.

Solid silver through and through or so I have been told
  prevents the shiny surface from ever getting old.

When I gaze upon this shining love stirs from deep within
  lifting up my spirits to heights they've never been.

Life takes a different meaning as I start to count the days
  as what I once saw clearly has taken on a haze.

Images of love undying stay fresh within my mind
  kept in focus by my ring as youth is left behind.

Growing old with someone you love with all your soul
  is all that's necessary to reach that final goal.

Heaven holds a special place for angels like my wife
  who dedicates her every breath to beautifying life.

Destiny, no, God himself, brought Thespina to me
  and with this ring my love is bound for all the world to see.

When time comes to leave this earth, my body laid to rest,
  upon my withered finger my ring resounds the best.

As I appear at heaven's gate, the keeper may ask why.
  I'll simply lift my hand and say, "Could this ring ever lie?"

E. H. Holliger

Peace

It's time to break open the gates
   that hold us to our hate
Let out our rage
   and come out of our cage
Forget what they say about color and race
   because in this world we are all at the same pace
We need peace to bring us together
   understanding hearts that will put up a fight
Family and friends cry as their loved ones die
Oh God I pray for you to open their eyes
   change their ways and come out of their lies
For our little one that will be grown ups one day
In all this hate and sorrow I hope they won't have to live there
life's this way

   Debra Thacker

Who Made It

Who made the oceans
Who made the seas
It wasn't man and it wasn't me.

For I do not know how to gather the land.
And whole the earth with in my hand.

Who made the ski, so high up above
Who made it possible for everyone to love
It wasn't me and it wasn't man, because
Love is something he'll never understand

This is his earth, this is his land
We are his creatures, and he gives
the command. He is the greatest,
and will always be, because

He is God, and that's not you,
and that's not me.

   Lillie Gregg

In Memory Of President Kennedy

Sad and sudden on a cold November day
A call came from heaven to take our leader away
Sad and sudden was the call
For a leader loved by all

Come up higher said the Savior
On that cold November day
Come up here where there's no sorrow
Come up, up this way

Do not ask if we miss him
For there is such a vacant place
Oft we long to hear his speeches
And to see his smiling face

We must not say that he is dead
For he is just away
We must not say that he is gone
For we will meet someday

   Dorothy E. Pickens

I Can't Stop This Feeling

   I can't stop this feeling, this emptiness I feel,
God called my dad home, it still doesn't seem real.
   My dad is gone, he's been set free, there's such an
emptiness inside of me.
   The Lord took him around 10:00 one night, that's
when he left on his heavenly flight,
   To be with the angels, to watch and keep us from
harm, till someday we're with him in his heavenly arms.
   If heaven has angels that watch over me, I hope it's
My dad, cause he'll take care of me.

   Janet Huskisson

I Am Free

I am free, do not worry
I know you cry and weep for me
Don't for I have gone to a place I have dreamed of
My garden says it all
I chose the path I took
I saw the light and God himself called me
I took his hand and left the world behind
I didn't expect
For this I know
It was awkward for all of you
I am sorry, but I took the path and left
Now I am free.

   Jennifer Susannah Gee Lopez

Dream's End

The river winds
To worlds hidden —
Dark caverns
Where men slump
Over tiny pools
And women holding melons
Pass between rooms,
And everyone whispers . . .
Like the cooing over rocks,
Turbid, deep
And winding
Farther, farther,
Where people go when they're at the end
With two rounds left and no more money to spend
At the bar stool,
With one leg shorter
Standing on two quarters to balance
Almost.

   Mollie Murphy

the exchange

the old man in the dungarees who whispered he was

a father to the golem on the gurney draped in my
skin leaned close — so close i remembered by
his smell handing wrenches beneath a certain faded mercury

in the melted middle of july while gregg allman talked
to sweet melissa in the radio and

all i ever wanted to be was a guy who climbed poles to fix wires.

the old man in an attempt to make me
blink said he never meant to yell so much, to hit

so much, but of course i would have blinked anyway
and the tears on the pillow said as much, the old
man seemed very gray. we held hands, smelled ten years

of dirty oil together, and the fact of his grip ever after said so much.

   B. W. Carter

Dear Chris

I can't express how bad I feel
Seeing you lay there was just unreal
I miss you more than I can say
I wish you were here for just one more day

I say to myself that it's not true
But then I find myself crying over you
My heart is like one empty hole
But I know in Heaven is where I'll find your soul

Someday, someday very soon
I'll be rejoicing in heaven right beside you
But until I see your smiling face
In my heart you'll have your very own place

   Nola Hill

Heaven Will Be More

The beauty of sunshine in the clear blue sky
The colors of flowers that catch our eye
The highest mountain, the oceans to the shore
All of this splendor — can Heaven be more?

The snow of winter, the rain in spring
The green grass of summer, the leaves fall brings.
The tiny blue bird and the eagle that soars
All wonders of earth — can Heaven be more?

The tiny child all wrinkled and new
The man and woman whose love is true.
The grandma and grandpa at retirements door
All sizes and ages — can Heaven be more?

Street paved of gold and robes of white
No more sorrow, no more night.
Angels sing praises, we'll live ever more
At home with our Father — Heaven will be more!

Linda Coldiron

My Angel In Heaven

The no. 1, angel in my life is now sleeping peacefully
But he will always be down deep imbedded in my soul.
He was the smartest angel always so lovingly
And it hurts so much to feel him, so very far from me.
How do you keep from dreaming the one who cannot be
forever here beside me always smiling lovingly
Some day I will be near him and God will grant me
To hold him close to me and never let him be
So very very far from me.
My no. 1, grandson
Who God made so lovable
be waiting for me in heaven
When I will be sleeping peacefully.

James F. Lorence Jr.

Wedding Memories

This is the day one year ago now, that we became as one and
pledged our solemn vow
To stay together no matter the reason, to grow closer throughout every season
To mature as we grow, and to improve the quality of the things
we already know
To be strong and weather every fight, and do whatever it takes
to always make it right
To remember all the feelings we had on our special day, and try
to recreate them each in a special way
To not only live in the past but tomorrow and the day after, to
share in tears, anger and laughter
Marriage means two, a team to work together as one, and then
life's problems will seem as none
If you truly love someone then there's not much more to say,
you just know it each morning, night and day!

Sharon D. Eppihimer

It's Me

I have a dance I like to do
I am so different from all of you
I think my steps are very fun
But they can't be learned by just anyone
I dance alone and alone I be
But that's the only way that I feel free
If I lose the beat or fall
I don't scream or cry or bawl
I get up and check to see
If I can handle what's happened to me
In times of pain I smile easily
I can't help it, I'm just me.

Angela K. Geyman

Christmas Season

Christmas day is coming soon, and everything seems swell.
The house is all lit up so
nice and the tree is decorated well.

The Christmas songs are playing
loud, and the mistletoe is hung
high, it will only be a couple
of more days until we get
to eat that yummy christmas pie.

Wrapping presents and sending
cards, is all so very fun, we
can all sit back and relax,
after we get that christmas shopping done.

Sleigh bells are ringing loud.
Listen! Can you hear it? Every
one around is happy and in the
Christmas spirit.

We will all spend christmas
day, with the ones we love.
And we shall all have a
merry day as the angel sing from above.

Heidi Lewis

Wanderer

Wanderer, sweet, like the sweetest thing.
More sorrowful eyes I had never seen.
She was wet from the rain . . . or was it her tears
That fell from her face . . . that summoned me here?
Wanderer, sweet, like a sweet refrain.
She lied with a smile to hide her pain;
And I knew in an instant I was taken in
By her childlike sadness that seized me within.
She spoke, I listened, of her dreams deferred;
But to speak of hope she hadn't a word,
Except to say "it's for you, not me.
I'll not afford such a luxury."
Her future, it seemed, was four blocks square.
And I, of her past, am unaware
Save the knowledge of her grievous pain;
Tho' unspoken I knew it the same.
I wonder today of my wandering one.
Have you warmth? Have you love? Have you none?
Do you know I still search for you out in the rain?
Do you know in my heart you remain?

Daniel L. Nichols

Untitled

Suicide, you are not a solution
You are more like a cop out
Wake up — this isn't me!
Where are these thoughts even coming from?

Suicide, am I going crazy?
Why are you following me?
Why are you catching up to me?
Why are you looking me in the eyes?

Suicide, why do you want me?
Why do you want to be a part of my . . ., an end to my life?
How dare you get close to me!
Get out of my space.

Suicide, I've seen you try to work in others.
You are evil, you only know harm
Stay away from me, you are not invited.

Suicide, you are so manipulative.
Thriving off of vulnerability, looking good at times.
But deep inside I know you are not a solution
But a permanent escape from reality.

A. M. Cavallo

True Love

True love is so hard to find,
But, I know, that our love is the kind
that will never grow old,
no matter how the story's told.

I've never felt this way,
but, now today, I can gladly say . . .
I've fallen in love with you,
and I can assure you my love is true.

I think about you night and day,
'cause from my mind you'll never stray.
I can't stop thinking about,
the way you seem to wash away my doubts.

In you, I've found everything I've ever dreamed of.
When I'm with you, life doesn't seem at all so tough.

You wrap me in your arms,
and automatically, I'm overwhelmed by your charms.
You're my every dream come true, and I love you!

Lisa Marie Nila

Sunrise By The Bay

Darkness lies against the hill, silver streams touch waters still;
Sea gulls squawk as they fly by, silhouettes against the sky,
Egret stalks, with bill so bent, on his breakfast, eyes intent;
Swallows swoop, dart here and there, to and fro without a care.

Seaweed strewn from tide before, oyster leases by the score;
Periwinkle, black sea snail leaves behind a slender trail.
Puffs of grey float, touched with pink. Has man ceased to sit and think?
Soft orange blaze, than light so bright, finally dispels the night.

Sun comes out, man is about to enjoy his day, no doubt,
Shattering in motor boat scenes that shroud like overcoat;
Reviving motors spew their fumes — stark contrast with nature's tunes.
See, a touch of blue comes through, boy with dog completes the view.

Grace V. Knight

The Far-Off Barking Of Dogs

They chased me here. Through the Night Forest,
The rotting vegetation, the wormwood of fallen trees,
The wetness that stunk like a corpse, bleached
Green leaves white.
A spider the size of a dinner plate, barnacled
In red and white parasitic fungus digesting it,
Plunked down from the trees
While I fled. It was devoured before
My eyes.
Now the Moon like a ringed bag of pale bone
Illuminates the falls of the Hushed River.
A ribbon of silently screaming milk-white faces that twists,
Splits itself on the forehead of rock which stands
Above the falls.
A young deer, startled, listening, turns in the sand
Behind me, sprints over the dunes. Panting, frozen,
In a turmoil of fear, I am trapped between deafening silence,
Or the far-off barking of dogs.

Philip G. Banning

Untitled 2

One summer day the soil was dry,
Then all of a sudden the clouds started to cry!
The earth opened its eyes,
To the heavens and the beautiful skies,
And the field of flowers woke up too,
To a world so beautiful and new!
When the blooming flowers opened their eyes,
They surprisingly asked: "Isn't this paradise?"

Beatrix Kaldor

The Grim One

The Grim One stood beside the road,
And grinned in pleasure through the mist.
As with one fleshless finger crooked,
He watched the weaving lights that pushed
The night aside, but could not see
The sudden curve.
Too late the speeding wheels swung left.
And tortured tires ripped the berm,
Then lunged across the road to veer again.
And graze the railing of a hidden bridge.
The Grim One, motionless but grinning still
Watched lights receding in the murky night.
He shrugged and turned away with silent tread.
"Some other time will do as well," he said.

Ken Sears

Our Twenty Years

To my dearest wife,
and only Love of my life
I am sorry for all your tears,
Even though I am going to be here twenty years
once I'll go home to you I'll conquer all your arms.
I might be here in this cell all alone,
But because of your love and letters,
I always feel better and strong.
I know because of me you are suffering too,
But once we get together again,
I will show you love like you never knew.
I pray for our daughter and every night,
Because I love you both with all of my night.
I am loving you so much with love you could bet.
I wish that about me you'll never forget.
Twenty words are not enough to express my love for you,
twenty years from now you know . . .
I'll still be in love with you.

Enrique Aragon

Winter

Icy cold chilly feeling
In my toe's and on my nose
Hair as frozen as dinner rolls.

Cat's frozen in the alley, Chicken warming in my belly
Finally winter is over as can see,
Spring time is blossoming.

Jennifer Ortega

Pondering

Our lives are like the Dakota Seasons
Family and friends can come and go without reason
Why do we break each others hearts like glass
With time and hope and this too will pass
We are like our pioneer fathers before us
We do our work and about the weather do fuss
Days and seasons go like fallen leaves in a wind
Our daily habits are like a pattern that has been pinned
All ready to put together and try
If we do everything right we don't cry
Staying on the right course of life

Will not cause any tears and strife
Our babies may grow and go

But they forever have our love they know
Through the years our partners are like a hand and a glove
We conform and protect and still have love
The rains cover our faces like tears
Snow can cover all but hurt and fears
Secrets and dreams sleep on
Will they come awake with a yawn?

Crystal Hanna

Just My Dream

One night I was walking, a stranger I did meet,
With ragged jeans, a flannel shirt, and nothing on his feet.

He was sitting on a park bench, staring out into space,
I wonder what he's thinking, with that expression upon his face.

"Hello Mister" I said to the man, and gazed into his eyes.
The sunken lines of blue clear dreams, has left this man behind.

Without a word spoken, he pointed to the sky.
The ocean of stars overwhelmed in blue,
The color of dreams I saw in his eyes.

"I'm a captive to the systems game," he said,
"Prisoner in this world of free,"
"You've got to have a number," "Or system says You just can't be."

"They work you in the morning," "Till the day is done and gone,"
"And what do I have to show for . . ."
"Nothing — Just my dream lives on!"

Tina Gates

Much More

With me from the very start
You cradled me in your loving arms.
A sweet caress or gentle touch
Could dry my tears and hush my cries.
You nurtured me through both good and bad;
And with each new day, I look above
And give all thanks for your endless love.
Together we face our uncertain future.
Although scared, we are never alone.
Through scornful fights and bitter resentment
I love you more each day.
For you are so much more than my mother,
You are my unfailing best friend.

Catherine Ann Randolph

Messenger

The son of God will not be coming today,
although his mighty words we must obey.
Words of the good book says he's coming soon,
could it be tomorrow? Or maybe today at noon.

If he should appear well let's just say,
would you be ready come judgment day?
Oh the time grows near my loving sheep,
tears from eyes of those who weep.

Our father holy words are all we need,
for eternal life we shall succeed.
You must love thy neighbor and be true to all,
if you feel the passion heed his call.

We are messenger sent through out the land,
backed by angels and God's right hand.
For we must live we will say to his sheep,
there are souls to be saved, no time for sleep.

Richard Allen Libby

Puzzle Of Poetry

Captivation is the picture on the box
Desire opens the vessel of mind
Will pours the pieces (words, phrases, lines)
Knowledge and contemplation turn and sort them
Order from chaos begins
Piece matched to piece — only one possibility
Obsession holds the view till the puzzle is complete
Inspiration the process
The puzzle the poem

Trisa Baltgalvis-Lindsay

Through Thorns To Roses

Sometimes the path of love,
Has thorns in the way;
At times these thorns cut you,
Leaving you hurt, with nothing to say.
As you stand there wondering,
The tears begin to fall;
Did you choose the wrong path?
Did you cause this all?
As you ponder the answers,
Your tears fall and soak the ground;
Then suddenly, the answer is before you,
A rose so beautiful and perfectly round.
If it wasn't for the thorns,
You would have never cried the tears;
The tears that have brought,
So many roses through the years.
Now you understand,
That thorns will always be there for you and me;
But if you are strong enough,
A beautiful rose you will see.

Rebecca Combs

Weeping Willow

Years of gale force winds, and
many driving rains
    Snow piled up to her limbs, yet
stoically she remains
    A support for the many around
her, while she blends into the crowd
    Doing nothing at all to be noticed, but
her silence screams aloud
    The weeping willow tree, so careful
to hide her fears
    Never unleashing her sorrow, and never
unleashing her tears.
    They think her such a strong one but
Lord, if they only knew
    That the weeping willow tree,
underneath is lonely and blue
    Would they still respect her
and love her just the same
    Or would they shy away,
thinking only of how she'd changed

Sarah Minnick

America

America the strong
America the weak
America the overbearing
America the meek

America the understanding
America the vengeful
America the saint
America the sinful

America the rich
America the poor
America the pimp America the whore

America the caring America the cold
America the reserved America the bold

America the scared American the cool
America the wise America the fool

America the manipulator America the pawn
America the wolf America the fawn

Land of the free home of the brave
A nation in turmoil can it be saved?

Christopher M. Kennedy

There Is Hope

Dark, depressing clouds cover the sky
All the wetness amid the ground
A burst of color, stretching far and wide

Nine months of trial and pain
Will it ever end?
The faint smile and giggle of a newborn

All the fights and disagreements
Cruel words, not able to be taken back
But forgotten by two other words, "I do"

The pure white blanket hugging the ground
Icicles align in formation
The first chirping robin signaling its return

There is hope
Katie Sternberg

Showdown

He steps cautiously through my life as if a cat
Looking for prey in the dark
He steps cautiously on the branches
Surveying his prey
Unrelentingly as he goes, carefully treading
Carefully looking into eyes that wonder
He looks and searches along the way
Eye to eye, knowing a lie
Knowing that in his sights comes easy prey
And there, with one shot, meets his mark
All is blown away . . .
Sheila E. Mathon

One For The Highlights

The ball discharges from the chief's retain,
with fluent velocity towards the plate.
The ball is struck onto the stable terrain,
with rapid hail speed it looked like a date.
The shortstop shifted fleetfully to his right,
with outstretched arms across the infield line.
Then swiftly dove to it composed in spite,
he sprang to an abrupt controlled incline.
With graceful hands he flipped the ball to Chip,
who caught it, leaped, well throwing a dart to first.
The awestruck crowd awaits the umpires quip,
then silence broke, pandemonium burst.
With joyous admiration the crowd cried Ozzie,
someday I pray that shortstop will be me.
Marty Griffith

Storms Of Love

Love is something that comes and goes
Often like the winter snow.
Love may be as red as the reddest rose
It may be as warm
As ones toes
Love will come someday to stay
If that is your desire,
If it will please you that way
Love is filled with lots of pride and joy
Like a baby girl or boy or even perhaps a new toy
Love is something that comes and goes
Just like the cold wind that can blow
Love can bring lots of thrills it can
Also bring on those bills
Love if filled with times of sorrow sometimes
Ones wish is that there's no tomorrow
That is the way love goes even through the
Sun, rain, sleet and snow
Brianne E. Dani

Papa

I remember Papa.
With his old bib overalls and big black lunch box.

I would say "Is it time for Papa?"
Then I would go watch for Papa's old pickup truck
to come rolling through the gate.

My Papa always smelled of sawdust.
He always had a hammer hanging from a loop in his overalls.
And you could always hear the jingle jangle of nails in his pockets.

I would always say: "Hey Papa, got anything left in your lunch box?"
He always seemed to have a Debbie-Cake that he was too full to eat.

My Papa made lots of great things for me down in his barn.
Sometimes Papa would let me make things too.
Papa would look and say "Well now . . . that is something."

When he would go upstairs too "wash up"
he would splash on his Old Spice,
put on his "Papa" shoes: (Old brown slippers)
and ride me down the stairs on his shoulders.

My Papa was the best to me.
When I was a little girl I loved him so very much.
Years later he is still the best to me and I love him even more.
Wendy V. Tippens

Just A Shell

They say our body is just a shell,
The flesh we see and touch and smell.
The bodies of the ones we love so much,
Are gifts from God, and more, like such.

The precious force within our hearts,
Is truly the most important part.
For it's the force that transfers on,
To give still more when our shell is gone.

It transfers to the ones left living,
Stays in their hearts and just keep giving.
The memories of the good times past,
The love we shared will always last.

So when our loved one passes on,
The lesson is they are not gone.
We only lay their shell to rest,
Their force keeps living in "Their Best."
Lucinda Hart

The Conquest Of Hunger

O Nations, Nations unite with emotion
Save the millions of hungry generation
Show heart full of compassion
Upon every child with veneration.

'Die in hunger,' O what a sin and shame
Greater sin than any other one
Every nation should know how to get fame
By providing food and shelter to everyone.

Continue the war on hunger
Attention, march, modernize agriculture
Stimulate industry, Produce fertilizer
Stabilize population, Accelerate human culture.

A great strategy for alleviation
Of world hunger — Love and Peace
Must work successfully in every nation
Bring out the divinity in human race.

The world is a family of ourselves
Work with persistence to avoid danger
"Love thy neighbor as thyself"
The secret of the Conquest Of Hunger.
Jacob R. Godi

Through The Night

As I place my head gently on my pillow
I pray my Lord my soul to keep
and that is when my eyes close tightly
and I begin to Dream

What I see

Soft lilies in a field of green
My toes are in the grass
The sky a crystal spectrum
and there, salvation at last

No one shows a face
Yet, a presence still exists
and no one holds a judgment
Yes, Innocence is bliss

Here is childhood perfection, held by those most high
and though I Dream, I am at ease
For all of this is mine

Then awakened by a chiming clock
My vision here does fade,
and now I pay my Lord my gratitude
For the Dream and world he made

Allison M. Burns

Life's Lonely Road

I traveled down life's lonely road
With all its crooks and bends
Adversity had shown me
It never seemed to end.

I cried aloud to God on High
"I know that you are there.
Please lead me to a better place.
Relieve my deep despair."

Then in a moment came a ray
Of sunshine from above.
I heard a knock at my heart's door.
I felt the warmth of love.

It was a time when destiny
Reached out and took me in,
Revealing feelings never known . . .
A new life to begin.

And now I know it wasn't God who didn't care for me
He put the pieces into place which now I clearly see.

He led me to a promised land of love I never knew.
The day, the Hope of life fulfilled . . . the life I'll spend with you.

Don Edwards

Dedicated To Love

Set in a state of the love test, suffering is distinctively featured best.
Your peace is held, thoughts are fully swelled
because you're **dedicated to love**.

Deep within the aching heart are vibrant beats to sustain its parts.
Peace is wrapped in gales, confusion attempts to prevail,
as you're **dedicated to love**.

Doubt increase with time, grasping faith to focus the mind.
Temptation is eluded, despair continually disputed
when you're **dedicated to love**.

The hollowed will of what's right, is the single coping light.
Incased in a vault of involvement, reaching up is the resolvement,
knowing you're **dedicated to love**.

Because the stench of wrong is imposed, what's right now unfolds.
The difficulty of pain and distress is commonly what's known best
but forbearing, because you're **dedicated to love**.

Marcia R. Carter

Remembering The Past, Observing The Present

The children are playing, trying to behave, all along falling
for the imp and his way. Deceitful and cheating, lying for games,
keeping the truth hidden, out of your way. Like a bully who steals,
they snatch you away, leaving you dead, of passion and play.

You've got to learn the rules, in order to play, but you can't
figure it out, and home you will stay. Luxurious slaves, the way
you get paid, a pat on the back, a nickel to save. "Benefits and
protection, for you," they say. Homeless and broke, tax sure pays.

"Got to learn a trade, advance our ways, so I can live longer,
when dead I'll stay. No time to love, play is lame, I've got an
important meeting that can bring me pay."

Rolling in a chair, playing on the net, thinking how nice it
would be to leave this desk. I need some love, I'll try the phone
book, but Mom's talking to Dad, making plans for divorce. My
parents I love, I need them a lot, but things are not what they
were, decades before. I want a mission, a passion for life, I need
to sow and reap my garden, my life. I miss best friends, the
laughs we shared, the time we spent, will last forever.

Kevin Crane

Night Scene

Its suppressing sleek black coat
Shines in the moonlight.
His lurch lubricated the wild.
Back arched, body poised
And exuding confidence,
He leaps high and lands elegantly.
It gambols at the ground glaring foolishly.
Only to slip away
As quietly as the night.

Christina E. Castleberry

Humans Cry

Humans cry, day by day, then express their feelings a different way.
All the pain locked inside, trying to find a way to cry
    without saying goodbye.
Friends and family, from coast to coast, please tell me which you
love the most.
I hold my feelings in, it's not a sin, where you've come from
    and where you've been.
My life is empty without your love; you were always beautiful
    like a soft white dove.
Humans cry, your hair blows in the wind; your smile, eyes, and face
    are all the emotions that you send.
Your family and friends — we miss you so; we will always have
thoughts of you though.
Humans cry, and you are at rest. All I can do is wish you the best.

Brad Arndt

Your Love Is Killing Me!

You're the cholesterol in my veins,
you're the acid in my rain,
and you have paranoid my brain
your love is killing me.
You're the wrinkles in my skin,
You're my hunger's never end,
You're my double double chin,
your love is killing me.
You're my sinus constant drip,
the fever blister on my lip,
you're my code without a zip,
Your love is killing me.
When you're near my hormones seem to splatter,
and I can feel some pressure on my bladder,
Then my heart knows what the hecks the matter,
I love your love that's killing me.

Charlotte Royal Moskowitz

As A Story Told

Limply it hung on the kitchen door
Its buttons dull its pockets tore
The cuffs were frayed and the elbows patched
And the buttons in front didn't match.
A young man wore the coat when new
The buttons shone and the color blue
But the years were long and the labors hard
His hands grew calloused his features marred
By times own brushes as a writers pen
Tells life's story again and again
Now the young man's frame is bowed and bent
Under the weight of years well spent
Plowing the fields and reaping the grain
Thro rain and sunshine and grief and pain
Just like the coat the ravage of age
Had printed its story as a written page
Through love and labor all things grow old
We live our lives as a story told
And then some day when our race is run
The Father will say "My child well done."

Willodean Staggs

Year After Year

Another year has passed on by
The truth of the matter is time can fly
Without even knowing or realizing when
A moment is gone and another begins
Each life you have touched both now and then
Will always remember their teacher . . . their friend
Some days were hectic, others relaxed
Stress is an issue with children at best
Their questions
Their answers
Their honest intentions
The games and the mischief
Some days seemed so endless
One thing you should know
Maybe you've heard it before
Year after year as they pass through your door
The fun they've all shared, the stories you've read
Friendships beginning, their futures ahead
How very special you are to all of us now
Year after year, child after child

Cheryl Jackman

Her Behind

Caravan of twinkling diamonds
rushing by bring tender hums
breathing life into her spirit form

*I've gotta slow ridin' mind and a fast drivin' foot
on a cold dark highway
a way away from you*

With every mile I make
my heart cuts a little more
Piercing light through tunneled dark
I don't know until I'm gone just how much
how much she makes me cry
Why I leave is all for her
but that girl mocks, my steady drive
So I steal the night and curse her soul

*Another sip of brown bagged blues helps the pain
Another drag of sweet white smoke blows her gone*

Endless road
in front of prying eyes
and all I see is that stoic face
of hers moving at eighty down that road

Robert Elder

Listening Stranger

When I felt no one would listen along came a stranger to hear me.
When I felt no one could see my grief, this stranger has come
and noticed my sorrows.

Someone to listen, someone to care, someone with whom my
thoughts I could share.

Why has this stranger come and offered an ear to hear?
My dreams, my desires, my need to succeed, my hopes, my joys,
and my inner-most feelings.

Unbelievable it seems, who could this person be? Someone of
the opposite sex usually only wants to see; your weaknesses,
and wonder how he can uses them to get you into his bed. But
this one just asked me for a hug instead.

With words so encouraging, thoughtful, and sincere.
He has touched my life and in my heart he is dear.

Listening stranger we part with a smile. No longer a stranger,
For you are now my listening pal.

Ta'mara H. Tobin

We Are Arrested . . . And Forgotten . . .

Day in and day out I sit here wandering when will I see my
freedom come about . . .
No one to care, No one to share — my hopes and dreams . . .
My body is longing for some fresh air, my mind is thinking I
have already gotten the electric chair.
I am already guilty, as it seems — took from my family, my hopes
and my dreams . . . No more late night snacks, only left over food
I saved from hours back I sit and await for the courts to call, but
instead I receive a paper saying, "We have no information at all"
. . . Long restless nights, day in and day out — it seems as if I'm
losing the fight . . . I won't give up, no my friend, because I have
a savior who's from within . . . As I bend my knees for a little
prayer I ask Jesus to keep me in good care . . . Lord only you
knew my beginning and only you know my end . . . Although I
am locked up, I know that I'm never locked out from the ears of
my father whom loves me without a doubt . . . Bless you my
persecutors, my enemies and my foes because I know Jesus will
soon open these iron doors . . . I will be free in my mind, in my
spirit and in my heart — no longer forgotten — no longer apart
from my family and friends. My savior is at heart . . .

Cassandra Hefflin

Road Of Life

As I was walking down a wooded path one day, feeling so
alone and full of despair, I came to a lake.
As I stopped to take a look I saw a reflection of my life, from my
birth to the present day. When I saw what I had become it
scared me and I started to cry.
As I kneeled there, by the lake, I heard a voice that was sweet
and gentle, like a breeze, telling me that I wasn't alone. As I
turned around I saw the Lord Jesus reaching out his hand to lift
me up. I took his hand and told the Lord that I was a sinner, and
as I told the Lord my sins the feelings of loneliness and despair
were replaced with the feeling peace.
As the Lord and I started walking down this path together we
came to a fork in the road. One path was wide and smooth but lead
to certain death. The other was narrow and rocky, but lead to life.
As we stood there the Lord asked me which path I was going to take,
the narrow path or the wide path. It was then that I put my Faith
and Trust in the Lord and walked down
the narrow, Rocky Path . . .
The road less traveled with the Lord as my guide.

Jeff Detwiler

Dinner Table Companions

While sitting by myself quite alone
Two strangers came by and sat down to share
With a mumbled "May we?" then glanced around and
Spied another place and murmured "Excuse me."

The place was not free — there was no space —
The empty place was not.
Filled in every seat there sat the old familiar faces
Who sit at my table from years bygone.

They genially nod and smile and bob their wise old heads.
Their knowingness laughs a little and quietly reminisces among
The current topics over and above the general melee.
Their voices rise and fall never ending always there.
My dinner table companions.

Watching and waiting, complacent in place
The unerring eyes viewing life's surrounds.
Until rudely jerked awake and pulled so hard
They lean precariously in their seats and almost
Fall out of the way.

Into harmless dust.
My dinner table companions.

Joy Smith-Babbin

To Shed A Tear

To shed a tear
could there be something more noble?
To declare ones love with eyes rather than voice
staining ones cheek with heartfelt fire
deciding to share from the deepest depth of desire

What of a tear?
is there a gift more complex with simplicity?
Does it not stand in singular stature, grandeur, and glory
as one, 'tis more noble than a king
as many, 'tis no less worthier of a thing
by definition, a thing of lamentation
by poetic recognition, a thing of exaltation

To shed a tear,
to metamorphose love to a tangible fashion
to state with the grace of breeze, with elegance and passion
the simplicity of child, with mindless extraction
all the beauty of virtue, in one tiny tear
I cry for but one,
'tis you my dear

William McDowell

Looking Window

And through the glass
And through the looking window
Her breath forms a cloud
Her tears form a stream
a looking window
Looking down on the sweet spring
wishing it wasn't so cold from her
looking window.
Watching the faces smile, seeing jelly
bean castles, she sat, she sat crying,
from her looking window.
Now, a girl who no longer looks
at the summer or even spring even
though it's ever so close from her looking window
From now on, she stares behind her
into the bleak, white winter
not into her looking winter
Gradually, her looking window
fills with white, bleak, and permanent snow.

Lise Nicole Baillargeon

Wonderful Memories

I wish I could go back to those wonderful years
Where I hardly knew of any heartbreaking tears

To see the face of my Grandmother with her gentle smile
Today I'd even walk through a thorny, hellish cruel mile

The years of innocence that took great pleasure
Of being with the woman that love cannot measure

The lady who taught me the good from the bad
When everything to me was just a simple fad

So much love was put with all that she made
Today that precious memory will never fade

Those wonderful, happy unending years, cannot disappear
For in my heart they will somehow and someday reappear

Grandma, you'll always be in my thoughts, words and heart
And forever and ever those wonderful memories will never depart

Ruth Madrid

The Love Of Life

They say the strength to your body is in your mind.
Reach way inside and feel yourself unwind.

Fight for your life because it feels right, know loved
ones will be there holding your hand through the night.

Life is good and you'll feel that once again.
Your heart and soul will soon mend.

Think of the song birds singing every day
and the love of life will guide you on your way.

Laurie Antfeld

Untitled

she's not as tall
    as our kitten thinks
but she carries him over the world in a blur
in arms with bare cradle comfort
I'm not so sure
that I know her
    or that our kitten thinks
she's not as tall
    as me at her side
she raises a smile that steals my heart
    with the eyes of crisp child passion
        demanding and hard
    like the love of a child
    but she let's me decide
in arms with bare candle comfort
her hair is fair
    with points of pink
but she's not as tall
    as our kitten thinks

W. T. Buller

Remembering The Forgotten

This poem is written with great fondness and desire, to remember those who history forgets but I choose to admire. Each time I see our flag waving so high in the sky, or hear our anthem played like a sweet lullaby. My eyes fill with tears and my heart swells with pride, as I remember the men and women who fought bled and died.

People so quickly forget those who gave great sacrifice our freedoms we enjoy today came with a very happy price. Separated forever from family and friends, dying, cold, alone, meeting bitter ends. Many nameless faces in dark prison cells forgotten and mistreated, living a terrible daily Hell.

Lets not forget them though nameless and many, we owe them our lives, our liberties, and freedoms a plenty.

Robert Horne

Happy Anniversary Sweetheart!

It is one this day
Two years ago today
We pledge our love together
To cherish each other forever.

Your perseverance
Is through your experience
From fortunes
And misfortunes, of the past.

Your courage and drive
Always makes you strive
To leave behind the past
And take control of your mast.

Your positive thinking, gives you the inkling
To see good in all, instead of a possible fall.

It is for these reasons, I enjoy sharing each season
With a man of your fashion
With such tremendous Compassion
For life as it appears
Without any fears.

I Love You . . .
Katie Critz

My Favorite Time Of The Year

There is a certain time of year
I seem to like the best
When birds migrate south
To live in a warmer nest.

The air outside is crisp and clean,
The sky's the bluest I've ever seen.
The mild chill is just enough to tease
The leaves to change colors as they blow in the breeze.

The coming of this season renews the landscape
And projects summers end.
It produces the holidays
We share with family and friend.

We dress-up our children for trick or treat
While in our minds we see our youth repeat.
Take not for granted the gifts that God's given,
Stop and give thanks for the life that you're livin'.

As the season I love nears the end of the line
We celebrate Christmas and sing Auld Lang Syne.
Reading these words it's quite clear
That fall is my favorite time of the year.
Buck Collomore

Sad Eyes

Upraising in silent pleading
Looking for the light.
Searching through the darkness
Gazing at endless night.

Brimming in sorrowed moisture,
Shimmering with silent tear.
Wetting with helpless dew,
Mirroring windows of fear.

Shining light of morning,
Dissipating fog of night.
Welcoming a new dawning,
Pulling sad eyes to the light.

Refracting light through tearful moisture,
Bending rays of brilliant hue.
Widening eyes of filling hope,
Promising colors, life begins anew.
Debbie Evinrude

Onset Of Winter

The days are getting shorter . . . as evening comes.
The darkness comes a bit earlier . . . soon Winter's storms.
The fresh air flows . . . whispers and blows.
Where does the wind come from? No one knows.

Mom and Dad coming home from the "work day".
Making sure chores and homework are done before play.
Children sample the last of warm days . . . with their skateboards
and bikes. Unlike Spring . . . not flying kites.

Out the window we see neighbors with recyclable bags,
wheelbarrows, and rakes. View the debris trees and bushes make.

With onset of evening, we hear Mom say,
"Where are your jackets and sweaters? There is a chill in
the air, put on your hats and mittens, for your skin will
chap if your face and hands are bare."

And now we are aware with night comes day. With dark comes
light. With Summer comes Fall, soon Winters snowy delight.
All wrapped up with Mom's and Dad's warmth, love, and care.
Virginia L. Burriss Watson

The Pisces Princess

Golden hair has she, long because it has been left to be
Her eyes hold a thousand lifetimes or you cannot see yesterday
A big white house she lives within
But a horse drawn carriage perhaps at midnight
Will be only a mouse and a small safety pin
Alas a man who came to stay
And since that day the Princess has never been allowed to stray
A man that reigns with fear, a lust for power, at other women he will leer
Was he the troll under the bridge
Or is he the innkeeper of a deserted motel
Lost in the middle of the desert
Perhaps he is the Devil or Father Time teaching the Princess a way to rhyme
She waits in the castle for her prince to come
Maybe he is already there from the past or the future that has come undone
Ellea Sands

Vile Volcano

Vile volcano, erupting today,
Oh, Lord, make it stop, this that I pray.
Lava and magma spurting from the earth,
Chaos and carnage is given birth.
Another evil arrives which is an earthquake,
Nightmares enter, which from I may not awake.
Oh, vile volcano, erupting today, Lord, it has ended, that's what I say.
Adam Smith

The Open Sea Of Life

The end is just the beginning,
as I bid you farewell.
Set your sights forward
as you unfold your destined sail.

While dreams may seem nightmares
and your destination, impossible to most.
The guided image will take control
as the possibilities are unlimited from coast to coast.

For once you become aware
and decided to self-change.
You! Determine the limits
of your possible gains.

When the decision is made
to be the best you can be!
Nothing can hold you back,
for your destination becomes endless, as that,
Of An Open Sea!!!
Paul T. Pratt

Seven Ages Of . . . A Tree

In the sweet earth now the seed lay.
The bright new birth of a tree starts this day.
Soon the earth it will leave behind,
up from the soil the baby tree will wind.
It looks to the sun, as I to my mother;
this is the stage the sun will smother.
Soon a leaf sprouts up from the skin
Down to the young tree a drop will spin.
The rain will nurture the roots it owns.
Out comes more leaves as the wind moans.
As winter comes the leaves drop to the floor;
they always come back as the spring before.
The tree always has friends coming in and out,
helping to deliver seeds that soon will sprout.
Everything is happy till the day . . .
The man hurts the tree and takes it away.

Colleen Catherine Connolly

Carolina Dawn

It used to be aesthetic; now it is gone.
  A love which once existed in a time
glass, has drained itself dry.

Memories of days before, reflect like
  a prism in moonlight.

For every star that lights the sky far
  abroad, there truly has been a life to behold.

I used to hear the sun awake; beaming down
  upon me, stretched out on the 32nd parallel.

I must be moving in opposite harmony; 'fore it
  is but a dream to see another Carolina dawn.

Bruce Rabin

Grandpa

Oh, Grandpa I miss you so much,
The smile on your face, the warmth of your touch.
The many hours you'd spend entertaining me,
Playing cards, dominoes or just watching T.V.
All the nights I'd spend sleeping in your bed,
The stories you told that filled my head.
We'd spend hours in the garden working so hard,
And then you would try to cheat me at cards.
I guess you know how much you mean to me,
I wish you could see my two boys, how happy you would be.
I spend many hours thinking of you,
And of all the things we used to do.
But I know you're happy now without the pain,
Just remember my love for you will always remain.
For in my heart you will always be near,
And my memories of you will always be clear.

Sandra Dossey

Mothers

There's a certain group of women who are so very sweet.
Without these women, your lives would not be complete.

They will always love you, never leave your side.
They fill you with goodness and a sense of pride.

No one else can do this, not a sister or a brother.
But someone much more special, you call them your mother.

The love of mothers can never be surpassed.
They will love you every minute, up to their last.

No other cared or nurtured you from the very start.
There is no other with such a loving heart.

They are very protective, but peaceful as a dove.
You will not find someone else filled with so much love.

Austin Miller

As I Walk In The Street

As I walk down the street, I can't help to ask
If there is someone lost and needs a helping grasp
someone so young with a future ahead
or a man wandering the street because he has no where to go.
As I walk down the street.
As I walk down the street I can't help not to think
of the things that are happening on a night like this
how the devil can work on a night like this.
as I walk down the street.
As I walk down the street I can't help to look
at a sleeping family out on this street
no where to go, no where to hide.
As I walk down the street.
As I walk down the street I can't help not to hear a whisper
of the gloomily place where I stand
where I look out on the world
to see how hateful we are
as I walk down the street

Marc Di Francesco

A Poem For Bill

An ode to an eyelet bent and broken,
A tattered lace another token.
A rusty blade with shabby shoe,
Remind me of your love so true.

Abandoned pucks and well taped sticks,
Your worn out bag, I could not fix.
A blemished helmet, your gloves forlorn,
My child, my child, for you I mourn.

A Red Wing's jersey tossed on the floor,
Your Nordic's cap and so much more.
Smelly pads, your grungy jock,
"Remember me?" they seem to mock.
Your pictures and pins stashed all about,
"Remember me?" they seem to shout.

With grace and beauty my son you'd fly,
Across the ice instead of sky.
Your numerous trophies upon the wall,
Forgotten victories big and small,
Could never show your courage true,
My son, my son, I so loved you.

Rita Monzon

Psalm About Pain

We don't like pain Lord
It's true
But with it you can bring us through
Through good times, and bad times come our way
For without pain how could we gain?

For with it comes happiness for tomorrow
Even though we might have to bare sorrow
For with it I come to know my Saviour
Both now and forever.

I love you Saviour, Lord forever
You raised us up and brought us up
From the pain you went to the cross
To keep us sinners saved but not lost
This Inspiration came when God had brought the rain.

When we suffer that's pain
But when God wins our battles, that's gain.
God used my hands to write it, but He designed it.

I believe God has this psalm in Heaven,
Because, where the Bible ends on earth
That is the beginning of Heaven.

Mary Catherine Gordon

To My Shooting Star . . . I'm Sorry

In your arms I'd like to stay forever
The feelings are there, but said . . . almost never
Sad and wishing when we are apart,
That I will say whats truly in my heart

For you the words come easily to say
But still I can't . . . and just walk away
I can kiss your lips and feel your heart
But when you're there, I fall apart

The words are becoming harder and harder to say
Because I'm falling more in love with you everyday
One day I will learn, and I'll easily say
The words that crush my heart today

Maybe after this poem you'll understand
That for you I hold my heart in my hand
Writing the words is easy to do
I'm sorry I can't say I love you, to you.

    Gillian Clair Witter

Only Human

There are those who strive for glory
There are those who strive for fame
There are those who always have to have
Their name on everything.

There are those whose truest aim
Is service to their fellow man
To give unselfishly, and not for gain.
Those lives will not have served in vain.

    T. McDonald

Family Christmas Habits

Christmas is the time for praying, serving and giving
A practice we all should be doing,
Christ gave His life for the living and dying, giving
Our lives an experience of the vastness of his love showing
The sun, moon, stars, the seas, lakes foaming and roaring
The beauty of the autumn woods, farms, and crops agrazing.
The bible tells us what is done rightly or wrongly.
Sadly that has not been the life style of so many.
Our schools, home, work places, laws, family would be reaping
The great benefits of going back to serving and praying
A very merry Christmas to all people and family.

    Helen T. Fisher

Eve, Did You Listen?

While the serpent's tongue caressed you,
Did it stir the blood within you?
Did it bid you, exit Eden?
Seek your Mother's garden.

While the serpent's tongue caressed you,
Did it plant a seed within you?
One to grow beyond the garden *Felix Culpa*,
That happy Fall that found you the serpent
Found you guilty of all sin and sinning.

While the serpent's tongue caressed you,
Did it scorch and heal you?
Did it lead you past the *culpa*,
And the awful word of Milton?
Did it bring you to your Mother's garden,
Wherein grows the serpent's seed, the self?

While the serpent's tongue caressed you,
Did it stir the blood within you?
Did it bid you, exit Eden?
Seek your Mother's garden.

    P. Kaiser

Last

I had hoped for pain.
All I got was bittersweet agony.
I had hoped for joy.
All I got was a brief respite from pain.

A circle. Eternal hell. In
wanting, having, knowing.
Above all — knowing. That
greatest of sins when the
arrow was turned within and
left to exit and enter again.

Too far below . . . estranged from
the matter of truth. I've
turned my father from my
door to scrape within the
walls of loneliness.

He left dejected . . . and I stayed
. . . dejected . . . again. Return to beginning.

    Chris Wilke

Loneliness

Loneliness is when you have but one friend
    and you and her are in a fight.

Loneliness is waking up in the middle of the
    night and having no one to talk to.

Loneliness is when the enemy group turns the whole
    school against you and you don't have any
    friends because of all the rumors they started
    that weren't true.

Loneliness is when you're stuck in a room where
    everyone seems to have a friend except you.

Loneliness is when you have no one to share the
    holidays with.

Loneliness is a shadow that you sometimes stand in.

    Kira Lynn Erickson

Nostalgia In California

I miss Midwest life that I once knew,
And hot, humid days with nothing to do.
I miss Mother's home-baked bread and pies,
And warm, starry nights and the fireflies.

I miss the robins that come in the spring,
And the birdhouse where wrens nest and sing.
I miss the four-o-clocks that greet the morn,
And the garden with red tomatoes and corn.

I miss the May Baskets left at the door,
And penny candy from Predmestky's store.
I miss quiet living and old-fashioned modes,
And 'phone lines that "sing" along country roads.

I miss the park where the violets grow.
I miss playing "Fox and Geese" in the snow.
I miss the lilacs and the peonies, too;
But most of all, Family, I miss you!

    Blanche A. Miles

Untitled

God will be here he will be here soon.
He is only coming because the world is doomed.
He heard a cry from our children eyes
from the unborn heart that beats inside.
Some are perfect most are fable.
God only hopes that we all are able to walk with him
"He" guides the way. I only hope it's not today.

    Susan Nesseralla

Untitled

A seagull flying, light as paper
Over the clear, blue sea.
In his throat there's a scream
In his heart there's a dream
   A longing to belong.
   A place he cannot see.

His wings are tired
His eyes can hardly see.
He flies through night and day
From the moons first glow to the suns last ray.
   Gliding through the air in despair.
   To become the gull he longs to be.

The seasons are changing
The sky turns grey.
He pauses, he looks, he listens.
Gentle snow begins to fall. His whole body trembles.
   He opens his beak in a silent cry.
   Quietly lands. Quietly dies.
   Patrick Coughlin

Word Unfurled

I told you once, Diane, that
I could never write a poem
about you. That there are things
that cannot distill into language,
moments that cannot crystallize
into a sentence. The idols
I have built totter precariously,
balanced on the grainy surfaces
of prepositional phrases.

Sometimes I feel that I am more of a taxidermist
than a poet, and you, the great anti-muse,
play my foil — siphoning the ink from my veins,
   transfusing blood.
   Ravi Shankar

Moment With Nature

We find ourselves beside a beautiful moon-lit river,
with millions of stars as a background to the sky.

(Shhh), Listen, can't you hear the wind whispering,
as the river ripples softly against the rocks.

Trees dance in unison, as the raindrops beat a tempo,
and nature harmonizes to the rhythm created by all forces.

Thus allowing all of us that hear, to become as one, and
as we focus to the heavens, we can see the face of God,
smiling.
   Darryl Thomas

As Free as the Wind

As free, as free as the wind.
To be free, as free as the wind.
To drift over all of earth's wonders,
To blow where I want to be.

As free, as free as the wind.
To be free, as free as the wind.
To see all the wondrous miracles,
Just one time before I go.

I realize, it's not the fault of man,
Please try and understand.
That someday you'll be here with me,
In a lovely world, a wonderland.

And we'll be free, as free as the wind.
We'll be free, as free as the wind.
We'll be free.

   Michael R. Turner

Black And Red

Mysterious yet revealing,
   obvious yet concealing
     Beautiful and flamboyant,
      they compliment each other.

Bound in abyss
   Freely dancing in the spotlight . . .
     Incognito in black, cruising at night
      Fabulous in red, speeding down the highway
      Dark and sleek, bright and shocking

The color of midnight
   versus
     The color of roses at dawn

Like love and war,
   death and life,
     blood and raven
      like the song of the nightingale,
       district harmony
       like man and woman
        and black and red.
   Lynnee Archie

One Night . . .

In the moonlight lit sky, I see your beauty.
As I feel a draft, I turn my head.
It makes me think more and more.
How I want you, how I think of you, what I want to do.
You just don't understand, I would give my heart for you.
The dreams I've had, of making love to you.
It seemed so real, I could feel your inside.
For so long, I have tried to hide.
But now, my feelings are ready to subside.
I can't hold them in anymore.
I want to fall in love, but it takes two.
I don't want anyone but you.
As I've thought of kissing your sweet lips.
I sank deeper and deeper into your trays.
The trays of passion in your eyes.
I wont to lay you down in a bed of roses.
I'd do as I please to please you.
Give me one night, under the moonlight.
I promise, . . . I'll be a night to remember.

   Kristofer Linde

Nieces And Nephews

I have nine nieces and nephews
Good kids all are they.
That is to say they're all normal,
and from the rules they sometimes stray.

Justin used to skip to school
Happy all the way,
Aaron told his mom
At home he would like to stay.

Sherri attended many schools
moving from town to town,
Ethan decided pre-school was good
and finally settled down.

John and Katie attend Light and Life
and participate in many activities there.
Jimmy started Kindergarten
and rides a bus that bears him there.

Autumn is getting through 1st grade
and I see an honor student.
Juli has started high school
and with her studies she's very prudent.

   Roseanna Rogers

Life

Living each day one step at a time
  Interchanging feelings of joy and pain
Forever forgetting, and forgiving the good and bad
  Eroding away ever minute of the day.
  Yamonte Kee Lister

The Measure Of A Man

In truth, it never matters what anyone thinks of you.
No one is ever in position to say who you are other than you.
And why should you believe emptiness is too great a price to pay
  for your dignity?
When you stand before the sun when your day is done
You know if you've lived your full measure.
Let the words of your song remind you whom you must learn to treasure.
As you look to the heavens above let no man tell you who you are.
Breathe in of what life offers for too soon comes the night.

Above you shines the night star
Reach out your arms to the beckoning breeze and take flight,
Rising like a phoenix from your ashes into the chill of the evening air
And never deny the wonder of you.
Use freely of what you are given and arrive at a plan to take you there
Be gentle with others, be gentle with yourself,
  and always be true to you.

For there is no one,
Never has been,
Never will be,
Who can tell you the measure of a man.
  William W. Fox

Untitled

Tell me that you love me.
Tell me that you need me.
Tell me that you want me.
And tell me you believe me.
Tell me that it's all right.
Tell me you won't leave tonight.
Tell me that you'll love me forever.
And tell me that we'll always be together.
Tell me we won't fight again.
Tell me all this hate will end.
Tell me how the bruises heal.
Tell how I'm suppose to feel!
Tell me the hurt will go away.
Tell me what you want me to say.
Tell me how to love you but never care.
Tell me how to give you space, but always be right there.
Tell me how to believe you when you lie.
Tell me how to live but also die.
Tell me it'll be all right.
Tell me how to make it through another night.

  Kelli Hightower

Longing

Along the crashing shore I walk,
the current crimson in the sun.
I strain to peer beyond the locks
that bind my search for sight of land, my vision won
not by powers of earthly sight.
Nay, forbid it be for me to see
beyond far horizons by my own might.
A spirit spans distant sweetness, a honey
sweet comprised of heart and mind;
ethereal it is, a longing tempered by fire.
Invisible the flame, unlike the kind
that blinds with light and raging ire,
yet far worse the burn, for as a spark
is soon gone, so a pining soul is consumed and left dark.
  Tim VanDyke

Morning In The Woods

From the porch swing, one can see;
  the sun as it glistens through the trees.

The peaceful quiet of early morn;
  Morning Doves cry so forlorn.

The dew as it drips from the leaves;
  the magic spell of the wood, it weaves.

Creatures as they slowly wake;
  as they call to each other, the silence breaks.

Animals of every shape and size;
  Some go to bed, yet others rise.

Woodland creatures and all their kin;
  Another day in the woods begins.
  Natalie Anne Bellando

The Day My Papa Died

I was sitting on my bed when . . .
I saw my mom come in
She was crying
She was sad
My papa had gone to heaven.

My mom smelled like white diamonds
The roses were red
Everyone was sad
The clouds cried tears of rain
One last good-bye
Before my papa went to the heavens in the sky.
  Heather Whipkey

Sadness

Sadness deepens, the candle burns slow.
My grief is heavy, my feelings now show
I cry at night and I don't know why.
My feelings are never cheerful no matter how hard I try.
My tears fall, they fall like the rain.
My soul, my spirit, my feelings, my pain
My life is dead, no ups only downs.
Someone release these sounds.
One day my happiness will return,
The day I see you, my hatred won't burn,
My gladness is due.
  Michelle LaMere

Rendezvous

The rainy dawn. Cold and unpleasant.
Highway, from which not long ago
I watched happy autumn:
A rising sun, the mountains covered by snow,
and smiling flowers in a valley.
They are sad today.
Somewhat faded or perhaps shrunken from cold?
Fog that does not lift today.
Keeps up on the rainy strings, which weep on our window.
The rainy-thoughts. Hollow out a road, dripping inside.
Humdrum small town. Cobble road. Tea with a rum.
Table-tale. Full of confession scratched out with notch fork.
Another small town. Under an umbrella.
The church. For Sunday's believers.
The brothel, across the way.
For faithful on Sunday.
There is one over there. Truly feminine.
Quite beautiful not long ago.
Fully-grown today. With sorrow and wisdom.
Believing in sense of being without repetition.
  Miroslaw Wlodowski

I Am Not . . .

Dark sorrow binds me. I cannot see, nor hear, nor feel, nor love.
I am worthless in my own eyes.
I hate to think what others may see me as.
If I can see no worth in myself, how can others see greatness
when most know little about me?
Does anyone else see something wrong with this picture? Am I,
again, being left behind?
Am I, the one that you find so great, being left behind by you,
the one who sees greatness in things they don't know or
understand? Or is it I who doesn't understand you?
Maybe we should switch bodies for just a day. I would see
what you see; and you'd see what I see. Maybe then each
would understand where the other was coming from.
Would our views of each other change? Would you be able to
see me the way I see myself . . . *worthless*. Or would I be able to
see myself the way you see me . . . *angelic*.
But could that actually happen? Of course not. So why change
the obvious to something it can never be? So while letting the
obvious alone, do so with me as well, for I could never be as
you'd like me to be . . . *perfect*.

Marissa Rulez

The Best Thing

My perceiving images ideally glide
Peace, love, and happiness I feel inside.
I stand upon this rock, in the middle of the ocean.
Examining my thoughts which are full of emotion.
Sunshine arches glare down on my face
The wind is whisking in this peaceful place.
A deep breathe I took made me feel so clean.
If I were a painter, I'd portray the scene
Fierce water runs much stronger than a ripple
Autumn still trees, seem to be crippled
Life as I know it is left back behind
With all other pressures known to mankind.
Here I am at peace, myself I can be
On top of this rock in the middle of the sea
I can't help but notice, the silent birds fly
Where are they going, soaring in the sky?
The crash of the water, puts my mind at ease
The wind says, a prayer, I call it "The Breeze."
The moon now glows upon my face
The stars now dance with a gentle grace
Peace, love, and happiness still lingers on.
This is the best thing, this rock I am on.

Rob DeFrancesco

Slowing The Grasp

The extreme speed of sliding
From one discussion to the next
A supreme thought is gliding
The sounded percussion to the perplexed

Sighs of breathing leave me believing
That illusions are on their way
Lies are regularly about relieving
Disillusions of what will come someday

Entertainment being first bliss then tedious
Channel changing is indigenous
Exchangement is no longer expedient
Panel textures are plainly evident

To escape to what is not there
Leaving fruits passion on the table
Now rape can be hardly fair
Cleaving a pies cherries with a label
The knowing power of our prejudice
Can be all ignorant or a forgiving disguise
A glowing showering is left capricious
The plan is the sea and oceans rise.

Don Kennedy

Darkness To Light

Here I am, in my bed
Praying to God as I lay my head.
I pray to get through this endless night
I hope when I awaken to see the light.

But there is so much darkness all around
The light could get lost and be seen as sound.
My world is distorted due to the pain inside
The pain is so deep, even darkness can hide.

As my distortions get bigger I begin to shut down
Because the pain and darkness won't bring me around.
If God is listening, hear me say
Please help me through another day.

Please give back my colors to me
And feelings with each appropriately.
Blue is content; lilac serene,
Red is wild; white is clean.

With these colors I'll have light
And inner strength for my next plight.
Give me the rainbow, I want them all
For the darkness to fade, and for the light to call.

Judith D. Baker

The River Of Insanity

I'm paddling down the river of insanity
    bordering on the shores of narrow-mindedness
Endlessly fighting the doldrums that prevail
    heading towards my total obloquy

Rowing towards no man's land with trepidation
    my eyes scorn the spindrift excruciatingly
The icy cold wintry burst of the wind's endeavor to displace my
    bearings with its dissonant sounds from off shore try to thwart
    me forthwith

I'm paddling down the river of insanity
    evading countless shock waves intellectually
A stone's throw closer to the inner littoral of my imagery
    the jagged rocks cast their sorcery towards me

Many ripples alter my inner thought waves
    my deepening fears make the oars seem heavier
This river of insanity and it's many thought currents
    have caused me a perilous journey in life

Leonard Salters Jr.

Pondering

Thoughts keep coming back to me
Of things I feel, or think about, or see
One, in particular, comes at various times,
And fuels my mind with words for rhymes . . .
    . . . as I ponder . . .

I think of a simpler time in life.
A young immature man, a beautiful wife
Three wonderful children, good job, good pay
Putting food on the table every day . . .
    . . . and I ponder . . .

Days into weeks, weeks into years.
Time passes quickly and disappears
Children grow up, marry, move out.
Then it's just husband and wife to worry about . . .
    . . . I still ponder . . .

As the changing seasons quickly fade.
They join that disappearing parade . . .
And, it seems, it's come much too fast
When you realize, your time is past!
    . . . While you ponder . . .

Bill Stogsdill

Escape

Sometimes I wonder if the mountains grow tired of their majestic heights, or of the cold, bitter snow which seems to stay forever.

And sometimes I wonder if the sea grows tired of the countless vessels who have tread upon its waters, or of the unseen depths yet unconquered;

Sometimes I wonder if the wind grows tired of blowing, and if it wishes its travels would end.

And sometimes I wonder if the fire grows tired of destroying, and if it would like to repay the countless debts it owes;

Sometimes I wonder if the clouds grow tired of crying; if the melancholy is too much to bear.

And sometimes I wonder if the thunder grows tired of crashing, and if it seeks a tranquil, silent, resting place;

Sometimes I wonder if the sky is tired of being blue, and if night's darkness leaves it lonely like me.

Adam Pedersen

Feel Me Or Fill Me

How could a look, a mere glance
reach into my soul and claim
untraveled roads by another human?

How can a voice, a mere tone
open doors and extract emotions
that have been buried far away?

Already it's too late, you run rampant,
looking for every scar, every fantasy.

As each fear, want and desire
is uncovered, you must ask yourself;
What are the rewards? What are the dues?
Will the reaction satisfy the cause?

As hidden dreams unveil before you
only you will set the limits.
For you have entered where no exit exists.

The well waters whisper your name.
Dare you take a sip? . . . Oh Yes, Partake!

Is it paranoia? Desire and Passion?
Aren't they the core of all emotion?

I want to feel you . . . fill me?

Judith Ammons

Life's Reflections

One day as I walked by life's troubled stream,
I saw the reflection of a perishing dream.
I saw this dream being torn apart,
and I felt deep inside the sorrow in my heart.
It was young and free. It was beautiful too,
and I knew there was something I had to do.
I talked to this dream and said, "Give it some time.
In a day or two things will be fine."
The dream said to me "Just leave me alone.
I've tried all I can. I don't want to go on."
I said to the dream "Well you can't just die.
You're important to me!" And I began to cry.
"Your life is important. Don't throw it away.
You must be strong and face each new day.
Don't be discouraged for people do care.
Just take my hand, and I'll lead you there."
I realized then there was nothing more I could say
so I began to walk away,
and as I turned and looked to see,
I saw that the dream was following me.

Richard Schreiber

The Lady In The Chair

When first we met, she was in her chair,
a smile on her lips, a twinkle in her eye,
this look she gave me, I don't know why.

I came for her daughter, to go on a date,
a movie, dinner, maybe a dance,
as we walked out the door, she gave me that glance.

As time went by, we became good friends,
she called me her baby, I asked her why,
my daughter's not lonely, she doesn't cry.

She was always there when I was ill,
chicken soup, hot tea, a kind word or two,
nothing was too good, there was nothing she wouldn't do.

Now she was sick, and I was confused,
in the hospital, in a really bad way,
please Lord don't take her, please let her stay.

I miss her so much, I think I know why,
she's in heaven, giving the Lord my stare,
she's in heaven, the lady in the chair.

Thomas S. Wallace

Walking At Dawn On A Winter Day

I walk at dawn on a winter day;
    breathing crisp arctic air,
    my fingers and toes numb,
    watching night shadows there.

Anticipation keeps me moving;
    to view a radiant dawn,
    laborious steps in deep snow,
    not knowing the way so long.

Finally I see a cool dawn light
    then watch it grow pink and warm,
    raising to touch the pathway,
    caressing my cold stiff form.

Now, seeing night shadows bolt and blend,
    lavender to gold pink rays,
    pushing aside frosty currents,
    at dawn on a winter day.

Jeannine G. Stone

Divorce

With letter she came . . . I stood in awe.
Not of her script . . . but an academic in law.
Gratuitous contents of unredeemable time.
This was hers . . . that was mine.
He writes with detachment, and the eloquence of a drone
while my son wonders, which house is home?
Soon He'll say, you're divorced, happy anniversary.
But he's never seen my son's face . . . when she
drives him, away from me.

The attorneys ink . . . like a narcotic to abscond.
I find myself without the intellect to respond.

Having been given the opportunity to be a prince.
I find myself without the formula for changing back into a toad.

Having been given the opportunity to reach the end of the tunnel . . .
and step out into the light. I find myself without the courage,
to climb back into the tunnel.

Having been given the opportunity to experience . . . "A dream
come true . . . a dream that wakes up, when I do.
I find myself without the fortitude to sleep.

Having been given the opportunity to be
rescued from a raft, adrift in the ocean.
I find myself without the strength, to climb back into the raft.

Glenn Millar

Untitled

To: Melitza Jimenez
Little by little I will love you
in silence I will think
that every second is ours
that every second my soul to you I would give

Nor time nor distance would matter
once always to you I would come.
To you I would come every moment
in each breath, kiss and caress.

In a poem with its letters
in that peace, so comforting
found in your arms in your lips.
When your eyes follow me.

Little by little I will love you
one hour or a million days
lasting years, months, weeks
giving you love, tenderness and life.

Little by little I will love you
in silence I will think.
That every second is our.
That every second my soul to you I would give.

Juan Carlos Meza

The Tattertorn Bride

The vineyards of mischief are never tramped gentle.
Oft sparing the flesh, fools' tortures are mental.
Love vinted in lune-light, so devils declare,
Is mistress to madness, and passion au pair.

Labored twin-tapers glaze the altars tonight
But the eye of my raven spits the only seen light.
Hearts in a dungeon know colder no chains.
Mine, thought to be hardy, moves ice in my veins.

Departed saints, come! Free what she's bound!
Surrender my tongue to make audible sound!
For she lifts me her palm and vows me a curse.
No martyrs arrive. And it only gets worse.

With the ring comes her dower of linens and shade,
In tattertorn garments, the bride is arrayed.
In the darkness of dark near the brattice abode,
Her body is laid at the cross of the road.

The angels change guard who watch o'er the world
But leave me to keen for the tattertorn girl.
Among wizened elders, here's proof, as they say.
Fearing weirdlings in wedlock, you'd best stay away!

Michael Duane

In The Middle Of Heartland

Have you ever heard about a place
where they try to keep face
because the seeds they were sowing
somehow stopped growing
'most everyone comes, then moves away
'cept a few whose destiny is only to stay
if you have never been
you won't see what they have seen
hope you'll never know
and have no reason to go
because it's someway past dusk
and a time before dawn
alongside tear lake
deep in the valley of heartbreak
just past where the ways part
you'll find the broken heart
well it ain't easy to stand
right there in the middle of heartland

Alan Moroney

Never Lose Sight Of The Dream

To dream, there is no chosen hour that it will drive itself
through our veins.
For it is a gift given to man by God, it is the very lifeline of our souls,
Never lose sight of the dream, for it is the pathway to our tomorrows,
Take hold of every hope within and with every breath,
you take, make it happen,
Never give into the halfway mark, if you can see it, it's already there.
Without our dreams we lie in a lifeless state, waiting to be
plucked off with the rest,
Never lose sight of the dream, for if we do, there we'll sit,
hungering for power which never left the palms of our hands.
The desires of our heart, manifest itself, through our belief
in ourselves.
A mind that is built upon defeat, is death to the heart, our dreams
give us reason for being, kept alive, they make us complete.
It is an open door, swinging back and forth with each foot that
is placed in front of the other.
Never lose sight of the dream, for a man's dreams can take him
to the top of a mountain, just because he saw himself standing there.

Marsha Renee Evans

Divorce

Most stay together six months or more
several stay together one year or more
some stay together five years or more
few stay together at all.

The engagement ring was a surprise
the happiness was alive
then came the shower
no time to think alone
together was to think

But it was that winter
not only did the trees go limp
such wanting togetherness grew slim
it must have been nature.

One disagreement lead to,
then another, it lead to;
problems and more

They divorced each other maybe in search of a lover
or perhaps an uncommitted affair having little if any care
it wasn't the same can't find the kind of love for another.

Sharon Sykes

Inspiration

I am looking at the rainbow
That is there for all to see.
The hope and the joy that it gives to the soul,
The spark of God's love when we gaze
The beauty of its splendor, can
Always bring tender the moments of
Now to endure.
We will always have rainbows to
Look on and dreams of the future evermore.
To have and to hold them and cherish
Our whole life through.

Ann Guarino

Gravity

How to get there from here
Is the catch on the screen door of possibility
For dreams are nothing more than instruments of torture

I, for one, have soared the heights of grandest aspiration
To have my wings melt into mud
And plummet helpless back to earth
Maddened by battles lost
To gravity, the king of mediocrity

Robert E. Lipetz

Vacant Eyes

Staring blankly into space
Existing in many forms, your words belie
Vacant eyes.

Poisoning your mind in the clubs
Is it false bravado or simply an escape
From the life you lead behind
Vacant eyes.

If the eyes are truly the window to the soul
When the glow has diminished
I see the pain in your
Vacant eyes.

Take cover from your lover
Fantasize about how life could have been if only . . .
The blame and shame are masked by your
Vacant eyes.

Go to the mirror many a day
I've had to turn away from
Vacant eyes.

Is that a tear I see, don't cry for me
As I leave those vacant eyes behind.

Michael R. Byers

It's Time

It's time to renew old friendships in the New Year,
It's time to forget the bad things of the past,
It's time to start anew!

It's time to love in the New Year,
It's time to forgive others,
It's time to start anew!

It's time to be happier in the New Year,
It's time to become a new you,
It's time to start anew!

It's time to start praying in the New Year,
It's time to get closer to God,
It's time to start anew!

Joan C. Cox

Palm-Prayer In Haiti

Palm branches, catherine-wheeled, fan-ripple against
washed azure as they neck-stretch. Earth-fast, they lean
and yearn for shoals and breakers. Garrotte rocks dispute
the juice that thrusts through slender trunks that thirst for
height. It births sky-holds that gape, grapple, languish
for the ocean's surging passion that, in turn,
gropes for the shore.
            So man, also earth-fast, heart-stretches!
Clutching for soul-holds, he wrestles, another Jacob,
with emasculating agent provocateurs.

Miriam Clare

An Empty Glass

Three men holding the last glass of water,
Arguing the crisis and the causes,
Each blaming the parent, son, and daughter.
But as they dispute each one pauses
And from the glass they take a drink.
Which causes one to stop and think,
That in the end it does not
Matter who is right
Or who may be wrong,
But that the water
In the glass
Is now
Gone.

David Currey

To: My Little Giant

How can I describe you?
The best part of you, is knowing you.
You have given me and shown me love.
You have not only shared yourself with me.
You have shared your children and grandchildren also.
You have comforted me in my time of sorrow.
You have made me laugh when I was sad.
You made me dance because you knew I loved dancing.
Many people could and many people could not understand you.
I thank God that I had the privilege to spend the last
days of your life on earth with you.
I will always remember your funny little laugh. (Smile)
Little giants like you do not last.
God has prepared us a place.
Some day with him we will dwell.
Let the hope of joys to come.
If God be ours we are traveling home.
Go on, My Little Giant and keep blowing
your horn along with Gabriel.

Doris Gadpaille

Undo The World

To see you again for the first time
Your eyes, your hands that hold tight breath
    and life and beauty
I can see you holding a flower
Delicate but life
And walking across long ways
To lay your head upon my shoulder
And we undo the world

Palm to palm, face to face
Your lovely lips lack no life
Speak like floating butterflies
    Flutter and soar, lingering
In a loveliness you own
That's always inside you
And you undo the world

Sky blue eyes and violent but innocent love
You push the stars to the side in wondering
And fall to the grass shaking
To look up and stare into the heavens
And we undo the world

Deese Watts

What Will Your Child Remember?

As children, we will remember what our parents say and do.
Oh, we will remember alright; our whole life-time through!

What do you say, and do to yours when they are so very small?
Have you said a lot of things that perhaps you can't recall?

Well, maybe what you can't recall, or just can't seem to remember
is very real and causes them to stand there . . . shake and tremble.

As a child, I don't know what you know; only what I see.
And when I see you lose control, I learn to be like you — not me.

I want to act like God intended: be loving, considerate and kind.
But when you share those hurting words, it mixes up my mind!

Yes, I hear your "I love you's," and know you mean what you say.
But then you yell and hit me, later on that day.

You say you're only correcting and teaching me to mind.
But mainly I'm just learning to be hurtful and unkind!

I guess what I'm trying to say: We don't know what you expect.
But all we're asking from you is some dignity and respect!

Larry D. Taylor

The Gingerbread Boy On The Christmas Tree

There was a gingerbread boy on the Christmas tree,
I looked at him and he winked at me,
That was an unlikely thing to do,
It surprised me, it would have surprised you.

Says I to him, "haven't you heard
Ornaments don't wink." He said not a word.
He just kept hanging there on the limb
Which must have seemed quite high to him.

I left him dangling with the decorations and balls
Still trying to figure out if I saw what I saw,
When I looked back he was still there of course
Trying to lasso a red hobby horse.

Viola Mae Baker Rippeon

Omniscient Nobody

There's a big hole in the path
no one can see it
except me
everyone who passes falls in
except me
no one can explain why everyone falls into eternity
except me
no one can stop it
except me
if they would only ask, I would fix it
but they won't ask
because no one can see me either
except me.

Rebekah Michael

Dreamer

Lying in the summer grass,
my child toes are dirty and naked.
It's silent in the orchard, I am spread out,
on the cool grass in the shade.
I talk to God here
we have one-sided conversations.
I watch the shapes of the clouds' shadows move across the
ground and
I think about winter — the thought makes me shiver —
so I roll back out into the sunlight,
this time on my stomach so the brightness
doesn't blind me . . .
I lay my head down, dark, buried
in the blades of green,
and I dream of me and Jesus
climbing trees and laughing.

Jeanette McJunkin

Child's Cry

Now that I'm here, are you ready for me?
Or should I prepare you for what will be?
Ages, for me, will come and go,
how will you teach me what I need to know?

Do I ask of you all my question now,
and wait for your wise reply?
Volumes of wisdom I know you possess,
in time, what you reveal will grow in me,
do you know, will I pass your test?

Someday all my question I'll ask you for sure,
however, will you help me keep my heart pure?
In days to come will you lead the way,
be by my side through the cloudiest day?
Life, for me, is now at its start,
eventually our paths may have to part,
yet, for now, can I be what fills your heart?

Terri H. Davis

Until the Time Comes

Until the time comes . . .
    I will remain standing, strongly like an
oak next to you.

Until the time comes . . .
    I will be your Gardner, fertilizing you
with my strength, nurturing you with my touch.

Until the time comes . . .
    I will be your sunshine, shining rays of warmth
and light to help you grow and prosper.

Until the time comes . . .
    I will be your rain, gently pouring my love on
you to quench your thirst.

When the time comes . . .
    I will be a weeping willow, shedding branches
of tears for love lost, yet not forgotten.

Cathy Stech

Untitled

I see the thoughts as they are now
in anticipation of what they are becoming.
As a hardened face breaks into joy
so a hurting heart mends with love's gentle touch.
For so long a time waiting for what might never be
with a faith that fades with the wind;
like grass that has been trampled upon.
So you came . . . dancing with an angel on heaven's wings,
descending on my plain with a spirit so unknowing.
Caressing my soul,
dusting away the cobwebs of forgotten passions,
Pulling out what I only dreamed was there.
The thoughts, as they are now, are searching,
stripping away the old . . . weaving fresh patterns of life into my soul.
Learning how to live with new dreams . . .
Waking from the dead . . .
How full it feels.

Melissa Curtin

Octopied

While standing still with puzzled gape,
Escape now, but he's not so brave.
With fickle heart he'll forsake
Camouflage he thought would save
His life from this headless snake.
As he cogitates "I wonder why?"
Becomes another tidbit in Nature's Wake.

Paul Koontz Jr.

March Thundershowers

Sun oh sun it filled the whole day,
Till it hit 3:00 mid way,
The sky was now rolling gray,
The strike of lightning sparked my plug,
Up the 1 mile hill I went with a chug,

It's been so long since I've heard thunder and seen a flash,
I felt a scare slither down me with a sweaty, red rash,
Dark clouds with virga nearing and thunder did gnash,
I was shaking, so I flipped and fell when I attempted my dash,

When I was 400 meters from shelter I let out a thank you prayer,
I went to the rain-rinsed window and took a silent stare,

I enjoy, yet fear, thundershowers as I was told,
So few March thundershowers, but the ones that come are always bold,
I appreciate them because they bring a fresh fragrance and many
    May flowers to hold.

Alicia Weber

The Reason It All Began

I will not mourn my departure for from my deepest solitude shall come my finest escape.
And while those who have given me the components of company are no longer with me,
   their test to see what I have truly taken will now be known, and
   told by how well I allow them to remain in my mind.
A brick alone could trip someone, while one combined with many
   others could help support someone.
Assumptions result in enemies while curiosity creates sensibility —
   and interruptions are merely interferences of the truth to come.
No one understands me but you, and we should all just be steps in a ladder,
Helping the less privileged make it one step higher and achieve
   something he has never had.
A loss of innocence comes from a gain of intelligence and no longer am I innocent,
For when I surrender my castle to the child I've molded, I cry not for my departure
   and the moments I've collected, but instead for the walls the child has inherited.
My words are the product of my talent and my misery,
And that which I have written in my greatest distress the world seems to like the best.
Be you, for in the end we are all alone, and if you don't like yourself,
   your loneliness will overtake you.
Own the path you're on.

That Which I Cannot See, I Cannot Be.

   Richard Goldman

Fly Or Die

Tho she keeps growing she'll never see the sky
Resting upon this tree, screeching and rage
wanting so to leave
to be free of this cage,
why just me and not the rest?
Why one little bird, alone in this nest?
watching others "fly" she longs with her eyes
Eagles on high, how they soar!
Strong, brave, and sure!
Fly down eagles take me away
in this nest, I can no longer stay.
child, use your wings! Fly!
you had wings all along
who my child — stole your song?
Fly, don't you know?
you always had power within to go
join the flock!
Leave the nest!
I gave knowledge
you do the rest.

   Mary Ann Modes

The Posed

A moment captured in a white frame
where parents steal children from play
moving them like a sculptor molding clay.
A boy's face crumples into a scowling mask,
his touchdown stolen by a flash.
Two onyx haired brothers stand on each side
wearing shorts outfits with white zigzag patterns.
A brother and sister stand in the middle,
two blonde books between two dark bookends.
The victims of the camera squint
and wait for the photographer to shoot.
The girl smiles — she enjoys attention.
The boys look for a way to resume their game of cowboys and Indians.
The boy on the left — the one with the tragic mask — wears a cast.
His grinning brother assisted him — the creator of the break.
The grass blurs in the wind
around a building with flaking paint that stands to the side.
Electric lines invade the surrounding hills
jailed in this memory of a distant relative.

   Rhiannon Iha

Autumn 1996

Every autumn I feel a change
the wind stirs, restless in my aching soul,
I try to restrain the demons
which would crawl from beneath my skin.

I swallow hard the acrid pill,
designed by the authorities
to perfect me and protect me.
Or to protect themselves from me.

"How nice," the antiseptic people say.
"You do so well."
My life fits me like
someone else's suit.

See the expression on their faces
as I spit the pill upon the marble floor.
I will not let it eat me.
It is autumn, you know.

I will stand and let the wind
blow through my uncombed hair.
See the expression on their faces,
while I let the demons dance.

   Beverly Alspaugh

Look Into My Eyes

Look into my eyes
What do you see?
Visions of a nation
Not yet free
Warriors born
Untrained soldiers fighting in the streets
Who won't give into inevitable defeat
A world so cold
Not caring for another's needs
Poverty, ghettos, racism, lack of education
The foundation of a violent nation
Look hard; look deep
Now, tell me, what do you see?
Just a little more of me
Look into my eyes
Please tell me
How can American's such as me
Stop the corruption in this nation?
For teens to have better diversity
In our corrupted society

   Judaea L. Willis

Skin

Open your mouth,
take that cotton out of your ears.
Repeat after me,
in the mingling of blood
from Norway to South Africa,
in hellholes and paradises
there is a shared knowledge of the gene,
the chromosome, the DNA of a rip tide.
A slide into the mysteries
of a fathomless darkness;
a bursting of a bubble
of light found thrown
around a universe
like a sun unknown,
unwanted, even in death,
not knowing it had life.

As two children bounce
a ball across a sidewalk,
there is no telling of skin,
in their laughter.

   Keith Rhodes

Ven

You remembered me like a seasoned melody
How I sparked in you a deep memory
In my dream you spoke of a sweet but sad story
You whispered in my ear so truthfully
But you lighted that wintry candle of jealousy
That buried seed you long ago planted inside of me
Strange that all this plagued me subconsciously
Hindered in this mythical setting of confusion I be
Sending blazing emotions as if thou were my enemy
Though you were my twice lost love it was obvious to see
My other half and bonded soul ripped away so savagely
But in my dreams you came back,
You came back to haunt me.

Kristen R. Wellman

The Lost Little Girl

One day as I was wandering around in my mind.
I saw a little girl, a very lonely and sad little girl.
She seemed to be lost in a troubled soul filled with guilt and shame.
I felt instant compassion for her. I wanted to save her; to save
her from her own despair. She looked back at me with big green,
hopeful, begging eyes. Eyes that had seen pain,
eyes that had seen nothingness, eyes that knew someone,
somewhere could help her come to the surface. I reached out to
her with my hand; she didn't respond.
I called to her with my sweetest voice; she didn't hear. Oh, how
I wanted to touch her, to touch her with the compassion that I
felt toward her. I needed her help to overcome a lifetime of fears
and anger. I somehow knew she was the one with the answers I
was looking for. I reached out to her with my heart, to my
surprise, she responded. That little girl came alive with happiness. She became the flame, that lit my fire of love and self
discovery. That little girl came to be me.

Raelene Barnes

Untitled

I was mournfully disheartened by your callous farewell
which was no farewell at all
I became disinterested in myself and that which surrounds
the fairy tale which was told was a dream
therefore, I gave up struggling for that which was not
and would never be
Yet, to live as one seems an eternal sentence.
Two, even when one is gone
at least be in the grave together
Where will one be laid? In a cold plot of dirt alone
And it will be said "she had so much to give,
but alas no one wanted it."

Kimberly O'Connell

A Part Of Me Dies

How do I explain the feeling that I had?
When I found out that I was gonna be a Dad.
I was filled with happiness, I was filled with joy.
In a matter of months I would have a little boy.
But as the weeks went by, little did I know.
What she was doing to my baby, causing him not to grow.
I don't know how she could do it, what happened to her heart?
Before my son was even born, she tore his life apart.
She kept doing all her drugs, she didn't think of what would be.
How could she do this to my baby? He was also part of me.
She was smoking cigarettes and marijuana, and drinking all the time.
But she never once thought of what she was doing to his mind.
The day he was born is a day that will always haunt me.
My baby was five pounds smaller than he should be.
The doctors did all they could do, but it was too late.
His little heart was beating at a too low rate.
My feelings toward her now, are feelings that I'll never be able to shake.
The first breath my baby took, was the last he'll ever take.

Nicole Mayer

How Strange It Seems!

To walk through the silence,
to lay awake at night
thinking of you
knowing that you are gone,
yet, still catching the glimpse
of an airy presence that
now represents you.

How strange it seems!
Calling your name
and you are not there to answer reaching out,
and not having you to touch.

How strange!
For I now celebrate with myself 'cause I am alone.
I am mad 'cause I know
in my heart I miss you . . .
I need you near.

And even if we both know what is, what must be,
I am still assured of my love for you.
Every part of you belongs to me.

Joseph Hinds

Dream Away

What is a dream?
A dream is something not far away
sometimes you can capture it, making your day.

A dream can be especially sweet,
something real tasty like a chocolate treat.

A dream can mean floating way up in the air,
or bravely entering the dragon's dark lair.

A dream could be found in a book that you read,
like performing some kind of heroic deed.

A dream might be in the ocean so deep,
or cruising the beach in your old Wrangler jeep.

A dream might be sleeping in sweet smelling hay,
or relaxing a little on the dock of the bay.

A dream could be a happy crowd's smiles,
carrying you on for miles and miles.

A dream might be hearing the gentle rains fall,
or just hearing nothing, nothing at all.

Jennifer L. Chappell

Grandma's Peace Lily

When I needed strength you were there.
When I needed encouragement it was given.
On the day you left me, a Peace Lily was given in your name.
Yet I never gave it much thought when I brought the Lily home.

> You felt my sorrow.
> You heard my cries.
> You saw my pain.

You heard my frustration when I was trying to find a job.
For three years, you saw and felt everything I was going through.
Yet I never gave it much thought when I brought the Lily home.

One day, I asked you to help me and you gave me what I needed.
On the day I found my first job, the Lily began to grow a flower.
The flower was your sign showing me how happy you were for me.
Yet I never gave it much thought when I brought the Lily home.

This gave me life again and it is budding with the wonderful flowers
   the Lily is growing.
Now, I am realizing that your spirit never left me.
Your spirit is with the Peace Lily and I am glad that it has inspired
   me to make my dreams come true.
Yet, I never gave it much thought when I brought the Lily home.

Denise K. Marine

Your Still With Us

Your face was so pale,
your lips were so blue.
Your hand was so cold,
how could this be true?

You now lay so still,
your heart does not beat.
No more throwing footballs,
or teams to defeat.

Although you are gone,
I still see your face.
You watch from above,
in the better place.

We are still morning,
you're watching us cry.
But now you have wings,
and you're learning to fly.

You're still in our hearts, and never will die.
I would have felt better, if I could just say goodbye.

We must face the facts, we know you're okay.
And soon we will meet again, on a wonderful day.

Amanda Anderson

Mother's Day

The day my Mother rose above this life,
My feet grew roots in mud and could not move.
The streams and rivers dried and ceased to flow;
The clouds wept, but the rain froze into snow;
And birds, encrusted, lost their frail wings to
The wind, a heartless, slashing butcher knife.

The day my Mother climbed God's sequined stair,
I dropped into a well, cold, dark and deep.
Green forests browned in drought and crashed to earth;
The sun chilled and could warm no seeds to birth;
And birds, with no more boughs on which to sleep,
Flew until, spent, they fell out of the air.

In time these cataclysms went away;
I uprooted my feet and struggled free.
The natural world resumed its old routine.
Except the sky, which since her death has been
No longer blue, but silt grey like the sea,
In sad, silent honor of Mother's Day.

Peter Sipchen

Repeated Trips A Trip To The Fair

An old man sat on the bench, taking in the sights and sounds of
the park. With a smile on his face, he reflected on his youth.
The dancing, prancing horses in their never-ending race to
nowhere stayed in step, as the merry-go-round pushed forth
the streaming sounds of the calliope.
In his mind he mounted the tallest horse, as he had done,
so often, so long ago. Then something interrupted his ride.
A very large pink cloud was moving toward him,
a picture so familiar and yet so distant.
Suddenly the sugary air was melting on his tongue.
It seemed as the fruity taste came from the aroma
that emitted from the web spinning cooker in the middle of the park.
The sounds and voices of the happy children,
tired parents, and inviting calls
coming from the long rows of venders echoed his memories.
But, now he faced an anxious moment, he was lost.
Where was the rescuing hand of his father?
A tug on his sweater brought him back to the moment.
A tiny hand reached out from a replication of himself.
Hand in hand and bound by inherent love, they melted into the crowds.

Linda F. Herring

Life Support

Would it seem possible? Would it seem real?
That twenty-one seconds ago I could still feel

The roof of my mouth, the bottom of toes,
My knee as it bends and brain as it knows,
The wind as wind whispers across the expanse,
And closeted skeletons in darkness that dance.

Was it really a short twenty-one seconds or so?

When my eyes slipped shut, my pulse left town,
My soul drifted up and my body shut down,
My throat stopped clearing, my ears quit hearing,
My time had expired — Aahhh — I knew it was nearing.

But I never knew twenty-one seconds could go,

By so quickly, for me, now my immortal remains,
Bear a vague semblance of life, but I still maintain,
That my hold on this realm though reduced to mere thoughts
Is far better than the awaiting pine box.

Johnny Polk

My Tears

I sit in bed thinking about you as I lay on my pillow.
Although I know it's coming, I can't stop it;
a tear slides out the corner of my eye.
The pillow soaks it in.
Then my eyes are like a waterfall spilling forth.
I watch with a saddened
heart as my tears fall to the floor to collect in a puddle.
Everyone is asleep, so one is there to dry my eyes,
nor is anyone there to wipe my puddle of tears.
Then I fall into a slumber . . . full of dreams.
I dream, you touch my face.
When I wake up the next morning . . .
my eyes are dry,
my puddle is gone,
and in my heart,
I know!!!
You were there.

Victor Hill

Not Amused

Huddled in the night
I sit and stare with wretched despair
At the insignificant life that I hold so dear
I pray to anything that will listen to me
That I will soon regain my own sanity
But all I hear is lies
There's truth in everything
There's truth in those lies
There's truth in why I must die.
I'm just not amused by it all.

Michael Grace Jr.

Femme

What are daughters for
  except to grow too early into vexing women?
Contentious and cantankerous as a sweet lunar wind
  is what they are.
They blow hot and cold in the same breath.

That plodding creature man
  is so dazzled by their luminesence
that he is ever unaware of the wayward breeze
  and forever surprised
to find the crossing of their knees
  has changed his life
in a way he never realized
  was forever.

J. T. Cummins Jr.

Love

Love is warm, love is cold, love is there for all to hold
Love is two, love is one, love is being with someone.
Love is bold, love is shy, love is never knowing why.
Love is high, love is low, love is helping us to grow.
Love is soft, love is hard, love is sometimes in a card.
Love is white, love is blue, love is giving all for you.
Love is strong, love is weak, love is something we all seek.
Love is a flower, love is a rose, love is that way, why, no one knows.
Love is false, love is true, love is in the heart of you.
Love is danger, love is chance, love is sure to make you dance.
Love is square, love is round, love is something to be found.
Love is family, love is health, love is a special kind of wealth.
Love is a hammer, love is a saw, love always comes from my grandpa.
Love is coffee, love is tea, love is there for you and me.
Love can hum, love can sing, love can make you buy a ring.
Love is nice, right form the start. I keep it always in my heart.

April Milgrove

Mother

When my mother died,
it hurt.
Not just my loss,
but the fact that no one seemed to care.
The world businessed as usual.
Mom was gone and her passing ignored.

Then,
one night on a mountain top,
I looked to the stars
and counted one fewer than a trillion.
A star had died since last count
and the sky would be different
for the rest of eternity.

The loss of one little star
changes the universe . . .
forever.

Janie Kent

Death Of A Dancer

The end of my dancing is near
I must face this and control my fear
I have lived life my way
The bill is due, it is time to pay
Why one's spirit fails is hard to know
But I have weakened and it's getting hard not to show
As the old reality falls away
all I can do is watch, what can I say.
It's gone too far for me to stop
The pretense of control I must drop
I have loved life and the people as they pass by
As the dancing ends it's hard not to cry.

Roger DeVito

Moving Around

When you are moving you end up proving
how it is tough and how it is rough
to make friends and then make ends
you make friends one by one then some by some.
When you grow up in the military
you begin to feel a little weary
about moving to another town
because when you get there, you feel down.
You don't know anyone, but the sun
and when you feel as though you are done
and when you start to get used to the place
you move again, getting smacked in the face.
When you retire from moving around
you find yourself finally being found.

Kimberly McKnight

Reality

What is my reality?
What makes me . . . me?
I never get any answers to my questions.
Why is that?

Is reality unexplainable?
Am I really me, or a figment of myself?
Do my questions have any answers?
How will I ever know?

Is reality real?
Is it being written as we live it?
Are questions really questions?
Or are they a figment of reality?

So, what is reality?
Who am I, and why?
If I don't know, who does?
Not me.

Do you?

Susan Marie Willems

Room Revealed

A flower beside a candle
The scent of sweet perfume
The smell of potpourri near the open window
A black cat resting on the rug
Beautiful blue eyed Susan
Red roses in a vase
A dress laid on the bed
A novel waiting to be read
A picture of Mary
And in the wink of an eye
The candle blows out

Marcie Plyler

The Humble One

The time is now. One walks — his head is bowed.
We live and strive to be — be all but proud.
A watcher — he, in shape and form a blot,
knows all in that he knows that he does not.
The place is here. One looks — his mind is clear.
We are so far from knowing we are near.
A mirror — he, of sense and will a light,
progresses for himself in every right.
The one is he who, in the end, shall thrive.
We strive to live, but first we must survive.
A pupil — he, with ever rungs to climb,
succeeds in being one with space and time.

Eric J. Apodaca

Memories

The morning mountain air was fresh and clean.
Winter's shadow was turning dim and lean.
The season's icy grip was not away too long.
The stream was free to sing an old quaint song.

New life emerged from every hill and dale.
Mothers cuddled their helpless, weak and pale.
What price this new life will eventually pay
Was guaranteed by what occurred that day.

This was not a new or unfamiliar place.
Not so, was the look upon his weathered face.
Without a word, we knew the time was near.
Life's love is worth the price and that was clear.

It came to pass I lost a friend — a Dad.
Today he lives in memories that are never sad.

Henry A. Long Jr.

Beauty And The Beast

Within the sanctuary of love
In front of the alter of life
Kneels a man empty with sorrow
The heart it beats, though he lives not really alive
He prays for your love and trust as the shadows of
Yesterday give break to the dawn of tomorrow

Anxiously awaiting the future
While forgiving the past
It is for your love and sweet, gentle touch
That I long and I last

The oceans of my desire
Overflow their boundaries with the passion
Of a burning heart a fire

Deep within the depths of my sacred heart
Hidden from the wolves of the world
Burns the holy flame of my love for you
Guarded by angels with lions mane
Forever fed by the slaves of my soul

James Damon Simpson

Come Child

Come, child sit while I tell you a story
While you wander aimlessly . . .
Of a journey in shackles and chains

While you abandon your loved ones . . .
Of being snatched from your homeland and your mother's arms

While you take your brother's life . . .
Of having no life to call your own

While you cheat your fellow man . . .
Of being sold for profit

While you miss your opportunities . . .
Of laboring from dawn to dust without pay

While you lose you way . . .
Of stealing away by moonlight

While you refuse to learn . . .
Of laws against you being taught

While you sing songs to degrade . . .
Of song of pain and humiliation
Child, sit while I tell you a story of a life long struggle without
   a happy ending . . .

Elnora Wright

Dreams

A dream is an unknown wish
that your heart whispers to your thoughts.
A dream is something so strong
but yet so inexplicable.
Dreams are made up of the mental power
and the intelligence of your soul,
not only the principle of reality.
Sometimes when you think it is impossible to convey
all of your thoughts and emotions into words,
a dream will show you how.
Happiness can be found from undiscovered dreams,
dreams that go beyond the limit of what is expected.
There are some people who dream nonfiction,
and there are some who's dreams overwhelm reality
causing the birth of the dream never to occur.
Some people dream undecided,
and some connect en bloc with their dreams.
But what earns the title of a dream?
Your heart and soul will answer that question
using more than just words.

Janelle Peterson

Secure In The Arms Of The Master

As I often look to the hills, I know all my help comes
from my God in heaven above. Never, not ever will
he abandon or forsake me. I am one of his very
own, hand picked and molded, shaped and designed
in his very image. Oh how I love this wonderful
Master of mine. Words are not comprehensive
enough to tell you just how wonderful and
marvelous he is, this master of mine.
He's compassionate, he's awesome,
he's forgiving, he's faithful.
He's an all consuming fire of radiant splendor and
glory. Someday I'll go to live with him in paradise for
eternity in a beautiful city where the streets are paved
in gold. There I will bow down before him, and sing
wonderful hymns and praises to his blessed and holy name.
"Holy, Holy, Holy," worthy is the lamb of God Almighty . . .

Evangelist Sandra McMillan-Cato

Taylor

Well Taylor you're one year old.
You're something special for Grandpa to hold.

Your curly hair, your beautiful face.
Memories like these you could never erase.

I pray to God every night,
To keep you warm and bundled tight.

Take your time, don't grow up fast,
your childhood will quickly pass.

Take your time, and grow up slow.
You have your whole life, with places to go.

All I ask, is do your best,
And God will do all the rest.

William John Jarvie

The Wounded Heart

Lonely nights filled with tears
Lonely days filled with pain
No one there to take away the fears
No one there with me in the rain

Where is love so beautiful and gay
Where is he? The one who will love me
Is there no one who can truly say
There he is, look across the sea

Look at the sun shining so bright
Look at the stars glittering above
Why does not my soul warms from the light
Must my hopes and dreams flutter like a dove

Sing, sing, heart of mine
Sing, sing, lips so sweet
The misery will stop, give it time
Your true love, you shall meet

Dorothy Thomas-McCall

América

Cada año there are many muchachos who write to me
You've been a good girl de lo que yo can see
I'm checking mi lista y checking it dos veces
Para little girls who always limpia sus messes
I know that sometimes your mama says
"¿Caramba, que pasa?"
But, you know that
I will come to your casa!
After you fall asleep, in your cama
En la noche I will come, by la mañana

Love, Santa

Beatrice R. Guzman

My Tolerance Is Limited

If I were a bird, I would fly up
Up where the air is dark, and the stars are bright
Up where I will be safe, and where I will be secure
Up where I will have peace, but not be alone.

If I were a snake, I would slither down
Down to the deepest hole there I will be shielded
Shielded from the heartlessness of the people around me
And there I will escape, escape from the boulders that still me
I will be free, free from my past times
Times of mental abuse and times of suffering.

If I could escape, I would but now I am trapped
Trapped forever in this world and with my peers,
Peers who abuse my mind, and tamper with my emotions,
Peers who see that I am vulnerable and then attack my soul,
My soul which has already suffered severe pain,
And lacks time to build defenses, these peers will never understand
What needs to be understood, they will never say
What needs to be said, as I go on I begin to believe,
That it is not I who is trapped, but it is they,
So I must learn to be tolerant of the fact that they will never change
Or realize how ignorant they are for as of now I must wait for an escape.

Albert Pickens

Old Things

Old houses, old towns, old people, these seem to draw me in;
they cling like vines on a trellis, why do they appear so inviting,
unless it's because I'm old, I don't know because I'm only a child

Sandra Risner

Brother Sun And Sister Moon

Brother Sun and Sister Moon
have blessed us and will again, soon.
As we've laughed and as we've cried,
as we've lived and as we've died.
And Mother Earth hold us in her love
and father sky looks on from above.
Protecting us their children dear,
helping us because they care.
Each shows their love and affection in many ways
and for that we thank them all of our days.
And we shall hate them not now nor never
for only the Earth and sky last forever.

Clay Rylee

Black Traveller's Cabin

It took a long while for the wind
to sigh through this decrepit doorway.
Inside, old news was trampled in rat-play
and Packer Creek ripped up by hands
groping for luck. We couldn't wait.

There was a king, long ago
who carved these cabin walls
now he's seeking cellars below.
Aside from us, no one who had seen the remains
of what hands can do understood.
But there was still life here . . . tamaracks raving in the wind.

When we spoke of gold, weighted tins would swish
and chink along the creek. Lonely ghosts drinking wine
whistled and roared when the storm blew snow
through dancing whores. We both loved the cabin.

Were we only dreaming? No, we had found
the rusted wheelbarrow alive and moving.
Packer Creek had not yet become pan-fried fish
and Dutch-oven biscuits, but thee were hinges
and painted faces and wintry dust . . . telling what photos cannot tell.

J. D. Zindler

Space

Space, a black void of the unreal.
Pricked by shafts of unfeeling light,
scarred with the breath of the unmerciful.
It is an oblivion of unseeing darkness.
Chilled by death and burned with fear.
Singing a song of untold woe, heard only by the deaf.
Shrouded by dust of forsaken hope.
Stars pierce the silent sky.
Spears of cold, unfathomable whiteness.
They dot the darkness with lifeless light.
Shining orbs cast their lambent amber, the power of a hidden fire.
The realm of Uranus, it is ruled by a blind hate.
Space is an unending night, like a death of total life.
It twists the mind of the righteous.
Alienated from life, it lives for death.
It is a calculated insanity, a murder of all hope.
A tomb of warmth, it chills the mind.
Unperceivable loneliness, the predator of life.
The unknown, from which we hide.
It is the chill of a forgotten fear.

Kathryn Giblin

We Are Here To Serve The Lord

We are here to serve the Lord
In body, mind and spirit
Yet we seem to close the doors
And ignore our chores

Children crying, people dying
What is this world coming to
I want to make a change
How about you

This country was set up according to his word
Now we are changing our minds
And look at the crimes
What was right is wrong
What was wrong is right
The people are confused
Yet they choose to ignore the calling of the Lord

Wake up people, learn his word
Do your duties and serve the Lord
Heaven is waiting with great rewards!

Aronette Clayton

Through The Glass

A soft breath of wind, brushing gently against your face, a savage
storm of thunder rumbling, lightning striking your very soul.

A gentle smile, soft laughter, that lights your very being
a torrent of tears which threaten to rend your heart
from this body that houses it.

When love comes to you, look not through the rose glass, instead,
look through the glass darkly, for to give your heart, is to give
your soul. To look blindly, with eyes covered
in the soft blush of loves first stirrings
is to perhaps be shattered.

All falling, as illusions turning to dust at your feet,
your tattered dreams, the bottomless well of your tears.

Judge not the other, that is not your domain.
Better to remember, look through a glass darkly.

Continue to believe, to dream, for to give up
would be to allow your essence to wither.

Remember your pain, be cautious, take not your innocence with
you into your new world.

Crush the rose colored glasses, beneath the illusions already
given and see with your soul, what is real, and what is not.

Shirley M. Breznai

Observations A Poem

I've spent a lifetime
reading children's faces,
hoping the lights go on.

I change hats often during the school day . . .
building self-esteem,
smoothing ruffled feathers,
somehow managing
to make the unknown less threatening.

Thirteen should be fun, but it isn't . . .
too many hormones,
too few hugs,
pressure from peer groups,
sudden tears, realistic fears.

I wish parents would offer time, instead of money,
demand a little less, praise a great deal more.

I wouldn't go back to thirteen again if I could,
down their same road.
Better by far to nurture minds and bodies
for challenges that lie ahead.

Judith A. Kalinowski

Love

My addiction grows stronger,
with each passing moment we are separated,
together as one, the euphoria is overwhelming,
each time I use her my desire increases,
she fills my every thought, I crave her touch

Without, there is no joy,
emptiness festers in the depths of my soul,
the longing, my mind cannot escape her call,
she's there inside me beckoning me on,
how I need to feel her passionate embrace

At last she is mine once more,
pain ebbs as my veins pulse with her presence,
my senses dull to everything but her,
she is my world, her texture, taste, and smell,
until we are separate again, then pain is all there is.

Eric Weiss

A Tribute To My Brother, Tim

Timothy Michael Estes 7/26/58 - 8/5/91
We say you left too soon it wasn't your time to die,
We drown ourselves in sorrow we think of you and cry.

If only you were here
You could wipe away our tears,
with your joyous-lively spirit
Your love and your good cheer.

God had a better place
A brighter smile for your face.
Where all is peace and love
God took you to heaven above.

We miss you so much, Tim,
You were, by far, a heavenly gem.
To all the lives that you touched
Your memory remains, as such.

We pray for God's guidance, throughout our lives
Forever and ever to serve him.
To someday make it to heaven, bow down at Jesus' feet,
And once again, we shall meet.

A glad reunion in heaven we'll spend eternity thanking him.
reuniting with our loved ones especially, my brother, Tim.
In everlasting memory and eternal love.

Gyl Estes

Waiting For Someday

This is me short and gruff.
You think you're happy, I call your bluff.
Life is hard, I know it now.
Work is scarce and money poor.

This time of year still gives me hope.
I have great family, good friends too.
For them I'll keep on keeping on.

At times I feel like giving in.
This life on earth my only sin.
My lonely heart is open wide.
These empty feelings I can not hide.

They say all good things, come to those who wait.
I wonder why, I wonder when.
Loneliness my true real friend.

I know my life will turn around.
Love for me, I hope I'll find.
Someday my sins will all be forgiven.
Someday my prayers will all be answered.
But for now, I just keep on living.

Jerome Cervalli Jr.

Outer Banks — August 1995

rose-colored swirled clouds drift far above the dune's grasses
the sun begins to settle into the sound behind me
a warm humidless breeze blows up the corners of a beach towel
upon which my ebony wife sits quietly with broad rimmed straw hat
eyes gently closed
head bowed
a little tern squeals zreek-eek and stands patiently next to me
waiting for a dropped piece of cut bait
a family of porpoises swim the horizon
to my right, my daughter writes emily in wet sand left from the
previous high tide
to my left, my son scurries
diaper torn off
a little naked creation
many sand pipers, large and small, surround him
altogether they chase and run from the warm surf
I lean back as water splashes my shins and knees
I make my last cast of the day
looking all around me again, I quietly say aloud
thankyou GOD

James Nagele

Exercise Your Rights And Options

As citizens of this fine nations, we should take
advantage of our many rights;

Should we not take time out to vote for the
candidate of our choice?

Take pride in choosing the religion that we prefer.
Exercise the right of choice in choosing our
lifestyle, our bride and our friends.

Having the right to follow or not follow a new trend.
Should we be open or reserved can be determined by you.

The right to make a hastily choice or to think things through.
Going through life in the ultra fast lane, or
pacing oneself on a much slower plane.

Choose to better life through opportunity and
constructive change or be complacent and limit one's range.

Choose to love or be loved, depend or not depend
on the good man above, decide to agitate, instigate or hate.

Or decide to create a tranquil climate with our chosen mate.

Robert E. McMahan

Birthday Reflections At Middle-Age

"You're not getting older, just better," they say
I've heard that slogan on many a day
Yet, I've seen my youth before me pass
And I wonder if age really has any class.

My hair has become as shading of gray
The facial lines deepen to my dismay
And as I look back and remember the past
I wish that time had not gone so fast.

The man I married is still here at my side
I sense in his eyes the deepest of pride
Though we have grown older, our love has withstood
The years that were hard; the years that were good.

As I blow out the candles — one for each year
My children around me, my husband so near
I know that life will always be
The greatest gift God gave to me.

> *Marie Tedesco*

A Vision Of Natural Beauty

Who could ever imagine
that a woman of such great
intelligence would be chosen
to be my mother . . .
 She has beautiful blond
hair that naturally parts to
the right side.
 Her bangs reach below the
brow above the top of her eyes.
 The color of her eyes are a
beautiful color of autumn leaves around the center
with a cloudy blue gray sky around the outside.
 Her lips are the color of red leaves before they die.
Her smile is as bright as the sunset.
 The sound of her laughter is like the wind
blowing through the trees.
 As her words are being spoken
the sounds of leaves falling and
birds calling. With a vision of natural
beauty forever seen.

> *Marie A. Romero*

Were It Only Up To Me

Were it only up to me, my love,
 You'd never be sad,
For even the moon would wear a smile,
 And your riches would stretch a mile.
Were it only up to me, my love.
 You'd always be well,
For there'd be no hell.
 You'd always be young,
And wear the sweet blush of youth, my love,
 Were it only up to me.

> *Ann Possemato*

If I Have Died

Lookin' down,
I see my family hurt
Everyone is cryin'
I look around, why people are crying?!?
Than I see myself! Amazed!
I turn around, walkin' towards to dad.
Telling him, that I'm sorry,
But he can't hear me!
Started cryin', wish I could give him a hug.
Than I looked at myself, in the coffin.
Walked out of the room.
I realized, I was dreaming!!

> *Eliza Mark*

The Assassination Of Medgar Evers . . .
A Work In Progress

Excuses used to come easy:
"Ill educated." "It's their tradition."
Then a shot in the night . . . in the back.

Crack shot. Crackpot.
How comfortably those credentials commingle.
But he woke us up our shame!

Bile in one's throat sent a message.
We are better than that!
We are men!

Yesterday. Stood next to a man at the deli.
Ordered: "A pound of white American."
He conspired: "A disappearing commodity."

This morning. Another fellow villager offered:
"Blacks are burning 'em.
For the insurance."

The jury of the common man is speaking.
The assassin vomits hate creeds from his Jackson cell.
And people read them.
And smile.

> *Charles Fryer*

Children — Parents

Children are a special thing
and they should be treated like a gold ring
they should not be used
and they should not be abused
parents should be a child's light
not the one who makes a fight.
Children remember what they see
so they should see the right things more than three!
Teach children to follow Christ and his goodness
and to avoid the devil and his badness
children should be taught education is important
because the results are permanent children should be made happy
so they stay and a they should be made miserable and so they
run away children should eat until their hunger is gone parents
shouldn't let a child's hunger linger on and on
children are a special thing
and they should be treated better than a gold ring!

> *Bret Silva*

Wonderland

Whether you have love
or whether you have hate
will depend on your own fate
nothing is right in this crooked world.
Nobody knows how their future goes.
But you can be sure of this,
something bad will happen by
the end of the day,
there just is no other way.
Nothing is ever right
so people just break into fights
and if you've had a childhood like mine
you just can't stand the sights
people come and people go stop the clocks
and turn them back to where
everyone is in utopia land
everything that is good there is no
recollection of. Whatever happened to that land of love?
Love is gone on this earth as we now know it
love is gone and we can't help but show it.

> *Danielle Debrita*

Special One

While being tucked in her little bed
A little girl once sadly said,

Mommy, I wish that I could be
Like you — more pretty than me.

That is something you must never say.
Everyone is beautiful in their own way.

On her freckled face was pain,
So her mother sat to gently explain.

When God was done, He looked at your face.
There was something else He wished to place.

God took his time and was in no rush.
So He picked up a tiny artist's brush

And carefully mixed some freckle paste.
Not a portion did He wish to waste.

He painted some very special dots.
On your face they were such lovely spots.

When the angels asked why this was done,
God answered that you were His special one.

The mother was satisfied, her job was done.
They both knew why she was a special one.

Cindy S. Bond

My Literary World

How can I make people see,
literature means the world to me?
Books are my fantasies, my imagination
makes them real,
Every time I open one, a new adventure
is revealed.
Poetry soothes the soul, it lets the
mind fly free,
each time I read another one, it
truly relaxes me.
Writing is my favorite form, I've always thought it best,
it's so much fun to write something, much better
than the rest.
Literature can and will take me far away,
sometimes when exceptional, I won't return
for days,
I hope that I have made you see,
why literature means the world to me.

Holly Atherton

Eyes

    Oh eyes, all that I remember,
Pierce me like a cold frost of December.
Baby blues that I remember.
    I remember you looking into my eyes and I into yours.
I could just stare for hours and hours.
    In your eyes, I saw how they sparkled and burned.
Now, it makes my stomach turn and churn.
    They showed me when you were gone and when they rained
And now I know you'll never open them again.
    Oh hopeless! Oh Why!
Didn't anyone report it, so you wouldn't die?
    My blue eyes weep.
As I watch your casket seep,
Into the crevice of your grave.
    I don't believe!
I won't believe it!
    Do you blame me?
Just yesterday you could name me!
    Ashes to ashes, dust to dust,
I know our love will never combust.

Katie Horahan

Unforgettable Loss

My life was normal and going OK
When a telephone rang and changed it every which way
Not imagining the news I was about to hear
I picked it up and heard a voice filled with fear
Three words were spoke and a tear rolled down my cheek
I don't understand I was just with him last week
I scream out loud in unbearable pain
It seems my cousin went too fast in the rain
Taken from life he's lost so much
A family, a wife, an American dream
The love of a friend, and his boyish like gleam
I say it ain't true and it's all in my head
But the three words he spoke were Brian Is Dead

Russel Blondin

The Hopes And Cares Of Yesterday And Today

The hopes of today come and go,
and nobody stopping to even care.
Our minds are too high and our hearts are too low,
caring and helping turns out medium rare.

We are to caught up in ourselves,
caring only about the big me and how I look.
But knowing inside we look glum and are about as big as elves,
and now can only read about our cares in a book.

It seems only yesterday when everyone cared,
caring about the needs of others and helping them out.
Now today nobody even dared,
only thinking of themselves and their route.

Now all of a sudden we try to grasp it,
the hope and care that we've forgotten.
That love and encouragement in that dark pit,
all of it now rotten.

The Hopes and Cares of Yesterday,
slowly ripening for Today.
They are shared with others like a sunshine ray,
it'll be a struggle, but that's what we must pay!

Ashli Hanson

I Love You Daddy

    When I was younger, my daddy meant everything to me and still
does today. But as I got older, I matured into a young adult, and
I've come to realize without a great father which I have today, I
would not succeed in today's society. I now know I have passed
one obstacle of my goal: To become an intelligent person just as
my father is today. I wish for the best between us in the future
and I hope we never drift apart, because not only is he my hero
and I want to follow his footsteps to be just like him, but also
because I love him. My father is my everything and he should
know, whatever may happen, I'll never let him go.

Johanna C. Portillo

I Wonder

It is a lonely world we live in
With love, and hate, and sin.
I wonder where lies the happiness I used to dream.
Somehow, yes, somehow — gone it seems.

The longing grows much deeper — to be a child again.
For then there was laughter; before this life began.
I wonder, oh I wonder, what the years have done.
It is said education makes the battle won.
But I wonder, oh I wonder, the sorrows it brings to some.

These are but thoughts in writing,
How I wish they'd show the lighting
To a bright and clear new day.
Perhaps, perhaps — someday.

LaNeta L. Carlock

The Double Tree

There was a tree in the parking lot,
It made such a cool and shady spot,
Part time it was green and part time bare,
But it looked so tall and majestic there
Spreading its arms every which way,
As if to say God Bless This Day.

The tree is gone, progress the cause,
Now, when I look out I seem to pause
And see only in Mind's eye the tree
That reached for God and gave peace to me.

Phyllis Parente

Hold On

Sometimes in our lives, we feel so all alone
with thoughts that have shattered to unknown.
Our hearts have been battered and broken,
With words that are unspoken.
Often, we feel our desired dreams are far away,
But the memories of having them are here to stay.
So each lonely and passing day has gone
By faith and hope you can have it all if you hold on.
Sometimes we may say a prayer
And in our hearts God will let us know he is there.
He'll take you by the soft hand
And let your happiness begin.
Sometimes God may seem away and apart
But he'll always be in your heart.
He'll help you to be strong
When everything seems to be wrong
And help you to realize that it only takes you to
            hold on.

Lindsay Rachelle Bays

Valentine For Shirley

Years past when we were in our prime
And life flowed smooth in careless rhyme
It was an easy thing to see
That I loved you, and you loved me.

But high winds and rough seas came to force
Our hopes, our dreams, our lives off course,
Making us cling to shredded hope
As in the storms we strove to cope.

Now it's a wondrous thing to feel
You still beside me at life's wheel.
I'm thankful that God made you mind
And that you are my Valentine.

Keith P. Kirby

I Wish

I wish there was a place for me
Where all the flowers grow
And life was treasured as a valuable
A price far more than gold.

Where children played and sang of joy
Of what love meant to each
A mountain higher and steep to climb
But not far out of reach.

And in this place the days were as infinity
The nights crept by unnoticed
For happiness was an abundant reservoir
And peace was its caretaker and hostess.

So much for my dreams or desires
It's hard for me to visualize or insist
For what I'm speaking of in terms of life
Is not much more than, a wish.

Jacqualine Williams Rippy

Over The Hill Romance

Over the hill romance, may have a strange ring
But to those of us who are, I can tell you by far
It's a very very real thing.

Over the hill romance, may be 40, 50, 60, or more
But when it happens we sense, can be just as intense
As that which happened before.

Over the hill romance, can be even better than before
The children are gone, you enjoy being alone
You're reliving the days of yore.

Over the hill romance, rekindled with your mate of old
Or with a new friend, or with one who might have been
If you had been so bold.

Over the hill romance, is filled with as much fire
The flame is still there, even if you become unaware
The heart can be filled with desire.

Over the hill romance, for those who don't know
Includes — just as when younger, feelings sometimes stronger
The heart, as well as somewhat below.

Over the hill romance, in conclusion I'll say
Happening under, on, or over the hill, includes the very same thrill
as that of a former day.

Sheila L. Davis

The Commute

Early to rise each morning before the crack of dawn,
stumble into the closet for something warm to put on.
Then a quick dash to the bath,
hoping this will awaken me at last.
Next a visit to my dresser, to make me look alive,
then dress real quick, to make that door dash at five.
Now in my vehicle and headed South on 1-5,
wondering why all the bad drivers,
have the same work schedule as I.
Hope to find a good spot to park in,
one that no one can block me in.
A block or two to walk,
before I have arrived.
Safe and sound I feel,
with another rainy day down.
It's no wonder that I feel so blessed to be alive.

Shirley A. Baylor

End Of Love

It was one big day we met each other
You wanted us to be together
You called me every night and day.
There wasn't anymore sweet words left for you to say.
One night you called the time was one.
You said you couldn't sleep you felt alone.
We were still talking the time was 2. You said I love you.
You said for the love of ours you could always be there.
You said that for me you really care.
The love that we had was so tender.
But no-matter what, our love, I will always remember.
It was just your words that made me believe you.
Your love was empty, if it's love it can't do.
I hope I never gave you a chance.
But my love with you was an experience.
My tears fell like water everyday
But I realize that you could love anyway.
The times with you were meant a lot.
I hope our love lasted oh so long.
It was one night the tears went dry. We said good bye.

Hasmik Mamyan

Untitled

Cool breezes in the morning as water rushes by our side
Like the sinking of sand from our footsteps our love shall deepen
For each step we take will bring us closer to love's happiness
Our hands swinging together thru the motion of air as we rest
along the beach our thoughts we do share.
Secluded alone together. Paradise I'll give it to you
because you alone are my treasure ready to be cherished
To unlock the mysteries in your heart as I press upon your lips
the lovely pattern they impart. Our minds come together
as our bodies accept one another, a celebration of love
poured out like wine from the rainy weather.

Demond Ross

Why

Why do I love someone who doesn't love me? Why do I fall
in love so easily? Why is love blind? Why can't I control
what is going through my mind?

Why when you're in love you can never see the bad parts?
Why can't you see it's going to end with a broken heart?

Why does love block your vision? Why when you're in love
you can never make the right decision?

Why can't you make the decision that will save you from
another heart ache? Why can you only sit and wait for your
heart to break?

Why does love even exist, because if it didn't I would never
have to feel like this.

Rachel West

Autumn Leaves

And in a black power suit, she
on a summer shuffle
stops for the smell
of steam and urban crisis
(and one guitar, crucifying)

What large eyes you have

Oh, politics
it's all the same thing
the deconstruction of an evening
in early fall, when
the fences are down

Yes and the ethics of the thing
will stick to the wall like spaghetti
if you let them;
saved by grace which, impromptu
spins up off the yellow-slickered streets

inevitable as sunrise

Constance Adams

The Hero In The Town

An overwhelming litany of pictures keeps flowing through my mind,
    Seeing birds and branches exalted above the ground;
Yet, underneath the soil, without the worms of kind,
    Nature, the same will not remain, and would of course,
                completely change the town.

Except for one, no heroes you will find,
    All things great and small share honor in the town.
Whether strange or not, we hold the answer in our minds,
    The idea seems so simple, reminding us of clowns.

You see, there are no perfect people, all folks are of one kind;
    Not the answer but the question keeps floating all around.
Why can't we do for others the honor we hope to find.
    All things work together in honor of the other,
                if you hope to find the hero in the town.

Louis C. Kramp

A Tragedy

Beat after beat, scream after scream. Swimming in dirt,
tasting their thoughts. Entering the light, and falling
through darkness. Word after word smiling at me. The flesh
poured swiftly submerging my soul. My ears were on fire
though the sounds seemed empty. Catching and grabbing my
breath was extinguished. My eyes reflected the waves of the
sea. Seeing a memory of hopelessness and dreams. Rising and
falling, crashing and pulling, thrusting and taunting. Can
you hear me? I answered with a smile, an utmost deception
of the truth known by all. A transformation for none.
Talking a tongue upward to the darkness. Flashing
differences a show with everyone. Join this embrace
of mockery and deceit. Spread this disease, and contaminate
all. Feelings of betrayal, an overwhelming sensation through
this transcending enlightenment. Water begins to seep
through the cracks, bonding with the blood.
. . . drink this wine . . . Please quench your thirst . . .

Ralph W. Braden III

Alone I Stand

Alone I stand,
waiting endlessly for your love to return.
Tears fall from my eyes,
as thoughts of you drift through my mind.
I stand a prisoner of my own dreams,
Waiting and watching as each one turns to dust.
Having to let go, only to find
myself holding on to something that will never be.
When I look back at the love we once shared,
It was than that I realized,
Alone I stand.

Tanya Sewell

The Night Is You

The Moon is bright at night
The Moon is bright, like you at night
Your face is nice like the moon at night
Your eyes look like the stars at night
You are beautiful like the blue sky
Everyone can see you
But they can't see you at night
Because you're like the blue sky.

Carolyn Joan Thaggard

The Miracle

Days come and go as they always do
each with a new lesson or an obstacle that pops into view.

When this happens you need to remember that it's just a small stop
and soon you and your soul will be back at the top.

Look for the strength that is given from within
and free your soul from all guilt and sin.

Allow the angels of God to guide and teach you
as you find peace and harmony to flow as it should do.

Your mind and body are searching for what it deprives
so soon you won't have to fight so hard to survive.

When the end of the tight rope
your walking has come to its end
take all your strength and what
you've learned and begin to amend.

Soon you will see the victory you have
always dreamed would come true
because you yourself have become
the Miracle that you thought you couldn't do.

Salena Arbour

Love From Birth

Raising kids is the hardest job on earth,
It begins conception and starts at birth,
You see them grow and begin to crawl,
Having children is the greatest gift of all.

There's hard times but you'll see them through,
with a little love there's nothing you can't do.
So do your best and have a little fun,
before you know it they'll be grown and gone.

The birth of a child is a miracle from above,
so feel their hearts with lots of joy and love
for some day your child may be a parent too,
And from the beginning, it's up to you to show them what to do.

A family is a great deal of joy
And happiness to me is my little girls and boys.
Make your child's life wonderful and show them that you care,
And please let them know that you'll always be there.

Jeannella L. Terry

Blessed Scrutiny

It's easy, and often sensible, too
To assume that as you come to view
Or know someone better, what tends to show through
Is ugly, or selfish, disappointing to you.

Why try? Why even bother with love?
To deal with suspicions listed above —

Even so, I must, with indulgence, submit
Though the past has scarred up my own heart a bit
That sometimes a longer look can reveal
A bargain, great value — a wonderful deal!

Where security brought pain in the past, I surmise
That you might find the love of your life in disguise.

Marty Marks

The Blues

Through trees and water, we hear the blues.
In the children's laughter at play on the streets of Harlem.
It screams inside our voices like some living thing trapped
inside an ice box.
The old man sits on the porch one summer afternoon,
playing the guitar and singing his blues but with a
smile on his face as he plays.
How ironic. The band downtown, the
"Blues Brothers" sing the blues, their voices
like cold iron and splintered feet. The blues
runs through the African dancer's souls
and is heard clearly under their feet.
Blue moon blazing on a hot night, lights the eyes of ebony escapes.
Beautiful red, wine lips sing her child to sleep.
Mother and child under the blue night.
She kisses the sky good night and falls asleep into
the depths of blue water.

Lydia Parham-Brown

The Lonely Day

Do you remember that night
When you came to have some red wine,
We drank it out of beautiful crystal glasses,
That night we laid in the clean cut grass
Now it's all gone because you have found a new love,
When you left I cried like a sobbing dove,
Cause I remember you giving me chills up my spine,
And you using your same sweet old lines,
Since you left my heart has been broken,
You left with no words being spoken,
But that's OK cause I'll forever remember that lonely day.

Cassy Campbell

When Children Grow Too Fast

When the children no longer know how to play, it's as if our dreams are passing away. Dreams are our future and we all will pay, for their innocence taken away by our greed. Little people reflect the ills of our deeds. Bad guys once were the ones to watch, not it's the children with guns against the cops, and streets are the turf where hearts stop.

When we lose our dreams, we lose our light. Dreams guide us to our quest each night. When the children no longer know how to play, then where do our dreams go when we lay? Dreams are our future, they are our past. The light gives us strength we know will last, but where do the dreams go when the children grow too fast?

Children are our future where we plant our seeds, and the balance of our planet tips against their needs. Why do we steal their future with our greed? Life to spinning . . . spinning out of control, there will be no dreams when they grow old, 'cause, the children were never children in their day. They are only children having children and we all must pay. Where will their playground be when we've gone away?

When we lose our dreams, we lose our light. Dreams guide us to our quest each night. When the children no longer know how to play, then where do our dreams go when we lay? Dreams are our future, they are our past. The light gives us strength we know will last, but where do the dreams go when the children grow too fast?

David R. Sanders

Jennifer

Gentle, thoughtful silence,
    contemplating . . .
        your body, soul, mind — the way you might love.

It is amazing how many
    of my thoughts revolve around you.

You . . .
    are where my perceptions of what
    a woman should be swell from —
    are where my thoughts are, when I feel
    love, or desire . . . Or
        pain, loneliness, and insecurity.

Gentle, thoughtful silence,
    contemplating . . .
        . . . your body, soul, mind —
    the way you might love —
        If you loved me.

Travaleothsis Johnathon Trites

The Forgotten Child

There is a child with an innocent heart
He is hidden from our sight
Yet he has three friends that abide with him
They linger both day and night

The first of his friends is hunger
The pain that will not subside
The wrenching existence of emptiness
Its effects he can no longer hide

The second of his friends is homelessness
His domain is on the street
Here he has all the freedom he needs
To be abused, exploited and beat

The third and the last of his best friends
Is the loneliness that sings him to sleep
No one to care if he lives or dies
No one to hear him weep

The hunger at last has subsided
The loneliness has at last gone away
He no longer yearns for a place called home
Society killed him today

Susan W. Schuchter

It All Happened Just As He Said

It turned night in the middle of the day.
Jesus in His agony began to pray,
"Father, if it be thy will, let this cup from me pass."
Yet, He must die, alas.

They mocked His title as King of the world.
Ugly words, at Him, they hurled.
To a rugged cross they nailed His hands and feet,
as people gathered along the street.

They pierced His side for pure spite.
He prayed then with all His might,
"Forgive them Father for they know not
the blood I shed will cleanse each spot."

They beat Him so badly that we could not recognize.
They crowned Him with thorns 'til blood ran in His eyes.
Is there any hope for those that treated Him this way?
Did they treat Him any worse than we do today?

He suffered it all . . . His life He gave.
He arose the third day . . . the world to save.
It all happened just as He said.
He confirmed the fact that He wouldn't stay dead!

Wanda Ford

Twenty Years

The rush and the roar of the ocean
And the heavy beating of this heart in my breast
And the turning back of my memory
Will never give me rest.

My memory turns back to days that are gone
And to the years that have passed too
Then I keep remembering how beautiful you were
When you said, "I love you."

But now you are sleeping on the hillside
And the flowers on your grave are fair
And I'll live in a shadow forever
For I long for your beauty so rare.

Twenty years ago my heart was happy
For you and I were going to wed
But an angel softly called from heaven one night
And now you are dead.

Now today the change in my face is great
But my heart is still the same
I keep listening for the angel who called you
Thinking perhaps He'll call my name.

Dorothy Jackson

On The Wings Of Doves

Our fallen hero's the nation's pride,
On wings of doves they still ride.
They're still on guard both day and night,
To watch over them the nation's might.

The nation's bird shows courage and strength,
But the list of fallen goes on in length.
The flag of our nation is a symbol of pride,
But on the wings of doves the fallen still ride.

The fallen are memories both present and past,
But yet it seems we forget so fast.
They stood and fought for you and me,
But from wings of doves they keep us free.

From wings of doves God sends His love,
From all of them I've mentioned above.
When duty calls they're by our side,
From wings of doves they're still our guide.

James W. Johnson

Season's Greetings

This time of year is nice enough,
despite the frost and other stuff,
The fireplace is cozy,
and the coffee tastes much better,
makes sense to spend more time indoors,
and stay out of the weather,
a season's change is good,
for both the soul and motivation,
the holidays approaching,
give cause for jubilation,
aside from goblins, turkey, and a spate of
yuletide cheer,
There's one thing more important,
I have come to realize,
"My" cause for celebration is,
there aren't any flies!

Ed Aragón

You Are Not Alone

Ajar, the door, must be — as I sense a spirit that's oh, so free,
A ministering angel to comfort me!
Though you may misname it, a pest of a creature wee . . .
I dare to differ, you see; heaven, surely has sent it to me
As I was a friend in need . . . for in the dark of the night
When death rattles emit fright — ministering Angel is my friend indeed!
"You are not alone!" There is a presence as God within.
Lately, though scoffers still abound, do-gooders cast numerous doubts
My hope is rekindled: There is life about! . . . why?
There is a rhythm of sound in my lonely room as I lay awake,
I hear the wondrous of a cricket's chirp:
"You are not alone!"

Jessigrace Blankenship

Lover

A lover is all I need.
Someone with a heart that cannot bleed.
When will I find you here?
When will I loose my self in your love?
Can you hear me?
Do I need to scream a little bit louder?
Hope and faith.
Life and love.
What the hell am I trying to say?
Oh I remember now.
I love you.
I hate you.
I want you.
So let me die,
and let me cry,
and kill my soul dead.
You know you want too.
We all do.

Tillie Stiffler

A Christmas Cheer

Christmas is a time to spend with family and friends
And singing Christmas carols and having some gin
Presents under the tree
Startle children on Christmas Eve
They unwrap their gifts and play with toys
But they forget the true meaning of Christmas is about a baby boy
On Christmas day he was born and well
Until the Devil cast a spell
They sent him the cross to die for our sins
For that which we might not be here with our family and friends
So come celebrate come celebrate all
It's not winter or fall
It's Christmas Day
So children after you pray go out and play

Missy Stefko

Colors Of Life

Miles and miles of desert sand
Visions of mesmerizing color
Color that runs through your unfocused mind
Color that blinds you like the sun when looked directly upon.

Uneven lines of everlasting dreams
Visions of the afterlife and the deepness that follows
Color that deepens as you trudge further along
Color that binds you to the soul within.

The golden eye of eternity
Visions of the trip from your past
Color that runs through your unfocused mind
Color that blinds you like the sun when looked directly upon.

Leslie Horney

A Child of Abuse

A child that cries inside she dies, as her
tears drown her soul. A child of abuse to
her the world is so cold. She builds a shell
around her to protect from most of the pain
trying not to go completely insane. A world
of abuse a world unexplained,
    A child that cries inside she dies, as the
tears drown her soul, as anger takes control.
As the years go by her body grows, but the
child still cries her heart still knows.
    A child that cries inside she dies, as she
wonders where her purpose lies, in a world
that cuts like a knife, continued abuse
through out her life, trying to survive in her
world undenied, but the child has
depth deep within, and empathy to show
formed from a world so cold.

Eva Mae Lane

Forever Friends

You are my inspiration, my forever best friend,
From the first day we met, until the very end.
Fate, I believe, is what brought us together,
Now our lives can only get better.
I cannot imagine you not here with me today,
Friends comes and go, but I know that you are here to stay.
Maybe time took its toll and we were strangers in the past,
But now we have a friendship that will forever last.
I can feel in my heart that we will be at each others side,
To laugh with, cry with, and always to confide.
It means so much to know that I have this friendship with you,
That I did not know was possible to be so true.
The sense of security that we have established is so easy to feel
And I believe the reason why this friendship is so real.
I know you'll always be there to guide me and defend,
You will always be my inspiration, my forever best friend.

Lorraine May

Now We Will Be Parting

A friend always on the phone,
Larry knew of my problems and complaints.
Great times together, sometimes unexpected dates,
I always felt comfortable with him, like I knew him all of my life!
He shared a lot with me about his past life on a farm.
I will miss you, Larry, so much!!
You were my shoulder to lean on, and I loved our time together,
Although the time went so fast, it never seemed like enough,
even after hours together, we felt so close!
Yet, the time came to go our separate ways,
out of my control, because of your career!
I hope we share special moments someday again, and have
A Déjà-Vu of how beautiful it was before!

Pamela Katz

Sheep

In my opinion, for what it's worth.
Sheep are the dumbest animals on earth.

One sheep will start to wonder, and the rest will fall in line.
Wherever the lead one wants to go, the rest think that's just fine.

Now sheep don't like the water, just to drink a little bit.
If you try to get their wool wet, they'll likely have a fit.

Sometimes they will lay down to rest, and stay right where they lie.
If you don't go and kick them up, they'll lay right there and die.

I guess that's why Jesus, was always telling his crew.
Feed my sheep and watch over them, and see that they don't stray too.

He was always calling us humans sheep, and sometimes I think it's true.
'Cause humans can be pretty dumb, in the things we say and do.

One time we had a dumb old ewe, she thought she was a cow.
She followed our milk cows around, even swam the river some how.

Her favorite cow we called Old Red, she was red as she could be.
Our holstein was a big old thing, and we'd named her Old Tiny.

Well, we finally had to sell Old Red, she was getting up in years.
The way she started wondering 'round, I think she'd stripped some gears.

Why that dumb old ewe laid down and died, now I don't mean to be blunt
But I think she found out she was a sheep, and died of embarrassment.

Connie B. Packer

Untitled

When I was little I had a dream, but I was not asleep.
I dreamed of being a really special person, someone you'd like to meet
A person who was happy and humble.
A person who was wealthy and cared.
I wanted to be this person, but didn't know how and was scared.
I don't know the reasons why I pushed my dream down inside.
I pushed it into a corner that was dark inside my soul.
I thought it was not possible. I felt it was not fair.
I decided not to talk about it and act like it wasn't there.
For many years I lived this way, denying what was mine.
The dream that I was born with was getting harder to find.
Then when I turned twenty-four, I made a real big change.
I stopped using drugs one day at a time and turned my life over to God.
It was not easy and I was so afraid.
My life is so much better now because of the decision I made.
Now I share my feelings, even hopes and fears,
with people that really love me in happy times or tears.
My dream has come back to me and now it's plain to see, that as
I pushed my dream down, I also pushed down me. I am back.

Felecia Sovereign

My Outer Covering

I have been given this outer covering
So that my inner self can become the best that it can be
The road I am traveling is not easy
Nor do I want it to be
For if my journey was easy
Then that which I should have gained would be lost

Many a time I may stumble
But I know I will not fall
For this present route I am traveling
Does not last but for so long
A helping hand will always be appreciated
But those who offer pity are themselves to be pitied
For in their pity they lose out on what they could have gained
As their focus is centered on my outer frame

So the task of my outer covering
  Is to make of me
    The best that I can be

Barbara Y. Mair

Twice Was Not Enough (Whitley)

How can I have the best and worst
My faith in God is all I trust
I try each day to just get through
Twice was not enough of holding you

I held her twice, once when she knew
I was her mom and love was true
The second time she was with you
Up in the sky above the blue

You took her up to Heaven above
And left me one down here to love
How can a heart take such joy and pain
No one can ever seem to explain

It's so hard each day to face the world
Without my other baby girl
No one can feel what I've been through
I'll always know there should've been two

I see each day what she would have been
In the eyes and smile of my other twin
She must have been special to you too
Because you took her home to live with you

Sandra Kay Peden Cox

To My Pooh

Such a crisp autumn afternoon,
And I, my love, think of you.

Your devilish smile sets me free.
The glimmer in your eyes recapture me.
Your arms, so strong and tough, are gentile, and giving but not rough.
Your heart, so proud and true inside your chest,
Softly beats, for me, a love song unlike the rest.
Your voice so bold and warm,
Soothes me and calms me so I worry no more.
Your mind, thoughtful and wise,
Comes to my aid whatever the time.
Your untamed and wild, so strong and tough,
Yet so thoughtful and caring and filled with love.

So I sit here and think.
Out of all the bears there are in the world, I have two,
You're strong like a grizzly.
But loving like Pooh.

Trish Lund

Winter In The City

In the bleak dismal city, all I see is despair
People walk by and don't even care
For the homeless in doorways or on the street curb
Nor a starving pigeon . . . hell it's only a bird

This winter's been wicked, it's taken its toll
People and pigeons have died from the cold
Aside from my empathy, I do what I can
Spare clothing, some seeds, or money at hand

But nothing changes, I still see the gloom
Everyone's too busy, that's life I presume
But why does it have to be so cruel . . .
When it can fade so fast, it's rare as a jewel

Can we open our hearts to the helpless and needy
And open our pockets, and be a little less greedy
Or offer a smile or a hand to hold
Or a sweater or shelter to escape from the cold

It doesn't seem like it is too much to ask
It should come from the heart and not be a task
Wouldn't we want the same for ourselves
And our family and friends, to escape from the hell!!

Traci Lee Geary

Keeping Christ in Christmas

'Twas the season to make ready, for the holidays were near.
Make the lists and buy the presents for the ones that we hold dear.
Drag the tree down from the attic, haul the boxes in, but wait —
Where's the one that holds the lights, the ornaments to decorate?
Strip the house of normal knick-knacks, get the seasonal ones out
Fill the closet with the presents and the things that were about.
Get to work our in the kitchen, bake the cookies, make the fudge,
Fix the casseroles and freeze them, plan the menus — what a drudge!
Wait a minute, something's missing, where's the joy, the peace, the love?
Where's the singing of the carols and the message from above?
Where's the wonder of the story of a Child born long ago
To a couple in a stable, for the Bible tells us so?
Where's the thanks in celebrating life and blessing in His Name,
Knowing since His first appearance, nothing's ever been the same?
Tears of grief now mar my vision as I realize my sin:
It's the sin of poor perspective that I've let my mind get in.
Change my heart, Lord, give me balance, in a new and steadfast way.
Let me see the Christ of Christmas, live for Him, Lord, everyday.

Lois Sharpe

Yesterday And Today

(To my Mom with all my love)
Yesterday, you held me within the safety of your loving arms.
Today, I carry my own precious child with the same love you gave.
Yesterday, you held my hand and walked with me
through all the hard times in my life, never judging or condemning
but giving me all your love and strength,
in order for me to make my own way.
Today, my hand is out and ready
to take hers with all the same love you taught me.
Yesterday, you listened as I cried over my first broken heart
your eyes filled with the same pain
letting me know that you did understand
Today, I try to be like the person who sat beside me then.
Yesterday, you let me make my own mistakes but you were always there
to help me fix it, never saying you told me so, but instead telling
me that you still love me.
Today, I am ready to give the same unconditional love that I received
Yesterday, I walked away going to make my own place in this world.
Today, I am a woman walking in your shoes
trying to be like the mom you were to me.
Yesterday, we were mother and daughter, today, we are best friends.

Tawana Kelly

Whispers

The silent trees whisper to me
listen closely
They tell me winter is here
Christmas is near
The trees whisper to me, listen closely
The children play free
Laughter echoing from sea to sea
Their excited, and happy
Dreaming wistfully of peace, and plenty across the land
with love, and care they'll lend you their hand
Spreading whisps of cheer
with a grin ear to ear
The trees whisper to me, listen closely
This is the season we're all free
And so happy to be
We give, and receive joyfully
understand
Fill our hearts with all we can

Wendy L. Brubaker

1 Day Of Passing

As moments slip away and <u>OUR</u> time winds down,
<u>I</u> can't help but 2 frown over just what happened in the
Passing of 1 day. It seems easy 2 plan how <u>I</u> could
Withstand trials of being human throughout the
Passing of **1** day.

Even though unseen emotions never let <u>US</u> <u>K</u>now,
if they should stay or go with the <u>F</u>low.
1 day shall be measured by small amounts of completed tasks
as if no one had even asked why do <u>WE</u> rush at All?
Against possibilities of a <u>F</u>all.
<u>MY</u> body longs 4 a moment **2** Lay, somehow ignored during the
Passing of **1 Day.**

When clocks upon the wall has ticked their last Tock,
then will <u>OUR</u> thoughts run **2-gether** like birds of a Flock.
Doors closing and <u>MY</u> mind opening causes <u>ME</u> 2 say
"Thank **GOD**! **4** living the Passing of 1 day."

Lewis V. Wilkerson

When I Close My Eyes

When I close my eyes,
I think of you
You may find it hard to believe,
but it is true.
My dreams fill my head,
Like the dragon mist
casting magic across the living edge.
Swirling in fever,
so hot it ignites
flaming desire burns on through the night.
The world of wisdom cannot explain
this love that flows within my veins.
Though the thorns of love cause great pain,
and the arrows from Cupid's bow
can cause a man to go insane.
I would risk it all,
I would spill my blood
to be with the one I Love . . .

Kirt Kristian Draven Alarcon

Parents

Often forgotten and overlooked,
Decisions made with tears and hurt.
Their job can not be taken lightly,
To forsake them would be a mistake.

Acceptance of the decisions made,
Children, please, grow to understand.
Love and cherish them all their days,
For one sad day nothing, but memories, will remain.

Cheryl Strodtman-Anderson

The Hands Of Death

The hands of Death take away the very reason for living
And makes us come to the reality of our mortality
And the futile fight to stay alive.

The hands of time help heal us and bring us closer
To the hands of Death.
But time can be stopped in each thought
And in each fond memory of those who have been caught
By the hands of Death.

I know how it feels to have someone taken away.
Time is not good for me,
It brings the hands of Death.

The hands of Death bring for me a friendship
That outlasts the hands of time.

Chris D. Wilson

You're Worth A Million To Me

I write you this poem to which there is No End
to the number of toys, hopes, dreams and hearts that you will
Forever
Mend
This list is so Few of all the things you do
that pick me up when I'm feeling blue:
The singing of your voice as a lullaby to soothe me
The way you rocked me to tell me you will always be near
The way you kissed the "boo boos" even when they didn't hurt
The loving smile in your eyes constantly telling me you love me
The hug you embrace me with to give me assurance
The way you lend your ear to listen to my troubles
The purr of your "yes" to confirm I am heard
The encouraging words you speak to press me forward
The way you pick me up whenever I fall
The sound of your laughter to remind me to laugh
If it had not been for your guiding hand I would not be the person I am
From your careful molding and tender scolding
I am able to be what you are to me:
A Mother worth a Million in Gold

Robin M. Gum

Down The Aisle Of Time

I wonder just what my heart will feel,
when we walk down that wide, long aisle?
You on my arm, beautiful with charm,
with that overwhelming, little girl smile.

As we proceed on, step by step,
to the point of separation in time.
We both will be thinking of future and past,
then, awakened by the wedding march chime.

People on the left, also on the right,
will be giving their aahs and their oohs.
We will continue down the aisle of time,
knowing, one will gain, the other will lose.

When we reach that point of separation,
in front of the altar we will stand.
I'll kiss you good-bye, with tears in my eye,
to another man, give him your hand.

So, for the little girl of yester-year,
grown into a woman sub-lime.
Proudly walked down the aisle of happiness,
onward, into the world of time.

Neil O. Face

A World Unknown

The life they now will never see,
So beautiful and peacefully.
A world of love from here to there,
My love for them is everywhere.

I only wish there was a chance,
For both of them to take a glance.
To see the sun shine in the sky,
And watch the birds fly way up high.

There is so much that they have missed,
All the girls and their first kiss.
Being able to hold them tight,
Telling them it will be all right.

I really wish that they were here,
So I could show how much I care.
To hear again their soft little cries,
And wipe away the tears from their eyes.

My love for them will always be,
In my heart, you will see.
And someday I'll be way up high,
Saying hello, instead of good-bye.

Jacky Lee Moses

The Changing Of The Seasons

Winter starts off the year with its darkness and its chill
Before very long, most of us will have overcome its thrill

The constant shoveling and scraping is enough to drive you mad
The shorter days depress us while cases of arthritis turn bad

Spring follows soon after when the whole world comes alive
The days grow longer as another cold winter we did survive

Aromatic flowers bud then bloom while brown grass turns green
Birds of all kinds sweetly sing; it's a whole different scene

Summer arrives next as the school bell tolls for the last time
Vacation plans are made and kept till the bell again does chime

All the beaches are crowded with sun worshippers as they lay
Outside activities of all types carry on throughout the day

But then the fall season sadly creeps in and brings summer's end
The fun is all over; it's back to hitting the text books again

The leaves on the trees change from green to yellow and red
Warm weather is rapidly replaced by a nip in the air instead

The changing season's cycle starts over again in a month or two
When carols begin playing and the christmas shopping comes due

It's really amazing how the earth knows when it's time to change
From winter to spring, summer and fall; it knows the whole range

Marcia Bargnesi

Orange A La Ogden Nash

In all the English language nothing rhymes
  with Orange,
Unless it's something like Borange.
But to say that Borange rhymes with Orange
  is absurd,
Because Borange isn't really a word.

(Many have attempted to emulate
Ogden Nash, but have never quite
hit the mark. I believe the
above verse comes close.)

Charles L. Sigman

A Piece Of The Puzzle

These are the ways of counting . . . September and lost April days.

A smile lost somewhere in yesterday's moment and then again a tear.

But this is the day for which all lost tomorrows were spent, a
last goodbye for all things unsaid and deeds undone. A life complete.

One piece is left and a question. Is it for the end or the
beginning of a new puzzle? New moments to count or old ones
to place among the ashes of regret.

Is it too late to undo completion? Is there another September,
another April somewhere waiting?

Norma Smith

The Plowman

I stopped to rest mid furrowed field and changed upon a dream
  the plow, the team, the earth so rich in memory do cling.
Wife and sons forever mine with ties of love do bind,
Oh sons who bad a fathers care grew straight, grew tall,
  like redwoods grew,
Oh daughters who've spread wide and fertile like soil, where now I do
  lie in repose,
Oh heavenly father may it please thee now this burden to lay down.
This care, my part, this earthly lot to you favor in trust,
That they may know you great Lord, as I know your mercy, power,
  and love.

Rodney Morgan Brown

Tearful Oration

Hallelujah heavenly harmony heals heavy hearts,
  Will the tears ever end.
An amiable aura affectionately adorns angelic angels,
  Isn't the tears to ever end.
Zealously a Zephyr zapped a zaftig zionward to Zenana,
  The tears never seem to end.
Every evening end each enduring effort efficiently,
  Have the tears no end,
Love lifts large lingering loads lightly,
  Let the tears come to an end.
Time and tears trace the trail to tranquility,
  Obviously the tears have no end.
Inherently inborn intelligence intrinsically
  Interrupts ignorance,
  Volumes of tears find no end,
Nature naturally nurtures the nordic nocturnal night,
  Each fallen tear has found its end,
Eternity ends the ebbing of every erratic or
  Enlightened emotion.

Wilbur Larson

To My Little Angel

In Memory of Brooklyn Paige Fugitt
  God sent an angel here on earth for all of us
to see and love. Then with a twinkle of an eye he
took her back up into the sky. We were blessed a few
short months and got a taste of his pure love. Oh,
Lord! Oh God! Almighty High! We just can't seem
to understand, what's your purpose, and what's your plan.
  How much longer shall we wait for our calling to
take its place. We wait patiently for your sake, and
love each blessing that you make.
  For we all know that there will be a time of glory
for all to see. We love, we praise you God Almighty
High we love your blessings in the sky.
  Someday we will meet again and oh what a glorious
time with no end.

Paula A. Fugitt

In My Dreams

In my dreams I find you.
I hold you close to me.
To see your familiar face, so beloved by me.

Each day I gather pieces, to keep you here with me.
Night is the time, we move in harmony.
We walk a busy street or sit on a breezy shore.
What life has taken from me, my dreams give me more.

In my dreams I find you.
I hold you close to me.
It is your voice, that haunts me in my dreams.
The silence is never-ending and soon my dream will too.
So till tonight . . . I'll be seeing you.

Annette Joy Ehrlichman

A Season Of Merriment

A child's eye twinkles,
As from the sky sprinkles
The dancing, sprightly snow.
It's not just the child,
The whole town's gold wild;
Each window does cheerfully glow.

Sweet carols to hear,
When Christmas draws near,
For both young and old are singing.
A crowd gathers round,
To rejoice in the sound,
and the fresh year the season is bringing.

Sonja K. Erickson

This Room

I now can rest in the vision of what used to be,
While darkness cradles your ghost all about me;
Wrapped in the blissful arms of countless tears gone by —
Agony's storm has passed, leaving but a yearnful sigh.

The sweet scent of your body is as present as the air,
Calling ancient memories to rise and dance with your ladyfair
Weightlessly, two spirits drift about this room,
Like the mystical enchantment of an elegant perfume.

Music plays, but no one else can hear,
The tune of our bodies entwining this invisible atmosphere —
Your breath spilling upon my skin like a gentle breeze,
Whispering across wind chimes, moaning passionately to please.

And I will rub the fragrance of your memory on my skin;
The beads of sweat remembering where I've been —
My own hands replacing your once wanton touch,
With but a few remnants of you to remind me of such.

How my heart aches for the love slipped away;
Knowing our journey would be different if we first met today
But the forest between us offers no path to lead you here,
So I must comfort myself with the trinkets of yester-year.

Gayla L. Pledger

Gingerbread People

Gingerbread people have a life of their own
Playing their games and answering the phone
Climbing up and down kitchen tables and chairs
Cute as a button, they never put on airs
Eating up all the gumdrops and candy
But they're really only trying to be handy
Jump and tightrope walking with garlands and swags
And waving for all to see — Christmas flags
Scampering in and out of hallways and maybe a stair
Living their lives with nary a care
Swirling and twirling candy canes and such
And riding on a Christmas train, but never too much
Dancing under twinkling Christmas tree lights
Humans will never see — try as they might
Swinging on ornaments under the tree
Give them a break and let them live free
For gingerbread homes are not just for show
They house these little people in love, don't you know.
(So remember when you see a small ball of dough,
It's a baby Gingerbread just waiting to grow).

Melanie Jean Anderson

Snow Dreams

Sister, wife, mother, friend to all
Why must you answer death's bittersweet call?
It seems you lived your life in a glow of sunshine,
Amidst the ice or dangerous wind you were never one to whine.
When there was trouble no one would venture to tell,
Your smile was like heaven when situations were hell.

Those sweet boys — and a girl —
Life's strangest mysteries you'd help them unfurl;
Of flowers and deer and troubles of the world,
You'd feed them and walk them and magic batter you'd swirl.
Rolls come from magic dough and chocolate milk from brown cow,
They loved you much then and they miss you so now.

Let's go pick some berries and go for a walk,
Work in the garden and have a nice talk.
We'll visit on Sunday and we'll let you cook,
We learned of your secret youth by reading your book.
Now here we live,
You taught us all to give.
Even though you have gone on,
Much grace you have shown.

Darold A. Mathews

Three Strangers

Three strangers came upon my house.

The first looked at me and said, "My, what a wicked soul!
Let me offer you salvation by means of Christianization."
and with this he held out a cross . . .
and with this he held my soul.

The second looked at me and said, "My, what a savage beast!
Let me offer you civilization by means of education."
and with this he held out a book . . .
and with this he held my mind.

The third looked at me and said, "My, what a worthless fool!
Unlike the others I won't tell you lies. We came to enslave, not
to 'colonialize'."
and with this he held a gun to my head . . .
and with this he held my body.

Now these Three Strangers have left my house . . .
and with it they have left their gifts.
But instead of salvation, I received desperation,
instead of education, I received deception,
and even when given the truth,
I received nothing but destruction.

Now I'm left alone . . .
to uplift my home . . .
from its devastation.

Julman A. Tolentino

College Memories

Oh the moon shines tonight through the pine trees,
And its beam lights old main, so tall and true,
Where she's ready to give of her knowledge,
To all those who enter N.A.U.

As we stroll through the halls of Alma Mater
We hear voices ringing out so loud and clear,
Of the students and friends and our loved ones,
Whose future is carved while we are here.

May our praises ever be to our instructors,
For the lessons they teach so faithfully,
As they give of their knowledge and guidance,
To bring out the best in you and me.

As we live out the years that roll before us,
May our gratitude and thanks forever be,
To our wonderful Alma Mater,
Northern Arizona University.

Mason H. Fitzgerald

Jesus In Bethlehem

One night Jesus came to Bethlehem
Heavy snow falling down
On Christmas Eve night. He saw bright lights
in Bethlehem.
He was there praying for children of the world
To His Kingdom of Love.
The children went with Jesus for A
Walk in Bethlehem.
They saw most beautiful places
Kids call it Bethlehem Christmas
Jesus And his angels come down
into Bethlehem.
Jesus said come to us with
faith inside of your heart and soul
then pray for me
faith and love
shared Christmas day
with your family and friends
always forever amen.

Sheila K. English

Prophesy

So close to light
    Fallen into the black night
Like the impetuous Icarus,
    The wings of hope have melted
From the suns of forgotten dreams.
    The nights of love
Of warms caresses
    Of mind reaching touches,
Have become dark as the eyes of hell.
    The labyrinth of escape has closed,
And the ears of a deaf Jesus remain waxed with earthly fear.
    The cries of crippled angels,
Their wings cut from their sides by
    The sharpened tips of a broken crucifix
Suffocate little children.
    And their feeble cries of anguish
Are muffled by the sounds of a muted priest
    Whose laughter is cut short only by his own death.
    David M. Silberhartz

Let Me See

Let me see; said the blind man;
as he gazed upon his life.
The more I look, the less I see,
The more I learn, the less I understand,
The more I believe, the less I trust,
The more I listen, the less I hear.
    Sometimes less is more and
dark can turn into enlightenment
on a warm and awakening day.
    Understanding life will take a
lifetime to learn. For all we
really can pray for, is, the time we
live and a place to die, and then,
we will be granted eternal life.
    Donna Hornsby Rush

The Lightest Light

From the brightest light that ever
    shone, glowing streams of love divine

I caught a glimpse of love
    pure, even the hardest heart could
find a cure.

Wrapped and cuddled,, soft and sweet
    tender kind eyes do meet.

For a moment time stood still as
    all around me the love did fill.

Never more will life be the same
    for life as we know will not remain.
    Janie Heiken

Officer Pete

On patrol, through snow, rain and sleet,
Let me introduce you to Officer Pete.
In his uniform he stands tall,
Preserving peace and law for one and all.
Call him a friend or call him a cop,
Service to his community will never stop.
Rescuing a kitten in a tree,
or helping Johnny find mommy and daddy.
He hugs his kid and kisses his wife,
And hopes to return home with his life.
For the next bad guy he may meet,
Could put him under . . . six feet.
So when you see him on the street,
Smile and say "Hi!" to Officer Pete.
    Peter M. Culafic

The Men In My Life

I look at his old chair, but he's not there.
I wear his old shirt, but it makes me hurt.
I look at his picture on the fridge.
I miss him like he were my own father.
My father, what happened to him?
I guess he was lost from the start.
Or was it me who lost?
Tears come easily to me.
His shirt is getting wet, I'm sorry . . .
It's almost been a year now.
He was so virile, so talented.
His white hair was premature.
He really seemed ageless to me.
Why did he leave us so suddenly?
I look at his son with his graying hair.
How long will it be before he is there?
Some of us should live forever.
It really isn't fair.
They should always be there.
    Sheila Thomas

Sports

Sports are fun,
You play in the sun,
You sometimes run,
The whistles blows, the games begun.

You play in many different places,
And run at many different paces,
But in so many cases,
Everyone goes away with happy faces.

All players always fight,
For the one and only right,
To have the one great light,
Spotted on them every night.

The fun never runs out,
So there is no need to pout,
Because everyone loves to shout,
While they watch the bout.

At the end, all the people go,
Some games are like a show,
Others go ever so slow,
But no matter the outcome, nobody feels low!
    Daniel Nelson

I Don't Know Who You Are

I don't know who you are,
I've met you only once.
Our first encounter was, something of a hunch.

We met with eyes of wondering, of color, smell and touch.
Earning for that special love, we all need so much.

The hardest things we learn in life,
that take all our strength and time.
Are our most rewarding loves.
We keep and hold in time, you don't know me from Eve.
But people say I'm real, they feel my inside optimistic
and know I'd never steal.

God told me once he'd make me strong
to feel the Angels all night long.
With alleys dark, the path unknown.
I never once feet alone.

You are unique with much, indebtedness to explore.
And if you feel the need to give, you can give me more.

If you feel a journey with respect, love and trust
I am a person worthy of a friendship full of lust.
    Lynn Morley

Tell Me Why?

Tell me why?
Your mind is like a bull's-eye
if you aim at the target you will hit it,
For,
The future is that time you'll wish you'd done what
you aren't doing now.
Tell me why?
Hard work is the yeast that rises the dough,
Therefore
The highest reward for a person is not what they
get for it, but what they become by it.
Tell me why?
Achievers don't set limits they set goals
Because
Life is generally empty for those who put nothing into it.
Just Tell Me Why?
Why? Because all of us are born for a
reason, but all of us don't
discover why, success is what you gain in life and
accomplish . . . that's the reason why.

Fatiya Anima Ilegieuno

Don't Wait Too Long

Once upon a time in the not too distant past
never would I regret anything of me that was asked
You asked me to take you as my wife
to exchange vows of love, lasting forever in our life
At first I said I didn't know if I could,
waiting for so long for someone like you to come along
Memories of the last loves and hurtful lies
one more broken, heart would surely make me die
But the beauty of your love had possessed my heart
at that very moment, from your side I would never depart
Now that the moment we had has come and gone
I know now what fate can do and what must be done
I will wait for you till time has come and gone
then our love shall be the beginning of a new dawn
But loneliness can take hold of even the strongest heart
closing in on itself, causing the soul to fall apart
So don't wait too long my love
for soon eternity will leave its empty mark
And I shall be lost somewhere alone
with nothing but my love for you and a broken heart

Thomas B. Rogers

Hard And Cold

Outside it is raining;
    inside the loneliness eats at my soul.
Innocence is lost — gone forever;
    my heart has turned hard and cold.

Nothing lasts; no longer am I the person I used to be;
    but, never look back — that was so long ago.
Beaten down are my hopes
    and my dreams that never turned to gold.

How can I find my way back to where I was before?
    Hopelessness has taken control.
And the future I wished for fades slowly
    As I watch my body grow old.

Memories are all I have as I close my eyes;
    but what about the things I never got to know?
Reality overtakes me as I begin to die;
    to depression my happiness has been sold.

Outside it is calm,
    but the loneliness continues to tear at my soul.
Once something is lost, it is gone forever . . .
    and lost love can make a heart turn hard and cold.

Linda Williams

Our Son

Our son was always loving, always true,
there wasn't a day went by he didn't say, "I love you."

At three, he was up early, he had a lot to do,
he'd be taking cars apart in the middle of his room.

When he got a little older, baseball was his game,
he played and hit and ran, but standing in the outfield wasn't a part of his game.
So, he'd look up at the sky or kick a blade of grass,
he had to keep busy, just couldn't stop, his life was moving too fast.

Mud puddles were the greatest, he just couldn't resist,
his bike and he had more mud on them than the street had in its midst

He'd take a bag of marshmallows and go down to the creek,
he'd get so excited to bring me a treasure, a piece of glass I could keep.

He brought a lot of pleasure, always laughing, always true,
If you knew him, you were laughing too.

We had a lot of boys here, he would always say, "come and stay
at our house, my folks will take care of you."
And they'd stay. He thought there wasn't anything we couldn't do.

Then he went away to make it on his own,
but every once in a while he'd say, "I think I'll come back home."

God's plan for him was unfolding, a child he'd have to save,
oh, how we love the life He gave!
God will take Todd home to rest, We'll always think he was the best.

Janice Chelton

The Ten-Minute Christmas

Hospital regulations
Visit one person
On Hour
    Ten Minutes

The dress is important, bright, best if it
    holds a remembrance of happy times.
Perfume — long time favorite.
Lots of pats and kisses, if permitted.
Pictures of small neighborhood children
Talk of Christmas celebration postponed — later — when.
Packages of love
Boxes of tenderness
Baskets of concern
A pillow plumped
A blanket brought up around thin shoulders
A goodbye.

Lois M. Arthur

Us

The stars glistened with the twilight of a thousand years
As we walk this path of no end
We are asked of what for
If no end
Then where to go
At what length
An eternity, as it is
Tis no boundary of ours
Ours is, as it was meant to be
Indefinite
Never to be marred, nor shaken
For in this, we have all there is
One to one yet, one in whole
without seam or difference
Oh witness this most blessed event
For this event is ours
And as it is ours, we should embrace
For it can belong to no other
As we said it would be from the beginning

Wayne W. Cox

Battered

Have you ever heard the scream of a silent cry
Listen carefully, for the noisy pestilence has
rendered me speechless
Trapped deep within an abyss, I silently scream, freedom
Sing a song of sick sense her body lay black and blue
Seven times eleven she felt the choke hold deep within her womb
Come close, look into my eyes and feel my heart
you'll hear the scream of a silent cry
Beautiful butterfly born to fly, high high high or die!
Why does Cupid's bow sometimes shoots the fatal blow
Low low low
Listen closely and you will hear clearly
the voice of a tortured soul
Now you have heard the screams of a silent cry
In the distance, help somebody, anybody help me!
Hear the cry of those who silently scream

Charmaine Michelle Suazo

Nacht Lüge (Night Story)

As lightning ripped open the sky,
out of the dark came a single cry,
"Another day, another time, another riddle, another rhyme!"
On this night, lay a boy in the fields,
not knowing what the night, to him, would reveal.
With the sound of thunder coming through the
woods the boy suddenly understood.
Through the fog came a wise, old griffin
whose very presence made the boy stiffen.
Through those old lips, the griffin said,
to the boy whose face was as white as the dead,
"To you, young boy, I present a token and with
it the hold of Evil shall be broken!!!!!!"
"Peace and prosperity, people will find and all
creatures shall be cleansed of body and mind!
From then, forever, beyond that night
never again was there Evil or fright!!

Edward Drummond

Untitled

Voices coming from every direction,
Thousands of thoughts running through my mind.
My heart is empty,
My head is full.
Feel like I'm crazy,
I'm out of control.
Don't know what to do or what to say,
Don't understand why I feel this way.
Upset for no reason, depressed . . .
don't know why.
Angry at everyone,
when I'm happy, I cry.
Things really aren't funny yet I still laugh.
I just can't figure out these feelings I have.

Kelly Tease

Rough Whispers

Rough whispers glide down my throat,
they circle and cling with impenetrable grace,
slow death runs its hands through my hair,
we don't mind, we invited it here free to run rampant,
and circle us in, to consume us, and calm us,
save us from all that has been.

Soft silence around us, turmoil within,
guilt in our minds, those who have hearts,
relief is our object, the calm our inspiration,
gone is our immediate conscience,
lost forever within the hazy river
rising toward the clouds and sky.

Melissa Girton

Too Late To Turn Back

You think you're so mature but you're really just a child.
Don't you understand that you're not that great.
Your self esteem is low.
You run for sympathy, and of course you get it.
You pull your blanket over their eyes.
But me, not a whimper, not one comforting word.
They say you learn from your mistakes but you just feed off them.
Don't you know you can't live like this,
you've been doing it much too long.
No love to be seen, your friends are all gone.
But you brought it all on yourself.
One year, two year, I could count so much higher.
And this isn't how to win them back.
I thought you learn, you just ignored. This time it's too late.
I condone your acts, I turn away from your face.
It's so sad I can't look you in the eye.
You're so immature it's disgusting. All the words, all the phrases.
They role right off my back. It's our friendship you destroyed.
It's all hacked up into pieces. But now lets just forget it.
It's so far gone, it's like it's all an act.
It's just so pathetic. Too late to turn back.

Sheena Montecalvo

And Out Of The Darkness

I touched his hand, and it turned to sand
And slid down the sleek hour glass
And into the depths of blue
Stars they became, sparkily fragments of light
Brightness in night
A universe gone with the wind
Welcome to the grasping world of nothing
Where what you see, isn't
And what is, can't be seen
What an awesome thought
That God is a scientist
And in His hands, He holds the power
To destroy every man
And every thing seen
The stars and sky
Everything that is, isn't in His eyes
In His hands
That turned to sand
And made our vast night bright

Seadra J. Cronk

Something

There was a deep nothing.
No feeling at all.
No hurt
No anger
Nor passion
or trust
Nothing.

Then you looked my way.
Things started filling.
I could no longer feel nothing.
Now there was something.
Passion
and pain
Trust
and Jealousy
Something.

Then something happened,
something turned into everything
Everything pushed its way into my heart,
Everything became — Love.

Karen Strack

Eternity

I climb the wind swept steps of time . . .
Towards an unknown future void . . .
Behind, the past is fraught with care,
joy, pain; a lifetime stored.
Ahead, and yet through dark and misty fog,
a hand of light, a beacon shining,
touches my heart and guides me on . . .
And pulls me to eternity.

Thad Stevens

Grandmother

The angels in heaven look after her now
Like she did us while on the ground
Her words are still heard
From miles around.
The echo of her laughter, joy, and tears
Will ring happily throughout the years.
A woman loved
Both far and near.
Even though she's gone,
She'll always be here.
Safe and sound,
In the clouds,
We won't forget.
We never could.
The woman we loved
Will always be Ma.
As the wind whispers,
We hear her say,
"Good-bye my loves,
I'll see you again someday."

Rebecca Yokeley

Majority Rules?

Once upon a time, in a far away land, 3 out of 4 people were color-blind. Since 75% of the people were color-blind, they thought they saw things correctly. They said things like, "We can't all be wrong." "If most of us see it this way, then it is this way."

The ones who were not color-blind, did see things differently. But many were told they were nuts or wrong when they said what color something was.

Now days, of course, we know what color-blind is and who could see correctly and who couldn't.

But, what blindness do many of us have?

Can we see light waves, oxygen, or electricity? No, but we know they are real. Who knows what might be discovered.

We may find out that a lot of us cannot see things that are there, and we've been telling people they are crazy because they say they see things others don't.

Next time someone tells you they see something you don't, ponder the question, "Is he seeing something that is there, but I cannot see?"

Donna VanSickle

My Mother

The Woman bends over the machine,
whizzing and whirling about her.
The thread pulls through the fabric,
and pieces together the strips.
Needles are held betwixt the fingers,
poking through the fibers to stitch.
Hooks, eyes, and buttons placed
exactly where they should.
She creates something that wasn't there,
a dress, a shirt, or a hem.
To clothe her loved ones dear,
tomorrow she begins again.

Barbara Haas

Angels Of God

Angels of God come sit by my side
and tell me of God's sweet love

Tell me of old, old stories
of God's love and glory, and how
He has assigned you to watch over me

Speak of His Holy Spirit, of how He
guides me
to do what God would have me do

Tell me of those who's paths I cross
and how I might help them when they are lost

Take me by the hand
and show me what God has planned

Give me the strength, wisdom, faith, and courage
that I might do all I truly can . . .
to help those in struggle
to recognize God's gift of joy even when they are in
serious, serious trouble.

Bill Denk

Remember

She was the sparkle of life to all that knew and loved her, she was the teacher and the care giver to many, she gave advice to those who asked, and asked for nothing in return. For generations after her she told stories of the days of her youth and many before her, we all would listen and wonder of those days and we would remember and tell our children and they would pass it on to those who will listen. I speak of a wonderful and delightful person that there will ever be, she had a life that followed the lord, her bible would always be close and she would sit for hours and read the words of God her keeper and ours. She lived for many years and saw so many things in her life, I don't think there was a day in her live she regretted, I think the most wonderful thing she loved the best was to see all she knew grow and learn like she did. And for us who knew and loved this most special person will always remember her and listen to her words of wisdom, and carry the love she gave us all in our hearts, we will all love her and remember her as she was. She'll be missed but never forgotten, she's our light, our voice, and the most thing we will hold dear to our hearts, she's a mother to four, grandmother and a great grandmother to many, and for those who will not meet her now, will meet her someday in the heavens afar.

Shantell Noble

Endless Nights

He was a lightning rod man, who just loved to work,
a job he did well, what courage it took.
It was a warm summer day at a chemical plant,
an explosion occurred and ended his life.

He was a good kind man, gentle and strong,
loved little children and all of mankind.
A love that never can be replaced,
all other life moves on without skipping pace.

I cry each night and stay up late,
no sleep for me, just heartaches.
The love I once knew, has been taken from me,
only an empty shell is what's left of me.

On the outside looking cool and calm,
crying on the inside, everything's so wrong.
The hurt and pain won't go away,
how could, I lose my love this way.

You see in my heart a part of him stays,
but a part of me died with him that very day.
My true love is gone, and said no goodbyes,
he left me alone, only God knows why.

Ruth Sims

I Want To Be There

I would like to live to be thousand years old and stand tall like a
redwood tree. I would wish the tips of my branches like fingers could
touch the stars and the stars could reach back and touch me.
I would like to be able to talk to God so that he can tell me
mysteries of time and space. Everything so great and true, we will
travel to anyplace. I want to go below to the ocean so deep to watch
in awe the whale, the shark and the squid. I want to travel the
ocean floor and see all of the works he did.
I want him to explain why do flowers bloom and why do vines creep.
I want know the power of a thunderstorm, and to hear his
booming voice so deep.
I want to know how angels fly faster than the speed of light.
How does He know all of the stars by name and please tell me
dear God what brings on night.
I want to know how he created Adam gave Him the breath of life.
And when this man became lonely God saw to it that this man had a
wife. Yes 1 one day I want to be there when he shares that great
secret with you and me. I want to be there when he declares to
the inhabited earth I am the powers that be!

Teresa A. Winslow

Snowflakes In April

Snowflakes are falling.
Their beauty adorns the sky.
They fill the earth with elegance,
Jewels that money cannot buy.

Snowflakes are falling.
We gaze with pure delight,
And take in all the wonder
Of this glorious awesome sight.

Snowflakes are falling.
What a miracle to see!
Too soon the warm earth swallows them,
And they are hidden from you and me.

While the snowflakes gently fall,
A peaceful feeling surrounds,
As if God is saying,
"Be still, and know My love abounds."

Peace be still; peace be still.
Let our troubled hearts unfurl.
For God is at work in His wonderful kingdom,
And all is right with the world.

Doris W. Vaughan

Christmas

Three weeks away from celebration
Birthday of light, hope, salvation
Pertaining to the reality of life
Only begotten son of our creation, Jesus Christ

Bringing forth, birth, Spirit of Christmas
Greatest gift to one and all, today and time past
That of life, unconditional love
Of mother earth, the spirit of heaven's above

That still lives on
Even the hell, world today, called home
The blessings of children we conceive
Relatives, friendship there, when in need

Reaching, stretching, of a helping hand,
soft, firm, shoulder to lean, to cry on
Or just their present, their being, a bond
That hardly anything can compare, surpass in this land

Christmas, Eve of the New Year
Coming forth of new gifts of friends dear
Love's, life's hopes, dreams, joy of children
People whose essence is spirit of christmas of everyday living!

Steve Goebel

I'll Ask The Angels

I still write him a letter each and every night,
I need to tell him I miss him; somehow it just feels right.
This pile of heartfelt notes that I have no where to send
Are stacking high beside my bed; through words I hope to mend.

I'll never forget the pain of it all, that simply will never be,
But, hopefully, time will ease it some,
And the healing will start for me.
They say there is no pain in heaven, yet, I wonder if that can be true,
Because I know his feelings are mutual,
He must hurt as he misses me, too.

I don't know if he can hear me and he sure doesn't get my mail.
I ask the angels to tell little brother . . .
That my loving him will never fail.

Donna Earley

Innocent Eyes

Relationships are really simple things
Just getting along when you're little
That special pal, buddy, or friend
You play, sleep over, and lick the middle
Out of Oreo Cookies, not caring of physical
Seeing the beauty within with innocent eyes

Remaining unhazed until your voice breaks
Appearance of you and the pictures of others
Corrupts and clouds that once clear perception
The physically unattractive, fat, thin, white-skinned
Are ostracized and ignored — their inner beauty
Cannot be seen by a translucent mind

And maybe a man or a woman
Can regain their sight when older
To realize perhaps — if they're still alone
That the one they want with innocent eyes
Is the same one they pushed away.

James M. Laird

Untitled

White roses,
Yellow roses,
Pink roses.
They're all great. Especially when they come from
number twenty-eight. A football player so cute
and cool. When he comes around me I don't
know what to do. I love him. Do you think he
loves me to? Does any one else have feelings like
I do?

Kristin Gibson

Pink Elephants

What delirium lingers there,
Slightest of grins planted on waxy red lips?
Perched in a corner chair, jelly-roll thighs
tightly crossed, as ladies do. Pudgy pink
Enameled toes gape from shiny, white
Patent leather sandals. What business could the
Frocked creature purpose, uninvited on Mother's
Finest settee, grotesque in ruby toilette?
Lost in drudgery, Mother dusts by —
No notice or nod of the pink who,
Tongue poking out, traffics disrespect.
Is it only my horror so weightily poised,
As to crack the legs whereon it sits?
No. No vision of drunken acuity this
Awful specter; a familiar caller whose
Girth and painted facade balloon
With every pretense of ignorance.

Lynn Carver

He Let Me Live

Thank Your Lord, for letting me live.
Each breath I take, each step I make,
I cherish so much more,
Because you raised me up,
When I was at death's door

Malignant tumors nested on my liver.
One near the vein, others causing strain,
Good surgeons took their chances.
You guided their incisions
And gave them right advances.

The doctors knew that a greater force
Raised my blood pressure to right the measure
And helped me to sustain,
Some necessary vital signs
For good health to regain.

A total healing in body and mind,
All pain has ceased, deeper faith increased,
The richness of living each day,
Allows me to encourage others
And to Your Lord, always pray.

Barbara L. Bell

Note To Them

Speaking of the world in general — when mind thoughts collided
with others into a path of abusive mental behavior where denial is
an unaccepted manor, but the true reality of the time.

Mini organizations of robotic like disapproval growing like
fungus until open mindedness is a down looking trait ripped
upon by faces of scorn and fear until seclusion is not a choice —
just the starting of a new faction.

Supreme survival of the fittest begins in the tiniest
light bulb of your mind

Do you have any true ideas or thoughts of your own? Do you
have to be walked around life fearing what pops into your mind?
If you know what I mean speak your mind, I would rather be a
creator than a clone!

Acceptance is not an issue that will bog you down or make you weak
It will make you create and believe not in the words of
others but in the truths that lie in environment and
instinct. Your truths!

Tom Slatt

A Survivor Asks . . .

If you want to know me . . . listen . . .
Please, don't give me advice.

If you want me to express my feelings,
Please, don't trample on them, nor deny them.
They are my feelings.
Accept them as they are.

If you would have me walk on . . . walk with me.
If you would have me forget the past, be patient.
It took me awhile to say, honestly, to a trusted person,
"This is what happened to me . . ."
The trusted person assured me that the harm had been grievous,
extreme.
I had been covering it for a long time with shame,
Protecting those close to me, from the shame.

The trusted person taught me that the shame is not mine to bear.
The persons who did this to me own the shame . . .
This helped me, then to look around and to realize that.
Perhaps, I could live,
In a different way.
But, beyond that . . . I can want to live!

Julie Verrette

Time Immemorial

When we know something to be true,
Deep in our hearts, our soul, our mind;
Why then is the way to express it
So difficult to find?

Time is not the great thief
Of our lives,
Nor our master.
As so many seem to strive
To catch up with time as the wind.
Behaving like squirrels in heat;
With tails flying.
If only these scurrilous beasts,
Arrogant, avaricious, haughty,
Would stop all their scamper
And banter:
Just stop!
Be still . . . look within.
There you will discover
Time without measure. No beginning — no end . . .

Thomas M. Gray

Donté

Dear boy you growing strong
    Mama has so much pride
Prove to the world it is your throne
    You hear the lies, yet you let it ride

She took time raising you
    Having all your needs met
Loving her was all you had to do
    Times was hard she fret

If you listen long
    The wind tell their story
Mama knew you did little wrong
    As long as she had faith and glory

In her eye's you were a king
    You were never once doubted
I suppose it's a personal thing and she sang out and shouted
Could not believe it was him she said my son it could not be
Suddenly the sky grew dim I held her hand, and weep with thee

He was no longer here to much pain to bare any sorrow
As I reminisce I drop another tear
    Wishing yesterday can stay and never come tomorrow

Nyla Drayton

Lost Love

The lonely days I sit alone,
Wondering why he's not home.
I can't imagine me like this,
I look at myself, and I'm a mess.
My hearts torn apart and in despair,
As I ask myself, why I must stare?
He's the one I want forever,
Even though that's a never.
I wish it all could be changed,
But then my mother would be in a rage.
I think I know my decision I have to make,
But is that the right one I must take?
I'm so confused I'm in a flutter,
You can tell when my rooms a clutter.
Maybe the only way out is to die,
But then my family would cry.
It can be fixed I'm sure it can,
But if not, I'll just keep repeating,
Love has no meaning to me,
If I cannot be with the one I love.

Tammie Frank

The Birthday

When I was 40, 40 years ago I could clean the house, shovel the
snow. I waited for the early spring so I could walk in the forest
so green where God can be heard and seen. Life is like the forest
so green and cool, with a river running swiftly to a shimmering
pool. If we are lucky we can look back, and see the beauty of
the forest, and what it represents on our life long track.

The river is the forest's soul and is the reason all things grow.
The wild flowers are children who have been in our lives first,
the pool is the water that quenches the thirst. The fish in the
pool helped feed the hunger. If in our fast moving life we have
done our best, I know that God will do the rest.

80 is really not so long, although, we think so after it is gone.
80 is just days of memories past, memories that will last and
last. The river, the flowers, the pool, and don't forget the forest
green and cool, at its best a wonderful place for me to rest.

Yevett Forester

Autumn Fire

The fire swept across the hillside, alighting tree and bush alike.
The fiery red crowning the tree tops
the orange-yellow licking across the limbs and brush.
It rushes across the hilltop and over the crest and sets the valley ablaze.
Nature has started her autumn fire.

Nature begin with hints, here and there among the bushes and trees.
Then with full raging blaze she set the trees and bushes afire
with autumn color.
The colors shimmer like a heat wave,
And leaves fall like dying embers of a fire.

The leaves in the breeze are swirled like the flames of a fire.
They sweep across the grass glowing like dying embers.
The trees bare and naked, consumed by the fire in their branches.
This is nature's way to prepare the world for the healing death of winter.
She turns her green world into a blazing inferno so that it may go
quietly into winter.
Then nature will again paint the world green, the spring.

Jan Quinn

Heart Sounds

When you hear the mournful cry of the wolf,
is his heart broken?

When you hear the lonely song of the whippoorwill,
is his heart broken?

When you hear the Loon's soulful call
is his heart broken?

When you hear a puppy's whimper in the night,
is his heart broken?

When you hear my silence,
is my heart broken?

Ruth Ahl

Stair Steps

Wish all of my children were
still stair steps getting in my way.
I was always busy throughout the day.
They'd laugh — they would cry.
They would fight and words would fly.
But at the end of the day
they would be tired.
Especially after being wired.
I sure miss those little dirty faces,
and taking them with me to all kind of places.
But they grow up and time goes on.
So I look forward to the
Grandchildren born.

Sharon Cunningham

Shades Of Reality

When night time comes
And realities fade
When truth's edge is dulled
By the evening shadow's shade

When passions are set a fire
And hearts set a blaze
And the weak run for cover
From the midnight sun's rays

When what's wrong seems so right
And what's right a pain too true
When longing overrides control
And lines blur between me and you

When one's embrace brings so much solace
And one's touch so much bliss
And time's ticking stops for hours
As two share the sweetness of a kiss

Alas sad as it is
This stolen love lost
For daylight always comes
And reality's return . . . always the cost

L. Scott Palazzo

The Window Of Love Grand-Mother

As I looked through the window, what did I see?
It was Grand-mother, sitting in a chair and shucking the
peas, while telling a story to you and me.

As I looked through the window, what did I see?
It was Grand-mother, piecing a quilt and mending things.
Full of wit and love, sharing everyday things with you and me.

As I looked toward heaven, what did I see?
Through the reverse of the window and looking at me.
It was Grand-mother, smiling and waving at you and me.

Through the reverse of the window and looking at me.
Who's this on Grand-mother's knee? Is it Dorothy?
Is that Edward standing near? And other's she loved?
It seemed to me, that her life had just begun.

Through the reverse of the window and looking at me.
I couldn't hear Grand-mother, yet I know what she means.
For her love has no ending and on any given day,
you might see her if you remember her this way.
For Grand-mother, will always be there for you and me.

Jacqueline Russell

All Alone

Do you know how it feels to be all
alone, behind bars of steel and walls
of stone, with no one to write or call back home
    Yes I know how it feels to be alone
I was like a king sitting high on the throne,
Now reduced to a jester with a heart of stone,
    Wait each day for Mail from home,
but no Mail ever comes I'm so all alone
    I am a good person if you look
into my eyes, you will see pain and
confusion that even I can not disguise
caused from false friendships and relationships
of lies, come have a look into my very sad eyes.
    They say a heart that has been
broken only time can heal
believe me I have had one I know
how it feels, as I look to our
future that is still unknown,
I hope and pray that never again will
I be all alone.

Archie L. Clausen

Amorously

Tree talks with jungle grass with field
star with galaxy and I talk with you.
Tell me your secret give me your hand
tell me your word, give me your heart
I have found your roots
with your lips I have talked to all lips
and your hands are familiar with mine.

I have cried in the brightest silence of my solitude with you
for reason of living people
and I have sung in the darkest nights with you
the most beautiful songs
because, the dead people of this year
have been the most loving living people of all times.

Give your hand, your hands are familiar with mine
hard to find, I am talking with you
like grass with field, like cloud with storm
like bird with spring, like tree that talk with jungle.

Because: I have found your roots
because, my voice is familiar with yours.

Ahmad M. Koulakani

Games

I remember nine year old toy gun
war games in the woods, behind my house,
air-mind bullets to kill not to stun.

Lying on my autumn leaved chest, mouse
eyed, cocked plastic, pricker bush cover,
afraid to run, but ready to pounce.

Boy armies, friends, civil war soldiers.
We pick teams, set rules to break,
I see feet, hear Chris and John whisper.

Excitement, they don't see me, I make
machine gun spit sounds like on T.V.
real movie action, make my gun shake

as my friends turn and fire back at me.
"I got you, I got you first, you're dead!"
"No we got you first, you cry baby!"

Argument every time. What we said
mattered. No one wanted to be dead.

Matt Canetto

Blue

Blue is a person who is a giver
spreading peace and joy to the world.
Blue is people who don't bother
hitting, smacking, or spitting on each other.
Blue is for people who never give up
who strive and face their fears.
Blue is for all those lonely people
who cry and are not ashamed to shed their tears.
Blue is for people who have families of their own
who care and share and have happy homes.
Blue is not to be tolerated and is
and never really supposed to be hated.
Blue is something that I sometimes see
where all the peace in the world comes into my dreams.
Blue is to be shared with joy making
people happy especially girls, and boys.
Blue is the one who always stands by my side
So I really don't have a reason to hide.
Blue is something that I will always like to see
No matter what day it is doesn't matter to me.

Michael T. Marsh

The Rose

As my green coat smothers and holds me
in my perfect shape, I feel locked in and long
to be free. So I begin to fight, and soon my
yellow face starts to show. Within a few days,
I am totally free of my coat, and many
people stop to admire my short lasting beauty.
I am fully blossomed within a few more
days, and on my way to my death. I am
still very lovely, if you look deeply; but my
yellow faces is withering, and soon my silky
petals will be falling out. My life as a rose
is always one of virtue, no matter how
short and sweet.

Leah Phillips

If

If you could fly, where would you go? Would you go to Paris,
the desert or do you even know? If the sun didn't shine would
you still see the light? Or would you be blinded by the moon at
night? If it snowed in June and was 90 in December, what about
summer would you remember? If water was scarce and tasted its
worst, would you drink it anyway or die of thirst? If the could
caress me with your fingertips, would you hold me tight and kiss
my lips? If the world was peaceful and a great place to be, would
you want to be here? Who knows! Maybe, we'll see.

Gale L. Higgs

Illusions

There was something desolate in the stillness of the tears.
Something eerie in the sound of the solitude.
Not a feeling of hysteria, but a cold clarity coming from silent years.
A reverberating into the darkness through a useless and empty mood.
Bewildering, bantering, ungentle and ruthless-each a misleading word.

Like a stretch of placid water seen between the sycamores.
There remains a symbol of the unknown where sounds of
dismay can be heard.
Perceiving a clear and smooth looking destiny, which lurked in
the shadows before.
Things seem to be a mistaken perception, discussed and
debated in a state so remote.

Indicating the probability of a disturbing sadness, but yet lifted when done.
Who will chase an innocent phantom?
Who may ponder this overwhelming surprise?
As of the sultry solstice of summer — a speechless wonder in all eyes.

When civilization must have perceived the joy of self-sacrifice.
Looking sharp and almost grim, but obviously bent.
To remain in effect, the matter is not of our own choosing.
When our illusions will always misrepresent.

Madeline S. Carlin

Ashley

A little girl was born here,
almost six years ago.

An angel sent from heaven to
delight those she would know.

Ashley didn't get to stay here long,
and yet she touched us all.

With beautiful smiles and bright blue eyes,
we couldn't help but fall.

She played and danced among us
and remains in all our hearts,

And now she's back in heaven,
Where all angels really start.

Karen Lamb

When I Consider Sirius

Revolving drunkenly on her course
Through the dark depths of space
With her traveling companion, Dwarf,
Microscopic beside his mate,
Yet terrible in density;
How he pulls and tugs her
As they streak a wavy path
Through the firmament;

How she steadfastly pursues her course,
Continues her mission,
And still shines brightest
Of all the stars in heaven.

When I consider Sirius, I question:
Should Man, noblest of all creations,
Burdened with the density and pull of evil
On his terrestrial tour,
Perform with any less splendor
Than that tormented star?

Evelyn Blair

Somewhere Beyond The Deep Seas

The frost is such a pretty sight.
It's a shame it has to come at night,
When I'm asleep in my little warm bed,
Snuggled beneath the covers red.

But I can see it in the morning light,
Even if I can't during the cold black night.
It glistens and sparkles and oh you should see,
All the wonderful things that happen to me.

First I am mounted on a shinning white steed,
Galloping along at a furious speed,
Toward a beautiful castle mounted so high,
On a smooth glass hill that it touches the sky.

As I draw nigh its doors unfold,
And wondrous beauty I behold,
Of Aladdin-like caves and sugar plum trees;
In this land of somewhere beyond the Deep Seas.

Then my little pink toes are nipped by the cold,
As my nightie around me tightly I hold.
So I crawl back in bed and snuggle up tight,
To study the picture and dream in the night.

Shirley A. Evans

A World In Need

In a world filled with madness and confusion,
It tends to paint a grim illusion.

There's a lack of kindness for our brother;
Shouldn't we learn to love one another?

A baby cries for its mothers touch;
Why not hold it, or is that asking too much?

We work hard for the fruits of our labor;
What's wrong with lending a hand to help our neighbor?

Many are hungry and need to be fed;
So how much could it cost to share a loaf of bread?

People are homeless, left out in the cold;
Is there no warmth in our hearts to help cover them,
without being told?

Our world could be such a beautiful place;
If we would only give a little compassion and grace.

Vicki J. Shelton

At The End Of Another Day

At the end of another day I find my
thought's drifting away.
    Drifting away to realms unknown.
Another place which I call home.
    A place I hope some day to reach
when my burdens here with me shall comely fall asleep.
    Fall asleep in death and wake not
dearest friend for me don't weep.
    In that home away up yonder where
no misunderstanding ever come, where
the body know's no sickness. I have
friend's who are becking me home.
    In that mansion I am certain
I have for me prepared, a place
some day I am going and leave
these earthly cares, and when you stand and look upon me.
Over me shed not a tear, far the form you
are beholding is only a form molded here.
I shall rest beyond the river self contented I shall be — where all
is peace and happiness, I would not exchange will thee.

Emma Moncrief

Luck Is The True Key (The Cry Of A New Immigrant)

Is American dream kept alive by new Americans?
Is America a ship built by immigrant labour?
Is the liberty statue still the new hope for immigrants?
Is America still a welcome home for the dejected,
    tired and famished of other lands?
Is the Chinese immigrant forgetful of the rail roads?
Is the African, sold out of his free will, forgetful of
    the Civil War, fought for his value?
Is the language and the face still the key that opens door?
Is there still two different world?
Is the new immigrant really welcome?
Is the new Chinese immigrant still looking for jobs of
    the rail road of the west?
Is the new African voluntary immigrant really buying
    his own way for modern time enslavement?
Is there a conspiracy to glue a group to the bottom of the bag?
Is it education that can really unglue to mainstream success?
Is it really true that considerable effort, ability,
    persistence and luck is the true key?

Chris Obi-Rapu

When A Sunny Day Turns To Rain

When you've looked into those eyes of blue
They looked like the bright clear sky to you.
And now they have turned so dark and gray
You watch their anger as they turn away.

That's when a sunny day turns to rain.

When you've felt the touch of a lover's hand
Like the warmth of sun that envelopes the land.
And now that embrace turns suddenly cold
Like a northeast wind blowing in so bold.

That's when a sunny day turns to rain.

When you've heard a sweet voice call out your name
Like birds sing in fight out over the plain.
And now that voice sounds harsh and shrill
Like a boom of thunder rolling in from the hills.

That's when a sunny day turns to rain.

When you've felt the rapture of love in your heart
Like the sun and the sky, never to part.
And now the Gods have turned their backs on you
Looking for someone else to renew.

That's when a sunny day turns to rain.

Kathleen M. Marcin

"For Us"

You died on the cross for our sins
walking me through the darkest ends
showing me truth and the path ahead
making me believe in all the good you did
I prayed to you many times
to give me strength with in my mind
showing me all the ways,
to make my body and mind feel at peace
as my love for you is now released.

David Wieber

Put On A Happy Face!

Mrs. Potato Head selects from a variety of eyes, ears, noses, eyebrows, and mouths when "putting on her face" before going to work each morning. If she is congested, she inserts a large nose into the hole in her plastic face. If she feels tired, she inserts red, irritated eyes. She uses her broad, smiley mouth when she is happy and frowns when she isn't quite up to putting on a happy face. Finally, her selection of ears and eyebrows is on a rotational basis, to allow the canals of the former and fibers of the latter to dry properly after being washed following each use. At night, when Mrs. Potato Head is ready to go to sleep, she removes all the accessories of her diurnal complexion and has quite a blank expression when she snuggles under the blankets with Mr. Potato Head.

Alan M. Dutka

Defining Me

My life is not perfect
   but I am somebody
I am, I really am
I tend to do things
   most fail to understand
      confused

Standing, peering into the looking glass
Pseudo reflections glaring at me
   looking through my soul
      thinking

Who are you
   Judging me with your disapproving glares
      controlling my inner child
         depressed

Derwinn Green

The Roses Of Love

The love of life is everyone's passion.
The everlasting fragrance of the rose.
Someone who is in your every thought.
The symbol of love to hold dear to your heart.
The rose bud emerges from the stem, bringing a desire to nature.
Their eyes met across the room, bringing an enchantment to their hearts, as if it were a poet's dream . . . their destiny.
The rose bud opens her eyes to give off her passionate red color as if their hearts opened to one another.
They met for the first time yet they've know each other an eternity.
Her smile, his eyes, her laugh, his charm so perfectly matched; as is rose to nature.
The bud has blossomed into the rose as has love into obsession.
As his knee touches the ground and a tear comes to her eyes she whispers, "yes." She is dressed in lace as he awaits their joining.
As he slips the ring on her finger, he hands her the symbol of his love.
The rose sits in the fragile glass vase, a witness to their love.
The diamond day has come.
The rose's scent has never been stronger nor its beauty more.
She hands him the rose as he had some years ago.
As they fall into one another's embrace, it cascades to the ground.
The fragile rose, the symbol, the witness of their love.

Tasneem Rukhsana Yacoob

The Attic

I tiptoed up the dull and dusty stair, sunlight filtered through the air.
Cobwebs hanging from ceiling to floor, there's an old cupboard, with one very large door.
In it were letters yellowed with age, and with a ribbon they were tied
Music sheets tattered and torn I spied.
There were dishes and old books upon a shelf, and nestled in between was a whimsical ol' elf.
I picked up an album and sat in an old chair.
Next to a floor lamp, an tasseled shade so bare.
I looked at the pictures so brittle and curled, one in a frame that was heavily pearled.
I sat there and rocked, looking about the room.
Hanging from the ceiling was an old lantern, and a loom.
In the corner sat a teddy worn with age.
If only someone could tell me the stories, page by page.
Generations should keep their histories alive, just so the stories can go on, after they have died.
I know my roots as far back as the czar, and I will keep the legacy to be passed on, by far.
So don't let your stories slowly vanish.
Some will be great and others a bit tarnished.

Linda F. Goltz

Why?

Why did he have to leave?
Why did You call him so soon?
I know that I don't have any right
to question You,
Maybe because it hurts me . . . so much
I know that the gift of life is ours, . . .
Until you want it back.

But, why Johnny?
And why this way?

He was so full of life, and with so much
Love to give.
I'm so lucky to have been one of his
many friends.
Yet I feel like I not only lost a good friend,
But an older brother too.
At this point, I'm going to end by telling
You Johnny I love you and you will
Always be a part of our lives.

Kennia Ramirez

Only Human

Sometimes I want to say things to you
that I never even say at all
because you see I'm human too
But you can make me feel so small

I try to do the best I can
at whatever task I do
and even though I'm just a man
please remember that I'm human too.

So if you can please understand
these words I'm writing you
are from you loving husband
who is only human too.

I make mistakes I don't deny
we all do including you
But that's not a reason for me to try
to not be human too.

I can't help the way I act
as the little things that I do
Because you are the courtesies I lacked
are by God's grace, I'm only, heaven too.

Paul J. Hofstod

Childhood Ending

I knew the day my childhood ended, I was nine.
That's when I took a beating that no one should suffer, not even
an animal.
Much less a child from a man I loved dearly, "My father."

When the beating was over, he said nothing.
I stayed in my room silently crying.
When my mother came home, I could hear them talking.

They walked in my room were I was lying,
not having moved an inch from where he last left me.

He came up to me and said he was sorry, but it no longer mattered
because at that moment I knew my childhood had ended . . .

Mischell Bowen

The Forest

Deep in the forest is a lovely tree
    its branches hang so low.
This is the way it was meant to be
    to hide the lonely doe.

Deep in the forest is a tiny brook
    its rocks shimmer so bright.
Come very quickly and take a close look
    before the dusk turns to night.

Deep in the forest is a beautiful deer
    its life such a peaceful sight.
Walk very quietly and don't come too near
    for the deer will surely take flight.

Deep in the forest there is life so great
    it's truly a breath-taking vision.
But we must act now before it's too late
    to preserve this wonderful mission.

Shelia Green

Untitled

Unbelievable, don't know my own hate.
Stresses come up at any given time.
Constantly trying to blame it on fate.
Up some social ladder, trying to climb.
In my world full of doubts, no grip at all.
Comprehending problems that have to be.
Finding it easy to give up and fall.
Don't know what is going on inside me.
Spiraling in a void of confusion.
Only me, myself and I can stop this.
Wondering why I have this illusion.
Trying to make contact, but swing and miss.

Every day pondering why I don't try,
Only to find out to myself I lie.

Ryan Kerby

Get Away

Get away from all the bustle of the city,
And settle down into the quiet country.
Forget about your problems,
There's better things to do,
Here there is peace that fills the air,
Which brings back old memories,
Memories that linger,
Are blossoms of the past.
A life is to be worthwhile,
So sit down, rest and think about the world.
Think about that special dream,
Which someday may come true,
Just try your best and you'll do fine,
Be happy and live.

Bonnie Proesel

Is This The Way

The silence lies over the hill.
There the sudden sound of death
Lingers and invades his will,
As man breathes life's last breath.

Another life is lost, another battle unwon.
Is this really as it should be?
Must this be the way things are done
To keep our country free?

Frances Katherene Mott

To Speak With Your Heart

I was always told to be sure to speak with my heart.
It was always said that if I did so, I'd never go wrong.
Oh how wrong that was!
I spoke with my heart more than once and both times I felt
so dejected.
I felt as if I was turned away and like I was insane.
I was called numerous names all because I spoke with the heart.
I have just one question for you . . .
Why should I speak with my heart, only for it to be
shattered and broken?
Oh, to speak with your heart . . .

Laura Nicole Lanzone

Untitled

A woman full of warmth
bright as a summers day
with the sun in her eyes and the wind in her hair
brings love to the world in a beautiful way

Armando D'Accordo

Mr. Beck's Evergreen Tree

Mr. Beck planted a beautiful tree!
For all of us and others to see.
It is unique and one of a kind,
It's small and straight and one of a find.

This is a proud little dancing tree,
Has a round top knot that you can see.
It's spreading fingers reach out with love
Hoping to attract a live white dove.

It has a top knot round and light green,
Like a leprechaun that's seldom seen.
Every day gives thanks to God for life
Do we think to say, "Thank-you for life?"

So little tree grow up straight and tall,
Let the birds nestle and seldom fall
And in return from bugs protect you,
Raise their young and sing happily to.

This moment in time has come so right
The sky is so blue and the sun shines bright.
God's pattern is hidden in the seed,
And it's always there in time of need.

Bertha Baker

The Battlefield

As I walked out to the battlefield,
I raised my musket to my chest.
A speeding horse hit the field,
A silver bullet battered my breast.
I fell to the ground with a hammering shock,
Nobody there to see me fall.
I yelled and screamed to solitary rock,
But only the horse saw it all.

David Libertson

Invisible, Divisible, Unfound

Smart. Good. Righteous.
  Old eyes, of another age, sightless see.
Sweet cherry. Delicious moods. Easy lay, in back-roads woods
  Limited male eyes assume.
Stupid. Lazy. Thief.
  Behind sun-glasses, biased strangers gaze on.
Loving. Obedient. Kind.
  Mother's hearts have no eyes. No minds.
Liberal. Traitorous. Vile.
  Brown skin of the old heritage,
  Closed, Latin-Black eyes accuse . . .
Yet all eyes, do identity abuse. Refuse the face
Dilemma of a new-breed — misunderstood

Invisible.
Divisible.
Unfound.
  Brown eyes search in the mirror.

Guadalupe Kautz

Is Love Enough?

A tear runs down my cheek, and you wipe it away.
Another tear runs down my cheek, and you wipe it away.
I start to cry, and you hold me tight,
telling me everything is going to be all right.
I look up at you,
and tears run down your cheeks too.
Why can't love be enough?
We dance under the stars holding back tears of sorrow,
remembering tears of joy we once knew.
Why can't love be enough?
I lay here with tears running down my cheeks,
and you're not here to wipe them away,
or to tell me everything is going to be all right.
Why can't love be enough?
One day, we won't have to hold back our tears.
We will only have tears of joy,
for a love rekindled,
after time apart.
Then, love will be enough.

Danielle Daddino

To My Children

At times the world may seem chaos,
And you feel you are tossing about.
Just remember — each generation
Has been faced with its own strife and doubt.
Try to keep in your life sense of balance;
And weigh carefully right from the wrong.
Take with you the love of your family;
Keep the home ties about you, and strong.
As we send you away to your schooling,
Or to service — wherever you roam,
Don't forget that your real base for freedom
Lies in God, and your Country, and Home.

Rose Emma Hutchinson

It Was A Dream

For many years, and still today;
Gently it taunts me, and in the dark we play.
Arousing inner senses, awakening an intensive desire;
Toying with secret passions, setting my soul on fire.
Deliciously it seduces me, repeatedly day or night.
Its sensual charm I find unable to fight.
I'm completely defenseless, caught up in the fantasy;
Surrendering in a sigh, engulfed in sweet ecstasy.
It tremendously excites me, giving pleasure so extreme;
Awakened in the afterglow, once again it was a dream!

Jody Lingerfelt

Untitled

Saturday morning again alone on the porch swing rocking
my heart and rocking and rocking and rocking, have to
rock, and rock, and rock again

Sheila my inspiration calling me to trees in sun
and breeze; every sound: every katydid, bird song, and
brushing leaves calling me, calling me.

The Yellow faithful sun reminds me she's alive
and trying and she will not stop treading. Nor
will I nor will I.

This grieving will not be the end, but a passage
must be travelled, and this grieving is the
only way, through to another day.

Saturday morning again not alone, not so alone,
but being in this beingness, so glad I
paused to see all this.

Melissa Bentley

One Morning

I was sitting with my coffee and cigarettes
Feeling lost and lonely in the sun
Worrying and wondering why I was so afraid
And when was the last time I had any fun.

Then, I heard a wild bird call . . .
And peacefully remembered . . .
A mighty, magical waterfall
Beneath ancient redwood trees, so tall.

Mary Michele Golden

Friendship

Faithful Friendship is not about one thing but many,
It is about respect,
  Being a sincere friend when needed but also
  knowing when it is essential to let the friend
  have privacy,
It is about caring,
  Always having a shoulder to cry on always
  having a hand to hold,
It is about awareness,
  Feeling the same thing almost naturally,
True Friendship is the superior thing about life.

Anna Alexander

Fireworks

Every time my parents say,
"We're going to Grandma and Grandpa's today!"
Fireworks go off in my heart.

Whenever the phone rings,
my eyes open with a start,
for hope it's my elders to talk of things,
which will set my mind apart,
from, dank, things in a blanket of dark.

As I'm walking through the park,
when I see a lovely spark,
I think of fireworks in my heart.

Every time it's dark and gray,
I think of you,
which always lights my way.

As I write this heartfelt poem to you,
I hope it makes you happy and gay.

Now that I must say goodbye,
and end this poem today,
that expresses my love to you in immeasurable ways.

Ryan Shissler

There's No Limits

How high can I fly said the little bird
To his Mama trying to teach?
As high in the sky as your dreams allow,
There's no limits to how high you can reach.

How fast can I run asked the little gazelle
To his Mama who watched him race?
As fast as the wind or a falling star
Or the speed of light through space.
　　There's no limits.

How far can I swim said the little whale
To his Mama swimming nearby?
To the east and west, north and south,
Wherever oceans lie.
　　There's no limits.

What can I be when I've grown to a man,
A doctor or lawyer or pilot a plane,
A merchant or banker or run a train,
Work with my hands or work with my brain,
　　There's no limits.

　　Madge Millward

Awake Child

Head so still. Brown eyes that gaze skyward
Hospital room so sanitized.
Awake child, awake.
Doctor's face seemed so concerned.
Nurses monitor your every move.
Awake child, awake.
Needles, I.V.'s, tubes; do you feel these things?
Awake child, awake.
Your cry I hear; my prayers I give.
God will answer.
Awake child, awake.
Student doctor tells me, you will never be the same.
That's when God steps in.
Awake child, awake.
Midnight hour, when you think no one sees,
You reach for a balloon.
Awake child, awake.
Doctor said you might never walk again.
Yet on christmas eve you walked the hospital floors.
Awake child, awake.

　　Cynthia W. Mickle

Our Society

Our Society, full of hate and blame, not caring for anybody, not feeling any shame.
The homeless selling dope, just to keep their family fed.
Kids who feel no hope, so they kill for the colors of blue and red.
Everyone in their own little clique, making fun of each other just to get a kick.
Husbands beating their wives, some stabbing them with knives.
Girls selling their bodies in the street, to get some money, trying to make ends meet.
Kids snorting coke and crack, some selling marijuana sacks.

Our Society, is there any hope or care, if there is please, please share.
Some think they have the answer, but they don't follow the One, true Master.
Some of us who know Him don't ever share Him.
You might think you can't share to all, but if you don't, you, yourself might fall.
Heed these words I say, follow Him, and obey.
For in the end, there is going to be one huge battle, against the one who rides the pale horses saddle.
Yes, we will win, those of us who have forgiven sins.
To be on the winning side, you must ask the Master and then decide, whether to follow Him and all His glory, so one day, you can tell of His story.

Remember, Jesus Christ you must choose, or in the end you will lose.
So make a decision and stand beside me, or die with the rest of Our Society.

　　Josh Hadley

If I Had Only Kissed You

If I had only kissed you,
Why did my body tingle in spirit?
If I had only kissed you,
Why did you let me kiss you twice and again?

If I had only kissed you,
Would you have spoken of soul mates?
If I had only kissed you,
Could you have mistaken me as just another date?

If I had only kissed you,
I could understand how I let you walk away.
If I had only kissed you,
I would not question the tear drop against my face.

If I had only kissed you.

　　Michael D. Correro

Black

The sound of a graveyard cloaked by the night.
The hue of a raven while in flight.
The melancholy mood of a sad love song.
The scheming villain plotting along.

The foreboding panther stalking its prey.
The terminally ill cursing the day.
The diabolical assassin and his sanguine mind.
The rotting carnage that was leaves behind.

The razor sharp sickle of the Angel of Death.
The suicide victim struggling for breath.
The accident that takes the life of a child.
The graves of Auschwitz where bodies are piled.

The lethal dose of a hypodermic injection.
The airplane bomb that escapes detection.
The pickpocket's limbs pulled apart by the rack.
All these things can be described as Black.

　　David L. Hoffman Jr.

Question

What is love?
It is not something that can be seen, heard, or touched,
Yet everyone knows it exists.
It is a feeling,
But what does it feel like?
Love is described by different people,
In many different ways . . .
Who is correct?
Is falling in love
The same thing
As loving someone?
Who can answer the question?
Maybe the question is the answer.
Love is full of questions
And
A question itself.
What is love?

　　Alison Thayer

Dreaming

My feet are on the earth but my head is in the stars.
I can play with all the planets, and touch the dust on mars.
The twinkling in the night, is but happy faerie glow.
I coast the solar flux, letting lights around me flow.
To skate the rings of Saturn, and picnic on the moon,
would make me happiest, but I must leave this soon.
Rings of light I wear, as I expand upon the wind.
Happy, airy, free to dream; I can feel my troubles mend.
Yes, my feet are on the earth, and my head in the stars;
but I must stay at home, and only dream of mars!

　　Marci Swaine

A Valley

How quiet and serene this valley lies,
Breathing sounds of nature beneath its sky.

The sweet smell of flowers fills the air,
A freshness of life for those who care,

Its hills and meadows whispering words,
Answered in flight by soaring birds,

A walk through this valley of sweetness galore,
Is like reaching for life through an open door,

The rapture and beauty that's renewed each spring,
Reminds us all of the joy this valley brings
Ron Giordano

Father Time

A year is a day, a day an hour
I dance the slow waltz as time jitterbugs by
Watching helplessly as the wrinkles of time
Etch their birthmark upon the corners of my eyes.

I sleep in silk, on satin sheets
Relishing the softness of their touch on fallen breasts
I frequent boutiques, covering my age with designer wear
Hoping to defer my destiny with Father Time.

Karen Alexander

Dad's Dilemma

I can't believe there is a day without a new tomorrow,
So I'll just slip beneath these covers, hunker down, and wait.

Blissful sleep you've taken me so often on your boat,
Cross pillowed waves, through ocher caves, to castles with a mote.
I followed you with strength unmatched, a pillar of pavilions,
To kingdoms where there's no despair and chances by the trillions.

They blast me with hot magma, then brace me with the cold,
My memories are fading fast, my eyes are growing old.
So much to do, much more to say, can they make it on their own?
They need my strength, my song in sync, when flush with their alone.

Stop your Plan, I'm in command, I'll break this retched reverie,
But thoughts of pain still remain, a bulwark during the reveille.
I'll call to task my stiff strong mast and present it without a sail!
Winds that carry me, stars that guide me, won't fail this vessel pale.

It seems I've won, or did I lose, or did I even fight?
Darkness moves in mysterious ways when standing in the light.
Slim are the chances of success, but driven by all that's fair,
I'll hesitate, then contemplate the option of repair.

Tomorrow is a day anew with roses spilling o'er the gate,
So I'll just slip beneath these covers, hunker down, and wait.

Dennis N. Lorenz, Ph.D.

True Love

True love is . . .
  As beautiful and delicate as a butterfly . . .
  As wild as a mustang running free . . .
  As warm as the sunshine on a summer day . . .
  As refreshing as the sparkling morning dew . . .
  As exciting as a child on a new adventure . . .
  As content as a kitten snuggled by a warm fire . . .
  As caressing as the breeze blowing gently through the trees . . .
  As passionate as the heat of blazing embers . . .
  As unending as a brook rippling over the rocks . . .
  As vast as the deepest ocean . . .
True love encompasses . . .
  Beauty, gentleness, passion,
  Sensitivity, warmth, and freedom.
True love is a treasure.

Lola Y. Corbett

We, The Clouds

You study us often and intently
and believe from our size and hue
that you can foretell our intentions
but we often have a surprise for you.

If we are the towering cumulus type
it may seem safe for you to surmise
that showers and even hail will result
instead, there is sunshine in your eyes.

The experts have analyzed us for centuries
and gave us names according to shape and height
but we owe allegiance only to the sky
we do care that you marvel at our sight.

We admit being quite unruly at times
causing discomfort during some of your flights
These acts are to surely remind you
that the early tenant has inherent rights.

We are pleased to play a part in forming a rainbow
and for adding to the sun's aura as you see it rise
but we insist on being fickle and independent
we thank God for allowing us to dwell in His skies.

George L. Volk

Stones

There were no clouds in the sky that day and
There was no threat of rain or thunder, but
We were all hit by some streak of lightning
That came bursting from the heavens above
And reminded us that there was a God.

I'd like to recall running away from it all
Or bursting out some bitter objection,
But when the others yelled the word timber,
I had my hand on the slippery axe.

I knew the color of blood and its course —
Yet I didn't know the color of pain,
Until that day when we threw those stones.

When he fell to the ground, I felt the earth move.

I was the one who took my hand off the axe.
I saw the color of pain mixed with blood.
I saw God take that Boy's spirit away.
I saw blue, gray, and a puddle of red.

And I knew that these were the colors of pain.

Eric C. Waldemar Jr.

The Well

I am just a well, you see.
From looks alone many misjudge me.
The stone and mortar create my steadfast foundation
yet I am open to all who approach.
To some I may appear romantic,
others view me as dependable.
Once in a while, I may be life saving
though most merely pass by
never noticing my continuing existence.
But my real passion, and yes, my value,
lay deep within me.
Those who take time to sing a song
while exchanging refreshing life with me
are rewarded with overflowing buckets.
Sometimes I hear the sacred wishes and dreams of secretive people
and at times I am the backrest for a lonely heart.
I can catch the wind, rain, and sun
and I have softened the fall of a shooting star.
Come sit on my ledge for a spell, for you see,
I am not just a well . . .

Jason Umemoto

"My Mom"

My Mom was someone who was always there . . .
for comfort and love and to say that she cared.

My Mom has always been a big part of my life . . .
even after when I her daughter married and became a wife.

My Mom soon adjusted and began to share . . .
to make things easier as Steve and I had become a pair.

My Mom was soon filled with more love and great joy . . .
when we presented her with a cute Grandbaby boy.

My Mom continued to enjoy her family and do what she could . . .
and many a time it was much more than she should.

My Mom was stubborn and determined and this we all know . . .
but this kept her going even though her list of illness began to grow.

My Mom later seemed to know that her life wasn't to go on . . .
so she began to prepare her departure down to what clothing and what song.

My Mom tried to make things easier for me so I would know what to do . . .
and my list with her instructions and helpful advice just grew and grew.

I didn't always appreciate when we had to spend our time this way . . .
but deep down I know she was getting me ready for just this very day.

My Mom will always be a special lady a friend that I'll always love . . .
even though now I have to do it from a distance and wish it to her up above.

Thank you Mom
Love, Cindy
Cindy Yager

Majestic Soul

Beautiful eagle, soaring, soaring high,
Feathered fingers touch the sky.
Above snowy mountain tops so free,
Eagle, gliding, gliding on life's breeze.
Over fields of wheat and rocky hills,
Whispering feathers pass lakes so still.
Grassy acre's filled with wildlife,
She soars above all, with no gripe.
So sad I feel for her majestic soul,
That she must rest upon a . . . telephone pole.
Tammy L. Marko

Some Things Are Meant To Be Cherished

Things are seen differently through the eyes of each person.
But what you see, others may never have the chance.
So cherish each waking moment of your life, no matter how
long or short.

Things are felt differently through the heart and soul of
each person.
But what you see and feel are very powerful when together.
So, remember each touch and feeling, because one day you may
not have that gift.

Things are done differently through the thoughts of each person.
So it ends where it began, and a simple thought started it all.
Lanette Andrews

Countless Sorrows

Unspeakable pain hidden within,
Shreds her insides with teeth that grin.
Claws it's way up her throat.
She wears indifference as a coat
To keep her warm against their stares,
To insure herself no one cares.
The monster grows nourished by tears.
She awakens from dreams fed by fears,
And realizes there are infinite tomorrows,
If she gets past the countless sorrows.
Lauren R. Silver

The Pancake Maker

The pancake maker mixes the batter
while he flips the other batch to make them fatter

1, 2, 3, the pancaked flip in the air
They hurry back down and fall in his hair.

He flips them off with the pancake turner,
and they fall right into the pancake burner.

He scoop's them off with an ouch,
and they fall in between the cracks of his couch.

He hurries back to get the other batter
Then he see's that something was the matter

He had forgot about the other 3 pancakes he flipped
they had fallen on the floor and he slipped.

As he packed up from the shore,
he decided he wasn't making pancakes no more.
Juliet D'Angelo

Midnight's Moon

Glistening under midnight's moon,
snowflakes fall so silently;
as quiet whispers of God's grace
bears the light of winter's face.

There's no destiny to where they fall.
Winds sweep the blanket fresh;
a stage of splendor to behold;
the earth and heavens conjoin as whole.

Bring forth these bodies and souls,
connecting them to form as one;
a creation of unity few imagine,
this passion so grand, too much to fathom.

This blissful wonder a vision in bloom,
underneath this midnight moon.
Joni Gautney

What Is An Uncle?

An uncle is more than just your mother's brother,
he is more than just your grandmother's son,
he is a loved one,
and a loved one is someone you love,
It doesn't necessarily have to be a relative,
It is someone you love and care about deeply,
And although we may not show it in our actions.
We still mean it in our hearts . . .
Patty Gibson

Cruel Memories

He was to me my major illusion, my first
greatest love, he was everything. And I
never understood why he betrayed me, if
I truly loved him in millions of ways,
and now in hands of her I saw him
walking by, really happy and a cloud of
beautiful memories made me cry.
And now he knows of his mistake because
she abandoned him,

I would like to have her face to face to
congratulate her for making him suffer
with her kisses because he only deserves
to be rejected, he has played with my heart!

I congratulate her because one day for
him I almost killed myself and at nights
when looking at his picture like crazy
I cried for his love.
Zoila A. Florentino

278

The Janus Trees

Vermilion sparks from flaming trees, maple leaves let go,
float down, swirl up against the window glass.
Sink-bound I duck — red-feathered birds about to crash?
Just boomerangs of red and gold, kaleidoscopic whorls.
I am a figure in a shake-me globe of wind-tossed leaves,
Crimson caracoles stirred up by whipping boughs.
Bright embers cover the ground, bed down the lichened trunks.
High wind and rain night-long soon blacken my window view.
In morning gray, dark skeletons stretch bare fingers,
toss and weave their brittle web outside the glass
as hempen nets entwine green globes bobbing in a leaden sea.
Banked embers, muted ash, blanket the sleeping trees.
Leaf warm, the maple giants rest,
resilient, naked, ready to survive the winter snows
and yield lifeblood to sugar taps come promises of spring.

Pepper Mainwaring-Healey

Precious Love

When you're young you look to see
A smile so tender and true.
And notice that it's coming
From the two who love you.

To them, you seem perfect and serene
In each and every way.
And always hope the best for you
Each and every day.

This precious love will last
Through all love, joy, and stress
And in the end you shall always remember
Your parents loved you best.

Brian T. Gordon

Fun Fantasy

Oh, fantasy of fun and work . . .
Of fickle lives and tickle
Our toes and ribs, our laughter rings
On the winds of our words that sing!
Oh, joy of laughter and sweet repose
Fill our thirsty souls with glowing prose!
Come, hold our lives in your beautiful hands,
Suspend us on tiny strands
Of feathery strings, of yards of pearls,
Up high above the sea
Where sun and stars and beauteous things
Await our wonder . . . and furls
Us . . . up and out and back again . . .
Till we reel with giggles and glee!
Oh, joy of living and dancing wild . . .
Oh, calm on the breezes above . . .
Oh, march to the drums of a thousand boys . . .
Oh, seal our hearts with love!

Joanne Bales

The Big Blazing Ball of Fire

There is a big blazing ball of fire high up in the sky,
Watching the airplanes, jets, and eagles racing right by.
That big blazing ball of fire gets burned out by night,
He goes to bed, tired, from giving everyone his light.
He gets up nice and early, ready for another hard days work,
He sees every move from everyone, while behind the cloud he lurks.
He gives us light and he gives us heat,
Out of any planet he couldn't be beat.
He makes a beautiful sunset far out in the west,
He shows off his beauty before he takes a rest.
He is a fire burning in the campground in the sky,
He is a fire burning in the campground in heaven, oh so very high.
He sees everything from people at work to children having fun,
That big blazing ball of fire is the sun!

Sarah Croll

Africa — Patterns In The Grass

The trees older than history — who even in death point their
gnarled fingers to the endless sky in defiance . . . the bush —
dark shadows where unseen eyes peer back — tensing to any
movement that could mean prey or death . . . the stillness, the
clouds, the promise of a brilliant sunset, the eerie danger of the
moonlight and the hope of survival until another dawn . . . the
vital struggle of the strong life that has never known the harness
or the limitations of boundaries . . . the wild — where eagles call
and vultures wait; where all walk quietly; where delicate herds
peacefully browse; where the great buffalo, rhino and big cats
look with disdain; where soulful elephants savage the thirsty
forest; all making patterns in the grass . . . the freshness of the
evening breeze; the freedom and harsh fairness of the cycle of
life and death; the sudden reality of nature that our own daily
life hides behind many masks . . . there are hardships beyond
feeling; there are valleys unpeopled and still; there are vistas
that go forever to the horizon; that beckon and beckon . . . this is
Africa — dark and beautiful cries of death and chants of
happiness; all these memories bring me back; and I want to
return — I will return — to add yet another pattern in the grass.

William E. Crisp

Leaf

In winter's dormant state,
I lay sleeping within the warmth of the branch
Anticipating the arrival of longer days.
Where the warmth of the sun awakens life.
As I bud forth to reach the bright rays,
I watch the lives of creatures bud forth as well.
Birds in the nest near me, squirrels that run playfully by.

As I grow, I see more of the forest, and the beauty surrounding me.
The wind tries desperately to sever my link
To what I know is safe while I am still young.
With determination, I stay where I belong, as the days grow warm
I reach my peak of growth, and with it peak growth of the forest.

All to soon, the weather grows cool.
With some regret and fear, I begin to change. My color begins to
lighten, and with it my attachment to all I know begins to fade.

Once again, the wind tries to remove me, but this time it succeeds,
And as a gently fall to the ground,
I realize that even if only for a brief time, I experienced the
beauty of nature,
And not even the wind can take that from me.

Estella Hornaday

A Memorial Prayer In Gratitude Of Mary's Life

Thank you Dear Heavenly Father
For sending Mary Alice into our lives
She has been such a blessing to all of us
Her beauty and charming smile
Gave us a loving greeting always

She was a loving, caring Mother and Grandmother
Her perseverance in adversity was unrelenting
Mary knew the joys of achievement
Experienced the grief of loss
A measure of sacrifice for the good of others

We will always remember her warmth and kindness
Her endearing personality we will miss
The soft spoken words
"I love you, I love all of you"

Dear Heavenly Father
Hold Mary Alice, lovingly and tenderly
In your care . . . "Precious in your sight"

Thank you for Mary's life
The blessings of knowing and loving her
As a sister, a friend, and confidant

Jessie McWilliams

Vade Me Cum

I'll be your tour guide
and reveal truth
about Polish castles.
They cost light
upon the unknown
history of the land
known less
with polishness
one could hardly
expect from ruins.

If you need a lift
I'll elevate you
up to the skies
and we'll ski down
the clouds . . .
. . . a field of sunflowers is our destination.
Be like a castle and cast the light
but first become a sunflower
and follow it.

Andrew Jaroslawski

Untitled

In the mists of Time
Your deeds of valor past
soon will be forgotten today chimes and what once was cast
clings only in a memory of one
today the battle will be fought anew
and warriors wage for fleeting glory
heroes soon forgotten enemies once rued
with fear your presence time's story
however does not end with a single deed
victorious valor once achieved today
like the sand through fingers spread
returns from whence it came and the rays
of light tomorrow shall shine singing
the praises of the youth who felled
with might enemies to our light
but brave warrior of the past assail
not against the youth for bright
are his deeds today but time
the conqueror of conquerors, vanquisher of the victorious stymies
slaves and enslaver and all are extinguished.

Harvey Decker

A Tragedy

Lifeless fell to Earth below
Her insanity I captured, grasping strong —
Life I drained, Fool — let go.
Infatuation drew me there, love controlling no time I did spare.
For fear felt heavy to mine soul . . .
Scared she gasped as I gained, my treasure there at last did hold —
Then ivory skin grew morbid, cold.
Rattled mind and shattered soul; In love I killed her body whole.
Separation once more I refuse to accept —
No meaning to survive, beauty deceased, I am alive!
Hatred within tearing — existence I wish to be sharing —
Ignorance. Ignorance. Death . . .
Now I ponder as I did once before —
I stood through eternity outside her door.
Opening slowly no latch to break,
Premeditated. I found her lying awake.
My emotion flowed, she responded with rage I pleaded to persuade . . .
She refused me with certainty — now I do bleed.
Soon I shall ponder in morbid light —
To win in death, my life's delight.

Carrie Ellen Cotter

The Beautiful Bird

Only a fool would continue to hold on when a bird prepares for flight.
The wise let go because they know what the bird can do if we
just lead it towards the light.

Only someone who does not understand that some things
cannot be delayed would hold on so tight until this beautiful
bird's feathers are frayed. No, we must love it enough to let go
and to trust that we have taught it how to fly and when it starts
to spread its wings we must stand back and pray, not cry.

For we always knew that this day would be that the beautiful bird
would want to see this world she's only heard about thus far.
We must let her go to experience this first flight being careful to
never let her out of our sight —

Flying behind her in the distance so that she may test her wings
once and for all — being ever ready to catch her should she fall.
Knowing that in the end all birds return safely home no longer
having the need to roam because they have seen, heard, and
done all they longed to do and in the end they know for themselves that what mother said is true that all you're searching for
can only be found in you.

Freddie Burnett

Black Eagle

Rain soaked habitation;
Lightning struck the creation;
Thunder roared in anger.
During this storm
Black Eagle was born.

Black as night, bright as day,
Foaled during a storm in the month of May,
She fits her name as we fly o'er the ground;
Black Eagle she was crowned.

Lightning swift, yet gentle as the breeze;
Strong in spirit, though always aiming to please;
Forever a constant and unfettered friend as the eagle;
Lifting high her head, as she does quite often, she is most regal.

Even in death, nothing will match her willpower;
She will fight to the very end of her last hour.
Though I know she eventually must pass on,
Nothing will ease the pain in my heart
Of having so great a friend as Black Eagle depart.

Kathleen M. Kossey

A Twinkle In My Eye

Upon a dark day I walk in the mist of my tears.
Within I see the evil that lurks, and the sores that tear.
I see the undesirable all bundled in a bag.

The time has come to dispose of such things.
My journey takes me up a hill to a place of cruel hate.
I see a man upon a beam his head bowed low.
I see the blood so pure running down onto the ground.

I can't do this thing I need to do; this is my burden to bare.
I deserve the pain He feels and gently tacked my burden on.
My heart ached and through my tears I heard Him say.
"Father, forgive her, she knew not what she did."

My tears mingled with His blood to form a stream so rare.
It flowed into a river: my heart, pulse and blood did
jumped, meshed and merged into the rhythm's flow.
Out of the River Of Life I came into a garden so fair.

I saw in the center square a statue so white and pure.
I saw the face, my face, looking up to Him.
How cruel I thought to put my ugly on art so rare.
"Not so my child," I heard a voice around me say.
"I have formed you into the person you are; a twinkle in my eye."

Jean Even

Walking In Dreamland

Come walk with me into Dreamland
Where there's only one woman and one man
Where all dreams come true
Just come my way and take a step or two
Just think of all the fun we'll have
Laying on a sunny beach
Building sand castles in the wet sand
Maybe stranded on a deserted Island
Wouldn't you like to take a spin around the moon
To dance and sing out loud
How about making love on top of a cloud
Then sliding down a rainbow and
Splashing into the pot of gold
Yes, yes, my love come and walk with me
Into dreamland
Where there will always be one woman and one man.

Sharon Dianne Sloan

Time Is Running Out

As I lay here in my death bed
A lot of things are going through my head
I worry for my wife and kid
And all the wrong I did
My time is running out
Yet I don't know what to think about
If I hadn't told that lie
I probably wouldn't be preparing to die
But it's all in the past
So my time left is going fast
Should I cry
As I die
Only one thing left now
Time to make my death vow

Brian Henry Raymond

Tornado Warning

A siren shrieks and I scorn the weather eye.
I know my enemy time
And am merciless in my attack.
Today and now, the law suspended hangs,
And I am fiend, frenzied and indifferent
To the tortured scrape of street and metal.
Reason wins or reason loses,
Who can care if faith is victor over all or instinct.
For I am dumb, a creature driven to the nest
As hostile, dark-tailed birds dip low to fall.
And I, lone savage tangled in some primal growth,
Keen mindlessly for open brutish cave and dying young.
And when I run the yard to find them safely hid,
There's nothing left for me to do but weep. I weep.

Marie Talley

I Wish I Was Beautiful

I'm walking down the street and
my boyfriend turns his head and looks
the other way.
  I've always wished before that,
wishing to be beautiful, but it just never
came true. Everyone says, "you are so
beautiful," but they don't know how I
feel inside.
  Even when I'm walking down the street
everyone turns their heads and walks
away from me.
  I've had so many problems in my
life and now, when people look at me
they just turn their heads and walk
away.

Jennifer Strelec

God: The Greatest Teacher Of All

As I laid my head down
to fall into sleep,
I tried counting dogs,
cats, even sheep.

I had forgotten to pray
and the Lord ask me "Why?"
I couldn't say a word
and started to cry.

He made it clear
that he was the one.
In this he said
he gave his son.

His son was a teacher
of all mankind.
A greater teacher,
no one could find.

He was perfect and taught his children well.
The ones who never knew him were caught in hell.

The Greatest teacher of all is found sitting above,
looking down upon us with open arms of love.

Jana L. Johnson

It Could Happen

It could happen if you're happy or sad.
It could happen if you're healthy or sick.
It could happen if you're young or old.
It could happen if you're rich or poor.
It could happen regardless of your race, color, size, or looks.

You could die if you're happy or sad.
You could die if you're healthy or sick.
You could die if you're young or old.
You could die if you're rich or poor.
It could happen regardless of your race, color, size, or looks.

It could happen if you're happy or sad,
It could happen if you're healthy or sick.
It could happen if you're young or old.
It could happen if you're rich or poor.
It could happen regardless of your race, color, size, or looks.

You could fall in love if you're happy or sad.
You could fall in love if you're healthy or sick.
You could fall in love if you're young or old.
You could fall in love if you're rich or poor.
It could happen regardless of your race, color, size, or looks.

Scott Miller

Love Around Us

Soft, tender, moist, wet, loving lips give a kiss,
Cupid's arrow, shot straight, did not miss.
Two hearts, with love, intertwined for life,
He, the loving husband, she, the loving wife.
Together forever, as birds in a cage,
Love is forever, at any age.
Age in their hair, years in their eyes,
Love still blooms with dark blue skies.
Their steps may be slower, but there's a quickness in their smiles,
The love they share could take them yet, many miles.
Teen love flourished in these hearts with age,
Love, strong and wild, ready for the next page.
The young, they know how love abounds,
The old, they know love is all around.
With the love they know, stronger by far,
They can reach up and touch that star.
With love all around us, there is one thing to do,
We should celebrate this love, between me and you.

Bobby R. Gardner

Rainbows In The Night

The room is almost black but for a few dimly lit candles
flickering a bed is the center of focus. There is an aura of quiet,
and solitude, and ancient wisdom. We speak in low, hushed whispers;
we speak of Heaven, angels, birds, and of the spirit being set free.

Many hours have passed by; weeks and months; I've held a hand,
talked, listened, and comforted, almost beyond my human endurance.
The night is quickly growing darker; the stillness encircles and
surrounds us like an enveloping shroud.

Tears shower my face; I clutch the hand tighter as we say a final
goodbye. The sadness I feel and the burden I bear overwhelms me
to my uttermost soul; I close my eyes and raise my head in prayer.

My mind imagines a bird, where as before it was imprisoned;
long trapped in a cage of pain, loneliness, and suffering; it has
now been set free. This ethereal bird with wings spread wide
and glistening in the sun; is now rising, dipping, gliding, full of
enthusiasm. It glances back at me for one last look of farewell; it
tips its wings as if giving a final wave; it soars with great
expectancy, over a glorious and radiant rainbow.

Patricia Swindell

Nobody Dares

I'm a branch, a leaf
I've got lots of bugs
I can grow from here to there
With lots of pairs
But when I grow
I miss the crows
I get lots of fresh air
But nobody dares to come near me
But you know why because I have mostly fleas

Markus Marqui Liner

A Parent's Love

As the years, days, hours, and minutes tick by,
your love seems to grow.
Even during the biggest fight over the smallest thing,
your love never ends.
When everything is going wrong and life's a struggle,
your love is at its best.
During frustration and hatred,
your love calms my soul.
While sitting in the dark alone,
your love is my best friend.
When my tears of sadness fall to the ground,
your love is there to break their fall.
And when there is a call for celebration,
your love is there to throw a party.
As I finally accomplish a long-awaited feat,
your love is there to give me praise.
When I must make a hard decision,
your love is like my guiding light.
No matter how hard life's pressures get,
your unending love will pull me through.

Nikki Wruck

Daddy's Girl

Dear Dad,
Just a note to say I'm okay;
the terrain here is beautiful/full of turquoise
and jade; I'm excavating a new life.
No jail cell for me/ no more bad trips.

Daddy, I'm sending along a pearl I've found.
a round, pink dot that I've swam hard to meet/my feet
are sore/I'm hungry, yet satisfied, for I've crossed
a border. From here I can glimpse the tall cactus
under a burning east sun

And a wandering mirage of a lost little girl
who still looks for you.

Pamela Partin

Untitled

It passes through my mind like the sun through a stained glass window.
Caressing my thoughts like the mother of a new born babe.
Whispering in my ear like the gentle blow of the wind.
Staring me in the face like a reflection in a shimmering pond.
Love's gentle embrace.

Kristen Geske

Untitled

There's no one left to depend on,
they have all flown away,
some have been ripped from the desperate
clutches of my heart,
leaving me clawing the dirt,
crawling around in disbelief, trying to find them,
not knowing where to turn,
shall I die like this? Lonely, desperate, blind,
only one can save me now,
that has never let me down,
he must help me embrace this fear of loneliness,
the only fear I have,
this vortex of hate and sadness is pulling me down,
and remembrance is everywhere,
remembrance of those who can no longer save me,
don't be a hero, let me die of my own damnation,
for upon this black cross I have suffered, and they try to form me,
but I am one, in myself, and the young must never fade,
for our secrets will forever be wax silence,
and I shall forever pay a penance for my sin.

Rachel Lee

The Beauty Of A Rose

Have you ever stopped to smell a rose?
I'm not just talking about the fragrance that fills your nose.
Once you stop to smell you can't help but notice the power
of this magnificently lovely, beautiful flower.

It is quite likely the rose bush is in a flower bed
surrounded by bushes of roses colored pink, yellow and red.
Might you notice, too, a few rows away
Birds, bees, and butterflies frolic and play.

One might wonder why a rose bush has limbs so prickly.
Perhaps, God, when He created our great world and all of nature
meant for the rose to go undisturbed. If you pick it the sticky
feeling in your fingers might make you wonder if your action is
immature.

In many instances you can be rewarded, in both sight and smell,
by looking around you notice, other lovely flowers also dwell.
Are there very many other ways to spend better time
than to admire the rose's sight, smell and appearance so fine?

George A. Sassano

Dedication Day

The carpet now is all in place
Though the painting's not complete.
The steeple can be seen from far,
And the pews are lined up neat.
We're here to dedicate our church
For the glory of the Lord,
And we'd like to thank the volunteers,
That helped with all the chores.
May this church grow stronger bound by love,
And may our family grow;
As we share the love of Jesus Christ
With everyone we know.
And when it's all said and done,
And we see Jesus face to face
May he tell us "I did bless your church,
For I dwelt there in that place."

Florence Sullivan

And I Have Words . . .

I walk in a world of strife
  I search for a world of beauty
hidden by the ugly.

I try in a world of despair
  with each step I come closer
for in my being lies a world or peace
  a world or beauty a world of hope.

I have the serenity of
  one moments contentment,
because I am loved and I love.

I have todays and tomorrows
to carry life's burden,
  travel the roads of humanity,
leaving justice in my shadow. And I have words . . .

I am rich with these things that are life
  but the sand of time
flow swiftly through my fingers.

The trail I must blaze
  is long and rough; to waste but a moment is,
to fall back and be poor.

  Anne Ayres

Gradual

Moon outside my bedroom like part of a dollar
a pyramid eye the color of sanded bone.
I am beneath this and the blanket,
and whatever I try to do.
Slow log moving with the current, so still —
wood eyes don't watch the bank flow by,
just down, more water, and air above
smooth as a water moccasin's footprint,
as sad and funny.
I don't look at the bureau, batter
absurd Andean images of maize from my head.
This is cotton, blue like a lake
floating reflected in the sky
like a reed mat with a leaf flag,
a green idea,
and a tiny stick man lying down.
He is thinking of stroking like mad
or calmly
toward a winking stone
below there.

  Phillip Dryden

You Can Run But You Can't Hide

You can run but you can't hide
  from the demons in your mind
The demons tearing you inside.
You feel the demons gnawing at your bones
You can feel the demons tearing at your soul
You wish they would go away and leave you alone.

To your demons consumed with rage
  your mind has become a cage,
The empty feeling is making you insane
You feel the demons eating at your brain!
How much longer must you live this way
Will you ever set your demons free and
Even if you face them
  will they ever let you be?

You're tired of running — besides, there is nowhere you can go.
Until you face your demons there is something you should know:
You can run but you can't hide
  from the demons in your mind
    The demons tearing you inside.

  Jesus F. Gomez

Woman Of Courage

I am a woman with courage, I am so strong
I can run as fast as the wind, I can walk miles and miles long
I am a woman with determination, any battles I will fight
I may be a small woman, but I explode like dynamite
I am a woman with class, just watch me when I walk
Watch the way I move, and listen when I talk
I am a confident woman, I'm always standing tall
When I hold my head up high, I don't ever feel small
I am a great woman, I can concur anything
I believe in myself, I have high self esteem
I have confidence in myself, no one can take that away
I am a magnificent woman, in each and every way

  Joaquina L. Dickerson

I Am The Course Of Golf (Of Course)!

I am the omnipotent, the bold, the
  beautiful, the challenging, the
  forever forlorn!
I awaken to the gray morning mist, the
  quiet, the solitude, the pale loneliness
  of what I was not meant to be!
But now my ways feel the soft footsteps
  of a carer, a giver to my green, a
  keeper of these gentle flowing by ways,
  a soul, this one of four that tend
  my forever needs!
My greatness is from their toil, sweat,
  wellness, love and admiration aimed
  at a perfection that I truly was
  meant to be. Hail to these!

  Edward J. Desautels

Jump-Start

You are my jump start
  every morning
You are my chow fun during
  the day
Your sparkler lights the way in
  the evening
And your prayers see me through
  the night

  I used to be a runt of a tree
  The biggest wart on a toad
  Knew little more than what was
    on the tip of my nose
  I stood for naught and cared less

Now I am almonds, cashews and pecans
Because you are chocolate, caramel and fudge
I am!
Because you are!

  John H. Fong

Stress

We all have it that damnable stress
It's the system of all distress
Strikes when we least expect it
Takes away our loving spirit
Throws us into a violent mess
This violence named stress

No medicine can cure
Only cure is to think pure

Loving-caring for others who
Yes, who have stress for me and you
Put your trust in Jesus name
And go out without stress in heaven's name.

  Leonard A. Miskiewicz

My Garden of Friends

I live in a garden, exotic and fair,
   for I have many flowers blooming there.
The flowers are friends I see each day,
   who brighten the path along my way.
God has planted them upon this earth,
   rooted in the World of God, without weeds or turf.
Nothing seems to choke them out or cause them to wither,
   but they're always standing tall in all their splendor.
When I feel oppressed and need words of cheer,
   I look into my garden and find one near.
My spirits are lifted just knowing they will pray,
   and ask God to help me along life's way.
Then, He reaches down and ministers to me,
   assuring me of His and giving victory.
May my garden of friends forever bloom,
   for they help drive away all fear and gloom.
And in their garden may they find many friends,
   who will be blooming until life's end.

   Juanita Carter

Our Love Divine

I want the pain to end.
I'm past the confusion already and I'm dying inside.
I searched far and wide to find you,
Only to sport a lifetime of memories
Now that you've passed away.
How am I to overcome the torment
Of not being able to kiss your lips once more?
Did I stay to watch over the endless nights
And have the beauty of your face
Look upon me from the stars above?
I pledged my life to you once.
I prayed for you my soul to keep.
You may take it with you wherever you've gone,
To remind you of the man that loves you.
I too will one day pass on life,
To be with you as I promised.
And our love . . . everlasting will remain.
Just as the stars shine bright,
So will you and I.
So will our love divine.

   Jerzy A. Vega

For Freedom

Martin Luther King was the man you know,
he helped our people to learn and grow,
for freedom

There was a big problem he could see, and Dr. King
changed society, for freedom

Violence was spread all over the land, aimed
at every African American man, for freedom

Dr. King said, "Hey let it lay,
violence is not the only way," for freedom

They walked across the promise lands,
all Americans locking hands, for freedom

With determination they took a stand,
and changed the laws throughout the land,
for freedom

In the marches you could hear them say,
"Freedom is the only way," for freedom

Dr. King has since passed away, but if you listen
hard you can hear him say, for freedom

"I still have that dream today," for freedom
For Freedom

   Amber Helphingstine

Love Through My Eyes

Love is as gentle as a dove, bright as
the sky above.
   When cupid takes aim, we hide for it is
him to blame.
   Love makes us all tremble inside, despite
our color race or pride.
   We have all been hit at least once, it
leaves us silly, feeling like a dunce.
   But it is for love that we lust from
the second we were born until dust.
   For without the need to love in our life
we would have no purpose, only strife.
   Love is the force that keeps us up at
night, that makes us laugh and tremble in fright.
   Love can make us cry, or even kill
leap for joy or just sit on a window sill.
   And gaze away in our own world,
instead of seeing straight we only see swirled.

   Frederick Gunning Jr.

Lost Memories

I look in and see that you have left,
And I know there is no one here except myself.
I see our memories on the wall,
As I walk down through the hall.

You left me a short letter
to try to make things a little better.
But the love we once had
is lost now, and it's sad.

I thought our love was real
but now my heart must heal.
Neither of us are bad guys,
But you told many lies.

Trust is a hard feeling to behold,
and when you get betrayed, your feelings are cold.
Trust is not love; it's respect for someone.
I had it for you, until what you went out and done.

You deserve the person of your dreams,
and I hope that someone comes down your life's streams.
Goodbye; I wish us the best
Now it is time for me to give love a rest.

   James Odom

Ian

"E" — I haven't written a poem in years
But today, the urge came through the tears
My brother I loved you, and love you this minute
Will love you tomorrow, mere words cannot say it.

As a young man, we all knew were destined to be "the boss"
Now our aching hearts are suffering your sudden, painful loss.
Handsome, tall and arrogant, you knew you were "the man"
But inside I saw a yearning for the world to understand . . .

That your laughter was a gift you hadn't always shared
An ambition to succeed from depths of turmoil that ensnared
Oh, but you were valiant, a hero, one who did not choose to settle
You grabbed the horse of life and rode through many a battle.

The sun is set, I see your frame, your winning silhouette
The war is won, the cause was just, the challenges are met.
Ian, I cannot but salute you, though my heart is weighed with clay
You stared at Death, made up your mind and did it all your way.

Larger than life, my baby brother, commanding our respect
Your final words, your final deeds projecting selflessness
I feel so proud, I am so proud — I say it clear and loud:
You play the cards dealt to your hand — in life and death a Man.

   Hyacinth Byron-Cox

Mother

Dear Mother, I lay this flower upon your chest
With never a regret that I knew you best.
My goodbye is not scornful
I shall miss you I know
Especially when rain falls and with winter's snow.

When I was a little one you took care of me
I have long since remembered and now I can see
That to be a mother
Takes time, effort and love
And yes, it comes natural with help from above.

Though the years went by swiftly and we grew apart
Never a day went by without you in my heart.
So now I am a mother
Just like you were to me
I want my child to grow proudly as you wanted me to be.

And now as you lie there in your final rest
I shall never forget you, for I knew you best.
And as days surely go by
I know I will see you again
When we walk together in the promise land.

Brenda G. Adams

Irish Dream

Sometimes at night I sit and dream
    of Ireland and an Irish queen
Lying out in fields of green
    in places no one else has seen
I see her skin as white as cream
    so vivid is this Irish dream

In a small cottage we would stay
    and share our love each golden day
While we're young we'll run and play
    then under Irish trees we'll lay
And when our love is aged and gray
    it's in these Irish arms you'll stay

So that's where my Irish dream must end
    with fantasies of fields to tend
It's all my love to you I send
    in hopes this broken heart will mend
To me these hopes and dreams you lend
    of which I'll neither break nor bend
To this I pledge my Ireland

Patrick P. Knapp

By The Way . . . The Way It Was

Idols always have feet of clay,
God is always miles away,
Truth will cause one to lie,
While reality to break down and cry.

A stubborn will is hard to bend,
A broken heart yet harder to mend,
I flee from the tears of unswallowed pride,
But the shame of the past keeps up with my stride.

The absence of God,
Today it is present,
And the presence of death,
Tomorrow will be Heaven.

The angels now cry, but oh! How they once sang!
The devils did flee, but soon they shall reign,
The flag that had flown is fallen away,
The king that had led is now in the grave.

Natasha H. Clausen

Let Me Be There

Let me be there for you —
Help you through the bad times —
Share in your joys and triumphs.
Don't keep everything closed up inside —
You can trust me you know —
I'd never hurt you.
Let me do things for you —
Lend a hand when you need it —
It's not a burden — really.
It makes me feel good to be there for you.
Let me be the kind of friend you deserve to have —
The kind you always are to me.

Marycarol Beth Soistman

Can't Find The Words

I sit here alone, thinking of you
And how I could get lost in your eyes of blue
The days are short the nights are long and sleepless
I lie here and wonder how you can cause me to be so restless
I don't know how to explain the way I feel
All I know is, this time it's real
When I'm with you, I get that wonderful feeling, like when you get your first kiss
The time has come for what I was so afraid of
It finally happened, I've fallen in love
But what hurts me through and through
Is that I can't find the words to say I love you.

Brian Frensemeier

Earth

There once was a planet called earth
composed of water of air and of dirt
and people who were not so alert

They got kind of careless and soon became airless
the water is stunk and could not be drunk

The oil and the gas were pumped out pretty fast
the woods they were chopped and turned into slop
to make products they soon threw away

The ores were extracted processed and smelted
and turned into things that later were melted

The good dirt was covered by concrete and asphalt
and buildings so high

I guess after all it was all their own fault

The earth disappeared with everyone on it
they probably could have saved it
but didn't — oh darn it

Robert A. Martin Sr.

Heavenly Companion

Unseen by men during the hours of day
Your tiny, glittering body comes out
At night, if nothing hovers in your way.
You appear above when few men are out.
And express your glow to light up the night.
Your light can make the darkest gloom seem warm
And protect children from all kinds of fright.
From far distances, you show us no harm.
Many songs have been written for your sake;
You have touched the hearts of many mortals.
I've seen your light reflected in the lake.
Sometimes I think you guard Heaven's portals.
    As long as you appear up in the sky,
    I will feel comforted until I die.

Jeff Campbell

From A Garrison Soldier Boy

Perhaps you have heard the song, when I leave the world behind.
I am going to try my luck, although it may not rhyme.

I am not going to leave the world, but I shall leave the old U.S.A.
And since I know that I shall go, here's what I would like to say.

I want to go and do my part, I want to be on time,
The only thing worries me, are the friends I leave behind.

There are others going too, but most of them have Mothers
To speak a tender word of love, and share all of their troubles.

I have no one like this you see, she left me when I was small,
And now you see how hard it is to go and leave them all.

Someone may think that I am a bonehead, and that my brains lay shallow,
But thanks, I am not one of the boys to show my country yellow.

I now have joined the Army, to serve as best I can.
I don't expect to be a hero, but just a fighting man.

My country called, I volunteered, I did not want to be a slacker,
To walk the streets, and wear silk hose, or smoke R.J.R. Tobacco.

When I have spent my time at training, and to the battle front I have gone,
Then again I will remember the ones that are still at home.

Now I could say a whole lot more, but I fear it will not do,
so I will make this my last line and bid you all adieu.

Bertram Ashby Patterson

December Blue

Tell January he'll have to wait. I'm all December now.
And I'll cling to him in February, until May comes back around.

I could forget the green from yesterday, if only all I saw was blue;
But even in October's rage, April's color still shows through.

Though Autumn's colors fight with fire, against Spring's
seductive stare,
It's the ice of my December that I pray will fill the air.

Please July just leave me, let this Winter stay awhile.
I'll call you when I want some green, but what I need is blue, for now.

Monica Mash

An Only Child

A lonely child feels isolated and confused
Doll and stuffed dog thrown aside, she no longer is amused

Wonders why mommy and daddy don't live together anymore
Packs bags every weekend but wonders what for

Sense of family togetherness was once strong,
Blames her mother now for what is wrong

No faith in church for her to claim,
Detachment from others because she feels not the same

Declares to be somewhat of a loner
Remains oblivious to those who might have known her

Friendships failed many times and the trust is lost
To give into emotion seems now to be a huge cost

People go out of their way to make her smile
But to her it is always a major trial

Cries at night when feelings are too great
Would rather hide what she thinks and feels, deny her mental state

Travelling to England and Australia were her dreams
All she did was run from problems, so it seems

Sometimes questions if maybe she has a heart of stone
Fears that in the end she will always be alone

To love and be cherished remains a mystery,
she hopes the future will not repeat her history

Dawn Dickey

The Forgotten Face

Evasive, but persuasive
He is
A man of many faces
And yet, I know the one that's really his

I can hear his pain
Scream out through all his laughter
I can feel his loneliness
Above all of the rapture

I can see the sadness
While others see the joy
And I can touch his softness
That others just ignore

I can shed his tears
And be what he cannot
And so, I am the face
The face that he forgot

Gina Camardello

Why Am I Weeping?

As I lay with eyes not seeing
  blinded by tears falling down my face.
Tell me, why am I weeping?
  The stars, the moon, up in the sky
They say it's not nice to tell a lie
  Somebody, tell me, why am I weeping?
They say, prayer, prayer, keep it out
Please, dear Lord, work it out
  Why am I weeping?
  You see I lie here as those dead,
With all these words running in my head
I know you turned the water red.
  Can you, dear Lord, so full of grace
Help me run this wicked race
  Why am I weeping?
It's the joy, the peace of mind, knowing
You'll be with me until the end of time
  Hey!
  Why am I weeping?

Ivory D. Carter

The Gift Of Life

The gift of life is so special that no price would be worth the value,
To be able to live is to move as you please, to be able to hear the
wonderful sounds of the world, to be able to fill such great feelings
as Love, Happiness, and fulfillment, to be able to live for even a
short while is the greatest privilege the Greatest Honor in the world!

Jamie Tripp

The Rose And Life

A single rose is like life.
You start out as a . . .
Seed,
Root,
Stem,
Bud,
Last is the most magnificent rose.
The seed means,
. . . beginning of a new life.
The roots means
. . . where you stand in life.
The stem is to hold you up
. . . never letting you fall.
The bud is a buddy
. . . who will help you along the way.
And the beautiful rose is you after
. . . after you have accomplished your goals.

Annette Romano

. . . And Eden Perished

See the fall of His creation . . .
Like a flower, withered bloom;
Rest upon a mound of sorrow,
Judgment passed, impending doom.
　Weary traveler through destruction
　Smoldered ruins, passes by:
　Sees old faces, joys remembered.
　Gazed upon through watered eyes.
　　Cross this plane that once was Heaven,
　　In your mind, shall ever be;
　　Mankind falls in blinded darkness
　　Down into forbidden seas.
　　Close your eyes with weakness.
　Silence.
　Now you see!
　"Death!" You cry.

　　Wake from a foreboding vision,
　　Quickly fading from your mind;
　　Painful dream or recollection
　　Of the garden left behind?

Justin Scott Van Kleeck

My Pearl

My Pearl, your light is too big for my eyes
expanding more than my vision can bear
You glow as the fiery lamp of dreams
where the sun stands dim beside you
My heart, my ears cannot hold the sounds from your mouth

Surrounding me like air and water and fire
Sounds which cut through my heart of hearts
piercing me open for the world to see

Beloved, the word is no use to me
it does no justice where you are concerned
Beauty stands embarrassed by your light
hiding itself in shadows and doubt

My love, the sound is not enough
or even the word which holds so much
How can my lips form the words which do not exist
Those sounds most luscious stand strained beside you

What my soul knows my lips cannot tell
the words fall shy and alone like faithless prayers
Powerless and futile and crying in despair
Like the ramblings of madmen baying at the Truth

D. Christopher Gomez

We Must Have Been Drinking Love Potion

Me and my new love
Were sitting underneath the stars above
We must have been drinking love potion
Cause our hearts were set in motion

The passion started to burn
And soon we both learned
What's been hidden all this time
Cause it was never in mind
To fall in love with each other
Or to spend time together
Or even become the best of friends
And stay that way from the beginning to the end
For true love we both fought
So we didn't gave it a second thought
We took love by the hand
And swore to love till the end
Now we don't have to worry about pretending
Or dreaming of a happy ending
Cause we can finally feel
True love for real

Jason B. Anderson

My Unseen Friend

I stood on the bank of the River Styx
Awaiting the arrival of the boatman in black.
Old, so tired, ever cold, alone — all fearfully intermix,
Dreading to go forward, longing to go back.

Around I turned observing the road just passed,
No accomplishments, no heroism, battles not won.
Only a faulting, stumbling, failing human in distress,
Journeying thru time, now nearly done.

Yet within this madding frustration of all mankind,
I sensed a Presence, a loving extended hand,
Lifting spirit and soul, deep wounds readily to bind.
It was the hand of my unseen Friend.

Then with hesitation turned I to the river's dark edge,
Expecting the black of night, but low a radiant light instead
Was One beckoning, with authoritative command . . . Come!
Yet with voice as soft as a mother's coo to a new born son.

Rushing to embrace into his arms extended,
I saw the scars on His feet and palms of His hands.
Like Him my countenance instantly transfigured,
And in that moment, I knew here was my unseen Friend.

Charles Edward Yost

Thank You

So often we complain, feeling we've been wronged
So often our children, feel they don't belong
Sometimes they drive us crazy being rude, rebellious and lazy
But as parents we still care although we've had our share
Enough is enough of all this crazy stuff
Not wanting to see our kids in handcuffs
Principals and teachers, counselors and preachers
God's hands created all so our children would not fall
We see how hard you strive encouraging them to try
To make them give their all to follow towards their call
The seeds you have planted so often take for granted
It only proves you care in all you do and share
It is of no surprise your input on young lives
I truly must confess you've made a great success
In preparing all our children for a brighter tomorrow
Where sometimes it may seem only pain and sorrow
So as I take this time to really speak my mind
From one to another thank you from a mother . . .
May God Bless You All!

Kathy Mansfield

Bedtime Thoughts

As we lay asleep in dreams,
Of places left behind,
Of people and friends, it never ends,
That is what we find.

As we lay asleep in thought,
Of materialistic things,
Of books and clothes, which everyone knows
That only money brings.

As we lay asleep in silence,
Our heads all full of thoughts,
Of people we love, and always dream of,
Because they cannot be caught.

As we lay asleep in sorrow,
For innocence that's lost,
For childhood days, and carefree ways
Of which life will pay the cost.

As we lay asleep in hope,
Of better days ahead,
Of happy things, that tomorrow brings,
As we lay asleep in bed.

Susanne Rieth

Suicidal Leaf

The soul of a suicidal withering up changing not only form,
but color; from orange to yellow to a dark ugly brown.

A brown with no feeling . . .
Or, possibly too much.

It's only a matter of time before the soul dries and starts
developing holes. Starting small, slowly growing larger until
the stem is so fragile it can no longer hold onto the branch.
Screaming for help the whole time, it endlessly falls.
While the world watches;
lit match in hand.

The stem crackles at the touch of the flame, not wanting to
burn. Resistance is futile because the world continues to strike
match after match after match until there is nothing left but
smoldering ashes.

(And) the world watches as another soul begins to wither and
change color.

Lisa Blanchard

Hide And Seek

Three branches hang low overhead,
their pale green leaves a sickly cloud
raining dark shadows over sparse
back yard tapestries.

Scarlet crab apples like hot air balloons
lie deflated. Their bleeding intestines
seep onto burnt spires and red clay dirt;
crushed by twelve year old ruffians
whose screams rise and fall like crashing
tidal waves against silent beaches.

A novel in hand, I surrender to
make-believe towns and wheat
fields, safe in my serenity; a game of
hide and seek from those playing
in another world.

Benjamin Norman

My Treasure

He listened when no one else would.
He cared as no one else could.
He touched my heart so many times.
I was always first, never stood in line.
His love carried down past my soul.
He understood the pain, that I never told.
He dried the tears others never saw fall.
He gave me hope, and made my problems small.
He loved me enough to let me be me,
While being myself, him I could see,
His love is so precious, only happens one time.
He is my treasure and one of a kind.

Patricia Edmondson

A Gentle Hand

Once when I was going astray, a gentle hand showed me a
better way . . .
And then when I was in my teens, a gentle hand helped hold my dreams . . .
And when I lay sick in bed, a gentle hand caressed my head . . .
And when I thought the end was near, a gentle hand held me so dear . . .
And when my thoughts ran wild with fear, a gentle hand helped
make things clear . . .
And now that I feel so secure and so loved, I know that gentle
hand still guides me from above.
And so when you feel down and out, and like the child the
world forgot . . .
Just think, the gentle hand is always there,
no matter when, how, or where.

Geraldine P. Daniel

The Dog With No Name

Spring had come dry for three straight years in West Texas
The wind blew
The land was a desert

Then a white Dog came to our farm
slick-haired, bob-tailed, bird-dog
Peaceful as a dove, gentle, like a lamb
The kids tried to think of a name

I ran him off, but he returned
bringing me a token, wagging his stump
A Green Twig

The kids and Dog frolicked like the drought was over
leaving their prints
They still couldn't think of a name

Then one morning the Dog ran under some wheels
We buried him on a hill

The rest of the day was too quiet
Sadly I looked at that token, those prints in the sand

That evening the clouds moved in
Heavy rain fell in sheets
and washed away the blood of the Dog with no name

Kent Rinewalt

What Would It Be Like?

What would it be like if there were no sin?
Where no one had to wonder what might have been.

What would it be like if there were no fears?
Where no one had to tremble or shed fearful tears.

What would it be like if no laws were broken?
Where the only things that broke were hearts where God had spoken.

What would it be like if no lives were shattered?
Where our love for Christ was the only thing that mattered.

What would it be like if there were no hate?
Where no one was left in Egypt and everyone had faith.

What would it be like if there were no anger?
Where children weren't abused and Jesus was never a stranger.

What would it be like if death was no more?
Where everyone faced each day by walking with the Lord.

What would it be like if these words came true?
Where evil didn't exist . . . Oh Father . . . we'd abide with You.

Courtney Ann Seay

When Does Love Occur? Or The Meeting And The Kiss

Love does not occur without a meeting first
It is not of just two a feeling that bursts
There must be sincerity and compassion, joining as one
Mercy and truth make a relationship fun
The faults of the lover or love must take at least second place
If there will be a unity in the love race
Truth is the shining knight that sits at the head of the table
Falsehoods are like a horse without a stable
Never able to find a dwelling place
They are always roaming forever
Searching, lurking and looking to sever
But every love must always be sealed with a kiss
It is the glue that does not miss
Righteousness and Peace one day did meet
Righteousness came down to find the bride, fair and tender
It is Peace for whom he was searching and to whom he did render
All his love, sincerity, compassion, truth and joy
Complete with angelic music to enjoy
A plan of love that succeeded in great measure
When God gave us his best Treasure

Charles J. Toth

Destiny Of A Selfish Person

The Destiny of a selfish person is like sinking into hot quicksand.
Stuck on yourself with no humiliation, not realizing
you have no foundation. Making progress, so you think. The more you
struggle the deeper you sink. Too proud to cry out for a helping hand,
will you continue to sink in that hot quicksand?

Fate comes along and offers a rope, but you're too blind to see
it's your only hope. You failed to see that the rope was divine,
Spent your whole life saying I alone can get mine.

God can deliver you from your quicksand. Won't you trust him right now?
Cry out by faith and open your hand. Experience God's love through
another person's hand. Invocation is the answer but you don't understand.

Living your life refusing to care, grabbing all you can, not willing to share.
Fighting the quicksand while grasping for air, you need a friend
now yet no one is there.

Your Cries for help really are sincere, and unfortunately now no one will hear.
These words of wisdom come straight from the heart, if you haven't been
giving, it is time to start. Show some humility when you're
under immersion, and you can avoid

The Destiny of A Selfish Person . . .

Ralph E. Fulton Sr.

Perpetual Abyss

I never thought there was darkness such as this,
Until I entered the perpetual abyss.
A realm of thought and blocked out sun,
Where time hasn't ended, for it's never begun.

Sinking deeper into perpetual abyss,
Tasting the succulent lipless kiss.
Thoughts bring pure madness and overwhelming vain,
That guide me along the path of the dying insane.

No doors or windows in this perpetual abyss.
No words to start quarrels, no fights with fists,
Odorless air, standing on unfeelable ground,
All conversations consumed in self, with only words for sound.

Self-implied death crosses the mind,
But there are no guns or knives to find.
Only a letter-carved plate lies way up above,
That makes me cry for the ones I loved.

Heavens is the only way I'll be saved,
I've come to perpetual abyss, and am lying in my grave.

Alex LeClair

Gem Of The Earth

If you found a rock all pitted and gray
Would you think it not special and throw it away,
Then search for a diamond, ruby or gold
Or rocks with the value man seeks to behold?

Listen while I tell you how wrong you can be
To judge value only by what you may see.
We know there is value in a crystal or pearl
Then wonder the worth of John, Mary or Earl.

Mankind's like a rock, a rare gem of the earth,
Which increases in value each day from its birth.
Then someday we're found all pitted and gray,
Just as the rock you once threw away.

But just as that rock we're special inside
For we've withstood the pressure and weathered the tide.
Rocks form very slowly under pressure through years.
Man reaches perfection with the laughter and tears.

Each part of creation has a purpose foretold
From a little gray rock to a mountain of gold.

Bev Marben

Ode To The Moose

In the far north region of America, and farther north still
roams the Moose
a creature who grows to over a ton . . . the size of a damn caboose!
But the Moose is not red . . . oh dear no; nor, for that matter puce
he by no means was created, on canvas, by Toulouse
He's a wonderful creature big and strong, with antlers which come in twos
not a phantasmagoric, mythical beast created alongside of Zeus
Although wise the Moose cares not for world affairs and news
he couldn't give a nocturnal squat about Sinai, Arabs, and Jews
His spiritual calm is gleaned it seems from savoring nature's views
you'll not find our fur bound friend among a churches pews
The moose is moral, he gambles not . . . he's never held a deuce
he'll never fold or hold a pair or accept an IOU
There was some trouble years ago from a black sheep cousin named Bruce . . .
seems he got liquored up, gored a man, and for that
he swung from a noose
And yet the Moose lives in regal obscurity, forever on the loose
while we pay homage each holiday season by dining instead upon goose

Mark Burger

Polarization

For those who've heard the trumpet's sound
for those who've prayed for sacred common ground

The drift to poles of black and white
seems to recall the darkest night

We once lit candles, bled in the park
how again can we stand
to stumble in the dark

I fear the work by Kings begun
eroded by time may came undone

A child of the south
a prophet in my youth
broke the chains of my ignorance
opened my eyes to man as man
regardless of religion or color of skin

Do not let the dream die
do not feat to be free

I am your brother
do not turn your face from me

F. S. Gamel

The Candle

A warm summer breeze gingerly blows through the window and
the candle flickers in the night

Bittersweet Nostalgia floods through me and I remember
I remember the way this candle once cast long shadows that
fell on your warm smile

The wonderful smell of your beautiful flowing hair as it
danced around your neck in the gentle wind

I can still hear your youthful laughter and child like
innocence that once filled you

I remember moments of intimacy as I stared an infinity into
your soulful eyes and how they made me at peace

How we believed nothing could come between us
foolishly, I concealed my heart as men often do
too much taken for granted, too many things left unsaid

Though in your heart I believe you knew the feelings
to be true, your undying love deserved the spoken words

If only there were but a way to turn back the hands of time
you would know princess that I love you now as I did then

In a moment — the candle flickers and is blown out by the wind

Michael Keith Drummer

You Are

You are the blooming rose in the middle of December,
The yellow moon that shines so bright in the
month September.
You are a wondrous shade of purple
across the evening sky,
A multi-colored rainbow that smiles
as clouds roll by.
You are a cherry pie smelling sweeter
than the sun,
A daffodil dancing on the hill when
morning has begun.
You are the single rosebush that does not
bear a thorn,
The smiling face I looked into the day
that I was born.
You are the wisp of summer breeze
that blows just like no other,
I love you dearly with all my heart,
you are my mother.

April D. Shifflett

An Ancient Vase

As I look upon this ancient vase,
Through its potter's eyes I start to gaze.
Its molding in his hands I feel,
And hear the whirring of his wheel.

I ask just why this shape and height,
And why this color, to be honored by what light?
As with a person, was't born for joy and beauty,
Or to humbly serve some daily duty?

Who first bought it, and placed it where,
To receive beloved or less anxious care?
Where lived it through the storms of time,
To stand before these awe-filled eyes of mine?

Where will it travel, and touch upon what shore?
Until at last, in fragments on some cruel floor,
Beyond man's and muses' power to restore,
Its long life's ended, its soul has fled for evermore.

Roger Mather

We Miss You Momma

We look up to the sky and count the stars and we say to ourselves,
  We Miss You Momma.

We know you are with your mother, father, two brothers, and
seven children, but we love you dearly, and
  We Miss You Momma.

All your children, Evelyn, Gertrude, Wallace, Randolph, Patricia,
James, Charles, Phyllis, Thomas, LaConyea, Celestine, your
Grands and Great-grands,
  We Miss You Momma, Grandmomma.

We hope and pray, since you had a very special way of making
us each feel like your only child, that we never forget your voice
and especially, your tender and warm smile.
  We Miss You Momma, We Love You Momma

Phyliss Hubbard

Let Me Tell You!

  Let me tell you how I feel, the twinkle in your eyes, the warm
touch of your skin, the way that you hesitate when your lips
meet mine. The way you call my name in the middle of the night,
when you suddenly wake up from a dream and realize that am
laying right next to you! Holding you tightly in my arms, wiping
the tears from your eyes, comforting you, reassuring you that I'll
always be there! Let me tell you how I feel! Let me tell you that
I love you!

James Starchild Smith

Stress

Sometimes you feel it
Sometimes you don't
But, if you just sit
And say you won't
Let yourself get tense
And you wonder from whence
You can learn to truly feel
A feeling quite so real
As achievement and joy
And not just feel anger and destroy
What others build through hard work
And cutting your work short
Because you feel stress
And you must realize that without stress
There is no success.

Robert Turley

Fruitless Labor

Energy levels seem to dissipate, as the day winds down to a halt.
Tired souls, exhausted efforts never ceasing, become the crux
of frustration
The almighty dollar, causing this scene, becomes a comedic thought
Meanwhile . . . we waste away . . . mentally, physically . . . waste away . . .

Different reasons, different intentions and different purposes
bring us all here
Smiling faces hide truths, as we strategically play the game
To the Superior's gratification
Meanwhile . . . we continue to waste away . . .

The day's at its end
Lights go out, systems disconnect and farewells are said
A final gasping sigh assures us it's time to rest
But tomorrow will begin again . . . as we begin again . . . to waste
ourselves away . . .

Millie Rodriguez

Reminiscence

Silently I shiver as my fingers dangle
in the cool waters of the pool
Made to reminisce of my lost love,
oh how may a heart be so cruel

For two lover's past,
it has been too many a year
With each passing of time,
I am allowed to shed but a single tear

To gaze upon this saddened face
in the reflection of the moonlight water
Is to stare into the mirror of the darkened eyes
of night's lonely and errant daughter

For this is the truth,
and in my soul I know it to be
My sweet child of the broken-hearted 'tis the irony
of the world that makes this so sorrowful —
for she is none other than me

P. Lynne Taylor

Gentle

Gentle is the peaceful breeze in the soft sweet summer light,
  Gentle is the moonlit sky with stars shining bright
    Gentle is the blue bird's song with a quiet lovely tweet,
      Gentle is the roses scent so genuinely sweet.

    Gentle is the rivers flow with beautiful divineness,
      Gentle is the mothers touch with loving care and kindness.
    Gentle is the heavens song slowly drifting from the sky,
Gentle is the angels wings as it swiftly brushes by.

Breanna Johnson

Search For Answers

People crying, people dying when they were just here a minute ago.
Lay in caskets, never flinching, lips like ice and skin like snow.
Caked in make-up like an actor in some expensive Broadway play.
Eyes closed, hands crossed, staring upward trying to see the light of day.

Endless meaningless radio songs and tired television shows
Watch me turn my nose up at them, I'd rather read a bit of prose.
Where are we going, what's our goal, are we just on this earth to live.
When we die where do we go, doesn't anyone have easy answers to give?

I'm just a confused and thirsty teen with nowhere else to go to.
And I'm searching for my reason to be here, so now I'm pleading with you.
So tell me what I long to know and whatever else you can,
Because I wonder where I'm going, my life needs some sort of plan.

And why do people care so little about themselves and others.
They do such bad things to their bodies, and consistently abuse each other.
They seem to understand themselves, yet do not care about consequences.
And then in the end when they leave us, all that's left are remembrances.

With new discoveries and a fast paced world, we still can't find the time
To spend a little with a friend or just sit back and listen to a rhyme.
The world goes on, and we need cures for new kinds of cancers,
And meanwhile, I'm just sitting here and trying to search for answers.

Stacia Dickson

The Truth

When truth is found, the only sound it makes is silence
Pomp and circumstance, like sweeping dust under a rug,
Hides that which we do not want others to really see.
And for a time, we can pretend that we do not recognize
That what is around us is not the truth.
But eventually, the truth will find us.
That deafening silence that rattles the very depths
of our souls
Waits quietly.
Yet in its hushed tone screams louder than the
eagle cries and deeper than the waves that crash
upon the sand.
I feel it.
I am not afraid, but in awe of its reality.
It does not embrace me or love me
But goes right through me.
I know it is real because for the first time I
don't try to explain it.
I can't - it just is.

Mary Helen Hensley

The Awakening

I planted a tree, and it grew
An inconsequent action of dissatisfaction,
I didn't mean to.
The light wasn't right and the climate inclement,
Yet wrestling with rocks with a spirit the heart lent,
The tendrils broke through,
And it grew.

I've no choice but to enter the fray
Awed by problems I face in the limitless space
Of a day.
With no pilot to guide, it's a rudderless ride.
While the world waits outside and I've no place to hide,
And no one to
Show me the way.

I now have a vision on which to rely
Despite darkness of night, I at last see the light,
And know why.
God's love is the ballast that allows me to cope
And live life abundant in promise and hope
'Til the day of redemption draws nigh.

Darthea Greene

Winters Unsung Beauty

Across the lawn two leaves play chase,
Others cling to trees — sleeping with grace.
There's a magical appearance to it all,
When winter comes — to overtake fall.
With no help from any mortal man,
A blanket of white — envelopes the land.

Out beyond the frosted window's pane,
It's amazing — what can form with rain.
After cold winds blow throughout the night,
Behold the changes — with dawns first light.
While diamonds adorn the windows seal,
Crystal stalactites — drip with appeal.

Everything seems so innocent and pure,
A sight to behold — that is for sure.
Sing of these wonders so others may know,
There's more to winter — than simply the snow.
Beauty is brought forth by a winter's day,
To be enjoyed — as it melts away.

William Brewster

The Desert Flower

As the sun sets on unhallowed episodes in
this Chapter of your life,
Remember those who appreciate your fragility
and your moments of strife.
Do not wilt, but fill the air with the
warmth of your fragrance, so sweet.
Let your tears be the cleansing nectar of joy,
not the salinity of defeat.

Reach upward through the darkness to the
celestials, let them watch and see
You breathe deeply the anticipation of tomorrow
on this very hopeful eve.
As you bathe your delicate petals with the
sparkling dew of this evening hour,
Let the universe witness the spectacle of the
unleashed beauty . . . Of a Desert Flower.

Bennie A. Fontan

The Touchstone

I am an old woman, my husband is gone.
My home is in Georgia, but I'm leaving at dawn.

For in my early days, when my marriage was young
My husband was a homebody, our love had just begun.

Tho I dreamed of visits abroad, Italy, Ireland . . . Venice, too.
My lover staid my place for me, a blessed home he construed.

I've led such a happy life, there's only been one limit
My life — nearly heaven . . . but there's been no travel in it.
The years have passed, the children grown
My lover passed, I leave at dawn.

Adventure and exploring, for now total freedom is mine
I'd trade it all for a moment, to hold my lover divine.

Isn't it funny, these life long dreams
Without my lover, don't mean a thing?

I think I'll call the airline, to cancel my flight this morn
So old and feeling tired now, so lonesome and forlorn

Looking out my window, hearing the birds singing
I search my soul for hours, my heart has needed mending.

Flower garden in the front, vegetables growing out back
Inside the homestead are, warmth, memories, bric-a-brac . . .

Alas! I'll stay home, gather friends family 'round
For here lies my touchstone, it's nowhere else to be found.

Jerri Peachee

When I Dream

When I dream, I can be anyone I choose to be.
Fairy tale princess, goddess of love, a fearless,
hungry tiger or a gentle, white dove.

When I dream, I can be any place I'd like to be.
Sitting atop a huge golden throne or out on my
patio of red cobblestone.

When I dream there are no angry words or accusations
or demands. There are no regrets, no
mistakes or punishing hands. No razor sharp hisses
or poison laced kisses.

When I dream I only see a field of roses stripped
of thorns and what I imagine to be the face of
God, without malice, absent of scorn.

In my dreams I can hide away my anguish and
fears and wipe away the painful tears . . .

. . . When I dream . . .
. . . But, when do I dream?

Tina Conklin

A Day In The Life Of . . .

So close to the top, I forgot my purpose
I rest, not climbing up or down
They whisper in my ear, and I hear them well
My mind ceases, and I am lost in confusion

Slowly I fall from the highest mountain
The drop comes fast as I near the bottom
From the top the world was clear
Now I look up, and must start once more

Once again I move to my journey
So near to my goal, so near to perfection
Wishing I was somehow near to end
Step after step, hold after hold

My heart will not allow me to believe as I should
My mind remembers the cause of my fall
A tear drops as I think of the pain I caused
Things in secret places, only we share

I feel alone, and my countenance fallen
My strength seems gone, 'cept His promise
"I will never leave, nor forsake you"
It rings in my ears and I know I am close . . .

Samuel Marzioli

As I Stand There

As I stand there watching in horror
watching him lie there motionless, lifeless; as if
my whole world came to a halt and I realize he is no more.
I will never be able to see him, to talk to him,
I can only remember him the way he was with me,
the way he lived, the way he was before his dying day.
I look around to all the old sad faces wondering why and how
this could all be. The tears fall from my face and all the pain
seems to stay with me. I try to think of what he would want me to do
but my thoughts are washed away by the pain that follows me.
We can only live on each day without him
and keep the memories of him locked in our hearts
never to be free but to be with us forever.

I wonder if he's watching down on us
watching us live on and if he is protecting us.
I want to close my eyes and scream and open them up
to see him laughing and smiling like a happy child
but I know that will never happen so I let the pain go;
and let him start a new life and
just imagine how happy he is knowing he can't suffer anymore
as I stand there realizing, he is no more.

Veronica Scuccimarri

A Child's Lament

See the needle shiny bright
We will party late tonight
No job, no friends, no home, no hope
This is the way we choose to cope

We know it's stupid we know it's wrong
What's it to you if we own a bong?
I'm tired of hearing I'm of society's dregs
Something's wrong! I can't feel my legs.
There go my arms and next my sight
Can't see the needle so shiny bright

Lying on a hospital bed
Thinking of tomorrow with tremendous dread.
I guess I'm lucky to be in a bed.
Lift your voices myths to debunk
as it's never safe to cope with junk.
Rely on your inner strength and friends so clean
Don't act innocent you know what I mean
Toke by toke my grave I dug
as I tried each party drug.

Pat Sanders

Why Christmas

The reason for the season is Jesus who died
And was born on this day and for your sin crucified
So your salvation could be decided right here
The decision for heaven or hell is yours to make
To be assured your soul is not Satan's to take
Ask Jesus Christ to rule and reign in your life this year
He provided you to heaven a way
Make your positive decision for Jesus today
To the Lord in heaven your life will be very dear
Freely your life over to Jesus you give
So satan cannot take your soul to hell
When we at last hear that final bell
There is no sin so great He will not forgive
I hope and pray in heaven to see you one day
For through Jesus Christ to heaven is the only way
And the remaining years you will live
Will be the best years I can guarantee
They sure have been since Jesus came to walk with me
Jesus to you the best of himself He will give

Dwight D. Baker

A Spirit From Within

When the sun don't shine so bright . . .
That's what makes the night so right . . .
And it's all because my heart is full of light . . .

Your grace and the way you strive,
Keep me happy inside.

I know that it was destiny when we first met . . .
For if it wasn't, we would forget . . .

Our lives have so much in common,
It could be that, we are soul-mates . . .
How else would we relate . . .

The stories and events that have happened in our lives,
brought this tribulation so that we may rise . . .
You're the first to know how I feel inside . . .

That's why when you come around I'm so alive . . .

Yes it hurts when you go . . .
For only God knows when you'll show . . .

During the times that you don't call or show
I'm thinking to myself has someone stolen you from me?

They say, if you love someone set them free . . .
If you come back then, you are meant for me.

Carolyn Merriweather

His Lady Sullivan

Within the dawn
her song takes flight
and tarries long the day upon these seas
heir she calls to me
in slight for I now lament
draw near the days yet so numbered
for marked them footsteps three

Of olden Lore her verse does sing
of Warrior's Valor and Maiden's fright
of love reborn and harden die
accursed beneath the Battle's Skies
of dragon's bane and Longsword's woe
the wraith of loss is yet to come
for He alone be claimed my foe
fell watchmen in the night

O Watchmen, Watchmen through the night
fall quickly in our troubled time
and know no victory cry this day
Oh, Fell watchmen, Watchmen
thief within my night

John Harris

Guide Me Home

The sun peaks over the hill
casting light upon a large body of water

A beat up wooden boat dances with the current
as an older man casts his line

A worm flies through the air
again and again
the same worm tries to grow wings

An old man's eyes open to complete darkness
not a word
for he knows mr. sandman has come too early

The moon covered by clouds
not a star in sight

The only light from the tiny insects with wings
"guide me home, oh, guide me home"
desperately asking insects that don't understand

They pass him by
one by one
again and again

Michael A. Marcavage

Mother . . .

Whenever I am feeling low, you make my spirits rise,
All the times that I was sad, you wiped the teardrops from my eyes.
When I need someone to talk to, you always lend your ear,
And if I need a hand to hold, I know that you are near.

Through all the times we shared together, the laughter and the pain,
And everyday you spent with me, in sunshine and in rain.
These times have made the memories, that I'll forever hold,
They made me the woman I am today, and my future they will mold.

In case I never said it, or forgot along the way,
Mother I'd like to thank you, for each and every day.
For all that you have done for me, and all you've seen me through,
I hope you know if you ever need me, I'll be there for you.

So even if we're far apart, or if we are close by,
Remember how I feel for you, and please remember why.
I love you more than you could know, and that will never end,
Because you are my Mother . . . and truly my Best Friend.

Leigh Ann Wood

Perspective

Still dawn in Naples Bay decays,
Night's brooding gray promises another hungry day,
Whispers brutally, you've gone away!
Its robbery twice your presence lost,
An emotional bill of cruel cost.
I'll pay it though with due regret,
And lay-away old memories like some postponed debt.

Gone? Well, you're not here. No wait. There you really are.
The irony of change is simply in my perception of far.
Not near or close or somewhere out there,
At this moment I understand you're everywhere.

Funny how earthbound we think we are,
Out of mortal vision, but in truth never very far.
Never mind, no need to convince the doubting few.
That light, the one just over the bay, will expand their view.

Elizabeth Addison

Without Jesus

Without him I could do nothing
Without him I'll surely fail
Without him I would be drifting
Like a ship that has no shame
Without him I would be dieing and
Without him I be in slave and
Without him life would be hopeless
But with Jesus thank God I'm save
Jesus oh Jesus I'm so glad I know you
Today I did you not turn you away Oh Jesus
My sweet Jesus without you how lost I would be
Jesus of Jesus you know him today
Please don't turn him away oh Jesus
My pressure Jesus without him oh how lost I would be
Oh Jesus my sweet Jesus without him oh how lost I would be
Amen

Virginia Carol Shanks Fields

Drain The Time

Drain the time, split my sides, out steps a new person to live my life.
Not the same, play a new game, everything's changed except my name.

Until one day I stay the same, until one day we remain unchanged.

Dawn has broken and so's the mold, the games you play are getting old.
You've got to change how you treat. Want true love? I'm the one to meet.

So many moons gone by with the way you've been. Never
knew the real you until now, got a new friend.

Until one day I live my life, until one day I point the knife.

Catch the sun casting shadows in my mind, born to a colorless
world long before my time

Waiting around chilling my spine, running my blood cold.
Disconnected from reality, breezes of air remembers seasons untold.

Until one day we lose our time, until one day all keep their mind.

Michael L. Tucker

Sigh Of The Lost

Bag lay on, weigh on
Don't stand it no more
O levee hold a minute to pour
We tried an muscle up ya frame
When ole muddy upped his game
Tired tracks did laugh . . . but then
A flow upon surge, yes . . . the worse began
And the trouble with mud it's got
No heart for the blood
and no mind whose thoughts are kind

F. Michael Fischer

Ode To A Child

There is a star in the cold night sky so radiant and bright that
not even the darkest of clouds can disguise.
There is a song in the air so soft and sweet that not even the
loudest crack of thunder can quiet.
There is a dance so delicate and flowing that not even a
butterfly floating on the warm spring breeze can duplicate . . .
and there is happiness and joy and laughter in heaven that only the
innocence of a child could have brought but there is emptiness and pain
chiseled in our hearts there is a river of tears raging in our eyes
There is a valley of darkness that we walk through each day
where hope seems hopeless and love is lost.
But there are the memories painted in our minds never to be
forgotten. And there is a space in our hearts that will always be
Taken by our sweet little boy whose now up in heaven
and yes we know dear Lord that he is in the greatest of hands
but we sure are going to miss him; his family and friends.
so please sweet Jesus on our difficult days
when there seems no direction in our walk through life's maze
please send down to us some sort of a sign
that our sweet little angel is doing just fine.

Sheila Guralski

The Season's End

The field hockey field lies quiet
as the goals are dragged away
The deep freeze of December is upon us
No more exciting games or long practices
It seems like only yesterday, we
heard our fans cheering us on, and the
loud thwack of the ball against the goal
Now all we hear is the crunchy sound of snow
Far below the surface the field slowly freezes
but next year the grass will grow green
ready for another season of long unbeaten streaks
Smiles and stickwork during pre season
will wake up the field from its frozen sleep
Then once again we will hear the cheering
of our fans and the loud thwack of the
ball on the boards
We will beat every team and go to state finals
where the field will once again
Save us from losing
State Champions will once again be ours

Arwen Somerville

Baby Joshua

Darling little sweetheart, I was there to see your birth,
What a holy moment when you made your presence known on earth!
You're truly a miracle from God, a tiny, healthy baby son,
As you live your life, keep Jesus number one!

You're Grandma's little angel with ten tiny fingers, ten tiny toes.
You have sparkling blue eyes, an adorable button nose,
You were only moments old when I held you the first time,
What a privilege and honor and joy sublime.

To old men and women, grandchildren are a crown!
You're a special blessings from my Lord that He has sent down.
Timothy's Grandmother Lois had a faith in God that was real.
As your grandma, I too have a faith that no one can steal.

Being a Grandmother is indeed a privilege and pleasure.
A God given responsibility that I will always treasure.
Jesus, help me teach Joshua all about you, the King of Kings
And the eternal reward that serving you will someday bring.

Little Joshua, you will always be in my heart and prayers.
May you always know that I love you and I care.
As much as I love you, Jesus loves you more,
In your life, God's richest blessings to you He'll outpour.

Susan E. Pelis

Searching

Give me words to speak that will reach inside of you,
to the deepest knowing place where all things lie true,
Give me gestures to make that would carry your every being,
stroking soothing, healing, enlightening you with meaning,
Give me strength to stand as you utter the untruth to be,
steadfast to the ripple of the waves emotions tides rushing at me,
Give me the gift of listening, my loved one speaking in pain, with
eyes shut and mind shifting, tune into what remains,
Give me compassion, to feel what is unfelt, arms lifting and
encompassing, surrounding your soul that melts,
Give me wisdom to know where the fires of growth lie, kindling
stroking, tending, where hungry embers long to fly,
Give me meaning, this kaleidoscope of life attacks, you're
surrounded by thorns of color and light, with definitions and
perceptions they lack,
Give me love, I know not what its truth be, mistakenly masked in
our world, my friend, myself show me . . .

Edith LeMay

Keep Me Warm

A cabin is imbedded in a tangle of pines, in the
ancient woods of Kentucky.
One candle is lit, but the fire in the fire place is
what gives the house life
A man, feared by the town, sits in a dearskin
cuddled up by his protector, his friend — the warm
trickle of prickly heat from his enormous grey rock fireplace.
He is old and sick, his hot cocoa in his hand.
The fire blesses the old man on this fatal night.
It kisses the man's feet.
The old man does not fight death, he lets it come
as the fire soothes his fear.
His eyes close slowly and he slumps over in his chair.
The fire rises and roars with fury, igniting chairs, desks, and the roof.
Smoke rises out of the house, creating a tunnel as it
lifts the old man's soul into the sky and — snaps
back to the cabin, and is blown out by a breeze from
heaven, thanking the fire for its help.

John R. Jones IV

No More

No more Negro, No more chains,
No more doing 300 hundreds years of sweat and pain.
No more guns, No more violence, This is a time for peace and silence.
No more signs, No more judgment, Everyone has his or her own substances
No more hate, No more pain, Love is a word that you learn to gain.
No more of this for I am trying, My children of the future are tired of crying.

Veronica Shorter

Retirement

Retirement is: When your working days are over,
    When it's time to say good bye,
    When leaving is never easy,
    When no matter how hard you try.

Retirement is: When many years you have worked,
    When you done your very best,
    When the time has finally come,
    When it's time to put up your feet and rest.

Retirement is: When a new era of life to begin,
    When no more money worries,
    When your pension and social security
    When they now kick in.

Retirement is: When your last working day is over,
    When it's time on past memories to dwell,
    When a part of your life is ending,
    When it's time to bid your co-workers farewell.

Margaret Powell

The Best Friend In The World

Short sandy blond hair with eyes that
are tender and sweet.
Came along a girl I thought I
would never meet.
A tender smile, and caring soul
would get me through the times of sorrow.
She was truly the friend of tomorrow.
The qualities of a friend.
She always had a smile above her chin.
Loyal, responsible, kind, and sweet.
She was always there with a little treat.
The best friend I thought I would never meet.
Turned up in front of my own two feet.

Stephanie Hughes

Unsure

For some it is long and endless
For others it is short with an abrupt end
For some it is curvey with sharp and narrow turns
For others it is straight with an easy path
Gray black and shades of brown
It can be hot and cold
Sometimes just fine
Some can be smooth
Others rocky
Yellow dashes here and there
Yet somehow it is a straight line
I look up from the window
Almost home.

Phyllis Snyder

Life Of A Bear

There once was a bear who lived in a den;
    He had a wife and children.

He had no food
    and didn't know what to do.

He went outside and looked around,
    all over the ground.

He walked and sniffed all around.

Then he smelled something in the air;
    there were fish everywhere.

He went back to the den;
    and brought back his wife and children.

They ate and ate
    until very late.
Now they are ready to hibernate.
This is the life of a bear.

Cynthia Burkle

Grim Reaper

His black cloak is all I can see . . .
Save for the bony hand holding
What will be

The worst and last pain
That I shall feel.

He enters my room and I kneel.

He beckons me, beckons me . . .
I obey, for there is no way out I see.

He takes my hand and out we go,
Into the darkness of death's black hole.

Oh, Grim Reaper, must I die?

I guess it is so, for he does not reply.

Kendra Schott

Rapturous Sentiments Of The Heart

As lofty as a kite that is how I feel,
    the happiness that you create is so intense, so unreal.
No words can possibly describe this feeling of utter bliss,
    the only feeling that comes close is that from your kiss.
In your absence the tenderness of your lips lingers on mine,
    your sweet kiss propels me from reality to cloud nine.
Along with your kiss, your eyes affect me to,
    I seem to rapturously emasculate into their deep green hue.
Each time your eyes meet mine my heart begins to melt,
    the emotions that you inspire within others have rarely felt.
With each smile that you surrender I feel so young, so free,
    the moments we share are as priceless as the pearls of the sea.
The companionship and friendship you offer I would never trade,
    the way that you make me laugh dispenses clouds of gray.
Our discussions cover any topic from Rush Limbagh to favorite foods,
    whether bowling or studying we have fun at whatever we choose to do.
The feelings that I possess for you are so profound yet so new,
    feelings of contentment that I do not want to lose.
I am always here for you and will never cause you pain,
    you are my paramount inspiration, my beloved soul mate.

Antonia D. Cleveland

When Will It Be Too Late

When will it be too late?
When sun has risen
When dawn has come
When moon is shining
While stars are bright

When birds stop chirping
When leaves stop falling
When animals stop fighting

When will it be too late?
When kids stop laughing
When tears fade away
When days seem shorter
While hours roll away

When people stop moving
When sounds are heard
When love turn hate

When will it be too late?
When Jesus comes
When he cracks the sky
While sinners cry and rapture takes place.

Timesha Blount

Untitled

Blood is thinner than words, when two people are
fighting in a world of hate — nobody wins
Water is thicker than love — when a weak soul is put
in the middle to choose — nobody thinks
A whisper can be louder than a scream, when words
cut through to shatter a dream — nobody cares
A past can be forgotten in two blinks of an eye
Actions are denied — when someone was scared for life
Looking for someone to blame, the cycle never ends
Only starts when someone sends a hateful word down used lines.
A church filled with people — only there for
them to see the surface, no hearing or understanding
a word spoken not caring, only there to socialize
but not with God — preaching the word, but not choosing to
follow the words that fill ears — it only makes you
sound good. Sitting on top of the fence getting the best of
both worlds not knowing which side to fall off on.
Creating something not cared for and calling it your own.
Not understanding selfishness the way others see it.
not to feel the meaning of unconditional love — worried about
how others see you. Take a look at yourself — you could
be wrong — even for the first time.

Jody Bukey-Jones

To My Mother

At eventide when ghostly shadows fall,
And little stars through twilight shadows peep,
Just as I hear the little crickets call,
Then I take time before I go to sleep
To think of her, the one whom I adore
Whose cheeks and hair show signs of toil and strife.
I realize that I love her more and more
And wish her to have a long and happy life
Actions or words cannot express my love,
For she means more than all the world to me;
She means more than the heavens high above
Or all the water that is in the sea.
For this of whom I speak is no other
Than my own dear, kind and loving "Mother."

Myrtle Eugenia Rider

Searching For You

On an island far away
I was a castaway
Then an image of you
I saw in the moon
That started my search for you
I prayed that someday soon
I would find my love so true
So, I've searched day and night
Then to my surprise, to find you by my side
Never to let you go.
Life together we will hit and I know we will not miss,
For now you are mine.

M. Brajkovich

Today . . . Make It Count

We take for granted what God has given,
The ones we love while they are liven.
"I love you!" And then, "Goodbye."
"I'll see you later!" Is their reply.

You never know when someone's near,
If the next day they'll be here.
Their company you treasure so very much.
Their smile, their face, a single touch.

Don't wait to say what's in your heart,
Weather you're near or far apart.
Kind words will brighten up their day,
And lots of love will come your way.

Remember someone dear to you,
Share goodness all day through.
Don't wait until this day is in the past,
Cause you never know whose day is the last.

Elizabeth Hope Snow

An Angel's Poem

Grieve not — for I am at peace
Worry not — for I am in a better place
Fear not — for I am with you
You only need think of me and my spirit will be by your side
To comfort and watch over you
Be not dismayed — for you will never be so lost that I
Cannot find you
Why — you ask?
I chose this life — my time with you was precious, but I have
To leave now
I have accomplished my mission here on earth
My body rests in peace
My spirit soars high and will always watch over you
I am your guardian angel

Barbara L. Elliott

Midnight Music

Midnight music surrounds the night
With every chirp and every sound
You gaze around
But nothing's in sight
As midnight music surrounds the night.
The water is still and the wind is quiet.
The moon is full and intended just right.
Midnight music, loud and clear,
Will fill the earth with certain cheer.
Each creature has a muse to make
While the moon and stars dance with the lake.
Midnight music, peaceful and soft,
But at dawn,
The music is gone.
As the sun rises high in the sky
They bid a farewell and a goodbye.
The moon and stars and others too,
To midnight music that once performed the night through.

Heidi M. Grolemund

Suspender Man

I cleaned up his welcome pile of magazines with numbers
And his chewed cigars, the ashes always missed the tray
He shakes and shakes, sometimes when he dances or eats or just sits
He takes every pill in the Monday space

He's a polka man
Wearing colored suspenders and gray dancing shoes,
Smiles with silver teeth
A hula man in Hawaii, a gambler in Vegas, a bargainer in Cancun
Faithful in church every single day

I will kiss him every time I say goodbye
He may not pucker
And I'll tell him "don't smoke those nasty cigars"
And ask "do you have a date?"
"I'll escort and sit between you and her."
I'll cook for you, Grandpa, and clean for you
no charge
And I'll love you
Suspender man
And I'll kiss you when I say goodbye

Jennifer Mohler Geary

Long Ago And Far Away

Long ago and far away
In a crowded stable He lay.
Born is He meek and mild
Born is Jesus the "Christ Child."

Long ago and far away
Mary and Joseph pray.
Husband and wife hand-in-hand
Kneeling on the "Holy Land."

Long ago and far away
Shepherds watch their flock by night and day.
Then they saw a peculiar star
Whose light could be seen from a far.

Long ago and far away
Wise Men come before the day.
Carrying gifts they traveled so far
Following a yonder star.

Long ago and far away
Jesus was born on Christmas Day.

Melissa Stover

A Rose From Heaven

I feel like a butterfly. Fluttering all around.
Looking for a flower. So I can settle down.

I see green, blue, yellow and gold. But I can't find a red rose.
Then I turned and saw your face. Blooming from the sun's rays.

Your hair is spun a yellowish gold. Your eyes are radiant, full of glow.
Your fervent caring loving smile. Will keep me warm. All the while.

I lightly sat, on a petal. How delicate it felt.
Strong enough to hold me. Yet sensitive to melt.

You seem very tender and delicate to touch
And yet you are strong. I admire that so much.

A gentle breeze rushes over. Caressing you and me.
The feel of your swaying is rocking me to sleep.

I close my eyes and dream. I'm floating in the air.
For heaven, I perceive. I know I'm going there.

Then I awake from my dream. And realized, I was asleep.
And became aware, you weren't real. And didn't know, what to feel.

But there is, something real. To make me feel better.
To have Jesus Christ. As my Lord and my savior.

I'm your butterfly. And you are the rose.
Your feet are my petals. I'm resting on your toes.
William P. Carrick

The Stars In Space

The stars twinkle, oh so gay
Only at night, not in the day
They shine and sparkle all through
The night, and leave the world lit so bright
When a star begins to fall,
It makes you wish your wish of all
When a star stays in its place
It makes all lovers stare into space
Space is world that is afar,
With trillions more than just one star,
It's a place for two to share,
When they're not in dark despair,
When they're in love with all their might,
The stars in space will shine that night
Lorraine Green

Soundrous Earth

Dressed in sound with it's flesh of amber,
from within the light of day comes my life remembered.

Oft not in a mist you'd see a lazy fallow,
under the power of the sun I can share my shadow.

Without lacking my rivers,
    or concealing my mountains;
With the complete skies,
    with my waves, beaches and fountains.

In front of a soundrous earth,
    the silence of your souls.
Louis A. Marrero Jr.

Where Is The Fear

Oh dear, oh dear,
Where is the fear I felt when I started here?

It's not here, not there, not anywhere,
Where could it be?
Could it be up a tree?

Or still in me?
But, I'm glad I lost the fear I had when I started here.
Sarah Ewing Sutterfield

Love Is God

God was made flesh, and dwells with us on earth
This we know and have felt
By love and loss of dear ones
And new generations of birth

For the peace and calm, that in our lives grow
And confident reassurance
Of love's presence
Our hearts with thanksgiving overflow

Though we may sometimes feel sadness and strife
And even inclined to doubt
We can love today, and be assured of tomorrow
In the cyclorama of love and life

In my heart there is a song
Love is God, made flesh that christmas morn
Our strength today and hope tomorrow
And love the whole year long,
Emily Boegli

The Traveler

First I went to Paris
    Parlez-vous français?
I certainly wasn't an heiress,
    But I didn't intend to stay.

Next I went to Mexico
    Se habla español
I felt just like a loco,
    But came back a lost soul.

Then I went to New Orleans
    to her the wonderful jazz;
Filled myself with okra and beans
    but only got the razz-ma-tazz!

So I'm "Back Home again in Indiana,"
    as Jim Nabors is wont to sing,
Why here, you will probably ask?
    It's the only place I can do my thing!
Rebecca Rosado

I'd Be . . .

I'd be an eagle, racing the whistling wind, flying fearlessly
into the face of the sun, then drifting gently with billowing
clouds . . . gazing at earth's wonders from afar.
But, be a woman? No, never again . . .
I'd be a wolf, lifting my head to the midnight moon, filling the
blackened stillness of the night with the lonely outpourings of my soul.
But, be a woman? No, never again . . .
I'd be a butterfly, a whisper in time floating on painted
gossamer wings over fragrant flower gardens, sipping sweet
nectar, bathing in dewdrops, resting on rose petals.
But, be a woman? No, never again . . .
I'd be a raven, a ball of feathered mischief with twinkling eyes
and a pirate's heart, bullying sea gulls and hoarding glittering
treasures in secret places. But, be a woman? No, never again . . .
I'd be a stallion, wild and free, thundering my hooves along the
floors of distant canyons, eluding those who would place my
spirit in shackles.
But, be a woman? No, never again . . .
Carole Judge

My Wish

I saw the angels in the sky
I wonder if God keeps them warm
I wonder how the angels fly so high like the birds
I wish the angels would sleep on the stars so I could see them
Angels put the sparkles in my eyes
I wish they may, I wish they might
Kileigh Alysabeth McKinley

Gypsy Cat

Genny was a drifter, a gypsy cat
Who roamed the neighborhood, aloof and proud.

Genny trusted no one,
At times she'd fearfully approach
Then turn to run in sudden flight.

Paul befriended Genny, enticed her
With soft-sweet words and tasty treats.

Slowly — cautiously she acquiesced.

He was her guardian, calming her fears, tending her young.
The only human she ever loved.

They're both gone now, Paul my son,
And Genny, the proud gypsy cat.

But if I listen close I hear a plaintive mew,
And in my reverie his blithe response,
"Hey, Gen, how 'bout a treat!"

I miss them so, but then somehow I know,
They've found each other once again.
Paul, my son, and Genny,
The proud gypsy cat.

Lily De Lauder

The Letter

She feels the wanting once more for pain,
the knife slices and the blood drips leaving a stain.
The craving was satisfied as her heart aches,
she's better now but her soul hates.
If only life was good or could be better,
then maybe she wouldn't have to write this letter.
She paused and dropped the knife,
and started to write why she just decided to end her life.
Everything was now meaningless and had no point,
then she dug deep into her pocket and lit up her last joint.
Her eyes burned,
and for comfort she yearned.
The blood stain began to grow,
and the blood still would flow.
For her letter no words came to mind,.Right now everything was
in a bind.
She took in her last hit and laid her self down,
in her sorrows and blood she would drown.

Amanda Johnson

The Future Of The World

I feel like a heroic coffee shop dweller,
Tiger-like in my quest to open up.
My lines instinctively fit into place
On my heartfelt strand of DNA,
And replicate my innermost feelings
On the universal pages of intellectual poetry.
The poet is free to give
And yearns to receive his own thoughts.

This blissful sickness will pervade
Across the monarchial states of others,
And this form of symbiosis
Will be the status quo of new writers
In all scoped races.
And all minds will blossom
In our eternal flower of interaction.
Sovereignty will no longer be the minority
And all extremes will be one.
This is no longer a dream, but a premonition
Of beautiful chaos which all hermits will be suspect to,
And this nation of dreamers will manifest a new age.

David Buckman

My Wife

Over the years that loving wife
  Became nothing but heartache and strife
Thinking back she was my support
  And now we stand together in court

She was my love, my life, my all
  But now I find my back to the wall
Finding it hard to be civil
  Cause she's positively evil

I spent my time, love, and money
  On this woman and it's not funny
She's after more and I'm afraid
  I will never live to see her paid

Regardless of the price I face
  She will be quite easy to replace
Will things get better in my life?
  Oh yes, the day she becomes your wife!

Anita Graves

Searching

What can I say, more than I love you?
Searching for the right words to make the tale more complete.
I've asked the silver stars, and the golden moon,
That shines above you, like the ebony night that goes by
On swift slippered feet, and still I search for the right words.
I've asked the little brook whose gaily laughter spills down the green valley,
Under arching trees reaching out to catch the rain.
And I've asked the sweet winds of spring that follows after a
lusty shout of march,
Letting April run free, embracing the coming of spring.
The bluebirds will not tell, for I cannot wake them,
Nor will the robins keeping house in yon tree,
Nor will the wise old owl, who grumpily ask that I not disturb him,
None giving their confidence to me, so I search on.
But alas, now I can hear it in the songs the birds are singing,
And if I would tell and had my way, it would be written,
With sweet bells ringing, about amber skies when dusk ends the day,
With magnolia trees in bloom telling the tale,
In lovely fragrant words for you to hear,
Written in the sky in deep emotions, this tale of love,
And now I shall have to search no more.

Etheline Goforth

Untitled

Listen to me children one and all
See that picture on that wall
Well that's really me that's the way I looked
Come sit down and listen I could write you a book
I giggled when I talked, I wiggled when I walked
And I turned the mens head when I walked by
I was so full of joy and laughter that some of the girls would envy me and cry
I walked through this world with James hand in hand from early
morning to night and into bed
There were times we were happy and times when many tears were shed
We had happiness and we had pain
But very little we did was done in vain
In our minds and hearts we knew our love would never end
We worked by day and we loved by night and made our way around every bend
I made my name in this world, worked hard and gave it all
I've had love, romance and children and my life has been a ball
As you can see I'm cripple now and I sit here in this chair
I must ask you to wash my face, feed me and comb my hair
When you visit and talk with me, you still find a beautiful woman
with a happy heart and a sensible, sensitive and loving mind
Once again see that picture on that wall, well that's still me,
heart, mind, beauty, and soul
If you total all the good things I've done in this life it couldn't
be bought with silver and gold

Gene Buck

Slipping Away

He's slipping away he's leaving me
he opens his eyes but what does he see
his world is now vary different from mine
he lives with the birds up on cloud nine . . .

There are so many things I needed to say
before my father slipped away
I didn't take my chance to tell him
what exactly I think of him
he was the strongest man I ever knew
to go through the torture that he went through
I don't understand how God will choose
how so many men like my father lose
I should have said what I needed to say
because now my Dad is so far away
I will not see his face tomorrow
and in my heart I feel that sorrow
I know someday we will be together
and his love, wisdom, and courage will
be in my heart forever.
I love you Daddy . . .

Ann Luzier

Lost

I see so many faces
  in all different places,
  joking, laughing and smiling.

Why can't they see
  the people like me,
  who's insides are truly crying?

My face may smile, laugh and shine,
  but if they looked deep down inside,
  they'd see that I'm not "just fine."

They'd see all the tears
  of the past few years,
  and the lonely nights that I've cried.

Oh, how I long for someone to find
  the fun-loving spirit
  that once was mine.

But, I know in my heart
  this will never ever be.

At least not until
  I can find that in myself,
  just for me!

Lori S. Wuthrich

Perfect Partners

The Hermit Crab moves into a beautiful,
  but very lonely, empty shell.
Suddenly, a heartbeat echoes once more
  through the complex spirals within,
and the shell's beauty becomes radiant
  as long-lost, cherished feelings waken.

No more will it be lonely,
  for now it has a companion.
The emptiness is felt no longer,
  for now they share each other.
Two of God's wonderful creations
  have become perfect partners.
And silently they teach us,
  in such elementary fashion,
  what love and respect really mean.
For you see, the Hermit Crab,
  by improving his own life,
has given life once again . . .
  . . . to another.

Capt. Hunter Donaldson

Like A Bird

One cold day you flew away,
To a sweeter place and a kinder face.
I know He'll take good care of you
For you see, I asked Him to.

  I miss you now
   More than words can say
  Ever since
   That sad, sad day.

I never knew just how much you meant to me
But now I see it clearly.
No more seeing that wonderful man
Or even shaking that feeble hand.

  'Cause like a bird
  You flew away,
  That very cold
  Sad, gray day.

Lauren Murray

Yellow

Yellow is the color of the future
Yellow is the color of the sun
Yellow is the color of peace and happiness
Yellow makes me run
Yellow is a color of a person's hair
Yellow is the color of a sick sick bear
Yellow is the color of a smile on a face
Yellow is a color of a big big race
Yellow makes me happy when I am blue
Yellow makes all my dreams come true

Beth Kingston

The Dancer

I saw her walk across the floor alone,
Her silent mourning flashes in her eyes.
The window to her soul within her shone.
I stop to see what hidden in her lies.

We dance; a couple gliding o'er the floor
While searching, seeking that which others lost.
A pair together look for something more,
He seeks to find, and she to show the cost.

Her hidden thoughts lie deep beneath her gaze.
Interpretation's hazardous at first.
For one can never tell where leads the maze,
Or whether finding out displays the worst.

The dancer, intricate but solace finds,
Forever dancing; lost to others' minds.

Matthew S. Beck

The Olympic Flame (June 10, 1996)

We were all awake by seven o'clock
Dressed and ready our chairs in the trunk.
Down to the Boulevard we took our seat
Flags in our hand and coffee at our feet.
On the day the Olympic Flame graced Euclid.

Most were dressed in red, white and blue
And by eight thirty the excitement grew.
The torch bearer ran proudly
As the crowd cheered her loudly
On the day the Olympic Flame graced Euclid,

And now it's over the Flame gone through
The excitement gone the crowds are too.
We have the memories locked inside
Some bought souvenirs to own with pride.
The day the Olympic Flame graced Euclid.

Delores C. Swider

Homeless Soul

Oh say can you see the city,
In the still of the dawn's early light?
Dirty and grimy and gritty,
Is the face concealed by the night!

Soon from an eastern direction,
The sun will light up the day,
Denied any kindness or affection,
We stir . . . we make our way.

A cardboard box for shelter,
So easy to dispose,
And it matters not the weather,
For each day a challenge holds!!

"A penny, a Nickel, a dime," I implore,
"Please do whatever you can!"
But my brothers and sisters
So often ignore
This invisible . . . this homeless man!!!

Willie J. Jordan

along a flowing river swiftly moving — nepal

above —

pale blue sky
touched by tilting jagged peaks
sailing through a white sea
billowing over
curving green terraces,
which wind down impossible hazy hills
licked by the golden tongue
of the late afternoon sun.

below —

the cries of naked nut-brown children
running to river's edge
pressing tiny hands to forehead calling out
"namaste" "hellobyebye . . ." float to my ears
as i float along a flowing river swiftly moving.

inside —

bubbling tranquility rises through my limbs,
through the limbs of the great straight tree
standing alone, dropping red petalled flowers
onto the waterworn stones inclined all downstream.

d. johnston

Untitled

The best thing that ever happened to me
Was this one man I'd found destiny.
He treated me perfect, said everything right.
He was the one, I knew at first sight.
He made my stomach turn, my temperature rise,
I fell in love with his beautiful eyes.
My love was so deep, so pure, so clear,
When I was with him I had nothing to fear.
My worries were gone, my life was complete;
But there was this girl who would always compete.
I was in love with the one that she'd take,
Never before had I felt such heartbreak.
He was my man, my heart, my soul.
My love was so great for the man that she stole.
I still want him back, but now it's too late.
I must let go of the love and also the hate.
Our first night together we had such a blast,
Love at first sight, I guess, just doesn't last.

Jacquelynn Faye Buchelt

Goodbye

Dedicated to Derek Dewey Thomas
First you think he'll always be there
his bright shinny eyes
his short blonde hair
Next you look and then he's gone
You don't understand how things could go so wrong
That's the way things end when losing a friend
You wish the pain would just go away
and that you'd see him another day
It seems that all you do is cry
then you realize it's time to say goodbye.

Jerilynn Ensign

Confusion

When the wind blows,
and the sun shines,
and there is confusion in your mind,
which would come from
the exotic world of our time.
The longer you live,
the harder times get.
The younger you are the confusion goes far.
The good times and bad times always come and go.
Friends you thought would always be there
could be gone tomorrow, you never know.

KimMe Scripter

The Blind Man Sees

I once saw a blind man cry,
and I thought to myself why?
He has seen everything through his
hands, with touch and not through his
eyes, but yet I think he knows the world
better than you and I.

So I walked up to this man and asked him
why do you cry? He said I cry for those of
you who see with your eyes, you don't use
your soul as God meant you to, your sight
blocks the beauty that's inside of you.

Just close your eyes he said to me and
maybe just maybe your soul can be your
guide. And forepass all the temptations
that comes through your eyes.

Ronald D. Flye

Do You Know Him?

Arms opened wide, head bowed
A crown of thorns around his brow
On that day he drew within him
The weight of the world, and all our sins

He cried out, "Father Forgive"
"They know not what they do"
His body was buried and a stone
tightly sealed the tomb.

Mary wept and Christians mourned the day
But, early Sunday morning
she discovered, the stone was rolled away
Crucified on Calvary
He died for humanity
Resurrected, He Lives Again!
Our Saviour and Friend.

Do you know him?
He knows you; each and everyone
Thank you Lord, for sending us
Your precious Son.

Barbara Veeney

Peace Be With You

Winter abounds with all its glory,
While the angel choirs sing above.
Friendship blooms like a fabled story,
When in the sky soars a white dove.

Peace filters through the sunlit air,
And a gentle breeze blows through the trees.
By the grace of God will he share,
The smooth tranquility of the calm seas.

Only those who have been through strife,
Can grasp the meaning of this tale.
We are all in search to a peaceful life,
And by this undying love, we will prevail.

Thank you from the bottom of my heart
For sharing your compassion and care.
Through your kindness survives a part,
Of the spirit of Christmas found so rare.

May the Glory Of God shine upon you,
in all its splendor, love and grace.
For you, my friend, are kind and true,
And may you find peace in his embrace.

Kelley D. Rubottom

Parallel With Two Hands

Wither the Old Blue Eyes
    that demeanor the tempest sky.
Burn the new fresh flower
    that grows from the sensual earth.
Tis faith that sees thou the other way.
Not that grass grows from the sky and
    clouds float on the land.

Earthened!
The heart has awakened.
The wrinkled hand has grown straight from
    its twisted augmented shape.

Earthened!
The eyes are open . . . all is gleaming
The twinkle is the wink sparked by desire.
Tis faith that sees thou the other way . . .
Not that flowers bloom in December and
    Snow falls in May.

Kristina Gish

What Is A Friend

    What is a friend?
A friend is a friend that knows how to lend.
Who cares when you do stupid dares.
Who likes to take long walks and enjoys having girl talks.
A friend is a friend you can trust until you die and to turn to dust.
A friend is a friend who writes a calls.
It does not matter if the friend is short or tall.
A friend is a friend you sit with at lunch when eating cookies
    and drinking punch.
A friend is staying up all night making pranks.
A friend is a friend who's with you when you cry.
When it's probably over a guy.
A friend is a friend you tell secrets to.
And it should not matter if you're new.
A friend is a friend who's with you all the time.
And thinks friend who likes to eat pickles.
And you laugh so hard it tickles.
A friend is a friend who's with you to the end.

Sarah Marie Skopick

The Rain And I

As I walked down my lonesome endless road,
the rain began to fall, gently.
I began to wonder if my life washed away just like the rain did.
Then, I was hit by the realization that you were gone forever.
The memories crashed down on me like the lightning bolt above,
I sat on the cold damp ground without thought.
The tears started to flow like blood,
but the rain washed them away,
like a friends hand.
The notion came to me that the rain and I were alike,
we are both looked upon as dark, gloomy, and depressed.
The rain can be furious, as well as can I,
the rain can calm and gentle, like myself at times.
After I figured this out,
I thanked the rain for helping me see,
in good times and bad the rain will always be there.
Anytime I'm down or hurt,
and even when I'm happy or angry,
I won't hesitate, when he's willing, to walk with my good friend,
the rain.

Jay Buchwald

Someday

Each day by faith — we walk the path,
That leads us home, where we can rest;
Let us never stray from God's true way,
That guides each step to eternal life.

Each day by faith — let us praise His name,
The Lord, the Savior, the God of love;
He gave His all, His life — He cried,
He suffered pain to save us all.

Each day by faith — let use live for Christ,
Old Satan is out to destroy the just;
Be strong! Have faith — never let evil near,
Keep praying, hold fast, God will save your soul.

Each day by faith — lift hands and heart,
Be thankful, praise God for life as it is;
We are pilgrims here on earth below,
Someday, we will walk the streets of gold.

Opal Blevins

Fallen Dream

Tess' body was curve and slender.
    Her perfect shape drew vast attention.
Her mellow breast was both, sweet and tender,
    And to tantalize further, was not my intention.
The time for teasing was past.
    The time was nigh for participation.
And I knew, at last,
    My beloved had a burning desire for sensation.
All of my sexual desire, and manhood pride
    Had been crammed into this one visionary night.
At least, I thought to myself, my intended bride
    will have experienced the pleasure of coming nights.
Morning came, and I expected to reign as king,
    But her eyes had no more beam.
Promptly, she gave back her engagement ring,
    And brought to an end, what I had considered a dream.
If the night had been any kind of test,
I had certainly failed with my beloved, Tess.

Joe N. LuVert

301

Forest Green

There's a place I know like a paradise that's mystic and so serene
With a moon so yellow and stars so bright where I travel in all of my dreams.
It's vague and listless as a summer breeze or a whirlwind in the frost
And lies somewhere in those woodland trees beneath that southern cross.

I still can see that yellow moon with a million stars at night
And pale blue skies with giant clouds that tower out of sight
And flowers that bloom in pastures green while meadow larks sing of spring
And cottonwood trees in the bottom land with the blue jay on the wing.

Who said that I can't go home 'cause I'd be there all alone?
I'll do whatever I please — I just smile, close my eyes and leave.

I've searched for those childhood friends and the vines at the swimmin' hole
And I still go home to that dreamers land where I lived so long ago.
Now I guess I'll rest with my cane in lap and close my eyes and dream
And dream of a place like a paradise that's mystic and called —
Forest Green.

William H. Leach

My Doggie

There is a pretty place up in the sky,
Where special dogs go when they die.
A place to stay and wait all day
Until their master comes their way.

For some the wait is short and sweet,
For other time drags on leaded feet.
Row upon row by heavens gate
The noble furried creatures wait.

Far a certain foot step that they know,
For a certain voice to say "Lets go."
And so you left us on this day
For a place of no pain, to run, to play.

But keep your eyes upon the gate,
I'll try not to be too late,
I'll softly call your name and then,
Together, life will be good again

Frank. G. Nuanes

Pages Of Time

Down through the pages of time
Jesus walked on this earth that I now call mine
He loaned it to us for just a short time,
Down through then pages of time.

He gave us the hope of saving our souls,
So we could live forever and never grow old
And He warned us, that it was just a short time
Down through the pages of time.

Martha Sue Crabtree Parker

Mindless Talk

The problems of the world and the fate of all mankind
is not the focus of my consideration.
I prefer to let go of my mind
with no specific destination.
I'm often referred to as quiet and quite reserved,
I like to think of myself as an observer.
Tell me my gaze can be disturbing
and I'll analyze you further.
I don't mean to come off cold or prudent
in my solitary contemplation.
I'm unaware if I'm being rude,
not participating in conversation.
I've even been accused of being vain or shy
but I'm merely in deep thought.
You see, I prefer to use my time on thinking
and not on mindless talk . . .

Gene M. Walz

Love

Love is a bridal kiss and a baby's smile.
Love is holding an invalid's hand for awhile.
Love is undying parental care.
Love is the time with others we share.
Love is our care for our planet earth.
Love is our respect for all at birth.
Love is the irresistible attraction of youth.
Love is growing old together in truth.
Love is a rose, a letter, a song.
Love is knowing that you belong.
Love is moonlight, a sunset, rain, and snow.
Love is a good book and a fire's glow.
Love is the happiness of a child who can read.
Love is believing you've done a good deed.
Love is pride in the place we live.
Love is joy in what we can give.
Love is our thanks to God in prayer.
Love is concern for people everywhere.

Mary Cortes

Welcome

Welcome to all the newborn children of the World. You are welcome by family and friends. The family and friends who have imagined your face, know already the light you will shed upon this world. Just the light you have shined for the past nine months has brought smiles to faces of people who will never know your name.

Your Mother and Father have imagined your smile, the color of your eyes and hair, the shape of each hand and foot. For you have been loved since before time began and will be loved till time no longer matters.

The times ahead will not be easy, but for every stumble you make, know that there will always be loving arms to break your fall. There will be heartbreaks and joys and always the hands of your Mother and Father to get you through.

May God keep you safe, in the arms of your Mother and Father, until you are ready to take your place among the stars. Yet, let it be known, that the light you shine will always be brighter than the stars in the sky.

Maria D. Flores

January 28, 1986

A Tribute to the Challenger Crew
Delay after delay, but today was the day
As we watched them happily single filing along, boarding the bus,
We all knew they were proud to be representing all of us.
As the Shuttle takes off into the sky,
We all waited and watched with an eager eye
All excited about sending astronauts and a teacher into space
Thinking about all the wonderful things that
science has made possible to take place.
Within fast a minute, the horror on each face.
The Shuttle! The Challenger! Has blown up in space!!!!
The confusion, the disbelief
All of a sudden our happiness had turned to grief.
How could this be, 7 healthy people in their prime
So full of life, so anxious to learn, to teach and give all their time.
Not to mention the unselfishness of all their families.
In one fleeting moment this was all gone.
Now it's up to NASA to see what went wrong.
Now our prayers go out to families bearing such a great pain.
However we must make sure they continue the program,
So the loss of these lives will not be in vain.
So bless them dear Lord, these heroic 7
As they make their journey home to you up in heaven.

Donna Lee Simone

All These Places Were Bruised On Calvary

High on Galgotha's hill so very far away
Stood three old rugged crosses that day
Two laden with thieves, one with our Lord
A cruel world no longer could afford

On the cross his accusers crucified him
Spiritual cup of tea filled to the brim
Our Lord hangs there totally in shame
Not one would think of taking the blame

On that old cross of shame without blame
Jesus Christ died in Jehovah's name
Accusers bruised his head, hands, side, and feet
Dying his father in heaven to meet

But then our Lord on that faithful morn
No feelings of sorrow nor forlorn
Ascending to heaven his father to meet
Glorious resurrection complete

Dan Watson

Believe

When things go wrong as they sometimes do
And you feel so all alone
Cast your eyes to the heavens above
To God upon his throne
Ask him for his guidance and
The strength to see you through
Ask and you will find he's
Always there for you
Lift up your head and call his name
Believe and you will find
An inner strength within yourself
And peace within your mind

Bea Meeks

Untitled

As I see the big white fluffy clouds
in the sky that seems so soft and gentle,
I think of holding you.
As I look out over the water I feel
so comforted and relaxed,
I feel you.
As I hear the winds blow softly,
like a gentle voice whispering in my ear,
I hear you.
As I see the beautiful white
snow that coats the ground,
I think of you.
As I combine all of these
elements of nature's beauty,
I see you.

Sam Spano

Blanket

Loved ones dying, people not trying, babies crying,
Death is near, right around the corner from here
Rapist, muggers, drug smugglers, Ladies of the night,
it's not right
The world is weak, some people can't sleep, some people
liven on the streets, no clothing, no meat to eat
Affliction across the land, brothers and sisters gettin'
canned, jealousy and envy, as far as the eye can see
God help us children, in Jesus name, help us to stop this
unselfish pain, hunger, greed, murder, jealousy, poverty
God send out your army, your army of angels, to lay down
your blanket, unknown to them, the blanket of love and trust

Amen

Terry Nickson

African Safari, Fun

You might be, morning, noon, and night,
over seas and out of sight,
But just remember you are not alone.
For all we need is someone of our own,
And for me, you are just that one,
Have a whole lot of fun, in the sun,
So, just remember son,
Mom loves you very much and misses you such.

Lynne Peters

The Other Species

Oh hear that call, a call
That soulful, plaintive call.
Listen close and long and well —
Oh hear that message and do tell.

Tell of the longing in that voice of calling
The cry oh ever so haunting —
Tell it clear, don't tell it wrong
Even turn it into a song.

Hear the music in the call,
Don't forget you've heard it all —
Whether from bird or spirit its tune,
The magnificent symphony of a Loon!

Glennis J. Lloyd

He Was Whispered To Me

Dear Lord, you alone know what lies ahead for me
and you alone know all that I have been through.
But if I can have another child and raise him well, please send him to me.
And if you feel I can't, for all that I carry, I will understand,
and always be so grateful you sent me Carl.
Let you will be done and I will understand and accept.

And in an instant I knew . . .
I heard a whisper so silently clear,
Softer and lighter than I can imagine any fabric feel.
Powerfully gentle not to be explained . . .
   The Whisper Came
With a breeze on my left ear soft and warm;
My mind heard . . . He Is Yours Now . . .
It was whispered to me by an angel.

Let all know how Nicholas came to be.
Whispered to me by an angel.
He was brought to me an angel's wings.
I will hear that silent whisper forever.

Carla D'Andre

Risk Takers

To the world we appear naive,
even foolish
but we must be true to our hearts.
The price for trust and faith
is often pain,
but when that faith is proved,
the rewards are immeasurable.
Fear
makes many hesitant to open their souls.
I believe
fear makes you stronger and treasures found that
much more precious.
Past disappointments warn my mind
to be cautious.
God, don't let my heart listen!
Perhaps,
risking it all is my way of breathing.

. . . Take that risk with me and breathe in Love . . .

Nora Sutton

The War

A stare-down between good and evil,
two world far apart.
Separated by the thinnest of lines.
hatred gone too long
not a word until this day.
One will come out a champion
one will never come out again.
This eternal battle must now end,
we all know the battle's outcome
everyone knows who wins
even the players are sure.
In this final battle, casualties will occur.
Secret weapons,
double agents,
allies lost, and gained,
all secrets revealed.
The armies are distinguished,
those who may win you over
without a word,
without a fight!

Tiffany Block

Wishes

'Twas a Christmas wish, I wish, I'd had 40 years ago. Peace on
earth and goodwill towards all, is a hope that we all know.

What I wished, hoped and prayed was for all the toys that were
ever made, a selfish brat I must have been, for kids were even
starving then.

Now, I wish for food and things for all, who need them to survive,
and give them God's gift of will, just to keep them alive . . .

So while you wish for what you want, please let your heart be free,
to wish a little wish for those who need a bite to eat, or for
clothes to keep their bodies warm and shelter from the cold.
Please oh Lord, help me do my part, that's all I can hope. Please
give to us the peace on earth that will always last, and give to
every man, woman and child my wishes of the past.

Louis M. McCartney

Celestial Guidance

Standing a foot of this grandiose wonder,
I cannot imagine any place more spiritual or mysterious.
I begin to feel a sense awe as I begin my climb.
The steps, weathered by thousands of years of subtropical rains,
incredibly has kept its shape for its intended purpose.
I cautious reel upward, up these historic filled steps.
Where the aztecs and ancient civilizations before them
sacrificed and fed their Gods.
I finally reach the top, feeling no real repercussion
from my two hour journey, but a sense a home and a oneness
to my God.

Ted López

Cara's Sonnet

To those I see, I'll say "I'm over him!"
But still this pain inside my heart burns strong
Until the fire that burns the bridges dims.
I'll shield my heart and know that trust was wrong,
My best friend warned me to protect my heart.
I laughed and thought our love would never die,
And now I feel my heart has been torn apart.
By chance, not broken promises or lies.
Then through the clouds there shines a single ray
To break upon the mist and form a light
A voice of many wisdom's speaks to say
"In time your heart will heal, you'll be all right!
Although hearts may break and love may perish
Lessons learned are lessons to be cherished.

Cara Lyon

The Wall

How many comrades, dear to heart reside in name and spirit
On its death black granite panels
Their souls stare out at you and meet yours across the narrow walkway
Which separates today from the past
And in confused unison, we ask each other the question, "why?"

So many years removed from the northern jungles' madness
A wife and family, home and job
But for the grace of God and pure and simple fate
I could be staring out to you from behind that death black slate
Is it guilt I feel for being on this side
While you, my brother, forever remain within?

We didn't understand it then; to great degree we understand it less today
So young were we, in innocence led by men whose power and pride
Would not allow the compromise which would have lessened masons' tasks
In building this long testament.

My children ask me why I weep when confronted by these names I see
Son, I look into the past and pray for you, the future holds
No memories like these I keep
I am dearly sorry, friends that we must meet again like this
In silent sadness, comrades, we are at long last together, Home

George J. Cargo

Lonely Days

Love is a blossom, blown in on the wind,
Given from the heart of a true best friend.
It needs to be kindled and reignited,
On lonely days when it seems one sided.

The wind makes you scared, and afraid to dream,
Because then you have to think of what life truly means.
That gentle breeze can confuse your heart,
It races in every direction, without a start.

One day you wake up and wonder "what is this — Love,"
And question if it came from heaven above.
The valleys widen and the mountains grow,
And emotions are lost that you can't show.

The blossom fades with tinges of brown,
In an endless spiral, it seems to fall down.
'Til the breeze that blew the love your way,
Echoes soft memories of a heart meant to stay.

Teresa Chisholm

Those Boys

In ripples caught frozen
    in the timeless pool of youth, those boys play.
    It never ends.
        On and on forever they play down paths that will never part.

        Solemn vows of youth far stronger than steel,
and more honest than the blood, over which they were made.

Brothers of soul . . .
    . . . and of heart.

        A simple promise of friendship that has outlasted who we were . . .
            . . . or what we've become.

I've watched them play, those boys,
    and I've heard them laugh, and I have heard them cry.
But always boys, they play unchanged, by the mere presence of time.

Bankers placing money in vaults could never match the value
    of what is locked in the hearts

        of those boys,

    And still they play.
        In ripples caught frozen,
in some timeless pool
    of youth . . .

B. Kline

304

The Fortress

They hold me still in the dungeon of my hell
Denying the very things I've called out for, beliefs and values which are sustenance to my soul
They are denying me the water so craved by a man in the desert heat
They are the sun beating down on him, me, incessantly
Harsh, cruel, immutable in the barrier of their beliefs
Like the sun who would claim even the bones of the dead man to add to its plentiful sands
They repress my will in order to add my self to their bastion of cultural identity
The structure of their fortress must be followed with no stray mark or subtle shift to the age old pattern
So they deny me a free will like the man is denied his life giving water
There is only one thing that the man, me, has left
The small bright light within that drives him, me, on
It tells of the utopia that is seen across the desert sands
The man staggers to it, unerringly knowing he'll regain his life there
Then he reaches it — it is only more of the desert sands, more of an insurmountable fortress
Everything is false a cruel trick played by his burning antagonist
The flickering candle that had driven him is extinguished by the harsh wind of reality
He lays down, closes his eyes, and waits for his enemy to do with him as he will
The sun laughs and adds him to the unchanging desert pattern
They wait to laugh in victory like the sun
And me? I am nearing the mirage

Aswini Anburajan

Remember When . . .

Remember airplane rides, feet never leaving the ground and "shhh, listen" when there wasn't a sound.
Remember grandmas and grandpas with us on their knees and black licorice cough drops if you say please.
A trip to the ocean, digging for clams; hiking and playing; discovering dams.
Sipping of water from that warm burlap bag, while soft breezes above stirred trees like a flowing flag.
Trips out of town, calling home "accept the charge"
and that small voice on the other end saying "no." Oops, she wasn't very large.
Remember the camping; poison ivy and lake itch and the spooked wide-eyes the night is stormed at Lake Fish.
Remember the teamwork it took all those years, when smooshing spiders were the biggest fears!
Remember the golden carpets on the ground which I gladly picked if priced by the pound.
Dying eggs and leftover colors were to shade our favorite rink.
You'd create it and ask what we think.
Wool skating sox at Christmas full of popcorn balls, fruit and nuts were surely enjoyed, no ifs and or buts.
Sleds in the snow—climbing those hills seemed so far. Remember the sled made from the hood of a car?
Early morning at Little Bear wetting a line. With fish swimming below our feet, this must be a sign.
I was in my glory, cuz now I would have yet another fish story.
Remember the one about milk and cookies and a sandwich . . . Boy do I remember when!
Late nights out, coming home feeling like an ass. You handled it well, with a touch of class.
Remember the days that we married. Grown up lives of those you fed, changed and carried.
With happiness now, I remember the past, being touched by our parents with a love that will last.
I truly remember when.

Cheryl Lynn Brehm

Love Isn't Love Until You Give It Away

I was sitting alone as I gazed at the lake and wondered the meaning of life,
When I saw a sunbeam just dancing away and joyously giving its light.
And it seemed to say you will find today the secret of life is not power or gold
But it's truth and love all the way. But love isn't love until you give it away.
Love isn't love, love isn't love, until you give it away.

You must find in each one the good that is his, and judge not his faults.
You may not like her but she's part of your life and longing for truth and for love,
A friendly hug or a kindly word to brighten the day and give freedom to love.
But you can not love all the way unless you love truth and light that guide the way.
Love isn't love, love isn't love, until you give it away.

There's a world out there just crying with pain and people with nothing to eat.
There is work to be done and children who need a doctor to ease all their pain.
All war is cruel; you must works for peace and find a way out with real truth and with love.
When you reach heav'n's gate he will ask what you did in life, then you can answer him well.
I learned to love. Love isn't love until you give it away.

Marian Lewis Appleyard

The Poor And Homeless

One so soft,
one so sweet,
one someday,
I'd like to meet.
As I watch,
as I stare,
I wonder if,
some do not care.
They have nothing,
they need more,
as they sleep,
upon the shore.
Under blankets,
made of rags,
they store their things,
in dirty, old bags.
Please help them,
before it's too late,
unless you are,
just full of hate.

Sara Vorndran

Untitled

The yellow flower catches a peak
at the morning sun about to speak
it opens in glee at its very touch
others join in, wanting too much
and as the little gem disappears
the on rushing crowd covers its tears
for the flower weeps as it's swept away
and hopes to be first yet another day.

Jason Zaworski

Untitled

It's night time in the barracks
And I lie restless on my bunk.
Sleep evades my clutches
Till to despair I've sunk.

Your image hovers in the air
Closer, ever closer.
Soon I swear I can feel
Wisps of silken, amber hair.
Alas, the fantasy dissolves,
Returned to its ethereal lair.

The blaring notes and glaring light
Disrupt the anguish of my thoughts.
Another day; now all is right,
But alas, soon another night.

Irving J. Labes

Winter Musician

Snowflakes like fragile crystal
  Break against my cheek
  Shattering into notes of cold
Attuned to Winter's whim.

Swirling,
  Swirling,
    in
Silent crescendos
Note by note their
Symphony quells
The blatant tones
Strummed loud and strong
By tons of ghetto litter
Left by the strolling throng.

Betty J. Hicks Lee

Questions

I wonder if the world minds
being frozen on both ends
and sizzled in the middle?
Do trees grieve
when they lose their leaves?
Does the ground frown
when it's covered with Autumn's brown?
Does the sky really mind
being painted blue
instead or red, green or
some other hue?
Does water mind flowing?
Does wind mind blowing?
Would mind going?
Can't you see the love lamp's glowing?
Can it be extinguished
by the night

Luellahj Darshanon

Big Al

I close my eyes and he is near
I hear his whispers in my ear
I feel the softness of his touch
I know he loves me very much

He wakes me up sometimes at night
And lets me know that it's all right
He wipes my tears when I am sad
And makes me smile for what we had

I miss him so he knows it too
He says don't cry I'm still with you
I touch his hand he leads the way
And helps me face another day

But when I awake and he's not here
I still expect him to appear
And say "it wasn't me who died"
"And if they say I did they lied"

Anita Allenby

Dreams

Dreams are like vacations,
They let you get away.
Others are like nightmares.
Making you work, night and day.

Dreams can be fantasy,
Or they can be real.
No one ever knows for sure,
If you'll get a movie deal.

Dreaming is like a recipe,
In which you get to write.
But be careful when you dream.
Or you'll have to turn on the lights.

If you like your dreams,
You'll help to make them true.
But if you just sit there,
You're going to feel blue.

Jenny Ashman

Getting Up From Bed

My head is swollen and red,
My legs are totally dead,
My stomach is empty,
My arms feel limp,
My neck is cramped,
My brains are stamped,
My whole body is tramped

Scott Robinson

AIDS

There a deadly virus out there
and it is called AIDS.
It kills and it makes
people very sick.
There is no cure
and any body can get it.
So many people are dying
and going through suffering
because of this virus.
I wish I could make a cure
and make it all go away
but for right now there is no way,
there is a deadly virus out there
and it is called AIDS.

Kristin Wilcox

Dragon

Let me tell you all about me:
Children love me; you're a child.
All my heads are green and horny,
All my eyes are red and wild.
All my toes have claws upon them,
All my claws have awesome hooks.
I blow smoke through all my noses,
It is hotter than it looks.
All my tails are diamond-pointed,
All my teeth are sharp and blue.
I won't bite you very badly:
I am rather fond of you!
All my scales are shaped like arrows:
They will hurt you if you touch.
So, although I know you love me,
Do not pet me overmuch.

Charles R. Ramey

Colors

I am blue
so full of love
and giving it out.
I am green
so full of envy
of my surroundings.

I am yellow
so full of happiness
and showing it.
I am purple
so full of hope
for my future.

Jackie Castro

Untitled

Rest now, oh, sweet child of God
In your saviour's arms
No pain or fear, is there to feel
Within his loving arms
Life's journey has led you
To the green meadows
We've heard so much about
Where he shall tend to your every need
As a shepherd to a lamb's
To thirst no more, it shall be quenched
By streams of life everlasting
To hunger or want, it will not happen
Within this holy land
Fear not, oh, sweet child of God
For you are now just passing
Into his promised land

Jo-Ana E. Lester

Untitled

I watch the big oak tree, its
    boughs bending in the breeze.
With each breeze the bough
grows weaker.
I wonder, "How far will she
    go before she snaps?"

I am, but a bough on the tree
of our relationship,
always bending.
and inner strength helps me
to bounce back after each breeze.

Hoping . . . I can withstand the
one that will snap me,
then . . . there will be a
space on that tree, never
again, to feel the warmth
of the sun.

Valerie Boccadoro

Crystal Shores

Red sea of blood
    On the crystal shore
Light the candle
    And it'll bleed some more

Red sea of blood
    On the crystal shore
I hold on to the crystal
    So I'll bleed no more

Red sea of blood
    I don't want to drown
I hold on to the crystal
    So I'll never go down

Red sea of blood
    Show me love and not hate
That's why I cling to the crystal
    It shows me my fate!

Bob Saulski

Tamiboom Bay

Just where is Tamiboom Bay
except in a place in my head
where winds must be raced
to enter that place
first where in the world
is Tamiboom Bay
a place where and once did go
as a dreamer in childhood
to race the wind once again
upon a sailing ship
to reach the bay of Tamiboom
and daydream once again

Mark Twain the III and Last

Remembered

The times we shared
    Will never grow dim
For tho you are gone
    The memory's within

The good times remembered
    The bad times were few
The time is coming
    When our friendship's
    Renewed

Dorothy I. Bjur

A Vision

When I look through the mirror,
I see you,
   your image,
     your features,
      your facial expression.
As I gaze through this reflection,
I see you as the destiny
   that has come to me.
I look beyond the silhouette.
You are the one I most respect.
Amazed by your shadow,
   You are
     the eternal life
      I didn't know.

Diane Jeannette Vislar

Julie's Theme (No Way Out)

White lace.
Long face.
Blank stares.
Who cares?
Should wait.
Too late.
No way out.

The shame.
The same.
Dark streets.
Heartbeats.
Can't fight.
Tonight.
No way out.

Should wait.
Too late.
Black lace.
White face.
A sin.
Amen.

Linda Hollingsead

Todays

In an insane society
an insane person
might seem very sane,
and yet,
that insane question
still remains,
are you sane?

Daren Sarcione

Husband

You are the beauty
Of each sunset
The warmth
of each sunrise
The tenderness
In each tear
You are the newness
Of each beginning
The comfort
Of each ending
You are
The one and only
Love of my life
Life of my love
Forever

Shelli Anne Childson

Simple Yet Genuine

He is a man.
That is all.
He moves with swiftness
and always
achieves his goal.
His face
appears to be
hard and cold,
but his penetrating gaze
reveals the benevolence
that lies beyond his exterior.
He is entitled to his share of respect,
but in turn
he is criticized for his judgments.
He feels compelled to improve
an adverse situation into
one of excellence.
As an individual,
he is simple;
as a man, he is genuine.

Katie Slinkard

Solarius

As I look through my window pane
One summer morn,
I see your invisible grin.
Oh yellow-faced man
Shine brightly on me,
For I am your biggest fan.
Your light comes day after day
Like a persistent child,
Trying to get its way.
Some days your light is mild,
Hiding behind the trees.
Your yellow face then turns to gold,
And starts its journey home.
Each evening I watch you grow old,
Slowly I see you sink in the sky.
My window pane and I
Then softly say good bye.

Sarah Kernan

Love Me

It seems to me,
I have to be,
how everybody wants me.

But it is said,
that in your head
is the only way it should be.

Cause I'm my own
and you are yours
but I love you anyway.

Can't you love me for what I am
and not for what you see?

Christine Gougeon

Joy

With my children on my mind
my heart is filled with sorrow
my eyes heavy with tears.

I prayed to God
do you love and miss me?

He answered
my heart is filled with sorrow
my eyes heavy with tears.

Joseph Francis Vialpando

Anticipation

To be able to savor
Your delicacies
Hidden treasures
Promises excitement
Primal instincts
Tamed by appearance
Unknowing knowledge
Platonic urges
I'm barely breathing
Unable to eat
Can't hardly function
My mind often wanders
My mind often wonders
What gifts of our souls
Lay there unopened
What physical joys
The future is holding
What two hearts share
When spirits are willing

Rhonda L. Frazier

Home Sweet Home

That place you call home;
The drapes are hung
Your pictures slant
The dusted table
The old dog's pant
That sweet apple pie scent
Mixed with the collard greens
The sweet water corn bread
And black-eyed peas
The T.V. still on
With the same old show
With a ha ha he
And a ho ho ho
Your mother looks at you
And gives you a smile
That makes your home
All worth the while

Tiffany Irvin

The Rose

The rose is a flower from above
A sign of friendship
A symbol of love

One man gives it to his mate
They say it holds their fate

No one knows where it'll go from there
But the couple really has to care

It depends on the couple
It depends on love's power
More importantly, it depends
on the decision of the flower.

Mandy Jay

God's Way

I don't need to live fancy
I just want to live
I want to see the earth and sky
all that God has give.

Don't need diamond or rubies
or that mansion on the hill
just want to love and share and care
for that is our God's will.

Betty Elstad

Before the Great Darkness Falls

What is the world to me?
Though inviting and charming may it be.
Its wanton pride and Vanity
doth not pleaseth me,

What is God to me?
A king of love, hope and life is he.
Yield! Yield!
All ye sinners to his gracious calls
before the great darkness falls.

Bessie J. Voytko

Explanation

Let me explain this
Very carefully
The circle is the universe
All three coins are the same
And the bad humor
Of us and others
Is really just a song

Believe
It is your only chance
Just remember
This is bigger than you think
And nothing really ever
Stops moving

Joshua Mertz

My Shepherd

As I walk the road of life
and I know not where to turn,
I ask the Lord to guide me
for this journey I have not learned.

When I travel down a road
that He knows is wrong for me,
He somehow let's me know because
He's always watching me.

If ever I get weary
and I stumble and I fall,
when things look there darkest
and I can't see light at all,
He's there before I know it
as He has been all along,
I just have to let Him handle things
and everything gets calm.

He only wants to help me
through this life of twisted roads,
till He comes in all His glory
and He calls to take me home.

Kathleen Harper

It's What We Make It

We make it so complicated
Giving gifts we can't afford
Making promises that'll be ignored
Living life, with which we're board

We make it so complicated
Living just about the law
Wanting all to take our fall
Robbing Peter to pay Paul

Yes, we make it so complicated
Whore ourselves for security
Sneak a peek at impurity
Hope to die with dignity.

Rosalie Armstrong

Second Thoughts

I'm listening to the falling rain
as it taps upon my window pane.
I'm lying on my cozy bed
and glad I'm not outside instead.

I'm dozing off in sheer content
not caring when the rain is spent,
because my errands are all done
so let it rain, who needs the sun?

But then a nagging thought steals in
and starts me to a-wondering
what of those who have no home
to keep them comfortable and warm

Those who must find some place to stay
until the rain has gone away
Those who must find a place to eat,
never mind the sodden feet

And then I say a fervent prayer
for God to keep them in his care.
The rain now plays a somber tune
and I pray it's over soon

Caroline M. Niklas

Untitled

"Odd, the many shapes
That shadows form,
And when they go,
They leave no marks."

Woodbury A. Palmen

The New Year!

The new year is here for us
to see, to love and enjoy life
and to have fun is the Key.
We need to guide our children
to build on what we left behind,
we need to teach them more so
that we can better their minds.
The new year is here for us to
change the things that we can't
no longer arrange, let's make
do of what we got and turn
our dream's into a melting pot,
that will always remain full
through all our lives and give us
happiness and wealth as we survive.

Elizabeth A. Dowdell

Silence

I am alone and tired
In a big place that I once enjoyed.
Now there is no one
Silence surrounds me
I long for human contact
  A voice
  A whisper
And I wait . . . Wait . . . nothing

This was a different place,
  full of noise, laughter and tears
Now there is nothing

I sit in my silence and wonder
  where is the noise?
  Have I ever heard it?

I fear that I have not.
I weep in my silence.

Crystal Osborn

The Book Of Truth

The book of truth lays in wait
down through the ages,
waiting for a friendly soul
to come and turn its pages.

To study the word
that God is giving
that will take your soul
to eternal living.

Heed what I tell you
for it's all true,
but reading the book
is up to you.

The laws he lays down
are plain and straight.
Learn and understand them
before it's too late.

Nathaniel W. Harbour

Remember

The blankets of snow,
the bright, starlit sky,
children watching for Santa,
and his reindeer high.
These sentimental things
remind us of Christmas,
but, we must search deep,
within ourselves,
and find the reason why,
it's not Santa and his elves,
that we have this wonderful day,
it's the precious baby
that was laid upon the hay,
our savior that was born on
Christmas day, that died on the
cross, much to our dismay,
but, raised again three days past,
and we praise him until
our day is last.

Alyssa Caldon

Wind

I feel a deep wind blow my hair
In came all my pain and fear
The pain of when you scratch your arm
The fear of when the lights aren't on
The wind won't stop, it blows a lot
It makes me quiver in this lot
Then it stops the lights are off.

Aubrey Michelle Kinyoun

The Sea

When I walk by the deep blue sea,
I can hear the waves
rushing and crashing.
And when I walk down
that beach, I can feel
the hot hot sand across
my bare feet.
As I looked up, I could
see a precious sunset so beautifully.
While standing so silently, it
was gradually hard to breath.
When it came as it did, it was
late and the end of a hot
and very busy day.

Laura Foley

Drudgery

Slop, muck, swamp life
  my thoughts

Perverseness, blackened chastity
  my heart

Mucus, corrupted bile
  my soul
Human portrait of drudgery.

Nicole R. Henderson

It Could Happen

The world could be a better place,
fit for all the human race.
We can all make it so,
for everyone to learn and grow.

It only takes you and me,
to make people want to see.
The hate and violence will disappear,
just try not to have fear.

All it takes is a little kindness
and love to remind us.
No more drugs and abuse.
We have the choice to refuse.

Just take the time to think it out.
That's what life is all about.
It could happen here today,
knowing there is a better way.

Amber Millon

Three Branches

Three branches on a tree,
in strong comparison to me.
How in thy Father, Mother,
and Great Lord on high
they all help me to make it by.

To repay them enough would be
a task so impossible for anyone
to complete especially me.

Three branches on a tree,
in strong comparison to me.
I thank my Father, Mother,
and Great Lord on high
for all the work to get me by.

Pearl Marie Phillips

Love

Love;
a passion gift God given.
  A sensitive feeling toward
a couple.
  A caring feeling toward
parent and child.

  Love,
A strong motion in your
  heart.
A way of forgiving.
  The goodness of your
soul.

  Love;
A special feeling.
  The life you carry on
forever.
  A dream of peace.

Lauren Rea

Make-Believe

Real is not real
Now is then
Post is pre

When I see it now
Before it, I saw
In a past it didn't exist
In a future that won't be

A world that never existed
A world created by men,
A God of make-believe

Virtual reality, I was told
Still I don't know
It's virtual
Or it's real

Jaime Imoto

Chinese Paper Flowers

Still and white
With long translucent stems
they catch the sun
with their peek-a-boo faces

A mesh of opulent fibers
glowing as if diamond dust
enhanced their beauty
like fine jewels

Standing guard
ready to take on
their regal place in
God's garden

Erica I. Hidvegi

Etching

Happy memories form
  The spirit's frail protection
Against corrosive time.
  And, when these fail, possess
Plastic flower replicas
  Of gardens in a dream.

Or, brave and foolish, let
  Time's acid etch entire
Its story on the soul;
  Terrible, unsparing
Admission to art's truth.

Ink the wounds with soot
  From all the burning lamps,
Lay the soft white paper down
  And pull me through the press.

Roberta T. Griffin

Who Am I?

As I sit by the dock
I see four pelicans
I have to watch my clock
I'm only an American
Or am I
maybe I'm something else
my eyes only see what they
want to see.
Maybe I'm a pelican too.
Pelicans have eyes that see
Just like me
Now I ask myself, who am I?

Lacey Tregembo

Love

The old man of the tree
looked down at me and said,
"I know you belong underground."
This said with a frown!
"Just look at me,
starting from the Earth
which gave me Birth
to the sky,
for which I've spent my life,
to try I must!
Get back to the ground,
the root of all evil,
the roots of my life."
"OK" I say,
"I'll meet you there."

Jeffrey Winston Brayne

My Time

The time it seems is never enough
For the ones we love here on this earth
The good times go by, quick as a flash
And only the bad ones seem to last
Each dawn begins a day that is new
We're never promised tomorrow
Our days are few
But caress each day as a newborn
Because we have all been warned
For tomorrow is never ours to keep
Only the memories are ours to reap
The love in our hearts is ours to share
With all our loved ones here and there
So mourn me not loved ones behind
A full life I've lived and now
The Kingdom is mine

Mose E. Harrison

Pain

There's an emptiness inside me
No one could ever fill;
A hole in my heart
Not to be solved by a pill.

I'm hurting deep inside
But there's no one to tell.
I've made myself a prisoner
Inside a burning hell.

I have to vent it soon
Because no one can see
The pain and anger I hoard away
In this body I call me.

I do not want to lose him
For one will never know:
The feelings I still have for him
I shall not outgrow.

I cry myself to sleep
'Cause this heart of mine still yearns
For what I once called love
And a flame that forever burns.

Alexis Smith

Gifts

Love is a gift every
one should have. A gift
filled with joy, happiness,
and wonderful memories.
Only loved ones would
know of a gift.

Jessica Moreno

Children

Where have all the little ones gone?
I've heard it said before,
we really miss their laughter
as they passed by our door.

So as each fleeting day
soon becomes another year,
the little ones of yesterday
have flown away, we hear.

The curly blonde that we just loved
is now all dressed in white,
to carry on her service
well into the night.

That little lad just down the street,
the one that we all knew,
is guardian on the high seas,
now he's dressed in blue.

It is such comfort
and puts us all to rest,
to know that our great Nation
is still seeking out its best.

Ralph Neldon

Think Of Me

When the golden sun is sinking
And your mind from care set free
When of others you are thinking
Will you sometimes think of me

When the leaves begin their turning
And then begin to fall
If away from you're walking
Will you turn and hear my call

When white snow high is drifting
And storm clouds fill the sky
When you sit alone and listen
Will you listen for my cry

When flowers start their blooming
Waving petals in the wind
If alone I have been standing
Will you come and my friend

The stars have begun to twinkle
The grass will soon have dew
As I lie asleep and dream
Remember that I dream of you

Kristin K. Bickerstaff

God Is Love

God is love,
He's the leading pathway,
And the brightness like the
stars above.
He'll never let you down,
For, deep, in your heart,
God is love.

He's the answers to your questions.
The fathers and master of
All creation.
The willing and hope of your future.
For, if you need anything,
Just call on the Lord,
And he will answer your prayer,
Don't ever feel down,
Because he's always going to be there.
For, deep in your heart,
God is Love.

Kamilah A. Young

Dawn's First Light

See the clouds so far below.
    Ever changing as they come and go.
Flashes of lighting over the horizon.
    Bolts of lighting across the sky.

All along the bluffs.
    Illuminating the landscape.
So far below.
    Down to the valley below.

At dawn's first light.
    Rays of Sunlight.
Glow in the dawn.
    Of a new day.

Wilks Oren Reese Jr.

The Widows Lament!

I look around, and what do I see?
Something is missing,
Something very dear to me.
My love is gone,
The time stand's still
How can it be?
I know it is God's will!
The wonderful years went by so fast
Tell me my love
Why did it have to pass?
Now you are gone
I am alone!

When the time comes for me to go
Will you be there to open the door?
Will you be there for me once more?

Erika R. Hindel

A Toast

Let's drink to us
For all those years together
Let's drink to happiness
And let us live forever.

We pray for better
To stay together
Let's drink to us
For all those years together

Let's find the right course
To our happiness with joy and pleasure.
Courageous deeds of you and me,
Honey we'll be in heaven.

I pour the wine into my glass
With words of wisdom.
Let's drink to us
For all those sweet years together.

Robert Buryakov

For All Seasons

Love is for all seasons,
Not fading away
When Winter comes.

It endures the cold air,
The early nights;
The Snow.

Ice once tried
To freeze poor love,
But Love melted it away.

Randall Pederson

Individuality

I'm a freak,
Someone different —
Not to be trusted.
Stop!
Don't come too close.
I might be contagious.
My thoughts could enter your head
And give you a new perspective —
One that you never knew of.
So don't come too close
Or else you could become,
God forbid,
An individual.

Michelle A. de la Vega

The White Mountains Of New Hampshire

Ancient bed of glaciers.
Realm of gray stones,
Clouds and sun.

Winds tug at hikers
Rejoicing in solitude
Or companionship.

Aching muscles.
Slippery roots
Lying in wait
For incautious boots.

Long views,
Or none, in rain.
Bugs and moose tracks,
The occasional bear.

Flickering leaf-shadows
On cascading waters.

Vein-cleansing
Heart-restoring
Talk-begetting
Soul-soothing.

William E. Knight

My Wish For You

I wish for you so many things
    too many to,
    put down on paper.
I wish the stars, the sun, and moon
    to shine on you forever.
I wish for you
    happy days
    and dreams that will come true.
I can only wish so much
    for,
    the rest is up to you.

Julie Blew

My Window

Poetry floating by my window
snow
falls gently to the ground,
first winter coat.
Sleeting thoughts of grieving hope
kiss the minutes
which drift like snowflakes
onto the lawns of my eternity
melting,
till gone

Jeremy Sherr

It Could Happen: Racism

What do people think about
when they sit and dream about
Racism?

Racism hurts inside our hearts;
Racism blinds us from seeing the truth;
Racism we do not respect for it is
a bad thing;

We can't share our feelings,
if we keep getting hurt;
We are dying because of
Racism in our world;

Why can't we arise from our
differences and love one another?
I don't like going to sleep
knowing our world still has
Racism.

Kimberly Nicole Andre

A Mother's Loss

(In Memory Of My Son, Devin)

   I look into her face and see
only sadness in her eyes,
not exactly sure how to act
or how to say her good-byes.
   She looks so lost with no
where to go the pain in her
heart that hurts her so.
Looking back on how happy she
used to be, knowing that her
son is what held the key.
   A beautiful face and shiny
black hair, holding him in her
arms with such loving care.
His tiny body and little fragile
smile was enough to give her
strength to walk that extra mile.
But we held on to the memories
and so does she, and the
suffering she goes through
will always be.

Samara Anthony

Vending Machine Syndrome (V.M.S.)

I'm tired of being a vending machine,
I'm fed up with the slugs.
I'm tired of always putting out,
Still having to beg for hugs.

I'm tired of all the time,
And energy I've spent.
I guess my chance at love,
Must have come and went.

So now I hide in a closet,
My bitterness makes me choke.
Go find yourself a new sucker,
This vending machine is broke.

Tracy Noonan

Night Sky

The sky looks bigger by night than day.
With so many stars so far away.
Glitters and glow balls of light.
Shine so bright every night.

Molly Scholl

Today

Today as a person we take
our life for granted. Not just you,
me but everyone. But just once
in our lives we lost faith in our
selves, each other and worse
our Gods, today we don't look
at life as a treasure. Today
we see it for other personal
reasons, to gain wealth, and
other devilish deeds. Today
many of us lost meaning to
the ten commandments within
ourself but I guess you have to
do it in today society. Today as
we look back in time God gave
us one special gift to have
life give life and to be superior
and we took advantage of that
by being cruel today. What
became of us? Today?

Robert Scoby

They Don't See Me

When first I wake, I give my all.
I'm at my loved one's beck and call.
I try to think of ways to say
How much I love them everyday.
But they don't see me!

I try to make them happy,
With the little things I do.
To smooth away the wrinkles
And make each day brand new.
But they don't see me!

Yet in my heart I'm happy still
Because I know it is God's will.
And when he lays me down to rest
I'll know that I have done my best.
Maybe then they'll see me!

Carolyn Eaker

Longing

There was a kiss
urgent, deep
a merging of two into one
I could live there.

A moment in time
wanted, needed
swept into his arms
It's warm there.

Time is fleeting
walls, wounds
keep love at bay
I'm cold again.

Chris van Soolen

Untitled

This love of ours is like
The universe

It holds no boundaries
But forever bounds our
passion

Truly a love of celestial
proportions

Ernesto Bevilacqua

Forsaken Love

I used to love,
I used to live,
I used to care,
I used to give.

Now my dreams are
Shattered
All my love
None of it
Mattered.

Who now will
Here my cry,
Will it matter
When I
   die?

Chris Neer

The Seas

Disturbing power
Yet Serene . . .
Continuous in its motion.
Forever pounding, stirring the earth.
Since birth.
Overwhelming in its vastness
In its beauty.
Connecting me wholly with Infinity.
Leaving me calm, complete,
to the center of my being.
As I bathe this morning in its warmth.
Watching as the sun rises
From blackness . . . into blueness
I feel newness.
I feel time . . . passed.
And for this brief moment
I feel its cure.

Diane Goldman

Untitled

There was a little girl
Who had a little curl
Right behind her left ear
She's as sweet as she can be
And you'd better believe me
'Cause if you don't, you're weird
She's as cute as a bug
As she plays on the rug
With her toys that she got from Santa
She's her daddy's best girl
The girl with the curl
And this is God's truth, I'll grant ya!

Margaret H. Poil

The Sun

I rise in the morning,
I fall at night,
During the day I shine so bright.

When the clouds are thick and gloomy,
People can't see all the way to me.

When it is real hot one day
People wish I would go away,

I will not leave or go away,
For I will stay day after day,

But when I do finally go away,
So will all that was here to stay.

So now you know how I feel,
If not for me, no one would be here.

Robby Starner

The Circle

Life is an endless circle
repeating itself as it in turn,
 is repeated by the unwary
traveler who tries to avoid its burn.
 When the summer heat becomes
unbearable for a length stay,
 winter will come to bring
around a cooling day.
 And when the chill has set
inside a body's home,
 summer will come once more
for the seasons never roam.
 If the human race could look
ahead to a future time,
 would their winter be as loyal
or a summer in its prime?
 or would we see our past
coming back with haunting greed,
 our circle of life ending
for signs we would not heed?

John Steele

My Mother

There is a lady that I have known,
all of my life.
She is sweet, kind, loving and makes
my father a perfect wife.

She has been there for me through
good and bad times.
The many moments I think of her,
my heart sounds like chimes.

She had a very tough job raising
two rowdy boys.
But, she never lost her cool when
we were really making noise.

She was tough, but understanding
and took nothing light.
And, with all of her love and guidance,
I turned out all right.

I was really blessed when God gave
me such a precious gift.
A wonderful Mother that has given
my life such a lift.

Glen E. Coyle

Climbing Stone

Glacial Stone of empyrean birth,
All life's secrets in its girth.
Looming massive, grey and bleak,
Black striated and silver streaked.

Strip off your shoes.
Risk a climb.
The toe-holds are . . .
Extremely fine.

Turn now, stop.
Lie back and feel
The grooves and ripples
Of life's wheel.

Coarse and pocked,
Serene and calm,
It holds your life
In its cold,
Broad
Palm.

Anne Burke

Tornados

Crashing cars
Smashing trucks
before it was
silent
dangerous lightning
scary thunder
before it was
silent
when it's over
the sky is clear
for upon that
day the
tornado
struck!

Matthew Berlin

Traffic Light Poem #6

Pillow drifts on autumn sky
bed of cobalt hue
winter looms o'er faded land
summer bids adieu

Corn soldiers guard the greying fields
pumpkins dot earth's cloth
arctic wind and icy sea
swiftly plight their troth

Haste to wrap the shroud of love
against the barren night
seed pod cloistered in the tomb
awaits spring's morning light

Priscilla Holmes

Lost Love

As I watch the sun
Go down each night
I can't help thinking how things
Could have been so right
From the sound of your voice
To the touch of your hair
All the way down
To the last deadly glare
You had no reason
You had no right
I should have stood up
And put up a fight
All I wanted
Was to be great
I know now that
I started days too late
I'd have fought this thing
All the way
If only I'd known
I'd be yours someday

Lynda Wright

A New Day Is Born

Sunrise in the morn
Another day is born
The grass is wet with dew
It sparkles like bubbles blue

The sky is clear
Not a cloud to be seen
In the meadow the deer
Dine on grass so green

A new day is born
So early in the morn

Ruth Steinhilber

Precious Gems

Crystals and diamonds
Precious gems so rare
Can never compare
To the light of Jesus
The garment He wears
Blinding, beautiful, magnificent light
The love of Jesus
Is brighter than white
Pure, exciting unending love
Shines from His face
In heaven above
Righteous and pure
Holy He stands
It's he who keeps us strong
By holding our hand
Leader in truth, a teacher to me
More precious than gold
Is Jesus to me.

Vicki Beal

Friends

Thank you for your kind words,
And the sweet things you do.
Thank you for the sacrificial deeds,
Thank you for being You!!!!

It is without a doubt a great
blessing to have
A friend you can count on in
good times and bad.

So He gave you, me,
And He gave me, you,
At a time in our lives when we
needed to be —
A friend among many, but special
among few.

Deborah G. Howard

The Death Of Death

I wept upon a desert land,
of life that death became,
an ill-kept grave of fertile man,
betrayed by fear his name.

My soul from out me streaming sought
my seed to sow once more;
perhaps to stir this morbid sand
to life begun before.

Of hope, the whiteness pleaded had,
of love, it thirsty cried.
I know my stream of sadness pleased
the ever-crying pride.

A grain of trembling happiness,
stirred twice upon the tide;
beneath this crusted emptiness,
yes, there death is, but not alive.

Barry J. Chasen

Rain

God allows rain to fall
In that, it is a sign of cleansing
Every rapi, tat, tat, is a call
To all of His creations
Remembering the feeling of His love
we ask for restorations
warmth and peace from above
leave us free from all persecutions.

Elizabeth Gutierrez

Young Mother

A perfect child God sent my way.
To mold and fashion just like clay.
But I too am just a child,
And I need growth which takes awhile.

Frightened as I could be. I
wondered throughout life aimlessly.
Then it came to me one day.
Why God sent that child my way.

Now he is older, yet I am still young.
And still another life has begun.
Now my life is more content.
For I know my child is heaven sent.

If I humble myself to him.
He returns it with a grin.
And through my child I found life,
And a purpose without strife.

Now I know God loves me.
And now I know my place to be.
A teacher, friend, companion too.
For this I pray my whole life through.

Iris Caudle

Flowers

They come after April showers,
The variety is endless,
They grow in shady bowers,
Under a rock it cowers,
In a field they stand fearless.

Jana Fullerton

Roses

Roses are blue,
But are mostly red,
And usually always
Stay in a bed.
But when they get sick
And lose their head,
Then they really know they're dead.

When they shed and
They lose their petals,
And it starts to rain,
They don't run in pain,
Because they know they
Don't carry bicycle pedals that
Are made out of metal.

Nathan Todaro

An Execution

The night before
I know tomorrow what will occur,
and yet I still think
those hours are far away.
When I awake,
alarmed
I push to gain some peace
again and again.
My mind searches for a way out
Sick thoughts.
But I'll get up, like always
and the noose will tie
around my neck.
Sentenced to another
day of work,
and a slow death.

John Perella

God Is Love

As God looks from high above
I rejoice Him with love

Looking down from above
As He sends all His love

As we return out break of day
All our love pass away

As I live from day to day
He will guide me in the right way

He loves me yes He do
I love you the same way too

God is love all the time
He's never far far behind

He loves me in the morning
He loves me in the day

He loves me, loves me, loves me
And that's no other way.

Keiosha S. Pitts

Christmas Love

Christmas season is best in the world
As the snow, around us swirls
It is great, to a child's delight.
To see the snow flakes, in their flight

There's nothing like a girl or boy,
To fill your heart with Christmas joy
They put on airs with all their charm
As Santa, encircles, them in his arms

In their gay world, of make believe
Playing with dolls, and trimming trees
You can hear their happy little shouts.
Excitement, and merriment are all about

Bell are ringing loud and clear,
Christmas now we know is here
From the beds, the children hop
To see, what Santa's put in their sock

On the laughter, and joyful sounds
In the mystery that abounds
Christmas wouldn't be complete
Without children's love so sweet.

Edith Spurgeon

Now

If I could hear you now
　　I'd demand a song
　　　Something slow and sweet
　　　Not too sad, not too long

If I could hear you now
　　I'd ask for what I've missed
　　　All the words and sounds
　　　That others just dismiss

If I could hear you now
　　You'd never need repeat
　　　All the words I didn't get
　　　I'd never miss a beat

If I could hear you now
　　I'd have you listen, too
　　　Identify strange noises
　　　And teach me all that's new

If I could hear you now
　　I'd ask for whistles and a vow
　　　Kissing and whispering in my ear
　　　If I could hear you now

Charlotte Schamadan

No Strings Attached

In Memory of Lonnie Straight
A warm hand to hold
A soft arm to touch
This love that I have
Can hurt so much!
But I don't care
No tear will fall
I will come running
When you call.
My arms will hold you
All through the night
As long as you hold me
So very tight.
I will be yours
And our love won't be matched
I will be your puppet
With no strings attached.

Tammy Lynn Pape

Darkness Brighten

The Stars are bright,
The earth is dim.
It's the little spark of love.

Beyond the rainbow's rim,
That my heart longs for.

Oh little Shane you're not gone,
Only awaiting for us.

Oh death a sweetness,
of life everlasting.
For we shall behold one another.

For together we shall enjoy a peace,
In the love of God.

Iris L. Hubbard

Book Of Poetry

A very dear love to me
Is my book of poetry
I read them day and night
They keep my world bright
The verses are so dear
They're good any time of year
The peace of mind they bring
Make my heart sing
Poetry the words are hurled
The language of the world
Time set in print
All the hours spent
And you can depend
I will read them to the end

Marie Elizabeth DeMoss

Searching For The Light

Even though I walk in darkness
I search for the light
that is, the day when we shall
reunite,
My face stings
from the tear's and winter wind
as I search for that, one friend
that I had once up on a time
though I search I can no longer find.
I can see you out of the corner
of my eye.
but you are never there
yet I still will not let my search end
in despair

Henry Ellis Duvall

She Cries, But He Can't Anymore

Salt rushed down from
The crystal pools of mirrors
Filling the bed of the sea
With black tainted water.

Waves rolled in, as yet,
Another stiff breeze blew in,
And the water stirred up
things it thought had settled.

These pools eerily shimmer
Confronted by a reflection they
Have seen before.

Don't drown it.
It was once a rapid.
But now is a dry river bed.

Ryan J. Stradling

Sunset

As the sun sets,
hazy shades of
pink, purple
and cerise
float across the
sky.
As the colors
spread themselves
across a
golden sky,
night falls,
and the colors,
fade into the
darkness.

Blair Albom

Untitled

The average street glows dimly
with a slight few street lamps
sparsely decking corners roundness.
Lights out
inducted by the female touch
upon his playfulness.
Black skies
hung dark clouds about.
The satisfying view.
Eyelids tenderly joined one another.
Entering powerful imagination.
Bubbling springs dripple
with plush greenness covering all
and bracing the pads of their feet.
The sound . . .
None.
The magic fine as an exploding star.
In an infamous lock
Their dreams begins sweetly.
With no end.

Nicki Roseman

Images

The lion of the mountain
Looks down on civilization.
The Indian Warrior returns
To his village, with no idea as to
How close to me he really is.
The buffalo on stampede
Kick up dust from the
Wide midwest plains,
In my living room.

Richard L. Smith

If You Could Only See Through My Eyes

If you could only see
through my eyes, you
would see a whole
new world.
A world of sadness,
a world of fear, a
world of confusion
If you could only
see through my
eyes you would see
a world that is too
scared to see, to
hear, to talk, or to
touch anything or
anyone that is not
the same as themselves.
Maybe if people see
the world the way
I do, maybe it would
not be the way it is today.

Diana Ruiz

Untitled

She was born on the dawn
Of a beautiful spring;
We could never have known
How much joy she would bring.

From her first ballet shoes
To the softball glove small,
From beginner flute
To best flautist of all.

From nursery school
To old Aggieland;
How could we have known
That someday God's hand

Would carry this daughter
Of two Cougar brags,
And plant her with care
In the kingdom of Ags?

Gig 'em, Kristin!

Kenya Magee

Disappear

I gulp a breath of dew
and surrender to my surroundings
praying for deliverance

Swallowing thistles as I am
suffocating with this suffering,
I hope for hope

Slammed against metal walls,
I wonder,
is there no way out of my mind?

Deliver me! I scream
(or at least cause me to disappear
like stardust)

Salvation leaves my soul
as I extradite the past from my heart
and transcend the mortal realm

Belief. Delusion.
One and the same.
I just can't get away from myself.

Mary S. Uddin

Mothers Know

Mothers know everything
Or so I'm told.
They know why birds sing,
And snow is cold.
They know why girls are pink,
And boys are blue,
They know what you think
Before you do!
Mothers know when you tell a lie,
And they say they even know why.
With all their wonderful might,
ESP and second sight,
Why is to so hard for a mother to know,
How much their child loves them so!

Loretta S. Kirkpatrick

My Greatest Fear

When I'm gone
May I be remembered for who I was?
How I got to be who I was?
May I be remembered for my
contributions to society?
May I be remembered by my
family as a caring and loving person?
May I be remembered my friends
as a good friend?

Because when I'm gone the
thing I'll fear most is to be forgotten

Crill C. Warner

My Dream

Last night I had a dream
it was of you.
When I woke up this morning
I found it was not true

I guess we all have dreams
a night or two
it just seems so real
your heart I will steal

So I'll go on dreaming
I hope it will come true
if it don't I'll go on
knowing I still love you.

I would sit on a post
and all I'd do is dream
I didn't hear my mom calling
I was in dream land it seems.

Violet Oard

A Kiss For The Dying

Kiss me
But not goodbye
If this be my last kiss
Make it with passion
Not with tears.

Kiss me
Arouse my spirit
Make me long for another
Inflame my heart
As with a hot arrow.

Kiss me
Make me hope to live
But beg to die
That I might never
Endure another such kiss.

Dale Hanna

The Angel In You

Dedicated to Lisa Elliott
What a wonderful day,
when you were born,
for there was an Angel,
in the youngest of form.

As you matured,
you had a certain way,
of touching many hearts,
each and every day.

Wherever you go,
wherever, the place,
you bring a smile,
to everyone's face.

Now as an Angel,
still to this day,
You shine above all,
in every kind of way!

Raven Owens

Baby Unknown

She was left for dead
But she survived,
Cause God was there
To watch and guide.
To keep her safe
And out of harm,
Into a warm
And loving arm.
So she may know
That life can be,
Full of love, and
Probability.

Cynthia Cain

Forever

If my love was a flower
It would be a perfect rose
With petals soft as velvet
And would be only for you.
If my love was the rain
It would fall and never stop
With endless showers forever
And for you would be every drop.
If my love was the sun
It would shine all the time
With warmth and light forever
And protect you from the night.
But my love is only love
It is all that I can give
And it's yours forever
Forever, as long as I shall live.

Brandon Potter

Simple Pleasures

A cosy nook,
A cherished book,
A copper kettle singing merrily.
A sunny place,
A friendly face,
And jam and scones for tea.

Autumn leaves,
Grain in sheaves,
Are some of Life's Simple Pleasures.
The moon in the skies,
My dog's loving eyes,
Are all of the things I treasure.

Marise Marken

Untitled

The object of our desire
the reason for our distress
the source of our sadness
the reality of our dream
the breaker of our hope

Our loneliness and deeper despair
eating us alive
our eyes turn inward
soon we will arrive
our purpose undiscovered
our lives unfulfilled
the cold black beckons
its wonders carefully chilled

Jason Rivera

Every Inch

With every inch,
of every mile,
the road I travel is empty.
With every pause,
of every word,
the thoughts I feel are tempting.
Through all the tears,
and all the pain,
the smiles I show are few.
And with all the blame,
of all the world,
my heart is sad without you.

Jessica Frisinger

The Cherokee Nation

I love this land that my
ancestors ran. Through the
open door of spoken war, I am
willing to restore that is no more.
we loved to trade for schooling
aides to help promote our new
hope. With our new ABC, it helped
me see the new me. We left
our name land to search for
greener land. When we arrived
we were surprised there was
dust flying in our eyes. We
took a dust bowl and found
black gold to help restore our
ancestral hold and now the
Cherokee story has been told.

Robynn Butler

Mourning Showers

Like an ancient river
The emotions flood
Standing under the waterfall
Diluting the spirit in my blood
A thousand drops a second
Beat against my shell
Unable to reach the soul
Or find the bottom to the well
Naked and shivering
I stand in the mist and cry
Tears becoming lost
As the water pollutes my eye
Obscuring things once seen clearly
Things defined now shades of grey
Morning ritual now complete
I wrap my towel tight
And prepare to face the day

J. Charles

Love

Spring
Young Hearts glow
like neon lights shining
through the darkest day.
Summer
Tamed Hearts beat
to a different drummer slowing
the pace to a steady walk
Fall
Steady Hearts woven
by the silver threads
of life never to be broken.
Winter
Aged hearts
still
have the glow of spring
growth of summer,
endurance
of fall and winter —
love everlasting.

Rosetta Austin Gurtina

The Promise

"We must not fall in love",
is what he said.
"Ours is to be a happy thing,
a little wineing, a little dinning,
a little fling."
"We must not fall in love", is
what he said as his arms so
strong and tight held me close
throughout the night.
That is what he said and I, I
agreed. But my heart knew that
my lips lied. I could not see
as my eyes cried.
I feel his arms around me yet
and his kisses when first we met.
"We must not fall in love" is what
he said and I, I agreed and then
I wept.

Bonnie Jean Nelson

Untitled

Unlike a dream, unlike anything
it came to me.
Unlike a gift, but yet a great
surprise, it came to me.
What was seen was wonderful,
beautiful, poetic . . .
A poet, a lover, a romantic,
an artist.
An art, an extravagant work.
An actress, is it an act or an
act part of?
A sad act ever on my mind —
Yes, so like a dream.
Sad act too, so like a dream
shattered.
At a time an action acted on a
fear, an acted need.
A masked fear, will it ever be known?
Will anything ever be resolved?
Will it come to you?

April Dawn Miller

Eureka

Still my thoughts and let me muse
on subtle meaningless things,
to be swept in the momentary
softness of time, of place and mood.
Beauty, light and distance are
attainable, fueled by desire and
tempered by patience.
My life.
Eureka.

Martin Crossnoe

Sisyphus

Sisyphus
You are my patient twin.
How many times
Must you have
Questioned your God,
And heard nothing
But the sound of the stone
Rolling
D
 o
  w
   n
    w
     a
      r
       d
        s,
Silencing
The fragile voice
Left in Pandora's box.

B. Chamberlin-Yates

House

The curves of your path,
So perfect.
I cannot fix them
In my mind.

The red of your brick,
So glaring.
I cannot see you
Through my lids.

The edge of your garden,
So clean.
I cannot crush leaves
Underfoot.

The order inside,
So quiet.
I cannot hear blood
Fills my veins.

Barbarie Rothstein

David

The times we had were
very special to me, and
I know that you'll agree.
For you there is always
a place in my heart
but that's only a start.
When I see your face
my heart begins to race
Being with you was so divine,
but now you're not mine.
Oh, this can't be the end
will you ever be mine again?

Amy Lynne Bowen

A Grandmother's Dilemma

A child was born on Nov. seven
You might say that he came straight
from heaven
He has brought me so much joy
At times to me he is like a toy
But I as the adult must learn
That with this child I must be firm
Let him know the boss he's not
even when he cries a lot
yet as we grow older
we do have our druthers
Did I mention I'm
his grandmother

Socorro Rodriguez

What If . . .

What if the grass wasn't
    green?
What if the birds didn't
    sing?
Would I still be me?

What if happy meant
    sad?
What if love meant
    hate?
What then would be
    my fate?

Why am I here?
Where do I belong?

Oh dear Lord don't
    let it be long.

Anthony Tingelstad

Another Innocent Homicide

Looking down the barrel of a gun
You start to run
Right as the bullet comes your way
It's too late it's swayed your way
Another Innocent Homicide
Just like the Holocaust
Everyone dies at no cost
Right when you think everything
is going to coincide
Another Innocent Homicide
Are we all a statistic
But let's be realistic
We are all part of the death toll
Everyone pays, but it's out of
control
Another Innocent Homicide

Michael A. Pfister

The Power Of Animosity

   In the distance I saw Animosity
coming toward me,
   In looked menacing like a serpent.
   As it slithered closer and closer
I heard it roar.
   A reeking breeze carried its ominous
odor to where I forlornly stood
   It crept closer and closer until
it was next to my paralyzed body.
   Feeling very paranoid I hesitantly
reached out and touched animosity.
   It felt like a long winter and
made me think I was invincible.

Marlena Kay Weisbrot

A Gentle Passing

Through the night the angels gather
Softly woven veils of gold
Whisper in the darkened silence
As they have for time untold.

Gentle hands as soft as snowflakes
A worn and weary heart caress,
Free it from its earthly anguish;
Guide it to eternal rest.

With but a hint of peaceful wonder
Left upon the wizened face
They slip away before the dawn;
The essence of ethereal grace.

Heidi Bauer

Rebirth

Gold and silver lace
Red velvet, soft snow
Pretty packages
Covering ugly truths
Pretty boy and girl
Grow into ugly lovers
At the Advent of the New Year
Sweet smells, lingering perfume
Sickening ambrosia
Orchestras of angels
Sing me a song of Christmas
Melodious love
A song unheard
As my heels clicked
And my lipstick wore thin
And my smile grew tired
And my body fell weak
Like my pretenses.
Oh Jesus, let me know a better birth..

Natalie Lockwood

Evening

Now the day is done
Our labor's finished
The night's for fun
No strength diminished
A drink with friends
A lovely dinner
Your mood is set
I'm no beginner
Some loving arms
Some whispered nothings
Praise for charms
Now life's worth living.

Dorisanne Swanson

My Sister Stelle

Yesterday, today, tomorrow
I feel such sorrow, Stelle
We talked and walked away
From things we wanted to say
We flirted and skirted and
Yes we prayed
We wouldn't and couldn't.
Finally a moment "I love you"
"I love you more"
"How much?" "More than I can say"
"That's not enough," said I
It is, it was
I didn't know it was our goodbye
And now I cry and cry.

Josie P. Vitkus

The Wonders Of Water

Water is swift, gushing,
glowing, and flowing
It glides like a snake
ready to strike
with all its might
It's as shiny as a crystal
grabbing your attention
So clear, pure, and glistening
Water is so bubbly
So full of life
You want to pull back
but you can not
Water is full of wonder

Patricia Anne Sera

Mama's Love

She was always there
To catch me when I would fall
The times I couldn't bare
She made them seem so small

Oh, how I miss her
So tell me about this pain
How do I put my world
Back together again

It's hard to believe she's gone
Nothin's the same anymore
I feel all alone
I wish it was like before

She won't be forgotten
Her memory will live on
She's in my heart to stay
Each and everyday

Mama's love
So sweet and tender
It's a sure love
Mama's no pretender

Lavonda Kay Wilson

Is It True . . .

Is it true that a rose never dies
Is it true that the sun will rise
Is it true that a face can't lie
Is it true that it's okay to cry

Is it true you can stay together
Is it true it will be forever
Is it true the past is gone
Is it true that life goes on

Is it true what they say
Is it true that people pray
Is it true I wish I knew
Is it true I'm asking you

Natasha Reutov

The Moment

We do not "catch" the moment
not even in that moment.
It can not be caged
like some laboratory animal
to be observed for cause and effect.
The moment "escapes" us.
Fast it flees . . .
recalled is little of what it truly was
but rather the desire of what we wished
or needed it to be.

Jennifer Parrish

Daisies

I'm a lovely, pretty thing,
I cannot dance, or sing, or swing,
But I'm always fit with spring.

In the pretty meadows I'm found,
Sneaking just above the ground,
my stem is cover'd flat,
with a bright and yellow hat.

Little Mary as you pass,
step gently over the tender grass,
Skip about, and do not tread
on my bright and pretty head.

Bettina To

The Quest

A vision slowly rises
On a foggy, blue horizon;
Comes a man with eyes of fire,
Secret whisper, one desire;
Captivating all with stories,
Buried treasure, conquests, glories,
Far countries, bloody battles,
Royal brains he has rattled;
Nearly slain, but by a breath,
Eluded twice the jaws of death;
Spears the night in youthful ardor,
Careful not to play the martyr;
Slaying vice with saving grace,
But years of torment line his face;
He breathes his last, his soul at rest
Finds the object of his quest.

Janet Pringle

Shadow Lover

All night I lay and wait.
When I'm about to fall in
to a slumber, someone awakes
me. I look into his baby blue
eyes and I melt into his arms.
He carries me outside and lays
me on a soft bed of rose petals.
He lays beside me and whispers
in my ears how beautiful I am
and how he will always love me.
Then he leans over and kisses
me so softly and gently. I wish
this to never end, but everything
comes to an end. He carries me
back and gentility lays me in my
bed. Kisses me and disappears.

Melissa Matovski

The Night

The night is dark,
but also bright.
The moon and stars
make the light.

The night is black,
and all so weary.
I look around,
and around and around.

In the night I get so scared,
cuddled up in my bed.
I wonder why the night is so.
I guess I'll never know.

Michael DeMato

Mold Me, Lord

Oh God, I am so tired
and have failed so often too.
Why is it so hard for me
to stay humble and look to You?
Although my heart's desire
is to trust You implicitly.
Don't you have an easy way,
a plan of pure simplicity?
Isn't that just like me, Father
to want the easy way out.
However, from the past, I know
that's not what life's about.
I know You want me to struggle
and let You finally take control.
Because then, and only then
can You truly make me whole.

Patti Bibel

Muscles From A Shell

For as I walk,
I also seek,
For this passion,
Buried oh so deep.

It's nothing that's explainable
I don't know what to say,
I feel my body quiver,
When I think of her in that way.

From the moment she approaches,
Till the time she fades away,
I feel this hunger everywhere,
But it just won't go away.

So from dusk till dusk,
And dawn till dawn
I guess I will go on searching
For that princess in my dreams.

But if this is a dream,
And I should awake,
I hope she remembers,
I'm for her, to take!

Todd P. Danni

The Sybil

She stretched out for him.
His absence echoed her chimera.
Then —
the hand cast its shadow,
and a silent stroke
held back
her last bunch of lies —
unworthy.
The chain broke.
For a moment
its shivering rustling
tore the Time
through a long instant of indecision.
Then —
the cage crashed,
and her ashes shook off.

Elisa C. Ravella

Time

Time the enemy
Time the friend.
So will it ever be
Time without end.

Adelaide G. Cole

Dream Solace

. . . And if I ever get the chance,
And if it should come by
So many things that I have learned
No matter how I try —
This sage knowledge I have attained
I've garnered much too late
Though now I've let you see inside,
The past has sealed my fate.
And it's like I have awoken
And my thoughts are all anew
Though I realize, it took too long
For you to share my view.
And I hope that you are happy
And I hope you're never sad
And though now, there's no connection
That we touched, still makes me glad.
And if there is, no way to fix
What is beyond repair
Then as we sleep beneath the same sky
In my dreams — please be there.

Michael V. Morizzo

dress me not

why do you dress me
in black
and . . .
why do you dress me
in black
when you know I am a rainbow

when you know
I have become forever
whole and eternally fulfilled

when you know
I have become forever
complete joy and love

why do you dress me
in black
when you know
I am now uniquely in your heart
as an undying resplendent rainbow

if you dress me as a rainbow
I will forever be
your bridge to tomorrow

richard armstrong scheyer

Mom

You fall down,
hit the ground,
see some blood
and start to frown.
You scream and cry,
it starts to hurt,
your mouth is dry
cause it's full of dirt.
You are scared,
your knee is throbbing,
you are hurt,
you start sobbing.
Mom comes running
out the door
and comes and kisses
your bloody sore.
You can count on your mom
every minute of the day
to kiss your sores
and take the pain away.

Glenn Snider

Memories Of Love

Vivid colors of the rainbow
Slowly fading into the blue sky
Like memories of love
One thought could never die

I struggle to hold those colors
in my mind
but there is no sunshine
from your smile,
no ray of love
from your eyes
Only memories of love
one thought could never die.
I sit alone with fading memories
and I thank God, that in their place
is a blue blue sky.

Lu Rose Lacovino

The Hunter

The Hunter is a Prince,
or maybe King.
To whom all will bow,
become prey.
To fear is to paralyze.
To accept, life.
Appease the Hunter
and torment waves.
Defy, tranquil peace.
Though all succumb
to the Hunter's rule.
The defiant,
the victor will be.

James G. Bender

Nancy Ann

Colleen wants to know, Nancy Ann,
About your brief life.
Was it happy or filled with strife?
Your short life! Your short span!

Did you merrily go
Unforeseeing the future?
Or was it knife and suture?
Or did you not know?

These are questions we ask.
Such a great desire
To know of the dead fire
Which now remains as Ash.

We ask the unanswerable.
We hope you will be forgivable
For our prying,
For your dying!
Nancy Ann! Nancy Ann!

George B. Viele

Nature Made

Choir of the fire
Melody of the birds that sing
Caressing moon upon me
Loving . . . leaving . . . heat
For the wind then soothes me
Melting down . . . anything
Then gently she rises
The sun
Kissing my lips
Moisture forming
As I taste what nature made
Forever more

Brenda A. Coleman

Solemn Oath

When I wasn't looking
You came along
You took me dancing
We shared a song
Together we walked
And shared our past
While we talked
I hoped it would last
You told me you cared
That night in the park
You opened and shared
Your feelings in the dark
You made me want to stay
Forever in your arms
Never going away
And never being harmed
Now what we feel
Is special to us both
So let's keep it real
With this solemn oath: "I love you"

Julie A. Zemke

Freedom's Key

Heavy chains are weighing me down.
I feel like I'm going to drown.
Got to get loose, must get free.
Can't let this feeling overcome me.
Where's the key to open this lock?
The time is ticking on the clock.
An angelic voice I can hear,
Telling me he is always near.
He has the key to set me free,
If I have the faith to believe.
"Believe in what?" Ran through my head.
In Jesus Christ raised from the dead.
He is the key to set you free.
He won't let you down, guarantee.
Put your life in Jesus' hand
Let him be in total command.
These chains can not keep you bound,
When his love and grace you have found.
Go ahead before times runs out.
You have the key, no need to doubt.

Julie A. Gehman

Birth Control

Whenever the topic of abortion comes up
people talk about the right to choose
but no matter what decision you make
someone is going to lose

There never would be a decision
if you use birth control
not to mention over population
which should also be a goal

Think of all the children
abandoned in this world
it will break your heart
and make your stomach curl

This is a message to
men and women alike
before engaging in sex
think about the little Tyke

If you practice birth control
the world would be a better place
and it would solve so many problems
for this. Our human race

Sue Johnston

Time

The years go by.
A rush and bustle of confusion.
No time to sigh.

The children leave.
The years of going shatter fusion.
The time to cleave.

The quiet years.
One final loss completes diffusion.
The time of tears.

Now all is gone.
The love and laughter seem illusion.
But life goes on.

Jean Blood

Untitled

The beauty of women
is the nature of life
I see the lightness of the
Blueness of her eyes as
I face the day goes
on, the light of the dawn
goes on with blueness of
her eyes.

I saw the scenes
of a jail that I was
sentenced to without
a godless trial
I blast the days
through dramatic
experience
wish I was born
with living or dead

David Brenner

Chilly Tornado

As she floats out
On the flowing breeze
You can't quit your care
So beautiful.
Wishing more fragrant breezes
So much that you stare
Being entranced here
And she's there
While the mountain cold encloses
Making people cease their vacation
On another breeze
Ignore and watch the escape
Is easy some say
Mingling with the hardening clay
As the clay forever shows itself
In the already past upcoming days
When you go there
Finding she's everywhere.

Carl D. Schultz

Why

Mother can you tell me why,
any child should need to cry?
Can you help me shed some light,
on why we humans have to fight?
Can you make me understand,
why some people rape the land?
Mother please, I cannot wait,
tell me, why do people hate?
And Mother can you help me see,
what it has to do with me?

Sabra Ray

For George Cobb, My Dad

My life is almost over
you see I have no fears.
God will come and take my hand
and wipe away my tears.
My life has been a good one.
I couldn't ask for more.
It's been full of love and laughter
as I opened up each door.
Sometimes we had bad times,
and sad times we have shared.
Good times overtook them all
because my family cared.
Don't cry now I'm at rest
Just smile and go your way
For I'll walk slow and wait for you.
See you another day.
We'll meet again in Heaven,
and happiness will be
as good as it was here on earth,
all my loved ones and me.

Gloria Townsend

A Thought

Although tonite I sit alone,
Tomorrow I shall rise
And don a gown of scarlet silk
And paint my mouth and eyes.
I'll toss aside my woes and cares
And dine and dance and wine;
And break the hearts of all you men,
Because a man broke mine.

Norma J. Davis

In The Shadows

I stand in the shadows every day
No one listens to what I say
No one asks if I want to play
All they say is 'go away'
I'm all alone in the dark
In the cold windy shadows of the park
I know I should — but I don't mind
It's part of my heart I hope to find
And then — there it is
What I've been looking for
It's like luck knocked at my door
What I've been looking for is you
And then it hit me
You were looking for me too.

Kelly Lynn Ross

Feelings

Your eyes are so deep,
deep with much emotion,
Yet your mind keeps it tight
All bottled up inside.
To see you smile,
Is to see your soul.
Your physic is so strong
Your presence is so dear,
So wanted
So needed
So be it near.
To think of you as I do
Is to want to know you as I could
To make you feel the way you need
To be fulfilled only by me,
Is the way I want it to be.

Sherry L. Frederick

The Thief

The house where I grew up,
all the comforts of home,
but the woman who lives there
is now an unknown.

To stretch to arms length
but be just out of reach,
a lifetime of memories
I would love to reteach.

The sweet gift of life
can be such a cruel thing;
when the body can dance
but the soul cannot sing.

Blank stares, no affection,
is now all I find,
a disease left her body
but has taken her mind.

Age is the culprit;
alzheimer, the thief,
pray for life pray for death,
on which road is relief?

Lois E. Bailey

Downfall

I turn my head,
    I don't want to see
        What you've become,
        I refuse to believe.

        The one thing I saw
            that I could not deny
            The look in your eyes
            That fourth of July
            At the carnival
                Where the lights dance
                I met you there,
                    purely by chance.

I gasped
    I stared
    I knew
It was all wasted.
    So many dreams, so many hopes
        All thrown away
            Not much I can do
            I can just pray.

Abby Lea Pickens

A Note For Mama

How I wish I could remember
those nights of lullabies;
when you cradled me to sleep
and kissed me good night.

Your voice so sweet and tender
caressing me to sleep;
in your arms safe and warm
I had no fear of the night.

Your love has kept me strong
all through my days.
Your constant prayer
and your loving care
will be my joy forever.

Mama, I remember still
your gentle hand on mine;
when you kissed me and said
Goodbye.

Patricio R. De Los Reyes Jr.

The Turnabout

I remember as a youngster
My mother saying to me
"Take time to visit Grandma
She so enjoys your company,"
I had the best of intentions
But friends and plans got in the way
I can only hope for her forgiveness
For the shame I feel today.

Now that I'm a Grandma
And am in a Nursing Home
Time has a way of standing still
For I feel very much alone,
There's nothing I can really say
To my very busy family
But in my heart the turnabout
Has really come home to me.

Jean E. Hayes

Friendship Begins In A Garden Of Roses

Roses, Roses everywhere,
    yellow, pink and red.
Look and see how beautiful
    They make a flower bed.

I care for them morning,
    noon and night.
So we can all enjoy
    them and smell them with delight.

The gardens is a sight to behold,
    As we watch them bloom,
they will need more room
    to share their beauty and color.

Friendship forms in a rose garden,
    no other can compare.
With thoughts and lot's of memories
    If only I could be there.

They bring great joy and happiness.
    The lasts forever and ever.
We give thanks to God above
    To show us such great love.

Kalynn Michelle Miller

American In Paris

The music was very nice,
the show was still going on,
when he arrived with a friend,
she was going home.

He took the cab to come,
faster than the wind,
she was a dancer,
she got a free drink.

Both together in Paris,
Paris is a dream,
champagne, caviar, Monseigneur,
dreams in a dream.

New York, Paris, heart to heart,
the roses for a gift,
they fell in love with the wind,
Paris is in a dream.

Life is like a painting,
believe it or not,
they are still together,
loving each other just as strong.

Ljubica Straus

The Beautiful U.S.A.

Our country and our nation,
Depend of young generation.
Every night and every day,
I pray for our U.S.A.

From the South to the North
From the East to the West,
Our beautiful U.S.A.
Is always the best.

I like our fifty states
From the bottom of my heart,
Forty Eight are together
Other two are apart.

You and me, you and me,
We like our capital Washington D.C.
Every night and every day,
I pray for our beautiful U.S.A.

Mike Solunac

Tresses Golden Round

Your hair is special to me
tresses falling golden round
spilling onto your shoulders bare
it is remarkable
the attention I give
to running small strands
delicate around my fingers
you pose a questioning look
with your eyes fixed
steadily on mine
I just love your hair
specially when I feel you mine
announcing it
with your flowering
shade rare

Brett A. Holloway

Poem For Future Poets

This
is a
mechanical
poem.

It can
walk run
teach
play ball
ball
ball.

A sundown
of stiff
starch
words.

Jerry Jenkins

My Protector

The evil makes me shiver,
The danger makes me quiver,
My stomach churns,
My senses burn,
I'm scared of what I cannot see,
Fear is stalking me,
Suddenly my terror fades,
Why should I be afraid?
Heaven is above me,
    and His arms are beneath me.

Stefanie Spitilli

The Mists Of Dawn

Tall trees reaching for the sky while
Gray mist hangs between the leaves.
In the silence of dawn, I hear the
    sparkle of dewdrops.

Light flashes . . .
And in the wonder of that moment
    I see a rainbow of color
And know the pain of too much joy.

In my frozen lens of timelessness
A gentle doe raises her head . . .
    a rabbit pauses,
And in that moment we know
    that we are One.

Mary Horan

Holocaust

Back in the past
    there was a holocaust.
People were killed
    and family members lost.

Both father and brother
    were worked to their death.
And child and mother
    were beaten and wrecked.

There were death camps
    and a gas chamber.
But that's for the people
    who couldn't do labor.

Be thankful you weren't alive
    to see all this terror.
You could have died
    or lived to remember.

Dannielle French

Gabriella

There is a God, this I know,
for on the day you were born the
winds did blow.
    The sun did shine and the
stars were bright.
    For the first time in my life
I felt what heaven must be
like.
    For on that day my life did
change,
    Everything I thought important,
all got rearranged.
    I think back to that day, I
saw you take your first breathe
your very first puff.
    And now I truly realize that
once you have touched heaven,
you can never get enough.

Patrick Panella

In My Life

In my life, I can't stand to fall,
by being content that I have it all;
when life and death is o so real,
there is no wonder that I feel;
don't disrespect men for man,
when men will;
but man don't understand;
in my life! Without strife.

Menieli Meli Inin

Flame

I
Now
Fighting
To burn
This light
Within me
Glowing
A stinging flame
One burning candle
Upon slamming doors
Icy air in deathly gusts
And chill of rain sent to snuff
This light within me,
Glowing.
And in my heart,
A flame,
Integrity brings
Brilliance.

Stephanie Mitchell

Last Time

He was there,
So was I,
At the right place,
At the wrong time,
My mind said don't do it,
My heart said go ahead,
How could I still love him,
After all he said.
He was the one I fell in love with,
And the one who broke my heart.
I just can't stop myself,
I have to take part.
So I go out to see him,
It happened once again,
My heart is broken,
And I ache once again.

Alison Gravley

Ocean

Floating on a saline current
heading towards the infinite blue
a void were elements collect to become.
A whirlpool - a house
different rooms,
different doors,
different windows.
Quietude interrupted
contained inhabitants perceive essence
creating different speeches
emphatic symbols overlapping
hieroglyphic distortion
throughout continuum
Announcing The Arrival.

L. Moreno

This Country Road

To pass down this country road
Sends me back to somewhere
I've never been before
In some other life,
I suppose
The leaves move aside
For our car to reach the destination
That brings us messages
Of other worlds

Shannon Lawless

Questions That Need Answers

How can I love you?
Is this what you ponder?
If I tried to hold your hand . . .
Would you sit and wonder?

You said you haven't reflected,
the relationships of my past.
But you shouldn't have neglected,
my presence in spite of my past.

The questions that you ask,
require answers I don't have.
So I'm taking off this mask,
questioning the answers that I have.

Why do you wonder?
Is it fear of my trust?
Why should you bother?
To deposit faith in my trust.

Where is your answer?
I'm trying to find it.
Why should you need this answer?
Are you so blinded?

Frank Kane

To Love God

To love God
   is to be loved
To be loved
   is to be happy
To be happy
   is to be at peace
And peace is the center
   of life

Jay Kern

Loved One's Decease

You were my loved one
You'll still always be,
I'll never forget you
I hope you won't forget me.

We fought sometimes
We disagreed,
But I'll still always love you
I know I will.

Since this is our last day
my heart you'll still be a piece,
But hey what could I say
This is a Loved One's Decease.

Linda Berti

Forever

Love can live forever
   unlike me and you
Love remains forever
   as only it can do
I will love forever
   a love fresh and new
Love that lasts forever
   bold and strong and true
We have loved forever
   we the lucky two
A love that lasts forever
   that time cannot subdue
This love will live forever
   between me and you
And we will live forever
   in our love so true

Melissa Harrison

The World Is My Home

The world is my home
The sun is my warmth
The grass is my bed
The tree is my shelter

The world is my home
The bird is my song
The flower is my scent
The rain is my growth

The world is my home
The star is my knowledge
The moon is my light
The wind is my spirit
The world is my home

Paula Franklin

Masquerade

The face has changed
The mask is ugly,
Tarnished.

The fish seem nice
They do not bite,
Yet.

Being someone else
Nobody knows this,
Never will.

The whole world is gone
Caught in a flash puddle,
Drowned.

Chicks are dead in the kitchen
Can't blast off to adventure,
No fuel.

Do not keep the mask
Think about the fish,
Migrate.

Karre Overkamp

Truth

Where is truth?
She went out to play with wisdom
And got caught in doubt.

Where is doubt?
With unbelief.

Where is unbelief?
In the pits of darkness,
The shades of night.

Alice May Bookout

My Bicycle

I like to ride my bicycle
I ride it all day long
Around the curves and up the hills
It makes me feel so strong.

The fresh air blowing on my face
The scenery gliding by
The pedals spinning round and round
I feel like I can fly.

Then in the evening when back home
Beginning to feel sorrow
I close my eyes and think with joy,
I'll ride again tomorrow!

Tim McClelland

Dare To Dream

Dare ye dream,
while reality's awake?
Call it noble,
the chance you take?
Give some time for
reality to sleep.
Then escape to dream land,
and your dreams you'll keep.
Reality is torture;
it'll ruin the mind.
I'll go on dreamin',
while I have the time.
It is a risk,
I'll take that chance.
The danger makes
the dream enhanced.

J. Edward McNeill

Season

White, brown, and gray
crispy cold
blaring sun

emotional state
Having no peoples once
having it all again

Trees and gifts
Coming together with art

lead by a master
time to let your muscles go

Sip, smoke, and consume
guiltless

Reflect and compare
the beauty of a family.

How do I call you,
Brother, Sister, Teacher, Friend

Who are we?
All together

Peace of mind for all our suffering
Respect, love

Gavin Markiet

Untitled

Mothers are a special breed
God gives to each a like
Sometimes it's an awesome task
when you've a little tike

Each mother has a special job
given lovingly by God
To lead her children down a path
that she has never trod

The dangers, snares and many curves
are an ever present foe
and with no map or guarantee
which way is she to go . . .

But of all the mothers in the world
God chose you for me
He knew that you would shape me
into the woman I was to be

So, I thank you for your constant care
your wisdom from above
your wondrous way of teaching me
that I am free to love.

Teresa Elkins

A Child's Pain

Though life may not be fair,
and at times your pain is great;
While you feel all hope is gone,
and tragic seems your fate.

Remember it's within yourself,
that all the answers lie;
To help release your hurt and pain,
allow yourself to cry.

Every tear that you hold in,
will only turn to rage;
Yet all the hurt will stay inside,
no matter what your age.

Allow yourself the time to grieve,
for all the loss you feel;
From infancy up till now,
your hurt inside is real.

Please give yourself the comfort,
you'd show to a child in pain;
You have to learn to love yourself,
before you can hope again.

Mickie T. West

Imperfect Mirrors, Distorted Reflections

Tighter, tighter
tighter.
Rules, mysterious dictates
given without regard.

Compress, compress
compress.
Shapes and forms and
definitions that won't fit.

Smaller, smaller
smaller.
Childhood diminished, then denied,
denied.
Adulthood undefined.

Ill-fitting, ill-feeling.

Striving, striving
striving.
She must always
walk her path in
shadow, never in light.

Scott R. Bartl

Stone Temple

Stone temple in the stream,
still.

As petals flow
with fallen feathers to this site,
a quiet mirror.

Pebbles, a constructed shore,
a slim shoal
where no one treads.

A bird's wing strikes
the stillness of a pond:
A silent cymbal,
liquid rings,
marking time,
growing outward,
a fading imprint
of the hour.

Lois B. Cooper

Dreaming

Did you forget how to dream
or do you know how
do you know that dreams
breed hope and unity
and a wish for harmless togetherness
How things could be because of a dream
a life of warmth
a life of peace from within
a life where love erases pain
a life where support rubs out isolation
Dream to touch the sky
Dreams becoming a reality
Dreaming for the future
Dreaming for life

Wendella Van Rossum

Song Of The Sea

On warm golden sand
I dreamed by the sea
As laughter sparkled water
Danced all around me
I captured a beautiful seashell
Tumbling through the spray
And held it very close
To hear what it would say
It sang softly to me
An aria of the deep
Of mermaids' escapades
And lost sailors' sleep
Of ancient treasures buried
Amid skeleton ship graves
Lost, lost forever . . .
Below icy emerald waves
My soul fell enchanted
By that lonely song
Adrift forever within me
It plays on and on and on

Jerri Mohr

My Best Friend

I will always love my teddy bear
I take him with me everywhere
He sits beside me on my swing
We laugh and talk of everything

Sometimes when I am sad and cry
I see a teardrop in his eye
But when I'm happy as can be
He turns his head and smiles at me

Sometimes at night when I'm in bed
I turn and pat his fuzzy head
It's nice to know he's always there
My favorite friend, my teddy bear

M. Jean Heine

Unforgotten One

It broke our hearts to lose you
But you did not go alone.
For part of us went with
you the morning God called
you home.
A precious one from us has
gone, a voice we love is
stilled. A place is vacant
in our hearts which never
can be filled.

Lena McClendon

Father Time

It seems You come calling
In funny little lines
At the moment of life
You rush in with Time . . .

Tho we don't appreciate You
Or the passing of Your signs
Till the clock says we're late
And we've run out of Time . . .

Yet People are so funny
Trying to capture Your rhyme
To be just like You
Young all the Time . . .

Hidden in Your secrets
It's we who are so blind
We can't see aged beauty
We want Young Father Time . . .

But the ages are so beautiful
Filled with treasures I find
Walking through the Ages
With Old Father Time . . .

Connie Ivous Caldwell

The Pessimist

Dreams are self-destructive,
    Hopes will only mislead.
Happiness is fleeting,
    Pain pushes it aside.
Love is just a myth,
    You get who you do not annoy.
Faith is for the naïve,
    Trust is always betrayed.
Confidence is pointless,
    Someone is always better.
People never stay,
    The party always dies.
Solitude is forever,
    One man, one soul.

W. Michael Alden

Jumping On The Bed

We jump, jump, jump
Up in the air
We never stop
We just don't care.
Our Mommy yells
For us to quit
But we don't hear
'Cause we're just kids.

Erin Barr

Emptiness

Alone and scared
Nowhere to turn
Nowhere to hide
To let the emptiness go bye
There is a world of empty lost souls
    out of control
Looking for that outlet of some
    hope
To show them the way to a fuller
    and more exciting life
To take away the emptiness of the
    lost hope they feel inside

Stephanie Pingel

America

America, America!
Land of the free,
Our forefathers fought,
And struggled for liberty.

America, America!
Land of the free,
Where justice prevails
In a democracy.

America, America!
Land of the free,
With freedom of speech,
And brotherhood with equality.

America, America!
Land of the free,
Regardless who you are,
'Tis a land of opportunity.

America, America!
Land of the free,
Free to worship God,
As each of us see.

Mildred Zimbelman

A Child

I didn't mean for it to
    happen, Mr. Sir.
Please, try to hide
you are like me, your son
Air sealed that with lust. A
kiss was involved, (Maybe one or two.)
Under a tyrant blue abyss full
off stars and needles, it was
better than any dream I'd
ever had yelling and screaming
at the punk walls of his ears.
Please, don't cry Mr. Sir.
He would laugh at you right
now, your son's wishes are bastards,
yes, I know. They stay in memories to
far for us to imagine and far more
closer then we want to realize.
He told me,
your son

Katie Smith

I'm Painting Pictures

The night is black as ebon
Not a star is shining through;
But not my mind I'm painting —
The sky is always azure blue.

Beneath the skies of summer
Lie the mountains reaching high
To touch God's heavens gently,
Up there where eagles fly.

I can hear the breezes whisper
As they dance among the pines,
They tell me God still loves me
As I paint pictures in my mind.

I will paint my children playing,
Their happy laughter I can hear
As I recall those memories
That are a part of yesteryears.

Yes, I am painting happy mem'ries
And all darkness leave behind;
I will remember only happiness
As I paint pictures in my mind.

Lillian O. Long

Confessions

Could there be a sound
sweeter than your name
Whispered in your ear
screaming out in pain

Could there be a scent
softer than your breath
Escaping from your lips
buried in my neck

Could there be a touch
stronger than your kiss
Holding my attention
resting on my lips

Could there be a time
more powerful than now
Consuming every moment
no question as to how

Tami Jones

Him

So much I cannot say
Thy heart full of unspoken thought
The love in which thou portray
From it cannot be bought

Two lives in transform
Extinguishing lonesome pain
Thou was sent to calm thy storm
Believing truly this be thou gain

This love is as the earth
The honor of receiving
This is promise oh, so true
Natural as self its birth
Flown down from believing
Still only to say, I love you.

Linda Stout

Lonely

Lonely, I am lonely.
He is gone and
I am lost.
I am without direction.
He became the focus of my life.
I pulled from his strength
and got energy from his smiles.
Now I am alone and lonely,
how painful, how hurtful.

Patricia M. O'Toole

God's World

A stroll through the woods on an
early spring morn, gives such
a peace within that it makes one
feel like one in being with God.
The smell of the earth, the birds
singing, the sun shining through
the budding trees, the little animals
chasing each other in the light of a
new day, and to witness the cycle
of birth and death in a little
corner of God's world, showed
me that no matter if the sun
shines or the rain falls, giving
of ones self and living every
moment to the fullest, in hard
times as well as good, is a true act
of love.

Delphine Kondrat

To Buster

Buster is my favorite cat
  Because he is so soft.
Buster is gray and black
  And a little white.
Buster is a long haired cat
  And he snores a lot.
Buster has a gray nose
  And green brown eyes.
Buster has pink ears
  And white tippy toes.
Buster is so cute that
  I just want to hug him.
Buster sleeps so soundly
  Until sassy pounces on him.
Buster is a little pudgy but
  That only makes me love his
  Little Tummy.
Buster is a peaceful sleeper
  And quite good at it.

Dezarai B. Fisher

Fine Wine

I'm submerged in your essence;
Your presence produces pure bliss.
For a kiss from your perfect plush lips
I would give up my life;
Any type sacrifice would suffice
For your spice, meaning flavor.
You bring out behavior
That some would call naughty;
Thank God that you taught me
Love is what matters the most.
So for you, Love,
I raise up this toast.

J. Griot

Death And The New Life

Death comes after life
Then gives birth to life
Our life
The new life
The new dimension

Death for mew life
It comes for all
For life is to die and still live

Death and the eternal life
Living death as life
Death makes angels of us all
And gives us wings
Smooth as ravens' claws

Brad Johnston

Cigarettes

The only thing I have
are my cigarettes.
They are there when
I go to bed, they are
there when I wake.

Only my life
can these cigarettes take.
Breath filled with pain,
smoke rings of sorrow.

The only thing I have
are my cigarettes for
tomorrow.

Chad Meachum

Sounds And Feelings

Went to the county shore
Never come back for another 3 years
wanted to stay so much more

Hear the waves crashing on the rocks
almost hitting the very large docks
Hear the wind roar
while it brings the waves a shore
Sitting in the sun
having a whole lot of fun
Watch the moon
hopefully not at noon
Sitting at the edge of the land
on a whole bunch of sand
Jumping in the water
is better than a whole quarter
I'd like to win a raffle
but I rather be building
a great big sand castle

Jessica Basso

I'm Fine

You ask me how I'm doing
Well, I'm doing fine
Got a little ache
In this head of mine.
Must be this weather,
And for better weather I beg
It might get rid
Of this pain in my leg.
My stomach is empty.
I'm hungry as a bear.
I really need some food.
Just anything, I don't care.
And it's been a busy day,
Not one of my best.
I am so tired,
I need a little rest.

Joyce M. Frederick

New World Orders

Hazy greyness hanging around,
steely sharp neon lightning future.
Methodical relentless cycle,
darkly shadowing into a season unknown,
quietly tracking thru the universe.
Padding world, a bear on crystal snow.
Eternal void so coldly observing
the passage of eons.

Scott Levi List

Untitled

Albeit dark skies
rivers of light belie

A calyx forms in tide
camelot takes
soul in bide

Companions bear an order
of knighthood
Raise the light from darkness
Cover the soul in lightness

All are gone the sadness
joy before man, came
with light.
Raise your face and
see your life.

Albert H. Beck

Tornado

A tornado picks up stuff on the
ground and throws it down. It rains
and blows and lightening goes around
and around until it is done and then it
goes away.

Run it will get you!

Robbie Hixenbaugh

The Last Rose Of Summer

In the latter part of October
  a rose faded on the vine.
It was the last rose of summer
  This precious mother of mine.
God has a special place in Heaven
  For the last fading rose.
Where it will live and bloom again
  In a garden where it grows.
It will meet with loved ones again
  a place of no pain and sorrow.
They will rejoice together
  Forever and tomorrow.
Until we meet again someday
  and never more shall part.
I'll remember this fading rose
  always in my heart.

Myrtle Ballow

Stormy Weather

On stormy days I like to sit
upon the beach nearby
and listen to the ocean roar
invectives at the sky,
as shrieking winds dive from above
with terrifying might
to scare the waves that lie below
until their hair turns white.
I like to watch the sky turn black
with rage and then reply
by shooting off her long-range guns
with such a practiced eye.
At first I see the powder flash
and then I hear the sound.
It seems so loud that I am sure
it's heard the world around.
And then the sky bombards the main
with raindrops for its shot
until the sun returns once more
to end this warlike plot.

Lester I. Leonard

Shattered

  A baseball strikes a window pane,
this is what it's like to be insane.
  Fragments dropping everywhere,
as you fall into despair.
  Like a spider web it breaks,
wondering how much you can take.
  Life is limited to the confines,
to the world inside your mind.
  You become an empty shell,
while watching all the glass that fell.
  While picking up the broken glass,
you remember all your past.
  Broken pieces here and there,
as you have an empty stare.
  At the shattered window pane,
broken memories still remain.

Bart T. Brennecke

324

Portal

The angry stirrings
of remembered accusations
fester
like an unhealed sore.
A deep wound
that eats away at
my flesh.
Go ahead! Cover it over
with sweet smelling antiseptic.
Hide it from memory
with beatific muse.
I'm the one who will bare
the scar . . .
a heinous cicatrix
from your cancerous touch . . .
    touched . . .
touching.

        Always touching.
        Jeanne M. Morrison

Mother, I Honor You

Through hurtful birth pangs
Sorrow and tears
Mothers have birthed
Many through the years

They are God's appointed
Vessels of birth
That keeps replenishing
Man's seed on the earth

It was through birth pangs
God let Jesus in
So he could redeem
And atone every sin

So, on this Mother's Day
Let me give you your due
For all the birth pangs
Mother, I honor you
        Sam Weaver

Self-Portrait

Jubilant
On top of things
He is a nice guy
Not a jerk.

Very good grades
Emanates "good" (I hope)
Radically weird
Obvious
Nearsighted.
        John Veron

A Truck Is A Duck

A truck is a duck
With four wheels
But no beak.

A duck is a truck
Without wheels
But two feet.

Each honks and each waddles
And they sound
Quite the same.

A truck is a duck
With two letters
To blame.

        Diane Young Uniman

God, Make Me Your Soldier

Make me your soldier
Prepare me to fight
Send me to battle
What lies out of my sight

Arm me with wisdom
Strength and peace from above
And walk with me daily
In thy perfect love

Let no man destroy me
Please sharpen my eyes
By faith, let me handle
Whatever may arise

Teach me the knowledge
Of what's good and what's right
Then I'll be your soldier
I'll be ready to fight
        Stacey Rainey

Petals In The Snow

What's my destiny, what's my fate
I'm awake now
I think I'm too late
As I arise — I feel renewed,
But as seasons change
I lose the mood
Here in life — I must stay
I wonder, always
Will it be this way
Tomorrow opens — as a new day now
happiness fading
please stay somehow
Now I understand, it becomes so clear
My life is gone
without you here
Petals fall
red, in the snow
you turn away and start to go
Do you see me, please turn around
Tears turn to ice, as they trickle down
        Melanie F. Vicknair

Sports

Brave basketball
Famous football
Serious soccer
Memories from the hospital.
        Taylor Hale

Inexplicable

Why do some of us, momentarily
    forget about God.
Yet He's the first one we
    cry out to,
When we're desperately in need.
Save him! Save him! You must —
    Save him, my heart yelled.
There was silence, as the doc
    tried to find a vein.
Then it happened!
His head slumped back, and
    fluid drained from his little mouth.
Then there was darkness, as I
    fell to the ground.
It was over.
My baby was gone too soon.
And deep down, I knew a part
    of me, was gone too.
        Yvonne Daye

Enormous Iron Petals

Enormous iron petals
floating in the cool breeze
of the now ending day
with a twilight setting in,
washing over the rusted metal
turning it a golden
sheen of pleasure.
I hammered it home,
made to withstand any hammer's blow
and mold to that heat
corrupting of our eyes.
A tingle,
a jingle
in the night as the petals
chime the hour of witching.
Tonight I do not hear them
without a word to my mistress
for they were made for her adoration
and my ears.

        Tim P. DiMiceli

Childhood

A poet writes
and his words
send childhood pictures
racing through my mind.

Scenes long past: Hot summer days,
lazy creeks, crayfish skittering
backward away from
probing fingers.

Sun-drenched hours,
lazy afternoons in cool woods.
Swinging on grapevine swings,
resting in moss-covered lean-tos.
Initials carved high in pine trees
Surprises for a future climber.

Childhood . . . memories of
loved ones gone.
Now
I help my grandchildren
make memories.
        Shirley G. Turner

Weather!

Drippy! Droppy! Noisy! Loud!
Monsoons are coming down
Hurricanes are starting now
So crazy crash! Boom!
It's really loud
Oh My Gosh!
The tidal wave, from the hurricane is
coming towards me
I've got to go
And by the way someone help me
Because I'm drowning
Gulp!
Gulp!
Gulp!
Gulp!
Gulp!

        Hope Fisher

My Mom

My mom is always there for me,
she helps me when I need help.
My mom loves me no matter what I do.
My mom will always be my friend.
        Melissa Spencer

For Karl

Planted in my body;
a seed of love.
You
my son.
A gift from God.
Life has been
questioning my body,
my soul, my mind,
my ability to deal.
My seed has been
planted many a time;
and yet you are
my only.
A gift from God.
Love of my Life
Life of my Love.

Veronica Scott

Do You Hear?

Do you hear
The sound of my cry
Howling out in the dark
Do you hear
The sound of my heart
Breaking apart
Do you hear
The sound of my soul
Drifting away
Do you hear
The sound of my mind
Screaming in pain

Natalie Wiberg

Untouchable Memories

I love you so
How much you'll never know
If you went away
My life, it'd be filled with rainy days
Untouchable memories
Are those you can't let go
I want to let you know
That I will never let you go
I don't know how to express
The love I feel for you
except to say a few things
I love you and you are appreciated
For everything you do.

Tiffany Peterson

My Christmas Wish

If I woke up on Christmas morning
and found you under my tree,
all tied up in tinsel and bows.
How happy I would be.
I'd thank dear old Santa Claus.
For sending you to me,
if I woke upon Christmas morning
and found you under my tree

Roger W. Giffin

Jealousy

Jealousy is a knife
It stabs people in the back
Cutting off friendships
Piercing people's hearts
slicing up their lives.

Heather Quirk

Blessings

Always, when I pray
My burdens, seems relieved
And that's, when I know
There was, a blessing, I received

Dear Lord, I thank thee
Each and every day.
For always, being with me
To guide me, along the way

When pains, of my worrying
Somehow seem to cease,
I know though a blessing
Has brought, enduring peace

You've more than protected me
As I travelled, through life's way
So I want to thank you for
The blessings, I got today

Charles E. Taylor

Second Chance

A memory rings
And time's erased
In velvet dreams
My fortune's place

A bitter fruit
Sometimes regains
The sweetness lost
From love's refrain

How will I know
If past is past
The answer's lost
'less the question asked

And if the answer's
Not the one
That parts the clouds
Lets in the sun
Then I am where
I started from
Two divided
Equals one

Jeff Stratton

One Special Wish

I think of you often,
   more often than not
memories are flowing,
   in them I am caught.
No other person is like
   you I know
and the feeling I have
   is you're watching below.
You're up there in heaven
   with God side by side
Knowing this, Mom
   really fills me with pride.
There's no coming back,
   of course we all know
But someday I'll see you
   when heaven I go.
If I had one wish
   I know it would be,
To see you again
   Just you and me.

Kathy Moreau

summer

The summer fades,
and the winter sets in.
I stand alone outside
bearing the cold, cold wind.
A desolate view
of the future to come,
would be nothing more
than apathy to some.
But I have a different view
of the future to come.
Because between those
dark, heavy clouds,
brightly shining
lies the sun.
For I know deep down inside,
through all the howling of the wind,
the snow will melt
and the sun will shine,
and it will be summer once again.

Trevor Brown

Farewell Is But An Illusion!

A time of juncture looms near
And wishing not bid farewell;
Rather to give thanks for friends
And acquaintances as well.

Perchance we'll stop a moment,
When fellow spirits we see.
On occasion that we touch,
A special time, will this be.

Into these heart-strings came few,
Bringing life-change in short while;
Soft words, kind gestures — the keys,
For one, her delicate smile!

You few who tugged these life-threads
In heart's hidden chambers deep.
Forever, you're now part of me,
Memories . . . precious — I keep.

Raymond D. Miller Jr.

The Sale

Down the twisted, darkish path,
Chasing dreams from years gone past,
Long and cloudy corridors,
From every crevice horror pours,
Wishes wasted, hopes denied,
Endless despair multiplied.

Down the tangled lanes of fate,
Illuminate, illuminate.
Pay the price, your life is rent,
For briefly flashed enlightenment.
Was it worth the price you paid,
Insanity from day to day?

Down the faded cobblestone,
Strewn with rust, decay and bones,
Can you find your own face there,
Amid the foully laden air?
Was it worth the price you pay,
Your soul bespoken from that day?

Heather M. Taft

Wondering

I wake and lay in bed,
What to do?
I think I will wonder.

I wonder if . . .
One day I will walk outside and see a poor family,
Living in a box and all they wanted,
Was just two more weeks to pay their house payment,
And I won't have any money to help.

I wonder what . . .
Will happen in the future,
If the future is happening
Right this very minute.

I wonder why . . .
I am wondering about all this right now,
And not yesterday or today.

And I just plain wonder.

Ashlee Priddy

Schizophrenic

Could you imagine sitting alone
In the dark by yourself
No lights, no friends
Just darkness all around
Wondering, hoping someone would come and rescue you

No one would, you'll be all alone
Talking to yourself because it's your only friend
Secrets told, but no one to hear
Listening though it's only your ears
I'm going insane! I'm going insane!
Though no one cares

Weeks even months have passed
I'm all better now I understand
My mind was running and so were my ears
They told me things about earth, space, even you

Though I believed them I don't know why
Even though they told me lies
My mind was dark and so was my soul
Now I have real friends so, I'm not alone!

Sherita Jamison

To Our Kid At School

You need not be an Elizabethan Bard
To drop us a line . . . send us a card

We've heard you whine . . . "It's oh so tough!
What with tests, societies and complex stuff."

"Why even Yalies . . . (or so you say),
Grunt n' groan to pen an essay."

Excuses feeble . . . sure do swallow hard . . .
More'n likely . . . you're full-o-lard!

St. Paul found time to write as well
Even from a prison cell.

I hope we don't blow 'eighty grand'
For a kid who can't take pen in hand.

It's a 'breeze' to write since you're PC lit . . .
"Word-For-Windows" even makes the spelling fit.

The Web, a Fax, and E-mail too?
To us they're all a bit 'taboo'

And you know we ain't no 'Techy-Nerds'
Just put a pen to paper and some loving words

The moral we can't stress too much
"Is write more often . . . please keep in touch!"

David Craig

Transfigure

Why do I wander like a nomad?
What am I searching for?
Why do I feel so very sad?
Why can't I open the door?

Why is what I want so elusive?
Why do I feel this awful, awful pain?
Why do my dreams turn out to be delusive?
Why does everyone see them as mundane?

This time I won't silently cry.
No, I will not shed another tear.
This time I will not just comply.
For I am sure this must be my year!

Karen Cavanaugh

The Pussy Cat Declares Listen Up Drunk Dude!

Listen up drunk dude! Thus purrs the cat.
Like shalom my purrs also have many
meanings. Be on guard! Do not waste words or deeds on me?
They have no value. Frankly Dude, I could care less. Belief is the ticket;
that miraculous seed that represents your love for me.
There is no other beast who would dare challenge me —
not even you Dud Dude! Your daily food offering I truly despise.
I depend not on you, Dunce Dude, but you depend on me.
I do not toil for my keep and unlike you, I am never politically correct —
slow to anger, my vengeance is swift as lightning.
I come totally unexpected. My countenance I keep invisible.
This right is mine, brave or coward, judge me not.
I am the judge, not you. At crucial times, I may seem to retreat.
I do this so that my diamond valor is not exposed.
It is said, I sleep too much; beware of such falsehoods. I sleep not!
Repulsive or beautiful friend or foe, you are either for me or against me.
Unless your belief rises up to meet me, your only vision of me will
be that of a cat. Remember, I own you Duke Dude. You don't own me.

Dave Hayes

Not Fade Away

How do you pick up the pieces if you can't see where they are
It's like making a beautiful wish without even seeing a star
How do you put things back together when they are beyond repair
all you do is wonder, does anyone even care
How do you tell a friend from a stranger on the street
Why should you have to study everyone you meet
Why is it right for you and so wrong for me
Suffering is all I have and it won't let me be
How do you see the light if there isn't any day
How do you pull yourself together and not fade away.

Athena Papavlo

Sand

Hot simmering smell of meat cooking flows through his nostrils.
The piercing hot golden rays ferociously pour over his numb body.
Lying in the scorching hot sand, his flesh slowly burns with the
intense summer heat. His tongue swells with dehydration,
leaving only the taste of clumpy white school paste. Boiling
blood seems to rush throughout the shriveled up veins. Only
blood isn't actually rushing it is slowing down. With each
thump of the heart, less and less blood is released. His brain
throbs with pain, causing his lying eyes to see all the wrong he
has committed. Red veins cover his dilated pupils, making them
resemble a demon's eyes while he eternally burns in the flames
of hell. The soft gentle wind covers his body with a blanket of
sand like a mother covering a child.
Soon the preying animals of the desert will feast and the
leftovers will be buried by billions of little sand crystals; leaving
no clue of this event, unless he is somehow saved.

Stephanie Furguson

Beyond The Tears

Beyond the tears, is an ideal plane.
It's beyond any hurt, it's beyond any pain.

Beyond the tears, lie all the truths.
They will carry us to the grave, they will bring us back to our youth.

Beyond the tears, is a world we all seek
Getting there is not easy, that road is not for the weak

The road take commitment, it takes understanding
This road requires strength, it can be very demanding

Two people are required, to walk that road together
With faith and honesty, each step will only get better.

Tears of happiness, tears of sorrow
We cannot change the past, we must look to tomorrow

Beyond the tears, is a world of strength
That two people have built, and time knows no length

Beyond the tears, is a new way to view
This life we will share, may I go there with you?

Don DeYoung

You Are That Fire!

A fire! . . . a great ball of fire burning under the mantle
Bon-fire, brush-fire, a great ball of fire . . . You're that fire!
Your bright glow flowing from the meadow,
From the distant meadow nobody knows.
Your blooming brightness, the love you bestow.

A sunshine! . . . the radiant sunshine beaming into the shadow,
Gleaming from the distant light glowing from the meadow.
The smile you beam, your love is so real.
It is that great ball of fire which gives life to the world,
And color to the flowers, the flowers that flourish.

The burning fire, the radiant sunshine, the smile you bear.
Day change to night, night to day, day to night and to day again.
A result of the great ball of fire burning in your depths,
The depths of your soul; but no one reflects.
No one . . . no one but me adore.

From afar you're bright, ajar you're a delight . . .
From nigh you're hot . . . hot . . . hot . . .
Hot so hot no one can touch you. No one to touch you,
Who's to touch you but me?
My love for you is real. Can't you tell?

Caswell Foreshaw

Untitled

A heartbeat away you read these words,
these words that can only start,
to whisper deep into your soul,
what I'm feeling in my heart.
A deep and dark fantasy,
of a secret, hidden place,
where your eyes shine like two precious jewels,
when the moonlight falls to your face.
What are your wildest dreams?
Tell me, I want to know,
let's follow our hearts and run that way,
let's make this fire grow.
Holding you dear to all that I am,
my heart starts to pray,
You know how much you mean to me,
please don't ever go away.
So remember when life is unfair to you,
when the problems seem without end,
remember the one who cares for you,
your lover, and your friend!

Tom Johnston

Paused In The Still Steel Posture

I paused, held my breath and listened to my throbbing pulse.
My spinning head bowed low in the dripping freezing rain, I forced
my heavy eyelids open. Open to look again at the world's violated,
bloody wounds, the ethnic cleansing, the ravaged parent's child,
the grip's many-fingered strangling power — not caring that infant
brothers starved and baby sisters feared before they died.

The Holy World condemned and laughed, cuing the politician's
posture, snort and loud hurrahs. I looked and saw the cities'
hopeless, finally all locked up, education and opportunity finally
all locked out. I dropped to the frozen icy mud, and despaired.

Over to the leafless woods I bent and tripped and fell — feeling
the winter now and the cold hard wind — an icy snow was falling.
I re-felt those forgotten feelings of being so very far away and
so very much alone.

Stooping and bowing, I limped over to the surrounding dreary
forest with trembling cold and gripping shame, sorrowing for all
the lifeless partitions that bind and blind our love.

I paused in the still, steel posture, bent over like a covered limb.
Head bowed low and choked with tears, I wept and prayed until
evening's darkness lit the path up the slippery frozen hill to home.

Larry Waldron

Christmas Night

Under the sprawling walnut tree,
The squirrels leap from branch to branch.
This proud tree stands a Coffee Creek Ranch.
They steal our nuts
Sometimes dropping them on our "mutts"!
The nuts are sweet
If you can find any to eat?
What a shame when worms prevail
And the leaves do fall
At the coming of Winter rains, the end of the trail.
Letting down its shaded wall,
To await the next new Spring;
When leaves will come again to cling
Under the sprawling walnut tree
God breathes life into me;
As the blossoms begin to bloom of a Spring that will be doomed
As the leaves begin to unfold, their Summer wall of shade,
Until the nuts in Fall are made.
The loss of green dares you to dream
Through Winter white of Christmas Night!

Ruth G. Hartman

For Yourself Alone

Dear Lady of unquenched and youthful fire,
    How long will thoughts of you remain the best?
Shall years erase the love that does inspire
    The beating of the heart within my breast?

What is the reason that the feelings soar,
    Emotions springing forth from wells unknown?
The answer echoes back from heaven's shore:
    "I love you for yourself — yourself alone."

And when the quickly passing years shall trace
    The wrinkled signs of aging on your brow,
My love will not increase at slower pace
    Nor be of less degree than it is now.

So when your days of youthfulness have passed —
    Swift, transient scenes of ne'er retreating time —
E'en then, among the wondrous sights that last,
    Your timeless beauty will remain sublime.

Though Nature's landscape's painted all anew
    With loveliest of every tint and hue,
No lesser then will love in me have grown:
    I'll love you for yourself — yourself alone!

Thomas N. Thrasher

My Wonderful World Of Old

Where has my wonderful world gone?
The world I so fondly recall,
With plowed fields, forests and meadows,
Where I played when I was so small.

Where has my wonderful world gone?
The world so warm and pristine
The one I remember so fondly
A world without smog and the air so clean.

My wonderful world is fading away.
They've replaced the old family farm
With highways, tall buildings, construction galore.
The world of old has lost all its charm.

What is this thing we call "Progress"?
Oh, how I wish that I could return
To life as a child as my memories are filed
In a time warp for which I now yearn.

My wonderful world shall never return,
Still, my memory yet holds it so dear.
Should my heart ever yearn for that time to return
Vivid pictures from memory will bring it back here.

Doris Landis

Forgotten Warriors —The Glories Of The Past, Indomitable, Used To Be Forever

It seems as if I turned a page;
The fire of youth has lost its rage.

The walls of time are closing in;
The mirror shows a fading has-been.

The Fearsome Foursome only a dream;
Lombardi, Hallas, Landry, barely a gleam.

The heroes of today cannot match the past;
Nitschke, Butkus, Mean Joe Green, men made to last.

Y.A., Sonny J., Van Brocklin too;
Gave it their all for praises so few.

Salary cap, coke, and funky rap;
Don't compare to Deacon Jones and his helmet slap.

Modjelewsky, Katcavage and Night Train Lane;
Heroes all with Otto Graham, Broadway Joe, and Dandy Don so vain.

All seem to fade like fires on a hill as sunset falls;
The glories of old become memories in hallowed halls.

Undefeated Miami, The Steel Curtain and the Green Bay Packers;
Eclipsed be agents, buy-outs and corporate wise crackers.

There used to be guts, brawn and courage too;
Today, it's forget the point after, let's go for two!

Valentine Huegel

Catfish Joe

What do you know, there goes Catfish Joe.
1 cents, 2 cents, sometimes 3 cents a pound.
Dragging them big old catfish from the river
and flinging them onto the ground.
Up before dusk and back before dawn,
if he's going to feed his family,
he must fish on.
At the market in front of City Hall,
trying to sell a few catfish,
hoping to sell them all.
If you should stand next to him in the market place,
never mind the smell,
because he's Catfish Joe,
that's what sells.

Terry Harris

Cicadas and Untied Shoes

Cicadas are making love on the trees
screaming and fluttering their transparent wings with delight
The greyness of the day is killing me softly
Stagnant air pregnant with humidity
drifts around aimlessly like a drunken man
kissing everyone's face with glossy sweat
And the girl with the New York accent talking to me
is playing with her untied shoelace
as she squeezes out tears and tales
coated with bittersweet love and squalor about a boy she once knew
And I am thinking of you
how I cradled you in my arms and whispered your name
Gave you my heart bare and trembling
beneath the pale blanket of the moon . . .

The cacophonous moans of the cicadas die down
And they fly zig-zag lines from the trees dizzy with satisfaction
The grey misery of the day is falling all over me
The girl with the New York accent and I are dying softly
as we sit alone
staring at her untied shoe.

Alyssa Curry

Open Your Heart

True beauty in the world, isn't hard to see.
But it is only revealed,
To those that seek.

There's beauty in a little child,
So trusting and naive, they know not how to hate,
And love is all they seek.

There's beauty in the dream,
To reach for the stars.
Our dreams keep us going,
Without them hope would die.

There's beauty in two friends, walking arm-in-arm.
A special kind of love,
That doesn't take . . . Just gives.

There's beauty in a moonlit sky,
So peaceful and so calm, if only we could do the same,
Stop all wars and carry on.

If only we would take the time,
To stop and look around,
True beauty would go free, and love would abound.

Hope Lemus

Control Me

In prison I be
Though no bars or cells there are
Just a band of gold and piece of paper
Slave that I be — Tear me down
Smack me — Hit me
Break my very soul
Beast though and Ruler that you are

　　You'll never win

My spirit is strong
　I will conquer
　　I will soar like the eagle, wild and free
　　　Just you wait and see

God and love will set me free
　I have found a purpose
　　Love, not hate, will set me free
　　　True love I have found
　　　He will lift me up

Out of darkness and into sunshine, he will carry me
　Shine on me, My Spirit is free
　　I am soaring like the eagle wild and free

Patricia Sheldon-Johnson

Untitled

A time a place
Beyond our grasp
Yet so close
While hope still lasts stretch out to touch
What you want to feel
So much
And touch it you must
Before dusk
After dusk it is no longer real
There is no need to feel

Randolph Croson

You Are The Soil

I am planted there.
You hold my roots strong and steady.
You give me all I need to grow and blossom.
Embrace me, surround me with your warmth.
Nurture me with love, compassion, trust, and passion.
We will grow together as one; but separate.
Sow kisses and hugs, reap their rewards.
Grow ever strong and steady.

Paula Mendenhall

Best Brother In World

Nobody's concern counts
as much as yours.

Your care and concern
places your love in writing.

Sorry to question your concerns
but the pressures upset my mind.

Your command in mornings
consults till the evening.

All we hear today
is to thank you in future.

All the sis (s) in the universe
would love to have you as their commander

I am very lucky to have you.
Thanks for all, Bro.

Sameera Rafi

Say We've Begun

How is it possible in such a short time
Our Nation is facing this hatred and crime
Whatever happened to compassion and love
From friends and neighbors as well as above.

Many people are giving and loving and kind
And live each day with one purpose in mind
To earn an honest living and provide for their own
As an example to children not yet fully grown.

But times are not as they once used to be
Today it's guns and violence and much tragedy
A new generation of nothing but fear
Which seems to increase with each passing year.

It appears we failed by not looking ahead
As can be seen from statistics of how many are dead
So let's teach and repair what's already been done
Then maybe tomorrow we can say we have won.

With vision and awareness and promise and hope
Say no to the guns and the crime and the dope
Let's rally together as a nation of one
But let's do it now and say we've begun.

Nancy Geist

Frozen Fantasy

Dedicated to Pat: I'm sure you'll make a wonderful teacher.
You have enriched my life and will never be forgotten.

The only barrier between us and the glass-like earth was a
spectacular window draped in frost through which we could see
only when the warmth of our breath melted a spot as we spoke,
but we had to break out of warmth and protection

It was a night so sweet that the earth seemed to be covered in
frozen coconut. The sky was brush painted with streams of color,
as the sun sank into the depths of the earth.

There we stood on an old rustic bridge that arched across a small,
frozen but glittering pond. The air was fresh and exciting, seeming to
carry us over solid sheet of slickness the sidewalk was offering.

At dusk, all glowed in radiant blue. Sparkling snow jewels pretty
enough that, if captured, a brilliant frozen crystalline necklace
would be created for me.

Trees rimmed in snow lace for the holidays, sheltered a small bunny
a he scampered away into the stillness. The snow fearlessly tingling
our faces, glistening on our lashes beneath the towering street lights,
which produced a magnificent orange glow during this heavy snowfall.

Not far off, the voices of carolers, carried merriment through the air.
We sang with them, while approaching the ice rink. It was a night made
for beauty and innocence, a place where all seemed new and wonderful.

Dana Christine Kowal

What's A Million Of Anything?

What's a million of anything, have you ever thought about it?
Bet it'd make your ears to ring, had you to count and shout it.

But let's find out what it can be, if we try to make a gauge.
A million hours adds to thee, a hundred years to your age.

If a million times you did sneeze, and ten seconds between a start,
Two years later the final wheeze, would blow your nose apart.

A million days gone by, my friend, is a very long time, I'm told.
If on your birthday it did end, your twenty-seven hundred years old.

If a million dollars you did earn, at ten dollars by the hour,
It'd take near 50 years to turn, if the job didn't go sour.

If you ate three meals in every day, and never did miss a one,
Over 900 years must come your way, if you intend to get them done.

So why this abstract concept ponder if we haven't got a clue,
Its measure seems way out yonder, lest you've nothing else to do.

Edward Yrisarri Jr.

Jordan

Jordan was my pride and joy
When you laughed and played with your toy
But now you're gone
It has not been long
When you died
I really tried
My family so sad
It has been really bad
Don't cry don't shed your tear
For Jordan is gone but no he is here
Only in one place
So don't put on a gloomy face
In my heart in my soul
Nobody knows how much I cared
When you died I was really scared
So Jordan my baby cousin
You died when you were one
I miss you a whole ton
So you see in this poem
I describe how Jordan was so special to me

Lacey Smith

The Treasure

The only thing in this world that makes me feel secure is my lock.
The lock was meticulously fashioned of gold
That shines like the first ray of the sun on a brisk spring morning.
The mechanism,
Still in perfect working condition after 14 years of relentless abuse.
  Is crafted of the finest silver.
Around the key hole there are tiny gashes and scratches
From the numerous times people have tried to deceive the mechanism
  With a false key.
Nevertheless, the lock still shines with an iridescence all its own.
Engraved in the lock in faint, delicate manuscript is the ominous maxim
"All who enter this domain will never leave its vast realm."
This lock guards neither my door.
  Nor my safe.
No.
It protects a much more valuable and cherished treasure.
It is
  The sentinel of my heart.
  Eva-Marie David

Germ Warfare

A vast army of viri stood poised on my launch pad Tongue.
On command, they parachuted into the dark cavernous Esophagus.
They seemed like harmless, floating feathers
Landing undetected on my Epiglottis.
There they established a beachhead!
I never felt a thing.

Two days later, it seemed a nova had exploded in my Larynx.
A command post had been set up on my Tonsils.
A battle raged in the Sinus Cavities.
I waved my Kleenex like a flag of truce
Over Swollen Nose and Watery Eyes.

I was undone.
  Belva J. Warren

Soul Rebirth

To every man there is open;
  a way, ways, and a way,
The high soul ascends the high way,
The low soul descends the low way,
  In the midst,
  On the misty flats,
The rest just drifts to and fro.
But to every man there is open,
A high way, and a low,
And each man himself must decide,
  The way his soul shall go.

I don't cry for precious moments passed away,
I don't weep for a "Golden Age" of social reign;
  Each night I burn
  The records of the day,
And at sunrise, my soul is born again.
  James C. Hall Jr.

A Patients Prayer

"Hear me "O' Lord" above my many
  other voices I hear.
Help me to walk again using my crutch
  of medication.
I fear of using my crutch of medication,
  even tho, all those that care for me encourage
  me with all their love
I fear that when I leave here, others will
  shun me as they have before.
Help me to regain my life using my crutch
  of medication, that I might walk with
  my head up among others of my kind.
  Melva A. McKinley

Growing Old Alone

Like an ancient oak standing all alone, in a field
that I call home. My leaves are shed there are no more
and my limbs begin to break. It's time to leave this old
Earth when the last breath I shall take.

For the acorns I leave behind my roots will still be
here, I'll leave this world with great joy and haven't got a fear.

In the passing of each day, I think of the day before,
not of tomorrow that's coming, but of the memories I adore.

The future is yet to be, and the past has came and
gone, so remember those special moments, and you won't
"Grow old alone."
  Billy Grant

His Presence

Relationships come and go, breezing through
my life, just as the wind blows.
Hardships and disappointments was the raging
tide, that pounded my very soul.
Drowning in self-pity, He reached down
touching the heart that was dark and cold.
My burdens captured the spirit that once was free.
And, at times, the unworthiness overwhelmed me.
Then one day, a seed was planted by an unsuspecting friend.
The roots have grown deep, soaking up the tears
that have fallen at His feet.
Once again, I realized, He died so I could see.
The dark nights have turned to brighter days,
as I stand in the midst of His ceaseless grace.
His love permeates forgiveness, comfort and peace.
For He, holds me, in His everlasting embrace.
  Lisa Ann Switzer

A Letter

  A letter is the warmest way
To bid a friend the time of day
To keep in touch that brings the smiles
Across the very longest miles.
And what a wealth of strength and hope.
Is tucked inside an envelope,
Reminding loved ones that you are,
At least in heart not very far.
In no country, state, or camp, is
The wealth beneath a postage stamp.
For memories that never age,
Are written down upon a page.
And though it's nice to telephone,
One of the sweetest pleasures known
Are moments shared through thoughts we send . . .
That can be read and read again.
  Randy Owens

I'll Miss Her

I'll miss her when she goes
To another place, well, who knows
She might change her confused mind
And will not bear leaving me behind.

I'll miss this person who makes me happy
Trying to cheer me up when I'm gloomy
I hate being left but that's how life is
But I don't expect it to come to this.

I'll miss her, I really will do
She said she'll miss me badly too
But no need to worry, it's not the end
I'll keep in touch with her, my dear friend.
  Ruth S. Gonzales

Just One More Time

In memory of "Our Jason"
If I could say just one more time,
just what you mean to me.
I first would start, straight from my heart,
and thank you for loving me.
I'd thank you Mom, for the countless
times you cared and were my friend.
And Dad, I knew down in my heart,
you were preparing me to be a man.
I know that life isn't perfect, but I now understand,
We won't get to Heaven, without,
nail scares in "His Hands."
I know you both miss me,
there was so much we needed to say.
Please, rest a sure one day soon,
We'll meet at "God's Pearly Gate."
So hold tight to each other,
and always remember one.
For when that glorious day comes,
and there's no memory,
Once again, Mom and Dad, we'll be a family.

Lisa Walker

Wind Of Change

Who's tapping at my back door? It's Wind of Change.
He creaks, he rattles, with his icy fingers,
He seeks out the frame of every day living and mediocre
thinking.
Shaking up our minds.

Topsy, turvy, life is blown,
What will happen no one knows.
Like leaves from a tree we twist and spin,
As Wind of Change blows at all held within.

With a breath, all is clear,
Leaving room for new ideas,
Bright, refreshing, not all are without fear.

But each are tried, some tested,
Lots of them are rejected.
Soon the frame fills as one by one,
Ideas are accepted.

Now we grow, expanding our minds,
Soon, we become complacent.
Then what happens?
We hear a tap, tap, tapping.
It's Wind of Change.

Deborah Pinson

Prison Experience

It's really hard being locked down
Almost everyday you wear a frown

You sit around with nothing to do
And see exactly who cares about you

For visits every week you chase
And smile when you see an outside face

You often reminisce about things you used to do
And blame the white man for what has happened to you

You try to keep your head up as the years go by
When deep down inside you really want to cry

You view life in a totally different way
And pray in the future you'll have your day

When your day comes you'll have a plan
Each one different depending on the man

So listen blackman and take my advice
Don't ever make the same mistake twice

Umar Yasin

The Endless Circle

To misunderstand is a human frailty
To act on misunderstanding is a human error
To apply this act to another is a transgression
To identify the cause is to be self-analytical
To deny an explanation is to hide in obscurity
To hide in obscurity is to avoid contradiction
To avoid contradiction is to elevate one's self esteem
To elevate oneself above error is to assume perfection
To attain perfection, one cannot be wrong
To not be wrong, one cannot misunderstand
But misunderstanding is a human frailty
And acting on it is a human error
To gain understanding, one must be self-analytical
For in self-analysis, one can reveal the truth
But only if one is honest with oneself
And with this revelation, one cannot misunderstand
For one cannot live in truth and be in error
Without the truth, there can be no understanding
Without understanding, there is only misunderstanding
The human frailty in this endless circle.

William E. Kahler

Fear Of First Love

You are tough and unafraid
Fear is a thing of mystery.
A huge german shepherd, not a problem.
A knife wielding maniac, a breeze.

Then you see her and all is different.
Suddenly you are a mortal
You feel strange churning emotions.
And you feel something else. Fear?

There before you; a dream made real,
A beautiful smile, a warm laugh.
Truly, an Angel visiting earth.
And you, have suddenly turned to stone.

Frozen! How can this be?
Nothing can make you even pause,
You are indestructible.
You must move! Move!

You must say something, say anything!
You must speak! Quickly before she leaves!
Talk! Open your mouth and say the word!
SAY IT! NOW!! SPEAK!!! . . . Hello . . .

Justin Scott Henley

Spring

It is a time for airing the house, cleaning the floors, and
washing the doors. Cleaning the house and getting rid of that
last little mouse. A time for planting and a time for panting
for that last bit of air at a country fair. Digging a garden and
having fun, basking in the afternoon sun. Spring is a refreshing
time of the year. People are looming, flowers are blooming, and
dog's get grooming. What a beautiful time of the year.

James E. Pickard

The Single Red Rose

I opened the door and there you were.
Like a little lost puppy.

I held you, I helped you, I gave you
Everything you've ever wanted or needed.

One single red rose, you gave to me.

There was no need for words. That single
red rose told me everything.

Molly Gipson

A View From My Window

I will do this for me every day
it is very simple, it is very powerful, it is pure love.
I sit quietly, breathe deeply, I relax.
I insist on being in the now.
I visualize exactly what I wish from this life time.
I do not limit myself, nor do I let others limit me.
I feel calm and balanced within.
I desire to experience a harmonious life style.
I desire to experience great health, and energy,
   that leads me to creative adventures.
I desire that I am well provided for with food,
shelter and all the things I need to experience
Life abundantly.
I desire to give this great abundance to others.
Everyday I will give a small portion of my
time to read this.
I call for the power of the light that is mine to
fill me with love and enlighten me.
I am breathing deeply . . . So be it.

Anita V. Woyda

You're Dead

Black with no sight,
Pale with no color
No longer able to feel the sunlight.
No longer able to hug your mother or brother.
Death with no breath circulating in and out of your body,
You're dead with not a thought flowing through out your head,
Now laying in that casket only a frame.
You'll never ever be the same.

Silvia Bailey

My Soul's Plea

O fading moon, sweep across this desperate sky and pick up the
pieces of my shattered soul.

Please, let your light burn a pathway through my mind that I may creep,

Finding what secrets are buried within my tattered spirit.

Don't let the violent sun come and sting my eyes with its flames.

Instead, let me behold your brilliance one last time before
I close my eyes.

I will dream of you while searching for a distant echo of
childhood or an answer to my questions.

You caught me again, alone, seeking my own destiny, my own
gateway to years lost, memories forgotten.

Melissa Toney

Who Needs Love?

People say love is in the air.
Well if you ask me, I don't care.
There used to be love in my mind.
Now there's no feelings of any kind.
To me cupids nothing but a devilish little boy.
He's nothing but the devil's play toy.
There is no affection in my soul.
Love's turned my heart black as coal.
My heart was broken by only one girl.
It won't happen again by anyone in this world.
One girl had the key to unlock my heart.
That key was lost when we split apart.
I'm going to live out my life as a single man.
Why you ask me because I can.
That's why I ask this to the heavens above.
Who in this world really needs love?

John D. Gregory

Missing You

As darkness spreads throughout the land,
   thoughts of you are close at hand.
I lie awake unable to rest,
   fighting the pain since you left.
Although I yearn for you in my heart,
   I love you enough to be apart,
Gathering your thoughts is what you need to do,
   slowing down is better for you.
Stifling the pain which pounds in my head,
   needing you more than as just a friend,
I tolerate the emptiness deep in my soul,
   . . . oh how I miss having you to hold.
So as you lay down for the nights rest,
   . . . remember the guy who's doing his best,
To hold back the tears that come crashing down,
   every day and night that you're not around,
If starting slower is what you need to do,
   let me know and I'll be there for you.
If not, I guess will just be friends,
   torturing my soul without end.

Daniel Heffelfinger

The Light

Unwanted . . . yearning to be loved
hugged and kissed and cuddled.
Hard to escape this loneliness,
wanting, searching daily for the delightfulness.
The real her, she longs to express.
Screaming in pain . . . looking for anyone to blame
slowly going insane.
Drawing some attention near
like that of a fallen star,
but not enough to cause the world to stir.
She lets out silent cries,
causing gentle tears,
sobbing hard for many hours.
Shrinking, vanishing . . . losing faith in the surroundings.
Living yet dying
from the harsh world outside,
where war corrupts and peace to all is set aside,
and her will to go on is crucified.

Slowly she is swallowed by the earth, so deep down, that there's light.

Suddenly hope!

Kimberly A. Norton

Happy Birthday To You, Mr. Clinton

The years passed . . . square your shoulders
Behold, you fifty years, indeed
Forgotten be your griefs and sorrows,
Let's shoot a glance on what you did.

No thing, o ye, can be forever
Don't worry, Mister President —
But the winner is that guy who's clever
And who posses the true friends.

We trust, o Clinton, in your justice,
We trust in you and, witness God,
We want be friendly everlasting
And be devoted to the blood.

We wish you, dear Mister Clinton,
To reach your golden marriage date,
To see your country very fruitful
Without poverty and hate.

Make all the goblets full of liquor,
Let be the light and will not dark!
For happy days, for our victor,
I ask you, drink, but not be drunk!

Grigoriy Libman

A Photographer's Dream

When my journey through this life is o'er,
And I step into the uncertainty
To another world, beyond that one way swinging door
That promise an opening
Into a world of unchangeable peace.
The kind that surpasses all understanding:
Where forgiveness and friendship
Will never cease.
There will I pick up a solaroid camera
With never-ending film,
And take perfect pictures
Of things so ethereally beautiful
Everywhere one can see.
I know for just a brief moment
It will make just a wee-bit sad,
I can't share them with friends
To let them know of the beauty
In this land that will never, never end.

Adeline Woodward

A Child's Mind

A child's mind
small but remembering,
my brothers and sister are dead,
I am in dream land but I have not reached the grave.
When I see the ground drawing
closer, my eyes grow wider,
my screams are held back by the
gushing wind upon my face.
Why Mommy? What I have done or not done?
How can I please you?
I know the man that came yesterday left tomorrow.
Did I drive him away?
Grandma has been released to torment
you, maybe she'll go away.
Why can't we stay?
Do we have to go? Why?
I will not forget you Mommy.
If I wake from deep dreaming,
I will always remember you loved me
enough to take me with you.

Christina Hatcher

Never Enough Time

There's never enough time to be young and have fun.
Never enough time to be with one you love.
There's never enough time to meet childhood dreams.
Never enough time to meet your wants and needs.
There's never enough times to find out who you are.
Never enough time to thank the ones you love near and far.
There's never enough time to say, "I love you."
       Never enough time.

Nestor Martinez

Images Of The City

A couple holding hands.
Stolen Merchandise worth twenty grand.
A cop walks their beat.
Drug peddlers on the street.
Babies being born.
Exasperated drivers honking their horns.
Chefs cooking up culinary delights.
Prostitutes wearing tights.
Buildings that touch the sky.
Park benches where the homeless lie.
Street artists who perform for all to hear.
Locations ruled by fear.
Images of the city have been told.
Images of the city, watch them unfold.

Paul R. Saltzer

Guiteau The Assassin

"Guiteau the Assassin" of disorderly mind,
   A lawyer of surly reputation.
A self proclaimed Messenger of God,
   Preaching socialistic ideas to our Nation,
Stalked Garfield, the Great Warrior and President,
   In a murderous sneak attack.
Crept behind the Berean with revolver drawn
   And fired a bullet into his back.

"I am a stalwart of the stalwarts." The bloody assassin cried.
"His death was a political necessity, it matters not how he died."
Taking aim he fires another bullet into the warrior at his feet.
Then the cowardly assassin hastily fled the carnage in thestreet.

Sept 19, 1881; over waters of Big Sandy River,
   10:36 this night appeared a brilliant star.
The Mountain People stood with heads bowed,
   Silently watched the shimmering light from afar.
The Heavenly star burning brightly, ascended
   Swiftly upward and vanished in the firmament.
This star was sent by God our father to bring home
   James A. Garfield, Soldier, Statesman and President.

Perry T. Hall

God

I will not let the times we've shared fade into my thoughts.
I will take secrets I have shared with no one but him to the grave with me.
My love for him goes beyond a teenage infatuation.
I know his tortured thoughts, and feel the pain.
My thoughts never leave him.
I have never cared for a single soul so deeply.
It is likely that I never will again.
Though others may stand before him,
I hope that I will stand out.
I want desperately for him to love me, but I know I must share his undying love.
I will enjoy what we have so timidly shared.
Forever will he be etched in my mind.
Swirling, dancing, smiling . . .
Why must I care so very deeply?
That very question is mounted in my mind.
I cannot erase his presence from my breaking heart.
I want him to be mine.

Brenna Faull

The Actor

With the wisdom of age.
Comes the filling of the page.
But now I can read every line.
Because it is my time.

When I was a child so young.
The only thing important was having fun.
Each days horizon held only the sun.
This is the way it was, when I was young.

But future days now have past.
Now I play the lead in the cast.
As I read the lines upon the page.
It is for my children in their young age.

It is for me to play the scene in their eyes.
If hero or villain here in lies.
If inflection of voice is but changed.
They will surely believe I am deranged.

If the sounds of love are but sounded.
Then all of their fears will be unfounded.
When the play is finally over and the curtain falls.
I will surely receive good reviews from one and all.

Patrick A. Carney

A Genetically Altered Apple

"Humanity, you never
had it from the beginning." —Charles Bukowski

. . . and then God created the Sabbath
and rested
and humans took their turn at creation
and now the world suffers from poverty
of the sperm
and grain is squeezed in flow
and it snows on falling cedars
and healers pass placebos
and puke science and scientists
and archaeologists fight over who is right
and who is wrong
and churches rise
and fall with stocks and bonds
and the last good man
meets the last good woman
and they share a genetically altered apple
and ponder why Barbara created the missing link.

Brian O'Neill

Just My Imagination

I looked for someone to walk with me
so I wouldn't have to travel alone
I wanted someone to share with
that would make a house a home

I wanted someone to stand beside me
through all the thick and thin
and support me when things go wrong
to truly be my friend

I had someone to walk in the sand with me
and bask there in the sun
then when the gray clouds formed
I found the footprints of only one

When the rain ends
Will I again have my friend?
Or with the loss of the sun
Did I too lose him?

I stand there contemplating
as I was drenched to the bone
Did I really have a forever friend,
or did I just imagine I wasn't alone?

Patricia Elaine Marie Schaffer

On Our Wedding Night

To what shall I compare thee, my love,
And how shall I describe thee?

Thou art as beautiful as any jewel,
But a jewel's beauty is cold;
And thou art warm and passionate as fire.

Art thou, then, a fire?
Nay: a fire would burn me,
And thou art as gentle and harmless as a dove.

Art thou, then, a dove?
Nay: a dove would flee me in fear,
And thou art as brave as lioness.

Art thou, then, a lioness?
Nay: a lioness would rend and tear me,
And thou lovest me.

Aye! Love is what thou art!
For thou knowest all about me,
All my faults and flaws,
And lovest me still.

Michael R. Cotterman

Loving You

I love you as you can probably see.
I'm dreaming of how it should be.
I'd show you my wounds but I can't show you my soul.
It feels like my heart has a big black hole.
I broke down inside.
It seriously feels like I have died.
I guess I'll give up loving you before I go insane.
It really makes no difference, except for all the pain.
Your love has taken over me,
I'm living off a fantasy
I loose my breath when I look into your eyes.
It really hurts when I keep telling myself lies.
I don't know if I can face the night.
When I cry these tears I cannot fight.
I wish for once our love to stay,
but my only hope is to get on my knees and pray.

Shelly Stinsman

Chickasaw Warrior

Down in Mississippi along the Natchez trace
We strolled hand-in-hand through an
Indian resting place.
The Chickasaw chief awoke and he said,
"Look who's back, he's one of our sons,
he's one of our own."

Many moons have come and gone
since he went away,
Many eagles have soared high above us,
But none so high as our son of
the Chickasaw tribe.

The winds sing a love song as he
stands before us
The magnolia trees stand in awe of his strength.
Welcome home, my son!
Welcome home my Chickasaw Warrior!

Maxine Jennings

The Christmas Birth

On one glorious night
there was a birth of a king who
gave the blind back their sight
and made us without a word sing
a song of praise. The angels
appeared and gave us the news
of the birth and the shepherds
sung to the baby child who was
born in a stable, not a comfortable inn.
This child grew without sin
but was tempted by the devil.
This child, who is Jesus, saved you and me.
He was crucified on a cross.
He rose on Easter and returned to heaven.
That is the life of the Christmas birth.

Jennifer Beasley

The Audience Of One

Actions stretch the boundaries of attention.
Thoughts that of which He can't mention.
Sorrow is fueled by doubt,
Questions begin to sprout,
What would life be like without,
I, as one without an audience.
Drifting through this void without reliance.
The questions that rise order defiance.
Is it the audience I am to please?
Or is it now time for me to leave?

Scott Stangler

The Seeker

With a flash of searing heat,
   the image of you before me
   screams to my soul,
Throwing into abandon
   all that I conceive to be me.
Seeking, seeking — but desperately hoping
   never to find,
   the one reason
   why I should not let you look,
   upon the depths of my heart.
Fear, Fear — The last defense
   of the Seeker;
Fear of being lost in the aftermath.
For I, the Seeker, am unconquerable,
   except by one.
And when she comes —
   the Seeker will find,
   and I will rest.

    Jay D. Testerman

The Dreams

When I was five the dreams I had were simple, neither good nor bad;
I dreamed of ordinary things like teddy bears and toys and swings,
And eating ice cream for dessert and making mud pies in the dirt.

When I grew to the age of ten, the damnable red dreams began;
I dreamed of cursed, mutated things, like nobody wraiths and headless
Kings, and unclean ancient hieroglyphs on crimson-tainted monoliths.

The advent of the cold black dreams came soon after I'd turned fifteen
I dreamed of dead, decaying things, like foul blue corpses withering
In furtive mausoleum voids on blasted, barren asteroids.

At twenty years, the dreams became kaleidoscopic, wild, insane;
I dreamed of shambling, faceless things like giant maggots blessed
With wings whose primal, cosmic violence sparkled technicolor pestilence.

At twenty-five, the dreams turned fey and came in dull, flat hues of
Grey; I dreamed of stagnant, crumbling things, like seas of fungus
Festering near endless plains of leprous mold, in aeon-long nocturnal cold.

    Loretta Glaser

Fluidity

Drink this liquid which has become my existence
it holds my likeness in its soft, flowing gestures.
Until this leaking orifice dies
I will continue to fall into this cascading landscape
where is the promised sun hidden?
It was meant to be the subject of all this transgression
now focused inward where the bleak aristocratic rules
silencing the voice of optimism
crushing hope.

    Morgan Burton

Someone Once Told Me That You Can

Tell a lot about a person from when they were a child
So your introduction to your heartache began as a child,
So it's no wonder you protected your feelings in walls.
But walls crumble exposing the frightened person.
In solitude you couldn't deal with your own existence,
The burning questions may still remain.
But if you ever need a friend,
We will be here to the end,
To show you how much we really care.
If you ever need guide,
We will help you see the light,
We will be right by your side,
To make things seem bright.
So if you're ever feeling blue,
Just remember we love you.

    Sherry Klutts

To Becky

Ease the pounding of my heart
   by the quieting of my mind.
Steady my hurried pace.
Give me, amidst the days' confusion,
   the calmness of the everlasting hills.
Break the tension of my nerves and muscles
   with the singing stream which lives in my memory.
Help me to know the magical restoring power of sleep.
Teach me the art of vacations,
   slowing down to look at a flower,
   to chat with a friend,
   to read a few lines from a good book.
Let me look up at the branches of a towering oak
and know that it grew slowly and well.
Inspire me to send my own roots deep
   into the soil of life's endearing values
That I may grow toward the stars of my greater destiny.

    Roy Wayne Huskey

My Rise To Fame

As a young girl I wanted to be
A wave in the Navy and sail the sea
Or an airline stewardess, another whim
But I was never that pretty or slim.

Oh! I had a career, a secretary I was
Til I got married — then a pause
I'm now a full time mother and wife
Happiness and love, a wonderful life!

After the children were out on their own
Sweet and lovely and oh! So grown
I pursued my career once more
As the years passed on I ask what for?

Now I'm asking what can I do?
The years ahead are all so few,
Then I realized as the grandchildren came
Being a grandmother was "my rise to fame."

    Dorothy Louise Kester

Intruder

   Crystal water ripples endlessly over stones worn smooth by the years, winding its way down the rocky pathway nature has created. The swishing, gurgling whispers grow to a crescendo of sound as the gentle flow meets the barrier of the stony wall and finding no escape tumbles, in a boiling foam, to enter the beauty of the pool below. The banks stretch wide to receive the pounding waters and calm the rushing tumult. Sunlight filters through the leafy ceiling high above to dapple the clear green pool, now deep and still. Only the flash of a darting brook trout, stealing its way from rock to rock, mars the mirror image.

   And I, perched upon the large grey boulder, dare not speak, move, or even think, lest my very thoughts disturb the tranquility of the moment.

    Joyce E. Farmer

A Love Subdued

I gave you not a second thought when at first we met
A fleeting, floating, wispy thing of no real consequence
But still you came in form of flesh and beckoned me to go
Down the well trod path of life in search of love's true soul
We tramped through fields without regard to where the road would bend
We had no guide, no star to track as we journeyed toward the dawn
But when we reached the darkened edge you stopped and turned away
I called . . . You fled and said to me you could not face the dark
The wooded grove calls me forth, it holds no fear for me
The breeze is cool, the carpet thick as I walk among the trees
I know not if the dappled light be sun, or moon, or star
The forest turns to open field as the shadows slowly part

    Marie Buschi

Shattered

The ice, the snow, the wind
blows across the barren stretches and it's
  cold, so cold, and so
are the faces that walk by, huddled under the sky too dry

To smile and cry for the wind
just blows it all away — away far away . . .
like life is gone, the sun is alone,
  far far away
and I'm not sure where to look
down below are only
shuffling feet, my own

Stepping slow, my tears frozen behind my eyes
I can't see for the blackness in front of me
and your face is lost in a haze and
  chopped up like cold snow
blown away in sullen wind
and shattered like ice under a hammer blow

J. Russell Woodman

Rage

Sometimes I feel like a lion stuck in a cage just so full of rage.
Hating everyone that walks by my cage.
Like I'm a freak on stage.
The sound of a tap will make me snap. And when
sometimes stands at the door all I can do is give up
A God awful roar. I want to knock down the door.
My rage it's caged. And when my rage gets our there is never
any doubt that blood will be spilled inside and out.
Whoever dares open my cage will surely unleash my rage.
And with eyes of flame he will know I am no longer tame.
At this point I bare down on him. He can't be saved by a
holy hymn. As I sink my claws into his skin and tear out
his heart and neck vain. He will begin to struggle and then
realize it is in vein. And right before he dies. He will stare
into my eyes. And see my rage. He will see my blood red rage.
He will regret opening the cage.
And in the end he will scream why did I open the cage?
Why did I unleash his rage.

Michael A. Blanco

Psychosis

I'm looking at a pink duck on wheels,
what has this world become . . .
what the hell is a pink duck doing here?
Is he trying to kill me?
Linguini.

Faith Liberty

Daybreak

As the mist lifts off Birchwood Pond
so does the last vestiges of a
cool and somber evening.

The crickets respond in a final chorus
of farewells to the dark wrappings of night.
The sunshine peaks through the eastern
trees with a warm glow against the early
morning sky.

Sleepy eyes stir, reluctant to meet the
incandescent intruder. Birds call out in song
proclaiming the coming. The plants which
bathe in the early morning dew reach out for
the warmth filtering the air.

A new day is beginning in a revival of spirit,
an initiation into a bright new endeavor.

Praise this start, for all will begin from here.

George Joseph Cohen

Paint Me A Picture

Paint me a picture of what Heaven must be
For I'm a mere mortal, and I cannot see
The realms that you dwell in, the places you know
So paint me a picture, and help me to grow

Into the knowledge that you now possess
Impart to me wisdom, counsel and rest —
Twirling around in the light of God's love
Give me a glimpse of Heaven above.

Yes, paint me a picture with guided hands
Of Heavenly hosts — Waterfalls — Angelic bands
Majestic mountains — singing saints
Places and scenes, which only you could paint.

And I'll wait for tomorrow to come
When we'll be united, together as one
Until then, while we must dwell apart
Just paint me a picture, to hold in my heart!

Dorothy Womack

Memories

To my brother, John Moore.
I thought of a rainbow today,
Of a blade of grass wavering in the breeze,
The bloom of a rose and the falling of leaves
And the sun slipping down.
No matter where I looked
I saw him standing there.
No small demands, no frets, no fears,
Just loving memories down through the years.
He taught us patience, he would say,
Stand still and see the joys around you,
You don't have to be reaching beyond this day.
Don't let these treasures pass away;
Sit here beside me and talk,
There's plenty of time to walk,
And not much time to be, here with me.
My ship is veering to the shore
I'm ready to climb
To joy and peace sublime,
He walks beside me.

Virginia Moore Marshall

Bud

In my heart you'll always be here, to light my path and guide my
step wherever I may go.

Though you're gone away to that heavenly home, you are never
really gone.

The love we shared, through all these years, still keep me warm
and calms my fears.

The hurt and loneliness I feel, and are hard to hear, but yet and
still, I would not change things if I could, for life with you bud
was precious and good.

The days go by since you are gone, and I sometimes don't seem to know,
What day, what week, what month, what year — it seems so
strange without you here.

Yet in my heart you'll always be, when things get rough, I'll turn
and see, something you touched, your presence seems so close
and oh so dear to me.

So even though God called you home and I remain, you're never
very far away. I guess God needed you up there to bring a smile
to him each day.

So be happy little daddy, mine and it won't be long before we'll
be together in that beautiful home.

Callie Spight

The Football Player

All the field's a stage,
And all the men merely players:
They have their ups and downs — their ins and outs;
And one man for his team plays many parts,
His acts having many stages. At first the rookie,
Studying and stumbling in front of coaches and players.
And then the moaning part-time player, with his note pad,
And wide-eyed anticipation, jumping at every opportunity
To willingly take the field of play. And then the loyal team player,
Setting the example, with poetry and grace
Made for his awe-struck teammates.   Then the veteran player,
Full of lofty goals, some unmet, and bearded like a beast,
Jealous in honor, quick to quarrel in defense of his role,
Seeking to maintain reputation and hold onto his job
Even in pain of injury and looking like a slob. And then the
reality of time, in glory days past with full round belly.
With eyes reflecting glory days past and scalp reflecting sunlight, his hair since lost.
Full of wise old schemes and fighting new modern ways;
And so he plays his part until he must say good-bye. The last stage
shifts into the day he executes no more, cut or traded he plots another course.

> *Kenneth A. Miller*

Family Treasures

In the corner of the attic an old trunk stands,
Carved, camel-backed, trimmed with metal bands,
Wrapped in faded memories;
The forgotten, the best — all of these.
The past, like flowers pressed in a book,
Safe, secure, hidden 'til some off-chance look.
Once, long ago with a new bride sent
To a strange new land the three they went.
His picture, lock of hair, still rests
Safe in the tatters of a wedding veil nest.
An ancient gown, a piece of twine
From a long-lost hat box it once did bind,
A feather from a boa of yesterday,
A small alligator of kindergarten clay.
"Japanese Bomb Pearl Harbor!," a flag in tricorn fold,
Service bars and "chickens," from a man never old,
One baby shoe, a wedding card, an old afghan,
A Boy Scout suit, a hiking boot, a first-aid kit in a can —
A family's treasured memories; their history resting there
In an old dome-top trunk by a broken rocking chair.

> *Margaret K. Handley*

Grace

Grace — gentle as the brush of the wind
in early spring announcing its arrival.
A rare jewel that permeated the
atmosphere with the brilliance of a
beautiful prism touched by the sun.

Nature acquiesced to her gentle beauty
as she pivoted forth in supple effervescence.
Ingenious and uncontrived, this unusual
soul came into the midst of my presence.

I stood afar and watched her as she
looked toward the horizon, remembering
things of old, things lost and forgotten in
the ripples of ancient waters.

Dream, my lovely friend of clear waters,
soaring birds, and songs of the chickadee.
Green grass, blossoming trees of Lilac and roses.

Remember always that I know you, and
I can touch the very essence of you by
remembering that God blessed me when
he opened the heavens and allowed you to touch my life.

> *Betty Williams*

Summer Days

The water sparkles,
playing along the shore
beside a child
with a red shovel.
Dancing in the rippling foam,
his laughter echoes
with the cry of a gull
as she swoops and soars
in the spray.

Gentle lapping waves
caress the shoreline,
singing Mother Nature's lullaby.
Ocean and sky
mirror each other —
turquoise capped with white.
Whispering winds
carrying sweet salt essence,
convince the sea grasses to kiss the Earth.

> *Nora McIntire*

Fire Fire

Lightning and his siamese twin
thunder were automatically
separated at their own natural birth
the crooked sun streak flash
made its mad dash to find
the tallest tree
Mr. Thunder rumbled and
grumped behind that famous
old wise crack now because of this pair's
antics we see much more
than smoke fire in the midst
of Green it's run if you can see
if you Mr. And Mrs. Inhabitants
of nature try and bring your offspring to safety
at least you tried most won't make that journey
nature is again thinning the
old and the weak and even the strong that hold the title brave
If Mr. And Mrs. Green lived by themselves without all
that fodder lying around dry kindred kinder maybe
its light show wouldn't be so bright with fear.

> *William O. Gould*

True Heaven

Remember when the snow was deep
    And we all sat at Grandpa's feet,
To hear him tell us with a sigh
    About his homeland long gone by.

The fireplace glowed so warm and bright
    As he would tell us of his plight,
How Irish people had to flee
    From lack of food and tyranny.

They left their loved ones, oh so dear
    To start a new life without fear,
The memories that they brought along
    Were relayed to us in merry song.

We never tired of any story
    Of his true heaven filled with glory,
We sat and dreamed about the day
    When we could travel all that way.

And now I'm old and I can see
    What grandpa prized so fervently,
For I have been to the Irish Isle
    Where Grandpa lived for a little while.

> *Wanda J. Ryan*

338

Mystic

Has a man yet conquered anything when sand shifts, conquers
cease to be like a maiden sweet blush clings to a countenance
claiming all.
Yet tomorrow grows sweeter nectar in the cup than today was drained.
How, says he, I have conquered this that blood has stained.
Does not the lips pressed tight, stand a greater crushing from another man
Tomorrow as the shower replenish flower bloom so soon again.
Not I to say, vainly say
That she who gave her love did not receive as much as first she gave away.
And more
   stand panting at the door
     for another shower of the same.
True,
  few
    can know.
    Ira Outland

Emissaries In Lonely Flight

I wonder at this midnight sky
A counterpoint of dark and light
Of emissaries in lonely flight
Cast in celestial blue

And if the eve is still enough
And the burdens of the day
But only for a moment are neatly tucked away
A simple truth emerges

The Smith that forged these cosmic vessels
Midst the furnace of creation glowing
Has sent each one adrift well knowing
The witness they will bear

As they wind their way
Cross frozen tundras of time and space
And come to rest at this distant place
Each a twinkle in my eye
    Ronald Graniero

Snow Dream

Floating drifts of angel's breath
settle down to rest on banks of icy blue.

Abstract figures in the distance
creep sleepily into the drab colors of night.

Vague ideas of warmth somewhere
touch the sky with the softness of a yellow light.

Frosty flakes of dove feathers
scatter wispily on the dusky trees.

Crisp howling wind
whispering amid the shadows
telling its secret to the hazy night.
    Lori Jennings Wright

Subtlety

In the potpourri of earnestness,
  I've encountered futile minds.
Gave way, at time, to hopelessness,
  To toss out unique finds.

Somewhere in the honesty,
  Of subtle thoughts passed on,
There lies foolhardy recklessness:
  The glimmer of a moment, soon gone.

Important messages, too often so misread,
  Become cliches, half right,
And interpreted as truth, instead,
  Where black can change to white.
    Evelyn M. Swenke

Snapshot Photograph

So desperate to see,
  to taste,
  to feel
these feelings that you have, unknown to you.
To take it with you, a snapshot of the past.
To hold it close to you, the feeling that could not last.

The scenery you see,
  you taste, and
  you feel
the beauty of it all, you absorb and you contain . . .
these thoughts that you have, unknown to them.

Separate, but once, twice is not enough,
to keep me away, it is never enough.

"Collision," you say, so calmly, like a word that is so nice,
or something I would love to hear instead of love on a beautiful night.

Once more, they want to see,
  they want to taste,
  they want to feel
something I cannot even explain,
something that is not even real.
    Sarah Reiser

Silhouette On The Hill

There is a silhouette on the hill,
  a silent and unmoving silhouette
like a statue he stands there . . . motionless.
There is a noise
  more like a scream of a banshee.
No, it isn't the wind.

Now there are two silhouettes on the hill,
  two silent and unmoving silhouettes
like statues they stand there . . . motionless.

Suddenly with hooves flying
  teeth bared
  they fight.
The challenger walks away,
realizing he has been beat.
There can only be one king to a heard . . .
There is a silhouette on the hill,
  a silent and unmoving silhouette
like a statue he stands there . . . motionless.
    Crystal Tracy

Listen!

I may be mongoloid, negroid, caucasian
or a combination thereof. But I am a person.

I come from the other side of the tracks.
My clothes are not of the latest style.
My thinking is sometimes different;
But I am a person.

School has become drudgery.
Classes have little meaning.
I am not excited by the ovine behavior of my so-called peers.
But I am a person.

I am expected to think like the others.
Regurgitation of "facts" is the accepted way.
Independent thinking is frowned upon — made fun of;
But I am a person.

I dream of exciting far off places.
Songs abound within me ever trying to be loosed.
I dance to drumbeats the others seem not to hear.
I'm called a non-conformist — a misfit — a troublemaker.
Yet I am a worthwhile individual — one of God's creations,
Striving to be me. Won't someone please listen?
    Lester Abbott

Back To The Future

Though my back is a problem, I've managed to find
The solution — keep the pain in the back of my mind.

To offer some background, I'll backtrack a bit
(Some back breaking work the causation of it.)

I went to the doc for relief of the pain
"Glad to see your back" he was quoted as sayin'.

"Surgery's required." I was taken aback
A setback for sure, but I started to pack
To go to a hospital, with fear of bacteria
But I seem to remember the back rubs are superia.

My doc as a back stabber takes a back seat to no one.
But I had no compulsion to actually know one.

When I'm back I'll lean back and turn off any rock
in favor of music of Bacarac or Bach.

    Mel Wade

Spring Is The Time When

Spring is the time when — most softball starts,
  and men ride around in little golf carts.
Spring is the time when — people fall in love,
  and sit in the park and feed the doves.
Spring is the time when — trees start to bud,
  and little kids love to play in the mud.
Spring is the time when — grass starts to grow,
  and most of the men go outside and mow.
Spring is the time when — flowers start to bloom,
  and there will be lots of new blossoms soon.
Spring is the time when — birds start to sing,
  and women go out and sway on the swings.
Spring is the time when — skies turn bright blue,
  and many new couples will soon say I do.
Spring is the time when — schools will soon close,
  and this is one real sign that everyone knows.
Spring time will always come to an end,
  and everyone will wait for its return again.

    Lois M. Helwig

Tranquility

Sitting here, taking in God's creations
Snow covered earth
The sun breaks through the gray cloudy sky
as snow falls lightly;
The sound of the wind as it gusts
Through the trees, blowing snow up,
and in circles, and then down;
How beautiful it is,
the simple things given to us in life;
Take in the beauty,
Feel the peacefulness,
Of these, God's creations

    D. Andrisani-Lopez

The Sea Gulls

A cast of weather lookouts keeps a vigil at the sea
To weary lost seafarers, and fishermen adrift.
Their eyes look toward the water
As they hover, soar and coast
When waves come from the crest
To meet the shore and rise and lift.
When sighted they are welcome as a friend of long ago
With guile, so knowing one only has to look
A charming sort those fellows
Enduring as the sky
To watch up on us is their mission
On wings like pages of a book.
The sea gulls

    Norma Morgan Vickery

Haunted

Thrust into a world unknown
Freedom descends upon my fingertips
I reach into this mist of life
To pull it in close to my breast
It is mine for the two lost innocence whose gazes befall me

Out of the mystery of days gone past
I sense a need for peace rising up
To greet my restless soul
I touch it with quavering palms it kisses my brow
I am awakened to the passions of life

Moments pass quickly by to find
An untamed spirit still and silent
Held trapped within clouded furores of yesterday once more

Brief yet present they are there ever more
Taunting and teasing my worried heart
It is here that the bittersweet token swells
Lest I be spared by hope

A cry in the dark
A long lost prayer upon my lips
To save my bitter heart

    Christine Greene

Winning And Loosing

In memory of my dear wife of 39 years
You gave love to me,
but stole away my heart.
I became shattered
You won and I lost.

You mesmerized me with your looks
You went away with a flicker of a smile.
I was blinded by your looks,
You won and I lost.

I was an earthen doll
which you broke to pieces.
Why did you play with me?
You won and I lost.

You were just a mirage
You vanished in the eternal light.
My dream was shattered
You won and I lost.

    P. K. Banerjee

Insight

I live in a world of darkness,
no flowers or children do I see.
My only question to you is,
"Why did this happen to me?"

I hear your voice.
It sounds sweet,
Like cookies and things you eat.

Do you love me for me?
Do you hate me because I don't see?
Tell me later, I must mourn,
For this is how I was born.

I love you, please love me.
I can't help that I can't see.
Be grateful for your sight,
It's not always night.

Thankful am I, for I don't need my sight.
I have you, and you alone.
With you I need nothing,
Because with you I have everything.

    Audra Rachel Beckett

The Force

The Awesome force claims the path it follows
Feeding on the turbulence of an angered wind;
Existing only to crush its aggressor, the winding spin approaches —
Challenging every form of life.

Day becomes night. the inhabitants of the heavens turn away
from an enraged neighbor; their terrestrial radiance diminished
as the force marauders through their sphere. The restless ocean
influenced by the ferocity of the force ravages her beaches and
raves beyond her boundaries. She caresses mother earth
unconsciously crushing, destroying and devastating.

The force announces his arrival demanding respect.
The inhabitant of the heavens shudder and turn in shame
Refusing to participate in affairs so violent;
The creatures of the earth tremble
Shrieking in fear they find comfort in none.

His fury is guided by the strength of nature yet he terrorizes,
mimics and destroys her glory. His rage is short-lived upon contact
with the concreteness of earth, yet only remnants of earth prior
remains; and the memory of his wrath is eternal.

Nicole O'Neal

Christmas At Our House

Some say Christmas comes too quick, tis time to get ready for St. Nick
The tree is trimmed with bulbs and a star, lights twinkle like stars from afar.
The stockings hang by the fireplace, and joy is reflected in every face.
Bedtime draws nigh, we try to sleep can't wait til morn to have a peek
But before we can think of morning time, the sun through our
window begins to shine.
We sneak from our beds noiselessly, not to waken the others.
My sister stumbles clumsily, and a laugh with her hand she smothers.
My brothers then waken with a shout, and from their bedroom
they scramble out.
My brother Jeff walks with dignity, and slowness to the Christmas tree
My mother watches with shining eyes, at our looks of joy and surprise.
My father then wakens, and fulfills his mission, of passing out
    presents, a family tradition.
When all is unwrapped and put away, or kept aside with which to play,
We all sit back and look over our presents, be they dolls, trucks,
    or a gun to shoot pheasants.
I shall always remember Christmas, no matter what year, all the joy
    expressed through a smile or tear.
I am sure it must be the joy of giving that keeps the Spirit of
    Christmas living.

Sandra Merrill Holmes

My German Girl

She became my heart's desire. And I became her man.
Our love did grow so strong, far not too long, we where to wed.
My German Girl and me.

I came home with a treasure to show. But she had to leave her
beautiful home, willing to leave her family and friends.
This my German Girl, did for me.

Then she took my home as hers and even made it better.
And there we shared it together. My German Girl and me.

We had some hard and trying times. Then the Lord we did find,
and put our trust in Him. My German Girl and me.

Jesus made our life anew, to renew our love like new.
Our love soon grew into a baby girl. My German Girl gave to me.

As time went by, we worked and served. The Lord, He gave to
us once more. A baby boy He blessed us with this time.
My German Girl gave to me.

It pleases me to see her smile, to see her do the things she likes
to do. She shares her life and love with me, this my German Girl
has done for me.

Roy L. Lindsey

My Faith Holds On!

I awaken in the mornings with a feeling of fear. I look to my God,
whom I know is near. My faith holds on!

When sipping late coffee, a sensation I feel. I know not its origin,
so to pray I just kneel. My faith holds on!

My telephone rings and I answer to hear, a dear friend's voice,
filled with cheer. Hi Addie! How are you? Fine I hope! I want you to
know I'm praying for your recovery full scope. My faith holds on!

It's mealtime again, not another morsel can I chew. My strength,
Dear Lord, I know cometh from you. I open my Bible and sit to read.
Your word just seems to answer my need. My faith holds on!

I sit in my recliner for a brief rest. Lord, the length of my day is
becoming a test. I close my eyes and take a deep breathe. I can
already feel you in my inner depth. My faith holds on!

My faith holds on, Lord, with each passing day and I realize even
more the many blessings you send my way. I know, Dear Lord,
there is a purpose in your way. So help me, Lord, to continue to say:
"My Faith Holds On!"

Sharon Griggs

Why Make The Effort?

You awake each day at the break of dawn,
try to get up, stretch and yawn.
Your legs and arms feel very sore,
Gee, how you'd love to sleep some more.
Then your neck begins to crack
Oh, my gally, a kink in your back!
Now try to get dressed, put on your hose,
fits of sneezing and blowing your nose.
You rush into the bathroom sink,
Look into the mirror, Your eye won't blink
Finally your favorite cup has started to brew,
It is ready and so are you.
"Election Day" is now here!
Ninety Seven, starts our new year.
Work the whole week through,
It all for taxes, nothing left for you.
Oh, I could get a raise there is no doubt,
Then they would take more money out.
So why make the effort for so little pay,
Just stay home and sleep all day!

Pauline Clark

The Legend

Notorious was his middle name,
You see he did help himself rise to fame,
Autographs, pictures, they all wanted the man,
It was obvious everyone was his #1 fan,

He couldn't walk the streets without a gasp or stare,
His head held high and proud in the air,
He would smile and say "Nice weather today,"
Then chuckling to himself, he would simply saunter away,

This was life, the way it was meant to be,
"It's so true," he thought, "they all want to be me,"
And as nightfall approached, he went through the day in his mind,
And counted how many autographs he had signed.

"Twenty-six," he thought, "more than day before last,"
His career was in tact, the Oscar was bound to come fast,
But walking towards home, he heavily breathed in the air,
A ten-bedroom mansion, yet no one would be there,

At the close of the door, the silence deafened his ears,
As loneliness crept up and awakened his fears,
"Perhaps just one drink, at the local corner bar,"
"For everyone there knows that I am a star."

Carol L. Gonzales

341

The Stars Of Tonight

What's in his smile, what's in his eyes
What's in his face, which reveals no lies?
A look to send me to the heavens.
A smile to send me to the stars
Looking closer and closer, no longer gazing far.

His humor making me laugh
Working his sweetest charm
Wanting to know more, never causing harm.

A touch which warms my heart
An embrace to hold me tight
Dark is the sky and bright are the stars of tonight.

A breeze to cool the waters
Sunshine to warm the land
The connection is growing stronger
Now knowing where we stand.

Walking hand in hand, through dusk until dawn
Gazing upon your eyes, gazing upon a fawn.

Standing here beside you
Realizing how right, this is here and now
And bright are the stars of tonight.

Lisa Sobala

The Unknown Adventure

I've come from faraway but, with a dollar in my hand,
Dreamin' about the future and travelin' through the land,
Distant light keeps a callin', while I blindly see the way,
towards the unknown adventure and its vision I obey.

Still I leave behind the darkness, without no sense of fear,
my path is only forward blurred with vision that's not clear,
There is no real direction, when searching for the truth,
I wonder about the driving force left behind with my youth.

As the journey is my keeper, and it helps to carry on,
I cannot lose the vision, or just chase the setting sun.
And with that final dollar, spent on the seeds of dreams,
grows the unknown adventure, or so in my mind it seems.

Charles Williams

A Child's Question

There she was with someone
  I'd never seen before . . .
    The gesturing of her hands,
    The tilt of their heads,
      was it a conversation with a foe?
  Or
Just my grandmother
  in her excited way
    telling a new friend
      about her morning bread baking?
Ruehame Louise Milligan Jordan

Untitled

Meet me in the mystery of a winter sunrise sky
A deep purple rosin in the eastern tip
Like a dove or a sea gull in love
With the see, here again I go
Alone for a moment awaiting reign
The harmony of a go-boy's heroic Love.
Skydiving never again but lying on a bed
Of interminable bliss soul capturing joy
Over arching wonder a masque of green hope
Listening, listening, Listen!!
I can hear the Bells of Dublin. Can you?
  I love you.
Austin Walsh

Times

Times have come and times have gone,
The children are grown and moving on.
Just yesterday we sat and played, and
Read stories out of the Bible.

Sweet little ones how I miss those times,
Your joy and laughter a ray of sunshine.
You'd reach for me and I'd be there,
Little hugs and kisses we would share.

Times have come and times have gone,
God has blessed us more than we have known.
He's guided footsteps and directed paths,
Helped us in hard times learn how to laugh.

Time will come we'll soon be home,
Don't let me look around and be alone.
Those little faces I expect to see,
Cause I told you heaven was reality.
Won't it be great when we get home?
Linda Faye Loudermilk

Parade

Swimming noiselessly in my thoughts
So often a shadow, brushing softly against me: Gratitude
For those who have paused to share life with me, talked to me
Without shutting off their ears
Looking into my eyes they have bent their faces down to mine
Lifting me onto their shoulders to see above the milling crowd
A perpetual parade flowing past in blurred confusion
Firemen, clowns and jesters
But dark apparitions too, the figure in the night cloak
Whose unearthly eyes stare momentarily into my own
My fever strains the limits of my brain as weakness invades
I am reassured by the weight beneath me, buoying me up
And I stare back

Always unexpectedly, the Light comes
Making the street shine like glass, so bright that I must look away
The weight beneath me dissipates
Around me people hide their eyes, burying heads into knees

As the last trace fades they all stand
It seems to me, though I can't tell, that they pretend the light
Was never there at all
Daniel Anthony Murphy

Wisdom's Call

Wisdom calls. Come to me, I am here!
From the beginning I have been, through eternity I will be.

You say, what is wisdom and where do I find you?
I say, search no more the shadows where evil dwells.
For those who are wise shun evil and seek light.

No earthly riches will buy me. No wicked or foolish man
will find me. Come to me! Search no more to the ends of
the earth, I am not there!

Don't look down, don't look around, for there I will not be
found. Come to me! Seek me with all of your heart! Search
for me as for a hidden treasure! For I will be worth your time.

In me you will find knowledge and understanding. In me you
will find honor and long life. I am here, don't give up!
Look up, to God and fear Him. For the fear of the Lord is the
beginning of knowledge and understanding.

Look to His Word and love Him! If it be His will, you will find
me! I am Wisdom and wisdom is God. So before you come to
me, go to God. He is waiting!

For in Him you will find all you need and more!
Michelle L. Hamilton

Solitary Rose

As I walk through this baron garden,
I cannot help but marvel to
find a beautiful flower
    standing alone; upright and tall.
New petals untouched by man. Alone in
their regal splendor . . . Innocent
    and pure.

Oh, to pick such a magnificent
and single flower. Oh, to
keep this symbol of love for
    myself! This flower so splendid, that
I want to alone cherish its
beauty and splendor . . . Innocent and pure.

Instead, I will selflessly water
and nourish her. Fertilize
her. Fertilize this beauty
    that grows alone; upright and tall.
This magnificent flower, perfect in her
shape and form! (So others may see her.)

    Innocent and pure.
    David Rudock

The Hero

He stepped into his plane
His mind was not on fortune or fame.
He was there to do or die
To ride the great blue sky

That early morning in May nineteen twenty seven.
When he was to ride God's blue heaven.
He wasn't all alone
For God rode with him into the great unknown
The distance it was far the Hero didn't mind
For this was his dream to conquer and he had time
And the Hero he was one of a kind.

The mold of which he was made, never again will we find.
He made his destination — thru rain, sleet, and snow
Thirty three hours of flying sometime high and sometime low
The hero never faltered for on his plane did go.
He landed at Le Bourget France the field all aglow.
The crowd was overflowing
He didn't know in what direction he was going.
They all wanted to touch and shake the hand of the man
Who flew three thousand miles to a foreign land

    Lawrence Jackson

Shine On America

I see the beautiful river that hurries by me
As it flows on to the sea
See the mighty mountains all around us
Their beauty for all to see
And there's the fields of grain
That wave like an army of marching food
To feed the hungry people of ours and other lands
As I travel down the highway
More wondrous sights I see
There's bridges and tall buildings and such
Put there by the efforts of many to make life better for you and me
There are rockets going to the moon and coming back again
A tribute to our courage and commitment like no other land
And let us not forget people
Who as one stand united with love and care
That no matter where upon this earth others may try to despair us
Our faith and determination shall rise and meet the call
For this great place is America
A country who finds love and freedom for all who choose to stay
Thank God for the U.S.A.

    Albert F. O'Toole Jr.
    Rifle, CO

A Song For Steven

In Loving Memory of Steven Dunn
They'll never write a song for Steven,
but he's someone we choose to remember,
A fine and gentle person was he
This young man, tall and slender;

He wore a smile every day, and treated all with kindness;
An abundance of compassion displayed
With a humor that was timeless;

As we knew him more, we'd appreciate all that he had to offer,
The love of the family, neighbors, and friends
Was something he always fought for;

Impressive in stature, so handsome was he
With a presence like no other;
Much too soon was he taken from us a friend, a partner, a brother;

A child was formed from Steven's love to carry his name forever.
But this child needed his father's love
So God saw that they stay together;

What you gave to us can never be measured,
You'll always be in our heart;
We'll miss you Steven, but your spirit's with us
and we'll never be apart . . .

    Jon-Michael Scott Duro

Beauty Is Bliss

Snow-capped grey mountains against the clear blue sky,
With elegance do they stand captivating the eye.
Streams of crystal clear water amongst these mountains race,
Froth and foam do they churn with increasing pace.

Flowers of sundry colors and fragrance we see —
Faint and fragile they are, a glory amongst to be.
From flower to flower dart pretty butterflies,
Flower or fly to be judged beauty — 'twould be a tie.

The towering trees in the green woods doth creak,
Many a bird nestling on them chirp and peep.
Merrily they relish the sway of the trees,
'Tis all a rapturous sight to watch in peace.

The hazy mist that hovers at dawn and dusk
Lends an appeasing moment for a stroll in the hush.
Dewdrops on petals and raindrops on leaves
Dazzle like diamonds in the sunny morning breeze.

Each tiny creation and each beauteous scene
Is the art of our Lord who cannot be seen.
Let us lift our hearts in thanks to what is His,
Lo! Behold! Beauty in bounty is bliss.

    Padma Palanivel

My Mother's Blue Afghan

Sometimes after you've taken your cup of coffee and
Left again at 6:00 a.m. for the hospital after a quick kiss and
After I've sleepily made you two salami sandwiches
And included those dills you like and a piece of
Fruit pie to please you hours from now
I take my cup of coffee back upstairs
To the king-size bed I've already made
And prop up pillows and get the blue afghan my mother made
Out of the wicker trunk to spread on top of me
While I sit on the bed in the still early morning quiet
Listening to the children breathing lightly in their own beds
And open a book of poetry just right for
Early morning reading with a cup of coffee
And the company of silent cats who also
Enjoy the comfort and warmth of my mother's
blue afghan.

    Barbara Kerr

Autumn

Autumn is a special time when leaves fall and dry.
When the Winter is cold and the sky is blue, and the grass
is brown and dry. Even though the Winter is cold the sun
still shines as bright as in the summer. Autumn is a
beautiful time of year. All the beautiful colors that appear. The
leaves turn red, yellow, and orange, and the branches look
alone, and empty. The kids play around the yard playing tag, or
hide and seek, with their hats and heavy coats, and boots to
match. You also see kids playing with Autumn leaves, throwing
them back and forth at each other. You also see the leaves on
the trampoline going up and down while the children are having
fun jumping. Autumn is also a very festive occasion because
we remember the Pilgrims and the Indians sitting together, and
enjoying a Thanksgiving meal. Breads, corn, fruits, and turkey
were enjoyed by the Pilgrims and the Indians, and their little
children. Giving thanks was very important to them, as it should
be for all of us. We should all take time out of our busy schedules,
and be thankful for the many wonderful things we do enjoy.
Remember Autumn is the time for beautiful colors, having fun
with friends and family, and being thankful for the many blessings we do have.

Marcie Wilkerson

Emotional Flight

The desire to be free, like an eagle in the breeze.
Enjoying the views, at any given altitude,
High above the ground, is the only way to get around.
Practice to perfection, maneuvers taught by instructor's direction.
Approaching the FAA test, you must give it your best,
Keeping your goal in sight, through the long and hard flights.
Experiences of good and bad can sometimes make you feel sad.
My biggest fear of all, the spin and then the fall,
Circles toward the ground, if only you could see, controlling
its own destiny.
My heart was beating fast, I prayed this would not last.
I started to cry, when I thought I would die.
Leaving behind all those whom I love was not something I
thought highly of.
Snap out of it and recover is what I had to discover.
Time to pull from what I had learned to accomplish what I once
had yearned.
Now, go rebuild your confidence and add to life yet another experience.
No matter how we travel around the earth, be sure not to let your
dreams burst.

Linda Daquilante

My Dream Guy

As I sit across the room watching his every move,
He turns to glance at me
I stare deep into his eyes searching for an answer,
as he does to me.
We blush by embarrassment,
for we always catch eye contact,
then turn our curious eyes away.
I glance again, making sure he doesn't notice,
and study every curve — every dent on his soft,
almost perfect face.
I yearn to someday touch his golden brown hair,
to run my slender fingers through the thick strands.
To someday hold his gentle hand
or kiss his soft, moist lips.
To have him hold me
pressing me against his muscular body.
To just be with him and be able to say that he's mine.
To have my dream guy love me as I love him.
That, I think, would be the best moment of my life
and I would treasure his love always.

Jessica Wheeler

Memory

A life before, a time gone by
A beautiful love that never will die
Time can not kill it, nor the passing of life
It lives on through war and strife
The darkest place, the brightest light
I'm calling to you to end my plight
I know you're near, you're never far
Now I need to be where you are
I call your name, I know you can hear
Though I can't see it, something I fear
This memory haunts me — to stop it I've tried
I lost you back then, and without you I died
You couldn't have stopped them, I knew that then
But life will bring us together again

Marjorie Cummins

Playing Above The Rest

As a unique great football player
myself, I am now demoted to only
watching football games. I see
players lose self-esteem when they
are having a losing season, but doesn't
ninety percent of the league have
losing seasons. You must play the game
as if it's your last play ever, your
last block ever, your last run or pass
ever. And, if that doesn't make you
give one hundred percent. Why are
you taking up space someone else can
produce. Remember if you have a tragedy,
you shouldn't worry unless it is shown
different on game films. Their loss
will be your gain. And others will
fall. Before you, there is no loyalty!
Playing above the rest.

Marvin LeDuff

Flowers

Flowers flowers here and there.
Flowers flowers everywhere.
Flowers flowers I could pick them for hours only if the sun will shine.
Flowers flowers they're nature's daughters lying in the meadows so high.
The birds that sing so elegantly lets the flowers sway in the wind.
So forever and always flowers will grow.

Lauren Steeves

Destiny

What if . . . what if things were different?
What if I had taken different turns?
What if all my faults became my triumphs?
What if all those years I wasted . . . were given back repaired?
Were given back somehow.
There are some things I'd change, I know it might seem strange . . .
but strange is stranger without change . . . when all you've got
is reasons why . . . you've failed.
Not at every single thing . . . just the ones that hurt the most.
If only I had listened . . . to those who loved and cared,
If only I had waited . . . till I was more the man.
Instead of just a child with countless hopes and dreams.
So I could understand . . . the things I was creating . . .
and how they were affecting . . . the Man I finally am.
All that time . . . and all those things I've done.
From child, to boy, to man . . . each and all three lifetimes,
growing towards and leading into one.

My Destiny and Birthright . . . my countless hopes and dreams . . .
today . . . are up for grabs.

Isaac Diaz Barcelona

The Pocket Watch

As soon as I saw the pocket watch in the window,
I knew I had to make it yours.
I could imagine you holding it in your hand
until the cool metal warmed to your touch.
I could hear your chuckle when you heard it chime
on the half-hour.
And I could guess your delight
when you slipped it in your shirt pocket near your heart.

For a moment I envied something that could be carried
with you wherever you went.
And I felt sure that it would be yours to possess
as long as you treasured it.
Yet I smiled even as I counted out the money
to buy it.
Because I knew deep inside myself
that you would know how like that pocket watch I am.

For I am with you wherever you are
and I belong to you
as long as you hold me close
to your heart.
Mercy Graf

Can You Hear Him?

Listen to hear His small voice,
   Can you hear the sounds of weeping?
Consider the hurt He's felt for us,
   The pain, the suffering, the bleeding.

One cruel day, He wept in pain;
   The bruises too many to see.
His love stands without measure,
   His love will forever be.

He's been in our hearts;
   Since breath in our lungs.
There in your chest,
   His songs have been sung.

He's here to bless and free you;
   Don't run from Him any longer,
Accept His love and forgiveness,
   And feel your heart grow stronger.

Time isn't on our side when we delay,
   Don't wait, don't wait;
Tomorrow may never come,
   For tomorrow might be too late.
Jennifer R. Tienken

Life

Life is great, life is grand
But when shall I know where I stand?
I'm completely enjoying this living thing
Someday I'll be soaring — an eagles wing,
Soaring high against the wind,
Wondering when this game will end.
Looking down on life below
Wondering to myself what have I to show?
My accomplishments my goals not met,
Of course life is not over for me yet.
I still have time to prove myself.
I can not reach that high, high shelf —
The one unreachable untouchable for all.
I will not jump too high for I might fall.
Crushing my dreams and all my goals,
Realizing life too has its tolls.
I sometimes wonder — is it really worth being here?
If in the end we all just disappear,
From the earth you are banned remembering forever,
Life is great, and life is grand.
Claudia Jansson

It Is Autumn

Brown the grasses wave upon the hills
As summer lingers, soon to meet its end.
Leaves flutter to earth like countless coins
It welcomes their golden carpet.

A pair of fat grey squirrels leap and tumble with gay abandon
The silence broken by their verbose chatter
And the cawing of a shy onyx raven
From his lofty perch in a pathless forest.

The misty mornings are cold, frost clings to the grasses,
Snowflakes tumble with the wind
Soon its fleecy blanket will tuck the earth to sleep
It is autumn.
Caroline E. Smith

Grandma

You've watched me grow from a baby,
into what you'd call a young lady
You've tried to teach me right from wrong,
so I'd live my life honorable and long.
If I ever needed anything,
you'd help me all you could.
I may not be the best grandchild,
though if I could change my faults, I would!
The love from our family,
and the love from you to me.
Is all I need to live
a joyous life, you'll see.
There's one last thing I need to tell you,
that's very important and true.
That no matter what may come to pass,
I will always love you!!!
Tiffany Cervantes

Opportunity

Life has so many, many choices
   yet we very rarely hear the voices
When opportunity happens to knock
   we find ourselves hiding behind a rock
We don't usually give any second chances
   eventually to find; we've passed all our glances
When we sit with a starving hunger
   that's when we finally begin to wonder
Why did we pass them all up?
   simply to have the very best cup
So when someone comes to your door
   don't play dead, rolled over on the floor
Just get up and stand tall
   and one day you may find; you have it all
Angela Weber

Untitled

Sway, Sway, Sway
The wind goes, as it brushes up
against the weeping willows.
Sunlight beams play peak-a-boo with the trees.
To some living souls, it is a perfect day.

But for one it is not.
Prayers are read
Tears are shed
As the Holy One sprinkles water,
the final lid of life is closed on one soul.

Darkness approaches in the sky and in our hearts.
Optimistic or Pessimistic are the choices of the day,
for the living as well as the deceased.
Is there a place in between?
Or do we call it earth?
Nancy Lee Miles

Frost

As the sun travels beyond our sight
The shadows start to appear.
Minute by minute comes the sky of night
Whispering songs of fear.

The tears freeze upon my face
As the silent voices fall.
Life is no longer an endless race,
Just a lonely, empty, silent hall.

Feeling the depths of hell calling my name,
I look the other way.
The frost came,
And I will never see the light of day.

My beautiful angel come and guide me,
To see all I have lost.
See only what I see,
The color of black on white, the feeling of cold . . . frost.

Debra Dougherty

To Dance With Love

When love comes my way will I know its name?
Will it embrace me sweetly
and beg pardon for delay?

Many a time has it passed me by
each time without regret of remorse,
but that's the way love is of course —
at least for me . . . for now.

Someday I will be loved though I do not know when
I suppose I'll only know then.

Till then I can dream and weave tales of romance
of that certain someone begging me to dance,
begging me to dance.

Adina N. Booker

Footprints For Children

I will take your trusting hand in mine
And lead the way a very brief time
I will pace my steps, I will make them slow
So you may learn each step we go
We will not take the easy road
For you must learn to share the load
When your steps are firm and wide
You will have the faith to leave my side.

Pauline Braswell

The Lighthouse

When tides crash . . .
sands will run, birds will flock,
leaving footprints on wet sand.
salt is in the air — mist is everywhere,
on the rocks, on the sand . . .
And the old lighthouse,
it still stands, it still shines —
even through the roughest tides.
The cliffs still take breaths away,
the sea still comes and goes . . .
but you are always there,
to hold, to care, to love . . .
And unlike the sea,
you will never come and go,
but instead, stand through it all,
like the old lighthouse.
You will be there, leading the way,
always showing me your love,
even when I'm lost at sea.

Brian Du Bois

Yosemite Bear

There once was a bear in Yosemite
Who saw a blue van and said, "Lucky me!"

"It smells like spilled soda, oh my, what an aroma!
Hey look, bran muffins just for me!"

"The owners were so lame to leave this fair 'game'.
I think I'll break in just the same!"

"A '93 Dodge, no problem with these claws.
I'll just pop out this window with my paw."

"There's glass everywhere, but what do I care?
Bran muffins are tasty to this hungry bear!"

"Stop yelling and clapping! You're ruining my snacking!
Watch out, or I may send you packing!"

"Just wait! I'm not done! Ok, so you've won.
But I'll meander, not run. You humans are no fun!"

Betty Hogan

Sunrise Memories

My alarm buzzed at 6:00 AM.
I pulled on a pair of faded blue jeans and a soft pink sweat shirt.
As I peered through the mini-blinds, I merrily sighed.
I had not missed it; The sun was yet to rise.
I slowly opened the creaky door,
For fear I would wake the not-so-early birds.
Stepping onto the cold brick porch I felt a sudden chill run through me
Tickling my toes and causing my excitement to rise.
I ran through the damp grass to an old, rotting tree stump to wait.
In amazement, I watched as the huge, round ball of fiery red light
Emerged from beyond the rolling hills.
The bold bright rays of the golden sunlight
Stunned my anxious, onlooking eyes.
I was captivated by the magic and beauty of the King of the Sky.
The breathtaking views of the spurting colors made me long to reach out
And be a part of their intense magic.
A sadness came over me as I realized it was rapidly slipping away.
The truth sank in like a setting sun and I knew it was gone for the day.
I then smiled intently when I remembered, I could look forward to many
More glorious mornings full of beautiful flaming sunrise memories.

Marie Tenny

Someone Watching Over Me

Look upon me and judge me not by my appearance
For my life is hidden within a human shell.
The magic within me cannot be seen, it can only be felt.
To live the life I have lived, you would have to be strong
To overcome the obstacles I have faced.
You would have to posses the will to live on.
I have learned many lessons well and hard,
But from these lessons I have grown wiser.
For you see, I have someone watching over me that gives
me strength — Christ my Savior.

Ricardo Gomez

Memories That Never Fade

Memories from a child of long ago
fill up my heart with thoughts of love.
Freedom abound in a world that cared.
And life held a promise that all was well.
Laughter from voices out of the past.
Bring a smile to my face though
tears fill my eyes.
Onward I march to the beat of my song.
For memories enslave me not.
But set this soul free to roam.

Mildred McVicker

Imprisoned Love

Patient: Love waits. Untouched it grows inside my heart like a
vine, clinging tightly to my soul . . .

Alone: Filled with desire. Passion burns like fire. Through
flames of emotions, testing my devotion. A victim of the
moment. Prisoner of my own design . . .

Time: When together. Two hearts beat as one. Perfectly tuned
to each other, they echoed like thunder. Intense was your
touch. I wanted you so much. How could a feeling so strong,
turn out to be so wrong . . .

Gone: Without warning. You took your love away. I could tell
by the look on your face, someone new had taken my place.
My heart broke in two when you confirmed the news. Taken
by surprise, forced to say goodbye, I cried when you went away . . .

Pain: slowly drains from my body, as I learn to set you free.
Hoping that someday, you will return to me . . .

Now, Always and Forever
I will look forward to times spent with you.
While cherishing the memories of this love that we once knew . . .

Michele Renee Rhoads

America We're Losing Our Children

America wake up!
We're losing our children.
Red, yellow, black and white,
all the same in his sight.

The white horse comes to town,
claims their lives disguised as a clown.
Made to starve on the street,
trading innocence for a bite to eat.

As liquid runs through their veins,
gives pleasure then trades for pain.
Promised a merry-go-round,
takes them up then drops them down.

Searching day after day,
lost not finding the way.
Without enough insight,
to determine the wrong from right.

Tell them they are not alone,
offering a peace filled home.
We must reach out in love,
guided by a greater force from above.

Anna M. Pelto

Dance Celebration

For those with courage to step out
Daring to explore
Unending variations of movements,
Life is but a dance.
For those who never try
For fear of being out of step
Life passes untouched, unexplored.
Let the music begin!
Move to the Universal heartbeat of Love
And the rhythmical ebb and flow of life.
    Improvise
    Harmonize
    Synchronize
Alone . . . Together
Till the dance, the dancer, and the music
    Become One.
In joyous celebration,
    Dance
The dance of life!

Jan Beaty

The Candle

Candle, candle burning bright, lead me through the darkest night.
In the shadows flickering light, heal my sorrow, hear my plight.
Days will come and days will go, some fly by and some go slow.
Memories in my heart so deep, there your love I'll always keep.
Like the candle in the dark, your love glows within my heart,
keeping bright the burning fire of my strong and warm desire.
In my heart I'll place your flame, knowing where to put the blame,
burning softly with no end waiting for your heart to mend.
Like a moth you hover near, your wings will burn is what you fear.
I will catch you with my hands and gently bring you in to land.
There I'll hold you still and quiet chasing day away to night.
I'll light the candle from the embers knowing that your heart remembers.
Heart to heart, fire to fire, ever burning stronger, higher.
Shadows dance in softened light, white hot candle burns tonight.

Connie L. Powell

Daddy

I love you, he said, as he stroked her head.
Yeah right, she sighed, you were never there
those cold, cold nights.

Yes, he replied, yes I was, I was in your
dreams those nights.

She took a ragged breath, sighed daddy
don't leave me in distress.

I won't he choked, I won't leave your side
even after you die, there'll always be a place
you can call home in my heart.

As she died, she finally cried, I loved you
all those years, I just couldn't say what
was on my mind, too much anger blocked the way.

I love you too, my little one,
now please don't go away.

But when she died, he did not cry,
nor did he leave her side,

For the words they spoke were too hard
to let go, and he claims she's still alive.

Audrey Byrd

The Vestibule

No gatekeeper at Kafka's? When I walked inside
The vestibule was one stave wide.

C Minor Prelude pillars two octaves high,
Modest and unadorned — they hardly caught the eye.

An entrance to a hut — enchantment round.
Those pillars stand outside of sound.

My spirit formed that hut: with my heart beats
I searched for it on Westwood streets.

A music student dreaming, through music lecture,
Of vestibules and architecture.

The fugue was dialogue; I wanted silent space
Inside a structure: simple grace.

Bach's conceit: Admit Mirage. Man's
    Estate: Persiflage.

And dialogue must sound — sound and resound
As walls to wrap bare spirit round.

The chords are solid — a mandala grail,
The magic structure where words fail.

The spirit bold, behind time's face
Forever caught in Bach's embrace.

Gloria Julianne Frandle

Safely Home At Last

There's a picture of you by my bed
A thousand good memories of you left in my head
Time passes on without you here but I still know you are near
Telling me not to shed a tear

It's sad that you had to go leave
I know now there's no need to grieve
I trust people when they say we'll all be together one sweet day

Don't worry about me on earth
Have a good time in heaven
Don't forget me or what your life was worth
I'll wait till he calls me home
Till then I pray that you're safely home

Safely home in his arms at last
Precious time has past
You're safely home at last

Melissa A. Bonnell

Morning Walk

Morning comes softly as the sun
starts its walk across the sky.
Shadows that were dark and tall fade
as day comes and night goes by.

Come, take a morning walk with me.
Let's listen to the sounds of a brand new day.
Birds are singing as they sit in the trees.
Hear the warning sounds of a protective blue jay.

Jar flies sending out their messages loud and clear.
Busy bees humming as they fly around.
Hear the barking of a squirrel as it
gathers nuts from the ground.

Come, take a morning walk with me
Breathe in the freshness of cool mountain air.
Feel the breeze upon your face.
Hear the quietness of the hour.

Sylvia Shultz

Morning Break

Morning break, rise a new day,
send through the wind a coded message
for the birds to sing perched up in the trees.

Morning frost, gentle rain shower,
freshly scent the air,
misty dew, sprinkle droplets upon crackling leaves,
refresh, renew.

Morning light, capture a shadow, bare your spirit unto the earth,
radiate magnificent beauty.

Morning dance, glide on a melody with the resonance of nature.

Morning air, whisper, whisper,
dancing petals; reaping blossoms; waltzing flowers; glistening sun;
setting moon; trickling streams; billowy brooks; vibrant mountains;
rainbow skies; birds; trees;
wake up,
morning break, rise a new day.

Crystal L. Blount

My Friend

My friend is always there for me,
to comfort me when I am sad,
when there is no one there for me.
But when I have these feelings,
she will help me battle through these,
feelings to the ones I want to feel . . .
feelings of love and forever friendship.

Janae Johnson

Tearfulality

Tear not the flame of a Broken Heart
Tear not the love that's torn all apart
Tear not the sorrow of a Star gone dim
Tear not the pain of a life filled with grim

Think of the Gentleness of a life span of a tear
Some drops are Bless and some are just dear
They slowly evaporate quickly gone and forgot

A factory of thought try to consume my pain
Unequivocally Reluctant to face a new change
The Heart demands emotion Recklessly with fright
It Beats without Rhythm nor patient nor sight

There's been an Emergency Breakdown in O' Tearfulality
Quick Quick Quickly as you can fill that tear with
Life and Love with the Smiles of Angels from heaven above

All is Well now "the Doves of hope" fly
Sightfully with Cheers to create a new tear
Of happiness deep within the Heart of the absence of fear

Cerdan Smith

The Land Of Humanity

I see the shadowings of long ago in the dark of a winter's night
I search for some sort of beacon but I cannot see a light

My loneliness is inconsolable
My heart is keeping still
My hunger for compassion has not yet had its fill

In horizons far beyond my sight
Where gruesome creatures lie
Open to the gaze of all yet they have drawn no eye

In the land where mountains crumble and the fire eats the sea
Look long and hard and perhaps you might see me
In a mythical body with no soul and a demeanor all my own
That is how you'll find me in a sea of broken bones

The moans of human suffering and the groans of human pain
Fall endlessly upon my ears like water in a rain
and while my misconceptions are misconceptions all my own
For all my misconceptions surely you will break some bones

Ah, the land of humanity where the dragons are here to stay
Where no one ever wins but everyone wants to play
Ah, the land of humanity just a land of hate and lies
Where everyone is what they seem except for their disguise

M. W. Landis

Whisper Along The Seawaves

Days are passing by
    You remain a dearly treasure
Rejection by others
    Such a way of unknowing leisure
Echo of the air breeze
    Like a tiny voice to be swept away
Along the seawaves
    That brought to where you stay
Mark the destiny
    When the wind blows the gloomy ocean astray.

A bright sunshine
    At beaming rays may find me there
Let gentle touch
    Awaken you from a sudden nightmare
Over the spacious sky
    Be not frighten to hear
Nothing will harm you
    For you have been blown out to draw near
Gone are the dark clouds
    When you whisper a simple prayer.

Edna N. Paguntalan

Parties

Parties are the light bulb at the end of a burnt-out week
The spark at 3:00 today
People rush home in a fiery heat
They arrive at seven; leave at ten
But all that's left is
One big pig pen.

Adri Archer

In Service To America

As we approach the summer season
May peace descend onto this earth
And to all men of courage, logic and reason.
America does indeed appreciate your worth.

I see the millennium begin to approach
We must all stand and work together
But violence and prejudice are trying to encroach
And this storm our country will weather.

To be free is our constitutional right
As our beautiful flag is unfurled
May God guide us and give us the sight
To work and pray for justice throughout the world

The challenges numerous rewards all too few
It is my honor and my belief
That America stands alongside of you
To say proudly "Hail to the Chief"

JoAnn Faris CPA

Class Ring

Close by the door he paused to stand
as he took his class ring off of her hand
all who were watching did not dare speak
as a silent tear ran down his cheek
all through his mind the memories ran
of all the times they played in the sand
but now her eyes were so terribly cold
he'll never again have her to hold
they watched in silence as he bent down near
to whisper "I love you" softly in her ear
in touching her face he began to cry
he put on his class ring he wanted to die
and just as the wind started to blow
they lowered the casket into the ground so low

Tamara L. Hines

Self-Portrait

Crump in every perspective.
His taste is great especially in friends.
Right choice in socks.
Is kind, nice, and easy going to a friend in need.
Schoolin' anybody, anytime, anywhere that tries to get the
    train off schedule.

Loving and caring to others, the Gentle Giant off the basketball court.
Assuring and insuring to have around.
Veering over anybody, that's why he's the BC.
Appreciative to any little thing done for him.
Never-the-less always trying to be the best.

Chris Lavan

Life

Life is like a house,
It must have a good foundation to grow on,
It must be showered with love and care,
It wears with age but,
With each day comes a memory.

Meghan Mize

Lessons

A nation met in gray and blue
across the summer-golden field
of Old Josiah Flander, who
farmed wheat, his eye on profit's yield.

The blue entrenched upon the hill,
defeated time and time before.
At Fredericksburg and Chancelorsville
they'd died, eyes wide to heavens's door.

The men in gray were led by one
who rode the white rose on the height.
Entranced by sultry sabre song,
eyes bright, eager for the fight.

"Hurrah, boys!" and the army broke into the storm of cannon crying.
Thirteen thousand clad in smoke of steadfast faith, defiant, dying.

The shadow crossed the valley then, the Old Man urging on the action.
Fewer now, and less again; the math of war is all subtraction.

The Old Man turned his eyes away.
The guns had reaped their wretched yield.
The future's bright gold harvest lay
among the dead in Flander's field.

John A. Friday

Seize The Grain

Seize the grain and chaff the wheat
soldiers came with no retreat,
saving up against the day
my children fled and ran away.
Justice has not been repaid.
Surface for a time again,
in boldness now, tis mine I send,
against the armies coming now
when caught off guard, to win I've vowed.
Sealed unto the day it is done
ancient battles we have won,
France at war with me again
mountains built against that day,
no hills nor mounds made out of clay.
Hear me as I speak this day
I have passed along the way,
"unjust reward", some think to say
as they break down my vow shall stay.
Is not all I see about to be
since dawn until eternity?

Barbara R. Sullivan

My Wish For You

I wish for you, a nice cool breeze
on a hot summer day
I wish for you, a field of
wild flowers along the way,
I wish for you, a crackling
fire to warm you on a cold
winter's night
I wish for you the joy of laughter
in a child's delight
I wish for you, the warmth
from a friends embrace
I wish for you always smiles
upon your face
I wish for you, a world of rainbows
and stars that shine from up above
I wish for you, a world filled
with joy, peace, and love
I wish for you, sunrises and sunsets for only your eyes to see

I wish for you a world filled with perfect harmony and
precious memories

Morry Donald Sher

Account Of A Stargazer

By the obscured stairs I gaze at the sky,
and nothing shines but twinkling stars.
Strange sensation sneaks by,
sending my emotions trots afar.

Like a star with burning flames,
I will flush at the end of dusk.
with fellow stars our radiance shone,
showing resplendence beyond morn.

The sky now masked with choice not mine,
gone the stars carrying my name.
Alone in the dark I quietly whine,
for who shall ignite my incandescence.

For every star yearn for a shine,
alone in the sky I sorrowfully sigh.
Never I wish be a lonely star,
forever drown in the barren sky.

Riady Gozali

Memory

We were so young that year,
The summer that you were here.
I think of what we had done,
Those long summer days were so fun.
You picked me flowers, wrote me rhyme,
We had it all, except for time.
We walked together, hand in hand,
We talked together, our futures we planned.
Now those days, once so clear.
Make me wish you were still here.

Kris Beatty

Untitled

Do not stand at my grave and weep.
For I'm not there.
I am the wind that blows softly across your face.
I am the tree that cast a giant shadow to free you from the hot sun.
I am a bird that soars over the land.
I'm a star that glistens in the night.
I am the flowers that dance in the fields.
I am the warmth in the sun on a cold day.
I am cool water that flows in rivers and streams.
Weep not for me. For I'm not there.
Feel me, taste me, see me, for I'm everywhere.

Thad Pinder

Time's Shadows

To fight your brothers
is your daily task,
but not on fields green
with sword or lance.
You must battle with ideas,
fight with your heroes deeds,
to be remembered by time
once your soul is freed.
The point of life is to mark your place.
To cast a shadow across time's face.

To do deeds that ignite the wind,
send fire through the air.
Soar over boundaries built,
and up times windy stair.
To speak words that spark ideas
in minds left dull and bare.
Fly over defeat's wall of flame
and lift another up from there.
To send shadows that pull from life's dead end
a man, to fight again.

Elizabeth Bly

Deprivation

Tracing the lines of an age never known.
A precious piece of work never called your own.
So you feel that you can't go on,
Pleading insanity of a mind that's not strong.
And you sing to me,
With the voice of an open sea.

Calling upon an era of a promise denied.
Falling beneath a world that won't hear your cry.
It claws at the depths of your soul.
A youth thrust in with the old.
And you sing to me,
With the voice of an open sea.

Laying underground in the cold of a world unheard.
A prompt destination only to be deferred.
Giving what was never received.
Wanting what could never be conceived.
And you sing to me,
With the voice of an open sea.

Dawn McNamara

Alignment Of The Planets

The Planets don't rest. They are always in motion
And wander in space like the ships on the ocean.
But once in millennium they should align
In total accord with majestic design,
The perfect design of Creation.

When Planets are ready it's time for the sun,
The great patriarch of this powerful clan,
To check them for proper arrangement and pace,
To aim at invisible target in space,
The space far away from the System.

It's only the perfect alignment, which yields
A sudden release of mysterious fields,
An impulse, which can for an instant erase
The gravity's overprotective embrace,
The jealous embrace of the Galaxy.

A blast! And the impulse is well on its track.
It never will stop and will never turn back.
It's carrying the Message. And like in the past
The Planets will wait for that answering blast,
The blast from a different Universe.

Isaac Bell

So Long

You think that we'll always be friends?
That our time together will never end?
Well then wake up!
We're gonna fight, but we'll always make up.

The worst thing, the one that hurts me most of all,
Is the fact that we won't really keep in touch after all.

We spent years building our friendship, "for what?"
Some day I'll catch up with you along the road.
We might say "Hi" and "Bye," but never like before.
Now, it's our last year and, to me, you mean even more.

I know I'm trying to save a sinking ship,
But I hope the captain won't go down with this Friendship.

There'll be days when things go wrong,
Only I won't be there to keep you strong.
These are the best days of our lives,
I've known you for so long, so long.

I've never had to learn to say goodbye, so, so long.
This poems makes me cry; so long my friend, so long.

Chrissy Hebert

Anything For Love

I would do anything for you,
If you brought back "Love" the feeling I once knew.
To feel a tender touch.
To love once again with a passion so much.
To give a kiss of lust,
And to never want to let go.
To hear those special whispers,
And to make Love slow.
To love once again like I never had before.
To love for love and go beyond more.
To live to be your life.
To live to be someday your wife.
Never to feel loneliness again.
To throw away the past sorrow and all the pain.
To bring dreams into reality.
To be your every fantasy.
To die in vain,
Just to have Love once again . . .

. . . The feeling I've lost in time.

Rosie M. Ramirez

Self-Portrait

Knowing and not knowing at the same time
Indecisive
Tiresome

Creative
Logical
Efficacious
Lazy
Apprehensive
Nonsensical
Dramatic

Kit Cleland

Love

Love is like a bonfire
It flares up now and again
The warm coals smolder in your heart
but love can be extinguished by jealousy
Like water on the fire.

Sarah Willis

Time To Say Goodbye

A kiss upon the cheek
A glance into his eyes
To forget his disrespect
To forget all his lies

For all the times he said I'm sorry
And wiped away my tears
For he's the one who's caused all the pain
And created all my fears

But no amount of diamonds
No amount of pearls
Could make me forget
All his other girls

I lay my head against his chest
Making a bet
That he's thinking of another
Love he's met

There's no time to worry
There's no time to cry
For once again it's come the time
For us to say goodbye

Missy Boney

Daddy's Little Girl

There's something very special about that little girl of mine,
I wish that I could keep her here — with me all the time.
I think about her constantly when she's not here with me,
I think of playing games with her; or just to watch TV.

My little girl is very wise, despite her tender years,
And all her words of wisdom often fills my eyes with tears.
All her fun-filled laughter rings throughout our large old house,
But then she goes away again, and it's quiet as a mouse.

The weeks that I don't have her — they creep along so slow;
Does she know how much I miss her? How hard it is to let her go?
Sometimes I have to make her mind. Have I been fair? I've tried.
But to see those tears well up in her eyes; just tears me up inside.

Memories we've made together, we'll keep forever in our hearts.
And when we think about them, we're never far apart.
So as I say in closing, with all my heart, soul and love —
To my beautiful daughter, Samantha, you're my God send from above.

Love, Daddy

Jeffrey S. Finley

Nick

Those big folk you went home with
Who seem bent on prodding you
Are friends of mine and as you'll find
Take time adjusting to.
But just like me, I'm sure, in time
With patience while you're weighing
The options opened up to you
Like leaving home or staying
I guess I've spent more time with them
It seems like quite a while.
Ten fingers, toes and button nose
You took them with your smile
You're new right now, I'm sure you'll take
Some time to settle in.
And you're just blowing bubbles
Warming hearts with every grin
Well Nick those smiles, those big folk make
Seems you're not all that trouble
You won both hearts with just a grin
A smile, perhaps a bubble.

Ed Houghton

Sunshine

Sunshine is a blazing chariot through the clouds
It is beaming intensely
It is a vigorous glow of light
That streaks away the darkness we have to bear
As the night passes by.

Jennifer Cohen

Gentry's Bluff

There is a place I love to go
A place where soft breezes blow
For there fear vanishes away
All my troubles and cares of the day

It stirs all the desires of my heart
A haven from which I dread to part
My fondest wishes seem to come true
This place I go when I feel blue

Hear the rushing sound of the waterfall
See the trees that grow ever so tall
I go there when life seems rough
This place called Gentry's bluff

Gracie Gunn

Mourn After Mourn

Missing the love of one so dear
Seeing her face, how I wish she were here
Time spent alone
With thoughts

Thoughts of mom that make me cry
Squeezing my heart
My stomach in knots
Aching, throbbing, pounding, head

Head too heavy to lift
I'm overwhelmed with
Panicky feelings of dread
How do I continue to overcome

Overcome
The fear, the tremors, the pain
To see the light
Through the night

Night
After night
Storm after storm
Mourn after mourn

Sharon Fournier

Can This Be Love?

Before, I had promised the almighty
Not to be in love with anybody,
Because a great hindrance it will be
Of my entering into the nunnery,
But then you came to me . . .

How can I refuse
The love in me you propose?
Is it because I find you being true,
Or I envy other girls too?
Or maybe I love you so . . .

Are you the sign to show me what's ahead
So I can take a different road instead?
Are you being sent from above?
To show me what is love . . .

Easter Omandam-Byrne

Ocean Blue

The ocean is a beautiful starfish
Reaching for the blue sky
With white cresting waves crashing like thunder
It holds great powers that can't be controlled
It is one of God's most wonderful creations.

Taylor Filo

Fran . . .

   Fran was a hurricane that we as a people won't ever forget, she came in and went out strong, it was only by God's grace and mercy that we were able to keep holding on. There were a lot of people that were in despair, but no matter how strong the storm, God was right there.

   It is written he will never leave or forsake us, if only in him we will trust. Fran was bringing a message that a lot of us did not get, if we don't read the handwriting on the wall, we will surely have a lot to regret. We are living in some hideous times, I am so glad that Jesus is mine.

   So let us hold our heads up high and don't forget to pray, having the reassurance that God will lead us and show is the way. There will be other storms stronger than Fran, oh Haleigh, God will and he can.

Hilda Antone

What Can I Say?

Dearest Emilie what can I say?
My heart aches for you each passing day.
At times I think I'll go insane,
As I feel my sanity going down the drain.
The future I see seems dim and lonely
But as time passes I know I'll love you only.
I long for the sight of your beautiful face,
And your body clothed in shimmering lace.
My senses yearn for the feel of your skin,
It becomes a pain I can't keep within.
My lips cry out for a passionate kiss,
Oh that's something I desperately miss.
I wish I could hold you in my arms again
And never let go even if the world should end.
I want you to hold me in your loving embrace
Until my palms start to sweat and my heart starts to race.
So until the day comes when we can meet once more
Shut up your heart and lock up the door.
Then I shall come and use my love as the key
To unlock your heart and hold it for eternity.

Zachary Stauffer

That Apple

When Eve took walks in Eden's lovely garden,
   She was undressed without a sense of shame.
She did not even ask for Adam's pardon,
   Because she felt he'd treat her just the same.

Then Adam tempted Eve to eat that apple,
   Which prompted her to change into a prude,
Knowing that henceforth she had to grapple
   With that disturbing problem of the nude.

This modesty has caused the men to worry,
   A husband might find reason to despair,

'Cause he must wait, although he's in a hurry,
   While she decides what she is going to wear.

But in these days the girls dress less discreetly,
   In fact they hide so little from the men,
Before bikinis disappear completely,
   It's time to pass that apple 'round again!

Elvin Ragnvald Heiberg

Hope

Hope is a snowflake tumbling down from the sky
Through the holes in the oak
Turning sideways in the crescent moon
Laying softly on the white fur of his coat.

Allen Henning

Our Love

We were brought together by God, and friends,
And now, we are finalizing our love,
In the sacred ceremony of marriage.

Our love has increased by leaps and bounds,
And we get to express our love,
On this day, our wedding day.

Like the ocean that changes the surf,
Our lives will be constantly changing,
And with that, our love will grow stronger,
With each passing day.

The angels in heaven are smiling down on us,
And with God's blessing,
Our marriage is going to be,
One of strength, faith and most of all love.

Kathy Pagel

Leave Something For Me

Take a look at the forest, it's our chemistry
Think deeply before you kill that next tree
Seven trees per person, it takes to live
You take from the forest, but what do you give?
The squirrels, opossum, rabbits, birds, and deer
Live every moment in caution and fear
They leave their habitat early each morning
Return at dusk without any warning
Only to find their homes all uprooted
To housing developments all just suited
You'll wait till the last blade of grass is gone
Then too late you'll ask "where have I gone wrong?"
A squirrel less, a bunny or two
Won't matter at all, because it's for you
To sit yourself in a house so fine
Such removal of nature should be a crime
Leave the forests for your children to stroll
Destroy no more, it has taken its toll
To leave only a pine cone and perhaps a tree
Selfish as you are, you've left nothing for me

Rose DeLia

By The Hand Of God

Sweet little Asian girl, with chocolate eyes,
at 28, young body riddled with cerebral palsy,
by the hand of God.
She pales a deep ash white,
once someone gives her a sour
distasteful stare.
Sometimes she is embarrassed
she is unlike the others.
Her right hand and leg cause her discomfort
at times by age.
She wants that gigantic huge black pit
to swallow her entire flesh.
Beyond is the deteriorating
and harsh world. The land with able-bodied
strangers.
She loves a challenge, but must work twice
as hard.
One day she will honor herself,
one day God will make her whole
again.

Laurie Fay Yoshino

Boot Camp Blues

I find myself far away from home,
And the kid inside me feels scared and all alone.

Stuck with a bunch of men I don't even know,
Away from their families and children stuck outside Chicago.

With one goal in sight, and that is to graduate,
And start my new civilian life with a clean slate.

We all came here for something to prove,
Stuck around females and we can't even bust a move.

I sometimes think why I signed my name on that line,
I'll figure it out in a matter of time.

Dreams and goals I have to set,
For there is a whole world out there I haven't seen yet.

Like Christopher Columbus I'll travel around the earth,
Waiting to find out what my life is worth.

Inside my mind I strive to achieve,
But to achieve, my heart and mind must believe.

I love my Mom, she means everything to me,
While I'm away supporting my country, the land of the free.

Andrew Jonathan Frerichs

Why?

Why don't you love me?
Why don't you care?
Why when I needed you,
You were not there?
When you said the things you said,
Did you feel my pain?
Did you feel these terrible words,
Imprinted in my brain?

Did you really love me,
Or was that just a lie?
Did you really love me,
Or do you just like seeing me cry?
All my life I've waited for someone just like you
Just to hear these terrible words, "I don't care for you."
I'll cry, and cry, and cry
Until my eyes run dry.

And forever I will ask myself
This question . . . "Why?"

Dawnyell Barnes

Addiction

Addiction is a vacuum cleaner sucking up your life
Little by little
Piece by piece
Like a dirty old carpet.

Jacques Badon

Essence

Essence of life, link to the stars
Of what reality the soul
Are we part of it, is it part of us
The question is who's in control

To some it's once and we're gone
To others it's time after time
Through karma we work because lessons we shirk
Or be cast to the pit for one crime

The soul is the ultimate prize
Sought by whom and for what
To hang on a wall, maybe set in a hall
For the tale of how it was caught

The vessel grows tired and withers away
As the essence is gaining its strength
Poised to fly free from the prison of thee
On a journey of much questioned length

D. Tex Gipson

Life Is Full Of Pain . . .

Now have you ever sat and wondered how life would be
with no crimes, no drugs and no poverty
no murders, no rapers, no wars, no disease,
no hunger, everyone living peacefully
but that's life you know be in it get with it
there's no turning back cause it's a one way ticket
now let's take a minute to talk about contortion,
distortion, leading to corruption
all this commotion, causing interruptions,
of the life that you try to live with production
stop the madness lets put an end to the war
with all the violence can we stand anymore
a girl is robbing — cause her head is throbbing
to get a rock for the ten minute shock
she can't begin to quit 'cause it's right around the block
we were put on this earth to live the best we can
to live peacefully and love our brother man
it's a long climb to fortune and fame
and on the way remember life is full of pain . . .

Anthony Craig Teasley

Goodbye

It's time . . .

I have to tell you how I feel.
You meant so much, for so long.
You were my first love, before I knew what love was.
You taught me to believe in myself.
To follow my heart . . . wherever it led.
To love unconditionally.
And to trust in others.
You showed me a lifetime's worth of joy and happiness . . .

Only now I'm left with emptiness and despair.
Shattered dreams and failed expectations.
A shadow of my former self.
Left to wander alone, and wonder why.

You've moved on, I'm sure.
Only I've been trapped back there.
Struggling to get free from you.
Fighting my fears, the pain, the agony, to finally break away.
So I'm saying it now, not for you but for me.

It's time I say goodbye . . .

Mark Borowiak

J.O.Y.

A special way of showing the things that you feel,
Assuring the world that emotions are real.
Maybe twice in a lifetime a chance will arise
To show to your loved ones the tears in your eyes.

Be not afraid, not ashamed or blue.
These tears are diamonds, and emeralds too.
For teardrops are Holy, and I'll tell you why.
Just open your eyes and look to the sky.

The good Lord had but one lonely Son.
He walked on the earth and loved everyone.
But evil temptation, hatred and strife
Spelled the end of the road and took Jesus' life.

I often have wondered but now I am sure;
What are the limits one can endure?
Maybe once in a lifetime these limits arise,
And you will display those jewels in your eyes.

The limits for God came one stormy day,
When evil temptation took His Son's life away.
So be proud to cry Dad, don't run and hide.
Think of our Lord — how He must have cried!

Dana W. Brown

A Crystal Moment Of My Life

In the middle of my autumn sun
I met two blue lightings,
a golden cascade,
a mystical pearl and coral,
an alabaster presence: You,
April bright
came to me (gray afternoon).

Suddenly, I know you know too.
You are not here but
we are tasting together
the four seasons as a beautiful weather . . .
though, they hurt me. I grow older.

If you still are coming down through the narrows
of the river of my life,
please let me know beforehand,
and my being will shut very beautifully,
as when the heart of my soul imagines
the power of your intense fragility.

Victor Betancourt

Jealousy

Oh! You poison jealousy
Hidden in the depths of my soul
Wishing only to reap
The spoils of my unhappiness!

You hoary seeker
Flowing passionately through my veins
How many conquests will you make?

Subtle — sleek — parasite
Slowly drain the life from my contentment
Hungry wolf in love's form disguised
Rocking the balance of my sanity
When will your triumphs end?

Russell J. Fetherolf

The Way

There is a way that seems so right
It promises day without any night
Beware that way is not my friend
Even wishful thinking comes to an end

That way leads one on a crowded road
With happy-go-luckies and shunners of the load
Dreamers who dream of a better way
And pass up opportunities day by day

The fear of God is a hint to the wise
Empowered with wisdom to see things in disguise
Though filled with challenges, don't you see
It leads to the path of reality

Take fast hold of instruction, let her not go
She is your life, she'll cause you to know
Life is beautiful, but life is a fight
Life is rewarding when you do what's right

Ethel H. Williams

Sure Dreams

My dreams came true the day we met
With you I've found not only my greatest love
    but also my very best friend
It was love that brought us together
    that joined our hearts as one
You're my life, my world, my forever
    always be by my side
I promise you a lifetime of love
    sharing and making our times together
        our special memories to fill the heart
My love we will move mountains together

Penny A. Tucker

Freedom On The Mississippi River

In the morning I look through my window
And I see the majestic Mississippi
running free and silent
and on his back he carries a
large barge loaded with
coal and oil without any turmoil.
I can see the beautiful eagle
flying free over the big river
he spreads his wings and surfaces
in the wind.
Boaters cruise free enjoying the river calm.
On the river shore I can see
beautiful trees of elm.
the boaters cruise free
the river runs free,
the eagle flies free
the wind blows free
why I can not be free?

Pablo B. Plunkett

Slow Burn

My reflection in the mirror is bittersweet
My eyes see directly into my soul.
What I see makes me grab hold then retreat,
My reality is encumbered, I loose control.
What kind of man allows fear to lead the way
Change his fortune, control his day?
What kind of man? He is the reflection of me,
Lost and alone without eyes to see.

My heart cries somber tears in the rain.
It's as if my soul simply walked away;
But lacking a soul means lacking the pain.
Reluctantly I must choose to stay again today.
When will I loose the ability to choose?
I simply take what life gives in fates bold move.
I saunter silently towards this inevitable end,
Only to be cheated by fear again.

Antonio David

Untitled

I wonder what makes one fall in love?
Is it the words one says without a sound or
is it the smile one's face shows after a passionate kiss?
It is all of this and more.

You find love inside and out.
Sometimes hidden, but others well shown!
It comes in all sizes, shape and designs.
If only love came easy, found without a broken heart.

Misty Smith

Legacy (An Ode To My Father)

The path he trod was long and steep, bricks of suffering paved the way.
A child born ill, a young wife dead, how much could one man pay?
But strength became his mortar and life's road did he repair.
While grief always traveled with him, he withstood winds of despair.

As he weathered all life's turbulence, he bent but never broke.
And though illness finally claimed his limbs, he still found time to joke.
Though wracked with pain, his tortured face never lost its gentle smile.
When with a rhyme he'd greet you, for complaint was not his style!

The wisdom of the ages shone from his weary eyes.
Thru decades he had seen all things, nothing now came as surprise.
So small and frail he lay there, as his final fight he waged.
And he battled, and grew angry — death's approach filled him with rage!

For so much he still had left to do, as his flame of life burned out.
But the legacy he left me, taught me what life's all about.
His philosophy of courage, guides my journey, so he's near.
While life's perils may surround me, I move forward with no fear.

Though he's gone, he's always with me like a candle burning bright.
It's the legacy of survival that remains with me tonight.
And now stars somewhere in heaven, shine much brighter every day.
As his love beams down upon me, and his light still guides my way.

Phyllis R. Stellman

Silence Is Deadly

As the soul slips into darkness.
We see no way out of the darkness.
The fear that surrounds the heart has only one answer
to free the heart and soul.
From the darkness comes the light
Then we are free to become whole again.
But to still not speak my name.
To still hide from the darkness.
To say I never lived or was part of your life.
You know who you are.
Because you are still in the darkness yourself.

Denise Nelson

Summer

Within her heart lay a dream
her future was in God's hands
she had a smile for everyone
even the people who were always mean.
She cared not what others thought of her
if someone said something mean she'd just smile and go on her way.
She was a sweet, kind, and gentle child who put her faith in God.
And now she is glorifying in the heaven's and has no more worries.

Jenni Kidd

When I Was A Child

When I was a child I owned
about fifty billion G. I. Joe figures.
I broke off all of their thumbs. I don't know why.
When I was a child I had a wart
removed from my finger
and brought it in for show and tell.
I lost it. It's probably waiting
for some girl to find it,
squished between the pages of a history book.
When I was a child I tried out for first base
on our baseball team.
The ball ricocheted off my head — twice.
When I was a child I spent Saturday mornings
watching Wile E. Coyote lose his eternal fight
with the roadrunner and eating triple-decker
peanut butter and jelly sandwiches without a napkin.
When I was a child I went to a boy scout
summer camp and learned what honor meant.
When I was a child I laughed and dreamed
and thought it would all last forever.

Daniel Hankee

Life's Simple Pleasures

Life's simple pleasures are the best . . .
like watching a shooting star stretching across a moonlit sky
or laying under a shady tree letting time just tick on by.
Like watching a rainbow form after a warm summer rain
or cruising through the country side on an old time train.
Like hearing your little baby start to repeat things you say
or watching snow begin to fall late eve into Christmas day.
Like sitting down for thanksgiving with your family members there
or meeting an old friend and talking about the times you both did
share. Yes, daily things you may do could be little hidden treasures,
I'm talking about things all around us . . . life's simple pleasures.

Ronald P. Olsen

Seasons

Somewhere in the mountains
where majestic beauties grow,
a man takes in the luster of
the freshly fallen snow.

Somewhere a field of grain welcomes
the spring rains, coming down
from the sky and washing over the plains.

Somewhere a flower waits for the
summers sunlight, to help it to
flourish and to grow up just right.

Somewhere as the leaves of autumn are
falling from the trees, a child looks
with wonder at the sight of these.

So you see it is good to have some
of each season, because somewhere,
someone appreciates them for all the
right reasons.

Rhonda C. Widener

The Morning Sun

My skin is old, my hair is gray, the years of
youth have passed away.

The sun comes up and all is sane, I have
arthritis, my morning pain.

I ask the Lord "please hold me tight," the
pain is gone, and all is right.

I thank the Lord for this beautiful day, and
before I know it, it's gone away.

The sun has set, the sky is bright, "please
carry me Lord, through the night."

Well, the sun comes up and the sky is blue,
thank you Lord . . . thank you.

Michael E. King

Getting Old

I am not the woman
In the flowered dress
And sturdy shoes
Leaning on her cane.

I am flying across the sky
Picking bouquets of peonies and lupine
Eating wild grapes by the water's edge
Wading in the creeks of the world.

O joyous flight.

But she calls me back, crying like a child
Clutching me with gnarled fingers.

"Don't leave me," she says, "Don't go."
I remove her fingers.
"I will stay . . . for a little while . . . old woman."

Maxine Clarke

Broken World

Wanting to be put back in place
By so many people, face to face
Can we fix it by a thing called race
So much hatred, so much pain
What would it take to fix it again?
There's so many ways I could think of
Two of them would be Jesus and love
No matter what race or religion you may be
We could all bond together and bow on our knees
Love one another as you would have them love you
You would really be surprised what that could do
Some aren't as fortunate as other ones are
But in the eyes of the Lord, we are equal, by far
If we could all join together on each other's accord
I believe we could help mend this broken world

Gary G. Lilly

Trees And Dreams

Would you come with me to a place I know
Where the trees are old and huge?
The sun filters down through wind fluttered leaves.
From repose as through a prism
You can see diamonds and fireworks.
The oldest leaves on the ground have lost all substance
Leaving only the lacy veins,
Often have I wished to weave them
Through the fabric of my life.
Could I trace the shadows of the leaves on your skin
So lightly with my fingertips?
Would you lay your head on my breast
To feel the words as I share my dreams?
Would you tell me yours?

Linda Lombard

Untitled

Sacred dreams, hold near to me.
The love of fond memories stay close and dear.
Sacred vows, a bond not to be broken.
A love that holds true to one's heart.
Sacred ground where he walked many times.
A ground covered by manmade construction.
Footprints exist no longer.
Sacred man, one who died to give life . . .
Sacred sacrifice.

Aimee L. Weatherly

Safe

White deceptive fog of death
Contaminating cells of born and unborn.
Trucks full and spewing the born splashing in fog.
The world decrying the mad men of Germany
Yet more slowly we were
Murdering our own born and unborn.
Windows open to the dreamy safe pest killer,
Clouds between the bed and ceiling
Safe was meaningless to the born children.
Safe little girls became women
Women with breasts deformed, useless, ugly but safe.
Women who cry in anguish
Hair gone, skin sallow, tossed away,
Carved and unwanted but safe.
Mad men profess safe for profit
Thus condemn their own children then and still.
Define safe
That humanity may continue with lungs clear,
Breasts beautiful,
Truly safe.

Mary Glenn McMurry

No Carrots For Me

As the school year begins, they walk through the door, looking scared
and a little unsure. They look at the toys, books and the blocks, find
their cubbies while their knees knock. They are shown their names over
and over again, but won't let go of their comforting hand. They wander
around, then look ready to go, but unfortunately the answer is no. They
are preschoolers now with their day ahead, for the parents who leave
them, we know their dread. To say goodbye, or watch them cry, often
they too have a tear in their eye. 9:30 is clean up, the families have gone,
now it's time for a story or song; maybe an experiment that won't take
too long. It's a time where we learn, listen, and sit, laugh a lot and hug a
bit. We then have snack "Oh, what could be?" "Pudding, fruit, no
carrots for me." They pour their juice and fill it halfway, there may
be some spills but not today; next it's playground time, big? Or
small? A great place to run or throw a ball. They can scream and
yell and swing up high, you can hear them say "push me to the
sky." It's story time, back to the rug. This time there's a push,
nudge, and shrug. They're hot and bothered yet ready to play as we
enter the last hour of our day. The centers are open, the children
scramble, in housekeeping you hear them ramble and ramble. Block
corner is busy building a town, then the sound of them crashing down;
laughter a tear then they build them again. It's all about coping and
being a friend.

Sarah Perkins Cortese

Gentle Lover

It is early dawn
The sun, like a gentle lover barely rises over the horizon.
The soft early morning light let's me believe as though we are alone.
There is a light breeze that enters thru my window.
And as I lay there, it gently whispers over my face and shoulders.
Caressing me, making slow beautiful love to me,
like a gentle and passionate lover.
Who will lift me to the heavens, just as the sun fully emerges
over the sky.

Nora Elia Guevara

Dream

In my dreams I prayed to God
for those who sacrificed in pain
and for those who died o'er gallows,
with the last word of freedom.

We defend our freedom from enemies
and from those who try to destroy
our dreams of tomorrow to come,
and for those, who will follow us.

Dreams are full of happiness and sorrows
that is in all of us around
we celebrate with joy and remember those,
who sacrificed for our freedom we love.

Otto Valnoha

Jealousy

Always using your peripheral vision to see what your friend has,
Creepy looks on your devilish face as you covet her new
Car,
book,
boyfriend . . .

Chaney Ferguson

Faith, Hope And Charity

Faith is the answer, trust is the key,
to all life's problems, whatever they be.

Hope for a vision, want of a dream,
sustains our desire, with our God supreme.

Charity's easy, just if we try,
to give of our substance, that money can't buy.

Faith, hope, charity, these three abide,
just stay close to Jesus, with him by your side.

Steve Strande

Our Little Girl

Sweet little baby soft and pink.
Sleeps so soundly not even a wink.
Dreaming of the heavens above, and all the beauties of nature you love.
When you awake you're active and gay, ready to explore
another new day.
Crawling and wandering about the house, keeps you busy and
quiet as a mouse.
A year has gone by and now you are one. Walking and romping
around in the sun.
Baby dolls that squeak and cry, have your attention as time goes by.
Mommy and daddy are proud of their girl, who brightened their
lives and set their heart a whirl. How beautiful you've grown as
years go by, winking and blinking to catch a boys eye. Even
though you're getting older, you're still our little girl and a
beauty in the eyes of the beholder.

Maryann Castardi

My Enigma

I walk as a woman, I have walked as a child
I close my eyes, darkness falls and I became the land
strong like rock, smooth as sand, I saw the waters of
the oceans, I dove into it and became a whale,
knowing all the secrets of life from time unending
I flew up suddenly towards the sky and became an eagle
flying high, seeing a flame of light it was the sun
I became a circle in the middle of this great heat
I was part of the eye of God and it all was made one,
his love has no walls, take in a deep breathe now and
know one gift of God.

Mamie L. Jackson

A Heart With No Home

Lights all a glitter, lights all aglow
Cold winter night, soft gentle snow
Lover's kissing quickly, underneath mistletoe
Couples talking and laughing, as they all hurry by
Their happiness only, brings tears to my eyes
All the shoppers and lovers, this Christmas Eve night
No goodbyes, just hellos, voices shriek with surprise
Echoing sounds of happiness, underneath Christmas skies
Seem's all's well in heaven, thru the glittering lights
And everyone needs someone, on a cold winter night
Nothing is lonelier, than a "heart with no home"
Nothing seems colder, than Christmas alone
Seem's everybody's got someone, everybody but me
To talk with and laugh with, to set themselves free
Lover's passing by, walking hand in hand
Only one lonely me, needing one special man
Seems somehow, I was left out of God's Master plan
It gets harder and harder, being alone
And nothing is lonelier, than a "heart with no home"

Phyllis Strong

Youth

Youth is a tornado spinning all over planet Earth
Tearing up the trees
Destroying our lovely homes
Making our community smaller
By age.

Thomas Lampson

How Small Are We Anyway?

Can you see me? Will they hear me, what I say. Because if they
cannot, it is fruitless my endeavor to please . . .

Like spring we blossom, so alive and fragrant. Like new life,
does the warmth bring us forth. Until we live the balance of our years,
only to feel the seasons turn. We, like the bright foliage of nature,
return to a freeze . . .

The loveliness of life, we stay but an instant, compared to the
rocks and dust of this earth . . .

First an infant, then a child, we grow to maturity. Sustain two
million heartbeats of existence, become aged, and wish we could,
in fact, return to re-birth . . .

Of life? Not necessarily. Not this one anyway, is the true
answer that we seek . . .

For only our legacies will inherit the earth that we leave. As say
the Holy Scriptures, I believe we are referred to as, "The Meek."

Ed Roth

Please Love Don't Walk Away

There's an empty place inside of me which longs for someone's warmth.
A place that's full of loneliness and fears so of being harmed.
It's the part of me that's the weakest — the part that's like a child.
It longs for tenderness and love — to be treated kind and mild.
So many times it's been broken — so many times abused.
Now it looks for shelter — so tired of being used.
It needs protected from the games so many people play.
Oh please love don't another time get up and walk away.
Can't take any more pretending. Can't stand another lie.
Can someone restore my faith in love and wipe these tear drops dry.
Can someone fill this empty place and rid me of my fears,
so my heart may once again be whole and my eyes shed no more tears.
Come show me that there's more to love than feeling hurt and pain.
Let me feel the sunshine so tired of all the rain.
Come into this lonely heart of mine and promise to always stay
Oh please love don't another time get up and walk away.

Debbie Scharbor

Listen!

Can you hear it, in the air?
Can you hear it everywhere?
In the slow roll of the sea,
in the droning of a bee,
and the soft purl of the rill
when noontime is very still?

Do you hear it in the drips
from icicles melting tips?
In the chinook's susurration
through the fir boughs cantillation;
from the marsh and damp lea peepers,
the resonant shrill chorus keepers?

Can you hear it as clouds pass, and zephyrs titillate the grass,
with its insect thin conclave singing in a soft octave;
while Canadian geese fly high honking defiance to the sky?

Have you heard the house finch thrill
matched by the peewee mournful trill,
when crickets merge their melody with mockingbirds flip threnody?
Winter's had its final fling . . . can you hear it? Now it's spring!

Horace S. Mazet

Wander-Lust

O'er land and sea I wander, 'tis the destiny of me
   To see enchanted places, where I oft did long to be.
The mystery of India, the sights of ancient Rome,
   The ruins of the Acropolis — the musty Catacombs.

The stately spires of Islam, the shores of sunny Greece,
   As Jason in olden fable did hunt the "golden fleece."
The tinkling of the temple bells in Burma's far off land,
   The Sphinx and the Pyramids on Egypt's shifting sand.

The timeless, cresting ocean waves that always seem in strife,
   The steaming jungles of Africa, her veldts that teem with life.
The ships that ply the China Sea, the road to Mandalay,
   The dawning of the rising sun, o'er China 'cross the bay.

The ice-bound land of the Polar caps, where the seal and walrus play,
   Where men amidst this frozen void, survive in unknown ways.
So, on forever wandering, until I find that place,
   That quells this thing within me, and I quit the weary pace.

William Keyes

The Execution

The mind of a butcher is rigor and dim,
A demon deranged in a dark world of sin.
He rests in the day and the night is his keeper,
He's a dealer in death, and a real-life grim reaper.
He crushes out life for some queer kind of glory,
And out of the blackness he flushes his quarry
Then back in his castle he sits on his throne,
The king of his carnage to rule all alone.
He grins as he waits, in his eyes a cold stare,
Sent into the blackness, when they turn on the chair.

Lance Gilbertson

Family Prayer

Dear Lord I pray every day
Please help my family find the way
Show them that you will enter their heart
Please let them know you will help them start
Make them believe you are the only way
Give them faith and strength they will need every day
Counseling and meetings are still ok
Only you can help them find the way
If we believe we will meet again someday

Gloria Smith

The Night

In the blackness, you an hear the crickets,
chirping their beautiful song.
The stars, that shine so bright, give more beauty to the night.
The full moon is shining bright,
smiling as if a man.
Glowing on everything he sees.
Grinning and keeping his secret,
hiding the truth from the earth.

All the beauty in this world comes out while we're asleep,
as if afraid of what we'll say.
In this world, there is another world inside,
a beautiful one that shows its face in the night.

Meredith D. Raucher

The Case Of The U Nation

Children to the U4 power:
Unhealthy, Unhoused, Underfed, Un(der) educated.
A nation Unable?
A nation Unwilling?
A nation Unconcerned?
A nation Unbridled in greed, inhumanity, violence, crime, corruption.
Fast becoming a nation;
Unfortunate,
Undermined,
Unnecessary,
Undeniable Unreal.

Rosie L. Winfield

Untitled

Society moves us at a breakneck pace
Stop the world I want to get off
To slow down would be suicide either way you die

I can't take this rat race, my wheel will turn no more
Why do they say time is of the essence
When it's already past

Things should have been done yesterday
Tomorrow is already too late
Today doesn't exist anymore and there's no time to wait

Someone show me an easier way I'm about to loose my mind
This world survives without us
Yet we're slaves to the core

Things should have been done yesterday
Tomorrow is already too late
Today doesn't exist anymore and there's no time to wait

Dennis Durst

Dear Mom

I remember skating down the street
with mom looking on.
I could hear her heart beat.

There were times when I went out
and got home late.
Mom was always waiting at our gate.

On the altar, those beautiful words were said so clearly,
mom's tears were falling,
on dad's picture that she held so dearly.

Our children are playing and having a ball.
Mom is right there watching them all.

I know she is looking from far away.
Mom, we all love you and miss you, each and every day.

Anthony Del Duca

Truth

What a wonderful accomplishment to experience!
We should not live in fear of ourselves,
But become more aware.
Sharing what we feel; not concealing:
Taking a chance.

If it is favorable, fine.
If it is not, that's also fine.
We always have another chance.

Stay aware.
Develop the mind.
Be true to yourself and others.
If you find it painful, that's okay.
For how would we realize pleasure if not for pain?
We were given a gift: Life.

I do believe we were put in this world
to assist the earth and each other.

All else is superfluous.

Jon Fortgang

A Gift

It comes out of nowhere like a thief in the night.
It makes you do things that are way out of sight.
Once you get it, there is no turning back,
It brings on great joy that turns light into your black.
You can show others this wonderful gift,
By giving other people's frowns a tiny lift.
It would not harm you to do some labor,
By offering to help an elderly neighbor.
Read a book to anyone you choose,
If you do this, the gift you will not lose.
Give a poor person a healthy meal,
After that the gift is what you feel.
Do not stop there because there is more,
Help a mother at the grocery store.
Teach a child how to count,
That's what this gift is all about.
The time is now — don't wait until the end,
Many problems of the world, this gift will mend.
I am telling you of this gift because I want you to share,
The wonderful gift I call care.

Nicole D. Smith

Stone And Beauty

Your eyes are a gateway into a mystical place,
Where the beauty and peace of the lagoon with
its waterfall, and surrounding high cliffs with
giant pine trees covering the area.

Your smile is a window into a world of heaven
on earth, and a gateway into your true self,
and personality.

Your hair's beauty and color is equal to the
northern lights, and a clear night with a full moon.

Your voice is that of the songs of angels
echoing in the mountains.

Your beauty is that of all the beautiful creations
of God, all the wonderful features of heaven and
earth put into one soul, which is hidden behind
a wall of "stone".

Your aura is that of all the colors in the
galaxy put together to form a giant cyclone that
transports your thoughts and personality into ones "heart."

David G. W. Clark

Farewell

I tried my best to believe you when you said your love was true,
but each and every time I did I found it so untrue.

I put my faith and trust in you when all you do is lie,
so I guess it's time for me to say my last and final good-bye.

I cooked, cleaned and washed for you, I tried so hard to please,
still each and every time I looked you said the hell with me.

The harder I tried to do things right, the more you turned and ran,
so do not worry anymore I'll leave you to your plans.

Your games are old, your lies are weak, there's no more I can stand,
I love you more than you'll ever know, but happiness is in command.

I said this many times in the past, but this is really the last,
it's time for me to let go of someone who put's me last.

I wish you all the best, I wish you all the luck, and hopefully
what you're looking for will be there I hope and trust.

My heart will break, the tears will come, this is how it must be,
this is my farewell poem to you, I must find happiness for me.

Sandra McKinnon

Season After Season

I cry for you on the cold Winter's wind
and wish that I could help you live here once again.
It was the dreaded dark one who led us all astray.
Then came Majaio to bring another day.

I cry for you in Summer, when all is parched and dry.
My tears will quench your thirst, so you won't have to die.
I wonder, do you see me cry, or hear me when I call?
And, do you know that it is you, I've loved most of all.

I cry for you when the moon is full and bright.
The fox is my companion throughout a lonely night.
I wonder where you are, standing proud and tall
when Autumn changes colors and makes the leaves to fall.

I cry for you when Spring brings the rain,
and sing a song of battle to hide my bitter pain.
One day I will join you on the four winds above.
There, we will have plenty, joy and peace and love.

Scott L. Pruden

I Have A Dream . . . Someday Heaven

It's been twelve months since God called you home . . . God promised,
never would I face this burden all alone . . . Tho I miss you more
than words can say . . . Great joy fills my heart, for God's
everlasting love is ours each and every day . . . Yes, deep sadness
still lingers in my heart . . . Many dreams have slipped away . . .
For you, I have cried a river of tears, each and every day . . .

A precious gift from God, tears are meant to be . . . To help heal
the wounds of both you and me . . . Tears wash and soothe the wounds
earth's journey leaves behind . . . For all of God's ways are ever so
gentle and kind . . . Listen to God's words, no greater comfort
can you find . . .

Yes, with death old dreams must pass away . . . It is now with great
hope I pray . . . All will come to know the healing love of Jesus
Christ for wounds big and small . . . I pray the great love, peace and
joy only Jesus can give will someday reign in the hearts of all . . .

Yes, someday Heaven Lauren . . . Jesus, you and I shall walk
hand in hand . . . A place where only peace, love and joy are
known in Gods promised holy land . . . And of the three, God
wants us all to see . . .
The greatest of all, he meant love to be . . .

I love you, Lauren Elizabeth, forever in my heart you and Jesus
shall be . . .

Mary Jo LeGare-Hoffman

Heaven Sent Water

The space scientists look for water on heavenly stars,
concerned about life on other cosmic shores afar,
yet we who live daily on earth's surface and below,
strive our utmost to secure water to bestow,
life in cells of living matter daily for all mankind,
conservation of heaven's rainfall every soul can find,
barrels, buckets, containers of all ages example,
giving every race and creed realization of pull,
lifting the burdens cited impossible to assure,
the ever onward demands of exploring our future.

Carol Sanford Hall

How Many More?

Standing in line, five thousand strong
shivering soldiers, together they mourn
one of their own has given his life
another brave soldier whose left a sweet wife

Heartbroken parents, a young widow grieves,
"What happened?" they asked, they cannot believe

Your soldier's a hero, you can be proud to be sure
But how many more must we lose in the war?

Robert Machate was cut down in his prime
by a punk, a drug dealer, a real piece of slime
just like Miller and Hoban and Ed Byrne before
oh, how many more must we lose in the war?

So many have died, the best of the best
they answered the call, they all passed the test
they are all heroes, our soldiers in blue
they're my brothers and sisters and they bleed for you

But dear Lord, I am tired
so I'll ask just once more
God, how many more must we lose in the war?

James Wallace

The Source Of The Light

We are not the source of the light, we are but a reflection of it
The light is infinite and cannot be controlled, only embraced
The darkness lies in fear of the inevitable penetration of the light
The soul lies in painful anticipation of the inevitable freedom given
by the light once the soul has absorbed the light the meaning of
its own existence is revealed
We are not the source of the light, we are but a reflection of it

Lance Teague

L.A. Bound

1995 unpublished work
Pack the bags, kiss the wife, leavin' this town tonight.
Down the road, on my way gotta get to L.A.
L.A. bound, L.A. bound gotta get my feet on West coast ground.

Twenty-six hundred miles to go
Hope I can make it this G.T.O.
Tires squealin' dust is flyin'
This engine sounds like a lion
L.A. bound, L.A. bound
Gotta get my feet on West Coast ground

Traveling across I-70 West
Gonna climb in the back and get some rest
The sun was bright when I came alive
Thirty miles to I-5
Travelin' South across Frisco Bay
The highway sign said to L.A.
City of angels what a sight
Nowhere beats L.A. nights
L.A. bounds, L.A. bounds
Got my feet on West Coast ground.

Lennie Miller Jr.

A Heart's Journey

Moments not meant to be spoken
  when words will never do
A look, a touch, a hug, a kiss says,
  we'll make it through.

The distance and time between two hearts
  yearning no longer to be apart
Fighting for independence
  yet longing to be one.
Set forth on life's long journey unknown
  not knowing which path to choose.
Entangled in webs of spiraling thoughts
  aching to be free.

At the end, a comfort and peace
When two heart's finally acquiesce
  there, they can grow and love and rest . . .
      . . . until tomorrow.

Colleen Harris

Blue

In the hollow absence of a warm autumn night,
the small abyss seems at ease.
The perseverance of illusion keeps at bay
the swirl and mischief of dark blue waves.
And an almost genuine glow arises with a warming flicker
of softness and sensitivity surrounding my chest
with arms of hope and hopeful insight.

The future, it seems to encompass the world.
An understanding profound, yet I wonder if such is narrow.
To start from the conception without need of the whole.
To move to two, a move from the most sacred center.
And how all the glass shatters as newly exposed rooms are entered . . .
That painful intimacy that takes the courage of a thousand valiant soldiers.

As the candles burn with intent, I see the simplicity of progression . . .
To allow all that is forbidden in. And voyeur at the extremity of the outcome.
So pure and exposed as fresh rosy skin. So reflective of the
beauty of circumstance, untainted and searing to the soul.

The duality of true age and sweet surrender to the enduring,
  blue waters of humanity, of life . . .
Of love.

Tara Louise Pitts

A Special Woman

She has big brown eyes, just like a young puppy's eyes.
Her hair jet black and soft like velvet.
She sheds no tears, for she has no fears.
With her intelligence she stands so tall, completely well above them all
She smells as good as a crisp mountain breeze, blowing freely
  through the trees.
She has a heart that bleeds with passions, to suit ones many fashions.
With her wings stretched so wide, she protects a child, so it can hide.
She makes my heart beat as fast as a humming birds wings,
  sometimes I think it sings.
So this woman holds a fire, and that's what I desire.
This stunning woman will never stumble, because she is so very humble.
She has much beauty in her face, and always moves with such grace.
Indeed this woman is very special to us all, for she's an angel with it all.

Andrew J. Spring

Saguaro Gypsy

she turns in tornado whirls
suspending the cool llano blackness
the bangles titter in shimmering kisses
wrapping into silken net skirts
and los ojos azulísimos flash beside the veil
as her dance swallows cries with the pulsating earth

Sharon Tseng

Which Goal Did He Choose?

One cold day in the month of December,
one thing happened I'll always remember.

We were all happy and laughing that day,
for it was Christmas Eve and soon Christmas Day.

A trip turned up my dad wanted to take,
and we never knew he would return unawake.

On that day death came to his face,
and he no longer lives at our place.

He is somewhere else I wish I knew of,
whether it's below or up above

I didn't know about my daddy's soul,
if it was the right or the wrong goal.

So friends and people with living dads,
see if his soul is good or bad.

For when he leaves you, you'll want to know,
if he chose the right goal and if you'll see him when you go!

Kay F. Carver

Forbidden Fruit

It was a long time ago
He was away and I was alone
You were young and filled with promise

I will never forget
The warmth of your breath
The longing in your eyes
Your sweet, soft and tender kiss
The electricity in your touch
The moist love spent in my loins

The hurt on your face when I was no longer alone . . .

Now you're back and scarred for life
Cold as a frosted winter
Your words sharp and cutting
Your eyes dark and fierce
A tone of regret, another love

No memory of the delicious fruit
That filled your passionate belly
Satiated your lustful thirst
And made your heart beat . . .

Norma Flores

The Gift

It was a gift, a keyboard,
Her only wish —
To play.

Uncle, the gift giver,
Now it was he who needed a gift.

Only a gift, but entered her heart,
And left it bare, the day of the accident.

When she saw him, lying on the bed,
It was all she could do not to fly,
And be the bird she desperately wished to be.

As she grew, great and grand, she still could not bear,
To see her uncle, helpless in the wheelchair.

The gift is lying somewhere, never to be found.
Like the innocence she lost that day.

The girl can still see it, even after all these years.
In her mind and heart, a child's little gift.

The gift her uncle gave.

Uthra Raghunathan

Hallucination

When you have a hallucination,
it leads into a sensation.

Everything you look at is all in motion,
it's like taking a magic potion.

You dance and sing and things are weird that you play,
your mind is much farther and farther away.

You may think you are superman and you jump off the roof,
but your tiny life ends in a loud poof!

This is the end of my poem and I hope you have learned,
not to kill yourself when someone is concerned.

Tara Pinizzotto

Still

Time passes by but I am still here
Alone me, myself and my fear
Friends have gone here and there
For some reason I don't seem to know where
Rumors I have often believed as heard
but I no longer know it truth is in their word
My heart hopes that happiness
has been found
But, when in need I will be around
whether it be to wipe away a tear or just to
lend an ear
Just look for me and you will find
I am still here

Anna M. Ochoa

Softly, Goodbye

How do you know when to leave?
How do you know when you've played the game?
How do you make it right for the ones left behind?
How do you say goodbye?

Is the answer there in your soul?
Is the answer in your mind, your spirit?
Is the answer in your heart?
How will you ever know?

Can you pray to your God?
Can you pray to your Messiah?
Can you leave the memories of you
for all to hold dear, and then
softly close the door? Softly, goodbye.

Patsy Privett

Betrayal

He used her love and broke her heart, and left her there with
nothing more then a tear and a dying red rose. Its petals
resembled the pain in her life, and as the petals fell apart
slowly she realized that this plant didn't resemble just her
life it resembled her soul. As she looked back on the past
when he said, he loved her, and when he said he would be
there for her forever, he made a vow that they would
walk through life holding hands. And as he turned and
walked away, he turned and took one last look on life
and faded into the moon lit sky. She looked into the sky
as she thought to herself 'why am I the one to be
misused? Why should I live alone and cold? Looking
into the sky the stars begin to speak to her as though
they were by her side as a person. As she turned to walk
away the stars all gave their message one by one but
before she turned away she made one last wish, which
was to be free from all her hurt and pain. And to be loved
again as she once was. Having said this she too faded into
the deep, dark moon lit sky.

Lindsey Martin

C-h-r-i-s-t-m-a-s Spells J-e-s-u-s

Oh Christmas it's the best time of the year,
Bright and full of holiday cheer

But as this season once again rolls around,
Let's take time to forget about reindeer and tinsel, and gifts that abound.

Because remember once, so very long ago,
A King was born — simple and clothed.

He was the greatest man that ever walked this earth —
Our God, our King — born of a virgin birth.

He was perfect and sinless, in a world full of shame —
Feeding the hungry, and healing the lame.

Yet he died on a cross, for both you and me.
Suffered our sin, like a prisoner not yet set free.

And so, as this Christmas holiday quickly comes once again,
I have but one question — what will you give to him?

Amber Nevin

Spinning On A Broken Axis

This world is spinning out of control
  Its axis is broken
  Its orbit's been crushed
  By questions whose answers are doom . . .

I strive to learn
  Though I really don't know why
  I strive to make peace
  Then I crave to crush it by war
How long can I hold on
  I'm not sure I can
  I've got to find help
  Someone who understands
This world is spinning around me so fast
  Day to day how am I going to prevail
  Will this spinning go on for ever?
  Is this confusion to become my doom?

I think I know everything
  You say I know nothing
  What I know for sure is the
  Knowing isn't everything.

Jasmine Yadon

Cry So Distant

I see your face; in my dreams you are there.
I hear your cries when no one else is aware.
Only I realize how precious you are.
I long to touch you, but I fear you're too far.
Your thought follows me through night and day.
I pray to the Lord that you're not long away;
A day never passes that I don't think of you,
A night never awakens without my dreaming of you.
No one could know how much I love you; you do not know how much I want you.
I see everywhere those unloved and unwanted,
and I try to understand why we must be parted.
I ask the Lord to help me, for it seems so unfair.
Please God hear me; please know my despair.
For the rest of this slumber let's dream on together. We'll reach into heaven and touch one another. Your skin is like satin; your face — so innocent. Your hair is like silk, but your cry is so distant. Something is happening . . . you're becoming unclear. Please stay awhile longer, for I'll miss you my dear. These dreams I have show how much I care, for you are the child that I long to bear.

Cynthia M. Nerness

Time

How precious
is the wild time that slips between our fingers
past the hours of our lives.
  How sanctuary
are the minutes we hold so close to our bosoms,
  but let them go one by one,
  or five by five,
and then wonder where they have gone.
Like a child who you can no longer hold onto,
and hold her in the heart of your motherly hands.
Slipping away to the realness of a freedom.
  So dear
are the stares that we capture under our skin.
  So restless
are the smiles we may hold but can never own.

Vanessa Fjelldal

Love Tinted Glasses

Give me love tinted glasses, so all I can see
  is the good in others and their blessing to me.
Simply blot from my vision thru love's mighty power
  the faults in the people whom I live with each hour.
May each weakness and failure disappear from my view
  let me see only beauty, what is wholesome and true.
For each soul has a value God planted within.
  If I search I can find it, make it blossom again.
All around me are treasures, tho often disguised,
  Give me love tinted glasses, oh Lord, open my eyes.
Give me love tinted glasses so all I can see
  is the good in others, and their blessing to me.

Vivian Bonnema Meade

Baseball Players

They can steal a base, but are not thieves.
They can knock the pitcher out of the box, but he isn't hurt.
They can catch a fly, but never see one.
They have numbers on their backs, but are not prisoners.
They wear gloves, but only on one hand.
They throw a man out at the base, but he can still play.
They have a cleanup man, but he isn't the grounds keeper.
They have a pitcher, but it won't hold water.
They play on a diamond, but it doesn't glitter.
They have fans, but are not always cool.
They play to win, but they sometimes lose.
They sometimes make an error, but who doesn't.

Ralph H. Roberts

Hands

Hands, vivid in my childhood memories.
Mom says that's where your age is shown
hands, nineh's are just film on bones.

Mom says she is not old at heart,
hands, great gramma's hands uncover mom's lies.

Mom, my grandmother, my great-grandmother,
hands, hers/theirs worked the flesh off gaunt fingers.

Mom says we married young-three generations,
hands, gnarled from cradling cold, starving babies.

Mom says they took their babies to heaven,
hands, blistered and chapped, dug mountain into grave.

Mom says we come from a line of yörük
hands, scratched into scabs from weaving kilims.

Mom says I will break the chain that bound,
hands, different form mine; thin, dry, scaled.

Mom says I am spoiled and ungrateful,
hands, unworked, young, plump, soft, grateful, and mine.

Ebru Bülbül

My Life

Ever since the day I gave my life to You
The morning is fresh, the sky so blue

I now have a confidence in myself
I can accomplish anything with Your help

I once was alone, frightened and torn
But when I prayed for help, a new strength was born

You're the Light of my life that shines so bright
In the midst of darkness I'm able to fight

Some days are harder than others passed by
But Your shoulders are there on which I may cry

As my friendship with You grows day by day
Your love reflects in what I do and say

My feelings of joy cannot be expressed
The pain I once had has been laid to rest

I'm pleased with what You give me and want to share
I know the price You paid with loving care

You did not deserve to die for my sin
With a clean heart this time I will begin

Where You are, You've got things ready for me
So I can be with You for eternity
        Sarah Jenkins

A Child At Play

It is so sweet to see a child at play;
It touches the heart one often say;
A heart so soft, like a sponge;
It wrings a tear, just a little one;
A tear of joy and hope for the cherished one;
Such a treasured moment to see a child at play.

        Stephanie Ulrich

Winter — Time of Long Nights

    Lengthening shadows slipping across
the blue whiteness of the snow — daylight
waning.
    Sun sliding below the horizon
the sky aglow golden against the stark
blackness of the tree branches — naked
cold.
    The dead of winter stalks the
land — icy-blue.
    The long winter nights are here
and the hunger moon bathes earth in
its pale light of want — empty darkness.
    It is a distant time and summer
seems but an illusion — winter reality.

        Carol Haney

Never To Be

Never to be a day without death or people who think they're better
than the rest color does not define the thoughts in ones mind.
Never to be a day where everyone is color blind
Never to be a day that is endless like the wind that blows beneath
our souls, there is beauty in truth so let it be told
Never to be music that calms the savage beast or stop the
violence within our streets
The struggles of life sometimes cut like a knife, but to those who are
Humble And Meek Life Is Often Sweet
Never to be tears unfallen from the pain that remain from the
world that drives us slowly insane
Never to be free as a dove that flies high up above and the world
to be filled with brotherly love
Never to be.

        George Bowen Jr.

Prayer To My Savior

God, I don't understand
Why this has to be Your plan,
To give up Your life for me.

I can not comprehend
All the torment and the pain, Lord, You suffered that for me.

Father, what can I do
After all they put You through? When will this guilt ever leave me?

Knowing you are the One
Who came to die on the cross, leaving all glory for earth.

The crown of thorns that mock
The purple robe does the same.
Those that blaspheme your name

Give nails that pierce Your wrists.
The great cry to Your Father "Why have you forsaken me?"

The Truth, You saved us all!
Though we roam in the darkness, your death became our only light.

And when the end does come
I know that I will rejoice!
For it is Your death that saves me!
        Amy Crawford

Circle Of Life

A drop of dew lands on a red rose petal.
The rose, like a mortal's time on this spherical blue planet.
A small life-giving bulb is planted,
It grows with love and care.
Blooming in spring, it brings so much joy.
The rose blooms through summer, into fall.
Petals float to the cold earth, back to the soil from which created its life.
It's not gone forever, oh no.
Deep rich soil of mother earth uses one rose in the birth of another.
A lone bloom in a field, soft, the odor sweet, dew falls lightly
from its petals.
A red rose picked for your Romeo or Juliet, is a symbol,
Of your true, everlasting love, yes,
But also of the short time you have here,
And the best you should make of it.

        Lura Huber

Skiing

I met four angels at Yawgoo's nest
North, South, East and West.

Though skiing was the part I liked best,
The angels came to meet me at TNT test.

The one from the west told me I'd make it to the end
The one from the east said there's just a little bend,

The one from the south laughed and gave a little grin.
I felt invigorated, my head began to spin.

The one from the north with hair golden brown,
Said there is no where to turn around.

So down I went, down, very slowly down.
I didn't look back till I was on safe ground.

Gone, they were gone, but their words remain.
There is power in their words, and courage again.

Like a soul that needs flat out quiet,
Like a spirit that needs a heavenly riot,

So are the crowds, the snow, and the hills
Are watched from heaven above with no ills.

Come! Catch some air, fly down hills, soar!
Be real nice and maybe, maybe you'll meet the four.
        Linda Jutras

The Old Home Place

The old home place looked so tired. It has lost its battle
with the unrelenting wild grasses, weeds, and brush it has
fought for so long. Yet, as I walked upon its soils, a peaceful
calm came over me I hadn't felt since I was a child. And it gave
a flood of memories of love, laughter, tears and sorrow.
The joys of childhood, and the warmth of loved ones long past on.
An era locked in time. There was feeling of safety, and security
within its perimeters. I could almost smell the home cooked
meals and hear the laughter of family. And as I walked within its
circumferences, there were memories locked in every corner,
under every tree, and around every dilapidated old building.
Some brought laughter to my breath while others brought a tear to
my eye, but all were warm to my heart. And as I came back to
reality I felt sad, as I realized as time goes by and we all pass on, the
old home place will have no one to share these memories with. And
just as the buildings that once held warmth and security fall by the
way side, so shall those memories that bring such comfort.

Sherene Digby

Our Prayer

Lord, You know our children
You call them by their name.
You've been with them thru thick and thin
And brought them thru life's game.

Just because they're grown and gone
Doesn't mean we're worry free.
They're just beginning on life's highway
Their own worries and cares to see.

Lord, take them in Your loving arms
And shield them with Your touch.
And when You can't — please let them know
You love them twice as much.

We offered them to You as babes
You took them in Your hands.
Now let them know You're there for them
When they will trust Your plans.

You've told us in Your word, dear Lord,
That worry is just a bother.
So again we turn them back to You
because You are their Father.

Mary Williams

Excitement

Ah! For the love of excitement
for the want of excitement, for the lust of excitement

Ah! For the allure of the ingenue
the innovative, the change from the routine, from the boredom
from the hum-drum that we allow ourselves to get into
that sometimes seems to take over us
envelop our very essence, our very being
the monotony that monopolizes and suffocates

In some cases we loose the battle
an become enmeshed within it's one way lure
Yet . . . For the fighter
who values more than the security the comfort
presented by the lure like a mirage
an apparition . . . The beat of excitement!

Come! Join the excitement! Your new found excitement!
Grasp it! Hold it! If just for a moment, it fleets
it wanes as times does; it too refuses to stay still

So fight, for your excitement! Cherish it! Brandished across your
chest emblazoned as it were for the fighter, his reward, his . . .
Excitement!!!

Sybil Ingram-Mack

Violence

Drugs, alcohol, guns and knives. All these things
have taken so many lives.

There are millions of new lives brought into
this world everyday. And at the same time, one
of them is being taken away.

Even young children are getting involved. And it's so
sad to think that this problem might not be solved

It's so hard to think someone could take a life
by pointing a gun or pulling a knife.

Nobody wants to spend their holidays standing
at a grave, thinking of how that loved one
could have been saved.

Sisters, brothers, husbands, and wives. So many
people. So many innocent lives.

So that's why we need to close the door to violence
And open the door to peace. Because that is
one thing that we must and will increase.

Well I guess it's up to us my friends, to
put all this hate and violence to an end!

Magean Ward

A World Of Peace

The rifts of immense depth and width begin to appear untraversable,
  unable to be mediated.
The divisions become grim and formidable,
Estrangement from families, communities, our very selves, our own souls.
Especially when confined in the claustrophobic closet of isolation,
I grasp at sinewy webs of connection that will (and do) lead me back.

Can we, like eager, young parents, claim, name, nurse our orphaned parts?
All those ingredients of our person, our life, our days, our society,
that surface so uncontrollably and shriek for attention like impish children?
Can we rock them gently,
singing soft lullabies before warm fires,
embracing our least tended to visages with genuine love?

To bridge that which divides in our world,
one must make reparation with one's selves.
Rainbows provide a clue.
In remembering the essence of rainbows — water, air, energy —
the very stuff of our bodies,
we realize there is within each of us its full spectrum of colors.

Gail Armstrong

Life's Garden

I came to a garden of roses
Just over a sea green brook,
Where angels could dwell so happily
I stopped for one brief look.

It seemed I lingered for awhile
And did not wish to leave,
In an instant a bright light shone around me
I suddenly fell to my knees.

The warm light embraced me
Just like a loving caress,
Such peace and love engulfed me
With a feeling of contentment and rest.

Then suddenly the light faded
And a sadness stumbled in,
Afraid to look, I closed my eyes
That's when my tears began.

I left the garden of roses
And I took the warmth of the light,
To guide and protect me
I hope for the rest of my life.

Harriet G. Albers

God? . . . Help Me!

Lift me up, I'm falling away
Give me your hand, don't look away
I've lied I've cheated, now I'm on my knees
I know I don't deserve it but God help me please!

I turned my back on you when the going got tough
I asked Jesus to be my savior but that wasn't enough
I wanted to do my own thing and my heart got hard
Because I received you as savior but rejected you as Lord.

Straddling the fence became hard for me
Striving not to lose friends and create enemies
All the while not realizing the sin and shame
my hypocritical attitude have brought to Jesus name.

Forgiveness, forgiveness the Cross stands tall!
Rejoice my child, for I have heard your call
Surrender, abandon and turn away from sin
My blood is available to make you whole again

For every friend you lose I will repay you twice
Both here and now and in the next life
I've felt you hurts and I've seen your tears
Believe me, my eyes were never dry when I heard your prayers . . .

I love you!

Dwight Stewart

Dreams And Hope

Dreams and hope seem to drift
Constantly through my mind
Hope that makes my spirit lift
Dreams that may happen in time

Without dreams there would be
No hope for a better tomorrow
Just today filled with reality
Today filled with sadness and sorrow

All yesterdays that have gone by
All tomorrows that became today
Would in some way seem a lie
Without dreams and hope leading the way

With passing days some dreams came true
While some still fill my mind
But with tomorrow to look forward to
Dreams and hope will fill my time

Frances L. Hebert

The Love I Found

Lonely days, lonely nights, crawling in comparison to form a torturous
The morning, the evening, blending together to form a torturous
collage my life a cold wind, blowing in a barren urban area
Then I saw the sunrise in your eyes
I felt like the sunflower on its endless journey to face warmth
And the child inside myself crawled towards the light
That was the love I searched for my life over and arms outstretched
I was embraced with love and security, the eyes spoke, the feelings
soared and the wind brought a blinding love with our coincidental
meeting with hands joined, conversation flowing and the time
ticking to the beat of my overflowing heart.
Wishing for time to cease altogether as to prolong this evening in
utopia you're refilling the cracks in my desperate heart with what
was absent for years.
And now I can sing and tell the days, the years, and all the couples
to share in the feelings of what I have found.
My pen and words couldn't possibly expense my raw emotions
I can say, looking to me and view my happiness, the shine in my
eyes when she is near.
And now, I have what I want and love what I have.

Hussein Mahmoud

Our Country

'Twas long ago our fathers
Lived in a wilderness,
And from their work and suffering
Came this land we now possess.

Our vast nation in its beauty,
Country of priceless worth
We've known more peace and freedom
Than any land on earth.

And yet where is the mighty faith
That our forefathers knew?
Where is the family alter
And His Book so sure and true?

Oh, must we lose this heritage?
Is it we will not see?
Lord, touch our hearts, our homes, our land,
And turn us back to thee.

Elva Fotter

Dear Dad

There is a gift for you that no one else can give
A gift for you that you will eternally live.
You will never experience anymore pain
With this gift, there is only gain;
Gain of freedom to laugh and sing
Joy in your heart this gift will bring.
You need to know and understand
This gift is Jesus, and to you He holds out His hand.
Just ask Him to come into your heart
That you realize He died to give you a new start.
He died on the cross, and was buried that same day;
Three days later He rose from the grave.
He says to you, "Matthew, my son,
Just let go, and to Me you shall come.
Don't be afraid just let go;
Trust in me then you will surely know" . . .

Doris Wilding-Yell

Eternal Peace

When peace is come
I shall not die
I and my savior shall sing praises
Praises of love and joy shall bubble
in my soul — Even the sun shall rejoice
For evermore — for it knows peace is come
Thank you kind master for eternal peace

Evangeline D. Russell

A Lonely Shade Of Blue

If I was a color, if I was a mood
I would be a lonely shade of blue
If I was the sun, I would stop shining
I'd be a fire put out by all my crying

But all I am is a lonely man, ever since you said we're through
And nothing's been right since you turned my life
Into a lonely shade of blue

If I was the clouds, I'd turn the sky into gray
I'd thunder and lightning, I would always rain
And if I was the stars, I would fall from the sky
I would disappear and never return to the night

But all I am is a lonely man, ever since you said we're through
And nothing's been right ever since that night
When I lost you

If I was a color, if I was a mood
I would be a lonely shade of blue

Jason Daniel Covey

January Flight

On a flight, not long ago,
My mind was drifting down below,
Below the clouds so thick and white,
The sun bathed Earth in brilliant light.
And for a moment in my peace,
I thought about both man and beast.
Who walked the streets so far below,
The billowed clouds, as dense as snow.
The villages lay with a pristine glow,
Covered in a coat of snow.
With silent drifts and flowing mounds.
That clothed the many midwest towns.
As west we flew, we travelled on,
And soon the winter scene was gone.
Replaced by scenes of mountain might,
And deserts full of twinkling lights.
The Canyons stretched majestic'ly,
And rivers flowed through mightily.
The hours passed and time marched on,
Until our time in flight was gone.

R. J. Krass

Moonstar

There once lived a horse,
so brave and so bold.

His name was Moonstar,
although never told.

He ran like the wind,
and galloped through streets.

He traveled through cities,
and people he did meet.

Poor Moonstar was put in a circus act,
with clowns and lion tamers with big top hats.

Moonstar escaped from the circus and still galloped through streets,
he runs like the wind, and looks as white as a sheet.

Although he is gone, his memory still lives,
forever and ever may his soul roam the old town called, Sidde.

Keara Monahan

Ominous Tension

Poised, ready, waiting their time to fly
Their long sleek bodies now supined
But soon, perhaps, yea, soon through the sky
An ominous target they seek reclined

Equipped, ready, waiting their master's touch
Their droning but static bodies now rest
How soon? Too soon perhaps yet perchance
Not soon enough their counter-type they seek and quest

Stored, ready, waiting in stock a thousand fold
Their bulky and deadly bodies shine
Not soon! Who knows the time untold
When from their toil the world will pine?

Numa Lee Everhart Jr.

Summer Splendor

The world is great within me
I feel her caressing breezes
Her skin the soft bounty of life and serenity
Kisses of summer air rest upon my face
Delicate is this lady of grace
Her passion holds me through the days
Her softness rocks me through the nights
These are the sweet moments of a summer life

Naika R. Malveaux

Untitled

Kindness, a smile, and a love for children
that could never be surpassed,
This reminds me.

To give of herself was honorable and could
never be taken for granted,
This reminds me.

A will that was so strong, could not
be out done,
This reminds me.

An angel in a human being's body is what
she was to everyone she met,
This reminds me.

No matter the age of a person, she made them
feel loved,
This reminds me.

Now she's gone.
To know she is pain-free, worry-free, and to be
home,
This comforts me — you were and are a true
inspiration!

Jan M. Foster

True Worth's Eye

They turn on the catwalk
bare erotica in a live gallery
Heart-broken, living hand-to-mouth
staking their hides to rent their lot.
They look to you, despairing hopefully,
getting up the nerve to ask
for their livelihood;
Sadly you slip her a bill for compassion's sake,
swallowing pained lust.
They smile through shot-glass eyes,
as anything that your fantasies can imagine
Chameleons of the night spent
in stranger's company.
A tease for small denominations,
$20's for your touch on their skin
A small price for adult pleasures
berated by dignity's bill of sale.
All distance and viewing surface
not an inch for what's beneath . . .
Where is true worth measured?

Robert E. Jaggard

The Beginning

Long awaited life begins
Caps and gowns are fitted
The last minute preparations are done
Announcements were sent out;
Our families are here
No more finals to take
Those anxieties are gone
The practice and rehearsing is over
On the horizon we can glimpse the future
With many different roads we could take
Bold, ambitious, naive, with so much to learn
We set out for our futures
To fail or succeed
Not knowing which will be
We follow our hearts
Hoping and praying that our choice was right.

Jeannie Marie Sapp

New Birth

The troglodytes have arrived.
They've stripped us of sun and leaves and lemon scented breezes.
The earth is cold, death is the cocoon.
Lean woodland creatures bloody their noses foraging in the
bitter ungiving land.
Perchance . . . they die,
curled in a white blanket of marshmallow fluff snow.

    Or they wait!!!

For the moment the fairies arrive
   with their magic seeds and saucers of sun.
To delicately sprinkle what is below our feet,
   and joyously toss into the blue abyss,
What we gently speak of as New Birth. Spring
    Jacqueline Ann Kielbania

Remembering

Two years have passed since the day
You went to that far-away land.
I remember how tightly you held my hand.

Our children and I kept the vigil all that day.

It was time for you to go and me to stay.

Then Jesus took your hand and said,
"Roy come with me you cannot stay."

The day was clear and cold when we
land you to rest.
The Lord always knows what is best.

God sent His angel to comfort me
As if to say you are never alone
Do not fear
"Just remember I am always near."
    Freda Holle

Love Your Child

A beautiful child was brought to me,
This I could count on you see.
Neglected or abused so needlessly.
So beautiful and innocent brought into this world,
Only to be ignored or abused or hurled.
A tear in my eye when their story was told,
To me they're more precious than money or gold.
I was a foster parent and so was my spouse,
We opened our hearts and souls and our house.
They're God's gift of love without a doubt you see,
So smarten up and love your child the way
they were meant to be!
    Judy Ames

My Train

As I hear the train passing by,
I hear a familiar scream.
As I realize it's me crying out,
I fall and I start to weep.
My salt-tasting tears sting into my face.
I gather myself together once again.
Just waiting to fall apart all over again.
I'm so cold, my fingers are going numb.
The train drowns out my cries every time.
The sound is making me crazy.
My ears start to bleed.
Why won't this loud train go away?
As I scream out again,
The train vanishes.
Leaving me in pain,
My train . . .
    Lisa Selman

The Open Road

Blue is the sky and green the trees
   The winding road, the hum of the bees
The motor's sound and swish of the tires
   Songs of birds, a symphony that fires
Tired bodies with new zest in life
   While riding the open road

Flowers blooming in the fields
Tracks with trains of freight
Towering mountains, roaring seas
Trees so green and straight

   Placid cows chewing cuds
Lambs gambol nearby
   I drive and look, my heart is full,
Loudly I sigh, this is heaven,
   out on the open road

Remember this when bored with everyday life
   Get in the care, take your child and wife
    and get out on the open road.
    Frank Binenbaum

Caged Escape!

   Oh Juliet, my one, my first only true love.
Tis I, only miss you so dearly, I feel as if I
should pass away from the torment of your caged love.
   This wall, this fern grown wall for that which,
it sets us apart from each other. For only I wish you a bird,
or perhaps maybe even a dove that could spreadeth its wings
like a falling leaf from the above, to gently
descend upon the earth as gently as a cloud from
the heavens, but the wall for that which it
maketh me think myself as a humble peasant
bowing down unto a great unconquerable Lord.
This Lord the wall, the bird the unescapable you.
Juliet, the earth the unmovable Romeo, but only left
in a barricaded silence of doubt, but yet to ponder
of the escape of my lovely bird in a cage, Juliet.
Come with me, and thou shalt have no pity of
Trapped Thoughts Of Escapement. This night we will
elope and wishes beyond your own wildest dreams you never
thought possible shall come true
    Levi James Cortez

The Past Is Present

"Live in the present moment, not the past," I am told.
"My past is my present," I reply.
As I walk through the hallways of a soul burdened with
painful memories of long ago losses, I open a door and
see a young girl-woman sitting alone in a dimly lit room.
Her eyes are filled with tears of sadness and yearning.
Yearning for what? Her joy; my joy. Her life; my life.
"I've been waiting so long for you to open the door and
   heal my pain," she cries out to me.
"Can I see my Beloved now?
Does he miss me as I miss him, or did he forget me
when he died and his life became another?
I die but the painful memories birth again and again.
Rachel; Mary; Anna. Three of my names, but not my name.
Who am I really? Will I know me when I find me?"
She covers her face with her hands and sobs.
"I am so weary of the sadness and lostness.
Can we go out and play in the sunshine now?"
    Allexandra Hamilton

Who's Choice?

Pilgrim you must go. Sail! Sail! The hunger the pain.
Are we the insane?

The Indians, they are there, they will know no hunger and
know no pain.

Sail! Sail! Sell! Sold! Another one of my strength you
must go. The hunger the pain.

Stop this madness, this is not my choosing. I will help
only if you let me. Punish yourselves. O.K. I will stop this war.

Listen my children. I given you knowledge, I given you strength.

Killing the president didn't stop me. Don't you understand
it was never your choice.

Now all my children sail! Sail! And if you don't, my Mother Land
will help.

Shelia Black

Gazing Across A Deep Blue Sea

Here I am standing — alone on the shore
gazing across a deep blue sea
Understanding more and more
what this picture means to me.

A red-orange sunrise in the distant sky
shows a new beginning, another day
Feeling my emotions multiply
as the heavens lose their gray.

Sea gulls soaring high above
motionless among the clouds
Represent my freedom — my freedom of love
not a captive, but high and proud.

The ocean begins shallow but gradually gets deeper
it is mysterious, exciting, and hard to resist
Like passionate love, this beach is my keeper
covered by the droplets of a mid-morning mist.

"Nature is beautiful," I've said since the day I first met her
I was gazing across a deep blue sea
But the one thing that would make it better
is to have you here with me.

Allan Bennett Manganello

Thorns

She comes in like the Darkness
On a cold winter night;
A child, pale, the consort of the Angel of Death
With lips as red as the finest rubies
And as crimson as the blood which runs through my veins.

Eyes, haunting; dark and mysterious
As the bottomless depths of the ocean.
Double faced woman in mourning and in laughter
Torn between the magic and the tragic
Essence of the realm of desire.

Uncharted, unexplored; a virgin
From the joys and pleasures of this world,
Oh, fruit not tasted, passion wasted
From fear of the wrath of some loveless God.

Inspired by her Beauty I lie awaiting the last beat of my heart;
I sank into the blood red lips in hopes that soon, as I expire,
as we embrace we may enter the world christened forever.

Our blood, mingled, spilled upon the earth like seed scattered in
passion dispersed on some impossible soil with one scream for pain
and one for pleasure two roses emerged to face the rising sun.

Gerald del Campo

More Memories

When my thoughts are cluttered and confused
You always seem to unscramble them with the answers.
I think back on the memories we've made,
When love was new and there were no limits.
The love filled fights
The hate filled love.
Now time has changed our feelings
And somewhere we ended up as friends.
You know what I feel before I tell you,
I hear what you feel before you say it.
The bond we've created is too great to break
But the lines that have been drawn
Are too thick to cross
Without stepping on each other's feelings.
I can't help but love our new long talks,
But I can't help but miss our long kisses.
Together we have made so many memories,
   Now let's make some more.

Leeanne Pittenger

Our Guide

The bells ring and gone the sun
They tell us that our day is done
Night is here tis time to rest,
And think of how today we were blessed.

The sun came up o'er the hill,
And told me not to stay still,
But to rise and start my day,
And remember who guides my way.

He watched me as I did start, and from my side ne'er did part
Even when I took noontide meal, by my side, him I could feel.
Then I toiled in the heat, and it was there that we did meet
I saw not him, but he saw me, and keep me working tirelessly.

At evening meal I felt him there, and knew then he was everywhere
Omnipresent, and always our guide
In his dominion we strive to reside.

The bells have tolled, and now we lay,
And think of what to him we'll say
One thing which shouldn't seem so odd
Is love mankind, and thank you God.

Richard M. Englander

Strangers

You've never met me, nor I you.
But I know what you're thinking; what you are about to do.
If you could hear me, I would say: With you forever is where
I want to stay. I know you are afraid; there's a lot to think about.
I know it will be hard to do without a doubt.
But I promise you, you'll never be alone.
When others turn you away with their hearts of stone.
You'll always have me to lean on . . . when you need a friend.
I will give you love until the very end.
If you would give me this one chance;
I know I could make your heart dance. The world is waiting.
Who knows what it will have in store.
I may be famous, or I may be poor. But you and I will never know.
Unless you let me stay with you and grow.
In my final hour I'm grasping for hope.
If you go through with this, how will you cope?
You will see me in the faces of others.
In little children as they cling to their mothers.
You'll do what you think you must. It's God now, that I must trust.
To give you the strength to do what you feel is right. I won't blame
or hate you for my plight. But mom, I pray you won't abort me tonight.

Darnell Appling

Who Cares?

The situations sticky, we're stranded,
born Black into a life of despair

Systematically cursed, before birth, but who cares?
A Mother loses her Sun in a senseless murder,
when I was a teen that was something unheard of

In retrospect do not neglect the preceding verse,
I said Sun, meaning light

Not intentionally excluding sisters who are the
Moon, beware! Teach the children who are
the Stars, prepare them for their fight

It hurts like hell Black people! White people!
my heart's in pain

Blindly, we play right into this dirty racist game

You're not my problem Cracker and this Ni**er's
not yours; it's the elite who have erred

Believe me we're suffering in the same boat
with misnomers like I just used,
Scapegoats, but who cares?

Alonzo Hill

Taken

The serpent's tongue
slithers in,
feeling all corners,
tasting . . . Tasting.
Like the arms of Satan,
the touch of the dragon
burns my skin,
silent and greedy
cracking and peeling.
Eyes of the God
glow red,
lighting demonic gateways,
watching . . . Waiting.
Breath from the evil one touches me.
Cracking . . . Peeling . . .
watching . . . Waiting . . .
slithering . . . Tasting . . .
In me he lays.

Jennifer Williams

Heroin

My name is Heroin, call me smack for short; I entered this country
without a passport ever since then I've made lot's of scum, Rich, some
have been murdered found in a ditch, I'm more valued than diamond,
more treasured than gold, use me just once and you will be sold.
I'll make a school boy forget his books, I'll make a beauty queen forget
her looks. I'll take a renewed speaker and make him a bore. I'll
take your mother and make her a whore. I'll take a school teacher
forget how to teach. I'll make a preacher not want to preach. I'll
take your rent money and you'll be evicted. I'll murder your babies,
or they'll be born addicted. I'll make you rob, steal, and kill,
when you're under my power you have no will. Remember my friend,
my name is "Big H" If you try me once you'll never be free, I'll
destroy actors, politicians, and many heroes, I'll decrease bank
accounts from millions to zero, I'll make shooting and stabbing a
common affair, once I take charge you won't have a prayer, now that
you know me what will you do? You have to decide it's all up to you.
If you decide to sit on my saddle. The decision is one that no one
can straddle. Listen to me and please listen well. When you ride
with heroin you're headed for hell!

Claudia Minjarez

Disguised Life

Poor Little Audrey:
Tangled in life's mess
moves away
from family, friends
to be with him?
A stranger she met one day,
hoping to be held and caressed.
His handsome fee —
her happiness.

Poor Little Audrey:
When will you learn?
Life is more than sex and guys,
hording your bed,
your innocence.
Your soul stained as each left
you red, bruised,
hanging from their lies,
the remnant of your heart
burning to be free,
To remove the Mask, your Disguise

Leslie Clardy

Ocean Pearls

I waited for you on the beaches of Vallarta.
The pearl of your existence lingering in my mind;
The sensual aroma of your sex surrounds me
And fills each of my breaths with sweet intoxication.

The wrath of nature is exposed with each crashing wave;
Two volatile worlds forced to coexist — earth and sea.
The foundation of Life is born from this coupling;
You and I, brought together to calm the savagery.

Two volatile worlds forced to coexist — you and I.
A union born out of the savagery of this world.
Drowning in a sea of despair, we saved each other
And were washed up along the beaches of the future.

The world is our oyster and Vallarta is the pearl.
I cannot open it without you My Love; I won't.
The sun promised to deliver you to me this day.
Even as I wait, the treacherous clouds block your path.

Deborah L. R. Shelton

The Fire In My Heart!

My heart is full of love,
Your eyes are its desire,
You are the only one,
That can quench its furious fire;

For the fire in my heart,
And the love that's in your eyes,
Shall bring us both together,
And in turn shall make us wise;

We will kiss a million times,
And love a thousand ways,
We will touch a hundred hearts,
And be happy all our days;

I will kiss you oh so slowly,
And look deep into your eyes,
I will find your heart's desire,
And quench the flame between your thighs;

Please show me your love my angel;
Please give to me your loving heart,
I will never leave you lonely,
And we will never be apart.

Marvin E. Young Jr.

Metaphysical Love Poem

In an infinite Universe,
    all things are true.
So somewhere my feathers aren't kept in a jar,
    but propel me through green lakes of bourbon.
Somewhere, I'm with Jesus's Mary
    smoking crack in a 7-11.
Somewhere, I'm teaching my Siamese twin
    how to construct a typewriter.
And somewhere, in some existence,
    you're in love with me.
So you might as well just love me
    now, here, in our own warped web,
        perfect as infallible pink possibility.
Love me like faith in infinity.

Martha Buckley Sullivan

Bittersweet Embrace

You took me for an angel when you looked into my eyes
No part of you could notice that my heart loves to despise
I'm your pretty little lover, and I'm quickened by your lust
But keep your eyes wide open, and learn when not to trust
Your crazy little beauty who sleeps upon your bed
Has dreams of wicked incest when she rests her pretty head
The lurid masturbation that you call intercourse
Pulls me closer to you with a claustrophobic force
And when you see the tears fall down my pretty face
Will you patronize me with your bittersweet embrace
And what will you do then, with your pretty little bride
When you find her naked sleeping with her suicide?

Krystal Parsons

Raped

I thought I would be okay, walking here at night.
If somebody tried to start something, I'm straight up ready to fight.

Was there someone behind me? I really couldn't tell.
The next thing I knew I was pushed hard from behind and I fell.

I felt someone massaging my body, trying to get inside.
Then he asked me a question. "Are you gonna let me ride?"

I knew something was about to occur. I felt myself starting to cry.
Then it happened, he ripped off my pants, and began squeezing my thigh.

I tried my best to scream, but no sound would come out.
Then this dirty man began kissing my mouth.

I tried to resist him, but he was too strong.
He forced me to have sex with him, and that was very wrong.

When he was finished, he ran off to escape.
But I could do nothing, I had just been raped!

Donya Gibson

Shadows

Out of the shadows she came like a nightmare,
She was very pretty, but the horror was in her stare.
She had legs right up to her neck,
When she walked by the limpest of things became erect.
I knew I couldn't have her, but I wanted her just the same.
She was very clever, but I thought I could play her game.
She was a cheatin', lyin', deceitful, little b*tch.
She had no money, but in beauty she was rich.
I am not weak, but she's very strong,
And wanting her so bad, I knew was wrong.
She stole my neart with just one look,
I tried to deny it, but I knew I was hooked.
I knew it was wrong, but I wanted her so bad,
She was the prettiest girl I never had.

James E. Barton

Untitled

Like an Aztec sacrifice
the heart torn from my chest
    I saw it beating once
as my body was tossed aside.

    My warm blood streaming down the arm
of the guilt ridden commoner in disguise
    Who gave him the power to do such a deed
as others line up for the honor

    Smoke rises from the pyre of empty shells
Don't mourn for me, my soul untouched by death
    As the celebration of the victors ends
Sweep the ashes from under your feet
    You'll walk on me no more

    Let the ancient God's whisper
Shake their heads in vain
    Where's the lessons learned so well
how many more will burn.

Melissa A. Bartz

Her Baby Lay Dead On The Ground

Clothes to wear or to go bare,
Is this the question here?
No! We say, it's a plea not to kill,
Those little animals we love so dear.

I heard the thud! As the club came down,
The voice of the little one as it cried,
And the sad sad wail of the mother seal,
As she stood helplessly by.

I felt the sting, the heavy blow,
As the club came crashing down,
I watched it all on television,
As the blood spilled red in the snow.

Then I felt something wet upon my face,
There was nothing else it could be,
My hand went up the wiped away the tears,
That were running down my cheeks.

I wish I could express the sorrow I felt,
Oh, how my heart did pound,
As I watched the mother and heard her cries,
When her baby fell dead on the ground.

William W. Wallace

The Living

Why should we live we've nothing to give
Always someone around to put you down
For what you are wearing
Or if you're swearing
You're really neat
So you might think
When you go out and buy your own drink

It's not what you are that counts anymore
But how you look and walk cross the floor
They'll smack you and beat you just for some fun
But what can you do can't carry a gun

The earth's draggin' on too slowly it seems but once in a while
Some child screams cause someone has grabbed her
And hauled her away to be found in a ditch

On some summer day it's to the point
Nobody'd care if you ever die cause you're just pigs
In a world full of pig sties
The world's about had it I'm sorry to say
Face up to the truth we'd all better pray
To who you believe in whoever he is everything made remember is his

Adam Stodola

This Day In December

A photograph in
Time Magazine
a face, a name, hazy but familiar,
Thurmon Scott.

My heart races with shame
large slices of pizza, chocolate,
handful . . . then handfuls of chocolates later
feeling sick, high, angry and scared . . .
I remember.

The warm summer of 1981,
he had been my acting teacher
and then became my therapist.
Steamy August night, my second therapy session,
he had sex with me.
Numb, completely numb was I,
as he entered me
and satisfied his desires, twice.

I told him, never, did I want
to see his face again,
and I didn't until this day in December, 1996.

Leslie Faith Harris

And The Pleasure Is All Mine!

You say you can not stay, it's too soon and though you may be right,
the pleasure is all mine. I reach for you hoping you turn to be my
forever-more, and you know the pleasure is all mine. When my nights
become lonely, I not only pray that you see my light being in flight
inseparable mighty love! But I show it and tell you it's safe, but
yet you say I can not stay, it's too soon and the pleasure is all mine
Please don't forget to pray for the same mighty insight even
when not the doves cry. The time is four-twenty-four, I'm more
than ready to be spanked for foreplay, flank for specific position,
drank for the taste of things and the pleasure is all mine. I
ebulliently appreciate the ascertainment of high class caliber
knowledge you exemplify and the pleasure is all mine. Over
night sensation continues to grow whether you stay, come or
go, there's more to empower behind my flower, the pleasure is all mine.

I don't want to fight just want to be your righteous light that
makes your nipples ripple of sweet-sweat and your nature rise to
my sensational dark ebony prize of contentment. I only ask of
you to feel my mood that craves for your impressionable touch,
and moan for the sound of your Beloved Bear in your striking an
accord within me. I do believe you know I'm true to you
impetuously and unconditionally without a doubt. True or dear
most heavenly sanguine the pleasure is all mine.

Jewel Jorge

Love, What The Hell Is It?

Who is love?
What is love?
Where is love?
Why is it here?
Is it here to torture me?
Why can't I experience it?
Was it ever meant for me?
How come I hear others speak of it but
I never known of its meaning?
Is it wonderful and phat as I heard or
is it a demon, a demon trying to tell me to get
into it so he can maintain my heart,
Was it meant for good from the start,
I'm confused because I've been used and
abused and battered down and up and
didn't give a f%$k, till I hear of love.
What is love?
Who is love?
Show me love!

Rajah A. Walia

Pear

Lust, all's black.
Sense of innocence.
Instinct craves her.

Blood and sweat
I've come to an end.
The flame is smothered.

Her neck is broken
Oh, God, help me now.
Run through the darkness.

Forever is a sin
Forgiveness is temptation.
Another light will be found.

It's over now.

Paulo Eduardo Evangelista

Untitled

The musty whispers waxed queasy upon my mouth
the foam danced timid, the sand clad in mourning afar.
With rapacious air my drowned eyes hunted you
yet they faltered, a brace of dead quail.
My fingers, loath to finding but misty shadows
when they went, somnambulant, in search of your hair.
Oceanic scent of a tired beach in my eyes
and my orphan breasts, smiling before the moon.
And your drowsy thighs, wounded with my lips
now meek, healed over upon the morning lightening.
In my navel the earthly taste of the hushed sea
where your kisses ran aground, awkward castaways.
Drunken with insatiability, with your spring of anise
the furtive mouths, filled with sighed kisses.
Forgotten in a delirium of rain, of moss
beneath the raspy murmurs of the weeping waves.

Diane Elizabeth Graves

Fantasies Of A Scientist

In the depths of the lab I dream of you my love,
Your hair is a million strands of gold wire,
Your body is the shape of an Erlenmeyer flask,
Your eyes are a pair of blue light emitting diodes,
Your lips are a set of greased o-rings,
Your breasts are ports on a vacuum chamber.
Surely my heart beats for you like a thousand cryo-pumps!
Your Gamma rays penetrate my inner being.
Oh for the funding to analyze your every molecule,
To quantify your proportions,
To observe your every reaction.
May our wave functions infinitely extend to the confines of the universe
in the absence of attenuation and our signals be in phase forever!

Peter D. Milewski

A Witness Protected

Here I go again
In my life of crime
Thanks to the feds
I'll do no time

Stoolie, stoolie the Don calls me
Say the feds — "cop a plea"
Then the Don is history

Set me up in a job — great pay
I'll live to see another day

Get a woman, roll in the hay
Murder, murder anyone in the way
Crime they say really does pay
I'll be free any ole day.

Richard B. Pappas

I Am Who I Am

I'm sorry I can't be the hero that you need me to be.
I'm just a little short of that order and all I can be is me.
I'm sorry I can't be the rich man that you would like for me to be.
I'm better off than my father,
So that says something for me.
I'm sorry I'm not the brain that you said I could be.
But I am smart and blessed with wisdom,
That's a plus for me.
I'm sorry I did some things wrong.
How am I supposed to learn?
The goals that I have achieved;
With honesty and hard work I earned.

Jay Cooper

T.S. Eliot put it this way, in 1930:

*"Let us go then, you and I,
When the evening is spread out against the sky
Like a patient etherised upon a table . . ."*
             from "The Love Song of J. Alfred Prufrock"

I put it this way, in 1996:

That late October evening,
When the whole world is
    a-tilt,
    a-slant,
When the long, deep, slender shadows,
Like rubber bands, are stretched taut and tight
'Cross faraway fields and highway lands;
When the whole world seems to be lying on its side:

    A horizontal El Greco!

When the sinking, drowning Sun reaches out
    and screams
For the whole world
To come and join it
For that long a-waited
Rest.

Frances H. Ellis

The Shrine

All the young boys at the park
the fun starts with the umpire's bark,
"Play Ball," and the crowd jumps to their feet
while the late arrivals scramble to their seats.

All the big players are knows as their team's million dollar man
they get paid all their millions to hit and run as fast as they can.
"Popcorn! Popcorn!" you yell.   "Over here, just one!"
Then crack, everyone stands and cheers for the go ahead run.

The one running around the horn is the MVP
you struggle to stand on your seat to see
A fast ball, "Strike three!" to make the last out
"We win!" is what all the hometown fans shout.

David Ross MacMaster

Love At First Sight

Eyes meet and
    suddenly
        out of the gaping wound of loneliness,
The red hot magma of love
    gushes forth.
The rock of stony hearts melt
    together
        in the fierce heat.
For a time
    the wound is
        cauterized.

Timothy R. Branson

Happy Birthday Aunt Grace

Where do all the years go
Is what we really would like to know
with maturity comes sweet wisdom you see
but the Physical body ain't what it used to be

When every thing aches as you get out of bed
remember we need to hear all you have said
we visit you today to bring you some cheer
Later you'll wonder where the hell have they
    been all year?

Enjoy today and do something naughty
remember don't let yourself be haughty
you are as tough as nails with an iron will
you try to hide your soft heart don't
    want to put it thru another mill.

Enjoy to day but don't eat too much cake
Remember we love you this is why we partake

Dawn Brown

K

    In the days of my youth I was entranced
    by a girl so fair, she reveled the purity of
    snow, as delicate as the first fallen leaf of
    Fall. For years my life was full of
impartial love and crippling shyness.

She gave so much joy and happiness, for as long as
the sun rises to kiss the sky, till the moon in all its
glory illuminates the heavens.

As the butterfly must leave the cocoon to radiate its
beauty to the world, she discarded the old for the
possibilities of the new.

She glistened with inner beauty more magnificent
than the brightest stars, catching the eyes of every
suitor that crossed her path.

The love that was thought gone from sight hast
returned, like the blooming flowers of spring.

Dreams captured my mind, emanating the heavens
on earth for mine own. The God sent beauty that
was to be mine has been taken on a gentle breeze like
the first fallen leaf.

William A. Sambel

The Heartbreak Of Psoriasis
AKA The Sinking Of The Bismarck

He stood there watching her sleeping form, her breasts gently
rising and falling as she slept.
Her face, relaxed, only showed peace and contentment.
Her slightly mussed hair framed her elegantly featured face.

He kissed her cheek softly, knowing this was the only intimacy he
could have with her. While she was warm and soft and gentle in
sleep, wakefulness brought a hardening, a defensiveness and the
kind of oneness that tends to exclude the world and all others in it.

It couldn't be, another love as great as his for her, nor a gift so
pure and new. They both were like that, not so long ago.

But she, huddled in the corner, still in her farmer's jeans, spat
upon him and all that he was,
all the while holding him to her breast with tidbits of emotion.

And he, naked before her, withered and slumped to the ground
as though he were naught but a pile of oily rags.

And there he died.

John E. Eastland

My First Love

You've given me goodness and mercy, My Lord
Something with money I could not afford.
You've given so freely your love and your grace
The light of Christ Jesus shines down on my face.

He carried His cross and took with Him my shame
That for my wickedness, I should have no blame.
He died on that cross upon calvary
Wonder of wonders He did this for me.

Now, knowing this truth, daily I pray
That should I falter along the way
He will me pick up gently and guide me once more
Down the path of righteousness to heaven's front door.

I will carry the cross now, that He carried for me
So when the flesh dies and my spirit's set free
And when my name's called from His book up above
I'll go back to my Father, with Him, my first love.

Sharon S. Wright

The Key

The hours almost over, the time has gone so fast
That I've scarcely had a moment yet the time is here at last
To send a note of Thank You for your care and great concern
And all the knowledge you have shared in hopes to help me learn

You've taken time with patience more than most I ever knew
The issues that I face each day, the tests I've put you through
To see if you would leave me within a drowning sea
Of shattered lives, hopes and dreams a perfect time to exit me

You've given of yourself you see in ways I can't repay
And for this reason I give to you this key I hold today
To crumble down the walls about that keep me safe and sound
Experience the hurt within that often lurks around

My life is mine and mine alone and yet it must be shared
The key that I have given you is trust because you cared
I do not want to leave you though at times it may seem so
It's just a test I put you through to see if you will go.

In the years that follow I will always wish you well
And pray that God will bless you more than words can even tell
For you hold a special gift that's often rare to find
You help me want to learn to live and educate my mind.

Kelly Jean Linde

Reflections

Child of the universe, from where
Do you come?
You are master of all that you see,
But you don't know your own soul.

Protector of the weak and meek,
You still water this earth with the blood
And tears of your victims.

Thinker, doer, healer, killer,
Who are you?

Your face is reflected through
An endless hall of mirrors,
Each reflection subtly different,
Slightly changed, rearranged,
Always new and always old,
Never the same for long.

You fill the universe with the melodies
Of your symphonies and the screams of your prey
Pray, who are you?
Ah! Of course . . . now I know!
Yours is the face that I see when I look in my mirror.

John Kozin

My Spirit

My spirit I'm looking for you, where you at?
Can you bring me my life back?
My soul went dead over these years
I'm not afraid of dying, that I do not fear
I shared my heart, balance my life trying to make it even
I sometime dream my life ain't worth living
Sometime I see my life goes by with my own eyes
Where so my spirit you leave my life paralyzed
But what can I do to make my life last?
All my memory haunts me, because of my shattered past
My spirit could you open my soul and let it see
My life ain't worth living without you inside me
I can't dream about the future anymore
Please come back to me my spirit, or I will close this door
Why did you leave me, and leave my heart behind
In the future what way of life will I find?
My spirit is this an realistic dream I can't escape
My spirit will I forgot this life in its right shape
My spirit did I do something wrong to make you leave
My spirit come back to me, I beg of you, please.

Dan Inthapangna

While Love Lays Silent

If life is worth living,
    then why is their loneliness,
     seemingly endless loneliness,
     which wrenches the depths of my soul?
Its identity possesses many faces,
    memories of loved ones lost,
     of broken hearts and dying hopes.
But the most unforgettable face,
    is the face of a mother,
     whom, when lost at a tender young age,
     suddenly turned what was innocent,
    into a stranger in a strange world,
    separated from affections held so dear.
And, no matter how many tears later,
    the void unexpectedly opened one dreary August night,
    remains empty still,
    while love lays silent.

Charles J. Conrad

The Snake

As we walk through life each day,
Removing stumbling blocks in our way.

Being ever so careful with each step we take
Sometimes we befriend, "The Snake."

He comes to you, and such a friend is he,
Cuts your throat and knocks you on your knee

Then he ask, "whats the matter my brother?"
At the blink of an eye he'll knock you on the other

The snake is cunning, conniving, and wicked
If you're not strong you get a one way ticket

Straight to hell and may never come back
If its strength and faith in God you lack

The pain is sharp, the daggers deep
The fall may be ever so steep

You say to yourself, "I should've known better
Dust yourself off, get yourself together

The Snake is mean and his blood runs cold
Even the best have traveled that road

No matter how careful the steps we take
Sooner or Later, all befriend, "The Snake"

Donna R. Broady

Faces

Sun bursts red hot flames of blazing rage;
Moon lies dull blue set in languid space.
Earth floats lightly through a sea of age,
And sheds to sun and moon its double face.

Under fiery clouds the sun does rise,
And renders moon unseen until the night.
When sun forfeits its beauty from our eyes,
The moon shines forth in sun's reflected light.

Earth without the sun is cold and damp;
Sun must sit upon its throne so high.
Without the moon where is our midnight lamp?
Its luring light with silver fills the sky.

Earth who's blazoned blue and green and white,
without these faces drowns in endless night.

Joseph P. Parker

Untitled

As long as I have dreams,
Bad things won't be what they seem.
My dreams keep me from crying,
Sometimes my soul feels like it's dying.
Maybe things will change around,
But then again, they might fall to the ground.
I wish bad things would change to good,
I'd change them, if I could.
Some things don't go the way we plan,
And it's too hard to understand.
I believe that it will work out at the end,
Because as we know it, we still have our friends.

Teresa Ramsey

The Lord Has Blessed Me

The Lord has blessed me in so many ways;
These little joys which drop in on worn days.
They fill my heart to its extreme;
Maybe by having a soothing dream.
I see these blessings in a child's smiling face;
Or perhaps while I'm sitting in my favorite place.
Knowing that God is close at heart;
I know that these gifts shall never depart.
Through the sweet sound of laughter;
And that feeling of happiness after;
I am feeling blessed once more.
Thank you, Dear Lord for all blessings in store!

Meghan McMahon

The Knock

The energy of that night I remember still
How it stayed the bite of December's chill
Yet spared the crystals of my frosted door
That froze her knock into my evermore.

Muffled came the sound of my siren song
Alluring my heart to forever long
To be the captive enslaved by her melody
And to crash on her shores for eternity.

Her silhouette framed by the glistening glass
Yielded a vision of beauty of heavenly cast
And by the rap of her hand was my destiny set
She was my master, I her marionette.

A more angelic sound shall never be heard
Nor more emotion aroused by a spoken word
Relished as the kiss of a butterfly's wing
Her knock has become my everything.

Chris Buchar

A Child Is Born . . . A Son Is Given

For unto us a child is born
On this blessed Christmas morn;
The angels sang "peace on earth"
To greet the babe of heavenly worth.
Begotten of God, His son Jesus
Became flesh to dwell here among us;
But there is a tear in Mary's eye,
Her precious son has come forth to die,
The hallelujahs would soon turn to scorn
And a glowing halo would become thorn.

But, I rejoice, for He came to be
My loving savior on Calv'ry's tree;
Forgiven of sin, I'm reborn to His glory,
Renewed, restored; I now tell His story
From the wonder of the Virgin's womb
To the wonder of the empty tomb.
Yes, a promised child is born today
Came on Christmas to show me the way.
In the family of God, I now am a part
As I celebrate Easter in my heart!

Iola W. Earl

Small Packages

You are responsible to see and behold
To clothe me and comfort me until I am old

Wise enough to see which is really right
To make my own decisions and mistakes in your sight

I'm a fragile small package to guide and to teach
To share accomplishments and failures, and dreams that I'll reach

Although features seem similar, my ears hear different sounds
My mind and soul are separate, though we share the same ground

For you alone are the window for the clouds, rain and sunshine
A purifier and a filter to the experiences which will be mine

You are my idol, my heroes and my friend
From the sandbox and the school room, to the world I am sent . . .

Even though I'm slowly becoming me, I've probably grown up too soon
I'll always be your small package, from my manhood to the womb

Stephen E. McCluskey

A Wife's Prayer

Oh Blessed Father above
Thank You for my husband and all of our love

I know that this marriage was all in Your plan
So help me be the best wife I possibly can

I pray that Thy will be done in all that we do
Help us in all things to depend upon You

May our love come from You and constantly grow
May it always bring strength when times get low

By Your Mighty Spirit may we always be led
Give us wisdom and courage to face trials ahead

Keep us faithful to each other and to You oh Lord
May we strive together for our heavenly reward

Bless us Father with all that we need
Speak to us through the scriptures we read

I pray that You keep him close to my side
That I can bring happiness and peace to his mind

Help me spread love and kindness throughout our home
That my husband may feel warmth and never alone

Please help us keep You the center of our life
Thank you Oh Lord for letting may be his wife

Sheila O. Thomas

Murmurs Of Gaia

This never ending river of lights,
Casting a shadow on natures rights,

Winding its way to the furthermore reaches,
And dipping its way to ocean beaches.

Craziness it will seem,
till the last of its gleam.

Has forsaken our short stay
but there is one other way

And one more chance
for the ghost dance.

Gather your thoughts and glean the best,
and put our conscience to its ultimate test.

Hobson Richards

God's Menagerie

Think not about the color of the hand stretched out to thee —
There's no such thing as predestination in the world of poverty.
Still not the haunted voices that beckon in the night —
Open the bowels of compassion, give love flight.

Think not about the origin of the one who asks of thee —
There's no room for prejudice in this land of liberty.
Shut not thine eyes against the lost, the homeless, the poor at heart,
Rather seek to enrich the world with a pledge to do thy part.

Think not about tomorrow, but learn to care today
There's no time for procrastination; a loss of life along the way.
We're but a specter in the rainbow; God's kaleidoscopic menagerie —
Passing strangers upon the path of life's grand odyssey.

Kathy Burrell Stokely

My Silver Spoon

Hi Becky, darling how are you? I hope you're doing fine, and also
Molly and Francis and your mother who's divine.

Sorry that I couldn't write real soon but I've been kept real busy
polishing my silver spoon until it made me dizzy.

I have been buffing it for months trying to make it shimmer but
the more I polish the damn thing seems to be getting dimmer.

The silver spoon I mentioned is really my endeavor to find myself
a dwelling place and bring my family together.

The polishing I'm doing is choosing the right place but I'm afraid
if things don't change I'm bound to lose this race.

Unless my God can lend an ear and listen to my plea and make
my problems disappear by knocking down these walls for me.

So I may walk on through real soon and put away my silver spoon.

Elias Cruz

Class Ring

Beside the door he paused to stand
Taking the class ring from her hand.
None who were watching dared to speak
A silent tear rolled down his cheek.
The thoughts that ran through his mind
were precious shared memories left behind.
Then in an instant his eyes grew cold,
For never again her hand would he hold.
As he was watched with a silent stare
He whispered I love you and I'll always care.
With the ring on his finger he kissed her good-bye,
Knowing she had worn it he began to cry.
The doors blew open and the wind did blow,
As they carried her casket away in the snow.

Crystal R. Isenhour

She

One day when everything was just like the ordinary
I saw her and I knew I saw something extraordinary
Something that I cannot find the word to describe in any dictionary
Innocent as child, beautiful as moon, pure as water, and very smart
She can never be imitated by any piece of art
Knowing her has brought new life to my heart
When she speaks, her words become the loveliest songs in my ears
My worst nightmare come true whenever I see her tears
I believe she's the one I've been looking for all these years
She is like a dream came true
A dream which I always want to go through
She's a friend I can always turn to to help me out
By now, she is one of those people I cannot live without
She give me the power to go on with my life
Cutting all that faces me with a knife
When I'm down, she left right up again
And if somehow I make a mistake, she'll never complain
That's how true she is, so simple and plain
Yet her favors can never be bounded by any domain
And just case you're curious, her name is Amy Lynne

Hussain Ashkanani

Over The Hill

Over the hill — over the hill
Debbie! Debbie! — o soon you will be

Gray hair — gray hair
A case of Lady Clairol — so no one knows but me

Fatigue, no energy — ambition gone
O Lord I just can't finish — cleaning this whole house

Memory loss — forgetfulness
O which direction is it — from my house to the mall

Support hose — girdles stiff
Way too many sagging parts — that need an extra lift

Alka Seltzer, Maalox — Pepto Bismol too
Try this, try that — when nothing else will do

Aches, pains — muscles sore
Bengay! O Dave — please rub a little more

Walkers, canes — crutches too
Just getting up — is sometimes hard to do

On top of the world — on top of the world
I pray God will grant you — at least another "Forty"

Roseann Yelles

Volunteer Clerk Senior Surprise Store

Well here I am, it's Friday once more.
So far only one person has come through the door.
She wanted a quilt, and I thought money!
But she went away without even a bunny!
The weather is perfect — they can have no excuse
The traffic on forth street, proves they are loose.
The parking lot on the corner will hold quite a few.
So come on people and see what we have new.
We've made all these pretties so we'd not have to starve
We'll sell you a necklace and maybe two scarves.
The news says we're hungry the president's perplexed
So out with your purse and write a few checks!
We have dolls on our tables and cushions galore
Quilts to the ceiling and toys on the floor
We have doilies and afghans and table cloths too
Dishtowels and pot holders — I mean not a few.
If shopping makes you tired
We have chairs for the weary
So come through that door and don't be so leary.

Ethel Richards

"Blues For My Mother . . ."

this song is incomplete —
but whose voice should I use?

    a quick crescendo calls out
    & tells me to come home . . .
        NOW!

    what is the mystery of the mother
    that makes the man want to leave
    yet always return to the warmth
    of a single solo flute
      playing in the background of spring?

    there are smells you cannot taste,
    like the melody locked in memories
    that make learning such a chore —
    that's why I'm 99 & 8/10ths percent sure
    my mother wanted a girl.

    Odell Montgomery

Only Daddy Knows

How can one say how much love they have in their heart?
  Only Daddy knows

Who knows of her hurts inside when she cannot say what
is on her mind?
  Only Daddy knows

Who has always shared a tender moment with this young
girl on her special occasions?
  Only Daddy knows

How can he ever know how very proud I am of him?
  Only Daddy knows

Only my Daddy know how much he means to me each and
everyday of my life.

  I love you, Daddy.
    Shirley Hughes Cottrell

To Miss Hayslett

relentless Love, end at last Your torment!
upon light wings You carry Her fair image to my bed,
prevent for all eternity the sleep there meant,
and leave a thousand thoughts of Her about my heavy heart instead.
then, at break of dawn when i arise
to my dismay Her gorgeous eyes again greet mine
as i curse and treasure the bondage which will lead to my demise
for Love at times is a one-way street as We will find.
i do walk to the pounding of Her name in my mind
as my heart does beat in unison with the blink of Her eyes
i search the air for Her words which my ears do pine,
and, if by accident, i catch Her glance, my eyes do cry:

"Love, angelic demon, what right have You to enforce my bondage
  sustained
with such a weapon that ceaselessly strikes with both
  pleasure and pain?"

    Leonard Tuanquin

Clichés Of Life

To many life is a cliches
Live and let live
Why do we take all things for granted.
  You live day by day.
Live life to the fullest — tomorrow is
  not promised.
Life is to short to be unhappy and sad.
  When it's all said and done
You've lived your life — according to the
  clichés of life.

    Sandra Robinson

A Special Call On Christmas Day

Son, your call today
Meant so much to me
To hear your voice
How happy it made me
God answers our Prayers
In his special way
I had ask God to let you call me
I had not your number
Or knew where you lived
One thing is for certain. God surely did.

    Mary F. Wells

School

Why school?
Why make me wake up at six to catch an ugly bus,
Why make school start at eight, why not nine or ten
Why give me hours of homework, why make me do it all
Why school?
The boring teachers and ignorant kid, the girls, the boys,
The hoards of kids, running and rushing to catch their next class,
Not knowing they're already late for their class,
We burst in the door, and eyes galore.
Starring at me.
And only me, the teacher pauses.
And then continues
About something we learned four years ago,
She passes out papers and stares at me
She waltzes over to me and says,
You're late, what gave me away?
That will be detention for you, you're two minutes late.
You're missing some valuable time,
Two minutes about something we learned four years ago

    Gabrielle M. Mirsaidi

You'll Know

When you hear a child's laughter
  and watch it at its play
  or hear a bird in beautiful song,
You'll know God made this day.

When you hear a loved one's voice say
  "I love you, Dear"
  and feel the warmth of that love,
You'll know that God is near.

When you look up and see a rainbow
  or see a meadow fair,
  or see the ocean waves comes rolling in,
You'll know that God is there.

When an evening sunset glows with fire
  and the stars soon shine above,
  then when you see the moonlight beam,
You'll know that God is love.

When you see the wonders
  of a golden fall,
  and see the beauty of the earth,
You'll know God make it all.

    Margaret LeBaugh

Untitled

Over the crooked cement,
I send more smiles unkempt —
hovering over to the corner,
shaking, burnt — the mourner.

The Ritual of Lethargy, drunk and devoured
I lay calm, wounds rudely soured.
Thawed hysterics elapsed in cold eyes
perpetuated with a frozen sigh.

    Mindy Yu

Nova

No power is greater than love.
But to obtain its unshackled strength
One must become as sensitive to the
Pulsing quivers of the heart as a
Candle flame is to the faint unseen
Breezes of a dark-filled room.

This control at the center of things can only be
Reached by humility, reverence, quietness, and a
Search for beauty. When it is found, the faintest
Touch can release untold energies . . .

Then a man can stand ten miles tall and send
Thunderbolts crashing through barriers of
Stone and steel. He can unleash ten thousand
Amazons to quench the world's great desert thirst.
With the serenity of Mount Everest in his mind, and the
Fires of Vesuvius in his heart, he can
Unleash the energies of his faith with the
Sudden brightness of an H-Bomb.

To find and master the delicate secret
Control can be the great quest of a man's life.

John McConnell

Islands

Take me somewhere
where the seasons change one day
at a time and the people are walking with two feet
behind the last, and the grass tickles the bareness
of their souls

Where they notice, unnoticeably noticing
what we choose to ignore through hidden cracks in cellar doors
and stained glass visions of tomorrow-

Take me to a place where the top is far
but near and people stretch five fingers out to touch
the untouchable and run their hands over the face
of the other — to trace reflections of entrenched destinies

Where the leaves always cling to the trees
even when the wood is deadened by the shift in the night sky
while efforts speak the sorrows of the side they can't see

But bridges — short, clumsy bridges connect
their inner linings with the outside world
that can't understand but only feel
the grace from their island that dances in the shadows of your heart.

Ann Frisbie

Cybernetic Savior

Drowning in a deep and endless sea of information,
Fighting for the freedom of a cyber pseudo-nation.
For better or for worse, my soul is bound to this domain.
I was when it was waxing, now I am to see it wane.
But I won't stand by helplessly, and I am not alone,
As millions unite to make their discontentment known.
"A Thousand Points of Darkness" and the graphics of blue ribbons
Show that there will be no peace until redemption's given.
Now the System tries to put a limit on behavior.
I'm a techno-rebel, I'm a cybernetic savior.

"Internet Indecency," a bill conceived in fear.
One way or the other, the engagement's end is near.
The only true democracy will either fall or thrive,
But I'll continue fighting for as long as it's alive.
What is there to die for but our freedom and our right?
Together we can triumph, for in numbers there is might.
Like a dragon, now our cause must spread its wings and wake.
Send their strongholds crashing down, and cause the earth to quake!
Now the System tries to put a limit on behavior.
I'm a techno-rebel, I'm a cybernetic savior.

Joshua Justice

Gentle Old Man

My eyes have seen this gentle old man
With sage blue eyes and smiling face as
    he walks down the street.
He softly stumbles along just glad he is
    still here
To feel the warm sunshine on his face,
To smell the green grass and watch the bees
    fly around the colorful blossoms.
How lucky I am to have seen this ancient jewel.
He has made me think of all the wonderful
    things he must have seen and done.
Perhaps I cannot imagine them all; probably not.
His tan pants and jacket,
His crumpled straw hat
    and his skimpy gray hair . . .
I bet he was a dashing figure in his youth . . .
This gentle old man.

Diann McPherson

Untitled

When his inspiration left
He constructed a wall

A place unto himself
Where he could stand tall

Like the House of Usher
his fortress began to fall
He desired to resist
He knows however he could not muster the gall

Like wexford
He destroyed what he made
Simply to prove a point
He had to be saves

Today when his soul mate calls
He heads to his palace
where there now stand
No Walls

Shaun McPhillips

My Mom's Dead

My mom's dead and I don't know why
Today by her grave I sit there and cry
Sometimes I feel like an uprooted tree
She lays dead in her grave and I wish it were me.
Now don't get me wrong I have life in my heart
And I know by her dying she has a fresh start.
Although she's gone and we no longer touch,
I want you to know I loved her so much.

Collins Anthony Smith

Spark Of Life

Above the sea gull, soars on high
Her numbers few, I wonder why

In her search, to survive
She wonders inland, to provide

If by chance, a feast of crumbs
Discarded by breeze, in our slums

Her home for which, she must not return
Is darkened and void, as it burns

Today the sun peeks, through darkened clouds
Touches her frame, and for a moment shrouds

Desperation, through her silver sheen
A spark of life, in a hopeless scene

Denise Crose

We Are

Wounded and broken are we,
the many that no one sees.
We are the ones that life forgot,
peace, happiness, joy we have not.
We are your sisters, your daughters,
your wives, even your mothers.
No you don't have to hear,
but we exist, we are near.
We are the abused, the neglected,
the ones who never felt protected.
The ones who don't belong,
the ones who truly are strong.
The other ones you see
no longer are here, with death they went to be.
We are the crippled and our lives are torn,
but we are determined to be reborn.
We are the ones some think fail,
but we won't give up. We will prevail.
Wounded and broken we are,
someday we will be the free.

Adriana Reed

Nocturnal

No sleep in 48 hours
Like a marathon but not for the record books
Mental and physical run together
Fiery sun at daylight
Gleaming moon at night
You want to stop
But the clock of the body won't let you go.

Robert Butts

I Still Regret . . .

You left me fourteen years ago on a warm, June, summer night.
How much I wanted to be there, once more, to hold you tight.
As fate should have it, we cannot stop it, I was going out of town,
And to this day, I still regret, and wish, I was then around.

The last time that I saw you, you were sitting in a chair.
I kissed you and said I loved you, you simply sat and stared.
You didn't know me, it broke my heart, I began to cry.
How was I to know that this would be my last good-bye.

Time has passed, and I hold dear the memories that we had.
And I always reflect on those memories, whenever I feel sad.
You made me laugh, you made me smile, with your funny ways,
If only we could have kept you with us, just a few more days.

They say that time heals all wounds, I tell them that they're wrong.
The hurt in my heart will always be there, an emptiness so strong.
I'm proud to be your granddaughter, and to you I always pray.
I miss you, Nonnie, I'll always love you, forever and a day.

Michele Guarnuri

The Lily Pad

Life begins on the cold, dark bottom of the pond.
The tender shoot grows and strengthens with age,
upwards, towards the surface.

The shoot encounters many obstacles that could block
its development.

But, the shoot has a strong desire to succeed.
Each obstacle makes it bigger and stronger.

It finally reaches the surface and unfurls its life hardened
cover in magnificent splendor.

The shoot has matured.
The lily pad deserves its rest on the calm surface.

Patricia B. Baker

What Did The Lord Do

I had a dream last night in the dream I started to cry,
I wasn't going to heaven, I asked myself why.
People were going through the gates yet I didn't get a chance,
Yet rather instead I saw my life pass me at a slow glance.
I thought what did the Lord do to receive all this pain,
I remembered he sacrificed his son and Jesus was His name,
Outside those gates parents were sad, while children were crying,
The pain I felt in my heart was like all over again Jesus was dying.

What did the Lord do to cause us to steal and lie,
Nothing, he gave His only son on that day at Mt. Sinai.

What did the Lord do to make us hurt one another,
Nothing, did we really respect Him and our Fathers and Mothers.

Why were we so quick to blame Him when all went wrong,
And never thanking Him through prayer and song.

I wished I'd remembered he cleansed me of my sins,
If only I'd changed, through those gates I'd be going in.

I awoke from my dream, to tears of reality
Thanking our precious Father my sins He set free.

I know what the Lord did, through this I hope you know,
If choose to follow and serve God first, through the gates of heaven
  you'll go.

John R. Pert

Thinking of You

Today from nowhere there came a thought,
  and I'd like to tell you what it brought.
It brought a smile to my face,
  it took me to a far-away place.
It brought a sparkle to my eyes,
  it made me feel happy to be alive.
It brought such a comfort into my heart,
  it made me realize this is my new start.
It reassured me I won't have anymore pain,
  it showed nothing but kindness is here to remain.
It helped me to see what I knew all along,
  it made me understand how I can be strong.
It showed me that life really can be fair,
  it gave me awareness that I have reasons to care.
It brought out the truth on how lucky I am,
  it told me to do everything I possibly can
to hold on to this thought that's so dear, so true
  this beautiful thought, my love, is you.

Julie M. Severson

Tears

Why do people have tears?
Is it something that falls
from your eye when a drunkie
comes home, but to the wrong
home or doesn't know his own children?

Why do people have tears?

Is it just water from your eyes,
joining the blood from your face
after you get beat up by someone
maybe your parent?

Why do people have tears?

Is it something that falls
from your eye when you hear
some relative just recovered from a disease?

Why do people have tears?

Is it just water from your eyes
falling on to a new born baby
and being parents for the first time?

J. Oliver

Eternity

One day with God is like a thousand years,
and a thousand years like one day of tears.
It took the eternal God to limit Himself to time,
to put a stop to Satan's sinful crime.

God inhabits eternity where time is no object,
yet He inhabits the praise of them who have His respect.
Praise is the only act done in this present day,
that will continue long after the end of this vessel of clay.

Just to think of the awesome miracle God performed,
when He caused eternity to manifest when Jesus was formed.
Eternity took on the likeness of man,
in perfection and glory like only God can.

How frail the human race when compared to eternity,
they fail even in their quest for sincerity.
Human righteousness has no part in the God of ages,
only redemption — as it is written in the Bible's pages.

Hendrik Horn Jr.

The Love We Share

Remember that day 15 years ago when we first met
It's definitely a day I'll never forget.
That summer day you came into my life;
A few years later you became my wife.
Nobody gave us a chance for romance,
But every time they saw us we were holding hands.
Sure we had our share of problems,
But together we have always solved them.
Nothing to offer each other except the love
    we share with one another.

May God continue to bless us
May Love continue to guide us
15 years from now may we continue
    to remember "The Love We Share."

Marvin A. Egelhofer

The Rose

Many poems have been written . . . about the powers of the rose.
From white that stands for purity . . . to black for all your foes.
There's peach and pink and purple . . . so beautiful as they grow.
But the colors that mean most to me . . . are the Red and Yellow Rose.
The Yellow stands for Friendship . . . a foundation on which to grow.
It's firm and everlasting . . . flourishing stronger as time goes.
The Red it stands for True Love . . . it makes life's river flow.
They say it happens once in life . . . it's up to us to know.
So I give to you my Friendship . . . and thus the Yellow Rose.
I give to you my True Love . . . and thus the deep Red Rose.
I give to you the Two of these . . . in hopes you'll Always know.
I give to you my Everything . . . May We Forever and Always Grow.

Jeffrey Sargent

Kaleidoscope

A kaleidoscope lights the wall in prismatic
shades, turns and interweaves.
Colors of life continually changing.
Darkness and light fade, then deepen
becoming one.
A pattern unknown forms, clear and bold.
Nothing is hidden, all is known, yet it is not.
A tapestry, a quilt; woven, created.
Smooth, connected, and complete.
As quick as a flash of lightning,
life changes once more.
A color lost; a new one gained.
Never ending, continual.
It will end, and begin again.
Arms open wide, a loving smile,
you.

Charity Angel

The Black Sparrow

Poor, poor Black Sparrow
Who has had to endure many hardships
His short life has been in constant turmoil

He had been captured and terrorized
Confined by his imprisonment in a cage
Lost the most important thing he once had, freedom

There is no family with him
For they have been sold to others
He is all alone, and has no one to love him.

The wings that he once used to fly so high
Has been clipped by abominable men
Now he is left to gravel in the dirt

But be strong my proud Black Sparrow
For your day is soon coming
When you shall once again take flight

Just like the Phoenix, you shall rise from the ashes
Strong and replenished, ready to fly again
And shall regain all the glory, that you have lost

Joshua A. McCann

The Coming Of The Furor

Someone opened the squeaky door,
Silence filled the tiny attic.
Foot steps on the hard wood floor,
Their stomachs churned with panic.

All they could do was sit and wait,
And kiss each other a last good-bye.
For they knew their awful fate,
And couldn't help but cry.

It had been two long years,
Of praying, crying and waiting.
Now they were living their worst fears.
They could feel their lives fading.

The foot steps grew painfully stronger,
All hopes of life were now buried in their minds.
For they knew they wouldn't live much longer,
Which is better then awaiting terrors of all kinds.

Then suddenly there was a hollow pounding,
Reality had never felt so painstakingly real.
It was sickening and haunting sounding.
Any remote thought of the future, the coming Furor did kill.

Angi Jean Stevenson

"Say A Prayer To My Good Friend St. Anthony"

Turning a doorknob covered with dirty rubber bands,
I step into the existence of Helen.
Armed with an apron and a pair of rubber gloves,
I find her wrestling with her rosary
and praying for the confused souls of Catholic Jersey.

Sometimes I walk her hairball dog Max —
the same animal she pets lovingly with rubber gloves.
When he runs away,
I find him and bring him back to her.

"Oh . . . I knew you would find him.
St. Anthony always takes good care of me.
If you ever lose anything,
say a prayer to my good friend St. Anthony —
He finds what Christians have lost."

Loss upon loss, through the decades,
and I still find myself asking that friend for help.
Whenever I need to look,
my prayers go out to Helen of Trenton.

Joe Shields

Autumn

Autumn remembers the joys of spring;
How everything was free, and could do anything.
But now it is over, and we must realize;
That winter will soon be before our eyes.

The leaves were touched by a nymph's wand;
They drift gently down, onto a clear, blue pond.
The leaves will dance as much as they please;
For the wind knows quite well, on how to tease.

The sky turns to an autumn blue;
With a certain beauty that is quite true.
With great, white clouds that pass silently by;
The vast, never-ending, clear, blue sky.

The wind knows that summer has finally ended;
That all of our troubles are peaceful mended.
I love Autumn for a very good reason;
For Autumn is a memory of all other seasons.

Jessica Lynn Artymiuk

Down By The Beach

The wind blows, like crystals dancing.
The waves pirouette on the shore
and leave a lacy snowflake pattern,
no two the same.
The sun cascades rays of gold upon
the sapphire sea.
Sea gulls compliment the pristine beach,
not a soul to see this God made
masterpiece,
except for a solitary manatee.

Jean Bush

Rain Music

Nothing feels like summer rain.
As an experience it stands alone.
Water warm and clean landing upon your hair,
And caressing your face as it rolls down to drip off your chin.

As you sit out in the rain,
You feel the lonely calling
Of music once heard and long forgotten
Yearning to be heard again.

As you feel the music pull
Your feet begin to move.
The rain washes your will away
And lightens your feet 'till they barely stay on the ground.

And while you dance out in the rain,
You just can't help but smile
At the feeling of joy the raindrops bring
To those who will listen and let the music sing.

Sean Bailey

My Tranquil Reality

My cloudy perception converts to a soft plead
    for the summons of silence to come.
Whispering echoes grieve of lost time;
    the cascade of entity has gone.
Present . . . are the deserted catacombs of mind.
The jingle of wind chimes dances through an empty home.
As I continue to grasp for the love of mine,
    the cycle of the vulture has begun.
I am ready to take a last glass from the buttery
    and be cleansed of all my iniquities . . .
        . . . Nativity
Once again, awaiting the innocent chirps of the land
    and view the shimmering sparkles of the sea.
A gentle resurrection is at hand.

Craig Tonkinson

Life's Recipe

When I was young I played a lot and thought of many things,
But as I grew the games were few, prepared for what life brings.

I did the things that children do, wish for toys or climb a tree,
I went to school not sure of me, of what to do or who to be.

It took some years to 'settle-in' to the shell God gave to me,
But when I did, or thought I had, I found it never could be.

Because it's a road without an end, a process of daily toil,
It's honor, truth and a dash of trust, thrown into life's pot to boil.

I steeped for years til cooked and cured, often burned-out and alone,
But maybe the measure of life's perfect recipe is the friends I call my own.

It's the handful of folks and family so dear, who enrich life's heady brew.
'Tis lucky am I, as I glance to the sky, that I'm daunted by
troubles so few.

Hilary Woodworth

October In Concord

White houses march up the block,
stately sentinels in an army of gray
leaves drift from the clouds
helpless to control their fate

A girl flows briskly up the hill
a drop of honey in bitter tea
One of the doors swallows her
and she is gone

The hole left by her absence
is filtered in and through
like molasses filling the gap
left by a greedy finger

A sparrow wings through unforgiving sky,
struggling to stay aloft
against the omnipresent pressure
of the dark canopy above

Mara Ginnane

Longings

Longings so intense — God can fill them every one;
but sometimes He lets them linger for reasons all His own.

Longings that are wrong — He can take them all away;
but often it's a struggle day by day by day.

Longings undefined — uncertain what's at stake;
a race to come to grips with them before your heart can break.

Longings that aren't bad — just never meant to be;
for in His wisdom He can know much more than we can see.

Janet Laudett

By Hillcrest Grave

My mother, my father
Lie side by side
Beneath this blanket of green,
Faces turned heavenward,
Hands gently clasped.

In truth, it is not they who lie there,
For they are here.
They gently scrape the cinders from my
    brush-burned knee;
They share the fragrance of a flower
    with me;
They mend my torn spirit and send me
    forth again;
They do not lie silent and unanswering,
My mother, my father.

Sally K. Donnor

My Life On The Road

When I was young, I would crawl down the road — and bump
into things as I would go.
Then I started to walk, and off I would go — but only to find I
had no place to go.
Now that I'm older, I started to run — but still I would trip all
on my own.
I would try to hurdle the objects in the way — and if I couldn't, I
would just go the other way.
My trip down life's road hasn't been easy, as you can see —
but I have no one to blame, it's all upon me.
So now it's time to get out of the road — but still look ahead to
see where I should go.
The road I've been on, has been a long, bumpy ride — but I'm
still young, and I still have my pride.
It's time for me to slow my roll — to figure out which way to go.
I'm getting off this long, sad road — but where I should go, I
don't know.
You know my story, you have heard me talk — the best thing I can
do is only to walk — But not in the road, but on the sidewalk.

Jonathan Daniel Bowers

Following His Ways

Believe in me and these truths I speak, follow
all my ways, trust in every word I teach as you travel
through these days. Listen as I call your name I'll
whisper through the wind, the Holy Spirit shall be your
guide, do not be afraid. Your prayers I hear, for I know all,
walk with me and you shall not fall. Silence and be still and
know that I am Lord, for God's word is sharper than any
double edged sword.

Listen when I speak to you and follow my commands,
for I am Jesus Christ God son, you are merely man. Be humble
don't speak so much so that I may speak to you, for at any
time now I may call, so be ready when I do. Your old ways are
gone forever no more shall they exist, nor shall any old ways of
sin ahead of you persist.

Your dreams they have not ended, your life has just begun,
for you have given your life to Christ, Gods only begotten son.

Robert A. Walters

The Walk

I walked alone upon a broken sandy shore
and felt the pebbles slip away like the time that is no more.

The graceful wind was playing with my hair.
I knelt in silence and offered God my prayer.

I stood and gazed at the waves rolling in
and thought of how the world is drenched in sin.

The water overcame me with a cold and startling shock
the next I knew I had been tossed upon a rock.

A lighted Being appeared and took me by the hand.

We walked upon a path made of gold
and suddenly I was no longer cold.

He led me to a fluffy glowing cloud
and knowing I had earned my way I felt so very proud.

Janice Nielsen

Grandpa

You were like a father to me,
You would bring me doughnuts while you drank coffee.
We would go to the Dairy Queen,
I would have ice cream that was green,
When the weather was nice,
We would sit on the porch quiet as mice.
I was sad the day you took your flight;
But I know you had to give up the fight.

Jenna Rump

The Proud Peacock

There stands a woman, proud as a peacock
Elegantly poised, perfectly manicured
A woman of class, a woman of grace
Will say the people, who look upon her face

But the woman herself, knows only too well
An image to uphold, a facade to portray
A martyr at heart, standing there in vain
Offering sacrifice, pretending no pain

Look at my strength, a perfection of sort
This message she sends, a plea for her worth
I will stand in snow, I will stand on rocks
I will be the woman, I will please my man

He looks at her in awe, stepping far enough
He captures her image, an etching in his mind
There stands the woman, a symbol of his wealth
The peacock of pride, worthy of his own very self

Ana Cox

Christmas Night

The stockings were hung over the mantle up high
While mother was in the kitchen baking apple pie
The children were fast asleep in their beds
And candy and presents are dancing in their heads
The clock struck ten right on the dot
All the children in the house wondered, is Santa Claus here or not?
So they crept down the stairs as quiet as mice. They forgot to put
on their slippers, so their feet were as cold as ice. They saw there
were no cookies or milk on the tray. So they knew Santa had been
there, and quickly sped away. They heard a clatter up on the roof
top, and quickly went to bed. And the candy and presents they
dreamt in their heads were no longer a dream. For there were the
presents right in front of them. And on their faces was a big gleam.

Ashley Taylor

The Woman

"Are you ever lonely?" The old woman said
Tears ran down her cheeks as she bowed her head.
"Nothing ever happened to me that is good,
I'm just an old woman who would die if I could."

She spoke these words as I sat by her side,
I felt so sad and the tears I could not hide.
I was filled with sorrow and could think of no other,
Except this lonely old woman, who was somebody's mother.

She talked and as I listened, far into the night
She told of years gone by, of troubles and strife.
Then she smiled a sweet smile as she fell asleep,
And left me with wonderful memories so sweet.

Dixie Lansberry

Pride In A Mother's Eyes

The pride in my eyes is for two small
boys. They fuss and they fight over bikes
and toys. They give you a rough time, but
who'd give it up. When one look they're
babies, the next they're grown up.

Where has the time gone since Bobby was
small. I turned around twice, now he's
six feet tall.

Brian's a bundle of energy too. He
corrects all his errors with "mommy" I love
you." So when asked "are these your sons?"
I can't deny. You can see that they are,
by the pride in my eyes.

Karen Rust

The Fall, The Fall

The fall is a beautiful season, so crisp, and so golden, so fair.
A time of great harvest and beauty, falling leaves fill up the air.

The wind just starts to get chilly, the trees all become bare.
The wind caresses the leaves with an eternal care.

Smell the color-kissed leaves, look at the sun-painted mountains.
Rays from the sun seem liker magic, turning leaves into golden fountains.

All this beauty, all this wonder, is under a curse.
Adam and Eve lived in ten times the bliss, yet they sinned,
    what could be worse?

Man, beast and earth would receive this curse,
By it there would be sickness, but there was no nurse.

Yet, God in His mercy sent a relief.
His own dear Son would ease all of the grief.

As spring follows winter, with life after death.
After Adam came Jesus, to give us all rest.

If you want to avoid frost after fall.
Listen, and answer to His beckoning call.

Chris Chesley

Choices

Daily, we are all faced with Choices.
Some Choices are more significant than others.
Some Choices seem unimportant at the time,
But may prove to be very important later.

Most of us have wished, on at least one occasion,
That we could return to the past with our
Current Knowledge and Experience,
And Choose Differently.

When wise Choices are explained to the Youth,
They don't want to listen, just as we didn't
Want to listen to our Elders.
They can't, (We couldn't), they won't,
(We wouldn't), be convinced that Elders
Have "Been there, Done that" and truly
Have their (our) best interests in mind.

We are forced to sit back and let the
Youth choose. We have to let them learn
From their Mistakes. We have to
Give them their Space.
We don't have a Choice in this Matter.

Pam Stevens

The Direction Of The Wind

I dreamed of my lost love of yesterday.
Then, out of the shadows, he came back my way.
Perhaps, this time, he would be eager stay
If I could change the direction of the wind.

He lingered a while, then he kissed me goodbye
And left me once more to wonder and cry.
In my anger and pain, I asked myself why
I tried to change the direction of the wind.

I was a fool to dream
I could bring back the past.
I should have seen
That the die had been cast.

You must face the fact,
Though you feel empty hearted,
There is no going back
Once your course has been charted.

I thought that I would never be free,
But my prayers were answered when fate sent to me
A lasting new love and, finally, I see
You cannot change the direction of the wind.

Annette M. Lavoie

Friend

Nothing stays the same,
In this world of triumphs lost and won,
Sacrifice proves inconsistent,
As loyalties shift with the sun,

I've watched you change as we've grown,
We stumbled, we faltered, we searched for what mattered,
I admired you every moment of the way,
As you put your soul into everything you did,

I'm separate from you now,
As you grow to levels I cannot reach,
But you gave me all I have,
In the ways of dreaming, believing, and confidence,

I look to you now,
With a heart full of love,
As we each become ourselves,
Pulling wishes down from the stars.

Kim Ruthsatz

Haunted Harry

A tattered old barn has been the home of Harry the spider
for many years passed.
Harry will still be here for years to come, like a devout
catholic attends daily mass.

On a dark and spooky day, Harry awoke to find his webs
hanging with dew all glowing.
The clouds looked frightening and the winds kept blowing.
Harry felt haunted on this day of not knowing.

His appetite was still borderline, but by noon he had grown
a little more stable.
He grabbed himself out of this stance and fell straight down
from the loft onto a table.
He stood up and looked all ground, and realized he had
fallen into a long know fable.

He immediately shot back up to the middle of the barn to eat
his lunch before it could go cold.
The beetles and winged insects tasted a bit old.
But he reassured himself that by nightfall the beetles were
sure to taste like gold.

The moon now shining and the pumpkin all a glow, Harry had
seen yet another Halloween!

Malia Hensley Cooler

Going, Going, Gone

Take me to the football game.
No, take me to the mall.
Wait, let me get my purse!
I think I have enough time to do it all.

Don't forget to get the gift
For the graduation party.
And remember to pick up my new dress.
I need it by six-thirty.

Make spaghetti for dinner.
With garlic bread, too.
I'd love to help you, dear,
But our son's waiting for me at the zoo.

I think I'll go to the cinema.
Mother, do you want to come with me tonight?
I wish I could,
But you know my schedule's pretty tight.

Where did all the time go?
Why does my life have to end now?
What happened to all my dreams?
Going, going . . . gone.

Melissa A. Minetola

The Broken Mold

God broke the mold when he made you,
because he knew you'd be the one that I'd look up to.
He didn't give you wealth or fame, he knew you wouldn't mind.
Instead he had greater things to offer you of a more humble kind.
He gave you courage to face anything and strength to make it thru.
He gave you perseverance, and peace to comfort you.
He gave you wisdom and knowledge and tools to heal the sick.
He made you a Christian doctor, so you could touch the lives you fixed
To me you are the greatest, not because of all your gifts,
but because your love is unconditional and sincerely magnificent.
God knew from the beginning what kind of father I would need.
And although I'm only a reflection of that mold,
it started with your seed.
I love you, Father.

Patricia D. Sabin

Halloween Poem

I like candy.
I like things hanging on trees on Halloween night.
I like witches.
I like cats meowing at midnight on Halloween night.
I like goblins.
I like ghouls yelling and screaming on Halloween night.
I like ghosts.
I like bats screeching and squeaking on Halloween night.
I like vampires.
I like skeletons clinking and clanking on Halloween night.
I like full moons.
I like pumpkins squooshing and squashing on Halloween night.
I like spooky houses.
I like trees whooshing and gooshing in the air on Halloween night.

Bonnie Rock

I Am

I am a curious person
I wonder if animals can talk to one another
I hear someone whispering in my ear
I see someone dancing in the wind
I want my own car
I am a curious person

I pretend I am a store owner
I feel like someone is holding my hand
I feel the air going by
I worry I won't get an "A" on the test
I cry when my family dies
I say we should be free
I am a sensitive person

I understand math problems
I dream of boys that are "cute"
I always try my best
I hope I get good grades
I am an independent person

Chelsea Ann Craythorn

Untitled

Wake up! Look around you as you go through your day
At work, at school or shopping, or watching kids at play.
Think of what they're doing — remember what you see
They're your family, friends and neighbors or some you call enemy.
Tell them that you love them — show them that you care
Don't wait another hour — they may have none to spare
Say "I'm sorry" or "I apologize"
really mean it — show it in your eyes.
An "enemy" is just another who thinks differently than you
Even though you disagree, his thoughts to him are true.
Make amends — cross the bridge even though it's quite a duty
Your world will be a nicer place — of love, of hope and beauty.

Dianna Hotchkiss

Clouds

We travel with the winds that blow, with all our cottony kin
And as we float along, we wonder where or when
Our tears will start to fall; on an arid desert place,
Or a rustic garden wall where flowers and butterflies embrace?

Maybe on a field of grain, after many days and nights
A farmer prayed for rain to end a dry and dusty blight
Or, will the wind take us farther to an ocean calm and blue
To aid a storm that is coming, fierce and wild the whole night through?

A cloud moves with no control as to where its rain will fall
But, we ourselves have every choice to make life better, and we all
Have today to do our best, to change at least one thing
And to some despairing soul some hope and comfort bring.

Deane Bruce

The Next Day

It is the next day. Though still a painful thought. A thought
that burns your soul when activated by one word as gesture. It rings
in your mind with the constant reminder of what once was and is not
anymore. Though you challenge this with heart, your tolerance
declines as though it were the sun revolving the sky and receding to
dawn. Your mind then wanders to the sun with a wish of halting the
universe. Only then to find out that the revolutionary effect is
to overwhelming to control.
You're faced with the same destiny, only not to know what is.
You're faced with the same purpose, only to know what is.
You're faced with the same dreams, only to know what once was
and can't be anymore.
The dark sky opens its doors to the sun. As you wake from
the dream to reality. It is the next day.

Tom Link

From An Old Soldier

Those months in the Pacific
    and those many front lines
They got to my being
    and corrupted my mind

    It was the war
        and those barges I rode
    That heaped on my shoulders
        that mind boggling load

        The war's been long past
            but the memories still clear
        All those campaigns stole
            the me I hold dear

            But now it's a thought
                one I must face
            And cut out all combat
                to save the human race

                The truth I must seek
                I must help me
                That goal's so near
                    and then I'll be free.

James Frederick Sedgley

Someday

Someday I want someone to understand
    Someday I want someone to see beyond this core of life,
to see what one is like before they make impressions

    Someday I want someone to see a blooming flower
and see a blooming flower and to see its magic within

    For there is a flower ready to bloom in each of us,
just be patient

    Look at someone blooming and they will change somehow.

Samihah Huq

My Father's Hand

We walk together Him and I
thru waters still and deep,

Tho' I think at times I might go under,
A hold of my hand he'll keep.

He leads and guides this willing
vessel, thru night and morning bright,

And with each passing day gone by;
My Father's Hand, I'm holding tight.

His love and mercy strengthen me,
When doubt may come my way,

He holds me up and gives to me,
Hope for another day.

I want to walk beside my father.
With his hand to show me the way

Up the path to the Pearly Gates,
and "Welcome my child" He'll say.

Peggy S. Liming

Untitled

For a moment in time,
I had a taste
Of everything I ever wanted
In intimacy

It was love and so right,
But only for a moment

For a moment we bonded,
Feeding each others hunger

I caught myself looking into the future,
And realized I was cursed for doing so

For a moment I felt light at heart,
I was tingled with his touch
The sweet queasiness in my stomach,
It made my body quiver

This moment was so perfect,
Why did it turn to be so wrong?

I'd rather been left to die of my hunger, than fed
only for a moment . . .

Paula Barrow Miller

Still The Willows Weep

The roses bow their crimson heads
   as ones in need of sleep;
Their fellow flowers all seem sad
   while the weeping willows weep.

The birds hide each within his nest,
   straw castles in the air;
Each earthly creature, friend or pest,
   seeks out his special lair.

The lightning snaps, the thunder claps,
   and all life seems to cower
As every inch of green earth traps
   a portion of the shower.

But soon the sunshine wakes each rose,
   the rainbow cheers each plant;
The shower has ended and each knows
   as birds begin to chant.

But though all else is lithe and gay
   and wakes from showery sleep,
There are those yet who rue the day
   for the willow trees still weep.

Irvin M. Citron

Struggle

There comes a time, when you have to choose to do or die,
When you have to put foundations to your dream castles,
And show the world that you are the best,
So come on brace yourself for the struggle,
One that is an ongoing and never say die struggle,

There also comes a time, when days of strife seem never ending,
When frustration starts to take its toll,
Have faith and say to yourself,
That the present times will not last long,
That tough times never last but tough men definitely do,

Then one fine morning like that of any other day,
Destiny unfolds its hidden treasures,
And you are the cynosure of all eyes,
And it seems that you have finally made it,
But it is only the start of another struggle,
   A never ending one.

Anoop Kumar

Show Me

Whisper not words of love. Tell me not;
Of a loving devotion. Speak not of warmth
And caring; for words spoken in the heat of
Passion, either in anger or joy almost always turn
Great swelling tides of emotion in the heart. Some
To rend and tear; while so few can mend the soul.
When angry words have been thrown in haste
And morning finds the hurting still with us; as tears
Fall like rain but cannot wash away the hurt;
Kiss me with tenderness and passion conceived
In our love. Smile that smile of lovers in love as you,
Cast a glance across the room for my eyes only that says,
"I need you. I love you." With loving tenderness gently kiss
My fears away. Slowly rock me in the cradle of your love.
Then, finding that place of dark fear where I hide,
Let your love's light dispel the dark and bring on the day.
With great gentleness touch my face; seek only my side when
Day is done. Wrap me in the warm circle of your arms
And as longing turns to peace and contentment;
Show me; what love is.

Rriel Cichoke

Regrets Of A Pluralist

Hidden secrets usually flaw what others view in open awe;
And if to live it all again, so many changes I'd intend.

I am not me at times it seems more than one occupant believes;
And though they'd come to count on me, twas no one's fault they could not see.

That I'd become an empty shell and headed for the depths of hell;
And fearful not of this outcome, an independent one I was.

But all in secret 'til one day when fantasies begin to stay;
In forefront thoughts as if to be my major principalities.

A fractures portion of the whole can leave the story half untold;
If no one ever knows the truth, what brought me to this self rebuke?

For if the fact was ever known that more than one called this man home;
The innocent would never be allowed to sleep a night in peace.

Although the years kept passing by as if the end were just in sight;
A wind would always come at last to change again the circumstance.

And take me to worlds far away, some upscale way to go astray;
The struggles that went on inside were battles of a raging kind.

I cannot ever hope to say what happened to me on that day;
When I acknowledged in my heart that right was light and wrong was dark.

Yet if that means I'm still not well, tell that to all my former selves;
But plan to stay with me awhile, my age-old friends might come alive.

Edward F. Hillhouse

A Mother's Prayer

I thank you God for blessing me with Motherhood on Earth,
and I adore and I praise you for the miracle of birth.

I pray I may be worthy of your wondrous gift to me
and that I may do my part for all humanity.

I pray I raise my children right and teach them what to do,
to grow in strength and character and always to love you.

For they belong to you and they are only in my care, to
comfort and protect them and to help them with a prayer.

That is why I make this plea for wisdom and for grace,
that I may do thy holy will and fill my humble place.

Lavera Cole

Life Dreams And Happiness

Life has always been for me to fulfill my dreams and they will
make me happy. As each year has passed I dreamed I would be
happy; somehow at the end of each year I find myself unhappy.
Life is dreams come true, I look up high above for comfort to
fulfill my happiness. Dreams are wishes we want to come true.
The things we dream seemed to be the things we want most.

Happiness is true feelings of yourself and others. Each night I
close my eyes and wish for the day one of my dreams will finally
give me happiness and I can take the wrinkles from my face because
God has finally answer the one prayer I have prayed for so long is
to give me true happiness that I always wanted and dreamed about.

The love and respect of others and allowing me to express my
true self because I have loved and helped to give others to fulfill
my dreams and happiness I want in life.

Life, dreams and happiness is being balanced with love like the
sun and the moon constantly going around and bringing light
and sunshine to give life a feeling of being happy and not sad.

Life, dreams and happiness is a combination of true feeling.

Doris Bickham

Pain Can Spell Any Name

I will visit you one day for I am part of life's game.
"I Am Pain, I Can Spell Any Name."
No one avoids my knock on the door,
    to some I knock once — to others many more.

Your money can't save you I like rich and poor,
    all names have letters I spell them for sure.

Both injury and death are good friends of mine,
    I use disease or heart break, whatever I find.

Matters not your inventions or that you cover your ears.
    I have made humans cry for thousand of years.

So look to the heavens from whence cometh some help.
    Pray for relief to blanket yourself.
A short or long title to me it's the same,
For "I Am Pain, I Can Spell Any Name."

Juan McMoore

My Grandfather's Clock

Up the stairs and in the hall,
The ancient time piece clings to the wall.
The face — like a ghost, glows in the night.
The Roman numerals glisten, luminate the white.

Like wakening echoes, stroke by stroke,
Upon the quiet the tics are broke.
They sound upon the creaking stair,
And in the hall; so long and bare.

I often pause as I go up the walk,
And listen to my Grandfather's clock.

R. Worthington

Six-String Guitar

A child pulls notes back through strings mischievously
Peeks through shyly —
— I know something you don't know.

This is my house.

Curling within the soundboard
Weaving melodies through the loom
Rhyming with drab olive and strong brown
Earth sifting through to my eyes, falling dryly to the wood
behind
Gritgritgrit —

Smooth oak skin beneath callouses
Shlurmy steel strings

It belongs to the holder alone.

Kate Chabarek

Untitled

Where do I go when the dream is gone?
When that bright flame that led me through
the darkness of self-doubt and the pain
of loneliness is extinguished.

Do I fall back to the lost and lonely world
I began to lose;
or continue to crawl towards the light
glimpsed in the distance?
Do I hang on to the memories that shine in my mind
even though the reality is shaded with emptiness
and the knowledge of days and nights without
the warmth of that flame?

March on! March on!
Though the flame may flicker and fail
the hope for tomorrow will never die!

Donna Kohlbach

Untitled

God is something you can't begin to explain,
Just like trying to learn the functions of your brain.
You can't define God in just one name,
Because he's too complex for the human brain.
Sometimes I ask "how could this be?"
But God knows, and to us it's a mystery.
Some people know a lot, but no one knows it all,
Just always open your mind and follow the Holy laws.
God never turns his back and believes in us,
So a close relationship and regular prayer is a must.
We don't put enough faith in God when times are rough,
But when we want something, we never hesitate to look him up.
He smiles on the good people as well as the bad,
And keeping him in our lives should not be a fad.
So when you're having a problem or feeling low,
Just say a prayer, let God and let it go . . .

Gregg Boyd

Tears

Once I swore that I would live and die for you,
But you ripped that wish from me,
Now you'll never know,
What true love is,
Because you left me here,
In the cold, dark rain,
To die all alone,
Drenched by the tears of my sadness,
And yet the madness overthrows,
my cries of sadness,
And turns them into,
cries of revenge.

Lindsay Dias

385

Dusk To Dawn

I shed a tear, but carry on,
Inspired by the persistence of dawn.
I'll find my way,
But I hold tight sanity everyday.
Full of dangers, I please strangers.
Do or die, to survive.
Turning cartwheels among the dunes,
Sea spray cleanses invisible wounds.
Sand tickles my toes, the surf resonates through my soul.
Sea gulls take flight above waves dancing in the morning light . .

Perfect conditions for love to ignite!
Stability would free me to nurture creativity.
My heart beating in rhythm with the sea.
No longer a dream, reality,
My destiny.
Kay Beeman

The Search

Some nights I lie awake and ponder,
about the microscopic world of one celled life
that are churning and striving for being
in the ebb and flow of the ocean and on
the span of the continents,
about the microscopic orbits of the galaxies
and the stars,
on the rhyme and reason for the existence
of mankind,
that seem to issue forth from my mind.
When I rise in the morning I am vexed,
mute with frustration and perplexed
as the answers have once again eluded me,
and I must again return to my Gethsemane.
Carl Vogt

Darkness

Twilight moon, snowdrop stars;
  did the night beckon my heart.
A destitute wanderer did I become,
  starved of that pure drop of incense: Love.

Valley and yonder did my heart search;
Through storms and thunder did my heart beat;
And in the darkness of my search did my eyes and body reach.

Ecstatic waves of pain did I roar;
For the soul of Satan had touched my heart;
For I was the child of darkness;
And darkness had smothered my innocence to ashes.
Saritha R. Venumbaka

God And Me

My God so Sweet, my God so Dear,
You are not far, but really near,
Residing here within my Heart,
For we have never been apart!

There isn't a moment that passes me by,
When I think of my Lord, I don't even try,
And for all that I need, I go to my Father,
Abundantly He provides for me like no other!

Light of God, so Bright and Pure,
Love of God, Forevermore,
Life of God, I do Adore,
I Am that I Am, and so much more!

To my Father, for counsel I go,
When in times of trouble to know,
Just what it is that I should do,
Knowing, all things Are possible with You!
Sandra Ann Mowery

Our Father

We all miss our father
He died the other day
73 years too young
He just faded away

But not our memories of him
Helpful, loving, caring
I remember him smoking
He was always a bit daring.

Pickle-nosed, hazel eyed, and pot bellied
but no one could say he looked like hell he'd
Drive a truck 65 miles an hour
A strong, strong man — you could feel the power

My father was a great man
We all loved him so
It was very painful for us
When it was time for him to go.

But he will always be remembered
The good times we've shared
When no one else gave a damn
Rocky Always Cared.
John Rocco Duardo

Resurrection

Life is full of countless resurrections,
Not self-resurrections;
One man alone, from agony to new birth,
But healing touches of another
The hand of God in one another
Forgiving — renewing — healing . . .

Tell me — when I
rebel and
wrong-do and
wrestle with my
restlessness
and fear the while
you'll never
love me again —

Tell me —
when I've run and died —
Will you touch me,
forgive me,
resurrect me?
Will you love me?
Sharon Sullivan

I Dreamed

I dreamed I stood in a studio,
I watched two sculptors there.
They used great clay,
it was a young child's mind,
which they finished with so much care.
One was a teacher,
using tools such as books, music, and art.
One a parent, whose experience showed,
using guiding hands, love, and a gentle heart.
Day after day the teacher toiled,
with touch that was deft and sure.
The parent labored right by his side,
polishing rough edges and smoothing them over.
The task had been acutely completed,
both were proud of the masterpiece which they'd wrought.
The things they had molded onto this child,
could neither be sold nor bought.
I woke to this dream's vivid conclusion,
seeing behind the parent a school,
and behind the teacher, a home.
Seth Andersen

Long Before Death Came

She lays in a fetal position —
Day, after day, after day,
Something has stolen my mother,
It has taken her "soul" away.

I'm told she is still alive,
Yet, I see no signs of life.
Where is the woman who once
Was mother, and lover, and wife?

Her blue eyes are open but she does not see.
And she has ears which do not hear.
Her mouth moves but it does not speak
Of the inward turmoil and fear.

Alzheimer's claimed my mother's life
Long before death came.
Now I am getting old —
   I wonder!
   Will my life end the same?

Clara Flowers McLaughlin

Sunset Over Love Canal

Feed all the little ones implanted to grow
and in a little while, you'll throw what you sow
far away
feed all the little ones
to restless indulgence
In tides the sun subsides to sprinkle the love.
and crash. The lunatic laugh from up above
sea of blood
in tides the sun subsides
and splashes the loveless
Give to the untrue a promise to lie
and to the who-are-you a reason to live
or to die
give to the untrue
four thornless roses
A scream inside a dream, a whimper to others
brushed off unending cough to sisters and brothers
awake
a scream inside a dream
would separate lovers.

Oscar Arias

My Love Is Gone

My Love is gone away from me, I feel his presence constantly.
I miss him so, both night and day, I can't believe he's gone away.

Through all the years I loved him so, he loved me too.
He let me know.
He was so much fun and full of life, I was very proud to be his wife.

He was known for his jokes and silly pranks
His circle of friends could only say "thanks,"
For being a buddy, a pal, a friend,
The memories they hold will never end.
They told me how much he had meant to them all,
Their lives were made richer and all had a ball.

For many years he could not speak,
His many strokes had made him weak.
He suffered so long and it hurt me so,
I had to hope he would just let go.
I knew he'd go to a better place,
In my dreams at night I can see his face.

He was a Daddy, a Grandpa and Great Grandpa too,
Our fifty four years were all too few.
We'll be together again some day
I still can't believe he has gone away.

Jean Atteridge

Untitled

Quiet of color — and quiet of sound — with a soft — soft glow
Warm — ever so warm — giving comfort — giving security
What it may be — from where it comes
I do not know — there is no need to know

It fills me with such serenity — that all else by it does pale
And it upholds me when all in life tells me I have failed

It has a small beyond description — composed of all things I know
And have ever known
From the beginning of my time — a tiny embryo

Quiet — only a whisper of sound
No need for anything beyond a whisper
For in the presence of millions only its whisper would you hear
As quiet as the brush of angels wings — as quiet as harp strings

When I am in its presence — or perchance its presence is within me
I am all I ever hoped to be

Only then do I transcend beyond this mortal ground
And for just a little while — rest in peace
Within the warmth — the glow — the sound
Of what I do not — nor need to understand
Resting in the arms if a presence beyond man

Gayle C. Arbes

Blink

Blink
When I see my shadow sunlit on the chimney
Maybe it's mine
Fine fluorescent fire flickers off my love light
Think
It's my claustrophobic mind
Caught in a candy shell
Dog sniffs at the smell of his own winter coat
Drink
Water to dilute the acid spilled on my rug
And in the sink
Coffee is God
Brink
Of darkness and light
Who fight over Bunker Hill
I stood and fired down upon you, from my roof
Yin fought with chided fists, as Yang stood steadfast in a misty meadow
Hazed over in a purple fog, that hushes my eyes with its breath
And causes me to
Blink

Rachel Soffer

What If

What if there was no tomorrow?
   All the days would be so sad.
What if there would be no second chance?
   Then maybe we would not goof up
   the first.
What if there was no love?
Then the world would be an endless tragedy.
What if there was no Christmas?
   Then there would be no need
   for us to celebrate.
What if there was no God?
Then there would be no hope,
What if there no tomorrow?
But there could be a good tomorrow,
   A forgiving and new tomorrow.
Oh but God only knows and that is
   the tomorrow we are living today.
Now what if there was no tomorrow?
   What would you do today?

Nina M. Shetter

Poem

I've always wanted to compose
The most beautiful poem that ever rose
From paper and pen and one's own mind.
One where there's only one of a kind.

A poem full of love and trust,
Of deep thought and lust.
One of fantasy dreams and darkest fears,
One of songs pleasing to the ears.

A poem full of love and everlasting joy,
A poem that words would employ
Not only the heart but also the mind,
For peace and fulfillment to find.

A poem so real it makes one cry.
One so deep, there will be tears to dry.
A poem so dear and full of meaning,
That it's almost worth believing.

A poem that shows there is light up ahead.
One that will be more over read.
A poem to be found in the annals of time.
In a book of beautiful verse and rhyme.

Janis Izzarone

In This World

In this world know that there is pain
But do not be angry

Know that is this world there is anger
But do not let it consume you

Know that in this world there is sorrow
But do not let it burden you

Know that in this world there is fear
But do not let it hinder you

Realize . . .

In this world there is love
Let it uplift you

Know that in this world there is peace of mind
Let it enlighten you

Know that in this world there is truth
Let it free you

Know . . .

In this world there is both Hope and Faith
Let it deliver you

As it has done and is so doing ; for all
Indeed in this world . . . Amen . . .

Melissa Kay Taylor

The Lucky Dolphin

There was a dolphin named Skipper.
She looked exactly like Flipper.
She lived in the river
Where the water did not quiver.
One day she saw a boat
Skipper thought how could that much weight float?
While she was thinking she got caught in a net
But she was too scared to regret.
She wished her mother could save her.
And she started to shiver.
The fisherman was too old to drag Skipper into the boat
He had no choice but to let his catch go,
Skipper was a free dolphin and never went near a boat.
But she never knew how that heavy wight could float?

Pratik A. Dash

Sometimes Like This One

Sometimes like this one,
my mind really flutters or rather tries to do so,
in order to unfurl its extraordinary energy and capacity.

Sometimes like this one,
my mind really points a questioning finger at everything,
putting on trial the validity of everything in this world.

Sometimes like this one,
my mind really inspires my whole self to position itself on a podium,
which is nothing close to any other podium,
to see and notice this world from there.

Sometimes like this one,
my mind really compels myself to believe in the extraordinary ie . . .
GOD the Almighty,
putting aside my nevertheless faith in Him,
thereby reassuring my faith in Him.

Sidhartha Misra

Color My World

Color my world you . . .
There is no other color that will do.
To color my world would be to color it with you.

A color of bright sunshine
That sparkles day and night.
A very splendid and fascinating color
That makes me feel just right.

To color my world would mean
That I would need no other colors,
Not blue, red, yellow, or green.
Only the special color
That you bring to my life would be seen.

Toney George Jefferson

Why, Why, Why?

Why are cabbages purple?
Why are blueberries blue?
Why should colors matter if we are friends?
Me and you?

Why are limes green?
Why are tomatoes red?
Why do people care what color you are?
And sometimes end up dead?

Why are oranges orange?
Why are Kiwi's brown?
Why must we walk down the street?
Always with a frown?

So look at all of these colors,
and ask yourself "Is this me?"
If you have looked over this poem,
you know how the hatred comes to be.

Carrie Austin

Triste

A dark cloud is but settled over the very
essence of my soul. The melancholy dream settles
in and revenges upon me. As much as I'd like to
fight it, I welcome it — it sets in as does the
numbing cold and within the bleak coldness of
winter it pushes all thoughts of summer — and warmth
away. I hurt from an undying need for those
thoughts for without them my very body shall
lose all breath and the cold shall set in upon me
It is only holding on to the very small amount
of warmth my body contains that keeps me from
succumbing to the cold and welcoming its very depths

Summer Rolin

I Think It Is Best

This is the hardest thing I have ever done.
But I am only doing it to show how much I love you.
I'm giving you to your father, because I know you miss him.
I think it is time for you to get to know who he is.
I think it is time for you to have the attention paid
   to you that you need.
I think it is time for you to be away from the short temper.
I think it is time for you to be away from the harsh words.
I think it is time for you to be away from the whoopings.
I think it is time for you to have the piece of mind
   that you are in need of.
I'm not going to be away for long.
I'll be there when you need me the most.
I'll be there on some weekends.
I'll write when I can. I expect to get some from you also.
I'll be there for you through the phone calls, when you need to talk.
There will always be a bond between the three of us,
   because you are my kids and I love you.
It tears me up inside to come to this decision,
   but I think it is best for the both of you,
   to spend time with the man who is your father.

   Cathrine C. Hayden

Running

Music flows from me
As I lift the magic to my lips
And let my soul out.

Just so softly I am running
Yet making no sound but the music.

And I keep running

The sun appears through the cracks between leaves
And casts strange shadows that dance to my rhythm.

And I keep running

In a field
The grass seems to quiver just slightly
As I pass through it.

And I keep running.

As I enter an orchard
An apple drops just in time to my music and rolls along the ground.

And I keep running.

Then on the beach my music gets swept away,
The waves take it while it echoes in my ears.

The sweet song, the soul and mind,
The running, and the flute.

   Sarah Williams

The Silent Intruder

How can one know when love comes in?

For it does not always knock upon the door
Loudly, unmistakably,
Announcing its arrival

Or enter with a rustle of skirts
Proclaiming its importance

Or leap through a window, suddenly,
With a shout, to surprise.

Sometimes, one does not know that it has come
Until there is a slowly growing sense
Of a warmth not from the grate
And a glow not from the lamp
And a happiness, deep in the heart,
Come from some unknown source.

   Elizabeth B. Grable

Flying High

Come fly with me
upon the wings of an angel
when your soul can take no more
soar high above the clouds in
the starry mid night sky.

For there will always be an angel at your
side, watching over you and me your angel
will make you delirious with joy, and
contentment.

You will feel like you have seen paradise
when you have been touched by an angel.
So won't you please, release those dreaded
feelings, and come fly with me.

   Lynne Fahrne

Be Strong

Be a warrior in this time of grief.
Keep a level head, and a strong belief.

Know no boundaries, and any level you can reach.
Be a strong listener, and you will someday teach.

Stand up for your rights, and live a joyous life.
Use your tongue sharply, like a double edge knife.

Just live life right and do no wrong, and
Whatever you do, just be strong.

   Sharrod Perkins

The Wolf

Would that I could be the wolf
Who hungers at the door
Rather than this timid lamb
Who looks for nothing more
Would that my soul could loose the howl
That's been drowned out by the whisper of civility
Would that my heart could thrash and wail
And show my true ability
Would that I could be the wolf
I've always longed to be
Would that I could shed this skin
And at long last be free
Would that I could be the wolf
But the wolf lies hidden deep
Strangled within, in woolen lambskin
Convinced to be a sheep

   Lisa Deason

Entombed

Your mind is like a mysterious vault,
locked by time who does not fault
The age packed memories of your life
That stored its pleasures — its strife.

What do you know — what do you feel?
How can you translate naught from real
Will some magic from within spare
my anguished soul
Now that I have assumed the
mother role?

I wait, I pray, I search for a clue
Never forgetting that you were once you

Oh my mother dearest, my bearer
of breath, love and hope.
Open that tomb, let me in —
let me cope!

   Frances Jean Adelson

The Intelligence Of Sin

Stardust flowing
through this stardust corpse
of regret.
How appropriate,
this pain of eternal creation
bestowed upon the creature . . .
the Creator.

Circular, cellular flow
of minute atomic fire
burning constantly
this memory
into new realms of the
same old tale, never
told the same way twice.
That memory —
  That is me,
   That is the universe,
    That is infinite; that is all.
     God's memory informed and inskinned.
     Intelligent Atom sins again.

Jason Carter

Mother

Mom — you were alone. Mom — I don't know why.
You pulled out the gun as you whispered good-bye.
Mom — you tried so hard. Mom — you didn't see.
You wasted your life away, and the blame is on me.
Mom — you should have waited, Mom I was there.
You put the 9 to your head, and you know it wasn't fair.
Mom — the pain will heal. Mom — I tried not to see.
You pulled the trigger, and the blame is on me.
Mom — I know you love me, Mom — we'll be together someday
The blood that ran beneath my feet has washed
the scars away.
Mom — I'm locked up in prison, Mom — I'll never be free.
You killed yourself and the blame is on me.

Chrissy Staggs

True Love Never Dies

God's true love came from on high,
It will never, never, never die.
For that love was shed for all of us,
If we'll only learn to put our trust.
For this love God gave is beyond compare,
It's a steadfast love it will always be there.

Now there's love for fortune and love for fame,
There's love for money and love for gain.
There's love for sister and love for brother,
There's love for dad and love for mother.
There's love for rich and love for poor,
There's love to be shared from door to door.

But the love that God commanded us,
Is to love our neighbor, and in Him put our trust.
So the love that hung on Calvary,
That love was shed for you and me.
Now each time I heard a new born baby cry,
I know that true love shall never die.

Emma Burress

My True Love

My one true love I left behind,
To pick up the pieces, I know you must cry.
But here is my legacy, watch them grow.
I hope your sorrow they keep low.
One day we shall meet in a far away place,
And we can start all over when we meet face to face.

Gwen L. Phillips

Creation And God's Kingdom

On this earth created for mankind
A variety of things you will find
To sustain our lives, creation employ,
Various activities we can enjoy;
For example take a Sunrise
Hues of colors to delight the eyes;
The birds so colorful and with song,
A beauty of experience all day long;
Then the mountains majestic and tall,
Canyons and cascading waterfalls;
And this is due to a Creator Grand,
For all of these workings is in God's plan;
And God will yet in a future day,
Realize his purpose and again say;
All my creations are as they should
Once again declare them very good,
So, when you see a beauteous sight,
And think of mankind present plight;
Just visualize what our life will become,
When to the earth God's kingdom comes.

Joan J. Posey

My Security Blanket

My little security blanket
is not a blanket at all
It's rather a heart woven pillow
that is very small

It brings back, every time
the sad child within
And yet tendering the pain
over again and again

It never gets tired of me
wanting and needing it so
with its torn material
it will never say no

Whenever I need it to hold
or kiss away my tears,
It makes me want to forget
about the rejection in my childhood years

Oh, I know that the love
from the pillow is not real
but the security and safety
is worth what I feel.

Ruth Street

My Sisters

My sisters black . . . like me
But different shades of beauty.
Strong . . . like me
But different paths of duty.
Year in year out, we struggle
To make our gifts and goals much better.

My sisters afraid . . . like me
But fighting different devils
Tired . . . like me but fighting daily battles.
Every day, in every way, we struggle
To keep our lives and loves together.

My sisters, loyal . . . like me
But supporting different causes
Giving . . . like me but sustaining different losses.
Every minute of every hour, we struggle
To protect our families and friends forever.

My sisters, all different from one another, yet the same.
Not all having same Father and Mother, yet the same.
Let's support one another and give love to each other
As sisters and the same.

Alonna F. Monegain-Arnold

390

The Friend Is Time

Looking out the window
Towards a desolate end
I hear a heart calling me
Is it that of a friend?
Or is it my own trying to make me see?

Trying times ahead as I try to hold ship
But with it comes a time of solace
Sighing in my arms her lips I try to kiss
As I have missed her, I've also learned this

She's more than I thought she'd be
Too late though, too late to see
Beginning to think the ship is sinking
Her fleeting thoughts are those I am thinking

Looking out the window
Towards resolutions end
Now, I see it calling to me
And with it comes the heart of a friend
The friend is time, I hope it does mend

John Polise

No Father To Look Up To

Born in eighty-one with no happiness and no fun
It shouldn't have been that way, but it's the way it
begun, you could say everyone else had one
I guess you could say too
I had no father to look up to

All my days growing up were black and blue
Cause I had no father to look up to
I guess he did what he had to do
"So why are my days black and blue?"
Cause I had no father to look up to

I would ask everyday
But they just would say, his name is clay
I think about him everyday
Asking myself is his name really clay

Born in eighty-one
my days black and blue
It all comes down to
I had no father to look up to.

Alicia Renee Gladden

With You

I lived my life and then moved on
It seems to you that I am gone
But through your life as you go on
I'm with you.

I've crossed the river and I am free
My pain is gone and I have peace
My soul has left and been released
Still, I'm with you.

In many ways I'm still alive
For in your memories I survive
And through your trials as you strive
I'm with you.

Life as we know it is but a dream
Where shadows fall in tearful streams
But sometimes things aren't what they seem
I'm with you.

And when your journey comes to a close
And life is ended, who do you suppose
Will greet you on your last repose
I'm with you.

Patricia L. Yost

Thanksgiving

Thanksgiving is every day.
Thanksgiving is a time to thank God for his son Jesus Christ.
Thanksgiving is a time to show Him our gratitude for his love
And mercy that we live daily by.
Thanksgiving is a time to thank Him for the seasons of the year.

Thanksgiving is a time to thank him for the air we breath, the
Light that shows the way, the raindrops, the flowers, birds, and
Trees but most of all the beauty that surrounds us all.

Vera Hall

Gold Of Life

As gold is set before,
We see it as shiny or something worn.
We think of gold to be something we hold;
To spend on things we think we need,
To only realize it was something to see.
The world's gold can come, the world's gold can go,
So listen closely so you will know.

The Gold of Life is the one true friend,
Who is the sunshine of your day;
The only one in hard times will stay.
That kind of Gold, we must realize
Will one day vaporize.
So keep your Gold close to your heart,
Because tomorrow it could depart.
When departure has come to measure,
You will always have memories to treasure.

Angela H. Calton

Safe On My Cloud Again

I hear the steps on the stairs, they creak.
I know he soon will be here.
His breath I know will reek.
Of coffee, cigarette, and Listerine.
I hear the swish of his overalls.
I feel the bed sag, as he sits down.
I feel the covers being pulled down,
The boys are in the other room.
This I know will not stop my doom.
I feel doomed once again.
They hurt me like a pin.
As he whispers my name, I pretend
That no one is home within.
Cause if I am asleep, me he will wake.
I am afraid my innocence, he will take.
No one is home within, I pretend.
You see I am safe on my cloud again.

Lucy Fegter

Trapped

I feel so trapped inside
I feel like I'm being forced to ride
my stomach churns with every breath I take
I think that I'm about to break

They say I'm not trying
but little do they know that inside I'm dying
I wish they could understand the way I feel
but I just don't think they ever will

Maybe someday they will see
that I tried to be all they wanted me to be
I know that they care
but the times I get freedom are very rare

I know this is their kingdom
but couldn't I have a little more freedom.

Emily Stillions

Dream On

Through my kitchen window dirt and filth I see.
Poverty, ignorance, squalor and it's staring
 back at me.
Below my bedroom window an alley lies in wait,
For tattered little children, as here
 they congregate.
They plan and play their childish games
 between the walls of brick.
They pick through garbage, rubbish, swill
They fight and swear and kick
They dream of wealth and grandeur,
So sure someday they'll gain it.
They have no doubts . . . they're children . . .
So maybe they'll attain it.
And so I sit amidst it all one thought
Can't be forgotten
I once had dreams so much like these
And look how far I've gotten.

Ann E. Griffin

The Little Boy That Lives Inside This Man

No one has been close to me in many, many years,
so please be gentle as I let you near!

You see I'm afraid as I reach out to you with my hand,
because I must let you meet the little boy who lives inside this man!

As you draw near me — you will see my worst,
my heart is a barren desert, the little boy dying of thirst!

He's not thirsty for water, but for a love that's true,
and he's hoping it will be the little girl who lives inside of you!

If she will be his true love, together they will see,
the barren desert in his heart changing into mountains, rivers and trees!

So lets let them bring back to our hearts the joy from years ago,
so that the man and woman we are today, might forever truly know,

That true love is a precious thing indeed,
and if we are to find it, we must let the children inside us lead!

Robert Acosta

Life's Current

A soft gentle whisper of the solemn ocean,
passes through the ears of people and caresses their souls.
It gives them serenity.

A wave crashes into their minds,
forcing them to think about and judge the wave.
It gives them light.

The ocean is their self.
Some days they are shallow
and other days they are in too deep.

They swim in the currents.
They float atop the water.
They drown in the sea of love; of wisdom.

The Ocean Gives Them Life.

Anne Szumigala

Holidays

Holidays are having fun. Dancing and prancing all day long.
Boys and girls all over town, never, ever wearing a frown.
Moms and dads taking a break. How much of this can we take!
If you're cold go by the fire. Don't start playing with a moldy old tire.
Having fun is what we do. I hope no one has the flu.
Christmas babies are being born. Come on everybody come
blow your horn.
Now we're coming to the end of my poem, so long, farewell, and
now I'm goin'.

Ryan Petrizzo

What Do You See?

What do you see in me?
An opaque mystic look in my eyes
Many years of trouble and to many tears I have cried

My eyes tell it all
Some what disillusioned but some what there

There is a sadness in me and a pain I just can't explain
A loss of my brothers was a loss like no other

Long nights in front of the TV
An empty chair next to me
Sitting up all night in a motel room
All around spirits and demons loom

My body goes numb and my eyes fill with tears
Every time I hear his name Duane
Oh God, here comes the rain

My face is hardened with many years of trouble
And my eyes . . .
My eyes tell it all

Every morning I get up and put on my working shoes
And each night to ease the pain
I sit down in front of my piano and sing the blues

Jeff Condon

Emotion

I'm bursting with emotion,
And I don't know what to do,
My heart feels torn in so many ways,
And it's all because of you.
Each night I lie in bed to sleep
but all I do is cry,
You've hurt me in so many ways,
I feel like I could die.
My hopes, my dreams, my happy thoughts,
They all have gone away,
And everything would be different now,
If only you would stay!
I used to trust so easily,
But you made that disappear,
When you left you took my heart, but now all I feel is fear.
I fear that I might once love again,
I might be caught in someone elses trap,
And in the end alone again, my mind, it might just snap.
Someday I hope to love again,
But none will be as special, as you have been.

Angela Meink

Myself

I didn't know who to turn to
I always though I was alone
I found my comfort in friends and weed
It just didn't seem to be enough
So I began drinking
Hoping to wash away all the pain inside of me.
I soon began to realize
My life was going down hill
I wanted to stop but just didn't know how
I was angry inside, yet so confused
One friend stood by me, and that was myself
I learned to find comfort in my friends
And stayed away from weed and alcohol
Cause the pain wouldn't go away
I found my way up hill
Found the love in myself
It seemed right to smoke weed at the time
I'm glad I was able to quiet
I did it for myself and no one else
And know you can to

Zelpha Metzger

My Innocence

I left your heart, and I feel I did no wrong, maybe a little, but
I promise I meant no hurt and the least bit of pain I caused you.
My intentions were sincere and honest, but my feelings and
heart were confused. I feel I have to regain my respect for love
and its values. In this game called love, I've heard words and
promises that I've held on to for an eternity. I felt my heart was
innocent and my words and feelings were taken for granted. Not
knowing all the hurt I could feel, would leave me crying in night.
But again I hold on to all words and promises to me and my heart,
and all over again it's the same pain I feel, that is left in my innocence.

La'Sayalli Jamille Lett

What If

What if — I said, I love you so much
That life would be nothing without your touch?
What if — you said, you feel the same
That there would be no meaning without your name?
What if — God said, I love you so much
That I gave My Son for you to touch?
What if — we said, we feel the same
That we give our lives to Him, in His name?

What if — the sun in the sky, did not shine
That there was just darkness in your life and mine?
What if — the stars were not out at night
That there was just darkness and no light?
What if — the sun and the stars were not there?
Then, there is no "if" — only despair — too much to bear.

Katherine E. Blomquist

Death Of A Husband

Where has he gone, the man that I married?
So virile and strong, the world he did carry.
The laugh, the smile, I still remember
His smell, his touch, his caress so tender.
Where once stood before me, a most debonair man
Now stands a shell of a once great man.
Did the weight of the world become too much?
His heart beats inside, but his demeanor is such
Hardly a word or smile crosses his face
The world has been cruel, with finger I trace.
Am I to blame for the changes I see?
I hardly thought I had it in me.
So what caused the change in the man that I loved?
I reach for the answer, if only above.
For now he is gone, as final as dead.
Sleeping alone, am I in our bed.
My tears touch the pillow, where once he did lay,
My husband, my lover, why wouldn't you stay?

Lois J. Brown

Beginnings

With my eyes closed tight I see a flash of light
like the white fuzziness of the last frames of film
Run threw the projector after the credits pass,
the beams of light over the horizon pan into focus
like the camera's eye the swinging of long reapers
in the late October Sun. Like perfect pendulums majestic
yet somehow medieval, the blades slash the landscape
a distant melody escapes, beyond the field
the dark cold forest lures like the curiosity of
a puppy, the light is devoured slowly disappearing
like the water patiently waiting for the end
of a slow circling drain, shocked by the
intrusion, the blocks of cold arctic cubes embrace
as the distant sound fades; like a slap in
the face upside down I see the stethoscope
hanging from the neck of a being who holds my ankles.

Richard P. Corcoran

You Didn't Leave Me

Another new day.
Another feeling of emptiness.
I know You're next to me
Trying to fill me up with strength,
    but the window to my heart is stuck.
You painted me a pink, warm sunrise,
Yet grief was blinding my eyes.
You sent the birds to sing me a song,
A breeze to cool my tired mind;
But ears went deaf, brain waves numb.
    Again, You didn't leave me.
Calm, peaceful, puffy clouds surrounded
Your sunset as darkness edged its way upon me.
As You nestled beside me, guarding my sleep,
You wiped the tears away,
    encircled me with love.
Tomorrow, Lord, I'll wake up with You
And we'll walk through the day together!

Joan Stroyny

Untitled

They are close in their spirits,
    inseparable, as if it is high above
In another galaxy, within the planets,
    and they soar to worlds of powerful love.

Yet, with their thoughts they do not meet;
    no togetherness, like their souls.
How can this be? What is the need?
    They must see to what their heart controls.

To walk in the clouds, as the fowls,
    to see what most only dream
And without understanding
    to realize that there alone can they find their place.

If, by chance, they stubble upon this place in time,
    with that breath of hope, and peace
Can they exhale into eternity for that moment.
    In which, time is sealed and dreams are dreamt, but not comprehend.

Though the mind of the heart they will spend
    life and eternity beyond enveloped
In the trust of being wholly
    involved. Can this be achieved?

F. Julia Miller

The Taming

From the granite cliffs of Montana
To the sandy pastures of Nebraska
He brings her with eyes flashing steel;
Her sleek form masking her strength.

Around and around, end to end
The lioness measures her new realm.
Patiently, the man waits, watching
His prize toy with the food he brings.

And somewhere upon the rocky heights reigns
The new queen who claims the spirit of the rock.
Her eyes flash the cold metal of her hunger and
Her voice snarls her triumph over her foes.

But, here, upon the lush, grassy plains
The man smiles at the princess at his side.
Her eyes show only the soft glow of contentment
And, at his touch, her throat purrs devotion.

Scarce a trace is seen in this queen brought down
Of the regal grace she wore like a crown.
She has come to depend upon the man who dared
To enter her rocky realm and tame her wild heart.

Blair Kirkpatrick

Melody

A poem is a song
Its mellow beats taking the pen along
Then the rise of the beats
Increases the pen movement
As it rushes across the page
Faster than the writer can think
So much flow of emotions
That the writer empties on the page
Like a spilled glass of milk
It continues, unstoppable and so quickly
Then the poem slows as the music slows
The pen gives the paper its last drops
For the pen knows the end is near
And as the song comes to an end
The writer finally exhales

David A. Paul

First Flight

Pushed from the nest, out of the eyrie
Into free fall
Gravity's death-grip crushing
Abandoned to terror and the abyss.

Wings never used
Flap in awkward desperation;
Earth's pull hesitates . . .

Wings stretch full to find the saving current . . .
Caught!
Lifted slowly from the depths
Riding the new-found wind-rush heavenward
Abandoned to glory and delight.

Susan Bedor

Perfect Love . . . My Dream

To reach the point of perfect love is . . .
My dream . . . my hope . . . my reality . . .
No fears . . . no demeaning words . . .
Dissolving the pain and anger of past with kindness . . .
To give twice for every once . . .

A voice inside me says . . .
Reach . . .
Search . . . Don't give up . . .
Love wi'l return, three-fold . . .
Higher than your wildest imagination can take you . . .
More brilliant than a billion stars . . .
More calm than the settling seas . . .
True inner-peace and abundance of happiness and loyalty . . .
For those who wait . . .

Pamela J. Eubanks

Four Seasons

The sudden summer
its sun of warmth for flower, insects and man
projects an inner heat of safety and security for me.

By contrast, the harsh winter
with its wet of rain and cold of wind
instills a feeling of uncertainty of time and events.

The cheerful spring
with the new hope of sprouts, seedling and young
makes life precious and individual.

Fall with its leaves of color and brilliant sunsets
seems casual and carefree
uncommitted to anything of value.

Helen N. Kobayashi

Did You Ever?

Did you ever love someone and know that person didn't care?
Did you ever feel like crying, but know you'd get nowhere?
Did you ever look into that person's eyes and say a little prayer?
Did you ever look into that persons heart and wish you were there?
Did you ever see that person standing when the lights where down low?
Did you ever whisper "God I love that person but I'll never let that person know" and when it starts you don't know why it goes on day and night. That you'll never have this person no matter how hard you fight.
Don't fall in love my friend. You find it doesn't pay for love causes heartache it happens everyday and so my friend don't ever fall in love. It'll hurt you through and through. You see my friend I ought to know.
"I fell in love with you!"

Kimberley Forry

Heart Strings Tied With Love

Best friends share a heart string tied with love.
If you have one you've been blessed from heaven above.

I've known you since you were Deedle Bee.
Now they call you Freddie D.

Best friends we've been for over twenty-five years.
We have shared so much laughter and many heart felt tears.

We've been there for each other just a phone call away,
to say 'Heah, I love you" just brightens our day.

So when you feel a tug, and there is no one to see,
You will know it's your heart string tied to me.

Marilyn Stepp

A Tribute

When we are born, were meant to die
But what I'm wondering is "Why"
A girl so full of warmth and charm
Someone who never did no harm
Could be taken from us, still so young
Who had lots of songs yet to be sung
We saw her growing weaker each day
We knew she soon would be going away
She is with God, for that I'm sure
We all loved her, but He loved her more
The pain and agony finally gone away
For this frail girl, closed her eyes today
She will be missed by family and friends
Who all loved her right to the end
Let this be a lesson to all who lives
Don't take for granted what the Almighty gives
For today he can give you all his charms
And tomorrow take it right fro your arms
Enjoy each day as if it's your last
For tomorrow is just a part of your past.

Erma (Pizzileo) Brown

Orange

The flame of the fire my eyes behold,
The colors of sunset and the leaves as the weather becomes cold.
I hear the laughing of children on Halloween night,
Pumpkins smashing, leaves, crunching, and the wet pit-pat of
    small feet running in fright.
I feel a fever rage through me.
The pain of inner fire — it causes blisters you cannot see.
Then, I taste the cider, it quenches my thirst.
Tang and caramel — but I'll have the pumpkin pie first!
I smell the autumn; the coolest of days,
Chicken and noodles, a state park, or even hay.
It is the color of an orange or the gourds that line the fences.
The color orange appeals to all my senses.

Brenda Dolph

The Lost Driftwood

There I laid on the beaches of Oregon hoping someone
would pick me up and keep me. I know not where I came from.
Perhaps, down from the mighty Columbia River
or the beautiful Rogue River, or maybe even from someone small
stream or creek such as Lost Creek in Trail, Oregon . . .
I know not what kind of tree I am. Maybe from a giant redwood,
a ponderosa pine or even a lovely willow tree.
It does not matter where I came from, for now I feel
I am a Family tree, again!

Richard W. Perry

A Cowboy's Wish

This is a cowboy's wish,
    for immortality.
But in this case I wish it,
    for you and not for me.

For me to live forever,
    would be a tragedy.
I would rather you would I live,
    and often think of me.

It would be no major feat,
    to keep this mortal shell.
But to live in your heart forever,
    is a heaven to surpass any hell.

So remember me as the cowboy,
    who rode trails around your heart.
Though I couldn't get in and build a fire,
    maybe I did set off a spark.

James F. Smith

Recipe For A Happy Holiday

One bushel of memories and a bowl of fruit
    Nuts with an old "cracker" in Great-Gramma's dish
Come, sit and chat awhile whenever you wish,
    Munch an apple — green, yellow, or red
It really doesn't matter . . . if your spirit is fed,
    Cuddle a baby, warm and sweet
He wasn't here last year . . . so that's a real treat!
    Feast on the smiles of a toddler, so full of life!
He has no idea yet . . . that this world is full of strife!
    Let's remember dear ones — gone on to glory
Everyone can think of an extra special story.
    Please take time to visit a lonely soul each week
        or, every day, if you can . . .
Then you'll be a "living recipe" for some lady or man.
    Help fill their life with a few more smiles
        It will be well worth going some extra miles
Then bring the joy you find there
        right back home to share
And show your own family how much you care.

Lucile Clancy

Breakfast

The smoke of her cigarette, like a fat white snake,
Slithers into my face no matter where I sit.
I'm not a smoker, but I'll hold my breath
As it coils around my head and keep smiling back.

The white snow swirling outside of the window
Is as white as the cream she pours in my coffee.
I like coffee black, but since she smiles as she watches
The black and white swirl, I don't complain.

I watch her reflection shiver in her coffee
and her black hair spill over her shoulders. I watch
The way she tilts her head like a pensive angel
and I hardly notice when I spill coffee in my lap.

Stephen J. Stork

Storybook Classics

We flew through the night, Peter and I, in search of the North Star.
The other stars seemed strangled by the midnight blue and forming clouds.
We were guided by the moon and followed by the children.
I remember the moon that night.
It was like the glossy white china that we ate from at Alice's party.
The tea was an odd color of a redwood, just like the angry giants
with green hair swooping down on us when the wind blew.
The rabbit rushing by was about as tall as the Dwarfs living in
the forest with Snow White.
Those Dwarfs had fat little noses and one had a furry beard,
like a bunch of dandelions pressed against his chin.
He had glass eyes that shone as bright as the floors scrubbed
each day by Cinderella.
The floors were so shiny you could see the reflection of her rags
as clearly as in a mirror.
The broom handle in the corner brought to mind Pinnochio's nose,
The nose that everlasting grew when he lied.
The fairy who granted his wish had the glittery shine of Tinkerbell.
Her wings had a rainbow tint against the moon.
That glimpse of her wing was the last I remember,
As I awoke to reality, leaving behind my dreams of the Storybook Classics.

Shane T. Mason

Closure

The silver tongue devil,
It rips at the soil
It produces a perfect six foot plot.
A lovely peaceful place for eternal rest!!
The red clay, my eyes never saw.
The box of unknown color or texture
Never for me to touch its shell.
The color of the satin where her head
Shall forever rest, never for me to caress.
No tear stains from my eyes does it hold.
No last kiss nor last good-bye!!
The silent lowering of the box unseen.
No witness have I bore to this final scene.
I saw not the first clay to pound upon the box
Nor the last grains of red soil to fill upon the end.
No long good-bye, no heart felt farewell.
Large colorful Happy flowers and a metal plaque
Were all I was to view.
Such a gay little package for a scene so morbid.
Doubt and disappear, such a heavy load for
My eight year old heart to conceive.
Damn him to hell, all this health wealth!!!
How easily he could forget the redness of the soil,
And the emptiness in my eyes.

Tracie W. Ellison

A Sunset's Love

As I see the sunset's kisses on the
sky, I wonder why our love had to die
    The clouds are stained with the suns
colorful kiss, and I remember when our love
was once sweet bliss.
    The colors neither last nor stay,
like our love they went away.
    I wait each evening to see what
color, the sun will kiss its only lover.
    Just like the sun I realize for me
there'll be no other, for you are my only lover.
    As I see the two lovers start to part,
I wonder if I'm still in your heart.
    That's when I stop and think about
the sun each day, and realize it always finds
away, to get back west, I love you Randy this is no jest!
    So come back to me my love, for the
sun's colorful kisses, are signs from the good
Lord above, and not just magic wishes.

Rachel Smith

Autumn

Outside the weather's blustering. The skies are gray and weeping.
Inside the weather's much the same, perhaps I should be sleeping.
It's autumn now. The leaves are dead. The branches brown and barren.
Inside the weather's much the same, as here I sit a-starin'.

Passers-by are dodging raindrops. Huddled close against the season.
Protected by umbrellas, they feel safe. Is that the reason?
Am I sad from the exposure to the autumn in my life?
Are the winds that blow internally, the reason for my strife?

The crossroads I am standing at no indication show,
The better road to travel. Do you learn that as you go?
So here I stand awaiting some small sign which road to take,
Wishing this decision left to someone else to make.

Outside the weather's blustering. It's autumn. Leaves are dead.
Inside a wife is dying. Could I save her? Is she dead?
Can she hold out through the winter? Will the spring find her alive?
Or will autumn winds blow through her heart and lose her in their drive

To clear the land of its debris, to signal summer's end.
This autumn storm grows vicious, as through her life it wends.
Outside the weather's blustering. Winter's calling to its bed,
All the casualties of autumn, all the sadness, all the dead.

Ramona Perlich

Saint Augustine And The Vandal

That old rolling of Chaos has now found
A shore: Poor Hippo, city of God's care

And mine. Time poises, waits now the error
Of future, soon passes mind, blood, the froth

Of a sealed witness. That old sword-point, wroth,
A-gleam, drowns the soul evermore. Unless

The Lord shout and stir men's old bones, blood-less
Now, but soon, as Christ's, raised from that great font,

Spoken — You jeer, jest, old Chaos makes grunt
Through your will, will but submiss, will not yours,

Not to old sun, wave, moon, rock, trunk, but His
He Who is Light, Good, Love, Lord three yet one.

The first blow rolls well: Sign of bright blood borne
From my side, rubriced as my lusts long dead.

My Lord, He died, agony, on tree held,
Held not, He Light, He bled to quell sin's roar,

Over dark casts Light new, covers deep bound
Now in Love, Lust all ebbed, Chaos no more,
To Love, Light, I rise myself Light unbound.

James Richardson Sprouse

Ruby

Ruby, sad and lonely
Walks the street at night
Never even knowing the love
She inspires in others
Who share her awful plight.

Ruby! Can you hear me?
Take comfort in the darkness.
It is kind and soft and gentle,
Quite beyond man's comprehension.
Accept its generous power.

It will smooth the jagged edges of the past
That jangle in your brain.
Soon, quite soon, I promise,
You can touch each one with trust
And marvel at the smoothness.

Jo Ann Forster Miller

Monkey Man

In Loving Memory of Kurt Cobain (1967-1994)
All alone surrounded by hate,
Trying to get out hope it's not too late.

Stumble along black becomes red,
Pools of anger monkey's ahead.

Straining to see gasping for air,
Gun in hand no more despair.

Heart is pounding a shattered bang,
Piercing echo two shots rang.

Sudden silence mind has decided,
Paralyzed by fear monkey delighted.

Sharp pain soul consumed,
Explicit thoughts forever doomed,

Monkey within no where to run,
Six feet under killed by a gun.

Michelle Baggett

Accidental Suicide

She felt so alone, so alone. That she could take it no longer.
Why was her life a jig saw puzzle that no-one could put together.

She wanted to fly like a bird, just once to be free.
So she ran to the empty lighthouse, holding the gun where no one could see.

Every step she took was another thought running threw her insane head.
Out of breath she reached the final step, thinking soon I will be dead.

As she looked out the window with the gun in her hand.
Thoughts racing, she threw it on the grassy land.

She thought, maybe I should jump, so I can soar through the air.
Or maybe just walk back down those creaky stairs.

Why am I here, what was I thinking about?
She looked out the window one last time with doubt.

She took one last glance.
Thinking this is my only chance.

She knew what she wanted, she wanted to live. Maybe people do care.
Then she slipped and fell down those creaky stairs.

Falling . . . down, down, down, on every step hitting her head.
Now she will never live her life because she's dead.

Sara Frasier

Untitled

My heart swells with the excitement going on in the room.
Even though I'm miles away . . .
I'm there.

The years streamed by with the blink of an eye.
All the memories of the "Oz" of my youth — you know
what I mean are being mused by all of you now.
I'm there.

Joy, sorrow, laughter . . . tears may fill your eyes,
but it was a beautiful part of our lives . . . I don't
ever forget friends . . . all
I'm there.

We are all older now.
Are we wiser?
I don't know
The curious blood of my tempestuous youth still
flows through me, like a dormant virus, rising up at I'm there

Gentle conversation, song, and dance . . . this night
will become another gem-stone to be kept in your
treasure chest of youthful dreams I'm there.
You're here.

Douglas Tutty

A Prayer Of A Vet

Dear God, I ask of you to-day
As this important role I play,
Give to me strength from above,
Fill my heart with your great love.

Please lessen pain I bear each day,
Help others too along the way,
Yet, not one of us will dare forget
Your blessings Lord, "The prayer of a vet"

There's many lives messed up by nerves,
Still contemplating enlisting in the reserves,
Some of us have lost a limb or two,
Others lost their life, it's true.

Yes, some of us have lost our sight,
Plenty fear the dark of night,
While some can not endure loud noise,
Remember the war, our girls and boys.

Don't forget we women Lord, who served in the war,
we suffer too, working long hours, 'twas quite a chore,
We had our cross to bear, it wasn't all fun,
We had one thing in mind, "There's a war to be won"

Geraldine L. Coleman

My Childhood Home

Tall and strong it stood,
    to comfort and protect.
Withstanding all it could,
    to gain increasing neglect.
If its soul could speak,
    would its heart skip beats.
As I listen to the tales from my childhood home.

It would tell of a young couple, full of dreams,
    facing the world head-on, full of steam.
Building a family without fear,
    as they grow older each passing year.
From cries of babes and children's songs,
    to the nursery rhymes we played along,
I'd listen to the sounds echo from my childhood home.

Older now it has aged alone.
No children left to call it home.
Its neglect increased by my age.
Now standing frail against life's stage.
As an adult we continually roam,
    longing for a piece of our childhood home.

Kristine M. Palmer

Is And The Tin Man

The cowardly soldier stands
She looks at the sky and she cries . . .
I am no longer made of tin
I am flesh and blood
I now have a heart and it bleeds
I am no longer a faithful guide
I am no longer a friend
I am that which I am
My heart is no longer purple
For purple is the color of kings
I have failed in my mission
All is a tangible shade of black
All about me is black
I never had a home and
I have no friend . . .
The sun then bursts through the sky
An audible voice says . . .
Soldier, complete your mission
And, she weeps as she goes on

J. S. Lowery-Malcolm

Forgotten

All the things that use to be,
are gone forever more.
I want to go where they are,
through the lost and forgotten door.
I am reaching out.
I am halfway there,
but it is all too far away,
even though I want to go,
I am forever here to stay.
I want to go,
I need to fly away,
I close my eyes and scream,
when I feel the pain of day.
I pray to sleep in darkness,
I drink the feel of fear,
as for all the things that use to be,
I will shed a shallow tear.
Every time I close my eyes
I become more like what I see,
which is nothing, nothing. God, I am forgotten.

Grace Russ

Beyond Today

Looking beyond this tedious day
I wonder what will come my way.
My life being guided by God's loving hands,
These are the things I certainly understand;
Without charity, faith and hope
Tomorrow may never come and that's no joke!

Linda S. Midwig

Kayla's Lullaby

Grammie and Kayla went for a walk.
And while they were walking, they started to talk
all about the animals and birds in the sky.
And Kayla said: "Oh, why can't I fly?"

Grammie started laughin' and sat in the grass.
Kayla spread her arms as the wind blew past.
Up in the air, Kayla did fly,
circling and swooping in the blue, blue sky.

Down she came without a sound.
Right behind Grammie she landed on the ground.
She tumbled so softly and lit on her bum.
Grammie had to hide her smiles and said "Now, let's run!"

Grammie and Kayla ran in the sun,
over hills and flowers. Oh what fun!
Later that night, when they tucked her in,
Kayla told Mom and Dad
"I flew like the wind!
(Grammie just smiled)

Cheryl Spagnolini

Those Eyes

A troubled soul those green eyes show,
Like a dirty old beat up backhoe,
The pain and trauma of a worm,
Squished and twisted from hands with muscles firm.
Hands gnarled in a gruesome defeat.
Sorrow and depression with no retreat.
No one could know these troubles,
the ones of your life, doubled.
With days and nights of endless regret,
And never stopping times of fret,
A troubled soul those green eyes show,
if the pain you could only know.

Andrea Utick

A Thanksgiving Poem

The first Thanksgiving was celebrated 375 years ago to be exact.
The Pilgrims and Indians celebrated peace — that's a fact.
The feast was made possible by Squanto and many others.
Yes, the Indians had accepted the Pilgrims as sisters and brothers.
Everyone had pitched in to make this Thanksgiving feast the best,
For the foreigners who crossed the ocean to the land in the West.
The meal consisted of foods such as vegetables, bird and beast;
It also included bread made of water, flour and yeast.

The Thanksgiving feast has not changed much in 375 years.
We still eat dinner with our friends, family and beloved dears.
Now we do eat our meal with our napkin neatly creased;
But you will find us still eating the vegetables, bird and beast.

Elizabeth Berilla

Grey Matters

There are nothing but grey areas,
I think;
And black and white are just
the unreasonable extremes of possibility.

The facts turn in the breeze of their telling,
truer and better with each new perspective.
No computer can count the number
of points of view.

Before you tell me that all is black and white,
because it is so obvious to you,
picture yourself a shade of grey between the two.

Pam Golwitzer

Friends

Money and health, slyness and stealth,
All are devoured by time and unhealth
But friends are always there
People will taunt, throw dare,
But friends are always there
When time and age throw you down,
And you feel shunned by the entire town,
Friends are always there
And when you pass on,
And the game of life is done,
Friends will still be there.

Andrew Seavy

Untitled

I sat by the shore today contemplating my life
Noting the happiness and the endless inward strife
It seems I've been existing on moments alone
Never clinging to anything just like moss on a rolling stone

I began to ask myself just what direction to take
But the paths are ever winding like the trails of some elusive snake
if I could but cast myself on the wind and simply carry on
Then it seems that my life should hasten toward dawn

There's been many facets and inputs from which to choose
When I let my heart overrule then my mind begins to lose
The battle's not an easy one between the two
One minute I'm smiling; the next minute I'm blue

Sometimes I even wonder if it will all be okay
Then I look back and remember one very special day
The day my little lady was brought into this world
Taken from my body was a beautiful baby girl

Now I know in my heart that whatever I do
I will do for us because we are one entwined around two
My world is hers to learn from and grow
No need to worry, it is time to go slow!

Debi J. Stevens

Grandma And Grandpa

You meant everything to me
But now you are gone
How can that be?
You promised me that we would, and could
Always be, but I guess you lied to me
You always said when I was away
Look at the star with the biggest glow
then, I'd know you were looking at it, too
Now you're gone, and none of us know what to do.

You picked me up when I was down
Made me happy when I was sad
And spoiled me when I was bad!
Thanks so much grandma, and grandpa
We all love, and miss you a whole bunch
Grandma always said "Nobody would live forever"

And, she obviously was very clever
the star we looked at, is still up there
And lonely because grandma, and grandpa aren't together any more
I will never understand
Why did it happen, and why were you taken from me?

Anne Laehn

Our Little Girl

Our little girl came into our lives,
So innocent, so precious, so sweet in our eyes.
We touched her little hand and she touched our hearts,
We bonded together with a love to never part.
She looked up one day right into our eyes,
With a look that showed something money can't buy.
To hold her in our arms so close and so tight,
To be there always to tuck her in and kiss her goodnight.
How simple things come to mean so much,
How a little girl yearns for our loving touch.
God has given to us a special gift for us to treasure,
As our little girl brings us a lifetime of pleasure.

Nikki Recker

Winter

Crystal cold high mountain night,
    star blanket in the sky.
The infinite surrounds and holds,
    but questions linger . . . why?
Rock ledges echo silence,
    no answer comes to me.
The past is gone, the future waits . . .
    its secrets yet to see.

Donna Marie Bowman

Treasure Of Love

If I could bring you silk from China
or rare old lace from spain.
The moon on a silver platter.
command the clouds to give you rain.
Give you all the gold in Ft. Knox,
treasures from beneath the sea
all the oil held by the Arabs
all the cars from GMC.

All the ceder on Mt. Lebanon
all the cattle on the hills,
the most rare exotic jewelry,
formed by old and secret skills.
You know I can't perform these miracles,
Just to prove my love is true
Would you accept this small token
Just three words dear, "I love you."

Millie B. Corbitt

Enchantress

In wooded glens, enchantress dreams a dream by
  Druids' Smoke,
As fog recedes, recoils from suns bright flame,
  sylph awoke
With forest eyes, brown-green, aglow, pierce the
  mottled shadows of this realm
Visions meld the memory fastly held, as the
  aged elm
Oh, enchantress of the brown-green orbs, granted
  of visions true
Sweet breath of Earth, embrace this child
  reborn unto
Secluded depths, beyond the reach of mortals
  hazard plans
Unscathed by patience trying hand — as mortals
  desecrate Earth's lands
Allow such wisdom as bequeaths enchantress
  to prophecies
So this sweet planet, orbit fixed, is ever
  mortal-wise.

    Joya Fairchild

Untitled

"One shattered dream is not the end of the dreaming;
One shattered hope is not the end at all;
Beyond the storm and tempest stars are shining;
Still build your castles, though your castles fall.

Though many dreams come tumbling in disaster;
and pain and heartaches meet you through the years,
still keep your faith, your hopes to muster,
and never should you ever cease to dream."

    Z. M. Scifres

The Desert

I shade my eyes against the sun to scan the burning sand . . . A
thousand miles of nothingness . . . A truly barren land . . . And yet
a beauty: hidden tho, is there for all to see . . . It rises up in
waves of heat to startle you and me, how can this mass of earthen
crust disgorge such lovely view? When all is naught 'cept emptiness
and cacti tho only few . . . Did it take the hand of a supreme one to
mold it bit by bit or was it cast aside for the searing sun a piece
that wouldn't fit . . . I think not, for if that be true then why the
creatures be? . . . There's life abundant even tho not much by light
to see . . . They sally forth when darkness falls to roam the waste
land wide . . . To feed and grow then at the dawn seek another place
to hide . . . And once again old sol comes up to chase away the
night, another day is dawning, just one more in the fight for the
desert's not too different from the rest of earth's great mass . . .
These creatures too scurry round and wait for life must pass

    Richard E. Welby

Autumn

As the time is approaching near
It is almost here
The leaves begin to turn a new color
Red, orange, and yellow leaves galore
The ground is now beginning to fill with leaves
Our raking days are here
So grab a rake and pull up your sleeves
Day by day the weather is as different as night and day
That even the weather man doesn't know what to say
Although these changes are coming about
We won't pout
Cause we're strong
And it won't last long
Cause winter will soon be approaching again
And it'll be a new season to begin

    Linda Logan

Just Waiting

I stand alone by myself I am fully
clothed but still I am naked. No one is there,
protecting me from the cold. I shake as
I turn blue. Protecting me from the rain.
I am wet; soaked. My tears are like the
rain. They only come when it's a cloudy
day. I Open my heart hoping that the
sun is going to shine through, when in
fact it is nowhere to be found.
Shining. Naive? Too trusting? Not
trusting enough? No, just waiting.
I waited patiently and I found the
sun one day. I stand. Not alone.
But with God. Never to be by myself again.

    Summer Mayhew

You Shine Like A Star To Me

The universe is large and O so vast — a question that
enters my mind is — will it always last?

An epoch is so long — a second so meer — the life of a
star is described in years.

The universe has light — the universe has dark —
It's the stars that we see and the rest is so dark.
The star is so kind — it provides for life —
because of your light and warmth — I asked you to be my wife.

Suppose I were a planet and you were a star — with you
by my side — I can go far.

You are so dear to me — even when you're not near.

You help remove the fears me — whenever I have tears.
You always bend an ear for me — when I need someone to hear.

So, in the last year for me — you shine like a star to me.

    Charles W. Kotorman

Under The Yellow Southern Sun

A tall gray crane lets itself in
through the screen door
to knock a question on the refrigerator
hopeful and at a loss
closer and closer to resigning itself
to human ways.

It the west
a room becomes one's own
when one remembers it in an instant
the smell of stained glass
a thundering of black cats down the hall;
when one has seen in the room a small picture
of oneself like the blue faded bird
tapping its beak against the unyielding icebox
a vague idea of what it doesn't have
while it walks through alien life
too cleaned or too much furniture
and there is no room for it here in the kitchen.

    Wylie O'Sullivan

Poetry?

Nature could not make us perfect,
So she did the next best thing — she made
Us blind to our faults, also knowledge
Is what you learn from others, wisdom
Is what you teach yourself, us education
Is proceeding from ignorance to
Thoughtful uncertainty

    Kate Koupo

Bluewater Bay Walker

I

Holding a bouquet of pine needles to your breast,
In your silvery, sequined satined-Bay dress,
With your skirt of stars and mantle of moon,
I remember you.

Stilling the night with your translucent white
Crinolines cresting, crescendos of light,
Iridescent girl.

II

Falcon feathers trailing at your neck,
Leaves, trees, moss, salt, and sand, your scent.
Dressed in doeskin,
Drumming the rhythms of your night,
My fires flame, sigh and die from sight.

III

Now my Reeboks walk concrete paths, but leave no print.
My scent is conceived by Yves St. Laurent,
But cannot lead to where I once went.

Holding a mirror of beige to my face,
I behold your disgrace,
Blue-gowned silk stained with brown-foamed silt,
And gilded with guilt.

I remember you, gentle land, dressed in your best.

Susan Crowe Lipnicky

Red, White, And Blue

There are many different types with many different colors,
However there is one that stands out from all the others.
History records all it's been through
from wars to brave heroes tried and true.
It stands for freedom and a way of life,
it's colors are red, white, and blue
It's the American flag, the best in the land,
And a lot of people died to keep it from a ruling hand.
when I look at a flag and compare it to our own,
I think of all the people that we have never known
But they gave their lives to keep us free
And I hope that's the way it will always be,
That's why I try to do the best I can,
So I can say I'm proud to be an American.

Sara Rae Maryfield

The Passing Storm

I looked to the skies and felt a raindrop.
   So I closed my eyes so it would stop.
But it started to rain as the clouds set in the echoing
      thunder came roaring in.
The lightning struck down, as I fell to the ground,
   And I could feel my world just spinning around.
I ran for shelter in self-defense,
   But the storm kept getting more intense.

My heart cried in silence, it was broken in two
   Until I opened my door and let you come through.

Release your heart without reserve
   For my chambers covet its preserve.
Just let it flow into my world
   for mine to have and ours to hold.

I love you more than I can say, even so a rainy day.
   In each and every passing day, I know our love is here to stay.

The storm is gone and I cry no more
   As the sun reflects upon the shore.
I love you more than ever before,
   Just give me the key to open your door.

Laurie Shear

The Country Way Of Life

The sky is bright as a new day is dawning,
Roosters are crowing, lazy dogs yawning.

Sounds carry so far across the land,
Children laugh as a new day is planned.

Woodpeckers tap on an old oak tree,
Other birds sing their sweet melody.

Deer wander through with their beauty and grace,
A squirrel packs acorns in the sides of its face.

Bees and butterflies flit all around,
Sipping nectar from flowers that cover the ground.

Spiders spin webs that are true works of art,
From under a rock a lizard may dart.

The sun slowly sets behind a mountain nearby,
And millions of stars blanket the sky.

Owls awaken and let their presence be known,
Felines are hunting in fields freshly sown.

Crickets serenade us each and every night,
The country way of living is such a delight.

Micki L. Wilson

Fly Away, My Friend, Fly Away

Don't look back for I'm Okay
I'll be looking forward to the wonderful day
When I too can come with you,
And we'll be together and all anew.

You have taught me more than you'll never know.
You have helped me through your life to grow.
You've opened up feelings so deep in my heart.
The memories and laughs will never depart.

Continue to help me as you look down now.
Stay by my side and show me how
To accept and love as is only right,
And when I falter, please show me the light,

Continue to smile and shine just like you have
And help me to understand that God loves us one and all.
No matter where we come from, or how often we fall.

So fly, my friend, and soar.
Soar to the highest and more
I love you; I thank God for you.
and most of all, you loved me too.

Fly away, friend, fly away.

Kaye Hunter

Breaking Up

I thought I would always love you,
And you would always love me too,
We thought it would go on forever,
You and I together,
Then one day came,
It just wasn't the same,
We started to drift apart,
That's when I realized we were going to part,
How was I going to tell you,
Because breaking up is never an easy thing to do,
In these words I write,
I hope that you can gain sight,
I want to tell you,
That breaking up is what we should do,
The pain may be hard to mend,
But hey, we can always still remain friends.

Keith D. Hoose

400

I'm Just A Girl

I'm just a girl,
Not like any other,
I'm special and privileged,
Not many have seen the romantic Venice in Italy,
Not many have great friends to go to when there is a problem,
Not many have a great supporting family like I,
I am different and I am happy,
I don't need any drugs to keep me happy and perky,
It comes naturally to me,
I am just a girl,
Not like any other.

Thalia Farshchian

The Match Holder's Hand

The crackling, the sizzling, a new spark began all with
the help of the Match Holder's hand. Etching its way, the
flame grew and grew until the tip of the wick was a
light honeydew. A brutal wind tried to break through, but
to its creator it had vowed to be true. The breeze
blew harder and it began to pursuade. The light,
getting weaker, flickered and swayed. Becoming
smaller and shorter it was only a glint of the
plan and the future its creator had meant. The
sad, little fire shriveled on down. But a spark
reignited and there was no more frown. The small,
serving light knew it would be brilliant again,
But only with the help of the Match Holder's hand.

Olivia Conkle

My Dad The Teacher

My Dad the teacher, with his hidden identity,
with his super values and hidden strength.
You taught me the values, of watching and learning.
For you could not teach me no other way.
You shared your wisdom, with its loneliness.
Sometimes wondering, why?
The teacher has left his loneliness for fear of love and hatred,
always away, but always there.
Your wisdom has stayed; for it shows.
My life has been hard and sad,
but through your strength, that you have shared.
My life has turned; to something of value for he who is not a teacher,
has taught me well.
Thank you Dad, for the hidden love, of my old man, My dad.

Donald A. Ramos

Love's Touch

There are so many ways to reach out and touch you.

With my eyes, I look into yours and see the person you are
and I like what I see.
With loving eyes, I don't see any faults or shortcomings,
only the woman you long to be.

With my hands, I reach out and touch yours and feel the
softness of your heart.
With loving hands, I will be there for you to help heal you
when the hurting starts.

With my arms, I long to hold you and comfort you when you are
hurt from problems and strife.
With loving arms, I place myself in front of you to shield you
from the arrows of life.

With my heart, I reach to you with as much love
as I am able to give.
With my loving heart, I long to receive that same love from you
as long as we both shall live.

Michael Pendergraft

In My Heart

Touched by the warmth of your body
Smitten by the smile you portray
All trouble dissipates in an instant
Whenever your love comes my way

But now I must put on hold
The one thing I cherish so dear
A love that keeps me alive
Whose heart I've grown so near

The unique bonding that's guaranteed to last
This rare intimacy and feeling so true
We believe tomorrow will always be there
Like I thought I would always have you

I never dreamed something so special
Would ever have to end
But I guess nothing really last forever
Except my love for you from within

And as each day goes by
In my heart you will always be
Because what I shared with you was "rare"
And no one can ever take that from me

Nimmie S. Hickman

To Zachary With Love

How do we ever explain it,
How do we make you see,
We gave you the most we ever could,
The Gift of setting you free.

Free from a teen-age mom and dad,
Who loved you with all their heart,
But who were persuaded by many of us,
You deserved a better start.

Although we don't know your parents,
We were promised on that day,
Your future would be so much brighter,
If with these people we would let you stay.

Babies raising babies,
Often times will lead to divorce,
We wanted you in a stable home,
Not with a single mom, or a dad who remained by force.

The greatest Gift we could give you,
Our Love — enough to set you free,
For a better and more steady life,
Our dearest, most precious, Zachary.

Barbara A. Ashwill

Fight For Freedom

When forces beyond reach
Threaten the happiness you seek
Stand up and fight, if for nothing else, so for the right
To make their efforts grow weak

If forces that do not show
Try to erase everything you know
Stand up and fight, if for nothing else, so for the right
To let your mind grow

When someone you never met, is trying to make you forget
The promises they made
Stand up and fight, if for nothing else, so for the right
To put their lies on parade

When forces beyond what you can see
Order you down on your knee
Stand up and fight, if for nothing else, so for the right
To live your life and be free

Hanne S. Bakke Talbert

Cananduigua Lake

In the stillness of the night,
as I gazed across the lake,
all was peace and tranquil,
all I heard was the water's wake.

The moon was full,
beautiful to see,
You could almost imagine you
were on a ship at sea.

Reflection from the moon on the water,
Sent images upon the wall,
Some looked like horses
standing in their stalls.

I awakened sometime later,
to see a burst of gold,
The sun was on the horizon,
a beautiful sight to behold.

You knew God's hand was in this masterpiece,
because it has been foretold.

Walter F. Gooding Sr.

The Dream Is Dying

"Oh" how I want to cry.
When we tell the dream good-bye.
Why oh why are we letting the dream die.

Dr. King had a dream that little
white boys and girls, would walk
hand in hand with little black boys and girls.

"Oh" my heart is sad, to see that
hate is so bad. That we as a
people would back over the
dream, because of the color of skin.

Why have we made such a difference.
In the color of black and white skin.
Don't you know God hasn't, we are
all Kin. Don't you know God isn't
offended by our skin.

Black skin, white skin who's
at fault. I hope we would see
the hateful work of the enemy.
The enemy in you the enemy in me.
That is why God's dream is dying in our society.

June Prieto

I'm Glad I'm Me

The years go by so very fast
Oh, my, if they could only last.

I turned eighty in 'ninety-six'
It's scary how fast that old clock ticks.

My health is good, I'm full of pep
Still lots of snap in my step.

I have so many things to do
Too many, I'm sure, in years so few.

The "Have-to's" give me such a pain
More "Want-to's" is the name of my game.

Being wife and mother did fill my life
Much love and happiness, sometimes strife.

And now I feel I've earned the chance
Last years to make my life enhance.

A Senior-Citizen, I'm proud to be
Life's so wonderful, I'm glad I'm me.

Irene L. Gregorio

Fleeting Moments

Once the world was quiet, lonely, and still,
Then came the light and the first fragile cry,
Breaking open silence, it echoed God's will,
Left here to grow, and soon after to die.

Like bright flowers in Spring, we're gone with Fall,
And when all grows back, it's never the same,
For life will go on and death claims us all,
We're reborn to the world from where we first came.

This world that forgives with no questions asked,
Shining with bright spirits, glowing with pure love,
It takes hold of hearts, freeing all that we've masked,
And brings back to God what He made here above.

So when this is done, we haven't truly died,
We've passed on to new hope and silently we've cried.

Diana La Verda

The Heart Of You

The years have passed so very fast
There's not too much that really lasts,
But all through times, both good and bad
Your love has made many hearts glad.
When things get hard or my heart gets blue
A boost for me is to talk to you.
From the compassion you've always shown
Your heart's bigger than anyone I've known.
The helping hand you've always extended
Leads the way to what God intended.
The thoughtful things you always do
Comes from the heart and makes you, you!

Wyona Pittman

My Walk With God

As I was walking down the road,
I thought of things I'd been told.
I kept on walking and wondering why,
"Did God create us to live or to die?"
As I was walking around the bend
I looked up to the sky and sensed a friend.
I kept on walking into the darkness of the night,
But then remembered, I had nothing to fright.
I came upon a shimmering lake,
And soon had to do a double take.
God was looking down on me!
I could not believe my eyes,
But it was not a so-called surprise,
he was there from the very start,
And he'll always be in my soul and heart.

Tracy M. Keithahn

Sometimes I Wonder . . .

She looks upon the midnight so clear;
Thinking of the one she loves so dear.
Wishing so that there might be a chance to share.
Might there be some time to spare?
She wonders how she lives a life of hope;
When every time, she knows the answer's "no."
For everyone she's ever loved is gone,
Away from her. She wonders what went wrong.
And is this really fair for her?

She smiles through a thousand tears.
She has her friends, but faith turns into fears.
When she finds a love; so pure and gentle and fair,
Maybe it won't be so hard to care.
Please, someone, to her heart, find the key.
This girl, she hides herself inside . . . of me.

Sara Puett

Honey

Please don't leave us, why do you have to go,
we have so much left to say and do;
Please don't leave us, not today nor tomorrow
Stay
Why do you have to leave us when we have family,
the sun, the sky, the earth and the moon,
Please don't leave us, not yet,
we need you so, please don't go.
You were doing so much to help others
and still had so much more to do,
please don't leave us, please don't go.
We all know you'd like to stay with us a little longer,
just a little longer, please don't go.
But we know God needs you and is calling you home,
we're just not ready to lose you
please don't go:
Goodbye my darling, goodbye,
the father of our children say Goodbye, we all love you so,
we're not ready to let you go, so until we meet again
we all love you so, please don't go.

Mary Ann Bies

Adulthood III

I am meshed between the lines,
the suckling of reason screeching from my breast.
Back and front,
side and side,
back and front it swings,
it slows,
it thumps into the walls I wander between,
a bloody dangling
from the soft pointed pink
i once loved to touch.

i will not stay between the lines
not for crystalline structures
or syllogisms
or four four time
or screws or plastic or computer generated lives
i want to make mistakes
i want to be seduced
i want to stay dead until i know
the sublime slashed and bleeding into my mouth
and die again when the first drop crusts between the lines

Susan Ignatius Paulovich

Why????

Why can't you admit the Devil's got you in his hand?
He's leading you 'round by the nose;
Making you less of a man.

Why can't you see why you're running in
circles, and never seen to get done?
How can it be you think you're in control;
And that this is all such fun?

I wish you'd open up your eyes;
See that this is destroying you.
And you're not the only one suffering
inside; you're taking your loved ones too!!

If you make it through this without losing
your life; you'll look back on this time and feel shame.
You'll never hide the fact from yourself;
That you have no one else to blame.

I think you should know — that I talk to God,
about you each night when I pray;
And there will come a time, when His
powerful hand, will send the devil away!

Debbie Coggins

The Call Of Nature

When you walk up a hill,
When you hear the birds sing to you from
the tree tops,
When you hear the bears roar to you from
the bushes,
When you hear the air planes hum to you
from the sky,
When you hear the snakes rattle their tails
from the rocks,
When you hear the wind whisper in
your ears,
When your hair slightly blows in
the wind,
When the coyotes call to you from
the hills,
And that is when you say it's the
call of Nature.

Lesa Erickson

Suzanne

Twenty-five years have been here and moved out,
thank God you never took that route.
You've seen trouble, seen delight, cliff hangers and indulgences,
they're all under your feet now, trampled into gentle fragrances.
Not much to be ashamed of, is there,
just the normal wear and tear.
You've been used and you've been had,
but You've never been mean nor bad.
Kids, you have some, but you made them all upright,
your skills are out of sight.
If you look down life's highway, with its uproar and its kick,
you'll see trouble enough to make you sick.
But I'll go too, and without much fear,
mostly because you'll stay near.
Silver isn't that bad, ol' partner, but just to be bold,
with Gods help, let's go for the Gold.

George R. Githens

The Cove

You can't recall this place you found
Where Quaking Aspen stands abound,
Singing with thrushes . . . near a hill
Which lake reflects when wind is still
But I returned to view its grace
And felt once more your gentle trace.

John H. McGowan Jr.

Danger In A Second

We sat and waited,
To know who had survived
In those awful hour of devastation.
Watching parents, grandparents,
Friends, and family identify their loved ones.
Not knowing what had happen
Or what would happen, the heroes
Responded without a blink putting
Their own lives in danger. The ones
Who survived will never get over
What happened that day. In seconds
Lives can be taken without a warning.
Still, one year later the American
People haven't put what happen
Behind them. Friends and family
Will never be able to respond to their
Cries for help or happy times spent
With joy.

Mary Bell

Fateful September Day

Beneath the sun I plowed the fields that warm September day.
My little girl — so sweet was she upon the grass did play.
My wife she died some time ago and left me all alone.
To get along the best I could and try to make a home
So carefully I'd always watched my child upon the green.
But woe — she must have wandered off for then I heard her scream.
It pierced the lazy dusty air, I dropped my plow and ran
And found my little girl face down just sobbing in the sand.
Two little red marks pierced the skin
Upon her dainty arm — and now it started swelling
I grasped her in alarm.
She lays there on her bed so still too brave to even cry.
I kneeled upon the floor and prayed, to God not let her die.
She drank the whiskey from my hand, I hoped to stop the pain.
The swelling turned from blue to black,
I nearly went insane.
All through the night I stayed with her,
Beside the bed till dawn.
But when the sun peeped o'er the hill,
My little girl was gone.

Thelma Anonsen

Night Life

Dimming sun light hung in the shadows at the end of a long hot day.
The children took turns in the bath tub, washing off the afternoons play.

Mom and Dad sat on the front porch enjoying a late evening breeze.
Discussing their daily problems in the fragrance of the lilac trees.
Quiet settled over their little homestead as the sun slowly
dropped from sight.
Darkness engulfed the lingering shadows as day gave away to night.

The children joined mom and dad on the front porch, to listen to
the crickets sing.
The frogs joined the chorus from their marshy home and the
night began to ring.

They sat together and marveled as the darkness came alive.
A bobcat called longingly to his mate from their forest paradise.

A small herd of deer wandered from hiding to browse in the
meadow with care.
Their young fawns darting back the forth enjoying the cool night air.

Mom rushed the children off to bed, where each drifted into their
separate dreams.
Of the animals that come out after dark, and play near the
bubbling streams.

Dan Parker

Tower Of Time

I sailed across seven seas
each held twenty four hours
The stones led on to build a structure
each structure contributed to the tower
And in its final completion
the tower stood brave and bold
Withheld many a storm from the seas
and many a story had it told
Nobody questioned its existence
and not many could stay on its path
Few knew of its weaknesses
or again of the power it had
Years had chipped away at its stone
though bruised it is still firm
This conglomeration of ideas
bread into life by a single sperm
Seven more seas will be crossed
more hours felt and seen
Time will tell the secret about the affair
between the tower and me.

Linda A. Kivenas

Black

Black is when the sun goes down.
Black is when I am alone. Alone, alone and away from the
bright colors that the day brings. The smiles that
the day brings.

Black is when it is peaceful. When I am peaceful.
When the world is in chaos black is peaceful.
In my world black is peaceful.

Love, love is a hollow black circle, just a myth.
No red in love. Black, black is love.

Black is terrifying, terrifying to everyone, but me.
Black is soothing, soothing to me, comfortable to me.
To everyone else black is different.
What is different is what people really fear. Not black.

Black is clear to me, but black to the world.
Clear in my world. Clear in my thoughts.
Clear to me.

Black is when the sun goes down.

Theresa Dicello

Sisters

Sisters are the best of friends;
We can share things with each other.
In the good times or bad times;
Sisters are forever.
We have done so much together;
Our lives are intertwined,
Though we live different life styles;
We still can get together and
Have the best of time.
Sisters are the best friends;
I think of you both all the time.
The memories that we have shared together;
Will stay with me for the rest of my life.
Sisters are the best of friends.

Jeanette Kratz

Autumn In Aspen

Solid blackness broken only by scattered pinpoints of tiny jeweled
stars envelope the Colorado sky.
Golden rays of early morning sunlight break through, bird calls echo,
ringing like bells through the lone wild cathedrals of the forest;
It's Autumn in Aspen.
Vapor rimming the turning leaves with diamonds of frost, the colors
of our "Artist's" pallet painting splendors of orange, yellow,
white and gold;
The brooks ring out their play, the early fog begins to burn away,
It's Autumn in Aspen.

John B. Rogers

Failed Utopia Style: Rondeau

A time ago the world was one;
All were at peace and sadness took none.
People were happy and united with all.
And the none day this peace did fall;
The world of perfection and equality was done.
Now we turn on our friends and run,
For fear the God-like power will be won.
Whispered in our ears is the beckoning call,
And we realize it's as if we're running from the sun,
And holding us back is an invisible wall
Too great to climb and standing tall.
The escape will never be finished, because the war will never be done,
And we realize our peace is gone forever.

Eileen Davison

Walking On A Rainbow

Magic in the air it seems as though
I'm totally free my soul has taken over
me and I feel I've sprouted wings.

I'm here to do whatever I choose, gliding
on the wind. Jumping over fluffy
clouds in this state I'm in.

Daydreaming about sweet things which
will never exist. For reality I've left
behind, on this wonderful trip.

Mind, body, soul, and all burns within me now.
For each separate dying ember a part of me asks how.

Exploring this wonderful dreamland, searching
through and through. Skipping over bright
lit colors such as purple, green, and blue.

I'm in a magical place now, shining with a glow.
I've left all reality behind,
I'm walking on a rainbow.

Jade Boudwin

Hummingbird

The mystical, magical hummingbird flies,
All through his life, until he dies.
His magnificent colors, so shiny and bright,
He wears so well, all through his flight.
With speed, he dances through the air,
and to think of landing, he wouldn't dare.
It seems he's always on the run,
and never stops to have some fun.
But maybe that's how he gets his pleasure,
these beautiful birds, I really treasure.

Julia Shields

The Triangle

He was 18, I, 28. Blue eyes, blond hair and skin so fair.
Straight as a pin, he walked with a flair.
Those eyes held secrets, and his frown gave away,
The internal thinking went on night and day.
 The years flew by, he, 28 and his girls came and went.
 I, 37 and worldly, then, saw less of my fair haired arrow, then.
The middle years had settled in and the friends met once again.
Changes brought them close this time.
A love did bloom and grew at fever pace. Together now, face to face,
Exchanging joy and living in grace, we gave our love in every place.
 Then winter came and a long lost flame appeared.
 She, too, talked of love and gave herself to the younger one.
The weeks came and went, her power grew.
The man, now man and man came together again. Their joy and
attachment knew no end.
The triangle still in place. Who wins in this three way race?
2 Samuel verse 26, Holy Bible, says
 your love for me was wonderful. Surpassing the love of Women.

Bruce G. Sparks

Lost Love

Our hearts were broken, for that I'm sure,
But the love we shared, tis the only cure,
You've been my lover, my mate and my friend,
And the mistakes I've made, will never be again,
I've never forgotten any of the times we've spent together,
My only wish, is that they could've been better
I miss your beauty, presence, your humor and wit,
Believe me, when I say, my love for you will never quit.
You are the love of my life, my eternal flame,
And my life without you, will never be the same,
I'm at peace with myself, more than ever before,
I may be alone, but I'm not lonely anymore.

Marc S. Dunne

A Loving Life

The joy and enthusiasm of looking forward to each new day
with glorious expectations of wonderful things to come.

The radiant curiosity that finds adventure in simple things.

The miracle of growing flowers the magic of snowflakes.

The courage that rises from defeat and tries again.

The believing heart that trust in others, knows
no fears, with faith in a divine father that watches
over his children from the sky.

The tolerance that forgets differences as quickly
as a child can make a friendship that holds no
grudges, never hates, and loves people for who they are.

Rochele Williams

Searching

Crying in the wilderness of my soul
searching for answer that are left
untold hoping that some day
they will all unfold
and peace will restore the unrests
that I have that sometimes I think is
driving me mad I look at
the short time I have and maybe I think life
hasn't been so bad.

Grace E. Curry

Security

 I waded in the angry ocean,
Rain drops felt like needles
Making some crude tapestry upon my vulnerable back.

 There seemed to be an unseen magnet
 trolling my body out and beyond,
 Into the dark abyss of the ocean
 whose intentions remained to be seen.

 Perhaps Poseidon should hold me in contempt,
 For my disregard of his powers were apparent.
 As I cut through the volatile waves,
Panic should have fallen upon me like an eager avalanche,
 Yet it never came . . .
 For the moon was the Cheshire cat,
 grinning amidst the dark clouds.
 Comforting,
 as the ocean turned green.

Derek Morch

Country Music Capitol

I remember a time;
when the hills belonged to the morning mists

The streams with sunlit beams
were kissed

Trees grew in an unruly fashion
harboring birds of all kinds

Who sang their songs and eased our minds

People moved at an easier pace and
wore soft smiles on every face

Each knew their neighbor and
cared for the same

And now we have a new name
With neon lights burning
But it nd can't fulfill the yearning
for mother nature's beauty
on an Ozark Mountain morning.

Mary Farris

Roses Of Life

If life is represented by the roses, life could bloom into a beautiful flower.
The bud of a rose is life beginning, the death of a rose is life ending.
When they are is bloom, it makes the heart bloom with happiness.
Death of the roses make the heart feel gloomy.

The roses represent different stages of life.
White roses are pure, and so is the first breath of life.
It also happens to be another beautiful creation of God's.
White roses are purity of the heart, with a pure heart life can be rewarding.

Pink roses represent friendship, friendship is very important through life.
Friends are needed when happiness and sadness need to be shared.
Life can be happier when it is shared by friends, and friends help the sadness of life.

The red rose is for the love in the heart.
The special person that will share the life that is meant to live.
The red rose will show the love for each other.

The yellow rose shows happiness in life.
Life can always be a yellow rose, but it is up to each person.
Make a happy life, and the rose will represent life the way it should be.

Of course roses die, and does life and happiness.
Therefore, every rose comes with a thorn, maybe that is why God created the rose.
Roses are beautiful and so is life, roses die and so dies life.

Diane R. Burkart

Car Trip Poem

Car Trip.
Bump bump goes the car,
Bump, bump, thumps your sister's hand on your back.

Your pillow, the only thing you can trust.
That strange yellow line on the road talks to you.

Skip, skip goes your CD, Garth Brooks now sounds like Gangster rap.
Your back hurts, the seat won't back any further.

A pillow is thrown by your sister.
Then feet, then nails, peace comes.
Thank you, Wendy's.

The smell of toxic fumes rises.
Gas Station, home of dirty bathrooms and junk food.

You are back on the highway.
But the smell persists
Suddenly you feel light and free and at peace.

You see out the window, stoned hippies in VW Buses,
Old people in leather on motorcycles.

The world comes crashing back, with a shake.
You fall asleep.
Bump bump goes the car, Car Trip.

Andrew L. Brown

Untitled

I came upon your empty room
Though darkened — breathing life.
Your shirt was there — upon the floor
And writhed to reach your tomb.
A sock within a shoe was rife
Within its wrinkled doom.
Your pipe of wood could not cry out
But, stately, held you more
Than any photograph or breath
Myself could then adore.

I flew to follow your ascent
Determined — heaven bent.
The gates of marble would not yield
Beyond, your voice concealed.
Cursing heaven I charged the doors to part.
In vain was my appeal.

Genevieve Mezzanotte

This Is A Boyfriend

A boyfriend is that special man you could write a book
about, the one you love to be with and couldn't do without.

A boyfriend is a gentle look, a hand within your own; He
always make you proud to feel that you are his alone.

A boyfriend understands your moods and laughs at things you say,
he see's you when you're at your worst and loves you anyway.

A boyfriend is the one you kiss and make up with again
when there's a little difference of opinion every now and then.

He is that Special Man who shares all that you're
dreaming of and gives a magic meaning to the wonder that is love.

Kelli D. Wilson

The Lover's Folly

I stand alone with my life in dismay,
Sometimes I just refuse to have some fun,
For I was relapsed to grieving all day,
And remain alone in need of loved ones.
My mind impenetrable and one tracked,
Many tries with no significant gain,
Though many lonely hearts and still I lack,
So many hearts stays empty, yet full of pain.
So used to rejection my heart is hard,
Yet another rejection is still feared,
But rumors get around and love is marred,
And one gets mad so the other is reared.
So now my lonely heart will try in need,
And this time I promise it will succeed.

Charles Wharton Jr.

A Path To Follow

Now and then I pause and ponder on life's complexities.
is it not better to go aware and comprehending into the lion's den,
knowing full well that you might walk off with the pot of gold at
the end of the rainbow, or if given a choice remain serenely in your
rose garden, content with the wafted scent of roses, hoping the
thorns will avoid you.

The young are devoid of complacency; the old secure within the rose
garden, willing to let all proffered experiences drift like petals
in a storm. Yet there is complacency amongst the young and
Dragon Killers amongst the worldly. Let each man decide for
himself which course to follow. In the game called Life, one
needs spectators as well as participants. If you venture forth
from your cloistered pinnacle, be prepared for upheavals as well
as joyous fulfillment. There are sorrows in both.
Be prepared to deal with human frailty and even bitter disappointments.
Be grateful for your ability to become involved. Challenge is for
the living. Serenity for the long time dead.

Harriet Hoffman-Stern

Without Her

The people shout today,
They say "hip hip, hurray!"
Celebrate this glorious day,
The fourth of July
Is now! Today!
So why do I feel
Everything is so unreal?
That I should try
To be happy, not cry,
Even though I deserve to die.
For I have nothing to live for in this world.
Without her face or gold,
Without her love as pure as pearls,
Without my angel, my girl,
Without her I shall never again be whole.

Biana Lupa

I Wonder . . .

I wonder . . .
About life . . . Hopes, promises, and dreams
about feelings . . . Some seen and some unseen
about friends . . . a Kodak moment, heart to heart
about family . . . Intensely, bonding from the start
about memories . . . Kaleidoscope of years gone by
about time . . . Ever questioning how or why
about love . . . nurtured through the years
about reasons . . . disappointments, heartaches, tears
about relationships . . . Broken at a whim
about honesty . . . Stretching very thin
about faces . . . Sometimes masking what's inside
about eyes . . . Showing hurt you cannot hide
about God . . . Watching over everyone
about faith . . Trusting that Thy will be done
about joy . . . Total opposite of sorrow
about yesterday . . . And what's in store for me tomorrow

I wonder . . .

Carol Jean Fernandez

May In A Wood

I will take time to note
each virgin leaf, each tender shoot
the bracket fungus moist and thick
the drooping whorls of Solomon's seals

I will watch a chipmunk scuttle
through a leafy thicket
near a fallen birch
and stop short to wonder once again
at the wind's music
as it plays the treetops bow to string
like a first violinist

I will catch the rise and fall
of the wild geese
recalling that December day
they skidded to a landing on the frozen pond

I will breathe the breath of life renewed
and imbued as my soul
and when the day's light pales
and a hush falls
I will remember

Bernadette L. Johnson

Turbid

Wandering dark hallways
Towards the empty rooms with windows
As I'm staring at the ground,
I see just what I conjure
Where my fantasies abound . . .

Finding light in darkness,
Not a habit but a need
I search the lonely midnight sky for stars.
I reach for windows, ladders, light . . .
But can't reach past my bars.

Angels tease and torture
If they always fade away,
But faith's destructive morsels are my bread.
Through dark and teary lonely night
I search my turbid head

For memories, the portals out;
The sole grace I can see
As I wander endless halls of empty night;
I need, I greed, I bleed, I need!
I fumble with my light . . .

Shawn D. Rodriguez

Another Day

Without love; we walk the warm
And sunny earth stone cold!
With all of our riches,
Money, silver and gold!

As we look and set ourselves;
Higher than others!
We some times find ourselves;
Looking down even on our own brothers!

Getting ahead as far as we can;
No time for children or the Son Of Man!
You never see the homeless eating out of our trash cans;
We find ourselves way too busy for such a nobleman!

Ask yourself how can I change?
What words can I say?
Will there be time?
Do I have another day?

Niki Mosteller

Elusive Peace

I've finally lost it, that elusive thing,
what is this peace of mind.

I've been searching all my life,
yet still I cannot find.

That secure feeling, being full,
resting easy in the lull,

Waiting for the perfect end,

Search forever, never bend.

Pamela S. Spina

Love in Glorious Bloom

Sunrise, with its robust tapestry of color, unfolds
With vivid splashes of sensuality
As love with its unbroken rhythm, its delicate harmony
The timeless supplication of divine succour
Her wild and unique beauty, visual magic
Like a cut-out against the cloud-torn morning sky
Her body twists and undulates
As a mountain stream flowing through the fertile wilderness
The scent is sweet, yet has a hint of tangy spice
She is a garden of earthly delights
With ceaseless buffeting of wind,
Her emotions stuck like a cork,
In the frothing bottleneck of regrets
An exquisite delicacy, beautiful and solitary
The empty sounds, huge vivid butterflies, dance overhead.

Norton Saidleman

My Favorite Place

Far across the meadow, just inside the wood,
Beside the rippling brook, the weeping willow stood.
On the hot days of summer, seeking a place of secrecy
I steal away to my favorite place beneath the willow tree.
Oft times I sit and listen to the rippling of the brook
Or lie down on the meadow grass and across the sky I look.
I watch the clouds chase each other across the deep blue sky
And watch in awesome wonder how the birds can fly.
Sometimes I just close my eyes and listen to the sound
Of the birds in the trees and the creatures on the ground.
Other times I see the meadow flowers swaying in the breeze
And watch the leaves dancing all through the trees.
When the summer days are over and the leaves begin to fall,
And in the sky above me the wild geese call,
I bid farewell to my favorite place beneath the willow tree
Knowing, come next summer, it will again beckon me.

Vergie M. Lovelace

City Winter Rain

The wind blows against
my face.
My skin prickles.
Glimpses of grey
as my eyes blink out
and ears burn with the cold.
I try to catch my breath.
My lungs ache
and my mouth is parched.
A building becomes
passing shelter from the wind.
I huddle down inside my coat for warmth.
Rumble, boom.
Rain splatters my face
before I can open my umbrella.
Tiny droplets
plop plop off the edge.
Colorful domes
bobbing, bobbing
people in the falling rain.

Tara Miller

Just Three Words

Last sunset shone into his eyes
as he braved his religion and followed
fought the demons straining his soul
but only let go to faith
he left the hearts of cherished behind
counted the second hand
faded from the life he came to love
but was going somewhere grand
I looked into his dieing eyes
ashamed to say three words
But somehow my feelings untrapped my heart
minutes before his death
I said what it took a lifetime to shed
in one moment that still echoes
I Love You
silence then filled the seconds ahead
and his eyes took on a glow
I regret I held these three words back
until it was time for my father to go

Michael Weinmann

Yesterday

Only in the eyes of yesterday
Do we have a chance to see

The things that maybe we should
Have done a little differently.

Like had a smile not been forced,
To have been more gracious in the past.

To have learned to calm our temperament,
Perhaps to help a friendship last.

To have listened to our children,
To have known their thoughts and fears.

To understand their hardships and wipe
Away their tears.

Now it's only in our yesterdays that
We seem to have regrets, with actions taken,
Words exchanged, how soon do we forget.

Now I know its not the things to do,
That is to dwell upon the past,

But maybe, just maybe it will help a friendship last.

Thomas A. Grundy Jr.

Arrival

We wait anxiously
My husband, son and I
Checking and re-checking the time of arrival.

We've done this before.
This time it's different
This time we're meeting
our first grandchild for the first time.

It's a long trip from Sweden
It's been a long wait for us.
Finally, we see her, our daughter,
tall, lovely, graceful,
Holding our grandson close to her chest.

We cannot believe it
We kiss her, then grab for our grandson
each in turn kissing him
And searching into his eyes
for some glimmer of recognition.

Who does he look like?
This unlikely combination of Swedish and Jewish genes.
He smiles — we melt. It was well worth the wait.

Gloria Rider

Just A Song

Anastasia . . . I wonder who you are
A tiny body, cold against my lips
My father cried
I listened, haunted by a sweetness I would never know

Knock, knock knockin' on Heaven's door
She waited to die
Brightness, care, loving; was it enough
I listened, questioning the goodness of God

Like a Rock, unencumbered by the weight
He ceased to be there
What shall I do, what shall I do
I listened, finding comfort in things never said

Just a Song
What melody will float on waves of air,
The ending of my life, once there
Will anyone recognize the winging essence

Oh God! Will I merit a song
Will my soul not float on the waves,
Perhaps . . . I am the only one to see
I listen; my time has not yet come

Vickie Barker

Death?

Does death leave an empty space in your world?
A space that someone special once fulfilled.
What is death, we all need to learn
Will the people once living ever return?

Where do they go, what do they do?
I'd like to know the person who knew.
Will the passed-away just leave us behind?
All they've experienced we have yet to find.

What they have done, what they have made
Will their shadow be forgotten and fade?
We don't remember coming into the world, so will we remember leaving?
So while you have time, make your life worth proceeding.

I guess the living will have to assume
Could this be the doorway that leads you to doom?
Is this a stop or is this yet another road with a bend?
Death is just like a book-you won't find out until the end.

Nicole Campbell

My Niece Miry

I witnessed a miracle on this awesome mid-night,
But, not just once I witnessed it twice.

It was December 4th, a cool and calm winter night,
That the test of faith would meet a spiritual fight.

Mommy was in "The Garden" with angles being courageous and strong,
When all of a sudden we noticed things were going quite wrong.

Now, mommy with Jesus and daddy with mom,
Made all stay as peaceful as a verse from the Psalms.

The staff was so efficient, attentive and quick,
In the presence of angles and the anointing so thick.
We barely took notice of the enemies hit,
'Cause you were back with us lickety-split.

Well, that nasty old enemy thought he'd try it again,
But, because of God's mercy was sent back to his den.

We all prayed believing in our own private way,
And in our faith remained on this miraculous day.

Yes — My Very Special "Miry"

I witnessed a miracle on this awesome mid-night,
But, not just once I witnessed it twice.

Donna Kautz-Sunder

Welcome Home

Parched, barren and desolated;
he came to the top of the hill;
the hot wind blowing around him,
the sun beaming down on him.

And then he saw it —
a sight for his sore eyes,
covered by his chapped hands.

Palm trees, huts, people, and a lake!

With a new surge of purpose, he stumbled, then ran,
his fatigued body zigzagging across the desert.

The sight came closer; now birds could be seen —
both flying over and floating upon the lake.

The man, tripped and fell.

Impulsively, he continued on, crawling.
the sight which was so near,
now appeared far away.

He stopped and with the force of his lungs, screamed.
his eyes watered, so the man closed them.

"Welcome home," said the voice in his head.

Daniel Joseph Goodman

Self-Destruct

Getting arrested so much
Mom's stopped crying,
She new it was too late
her little boy was dying.
It was the streets he wanted to know
And came too know them too well,
His final destination is "Hell"
All he knew is to
Lie, cheat, destruct hurt and thieve,
His innocence he can no longer retrieve.
Emotions could no longer be felt,
Using the same drugs that he dealt.
Never appreciated the sun
until it would rain,
Body and mind completely numb
from cocain.

Brian Dailey

Romance On A String

I am waiting on this string; waiting for just one thing
Like a spider hanging there, hanging out in mid air
I try so hard to reach the top,
But when I get close it seems I drop
I drop, I drop into the air
Always knowing that you're not there
Closer, closer here I go
I'm moving up, but very slow,
Will I make it; yes, I'll try
But it seems so far to the top
To reach the point that I want
I wonder, I wonder if it's true
That all of this is just for you
I see your love I see your care
But, my life is filled with tears
Can I ever forget these fears,
I want your love, I need it now
Please don't leave me hanging here
Pull me up, let me climb
I'll reach the top, I just need time.

Kim Atkinson

His Loving Care

Do not be troubled in your heart,
God knows all your problems before they start.
Jesus said, "Trust in God and trust also in me,"
With his purpose completed, He'll set you free.
If in your life, there was never a problem,
How would you learn that God could solve them?
During problems, people watch us, and that's a fact;
They are always curious to see just how we react.
Problems may come unexpected, many or few,
And they could result in His cleansing you.
When problems come, we need not evaluate them,
Rather consider, they could be to draw us to him.
Storms and problems hurt us even when they are our brothers,
But they could be for training us how we might help others.
The Psalmist was calm walking, not into the valley, but through,
Look up, remember the promise of God, "Never will I leave you."
Just trust in the Lord with all your heart,
Don't stop to worry, He will do his part.
Regardless of circumstance, you can have real peace;
Knowing that God's loving care for you will never cease.

Vivian Tate

One Never Knows

One never knows
What road life may take,
nor the love that it makes,
The feelings that may break,
Causing you to quiver and quake.

One never knows
How love can make you feel,
Left to wonder if it is real,
Bringing a knee down to kneel,
For a love, wishing to seal.

One never knows
What road makes the heart end,
Hoping to find one that'll mend,
Many messages left yet to send,
For a love, needing to defend.

One never knows
The changes that may go askew,
Dreaming and hoping we are few,
Only wanting to make the love fresh and new,
Because I know — I love you!

David Giles

Everlasting Love

I looked into your eyes so deep,
Little knowing that you would weep,
You make me feel like I can fly,
Like our love could never die,
I try to treat you like the shaman of love,
You're the one I'm always thinking of,
I love you now and shall forever,
But can you love me, now or ever,
I think about you all the time,
Your eyes, hair, and a voice like a chime,
The way you walk, they way you smile,
For you I would walk a thousand miles,
Our love contains our immortality,
To find it we change our own morality,
Whether it be as a lover or as a friend,
My love for you will never end!

Joe Alton

Sahara

Life is fun in so many ways.
Life makes you cry at the end of a day.
Life gives, you joy at the start of the day and
it takes it a way in a moment time.
Life is a challenge in many ways.
Life is a moment in every way and in my
life she is the challenge the joy the fun and
the tears in that one moment in my life she
is like the desert a challenge in a moment life.
She is Sahara the precious moment in my life.
The little life in one great moment. The biggest
challenge in one day. Sahara moments never end.
And the love grows in every moment of our lives.

Patricia Gallo

Ode To The Soul

Oh precious soul, hidden in man
Thy God, thy Creator is calling again
Lost out in sin, covered in flesh
He knows you are weary, He knows your distress

God beckons to you through the love of His Son
Whose blood was shed for you to overcome
Your sin, your weakness, your guilt and shame
His purpose is Saviour, Jesus Christ is His name

Look to the Cross forgiveness to find
Believe with the heart, not with the mind
Humbled before Him without reservation
Confessing Him Lord is the way of salvation

The Holy Spirit will come to guide you in faith
As a new creation to live by His grace
There is no recompense that you can afford
Just trust Him as Saviour, and praise Him as Lord

Larry J. Redus

Untitled

Oh dear Lord how You soothe me in my darkest hour
Bending down and placing Your gentle palm on my fiery cheek
I am Your child and I know that I am loved.
My tears pour out trying desperately to reach You,
You were mysteriously and lovingly there.
I know I am loved. I love You
Lord, I feel so clean and calm in Your presence.
So clean, so clean in my clean
white night gown and my clean, red hot,
fiery cheeks that boil the tears that run down them.
Feeling so small in the presence of Your pillars,
I search for Your eyes and cannot find them,
but I feel them in Your gentle palm.

Angeline Macak

Daphne Kay

My little girl . . . no matter what . . .
Though she is no longer a tot . . .

I know she's grown and all that stuff . . .
So what . . . Without her, life wouldn't matter much . . .
She is my diamond in the rough . . .

She and I together grew . . .
Mother-Daughter — Comrade-friend
. . . She has an unforgettable grin . . .

Those of you who are fortunate to know her . . .
are richer by far . . .
She is my radiant a star . . .

Her long chestnut waves and eyes of green . . .
Her moves . . . So graceful, as if upon the Silver Screen . . .

Daphne is the Dawn, as beautiful as the ocean's foam . . .
When it has touched the land, and rolls back to sea again . . .
. . . As if She reaches to touch your hand . . .
. . . Instead leaving treasures in the sand . . .

. . . Her gentle Spirit must be upon a Golden Chariot . . .
. . . For the Angels marked her when she was a child and gave her that . . .

'Alice In Wonderland Smile'
Nona Kay Johnson

Oklahoma Teardrops

I can't believe the Devastation I seen upon my set.
The building all in pieces, I never will forget.
They carried the children, Few alive so many gone,
Tiny little body's they carried in their arms.
I find myself standing outside amongst the rain,
To hide the tears I shed for them and feel the family's pain.
I reach out my hands, hold up my arms in hope that they will see,
The Love I send this Valentines is sent with love from Me.

So many dreams been shattered, futures torn apart, I hope that they
will see the Love I send them with this heart.
I've heard so often, the words too late in pain,
I wish I said I Love You, Oh Lord just once again.

You never know from day to day if someone you love will be taken away,
Open your heart, and reach out your arms wide, let them know now
how precious inside,
The feelings you show will last oh so long,
Please don't wait for them to be gone.

Send flowers or candy, A big bright red heart,
If miles are between you, a phone call will start.

To the families and children who's hearts are so blue,
I send all my love this Valentine's to you.

Lorna Thompson

Lady Of Fire, Man Of Stone

An angel in a shroud of flame flying high . . .
A man etched from stone, with an empty heart.
He knows that her fire can fill the void
And his strength can give her balance
. . . And solid ground to stand upon.
The messenger, the mother, the red-tailed hawk . . .
The hunter, the father, the brown cave, bear . . .
Unicorns and dragons, born from their love
The love and magic of legends foretold
. . . Lady of fire, man of stone, a world of life.
A union between earth and fire can form
This has been proven, look at the stars!
With cleansing flames and a stone foundation
Their love will be able to heal their world . . .
. . . And in turn each other's hearts . . .
. . . And the hearts of others.

Aric Slagenweit

Thank You God

Thank you God for being so good to me
For all the things you've let me seen
You gave me life for a many of years
So I know that time is soon to be near

You are here when there is right and wrong
And helping me to learn how to be strong
Taking me through the good and bad
Pick me up when my heart is sad

Never ever have you left my side
Also taught me I have to strive
God please do one thing for me
Help me keep my soul free

Dear God, I will always cherish each day
Because I have not pasted away
Many of family and friends have gone
God please hold me and make me strong

Patricia Russell

Hey Blue . . .

Hey Blue! — Did I hear you call that pitch a strike?
   Was it even close to the plate?

   What do you mean that pitch was ball four?
   From here it looked really great.

Hey Blue! — I think you need to borrow "my" glasses!
   Your call left our runners stranded.

   How could you call that hit a foul ball?
   Weren't you watching where it landed?

Hey Blue! — What do you mean he is safe at first?
   Didn't you see him throw his bat?

   How can you say the throw was too late?
   What kind of a call is that?

Hey Blue! — Wasn't he out at second base?
   His foot never touched the bag.

   How can you say he is out at third?
   I know he was under the tag.

Hey Blue! — What do you mean "You are out of here!"?
   I am innocent — can't you see?

   I don't know why you're in such a bad mood
   And then taking it out on me.

Donna J. Lawson

Be Encouraged

To be encouraged, what does it mean?
To some it's just a song and doesn't mean a thing.
You hear those words every where you go
From parents, TV, and even the radio.
It is a song that is sung by William Becton and Friends.
It tells you to keep trying even to the end.
Good doesn't always happen, bad times come around.
But you'll get through if you listen to my words as I break encouraged down.
   E — means to be "enlightened" in all that you do
   N — means "never give up" go all the way through
   C — means be "careful" with the choices that you make
   O — means that "obstacles are on the paths you take
   U — means "understand" what you read and what you hear
   R — means to "remember" those who are so near
   A — means get "active" don't just sit still
   G — means to have "gratitude" that you still have the will
   E — means to be "educated" don't be dumb, but smart
   D — means to "decide" to listen to your heart.

To be encouraged means different things to me and to you
Just make sure you are encouraged in all that you do.

Jerel Gadberry

Untitled

I'm left alone to cry my tears, and left
alone to face my fears. Friends and loved
ones are no longer by my side, to wish
me good luck and have their arms open wide.
I miss them so much, near or far;
but I know they are my guiding stars.
Sometimes I stare at the ocean so deep
and wide, it's equivalent to tears I cried.
Sometimes I think if I was in the still of the
night with no one to comfort me, I'd
reach out for them and them alone,
and if they turned their back no one
would be there to lead me home.

Tiara Da'Nette Randle

The Emerald Coast

Sacred of time and place
   White sand beaches, emerald green water
      breakers crashing,
      shore receding

Sacred of time and place
   Birds flying, flocks calling
      herons gliding,
      gulls crying

Sacred of time and place
   Wind blowing, gales howling
      dunes drifting,
      sea grass waving

Sacred of time and place
   Light changing, sky transforming
      water glaring,
      shadows beckoning

Kevin Ann Oltjenbruns

Dreams Of You

I had so many dreams of You,
   of things we would say and things we would do . . .

Yet since you were born, it seems only a day
   so very tiny and quiet you lay . . .

When I saw you there
   Machines helping with care,
My very first thought was "It's not fair!!!"

After the machines, were all taken away,
It seems that the price was too great to pay . . .

The dreams I once had, are now dimming today,
As I bury my dreams, further and further away . . .

I just never once thought, that it would be so bad,
to watch you suffer, and me feeling so sad . . .

I guess dreams aren't dreams, until they come true.
So I have to be content, with only my dreams of you!!!

Carolyn S. Montoya

Year End, Year Begin

After the Thanksgiving turkey comes the Christmas ham,
Along with safe wishes for the boys of Uncle Sam.
We buy toys for the kids, and presents for others,
Especially for close friends, and our dads and mothers.
Remember most important, the paper of the year,
To us is our calendar, my dear.
That's the way dates, days and the year goes,
So be safe, be happy, on these words I close.

Wanda E. Mayle

411

The Greater Power

When the walls of the world seem to be closing in on you, don't worry for there is a greater power upon which you can depend;

When every step you take is doubtful and unpredictable, don't worry for there is a greater power that will give you certainty and strength;

When the hardships and troubles of life bring you down and you cease to find zest in what you do, don't worry for there is a greater power that will lift and invigorate your life;

When every one you turn to betrays or forsakes you, don't worry for your greater power will never betray you;

When you are in your deepest woes and despair, don't worry for the greater power looks upon you with a tender and loving eye;

When you feel like no one is with you and your friends have abandoned you, don't worry for your greater power will envelope you with so much love and comfort that you will not yearn for that external love from others;

When you are not accepted for who you are, where you've been and where you are going, don't worry for you are a torch of light that stands tall over all and gleams with the knowledge that Christ accepts you for who you are and what you will become in his loving arms.

Yadira A. Ortiz

Christmas

Christmas time is coming near,
   hear the children shout and cheer.
Just can't wait to get their gifts,
   Mommy, Daddy, here's our lists.
As the days draw nigh it seems,
   thoughts of treats now fill their dreams
Thankful we as parents be,
   knowing soon we'll have that tree.
The perfect spot has now been found,
   to set all gifts and presents round.
Take a moment if you please,
   to recollect your memories.
Of all the joys of Christmas past,
   and of the one true gift that lasts.
When upon a midnight clear,
   was announced that all might hear.
Of the Saviours birth so rare,
   a precious gift beyond compare.

Joyce Jensen

Silly Rhyme

At this stage I have no hair
On my mind is nary a care.
I really look forward to dinner time,
Though to be hand fed is not fine.

At Diaper change I would dare to scold
For often their hands are rough and cold.
It's different when they give a bath.
Sometimes they tickle and make me laugh.

When I move it's only barely
To actually go somewhere happens rarely.
The best I can manage is a feeble yell.
The response I get is "now what the hell?"

Most of my time is spent in slumber,
Meaningless days march on without number.
I dream not of things that may yet be,
But only some of what I used to see.

I have shadows and thoughts of things long past.
I wait at the styx for a crossing at last.
I'm resigned to whatever will be, will be.
I guarantee it's not easy to be ninety-three.

Jack Mason

In Vain

Spores in the air,
nowhere to go but away.
Bird gets pushed out of its nest,
before it can fly.
People work hard their whole lives,
to catch an unreachable dream.
A dog chases its tail.
A worm crawls on its belly longing for the clouds so infinitely high above, to receive its wish one day in the beak of a robin.
Climbing over one obstacle just gives a better view of the mine field ahead.
A moth flutters frantically in a spider web,
Escape will tear off its wings, and maim it for life.
Remaining will put it in the spider's gullet.
Everyone falls down,
knowing they'll have to stand up to fall down again.
Coins at the water's bottom collect dirt and amounted scum,
the moral of wishes.
The sun rises upon another day.

Bryan R. Dennis

Bewildered At Dusk

Slowly the darkness has fallen upon me.
My vision has faded
I've lost sight of my dream.

To sleep but a moment
To sway in sweet sunlight
To rest but a moment
is too long it seems.

I hold to my vision of sun not far past
I search for my sunshine
I long for my sight.

I seek for my sun light
I find it at last
I seem to have lost it somehow in the night
I seem to have lost it somehow in the night.

I cleave to my sunshine
United at last
And now that I've found it shines twice as bright.

I seek for my sunlight I find it at last
I seem to have lost it somehow in the night
I seem to have lost it somehow in the night.

Beverly Sampson

A Still Small Voice

Sitting in the company
of unspoken words — uneasy and confused;
crowded by the silence in my heart,
I hear whispers
first soft, soon stronger in a voice
so foreign and strange
only tongues of fire can interpret.
I wait. And listen. —
for a time that seems to never end
stillness anxiously breathing its last remains
these words that speak to my heart.
This voice speaking in a tongue
I now am only beginning to understand
as the voice
which cries aloud in the wilderness
that echoes from the mountaintops
down into the canyons of our world
is the same voice
which speaks to me
even in the silence of my heart.

Gordon V. Jardy Jr.

Some Play, Some Pray

You can hope, wish and bet all you want to or be thinking
That money will fall out of an azure sky your way
You can gamble and dally each day, make that (now) twice a day
Skip playing at odds with many chancings, it's best to pray
Losing more times than winning, doesn't it seem a bit ill?
Need one long have to take such a bitter pill
Try looking from nature's very real point, if you will
You can run, rip and wander in the way
Just like an old grass-hopper — to just hop and play
And in the cold of winter, it's quite hard to find a sure way
Have'en made no provisions for yourself — where will you stay?
Depending on this person or that one only long as they so say.
You can keep on playing and I'll keep on praying — that your eyes
Be clearly opened — can't you see now that's its God, and you
And the world? And still it's easier to deal with any of them all
When you're faithful, truthful and just pray
Stop the much playing (here and now) and work and pray
Now is the time, yes, surely it's today
No matter how you look at it, no matter what you say
Look around yourselves, see!! It's truly not a time for much play.

Zamounde Stanley Allie-El, Sr.

A Father's Gift

When I was born into this world
I was a bouncing blue-eyed girl
I would dance, sing, play and whirl
With not a worry in the world

I would sit beneath the apple tree
Wondering what I would grow up to be
My Dad had bought me a ten dollar guitar
I wondered if I would become a star

This guitar brought me so much pleasure
To describe my happiness would be hard to measure
When I was feeling a little blue
I would just sing a song or two

My dad never realized what a gift he had given
I will treasure the guitar as long as I'm living
He also send me to music school
And taught me to live by the golden rule

I'm a professional singer and it's an amazing thing
What a father and a ten dollar gift can bring
The guitar was a gift from a father's heart . . .
The story of how I got my start.

Anna M. Travis

Soulful Trespass

Two spirits meet . . . and in as much
are not in love but based on such — unknowingly
they feel and touch to tell what they will find.
If found the fit is comfortable
and seemingly affordable;
it then becomes desirable . . . each soul responds in kind.

When timely motives may be true;
however actions were undue,
perplexes both with what to do
and so they come . . . undone.
Left and mired in true detest
to sort emotional unrest,
a wounded heart that goes undressed
will find its comfort . . . none.

Exceedingly, the price to pay
to find a friendship . . . drift astray.
'twas barely born and gone away . . . the sorrow never ends.
Dilemma of misguided love corrected by the Lord above;
I pray that peace, on gentle dove,
endows these spirits . . . friends.

Charles T. Cann

My Lady My Valentine

You are of a great quality, with love, understanding and not selfish.
You make me happy and keep me smiling,
You are that special someone that give me
love and accept mine in return.
You brings out every ounce of joy within my
soul to share with you.
You are that special person, whom I shall
always need and miss, whenever we are apart.
You have accepted my love with an open heart
and soul, to brighten up my darkest night
whenever they may occur.
You always have the flames of love glowing
in your eyes, to let me see that love within.
You kiss my lips so softly and passionate
you makes my heart start pounding loud
and my blood running through my veins
like a runaway locomotive on a track of no return.
I hope the flame in your heart will always
burn, I love you my lady, my valentine

Jacky L. Haynes

When I Am Gone

When I am gone,
    do not put me in a box in the ground.
For this would be dark,
    and close, and depressing.

Rather, please scatter my ashes
    in the woods, or along the ocean, or in the mountains.

For when I am gone,
    I want to watch a brilliant sunset;
    to see Spring bursting out in the redbuds and dogwoods;
    to hear the soft hissing of the waves,
    or the crashing of thunder as it echoes through the hills and
    valleys.

And finally, I want you to remember me
    not from looking at a marker with my name on it;
But in the sigh of the wind,
    the flash of the lightning,
    the smell of the rain,
    and the sight of new blossoms.

Do these things in remembrance of me,
    when I am gone.

Edsel D. Stewart

Between Friends

I never had a friend,
I could tell a secret to.
One that I could trust.
Until I met you.

You taught me how
to believe in myself
That I too had the courage,
not to give into doubts.

You thought me that strength
comes from the soul.
To always be confident
to reach for my goals.

I took your advice
the wisdom you shared.
I became strong
I was no longer scared.

Thank you my friend for believing in me,
you brought out the best that was hidden
in me.

Dora Kearney

He's My Little Bitty Buddy

He's my little bitty buddy, he's my son, and my pal
He helps me feed the chickens
He helps me with the cows
And he asks me daddy, can I do it now
He's my little bitty buddy, he's my son,
and my pal.

He's my little bitty buddy, he's my son, and my pal.
He gets up in the morning
and he hollows at the soul.
He wants to feed the chickens,
He wants to feed the cows.
He's my little bitty buddy, he's my sons.

Gerry P. Nail

So Why Be Afraid To Die?

Why? Family and friends let us rejoice this day
Why? This soul that past paid its way
Why? Because God took his life for us to survive
Why? So his people could live, so he was willing to die
Why? Fear no evil nor darkness enter into thy light
Why? Because all of God's children must pay the price
Why? To join him in heaven and begin a new life
Why? He said "My children" I'm coming to get what's mine
Why? My father took me for you, so you are for me
Why? I come for your sins, to set you free
Why? Your job is completed so rest thy soul
Why? My child "Come Go With Me" fear no more
Why? So don't be afraid to die a soul is taken every day
Why? You never know when he's coming your way

Tekakwitha Jefferson

Fly Away

Got to say "Goodbye!" to everyone
I'm going away,
gonna sail into the setting sun.

Have to climb the hill
and take a last look at the town.
One last look at the town that has been my home.
As I look, may face turns to a frown

Hung around all the hangouts for a last time
Most everyone has left anyway.
How I wish I could stay!
But I have to fly away.

Brian A. Sarge

Broken Dreams

There is nothing worse in the world
than to lose something you cherish
Or to come close to something you've always wanted
and to sit and watch and see it perish
Coming close to the dreams you've always dreamed
And watching as those dreams die
and are torn away forever more
With nothing more left in life
With no more dreams left in store
than those of pain and endless strife.

You pull yourself together
and try to dream new dreams
And try your best to figure out
What it all should mean.
But every time you reach a goal
You compare it to what you have lost
Wishing that you could restore
The bridge you burnt and crossed.

Amanda Lauren Port

Passing Days

And   foremost   is
   Confronting   the pile of
Massed failures that
          Preclude the   whole issue   being resolved.

   And   give   the permission   and find forgiveness.
Start   to produce   the most focused   beam.

      A western   wind ascends
Steps   into the   portal   salutes us
   Transform   all sorrows and   our
      Great-hearted   soul   soars.

The   vagabond   thoughts that   fetter flow
                              must
cease.

Nurture   green awakenings of
      the soul in our Tenure here
                         Adopt a vital   stance.
No   lead   pants.

Theodore Knerr

No Way Out

Stale air.
Starched air.
Nothing moves.
Nothing's there.
Clenched fists.
Enraged hands.
Pounding against, the empty air.
Pounding against, the nothing that's there.

Folding Fingers.
Thrusting knuckles.
Hitting the air,
where there's nothing there.

Struggling to break through the invisible barriers.
Struggling to get out from the inside.
Struggling against the emotions.
Struggling against the invisible barriers.
Only to find, that there's no escaping
what's in your mind.

Donald Eric Reynolds

Liberty

I'm alone . . .
In each instant, in all the fullness of my being
Project your beautiful figure — unforgettable image!
I feel the performance of your body, the heat that irradiates from
your bosom, wandering and caressing me . . .
I feel your absence, a sadness traces my face
My eyes bear lakes of tears

I'm alone . . . In each instant
I'll seed your love, I'll illuminate my ruined soul
I'll not let anyone sing victories of remote times,
In my broken heart, I'll turn my back
To voices against you and, I will trust you

I'm alone . . . alone, thinking of you; I can't touch you — alone! . . .
Only in this homogeneous dream, in morbid pleasure,
thrown in the bonfire of time; In the irrational world . . .
Those that believe in you oh, beautiful image!
Oh, beautiful premeditated dream! By those that believe
That the Liberty is the reason of human existence. By those that arise
the voices against those that devour intelligence, constructing a world
of terror. I'm alone . . . alone, In the world where war is the daily sustenance
Oh, beautiful image! Perhaps one day . . . Perhaps! . . .

Emmanuel Araujo

Memories

Can you remember when you were only a child?
    Days passed swiftly by, no sorrows, no sadness,
    no pain or tears.
Everything was happiness that happen in those
    early years.

Time passed — you grew older,
    Time changed then you began to understand.
Heartaches rolled up like mountains high,
    shadows filled the sky.

Oh, if I could live my life over, things would
    be so different now.
Things I used to think weren't important are
    the things I think are important now.

There is one who stands at the right hand of the
    Heavenly Father.
The offer he gives is free, the price he paid
    was on Calvary, that price was for you and me.

Sue Graham Hudgens

She Was A Nectarine

She was one among many
    Sitting in the glowing, warm beams of you
    waiting to be chosen in the market place.
She did not have the most perfect skin.
    It was discolored and had the roughest of texture.
She did not have the most perfect fuzz.
    For it was not soft and sensual like the others
    It did not have the purest of hues for high delight.
She did not have the most perfect form.
    It was a bit mushy to the touch
    It was of mutation and out of shape.
Before long she was secluded, sitting in the mellow tones
of moonlight. They say what you see is what you get. But what
they did not get was that beneath her less than perfect skin,
fuzz, and form was the sweetest taste known to existence.

Sara Lynn Nelson

In Search

Sometimes we walk down a barren path . . .
In solitude we take each step.
Driven by no focus.
Our journey out of reach.
Anticipating a darkened trail;
Only to view the light.
In search of the moment
Occupied by space;
And love.

Nina Franco

A Letter To Mom

Dear Mom this is something
that I want you to know,
I care, I love you and I need you so.
I know that you cry, and shed your tears,
I caused you pains throughout the years,
but now all those bad times,
are all behind
I'll show you new love,
and peace of mind.
So all the time that I made you cry,
you can be sure
that they've all gone by.
You are my mother
and I love you so
just believe me, I'll never let you go.

Joseph D. Lopez

Rhyme And Rhythm

A poem consisting of rhythm and rhyme
With thoughts from the inner soul,
Seems to withstand the testing of time,
Which is truly a poet's goal.

Poems memorized as a child in school
Gave us knowledge of things in the past,
With rhyme and rhythm as the artist's tool
Etched in our hearts to last.

Joyce Hopple Albert

Reflection Of The Wooden Cross

    This cross we give you made of gold,
Is just a small part of the story told
    The cross our Savior bore that day,
Was made of wood and stained with blood.
    So when you wear this cross of gold
Remember the love of the story told.
    He gave His life that we may live
His most precious gift . . . only He could give.

Loretta Buonamici

Songs For Paul's Tie (Save The Children)

Country towns and country spaces
Little lines are going places
Ribbons of washing pegged on the line
Crossing the valleys from your town to mine.

Teeming cities, foreign stations
Wire lines connecting nations
Our children's help depends on that line
Bridging the future from your land to mine.

Power lines are going places
War-torn lands our world disgraces
Let's reach out with understanding
A better life for all demanding.

Open lines, communication
Peace will heal our generation
Hands clasped in friendship it works every time
Pledging our hopes and our love on that line.

Kaye Cimini

Beautiful Pictures

I wish I could find the words to describe
    The beauty I see before my eyes.
Pictures etched on the window panes
    Jack Frost is the artist the children exclaim.
Scenes so beautiful yet icy cold.
    Such delicate beauty for all to behold.

Delicate beauty touched my heart.
    Creating memories, as soon we must part
For icy pictures don't remain long.
    The sun comes up and soon they are gone.

I remember when we still had our tree.
    How it looked after we had a deep freeze.
With drops of rain frozen like glass
    Sparkling like diamonds on the trees and the grass.
It glittered and sparkled, it glowed like a jewel.
    My spirit lifted, my faith renewed.

Only God could create so much glory
    The even a tree could tell the story.

Patricia Irene Weber Blake

Dogs

Some people like weenie dogs,
Some people like big dogs,
Some people like other dogs,
But most people like hot dogs.
Brandon Harris

Wales, My Father's Homeland

My heart is in a valley
So very far away
There are my roots, my father's home
There near to Colwyn Bay.

I saw them once, then had to say
My bitter, sad goodbyes,
And turn away, and leave them there
As tears welled in my eyes.

They're there across my native land,
Across a barrier sea
The valley, river, fields and bay,
The things so dear to me.

At last. I'm going back again
To have my hoped for dream,
To see once more with thankfulness
My valley still is green.
Grace Roglis

We Are Risen

Thought
talk
action
regarding
remains

Dissected
without
disruption
disruption
reigns

Ribboned
flowered
marbleized

Time
honored
discarded
recycled
remains

lovingly returned
Mother womb reclaimed.
Kathleen M. Regan

On The Other Side?

The river is to wide to cross
alone as I look at the pathetic
waves below and scream the
fears my soul is to only know.
I hate the wind that blows
these memories around in my
head while all I'm trying to
do is sleep.
I can't stop dreaming . . .
almost spring and in the
ground lies the hero. In the
depth of the sky I see his face,
hear the voice that calls me
while I forget. No longer do I
believe in the things forever,
I will leave the way I came in.
Shellie Goettsch

Me, Myself, And I

I'm naturally sweet
A guy you want to meet
If you think I am a shriek
You might as well be a freak
I'm so fine
I got more girlfriends than nine
I'm full of love and joy
I'm an extraordinary boy
Don't ask me why
I named this poem me, myself, and I
Since I wrote it down
I took it to town
But all I did was turn around
I wanted some money
So I could buy something for my honey

Thank you for reading
Me, myself, and I
At least I did try
Adrian Jones

The Four Seasons

Summer is hot,
summer is cool,
because there is no school.

Fall is cold,
fall is not cool,
because there is no
swimming pool.

Winter is fun,
winter is nice,
but there is a ton of ice.

Spring is warm,
spring is fair,
because there's love
in the air.
Rachelle Lutz

Spirit

Spirit is a stallion
Breaking all barriers
Helping defeat evil
It can be broken
Broken by despair and failure.
Ryan Chamberlain

Graveyard

Go inside a graveyard when
everybody is asleep,

Stay over night and let the dead
Get your soul and your spirit,

Let the dead take you under the
Grave and eat you up,

The dead will throw the bones out
Of the grave.

Only your soul will be left.
Robert Bissett

Medicine

Penicillin
Prozac
Tylenol
A hug from your mommy.
Sarah Hood

Death Of A Vine

What's life all about?
A seed begins to sprout
In soil that is fine
Growing like a vine
Reaching out to give
Happy to live
Changes in environment
Lead to being spent
Blown about
By winds of doubt
Confused, but clinging on
Abused, but determined
Injured, oh to be so firm
Rotting takes hold like a germ
It eats away the past
Destroying the present so fast
Looking for tenderness
Giving up on kindness
There is no one here to care
So why should I?
Laura Peterson

James' Song

To stand beside a running brook
that whispers a thousand tales,
running softly to the ocean's door
to catch a glimpse of sails.

To wander free across the hills
just to see the other side;
and hear the wind sing so softly,
"follow me, I'll be your guide."

To breathe in a thousand flower's
in the warmness of spring
or to feel rain falling softly
touching like angel wings.

To rest beneath the loving bough
of a great protecting tree,
while watching the great silver birds
glide majestically free.

To lay down in the dew strewn grass
and cool your tired brow,
to know that yesterday is gone.
That forever is now.
Trevia S. Elson

Dreams

There — some place east of nowhere
is the realm of all my dreams.
In sleep I drift out to there
far more often now, it seems.

For there my mind can set free
those images it holds in store.
Vivid scenes that I can see
much clearer now, than before.

In these scenes fate will cast
those that I knew in that day.
We meet again in times past,
they exist — then fade away.

Dreams are more than one quick trance.
Each is a gift sent to be.
They provide that desired chance;
to rest, while our thoughts roam free.

Each night to new dreams I'll wend
knowing when found each will share;
pleasant time for me to spend,
there — some place east of nowhere.
David E. Hubler

Youth's Bliss

Chaos
in the cerebral vortex
void of simplicity
empty of logic.
Whispered screams
echo in the loud silence
rippling in an empty pond
of hated love.
My friendly enemies
with angry joy
build my decrepitude.
I am full of emptiness
so starved, I can consume no more.
Thus, I fill myself to the brim
with a nothingness
that is something
like the hot, piercing chill
of loneliness.

Victoria Pitsker

Comanche Of The Seventh

Once there was a buckskin,
The seventh calvary he was in,
Captain Keogh was his driver,
Comanche was a sole survivor,
Of the battle they couldn't win.

Lindsay Nelson

Montana Winter

He stands there straight and tall
His hat pulled way down low
The wind cuts through him like a knife
He's boot deep in the snow.

He presses forward blindly
Against his better sense
He finds the missing calf at last
Entangled in the fence.

With the baby on his shoulders
He struggles to the road
His troubled mind is eased at last
He barely feels his load.

Cowboys have to love their work
It's surely not the pay
But he feels just like a millionaire
On this cold Montana day.

Larry Dubrul

Untitled

You know I love you
let's stay together forever
and keep things going strong.

We love much more
each and every day
I hope you never go away

You are mine and I am yours
We belong together
to love each other

We went out on a date
We came home late
then you told me you had
to go away

Someday we will live
to love again.

Reanna Burrola

X

A carefully folded cigarette pack
yields pearls of enlightenment.
Lightning paths to eager mouths,
my hair is reaching for the sky.
I look at you,
yours lies in repose, content.
We swallowed the sun,
flashlights beam from our fingertips;
hand in hand, we float down an alley
and by the purple door we melt.
My hands sink into your hair and face.
Your arms become my waist and
lips, of soft wax, are devoured.
Reality, with the light, creeps in
and the passion dies alongside the X.

Michele Kleineweber

Erasing Time

Dear forgotten time
So fair is your soul
outlined in silver
and eyes full of gold
Fragile as it seems
survives through its wander
of all concrete and cold
lives to be stronger
Your heart's silhouette
heard the luring Sirens
and scent of the candle
burns deep raging fires
The mind's illusion
is what make me whole
found far back in your palace
and chained down below
Now drown its feathers
to grow in the sand
the journey for its wonder
will lead my hand

Amber Hall

Moon Perfume

Words whispered across a pillow
light and lingering through
Sounds beyond the music
moon perfume

Rachelle Fox

Untitled

I am but a distant star.
Seldom seen in the universe,
but existing never-the-less.
Existing as a question
to which there has been no answer.
Light year by light year
my existence prolongs.
In time my presence will only
occupy the ebony of space, as
I will fall fate of all others
in the masses.
Until that glitch in time,
be cautious of the comets, and
debris passing by.
Take in the sights,
Maybe another galaxy beholds
an answer or two.
Tho it may,
gaze as you will
at the dreamy sky.

Pete Dickman

A Special Adult

My father is very special to me
But not everyone can see
That my father means a lot to me
And I know he loves me

I don't get to see him anymore
After that morning he went out the door
I was so mad I could have hit the floor
After that morning he went out the door

I visit him when I get a chance
A lot of people just stop and glance
But not when I get a chance
My father can no longer dance

My father is far away you see
He is in heaven with the angels not me

Cindy Miller

Wolf

The wolf is out tonight
It is not safe here
I can hear his cry
I can see his sneer

He creeps towards my house
Every night at twelve
Near me, he will always be
All alone, by myself

He was staring through the window
At the front door of my house
With his blood stained fangs,
And his snarling white mouth

So, the nightmares don't stop,
the terror doesn't end
the wolf is at the door,
He wants to come in

Alan Spalding

The Streetlight

My source of warmth,
my source of light,
it guides me to safe
places at night.
It keeps me going,
it gives me hope
But most of all,
it gives me strength.
It's my only true friend
And I'll treasure it
for it's "my streetlight."

Meghan Burke

Ode To My World Of Alzheimer's

Calm the heart that troubles me,
I want to hold on to a memory
that fades in and out,
A memory of my youth, my friends,
and family.
And to my precious dreams of the past,
I try to speak the way I use to,
but it is so hard.
Oh please tell me where I am,
And keep me there for just a while.
I long for a clear day and clear mind.
Unlock the door for me, with the
key that opens up my world
and gives me hope, freedom, joy
"peace of mind" and a quiet soul.

Carla Carrick

Journey's End

An ending to the journey,
An ending to the road,
The trip is almost over,
Victory we know.

An ending to our troubles,
Many things we feared,
Getting here we learned much,
And now the end is near.

We haven't finished learning,
We haven't finished yet,
The end we see before us,
Is just another step.

The journey's end is nearing,
We feel it in our heart,
And when we end our travels,
Another one will start.

John Jacobs

Rainbows

God gives us rainbows
    And not just in the skies,
God gives us rainbows
    Thru other folk's lives.

God gives us rainbows
    In each a little smile.
God gives us rainbows
    In the eyes of a child.

God gives us rainbows
    To enjoy each day.
God gives us rainbows
    Not to keep but to give away.

Mary Watkins

Heart Breaker

You loved me
"Sorry" was all you could say
I couldn't believe it
"Why?"
I kept on asking
But you wouldn't answer
I started to cry
You told me, "Don't"
But I couldn't help it
I tried to kiss you
But you pulled away
My heart was broken
But you didn't care
Although you are a heart breaker
I still love you

Sherry Peng

Shoes

Round laces
Smooth suede
Wonderful grip
Memories from the past.

Derek Brotherton

Water

The strongest force on earth
Tossing and turning objects
Enormous waves toss boats
White caps splash against the sides
The drain is pulled.

Eric Calvi

The Visitor

He came to me
In the middle of the night
Handing out wisdom
With proper insight
He told me the stories
Of Moses and Cain
He was spreading the gospel
To those blind and in pain
He said "fear me not"
For I am your friend
One who will never leave you
But who'll stay to the end

Shelley E. Fields

Triumph And Pain!

The days are long
and the pain seems strong,
but our love is stronger.

The days are lasting forever
but if we're clever
we'll get through the pain
stronger than ever.

The days are endless
and the time is all but painless,
but God joined our hearts.

So through all the hurts
he'll watch over us.
If we keep the faith!

Timothy Allen Angell

Rose

Something lovely must cover my supper.
Yes it's just some butter it cost a sum
of one hundred dollars. But I found
a number on the way home, that said
I won! So I shove my way home, and
my prize was a rose. Now I have done
all my stuff. And there's none left
to do. Except to give my rose to you.

Desiree Lacey

Elves

Elves are hard at work,
a tisk, a task, a jerk.

Busy making choo-choo trains,
busy making dolls.

While being as quiet as can be
when creeping down the halls.

The elves are watching you,
and Santa's watching too.

To catch a little glimpse
of what it is you do.

Nikki L. Hudson

Sky

The sky is smiling at me.
    I know it will be a good day.
    Sweet shades of crystal blue
    peeking through my blinds.

Now soft tears trickle off clouds,
    My poor feet will never forgive me.
Flat gray on my face,
I won't get out of bed today.

Caryn Melancon

How Things Are

You are the most polarized
fence-sitter I've ever met.
By nature you speak in riddles.
People miss the meanings
that I understood before
I knew your name.
This is as strange to me
as it is to you
and what can it mean?
Some might guess marriage
is the last fitting piece
of this jig-saw.
I can't hope so.

Everyone knows wedlock
of minds is stronger than
the wedlock of mere people.
I believe this so
you will not.
What perfect union.

R. F. Allen

I Belong In This World

I belong in this world
I refuse to believe
you are better than me
this is nonsense you see

When I came to this world
there was no one like me
the assignment I have
be the best I can be

There are things I should learn
to act right and achieve
to survive in this world
and contribute my dream

I will just be myself
in a world that's diverse
it is great to be me
I am something to see

I will reach out to those
who are needing my help
I will fight for the rights
that I need to be free

Horacio D. Lewis

I Hear The Silent Violin

The wood has seasoned
the shape is the same,
and four strings tuned to perfect pitch
only a master's ear can hear.
Technique acquired with practice
as each finger moves to various degrees
and vibration comes alive.
Vibrato, pizzicato and trills
thrilling those with trained ear.
They hear each note true,
"Caprice Viennois," "The Bee,"
"Ave Maria."
Fingers positioned
as the bow sings the song.
It talks,
it speaks,
with clarity of sound,
of soul.
The strad etched on the tombstone
beside her name, I hear again and again.

Beryl Elizabeth Todd

Immortal Ebb Of Sea And Soul

Sail the currents
of the sea,
Wave and foam
Infinity.
Soul spark to heaven
Capitulates,
Symmetrical tide
Regenerates.

Jeanne Mitchell

Lonely Lover And Darkness

Lonely lover sits inside.
Darkness waits in the night.
Lonely lover crying so softly,
As in the darkness, all is right.

Lonely lover sits and wishes.
Darkness covers everything around.
Lonely lover moans in woe,
As in the darkness, all is sound.

Lonely lover daring to love.
Darkness seeing with its eyes.
Lonely lover feeling so afraid,
While the darkness never dies.

Lonely lover knows not what to do.
Darkness, however, knows all.
Lonely lover screaming on the inside,
As the darkness grows tall.

Lonely lover wanting to die.
Darkness never weeps.
Lonely lover dying slowly,
As the darkness sleeps.

Matt Newman

Now She's An Angel

Now she's an Angel,
For her, I write this poem.
She took her Lord's hand,
He took her home.

Her struggle is over,
There was peace on her face.
She is promised eternity,
In a heavenly place.

Our hearts are heavy,
Our eyes full of tears.
Left are the memories,
She gave us through the years.

Always, we will love her.
Forever, we will miss her.
Time has come to release her.
Because, now she's an Angel.

Jean Connely

Winter Days Are Coming

Winter days are coming
it is time for winter fun
say goodbye to all the swim time
say goodbye to Mr. Sun
Get out your winter sled
and get out your winter stuff
you need to drink hot cocoa
and bundle up with fluff
But summer days will come again
and so will Mr. Sun
but winter can be fun sometimes
winter can be fun!

Haley Hopperstad

War

My way is right
And yours is not
A disagreement
A war is fought

A man calls for peace
With a fragile voice
The soldiers look puzzled
And say they've no choice

Man has fought
Since time untold
For fame and fortune
And power and gold

And still we fight
And still we die
And I sit here and wonder
Do we even know why?

Joseph Klein

At Eventide

I know a quiet spot
Above the valleys green.
Where the sun's bright ray
Casts its brilliant gleam
Upon the birch and pine.

The clouds, like tufts of cotton,
Drift across a sea blue sky
And a merry breeze
Slips through the trees
As a robin is soaring high

I often linger there at eventide,
When the sun at the end of the day
To the mountain bids a golden goodbye
And then gently fades away.

Barbara Goodrich

A Poet's Tribulations

As I sit here thinking,
of what on earth to write,
I find no sentence linking,
though I try with all my might.

The inspiration waves o'er,
and I receive nothing but naught,
My thought gage sinks even lower,
though Lord knows I have sought,

The perfect piece of literature,
seemingly never to come,
I'm very sorry sir,
I've gone completely dumb!

And as I look at what I've written,
without thought or tear,
I see I have written something!
Oh me! Oh my! Oh dear!

Tina Zuzek

Untitled

Perhaps in truth,
A service is rendered by pain.
If not for regret,
One could not grow.
Grief submits to emotions,
Facing one's fears.
In the end bringing wisdom,
The most precious gift
one could hope to acquire.

Rebecca Spencer

The Hare

An ordinary day in spring
While walking
Children's laughs faded
The only reminder of man.

Distracted birds twittering
    to themselves
As fragile flowers seek
    the sun.

In the bushes blended
A quiet soul, soft-eyed,
Flicked an ear,
And was gone.

Shanna Hughes

Untitled

I took the top from a jar today
To empty it out and throw it away
It smelled of jasmine, spice and rose
That took me back to a bygone day
of starry nights when our love was new
And my every thought was of only you.
Strange how a garden and a star
Can be imprisoned in a jar

Laveta Mohr

Dear Sweet Jesus

Dear, Sweet Jesus, One who cares,
Bless my life and my affairs.
Go with me, each step I take,
Be my guide, asleep, awake.
Should I face temptation's hour,
Gird me with Thy Mighty Power.
When my way in life seems lost,
With conflicting pathways crossed,
Lead me, Jesus, to Thy Way,
Ev'ry hour, ev'ry day.
Heal my body, mind, and heart,
Heal ev'ry cell of ev'ry part.
End the turmoil, calm the strife,
And bring me to Eternal Life.

Charles Brewer

Keep Your Head Up

Life is a trip.
You didn't know.
You walk around sad.
With nowhere to go.

Every where you look
trouble is ahead.
It's getting so bad
You wish you were dead.

Please don't give up
When your life is getting odd.
Just take a deep breath
and start praying to God.

One happy morning
You'll wake up.
Run outside
and say enough is enough!

The next day you are at work
Your friends say bad stuff.
Then they ask why are you so happy?
You say, I just keep my head up!

Michael T. Cary Jr.

How Cold Is The Snow?

Cold, cold lies the snow
Embalming the folks
In the earth below.

Mopsie Crawford

My Friend

I thought it sorta funny
when I saw you yesterday.
Who'd've ever known
you wouldn't be here today?

You were my best friend,
and forever our love shall last.
Your death has overcome me,
and my tears shall never pass.

You were my true love;
in God's hands thou does lie.
Finally, forever, free at last;
so I shouldn't cry.

For we will be together
forever, once again.
When the angels bring me
to you, my loving
Friend

Sean

The Beholders

His aura was deep blue,
like the clearness of skies.
It surrounded him forever,
And swelled within his eyes.

To look into his soul,
was to see a thousand dreams;
people near the ocean,
connected by many streams.

All can meet completely,
Within this large blue vast,
and see the web of life,
if your mind is sharp and fast.

For if you stare too long,
the image will be done.
The breeze will no longer chill you,
and he will close his eyes to the sun.

If you can catch the dream
before it drifts apart,
you will vision it forever
and cherish it in your heart.

Giselle Joy Gray

A Soldier Prayer

I was over seas in battle,
in a fox hole where I laid
when I heard a young man crying,
crying far away.
Does it show that he's a coward,
a coward afraid to die,
oh Lord, oh God in heaven,
why does that poor man cry,
Now that I'm home from battle,
I go to church to pray.
To thank the Lord in heaven,
that I lived from day to day,
I thanked the Lord in heaven,
I never had to cry,
I thanked the Lord in heaven,
I never had to die

Lawrence C. Pierce

Yesterday

Yesterday I saw a cheetah,
It was eating a fajeta.

Yesterday I saw a monkey,
It was riding on a donkey.

Yesterday I saw a kangaroo,
It has a friend named jump-a-roo.

Yesterday I saw a llama,
It was wearing pink pajamas.

Yesterday I saw a rabbit,
It was hopping with a wacky habit.

Yesterday I saw a toad,
It was sleeping on the road.

Yesterday I saw a gobbler,
It was eating cranberry cobbler.

Yesterday I saw a snake,
It was eating chocolate cake.

Yesterday I saw a zebra,
It was nursing a high fever.

Yesterday I saw a toucan,
It was eating from a food can.

Kayse Lauren Henley

White

How can you,
white
be so proud of your past?
Slavery, racism, genocide,
are these fine qualities?
Is it ignorance?
Or do you too hate?
Hasn't time passed?
Is it a choice?
Or something much deeper
in your skin white shaved head?
Genetic hatred driven into your bones
But I am white like you
but oh do I differ.
Your swastika ideals will never
Grace my lip
Star of David pressed to my chest
White,
will you learn?

Joshua Sapir

Cowboy

Cowboy is a word we use,
Sometimes too often I guess.
It congers up pictures of wild
fiery rides, eight seconds, and
all of the rest.

But cowboy goes much deeper than
that, to the very heart and soul
of a man.
It touches the place that makes you
who you are. And no one else can
understand.

It can't be pretended or just
put on with the jeans and the
boots and the hat.
But it has to be lived from the
heart, you know
'Cause that's where cowboy
is at.

Loretta Mason

Imagination

As I fly through the darkness,
On my golden wings,
I discover the most beautiful,
of beautiful things.

Islands of buried treasure,
Cities of gold,
In my imagination,
these stories are told.

Wizard, princesses,
demons and knight,
Merlin the sorcerer,
elves, ogres, and sprites.

Gnomes, dragons,
Pegasus too,
Emerald tigers,
it is all true.

I thought this all up,
and you can too,
if you have an imagination,
that runs away from you.

Audrey Davon Custer

Steel

The inside of vast skyscrapers
Safety belts for cars
Vast airplanes
Small deadly weapons.

Brett Goodwin

Tempest

The tempest came,
And I was tossed,
My wild soul to tame,
Else I be lost,

Amid life's enduring strife,
One must adapt to survive.

Here is pain and sorrow,
For things left undone,
I must look to tomorrow,
For better things do come.

All is not as seems,
When trials increase.

For within the storm is grace,
It comes,
And fields us face,
Give thanks to God!
Praise his name!

Marion Mills

Wind Song

The wind song blows upon
the Autumn snow

The black bird
sings in
a three-dimensional ring

But then was then
and now is now;

But what of snow
that does not fall

And what of the, bird
that will not sing.

William Blocker

Inspiration

Muses, Muses alight upon my shoulder
Let your light not smoulder
In the dark of night
Your beauty is profound
As you flit around
Alighting on my shoulder

Go now Muses, go
Share your knowledge with others
Who need it more than I
Fly
And alight upon another shoulder.

Guy Kemball Williams

All The Sides Of Hate

The snowflakes will fall,
   But the heart turns cold.
The ice will glisten,
   But souls will be sold.

In the endless night,
   A child will cry.
In deafening silence,
   Innocence will die.

Ten million voices,
   Shouting of this shame.
But another ten,
   Will just play the game.

Lives are torn apart,
   By slander we make.
Souls are rippled to shreds,
   But the lives we take.

When will we see all,
   Of the sides of hate?
I have no idea;
   Probably too late.

Douglas Smith

One God

Nobody knows him
He's peeking at us.
But who is he.

Kayla D. O'Brian

Snowflake

If I were a snowflake,
I'd never want to melt.
I'd fly all over Alaska
Throw a kiss to every pelt.
Land on every mountain peak
For a brief "good day,"
Float my shadow on the lakes
To show them how I play.

And when I feel I am getting smaller
A glacier I shall find.
And there I'll stay
Till earth runs out of time.

Dorothy D. Curry

Untitled

   Nana Banana, she's my grandma,
my mother's mother, Nana Banana has
good cookin', she's good looking,
that's my Nana Banana.

Miller David

Heat Wave

Conversation bores me;
social climbers leave me cold;
no longer go to parties,
I guess I'm getting old.

Satisfied reposing
and reflecting on my lot;
Boy! I enjoy this hammock
when old man weather's hot.

No more urge to travel
neither far nor wide to see;
seek no fame — I like it tame,
ambitionless, that's me!

Charles A. Lewis

Dust And Gold

Dust and gold
Gold and dust
Gold is a word that the miner's trust
They'll hunt the hunt, the day away
Searching, for the lode of pay!
A miner's life is hard,
It's true . . .
Busy the day, through the through.
You can see them in the morning,
You can see them all through the day,
The early dew doesn't keep them away!
Tailing piles can be found,
On roads and hillsides all around town.
It'd be such a delight
To find a nice round nugget
Out in plain sight!

Fran Prichard

Untitled

   My lovers hands run deeply,
down my spine while I sleep.

   His touch is soft upon my skin,
He whispers something sweet.

   He caresses me gently,
hoping I'll awake.

   He needs my body close to his
But, I hesitate.

Only for a moment.

I need to hear him say
   again, with such passion.

I will love you, always.

Julia A. Johnson

Thanksgiving

Blood trickles down His forehead
His arms are stretched out wide
His ankles are nailed together
His pain is held deep inside

Each wrist has a nail in it
Each eye holds a tear
That sort of pain was meant for me
How much more can He bear?

Now, That, is what I am thankful for
On this Thanksgiving Day
Just because of all my sins
He gave His life away

Crystal Pettit

Small View

Stand straight
Sit tall
Do it well
Or not at all

Pass high
Fail not
Don't you cry
You're no big shot

Work Hard
Be fair
Now don't act
Like you don't care

Whole life
Their way
No more time
To even play . . .

Nancy O'Keefe

Once More

Remembering
a memory
in my thoughts
only a dream
you can't touch me
I'm there
a whisper on your lips
a picture
in your mind
a scent in the air
a touch burning your skin
what happens what will be
is it what you want
it is still so
seek what you need
maybe just maybe
you need me once more

Sandra Zang

Facing Eternity

I can leave a part of me behind
To see the sun setting.
Yet, I shall rise
A new dawn to see.

Roderick Scott MacLeod

A Place

A place to hide
To keep the pain inside

A place the sin
Is held within

A place in the dark
Where you can't hear the dogs bark

A place in the field
Where you will be healed

A place in the water
Where the days seem shorter

A place in your heart
Where the love might start

A place to be seen
Where the grass is green

A face in the mirror
That takes you to that place

Steve Masi

Untitled

Cast into oblivion
I'll ride this
Cosmic Wave,

Aeons from eternity
I chance a
downward glance.

Below me the horizon
and, beyond,
the four corners
not one known to man.

Robert E. Clampit Jr.

Picture A Day

When two strangers meet
Let your heart take hold
Of something so sweet
Take the risk
Yet take with such care
Remember times past
And counting each tear
Frightened of feelings
So strong, yet unsure
Waiting on time to deliver a cure
Imagine a day God given and complete
Beginning with doubt
Never ending with defeat.

Suzy Marotta

Untitled

Walk with me
walk with me thru
the land of my soul
Walk with me
walk with me thru
the depths of my darkness
my land of unknown

Tremble with me
tremble with me in
joy and in fear

Tremble with me
tremble with me in
sadness and in courage
for I am evil and good
guilt and strength
love and hate

Walk with me
walk with me
in the land of my soul
as I come to know
my soul

Patricia A. Burns

Pettiness

No time to live;
no time to die.
Only the busy breaks in the dawn
and survives the dusk.
Only the incomplete death,
the deep drawn-out breath,
of one so pale
of one so sick,
and there is nothing new under the sun
but man-made trauma
and life undone.

Sara Berrey

Migration

Bluest sky, crisp lazy breeze,
Sun, still warm, on my cheek.
Monarch butterfly. High, then another,
One again, higher. And more . . .
Many orange sunbathers
Drifting slowly, on the air above me.
North to South.

Distant sparks
Catch my skyward eye.
Circle dark, then turn to glisten.
Sun lit fireworks,
Turn and gleam . . .
Turn and gleam, then
Form together moving South.
Snow geese passage.
Find a field, turn and gleam,
Again. Then again . . .
Ever lower out of sight.

Nature. I have shared these,
Your miracle moments.

Susanne M. Scott

A Little White Candle

A little white candle
just ready to burn out

A little white candle
shining its light all about

A little white candle
lighting up the whole place

A little white candle
sitting on top of white lace

A little white candle
almost to be gone

But no it's still there
still awake at dawn

That's the little white candle
that's all it was about

There is no more to say
because it just burned out.

Rachel Roman

The Alcohol Smile

Problems arise
More than once in awhile
It tends to bring the dreaded
And the awaited alcohol smile

One hour of peace
Is worth a hundred at war
This of the mind
Is what I search to adore

Waiting til dawn to find my smile
Just once, just once, just for awhile
I'd like to find my dimples
Minus the alcohol smile

A smile is a smile
Even if one is fake
If I can find a smile
The fake one I will take

But if the real one I can find
Just for awhile
I'd much rather have this
Than The Alcohol Smile!

Joel Edward Hopson

Sweet Summer Days

The long summer days
oh, how I remember the
sweet memories. The
swinging from deep brown
oak trees.
Smelling the soft pink
cherry blossoms in the air.
A blue velvet blanket
covering the sky above.
Our dangling heads watching
from below.
Fuzzy green sod laid
below to cushion
our falls
the sweet days of
summer still
lies in our hearts
for they are long sweet
memories.

Maria Deike

Cross Road

Narrow nose,
Pale skin,
Long straight hair,

A reminder that she don't
belong there.

Aware of her ancestors
Past of yesteryear
When they had to surrender
their bodies in fear

Now she stands at the
Cross road of life her
Decision, the next generation
will fight for their
rights.

Sean Golden

The Candle Glow

Against the dying light,
The candle glows
glow, candle glow,
The sands of time
Are fleeing, time and tide
wait for no man.

Glow, candle glow,
In the ebbing of your light.
I find a promise of
A bright new tomorrow

No longer do I fear
The night,
The deep and dark
Unfathomable night.

Wanda Greiner

Isolation . . .

I miss him out of desperation.
And hate him out of anger.
What is this?
Isolation or danger?

I shall never know,
With this on going cycle.
I love him because of solace,
But despise him in spite of failure.

T. Caraway

Father Time

Boy to Man, Man to
Old Timer. Passage of time,
reflections, reminders.

Ambitions abound, promises
forsaken, regrets chill the
soul while you awaken.

Knowledge lies in a mist of
yearning, as the spirit flies
endlessly learning.

Not yet there, the soul
contemplates as it dances
with fear.

Journeys slowly wither
away, as the hand of time
pushes each day.

Old Timer to Grave,
stand fast and brave,
for the promise of
tomorrow brings
a new day!

Steven Mark Sagendorf

Remember Christmas

Christmas come, and Christmas went.
Too much money we had spend.
For all the ladies and the gents
We must remember,
The "Christ" in Christmas.
Yes, the "Christ" is missed.
Though, we remember the child.
We still go wild, and "spend",
Oh, yes the burdens he did bare,
We must all be aware,
Remember the "Christ" in
Christmas.
Don't ever doubt, for this is what
Christmas is all about.
So when you're out shopping the stores
Remember the lore, of "Christ."
And love your fellow man.
You can, I know you can,
He did, only a man,
"Christ"mas.

Trudy Woollet

Untitled

You told me you were leaving
I smiled but wanted to cry
Without you here
I think I just might die.

    Cause once upon a time
    you said you'd always love me.

You smiled and hugged me
the warmth of your body, so inviting.
Outside I was smiling
but inside I was dying

    Cause once upon a time
    you said you'd always love me.

You turned and left
And walked right out of my life
As tears streamed down my face
I thought "How will I survive?"

    Cause once upon a time
    you said you'd always love me.

Pauline Valdez

Blame It On A Phase

On a personal cloud
Flashing sarcastic beams to
Strike anyone in sight.
Talk of the monotonous day
While thunder roars from the mouth
Violently shaking the attentive room.
Timidly apologetic —
The storm inside is calming,
But her tears begin to rain
And he can't find an umbrella.

Nicole Manning

My Friend

Time is deceiving near
my dear friend,
that you will be leaving soon,
going down that wood,
to places you have been before
maybe some day
we shall meet again.
While you were here,
we had fun.
I shall miss you.
Think of me sometime won't you
as the days and years go by
I won't forget
what good friends we were.
Someday, we will meet again
some place, sometime or where
so God bless you and
be on your way
until then.

Lorine A. Kautz

What's In A Name?

One called me "Ophelia,"
Another called me "Jade";
One bowed low and called me
"Silver Witch Upon the Glade."
This one called me "Dragon,"
That one called me "Whore";
The young one called me quietly
"Gentle Woman Wanting More."
An old man called me "Angel,"
A soldier called me "Hon."
The Cherokee looked me in the eye
and called me "Many Battles Won."
A friend called me "Morgana,"
A child just called me "Ma'am."
Now I wonder, as you look at me,
Who you'll decide I am.

Karen E. Davis

Rehab

Move a little,
Just a little,
To prove life exists.
Push hard,
Then harder,
On a memoryless limb.
Strain against stiffness,
Ignoring pain.
Lift unpliant arm
With unbending wrist.
Mind battles inertia;
Brain and spirit
Resurrect flesh.

Elizabeth Lee Kearns

Sports

Sports are fun,
a good activity to play,
especially on,
a warm summer day.

Basketball is cool,
Soccer is too,
There's so many sports,
That you can do.

A throw to the basket,
A flip on a mat,
A dive off the board,
A swing of a bat.

If you're lucky,
you might be on a team,
Hard and tiring
It might seem.

Roxanne Medley

I Know He Loves Me

As I kneel here beside Jesus
And He touch my hand.
He says my child I know and understand.
The burdens that you carry
just leave them with me.
And no longer worry for
by faith you shall see.
That all I ask is that
you bring them to me.
For I died to set you free
now live for me.
I know that He loves me
no matter what they say.
I'm going to serve Him
come what may.
In Jesus I will keep.
My spirit is no longer asleep.

Edna Mae Munro

Autumn

The tree stands
strong and sure.
The bird flies, free in the air.
From each one fall to the earth
The leaf and the feather,
both the same shape,
both the same size.
And they lie together on the earth
like sisters —
like death,
and like life.

Don Perl

Untitled

Standing by your side
That's where you wanted me to be
I don't know how many times you tried
Tried to make me see

Now we're apart
And I know how I feel
I'm listening to my heart
I know this is for real

Please give me one more chance
Let me do it right
Allow me to have this dance
I want to hold you tight

Shawn Christopher Cage

Short And Sweet

This poem is for a test
  so we must realize,
the rules specifically state
  keep it short in size.

Now everyone knows
  you can't do your best,
when you must keep it brief
  writing for a test.

It will be hard to write
  as I've stated why,
but never-the-less
  we'll give it a try.

Now for choosing a theme
  that is serious and quick,
it is like a sore nose
  it's kind of hard to pick.

As for different themes
  they are varied and plenty,
but now I'm out of space
  because this is line twenty.

Brant D. McKeever

Born

The day you are born
You enter a race
You can't always win
But you keep up the pace

Then comes the day
When you love and you care
And you finally realize
Life isn't fair

You meet a small child
Who's sweet and sincere
She can't talk
But can see and can hear

A three year old angel
Who's destined to fly
You pray everyday
And only ask why?

One day you realize
That love can be torn
And pray and remember
That's why you're born.

Lori Thornton

Angels

Babies and the Elderly
Both see Angels,
But not me.
Only those with special sight
Can see the Angels,
try as we might.
They stare at that empty space,
only those pure of heart
Can see the Angels grace.
Babies grow, and soon forget
Those beautiful beings
They once met.
Life goes on, be it short or long,
Then all too soon,
We'll once again
hear their magnificent song.
Angel's are messengers
from God above,
Given to each one of us
With unconditional love.

Linda Lou Kogut Thornton

Demon's Of The Mind

Shadows within the dark
Emerge from within a spark
Caught within our dream
Remembrance of what we seen
Enemies within our mind
Tries us for our crime
Seldom will we expose

Feelings that we oppose
Only within the dark
Recalls us to that ark

Under these stormy seas
Shelter is not a breeze

Tucked within our shell
Only creatures within us dwell

Kept within our ark
Enemies within the dark
Everyone forever will hide
Phantoms from deep inside

Jack H. Ridge

Untitled

Can't you see the tears
  falling from my soul
    drowning out life
      to fill an empty hole?
The feeling has come
  to corrode my brain,
    pushing me over
      to drive me insane.
It's dark and deep
  and riddles the mind,
    dug by broken dreams
      and shoveled by those unkind
It walks the tombs and haunts
  with a fight —
    it's the feeling that rips
      at your dreams
        late with the night.

Diana Bobb

The Ride

One bright morning
As he headed to the field.
He noticed a spider.
On the auto windshield.

Speeding to 45,
to put him to flight.
That little spider,
he held on tight.

On to 60.
to give him a stiff breeze.
The tighter the windshield,
That spider did squeeze.

Faster still.
To hurricane force.
But that little spider.
He is still there. Of course.

Turning on the wiper.
To give him a ride.
It was then he noticed.
He was on the inside.

Oakley C. Barrett

Life And Love

Life and love are bittersweet
And so is pain.
We learn from all these things
But not in vain.

For what we learn from life
We learn to love.
For all of these things
Are sent from above.

For what we learn from love
We learn to live.
And the things that are given us
We learn to give.

And pain comes in
Where love is found.
Where love is found,
Life abounds!

Mary Ann Raschke

Clouds

Fluffy clouds up in the sky,
A gentle breeze takes you by.
Up, up way up high,
Away, away, away you fly.

Jaclyn Ferris

The Ripples Revelation

What a picture of grandeur
  Mine eyes do see
Sitting by the pond
  Beneath the willow tree
What miracle of nature
  Caused this creature to be
With a ripple of water
  I realize it's just me

Chance Allyn Taylor

He's Really Not Here

As I watch my love slowly
walk out of sight, his love for
me grows dark as night.
  But now that he's gone it's been
different, when I said I
love you, I really meant it.
  I cry and weep, screaming
it's not fair, but his love
and memory will always be there.
  We stuck together through
good and bad, even when
everything got really sad.
  But now that he's gone
he's not very near, now I
am lost, he's really not here.

Ashley Doss

Morning Prayer

As I wake up to the sun,
tell me Lord what needs be done.
Help me seek Thy will for me,
show me what I am in Thee.
May Thyself be glorified,
cast away my human pride.
Allow Thy words to flow through me,
showing forth eternity.
Thank you for Your listening ear,
may I thus be true sincere.

Dwayne M. Potts

I Am

I am painter
the world my canvass.
Caribbean sea my blue,
lover's emerald eyes, green,
large sunflowers, yellow
juicy fat tomatoes, red,
mother earth my brown,
plump dove, white,
sunset, orange,
death, black,
joy, pink,
teardrops my water,
luscious lashes my brush,
God my inspiration.

Joanne Griffiths

That Little Hand

As a mother leaving her
youngest one at school.
The mother leaves to do her errands
or what ever. Realized that
she is all alone and she doesn't
have that little, hand or some
little voice saying where are
we going or I am tired and I
am tired and he hangs on light
and your hand has to find that
little hand so to hold on tightly
once in a while he wants to let
go and being a worried parent
you say give me your hand and
as the years go by you think of
that little hand that was

Doris E. Kokal

When Love Dies

How does love die?
A thousand different ways —
A partners frequent criticism,
Instead of words of praise.
Looking for faults — and finding them,
(For who of us has none?)
Doing things the hard way,
Instead of having fun.
Forgetting to count your blessings
When each day is done.

C. Rivard

Fall

Fall has come,
the leaves are brown.
Squirrels flee,
the sun goes down.
The world is quiet,
safe and sound.
The groundhogs sleep,
underground.
Then alive and full,
the sun arises.
Sparkling sunlight,
golden enterprises.
Life is full,
majestic and sweet.
Like candy corn,
ready to eat.
Excitement, excitement,
everywhere.
Full and thrills fill the air.

Emyli Volz

For An Old Love, Returned

Come, my love, and dance with me;
I'll sing softly in your ear.
You can hum the harmony,
And we'll have music, never fear.

Though you beard is getting gray,
And my hair's not long and brown,
We still hear the music play
As we waltz around and round.

Hold me tight and hold me close;
Rest your beard against my cheek.
Your touch so gently does expose
Emotions, and I cannot speak.

I think of us and of the past
And of the present, and I sigh,
For we are dancing here at last,
Or rocking to a lullaby.

What will be was meant to be;
We'll sing the song that we've begun.
Growing older, you and me,
Or maybe, we are growing young.

Marjorie M. Ivey

I Will Lay Beside You

When vows are whispered to each other
And night begins to fall
As we embrace each others love
    I will lay beside you.

New no more is love between us
But strong are ties that bind
Our love has lasted many years
    I will lay beside you.

I hold tight of love between us
And cherish memory's past
We feel the time that we have shared
    I will lay beside you.

No more are you to share by bed
Or tender love between us
But I'll be with you once again
    I will lay beside you.

Janet De La Torriente

A Special Friend

Dedicated to Louella M. Batiste
My grandmother is special.
She's one of the nicest women I know.
Every time she smiles,
she makes the whole room glow.

She treats me like one of her own,
so sweet and kind.
Whenever I have a problem,
she's not hard to find.

I love the way she makes me laugh.
It feels so good inside.
Her words and expressions
always seem to come alive.

But now she's very ill.
It's hard for this to be said.
It really does break my heart
to see her lying in a hospital bed.

I know that she won't give up.
Even though my sunny skies are blue.
But grandma all I want to say
is that . . . I Love You!

Eboni Anitra Williams

Tonight We Went South

Tonight we went south
I could have stayed here
We're innocent youth
To hell with my fear

We caress our vice
I murder virtue
We're but tiny mice
I could still hurt you

We'll fly up to heaven
I can't possibly fall
That was six, now we're seven
I'm not counting at all

We're cut! 'Twas the slice
of my sword, 'twas due
Our psyches on ice
My psyche is new.

Neil Prufer

Art

The power to create something
    no one else knows
The image of thought
    beyond everyone's but your own,
    letting your imagination go,
    letting it free to mold something,
    create something no one's created
but your own hands and mind
    body and soul combined
to make something so beautiful unique
It's what I know
It's something I can relate to
    something I need and thrive for
Addicted to the power of a creation
    never to be seen by eyes
    just seen by the heart and soul.

Tara Lindstrom

Snow

In the winter snow and ice,
we go sledding, it's so nice.
We sled until the day is done,
sledding is so much fun! Fun!
Fun!!!
We go sledding around, round,
round,
until we hit the ground, ground,
ground.
We go sledding night and day,
we play and play and play.
When it's time to go to bed,
we lay down and rest our head,
and dream about our little sled.

Kate White

Igneous!

Igneous! Thy name is rock!
From Earth's molten heart torn,
beyond a Moment's sight.

Let from the Hand you tumble,
tread Time's cloak, weathered star,
thy progeny, siblings all.

By sea's edge in sunlight glint,
'til a Moment's eye caught,
cherished stone now shelf adorn.

Steven M. Field

The Devil Does Not Wear Red

The devil does not wear red
His color is your skin
He is not a concrete being
He is not a tangible thing
But more an abstract idea
That permeates your fear
He does not ring your bell
With hell in tow
But rather shelters your thoughts
And smothers your love

The devil does not wear red
His color is your hate
He lives in your disgust
He dwells in your shame
But never is he seen, for he is
Rooted in things you crave and need
Yet he is felt more than life itself
He feeds off your pain
His color is green

Brian T. Heljenek

Threads

Clouds sprawl cheerfully in the sky,
as if lying on an invisible beach,
basking in sun's quiet shine,
seeming to hang by unseen threads.

Humans also hang by threads,
engrossed in need for desperate acts,
embittered by earthbound sacrifice,
oblivious to sky's enduring gifts.

What if we rose to sky's stillness,
caught by smiles, clouds' designs,
made sense of sun's clean warmth,
slid back to earth on threads of
sky's strong peace,
reconciled to nature's nourishment.

Simple things could be enough,
lives stripped of artifice,
threaded through with nature's solace,
filled with peace perhaps now on earth,
once found only in sky's hush.

Cynthia Robertson

Speaking Volumes

Within the library
Of the castle of our dreams
We awaken amongst the ancient tomes
Softly whispering
The annals of our lives

Touching tenderly
We muse within each passage
Speaking volumes
In the meter and movement
Of the verse

Lost in the dream
Each ballad a rhapsody
Each anthem an ecstasy
The poetess and the bard
The composer and the songstress
Alive in the expression
Of divine inspiration

Lost . . .
And found . . .
In a reverie with you . . .

Patricia Donovan

The One To Blame

Why am I always the one to blame
When other do their thang with no shame

They go here and there
And whisper things everywhere
They talk with me laugh with me
And even console me

But sometimes I think they
Love for me to be scold
And every now and again
I really do fill
As if you are
my only friend

It seems like if I succeed
Everyone's mad
Why can't everyone just be glad
Instead
They make me sad

Why does it have
To be this way
Can you fix it for heaven's sake

LaTasha Pittman

A Love Poem

How do you thank your sculptress?
Who so delicately with loving hands
created your very life;
The one who carefully shared her breath
and fed you with her body.
How do you thank someone like that?

What about your composer?
Who attentively guided you
through every note;
The one who listened to every sound
to make sure all was right.

And how do you thank your angel?
Who has willingly taken
her beautiful wings and given them
so you could fly;
The one who anxiously awaits your rise
but will catch you if you fall.
How do you thank someone like that?

Is it even possible?

Monica Landry

Dare

Dare, dare
Let's compare
You can do anything if you just care

Drugs and alcohol
Are not cool
And if you use them
You're a fool

Activities and games
Are offered at school
They're usually fun
And safe as a rule

Games and gangs
Are not the same
Because a gang
Gives you a bad name

So take a dare
And don't be scared
Because that is how
The winners care.

Rose Rinn

My Love For You

My love for you
I wouldn't say is through,
but since we've been
apart I've been blue

When you had to leave
You said we'd be together
It's been along time,
feel's like forever

You let me go
thinking I could fly
but without your love
I would die

You've found someone else
and so have I
but it has still
been hard saying goodbye

Ryan Garrity

Little Brown Monkey

When I was young
there was a monkey
as brown as he could be
eyes as big as saucers
looking down at me
he would climb
in a tree so tall
swing on a limb
and never fall
it frightened me
when I climbed that tree
that tree so big and tall
that little monkey
climbed that tree
and he wasn't
frightened at all

Brenda Auberry

Guinea Pigs

Guinea pigs are nice, soft, and furry
They are never in a hurry.
They sure can eat a lot.
They cannot be forgot.
Because when they squeal,
You have to give them their meal.
So you will never forget
That you have one for pet.

Alinka Flasinska

Precious Friend

If I walked a million miles,
And traveled across the land,
Tread softly over ancient tiles,
And sifted through the ageless sand.
If I searched the oceans deep,
And soared through skies of blue.
There is no friendship that I'd keep
More dear in my heart than you.
When God made you he broke the mold,
And sewed within a selfless heart,
Carefully sewn with threads of gold
Blessed with kindness at the start.
More than a sister you've been to me,
None other as strong and true,
I know that I will never see
A friend more precious than you.

Billie Holland

Something So Dear

It's your birthday,
   celebrate!!!
Birthday's come only
   once a year,
That is why this one
   is so dear.
People think birthday's
   are something
to fear, when all it is,
   is something dear.
Today is your day
   to relax, so kick
up your feet, there's
   nothing to fear,
for today is so dear!

Jennifer Buonanno

Bluebirds

As I watch the bluebirds fly
So very graceful through the sky,
I sometimes dream of worlds unknown
Where these birds have never flown.

As I watch them soar so high
I sometimes wish that I could fly.
To spread my wings and fly away,
For a brighter tomorrow and today.

I'd pack my bags and say goodbye,
Then fly up to the highest sky,
Leaving behind my worries and fears,
Shedding all of my sorrows and tears.

I would so much like to be
Just as calm and just as free,
As the birds that fly above
Which give me dreams and hopes of love.

Michelle Minutelli

My Father

You say that you don't mean it
When you hurt me with your hands
You say that you're sorry
But it happens again
You say you'll never forget me
When it is I who you neglect
You say I shouldn't fear
But what else could you expect
You say that you'll help me
Which I know you couldn't do
You say that you won't hurt me
When all my pain comes from you
You say that I need you
But you're destroying my life
You say you'll never leave me
Which forces me to say goodbye

Stephanie Leann Henry

Silver Tear

Somebody is watching
it has no face
it has no name

Somebody has power
it has no evil
it has good

Somebody is guiding me
it has not failed me
it has sent you

Yasmyn C. Puglisi

Untitled

Oh, this age
what has it descended to be
The ugliest of thoughts
Once foreign to me

And the horrors of doubt
That unsettled this mind
Speak not of sweet beauty
Once noble and kind

Oh, rage on this age
that has labored in wait
Used the years to woo fear
struck sudden and straight

Love so elusive
That was mine for a while
Was beaten by me
So silly and vile

And what of my hope
That fought bravely and stout
To this I warn sternly
Love spoke softly, rage a shout

William M. Johnson

Strand

A strand of hair
it is so queer.
It floats on air,
yet sticks on here.

A single strand
may wry your face,
yet form a crown
when twirled in place.

If one is found
upon your plate,
an appetite
will sure deflate.

As strands fall out
a man will worry,
and volumized
a woman's glory.

Strands to perm
or iron flat
from epiderm
atop our pate.

Gail Robinson

Father Forgive Them

Sweat rolled off his brow
Making his eyes burn like fire.
Each drop mixed with blood
And began its path down his face.
Gnats and flies flew wildly around,
Touching, landing, crawling
Anywhere they pleased.
His body, almost numb with pain
Felt each sliver from the hard wood
Pierce his already broken skin.
They spat, yelled, mocked and jeered.
They cursed and scorned him.
He might have felt anger,
He felt love.
He might have felt hatred,
He felt compassion.
He might have cursed, he said:
"Father forgive them."

John Haspels

You Make The Sun Rise

You make the sun rise,
You make the flowers bloom and grow.
Oh, Lord I want to thank you
for what you have done,
I love this world were in.

You make the birds sing,
You make the sunset like
A drawing of beauty,
Oh, Lord I want to thank you
for what you have done,
I love the world were in.

You make the sun rise,
You make the moon and stars shine.
Oh, Lord I want to thank you
for what you have done,
I love the world were in,
So be proud of what you have done.

Tamara Ann Barbaro

Love From You

The love from you
Is a big house
Without a mouse.
It is a farm
With a big barn.
Tis a mountain
Of fertile land.
It is a lake
Without a snake
To poison it.
Love could not get
Better than you.

Billie Jean Robertson

A Mother's Love

A mother's love is beautiful,
a wonder to behold.
A mothers love is more precious,
than diamonds, silver or gold.
A mother's love welcomes you,
when she hears your very first cries,
A mother's love soothes you,
you can see it in her eyes,
A mother's love will guide you
through those young and tender years,
A mother's love is always there,
to kiss away the tears.
A mother's love is steadfast,
if a child, should break her heart,
A mother's love is all the strength
you need when life falls apart.
A mother's love is unconditional,
as is our Fathers, up above,
Thank you very, very much,
For all your Mother's love.

Janet L. Brown

More Than Just A Friend

Indelible are those delights
Which harbor in my soul
And satiate eternally
Bestowing blissful joy

Long live the herculean nexus,
The bond between our hearts
Resplendent with trust therein my love
You are more than just a friend.

R. Sobala

The Hyphen

The hyphen
  Two dates on a tombstone
  only the numbers do tell
  when we were born
  and death's calling bell.

The hyphen
  A dash
   so fleeting
    so real
How we live our dash
Is how we do feel
  About Eternity.

Eternity
  continuous hyphens
Life here —
  Just a dash.

Pauline K. McColley

To Be

Oh thy dark which fills our eyes
All the fears despite the lies
Come to me in great ease
See me speaking on my knees
What to expect black or white
Is it life or is it fright
Is it the beginning or the end
Is it enemy or is it friend
All these questions we dare not ask
Leaves me searching in final grasp
Here it is my last breath dear
I am gone or am I here?

Jeff Nicolai

Your Love

Your love has helped me
through much struggle and strife
and because of this you have become
most important in my life.
With you by my side,
things will be forever right.
Our love together has made me
strong through the night.
We can build
a wonderful life together,
and stay that way
now until forever.
Promise me
our love is real,
because your love I need
and want to feel.

Jamie Fowler

Lost

As I sit and think of
our lost love, I wish you
would see how much I loved
you, and how much you hurt
me. If you have heart just
show it, let me know it's
there. Take me not into
your arms, your everlasting
embrace. Don't kiss my wounds,
my terrible heartache.
All you have to do is let me
know. Tell me it's there
are was once was long ago.

Batina Perez

Crow Flies

The crow flies high
Silently it sails
Bringing night along
Black as night with a cry
The crow flies high

Rebecca Diane Mayher

Mother

I admired you (from afar)
more than anyone I've ever known,
I strove to be like you —
failing miserably
I sought you out in strangers
faces,
Hated and loved you until my
feelings melted together
and left me numb.

Now you come to me only
in fleeting thoughts,
I no longer try to be you
(though your face stares
back at me from the mirror)
I am only me — yet I
find now that is enough.

Sherry Gerstenschlager

Death In The Shadows

What story does
The man in the shadows
Have to tell?

His gazing eyes as
He watches you pass;
You stop, look at him
His white teeth grin.

A match scratches the brick,
Flickers in the darkness
And its glow is like Hells flame.

He lifts it to his face
Bearded and scurry shag;
"Dear man, my soul has
Dried, my heart has shriveled.
My body wrinkled,
Lend me your soul,
As I pity you now, for I own all."

He reaches his hand
And lays it rest on your chest;
And his tale is all too real.

Jessica Lane

People From Far Off Lands

Many different people,
Many far off lands.
Making a world-wide circle
By connecting many hands.

People of many colors,
With feelings more or less.
Looking like a masterpiece
Not a scattered mess.

All different people,
Filled with peace and love.
What reminds me of an angel
Is a lovely snow white dove.

Rachel B. Funk

The Challenge

Never a contest have I won,
Many entered just for fun
If I keep trying will it happen?
The pen is quite a mighty weapon.

Thoughts so often to me come,
In lyric form quickly done.
If making money was this easy.
A winning place would really please me.

Sending my effort for your perusal,
A daring gesture, please no refusal.
A little quip may catch your eye.
Could see me in print, by and by.

Joyce Gottbreht

Reflection

Sometimes when I am all alone
I grieve for loss of those now gone
I wonder what my life would be
If they were still here with me.

Sometimes I feel that life is hard
And why have I been dealt these cards
What have I ever done
Why am I the lonely one.

But then I look around and see
So many people with less than me
And I realize that life can't always be
The way we would like it to be.

We still have family and some friends
Who we can count on to the end
Why are we so filled with greed
For material things that we don't need.

Isn't it better in the end
To be able to say
I have a friend.

Margaret R. Ibele

Personal Keepsake

Friend —
  Lost
   To
    My
     Present
Always
  In
   My
    Past
Forever
  In
   My
    Memories.

Debra K. Noble

The Words I Could Not Say

Remember me not as I was.
Remember me as I was young.
Remember me the way I laughed,
The way I sang.
I turned around my children were there.
I took your hand and away we ran.
Now the time as come for me to leave,
To the land of love so far away.
I turned around and forgot to say,
Remember my children *"I loved you all."*
Remember me as I was young.
The words I could not say, your *Mother*

Helen Wicykowski

My Shining Star

In the dark and dead of night,
I have a shining star.
And though the sky seems out of sight,
I don't have to look that far.
He's with me in the morning
And throughout each passing day.
He's with me when I'm mourning,
And to Him I'll always pray.
The devil creeps up on me,
And dares me to do wrong.
I keep my faith in the Lord, you see,
And that's what keeps me strong.
He is my strength, and my salvation.
He died on the cross for us all.
To Him I know there's no equation.
And with Him I know I'll stand tall.
And then the devil has to flee,
Because He has no power.
My Lord is always there for me,
Every minute, every second, every hour.

Rose A. Davis

You And Me

Smiles are forever
Tears they come and go
If I could only tell you
All the joy I know

Days gone by
And years we've known
The good — the bad
But how we've grown

All the years I've loved you
And stayed close by your side
Sometimes like the ocean
And the rising of the tide

Always trusting, always sharing
Always loving, always caring
God put us together
Apart we will never be

Somehow it isn't right
Not being "you and me"

Sondra K. Burnett

Soul Searching

A billowy silhouette emerges
Speaking prophetic verse.
Preemptory to Death
A predilection for your soul.

Serene preparatory dancing
As cathartic episodes commence.
To chaffer ensures finalization
So you belabor forgiveness.

Repent to no reprieve.
Surrender thyself to be reaped.
For it is inevitable and arrant
Behest by the omniscient.

Silent lucidity encompasses
The conscious mind asleep.
The immaterial entity extracted
By the one who reaps.

Entering his asylum
Where the tortured are set free.
Only to requite thy maker
To whom thy fealty is long overdue.

Velena M. Newberg

Memories

Violin's plaintive refrain
Echo like sweet spring's rain,
While woodwinds whisper of
A birch bark lovers' bower.

A piano tinkles tenderly . . .
Harps sing of secret meetings
As cool cellos murmur and
Deep bass drums throb and pulse.

Strange . . . And so wonderful
How a song breaks my soul
Into a thousand shattered mirrors,
Sweeping me away silently
Into the dim fragrant halls of
Bittersweet memories.

Jo Ann Waite

Floating Free

Bright balloons, sailing free
Traveling away from me.
Whisked afar by wind and sky
Dancing, whirling, flying high.

Swinging, swirling to and fro
I guess I know I'll never know
Exactly what balloons will see
Flying high and floating free.

Charlotte Nugent

A Lonely Soul's Cry

A heart beats slowly,
The spirit is tired,
The body is weak,
The soul cries out!
afraid, alone and meek,
Wanting comfort,
Wanting strength,
Wanting love,
Not to weep,
The wind sighs,
Carrying the tears
The heart cries out!
So many fears,
Echoes in the mountains,
"Why oh Why!"
"Come back my love
make me alive!"

Susan McFarlin

Dream

One hand to hold
Is all we need,
To rid the world
Of misery and greed.

One dream to dream,
And make come true
When the world has got us
Down and blue.

One voice to sing
The worlds song
Of hope, and joy,
And love so strong.

The hand and dreams,
The voice and song,
Will conquer the world
When the fighting's done.

Dru Weinstein

Mu

From her neck hung a gold Buddha
relic of her adopted country
the applause was louder than
the roar of the gym air conditioners
two decades for Rong Rien Bangkok
to receive a standing ovation
and a gold necklace
her face painted on the memories
of a thousand students
English lass to Thai matron
the Marginal woman
grasped two cultures
and united them
blending high tea and curry

Colleen A. Wylde

An Unforgettable Performance

It was an unforgettable performance,
As never before — or since.
The setting, the lights, the conductor
Were together in perfect sync.

The watching throng was breathless,
Would it be as they'd been told?
This was new, never tried before;
No one was ever so bold.

It began with just the faintest hint,
Then increased, they strained to see.
Almost imperceptible, ah, but yes,
There it was, it was going to be.

It started ever so slowly at first,
Then with speed it filled the place.
It flowed, crescendoed and climaxed —
Grandeur covered each face.

It went down as a moment in history —
The watching throng was right.
Never would they see such beauty again
As when God said, "Let there be light!"

Donna Bechthold

For Arrow

Memories are golden
Memories are true
Memories are light and happiness
Memories are blue
The first star in the sky tonight
I look at it and think
About the happy things we did
And how they start to shrink
If you can hear my sad song
I want you to know
I will always remember you
Through rain or snow

Zackary Colombino

A Child's Love

A gift of love and kindness,
is the way to start each day.
    Take the hand of a child
and lead him, a good start
will lead the way.
    Give him, love, guidance and
understanding, and teach him
each day to pray.
    As he grows up in life, with
love of family and friends,
    He will be happy and love
every day.

Meriam K. Sullivan

If I Had Wings

If I had wings and I could fly,
Across the whited winter sky,
And from above spy earth below,
As it twirled upon its axis,

Then I would from my place on high,
Amid that whited winter sky,
Call to all the earth below,
That in my life I knew you.

Mark W. McK. Bannatyne

Dispossession

You brought me seashells
in my Springtime
Kisses moist with wine
A song for my lips
you painted with Pink Grace
dissipating broken dreams
while you fed me
from your plate only
small bites of
Dependency

My Winter chills as
remembrance permeates
Age defying laughter
Shrieks through my aloneness
as I sit and rock
While time laughs and whispers
behind my head
wrinkled and warped

Leslie J. Hall

Natures Way

The Holy Grail
It's in the smell of the earth
After a spring rain
It's in the flight of the birds
High up in the sky
It's in the sound of the leaves
Rustling in the trees
It's in the feel of the wind
As it makes love to your skin
It's in the rhythm of your heart
Beating in your breast
It's in the depth of your soul
As you hunger to know
It's in the song of the angels
When you can let it go
It's inside of you
You know
It's peace

Diana Jackson

Snow

Snow makes its way
Through fields and trees;
Dropping, here and there, like popcorn.

The earth accepts it
In a calm, quiet way —
Drinking and quenching its thirst.

It comes drifting down
Soft and still:
Like butterflies on the wing.

It comes from above
Floating airily by:
Like tiny, white flowers from heaven.

Ruby Pearl Coffman

I Am America

I am America

I saw the Pilgrims
coming out of the horizons

I heard the guns
sounding for independence

I felt the blanket of
bodies over me in Gettysburg

I listened to the mother's
cries for their sons of Pearl Harbor

I am here now
I was here then
I'll be here to come

Heather Bigwood

Mail Time

So anxious I get,
    to hardly wait.
When the time is set,
    an hour past eight.

It makes my day,
    so very complete.
Seeing a letter lay,
    in my box so neat.

A letter from Mother,
    sure is a pleasure.
As one from another,
    I really treasure.

Of days that go by,
    with out a letter.
Makes me wonder why,
    the writers could not do better.

Clara Flink Taylor

Turning Loose

I found an eaglet long ago
Abandoned, homeless and alone
I bore him to my bosom near
And loved that eaglet as my own

With nurture, love and tender care
He thrived and grew, alive, aglow
I clutched him to my breast and yet
I knew I had to let him go

There came a day I set him free
Uncertain wings with which to soar
It seemed an arrow pierced my heart
To watch him rise above the shore

The hardest task I've ever had
The toughest job, bar none
Is turning loose to let you fly
Releasing you my son

Don Pottorff

Lord Thanks

For the morning of my birth,
and for our loving earth.
Thanks for health
and wealth.
Thank you for the love
from above.
Thanks for freedom, rights
and nature's beautiful nights.
Thanks for the flower and dove
that we truly love.

Saydi Chahla

Tear Of Hope

A tear fell today
When I looked in your eyes
I saw the pain
You so desperately hide.

I've been there before
I know how it feels
To live behind those closed doors.

The hurt that I see
Brings back old memories
Of the times I thought
There was no hope for me.

But the door will open
And in time you'll find
There's a special person
To give you peace of mind.

So til then, just remember
When I felt your pain
Just before you a friend become.

Melodie Campbell

Untitled

Your sweet words run through my heart
trickling down my body —
a cold drop of water down my spine
winding itself around
leaving me shivering
ecstasy

Words of torment
run through my head
settling down into my stomach
a hard stone
the weight of guilt interferes

I am torn
Between two worlds
one of passion, revelation
One of passion responsibility

Karen Amelia Conner

The Brook

The water moves slow,
A frog makes a sudden splash,
The brook is now still.

Sarah McCruden

Scared

At the beginning of life, there is a
    road we must walk
I was told to be scared and
    wondered why
But going further on, I stop to
    wonder how so many have tried
    to perfect this road on which
    we all will die

I have danced with success, I have
    cried with pain, and my greatest
    fear is still to face the way in
    which I will gain my respect

The beauty of life is what makes
    us succeed
Along this road that brings us all
    relief to this life of pure
    grief.

Stacey-Ann Nelson

The Photograph

I took your picture
I caught you off guard
But the smile was there
Not only on your lips
But in your eyes
It was freezing cold
But you radiated warmth
You were all aglow
Standing there in the shadows
It was a happy moment
It was a sad moment
I took your picture
It's with me always

Deloris Rickard-Hise

Untitled

I went out one morning
to shovel the snow
and I wondered
which way
the snow would go

As I directed this
frozen water
I said to my self
"I have nowhere to
dispose of mother nature!

My neighbor came out
with a grin - all a skirt
and said with a vengeance-
such a smirk
don't throw that
rubbish on my dirt!!

James Ellis Manis Jr.

A Fleeting Youth

And I was young and so alive
with the wonder of each day
I was carefree and lighthearted
I wanted life to go my way.
I wanted to live life to the full
wanted to laugh outrageously.
I wanted to love yes truly love
love with great intensity.
And so I did for all was well
all around me I could see
my spring for me was everyday
a good life was in store for me.
All was abloom I sang my tune
I was prepared come what may
or so it seemed just for a time
only good things came my way.
But alas my spring did pass
and so did youth it did not last
how strange indeed though far away
my youth it seems was yesterday.

Gwendolyn Clancy

The Trip

Heather, Heather, Heather
Riding on her bike
Where is she going
on her bike, bike, bike?
She went to the North Pole
She went to the South
Then she went home
and put cookies in her mouth.

Heather Anderson

Church Today

Church is fun since Vatican Two,
we hardly ever need a pew.
People are standing and shaking hands,
some Sundays, we even have a band.
Now we sing more than we pray,
and Grandma says, it's here to stay.

Priests and Deacons offer Mass,
preach, sing and communion they pass.
The ladies are no longer spectators,
but serve their Lord as commentators.
The Altar boys have little to do,
Latin is out, I'm happy, are you?

Matt O'Neill

Untitled

You loved me for a moment,
But only with your eyes,
Your lips I could not capture,
By storm or by surprise.

Your eyes I remember,
With a rush of sudden pain,
As one remembers a starlit night,
Or roses after a rain.

You loved me for a little,
I knew it couldn't be long,
Walking away, you fade quickly,
I try, but I cannot be strong.

You loved me for a moment,
Such joy we might have had,
For night and day it haunts me,
The kiss I never had.

Jeff Garrett

Moccasins

I will not go about
tracking you down,
but I will watch closely
the grace in your breasts
as you bend, the lines
a deer makes
as it moves,
how the water bends.
I will watch quietly
quiet bodies retaining
their childhood's music.
I will remember
my other women,
put as much faith
into these fantasies as can save me,
so when I see her
my elusive woman
I will recognize her.

Frank J. Antonazzi Jr.

The Knotting

Those days are but a memory
When you and I began to see
The morrow might be ours to hold
With laughter, joy, and love untold
Now our day is coming near
When both of us will make it clear
Our love from hence eternal springs
And wedding bells will loudly ring
Then will dawn a life anew
For both of us, just me and you

Daniel J. Onove

We'll Miss You

Roses are red
Violets are blue
You're gone now
What do we do?
We'll miss you so
Much it's gonna be
So hard to bear.
So I know we'll
All wish you would
still be here.
But now that you're
gone it's time to
let go and remember
the good times we had
with you. So I wrote
you this poem just
to let you know how
much we'll miss and
love you so!

Kassandra Mares

For Wilson

Time was

I wanted words to contain
Some label to explain
This elastic glue between us

Time was

I might have been your mother
Or your lover
Or the singer in your blues band

You could have been my rival
Or my idol
Or my leading man

Time is

Letting slip this tie that binds
Knots through my fingers

While I stretch past definition
Breathe to fruition
Deep delight
In freedom not to name

Debbie Green

Untitled

Never alone . . .
For he walks with me
And he talks with me
In the garden of my heart;
And the fragrance there
That he leaves with me
Is but the sweetness
Of his love.

Polly Ann Law

A Paradise Dream

Placid be the mirrored lake so serene,
Where I find tranquility, and dream.
Even before I awaken, whole-heartedly,
My eyes are open, yes splendidly.
Stars and sun reign over, eagerly.
A beautiful place peacefully.
Give your soul its restful reward,
And all spirits shall lift toward,
An endless harmony of joy and love.
Somewhere in paradise.

Elizabeth Serritella

When Away I Go To Die

When away I go to die,
I'll look not up into the sky,
I'll look not where the old men cry,
Nor away where birds do fly,
When away I go to die.

I lived my life without despair,
Saw many for whom I did care,
Die without their treatment fair,
Now their dust floats amongst the air,
I lived my life without despair.

When a beggar dies the rich care not,
He fits not in amongst their plot,
For a world where all is bought,
And for this world I do care not,
When a beggar dies the rich care not.

When away I go to die,
I'll walk away with my head high,
I ask for all ye not to cry,
For my pride they cannot buy,
When away I go to die.

Michael Fix

Raven

Raven, Dark Raven
Blacker than night
Let loose thy wings
and hasten thy flight

Raven, Dark Raven
Harbinger of despair
Mortals fear your call
Angels curse your flair

Raven, Dark Raven
Revel in your might
As deaths dread herald
Sound your caw of delight

Scott A. Taylor

Five times I have thought
what it would be like
to touch your thoughts.
Twice, I have wondered
how to embrace the
coils of your mind.
Would you let me,
ten times, soak myself
in the ocean of your soul?
Would I go mad to see,
two times, the sinews of
your heart? Or to
have one taste of
your identity? Or to
hear, twice, the very cry
of your spirit?
I desire only to know you!

Benn Gehman

The Dance

Dancing feet from side to side
    left hook
      a jaw of glass
        dancing feet are turned to lead
          falling
            falling
              falling
                the dance is over . . .

Lorna Marie Johnson

Wondering

I wonder what it would be like
    to know who you are.
I wonder what it would be like
    to have it real easy.
I wonder what it would be like
    to know you understand.
I wonder what it would be like
    to have it completely right.
I wonder what it would be like
    to know when it ends.
I wonder what it would be like
    to have it so short.
I wonder what it would be like
    to know what heaven is.
I wonder what it would be like
    to have you cry over me.

Mary Kalskett

Unseen Belief

Beauty rests within the hearts
    of loving people everywhere.
There is a sense of warmth around
    while among the ones who care.

Feel the strength within their touch
    like thunder from the sky.
Know the meaning of their thoughts
    before life passes by.

Let the peace of God enter in
    embracing heart and soul.
Believe that Jesus died for all
    by this your life's made whole.

Kathy Frock

Palm Sunday

After the storm,
comes the gift of life.

The storm is over,
and now there is life.

May there be peace,
for the world,
and everyone in it.

Share in this day,
the Lord has given.

The gift of the palms,
the sign of peace and victory.

Peace be with you all,
for the Lord has given you,
His life.

Nanette Resendiz

Arise

Sunshine on a moist green leaf
Arms outstretched from sleeps release
Sounds so crisp and tones so clear
Morning arrives and spreads it cheer.

Milford J. Talley

About You

I love to watch as you sleep
and wake you with my touch.

And hope that dreams you dream
are dreams of us.

James Mulcrone

Ode To Forty Years

When we met in school
Just two kids in the hall
Could we have known
That someday we'd fall?

We dated in high school
And were quickly a pair
Though not really knowing
The future we'd share

The years have gone by
How quickly they flew
But it didn't take long
To know I loved you

Time brought us closer
A great family we've had
We know how to live
With the good and the bad

We've had our share
Of life's joy and tears
But I still can't believe
That it's been forty years

Tom Fairless

The Storm

As she was driving . . .
    alone in the dark
Straight for the storm.
Waiting . . . anticipating . . .
    the storm . . .
Wondering what she will find
In the heart of the storm
Through . . .
    the wind,
    the lightening,
    the thunder,
    the rain,
Into the heart
As she dreamed,
She found . . .
    Calm,
    Peace,
    Happiness,
Just waiting for her
In the heart of the storm.

Tina Anderson

Wondering Why

Do you ever wonder
Why we are alive
Is it to love and nourish
or is it a test to survive
Do you ever wonder
Why the world is round
or do you ever wonder
why there's dirt on the ground
Do you ever wonder
Why the wind blows
or do you ever wonder
why the river flows
Have you ever wondered
why the sky is blue
or have you ever wondered
How much Einstein really knew
but my big question remains
Every time that I ask why
People shrug their shoulders
And there is no reply.

Jessica Hansen

Do Da Day

Smile with morning
Laugh with day
Clean some stuff
Pitch some hay
Tickle your friends
Let them tickle you
Open the door
There's more to do
Carry water
Chop some wood
Throw the bad
Hold the good
Eat some food
Smell a rose
Wash the dishes
Clean your toes
Close your eyes
Thank the light
For the day
And the night

Robert Mitnick

You

Is it you I have been yearning for?
A true companion . . .
Is it your arms I have stumbled into?
A long embrace . . .
Is it your touch I ache for?
A soft kiss . . .
Is it you I have found?
Forever.

Melissa Diane Brown

On Fall Mornings

The drive from Athens to Lerona
levels out over a black asphalt
highway that rolls over the landscape
with no end in sight.
On fall mornings, a multitude of leaves
color the cluttered landscape
and blind the eye.

In Lerona a country store
is run by two dry old men
who peek over bent wire frames
like two aging old owls.
Sing song syllables
mouth ancient words of wisdom
gleaned from years of hard living
and scraping together money
to make the rent.

Only the composer Copland
could carry the weight
of a drive down these American canals.

Michael Tyree Mooney

The Earth Is A Room

The grass is like a soft mat.
The wind is like a sheet
Who knows where it is at?

The sun is a light so bright.
The dirt is like a floor
which we soar.

The earth is like a room
so touching
so be happy it was found
and round.

Cody Robert Nolen

My Fair Maiden

Never to write a fair maiden
Of truth and brave events
Chosen from the plucked flower
A petal carries all of comments

Never to write a fair maiden
Of love and true feelings
Cut from the throat in agony
A cloud soaring, too revealing

Never to write my fair maiden
Of exactness and words of the heart
Stalling for time of which I gather
The essence of a new start

Never to my fair maiden
Have told my fears of love
Never to my fair maiden
Have worried of mine own love
for thee

Shannon Perry

The Darkness

Am I a sad woman?
Am I morbid?
Am I fully living?
And what is living?
Am I worthy of it?
Do I put on masks?
Who am I?
I don't know
but I am
continually looking for the
light out of the darkness.

Heather Staples

A Potpourri Of Love And Gold

Potpourri . . .
  A mixture of many things,
  Flowers and fruit or
  precious metals and gems

Mothers and Fathers . . .
  Blest with gifts from above
  Share a special kind of love

Awards and Rings . . .
  With jewels from the past
  Combine in a potpourri of gold
  meant to last

Bands of Roses . . .
  From this potpourri of gold
  Unfold as symbols of Beauty
  and Love untold

Lynda Lee Weller

What Is Life

We laugh, sing,
join life with life
flesh with flesh.
Two can be one
in thought and purpose
and share life's road together
for a while.
Yet at the time
death appears
we feel that on life's strand
we walk alone.
Or do we?

Florence Harris Abel

All

Spinning around,
Constantly churning.
A fire inside,
My mouth is burning.

A million questions,
Unanswered — every one.
Still, they try and help me,
After all that I have done.

The impacts of life make it hard,
To live from hour to hour.
My shoulder you may lean on,
I'll be a source of power.

The circus top is down,
The train has pulled away.
I hadn't let you know,
All I needed to say.

Love is very strong,
It's all one needs to live.
Promise me that one emotion,
You will continue to give.

Tim Larkins

Poppo's Dream

I like to reach 100
and bounce my grandkids on my knee
to tell them funny stories
or run with them upon a tree

But who can tell about tomorrow
who can bet another day
for all of us from life must borrow
and all of us to life must pay

So one thing I ask of thee
if my little ones I never get to see
tell them that their Poppo isn't dead

And when their eyes are sleepy
And they have gone to bed
I shall ride upon a midnight star
And kiss them or their head

Juan C. Gonzalez

Reply To: If You Knew Could You Love Me

If I knew, yes I'd love you
And our friendship would be strong;
Come and tell me your deepest secrets
I know you'll still belong.

If you talked about tomorrow
And the dreams that mean so much;
I will share with you my gladness
And give to you my trust.

If you told me of your feelings
I could not walk away;
I would have to stand beside you
And help you through the day.

I could love you and I'd help you
With your fear and pain;
I would treasure all your rainbows
Because I know you are quite sane.

If I knew, yes I'd love you
And our friendship would be strong;
Come and tell me your deepest secrets
I know you'll still belong.

Sharisse Duncan

Love Is Like The Wind

It starts out like a gentle breeze
Rushing through the willow trees
Where we stand, it's tousling her hair
As I bend to kiss her lips
The wind picks up
My heart does flips
I feel like I'm walking on air

The wind is in the eagles wings
Playing like the violin strings
Where he flies, he's soaring so high
As he turns to kiss the breeze
The wind begins
To play and tease
Carrying him up to the sky

Love is like the wind
Love is like the wind
It touches like a gentle breeze
With hurricane force
We're on our knees
Love is like the wind

Jeremy Ryan Hall

Why Did You Deny Me

Why did you deny me do
You know who I am. I can
give you all thing,
I can make your sick body well.
So why did you deny me for
I am the Lord.
I am the way of your life
I can make you walk again.
I can make you see again.
So why did you deny me for
I am the Lord.
No man or doctor can do all
the thing that I can do. I
rose a man from the dead. I
have made a man see. I have
turn water into wine. So I ask
you why did you deny me. Now
ain't that a good thing to ask
yourself . . . Amen

Ida Cooper

Untitled

The light and shadows
Make a dance in the morning;
Mountains touch the sky.

Lawrence H. Martin

The Other Side Of Dawn

Tonight my child,
close your eyes and dream.
Fly away on Angels' wings
Take Hope to guide you as you go,
and faith to bring you safely home.
And if in doubt you lose your way
and heavy burdens slow you.
Remember one who always waits
with heart and arms wide open.
Go with God in angels care
Anytime I can't be there.
Know that love always surrounds you.
So close your eyes little one.
Pleasant dreams will you have.
Drift gently through the night;
to the other side of dawn.

Sara Hurlebaus

Unconditional Love

You don't hit a child
That you say you love
instead of a hit, try a hug

You don't say mean things to a child
That you say you love
Instead of a mean word
Say nothing at all

You don't starve a child
That you say you love
Instead hold her hand and walk
Through the tough times together.

Margie A. Rodriguez

I'm Sorry

Does love equal
hate or hate
equal love

This is something
I often think
of

You make promises
you can't keep
then I cry
myself to sleep

I know I
broke if off
out of anger
and fear

But now you're
the only one
I want near

I pray every night
to the stars
above hoping I can win back your love

Amie Hicks

Reach Out

I think that I can sure relate
    To where you are right now
You go through all the motions, yet
    You're standing still, somehow
I've been there and I know the road
    That you must travel down
So I can say for sure, that you
    Will turn your life around
It isn't always easy, and
    Some days will last too long
But you will overcome it, then
    You will be twice as strong
So if you ever feel that you
    Are coming to an end
All you have to do, is just
    Reach out and find a friend

Paula Austin Bernard

Untitled

All I want is to be alone,
But alone with you beside me.
I need a place where I can go
And only you can find me.
I want to be a soul not seen
When I do not want to be found.
But I need to have you there for me
And always be around.

Sarah McEver

Someone Who I Love!

Someone who I love and
that someone who loves me.
    Someone who I care
about that someone cares about me
    This someone does not
know the way I feel about this someone.
    I don't know the way
this someone feels about me.
    I hope this someone
feels the same way like I do.
    I just know God sent
this someone to me. And God
Sent me to this someone
    that's why I married
this someone. And this someone
married me too.
    Love you!

Dalyla Davila-Ronda

Mountain Fever

Today I saw a mountain;
The air there was pure and clean.
The trees there on that mountain
Were colored a heavenly green.
There were blue skies and
Rushing streams;
And birds of various kinds.
Yes, today, I saw a mountain,
But it was only in my mind.

Gary Austin

One More Promise

The sun sets silently
Crickets serenade
A soft wind whispers
The promises we've made
To love and to cherish
Till death do us part
We were meant for each other
Right from the very start
I see us sitting quietly
Or walking hand and hand
When both of us are old and grey
Our love will never end
So lets make one more promise
When one of us is gone
Don't feel sad and smile
Knowing our love still lives on

Tammy Wildman

Untitled

I want to tell you I miss you,
    but shouldn't

The times I love you,
    but couldn't

The flowers I sent you,
    but didn't
My tears for you
    I've hidden

A simple glimpse of laughter
Does me no good
    there after

Understand perhaps
    you wouldn't

My love for you that shouldn't

Michael D. Weeks

Escape

White gray sharp rising imposing,
rocks,
Against a sea so serpentine;
Noise, Noise, Noise;
My mind cannot fathom,
Too quite such degree,
Of silence,
Of a soft rain cascading,
Dripping,
Falling,
From my roof on such a rainy day;
Turn off your television,
Turn off your car,
You can only guess how far.

Gene M. Horne

Beauty Of The Night

The lake is a mirror of glass
    The moon throws a sheen
The tall trees stand like sentinels
    In the path of its beam
Stars of crystal stud the sky
    On this enchanting night
What is man? Can he create so
    Magnificent a sight?

Muriel Hall

Black Panther

Darkness lurked the streets of doom,
Paws with mighty nails.
Horror about, the people scared.
Glittering his teeth like sabers,
Jaws like ivory traps.
Powerful is his coat of armor,
His tail as slashing whips.
Death sounded in his voice,
Thirst in his eyes,
Ears wind with mighty distance.
He has no soul, has no mercy,
Only temptation on his mind.
Alert is his sense of smell,
For enemies among the earth.

April Collins

I Like To Swim With Grandpa

I like to swim with Grandpa
Because he lets me play
When the serious stuff is over
Then I do things my way.

Grandma, always comes along
To make sure things go right
To help me with the "big girl" things
And keep me in her sight

To inspire and encourage me
And then of course to say
"You really did do well Darlin'.
I'm so proud of you today."

When swimming's done, we go for treats
Last time Grandma spilled her tea
I never said a single word
But I was glad it wasn't me

I love my Grandma and Grandpa
And I'm so glad they're mine
No matter what I choose to do
For me, they have the time

Jessica Mae Ehlang

Where The Angels Fear To Tread

I fear there is a certain place,
A place of fiery despair;

And I wonder why this deathly place
Was featured just to sear;

I fear the creatures that will rise,
And I pity those who go;

For some seemed great and noble,
But turned to be not so;

Not foot, nor hand, nor halo
Will touch these heated flames;

For the dear Lord's Angels
Play not the devils games.

Katherine E. Briscoe

My Grandmother

My Grandmother is special to me,
She has taught me so much.
How to crochet and make things
With her very special touch.

I always will be grateful
For the memories of her I keep,
Of playing cards and games,
Reading stories to help me sleep.

She is turning eighty-five this year,
The perfect time to say
How much she has enriched my life
And I love her more each day.

Cynthia Ridlon

Joy's Lullaby

In my baby's eyes
Souls of ancient wisdom shine
Limitless love
Laughter and beauty divine

Even though our bodies were once one
A shine of recollection gleams
Have we already met
Another life or in our dreams

In your innocence
Visions of eternity
Do you possess
Answers to life's mysteries

As you go to sleep my sweet baby
The dreamers kiss your tiny head
Hear joyful music as
Angels protect you in your bed

Tracey Weems

Colors

Red is for the color of
a red red rose.
It's soft to the touch and
sweet to the nose.
Green is for the color
of the various size trees
A home for many animals,
a kingdom for the bee's.
Yellow's for the hot bright sun,
or orange and red as one.
But many colors blend for
all to see.
A rainbow bright as the sun,
the night as blue can be.

Eleanor Pullen

The Sun

Spring has come
    flowers, birds, and trees
        radiate with joy
Rain melts hardened ice
    The land is alive with life
        butterflies dance with air
            flowers flow to the wind
Sun comes out
    warms up the sky,
        filling my soul
    rays filter through dark clouds
        penetrate rain
Gliding, hawk eyes expand
    melting into the beauty around
Trees feel whole
    raise their branches
        to the sun's warming touch
Clouds come
    and then rain
        you are the sun.

Melany Bush

Untitled

Crickets sing their song,
magic words heard by God as
stories from the past

Ronald Hanik Jr.

Untitled

I listen to my heart
On these days of mine
It speaks with a new tongue
Something so foreign
Yet not unknown to me
Speaking with compassion
Wielding strong conviction
Dedication to its perfection
And desire for its fluency
A tongue of faith
With the language of love
It talks to you
To your heart
With your dreams
Saying many words
None of which
Are more important than
Saying I Love You

Sheldon Brown

Not A Victim

You took away my purity
    my innocence
    my childhood
You expect to put back by
    one little story
    well now I'm dead
What are you going to do
    you took away my life

You took it away
    my purity
    my innocence
    my childhood
But now I'm surviving
    now I told
    now the pain is, fading
    now I am a survivor

Not a victim

Jaime Velasquez

Colors (Sing A Rainbow)

I'm feeling green,
while seeing red.
I'm white as a sheet
from being bled.

Not a purple patch,
nor in the pink,
but an indigo mood
that makes me think.

Is it black as night
or black as coal?
I'm black and blue,
which takes its toll.

The red and the dead.
The blue and the grey.
A yellow streak
gets in the way.

I'm feeling blue,
still seeing red.
I'm white as snow
now my colors have fled.

Neil B. Smith

One Step

One step toward my Saviour
Please let me take this day,
With holding not my feelings
In any selfish way.
One step toward my Saviour,
For I would like to be
Released from human bondage
And set my spirit free.
One step toward my Saviour,
One tiny step and then,
My Lord will come a mile to me,
And I can live again.

Beverly Solberg

Untitled

There shines in the darkness
A flickering light.
'Tis the flame of hope divine.
A renewal of faith in all mankind.
Strength in a world of despair.
'Tis given so freely,
That some may fail
To see the joy it imparts
But to those who perceive
It grants a wish
That shines in each ones heart.

Katherine Dietrick

Immigrant

I am sitting in the classroom
lonely and depressed
among the girls and boys
full of joy and mischief
looking at me
with kind faces but curious eyes
trying to read me
like an ancient book
full of strange stories,
odd cultures.

I feel like a prisoner
in a cage, on exhibition,
I am an immigrant.

Rafatullah Khan

sing cantadora sing

sing of seeing
sing of watching
sing of knowing

sing of seven oceans of the universe
sing of the night sky
sing of the rosy dawn
sing of the glittering sun

sing of the river below the river
sing of mists and rains

sing of music, laughter, dancing

sing not of tears
enough have flowed for centuries past
and those to come
from this woman alone

sing to
light the shadows
of the soul

sing to find the dream
    which has fled

sing to make the sad soul bloom

Mary Jane Nolan Kelly

Lorena

Lorena, beautiful Lorena
  So slender and tall;
Lorena, beautiful Lorena
  You're the best of them all.

You're the laughter and the tears
  The sunshine after rain
And everything that's lovable
  And I'll never cause you pain.

Lorena you're my happiness
  And everything I've longed for
And in my heart you'll always know
  You'll be mine and forever more.

Lorena with the sparkling eyes
With a love that will never die
A love for you that was meant to be
A kiss with every sigh.

Beatrice MacKnight

One Rib

'Twas in God's plan
Before I was born
Thoughts of constant loneliness
O' solitude I did scorn.

The Lord was to the task
His agenda well at hand
For that which I seek
Costalectomy demands.

My needs as the first father
Sole being of creation
For want of a help mate
Eve was his elation.

So after much searching
The Lord did open my eyes
The operation a success
That hushed my soul's cries.

Now I have a wife
Beautiful baby in a crib
Two gained with a loss
The loss of just one rib.

James L. Dillingham III

Life's Sunset

This evening I saw a sunset
Behind a mountain dim,
It rose from a beautiful cloud,
All gold around its rim.

There was a dark silhouette
Of tall and stately trees,
Reflected against the sunset,
Swaying gently in the breeze.

Nature stirred my very soul,
And gave me a desire to know:
Will my life measure up
To the glorious afterglow?

Oh, that our lives at close of day
Could be as supremely bright,
As this glorious, glowing sunset
That I have seen tonight!

Marguerite V. Knauft

In Love's Embrace

When I am down, I find it there
  to lift my spirits high;
To cast my worries to the wind,
  add sparkle to the eye.

When I am lonely, it comes forth
  to shed its warming light,
To fill my heart and soul with joy,
  to make my future bright.

When I am ill, I feel the touch
  that soothes away each pain,
And when I'm sad I find a hand
  to wipe away the rain.

When I'm away it comes with me,
  when I am home it's there;
Always present, always welcome,
  and always there to share.

I find myself in love's embrace.
  How lucky can I be?
The greatest gift a man can own
  has found its way to me.

Timothy J. Ives

Take Them To Jesus

When the burdens get heavy
and hard to carry;
Get down on your knees
and with Jesus leave
Every burden and care you cleave.
He will take over your cares
if you just leave them in prayer.
Trust Jesus to fill every need.

Pamela Branson

Mist On The Harbor

Through the haze of the fog
in the early morn, you can
feel the chill of the day.
We feel its touch as we approach
the shore in the silence of the day.
With a wisp of a breeze from
the sails above it brings us closer
to shore and there in the distant
haze we approach our port
submerged in fog.
The stillness of the time holds me.

Doris Swanson

Air Force Pilot's Dream

At night I lay in bed asleep,
Counting planes instead of sheep!

The first to pass, a sleek B-1,
Flashing toward the morning sun.

The second high in sky so blue,
Soaring slow, B-52.

The third an agile F-16,
Piercing sound and streaking clean.

The fourth a vigilant AWACS,
Guiding and detecting tracks.

The fifth a fully-packed C-5,
Keeping distant troops alive.

The sixth a "stealth" 117,
Striking sure and never _____.

This counting lasted endlessly,
All by all, camaraderie.

At last my gaze beheld a crowd,
Pilots marching in a cloud,

In chorus singing bold desires:
"Kick the tires and light the fires!"

Michael K. Fair

Dreams #1

Have faith little boy
    Have faith

Dream a little dream
    and live

For the future is yours
    and no ones to give

Change the feelings
    of this world
with a simple grin
    and talk to all

Cause all you need
    is faith little girl

Faith in the world
    Faith in all
and faith in the little boy
    Next to you

David C. Gorman

Give Me Solace

Give me solace,
Even dysfunctional peace.
Let me find creation,
And those who care
About thought, and art.
Give me the pieces
Of synapse, and dendrites galore.
Chase away the gun toting dragons,
And whores, and replace them
With space, and meaning, and milk.
Let us rail against both
the autocratic dynamic,
And the meaningless nought.
Build a house that we
All could enjoy,
And laugh in,
And play in,
And create in,
And Love in,
And not fear, or tremble.

Peter J. Fisher

The Accident

Three long weeks with
No bills paid
Mail unopened
Phone calls ignored
A letter not written to a
    friend far away
The last of the hydrangeas
    not picked for drying

Chores left undone
Books not read
Nor friends enjoyed
Appointments not kept
No work accomplished

Time to re-evaluate?
Or was this indeed a sign to
Practice omphaloskepsis!

Patricia Mason

Lost Love

And the tears in my eyes
distorting the way I look
at reality; through
that watery veil
having double vision
of things that were
and ought not to be again.

Until they fall,
and
the sight is restored
— just to be blurred once more.

Annemarie Monschein

Everyone Has A Special Place

Everyone has a special place,
and I find that very true.
Creatures live in trees,
and underwater too!
I know I have a special place,
and that is in my home;
Where lots and lots of people;
and lots of family roam!

Marva Brown

Untitled

Touch me,
Tease me,
Taste me,
Thrill me
With your
Body's soul.

I want, I need,
I want again
In time to
Your release.

Receive and
Give and
Love again
For my want is
Loving you.

Tasting you,
Teasing you,
Touching you,
Caressing you,
All hands and mouth.

Katherine Gregg

My Hollow Heart

Oh how hollow is my heart
My lamenting sorrows
things of the past and present
ring clear and true
weigh heavy on my brow
my countenance is hidden
deep in the darkness
at the bottom of my heart
awaiting a new sunrise
to brighten my sky of sorrow
then my hollow heart
will be full again
not with sorrow
but hope for a new tomorrow

James E. Hoemann

The Other Day I Saw A Black Man (In The Front Of The Bus)

The other day I saw a black man
he was working in a field of cotton
his life just like the waste land
for he lived in slavery
The other day I saw a black man
he was preaching in the streets
voting "no" for segregation
voting "yes" for all freedom
The other day I saw a black man
a scholar and an athlete
the owner of our business
the mayor of our towns
The other day I saw a black man
shaking hands with a white man
sitting next to a Jewish man
in the front of the bus.

Emilie R. Carson

Tombstones

The blades of grass behold
the memories of those who
lie beneath,
And later,
the leave will carry away
the thoughts of those
who stood above
Tombstones

William Hooper

Twenty-Eight

Twenty-eight is too young to die
You never had a wedding,
Never taught a son to ride a bike.
But what you did accomplish
In your twenty-eight years
Was more than anyone, even you,
Ever knew
You taught me about Tolerance,
Forgiveness, Equality.
You taught me Love.
I think of you
Every day of every passing year.
I will miss you until we can
Be together again.
How amazing that sounds . . .
To hear your laughter, listen to
Your words
To have my big brother back
My teacher. My hero.

Patty Gravel

Untitled

The sun entering the horizon.
A day beginning.
Yester years toys are new again
that have been stored.
Through a child's innocent eyes.
A life so precious
A smile so warm
Yester days bad news far from thought.
Laughter brings delight in hearts
to all that hear.
A new day beginning.
For todays child is tomorrows
leader.
And a brand new day
will begin!

Jennifer Cummins

Sometimes

Sometimes I lie awake at
night.
Wondering what I'll say,
in a song I'll write tomorrow
that I couldn't write today.
Sometimes the words seem to
tumble, and nothing seems to fit.
My mind is blank, thoughts
are gone, including all my wit.
So I'll stop for awhile, try
to sleep as I lay down my pen,
but the day before tomorrow,
will be facing me again.

Cliff Gonda

Lost Love

I can't think of life without you.
Your smile and touch
Just melts my heart.
But the love I thought
We shared,
Is not really in your heart anymore.
I am just your wife,
And not your lover.
For she holds that special place
In your heart,
That of desire!
I only get what's left
In a cold untouched part
Of you.

Anna Wade

Pain

Stop!
No more, this isn't happening.
The pain, the pain.
Another cut, oh so deep.
How can my heart withstand it?
Will my mind make it through?
Will I still be me?
The tears, oh the tears.
One for every second.
One for every pain.
Can I trust, will I trust?
Each tear a tiny cut,
And more pain.
One minute the sky is bright.
The next dark as night.
Why?
Why is pain always at my door?

Gail Williams

The Eagle

I saw an eagle soaring
Far above its nest,
Nestled in a crooked tree
Upon the mountain crest.

With awe I watched it fly,
So free and high above;
Yet I felt an empty sorrow,
For this fine bird I love.

One by one God's species
Disappear from earth.
Once they are gone, never again
Shall they bring forth new birth.

I saw the pollution from the city,
Creeping across the valley floor.
Just how much can we pollute,
Until we can stand no more?

Must we destroy all that we touch,
Or don't we really care?
Will our children's children ever see
An eagle in the air?

Wesley Scott

Love

Love has many powers,
It can bring you to your knees,
rip your heart like pain,
Then mend it back with ease,
can draw out tears of sadness,
and also tears of joy,
can make us smile at someone
whose trying to annoy.
Love is all around us,
no matter where we turn;
Love can be so simple
yet hard for us to learn.
Love's a soothing feeling,
That help us sleep at night;
love makes us grab a loved one,
and hug them oh so tight.
Love has many powers,
as I have said above;
the most important thing of all
to remember, "God is love."

Ann Whitaker

Snowfall

Silence fell as dry snow
on a cold winter night.
One morning woke
and it blinded our eyes.
I caught you squinting from the glare.

The sun was shouting through
the trees, speckled in white.
Our feet fell
lightly leaving little imprint
for all to see.

Who knew the snow
what day did it fall.
More sensitive to the chill
you knew it would not melt.

How long a season
which sees no thaw.
Bitterness, at the cold
in our hands.

Seth R. Sears

One World

Mother Earth, Father Sky,
Wherein doth the future lie?

Man's unholy game of war
Is no longer worth the score.

Battle scars on barren plains,
Broken homes, unbridled pains.

Some in riches, some in rags,
Borders, disorders, confusion flags.

Waves of rage (revenge!) repeat;
The earth rebels beneath our feet.

Famines, floods, and quivering lands,
Winds of change o'er sifting sands.

Mother Earth, O Father Sky,
Where does mankind's future lie?

Mother Earth contracts again.
Her labor pains progress and wane;

Intense and shaken, spent and worn
Until . . .
. . . One World . . .
is Born!

F. Katherine Edwards

A Gift For Skip

If you had one wish,
would it be a fish.
If you wanted a duck,
you're out of luck.
If you wish for a bird,
it would be absurd.
But if it's a fish, you
get your wish.

In the garage there is a
pool — so don't be a fool
enjoy the yule.
You'll find a tank
for a fish named Hank.
If you don't like what you got
Return the lot.
Get the cash and
Make a dash.
(The gift was a fish tank kit.)

Gerri Trethewey

Gentle Giant

So high on his pedestal
so strong are his hands
So gentle his touch
so warm his smile
so sad his heart
so long his past
so solid his word
so wide his shoulder
so soaked with tears
so unconditional his love
so willing to help the stranger
so lived his eyes
so tired his soul
so weary his body
so hard he's worked
so ready for rest
so big his heart
so gentle this giant -
my father . . .

Lizz Smyth

tahajjud

(muslim practice of praying late at night, after midnight)

the back of the chair is a cracked bone   a fissure like the edge of New Mexico

stiff daggers curling around powdery yellow buttons   colors of chinese water flowers   I was overwhelmed by the perfume and had to leave the table

the postman returned and finally moved his truck   opening my view of the crisp street   the man's coughing disturbed the thought patterns he kept coughing and hacking in rhythmic intervals and finally got up and walked coughing down the street

the staffed light of the lace   the patterns on the table   the sky swirling with those clouds we decided to take piano lessons   somewhere a river   murky   her veiled face   was tumescent in intervals of sharp wind

thought of black sand   absorbing the sun the volcano   the leaves seem plastic enormous and the drops of water sound like pellets hitting hollow veined walls there was a hurricane and we walked on the corrugated sheets of metal that were ripped up the tin houses torn up   remembered   catastrophe   the stars

something crawling on the wall outside   in the dark   cannot see the blinds the leaves frost covered the cars   bent the plants   tomatoes stinking like foul vaginas   in the bathroom stalls   the metal   tired the body   sinking baggage bottom of the pond   ghosts   seeking to suffer   the Mawlawis   salat   a killing praying as of animals   crawling with insects   divine light divine water

Irene-Marie Spencer

Nature's Show

Birds have to fly
As butterflies flutter,
Roosters will crow
And farmers make butter.
Cows will give milk,
Turkeys will gobble,
Chickens lay their eggs,
The ducks will wobble.
Flowers add beauty
And so do trees,
The flowers have color,
The trees make a breeze.
The sun has to shine,
The rain has to fall,
Blue skies above
Are prettiest of all.
The stars have to glitter,
The moon has its glow.
All this above
Is nature's show.

Marjorie Riley

My Brother

He is gone now;
This time it is for good.
He is never coming back.
Oh, how I wish he would.

For I never got to say
"I love you."
And we didn't get to accomplish
All that we wanted to.

We never got to get
As close as we wanted to be;
And now we'll never get to.
That is plain to see.

In a way he will be with me,
Like it was from the start.
He may have died on earth,
But he lives on in my heart.

Glenda Brooking

To The Man I Love

I knew from the start
That you had won my heart,
Just one look at you
I knew our love was true,
And now that we are two
Our dreams will all come true,
Standing side by side
Our love will never die,
Although we've had
Our ups and downs,
Our love has truly
Stood its ground,
Although times can be hard
And times can be tough,
I believe in miracles
Just look at us.

Sue Lehto

Essence Of The Holidays

At special times of the year
Families gather to spread cheer,
Warm hearts are full
And fond memories are held dear.

Candles with warm scents
Ribbons of satin adorn,
Hymns of glory ring out
To praise the Babe that is born.

Gifts are exchanged
Delicious foods are prepared,
Kind words are expressed
Great stories are shared.

Lights twinkle red and green
Hope and joy abound,
If everyday had Christmas cheer
Love could always be found.

Angela K. Guillot

So Thankful

I'm so thankful
    For your love
For everything
    You're capable of
Your warmth and passion
    Devoted care
Our endless love
    Will always be there
You've given my life
    A certain meaning
Being with you
    Is continuous dreaming
And if there's one thing
    I'm certain of
I'm so thankful
    For your love

Jennifer McBride

Untitled

A fair faced child with sunlit hair,
sits on a porch swing.
But is not there.

Young blue eyes watch butterfly's
But cannot see

Pale soft hands feed morning birds
A voice as sweet sings.
Without a word.

In a garden only angels.
Know of is a child of pure light
and true love
No longer earth bound this little one
Sits with God and is one.

Valerie R. Lucas

Inside The Darkened Room

Inside the darkened room
    there is despair and
        hatred — there is
            wrong doing and
                evil
Inside the darkened room
    there is sadness and
        racism — there is
            killing and
                war
Inside the darkened room
    there are all of
        us trying to find
            the only good
                hope

Amber L. Johnson

Crimson With Life

The being is so proud, so tall
withstanding anything
that comes its way.
Shielding itself, yet baring
itself, still in the change.
Increasing now, in tallness.
Expanding the wildness of itself.
Dust, brushing over its skin.
The light reflects off the
crimson rose. When after
dew has settled.

Brandy Domingo

Grandpa

I saw my grandpa standing in a golden ray of sun
As he looked at me I cried, "I miss you!"
He replied in a sing-song voice, "I know."
I could feel he was about to go as he pulled out a box
A box of bright yellow and golds
He told me, "this isn't a gift you can see, hear or touch,
but only feel within."

Shaking hands slowly opened the box
As the box opened a bright beam shot from the opening,
hit me then disappeared

While my grandfathers figure faded I felt that he knew
that I couldn't help him

Just as his face was about to vanish. A single tear
trickled down his cheek

It fell landed in my palm, slowly soaking in, explaining
the feelings of love he felt.

    Teresa Caven

God At Meadowbrook

It was at a house in a meadow, on the outskirts of town
When I first heard the Gospel preached, clear and sound
My eyes were gently opened as I understood the Word
I knew I was a sinner, so that proved there was a Lord

The Words the Pastor taught us, I'd heard them all before
Somehow they were different, not a bit like old Folk Lore
It's true we all are sinners, we've broken all the laws
But this man brought Life to God, who had not the slightest flaw

He showed us the Rugged Cross, where He suffered bleed and died
And took us down the path where He walked, prayed and cried
Then when He gave up the Ghost, it proved not to be in vain
For He gave His all, just to make us whole again . . .

When the sermon was over. I felt that I had been
Somewhere in the presents of my Lord, if only at the end
I knew that I was welcome for the World said, come again
And because God sent me to that house, I'll never be the same.

    Goley Smith-West

Compelling Impulsion

When autumn leaves begin to fall
Hear ye, hear ye, one and all
Sportsmen now shall come to call, And nature is the host
Tree stands made of lumbered pine
Store-bought rifle, high-powered kind
Tools they are, of modern time, To aid the sports man's boast

When autumn leaves are falling down
All ye sportsmen gather 'round
Tools of time are here abound, To make this sports more daring
Make your arrows, design your bow
Pursue on foot, as you well know
The Indians did, so long ago, For them, the need was faring

Then should you ever score a hit
With bow and arrow of your wit
Perhaps you'd pause to think a bit, Your prize was more than trifle
Boast ye may, and rightly so,
Perhaps you'd say, "tis quite a bow"
Boast ye may, when home you'd go, And throw away your rifle

    Hugh Buchanan

You Are the Light of My Life

You are the sunshine of my life, Lord.
You light my way, day by day
You take away my sorrow
Giving me a promise of a brighter tomorrow.
You are the sunshine of my life, Lord
I feel your presence day by day
Even when trouble comes my way.
I look up towards heaven and cry out to the Lord I know
A talk with Him always makes my faith grow.
Although I don't always get my way.
I know He always hears what I say.
He knows what is best for me.
Even though my prayers have not been answered
As I would see.
He has a reason that I do not know
Perhaps as His child He just wants me to grow.
As I lift up my eyes towards Heaven and pray
Thank you Lord for listening to me today.

    Irene Willcoxon

Rough Around The Edges

He's rough around the edges, my man
And I study him whenever I can.
His education is minimal
His sex appeal subliminal
With skin that's coarse and tan.

An evening at the opera is a waste
A rented video more his taste.
He's happy as a clam
With a plate of fried Spam
No clue what to do with caviar paste.

He's rough around the edges, my guy
But there's nothing I want he won't buy.
He works hard all day
And brings home his pay
The man doesn't know how to lie.

I look into his eyes every night
As he enfolds me in his arms so tight.
His edges are rough
But I can't get enough
Of this man who makes life feel so right.

    Christine Botting

A Day To Remember

On 2-10-96 it was too cold to play ball.
    We went to play pool at Table Steaks Pool Hall.
I entered a 9-ball tourney for ranks "AA" to "D,"
    And to rid the bye we entered you as a "C."

With your stick and stool you were full of excitement.
    Having just turned 7 this was your first tournament.
You had to win 2, your opponent 4, your match across the room.
    With no help from me it was your opponent who was doomed.

Awesome combos, banks and a shot behind your back.
    Though young and short you displayed it wasn't talent you lack.
Playing opponents your height only to their waist.
    Deciding each shot on your own never shooting in haste.

You challenged several men in this experience.
    Finishing a proud second earning 6 times your allowance.
Though losing in the finals you took it like a true man.
    Stepping down from your stool you shook the winner's hand.

Having so many talents with baseball and pool.
    You know what's important and remain excellent in school.
Striving for the best, your outstanding behavior is one.
    That makes me so very proud to have such a wonderful son.

    Richard Sabol

Sonnet On Youth

A girl walks the sands, and wrinkles up her toes
While golden is the sun that dares to set.
The roaring waves so high, the hill-sides wet —
The beauty that she knows.
The clouds above drift slowly down below,
Forgetting all the former weather bets —
The girl is running free from care and yet,
Where is there she can go?
Maybe if in search for life, she walks the land
And stumbles on a quiet ocean shell,
Life for her will be no more demands,
At last her heart will whisper "all is well."
So, wander little girl upon the sands,
You'll one day have the joys of life to tell.

Meg Richardson

Darkness

She once did live, she once did love,
The ground beneath, and all above.
But then did come a dank and dark
And hideous sun that brought with it despair.
And she was changed, and all that was given
Was wrenched away 'til she was driven
Just as mad as the Gods that she had worshipped.
And then she fled, to an evil place
And there she thrust into her breast
The dagger that she knew must
Bring upon her death.
Now all is quiet, and all is dark,
For in her eyes, no light shall spark.

Christina Davidson

We

Into my life you took a step quiet, unassuming and small
So soft and gentle your approach I hardly noticed at all

Your face a shadow in my mind every now and then
A face I began to love I can't remember when

A love returned a thousand fold as only you could do
We began to share a lovely thing which only grew and grew

All the sunshine that you brought when you came to my door
Would vanish the very moment you weren't there anymore

So you took my hand in yours and on my finger put a ring
and pledged to me your love with a lifetime of sharing

Now all the world awaits us and we'll set it spinning
For Dear, we have no end only a beginning

Janice Bain

The Special Bonds Of Love

Her eyes are care,
her touch is healing
her skin as soft as down.
Her smile a day of sunshine,
her laughter a sheer delight,
her wisdom ever present
a ray of blissful moonlight.
A silver crown rests in her hair,
the angel that she is.
The smell of time that lingers there,
through years that she has lived.
My teacher, my mother, my listener, my friend.
My grandmother loves me,
with all her heart.
And I love her,
with mine!

Christiane Davina Graham

Affairs Of A Pair

She's the vision on an angel, all dressed in white,
with just enough devil, to cause men to fight.
I must bid her wishes, to earn her favor,
the soft sweet kiss, I long to savor.
There's first a few things, I must put to rest,
before I am able, to give her my best.
I look towards the time that I will be able,
to shed my chains and become more stable.
For now I delight, in the time that we spend,
in hopes that the happiness, won't soon end.
She's been treated wrong, in the past by a few,
but that is something, I could never do.
At affairs of the heart she has been burned,
now trust is something that must be earned.
I'm happy for all the hours we share,
for as long as you want me I will be there

Ralph A. Lee

The Treasure At The Lake

It was a quiet Summer night.
The lake was clear.
Barely shimmering in the glistening moonlight
and the soft Southern breeze.
That rustled the leaves of the towering Oak trees
ever so slightly.
The distant sound of an owl tiptoed across the water.
The air still smelled of the bellowing thunderstorm
which had passed but an hour before.
Leaving a new sense of life.
Properly cleansed and awaiting the coming dawn.
The warmth from the crackling fire,
though not needed,
Somehow seemed to soothe the soul.
I could not help but feel my great fortune
as she softly laid her head against my shoulder.

Steven Michael Mott

To Tasha

I saw you standing, deep in thought, by the window's golden light.
How much you had matured and grown suddenly came to my mind.
Could you have changed unexpectedly, in an instant so it seems?
Has the little girl I have known so long stolen away into dreams?
A creature in her place appeared, beautiful, out of the blue,
As though she'd slipped from a cocoon, like lovely butterflies do.
This sudden metamorphosis, remarkable to behold,
At once caused me to realize you stand poised at life's threshold.
Eager are you to try your wings, to open them wide and fly.
Seize what life has in store for you, search, experience, try.
Now I know, as you grow older, I shall see you less and less.
Whatever happens in future years, continue to do your best.
May you always be contented in everything you will do.
Don't let adulthood change your sweetness is my fervent wish for you.
Do especially remember, wherever you may be,
That you will be forever loved so very much by me.

Gisela Myers

Infinite Intelligence

From aardvark to zwieback,
I'm more complete than A to Zinc,
a supplement for the cerebrum.

I stress about every word,
yet am a paregoric for every vocabulary,
a linguistic flotsam of the elite echelon.

I'm a quip for every query,
a denouement for every dilemma,
an apogee apparatus of alliteration.

Joseph H. Lyons

A Synonym Of Fiction Is Romance

How your hands held me still
a tiny bird shuddering in a small paper box
smoothed my turning feathers and whispered,
the first whisper I ever heard
that wasn't a secret or an insult;
it was my name.

The hair on my neck waved upwards
as if covered suddenly by the sea,
I believed the long list of words
knocked loose
by the mountains breaking
inside of me. I was very young
and you were very young.

We did not know the stars
were dead lights from a far away place,
the keepers of counterfeit
memories. A burned-out panorama
of past galaxies, a canopy to cover us,
two shining coins painted to look like silver,
composed of nickel and lead.

Nikole Hendricks

Lost In Time

Dark side of the moon and the hot spots of hell have left us withering on the floor's time. Wondering what has past us by and the things that have peered into our souls. Looking at a face in the ticket line of some forgotten bus station in the midwest. Trying to confront that long-dead demon.

A down-trodden man standing on a wooden porch of an old weathered trailer house in Lost Cabin, WY. Along with the swirling dust and blowing wind, he can't see the reasons why he came to a place like this for a women he lost and the black gold that still haunts his welfare paycheck.

Clouds block the sun on the beach of a nowhere place. Waves crash the shore in an unrelenting storm. Woman sits under the cover of pier-side tavern, watching, waiting through the rain drenched window. Wind whistling against the glass, calling her name. The past has left her alone in the future, looking for her sea-fairing sailor that has never come home.

Small boy quiet and still in a funeral pyre. Mother looking up to the heavens for an answer to the lost of her child. When no words come she will move on, looking for that lost word, phrase or look that has long escaped her. Shopping for groceries in the store, seeing children in every row. On streets, playing catch behind fences, in church squirming restless in the pew. She must bare the burden of memory, and stay lost in time.

John N. Esau

There Is No Part Five

1
You opened the festival of flowers that spring.
How could I know they bloomed for me?

2
Dawn never came that week.
We huddled together,
sentries around a fire.
You grew strong in my grasp.
Wake up, you whispered.
Come see the pale blossoms.

3
Only twice did we speak of later,
each time in low voices so later would not hear
and overtake us.

4
There you stood,
a sacrament of petals falling
shattered on the obsidian floor.
I watched, an arrow in a quiver.
No one disturbed the stillness.

David J. Weimer

A Friend For Life

Just sitting alone by the fire,
Never expecting to find a friend for life,
But you overlook the reality of you,
Why,
After all these years nothing but shame?
Can you really trust yourself?
If not, you might as well quit,
Go away and enjoy it,
Just worrying about who to trust,
Who to protect you,
You are your own friend for life.
Who else can solve your problems,
Clean your room,
Fall in love,
And even grow up,
Never thought that you could trust a friend for life,
Never thought that you could have a friend for life.
Think of what you and your friend have done.
You have lived together and will live together,
Forever.

Jill Stout

The Valleys

I travel through the Valley of the Dead,
and wreak of the victory of defeat.
I walk through the valley of the Dead,
and carry the burden of my doubts.
I stumble through the Valley of the Dead,
with the despair of a love lost.
I trot through the Valley of the Dead,
and know what it is to succeed.
I run through the Valley of the Dead,
and know what it is to fail.
I fall through the Valley of the Dead,
and have felt the pain of a life without love.
I have lived and I will die an uncertain death,
not knowing what will come next,
only knowing what my faith has told me to believe.
I have walked through the Valley of the Living,
I have traversed its soil, and stumbled on its stones,
I have run through its mazes and walked its uncertain paths.
I have fallen from its heights and,
and I have found that only Love lasts forever.

Patrick Patton

(what do i know?)

He paints a picture —
dark clouds and rain drops.
She sings a song —
words of love and life.
   They tell a story — listen while she weeps.

Youth out in the streets —
lost in tricks and treats.
A mother sits inside —
lost in all her life.
   Sun rises, sets for both — two worlds far apart.

Lonely stranger —
only bed's bench.
Ladies in next to nothing —
only love's strangely twisted.
   Funny how they're all over — even on your side of the street.

Child is starving —
eat your heart out.
Someone's Grandma's dying unloved —
live a little more.
   You're warm in that snug little bed — only sweet dreams for you tonight.

Adrian Lee Godbee

A Love Such As You

Warm breath of secrecy, whispers echo in heaven,
heard ever so sweetly, sincerely cures my soul.
A touch of warmth,
melting my heart,
heating my dreams
and creating a world.
Roses scattered in memory,
cover the path,
lighting the future,
guide its way.
A strength of weakness,
thoughts of hopefulness,
carry the power,
forever holds within.
Life of fantasy,
uncontrollable passion,
dreams are granted,
reality comes true.
Hearts in tune, eyes made of stars.
known of none so true, a love such as you

Kelly Chastain

The Flower

God sent us a flower, that grows
with beauty and with pain. Its petals
are delicate and silky, touched by colors
sent from heaven, like the sky after rain.
The sweetness of its fragrance. Is as
pleasant as a lovers kiss. It brings back fond
memories of things that we miss.
But while its blossoms only last for a
very brief time. The joy that it delivers will
stay always in our mind.
What ever is this flower do you
wonder or suppose. Just in case you
cannot name it. Then simply call
it rose.

Charles L. Baker

Calvin Calls The Dinosaurs

Calvin is a little lad no more than two feet tall,
who loves to play with dinosaurs that beckon to his call.
He eats his dinner late at night, about ten of one,
and then his mommy holds him tight as Calvin sucks his thumb.
She gently pats upon his back as if he were a drum,
Until he makes an "urrping" sound that bids the beasts to come.
And when he'd slowly close his eyes and dreams fill his head,
a green and yellow Burpadon follows him to bed.
And all night long, within his crib, as Calvin gently sleeps,
he thinks an ugly dinosaur's good company to keep.

Joel Hebert

Madness

In that dream within a dream,
in that sacred place,
images woozy-weird throb in calypso beat:

Portentous pygmies peek out indecently,
retreat,
in gardens of the dead;
snippets of picture-sound
fold, splinter, scatter-out,
become
chopped nothingness.

Now, rippled smooth broad *atria*,
the mind lies — endless;
waiting room for the dead.

Roberta Mendel

Your Smiling Face

The heavenly body we call the moon, is such a beautiful sight
It takes the darkness from the skies and gives the Earth some light

He has no brightness of his own, he shares from his mother the sun
And when the early hours come, he knows his job is done

In the waiting hours, it shines in some other place
Some people have even said, they can see his smiling face

At times he is such a romantic, he looks down at the couples in love
And we not only thank him, we thank the Heavens above

Celestial body so beautiful, no other can compare
And if we have any problems, it's with you our souls we share

You are always there to comfort us, waiting for our prayers to arrive
And if not for you listening ear, some loves would not survive

We praise you in so many ways, through books, stories and song
And never ever blame you for things that may go wrong

Having been with us since the dawn of time, your name I often hear
And as long as I see your smiling face, I know there's nothing to fear

When I take my late night walks, it's you looking over me
Because without your ray of light, I would not be able to see

So please stay with me till my time has come, and I will kiss your smiling face

For then there's nothing to restrain me, neither body, time nor space.

Nick Sym

Leave At Peace

Heavenly light in sky's dark night
Makes brightest stars with shame hide.
Ghostly shadows of clouds ride by,
'Tween earth and moon - dark and bright.

Warm currents of spring come forth,
With moon's rays from sky to earth
Dancing fairies 'mongst the trees,
Blond tresses blowing in the breeze.

Moon, as you travel cross the sky,
Are you happy with the world?
Have you knowledge of things gone by
Which no human can discover?

There's no record upon your face
Of things you've known on this universe.
Men are searching for even a trace
'Mongst rocks and dust from your face.

Will they not leave to quiet and peace
That heav'nly glow of your shores and peaks
Must they forever stir and trace
Even dark sometimes hidden in your face.

Margaret J. Wilson

Going Home

The sun comes up, a new day born,
The sun goes down, a new scar worn.
Windows of steel, walls of rock.
Nothing to do, but kill the clock.
Yard time, hard time, deals are made.
Promises broken, spirits fade.
The General decides who will pay.
Only luck can bring him one more day.
The bright turns dark, only seconds remain.
A pool of red, a body with no name.
The rush of war, the fear of defeat.
A soul is lost, and also forgot.
Outside is power to those with guns.
Inside the war is waged with none.
The sun comes up, a new day born.
The sun goes down, a new scar is worn.

Matthew E. Mattox

Untitled

I stand in the shadow of solitude
Withdrawn to my fate —
A transparent heart — the window to the examination
Of my soul's terrible lonesomeness

From which I watch with shallow breath —
The nearness of life's happiness
Wondering within the reality of thought —
There dwell other of God's creatures so unloved

I tear at my glass prison —
As one should pry the walls
Between truth — and lie's darkness
Within untouchable memories —

For the closeness of embracement —
The warmth of friendship
Taken for granted by free men-
Unrealistic dreams for its slaves

I reach for the lost child
With key in hand —
Fear grows from the past — they pity me,
Perhaps I — pity myself

Nathan White

Transient

Flowers in bloom is what we are
Fragrance of beauty that fills our world
Amid the thorns and thistled road
We smile, we love, we laugh, we cry
Emotions of sweet essence is what we emit
Embracing among the thorns
Our little seed.

Eloise Prado

Untitled

Someone calls me a Cowboy every now and then
I just tip my hat, say Howdy and give 'em a grin
A girl once asked me if I've ever ridden a horse
I just looked at her and smiled and said but of course
But I don't ride the horses as much as the other ones
the ones bein' the bulls, because they're much more fun
She said I was crazy and then called me a fool
but you just can't give up something you were born and love to do
I guess that's what separates a cowboy and just an ordinary man
and why cowboys are few, all across the land.

Chad Hert

Holy Ones

Holy Ones, Ancient Ones,
I send my prayer smoke to you this night,
for all whose hearts are empty and aching,
for those whose minds are confused,
and whose tired feet journey an untrue path.

Hear me, Great Spirit!
Warm and fill those hearts,
with the rays of our Grandfather, the sun,
that they might know love.

Clear those minds, with the healing,
cleansing breath of our Brother, the wind,
that they might know truth.

Strengthen those tired feet,
within the vibrant womb of our Mother, the earth,
that they might know the True Path.

Holy Ones, Ancient Ones,
walk this path with them,
that they might know peace.

Holly D. Murdock

Pieces

Tattered pieces of forever,
Lie in boxes on the ground.
Hollow footsteps in an empty corridor,
Now echo the only sound.

Plans and prayers of a lifetime,
Slowly become so remote.
As frustrations obvious, failure supreme.
Divulging their hideous gloat.

The uncertain road toward the horizon.
Leave a path of cinders behind.
A once intact heart heeds the leading,
Resentment though, encompasses the mind.

To have wasted one's life so vainly,
In a marriage that was never meant to be.
Flavor a world with distrust and denial.
Putting the rest under critical scrutiny.

Hope factors into a gradual beginning.
Based on raw courage and temporary scars.
Timid steps into the new direction termed "future"
Walk ever so slightly and dare healing not to be far.

Roseann Sloan

Ode To The Beast

It came from dust on the ocean floor.
    With lightening thrust, it strove for more.
Through walking fish it won the land,
    then made a wish and grew a hand.

It lost its tail and left the trees,
    then searched the jail and found the keys.
In magic fire it found a friend
    that did inspire both means and end.

It stood upright and made a spear,
    and with its might demanded fear.
"The Earth is mine!", it said to all,
    then drew the line to make a wall.

Its numbers grew, and sorrow spread.
    With every clue the Garden bled.
The billions teemed, their pride would show,
    and few, it seemed, would ever know.

They closed their eyes, and longed for gold.
    Embracing lies, their soul was sold.
In dark descent, their life force fled.
    This omen meant the Beast was dead.

Mark A. Nielsen

Son-Rise

I rose with the Son this morning.
The glorious Light filled my heart.
As I opened my eyes in the dawning
I was warmed by the bright Morning Star.

Son-beams fell all around me.
They brought a bright smile to my face.
With such glorious Son-light upon me,
I was ready to run the day's race.

Dark nights are forever behind me
For the Son has revealed a New Day.
No darkness can e'er overcome it.
The Son shines upon me always.

It's happy I am to claim it!
The Son has risen for me!
I'm free of night's darkness forever.
A Son-worshipper I'll always be.

Paula W. Roy

If I Could Write Music

If I could write music that spoke to your beauty,
its searing melodies would arouse uncontrollable passions.

If I could write music that spoke of your laughter,
its rhythms would tickle the spine and spur unbridled grinning

If I could write music that spoke with the warmth of your heart,
its radiance would entice listeners to hug themselves and smile.

If I could write music that spoke with the caring of your soul,
its sincerity would bring about the righting of many wrongs.

If I could write music that spoke of the dreams you generate in me,
its listeners would close their eyes and dance with rainbows.

If I could write music that spoke to the love that I have for you,
its timbre would compel sworn enemies to embrace.

If I could write music that spoke,
I might be able to convey the feelings that I have for you,
more accurately
than the piteous words of this language will ever allow.

If I could write music,
your symphony would fulfill me

If only I could write this music . . .
　　Michael W. Ferguson

Treasures

Daughters, sisters, treasures untold.
Mother, Father, pleasures unfold.

Distinct as the seasons that render each day,
The first gift in October, the second in May.

Restless and watchful our initial event,
Gave way to the hush of a darling content.

Each smiles so tender, tho' differently earned,
One peek-a-boo giggles, the other's tickled and churned.

Curious and unique their traits do appear,
We visit our memories to cherish them dear.

As days become weeks and months become years,
we yearn for the laughter and learn from the tears.

Daughters, Sisters, treasures untold.
Mother, Father, pleasures of gold.
　　Eric Trabold

The Wind Is An Unseen Messenger

The wind is an unseen messenger, and leaves
Made nervous by it wave cheer to floating condors
In playful contest with the currents.
These talismanic blessings give character
To our atmospheric friend and show the outlines
Of its presence. Come cool our brows and puff
Our sails, and waft our seeds, kind wind, unseen itself
Is yet seen for all its gracious goodness.
These emollients are the quiet breezes of renewal.

And when it chooses rage, it sends into battle
Hateful waters made furious by its madness
To capsize life, pound shore line boulders
And shred the house where innocence lives.
Unseen itself, in spiteful thrust,
It flaunts the might of lunacy.

There is no life to death. Inert and neutral,
Abstract, unseen — death does not exist except
For those who bear witness to its monstrous equanimity;
Except to grieve and vow that death is not the end of love.

Death has no message but that which we give to it.
　　Irving Gold

Love

Love enters the heart, like a young child learning to walk
slowly, at first, not yet knowing how to talk.
It then pierces our hearts, like a sharp, pointed arrow,
causing us grief, happiness, affection, and sorrow.
Love creeps into our hearts when we are unaware,
then all of a sudden we learn to care,
about people and things,
and all that love brings.
Love sings us her sweet song,
which makes us strong.
She rises like the sun each day,
helping us to find a way
to reach a goal of peace and rest
ultimately bringing happiness.
　　Ceres A. Krohn

New Year's

New Year's Eve, is the place to be.
At a friends house, but not near a mouse.
Kids are playing while saying "Yipee."
New Year's is so fun, for everyone.
No school, so kids can rule.
Watch the ball drop, at the sound of the clock.
Kids will have trouble writing,
and teachers will be shouting.
Things will be happening, because New Year's is coming.
Kids and parents will be singing
and more people joining.
People who are grumpy will be smiling.
Decorative houses, without little mouses.
Uh, oh, gotto go.
　　Zain Waqar

Guardian Angel

Guardian Angel, watch over your younger brother,
Guardian Angel, I couldn't bear to lose another,

I promise I will never argue over little things,
if you come back to me, give back your angel wings,

You were young and handsome and just nineteen years,
the angels took you, and now my days are filled with tears,

I waited up for you, I wanted to hug you each and every night
but that one night in August, I didn't get to hold you tight,

The night you died, I felt you gently touch my face,
saying good-bye as you journeyed to another place

A young girl sits at your grave, her words so softly spoken,
Don't leave me Shawnie, my heart is broken

There is a new star so high above in the sky,
it's so bright like the twinkle that was in your eye.

Guardian Angel, I wish you could have stayed with us forever
but, in our hearts we won't forget you ever.
　　Rachel Doheny

The Deer Are Leaping

In the summer the wind softly blows
To face the wide world and the places unknown,
　　To see if the deer are leaping.

In a summer lodge in the summer grass
A camping family leaves their task,
　　To see if the deer are leaping.

In a bubbling brook in a bright blue stream
A long-necked crane is waiting,
　　To see if the deer are leaping.
　　Tiffany Chezum

Beware

Feel insensitivity with every word she speaks.
Watch rage develop in her eyes and harden on her cheeks.

Pain will go unnoticed, for Love she has no time.
And God's the only one who knows what's on this lady's mind.
Pleasure, I don't think so it doesn't have a chance.
Her hardened heart has even thrown the devil off his stance.

Enter with a caution don't let her smile embrace.
Holding back the urge to touch the beauty of her face.

Woman they adore her. With men she has control.
Lady I will call her but she cannot have a soul.

Her voice will entrance you as she fills you with her lies
Then listens very closely with her understanding eyes

And when the night is over, her laughters all you'll hear.
Like lightning she came in your life, like magic Disappear.

Christina Prevost

Untitled

It is a cold winter's night. The rolling hills
slumber under the moon's luminous blanket
as the crickets serenade them with an
evening lullaby. Shadows move gracefully
in the deafening silence that embraces her
room. Tears are falling like droplets of rain
against a picture window. A loving heart,
stricken with sorrow and grief, beats slower
and slower as she lies quietly in the darkness.
A kind and giving soul makes one last desperate
cry for the warmth and tenderness it
once knew. With emptiness and loneliness
now beside her, her breathing becomes
labored and shallow. As she closes her eyes,
all is still. Abandoned by love and friendship,
the struggle for hope has ended and the
serenade is all that remains.

Casey Klein

Untitled

In North Dakota, it is sometimes
  Easy to believe in God.
  We are inured to vastness,
  Majesty of time and space,
  Horizons that go on to the infinite, boundless
  And beautiful North Dakota, where it easy to
  Believe in the power and majesty of God.

  Sometimes it is hard in North Dakota
  To believe. When rains do not come
  When the ground is hard and cracked
  When grasshopper swarms strip the
  Last green stalks along the roadway.

Evelyn Nack Olgeirson

The Cat

The transformation was startling
In just a moment he had changed
From indolent lie-about
To a dark furred feline not much different
    than a panther
Body taut with nose pressed against the glass
Tail alternating between undulating waves and
    stiff metronomic beats on the floor
Low growls, eyes of yellow gleams
Staring with the hunter's fierce intensity
At a trio of fawns grazing on the still green grass
Of early autumn.

Andree R. Wood

To Vicky's Smile

Vicky in every waken second of my life
You are always in my mind;
Your smile is the only source of light
Where from the sun steals its glowing shine,
The envy of the moon and every twinkling star
That brightens the worlds most darkened skies;
You are my morning star, the sunshine of my life
Of heavens how I wish before my ending comes,
That I just could in person most humble thank,
The almighty and all the great and sweetest beings
That graceful brought you to this life,
Impressing in your face that sweet and lovely smile,
That brings such greatest happiness to mine.
The budding roses with their scent are only witness
Oh how I've just fallen so deep in love with you
And my only greatest happiness is being close to you;
How much this passion hurts and prompts to desperation.
I only hope your beautiful smile will never cease
And make my love for you just grow with great devotion.

Dake Munoz

To The Flowers In God's Garden

The azalea, lily, and the rose have blossomed side by side.
Each is a symbol for today of love so proved — so tried.

The azalea blooms in springtime with colors rich and rare.
Its life though short is beautiful; its fragrance fills the air.

The lily tall and slender with head demurely bowed
Has a beauty strong yet tender as it towers above the crowd.

The rose is filled with wonder — its petals soft and free
A challenge to the loveless world — a joy for all to see.

The azaleas in our garden were with us but a while,
The Lord has taken them away. In them — He found no guile.

The lilies we have with us still; they're walking straight and tall
With a vision of the future and a challenge to us all.

The roses of our garden are a blessing from above.
Their perfume emanates abroad; they fill the world with love.

Though years have left their shadow on these blossoms so sublime,
They have not killed, nor have they chilled a spirit that conquers time.

The sixty-five's and over need no defense nor pardon,
And we today — a blessing pray on these blossoms in God's Garden.

Mary Mooney

I Wonder

I wonder if there is something out there in space?
Is there something alive in the dead of space?
Another world of sweet smelling rosebuds and cool
breezes by the beach.
Is there a place where the gift of grass and wild
flowers are cherished by the people who know it
was kissed by God and the Angels?
Are there people who sit by the beach, on all the
Amethyst rocks and Teal shells, who listen to the
crashing of the furious, curling waves time and
time again?
Do they look up to the Emerald sky and count the
twinkling, blue stars?
Do they gaze into the dead of the night and wonder
if there is something in front of them?
Are they amazed by birth?
Are they mourned by death?
Do they have any feelings at all?
Do they wonder about us?
I wonder?

Brandon Charpied

To Our Granddaughter Danielle Happy Second Birthday

Since you were born on that blessed day, we fell in love with
you right away.
Now you have teeth so white and bright, your strawberry blonde
hair that shines in the sunlight. With your pretty smile that lightens
up your face, and your cute dimples, that nothing can erase.
You always have a twinkle in your big blue eyes, like the stars in
the night skies.
You are learning new things every single day, reading,
counting, playing with friends, the knowledge you gain never ends.
With Mommy and Daddy at your side, they will always be
there to dry your tears, to comfort you when you have some fears.
We say Good Morning to you as we look at your picture
everyday, you do not know how much we miss and love you,
in a very special way.
You will have many more birthdays ahead of you, with
Gods help we will be there too.

Please remember, We love you very much.

Patricia Shean

Let Me Live

Mother, I am fruitage of affection.
But sometimes without your decision.

I am an embryo, youthful and limp.
Mother, you are superior than I.

I call to you, My heart is beating.
You are alive, let me live too.

Let intellect and senses prevail
pure and helpless.

I'm nowadays, an embryo,
Human being in the future
I will not close my eyelids prematurely.

I will always be your happiness.
You will be proud, that you are my mother.

Maybe times are hard, problems arise.
The People will help us, we will not die.

Or give me to someone, who wants me.
With happiness will accept me.

We will be together, to enjoy the world
Let me live, don't be an infanticide.

Wladyslawa Gozdera

32 Red Malicious

Hope is a liar — gentle and sweet, eager to entertain,
  Eager to trap the trusting souls of children in its syrup-sticky grasp.
It hangs on a vine, strategically placed —
  A bright red fruit peeping from the realm of shadow within.
Only I can see, from my perch high above the stupid souls below,
  The malicious gleam, the rotting skin.
  Only I can smell the smell that is Death itself.
I spy a creature below, on the ground, testing the vine.
  She shakes it to and fro, tugs it, stretches it as far as it will go.
  Too late, I see her begin a climb — hand over hand, ascending.
  Terrified, I give the vine a violent shake

Suddenly, she crashes to the harsh, cold ground . . .
  A crowd gathers, looking up at the bright red fruit where I stand accused.
The shocked silence is soon broken by an outraged voice,
  Hurling obscenities with perfect aim, the first of many stones.
I look down at the rotting slush to which I am almost irrevocably glued sinking.
  And it is a hell in itself, this climax of dreams, the eternal lie,
  Hope, that once attained cannot easily be escaped.
With all that is left of my soul, in a struggle for my very life,
  I twist, turn, snap myself free

And plunge to my death below.

Melanie Anne Hunt

A Joyful Moments On Wings Of Windy Skies

Forever near the moment of joy that fill my heart and soul.
My fate strengthen my guide on wings of windy skies.

When I sails I fold my hands in prayer.
My dearest friend (Jah) forever care.

My pains and sorrows feel my soul and heart
with wondrous sweetest of (joy) that fate
master my wings of windy sky.

That strengthen my sail and guide my wings
and set me joyful free. (Oh) by I fly on

Wings of windy skies. Free to fly on Windy sky of Wings.

Veolia Austin

May Some Father's Son Be Kind To Him

An elderly man rests weary feet
  'Neath a lonely bridge to escape the sleet
Of a winter storm at close of day
  For many have passed him along the way.

The speeding tourists ignore his hand
  As he slowly trudges across the land.
This father is weary, and grown so old
  That he cannot bear this driving cold.

Is this my father so kind and dear
  With neither friends nor loved ones near?
His days are numbered, his vision dim.
  May some father's son be kind to him.

Clarence M. Anderson

Untitled

To my little boy, who is now a man
I love so much and I think is grand.
I am so glad God gave "you" to me
you stand so straight for the world to see

Today you have a family of your own
it's so hard to think of you grown
everything you do, does make me so glad
I hope you the best and to never be sad

With two little girls, and you our boy
you made our life a circle of joy
over the roads, we've gone our own way
I just want to wish you, a Happy Birthday

Wadene Williamson

Moon Whispers

Away above the music of the sun
It felt delicate like a symphony blowing through
I dream behind the blue shadow of the sky
Dancing, prancing on the arm of the wind
Sea mist spraying in my hair
Swimming beneath the language of a storm
Sweet winter rain singing to me
Pitter-pattering on the walls of my world
Fairy dust falling from above
Drifting from the Heavens
It seems I have touched eternity
The clouds billow in white waves higher than the sky
Angels dance to the music of the night
Fluttering their gold crested wings of downy feathers
Stars twinkle brightly and light the way
The way to pure bliss — where love comes from
Where each moment matters yet nothing really counts
And people get along — no matter what the weather
My eyes are getting heavy so I settle in a cloud
Close my eyes and smile — now I am asleep.

Elizabeth Lokelani Ferreira

If I Could Cry (A Little)

Pride kept me from breaking down,
doing things that I was taught right.
I'm thinking today, if I could only cry a little,
things would be better in time.

Now, if I could only break down;
cry a little,
it wouldn't take nothin' from me,
just add to the spirits, moral upbringing,
I realize how much better off I'd be.

I was so used to bein' almighty,
where I was too good to shed a tear,
I've grown older; obstacles have become greater,
in my heart I've come to respect fear.

Crying a little really helps a lot,
relieves the soul; spirits and mind,
and to cry a little, don't make me less a man,
in fact, I've grown better with time.
"Yes," in fact, I've grown better with time.

Carolyn Buck

In A Big House

In a big house, people are there
Having fun, making noise everywhere,
Laughing until the hours are done.
I am there, but I am no one.

In a big chest, pain and sorrow are there.
They linger and are much too hard to bear,
Reminders of love that was taken.
My heart is there, and it is breaking.

In a big town, people rush by
To work or shop or eat they drive,
Too busy to smell the roses there.
Alone I walk, but nobody cares.

In a big world, countries ally
To battle and to war they fly
Over religion and boundaries of land.
Peace is there, they do not understand.

In a big house, the halls are silent,
Nobody is there and all is quiet.
The air is still and time has run.
I am there, but I am no one.

Mathew L. Hunt

Just Muddlin' Through

Life was not always easy for me,
For I never knew quite what to do,
And though I gave it a real good shot,
I always just muddled through.

I didn't face problems like most people can,
"Kinda stupid" would be more true,
And I believed until the day I died,
I would always be muddlin' through.

I was sure if I ever got into heaven
I would need a little boost or two,
And maybe I'd have to lie to St. Peter,
To get him to let me through.

But, when I arrived at the "Pearly Gates."
With accomplishments mighty few,
I knew that even if I lied like Hell,
He wasn't gonna let me through.

But, I guess someone up there understood,
And made an allowance or two,
For the "Gates" were suddenly opened wide,
And I muddled right on through.

William A. Gardner

Grandma

A woman so filled with laughter
Always happy and gay
No matter what came her way
She was like a light amongst us
Always shining brightly forever and a day.
The woman so filled with laughter
Her ship has sailed away
But her memory will always stay
Within our hearts and minds
Because she was so kind.
God has taken her away
To that place of heaven above
She will feel no more pain
Through the sunshine and the rain
As she still fills our hearts with love.
This woman so filled with laughter
Will never be forgotten as the years and months go by
We will each give a little sigh
Because we loved her so
And we shall never let her go.

Victoria Jones

Portrait of Love

On this day of great mourning for you, Mother Dear,
I praise the Almighty for your love and your care.

Mere words can't do justice to the beauty in you,
For such is the beauty possessed by so few.

Three sons you raised with true pride and joy,
Each one so different, yet each one your boy.

Your sweetness and love, and tender caress,
Were the nectar we sipped in our times of distress.

And the joy in our lives was your joy as well,
For your love made us one, and to share was so swell.

Rest peacefully, Angel, for each life you touched,
Was enriched and made brighter by so very much.

While your candle of time with us has now gone,
The flame of your love will glow eternally on.

The Good Lord is with you in heaven above,
For you, Mother Dear, are the portrait of love.

Steven Robert Radulovich

Dance With Destruction

My layers of skin are stripped. Like clothes torn from my body.
You, nonchalant and arrogant, are remarkable. Traits only a
conqueror can possess.
My body like my peoples' lands. You steal.

My master orders his demands: Shut up. Lie still. Or else.
His obsequious slave attempts to avoid further punishment. My death.
I contemplate his properties, conquests seized during a legacy
of land occupation. Lands of a people.

You continually pilfer yet dismiss your delinquency.
Accusations of inherent lunacy: Exotic. Savage. Barbaric.
I am faulty, you are blameless. Although my wrong doing is nameless.
You deem yourself judge and jury.
Your insolence and my obedience permit more reaping of my lands.
This time, my flesh is the soil.

I wait for you now. Spear in one hand and wine in the other.
I coyly tempt you with my felicity. I demand your repentance.
I carry souls of sisters sacrificed. Men obliterated. Children
corrupted. I nurture centuries of agony.

My gifts and my spears are waiting to pay homage. Waiting for you.
Patiently awaiting your arrival. Your sorrow frees the masses.

Melissa Sargis

What's Left Unsaid

The couple comes home from their daily jobs,
They walk straight through their house without any words at all,
With nothing on their mind but to sit down and relax,
They felt their aching feet and that pain in their backs.

As they search through the kitchen to find something to eat,
And pull out a chair to rest their feet
No words were said between the two,
Nothing was said, not even "I love you."

When three years later she became deathly ill,
Nothing could save her, not even her own will!
Nothing was helping, she was only getting worse,
Her days were numbered, it was like a curse.

Finally came the day when it was her time,
Not much was said but thoughts clouded her mind,
In their final "good-bye", not much was done,
Some emotions were shown, but silence had won!

Now he looks back every day of his life,
Wishing things had been different between him and his wife,
Why couldn't he say those words that he knew,
Those three precious words "I love you!"

Gina Osina

Do You See It Too?

When you see the wreath decorating my door,
I wonder if you see it too;
That beneath the pine, the pearls and bows,
Are the thorns Jesus wore for you.
When you see the tree adorned like a king,
I wonder if you see through it too;
To the cross that our king was nailed on,
When he was nailed to it for you.
When you see all of the presents under the tree,
I wonder if you see them too.
The peace, the love, the forgiveness and more,
Jesus has hand-made especially for you.
When you see the bright star on top of the tree,
Tell me, do you see it too?
The lights streaming down from heaven,
As Jesus was born for you.
When you look back under that Christmas tree,
Is there an unopened present with your name?
Just open it and receive him,
For it is for you that he came.

Brenda Popp

Untitled

I never realized life could be so hard,
Trying to stand tall and keep up your guard.
There are so many things to think about,
And there are so many things to figure out.
I though I was at the end,
Until I had a talk with a special friend.
And he said to me,
You gotta believe in what you can be.
There will be some hard times,
And there will be some rough climes.
But there is always a brighter side.
Once the sadness had died.
You just need to believe that everything is okay,
And you can't always believe what other people say.
You can have whatever you work for,
Even if the opportunity isn't knocking at the door.
So never give up on your dreams,
No matter how hard it seems.
If you truly believe in it,
Then you can truly achieve it.

Evelena Mason

Being High For Life

High off life
Life is fun
Especially when you're high
Gotta smoke warriors

I love being high being high is cool
Especially when you smoke it with your friends
I love smoking warriors when I am high
When you are on cloud number 9
that is cool being on cloud
Number 9 is one of the best
places to be I love being high
Being high is cool
Especially when you smoke it
with your friends people smoke it because
it is cool to be high when you are high
you float on air you act silly
It is cool to be high
being high is my life
smoke it you'll love it to

Stephanie Wise

Untitled

You know Lord, I've spent all year trying to clean up, trying to
sort thru and trying to maintain . . . My feelings are rapidly changing metaphors of menopause — should I put my life on hold? Is it
not yours to live? As I attempt to paint, I reflect . . . what do I see?
But the past . . . separate and far from me. Friends and broken
hearts, unexpected yet necessary and I'm not sure why things I
do coincide with people I spend time with.
Painting mark times, experiences, moods, periods . . . some have
a dozen in blue, for me it's true too! But I see each painting
as a world of many moods-stroke after stroke. To paint . . . after
2 years of not . . . to rummage thru hardened acrylic, smelly
mixtures of accomplished works. To bring all the tools together
out of boxes in the garage, and to risk making mistakes . . . to
spread myself out as the flat background color . . . to
in convenience my dad and brother as I prepare a place to make
my messes. A table here, a table there . . . only to confine them
to beds, chairs and TVs in their bedrooms . . . while I begin to
change the atmosphere. To worship God with creation,
with artistic expression, with brushes on canvas and paint,
mixed media. To encourage others that Jesus is the life, the vine.
To declare that apart from him I can do nothing. To keep faith alive,
to have an attitude of confidence, to say I paint.

Michele Ann Travis

I Wish A Very Merry Christmas For Me

I may look like a fool sitting on this bar stool
Tryin' to wink if I get the barmaids eye
But she's the cutest one I've seen
In her Santa cap and tight jeans
Sure wish she was under my tree
She'd make a very merry Christmas for me

Christmas lights and jingle bells
I'd like to make her one as well
I wish a very merry Christmas for me

But I'll go home alone and face a cold gray dawn
With Jack Daniel's mixed with iced tea
With no one around, the whole town closed down
She'd make a very merry Christmas for me

You can have your trucks and trains, your bow and arrow and airplanes
Sure wish she was under my tree
I'd love to untie her bows Lord I need one of those
She'd make a very merry Christmas for me

Christmas lights and jingle bells
I'd like to make her one as well
She'd make a very merry Christmas for me

Cecil Bryant

Patti

P is for the pleasing smile she wears.
A is for the auburn colors of her hair.
The first **T** is for two arms that wrap around.
And the second **T** is for two eyes, oh so brown.
The **I** is for inspiration, you see,
that she gives to you and me.
Because she cares, we can dare
be all that we can be.

Michael H. Belfry

Purpose

Purpose is the fulfillment of life
    Without which is hopelessness, frustration and strife

Many long to feel content everyday
    But without purpose, happiness escapes through a sea of maze

Some even dream to be someone great
    But without purpose, dreams are only a wish, O' what a waste

Few dare to try and even reach a goal
    Later to find they are still empty and cold

If I could leave you with a word of advice
    Seek the Master, the giver of life

Only he can make you feel at ease
    Because the destiny he has set is the only plan that can please

For purpose is the fulfillment of life
    Without which is hopelessness, frustration, and strife

Marilyn Smith Alexander

The World

The world is a very scary place
Turn around there is a gun in your face
Women beating men
Men beating women
Who could commit such a horrible sin
People using drugs
Others getting mugged
A teen has a child
There is not two parents
So the child goes wild
You see the circle keeps going on and on
Look at your world
It is all gone
Although all of this could have been prevented
Just one thing went wrong
Our world it just did not stay strong

Britany Beech

Silent Prayer

I guess you know what I'm going to say before I say it.
I guess you know what I feel before I feel it.
Yet this is my silent prayer.
Lord, help me see the light you hold for me at the end of my tunnel
Help me be strong against the winds that you send.
Please help me conquer the doubts that creep in my mind
For I know this is the path that you and I have chosen
And although this path is covered with weeds and thorns
I know you would not let me travel it
If it was not the right path to take.
I know that I am not alone in this journey
For I feel your presence at every obstacle I face.
Through my tears and heartache I still see your light
Yet I wish to make this small silent prayer of thanks.
Thank you Lord for not turning off your light when I strayed
from the path
And never leaving me to dwell in the darkness.

B. J. Thiesse

Need

I don't want to crawl into your bed,
I want to touch what makes you tick,
I want to feel what makes you sick,
I just want to roam inside your head.
Crowds scream your lyrics old and tried.
To feel your presence up on stage.
You must feel like you're in a cage,
Like something vital nearly died.
Your aura burns with mindless rage,
And so I itch with curiosity.
Is that the way it really has to be?
Or is this just my fatal phage?
    I want to step inside your mind
    And with one word, our frail souls bind

K. R. Gloystein

The Waves

Look at me. Tell me what you see. Am I merely the breaking
of the waves against the cold night sand. Lying under a single
lighted sky, wondering the beauty of the things you can never have.
If beauty is in the eye of the beholder, tell me what you are holding.
As I look at myself from the inside out, I am merely the shadowed
moon reflecting on those waves. A single lonely light in the sky
looking upon everyone, but, seeing its own reflection. Alone
again I could ring back the tides, but I let the waves crash, for
the longing of peace. So tell me are your eyes open, if so, do
you see the truth, tell me.

Brittany Cook

Bound For Unity

In life; . . . in time, we will become, that which is destined will
surely come,
I'll not be living for I will be gone. I'll not see the beauty,
when the world becomes one
Even the animals, our birds our deer will fully realize that we . . .
breath the same air; binding together so willing to share.
How!? . . . Oh how can I live to be with it all?
If I had the power my life I would stall. Living within that . . .
which will be done; enjoying it all when the world becomes one.
Just knowing, and pleased with this future to be, along with
realizing this life we'll not see. We'll share yes I'll pray, towards
this forth-living find.
That which is destiny most surely to drum.
When everything, yes all who lives becomes one.

John J. Sigala

Could It Be Love

Sometimes I feel as though
I wish you were more
than just a friend.
Could it be true that I'm
falling in love with you again?
I never thought that I'd be able to
love you the same as I did then,
but I feel like maybe I do.
How could I possibly feel this
way when you practically
threw my heart away?
After the terrible fight that we had
and the way that you left me
hurting so bad . . .
I knew that I'd always
love you inside
but that was something
I'd have to hide.
Now do you think there could possibly be,
a place in the future for you and me?

Heather Russell

Stormy Sunshine Days

I sit alone at the close of day
   beside a bright warm fire,
And think of days long gone by
   of dreams and hope and desire.

There were dark days when thunder roared,
   and cold rains poured down.
Bitter winds blew from the north,
   snow lay upon the ground.

Yet woven through those stormy times
   were days of sunshine bright,
And rainbows that touched my life,
   and stars that shone at night.

So as I ponder on life past
   I thank the Lord above
For all the stormy sunshine days
   that taught me how to love.
   Lucile Gieg

Prescription For America

Give/Take at least once a day:
A front porch place
that invites people to sit face-to-face,
in person,
unhurried,
sharing thoughts, schemes, needs and dreams;
caring that one another is there
for a friend taking time,
having time
to enjoy the company.
   Constance A. Smith

Capable Mind

It's just a small walk to ecstasy,
   or so I'm told at times.

Around the corner is your happiness,
   as well as vicious crimes.

They say that dreams become reality;
   if you follow a dream.

Some say life is easy to live,
   just by a single theme.

To believe in yourself is easy enough,
   the trick is believing in others.

Knowing exactly from whence we came
   is hard for my sisters and brothers.

So, to touch the heart and soul of people,
   we are determine and willing to find;

The love and the hate that engulfs us all,
   'cause we all have a capable mind . . .
   Brian K. Cribb

Acrimonious Humanity

Acrimonious humanity
and the beast was born.
Gentle in its last hour
it crawled through its final stage of deceit
saturated in portended visions.
A soft obedient credence dwells
suggesting a dead litany.
[Germane feast]
Subsided forgiveness to all who dwells
   inside the sanctimonious soul.
Give thanks to your creator, your muse.
Leave room for the twisted and aborted crucifix.
   Brian Vuyancih

Mild Epiphany

I've never felt so unhealthy —

My eye twists back and stills,
subsidiary visions afloat in a haze
As one thought blinks, another cries;
I begin to linger in helpless days.

My mortal coil bulges forth
and I feel my soul is bleeding dry
I look to the sky for a sense of worth;
her thick raindrops but pitiful cries.

I want these eyes to glaze over
with mucilage life repellent;
I want my lungs to flush out
each breath of hostile atmosphere;
I just want to be clean again.

There are visions unseen
Romanticized by conjectural consciousness, to satisfy vicious needs;
when we fail to consume this crop of fantasy
and not allow our minds to wonder, or to make believe
we feel dirty.

I've never felt so unhealthy . . .
   Eric Schwartz

For My Sister

To me, my sister's the best you'll ever find,
I also realize she may not be one of a kind.
We are just a few years apart,
but the strong love between us is true in heart.
We live different lives and both been thru hell,
and things for us lately haven't been so well.
We can usually talk and work our problems out,
but even lately we've had way too much doubt.
When one of us is troubled and totally down,
the other one can usually talk and turn things around.

She's given me courage, strength and understanding I never knew,
and all I can really say to my sister is "Thank You."
You've helped me along throughout all these years,
with calming my temper, heartache and fears.

I never thought we'd be as close as we are,
but I thank God for the love that has brought us so far.
If it wasn't for the love we were taught as we grew,
there is so much we would probably never knew.
Today I am thankful for all we have and love,
because I know all of it came from God above.
   Theresa E. Drdek

As I Watch The Sky

The sun is rolling high in the sky, as
birds fly by. I am in the meadow watching
the sky, watching the clouds raced across the
sky. I'm young and in my prime and time just
seems to fly by, like the clouds in the sky.
Each moment that I look up at the sky I'm
ageing by and by. Now I'm starting to
close my eyes and I'm seeing the sky. I ageing
more and more each moment I watch the sky.
Now my body is starting to ache but I just
can't stop watching the sky. My hair is turning
as grey as the old hay, that sits beside me
each day that I watch the sky. The sun is going
down and I'm having trouble breathing. Now
the sky is going into midnight, and a gust
of wind comes and carries me away. I go
up and touch the stars I go up very far.
And when I reach my destination I see a golden
cloud, and it says to me welcome, you're
here to stay.
   Jessie Kanagas

451

Frozen Webs

Awakening to an admission of need,
The stretching and bending to remain free
Remains unfulfilled.
So simple to fill the void with debris,
A true Murderer of blackness and despair
Remains unfound.
Rules and bounds shroud pure motives, yet
The search under hordes of mocking eyes
Remains undaunted.
Laid bare, every point of the soul reveals
Ravaged illusions, ragged emotions, stillborn desires.
Casting about frantically —
White knights upon white steeds upon white deeds?
Dark nights within dark rooms within dark arms?
Soft voices speaking soft words vowing soft lives . . .
Soft lies.
Shielded by faith, a light sparks, wavering at first,
Growing unfettered as only Truth can,
Sweeping away the doubts, the pain, the past
As a warm touch melts away frozen webs.

Todd Jordan

Rose Petals

Rose petals falling to the floor obscure the path she must follow.
The footsteps have almost disappeared
before her eyes, they've all gone.
Alone, standing at the intersection swept in a forceful wind
Winding down a well trodden path
The flowers are missing their petals
The ground lacks its green covering.
She is overcome by the brown drab cloak
A cloak her mother wore
weighing her down until her eyes died
Dead inside a body that lived
a sort of walking sleep from which she has never roused.
The daughter reaching out for the hand
the one that healed her kid scrapes.
She only feels the emptiness of open air
Her reach is met by uncertainty
Taking the first step over the rose petals
Fearing she will crush their delicate beauty
Realizing the petals upon which she now stands
have cushioned the fall for a thousand treading feet.

Emily Rogers

Fulfilled

I lived my life to its fullest, the only way that I knew how
By working hard, playing hard, and living by my vows

I vowed not to live in yesterdays, because yesterday was a
lonely place to be.
I vowed not to jealous, taking on peoples problems that I could not see.
I vowed not to settle — I only let myself down when I do.
I vowed not to be careless, I did with my life only what I wanted to.

I lived by these vows and I found it hard, I struggled every day.
Because one thing I never realized is to really live you have to pray.

So I had a conversation with God, and He helped recompose my vows.
The words you read below this line are the words I live by now.

I live for the present I walk with God, and He helps me through the day.
I am who I am that's who I'll always be, don't ask me to change
my ways.
I still refuse to settle, because what good is second best.
I still won't be careless, but now I ask God's advice and he does the rest.

I live by these vows and I find it odd,
that I know more now because I know God.

It took only asking him to understand,
now I live a full life holding God's hand.

Carrie E. Steel

In The Midst Of Pain

You share your life with someone, and it seemed like such a long time.
All of a sudden he's gone. And you feel, "But Lord; He was mine."

I gave him myself; I give him my love; I gave him all that I had.
Lord, I want to see him; you know that I do. I want to see him again.

Then to hear; "Mary, I know it's hard, and I know it hurts.
Believe me I do.
But through it all, I'll never leave you."

Just remember next time you're lonely, and you want to cry;
That you're my child and I love you; and when you hurt so do I.

So even though times seem un-fair and cruel;
Remember, I'll never never leave nor forsake you.

It may seem like a long time, maybe that's true.
But the time will come when you're together again, just the both of you.

So don't look back; but look ahead. To the time when you can say;
Sweetheart, if you only knew how I looked forward to this day.

Together forever, forever together. That you'll always be.
Never to utter those words again: "Honey I wish you were with me?"

Tamara L. Walpole

What He's Done For You

Have you ever walked in a forest early in the morn,
Heard the sounds of baby birds just recently born,
Seen the beauty of first sunlight glistening upon the dew?
All these things God has made for you.

Have you walked upon a mountain top ever so high,
Looked out and afar up into the sky,
Smelled the clean air, felt the peace in the blue?
God also made these things for you.

Have you sat beside a river watched the water flow,
Twisting and turning knowing just where to go,
Moving life throughout this wonderful land?
There is no doubt this was God's plan.

Have you cast your eyes upon the ocean tasted salt in the air,
Seen sandy beaches the new life everywhere,
Felt he waves caress the shoreline, the tides go in and out?
Just another part of God's plan that came about.

Always remember God did these things for you,
But most of all remember He sent Jesus Christ for us too!

Gary N. Hogg

Spring Morning After A Rain

Tree leaves bending low,
    Drenched with last night's raindrops,
My, how green the rain has made them grow!
    Rain — still dripping from the tree-tops.

Puddles fill the narrow pathway
    Winding through the orange trees.
The sun comes out to bring a new day
    With a refreshing spring morning breeze.
Raindrops falling one by one,
    Splashing all around me.
Like liquid diamonds in the sun,
    They glisten like a crystal sea.
Orange blossom on the ground
    Making a blanket of white
Bees humming all around,
    And rain — still falling since last night.
Oh, what a lovely day of spring!
    The birds seem to agree.
From their branches they gaily sing.
    While rain — still drips down on me.

David E. Bailey Jr.

To Laura

Gauzy blue ribbons
and sun-dappled dreams,
Calculus, bio and
boy-friending schemes,
Europe and back-packing
t-shirts and jeans . . .

This is what little girls are made of.

Pre-med and post-grad
and what should I do?
Religion and ethics
to thine own self be true,
Healing and learning
Life's such a coop!

This is what little girls are made of.

Creation, diversity
the weight of the world,
A pagan, a saint,
Snapping sails all unfurled.

That is exactly what little girls are made of.

Valerie L. Hall

Untitled

As I think back on the times that I shared with you
I remember a love so wonderful and true
You were in my every thought — morning, noon, and night
I really did believe that our love was so perfect and so right
All the moments and memories that we shared together
Will be in my heart beyond the end of forever
Each passionate kiss in my mind will always be
Along with all the romantic experiences that you have given me
Every love letter that you've ever written me I will keep
And remembering them with all your love I will often weep
It wasn't a girl that took you away
It was neither a car nor an argument that led you astray
Before I could ever become your wife
Someone would come and take your precious life
All of these things are just a memory now
Each day they tell me I'll get along somehow
I'm lost without you here to be my guide
How I wish that you never would have died
You were my life, my reason for living
And without you here I don't want to go on giving

Angelina Chapman

Mothers, Daughters And Love

Motherhood begins,
Mothers are love,
Love comes from Mothers,
Without Mothers, where is love?
Who will kiss your daughter goodnight?
Who will comfort her, when she is sad?
Where is love, when there is no Mother?
When there is no Mother,
Who will watch your daughter grow up?
Who will love her when she is sad?
Who will watch her when Daddy's at work?
Who will be there when she feels alone?
Without mothers, no one will,
Without mothers, life is cruel,
Who will put together her broken heart?
Mothers are love,
Without Mothers, where is the love?
Without Mothers, where is the hope, the happiness?
How do you enjoy life without love?
How will you survive life without your Mother, your love?

Crystal Raine Sharp

Friends . . .

If this world ever stops
When there would be no fire and no sparks
   to show the love when it hurts.
There will always be someone to care,
   someone to share the pain with.
Because there will always be friends
   who will care when you think there
Is no one there . . .
   friends . . .

Misty M. Steele

You Always Make Me Laugh

You have always been able to make me laugh.
No matter what my tale of woe,
You could turn it around with your
"But wouldn't it be funny if . . ."
And you would give it such a funny twist,
That we would have to laugh.
No matter how dark the day
You could make the sun come out
With your up-beat attitude
And your gift of gab.
Thanks for always making us
See the bright side.

Marie Coleman

Violence

His life was rough, he didn't have much.
the love he was getting left bruises to the touch.
His mother didn't care and he doesn't know his father.
Did she say, "I love you?" No, she didn't even bother.
She left him alone at the age eleven
for six whole days, maybe it was seven
He had no one to take care of him, he had to fed himself.
All alone in that small house, she left to please herself.
You see, bruises were not the only thing that left him sore of life,
the mother that gave birth to him left him with only strife.
Now, I know the times are tough, but with God by his side
he can make it through and within him he can confide.
But what about the quiet night when his mind is full of fear?
Thinking of what might become of his mother left hi eyes full of tears.
He knows he can not change the past, but in this lonely silence
he remembers when he thought it was love, now he calls it violence.

Tiffanie Gibson

Breathless Wonder

Behold a figure so intriguing
Lips that sooth and caress
Eyes that radiate

Leave one still and calm in rapture
Hair which glides effortlessly
And shines without help from the sun

Skin so soft
As if having been born
The daughter of Venus

With bodily curves
That defy Michelangelo's idea of perfection
An overall presence

That fulfills the deepest of dreams
Tames all that is wild
Provides the mind with fits of fascination

Mysterious, captivating, yet so gentle
A spectrum of human elegance
Woman - a Breathless Wonder.

Jason T. Low

The Answer

There I am listening for a sound,
Wishing, hoping, and yearning to be with you,
But alas as you pass I am not found,
How can you do this,
You don't even know,
You have no idea,
You are causing me great pain,
Every time I see you I wonder,
Will we ever be together?
But alas I know the answer,
My heart fills with sadness as I see you talk and hug someone else,
My body and heart wishes I was that girl who you hugged,
But my mind knows the answer,
My body rejects the answer that my mind always gives,
But my body and heart do not care,
They just keep praying and hoping that someday the answer will change.

Jennifer Toppan

Nature's Artistry

Nature is an artist
Her canvas is the earth.
She plans the season's colors
Long before their birth

For the spring she paints the vines
With buds of many hues.
She paints the rays of sun with gold
This sparkles the morning dew.

Her summer is a lavish green,
She painted many flowers.
They become more beautiful
With crystal drops of showers.

Fall leaves from the trees
Creates a plaided bed,
Nature uncovers the autumn,
Her painting in fiery red.

Whilst the winter there's a wonderland of snow immaculate white.
This painting by nature is truly a picture to behold with delight.

Nature is indeed an artist, her best works are the seasons
She painted them for us she explains her very own reasons.

Alphonso Dalton

Eagle

"Onward Christian soldiers"
is the familiar cry.
Ours is not to reason why,
but to do or die.

Society is really a treat,
hold your head high and shout equality.
Yet, each hates his brother
just because he's a different color.

America! Hear my cry!
Our once proud eagle
could really see
but, now he's got leprosy.

It's not only pollution that smears our bird
nor inflation rising high,
He's covered with scales of hate and fear.
Even the Indian sheds a tear.

Let's end all wars,
especially those inside.
Let peace reign throughout the land
and love for our fellowman.

Margot F. Clark

To Our Mom And Dad

We love you both so very much and you know this to be true.
We can never pay you back for everything you do.

You've given us something more valuable than gold.
It's your Love, Honesty and Faith that forever we can hold.

The best that we can do to get close to paying you back
Is to raise and treat our children with the same Love, Faith and Tact.

You must always remember that our successes and everything we do
Would never have been possible without the Love from both of you.

Love Your Sons.

Anthony Rosetti

Motives Of Life

The sound of the wind rushes round my mind
As all my thoughts seem to jumble
As well as I am and free as can be
The motives of life have shuttled in me.

The cares that I have seem so far out
As steps I take seem to stumble
As reasons go by and people can see
The hurting inside has huddled in me.

The loves and the hates of many a man
As the years flee to crumble
The waves of our thoughts, the means I can see
Is only the love that ponders to be

The wants and the needs that hasn't so shined
Wait only on in humble
As the winds will blow, the rivers will flow
The motives of life have shuttled in me.

And I don't know why I feel so high
As I watch the world go by
All I want is to help a little
Then maybe I'd be satisfied.

Ray Cameron

"Snow Eagle"

You have yourself an Indian guide, and "Snow Eagle" is his name;
He's here to lead you down the path, because you are one in the same.

Whenever you are in need of a friend, all you have to do is call;
And he will be there to take your hand, so you don't trip and fall.

You are his little "Heart of a Lotus Woman," and he is here to protect your rights;
So all you have to do is pray, and he will see you through your nights.

You have this strong young Indian friend, to hold you when you're weak;
He's so tall, dark and very kind to give you a kiss on your cheek.

So see Mom, you are a lucky girl to have a friend like him;
When you hear "Show Eagle" knocking, open up and let him in.

Roxanne Owens

Night (The Death March)

"Forward march" all stand in line,
I had no clothes; nothing was mine,
don't stop; don't slow down,
because if I do, I'll be shot to the ground,

Left foot right foot left foot right,
marching hungry and tired in the cold dark night,
Jews dead as far as the eye can see,
Jews falling dead all around me,

As I march I shed no tear,
I'll be saved, I have no fear.

Melissa Provost

454

The Last Rose

I paused to visit three generations of women,
a family garden of wildflowers,
Baby's Breath, Garland Chrysanthemums,
Toadflax, Virginia Stock and a treacherous
old rose bush

Sits folded into herself, desperately
blond, black mascara smeared
like a pansy's purple eye, and poppy
circles of rouge.

From this garden comes a hand,
bending me close to quivering
petal lips.

You are growing old
like the rest of us,
aren't you?

Tomorrow, I'll prune my
rose garden with
tender care.

Jacquelyn M. Spier

The Eyes Of Love

There is satisfaction in my soul
When I look into their eyes,
Just knowing they are a part of me — Satisfies.

Sometimes I see sadness there
Clouding happiness once seen
Or the new beginning of a — Dream.

At times I see their anger,
Unshed tears they try to hide
Or they shine when accomplishing — With pride.

With hurt or sadness, sometimes dulled
Or in merriment they dance,
Again I can see resentment in their — Glance.

They can convey a coyness
They smile or flirt and tease
Or can cloud to stormy tears — With ease.

Thank God I am so lucky,
When they look at me I see
A love and great devotion for — This Mother of Three.

Clarice Stafford Cummins

Epiphany

The song played over and over in my mind.
Finally, they played it, and you pulled me close . . .
Your touch erased the pain and suffering.
The rain no longer fell down upon my face.

The song blocked out my past with you — We started over.
It was our first meeting.
You swept me across the floor, and all eyes toward us
The princess and prince dancing on the starry floor.

The song came to a close, and as you released me,
The rain started again, the hurt filled my body
And I came to the realization that I should have known all along.

As I left you on the floor — alone, the rain fell harder than before.
I turned my back, and the rain streamed down my red cheeks
And fell upon my breast.

I closed my eyes and knew that you and I,
Would never be as I imagined.
We would forever be separated by your lies.

As I went on my way, I saw the light, reality,
Something that you will never know,
And I will not deny. Goodbye.

Chrissy Zmijewski

God's Only Son

There was a man
Who walked a long and dusty road.
Up to Calvary Mountain,
Is the story we're told.

He healed the sick,
He raised the dead and made the blind to see.
He said he did it all,
For you and me.

He said:
I am the one, I am God's only son.
I'm sitting at the right hand of the Father.

Won't you come with me,
And live eternally
And worship God the Father,
Throughout eternity.

Jennifer Pannebecker

Late Last Night And Early This Morning

Late last night and early this morning,
The last and first face I see.
I'm so grateful for this wondrous love
My dear Heavenly Father has sent to me.

Late last night and early this morning
It felt as though you were here,
Holding, touching, and caressing me
With your warmth and love that is tender and dear.

Late last night and early this morning
A tear came to my eye.
Not from sadness but from happiness
Because you are no ordinary love passing by.

Late last night and early this morning,
Together I asked the Lord to keep us
To have, to hold, to cherish this love
That is so full and miraculous.

Cynthia Townsend

Old Bob

A sailor at first glance, taking huge strides
Across the supermarket parking lot,
Tempting the imagination to dock a ship
Behind him, in a seedy coastal town
Where the air smells like salt water and bars.
Old bob wanders the streets seeking warmth
In the library, and coffee in church basements,
Which is given freely, but only if he'll leave.
At night he sails a cardboard box, in an alley
Off Main Street, and wrestles the waves
In a bottle of Wild Irish Rose.
I've met him. We've spoken. Another tragic story
Of another brilliant mind, ravaged
By alcohol, economics, and insanity, taking joy
In watching customers, coming and going with carts,
Or in the mystery of paper flapping in a puddle.
He's happy.

Sandra Atwood

Sunset Moon

Sunset moon you glisten, you wonder over the lake.
You make me bright and happy, you also make me cry.
I sit and wait for you.
You come but you can change my life.
Sunset moon I think of you as a charm, not a fighter.
I watch you dance across the lake.
You glide, not slide.
You wait when I'm late.
Please never go.

Sarah Bailey Hejma

Nature's Glory

Sun sets against the mountain side,
Birds sing in harmony,
With whistling trees
Swaying in the breeze.

Wild flowers and butterflies,
Precious sights,
Rainbow amidst
Beautiful colors of light.

God's creation of such exquisite glory,
No being around, nor, quarry sound.

God's hidden treasures,
Waiting to be found,
Natures, beauty abound.

Peacefulness,
Within the wilderness,
Nothing else, can compare to this.

Ricocheting roaring;
Of splendor soaring,
Eternal serenity
Overwhelming entity.

Kim Eileen Ritz

Clouds Unite Against The Wind

Memories like dandelions in an open hand
Scatter effortlessly in the wind's command.
Thoughts, like fleeting puffs, once held with a firm grip
Float freely with abandon on their endless trip.

A rocker made from fine old carved wood
By a yellowed lace, curtained window stood
Harboring a tiny fragile frame with head held high
Staring vacantly up into a cloud covered sky.

Clouds unite against the wind
Forming a face of one's own kin.
A face forms from an anxious cloud
Lightning followed by thunder loud.

Searching for a name to a face once vivid and plain
Brings arduous effort, despair, then pain.
Clouds disperse; the sky returns.
Relaxed now, still staring, brightness burns.

Memories like dandelions in an open hand
Scatter effortlessly in the wind's command.
Thoughts, like fleeting puffs, once held with a firm grip
Float freely with abandon on their endless trip.

Shelley Cooper

The Magic Of A Miracle

I found a special person who touched
my life, and believed in me so much
that I am and new person today.
Through kind words, good deeds,
and a heart as big as a mountains, she
transformed me, and my life completely changed.
Miracles happen when people believe
in someone. It makes them more creative,
productive and happier individuals.
After awhile this becomes contagious,
and other people share their goals, and
suddenly the world is blessed by the
kindness of others.
Conflicts and wars are resolved,
creating peace, love and harmony, where
it never existed before.

P.S. The world is blessed through
the kindness shown all over the world!

Joanne Mlodik

Move/Dance

Move, dance, talk with your feet
    show the world your rhythm.

The message of life is in your beat
    dance with the beat and jump high

Chatter, babblery, creates more strife,
    music is the sedative of life.

Let us not forget the music tonight
    or jab at the gibberish

Words of wisdom are in your beat,
    so move your feet.

Walk, dance and jump high,
    leap your spirit to the sky.

Did I hear you say that you cannot dance
    that your feet are grounded

Even if you rolls on wheels your heart
    beats and your soul leaps.

Paulette C. Rothenberg

Because I'm Getting Old?

Should I not love the smell of the ocean or the flow of my hair in
the breeze because I'm getting old?

Must I sit on the side and not enjoy the beat or act like I'm stone?
I must tap my feet!! Because I'm getting old?

Should I act like the birds aren't singing their hearts out
And turn away from my pet when she wags to get out?

Should I give in to pain in my back and my knees
And no longer enjoy quietly sitting under the trees? If I cry a
little more, should I hide my tears because I'm getting old?

There are a few more wrinkles and splotches and moles
And my memories are wonderful, but my memory has holes
My thoughts sometimes wander, the same as a child's
    But, is that because I'm getting old?

Must I never have a lover or a warm body to feel? Someone to bring
flowers and make me feel real? Must I cloud over the timeless
twinkle in my eyes? Only because I'm getting old?

There's talk of retirement, to what and to where? My fears of being
left behind, I can't even share, but my loving of living grows
greater every day — it's splendid because I'm getting older!!

Jean L. Embry

Why?

I'll never know the answer, so I don't even try,
why my son left this earth by choice and chose to die.
Perhaps to escape this world and find a better place,
so young, so beautiful and filled with amazing grace.
Maybe he was searching for the peace he could not achieve,
this brought great sadness as I was left behind to grieve.
I remember the good times that we shared,
He knew very well, how deeply I cared.
My prayers for him to find evolvement, are twice or more each day.
Filled with love, intelligence and sensitive in every way,
A child from God, how else could he be?
He had all my love, unconditionally.
I know I did all I could, gave him the best of care,
somehow for God to take him, now, seems very unfair.
I miss him more each day, as time passes by,
You might think by now, there was no need to cry.
We were the best of friends, now we're apart,
For my very own child, broke my heart.
I know someday we'll be together and share our love and joy,
What more could a mother ask for, than to see her little boy?

Janice G. Caronia

The Tiger

Tiger, he will search all day, looking for the scent of prey
In the light of two Golden Eyes, there are many darkened skies.

There was a time of fear of him, when men's hearts were dark and grim
The Hunter is The Hunted now, the victim springs, on the prowl.

He would slide on padded ground, in the jungle, not a sound
What was ancient Beast of Fear, soon, no longer will be here.

They would cower behind The Flame, cringing just to hear the name
Sun glints off of weapons bright, Tiger shivers, in the night.

They told tales of The Child of Death, no man dared to draw a breath
In the distance, they see the prize, the veil of death around their eyes.

Hear his call and one would scream, he is The Nightmare, out of
The Dream
The line of sight shall now turn red, the Endless Ancient One is dead.

Seen now is the pain of the stars, for what was there was taken as ours
But turn not in your human track, for . . .
The Ancient One
Will
Be Back.
   Lauren Zaworski

My Marvel

Mother's Day, 1995
I know that there will never be
Another as lovely to me
I'm writing of my love, for you today
And of the children God sent our way
God entrusted seven lives to your care
And when they need you — you are there.

A mother whose life has been spent
For our children wherever they went
Our family has been made as one
By your prayers and all they you have done
Poems can be made by fools it's true
But only God could make someone like you

   James J. Ryan

It's time to walk into the caverns of fear.
 No light. All dark. I'm afraid of
  what's here.
But now that it's dark, when I look deep inside,
 I can see the light guiding me, pulling me
  by, pulling me by.
         I AM
   Scott A. Freeman

Caterpillar

My strangely looking friend,
what a queer looking fellow you are.
To see you squirming around,
I tend to wonder about your life.

You must be content, to move about my garden, eating my plants
But that is only a fleeing moment;
Soon you will evolve into a majestic butterfly
But if faith conspires against you,
your life would briefly end.

Oh, to see the inhumanity of you being impaled and displayed
for someone mere enjoyment, frighten me.
Yet, in some strange way,
faith has brought you to lush garden.

My strangely looking friend,
your moments are fleeing;
Faith has already conspired against you.

   Alex Dixon

My Child

Though you were never born into this world
my child you will always be.
It didn't matter if you were a boy or girl
you were the one who lived inside of me.

I guess I could have gotten mad
and blamed the Lord above
for He left me so hurt and sad,
I felt robbed of your special love.

You were all I waited to hold,
to give the milk from within my breast
but instead my emotions grew cold
as I pondered this heart-breaking test.

Now I cry from within my womb
as an empty place will always be
will my life ever again bloom?
"Oh God, give my child back to me!"

As time passes by with hours and days
I will try to understand and see
that you are still mine in every way
and I swear will always be.
   Terry W. Wallace Sr.

Totem Park

In a trick with cigarettes and orange juice
Dropping light-headed as a soaked loon
Heavy hoped wings thrash loose
A hawk scanning yonder lagoon

Draining strangers listening to visiting voices
I wide eyed city line translating noises
Watching crashing from the treetops giddy with uncertainty
Whether horns released limitless linnets flapping in symphony

Or night bird descending on vacant greystone
Osprey squawking a curse
Everything more how I'd grown
Sadly better or worse

Blue skinned on indian rugs houris lessoned
On triple throat and joints rubbing spice
Coughing pansies humbling advice
Of pollination in an instant soaring on nectared insect

All are needy for all our time
Like serpents leaching a milky junky
Green sugaring jagged vomit in rhyme
With Eden's tongue silky in psyche

   John Ellis

Untitled

Why are women always smiling, talking or crying?
And are never ashamed of getting their feet wet.
There's nothing wrong with their water supply, as teardrops are good,
And so great for their ailments.
While the mechanical Lady, could never exist,
The mechanical man is quite common.
Quite soon after Eve first started to cry, her mechanical died,
As by drowning, I think, and it made her face,
Rust into place in a smile, but not so her jaws.
From her maker came teflon, installed at the start,
As a protection from wear out.
See! God's really smart, He has wisdom.
Well, how about Adam the fellow? Well with teflon in place,
He could not grit his jaw like a man. He might smile,
So Adam chewed his teflon and swallowed.
Can you imagine the stress it could have relieved at the start?
If Eve would have cried, then talked just a little.
Could be Adam would have had a reason to smile,
And I'm sure, He would have listened a lot.
   John D. Petty

As The Wind Blows

As the wind blows the world turns round
and autumn leave come spiraling down. The temperatures
begin to drop and the gentle breezes
never stop. Seeds are spread throughout the air
and trees are starting to go bare. We should
all appreciate the things that nature can create.
    Now the air has a bitter chill while
children ski down a snow covered hill.
The trees are white, the grass is gone, finally I
won't have to now the lawn. The wind
carries snow that tethers toward the ground
and a feeling of serenity engulfs you all around.
    The snow has all melted and temperatures
rise, life begins to sprout and bloom right
before your eyes. The wind carries pollen from
flower to flower and bends the grass just like
the leaning tower. Winds lift a kite and helps birds
fly and carries all the clouds across the blue, majestic
sky. So as the wind blows, so goes the earth, so appreciate
it for all it's worth.

Devin Lino

Out At Sea

I lost a friend, out at sea.
How lonely life is going to be.
I said goodbye at summer's end
How long does it take for the heart to mend?

He left one day at the break of dawn
"It won't be long till the fish are gone."
Out to the sea to catch a few
Would be home for lunch, right on cue.

The day grew late
No sign of him
A big yellow tuna — had done him in.

He had brought the fish up to the side
Took a look and felt great pride.
Then cut the line and set it free
    saying "It took a lot out of me."

Laying down he took a rest
knowing he had done his best.
But his time ran out; it was meant to be.
He left this world — out at sea

Margaret A. Dever

A Dream

Sometimes I see you in my sleep
You are like a shadow without a face
Voice without sound
Like a rainbow without colors
Hazy but clear
Near but, oh, so far
I can almost feel you but I can never touch you
I can see you but I can't find you
Can sniff you but cannot smell you
If I can suspend sleep
If I can somehow find the power to never wake up again
If I can hold the dream forever
Or maybe just a moment longer
Will I ever touch you, feel you, believe
Or will you remain forever a dream
A phantom
Drifting beyond reach
Tantalizing, exciting, deceiving,
Yet comforting
As only a dream, and only a dream can be.

Tryphine S. Ncube

Flight Of The Autumn Moon

Just leaving Jersey now, as the darkness is falling all around me
late autumn lays down its last carpet of leaves
the chill of December bays at the moon
a silhouette of bare branches in the light
almost full, almost home

I thought I saw someone I knew from long ago, the other day
I can't explain why I didn't know his name
my name and me are one and the same
what happened to the children we were then?

And the sound of time passing surrounds me, amazes me
I gaze in the mirror
the stranger knows where I am
I wonder where time goes when it is done

I have heard the echoes ringing clear, ringing true
so far away
all that remains now are faces that resemble each other
across the chasm of lives
here to dance again, again

Barbara A. Koch

The Love Between Mama And Me

The little girl listened defiant and proud as she brushed back the
tear from her eye . . . "Just look at these treasures our Mom bought
for us, the very best money can buy." "My stereo cost lots of
money!" He said. "My brother's game was expensive, too! My
Mom spared no expense on our high-tech gear . . . now what did
your Mom get for you?!"

The little girl listened, defiant and proud, her head high for the
boys to see, "no, my Mom doesn't spend lots of money . . ." She said,
"but I'll tell you what Mama gives me . . ."
"She wakes me each morning with a hung and a kiss, she tucks
me in bed each night. She tells me I'm pretty, talented and smart
. . . she loves me even when we fight."
"She volunteers to make cookies for the party at school. She checks my
homework to make sure it's right. She makes 'Ms. Bunny' talk to me
and my friends when they come over to spend the night . . ."
"She takes me to dances and to the movies. She holds me in her arms
when I cry. She shows me she loves me every single day and
there's some things that money can't buy
"So even though I envy the riches you have, I can make you this
guarantee, in my eyes there is nothing more precious than this
Love between Mama and me . . ."

Betty Burnett

The Cliff And The Eagle

The Cliff and the Eagle share a common resident.
Abiding together, as partners, in the same locality.
They provide a service, each to the other
and a mutual benefit is derived by both.
They are sharing partners in this grand Creation.

The Cliff juts majestically from the Earth with massive folds and dents.
The Eagle soars the heights with apparent impunity.
They both seem to exist as if Sister and Brother,
Yet they each receive benefits due a Host.
Together they exist as partners in God's Creation.

The Cliff provides a safe haven for its resident,
in its many folds and dents of its numerous principalities,
While the Eagle removes small rodents that tickle its Earth Mother
and gives the beauty of motion that it enjoys the most.
For the two have separate but co-joined parts to play in this Creation.

The Cliff is draped in multi-hued colors and many varied scents;
While the Eagle is clad in feathers that gives it mobility.
The Cliff resides in its spot as if it's a bother,
But the Eagle swoops and glides enough for both.
As they each fill their niche in God's Grand Creation.

Calvin Stafford Jr.

Dear Grandma

There are 3,000 miles between us but
I know you can hear me.
I'm telling you this because I love you.
Time went by fast, I'm almost grown up
Yet I'm still a little girl inside.
Coming to your house.
Sitting on your steps.
Playing with the dog.
Wanting to help you cook.
But that was the past
Now I think
Would I be the same
if you were here.
When I think about it I cry
But I have to accept it.
You've always been there for me.
Through tears, and laughs.
Grandma, can you hear me.

Stephanie Carmen

Bombs

Bombs are so mean
Some are disguised, so not seen.
Some are meant just to hurt one
Others hurt millions, when done.
Some are sent through the mail.
The people who send them are going to hell.
Ruin people lives.
Cause the women are somebody's wives.
Sobs, tears and heartbroken are all.
The people who get hurt, do nothing
at all.

Sydney K. Acton

Prayer For Talent

This I must do, Lord! I cannot say
That I will put my pen away,
Nor try again with what small art I'm given
To mold a thought, make words take fire,
Preserve a dream. This, Lord, I desire.
Let others work with oils or clay;
Let someone else the anthems play.
Each has talent handed down from Heaven:
An aptitude, a gift that gives delight;
Please add to mine! I need to write.

Martha T. Fugate

Day By The Sea

He is my constant and most dependable companion.
We begin our walk beside each other
At our favorite place, the sea.

He runs ahead crashing into the waves
I chase after him
He avoids me.
We chase one another
Disturbing the sea gull stay.

Finally we tire of the physical chase.
Both exhausted and soaking wet
We take our rest.

I hold him near and say,
I love you Griz.
He looks at me kindly.

Together we share the sun's last warming rays
and end our day by the sea
My puppy love and me.

Diane C. Martin

Memories Of The Old

He peers out the window with weary eyes,
So many things seen, so much gone by,
A child yells, laughter is heard,
But he hears only nothing, but the song of a bird,

A bluebird at that, chirping in the trees,
Marking the Spring that is felt through the breeze,
His wife at his side, content with the world,
Memories of bliss send his mind in a whirl,

Further back — he jumps through the woods,
Free as the squirrel which from above is stood,
Carefree he plays with no worries at all,
Except for the moon which increasingly grows tall,

Back by the window, he peers outside,
A tear escapes, from the heart it slides,
Years gone by, memories fulfilled,
Here stands a man with a sagging build,

I watch the old man with curious eyes,
Wondering what he thinks through those weary eyes,
A man he was, a man he is,
Forever living in the memories of his.

Seth A. Taylor

Intuition

Sitting on the rim
    of your canyon walls
I almost jumped, but I didn't.
I knew there was no bottom
    to your ice cream sundae,
    saw your cherries crashing down,

And somewhere in that dessert sky
I imagined myself
    falling in
Your oceans swallowed me up — I lost my way home

So I placed myself
In the safe arms of my own meadow
With my own fertile soil
And the precious flowers in my head
And I liked it there — so I stayed

Maybe there's another
Broken-winged butterfly
Who'll take the plunge,
But she won't come
    from my side of the garden

Jennifer Broussard

Father

I see, I say . . . and you know that you are,
Such an angry and bitter young man.
For the fire and smoke,
And the rage that you provoke.
It's . . . but a struggle,
That will defeat you.
For all that you know, and all that you are,
We after all, are all innocent at heart.
So heed to what I say, and, don't be dismayed.
For it's still not to late,
To know the truth about you.
So, surrender.
Surrender yourself unto thyself,
For your mind is the key,
That can unlock the door to your heart.
. . . Be still . . . and know,
With patience . . . love will gently grow.
And give all of what you've got unto him,
For then you'll know . . .
. . . You'll know, that he has always loved you.

Jeffrey M. Griesbach

Once

Once the feeling was there,
but now it is gone,
like a fire it burned there,
now it only smolders all alone,
the words you said caused me pain,
even though I didn't let it show,
a long lost memory still lingers in my brain,
and a seed of love I didn't let grow,
in the darkest corners of my mind,
all my feelings are safely stowed away,
a smile on my face you might find,
but on the real truth in my eyes give me away,
don't knock on the door to my heart,
I won't answer but only turn you away,
No one can tear me apart,
For my own dreams have taken my away.

Linda Hunt May

For Her

Such a sad feeling have I encountered.
I feel as if I may vanish into the universe,
Leaving but not a mere buff upon such a decrepit society;
Involved in a useless program of living.

Come and save my soul; oh immortal woman.
Pick me up and cast me into your
Paradise of satin silk and sea polished gems of pearls.
Whisper unto my feeble character of loving me
Till my burst upon burst cools your volcanic desires.
Touch me with tenderness until that time as to when a new era
Awakens me with the rays of suns and warmth of new.
Love me till I die of the ecstasy of your passion;
And let my will read: "And for her, being all he head, he leaves
Everything."

Ken Baker

Amazing Grace

The rose was a gift for my daughter Callie, she picked out the color and brought if home proudly. See Callie loves flowers, any kind any color, but this rose would be special among any other.

See nobody knew that my best friend was sick, the day she bought Callie the rose that she picked only God in his infinite wisdom aware knew that I'd need that rose to be there.

The rose took off blooming almost immediately. God watched over it daily for Callie and me. So fittingly Callie named that rose Grace. 'Twas Grace we would need in the dark hours we'd face.

He'd used that rose as a symbol of His love to assure me He heard all of my prayers above. God used Grace to bring comfort indeed. She bloomed constantly through my hours of need.

Cathy had cancer, the news was just devastating. The load was too heavy, I found myself praying. "God give me a sign to just help me cope," somehow I knew that in Grace I'd find hope.

That rosebud called Grace bloomed beautifully for so long. It beckoned to me assuring me night would turn to dawn. I looked at each rose petal and felt God was there whispering Grace is sufficient anytime anywhere.

God speaks to us always in mysterious ways to allow us His presence throughout all our days. I understand now He uses such simple things, to show His love, to give us hope, to soar on His wings.

I learned a wonderful lesson in Grace by my maker. I found hope in a rosebush blessed by its creator. God chose to heal Cathy and for that I am grateful and yes Grace is still blooming ever so faithful.

I weathered that storm in my life with some help from my God whose promises I've been shown are always kept. I truly found Grace in the face of that rose. Now "Amazing Grace" is the only name that she knows!

Lynn Miller

Why?

Why is it that you always feel that dreadful way after someone has died?
Sometimes you don't even cry.
You just sit there, staring into space.
Sometimes you get the chills, that tingling feeling up your back
Other times you feel sorry for yourself
Not the person that died.
Or you feel like you want to die.
But why does it have to be that way?
Look at this world.
They've been put out of their misery
All the stealing.
All the murdering.
It will never stop.
So why can't we feel good for them?
They have no more problems
No more worries
Why?

Morgan Bailey

Forever Friends

Once upon a time in a kindergarten room
A once in a lifetime friendship was preparing to bloom.
It was a chance meeting, I'm not sure how or why
But I am certain it started with a simple little "Hi."
Two girls in no time became the best of friends.
In one's important moment the other was certain to attend.
They had sleep-overs, went shopping, and wrote notes galore
and soon their friendship grew into something more.
They shared a special bond that nothing could break.
Even tho eventually their friendship would be at stake.
The sleep-overs and shopping have since ceased, the notes are no more,
But I still feel the bond as strong as before.
You see I was one of these girls and I never want to forget
I had the very best friend the world had in it.

Tammy L. Belcher

Forever Love

There are times when a woman
Has to let go and say her good-byes,
To control the flow of tears from falling from her eyes.
Holding on to the memories that she once knew,
Hoping that one day they will transform into you.

The days get darker, the pain never ends;
As she keeps waiting for her heart to mend.
His love is gone, while hers is everlasting;
But there is one question that her inner mind keeps asking.

How long shall I wait for that forever love
That I have been promised from my God up above?
He said,
    I am with you always as pure as a dove,
For within me is where you will find your forever love.

Karen G. Grosdaile

Cloudland

I look at the white snow
and my imagination goes
to the clouds where I see children play.
    They laugh in delight
    during a pillow fight
and the feathers float down as snowflakes.

The sun is their mother
who changes the weather.
This sight makes her laughter shine down.
    The kids run off to play
    and the light from her rays
sparkle the feathers on the ground.

Amy Baker

Sitting Under A Tree

Isn't it just so right,
   to sit under a tall leafy tree
on bright green grass,
   writing four line poetry?

Watching lies, happiness and depression,
   pass before my eyes
showing nothing from within,
   as they say their hellos and lament good-byes

And as they go on,
   with their noses still up in the air
they keep ignoring the fact,
   that a someone was even there!

Perhaps they can't get past,
   the shallow persona that I might uncover
because I know all they want,
   is a pretty face and great body in a lover

Or could it be what scares them,
   is my bag of 400 page books
that I use to substitute,
   for my obvious lack of ravishing good looks?

Steven Morales

The Sunrise Of Eternity

As day-dawn breaks each glorious morn,
   We summon blessings to adorn,
That all our works an entitlement may be,
   To the Sunrise of Eternity.

So as we venture out this day,
   We supplicate and earnest pray,
That those we meet may somehow find,
   Our deeds for them, most rich and kind.

May Charity exude our life,
   And in His name our service rife,
For as we do, it seems we're given,
   Most precious gifts bestowed by heaven.

At mortal end we'll rest assured,
   Unsought testaments by heralds, heard:
"We find this soul, a partaker should be,
   To the Sunrise of Eternity."

Don T. Peterson

I'm A Young Black Woman!

I'm a young black woman
Full of pride my brown color — I'll never hide.

I'm a young black woman
Full of grace — I'm proud of my people,
I'm proud of my race,
I'm blessed with good health and a pretty face.

I'm a young black woman
Trying to succeed,
Always doing my best to do a good deed.

I'm a young black woman
Trying to pave my way — I want a good life,
   Somehow, someday.

I'm a young black woman
Endowed with faith and hope,
Through road blocks and obstacles I can cope.

I'm a young black woman
Proud of my effort and my race,
World open your arms — take me — embrace.
I'm a young black woman!

Efie Bishop

Untitled

The sun sets and the sky falls black.
And the trees whisper to me as I turn my back,
On all the memories I knew,
Of how and when and why I loved you.
I look to the sky and I see
Stars that are reminders of you and me.
They twinkle their brightness for a time.
And slowly, yet surely, they lose their shine.
Dark shadows play stages for these memories,
As I look into them and you I see.
Darkness' arms engulf me to bring me the ghosts of love I knew.
I reach out to embrace them and fall right through
Transparent bodies that carry my pain from long ago,
And I begin to wonder if I will ever know
How to entwine my heart and love together
And discover a happiness that may last me forever.

Sandi Dykes

I

I was born in a one room shack
On sunny days the sun streamed in through the cracks
On rainy days showers came in through the roof
The morning after my birth my bundle of wrappings fell
   out of my mother's arms, before her waking,
I in them fell, into a rain puddle on the wooden floor.
I survived.

I am as a flower blooming and radiant,
   Today — this moment.
I am as a flower wilted and dying,
   Today — the next moment.

I am as a weed that grows today
   And is cut down tomorrow.

I am as wheat—gleaned, threshed and crushed.
I was in a desolate desert — destitute —

I was a clay pot — sooted and broken
I was picked up, shattered to pieces, melted,
   and restored by a skillful and loving potter's hand.

I was broken yesterday.
I am molded and not yet finished today.

Anna Maria Rios

"The Days of '65"

Does anybody really miss those days of "65"?
Do you drift away in memory, so glad you were alive.

The old gang gathered every night to laugh and play around,
But now we watch computers, and data entry is the "sound."

The children are attached it seems, to wires everywhere!
Have we all become computerized, and does anybody care?

The scenes in life flee by I fear, do we really ever see,
That there could never be a you, if there never was a me.

The home was simply structured just our Father and our Mother,
The word respect stood oh-so-tall, when shared with one another.

One day a week was set aside for God, and rest and pleasure,
Those family ties from bygone days, are memories we all treasure

A wise man gave us food for thought," walk just one mile in my shoes,"
If just one day we could go back, I know which time we'd choose,

Elvis still would surely be forever the real king,
And boys would still be asking girls to wear their senior ring.

We'd still be watching "Bandstand" on black and white TV,
And there would be no cable, we'd be watching it for free.

Thank God we had the chance to see the days of "65",
They keep our prayers and all our dreams, untouched and so alive.

Cheryl Canfield

Declaration of Love

Life first savored now ignored
Open thy eyes for thine to see
Vivid descriptions carelessly torn
Endeavored by some they carry the key

Cautious are some not to break their mirth
Avariciously, they plan to unlock the vessel
Rooted deep in the soil they cling to fresh earth
Revising their ways they're willing to change
Integrity inspires brand new intention
Exhibition of their love cannot be chained
Sacrificed the revolution a treaty declared new birth

Animation of their love has opened their eyes
Lost no more they pitched the disguise
Love shaped their life and that they won't deny

Jeremy Baldridge

Our Daughter

You came to us one bright Sunday morn;
    We were so happy the day that you were born.
Eyes so dark and hair that matched;
    So quickly your Daddy and I became attached.

Your smile will forever brighten my day;
    Your sincerity will always pave your way.
I want you to know how special you are;
    Do not be discouraged to follow your star.

The joy you gave us when you were small;
    Made all our obstacles not seem so tall.
We're so very proud of your accomplishments, dear;
    But don't be surprised when you see my tear.

Thru out the years we watched you grow;
    And now it's time to let you go.
Graduation day has come, you see,
    But our little girl you will always be.

Barbara McCoslin

The Heart Beat

I can hear your heart beat as it pitter patters inside,
A feeling of closeness one can't imagine or hide,
As your body and soul grows within me each day,
Not sure of your surroundings, but know that you are safe.

A warmth and security only love can give,
Is a will to progress and the strength to live,
To become a big part of our lives that will be,
A start of a new beginning for all of us to see.

Deanna Lynn Hansen

The Night

Pale and round the moon and stars are shining
The bright light from the moon shows the hard ground
Listening to the coyotes howling their finding
I marvel at the howl with its soft sound

Listening to the darkness I feel all alone
Wondering if I can follow in the night
I search the darkness and find I an known
I light a blue candle to clear my sight

The shining light fills the night with brightness
The wild wind whistles throughout the tall trees
When the flame flickers you become sightless
Hurrying on through many miles of deep seas

Looking ever so hard for your sweet warm house
Hurrying on through many hard troubles with spouse

Faydra L. Cannon

Even In The Darkest Hour

Even in the darkest hour when all seems gone — black and dismal
Like a dark rainy day cold and damp

And pain's cut can go no deeper — one even a friend couldn't mend
Thoughts raging within to get out like a caged wild beast

There is but a glimmer of light and life
Like rays shooting through an opening in the clouds

But somewhere deep inside — and hope's passion stirs
Like the red, hot boil of molten rock

When failure's crush has levied its blow
And dreams don't escape its pitiless sigh of no tomorrows

That far beyond death's apparent hold lies footstep's path
Of a once forgotten bold and adventures reason for being

For in the darkest of dark the grim raises its torch
To claim victory's dance in the sun's sparkling applause

Beyond the grip of fate's hold is the showering power
The light that floods out all remnants of age and sorry

And brings forth true beauty of life's victory song — of being
life's passion to persist into eternal age of the immortal

But even in the darkest hour know yet that one travels no further
Than one's own vision — even in the darkest hour.

Cary Goulston

She Loves Love

She sits and thinks about him,
but love is impossible by her standards,
she no longer knows love,
only hate feels her soul.
She hides her pain,
behind a quivering smile,
no one can understand her hate,
for fear of being hated.
She is imprisoned by the thought,
of someone loving her.
She wants to run,
but is scared to,
from fear of being forgotten.
She is frightened of him,
because he is tearing down her emotional walls,
that it took her so long to build,
and she's not really sure if she is scared of being forgotten,
or scared of being loved.

Michelle Monique Massey

I Am

I am what I am
Though I can but dimly perceive.
I am the sun,
The dew on green leaves.
All good and all evil does in me exist.
Not separate but in oneness I am all that is.
The warmth of summer,
The chill of fall air.
The vastness of space,
The smallness of despair.
My individuality is naught but a cover in a game
In which I lose myself
And go by the name given me there.
Wrapping myself so completely in the part that I play
That I can only see my reaction
To pleasure and pain.
Something less.
Seeing only the actor's reflection
In eternity's window glass.

Tommie Lee LeLugas

Someday

If perhaps someday your eyes shall see
that I'm unworthy in the sight of thee,

Moving into the forest's shadows would become my fate,
to watch you from a distance, a heart-broken mate.

I'd steal glimpses of you, my angel of bygone time
and make them pictures in the pages of my mind.

I'd seal them with a kiss to be reopened beneath a tree,
and once forgotten bliss would unfold before me.

And if perhaps someday you'd change your mind,
cover your eyes and make them blind,

To no longer see the unjust ways of my soul,
and call to the wind, "My sweet Joel"

Within but a few moments the trees above
would send down to me a snow white dove.

"Tell her I'm coming," I'd whisper to God's chosen one.
"You'll know when you see her, she radiates like the sun."

Beneath his graceful wings as he soars above,
his breast swells with the words of my undying love.

Joel De Lorme

I Am America

I am the child of Justice and Freedom
My grandparents are Honesty and Wisdom.
Married to Honor, I bore children, named
Fairness, Dignity, Compassion, and Valor.
I've lost some sons on distant shores
To rescue humanity from oppression.
But achieved my strength by drinking
from the bitter cup of errors
and hence attained a keen awareness
of the yearning of mankind.
The world through shadows of fear,
follow my eagle
there to the mountain of hope
where my torch of liberty flames
and my flag flies free against
the limitless sky
For I was given a golden rod to wrest
from bound seas the right of every man
no matter his creed or class.

I am America.

Gloria M. Anthony

What About Religion?

Why do we believe in it?
Is religion about truth?
If so,
What is right in the Crusades?
Or Bosnia?
Even World War II . . .
Who determines our destiny?
More importantly, who is correct?
Is it the Jewish?
Maybe the Buddhists.
What about the Muslims?
Could be the Christians.
Might be the Hindus.
What about the lesser known religions?
Religion has co-existed with us for centuries on end.
But was is for moral support?
The good of the world?
An explanation of the universe?
Or an excuse for war and expansion . . .

Hyung-Jin Won

Untitled

We used to fish in Puget sound
If we couldn't catch a salmon, there was perch, rock cod, and sole
We'd save the dogfish for the garden
Sometimes a starfish would jerk my pole

We used to hike up mountain trails
If we were thirsty, we'd drink from a nearby stream
We'd see foxes, bears, muskrats, and otters
Deer were everywhere it seemed

We used to marvel at the Cascade Range
On every sunny day
And Mt. Baker and Mt. Rainier
And the Olympics across the bay

You could see Possession Point
From the beach where we used to play
Now when it's sunny
It's the same as a cloudy day.

Mari DeClements

Absence Of Momentum

The wind is coming from the west, where
The moon bespeaks itself — "I beckon the stars
And gather them around me. I make of night
A spangled cavern where you may rest."
Eyes open, eyes closed, I sleep:
Icy teeth closed against my frigid breath.

I want to rampage through Spring, cut through dead trees
To the illuminating naked sun, break it open,
Cover myself in its warm drool, a big egg
Oozing Spring over the dead land — the goo of life.
But the sun is cold and small and the wind whistles.

What makes the surf beat against the ocean shelves?
Weak, my voice is a whisper lost in the wind. I am locked in,
I am barely conscious — there's not enough light or love
To warm my bones and keep me from sleeping.
Who can save one from the dead of Winter?

Pfelton Sutton

My Father

He lived upon the battlefield
He lived upon the plain
He lived to meet his maker
He lived with might and main.
He taught his children how to live
He taught them how to die
A kind and faithful father
Now lives beyond the sky
He walked patiently down life's highway
With footsteps ever to the right
His spirit is always near me
Leading, guiding to the light,
He went peacefully on to glory
In the dark hours of the night
Still clinging to that courage
With all a soldier's might
The ills of life have ended, the cares of life have passed
The way was sometimes weary but he was loyal to the last
He is gone but not forgotten, he has crossed the golden shore
He is safe at home with Jesus to be forevermore

Ralph Milton Sims

The Lord's Lamb

You shall never walk in darkness, upon God's golden path so bright.
God is your shepherd and you are his lamb. So look to him
when the light is dim. For He will watch out for you through
thick and thin . . .

Samantha Jankins

Mom

I'm writing this to let you know,
Some of my feelings, I don't always show.
I call you Mom, with the upmost respect.
You're my role model, teacher, everything I expect.
The love you have for family and friends,
Goes on and on, it never ends.
Your strength and patience are amazing to me.
Determined and caring, it's easy to see.
Most would be bitter, if your life they were dealt.
Anger, unhappiness for those around them would surely be felt.
Not you! Forgiveness and love is what you implore.
Your search for the best in others, this I truly adore.
I'm in awe how you deal with my frowns.
How easy you turn them all upside down.
Those around me will be luckier by far,
If I can be one fourth of the woman you are.
Anyone around can easily see,
I have a wonderful Mom, and I'm glad to be me.
I'm truly blessed to have someone like you,
In one person, my Mom and a best friend too.

Diana Jacinto

A New Fallen Snow

There is nothing quite as beautiful as a new fallen snow.
As the delicate flakes so softly swirl to the ground below.
It's wonderful to take a walk on this crisp cold day.
Look up toward the sky, let the flakes fall where they may.
They tickle your nose and lashes with a tingly embrace.
The chill in the air adds a radiance of red to your face.
If you close your eyes you can faintly hear the sound,
Of each tiny crystal as it flutters to the ground.
As you look out the window on this winter's night.
The darkness is illuminated in a blanket of glistening white.
No, nothing is quite as beautiful as a new fallen snow.
Each perfect tiny flake covers Gods earth below.

Jeanne Woodruff

Halloween

Halloween, Halloween, Halloween is coming.
Put on your costumes 'cause Halloween's on its way.
Halloween, Halloween, Halloween is coming
With witches, ghosts, ghouls and vampires,
Monsters in chains and people screaming
'Cause Halloween's on its way.
Halloween, Halloween, Halloween is coming
With gooey bulging-out eyeballs, sticky flesh of goblins
And damp dark shadows lurking right behind you
'Cause Halloween's on its way.
Halloween, Halloween, Halloween is coming
With wicked laughter and a witch's black cat,
An ear piercing shriek and a rattling skeleton
'Cause Halloween's on its way.
Halloween, Halloween, Halloween is coming.
Put on your costumes 'cause Halloween's on its way.

Insia Malik

Caring And Sharing

Little Charlie, Joey, Andrew and John were walking one day when they found a pear. It was yellow, rosy and ripe and was hanging low on the tree. Charlie said, "I saw it first, it's mine." Joey said, "I will pick it, so it's mine." Andrew said, "let's pick it and divide it in four. Each of us will then get a piece." John said, "I will pick it and it's mine." They wrestled with each other over the pear when suddenly it fell to the ground.

A little brown cow was lazing around and flashing its tail at the flies. Suddenly, the cow saw the juicy pear. Before the boys could get to the pear, the cow picked it up. He took a big bite, a swallow or two, and that was the end of the juicy pear.

Mary Burrell

God's Garden

If I could pick from God's garden
All the treasures my eyes behold,
I would pick faith, love, health and happiness
All that my arms could hold.

Faith sustains me in my darkest hour,
When it seems that all is lost.
And good health is such a treasure,
To be protected at all cost.

True love gives us a special feeling
So unselfish warm and kind.
But happiness is the only one,
Most people will never find.

There are so many treasures to see
In this garden from above.
I want to spend an eternity,
In God's garden, filled with love.

Margaret Ann Rondina

Jesus

I awaken this morning to bright sunshine,
with stiff bones but a clear mind.
I looked around to see my day's grace,
of God's forgiving and merciful face.

He takes me in his arms,
and protects me from all harm.
I know this man you see,
he's at the head of my family's tree.

He found me one day when I was lost,
extended his hand to help me across.
Remove the obstacle that stood in my way,
Giving me a bright and cloudless day.

He sits high, but looks low,
This man, I call Jesus.
He loves and cares for me,
By his death on Calvary.

Rosetta C. Rivers

Now

Something to be said for impatience
bad and good both have their way
always curious on the when and how
it must happen quickly it must happen now

Ill advised behavior some might say
several things lost on the short route
the quick route is a shorter one indeed
a path that sees one to succeed

The fine line that must be drawn
is one that binds our personalities
business is quick and must happen now
all personal efforts must time allow

Often hard this line we ease
mistakes we make long to forget
I practice the picture each day of life
if only time could be as might

A. Scott Woodrome

Highways And Byways

All the Highways and Byways but none going my way
they're all just passing me by
The dirt roads, the back roads, and the busy city streets
I wonder do the ends of them meet
And if I were to follow down one of them tomorrow
I wonder where it would lead.

Becky Holland Smith

Mamaw

Only you knew how I loved you so
It nearly broke my heart to let you go

Your laughing face and gentle touch
Is why I loved you oh! So much

From the day I was born until the day you died
You were always there and close by my side

When I was a child you always had time
To play games, tell stories and read nursery rhymes

As I grew up into a young adult
You were so understanding and never found fault

You taught me to sew, quilt and bake
Those cherished memories no one can take

I would sit by your side for hours on end
No matter how busy, you had time to lend

As time went by and you grew old
Our love for each other, no one heart could hold

I never dreamed I'd ever be so lonely and blue
But, I realize now you had to be with papaw too!

One of these days, together we'll be
Up in "God's Heaven" so peaceful and free

Mary L. Clark

Strong Enough

Views of distant revolutions,
closed eyes make the decisions for you.
Are we tied to the post of gratification
or care enough to speak of humiliation.

Bring on the depth of stored reaction,
a thought or two passing within reach,
or sweep the floor of eyes looking away
still overflowing of emptiness yet to be brought forth.

Choices rendered useless under friendly fire
overwhelmed by the rushing time of wrongful status.
Alone the Worlds visions lost in time,
are followed by the remains of silence heard.

Looks of desperation at words well spoken,
smiles of cobwebs swept aside to expose antiques.
Senses open the breath of strength and excitement
bodies uplifted in the celebration of strong enough.

Don Leehy

Daydream

Walking,
suddenly I stop.
We dance
gently gliding
almost floating
touching lightly.
Cabalistic winds
caressing gently.
The music
a trembling aura of mystic beauty
molding, shaping us together.
Our eyes
for a fleeting moment
have joined,
giving birth
to my mythical fancy.

A less desirable stage of being now engulfs me,
and a passionless reality pulls me into his grasp.
With help from the candid hypocrisy of life,
I walk on.

K. G. Riha

Time

Time is momentary and time is eternal.
Second by second and minute by minute;
Hour by hour and day by day;
Year by year and century by century.

Why doesn't time stand still and await me?
Why can't I keep up or finish what I've started?
Why is time always gaining speed with each step?
Why must I always adapt to this thing called time?

That time piece hangs above me on the wall.
It encircles me and ticks my life away.
I'm well aware, the fleeing of eternal time.
I must learn to accept as time marches onward.

I'm still behind that infinity of time.
I'm always checking time, but time runs on like a thief.
That face on the wall never shows me any emotion.
I've learned I can't control this element called time.

Elizabeth B. Loraff

Why Do You Hurt Me So

You claimed your love was true so
why do you hurt me so. You told me that you had no
love left. I hear from the rest you think I still love
you. I know deep in myself I was your one and only
love. Because sometimes when life would bring you
down I would try to pick you up no matter the
consequence. At times cheering you up made me sad
and at times it made our love grow stronger. Why
did you play those evil games. I'm sorry for calling
you all those nasty names. My love for you still
makes no sense. Could our passion have been that
sweet and romantic. Or was my heart too
sympathetic. A mystic curse you have placed on me
with a hug and a kiss. My love I shall miss you
so. But why do you hurt me so.

Edward R. Amirian

Poetry, Poetry, Poetry

A girl I once knew only wanted to write.
Poetry, poetry, poetry.
She wrote about love she wrote about life but
it all became the same thing. Poetry, poetry, poetry.
This girl told stories but shorter, she told the
truth about . . . Poetry, poetry, poetry.
Jenny, the name of this girl but people know
about her feelings, about her emotions, poetry,
poetry, poetry.
She had told herself at are time she knew
what she wanted to be, it scared everyone
because everyone knows poets don't make good
money, she didn't mind of the pay. Poetry, poetry, poetry.
She is only teenager but her young mind looks
for what could put her in a good place. Poetry,
poetry, poetry.
What she writes, what she thinks of poetry,
poetry, poetry and this I will say I can
hardly ever put my pen down again.

Jennifer Sullivan

Life

Life is it precious
or is life dumb?

Is it great
or is it full of rum?

Is it the best thing that ever happened to you
or would you rather die, is it true?

Carla Lynette Harris

The Butterfly

Once there was this butterfly
All speckled green and gold
That sailed into my life
Ever so bold and with the likes of which
I've never seen before
Grasped a hold of my heart and
Simply refused to let it go
I was shocked; I was surprised
Imagine me and this butterfly
He fluttered his wings gazing at me
He seemed content sitting on my knee, holding my heart
Lest it would flee but why, I had no wish to leave
Sweet little butterfly how lucky
you were to have found me
Together we soared my hand on his wing
Up over trees, flowers and things
Back on the earth standing on my own feet
Beautiful little butterfly
Who can you be, he fluttered his wings and winked at me
Jeffrey was the reply said he

Linda Johnson

A Love Letter . . . Forever

We were so very tiny when you brought
us to your home, but you've always loved and
raised us as if we were your very own.
I'll never forget the laughter and the tears
through all of those very influential years.
You've instilled in me morals, principals and
values that have and will continue to influence and
guide me through this long, strenuous journey
called life. But now the time has come for me to
return the gift of caring patients and time, for
you now need to depend on me as I once depended upon you.
As I look into your eyes, I see fear, the fear
of not knowing what has happened to that once stable, caring
and gentle person, now dependent and unstable. I
understand now the true meaning of love and dedication,
the kind of love and dedication you gave to me, I've now
given back to you. Your time has now come to an end.
You were so very dear to me and will remain in my
thoughts, heart and dreams . . . forever . . .

Kelli A. Case

Mom Was A Football Buff

Mom didn't know about Giants and Raiders,
Thought they were fairy tale invaders.
She never saw a football game,
Knew nothing of Dallas Cowboy fame.

A TV Set quickly changed her life,
Introduced her to football strife
"Them Coyboys" was now "her team"
"Go Cowboys" soon became her theme

She was not aware of the first and ten.
Field goals and such was not her ken.
As game after game progressed
She, with the score, became obsessed.

The Cowboys, famous, Big and Strong
In Mom's eyes could do no wrong
When some official a flag would throw,
"Can't be the Cowboys, that I know"

She knew the team members all by sight
They're "America's Team" alright.
How could a game so rough and tough
Make mom, so meek and mild, a football buff?

Kenneth Eck

All Of My Love

Sometimes I wonder, what I can do,
To let you know, how much I love you!
I think of the days, together we've spent,
The times alone and how much it's meant,
You are so special, so lovely you see,
There's nobody else in the world for me!
Any tears that you have I'll wipe away,
We're so close, we've got to stay,
Together forever, our love's so strong,
Maybe some day I'll make this a song,
If I could, I'd jump in a car,
I'd pick you up, we would drive real far,
Through the woods and towards the coast,
I'd have champagne to make a toast,
That our love would never die,
And to keep you forever, I will try,
Everything possible in my power,
You are my angel, my beautiful flower,
But sometimes I wonder, what I can do
To let you know, how much I love you!

Roland H. Westbrook

Numbness Like An Eagle Spreads Its Wings

Numbness like an eagle spreads its wings,
not in flight, but in stationary emotions,
the grace is not present
awesome impact resides alone
expansive stretch
tips touching corners
searching for foundation
lost . . . in a world of felt, feel and will feel
feathers and fluff.
Focus centralized . . .
ahh something substantial to grasp,
the sharp beak pokes and prods,
pointed pain
decentralized . . .
two enveloping eyes
questioning — accentuating
the pain reflected in a face
the eagle rests
waiting.

Kimberly Jantzer

Untitled

I can not see. Everything is dark.
Yet, I feel the obstacles around me
and know of their presence.
Yet, I can not see them.

I stumble over a chair.
I feel the desk in front of me,
the pencils, the paper, the pack of cigarettes.
The heat from the lamp that is lit.
Yet, I can not see any of them.

I feel the pictures on the wall and find a window near by.
I pull the curtains back and feel a breeze blowing.
I feel the warmth of the sun
shining through the open window on my face.
Yet, I can not see.

I hear a voice that is calling and I am afraid.
There is someone else here in the room with me.
The fears builds up in my mind.
I am afraid, so afraid.

The darkness, it surrounds me.

Maybe, if I open my eyes?

E. C. Royer

Seasons Behold The Mighty Tree

Standing tall in stately glory
Arms outstretched, dressed heavily in green
Reaching upwards embracing the sun
Strong flowing limbs intertwined gracefully
Offering shade to life below

Light and lively breezes
Slightly shaking branches, majestically moving to and fro
Feathery leaves drift quietly downward
Creating a colorful cushion to be walked upon

Obeying the command of nature
In stern and rigid stature pose
Petrified naked in snow and wind a gnarled silhouette
Glistening with ice patiently awaiting the thaw
A beginning of life

Small projections soon appearing on barren brittle branches form
Miraculously blossom into a haven, its identity confirmed
Anxiously greets the arrival of creatures large and small
Remaining eager to protect and overlook all

Continuing in its quest to endure the seasons
The mighty tree stands tall
Janice V. Kidd

The Stone

I threw a stone into a pond
and the effect it had went way beyond
The scope of what I could see.
As the ripples flowed away from me.
Growing ever bigger the further they went
I saw my life and how it was spent.
The ripples are the people I meet everyday
The words and the deeds that I display.
My influence spreads wider with the years
Through joyous times and through tears.
And each life touched through hand and heart
Start more ripples that go further and depart.
I thought perhaps I will never die
Because ripples touch you as they touch I
Ripples like memories live on in our hearts
And the legacy they leave will never depart.
For although I may not always see
The ripples that were caused by me
As they overlap with others and continue on
I know I will live this life and beyond.
Carmen R. Black

Reflections At Year's End

As we near the end of a blessed year
and find ourselves in a season of good cheer;
May each heart resound with a song and a prayer,
and praises to God for His wonderful care.

"Tis the season to be jolly" no doubt some will say.
And with an air of folly will rise to drink and play.
Or lavishly spend what our Lord has given
without one thought of the God in heaven.

But let us remember our Father above
who gives us His gifts to show us His love.
Greater gift could never be given you or me,
than that which was offered on Calvary's tree.

"For God so loved the world that He gave
His only begotten Son; that whosoever believeth
in Him should not perish, but have
everlasting life." John 3:16

If ever a gift would try to repay
the matchless gift that God gave away;
To give all we have is such a small part,
when we can do better by giving our hearts.
Lucille Williams

Firmament Of Heavens

One day I was given a deep personal
love, a ring my eyes filled with tears
of happiness.
     My heart burning a warm glow,
inside me I called it the "firmament of
heavens."
     The colors of the ring danced so
shiny and bright for all aglow.
     As they danced and danced so shiny
and bright a brightness of gifts of heaven.
     For every time I looked at the ring
fountains of color danced and danced
upon the rain drops.

     For they danced and danced into
new hearts and new heavens.
     My glow had a new place to go.
Judy Rhodes

Tylenol

The darkness is coming, swirling and twirling,
Flying so high, crying.
Tell me a carol, a story, a breeze.
Seems so far away, far away, grainy,
All so empty, flying.
The pain, the pain, it flies away.
Surviving.
Clara Fuchsman

Star Dreams

My eyes rise skyward upon the coming night
to wish, dream and gaze
entranced by the stars o so very bright.

They twinkle and shoot ever so bold
while holding the dreams and wishes of millions untold.

Ye many a wish is driven by greed
then there are those who's are simply a need.
There are some who are lonely and are looking for a friend
maybe even searching for a lost loved ones guidance again.

But then there are those who use it as a channel from within
to try and invade the subconscious of those sleeping and tucked in.

Could it be that wishes, dreams and stars are all joined as one
for as when the new day's dawn has started rise
why do I feel that I have been awoken by someone else's eyes.

I'll start my day with that boost from within
looking forward to casting myself to the stars again.
Michael A. Barr

Buckingham Fountain

Scorning accident, the multicolored fountain
geysers evenings in the greening park.
True to genus, the flowers of the mountain
shade the rough, pale, sharp-rising rock

With painted parasols, as if that withering height
were a sunny beach. And so the caved
front of ruined temples, the blinded sight
of antique eyes, is gradually lifted — saved

My love, for you — for you, my love, and I.
For others will circle the shooting water-fountain,
and others will pick the flowers of the mountain
to analyze the dream-work of the dye

But we shall be the multicolored rain
that stains the stonecrop of the sky.
Daniel Joseph Polikoff

Where You Fit In

There was a square peg who lived in a hole, but to live in round holes wasn't exactly his goal. He had edges you see, rounds never felt right, and his hole always was a bit too tight. Now, round is great, for those who fit, only when you're square there's nowhere to sit. He squeezed down just as hard as he could, but he flat didn't fit and never would.

Then he found a place on the other side of town that had square holes and very few rounds. There, he heard, square paradise could be found, where squares were the thing and rounds were drowned. He checked of the rent and found it quite steep, he knew if he moved he'd be in debt deep. He figured if he jumped he'd have but one leap, and if he missed he'd land in the street. So he packed everything in a little square box, right down to his top hat and three holey socks. Then he stood back, took a great leap, and to his surprise he landed on his feet! At last he was there in his very own square, and today he's still happy in the home he found there. So remember the story of my little square friend, home's not where you live, but where you fit in!

Veneta Pickett

Our Faithful Emblem

Proudly do you wave,
Oh, flag of this mighty land;
Fighting back the thieves
Who would take the freedom from our hand.

Flying high above the towns,
On poles that shine for thee;
Wilt thou let us down oh, flag?
That waves for liberty.

You are the emblem of this democracy,
You are the pride of we Americans;
What more then can you be?
Than the emblem of your liberty?

Oh, flag of the red, white and blue,
I'll do my part for you;
To keep this spark of fire,
Burning bright forever more.

If we each lend a helping hand,
To guide you along the way;
I'm sure this good old U.S.A,
Will be as free tomorrow as it is today.

Helen V. Boros

I Watched You

I watched you, with the inexperienced
eyes of youth,
observed, absorbed, learned
a slow gentle understanding style
rooted in limitless patience.

I saw the strength and fortitude
of your faith under trial
you stood strong, beliefs never faltering
from behind a face worn with years
you smiled at the oppressor.

A slow easy life style, peacefully serene and comfortable
like a well worn favorite sweater,
was just a guise, to cover up your daily struggle
and you won, grace given, grace received.
Eternal peace rewarded, humbly accepted.
Simple eternity for simple faith.

I stand and look at the stone,
the last remembrance of you,
recalling all of these things,
and hoping to live up to them.

Thomas M. Wallace

Mystery

As I walked a long narrow path, I stumble upon a fork
Lying right there in the middle of my path

As I stood there looking endlessly at which way to go

The road that lies to the right of me was lid up with the
Warmth of the hot sun shining softly upon my dark face

There was a beautiful smell of a wonderful spring day in
The country in my nose

And the most beautiful piece of land laid right there
Before my very own eyes

If you were to listen real closely you could hear the
Mellow sounds of mother nature

The road to the left of me had the nasty smell of a sewer
On a hot summer day

The blue sky was covered with a mysterious but pretty color
Of pink and gray

There was this loud noise that overpowered the sound of
The earth's natural inner beauty

Then came a cool breeze that brought nothing but hot air
As it passed me by

I just stood there and thought that life can be as simple
As walking down a road, but as hard as choosing which road to take.

Charlotte M. Crockett

Appetite For Love

People have an appetite for love,
but it seems to only bed to broken hearts,
and time and time again,
I find mine getting torn apart.

It doesn't do any good to fall in love,
because it only causes misery and pain,
yet I want to try and find love again,
only to find that my love for him,
I don't want it to end.

I don't want to loose him as a friend,
no one can control their appetite for love.

You and I search this world for the one we dream of,
but that one person is usually never found,
since we can't control our cravings when love comes around.

We can't control who we fall in love with,
so whatever will be will be,
maybe someday love will truly find me or you.

E. Roberts

Untitled

The night wind howls, the bats take flight.
I sit and wait for the arrival.
The dead rise, the ghosts take souls.
everywhere I can see, there is no one around but me.
I wait and wait, time marches on,
take no notice of me.
Who should care, for I know I don't.
The whirling spirits, fly around me.
But I couldn't see, I have always been blind.
Having no fear, I sit up, my eyes see nothing
my hand reaches outward, yet I feel nothing.
I lay back down, and the spirits swirl around.
No one to care.
No one to touch.
Another day I can't see.
Without anything.
Yet it is another day
for nothing and me.

Christina Kovinchick

If Only

See the blossoms — in the meadows
. . . Open their petals . . . wide . . .
They receive . . . the warmth —
. . . The moisture . . .
Our creator . . . provides . . .
If only — we could be more . . .
. . . like they . . .
Receiving the gifts he gives . . .
Spreading our arms to the
. . . heavens . . . with . . .
Total blinded . . . faith.

Mary Woodcock

Oh, There Was A Man From France

Oh there was a man from France, who did so like to dance.
He would dance all day and be very gay and sing along while he did it.
And the people would say he is so gay and then be on their way.
And oh, the people would say to themselves as they filled up
their shelves,
Oh, how I would like to be like him someday,
oh how I would like to be like him someday, someday!

Ashley Conover

Feeling Free

I climbed to the top of that mighty hill
    and found that all time seemed to be standing still
The wind gently whispered to the leaves on the trees
    While thoughts drifted off like a warm summer breeze

My heart asked to stay where I felt so free
    But reality kept pulling and tugging at me
My thoughts and my dreams just raced to and fro
    While I stood idle watching life continue below

The time just stood still on top of that hill
    As I gathered my strength and held tight with strong will
My breath floated free from deep within me
    As the feeling of freedom burst forth fast and free.

Caroline C. Wright

Christmas Spirit

What Christmas Spirit means, to me.
Gatherings of families round a tree.
Where laughter and love flow all around.
Forgiveness of past transgressions can be found.
Like small children we try to be blind.
To the faults in ourselves and all mankind.
Christmas Spirit brings miracles for sure.
Suddenly people see the sick and poor.
Christmas Spirit makes us open hearts and wallets to give.
So those less fortunate, for at least the season may live.
Somehow, someway we all must work and strive.
To keep the Christmas Spirit year round alive.

Patsy Mott

The Winter Night

The weather outside is cold and chilly
But inside I've got you to keep me warm and hot
There is a fire glowing in the dark
Candles burning in my heart
You are late and I wonder where you could be
Then, the phone rings and they say you are dead
I feel so empty and alone, I wonder how this could be,
because before you left, to come see me, you said you loved
    me, and that you would be careful
but now you are dead and I can't live without you
so I kill myself to be with you in eternity.

Brandy Hutchins

Butter Bay Image (1992-1996)

So much I wanted you to be, not just for you, but for me.
Your injuries were pretty bad, now we are all really sad.
I'd wake up each day and pray, for God not to take you away.
As I looked into your eyes, all I felt was pain inside.
I knew I had to let you go, but all I could say was no.
All the memories went through my head.
No, I couldn't imagine you dead.
Endless work never hurt your pride.
So tell me why are you to die?
The vet is here now, your pain is worse.
This is a damn curse.
So now is your last day, I'm crying as you eat your hay.
As I hug you one final time.
I realize you were worth every dime.
This is it, it's time to rest.
Just remember, to me you were the best.
You're breathing slower, your heartbeat's gone, I wish I could
have come along.
Your pain is gone now, mine is great, the biggest think that I hate.
I love you and forever more, be watching for me at heaven's door.

Danielle Peters

Tainted And Ill

As the darkness slips into the night,
some whispers are heard, there out of sight.

The silent breeze, past an old oak branch
the rustling leaves, some seem to dance.

But the shadow remains in the gloom of fear,
that not the end is coming, but the beginning is near.

So plans are made all throughout the land,
after winds and rains nothing stands.

The remains of things once now lost,
we futurized with human cost.

Are tiny plight now stands still,
the land we new, tainted and ill.

So for all of those who are blind to see,
were not the future, but history.

Go to work, and go to play,
for the next in line will surely say.

The things they did can't be undone,
now the end is sure to come.

So thank the ones who came before
the planet earth, it lives no more.

Anthony Funari

Balboa 1993

Bill stuffed his Toyota like a giant suitcase
    Chemistry notebooks, blankets,
    The family's old green dishes — the set he first ate from,
    Silverware from our basement,
    Bulging cardboard cartons, a worn duffle bag,
    Mountain bike body and wheels at mid-window,
    Maps, tapes, tour books.

Room for him only
    To drive across plains
        mountains
        and deserts —
        Balboa on his way to the Pacific.

Together we pushed to close the hatchback
    Tried again
    And again.

We didn't want it to close.

Nancy T. Zuercher

One Key Of Keys!

The non-achievers are but a curious people of sorts,
always being trampled by the achievers without there ever being
any retorts their unrefined skills, of not knowing which way is out,
blessed with the profound knowledge of not knowing how to correct
ones own self doubt, it being but a stones throw away, after
contemplating on it all day, an answer, and I kept it a secret, and
I continue to keep it sacred here to stay, or let's just say, to hear,
for now just for today: Be it so, that the paths, that you may cross
remind you of your own self life and you are what you are,
through your troubles and through your strife, and when I doubt
you must remember to remember, that it is the crossing of the
paths that one must correct oneself, and not the crossing over
out, and no matter what it is that you may do, you must find
change, and not let change find you, and that you must find one
key of keys to your hearts desire, and that bridge to cross, while
leaving, never should you set on fire, and that one key of keys is
to unlock the doors to your heart sinner most desire, and it is
held by you, but never to expire, and you, the keeper of the one
key of keys, which you hold is to unlock the doors to the many
gateways of the ever abundant floodgates to the footsteps in
the pathways to each and everyone in our life — this be true!

Dale Rivera

My Romeo

My Romeo where art thou
Romeo. Until thy take a kiss or
two? For I wait until nights
past that our lips will embrace.
Knowing the race will trace beyond
who follow in our dreams. Now
let us no longer partake of thoughts
of fears whatsoever happens, let
me lead the way as you fade mines.
Soon once meet and twice behold
again. As we pose how our love
frame a view. For let it not come
a dream but a reality. Give we
space to gain, so our love can be
stronger. I'm over the hills with
ills, but I can't have both; no
other. For my eyes is mainly gaze for books (race). When I
try to let you feel what I felt, to gaze in your eyes.
Farewell my love, still to call "Romeo where art thou
Romeo." For I shall die until I get what I want

Roseta Hunter

What Is Beautiful

Curling up in front of a fireplace during a cold, wintry snowstorm
listening to the howling wind outside, sipping your hot chocolate
That is beautiful!

Sitting on a swing on a bright, sunny morning, gazing at the
birds soaring high above you, when a cool, yet refreshing breeze
blows the scent of the newly sprung flowers towards you.
That is beautiful!

Walking along the ocean shore, with the waves lightly splashing at
your feet; waiting for the sunset to see what kind of day you
will awake to tomorrow.
That is beautiful!

Staring out a window watching in awe, wondering what alluring colors
you will see as the autumn wind allows the leaves to sail
gracefully to the ground.
That is beautiful!

Still though, nothing is more beautiful than a mother.
She brings you into the world.
Gives you life; gives you breath.
But most of all, she gives you love.
Now, that is beautiful!

Kellie A. Hepp

Christmas Eve

Oh listen and hear, the bells of Christmas ringing
It's the sounds of joy, praises and singing.

The spirit of Christmas is alive and here,
It's the exchange of love and caring, with those who are dear.

For these are the times, we cherish for years,
Sometimes, remembering, brings the sharing of tears.

But tonight as we gather making memories of fun,
Let's not forget where the spirit of love and caring begun

It began with our Heavenly Father above,
Who sent his Son Jesus, to us in love.

So, as we celebrate, the eve of His birthday,
Remember His love, and the price He did pay.

For all who believe, in what He came for,
Salvation is given, He evened the score.

We don't have to earn it, or buy it you see,
It's a gift of His love, He gave to us free.

Dar McBee

Untitled

Step outside and look above to the heavens God has created
On a clear night you'll be able to see a masterpiece being painted.
Bright lights, hand-picked, each put in their proper places,
To make a design, different each time to brighten up new little faces.

Tell me now, what do you see when you look at the stars above?
Could it be the artist tonight is painting a portrait of love?

When I step out and take a glance,
Look up at this bright, starry expanse,
My attention is fixed, not upon this view,
My thoughts have changed to memories of you!

Though far away right now you may be
It's as though you're standing here close to me.
In my heart I know that it's true
There's a star up there made for me and you!

Jennifer Igbonegun

What Is Love?

Love is something that we all need.
It makes us happy and it makes us strong.
Love makes everyone live long.
Love is something that we can't live without.
Love is a very strong feeling, that is no doubt.
Without love where would we be?
It would be scary for both you and me.
Love is the one thing that money can't buy.
Love is a very fragile power and that is no lye.
Love will be here forever and ever.
Of course, love is what brings us closer together.

Seeta Bhojwani

Sorrow In The Mist

Night has fallen upon all of our lives
Sadness prevails as the night mist arrives
With a chill in the air there is one last good night kiss
And all of us feel the sorrow in the mist

Yet lo and behold a glimmer appears
From the depth of the mist, from the sorrow of our tears
A light there is shining, we are not alone
For the Lord shows us the way, and guides us to home

The light grows ever stronger till bright in the sky
Giving warmth to our souls till we need no longer cry
We are embraced by the heavens and God's love is our gift
There is life everlasting out of sorrow in the mist

Randall J. Altenau

Life Is . . .

Life is a budding flower on a window sill,
a heart filled with love and laughter.
Life is a child's innocent smile and a mother's gentle touch,
a hurt emotion shared by all who know the pain.
Life is a sad teardrop in the middle of millions of happy ones,
a person with love in their heart and no one to give it to.
Life is a boy with an extraordinary talent with no one to see it,
a glimpse of the sun on a cloudy day.
Life is a child learning when no one is the teacher,
a mother who worries about her kids.
Life is a joke without a punch line,
a laugh out of thin air.
Life is a valued moment in time,
a reason for caring and sharing feelings with one another.
Life is . . .

Jana Crippen

Taken By The Wind

I dreamt I saw her on a hillside.
All around the Earth was snow.
With a gust of wind she tried to hide.
She was gone by the second blow.

The drifting snow settled and once again she appeared.
More wind arose, and pulled snow into the air.
She gently refrained to hide a fallen tear.
As the wind died down, she was no longer there.

I stared blankly into the white angelic flakes.
I stood there for a while, confused and alone.
She reappeared amidst the trees,
But this time no wind had blown.

She whispered "I'll love you forever."
In her eyes it had shown.
She gently rubbed my cheek.
Then with a firm hand, forever, she took me home.

Ryan Lagud

Insane!

You hear laughter, but not one is smiling.
You see tears, but no one is crying.
You looked in the mirror and you saw a
stranger, a vision of the evil that you've became.
You search for a reason, but find more questions,
so you go and create an excuse.
You ask yourself why, but get no reply.
You can't conceive the idea that man is
His own excuse for the evil, that he has become.
And you are your own worst enemy.
You dwell in life without thought, for you
don't remember.
You speak without reason, for you have no logic.
Shattered pieces of your life, are all that remain.
Leaving you wondering if you've gone insane.

Michael Bennett

The Moon

Shining bright in the eastern sky, the moon says
"Good evening" to us
Shining bright in the eastern sky, the moon relaxes
us; bids us a good night.
Shining bright in the middle sky, the moon watches
over us as we sleep
Shining bright in the middle sky, the moon stands its
ground as the keeper of the night.
Shining bright in the western sky, the moon gathers
its belongings
Shining dimly in the western sky, the moon says
"Good morning" to us and hands the day over to the sun.

Michael Keith Thompson

Truncations

There are times when the deep night will beckon,
From a place that has never been known,
But the echo fills up the distance
Like a beacon calling from home.

Onward, outward, on going,
Plunging, pushing for breath
Ephemeral madness, is madness,
It ends not simply with death.

It's the hurt in the heart that's so harmful,
Things that we do without thought,
Hoping no one will notice,
Strange, by ourselves, we are caught.

The light of the dawn is so joyful
God's greatest of gifts save for one.
But the muffle of fear in the blackness,
Seems often will never be done.

On the hilltop, the shadows are parting,
The light of the star is in sight.
Sleep deep the dreams may be healing.
Too Soon! — prepare for the night.

Eric Hayden

An Old Woman's Pain Of A Family

It doesn't seem like any year, had passed since a kind dear
whose only fault of her own, was 2 care for her family which had shown
When she became older, that some of them felt ashamed of their mother
Because she needed some help in caring, which made that thought 2 daring
Of their own time, it seems like caring would have been like a crime
Yet she didn't know that at first, what they had plan 4 her would soon B a curse
To have her committed and forced out of her home, so that some
Other body with some money, could live in her home with his honey
While some love ones continue to deceive, her to believe
That she would go back 2 her home 1 day, but no 1 said what day
As time when on while she was living, she could see the truth about the stealing
And also the lying, but if someone looked closely she was crying
About how members of her family contribute, to constantly dispute
Over who should try to care and feed, her instead of taking her deed
To the house and being completely in greed, since she was in need
Of a family to trust, B-cause 1 wants 2 B treated like dirt or dust
But I guess when U B-gin 2 forget your name, and some love
ones don't feel no shame
Towards your feelings or your mind, then they will try to find
A simple solution, to make a easy conclusion
4 the former mother, who was at 1 time my great-grandmother

Robert Antonio Butler

Untouchable

I thought I was something
But I am another.
I want to be one thing
Yet I am the other.
I'm falling, falling, falling down;
No one seems to notice,
No one is around.
But soon it will be over,
And my struggle will be fought:
But I am still falling, unable to be caught.
As the ground turns to water,
And the sky turns to fire
And I will tell the true story,
You may think me a liar.
You'll sit and you'll listen; you'll shrink and you'll cower,
And I'll laugh in your face as my id comes to power.
Then soon it will be over — the hurt and the pain;
The love that I feel for you has all been in vain.
I've pushed and I've pushed, but you continue to pull;
Why, why, why must you be untouchable?

Danielle Taylor

Earth's Warnings

The waters seem to be draining
and the forests seems to be dying.
The water is polluted that is raining
and everyone seems to be lying.
Our planet is in a lot of danger,
believe it or not, from the human race.
We have taken from our Creator
killing earth before His face.
Animals are dying out rapidly
And fish are less likely to breathe.
All they did was be friendly
and we robbed them of their home sea.
We all need to realize
just what our future may be.
Right now, somewhere, a child cries
In ten years what will we see?
If we don't try to fix things
and recycle the way we should,
every time a siren rings
there will be one less tree in the woods.

Kathryn Jensen

Shall I

Shall I love you forever, and hope you will, too?
Shall my life be on hold, while I wait for you?

Shall I give you my sugar for your sweet tooth of greed?
Shall I give you whatever, whenever you need?

Shall I be naive, and pretend to be weak?
Shall I wait in line until my turn to speak?

Shall I kiss your feet, as you turn to walk away from me?
Shall I be discreet when my love keeps you from running free?

Shall I dress your wound, when you fall running the other way?
Shall I be marooned when you decide you don't want to play?

Shall I cover your sins, as you beg to be pardoned?
Shall my heart remain tender, as yours remains hardened?

Shall I turn you away, cause it's you that's at fault?
Shall I be the one to put our "love" to a halt?

Shall I spit in your face for each time that I've hurt?
Shall I take what is mine, and throw you in the dirt?

Shall I be happy, and get on with my life?
Shall I find another, and become his wife?

Shall I find joy, and be loved till I die?
Shall I set you aside, make you watch me be happy without you?
Well . . . Shall I?

Debora L. Muntz

Life For The Lonely

As I sit and watch time go by,
I wonder, why, there is no life for the lonely
    Days turn into months
Months turn into years,
And still, I wonder why, there is no life for the lonely.

    All the vibrant colors of my youth,
have faded to shades of grey
    And still I wonder why,
There is no life for the lonely
    The warmth of a summer day
has now brought only dismay
    And still I wonder why,
There is no life for the lonely.
    But, as I wonder thru my earthy days,
and go about my humble ways,
    I know perhaps, someday, I may,
No longer worry about
    The life that is so lonely.

Kim Kostak

ONE
(I Have TwO I's, But can I see?)
A. $8 + 4 = 10$

Both are true, lines not crossed,
    though overlapping.
Awareness of things beyond we don't acknowledge,
    they fade away as words not
Said, they are lost. No things are beyond our
    custom's ability to
Encompass. 1 tell myself until 1 believe, even
    though 1 can see,
$X - I = IX = B = XI = 11$

II

B . . .?

MANY

    Jeffery Scott Annis

Leaf Of Life

Can life be compared to a leaf?
I wonder if it can feel,
but God said he gave everything meaning.
So I try to compare.

A leaf is decoration for the tree,
for I help decorate the earth.
It withers, and shows aging;
I shall grow old and then to have my own wrinkles.

For I am afraid to say we are some what a like.
But, I wish my life could be as simple.
Not a worry,
just a short and beautiful reason unto living
a life of a leaf.

    Nathan Aliff

Pogo Pete

Petey got his pogo stick and rode it down the street.
He looked at everyone he met but mostly at their feet
The policeman wore the biggest shoes of heavy shiny black.
The student rushed on loafers like the man that drove the hack.
The minister wore pointed shoes that seemed to pinch his toes.
The ones on a tiny baby were as rose as her nose.
A boy's shoes were wrinkled and run down at the heel.
A poor old man on the corner wore pumps about a peel.
His teacher's shoes were comfy to help her stand all day.
A flapper sported highest heels with pom-poms bright and gay.
Petey took a short-cut that brought him to his yard,
Happy with the shoes he wore, though both of them were scarred.

    Marginette Lassiter

Untitled

Unable to see your face I open my ears, desperate to hear a
tune that could remind me of you.

My eyes close, and I feel your warm arms wrap themselves
tightly around me.

Concentrating I even notice the gentle sensation your breath
once left upon my neck.

Going limp my head falls back, my emotions take over it's too
overwhelming to just imagine you here.

I call your name, painfully hoping like a magician I could
make you appear.

My heart cries for my thoughts to beckon you near me, but
like a teasing mirage you only fade into eternity.

I will never see the realization of you at my side, sadly it
shall always remain a hopeless fantasy

    Carmen Anita Gomez

Just An Old Dog

Just an old dog preacher, I heard someone say
  And it's probably a good thing he died today
Hasn't been able to eat much of his food
  And only got up when he is in the mood
But I remember when he was just a pup
  He would dig in the yard and chew things up
Never criticized me or put me down
  Happy just to stay close and follow around
He would guard our house all through the night
  Seems he could tell if things were not right
But I will never forget our final good bye
  I think he knew he was going to die
I fixed his bed and left him that night
  Hoping he would be better by morning light
But I found him next morn, cold and still
  His suffering was past, he didn't feel the chill
Just an old dog, he's better off you say
  Perhaps he is but I miss him anyway
Some day you may say the same about me
  He is just on old dog, longing to be free

Joe Walton

Final Struggle

As I stare into the dark abyss
Deep in silent wonder,
Is there something that exists
On this thought I ponder.

Sinking down in deepest sleep
I thought I saw a sign.
Unwelcome chills begin to creep
Up and down my spine.

I look around and see a light
Close my eyes and shudder.
This mysterious, ambiguous augury so bright
Causes my eyes to flutter.

As everything clears I look around
Overwhelmed with awe.
Incredulous with what I found
At everything I saw.

Now I know I've run my race
And passed my final test.
My own shoulders I embrace
And close my eyes to rest.

Alisha Payne

A Reminder To Child Abusers

Abusers are sad and lonely people
Hurting the innocent as they vent,
Though many abusers were themselves abused
The circle of pain must come to an end.

Tolerance and patience are gifts themselves
Love and understanding as well,
Gifts meant to be given with open hearts
To loved ones who desperately need them.

Remember how it felt to be a child
As adults we tend to forget,
Thoughts and feelings of the young are precious
So let us encourage and nurture them.

When a child is rebellious, try patience
When a child is crying, try consoling
When a child is sad, try smiling
And when a child is happy, try kissing.

But most of all let us not forget
As adults we are here to protect,
Children are the most precious gift of life
And meant to be cherished with love and affection.

Lisa V. D'Onofrio

Goodbye

In our lives
We say goodbye
To a lot of things.

When we are young
There is bottles, diapers, and pacifiers.

When we get older
There is parents on first days of school.

As we go through school
There is friends who move away.

Soon we say goodbye,
To pets, imaginary friends and others.

Through my life
I've had to say goodbye
To all of these but one.

This is hardest to say bye to
Out of all these things for one reason
I didn't say I love you before you left.

So grandpa here it is:
I love you and goodbye
I hope to see you again one day.

Maycie Adkins

Here I Am, Over Here

Here I am, over here
A room full of people and I am alone.
I don't have a car, and I can't use a phone.
I'm locked in my world with no one but me,
I need someone to talk with, can't you see!!!

Over here, just cast me a smile,
If you can, sit for a while
Tell me what's going on big or small,
It will interest me and not bother me at all.
I'm all ears even though you may have to yell,
I don't care . . . you have me under your spell.

It's amazing, what a kind word can do,
It is wonderful and very inexpensive too.
Here I am, over here, waiting . . .
I am aging . . . and fading fast . . . alive but still waiting . . .
over here.

Sandy Robertson

Regretful Good-Byes

One does not know why they would continue to
pursue such never ending sorrows in one owns life.
They do not take the time to questions, deny, or
define the feelings left behind.

You attempt to make the slightest change, in hopes
tomorrow will be much unlike today. But to your avail
all remains the same. Some may even ask, "What
have I done to endear such a grip unwilling to
release?" Feeling as if you don't belong. Empty, lost,
lonely and confused? These are well known in my life
since all has ended.

Uncertain as to where else you should be dwelling to
have the much needed happiness return. Only to
know in thought that even the next waking moment
will still not be soon enough, indeed.

The wishes for never ending happiness seemingly
continue to go unanswered, yet you try to remember
that one day at a time has gotten you thus far.
So you close your eyes and wake to a day a new . . . and see.

Kathleen M. Pullum

True Love

I saw something today I have wanted to see for a long time,
I saw the kind of love I long to one day find.

The kind that isn't unequal as a heated candle that bends,
But, it is balanced and strong on both ends.

A kind of love that could turn your tears into droplets of a sweet
wine, instead of the harsh, saltiness you were expecting to find.

This love will not rise and fall as the tides of the ocean,
Rather, it will stay constant as if it were the work of some magic love potion.

This kind of love will last forever,
No matter what happens this love will perish never.

It is the kind of love people say is to die for.
So if you ever find this love greet it with an open door.

You may find this wonderful true love with just a glance,
But sometimes you don't and you have to take a chance.

Then again sometimes it grows from a love you may have now,
It will grow stronger and stronger whether or not you allow

Let it grow, prosper, and strengthen as a great live oak tree,
Because it can take away your fears and worries and leave you happy.

Tracey Wetherington

The Boy I Love

Did you ever love a boy and
    know he didn't love you?

Did you ever feel like crying but
    what good would it do?

Did you ever look into his eyes
    and say a little prayer?

Did you ever look into his heart
    and wish you were there?

Did you ever see him dancing when
    The lights were down low?

Did you ever whisper "God I love him"
    But never let him know?

Did you ever wonder where he is and wonder if he's true?

One day you'll be happy, the next day you'll be blue?

And when it starts, you'll know when, you'll wonder day and night.

You'll see you're loosing him, no matter how you fight
Love is fine but it hurts so much, the price you pay is high.
And if you pick between love and death, I think I'd rather die.
So I say, don't fall in love. You'll be hurt before you're through.
You see my friend, I ought to know I fell in love with you!

Frances R. Lewis

From Now 'Til Then

    My fellow Leo's, I welcome you.
Have you done all the things that you would like to do?
Well, neither have I, but I'm trying to find
Things that will benefit all mankind.
Let's hear your ideas and let your inventions be seen.
More organized ways to keep the world clean.
Yesterdays ventures, good and bad, are the past.
We need more things that will last and last.
Things change every minute and so must we
To meet this world we cannot yet see.
I have lived with things borrowed and many things blue —
And I've found I need a little something new.
I respect the past and beautiful things — but
Our wisdom will determine what the future brings.
Either we correct our mistakes or simply throw them away.
Take the things that work best, sit down and start a new day.

Virginia Semple

Untitled

Beauty met its compromise with open arms and smile,
Not knowing that what it gave up would last for awhile.
Age her, change her, leave her with a name,
But through this she stayed a beauty, a beauty all the same.
I miss my old beautiful when I was young and she
I thought I was beautiful but now I'm just me.
I lost sight of it all; my hopes, those childhood dreams I had,
And if I lost them all at once it was when I lost my Granddad.
He loved me and I him and together we the world,
His spare time spent gazing at his oak and the busy squirrels.
It seemed so useless when he had gone, but life went on,
And we do, but it's different it forms, threatens, looms, lives, its death,
As so does beauty have a last breath,
It's as if one day beauty was nowhere to be seen,
That day they'll say I grew dark and mean.
Beauty did return but then up and left again.

I'm shocked, a dull pulsing surprise that your image may meet my eyes
But we'd not know each other love

Plagued with thought, silence never fills my head
I want to find beauty's compromise before I find my self dead.

Thaddeus Conti

The Voices From Wilderness

The loneliness! The loneliness!
Lovely it becomes — with
The voices from wilderness!
The voices so divine with pouring love — from distance
Yes — the voices from wilderness!
The lovable — devoting couple,
The tenderness they posses in the voices from wilderness!
The sweet couple — my parents of course,
The caring — understanding coming from — the voices from
wilderness!
Voices I still remember — though long ago,
As fresh as a moment ago, the voices from wilderness!
Calling me to wake up, for school to make up,
Those voices from wilderness!
Are so dear and near,
Calling for breakfast, lunch and dinner.
Those voices from wilderness!
Never hurting me, always talking of future 'Fizza'
Those voices from wilderness!
Pray and hope I soon be with
Those voices from wilderness!

Fizza Gulamali-Majid

People Are Sometimes

People are sometimes Mad,
When they want to kill others.
They want more money for nothing
So, they will kill other people for it.

People are sometimes become depressed,
When they can't make money,
they become depressed or go insane.
They also go insane when they lose their jobs.

Sometimes people will be happy,
When they get their jobs back,
and they are no longer depressed.
Then they are making money, so they
get out of debt.
They know that their money
will create interest.

People are sometimes are mad and depressed,
When they lose their jobs or have to pay taxes.
This changes when they have jobs and pay off
their debts.

Leland Van Valkenburg

My Gift To You

Saddened souls lose self worth,
So overcome with hopelessness.
Happiness seems so far away,
But hope continues day by day.
Friends pursue, showing they care,
Why do some make things hard to bear?
Faith is there, but so hard to find,
If only I can convince my mind.
"Forsaken" pains are tearfully expressed
Prayer so essential; can I be blessed?
Behold! I see, other's needs,
No more can life destroy me.
I can give so much, you'll see,
Love has just set me free.

Angela Wiebelhaus

"Life Through a Child's Eyes"

Life as seen through a child's eyes, should
not come as a big surprise!
For in their eyes they see, what a wonderful
world this could be . . .

But in this world of pain and strife, where
everything doesn't go just right, where
families are torn apart, never giving it a
chance right from the start . . .

Where people would rather fight their brother,
than try to work it out with each other . . .

Children, see a world without pain or strife,
where families sit down together.
Where brother to brother, we care for each other,
and yes, everything is alright . . .

Only then can we see, how the world could be,
as seen through the eyes of a child . . .

Renee E. Brink

Out Of The Darkness

Out of the dark forbidding soil
The pure white lilies grow.
Out of the black and murky clouds,
Descends the beautiful snow.

Out of the crawling, earth-bound worm
A butterfly is born.
Out of the black and dreary night,
Behold! A golden morn!

Out of the pain and stress of life,
The peace of God pours down.
Out of the nails — the spear — the cross,
Redemption, and a Crown!

Charles Dee Meiser

Momma And Daddy

Momma and Daddy, we hear everything you say
You fuss and fight almost everyday
Momma, you need to watch what you say
Daddy, the words you use don't pay
Cause, I can hear everything you say
Momma and Daddy, we hear everything you say
It makes us hurt in every way
You don't know how hard it is to play
When we can hear everything you say
Momma and Daddy, we hear everything you say
We need your love, so we're going to pray,
That you won't let us hear everything you say

Francine Tatum

Confusion

Am I going in the right direction?
Am I leaving from the store headed home?
Or
Am I at home going to the store?
Am I flying to heaven or fallen to hell?
Is where I start going to be where I'll end up again?
I swear I seen that boy before?
The beginning is not the end my mind has question marks
from the start!
Circles, circles
I run about not knowing where to stop
I'm getting, dizzy, I run about,
I don't know if this is where I'm suppose to stop?
Have I been here before?
Is this where I turn?
Oh!
Not around again!
Confusion, confusion,
Which direction should I go?

Tammy Dipple

Remembering

I was just 18 in '41
I didn't understand what those folks had done.
Where's Pearl Harbor? asked a friend.
We were at war, peace came to an end.

My life had changed on that day,
It wasn't long 'til we sailed away.
We couldn't wait, my friends and more,
To get overseas and settle the score.

They didn't realize their big mistake
For a sleeping giant they did awake.
With ships and guns, men and tanks,
They came from all over to fill the ranks.

The American people had gathered 'round;
"Let's give 'em Hell" was the battle sound.
Fathers and brothers, movie stars, too,
And the ladies asked, "What can we do"?

We all got together and did big things.
Then, one day, we heard Victory ring.
Remember the Alamo, remember the Main,
Remember Pearl Harbor, let's hear it again.

Now, today, memories are dim
And hope for the future look mighty grim.
Divided we are, united we're not.
It's real apparent, we all forgot.

Lucky Jones

The Revealing And Concealing Treasure Of A Smile

You rode the surf of life without a whining tide
You cross many bridges and made it just in time

You find hidden treasures with your humor and your heart
You were able to withstand when other fell part

You're a dealer in every sense of the word
You can hold them and fold them and whatever else you have in mind

You learn to be gentle and one know to be kind
And somehow you became a friend of mine

Wise men ordained it and fools tried
But you were able to do it simply with a smile

Then when life has ended and heaven bound are we
Oh what a day awaits us and oh what joy it will be

We stood with Saints of ages and you asked how did I make it over
And I said it's your smile

Eugenia Lamb

Grandma's Rose

The rose of Grandma's heart,
was her family and her friends.
Each petal of her rose,
had a very special meaning in her heart.

They stood for love, kindness, understanding,
gentleness and her ever willingness to give.
As the red rose bloomed through time,
Grandma pruned, watered and cared for her rose.

And with the rose came work and thorns,
which represented the struggles and trials of growing.
But with great reward and beauty.

Now she has a prize winning red rose,
that lives in the hearts of her family and friends.
We too must nurture the red roses of our hearts,
til they become beautiful like Grandma's.

The garden of Grandma's heart is different,
but she is still growing roses.
They are golden now, and have no thorns.

Lisa D. Haley

Good Old Pantry

Nostalgia caused it, I must say
My reminiscing on this day.
Quite vividly I see once more
The living scenes from days of yore.

A house with pantry — that's for me!
I miss those homes that used to be —
Long porches and verandas wide,
Faint perfumes from gardens outside.

A banister for winding stair,
With carpet soft for feet left bare.
There was an ornate chandelier
And high-backed sofa very near;

In bright, warm kitchen, one could smell
The fragrance that no words can tell;
For home-baked bread was then the style.
Aromas lingered all the while.

An outside cellar smelled of loot
Both juicy fresh and home-canned fruit.
But best of all I liked to stay
In good old pantry any day.

Lois M. Morgan

A Vision Of His Love

God gave me a vision, late one night.
His angels were involved in a horrible fight.
Satan's demons were attacking, so ugly and cold.
God's angels were standing, so strong and so bold.
The demons were making a frightening sound,
But God's angels were standing on Holy Ground.
Those demons were darker than even the night,
But God's angels glowed with a heavenly light.
Over and under, they were turning and twisting,
But God's angels stood strong, always resisting.

The vision faded, as I lay on my bed,
But not before the demons had fled.
Only the angels remained in the room,
And I praised my Lord, my Savior, my Groom.
His endless love, that I should see,
God sent His angels to fight for me.
I gave thanks for those angels, sent from above.
I gave thanks for that vision, a sign of His love.
It was spiritual warfare, that I did see,
And I thanked God, once more, for saving me!

Barbara Colchado

Love's Music

She found secret happiness in playing,
        And she played on . . .

Hands moving rhythmically, without conscious
thought or effort;

        Touching her hair, lightly, 'though not unnoticed,
        She plays on . . .

Movements becoming legato — smooth and connected,
        a crescendo — intense, then — a long, slow
        decrescendo — tender, no; subdued, almost calm;

        Kissing her gently on the nape of her neck,
        She plays on . . .

Suddenly, fingers striking with staccato-like precision,
        passion filling her heart, for that which she loves;

        Offering his heart, his most precious possession,
        She plays on . . .

Finally, turning, looking directly at him;

She smiles — knowingly, playfully.

Hands transcend black and white ivory

    finding his;

        And she plays on . . .

Don Fahrenkrug

Every Raindrop

God loves every person, that's ever lived upon this earth.
I want you to listen, then take these words for their worth.
To have them all reach heaven, without a doubt was His goal.
Could it be that every raindrop, is a tear for a lost soul?

So very, very many, are already beneath the sod.
Of these how great's the number, that never knew their God?
How many names will be absent, when He calls that heavenly roll?
Could it be that every raindrop, is a tear for a lost soul?

There are also very many, living on this earth today.
When they hear about my Jesus, they just turn their heads away.
By the sinful works of Satan, their hearts are hard and black as coal.
Could it be that every raindrop, is a tear for a lost soul?

Gary R. Arthur I

It's Christmas Time

It's Christmas time,
But what is your reason
For being excited
To celebrate this season?

Just think for a minute,
Why you're in a good mood.
Is it family and presents?
Is it candy and food?

The real reason for Christmas
Goes back many years.
When an Angel told Mary
God's child she would bear.

It was time for the birth,
But the inn had no room.
They put them in a stable,
For the baby was coming soon.

The word went out of the Heavenly King.
His name was called Jesus and angels began to sing.

Jesus is our Savior and He is the reason,
Why we should be celebrating the Christmas season!

Danell Meiss

Groovy

When we explain to one another
Where we are, we know
not two door disdain, conclude
mis-measurement we are there and
not on the edge.
Run, stop, go on the move, not
busy, not buggy, stupid, sluggish or slow
In the groove, with elegance as
a fine tuned machine does
with precision.
    With better moves, we make
bigger grooves, and decide where
and when to make better moves
always improving our points, our wares,
to subtract the flak, take out the bad
avoid the bummed,
became, the mundane, the best, no questions messed
Now if I had the chance to be just the one,
that's what I'd do be #1.

James R. Drisco

Patricia

Staring blankly at the screen knowing what to write
through the sheen afraid of what is wrong, or right
in my tortured mind

Many have gone through the process of duress
only to realize in time that it isn't a crime,
of the heart, but only a state of the mind

Love is a wondrous feeling; it's a shame though
that one starts reeling like a bow
that's expended its arrow.

Two beings in syn(k)ch with each other
can avoid the brink of disaster, and smother
each other with the balm of love.

This ointment of love is ne'er a terrible thing
for it is like the dove
carrying the burden of compassion on its wings
promoting peace around the world.

Why is it then
that women and men
    forget to
      love?

Paul v. W. Palthe

Lost Was A Foster Child

O how I've waited for this very day.
Goodbye foster home I'm on my way.
I'll work at Newberry's and the K-Mart.
The song I've got to be free I sang from my heart.
I'll continue to search for family of mine.
If only my little sister and dad I could find.
Dear Lord show me thy ways and teach me thy paths
Prepare me for a special moment with you I'll share.
The days went by and then a year.
I keep praying Lord my prayer you'll hear.
An elderly man came in to order candy.
He says peach blossoms and peanut butter cups will be just dandy.
I looked at this man shaking — what's wrong with me?
Is this my Dad? Really can it be he?
I cried "Daddy!" please replace my cry with a smile.
You have been away for along long while.
Yes my Lily you recognized me.
I wasn't sure that this really could be.
O dad I cried since you been away.
I've always prayed for this very day.

Lillian Julie Raymond-Provost

To My Son

You came into our lives on the first of July,
A gift from God above sent down for us to love.
You started out weak, but grew up strong.
We helped you to choose the right from the wrong.

Now you've reached a crossroads in your life.
It's time to make decisions.
The moment has come to move ahead.
It's too late for revisions.

We can't turn back the hands of time.
It's okay, son, you're now a man.
So take that step, reach for your goal,
And do the best you can.

If you stumble, or you fall, get up and try again.
Some of life's greatest victories came from fallen men.
Reach for the stars — don't settle for less.
Now you're ready for life's greatest test.

We're proud of you, you're on your way.
We love you, son. Happy Graduation Day.

Dana Bennett

The Time When Night Cast Over Day

The time when night cast over day,
Shadowed the Earth in a shade of gray.
The sun shone not to break a cloud
It blanketed the sky in one thick shroud.
The vegetation gave up trying
It ceased to grow and started crying;
"Mother Earth has placed us here,
But alone in the dark, we wait in fear;
To wizen, to wane, to wither, to waste,
The endurance of our existence must make haste!"
To see the world in a glowing bliss
Would be the termination of a spell — broken with a kiss!
The sweet awakening from a benumbed state
Is the awaited result, promised by fate.
The time when night cast over day,
Closed when darkness went away.
The sun broke through its iron cage;
Light sprung out with violent rage!
The greens now grow throughout the land,
And time passed by in the hourglass of sand.

Danielle DeSiato

Anne Waiting

Her paleness compliments
the silver ring and faded linen,
white cotton with wooden buttons.

Lengthy arms and legs and body
all move together with European airs
then, sit with a quiet severity under
sharp jaws, thin faded red lips.

The two bands of twisted silver
mark her, an allusion
to another. Captured,
with legs wrapping spirals.

Encircling the fire between
them. Flushed cheeks, reddened
lips, purpled patches on
vellum skin. Each melding
into one. Consummated like forged silver.

Now, the angles of nose and jaw,
arms crooked around a magazine,
pointed fingers grasping, hide everything
but the glint of cool silver.

Preston Pickett

What Father's Day Means To Me

It has always meant honoring one's older male generation no matter what went on the rest of the year. Here is the day where you give credit to your father and his father and your mom's father for making the tiny bit of perfection they now call "Charles." Nothing is more important then letting these men know just how good a job they did in making you for they are no more then the total sum of their humanness, each prone to his own share of mistakes. You were made a unique individual and for that any mistakes they make or will make in the future in the name of fatherhood are excused as you are the one sign that each man is capable of being perfect for a few seconds in each man's life.

Today we honor these men and their tiny bit of perfection for without these men, life would cease to exist. I for one want to thank my father and grandfather's for the 39 years I have existed, no I have not made history but not all of us are destined for such honor in fact most of us are destined for obscurity where we contribute in small ways to our father's honor by bring up our own tiny bit of perfection.

Charles E. Dignazio

Money, Money, Money, Money — Moooney!

Lie awake at night tryin' to think of a master plan.
Maybe get another job, if I can.
Baby needs a new pair of shoes.
Daddy's always cryin' the blues.
Poppin' aspirin like they're water.
Daughter poutin' cause of the prom dress I haven't bought her.
Christmas is just around the corner.
Mama's cameo, I'mma have to pawn her.
Pay day. May day, may day!
Gone before it even reaches my hand.
Guess I'll have to start returnin' them cans.
Go back to school, that's the rule, that's the ticket!
No financial aid, I'm just soooo sick of it!!!
TV's on the blink.
I Can't Think!!!
Walking on a tight rope.
Wish I was dumb enough to do dope.
Stress is high.
Can't even afford to die.

Stephanie Booth

The Special Person She Was

She had a special something at the age of ninety-two.
The turn of the century, was the year of her birth.

She lived a long time, and had many stories to tell,
of hardships, trials, and happy times too.

I remember sitting by her side, listening,
as she spoke in our language, for she knew no other.

She always thought, she didn't have enough to give.
But I think of the wonderful way, she cared for us.

She would remember the times, when food was scarce.
And replaced those memories, with over-abundant cooking.

She wasn't a hard person to please. The simple thank you's,
and I love you's would do. Yet she deserved so much more.

When her birthday came around, we would go all out with parties,
entertainers, the works. We never knew, when would be her last.

Until one day, it all began with a fall. One she could not endure.
One sickness led to another, and all too much to handle.

As she lay in her hospital bed, she signaled a simple gesture,
she let us know she would be safe now.

As she pointed to the sky, and folded her hands. She knew it
was her time. She was on her way to heaven.

Daniela Cambetas

The Candy Dish

I reach down
and choose one
from the dozens of colorful pieces
in the candy dish.
I unwrap the golden wrapper
to discover a transparent ball.

As I place it in my mouth,
I immediately taste
the sweetness.
I savor it
until it gradually becomes sour
and then unpleasantly bitter.

As I remove it from my mouth
and toss it away,
it suddenly reminds me of
our love
and I realize it's time to take
another piece of candy from the dish . . .

Laurie Lashomb O'Rourke

Tomorrow

You say you'll wait until tomorrow
To read John three sixteen.
You say you've "kind of" accepted Christ,
But there is no in between.

You say next week you'll come to church
And maybe stay awhile,
But you're not gonna sit in Hell
All eternity with a smile.

The point I'm trying to make
Is tomorrow is too long.
Jesus might come right now
With Gabriel playing his trumpet song.

You say you'll think about
What I've been telling you,
But I can promise one thing for sure.
What I'm saying is true.

So go ahead and wait.
I can't make you listen to me.
Go ahead and wait,
But the golden streets you may never see.

April Graves

The Goodbye

Pulling my jacket tight around me to quiet the inner chill
the wind and rain washes the tears from my face.
I feel strong loving arms wrap around my body settling my soul.
Looking up I see his handsome face with sweet loving eyes.
I cry out "I love you", nuzzling my face in his neck.
Lifting my face to his, he gently kisses my trembling lips,
and softly whispers "I'll always love you".
Then he fades away into the rain.
Through my tear-filled eyes
I see his grave.

Kerrie A. Freeman

Love's Moonlit Embrace

The moon shines down upon the two lovers.
And illuminates their faces.
They are in love,
Now and forever.

The moonlight caresses them and show them embracing,
They are sharing their love.
For they are together,
In Love's Moonlit Embrace.

Danielle Westhoven

Love

My body is as a house
And my heart as its treasures . . .
Thus, I know love must be a thief,
For every time love enters my house . . .
It leaves bearing a part of my treasures.

Mike Day II

My Good Bye

As I drive through the long, black gate,
I look over and see millions of grave stones.
And I think to myself that,
there must be a million crying faces.

As I go over to my fathers grave,
I think that I must be
one of those crying faces.

As I place the rose on my fathers grave,
I say to him in my heart, "I will love you forever,"
and "I wish you were here."

As I drove back through the long, black gate,
I thought of how he must have felt when he left me,
only I'm leaving him.
Good bye dad.

Jenafer Robichaud

An Autumn Sojourn

Her eyes shone like the summer sun.
The fleeting sun has now set, and our day is done.
Some say, "Why all the tears, it was only a cat?!"
But the love in her heart made her much more than that.
The illness would spare her for, perhaps, one more day,
So we went to the woods to find peace in some way.
In her woods, with the person whom she loved the most,
I know we were joined by The Heavenly Host.
She emerged like a butterfly from her earthly cocoon,
She frolicked and danced to a celestial tune.
Without weakness or pain my new kitten ran free!
She went across, up, and down, but always near me.
But finally she came to me with a look in her eyes
That said now it was time to say our goodbyes.
So I gently and tenderly held her up on my shoulder,
We both knew it was my last chance to hold her.
In that last perfect moment though my heart burst with sorrow,
A strange sense of peace gave me strength for tomorrow.
So as I stand by her grave in the crisp autumn air,
I weep 'cause I miss her, though I know she's not there.

Jane Cermak

The One You're Meant 4

The words of another sometimes just can't say
what they feel inside.
They can bring the joy back into your life
by the things they do, even at the time that it might not feel
like it is needed.
The love you have for a person will stay strong, not die because
what one says. If that person really makes you feel good
inside, treats you right, you shouldn't have to worry.
Sometimes people play too many games with each other,
they can lose each other. And if she needs love,
I'll be there to give it to her, from my heart.
There is one person out there that I am
meant to be with, I have found that one person.
But it is hard for each of us to say what we really feel.
So I just can't help the way I feel for her,
the love I show will always make her happy.
I'll just walk her home and say a good night.

Reginald Jones

Angel Eyes

She has the prettiest angel eyes,
And a smile that brightens the darkest skies,
Just a little bit more than four feet tall,
But she could climb the highest wall,
She fought with death and won the war,
At the tender age of four,
She told me once she saw a light,
With colors beautiful and bright,
Her angel kept her safe and warm,
As I held her in my arms,
Now she loves to run and play,
And I thank God everyday,
She has the prettiest angel eyes,
A smile which brightens the darkest skies,
And if you look into her gaze,
You will see her heart ablaze,
For when she was so small and weak,
An angel kissed her on the cheek

Frances Donegan

I Am

I am a happy girl who likes imagining.
I wonder if I will fulfill my dreams.
I hear the whispers of the wind saying my name.
I see my guardian angel taking good care of me.
I want to have peace in this world.
I am a happy girl who likes imagining.

I pretend I slide over the rainbow.
I feel the softness of the clouds.
I touch the stars in the dark night sky.
I worry about how the future will be like.
I cry because I feel no one likes me.
I am a happy girl who likes imagining.

I understand that sometimes I can't do all the things I want to do.
I say I will try hard in getting a good education.
I dream of going around the world visiting every country.
I try to have a positive attitude against negative things.
I hope I have a good purpose here in life.
I am a happy girl who likes imagining.

Patricia Torres

My Son

The day you were born we had a war far, far away
and I got so scared that you would have to go some day
So I was glad when you grew up and never wanted to join
But then one day, out of the blue, you decided you wanted to wear blue
So I thought back to that first day
the only thing I could do was pray
O Lord, you said to give him wings and let him fly
But as a Mother it broke my heart and I had to cry
I know you are not a child and my job is done
O Lord, I only pray that you watch over him each day
And bring him back safe some day.

Virginia Hill

Ritual

It's been years, five springs at least, since I've answered the
call of the trail to come to the stream's crossing, then off
through the thickening forest's tangle to a place where the
water's rushing smooths its winding tumbling to a pool, clear
clean and calm, shared only by a rustling breeze, winter's
debris, and me, alone and unanswered, winding tumbling rushing,
facing spring's revival, a baptism's cleansing as I slip,
stripped bare, through the water's surface touching me, enclosing
me, renewing, like Spring itself waking up, shaking off winter's
sleep and beginning the cycle of life once more.

Richard C. Wing

479

Ebon Wings

I lifted high on ebon wings
To soar beyond this world
To view the magic of the realm
Where dreams and imagination rule

The stars they danced before my eyes
To music I could not hear
The moon she called me out to play
Along with the tiger and bear

I flapped my wings to gain some speed
So I could race the sun
We circled round the milky way
And watched the clouds have fun

Then all at once before my eyes
Appeared ones who'd come before
Their beauty was beyond compare
And they spoke of things I adore

The nights are short and my time on wings
Came quickly to an end
But I know that soon I'll close my eyes
And spread my wings again

Cheryl Simonds

Hennesy

I love to curl around your magnificent chest
  and struggle in your arms engulfed by their breadth
I love the fit your head nestles over mine
  and the twinkle in your eye that sends away time.
I love your emphatically, upturned chin,
  the way you taste and the scent of your skin.
I love the delight of humor in your voice,
  and your multiple interests — eclectic by choice.

I love your polished tone and soft, earthly manner
  and strength of conviction you wear like a banner.
I love the funny quirk in your gait as you walk
  and the humorous pictures you paint as you talk.
I love our time thus shared, whatever pleasures unfold
  it mends and blends and enhances life's mold.
I love your ridiculous "Good Morning" on the phone
  regardless of the hour — it says I'm not alone.
I love the tingling from the thought of your touch.
  I love knowing you so very, very much.

Lyhnne West

Memoirs Of A Flag

I have flown o'er buildings majestic — with grace,
Softly fluttering in the winds of peace.
I have flown o'er bulwarks bloody and grey,
Of wars that never seem to cease.

From the towering heights of a battle ship,
I have witnessed the roaring cry
Of the thundering guns and the groans of men,
As they fought — and bled — and died.

My presence is felt throughout the world,
My stature invokes "don't tread"
My colors have served the living man,
And covered the box of the dead.

My solemn stars and furling stripes
Have looked down on the deeds of man,
As he fights in fury — or takes pen in hand,
All the world conflicts to end.

My stars of white on a field of blue
have changed as my nation grew —
But my status symbol of God and right,
Remains strong — everlasting — as new . . .

Leonard Earl Lockmiller

A Limerick

There once was a woman from Australia,
Who said, "If you don't move, I'll bail ya'."
But in one test yesterday,
She was asked to spell hay,
But replied by saying a brief, "Uh . . .!"

Ben Cohen

Shared Love

She is ours. She is mine.
How many times had you caressed her brow, kissed her nose,
marvelled admiringly at the beauty of her eyes, the serenity of
her slumber, the softness of her skin and how exclusively, she at
her most vulnerable moment, belonged to you. You alone would
love her; exclusively and eternally, and she would be yours, so
naturally compatible and happy to be with you within your quiet
and protective manner and domain.

I understand and feel too the depths of the emotion and love
you feel for her. I too have so caressed her brow, kissed her
nose, marvelled admiringly at the beauty of her eyes, the
serenity of her slumber and the softness of her skin. I too have,
at her most vulnerable moment, made a commitment within my
heart and soul, to above all, love her exclusiveness and eternally
within a manner without selfishness.

I know she is ours.

Randall M. Madderom

The Wish

I'll sew myself a cloak of grey;
To hide my body pale and fray.

I'll mount myself upon a horse;
And lose my worries on the course.

I'll let the wind blow on my face;
And keep at a fast steady pace.

I'll ride as fast as the wind has ever blown;
And seat myself upon a throne.

I'll hide myself in my cloak of grey;
If I were he or she none could say.

I'll ride by and by;
And tell all I'm Shadowfox to satisfy.

Then I'll ride under sun and moon;
To find my doom.

Alesia Peirson

Our Love's Strength

We started as two separate souls,
Our guardian angels brought us,
  together;
With Love, trust, and laughter
We became, one complete soul:
Because of circumstances
  the miles have separated us:
The love we had, has grown stronger,
  and continues to grow with each day
  we spend apart:
The trust has become faith;
The laughter has become loneliness and tears:
Yet:
Our guardian angels bring our
  souls together . . .
To give us the strength, we need to
  make it thru another night alone:
  I miss you . . .

Dawn Cottom

My Sister

This is a tribute to my sister so true
Who radiates with beauty from deep within;
Her eyes sparkle like the sky so blue
As she smiles though she may not always win.

She works so hard yet is always such fun
Her courage is an inspiration to me;
With her faith in God as bright as the sun
Truly her goodness we can readily see.

A sister so brave is very rare
And though her day may be sad;
She tells you that she hasn't a care
And never says that life is bad.

She deserve the best of that I'm sure
So I pray she will always have the best;
And like the brooks that run so pure
May I be worthy of her when put to the test.

    Lawrence A. Welch

Redemption

Be gone sinister demons of darkness!
Tempt me no more with your silver tongues and false promises.
Extract these blades of ice that have pierced my heart.
Take back your corrupting poisons of the flesh.
They merely dilute the relentless pain of reality.
I refuse to be thy faithful servant any longer.
My weakened soul longs for freedom from its captivity.
My consummation into the void of darkness ends.
The journey into the realm of light has begun.
I draw strength from my solitude and failings; they are all I have.
Give me the truth and let it chastise me for disobedience.
The searing pain serves as my humble guide.
Fate has shown me her saving hand and destiny patiently waits.
Redemption is within my grasp.
I have only to open my blinded eyes and see.
The fires of passion burn as my conception begins anew.
Beware demons, for I have returned from the claws of death and am
   eager to conquer the treasures of life.

    Raymond Willhoft

Untitled

If in your path you faced a brick wall blocking you from all the world's love
I ask you, would you try to tears it down?
And if you did, would it be brick by brick or all at once . . .
Trying to imagine what's on the other side.
You wonder is it something you often wanted but never had?
Do you worry about what you may loose?
Would you fear the thought of it being gone?
Tell me, is it worth the risk of pain, for all the beauty it may have?
And deep in your heart do you think it could be no different?
Would your life actually change?
Is there really another side? Or just another brick wall?
With everyone telling you
"Tear it down. Let yourself out!"
You question, is it so you can get out or they can come in . . .
And would you want them on your side?
Giving them the chance to know you and reject you . . .
Do you feel it you let them in you'll never get them out?
But there you stand before the wall; the choice must be made
  Brick by Brick; all at once; or not a all . . .

    Brooke L. Charette

A Child Again

Each day forward is a step towards the past
Each word spoken is a word repeated
Yet her smile bright, her appearance youthful
Relics of the past blend with the present
Indistinguishable night and day
Reality is ugly bringing forth tears to both our eyes and hers
But in dreams that smile reappears
And she is dancing in the sun
A little girl on a sandy shore like a child again
Surrounded by family deceased
Once she cried because she was left behind
Now she rejoices in what seems to have never been
And I come from another world
A time she has let go
My heart continues to break
With that wild look in her eyes
When I enter the room as stranger
Only a stranger

    Laura Richer

Wonder Walk

My walk brings me and my dogs
a new adventure each morning
Different neighbors are out
Joe stops his tractor to chat
Jane gladly rests on her rake
Different animals fascinate us
a new roan mare in a paddock
silly lambs in a pen
white egrets on black bulls
roadrunners in a pair keeping their distance
Different fields greet us each day
Some have become lakes during irrigation
Some look like lawns
the cattle having eaten them smooth
Some are close to being cut
and then we love to see the perfect bales
of hay in perfect rows waiting to be picked up.
Different skies arch each day
cloudless, overcast, artfully dotted or striped
I can lose myself in wonder at each day's show.

    Barbara R. DuBois

Sunday

The snow falls softly on this cold, gray, quiet winter day,
Reminding me of Sundays years ago when my life was sweet
and simple, as a child.
Winters and Sundays have come and gone, and now I am a
mother with a small child of my own.

I remember how I used to wonder how it would be, to be grown
up with a family of my own,
And I remember how I wished to know if it would ever be.

As my life unfolds before me, slowly now, for the baby is new,
I wonder what our future holds in store.
Somehow a cold, quiet Sunday makes me wonder all the more.

Now I dream of everlasting, ever growing love
That will be new and vibrant and fresh in spite of many years.
Our love and our family are still young and incomplete —
The structure of our lives is being formed.
We will not be the same ten years from now as we are today —
The cycle will go on.

Where will our lives take us?
Will I ever truly know my reason for being?
Will Sundays always make me feel this way . . .?

    Joanne Owczarzak

Once He Cried

There's a line between the blue sky and the red earth.
  There I walk, silently, feeling the sand that really isn't there
  Crawling between my toes. Spreading
Like the fear that engulfs the world after dark,
Feeding on emotions.
Screams like wounded souls start sounding in my head,
  Awakening memories better kept locked in their boxes.
I start running, fearing.
Oceans of tears appear out of thin air, making it hard to breathe.
  Waves crash down.
Noise, resounding off jagged salt mountains, like thousands of cymbals
  I reach out, seeking the water's source.
The smell of stagnant salt water blinds me.
I reach again, feeling with my fingertips, grasping.
  But I slip, missing, losing.
The redness looms ahead, spreading through the tears like blood.
  Like fear.
They know who has lost.

Mandee Perkinson

On The Green

I stand alone
with the wind at my back;
my thoughts beginning to race.
I have only one thought
and I know what to do,
but I'll take one last look just in case.

The water is still
and the banner is waving.
The excitement I feel is so great.
I hold my breath
while I get myself ready
but I feel I no longer can wait.

I keep my head bowed;
my movements feel right
and then I finally look up.
Following through
I carefully watch
as the ball rolls into the cup!

Larraine J. Redquest

The Journey

Cradling her gently against my breast, forcing her tiny hand
to let my finger invade its clutch, content in wonderment.
Looking for trust, her eyes drew mine to new depths of understanding
as I touched the newborn softness of her cheek, and
let my heart make a hundred promises,
our futures entwined.

Comforting her securely in my arms, stroking her hair,
her face buried in my shoulder, the gasping sobs slowly diminishing.
Looking for reassurance, her eyes drew mine to new depths of
understanding when through quivering lips she asked,
"Why doesn't God just turn bad people into butterflies?"

Softly touching her cheek, her eyelids limply lifting,
yet drawing me once more to new depths of understanding
through the rasping of her shallow breath
searching for a way to say good-bye,
without condemnation, without sorrow, she whispered weakly,
"Dying is an adventure I have to go on all by myself . . . but it's
O.K. Mommy, I practice seeing you smiling when I close my eyes."

Mary Johnson

Golden Days

A lone fence post, in a field of green,
Otherwise useless, but a beautiful sight.
Like a picture of a self reliant soul,
Setting suns distort the light.

Yellow skies, golden day,
Bitter reasons that remind me.
Troubled minds like empty fields,
Ships lost on a violent sea.

Little boy stares at the sun,
Never knew these were the golden days.
Beaming down to great a distance,
To reach a child who doesn't play.

A lone fence post, that used to hold,
Those who thought they had it made.
Now a man stands in a field of green,
Otherwise useless, where are the golden days?

Marc Hyatt

Rainchild

I am a child of the rain. I fall unexpectedly and don't come when
you need me or are prepared for me. The droplets drip down my
face leaving streaks of dirt showing my uncaring habits towards
myself. As I run through the tropical mist of life I can just barely
see the twinkling of the stars above. I go to the top of the highest
hill and shout out all my anger and rage. Then I go to the deepest
valley with the greenest grass and cry my sadness. After that I go
sit under the most sparkling waterfall and sing my joy. Joy of the
love I have for the people around me: my friends, the ones who
really care. I spend the most time at this special, hidden place.
When I was little I used to go to this one field and watch the wild
mares with their manes flying in the wind. I would pick the wild
flowers and lace them through my hair. I still do that when I am
not busy watching the new born animals or writing letters to God.
I love living on my own in the land that God created. It is so
unbelievably beautiful. You, dear God, are so unbelievably beautiful.

Vicki Herrmann

Detroit, R.I.P.

I grew up in the gilded Motor City
When everyone had good work,
Until the day politicos contrived to shirk
Defense of primal industry against the pirating huns
From the faraway land of the rapidly rising sun.

So now, because of this prank called Free Trade,
Hardly anything here is American made.
Consumption steadily rises while production trends down;
And the factories, as a matter of course, all close
Right under my nose,
As tumbleweed wafts through the ancient ruins of Motown.

Brett M. Decker

Untitled

Love has taken up welcome residence
Its new address within me
The vacant rooms of my heart now filled
The remaining echoes bounce off thoughts of you

I've hung my memories and hopes of favorite chambers
My dreams furnish the dusty corners
To hide the ghosts of the past and doubts of the future
Entwined in design

The barren spaces now filled
I overflow with excitement and anticipation
The charm of my reconstruction,
You are my love, my secret, and
The roommate of my heart

Val Eppes

Children Learn What They Live

If children live with beauty,
    they learn to see and radiate beauty out into life.

If children live with love,
    they learn to be love and give it to the world.

If children live with their inner light,
    they learn to radiate their light out into the world.
        Horus McNey

A Simple Touch

It's really very simple this soothing idea of touch
How it can and often does so very, very much

It has such power . . . such purpose too
Relaxing, calming, caring and sharing sometimes even revealing
Feeling or thoughts we often keep concealing

Touching gently with hands so firm
Listening quietly for a chance to learn
Tuning in for a glimpse within helping the stressful soul to mend

When muscles relax and nerves unwind
There's a refreshed body — a refreshed mind
A healing energy flows all through . . .
Awakening the senses . . . awakening you

So it really is simple this wonderful idea of touch
That it really does so very much
To improve your life . . . this "simple touch"
        Emily Mullings

Nature Of Friends

The branches swayed bare and dry
But spring was coming and new buds were on their way
A lonely bud decided to come out and play
Little did she know, some friends were coming out too
They were new friends she was about to meet
At first she was shy, with a case of cold feet
But as the chit-chatting began, these new friends became close
As they got to know each other, they grew
"These are my friends for life," she just knew.

They knew one day they'd go their separate ways
They went through a lot, thick and thin
Sometimes there were losses and sometimes a win
But the cold wind began to pick up
And as they blew away from their branches,
They wave goodbye . . .
and this was when . . .
She was sure she would see them all soon . . . again!
        Heather A. Scanlon

No Tomorrow

He came with the clouds and with a loud thunder,
I had no time to guess, to sit and to wonder.
The end is here! Which way shall I run?
For I'll go to hell with all the evil I've done.
"Oh Lord, please forgive me for my sinning and drinking;
all my wicked deeds, what had I been thinking?
I gathered my courage to look into his eyes.
Full of fire they raged; He'd hear none of my lies.
With one foot on the seas and the other on land,
He closed the death book and offered his hand.
I noticed the hole where the nail once had been
and I remembered he died to forgive me my sin.
Then he opened his mouth and lovingly spoke,
"Now follow my word child, salvage all you have broke.
For I'm really here although this is a dream,
and now that you know me we shall walk as a team."
I awoke with a start, my heart aching with sorrow.
Would I go to heaven, if there was no tomorrow?
        Teressa Nabors

Invisible Man

I lay down on taunt cool sheets that immediately stimulate
the warmest part of me to become the most moist.
My eyes search for that Invisible Man that I see so clearly on
the back of my eyelids.
I feel his hands hold me so tight
that it becomes hard to breathe
as I squeeze my pillow between my thighs.
My Invisible Man always satisfies me
because he knows what places on my body need caressing
before the thought comes into conscious.
My Invisible Man never lets me down.
Sometimes he even visits me when my lover has fast gone to sleep
in his exhausted afterglow,
to bring me to that point of tension-filled ecstasy.
My Invisible Man
always dependable, always satisfying, always imagined.
Sometimes I wish my Invisible Man would leave me for an
Invisible Woman
And the physical remains will bring their Imagined experiences together to
Realization.
        Gina Lillian Barrett

What A World

What a world, what a world.
    A world filled with crime and hate
Packed with people who discriminate.
    A world in which wrong seems right.
A world where people curse and fight.
    Hissing, scratching, cursing, screaming.
Children dying of AIDS for no reason.
    Homosexuals, homelessness, but yet nobody cares,
About the children starving and dying before their maximum years.
    Shooting, killing, smoking, squealing.
What a world, what a world.
Little kids, tiny kids, thinking they are ready.
    Eleven-, twelve-, thirteen-year-olds having babies.
Still everyone thinks of only themselves
and does nothing for their family and friends.
Lord God, what are we to do?
What a world, what a world.
        Stephanie Jones

Damnant Quod Non Intelligunt The Vibration Of Lustration

Most magnificent mother and beautiful whore
thy perfect presence is not mere fortuity
for my platonic mind is pure magical lore
our crystal coalescence proceeds in continuity

And they may conceive us as lascivious
when our astral lights are sattvicly saturated
because they habitually breed abjectly oblivious
to the pranic copulation that is consecrated

So let us not pursue a temporal passion
our perennial purpose is communion with Brahman
we shall escape samsara in festive fashion
after masticating mushrooms with a Yaqui shaman

To the sweet love I must diligently divulge
the theosophic secrets of my esoteric ceremonies
in my dharmic paradise ye must freely indulge
this is the domicile of immaculate matrimonies

I bring you to a blissful world without bounds
to manifest my profound mystical affinity
all of our sublime movements are dulcet sounds
that permeate the dynamical fields of infinity
        Ian Myckul Sigmon

Narrow Encounter

Finally: Every default was the reverse to what hadn't happen.
It was terrifying — of my character the lost and
briefly without much thunder to guide my feet.
Things were tight inside the ripe atmosphere!
While in verbal heat I slip to demand of my surrounding space
and dispose immediately what's overwhelming;
to implore my own lawful leverage.
Suddenly, coming at me a right arm,
which I had seized and turned into hand wrestling.
For me, the seething of my power missing earlier,
particles I should later run upon to escape which
now were the (path) for us both to rumble . . .
Instead we continued arguing.   Yet, restraints existed
on one or the others belongings; due to added implication,
we each held something belonging to the other.
Wait, I thought! . . . Hadn't I the finesse or dominance to
provide an assault, why not, or move-aside?

It's good probably that we'd kept on arguing,
because actually we stayed pretty good pals
   Ronald Allen

Untitled

We try to block the things in our minds,
the things we do not want to see.
But still they come, blinding our sight, from what is right.
We begin to swerve not knowing why.
It's hard to push them out although we try.
In the end we never win.
We just hold on, during our downward spin
   Rob Miller

My Prayer

I'm waiting, God, for that answer to prayer
for the desire of always having you there.
At times it seems you're so far away
and no one is neat to make things okay.

I'm listening, Lord, for the promises you keep
for the rainbow of happiness and joy that I seek.
I don't understand the trials I have
but I know you're aware and came make me glad.

I'm telling you, father, of the sadness I feel,
of the sin and unholiness that seems so real.
I want to be beautiful and have a heart like new
please cleanse me and make me just like you.

   Beth Ann Maples

To A Dear Niece Teresa

My thoughts are with you every day
Even though you are so many miles away
Hard struggles you have endured year after year
I know has brought depression, and many tears

But Teresa remember, there is help near by
Just talk to God he hears our hearts cry
When we think we are alone, and no hope left
Just reach out to God don't put him on a shelf

When nights seem long, and days drag slow
And you wish there was some place you could go
Get off alone, on your knees, talk to God and pray
He will give you peace, and a brighter day

There is many a day you don't want to move
Each step you take is like glue in your shoes
You just hang on, keep doing your best
And God is there to help carry the nest.

   Oleta F. Sparks

The Boyfriend

What is a boyfriend?
Someone who says they'll
treat you right but goes
out every night?

What is a boyfriend?
Is he a friend that's "just a boy"?
Or is it someone who
you can trust and
share your secrets with?

What is a boyfriend?
To me a boyfriend is
someone who you can talk to.
Someone who you can be friends
with. To me a boyfriend is
someone who's there for you
no matter what the problem is.

What is a boyfriend?
That I can only say like this:
When he sits down and tells you he loves
you, you know he's your true love.
   Jaclyn Gagliano

Martin Luther King, Jr.

A man of courage,
A man of hope,
A man who even met the Pope,
A noble peace prize winner,
A man who was not a quitter,
A man who spoke words that all men heard.
   Chasity Sharp

The Beach

The frothing waves chew away at the dry sand,
the iridescent shells suck up the fuchsia sun,
A "caw caw" swims out of a sea gull's beak,
the ocean is calm.
A splash breaks the sheet of glass
and a fish as white as a full moon
soars out of the water and plops back in,
the clouds cleave, and a sky,
as purest blue imaginable comes forth,
and one by one an opalescent
star leaps into its mothers arms.
The ocean is still, and the beach is silent.
   Paloma Lehfeldt

In My Dream

In my dream,
I dash to a steep cliff,
To gaze at the lovely sights.
I slip on a wet rock,
And tumble down, down
To my ultimate doom.
I see the ground getting closer.
As the ground gets closer,
I wake up,
And it seems,
As if I had just,
Fallen from my bed,
But I didn't.
I lie awake thinking about my dream.
I feel a little strange.
Like it is coming true every second of my life.
I'm thankful that it was only a dream.
   Jennifer Wilt

484

Sunshine Soldiers

We were friends or so I thought —
   the farm had not been bought.

I felt our time was well invested,
   we were prepared for war, battle tested.

Friends on paper not from the heart,
   they let go of my hands when trouble did start.

Not friends, but Sunshine Soldiers.

While the sun did shine they lined at my door.
   I did not have to look — I had friends galore.

Then the world rained trouble on me,
   using my hands for wipers I still could not see.

Surely my friends would not let me down. I yelled for them,
   they were not around.

Not Friends, but Sunshine Soldiers.

Left in the battlefield licking my wounds,
   I would recover, but not real soon.

They marched with me while the sun shown our way,
   replaced by shadows when clouds were gray.

Not Friends, but Sunshine Soldiers.

   Juan Jose

The Wanderer

I am a wanderer, I walk alone, I've been everywhere
on this troubled world. I've met lots of people
and helped them along, with smiles and prayers
and even a song, with housework and worries
I've helped them get along and now they are
happy and closer to God.

No one recognizes the deeds that I've done but that
doesn't matter God's will be done. That's my reason
for being in this world to help the people turn again to God.

I am a wanderer, I walk alone, no one walks with me,
they don't think it's fun, so I just keep on walking
wandering alone helping the people that need God's
love, I help them to learn that God is love.

I am a wanderer and I walk alone, the only one
with me is God and his love
Do you know who I am? I am a wanderer.
I'm the one nobody understands, the friendless
and homeless, the one nobody wants, the one that
carries God's light and shares it with everyone.

   Mirta M. Sonboul

Baby's First Snowfall

Snowsuit, scarf and boots, size two.
Clip-on mittens, soft and new.
Glowing cheeks and shining eyes
As he looks at the snow with great surprise.

He builds a snowman, mini-style.
He plops right down to rest awhile.
He catches snowflakes on his tongue.
So innocent, so very young.

He tumbles face first to the snowy ground.
Chuckles of laughter, the only sound.
Soaked to the skin, he is carried inside.
Pampered and powdered and towel-dried.

Content, he drifts off to sleepy land.
Sucking the thumb of his tiny hand.
A baby is beautiful, make no mistake,
If he can find joy in a single snowflake.

   Sandra Marie Jensen

Good Morning Baby

Good morning baby, I dreamed about you last night,
She said you did, Yes I sure did and I was holding you close to me,
Did you know you were the sweetest dream I ever had?
Good morning baby, so good to see you again,
I am your very best friend.

You know I love you baby,
You're not none of my sin,
I really love you deep within.
Good morning baby, I am always ready to see you again,
What made you think I didn't want you?

When you were the sweetest walking dream I have ever seen,
Good morning baby, it's always good to see you.
When you dream, I just hope you dream the same thing I do,
Cause you give me that fever.
If you think the same thing I am thinking,
There ain't nothing sweeter.

   Lem Poteete Jr.

The Last Strike

Would you steal from my heart
all that I have
with desperate words of hope?
If there is fault — it is mine.
If there is reason — it is I.
If I cut and torture, I suffer the pain
of demons too deep to be seen.
Yet they rise with no warning to defeat me;
I shall destroy them.
Chains forged by time
are not easily broken, but
do become weaker with age.
Although my strength is nearly gone —
let my last strike break all
that I have become
so her heart can love again!

   Douglas Scribner

Gabriella Elizabeth

You made your debut into God's world.
Do wish I could see and hold you.

We also could play peek-a-boo
Tis really a lot of fun to do.

How sad to live so far away,
Cause I'd like to rock you night and day.

My hope is that we can fly there soon.
Maybe even on the West Virginia moon.

When learning of your conception.
Our prayers went up to God.

He answered and formed you perfect.
This truly is his miraculous reward.

   Beverly J. Both

Malevolence

Seven hours running through voices in my head
Seven hours pondering through questions never read
A couple lost memories
A couple in a daze
A couple lead the way
A couple depressing months
A couple lost away
A couple fear the lies
A couple find themselves in the shadows
A couple know the truth
A couple hides their eyes

   Eric Ciechanowski

Iowa's Seasons

Winter is here, it's getting colder, even the days, are getting colder.
When you walk outside, it's not very nice, all that snow and plenty of ice.
Always press warm and button your sleeves, because Iowa
winters, are like a deep freeze.
Before you know it, winter will be gone, it's time for spring, to come along.
Melting the snow and all that ice, just thinking about it, sure sounds nice.
The birds will come along and sing their songs.
The grass will turn green and color our scenes.
Flowers begin to bloom, by the light of the moon, it couldn't
have happened, none too soon.
Then we pass over, from spring to summer, lots of rain, lightning and thunder.
No need to worry, it will pass over, it's the same every year, over and over.
It's starting to get hot, the grass is dying, the flowers are
wilting, you can them crying.
It gets so hot, so we all stay inside, the air conditioner running, ice tea by our side.
Then it lets up, the heat and all, here we go again, it's time for fall.
The leaves on the trees, they start to change, the wind picks up, it starts to rain.
The birds fly south, for the winter, the air it is, getting thinner.
Before you know it, you look around, and all the leaves, are on the ground.
The next thing you know, it starts to snow, here we go again, it's winter again.

Bryan S. May

Untitled

Let's go down to the river.
Where as children, we used to play all day.
Let's wade our feet, through the tender green reeds,
Lay our backs against the earth,
Feel the warmth of the morning sun, and
Plant the seed in our minds.

Let's run over to the railroad tracks
And watch the trains go by.
Wave and shout at the conductor,
Watch the wheels run over the ties.
Never knew where it was going.
Gone, far away, good-bye.

Let me keep these pleasant memories
Of a childhood gone by.
Let me close my eyes and pretend I'm home,
So far away, like the big blue sky.

Let's share each other's company
Let me be a friend
I could truly love you, no need to pretend.

Abel A. Alvarado

Dark Sky

I'm surrounded by a black cloud
I'm the rain maker
I'm the rain man

The rain that corrodes my very being
Rusted and stale
I rested in my cell
My cell in hell . . . the hell in my head

Now I dream I was dead, but
I already am . . . of the living dead

Force fed
I took the spoon to myself
I grin and bare it, choke and swallow
I feel empty, so hollow
Lost myself in myself . . . been filled
Still it wasn't me

The rain is pouring
Black and cold
It was drowning me
I came back up for air and was pushed back in
All because my guilt of sin

Keallian Oren Clark

Your Little Girl

I've lived by your rules
Since I was just a little child,
And just because graduation is near
Doesn't mean I'll go crazy and wild.

I've always been taught the difference
Between right and wrong,
But believe me mom and dad
I'll never give you reasons to sing a sad song.

I know you can't believe
How your little girl has grown up,
And even though I'm off to college
You still wish me luck.

I will truly miss you
And that's definitely not a lie,
For when I'm on my own
Where's your shoulder when I need a place to cry?

But let's not dwell on the future
For we still have seven months to go,
It's not like I'll never see you again
It's both of y'all's love I'll always know.

Felicia K. Cyrus

Alone

Alone versus lonely, are they the same?
There is no one to call out my name.
I survive on need, I survive on touch,
I don't think that's asking so much.
And now here I sit, all alone,
Thinking of who I could possibly phone.
My heart is weak, it's now quite frail,
I know with time, I will prevail.
The heart's a puzzle, and so is life,
Without every piece, there's so much strife.
I found true love, I got my taste,
I lost that piece . . . God, what a waste.
Though my heart is broken, it will still tick,
But is a wall a wall without every brick?
So now with careful needle, and gentle thread,
One stitch at a time, is how I'll mend.
But scars don't leave, they ever last,
And they make it harder to get feelings past.
And now here I am, alone I'll be,
Please, please, please . . . let her remember me.

Paul F. Nejeschleba Jr.

Follower

I am a follower of many
Who lead the way
The decisions we make
Day after day

Lost in the confusion
Of a life so cold
Seeking that rainbow
That rare pot of gold

I wish on the stars
And stare at the moon
Touching the flowers
Some days until noon

I think about colors
And the richness they hold
The moon, and the stars
And that rare pot of gold.

Sharon Broadway

The Thingamajig

The Thingamajig, it looks like a twig
and has a real long snout.

Give it a push, one or two
and it begins to pout.

Now, when you see the Thingamajig
remember not to shout.

'Cause if you do, the Thingamajig
will surely kick you out.

What's a Thingamajig you ask?
The answer is no doubt.

A Thingamajig is for me to know
and you to figure out!

Becky Sue Hougesen

Untitled

I held you in my arms
close to my heart.
I felt your life beating
in unison with my own.
With every succulent kiss,
I fell more in love with you.

I held you in my eyes
even when we were apart.
I breathed in every moment
we spent as one.

The bursts of joy
whenever I saw you,
the warm feeling
inside my heart,
That was always present.
I will never forget
the love we were
able to share.

You were my first love,
You will be the best memory.

Layne A. Beckman

Come Closer

Come closer
So I may see
The glow in your eyes.

So I may feel
The softness of your touch
And the beauty of your body.

So I may understand
The purity of your mind
And the thoughtfulness of your heart.

The love you have to share
Engrosses your surroundings.
Come closer
And embrace me
With your abiding love.

L. J. Gustafson

Empty Promises

Beware of empty promises,
The shallow songs they sing.
For empty rhymes
In empty times,
An empty lot will bring.

Bradley Schwartz

True Love

True love, pure love.
Does it ever die?

From time?
From the longing of its absence,
Each passing day
. . . each passing night?

Trying to forget
Fighting each moment,
When my heart stumbles
In the shadow of its sweet memory.

But in vain.
But in vain.
My true love is engraved
In the depth of my lonely soul.

True love, pure love.
Does it ever die?
Does it . . . ever die?

Josee Houle

Freedom Embraced

Throw them out to me
I'm eager to hide.
Receive me
accept me freely
and protect me with your heart.
Clad only in my skin
you shield me from
the shrill rain
and tormenting sun.
Keep me safe in your haven
of dreams.
But please
do not smother me
for I too need to be
released
and experience the
warmth and cold alone
in my nakedness.

Greta C. Hellums

Poet?

As I sit here on
my couch, a poet I'm
trying to be.
  I take life as it
comes 24/7 to me.
  I need not to
worry if a poet I'll
ever be.
  No matter what
a wife and a mother
I'll always be.

Janey Marie White

Not Ashamed

I cry out of pain, but no one
heard, I cry aloud but there was
no one there but Arthur, myself
and rheumatoid, I cry but
fibrositis, say I just want to meet
the rest of the family I met
Ashamed you see I'm undertreatment
Orthritis and Osteo are not ashamed
to there their claim to pain,
and crippling up the frame.

Irma J. Nowell

From The Forest

I can see the ferns growing
beneath the trees.
I can see the light beaming
thru the leaves.
I can see the forest the
way it should be
pretty as can be.
Please, please let it be.

Ralph Charles McDonald

High Wire

Teeter-totter,
tightrope walker.
Life is balanced on a high wire.
A breath of air could send you tumbling
to the cold hard floor below, so,
keep your gaze straight,
point your toes.

The crowds to whom you're playing
are intent upon your swaying.
And they seek the thrill of seeing
what it's like when you are reeling,
twirling 'round,
out of bounds,
hit the ground!

Teeter-totter,
tightrope walker.
Don't look down.

Janis Brown

Nostalgia

We built Greyledge
high on Puddling Lane;
we had 50 years
of family joys and sorrows.
One night, we saw bluebirds
fly in at dusk,
and feast on shad berries,
and then roost in a martin house.
Now others are creating their own
special memory book.

Edna M. Garneau

A Damsel In Distress

Where's the knight in shining armor
For a damsel in distress
Someone who will not harm her
But give his very best.

She's been captured in a cellar
For one too many years
She needs someone to tell her
He'll take away her fears.

For him to ride up on a horse
Would be her only wish
To take his horse off of its course
And save her with a kiss.

They'll live happily ever after
In a castle on a hill
With lots of love and laughter
While living in God's will.

For this is the story of a girl
Who's trapped in loneliness
Her life is suddenly in a whirl
She's a damsel in distress.

Lisa Sue Guernsey

Angels On High

Holly boughs that twist and turn,
silver bells that ring-a-ling,
Angels carry both on high,
and sing sweet music of Yule tide.

Bright red berries, dark green leaves,
silver bells that sing ding! Ding!
Carry on a special meaning,
to everyone this Christmas evening.

The day has come, and gone so fast,
we wish to make this moment last,
to hear the Angels sing on high,
but wait, for sleep is coming nigh.

Cerena Lynn Searle

A Yankee Reel

Hard flakes - cold flakes
Soft flakes - snow flakes
Drifting down - earth bound
Sifting, shifting - no sound.
Piling high - hear folks a sigh
Hearts despair - men prepare
Feet booted - ears lapped
Shovels grasped - snow is cast.
Workers weary - sky still dreary
Winter lingers - frost-bit fingers
Wait and wonder - will it cease
Hocus-pocus - there's a crocus.
March marches - away, away
April brings in May - nice days
Summer follows - sunshine glows
Heat's intense - man resents.
September's done - Autumn's begun
Beauty at first - then bubbles burst
Rakes are out - workers about
Crunch of leaves - end of dreams.

Constance C. Mathews

Justis

I saw you today!
Life in the womb
Once a secret
Now open to those who wait
My face lights up
My mouth opens and closes as yours does
The reflex of love wants to reach out, touch and hold you
I watch your Dad and Mom
They too see the miracle you are
And long to cradle you in their arms
You already hold your own special place in the family

Renee C. Rowland

Untitled

Tears of freedom chain us to unreachable desires
Passion of our souls blind us in fire

Swimming in our expectations
Drowning in our necessities

Binding us together
Dreams of want to be

Hopeless and full
This wicked torture with angels wings

Punishment or gift
A question to God above

A never satisfied appetite
This hunger we call love

Jason Pollock

Ah, Shucks, Miss Kitty

Don't think trouble's around the bend
When friends come forth to fawn
It's natural for them to gather when
A birthday like this sees the dawn.

You've reached 97, an enviable feat
With memories you've long sing recessed
To celebrate with you is really a treat
But to know you, we're truly blessed.

Should we uncork the bubbly, or just slice the cake
Possibly wrapping a big hug would do
No matter, it's your day, all day, to partake
We're all just proud of you.

So let's eat, drink and be witty; or hug, kiss or touch
Ah, shucks, Miss Kitty, we love you so much.

Charles Washburn

Wolf

Sacred Indian animal spirit, every
Howl has a message to it.

Strong of body, sound of mind, they
Remind us of the ties that bind.

Some have eyes that could pierce the
Soul while others just have eyes that
Look like coal.

They travel in packs in order to survive,
Feeding from others they seem to thrive.

Melanie Christenson

Sixth Sense?

I hear the rain on a quiet night,
    the screams in a child's laughter,
    the silence in each song.

I smell the pollution on a flower's petal,
    the stink of rain on a spring day,
    the death from a newborn baby.

I taste the acid in cotton candy,
    the bitterness in fresh honey,
    the venom in a glass of milk.

I feel the hatred in a friendly kiss,
    the crushing force of a handshake,
    the coldness in a warm embrace.

I see the pity in the tears,
    the menace in a smile,
    the darkness of the sun.

I sense it all,
    except how I can.

Jason Ellingson

Winter Moss

Autumn is lost in this winter of rain
it covers the ground and our hearts
colder than frost it covers the leaves
and smothers and grief like moss

To hide such a love and cape it in fear
To camouflage that it even exists
time does not stand still for such a dear loss
but speeds faster to remind us what we have missed

Autumn is lost in this winner of rain
it covers the ground and our hearts
colder than frost it covers the leaves
and smothers our grief like moss

Jules Dean

What Is A Mother?

A mother is a special lady
who loves you with all of her heart
and when it's time to say good-bye
she wishes you didn't have to part.

A mother is a very close friend
when you have no one else
she teaches you to be very kind
and live your life humbly and just.

A mother is a very dear father
when your father isn't there
even when she doesn't feel good
she always takes the time to care.

A mother is a very good teacher
and teaches you many things
and when you discover something new
she tells you what it really means.

My mother is all of these things
as well as a chauffeur too
and you should tell your mother each day
"Mom, I love you too!"

Alicia D. Miller

The Rose

I walked around the field,
thinking of my sorrow,
I picked up a red rose.

As I ran inside,
I noticed water beads upon it.
I stared,
I stared,
Until all around me is blocked out of reality,
Only to reveal imagination.

I looked around,
I stared some more
At a white luminous wall.
Soon,
Everything was white.
I heard voices,
Like bells.
Then all that was left of me for my family,
Was that red rose with water beads.
One for each of my dreams.

Sarah J. Higgins

From Afar

Aluminum clouds, they cometh,
as the skyline silvered . . .
A breeze convinced a garden to sway;

A midst a runny window,
a girl stood with her smile folded . . .
Fell tears, and raindrops, to the beat on the pane;

Upon a rod of light,
as her heart lost its pace . . .
A ray of love crumpled cluttering clouds away;

Her countenance did brighten,
as rays of gold enhanced her heart's pace . . .
She felt his warmth melt her heart's wall of pain;

His rooting strength, steadied the garden
His radiating compassion, unfoiled the sun
His touch shattered the pane of her lonely heart;

Over streams, and through dreams,
Over mountains, and through pens of fountain,
From afar . . . their dormant love still grows in its sleep . . .

Kina Carisse Cliette

Things That Makes My Heart Sing

Blue Jays and rainbows and things that makes my heart sing.
Bangles, ringlets, sparkles, and gliders, and jingles, and
things to make my heart sing.

An open space filled with blue skies, a bright green forest,
a smoky plain with prairie game, and a desert floor, who
could ask for more! An oasis of clear waters of a rushing
brook, or water falls, and these are the things that makes
my heart sing.

A sunny day, sittin on bay, to taste the earth sweet
grapes. To have all its rich bounty at my gate. To see
all it's beautiful lakes.

Bangles and jingles and things to make my heart sing. A
bouncing ball with the victory of sport, the flirting
glances of young men and women.

The passion for life, the zest and energy of youth. To live
life to the fullest, to have the comforts and contentment of
the golden age, these are the things that makes my heart sing!

Anthonette L. White

Keep Your Head Above Water

Good things come to those who wait their turn
Nothing come to those who wait too long
If you refuse to try you don't stand a chance
Because you didn't take it you'll lose it
Opportunity is waiting for those who reach
But you've got to be reaching, while the world is teaching
Keep what you have until you bet what you need
Your needs and inspirations are within reach
Just take a drink of the unpolluted or opportunity
And quench your thirst of taking a chance
Overcome all doubts and insecurities
By keeping your head above the water of failure
There will no need to look back while in the water
Life is hard and it'll have your head swim to safety
But if you keep your head above water
There is noway you can drown
Keep your head above the water as the waters let deeper
And you'll find that life is a whole lot easier
In the mind of a keeper.

Samuel Cooper Jr.

Asian Lover

Your skin of brown and golden hue of ethnic shade is strangely bold.
The silken softness of its kiss relieves and calms
    the tension of my anxious being and warps
    my turmoiled soul in quiet timeless bliss.

Against my white Caucasian flesh and dotted skin,
    a warming breath ignites a timeless sleeping fast of lost desire,
    absent in an ancient age and missing
    from an unsung, untold distant past.

A foreignness unknown and yet not uncompared consumes
    my character of rationality and sends my mind
    uncertain of its foremost source into a realm
    of dispossessed docility.

An Asian lover - you, of alien decent, have shattered
    every heartfelt strong and firm belief.
Astonishment explodes through each excited thought
    that I have found in you a source of disbelief.

Come lie with me and sear my white and spotted flesh to yours,
    a monochrome of muscle, brown and gold.
Possess my heart as only you have singly done;
    my Asian lover - you, a rebirth of a myth foretold.

Susan Molthen

Even If I'm Gone I'm Here

Even if I'm gone I'm here
Even if I'm away I'm here
Because I see you glittery in my eyes and
I can see you dancing in my heart
So I will always be with you O you
I'll always love you O you

Shoshana Akins

Winter Day

Sitting in a dark end room. Selling a
Shadow of a broom. The wind outside blows
and blows. How I wonder when it goes. I
Snuggle down in my bed with my pillow close
to my head. I close my eyes and go to
sleep. Without a peep. In the morning I get
up to dress for school. Without making life
look like a fool. At the school bus stop
Snow if falling light. And the grey sky
isn't bright. Sitting on a un-snow-covered bunch
I'm reading a book. I hear your voice and
Stopped to look. Beyond the snow, some one
I know. Looking I see you standing alone
Eyes that sparkle a smile that is warm.
Come on they say let's gather the corn. In the
spring when the sky is blue. Oh father I
love you. I really do.

Margaret Spencer

Friends

Difficult to define but easy to recognize.
Everyone wants them,
but they are few and hard to come by.
Acquaintances are easy, friends aren't not.
They are a rare bird,
with whom we rarely cross paths.
We touch many people throughout our lives,
but few qualify as friends.
We may not see them often.
We may see them almost never,
but we know they are there.
In memory we are together often.
The memories bring pangs of nostalgia.
In the trackless recess of our minds,
we find each other constantly.
The scenes of our friendship come back,
without warning.
We track each scene with fondness.
We replay the track over and over,
as the memories come back in full color.

Edmund Glenn Wagner

Freedom

What does it mean?
I say it means a car and an Education . . .
but, I don't think grades determine knowledge
I think education stands for what you know
on the inside of your soul
down the pit of existence
freedom from yourself
from your own disapproval and hurt.
Physical, emotional and mental?
No, just your own sense of morals.
In the past we were all unaware of our identity
sometime in your history
but rejoice . . .
if you understand this,
you have your freedom.

Marie-Claire Russell

Eyes of God

Read my poems, read my prose,
can you hear? Do you know?
The pain is real, through smiling eyes,
don't think it's a vision or a tricked disguise.
Believe what you feel, believe what you see,
though it's veiled, it's still plain,
there for decades — purgeless pain.

Think not I want pity
or grief or mute tears,
or a hand out, or a stand out
or release from my fear
these things would be fruitless
and temporal at best.

What I'd like is your soul to see truth beyond words,
to feel pain in the laughter that hides all the hurt,
to comfort the jokester, a kind word
have it heard

You can do this for your vision is beyond what you know
for I've seen it in your eyes and I've seen it in your soul.

William Schilling

Fly Away Momma, Fly Away

Momma, we love you, and will miss you, ever so much.
There were so many lives you shaped, molded and touched.
But, now the Lord has called you away.
Oh, fly away Momma, fly away!

Love, comfort, strength, and wisdom, you gave to your children.
We know it wasn't easy, but, on you, we knew we could depend.
We will cherish and honor your memory everyday.
Yes, fly away Momma, fly away!

Your earthly body had grown weak, and you had to depart.
But you left your precious spirit, for us to hold in our heart.
And, we know your soul is resting with the Lord, as we pray.
So, fly away Momma, fly away!

We thank God for you being the foundation of our lives.
And, being without you will bring many tears to our eyes.
But, we are happy, because we will be with you again, some day.
Oh, fly away Momma, fly away!

Karen Renita Jones

He Called You Home

You were a budding flower in our hearts and in our world,
touching us each and every day,

Capturing our hearts with your smile and charm
in more than one way.

But as you started to shine, God called you home,
ending your life here on earth;

So now you are in the kingdom above, living a new life a new birth.

We'll treasure the days we had to marvel at your
bright and cheerful personality,

You were always determined to make those dreams of yours
into a reality.

Friends and family were strengthened through your eagerness
confidence in yourself,

That's why we'll hold our thoughts of you close to our hearts,
for they are of precious wealth.

Sweetheart, we love you and we'll miss you a lot,
as in the fields of Heaven you'll roam . . .

Because God need another angel by his side,
so he . . ., so he . . .

He Called You Home

Vincent Watson

Lazarus Restless

From deep within a sleep he assumed was forever
He hears the voice of a twin, a murmuring mirror
of sound muttering, muffled at first, then gaining a sharp stick
of clear-pitched command: "Lazarus, come forth."
The cave, his mausoleum, is dark and thickly-stoned-cool like the
still clean black air he was just settling into, air of dark eternity.
No light, and only the deep bone sound of time out of time,
until just now.

"Lazarus, come forth," and the light slicing in like a clean chrome
knife blade makes his eyes ache through the tattered, loosely wrapped
linen. He feels the still oily unguents greasing his withering flesh
back to life. His hair has continued to grow on his head, arms, legs,
genitals. A large vein cutting across the hairline begins, again,
to pulse evenly.

Now in the echo of command Lazarus feels the warm welcome
life of the world opening into the cave as his words break the
seal that held death in a vacuum.

Ragged, bewildered, he steps shakily into misery and sees only dimly
His brother, covered in white linen,
between two astonished women weeping.
    Dennis P. Slattery

A Summer Night's Story

As a sunset fills the sky with all its glory
   It holds ahead a majestical story
In its trail a darkening sky
   While passion burns in a lover's eyes
Now as fog slowly crawls across the sand
   It caresses two lovers lying hand and hand
Songs of ecstasy in the night are sung
   As the sweat and flesh of two become one
And in the pale caress of a delicate moonlight
   Beads of sweat glisten like diamonds dancing in delight
Ever so softly the moon kisses the sea
   As bodies tremble in a passionate ecstasy
While they whisper words as soft as grace
   And steam roll from in between their gentle embrace.
Now admiring the stars and their orderly fashion
   The slowly walk the beach to cool the passion.
Once again two lovers give the sky a majestical story
   As a sun rise swallows the night's hidden glory.
    Peter E. Sisco IV

Our Free Nation

As an American I feel pride
That no citizen of basic rights is denied.
Through years of war and toil,
Liberty still remains on this soil.

As a people against British tyranny we fought.
Unity, as a free nation we sought.
Injustices called for revolution,
Which led to victory and our constitution.

Through Civil War our nation prevailed.
Freedom and unity as victors were hailed.

As a big brother to other nations, we lend
Our service — their liberty to defend.
Our desire — tranquility to instill,
By soldiers who sacrifice by will.

In this nation, countless freedoms we enjoy.
Our government leaders by voting employ.
Rights of assembly and free speech we possess,
To worship, and our beliefs to profess.

Remember our freedom is a gift from above.
Let us not forsake this land we love.
    Jason Havemeier

Untitled

And mountains enough to climb?
those are the only words from that
long ago song that I can remember,
or maybe they're the only ones I want to remember.

Well, I've climbed my mountains,
I've stood on the top and looked out
at a world I thought existed and
from up there, it does.

But from down here with my feet on
the ground, it's hard to recall what
it was I thought I saw, all I'm really sure of is, it wasn't this!

There were no razor sharp lines, no bottomless holes, no frigid block
or dirty glass. There were no hopeless glares or empty stares.

I thought there was color and warm, warm like the sun, warm like
the heart when it fills with love, warm
evening fire as it tries in vain to light the night.

From up there, I thought I saw reason mixed in with the swirling
color of green and gold and those things of earth, both new and old.

From up there, I thought I could see a friend I use to know and hoped
that somehow they would be looking up at me. Were you?
    Jon E. Anoles

Wondering If

Wondering if . . . you can reach the sun,
   Searching for the star,
     Looking beyond the horizon,
      Wondering if . . .

Wondering if . . . the skies ever end,
   Do the clouds ever stop appearing?
    Do new trees fail to sprout?,
     Wondering if . . .

Wondering if . . . the seed in a new cell begins life,
   Growing to be anything it desires,
    Continuing to exist in the world,
     Wondering if . . .

Wondering if . . . life is within yourself,
   Finding your soul,
    When you believe,
     You will stop wondering.
    Robert Morley Foon

Child's Eyes

The world to me as a child was innocent, the world to me was dark.
I could see through people as easy as glass sitting alone
as my days pass.
Outside my window I would peer pastures of green I found so dear.
My joy and my happiness peering at me, my horse Jack dear to thee.
A light brown silky touch,
I asked that I might have him, to me that was much.
My love for the world quickly decayed,
My pets I once loved beneath the world's cover laid.
Growing up on a farm wasn't easy to do with a garden enormous,
livestock due.
My peace I had, the peace I gave
Grandfathers so sweet, whom now lay deep,
Paid my working little hands so weak.
For generously rubbing their feet.
Why am I to bother?
Why must I say my childhood life may never go
But why must it never stay?
    Tiffany Anne Aslan

I Am Who I Am

I am who I am, I know no one else to be.
I am who I am Black, Beautiful and Free.
I am who I am spiritual, sensual, and sensational.
I am who I am through life's experiences and expectations I've set for myself.
I am who I am because of my beliefs and bereavements of life.
I am who I am because of struggles handed me and the solutions I chose.
I am who I am in Womanhood because of the knowledge of my
place in God's divine order to Manhood.
I am who I am because of love and loss of love.
I am who I am in Motherhood, uniquely Mother, Father, Friend, and Counselor.
I am who I am in the institution of family by believing we should
carry each other as much as possible in love and gratitude to that institution.
I am who I am in friendship more than expected or accepted in some instances.
I am who I am in humanity understanding the uniqueness of us all.
I am who I am in prayer for the simple joy's of life in every
promise given in Prosperity, Longevity and Creativity.
I am who I am by faith, love, and hope of making my eternal home sure.
I am who I am and just hope that it's leading to all God wants me to be.

Kathy R. Rayborn

The Walk

Imagine through soft blowing winds, you are walking
softly hand in hand with the one you love so dearly.
The moon shinning bright and there ahead lies a shadow
of two people; you stop and watch as the shadows move slowly
down a path through the moonlight, still hand in hand, talking
laughing ever so softly. As you stand there watching the
shadows change, you realize that what you are seeing is
yourself along with the true love of your life and the love you
share growing older together through the years.

Michelle Denise Hughey

P.S.A.   Commercial

The world talks about "Just Do It" like Nike because Reebok says
"This Is Supposedly My Planet." But when you find a woman
that will let you "Squeeze The Charmin," get like Bounty and be
a "Quicker Picker Upper" and pick up a Trojan. As a matter of
fact even if she get like the Energizer and "Wants To Keep
Going" to "Obey her Thirst" like Sprite, You better make the
"Choice Of A New Generation" like Pepsi and get a prophylactic
and let her "Have It Her Way" at Burger King, "Never Leave
Home Without It" like it's your American Express Card. Because once she gets that "Sensation" like she's been eating
Peppermint Patties, unwanted pregnancy and HIV will "Make
You Slow Down" like Roy Rogers. So get like 1-800-Call-ATT
and save yourself more that 44%, save yourself some time and
energy and treat prophylactics like that soul classic album.
(You Gots To Get You One.)

Absalom Phipot

To My Addiction

You took me to places where I have never been.
My mind wondering in the night wind.

I captured a sense of finding within;
all you are is a nasty lying sin.

Robbing me from all my life's dreams
leaving me mindless with nothing other than to scream.

You're trouble you're trouble you're trouble you're trouble;
I say this four times to keep me in line.

The fear of this path is more than I could bare;
so listen to me now I am much more aware.

It's war with you now the battle is on;
I will keep fighting you tell the end of dawn.

A recovering addict. Thank you dear God.

Dorene Marquis

Remembrance

I was but a mere child when I lost someone who meant so much to me.
His soul was taken and set to be free.
Everybody told me he was never really gone.
I thought of those words until finally came dawn.
Then the night suddenly came as I started into the sky.
Wondering where he was and how high.
I finally understand what I've been told through the years.
My way of expressing it is basically with tears.
If he just knew how hard it is on me
at this very time and the years to be.
It's the dream of him returning that keeps me alive,
I just don't know how long I could possibly survive.
I'd like him to know he's still in my heart,
Not a day goes by I'd wish to part.

Jenny Higginbotham

On The Sea Of Space And Time

Squeeze me, squeeze me   tightly, tightly
Kiss me, kiss me   lightly, lightly
Love me, love me   nightly, nightly

On the sea of space and time,
I'm a lonely bit of rhyme

Oh Lord, can you spare me a dime
Oh Edna, can you spare me some love

On the sea of space and time,
I'm a tiny bit of rhyme

_____ Repeat

Oh, Edna . . .

Christopher Steele

A Dwindling Flame

I once thought you loved me, but now I must know,
Is what you felt for me in the past, never again to glow?
Our love was made from a single ember, that grew into a massive fire,
A fire I thought to be ever lasting, never to retire.
Now that burning flame is down to a single spark that I hold tightly
in my hand,
And it seems, the tighter I hold on that tiny spark, the closer it
becomes to a grain of sand
Perhaps it is best that I let it go,
To find another place to bring a fire aglow.

I once thought you loved me, but what mended, you now unsew,
Leaving my heart ripped, with no love to knew.
It is now that I plead,
Pleading in a never ending sorrow for it is forgiveness I need.
I long to hold you in my arms, embraced around you ever so tight,
And give that cracking fire another chances, that again it may burn
ever so bright.
Maybe your love for me is gone, maybe it's no longer there,
But please tell me at least your friendship you will still share.
In concluding, I would like to tell you this,
I will always love you and it is you that I will always miss.

Jonathan Foster

BIOGRAPHIES
OF POETS

ABEL, FLORENCE H.
[pen.] Penelope Cutler Reid; [b.] December 28, 1941, Philadelphia, PA; [p.] Melda Beitzel and W. F. Harris; [m.] David L. Abel, D.V.M, December 22, 1983; [ed.] High Point University, NC BS, 1963, U. of Maryland School of Social Work, MSW 1972 and Capital Bible Seminary; [occ.] Certified Clinical Social Worker and Psychotherapist; [memb.] National Association of Social Workers, American Association of Christian Counselors, Dayspring Wesleyan Church of Bowie, Greenbelt Homemakers; [hon.] Who's Who of Women in America, Who's Who of Mental Health Professionals; [oth. writ.] The Beitzel Family a history of the descendants of Johann Georg Beitzel, The Shadow of His Hand a Biography of Melda Harris, Articles for; [pers.] To reveal truth as I know it to future generations; [a.] Greenbelt, MD

ABLIN, CHRISTOPHER
[b.] January 19, 1971, Glendale, CA; [p.] Kent Ablin, Rebecca Brown; [ed.] Glendale High, Glendale College, Commercial Training Services Inc.; [occ.] Professional Driver; [memb.] Harley Owners Group, American Bowling Congress, Roll'n Donkee Tour, Bowlers Tournament Club; [hon.] Glendale High: Most Improved Varsity Track and Field 1988, Athlete of the Week: 3-25-88, M.V.P. Field Events: Soph. Track 1986; [pers.] To my dear friend, Nancy Puthuff, for whom this poem was originally written. You inspire me! Love always, Chris.; [a.] Huntington Beach, CA

ADAMS, SARA
[pen.] Sara Elizabeth Adams; [b.] July 9, 1984, Kirkwood, MO; [p.] Don and Kari Adams; [ed.] Nipher Middle School - Seventh Grade; [occ.] Student; [memb.] Lagos Youth Group at Concordia Lutheran Church; [hon.] Honor Roll; [pers.] I am currently working on many short stories inspired by the writings of Judy Blume. My poems reflect my feelings and thoughts of the purpose of mankind.; [a.] Kirkwood, MO

ADAMS WHITFIELD, CAROLYN M.
[pen.] CMAW; [b.] March 10, 1948, Indianapolis, IN; [p.] Ernest and Anna Adams; [m.] Robert A. Whitfield, December 16, 1978; [ch.] Vernon L. Scott Jr., Lisa R. Whitfield; [ed.] Arsenal Technical High School, Martin University Class '95; [occ.] Communications Technician; [memb.] Olivet Baptist Church, and Press of Nurses, Martin Univ. Alumni; [hon.] Second place Martin Univ. Poetry Reading Contest; [pers.] I have the opportunity now to try to make a positive influence in the life of our youth. I hope to give to others a portion of the goodness that I have received in my life.; [a.] Indianapolis, IN

AGUILLARD, DAPHNE E.
[b.] March 9, 1968, Baton Rouge, LA; [p.] Eddie and Sandy Ellis; [m.] Jessie "Dusty" Aguillard II, March 2, 1991; [occ.] Office Manager; [memb.] Southern Poetry Association - Famous Poets Society - International Society of Poets; [hon.] Diamond Homer Award from Famous Poets Society; [oth. writ.] Currently I have quite a large collection of poetry that I have been writing since I was a teenager.; [pers.] My husband, Dusty, was my inspiration for this poem, but he is also my inspiration for so much more in my life.; [a.] Erwinville, LA

AHLMAN, LILLIAN
[pen.] (Lee) Nick Name; [b.] March 18, 1945, Baltimore, MD; [p.] Catherine Desfoge, Maurice Desforge; [ch.] Cynthia Ahlman/Michael Ahlman; [ed.] Waltham High (Mass.) Jr. High (Northeastern -Waltham; [occ.] Receptionist Secretary; [memb.] Work to learn Program (for Pinkerton Academy);

[oth. writ.] A Perfect Shell, Time, Comes The Dawn, There For I Am; [pers.] Always believe in yourself, for dreams can came true.; [a.] Derry, NH

ALDEN, W. MICHAEL
[b.] August 15, 1973, Hartford, CT; [p.] Warren and Susan Alden; [ed.] Middleburg High School, St. John's River Community College; [occ.] Allegiance Healthcare Distribution Employee; [oth. writ.] Numerous unpublished poems and short stories.; [pers.] I write to make people think and feel. You might find it stirs uncomfortable thoughts in you and so will not like it or you might discover some wisdom in my madness. Love it or hate it makes me no difference because at least I got you thinking!!; [a.] The Woodlands, TX

ALEXANDER, MARILYN
[pen.] TerRah; [b.] June 22, 1955; [occ.] Biological Scientist; [oth. writ.] Several articles published in local newspaper.; [a.] Pensacola, FL

ALI, KHALIDAH
[b.] Trinidad, WI; [p.] Frederick and Avis LaFleur; [m.] Bilal Ali; [ch.] Seven children ages 6 to 20; [ed.] Graduate of Everette High School Lansing MI 3 years of College; [occ.] House wife also sells Avon in Sparetime; [pers.] I started writing poems when I was twelve years old. I would like to write a book some day.; [a.] Riverdale, GA

ALIFF, NATHAN
[pen.] Nathan Aliff; [b.] April 27, 1978, Fairfax, VA; [p.] David and Denise Aliff; [ch.] Ashleigh Marie; [ed.] High School; [occ.] Construction; [pers.] Live each day to the fullest, appreciate your good health.; [a.] Sumerduck, VA

ALLEN, ANDREW CRAIG
[b.] December 31, 1974, Saint Louis; [p.] Robert and Betty Allen; [ch.] Ryan Alexander Staryak, Devan Andrew Allen; [ed.] High School Dropout, received G.E.D., currently attending college evenings, Eureka Sr. High School, East Central Community College; [occ.] Factory Employee; [pers.] I enjoy writing my own personal feelings down in my words. Having them published could explain someone elses feelings to them if they don't know to put their feelings into words.; [a.] Pacific, MO

ALLISON, DALE LEE
[pen.] Dale; [b.] March 6, 1944, Salem, OR; [p.] Vivian J. Story, Osborn L. Allison; [ed.] Twelveth (12) grade, High School, Graduated, 1963, North Salem High; [occ.] Factory Labor; [memb.] International Freelance Photographers Organization, Lewisville, NC; [hon.] Honorable discharge from United States Navy Services duties. Also an inventor of the product called, "Floor Scrubber" Patented 04/04/95. Have a certificate and plaque.; [pers.] Would like a copy of the "Looking-Glass." Thank you.; [a.] Salem, OR

ALSPAUGH, BEVERLY
[b.] February 13, 1965, Uvalde, TX; [p.] Billy and Joyce Faust; [ch.] Amaris Brett, Weston Ray; [ed.] B.S. in Interdisciplinary Studies from Sul Ross State University; [occ.] Reading Teacher - 5th grade; [memb.] First United Methodist Church of Uvalde; [hon.] Graduated Cum Laude Sul Ross State University; [a.] Uvalde, TX

ALTENAU, RANDALL J.
[b.] March 18, 1956, Cincinnati, OH; [p.] J. Eugene Altenau, Louise Altenau; [m.] Karen S. Altenau, April 20, 1979; [ed.] Elder High School, University of Cincinnati B.S. in Management; [occ.] Manager, Chesa-

peake Display and Packaging; [oth. writ.] Several poems (unpublished), and music, lyrics and arrangement of the song, "Today is Ours," which was awarded a certificate of achievement from the Billboard Song Contest, 1994; [pers.] My writings, though reality-based, tend to reflect the ideological sentiments of human emotion. My love and inspiration for the last 18 years has been, and is still, my wife Karen.; [a.] Pleasant Plain, OH

ALVAREZ, MARIA
[pen.] Maria Alvarez; [b.] March 31, 1927, Chicago, IL; [p.] Antonio and Gerarda Cordero; [m.] Divorced, February 11, 1947; [ch.] Rochelle, Juanito, Rueben, Sharon, Michael, Salvador Jr., Jerry, Donald; [ed.] High School, Import and Export Bilingual Interpreter; [occ.] Bilingual Interpreter, Amway Distributor; [memb.] The Latino Journal, The First Baptist Church of Hammond, Ind.; [hon.] National Library of Poetry 1st Award; [oth. writ.] Interpretation of a dream my life story Till Death Do Us Part, A Single Woman and Mexican - songs and a Spanish poem for Selena. Mi Angel en el Cielo.; [pers.] I love to put all my personal feelings and thoughts on paper, especially love for family and special friends and lovable musicians of Mexico and America.; [a.] Joliet, IL

AMBROISE III, FRANK
[b.] November 10, 1952, Cap-Haitien; [p.] Mrs. Lucette Ambroise; [m.] Yoklin Ambroise; [ch.] Marjorie Ambroise; [ed.] Two years college diploma in travel and business management; [occ.] Certified Travel Agent; [memb.] Tennis Club, Chairperson of Caribbean Union, Poets of Florida; [oth. writ.] Booklet Le Sucre Amer in French 1983 reprint in 1995 then poem of United West Indian in 1988; [a.] Hollywood, FL

AMES, JUDY
[b.] July 30, 1951, Athol, MA; [p.] Lucille Pratt and Paul Vinsant; [m.] Richard Ames, March 24, 1972; [ch.] Shon Ames, Jamie Ames; [ed.] Athol High; [occ.] Loving Wife, Retired Foster Parent; [hon.] Foster Parent of the Year Award, Achievement Awards in Foster Care; [oth. writ.] Poems, unpublished book about my Foster Children's Stories and my experiences with them.; [pers.] I thrive on helping children. I promote foster care. I encourage people to open their homes to children in care.; [a.] Orange, MA

AMMANN, GARRETT G.
[b.] March 28, 1953, New Haven, CT; [p.] Dorothy Sutherland, Myron Ammann; [m.] Carole Ann, June 24, 1995; [ed.] East Haven High, Westport Art School, Berklee School of Music, Boston; [occ.] Commercial Artist, Professional Musician; [hon.] New Haven Road Race Design Award; [oth. writ.] Poetic Voices of America, Reader's Digest, New Haven Register, New Haven Advocate; [pers.] Artists should reflect God's gifts in any and every way possible.; [a.] Northford, CT

ANDERSON, ALAN
[b.] March 1, 1980, Poway, CA; [p.] Lude and Harold Van Roy; [ed.] Junior at El Cameno High School in Oceanside, CA, Graduating Class of 1998; [occ.] Student; [memb.] Vice President of Associated Student Body of El Camino H.S., California Scholarship Federation (CSF) member; [hon.] Principal's award for Outstanding Academics and Citizenship, Honor Roll student since Freshman year; [oth. writ.] This is my first poem; [a.] Oceanside, CA

ANDERSON, CLARENCE M.
[pen.] Guy Anderson; [b.] June 17, 1913, Havener (Later Grier), NM; [p.] Nels and Elsie Nelson Anderson (Danish Immigrants); [m.] Mary Wier Harkins, October 21, 1941; [ch.] Janet Anderson Marriott, Fr. Ernest Anderson,

David Anderson; [ed.] 1st-8th grades, Grier NM, High School, Clovis NM, MacPherson College, MacPherson KS, 1 semester Eastern NM University, Portales NM, (2 Quarters) in Business Adm. - Legal Secretary to city attorney & studied law for 1 year, Journeyman carpenter, Patternmaker and Layout man in steel fabricating; [occ.] Retired Rural Letter Carrier; [memb.] American Iris Society, Grandparents Gospel Quartet, Ntn'l. Grange, AARP, Church Choir and Deacon, Senior Citizens, 3 Different Song Canary Breeders Associations (German Rollers - Waterslagers - Staffords); [hon.] 5 Grand Championships at County Fairs (oil painting landscape, acrylic landscape, flower arrangement, fruit, garden produce). More than 20 Blue Ribbons at County Fairs, 1st Prize Sr. Citizens Talent Contest - Baritone Solo, 1st Place Sr. Citizens Couples Dancing Comp. 5 yrs. Idaho Area 3 Sr. Citizens Legislative Coordinator to Idaho State Legislature, 1982 - 1987; [oth. writ.] Lyrics and Music (Religious) "My Saviors Feet", more than 50 poems (many different themes) several published in college and local newspapers. I spearheaded a petition to get a medical costs containment initiative on the ballot in Idaho (and into other states), but we fell short by 10,000 signatures on our petition in Idaho.; [pers.] "Get On Board", Don't let life pass you by. Live and let live.; [a.] Mountain Home, ID

ANDERSON, MELANIE JEAN
[b.] November 11, Poughkeepsie, NY; [p.] Jean Lucille Secor-Anderson; [ch.] 5 Kittens and 4 Exotic Turtles; [ed.] Roy C. Ketcham High; [occ.] Student, Aspiring Poet; [memb.] Singing Group, various Cat Clubs and Associations, President of Photography Club, Vice President and Secretary of Cat Club, several Dance Groups; [hon.] Local Bowling Trophy, I show my Cats - winning numerous awards; [oth. writ.] Several poems published in my high school's magazine, regular by-line column in my high school's newspaper; [pers.] Frequently I use humor in my poetry hoping it will brighten my reader's day. I most enjoy Robert Frost's poetry.; [a.] Poughkeepsie, NY

ANDREWS, CHERYL L.
[pen.] Cheryl L. Andrews; [b.] October 7, 1947, Milwaukee, WI; [p.] Ervin and Melva Mathe; [m.] Richard Andrews, August 30, 1969; [ch.] William Gilbert; [ed.] Random Lake High, Mt. Senario College/Bus. Admin. (No Degree, yet); [occ.] Nuclear Security - Access Authorization/Control Wisconsin Electric/Point Beach Nuclear Plant; [memb.] Manitowoc Historical Society, Nat'l. Geographic Society, Smithsonian Institute; [oth. writ.] Most are copyrighted but unpublished to date: Daughter-In-Law, Grandmother, Dearest Husband, A Wedding Prayer, Farewell Friend, 50th Wedding Anniversary, Ode To The Green Bay Packers, Oh Poor, Lonesome Me; [pers.] Some people we come in contact with play a significant part in our lives. I strive to dedicate a special poem to those who are important to me.; [a.] Two Rivers, WI

ANDREWS, LANETTE
[b.] October 29, 1981, Twentynine Palms, CA; [p.] Nanette and David Clawson; [ed.] Currently in High School called Fallbrook Union High School; [occ.] Student; [pers.] Poems come from your heart and your soul. It's a door way for the freedom of your most deep feelings, or desires. They let you share all that you feel and hope for.; [a.] Oceanside, CA

ANDRUS, JOAN DICKINSON
[pen.] Joanie Andrus; [b.] September 13, 1929, South Bend, IN; [p.] Russell and Mildred Dickinson (Davis); [m.] Donald F. Andrus, July 20, 1985; [ch.] Tom-Larry

- Glenn Eckert, Laura Blue; [ed.] Adams High School South Bend Ind., Business School South Bend Ind., Modeling School South Bend Ind., Cosmetology School San Antonio Texas; [occ.] Retired Nurse; [memb.] 1st United Methodist Church; [oth. writ.] Song lyrics (Tin Pan Alley), plays for School (P.T.A.), short stories for children, artist (draw and paint).; [pers.] I love people - have great compassion for others. Inspiration comes from God.; [a.] Escondido, CA

ANGELL, TIMOTHY
[b.] September 22, 1976, Corpus Christi, TX; [p.] David Angell, Debra Angell; [ed.] Richard King High School, Schreiner College; [occ.] Full-time Engineering student and Math Tutor, Schreiner College; [memb.] CRLA certified tutor; [hon.] President's List; [oth. writ.] Several poems and stories written for personal reasons only; [pers.] I write my poems for others to enjoy because I get satisfaction by making others happy.; [a.] Corpus Christi, TX

ANOLES, JON E.
[b.] August 8, 1954, Lima, OH; [p.] Mike and Mary Ann Anoles; [m.] Beth E. Anoles, September 16, 1941; [ed.] Whitehall Yearling High, Clark Tech. College, Upper Valley JVS School of Practical Nursing; [occ.] Nurse (LPN); [memb.] National Assn. of Practical Nurse Education (NAPNES), Springfield Chapter Fraternal Order of Eagles (F.U.E.), Springfield Chapter, Machinist Union; [hon.] Was recognized as Nurse of the Year in National Nurses' week at my place of employment by my fellow Nurses and staff; [oth. writ.] Numerous collections of short stories, Sci-fi fiction waiting for me to get up the nerve to do something with them, as so many people have prompted me to do.; [pers.] Be good and kind to all living things, a special place waits for those who are, we all matter!; [a.] Piqua, OH

ANONSEN, THELMA
[pen.] Roxy; [b.] July 31, 1941, Montpelier, VT; [p.] Edward and Bertice Bellmore; [m.] Paul J. Anonsen, January 31, 1971; [ch.] Three - Shane, Ardelle, Slade; [ed.] Boone High; [occ.] Retired; [oth. writ.] Two poems were published in my school newspaper.; [pers.] I have enjoyed writing poetry since 1953. Many events in my life were reflected in my poems, thereby becoming an ongoing poetic journal of sorts.; [a.] Orlando, FL

ANTHONY, GLORIA M.
[b.] March 25, 1935, Panama; [p.] Mercedes and Isidoro Samaniego; [m.] Roger R. Anthony, July 7, 1961; [ch.] Three - Randy, Eric, Shawn; [ed.] High School; [occ.] Antiques, Buy, Sell and Restore; [hon.] Honorable Mention Silver Poet 1986 World of Poetry, Golden Poet 1987 World of Poetry, Silver Poet 1989 World of Poetry, 2 Silver Poet 1990 World of Poetry, 2 Silver Poet 1990 World of Poetry, Silver prize 2 - 1974-74 Clover International Poetry Competition; [oth. writ.] VIA Vietnam - Piedmont Library Society - Honorable Mention "Echoes In A Shell", Orovan Book. Library of Congress Catalog Card No. 74-77317.; [pers.] When you look at someone and find him ugly it is because you are seeing your own reflection in the mirror of his eyes.; [a.] Dale City, VA

APODACA, ERIC J.
[b.] May 6, 1980, Montebello, CA; [p.] Lorraine and John Valadez; [ed.] High School Student Chino High School (Chino, California); [hon.] Who's Who Among American High School Students 94-95 and 95-96. Academic Pin, Honor Roll; [pers.] White fear is that which drives us to avoid exposure, it is also that which brings exposure about us.; [a.] Ontario, CA

APPLEYARD, MARIAN LEWIS
[b.] April 21, 1917, Panama, NY; [p.] Ray L. Lewis, Anna C. Lewis; [m.] John S. Appleyard, August 12, 1940; [ch.] Dennis, Jack, Wayne; [ed.] Jamestown High, Buffalo State Teachers College (Now SUNY); [occ.] Homemaker; [memb.] Plainville United Methodist, Plainville Woman's Club, Literary Club, Methodist Camping Club; [hon.] Valedictorian Jamestown High School 1935, Kings Daughters Chautauqua Scholarship, Kappa Delta Pi, Phi Upsilon Omicron; [oth. writ.] Other songs: The Hymn of the Vietnam Soldier, Winnepesaukee, Connecticut my Home; [pers.] I write folk songs with a message. The music comes to me in "tongues" (tongues is a gift of the spirit in I Corinthians 12:28) I am concerned about peace and preserving natural beauty.; [a.] Plainville, CT

ARBOUR, SALENA
[b.] July 23, 1970, Augusta, ME; [p.] Leon Paradis and Diane Bennett; [m.] Shawn Arbour, August 29, 1992; [ch.] Natalie Arbour; [ed.] Cony High School; [occ.] Disabled; [memb.] St. Mary's Church UPAPH Foundation; [oth. writ.] Several other poems titled: "Angels", "Sunshine", "Wedding Wish", and "Curry Jo".; [pers.] My goal in my writings is to inspire and to express feelings of hope, faith and forgiveness to all who need enlightenment.; [a.] Windsor, ME

ARMSTRONG, GAIL
[b.] October 1, 1964, New York, NY; [p.] Del Armstrong and Gloria Armstrong; [ed.] Old Wetbury School of the Holy Child, Bates College (BA), Georgetown University (MA), University of Colorado (ND); [occ.] Nurse - RN; [memb.] Bates Key, Sigma Theta Tau; [hon.] Sigma Theta, Tau, Dean's List; [pers.] My work as a nurse and perspective as a writer encourage me to see and understand the common, and unifying strains of the human experience.; [a.] Denver, CO

AROWOLO, AUDREY
[pen.] Audrey Nelson; [b.] Lagos, Nigeria; [p.] Shirley and Gregory Nelson; [m.] Ibrahim Arowolo; [ed.] Queen Amina College, University of Uyo - Nigeria; [oth. writ.] Poems and writings published in press journals while in college.; [pers.] I write about what I think and see, but more about what I feel.; [a.] Oak Park, IL

ARRINGTON, PATRICIA
[pen.] Buttons; [b.] July 16, 1983, New York City; [p.] Renee Arrington, Edward Brown; [ed.] P.S. 176/I.S. 59 8th grade; [memb.] Jibouti Cheerleading Team, Umoja Models, Student Government, Black Spectrum Theatre Youth Company; [hon.] Honor roll, 7th Grade President, 8th Grade Class President; [oth. writ.] I published in my Elementary and Junior High School Year Books.; [pers.] I don't use my head to write although I'm very smart. Instead I look closer inside and I use my heart.; [a.] Stalbans, NY

ARTHUR I, GARY R.
[b.] January 7, 1945, Linton, IN; [p.] Ruth and Yakey Arthur; [m.] Mildred J. Arthur, November 20, 1973; [ch.] Angela, Steven, Chris, Richard, Jennifer; [ed.] High School Graduate; [occ.] Truck Driver; [memb.] Moose Lodge, Eagles Lodge, Otterbein Methodist Church, Teamsters Union; [hon.] Numerous safe driving awards; [oth. writ.] Numerous poems and song lyrics; [pers.] I consider any talents I may have to be divine gifts and accept them as such.; [a.] Linton, IN

ARTYMIUK, JESSICA
[b.] April 8, 1983, Milwaukee, WI; [p.] David and Sandra Artymiuk; [ed.] 8th Grade; [occ.] Student at St.

Veronica's, Grade School; [memb.] I am an Editor of our school newspaper, a classroom representative for Student Council, a cadet, an allocate (server), and I'm in drama, handbell choir, forensics; [hon.] I have been on the All-star Excellent Honor Roll at school since the 4th grade. I received two scholarships for Christianity and my academics, also pins and ribbons for various activities.; [oth. writ.] I have written many various poems and a short story which I haven't yet sent to be published.; [pers.] I love to write and I am inspired by my feelings and inspirations. I value family, friendships, my independence life and love. I try to live life to the fullest.; [a.] Milwaukee, WI

ASTORINO, ANNETTE M.
[b.] October 6, 1970, Mahopac, NY; [p.] Louis and Rosa Astorino; [ed.] Mahopac High School, Marist College, Long Island University; [occ.] Bank Teller-Chase Manhattan Bank; [pers.] Love can inspire great things, my boyfriend Dave is my inspiration. Nothing is more important than love and family.; [a.] Mahopac, NY

ATHERTON, HOLLY
[b.] July 31, 1985; [p.] Emma Atherton; [ed.] Imlay City Middle School, Imlay City, Michigan; [occ.] Student; [hon.] Thirteen times on the Honor Roll; [oth. writ.] One poem published in a local newspaper and one poem written for the Reflections Program through the school.; [pers.] Inspiration comes to me from my mom and third-grade teacher, Ms. Warnars. They constantly encourage me to keep writing. They tell me my writing touches hearts.; [a.] Imlay City, MI

ATTERIDGE, JEAN
[b.] October 17, 1921, Minneapolis, MN; [p.] Charles and Helen Davis; [m.] Clinton D. Atteridge (Deceased), October 9, 1940; [ch.] Two daughters, Diane J. Jensen, Cheryl McCullough; [ed.] Graduate Roosevelt High School, Mpls., Minn. (1939); [occ.] Retired Credit Union Asst. Mgr.; [pers.] My poem is my first attempt at writing. My desire was to put my thoughts of my late husband on paper as a tribute to our long marriage neverending love for each other.; [a.] Bremerton, WA

AUBERRY, BRENDA
[m.] Carl W. Auberry; [ch.] Dennis, David, Daniel; [oth. writ.] I have poems on most topics I had one poem my Doctor donated for me hanging in the medical center in Louisville, KY; [pers.] I love to write, paint, carve wood figures, sew and other arts and crafts.; [a.] Lebanon, KY

AUSTIN, PATRICE CAMILLE
[pen.] Maverick; [b.] August 8, 1980, Illinois; [p.] Roosevelt and Sylvia Hudson; [ed.] Paul Robeson High School 11th grade; [occ.] Artist; [hon.] Honor Roll Certificate, Saxophone Player for Paul Robeson Band; [pers.] I was inspired by my most talented father Roosevelt Hudson who writes under the pen name Ric Velle. Much love to my immediate and outside family.; [a.] Chicago, IL

AUSTIN, VEOLIA
[pen.] Vea Skys; [b.] July 8, 1952, Arkansas; [p.] Earl Austin and Oradell Austin; [m.] August 7, 1970; [ch.] Denishola H., Donald R., Joseph R.; [ed.] Marvell High, C.C.A.C., College, Electronic Technetronic School and Business School, received Certificates from all Schools and Tractor Trail - School; [occ.] Tranportation - Patransit and Home-Base Business, Lifeplus; [memb.] J.W. and Heart Ass., Cancer Ass. and Children Abuse Ass. and Animal Ass.; [hon.] Certificate of Achievement, Most Valuable Performers, Contribution to Excellence and Quality at Port Authority of Allegheny County,

(M.V.P. Trophies, Plaques), Engraving with Achievement; [oth. writ.] (Black Bird Trapped), In White Sand of American! (In Book Form), "Black Bird!" Trapped In The Cave, Policies! (In Newspaper); [pers.] I strive to reflect my good ability to help mankind in a positive way so they can look at me as a shining light in their life and open their mind - and heart - to see good.; [a.] Pittsburgh, PA

AYE, DARRYL GABLE
[pen.] Darryl Gable Aye; [b.] March 11, 1961, New York, NY; [p.] Burl and Anna Aye; [ed.] Germain School of Photography; [memb.] International Poetry Hall of Fame; [oth. writ.] "My Aphrodisiac"; [a.] New York, NY

AYRES, ANNE
[pen.] A. Annie, Ava Anne, Anne Ayres; [b.] December 21, 1951, Maryland; [p.] Langdon and Edwardine Ayres; [ch.] Jennifer, Geoffrey, Robert, David, Jerome, Kristen, Beth, Andy, Joey; [ed.] 14 yrs.; [occ.] Receptionist; [pers.] A smile and a kind word can change a day, or even a life.; [a.] Arcadia, CA

BAILEY, CAROL
[pen.] Carol Bailey; [b.] February 20, 1933, Owego, NY; [p.] Jay and Caroline Schmidt; [m.] Divorced - Jerry Bailey, December 4, 1954; [ch.] Jeffrey, Cathy; [ed.] 15 years grammar, two years business, one year nursing; [occ.] Retired; [memb.] Union Presbyterian Church, AARP, other; [hon.] Several accolades personally, your poetry contest semi-finalist; [oth. writ.] Re- Treasures and Artifacts, several commentaries letters to wise editorials; [pers.] In my pain! I wrote to rid of "It", "In",!! "My", "Thought Pains!!; [a.] Endicott, NY

BAILEY JR., DAVID E.
[b.] August 5, 1917, Taylor County, FL; [p.] Mr. and Mrs. D. E. Bailey Jr. (Deceased); [m.] Eloise D. Bailey, August 22, 1940; [ch.] David M. Bailey, Randi Sue Cox; [ed.] B.S. from Florida Southern Education, from Univ. of Florida Graduate degree in 1955. Additional study at the Univ. of South Fla in Tampa; [occ.] Retired from the School Board of Hillsborough Co. Fla. as teacher and elem. school principal after 40 years of service.; [memb.] Historical Societies of local and state levels and Springhead Civic Club. East Hillsborough Retired Education Association - member of First Baptist church, Plant Cit, Fla; [hon.] Upon my retirement, the city of Plant City, Fla. declared David E. Bailey Day. "Citizen of the Year Award" by 10 Civic clubs in 1978, "Outstanding Service to Humanity," Award by Florida Southern College Alumni Association in 1993.; [oth. writ.] College, Lakeland, Florida, M.A. in 1949 Rank I Advanced winner of Essay Contest during World War II entitled, "What I am Fighting For". - Co-author of the book, "Plant City: It's Origin and History" in 1977 with the late Quintilla Geer Bruton. Co-authored play, "That Man Plant," in 1985; [pers.] Have been interested in drama and acting. Here appeared in several local plays. Have given a number of speeches, and have done poetry reading, locally; [a.] Plant City, FL

BAILLARGEON, LISE
[b.] November 6, 1980, Columbia, CA; [p.] Denis R. Baillargeon, Marie A. Baillargeon; [ed.] Junior, Woodstock Academy, Woodstock Conneticut; [occ.] Student, Woodstock Academy; [pers.] Everything that runs through my hand came through my ears first the music.; [a.] Pomfret, CT

BAINES, GEORGE
[b.] February 18, 1970, Philadelphia, PA; [p.] Diane Baines; [ed.] Camden High, Rowan College of NJ, BS in Business Adn; [occ.] Technical Computer Analyst; [pers.] I try to write about only what I have experienced

and then briefly touch on it so that someone would get a glimpse. I always put Jesus first in everything I do.; [a.] Williamstown, NJ

BAKER, AMY
[b.] March 2, 1974, Colorado City; [p.] R. W. and Donna Baker; [ed.] Glen Rose ISD Howard Payne University; [pers.] God is the light that can pull you out of any darkness. I'm proof. Thanks Lord!; [a.] Fort Worth, TX

BAKER, DONNA M.
[pen.] Donna M. Baker, [b.] February 12, 1936, Norman, OK; [p.] Loyd and Aline Vanderburg; [m.] James C. Baker, February 6, 1971; [ch.] Two (previous marriage) M. L. Brown; [ed.] High School Grad (and school of Hard Knocks); [occ.] High School Custodian, was Waitress 41 yrs. (13 was in Las Vegas NV); [memb.] Union Local #226 Las Vegas; [oth. writ.] The School Custodian This Day's Agenda OKC's Custodian F.B.I. and Ms. T. about Integrity.; [pers.] Always place principles before personalities and try to be open-minded.; [a.] Oklahoma City, OK

BAKER, JAMES ERIC
[pen.] Jim Baker; [b.] November 22, 1984, Korea; [p.] Russell and Cheryl Baker; [ed.] 6th grader at Mayfield Woods Middle School; [occ.] Student; [hon.] Jr. Black Belt in Togakure Ryu Ninjutsu; [a.] Columbia, MD

BAKER, JUDITH D.
[pen.] J. D. Nicholson; [b.] April 4, 1966, Millinocket, ME; [p.] Shirley Nicholson and Lewis Nicholson; [m.] Daniel F. Baker, September 26, 1987; [ed.] Schenck High School, Husson College (AS), College of New Rochelle (BSN); [occ.] Registered Nurse; [memb.] Mentor Program; [hon.] Sigma Theta Tall, Honor Society for Nurses; [pers.] Exercise to celebrate the body, pray to celebrate the spirit, write to celebrate the mind, learn to celebrate them all.; [a.] New Rochelle, NY

BANDO, ALEXANDRA
[pen.] Alex or Ali; [b.] February 26, 1986, San Rafael; [p.] Lorena, Barnett Bando; [oth. writ.] Soul, My House, A Wicked Old House.; [pers.] I am so glad I got to be picked for my poem.; [a.] Woodacre, CA

BANERJEE, P. K.
[b.] May 14, 1923, Salkia-Howrah, India; [p.] Manmatha Banerjee, Prabhabati Banerjee; [m.] Sova Banerjee, June 3, 1956; [ch.] Sumana Mukherjee, Paula Gangopadhyay; [ed.] B.SC. Calcutta University; [occ.] Retired Marketing, Executive: Free Lance Journalist; [hon.] Stood First in World Wide Competition for an Article "A Day In The Life Of A Salesman" sponsored by Ms. Philips of Nether Land my Employers for their Pharmaceutical Dept. (DUPHAR); [oth. writ.] Articles in Daily Newspapers - mostly Political Satire.; [pers.] 1. You can't be plus in every aspect of life, 2. From birth till death you have to adjust - adjust and constantly adjust.; [a.] Okemos, MI

BANINI, BONNY
[b.] December 15, 1980, West Africa; [p.] Miranda Odamtten and Festus Banini; [ed.] High School Student at Palisades Charter High School; [occ.] Student; [hon.] On the Dean's Honor Roll at Palisades High School; [oth. writ.] Other poems which has never been published including: "Reminders of the Past" and "America".; [pers.] My poems are a reflection of myself and they act as a mirror for the world to look into my soul and my inner being. My poems allow me to express myself lyrically.; [a.] Los Angeles, CA

BANNATYNE, MARK WILLIAM McKENZIE
[b.] May 22, 1952, West Chester, PA; [p.] Isobel S. Bannatyne; [m.] Tatiana Yurievna Bannatyne (Scherbakova), September 2, 1990; [ch.] Yuri Markovich Bannatyne (son, 5 yrs.), Kirill Markovich Bannatyne (son, 2 yrs.), B.Sc. Utah State University (1988); [ed.] M.Sc. Utah State University (1992), Ph.D., Purdue University (1994); [occ.] Assistant Professor of Secondary and Post secondary Vocational/Adult Education, University of Nevada, Las Vegas (UNLV); [memb.] American Vocational Association, Phi Kappa Phi Honor Society, The Church of Jesus Christ of Latter-day Saints; [hon.] Who's Who in American Education, Who's Who in the West, Who's Who in the World, Phi Kappa Phi Honor Society, International Friend of the Year (1988, Utah State University); [oth. writ.] "Focus '96: Russia Along the Volga (Technology Teacher, Nov. 1996), "Truth, Justice and the American Way: Our View of the Foreigner in American Comic Books (Popular Culture Review, 1997 January issue), "Current Trends in Industrial Education and Vocational Training in the Republics of the Former Soviet Union" (ERIC, 1996)".; [pers.] I believe that we can all be great for we can all give service (Martin Luther King). Indeed, I believe the quiet way is always the best (My grandmother). Chance favors the prepared life. (T. S. Monson); [a.] Las Vegas, NV

BANNING, PHILIP
[b.] July 11, 1975, North Tarrytown, NY; [p.] George Banning and Marylou Banning; [ed.] Forest High, Boston University, University of Montana; [hon.] Phi Kappa Phi, Dean's List; [pers.] Two letters keep resounding, K and B.; [a.] Ocala, FL

BARBARO, TAMARA ANN
[b.] July 30, 1986, Hartwell, GA; [p.] Mr. and Mrs. Steven R. Barbaro; [ed.] I am in the Fifth Grade. My mother Home Schools us.; [memb.] In the past I have been a member of Drama Club, Computer Club, Girls Scouts, and Cheerleading. I have won awards in Cheerleading, school and in track and field.; [oth. writ.] I like to write but this is the first writing I have had published.; [pers.] I believe everyone should love God and their family. My favorite music is classical. My favorite food is Pizza. I love to sing and dance. I enjoy outdoor sports and activities. I love playing with my little sister, Annabelle.; [a.] Buford, GA

BARR, ERIN
[b.] July 21, 1989, Fontana, CA; [p.] David Barr, Karen Barr; [ed.] Currently in second grade (Ms. Tucker's Class) at Plavan Elementary School, Fountain Valley, California; [occ.] Student; [memb.] The Great Pacific Nation Indian Princesses, Navajo Tribe; [hon.] Language Arts Achievement Award, Plavan School; [oth. writ.] Other poems.; [pers.] For my sister, Tara, and my grandparents.; [a.] Fountain Valley, CA

BARR, KAREN
[pen.] Karen Barr; [b.] September 10, 1957, Redwood City, CA; [p.] Donald Phipps Sr., Marian Phipps; [m.] David Barr, March 26, 1988; [ch.] Erin Victoria, Tara Lynne; [ed.] Covina High School, Covina, CA - 1994; [occ.] Manager of Budgets, Southern California Edison; [memb.] International Society of Poets, Academy of American Poets; [oth. writ.] NLP Publications: "Secret Garden", "All You Ever Were", also published by Anderie Poetry Press (print) and Blue Mountain Arts (electronic), currently working on a collection of children's stories in rhyme.; [pers.] "Destiny" is dedicated to my father.; [a.] Long Beach, CA

BARR, MICHAEL
[b.] August 21, 1959, Charles City, IA; [p.] Ronald R. Barr, Patricia M. Barr; [ed.] High School, Ottumwa, Iowa; [occ.] Furniture Installation; [memb.] P.A.D.I. - Professional Association Diving Instructors; [pers.] To truly be loved is to live, to truly love is to be inspired to have both is what our souls seek (Thanks Beca).; [a.] Seattle, WA

BARRETT, GINA
[pen.] Gina B.; [b.] November 24, 1963, Chicago, IL; [p.] Patricia Jackson and William Davis; [ed.] Whitney Young High School Cornell College, Truman College; [occ.] Registered Nurse; [memb.] American Association of Critical-Care Nurses; [hon.] Phi Theta Kappa, Honors List; [pers.] Poetry for me is an emotional catharsis whose intent is to teach, to touch and aspire to change.; [a.] Chicago, IL

BARRETT, KRISTA LEANNE
[pen.] K. L. Barrett; [b.] October 13, 1973, Memorial Hospital, Long Beach, CA; [p.] Stuart W. Barrett, Diane Barrett-Hickman; [ed.] Artesia High School, Lakewood Ca, California State University Long Beach (B.A. Psychology) (Minor Spanish), Master's Degree Student in Social Work; [occ.] Social Work; [memb.] ISP (International Society of Poets) Member, NASW (National Association of Social Workers), Member, Counsellor, Advocate for SuCasa; [hon.] Editor's Choice Award (My Dearest...); [oth. writ.] Poems published/to be published in the future, My Dearest..., Innocence Forsaken, No Ordinary Friday, True Love?, Natural Wonder, Transformation, Perils or Life?, Fluttering Heart, Believe, A Child's Glow, The Joy of Your Friendship, Mystery Man, Spiritual Trial, What Beauty Means...Degrees of Life.; [pers.] "I praise my Lord Jesus Christ for my life and His blessings. Inspired by God in 1995 (through the loss of my father) I began to write poetry. I hope to someday be a recognized professional poet.";[a.] Lakewood, CA

BARRETT, LORA
[b.] January 27, 1960, Lancaster, OH; [p.] John McCarty and Winifred McCarty; [m.] William Barrett, June 9, 1979; [ch.] Andrea and Roger; [ed.] Bloom Carroll High School graduated in June 1979, Carroll, OH; [occ.] I drive a school bus, for Fairfield Union Sch. Dist. Rushville, OH; [memb.] I belong to the First Baptist Church of Carroll, Carroll, OH; [pers.] A poem or story, everything I write is a reflection of how I'm feeling or an experience I've personally had. And if someone can read my work and relate to it. Then I've done my job. My biggest influence has been the people I've been blessed to know and love in my life.; [a.] Lancaster, OH

BARRETT, OAKLEY C.
[pen.] Oak; [b.] February 26, 1931, Columbia, IN; [p.] Wm. Barrett, Fayra Barrett; [m.] Clara R. Barrett, March 20, 1954; [ch.] Charles, Willia, Fayra Steven; [ed.] Kendalville High; [occ.] Retired; [memb.] VFW 4095, American Legion 807; [a.] Olivehurst, CA

BARROWS, JOSH
[pen.] The Dreamer; [b.] March 31, 1980, Fort Hood, TX; [p.] Mindy Barrows, Kenneth Barrows; [ed.] West Aurora High School (junior); [oth. writ.] A Lover's Thought, Beat, Words Spoken, The Earth, The Wind, Sweet Dreams, Her Utopia, Utopia 2, A Killer's Description and many more.; [pers.] Dreams are what hold people together. Hope is a delusion of reality.; [a.] Aurora, IL

BARSALEAU, RICHARD
[pen.] Richard Barsaleau; [b.] August 17, 1925, PA; [p.] Henry and Grace; [m.] Maggie, April 9, 1970; [ch.] Five;

[ed.] Colorado State University, School of Veterinary Medicine; [occ.] Doctor of Veterinary Medicine (Retired); [memb.] American Veterinary Medical Assn. (AVMA), California V.M.A., Sacramento Valley VMA, American Assn. of Equine Practitioners; [oth. writ.] Magazine articles: Western Horseman numerous poems.; [pers.] A working horseman, a lifelong student of the horse.; [a.] Loomis, CA

BARTL, SCOTT R.
[b.] January 11, 1957, Cleveland, OH; [m.] Rebecca S. Bartl, October 17, 1981; [ch.] Benjamin, Molly, Faith; [pers.] Tears are the rain that cleanse our souls. Poetry is the storm that brings the rain.; [a.] Bedford, OH

BARTON, JAMES
[b.] October 27, 1965, East Orange; [p.] Joseph and Patricia Barton; [ed.] H.S. diploma, 3 yrs. of College at Ocean County College for computer programming; [occ.] Struggling writer; [memb.] Museum of Nat'l History, Nat'l Authors registry, Iliad Press; [hon.] "Famous poet for 1996", "The Diamond Homer" 1996, (Famous Poets Society); [oth. writ.] Published in "Musings" (Iliad Press) book collection of short stories by Jim Barton (Watermark Press, 1995).; [pers.] Became a quadriplegic at 19. Been writing since High School.; [a.] Barnegat, NJ

BASHAM, GARLYN ARGABRIGHT
[pen.] C. W. Burke; [b.] February 20, 1913, Delano, CA; [p.] William E. and Bessie Argabright Basham; [m.] Dixie Mildred Basham, September 4, 1934; [ch.] Roger E. and Laurance A. Basham; [ed.] BA, Univ. of Calif. at Santa Barbara, MA, Univ. Southern Calif. Grad. Studies Stanford, UCLA, Fresno State Univ., Univ. of Nevada; [occ.] Retired College President; [memb.] Freemasons, Shriners, Scottish Rite, Kiwanis, American Legion, Veterans of Foreign Wars, Royal Order of Scotland, Nashville Songwriters Assoc., Int'l DeMolays; [hon.] Alumni Assoc. award in Education (Univ. of Calif. Santa Barbara), Patriot of the Year (Scottish Rite), DeMolay Legion of Honor, Commendation award from Adm. W. F. Halsey, Cmdr. Third Fleet WW2, President Emeritus Taft College; [oth. writ.] "Lord, We're Calling You at 9-1-1 in Heaven", "We Pray to You from Planet Earth", "Quest of the Double Eagle", It's a Lonesome Old Town", "Mail Order Catalogue Blues", "At the Parting of the Ways", etc. My poems and song lyrics are mainly related to spiritual faith and personal relationships in contemporary America.; [a.] Santa Barbara, CA

BAVOSO, EDWARD
[b.] March 6, 1961, Bronx, NY; [p.] Angelo Bavoso, Josephine Bavoso; [m.] Divorced; [ed.] Blind Brook H.S., Niagara University; [occ.] Owns a distribution Co, Freelance writer; [oth. writ.] Short stories, journalism, editorials; [pers.] To reach out to others who feel the isolation and despair of depression. I write as a native, not a tourist.; [a.] Somers, NY

BAYARD, YSEULT
[p.] Scherer Craan, Engineer, Francine Craan, Educator; [ch.] Victoria Bayard, Lawyer; [ed.] College; [occ.] Writer; [memb.] International Society of Poets; [hon.] Editor's Choice Award for Outstanding Achievement in Poetry, 1996; [oth. writ.] Poems published in Literary Anthologies.; [pers.] I was trained in the art of poetry writing by my mother who introduced me to the ways of the European Literary Masters at a very young age. My writings tend to capture the igniting feelings visiting man's soul in his yearning for oneness with his universe and to celebrate these intangibles which often act as a catalyst for his transformation. I also sometimes focus on current moral issues.; [a.] Manhattan, NY

BAYLOR, SHIRLEY A.
[b.] November 19, 1947, Camp Kilmer, NJ; [p.] Mary L. and Lawrence C. Dixon; [m.] Addison O. Baylor, November 5, 1988; [ch.] Ruben J. Scott and Jason F. Scott; [ed.] 1965 High School Graduate plus 2.0 years of Junior College and Computer classes; [occ.] Senior Secretary, University of Washington; [oth. writ.] Short story to Ebony Magazine in November, 1992; [pers.] Show respect toward others in all you say and do.; [a.] Everett, WA

BEASLEY, JENNIFER
[b.] January 17, 1984, Forrest County, MS; [p.] Sandy and Ben Beasley; [ed.] 7th grade; [occ.] Student; [memb.] Mathcounts; [hon.] Honor student, science award; [oth. writ.] Poems published for the Illiad Press and Anthology of Poetry by Young Americans.; [a.] Collins, MS

BECHTHOLD, DONNA L.
[b.] February 28, 1946, Vancouver, B.C., Canada; [p.] Harold and Myrtle Blize; [m.] H. Wayne Bechthold, August 4, 1963; [ch.] Christine, Brenda, Deana; [ed.] Univ. of Tenn. Nashville; [occ.] R.N., Vice President Pt. Care Services; [oth. writ.] Book published: The Colors of Prayer; [a.] Tillamook, OR

BEHRMANN, LEILAH
[pen.] Ashlee Taylor; [b.] August 5, 1982, Haiti; [p.] Josselyne and Clarck Behrmann; [ed.] Currently going to Hackettstown High School (Freshman); [hon.] Winner of essay contests, poem published in "The Star Gazette; [oth. writ.] Several other poems and essays.; [pers.] I enjoy writing, and not only to enrich my mind, but to also have fun and be creative.; [a.] Hackettstown, NJ

BELBECK, BOBBIE
[pen.] Bobbie Ann Belbeck; [b.] August 29, 1956, Chelsea, MA; [p.] Vie Oswalt and William McDonald (or McDonald); [m.] Randy Belbeck, July 11, 1987; [ch.] Keandra Porter; [ed.] Roscommon High, Spring Arbor College, Michigan State University, Psychology, B.S. Oakland University some graduate work in Dev. Psych.; [occ.] Homemaker; [memb.] M.S.U. Phi Kappa Phi Honor Society, M.S.U. Tau Sigma Honor Society Dean's List; [hon.] High School Valedictorian (1974) member of 1974 Blue Lake International Band John Philip Sonsa Award (H.S. Band, 1974) H.S. National Honor Society; [oth. writ.] Working on several books and copy writing research projects.; [pers.] My main goals in life are to serve God and to seek his wisdom.; [a.] DeWitt, MI

BELFRY, MICHAEL HOWARD
[b.] September 13, 1960, Lansing, MI; [p.] Wayne Theodore Belfry and Judy Kay Belfry-Verteuille; [ed.] Commercial Cooking, Real Estate, Computer Programming and Computer Operations; [occ.] Computer Operator with American Airlines; [memb.] American Airlines Employee Assistance Program; [hon.] Survivor of Polio and Cancer, have won awards for Paintings in Art Shows; [oth. writ.] Editor of company newsletter.; [pers.] Most important always keep God in your thoughts and a song in your heart couldn't hurt. God will only give you what you can handle - trust Him. Live today to the fullest and leave tomorrow to God, but do not forget your yesterdays.; [a.] Irving, TX

BELL, BARBARA L.
[pen.] B. Nefertari (on occasion); [b.] November 23, Atlantic City, NJ; [ch.] Four adult children; [ed.] BA Richard Stockton State College Pomona, N.J., AA Atlantic Community College Mays Landing, N.J., Ordained Local Elder African Methodist Episcopal Church Religious Studies, Lutheran Seminary, Phila. PA; [occ.] Zon-

ing Officer, City of Atlantic City; [memb.] St. James A.M.E. Church, Atl. City serving as Associate Minister, Fellowship of Churches, Atl. City and Vicinity, NAACP; [oth. writ.] Play, "Ruth," Skits for church school children. Poems for special occasions with a special person. Articles for local newspaper.; [pers.] Each day has a new blessing and a new poem that will lift us higher than we were yesterday.; [a.] Atlantic City, NJ

BELL, ISAAC M.
[pen.] Isaac Bell (Isaac Belotserkovsky); [b.] April 23, 1933, Kiev, Ukraine; [p.] Michael Belotserkovsky, Maria Turkenich; [m.] Valentina Bell (Semenichina), August 29, 1964; [ch.] Robert, Veronica; [ed.] MSEE from LVOV Polytechnic Institute (Ukraine); [occ.] Electronics Engineer, Thomson Consumer Electronics; [memb.] Institute of Electrical and Electronics Engineers (IEEE); [hon.] High School Silver Medal and College Diploma with Highest Distinction for Scholastic Achievements, 14 articles published in professional magazines, granted 22 patents, mentioned in 1993-94 Registry, "Who's Who Worldwide"; [oth. writ.] More than 200 original poems in Russian and English and translations from Russian to English, two dozens songs (Both music and lyrics). Not published.; [a.] Indianapolis, IN

BELZITI, RICHARD R.
[b.] January 26, 1961, US; [p.] Ivana Albanese and Salvatore Belziti; [ed.] St. Stanisluos Gramma School, St. Francis Preparatory High, St. John University College; [occ.] Laborer and tileman and mason carpenter; [oth. writ.] Time With You, A Mother's Reward, I Saw A Star Tonight, Trying Times, My Heart Is In My Hand, You My Friend I Thank You Lord, The Silence, over 100 other writings.; [pers.] A person's true life is within his or her heart, when alone in life a person can find him or herself looking within.; [a.] New York, NY

BENJAMIN, MARY M.
[b.] January 16, 1930, Youngstown, NY; [p.] Margaret H. Linneen; [m.] Lawrence D. Benjamin, January 28, 1950; [ch.] Two girls and two boys; [ed.] High School - 12 Months of Child Care.; [occ.] Retired - Volunteer Church Worker Singer; [hon.] Volunteers - two one from a School and one from Mental Health Orog. Ages 55 and over.; [oth. writ.] Alot of poems I am having typed.; [pers.] Yesterday's gone and tomorrow is out of sight. So lots you and I dance with Jesus tonight.; [a.] Margate, FL

BENNETT, CONNIE
[b.] October 31, 1944, Houston, TX; [p.] Mr. and Mrs. Coy Dowdle; [ch.] Two, son and daughter; [ed.] High School (Graham), Cosmetology at Pensacola Junior College, Pensacola, Florida; [occ.] Cosmetologist; [memb.] First Methodist Church, Graham, TX; [hon.] Honor graduate with A.S. in Cosmetology at PJC in 1980. Hairstyling competition - 1st place, in 1980. Judged competition in 1985. Class President '79-'80; [oth. writ.] I've written many poems, of all types - never entered any, just shared them with family members. My son encouraged me to do this one.; [pers.] I was inspired for this poem, as my brother was dying of cancer - it meant a lot to him - after his death, I added the last few lines and read it at his funeral.; [a.] Graham, TX

BENTLEY, MELISSA
[b.] July 22, 1964, North Wilkesboro, NC; [ed.] University of North Carolina - Greensboro, Southeastern Theological Seminary; [pers.] This bio should be about Sheila Wilson a survivor of Hodgkins Disease, she lives in Olathe, Kansas with husband Steve and sons Jacob and Samuel. She embodies true human courage and tenacity.; [a.] Asheboro, NC

BERGERON, RUTH D.
[b.] February 25, 1921, Lutcher, LA; [p.] Ricard and Lavinia R. Dugas; [m.] Clayton Bergeron (Deceased), September 9, 1962; [ed.] High School; [occ.] Retired; [memb.] St. Joseph's Church Rosary Altar Society, Telephone Pioneers of America, C.W.A. Union Life Member; [hon.] President of TPA Life Members 1991-93, TPA BAT - Ray - Mobile Award; [oth. writ.] Poems published: "Sixty at Last", "Seventy Five Alive", "It's Easter", "We Celebrate," "Thanks Mom", "Father Dear".; [pers.] Continued encouragement from family and friends.; [a.] Ponchatoula, LA

BERILLA, ELIZABETH
[b.] July 23, 1985, Washington, DC; [p.] Eileen and Paul Berilla; [ed.] 6th grade student at St. Mary's Elementary School, Annapolis, MD; [occ.] Student; [hon.] Creative writing contest winner (1994) for Archdiocese of Baltimore; [oth. writ.] "The Four Seasons," "A Snowy Morning," "A Christmas Poem"; [pers.] I love reading, music, lacrosse, ice skating, and animals.; [a.] Annapolis, MD

BESSIRE, ASHLEY
[b.] December 24, 1982, Fort Worth, TX; [p.] Mike and Gineen Bessire; [ed.] Kindergarten through eighth grade at Trinity Valley School; [occ.] Student at Trinity Valley School; [memb.] 1st United Methodist Church, Trinity Valley School, Mira Vista Country Club; [hon.] Honor Roll, Sports Awards, Piano Awards, Creative Writing Awards; [oth. writ.] Several personal journals and writings.; [pers.] I have always loved writing - I have made poems since I was three. My first journal was dictated to my parents.; [a.] Fort Worth, TX

BETANCOURT, VICTOR
[b.] September 17, 1945, Empalme, Sonora; [p.] Victor and Francisca Betancourt; [m.] Luisa Betancourt, April 7, 1969; [ch.] Corina, Dalila, Rebeca, and Lilian; [ed.] Language and Literature College; [occ.] ESL-Citizenship Liaison, Baldwin Park Adult School, Baldwin Park, CA; [memb.] OCAE: California Council For Adult Education, CSEA: California School Employees Association, The Mega Skills Education Center, BAC: Bilingual Advisory Committee; [hon.] CCAE award, First prize in the Los Angeles Literary Society's Annual contest; [oth. writ.] Several movie reviews published in local newspaper. Essays published in Adult School newsletters.; [pers.] Poetry produces within me a particular kind of aesthetic reaction to do my utmost to promote its value toward the creation of a world filled with love without boundaries.; [a.] Ontario, CA

BETTINGER, DION C.
[b.] February 21, 1963, Pottsville, PA; [p.] Ronald and Eleanor Bettinger; [m.] Sharon Ann Bettinger, October 10, 1992; [ch.] Regina and Liam; [ed.] Pine Grove Area H.S., Assoc. degree, Thompson Ins.; [occ.] Electrician; [hon.] Thompson Ins., Dean's List; [pers.] I enjoy writing about all human experiences: love, humor, pain, happiness, as well as the darker side of human behavior.; [a.] York, PA

BEVILACQUA, ERNESTO
[b.] February 26, 1970, Plainfield, NJ; [p.] Gino and Maria Bevilacqua; [pers.] Inspired by the love of Rachel Kohl, the brightest star in the sky.; [a.] Scotch Plains, NJ

BHOJWANI, SEETA
[b.] March 29, 1981, Birmingham, AL; [p.] Holly and Kenny Bhojwani; [ed.] I attend Milby High School, I am in the 9th grade, planning on graduating high school, then going into the military; [memb.] I'm in JROTC in High School; [oth. writ.] Poetry only. I am always happy

to send my poetry, so if some is needed notify me and I'll be more than happy to send some in.; [pers.] I love poetry. I put what I feel into it. I take my time and everything comes out perfect. I am also dedicated to poetry because it says what you personally feel.; [a.] Houston, TX

BICKHAM, DORIS E.
[pen.] Doris E. Bickham; [b.] November 6, 1937, Maryville, TN; [p.] John and Lydia M. Henry; [ed.] Hale High School, Green Jr. High Austin High - Knoxville College - Knoxville, Tennessee; [occ.] Receptionist Columbus Urban League (Ohio); [memb.] NAACP - YWCA United Way - UNCF; [hon.] Key to city of New - Orleans LA. 1973 Miss Elks - (Knoxville, Tenn) 1954, Miss American Legion (1955), Miss NAACP (1954), Band Sponsor (1953-1954) Austin High School; [oth. writ.] I always wanted to be a writer and artist. I would love to have a poem into a song one day.; [pers.] I have always stood for giving and helping others. I strive to be a real woman with class and appearance.; [a.] Columbus, OH

BIRD, ROBERTA G.
[b.] September 14, 1912, Lexington, NE; [p.] Benjiman V. Blair, Myrtle Blair; [m.] Reginald E. Bird, October 16, 1938; [ch.] Bobbie Jean Bird, Robert Blair Bird; [ed.] A.B. Degree from Phillips University, Enid, Oklahoma; [occ.] Retired teacher; [oth. writ.] My own collection.; [pers.] I write for the fun of writing, for my sisters, brothers, and for my grandchildren, giving them information about their heritage.; [a.] San Diego, CA

BISHOP, WILLIAM L.
[b.] March 26, 1955, Kings County, Brooklyn; [p.] Lettie M. Crawford, Leonard Bishop; [m.] Vivian McLaughlin Bishop, February 10, 1990; [ch.] Nichol, Demetrious, Leudvigg; [ed.] John Finley, Elem., Wadleigh H.S., Haaren H.S., Voorhees Tech., P.S.I.; [occ.] Cable Splicing Tech.; [oth. writ.] Political Satire, Feelings, Dreams.; [pers.] "Keep On! Never give up!" I feel what I write, I write what I feel. When I was young, I was told you can do anything if you put your mind to it.; [a.] Bronx, NY

BIVENS, JEFFREY
[b.] July 28, 1963, Raton, NM; [p.] Jimmy and Myrle Bivens; [m.] Stacy Bivens, May 27, 1994; [ed.] High School Graduate; [occ.] Disabled; [oth. writ.] I write country songs and have yet to be published.; [pers.] Through my own disability I have learned not to judge people by their outward appearance and what they cannot do, but to accept them for who they are and what they are able to do.; [a.] Bay City, MI

BLAIR, EVELYN
[pen.] Evelyn Blair; [b.] November 2, 1910, Sabine Co., TX; [p.] James Berryman and Helen Berryman; [m.] Edward Terry (Deceased), Edgar L. Blair, October 4, 1946 (2nd); [ch.] Marlene L. Terry, Venetia L. Terry; [ed.] High School, Business Courses at University of the Southwest, San Marcos, Lit. and poetry with Marjorie Morris, U.T.P.B. poetry workshops.; [occ.] Retired: Housewife helping raise grandchildren.; [memb.] Tau Lambda Club, Writers Club, Odessa, Texas Poetry Club, Baptist Church; [hon.] 1st place in Annual Contest of New York Poetry Forum, 2nd place U.T.P.B. for Epic, Song of Jenny, publication in Anthology of American Poetry, publication of poems in small local anthologies.; [oth. writ.] Boy's Book, Articles for newspapers, Child's poetry book, autobiography, short stories. Volume of poems, (Poetry volume, Search for the Blue Flower, never submitted for publication.); [pers.] My poetry mirrors the inner man, his struggle to pull away from the dungheap of evil, and to "perform with no less splendor than tormented star."; [a.] Monahans, TX

BLANCO, MIKE
[b.] November 19, 1980, Miami; [p.] Sonia and Oberto Blanco; [occ.] Student High School; [memb.] The Key Club, High School Football and Track.; [oth. writ.] I hope to publish more of my writings in the future.; [pers.] You only have one life to live, so make it count.; [a.] Miami, FL

BLANKENSHIP, KEVIN
[b.] August 15, 1976, Hardinsburg, KY; [p.] Dwight, Janice Blankenship; [ed.] Breckinridge County High School, seeking degree at Western Kentucky University (B.A. in English Literature); [hon.] President's List; [pers.] I try to look at the world through eyes cleared of any abstraction. I have been influenced by the neo-classics and the romantics.; [a.] Hudson, KY

BLEVINS, OPAL
[pen.] Opal Blevins; [b.] September 30, 1905, Decatur Co., IA; [p.] Charlet and Alma Poole; [m.] Howard Blevins (Deceased), March 25, 1928; [ch.] Five; [ed.] High School and study of the Bible and other good books. Taught Country School (1925-1928).; [occ.] Homemaker; [memb.] Church, New Salem Baptist, Pleasantown, Iowa; [oth. writ.] Many poems, some prose.; [pers.] I love the Bible (Holy Bible) and any good reading material.; [a.] Knoxville, IA

BLOCK, TIFFANY
[b.] February 9, 1983, Norwalk, WI; [p.] Kevin Block, Kimberly Block; [ed.] Harden Middle School; [occ.] Student; [a.] Salinas, CA

BLOCKER, WILLIAM E.
[pen.] Billy Edwards; [b.] January 25, 1951, Cleveland, OH; [p.] Edward Blocker, Ann Blocker; [ch.] Shilodge Blocker; [ed.] J.F.K. High (1970), some college; [occ.] Press Op.; [oth. writ.] Short stories, that I hope one day will be published.; [pers.] My inner strength, has given me spiritual peace, but I wish too, share with others.; [a.] Cleveland, OH

BOOKOUT, ALICE MAY
[b.] June 15, Clarksburg, WV; [p.] Fred E. and Daisy D. Beachy; [m.] Gary D. Bookout, August 5, 1957; [ch.] Craig, Reece, Laura, Fred, Scott, 17 Grandchildren; [ed.] Southern Garrett Co. High School, Alderson Broaddus College, B.S. Nursing University of Virginia, M.S.N. Nursing The Clayton School of Natural Healing, Doctor of Naturopathy; [occ.] Owner and Operator of ABC Health Center "America's Best Choice"; [memb.] American Naturopathic Medical Association, Nature's Sunshine Products, Inc; [hon.] Various Who's Whos; [oth. writ.] "The Little Sisters of Little Bethel," book poem published in Sparrowgrass Poetry Forum, publish, Nature's Way News (Soon to have name change); [pers.] I would like to see all the people of the world enjoying physical, mutual, emotional and spiritual health. There are many avenues to God and health is a main thoroughfare.; [a.] Philippi, WV

BOOTH, STEPHANIE
[b.] April 27, 1972, Norwich, CT; [p.] Terri DeBarros; [ed.] Katharine Gibbs School, Providence, RI 1991, currently attending three Rivers Community Technical College in Norwich, CT; [occ.] Secretary, Dept. of Corrections, State off CT; [oth. writ.] I have no other published writing, but I do have other poems. I also write the newsletter circulated at my place of employment.; [pers.] I try to write about things I feel or have seen, bad or good. Maya Angelou and Nikki Giovanni are big inspirations to me.; [a.] Norwich, CT

BOROS, HELEN V.
[pen.] Ginny Hines; [b.] December 23, 1925, Litchfield, MI; [p.] John, Alma Hines; [m.] John J. Boros, April 27, 1946; [ch.] Three daughters; [ed.] Michigan State University, Lansing Business University; [occ.] Retired Accountant, Private Investigator; [memb.] Catholic Church, Missing Kids Program, Timber Pines Golf Community; [hon.] 1) Numerous for my accounting ability, 2) Ford Motor Co Award - 1960's, 3) work with Missing kids Award 1988; [oth. writ.] Presently writing a book which will be titled, "Forty Acres"; [pers.] My poem was written at the age of 16 as World War II began. I was very touched by the futility of war and the strength our flag gave our beautiful U.S.A.; [a.] Spring Hill, FL

BOSTON-SAGAR, TONYA
[pen.] T. M. Boston; [b.] August 1, 1949, Williamsport, PA; [ed.] Goddard College, Plainfield, Vermont, BA in Bioregional Studies, MA in Social Ecology; [occ.] Bioregional Consultant; [memb.] (1) Associate Director Conservation District, (2) Pocono Northeast Resource Conservation and Development, (3) Susquehanna International Dancers; [hon.] (1) Permaculture Design Certificate, (2) Family Support Services Award; [oth. writ.] Conservation district newsletter articles, trail guides poems published in newspaper.; [pers.] Poetry dances and sings its way into being.; [a.] Benton, PA

BOURNE, PETER
[b.] July 9, 1923, Stockholm, Sweden; [p.] Karl and Mimi Bjornnefalt; [m.] Ulla, November 4, 1950; [ch.] Peter Jr., Anita; [ed.] Vasa Real Skola - Sthlm., Sweden, Koblanar Theatre School, Sthlm., Sweden; [occ.] Retired; [memb.] SAG; [oth. writ.] Motion Pic. Scripts: "Nothing But Blonds", "Man In The Middle", "48 Hours To Live", TV Scripts: "Bob Cummings Show", "Man From Uncle"; [a.] Los Angeles, CA

BOWEN, AMY
[b.] February 17, 1974, Bremen; [p.] Joan Tucker and Jim Bowen; [ch.] Miriah K. Bowen; [ed.] Bremen High School, 1 yr. of Cosmetology, Elkhart Career Center; [occ.] Graphics (Striping) of Motor homes Monaco Coach; [a.] Nappanee, IN

BOWEN, CECIL DE WAYNE
[pen.] C. D. Bowen; [b.] April 13, 1954, Clyo, GA; [p.] Gilbert and Marie Bowen; [m.] Cynthia E. "Hutchins" Bowen, March 2, 1975; [ch.] Charles, "Lil" Wayne; [ed.] 12 yrs. plus 21 yrs. of Military Schools, Retired Chief Petty Officer, U.S. Coast Guard; [memb.] Loyal Order Moose; [oth. writ.] Approx 85 other personal poems.; [pers.] Never worry about the small stuff!; [a.] Kingsland, GA

BOWLEY, BELA R.
[b.] Jalpai Guri, India; [p.] Deceased; [m.] Divorced; [ch.] Two sons, John and Simmie; [ed.] Holds 3 Master Degrees, last degree from the Ohio State University; [occ.] Associate Dean, Marion Technical College, Marion; [memb.] St. Mary's Church, International Club, Ohio State Alumni Association; [hon.] Excellence in Teaching (1989), Leadership in Coordinating Tech. Prep (1995), Innovative Ideas Award from Ohio Fed. of Farm Bureau (1988), and first place National Award for SIFEL Students in Free Enterprize) Advisor (1981); [oth. writ.] Occasional publications in local newspapers and college magazines. First poem published at age 14, writes in three languages. Won awards for essay writing.; [pers.] Admirer of natural beauty, believer in global harmony, strong faith in universal God without the confinement of religions boundaries.; [a.] Marion, OH

BOYD, GREGG
[b.] August 30, 1970, Chicago, IL; [p.] Priscilla Boyd; [m.] Sharmin Boyd, September 21, 1997; [ed.] Horace Mann Elementary School, Chicago Vocational High School, Roosevelt University; [occ.] Bank Operators Supervisor; [oth. writ.] Several poems written but never published. I just keep them. It's just a hobby. My mother convinced me to enter one of my poems into the contest.; [pers.] I write about how I feel, my experiences and what I see in other people.; [a.] Chicago, IL

BRADEN III, RALPH W.
[b.] September 25, 1973, Saint Petersburgh, FL; [p.] Hoa Smithson, Ralph W. Braden Jr.; [m.] Jane A. Braden, September 16, 1994; [ch.] Ralph W. Braden IV; [ed.] St. Petersburgh Junior College; [occ.] Student; [oth. writ.] Own personal collection.; [pers.] Enjoy free will and express yourself.; [a.] Pinellas Park, FL

BRALEY, RUTH A.
[b.] June 2, 1936, Versailles, IN; [p.] Carl and Myrtle Smith; [m.] Frank Braley, September 9, 1961; [ch.] Carla, Michael, Lena, Bruce; [ed.] High School; [occ.] Housewife; [memb.] First Southern Baptist Church, Ripley Co. Cancer Society; [hon.] Plaque for teaching Sunday School 30 yrs., Volunteer of the Year for Cancer Society, Volunteer for Ripley Co. Health Coalition; [oth. writ.] Poems for several funerals, obituaries, retirements, and own pleasure.; [pers.] Put God first and serve Him by serving others, specially my four children and ten grandchildren and my church.; [a.] Versailles, IN

BRANCH, BRYANT
[pen.] Bryant Branch; [b.] March 13, 1959, Bonham, TX; [p.] Jack and Frances Branch; [m.] Lola Branch, November 26, 1995; [ch.] Six; [ed.] Paschal High, Ft Worth TX., TCJC South Campus, Ft Worth TX; [occ.] College Student and Writer; [memb.] International Society of Poets; [hon.] Special Award American Collegiate Poets. 5 Editor's Choice Awards from the National Library of Poetry; [oth. writ.] Footsteps Of Faith, Smile, In The Mind Of A Poet, Old Tree Answer Me, Oh Lazy Day, Mothers Barden, Legacy, Reflections, Regardless, Silver Lining, Gratitude, The Poet of All Time; [pers.] Words are the beginning of a dream come true. Words motivate change in the heart and mind of the old man in order to bring fort the new man. Words are the inspiration of change and growth.; [a.] Fort Worth, TX

BRANSON, PAMELA
[b.] November 26, 1957, Columbus, IN; [p.] Edward and Barbara Huntsman; [m.] William D. Branson Jr., August 29, 1981; [ed.] Columbus North High School, Indiana Vocational Technical College, Indiana University, Purdue University of Indianapolis; [occ.] Registered Nurse, Private Math Tutor; [memb.] Thompson Road Baptist Church; [oth. writ.] Currently unpublished.; [pers.] I strive to give comfort, reassurance and joy to those around me.; [a.] Indianapolis, IN

BRASWELL, PAULINE MARIE
[pen.] Sometimes use the letters PB; [b.] July 24, 1925, Atchison, KS; [p.] James Q. Wedworth and Nora Rigby Wedworth; [m.] Troy Vren Braswell, May 22, 1942; [ch.] Edward Elton, Try V. Jr., Linda Kay; [ed.] Did not finish high school; [occ.] Retired Business Owner; [memb.] Docent Kern Valley Museum, Kern Valley Hospital Auxiliary (Pink Ladies), Daughters of The American Revolution (DAR), KRV Hospital Foundation, Calif. Federation Of Business and Professional Women; [hon.] Woman Of Achievement, BPW, Y.M.C.A. So. Bay Woman of the Year Merit Award, United Way Award; [oth. writ.] The Palos Verdes Review (Poem-Prose), New Voices In American

Poetry 1975, Endless Time pg. 84 and The Kite pg. 85, Columnist for The Bicycle Journal and The Schwinn Reporter; [pers.] Step lightly into each new day, always remembering to leave a soft foot-print for those who follow, as you build a foundation for your tomorrows...At eventide recall a warm memory, secure in the knowledge someone in the distant pass also left a clear, soft foot-print as a foundation for their tomorrow.; [a.] Lake Isabella, CA

BREWER, JEANNE M.
[b.] October 3, 1961, Endicott, NY; [p.] Robert E. and Mary L. Brewer; [occ.] Nurses Aide and Restorative Aide; [hon.] Art and Scholastic; [oth. writ.] "The Visitor," "Model Love," "His Room," "Highway Delites," "Shh! Listen!," "The Gray Cloud Pub," "Immortal Kisses," "Upon a Tree," and "Waiting for News."; [pers.] Be true to yourself. Don't change for others but for your own growth and maturity. Love always.; [a.] Charlotte, NC

BREWSTER, JANET BRADHAM
[b.] April 19, 1921, Manning, SC; [p.] J. Ingram Bradham, Elizabeth Allred Bradham; [m.] Marcus V. Brewster, November 28, 1942; [ch.] Marcia J., Carol A., M. Bradham; [ed.] G.W. University, DC and Suffolk Univ., Boston graduated Cumm Laude in Accounting. First job, docent Washington Cathedral, DC, then followed by 23 years with Fed. Govt. in N.E. area as administrator for F.D.A. Reg. Office and as Civil Rights Specialist and Investigator for Dept. of Education.; [occ.] Retired in 1981; [memb.] New Eng. Hist. and Gen. Society, U.D.C. Chapt. #1923, EPMR Chapt. D.A.R., Teige County Chpt. Colonial Dames, SC Hist. Society, and numerous Genealogical Societies throughout South; [hon.] First prize for Golden Years, by S.C. Southern Bapt. Literary Group, Winner of 1988 National History Awards Competition sponsored by Soc. for History, Res. and Preservation, Rockingham, N.C. for the Bradham Family History and Genealogy; [oth. writ.] Bradham Family History and Genealogy pub. 1986, editor for Mark Brewster of Hull, Eng., by Marc V. Brewster, 1990, co-authored Golden Years with Lila Bradham 1989, Allred and Newby Family History and Genealogy, to be pub. 1998. Misc. newspaper and mag. articles.; [pers.] "Precious Grieving," telling of my 52 yrs of marriage, was written in memory of Marcus V. Brewster. My sincere hope is that if read by troubled couples they might see that marriage is a covenant between two people, and with sincerity true love, and hard work, one's love grows deeper, respect and faithfulness are stronger, and with God's help it can always be worked.; [a.] Manning, SC

BREWSTER, WILLIAM
[b.] June 8, 1964, Beckley, WV; [p.] Robert Brewster, Flossie Collins; [m.] Donna Lynn Brewster, October 14, 1995; [ch.] Holly Michelle, Jacklyn Yvonne, Ashley Dawn, William Cody; [ed.] Davis and Elkins College; [occ.] Welder; [hon.] Seneca Trail Artists Guild; [pers.] Those strong enough to brave the storm eventually feel the sunshine upon them.; [a.] Beckley, WV

BRIGGS, LARRY
[b.] March 10, 1951; [p.] Jim and Cindy Briggs; [ed.] One year of college; [occ.] Student; [a.] Tucson, AZ

BROADY, DONNA R.
[b.] February 5, 1954, Charleston, WV; [p.] William H. Broady and Dorothy Broady; [m.] Divorced; [ch.] Thomas W. and Deshia L. Bradley; [ed.] German Town High School Phila., PA; [occ.] Retired Philadelphia Police Officer; [pers.] As an ex-police officer I write about the things I have seen. If I can touch one person's life, and let them know they are not alone, it's well worth it.; [a.] Charleston, WV

BROCK, BOBBIE
[b.] July 19, 1934, Plainville, GA; [p.] Augusta Shores, Ollie Mae Shores; [m.] Clinton Brock, March 3, 1976; [ch.] David Robertson, Karen Dillard, Mike Robertson; [ed.] Rome High School, Rome, GA; [occ.] Disabled due to back injury, several years ago; [memb.] Mtn. Music Club, Unity Baptist Church, AMVETS Ladies Auxiliary; [hon.] Was honor graduate from high school class of '52, worked in offices, dept. stores, direct selling, last job was in day care center. Raised 3 children and one granddaughter, active in church work; [oth. writ.] Poems for my children and grandchildren's birthdays, poems for my own enjoyment, short stories and anecdotes - never published, but I keep trying.; [pers.] I have been writing stories, poems, anecdotes since my teen years. I would love to have some of my writings published and writing is a very good emotional outlet for me.; [a.] Rome, GA

BROCK, SANDRA K.
[pen.] Sandra Sinclair-Brook; [b.] August 26, 1948, Houston, TX; [p.] J. P. and Eleanor Deramus; [m.] Gregory W. Brock, November 23, 1989; [ch.] Keri and Patti; [ed.] Graduated Klein Sr. High School, Spring, TX., 1968 Majored in Cosmetology and Licensed By State Board, TX; [occ.] Homemaker, P/T Sub-Teacher, O.C.I.S.D.; [memb.] 1st Baptist Church New Diana, TX; [hon.] Nothing Notable To Date Save The "Honor" of This writing Possibility! (I did win 4th in a signing Contest at age 16.); [oth. writ.] Several Songs, other poetry, 3 unfinished books (fiction and now - fiction) (I began in 1970's, current, 1994), Devotionals - All, as of yet, unpublished); [pers.] There's more than 1 way to "skin a cat" - but only I way to the heart of God - Jesus! (P.S. When the Cat is "Skinned", find a new cat!); [a.] Ore City, TX

BROOKS, DAVID W.
[pen.] D. W. Brooks; [b.] January 6, 1977, Winchester, VA; [p.] Mary J. Brooks and Kenneth C. Brooks; [m.] Tara L. Shoemaker (Fiancee), June 19, 1996 (Engagement); [ed.] Graduated Mountaineer Challenge Academy 1995; [hon.] A Volunteer Beyond Excellence by Hopemont Hospital Residents and Staff while in the Mountaineer Challenge Academy, also a certificate of appreciation for assistance in installation of the MCA Local Area Network calling project, on the Honors list at Mountaineer Challenge, Academy; [oth. writ.] None that had been published.; [pers.] D.W.B...Sometimes people are like wildflowers, they're strong and independent, but when they surrender themselves into another's hand they become very fragile and delicate.; [a.] Berkeley Springs, WV

BROTHERTON, DEREK DAVID
[b.] July 23, 1983, Houston, TX; [p.] John and Katherine Brotherton; [occ.] Student, Episcopal Day School; [a.] Lake Charles, LA

BROWN, BRYAN KENNETH
[b.] March 10, 1967, Nampa, ID; [p.] Kenneth and Barbara Brown; [ed.] Boise State University; [occ.] Accountant; [pers.] I finally realized that it's okay to forget one day out of the year, because its not that one day that made him the person that he was...and the person he will always be.; [a.] Boise, ID

BROWN, DAWN
[b.] April 7, 1942, Canastota, NY; [p.] Eleanor Rhinehart, George Cesarini; [ch.] Deborah, Tammy, Sherri, Amanda, Scott, Ricky; [ed.] Canastota High Graduate 1960; [occ.] Waitress; [memb.] YMCA, St. Agatha's Church; [oth. writ.] Poems, short stories; [a.] Chittenango, NY

BROWN, JANET L.
[pen.] Janet L. Brown; [b.] September 26, 1937, Lewistown, MT; [p.] Lawrence W. and Helen Koerner; [m.] Deceased; [ch.] Susan Christiansen, Pamela Neal (Cptn., USAF) Michael Brown, Burke Brown, Jr., Lawrence Brown, Theresa Brown, Michelle Brown, Helen Karnopp; [ed.] High School Graduate Associates Degree - Criminal Justice and Juvenile Deliquency; [occ.] Home Maker; [oth. writ.] Many poems for family and friends - short stories never brave enough to send anything to anyone until I received your application from my mother.; [pers.] I have 8 beautiful children and have raised them alone since their Dad died 17 yrs. ago. My writing come within my heart and knowing my Lord has been with me to help me every step of the way, is my guidance.; [a.] Lincoln, NE

BROWN, JOSHUA EUGENE
[b.] September 19, 1978, Alpena, MI; [p.] Betty Brown, Marvin Brown; [ed.] Senior at Alpena High School; [occ.] Student; [memb.] National Honor Society, 4-H, Odyssey of the Mind, Alpena Wildcat Staff, Alpena High School Jazz and Concert Bands, L.E.A.F.; [hon.] Honor Roll, Various Band, O.M., Academic, and 4-H Awards; [oth. writ.] Monthly articles in the Alpena Wildcat (Student Newspaper).; [pers.] I just want to make a difference in people's lives. I want to make them think.; [a.] Ossineke, MI

BROWN, JUSTIN
[pen.] Brandt Drake; [b.] April 13, 1982, Tyler, TX; [p.] Tamara Tarver and Charles Brown; [ed.] Troup High School; [memb.] Drama Club, Soldiers for Jesus, Spanish Club, Model United Nations; [hon.] Presidential Academic Fitness Award; [oth. writ.] Personal, non-published poems.; [pers.] I am not afraid of suffering, and I believe that our suffering as a race can eventually bring us to a place of great wonder. For all I have suffered, I am happy to be alive.; [a.] Troup, TX

BROWN, LOIS J.
[b.] December 13, 1960, Macon, MO; [p.] James Poshek and Wanda Lindley; [m.] Marion Brown, August 17, 1985; [ch.] James; [ed.] Bucklin High School, Hamilton College; [pers.] Life is not always pretty, but it is an ever changing process, allowing us to change and grow. Cherish the good, exorcise the bad, and learn from your mistakes.; [a.] Colfax, IA

BROWN, MARY E.
[pen.] Meg Gallagher; [b.] November 24, 1962, Scranton, PA; [p.] William R. and Elizabeth A. Gallagher; [m.] Andrew M. Phillips Sr., upcoming May 23, 1998; [ed.] Bishop Hannan High School Lackawanna Junior College; [occ.] Truck driver/Math Tutor-Elementary thru college; [hon.] Dean's List; [pers.] Children are the heart of our world. Listen to them and love them. Their souls are the souls of our future. They will show you what life is truly all about. Take care of them.; [a.] Olyphant, PA

BROWN, MELISSA DIANE
[b.] January 7, 1979, Woodstock, IL; [p.] Diane Doty-Brown, Dale Brown; [a.] Woodstock, IL

BROWN, RODNEY MORGAN
[pen.] Rod; [b.] February 15, 1949, Balto, MD; [p.] George Phillip Brown Sr. (Deceased), Eloise T. Brown; [ed.] Manhattan Sch. of Music, Univ. of Michigan, Howard University; [memb.] Who's Who in Entertainment, AGMA, Cambridge Biographical Society; [pers.] I greatly revere such writers as Walt Whitman, Edgar Allan Poe, and Peter Ilych Tchaikovsky whose music is in itself poetry.; [a.] Baltimore, MD

BROWN, VICKI LEE
[pen.] Vicki Lee; [b.] December 21, 1957, Rome, GA; [p.] Jerry Lee and Dorothy C. Lee; [m.] Frank Brown, February 14, 1997; [ch.] Mack and Scott Barnhart; [ed.] Tallassee High School, Tallassee, AL, Auburn University, ABAC, Tifton; [occ.] Publisher/Co-owner of the Southern Horse Connection, Inc. (magazine); [oth. writ.] Several other poems written to glorify the Lord Jesus Christ.; [pers.] My writings have been inspired by the holy spirit as a result of my personal experiences in life.; [a.] Tifton, GA

BRUCE, DEANE
[b.] February 16, 1919, Fannin Co., GA; [p.] Alvin and Mamie Hagood Cearley; [m.] Abraham Lincoln Bruce, March 24, 1940; [ch.] Joan, James and Rebecca; [ed.] Fannin County Schools; [occ.] Retired Homemaker; [memb.] Liberty Hill United Church, Order of The Eastern Star; [oth. writ.] Poetry for family, friends, special occasions.; [pers.] Appreciation for life and love and the beauties of earth can be expressed equally well in poetry as in art and music.; [a.] Morganton, GA

BRYANT, BRANDI L.
[b.] November 16, 1971, Millville, NJ; [p.] Bill and Linda Biggs; [ed.] B.S. Gerontology, University of South Florida, M.S.W., Temple University; [occ.] Graduate Student at Temple University; [pers.] "Thanks to my wonderful mother, who has given me the strength to accomplish all my dreams in life."; [a.] Ocean City, NJ

BUCK, GENE
[b.] December 6, 1936, Leachville, AR; [p.] Marion and Opal Buck; [m.] Bertha Buck, July 3, 1957; [ch.] Frank, Michael, Petti, Benjamin; [ed.] 2 years college; [occ.] Retired; [oth. writ.] Poems mostly elderly about their life as they see it and relate it to me.; [pers.] Anything I write is for the person it is written for and about and for their well being. No fee is ever charged. A few things I have written for myself.; [a.] Braggadocio, MO

BULBUL, EBRU G.
[pen.] Ebru G. Bulbul; [b.] October 26, 1978, Gainesville, FL; [p.] Remzi Bulbul, Serife Bulbul; [ed.] Graduated Wayne Valley High School, Wayne, NJ, currently 1st year student at Penn State University, PA; [occ.] Student; [a.] Wayne, NJ

BUONAMICI, LORETTA
[b.] January 1, 1939, Saint Clairsville, OH; [p.] Charles F. Fulton, Frances R. Fulton; [m.] Domenick Edward Buonamici, November 2, 1957; [ch.] Don E. Buonamici, Diana M. Twaroq; [ed.] Lafferty High, LPN (24 years), Pharmacology and Psychology courses to further my knowledge of nursing; [occ.] Retired from nursing, housewife; [oth. writ.] A written prayer for my daughter when she was born, a written prayer for my son when he was born, a written prayer for my family after my mother's death, and one other poem.; [pers.] These times of special meaning in my life had inspired me to write of my thoughts.; [a.] Bannock, OH

BURKE, ANNE
[b.] September 21, 1953, Waltham, MA; [p.] Mr. and Mrs. William Arthur Burke; [ed.] Ditson School, Billerica, Mass. Arlington High School, Arlington, Mass.; [occ.] Disabled due to a back injury in 1992; [memb.] American Legion; [pers.] "Climbing Stones," the poem, came about when I spent some time recalling childhood wonderings, most of which still remain as wonders to me.; [a.] Fort White, FL

BURKE, MEGHAN
[b.] June 15, 1984, Countryside; [p.] Elaine and Kevin Burke; [ed.] A student, 7th Grade; [occ.] Student; [hon.] Honor Roll; [pers.] "What goes around comes around!"; [a.] Countryside, IL

BURNETT, SONDRA K.
[b.] October 6, 1943, Anderson, IN; [p.] Lowell and Anna (McNally) Hewitt; [m.] Emmett L. Burnett, July 15, 1959; [ch.] Angel, Andy and Adam; [ed.] High School Diploma, Newport Pacific High School, Scranton, PA; [occ.] Retired General Motors Corporation; [memb.] Word of Life Church, Moose Lodge; [hon.] Many certificates from different classes I have taken and bowling trophies; [oth. writ.] I am going to publish a book of all my poems for my eldest grandchild Andy Michael Burnett Jr.; [pers.] My grandparents Margaret and Alva Hewitt, my parents and my husband have been my inspiration all my life. Without my trust in God I could not have made it through life.; [a.] Sebring, FL

BURNS, PATRICIA A.
[b.] July 7, 1936, Oak Park, IL; [p.] Audrey and Richard Rogers; [m.] Robert M. Burns, June 14, 1958; [ch.] Robert, Valerie, Edward, Linda; [ed.] Life; [occ.] Human being; [memb.] In planet earth; [hon.] Just being alive as a liver transplant; [pers.] Life is the most precious gift - cherish it.; [a.] Oak Creek, WI

BURRESS, EMMA
[b.] June 13, 1921, Cincinnati, OH; [p.] Samantha and Henry Evans; [m.] James Burress, February 20, 1941; [ch.] Two boys, three girls; [ed.] Stowe School, Lic. Beautician, Temple Bible Coll.; [occ.] Retired (Homemaker); [memb.] Mt. Zion Baptist Church Missionary Society (Chaplain) Sunday School Teacher Firm believer in the Bible, God's Holy Word. John 3:16; [oth. writ.] Book of poems entitled: "Showers of Blessings". Others not listed.; [a.] Cincinnati, OH

BURROWS, ELIZABETH
[b.] January 30, 1930; [p.] Leland and Ruth Frew MacDonald; [ed.] 25 years in Religion, Science, and Philosophy, specializing in interpretation of Ancient Christian Manuscripts and Origins, Transformational Psychology and Alternative Medicine. Bachelor of Religious Education-Christian College of Universal Peace. Doctor of Divinity-Christian College of Universal Peace; [occ.] International Spiritual Educator, Author, Youngest Grange Installation officer in the U.S., 1941 Credit Mgr. Home Utilities 1950-52, Credit Mgr. Montgomery Ward, 1952-60, Oregon District Plant Clerical Training Supervisor, W. Coast Telephone Co 1960, President and Founder of Christian Church of Universal Peace, President of Christian Church of Universal Peace, Archives International, cw/Author, Books, Pathway of the Immortal, Harp of Destiny, Odyssey of the Apocalypse, Covenant at Sinai, Crystal Planet, Maya Sangh. Published poet appearing in American Poetry Anthology, Publisher's choice of Poets for the New Era, 1990, Distinguished poets of America 1993, and Treasured Poems of America; [hon.] Who's Who in the West, Who's Who of American Women, Who's Who in Education, Who's Who in Religion, Who's Who in World, and Who's Who in America. Recipient of Caden Publishing's Presidential Award for Library Excellency 1994 and 1995; [pers.] The inevitable destiny of our planet is peace. Therefore, the ability of mankind to work toward this common goal is extremely important. In achieving peace, hatred, malice, war, pain and sorrow shall pass away as shadows of darkness. Then, and only then, will the truly great age of mankind come into expression.

BUSH, JEAN
[pen.] Dymphna; [b.] November 21, 1947, Phoenix, AZ; [p.] Harvey G. and Geraldine C. Bush; [m.] Former Spouse: Andrew C. Kobold, March 20, 1968; [ch.] Bernadette, David, Russell and Donald Kobold; [ed.] Graduate of North Phoenix High School, Phoenix, AZ; [occ.] Self employed referral service for care givers and prospective clients; [memb.] The Independent Order of Foresters; [hon.] Elitch Gardens Employee of the Year - 1993. Elitch Gardens Employee of the Year - 1995; [oth. writ.] "Waterfall", a poem published in "Waterford Press", "Ballet of The Fish" received the Golden Poet Award.; [pers.] Always count your joys instead of your sorrows. Life is a learning experience. No lessons is ever wasted. Always look for the sun rise as well as the sun set and remember we are all precious gifts to God, the gift giver.; [a.] Denver, CO

BUSTAMANTE, LYNNETTE
[b.] September 2, 1969, Oxford, England; [p.] Patricia and Norman Kevin; [m.] Juan A. Bustamante, April 8, 1989; [ch.] Marcus and John; [ed.] Peers School, Oxpens College, Oxford, England; [occ.] Housekeeper; [pers.] Gray skies or blue, live your life and be happy, life's too short to be blue.; [a.] Eveleth, MN

BUTLER, KAREN
[b.] November 4, 1961, Chico, CA; [p.] Lemar and Charlotte Butler; [ch.] Four; [a.] Hamilton City, CA

BUTOWICZ, ANTHONY
[pen.] L.T., Navanna McHale; [b.] February 15, 1969, Pittsburgh; [p.] Paulette Keesee; [ch.] Navanna McHale; [ed.] Self taught; [occ.] Song writer, poet, musician; [memb.] Musikana Productions, The Ohio Songwriter and Poetry Society; [hon.] Published article, Murryville Star, Sept. 1993, Poetry albums available locally radio air play from Pittsburgh Art Institute'; [oth. writ.] "Mother Beautiful" and "Carthartic" both are spoken word albums. Currently writing my third spoken word album, and completing original songs for publishing and selling.; [a.] Harrison City, PA

BUTTS, ROBERT
[b.] April 9, 1964, New Brunswick, NJ; [p.] Moses and Alberta Butts; [ed.] High School grad; [oth. writ.] Inspiritual Change, Death The End Mystery; [pers.] I write from personal experience. And I've always believed that God never gives more burden than we can handle.; [a.] South River, NJ

CADDLE, JACQUELINE
[pen.] Welwyn Starvelings, Z. Zinfandel; [b.] 1981; [p.] Glendene and James Caddle; [occ.] Student; [oth. writ.] Currently working on novels for publication; [pers.] I'm intrigued by the strange and unusual and that's what I usually write.; [a.] Willow Grove, PA

CAGE, SHAWN CHRISTOPHER
[b.] December 22, 1977, Kokomo; [p.] Deborah Raber; [ed.] High School Graduate, Taylor High School; [occ.] Army (Private); [a.] Kokomo, IN

CAHOON-JACKSON, ELIZABETH I.
[pen.] Elizabeth I. Cahoon-Jackson; [b.] October 19, 1935, Winchester, MA; [p.] Benjamin and Myrtle Cahoon; [ed.] The Principal College, Elsah, IL. (JC) A.A. Boston Univ. Boston, Mass. B.S. 1957, Boston Univ. Boston, Mass. Med. 1964, UCLA, Whittier College, Whittier Calif. Columbia Univ., (incidental Courses) L.A. Calif.; [occ.] Retired after teaching in Andover, Mass. 38 yrs. (Elem. and Jr. High), other assignments in Calif., New Jersey, Mass., and Germany with the U.S.

Army D.O.D.; [memb.] (Too many to list), Professional Organiz; [pers.] I like to live by the Golden Rule; the dividends are 100 fold returned.; [a.] Buena Vista, CO

CAIN, CYNTHIA M.
[b.] December 14, 1959, Milwaukee, WI; [p.] Marlene Cain; [ed.] Custer High, M.A.T.C. College; [occ.] Office Clerk at Manpower Distribution Center; [memb.] Received my majority from Jobs Daughters of America, with great honors, in 1981.; [pers.] I write from my heart, with an open mind, creativeness, emotions and a true love for whatever I write on any subject it may be.; [a.] Milwaukee, WI

CALHOUN, NIKKI P.
[pen.] Ponchita; [b.] March 21, 1970, Kingsport, TN; [p.] Hatha Garrett, Vernon Garrett; [m.] Roger M. Calhoun, March 17, 1990; [ch.] Whitney D. Calhoun; [ed.] Sullivan North High School; [occ.] Writer, Painter, Wife, and Mother; [oth. writ.] I have written some short stories and other poetry as a hobby.; [pers.] Inspiration lives in all of us and when someone reads what I have written and gets some sense of fulfillment that's when I know I've really achieved something great. Thank you God.; [a.] Kingsport, TN

CAMARA JR., JOHN R.
[b.] September 9, 1919, New Bedford, MA; [p.] John Camara, Catarina Rita Macedo; [m.] Luz Doceu Pinto Camara, May 29, 1986; [ch.] Nadine Corte Camara; [ed.] University - former teacher; [occ.] R.E. Broker, Notary, Income Tax Preparer, Translator, Ca. Teaching-Life-Diploma; [memb.] Sacar-Nar Member; [hon.] I am an average American; [oth. writ.] Three in edited books and 4 unfinished works. Plus over 100 letters and many essays.; [pers.] My background describes my philosophy of life: i.e. I grew up abroad fifteen of the first eighteen years of my life for which I wrote: My fifteen years Odyssey. After returning to the U.S.A. and spending four years in the military service during WW II, I attended the university and graduated five years later with a teaching general secondary credential in the fields of humanities, social sciences, history, and languages and taught for seventeen years, later becoming a R.E. broker, notary and income tax preparer. Generally, I enjoy reading, history, research and writing. I've always been an optimist and an eclecticist in life. John Donne's poem, "No man is an island..." describes me as, "...a part of the main..."; [a.] Fremont, CA

CAMBETAS, DANIELA
[b.] December 12, 1980, Rio de Janeiro, Brazil; [p.] Rui and Teresa Cambetas; [ed.] Clarkstown High School North, New York; [memb.] Aspira, Founded the Rampagers at Clarkstown North High School, Attended Angelo del Torro Puerto Rican and Hispanic Youth Leadership Institute 1997, attended New York State Governor's Conference on Youth 1997, and a Member of the Rockland Youth Council.; [pers.] Maya Angelou has been my poetric inspiration. My poems focus on real life, love, and tragedy. Days are time, friends are days, but families are eternity.; [a.] New City, NY

CAMERON, RAY
[pen.] Ray Cameron; [b.] Chanute, KS; [a.] Chicago, IL

CAMPANA, CHRISTINE M.
[b.] August 21, 1972, Sacramento, CA; [p.] Christopher and Anita Rhodes; [m.] Enrique Campana, September 7, 1991; [ch.] Antonio and Carlos; [ed.] Foothill High, Sacramento City College, California State University Sacramento; [occ.] Benefit Program Specialist, Public Employees Retirement, St. of CA; [oth. writ.] Dozens of

songs and poems written since 1986 to present.; [pers.] The gift of expression helps to heal my heart, and reflects my souls desire to give and receive love - unconditionally.; [a.] Sacramento, CA

CAMPBELL, DAVID
[b.] June 17, 1977, Yokuska, Japan; [p.] Arnold and Setsuko Campbell; [pers.] Becoming a published poet at age 20 was more than I dared dream for. I resolve to be more daring.; [a.] San Diego, CA

CAMPBELL, JEFFREY LEONARD
[pen.] Jeff Campbell; [b.] March 16, 1976, El Paso, TX; [p.] Kenneth Campbell, Karen Campbell; [ed.] Cathedral High School, University of Texas at El Paso; [memb.] National Honor Society; [pers.] In my writings, I try to incorporate the feeling of hope, the sense of stability, and the motion of overcoming adversity with the power of the human spirit.; [a.] El Paso, TX

CAMPBELL, NICOLE PATRICIA
[pen.] Nikki Campbell; [b.] June 28, 1982, Spokane, WA; [p.] Pat and Keith Campbell; [hon.] Vice President/ Treasurer of Student body, (8th grade), advanced classes, chairperson of Dance Committee at Middle School, 1st place winner of dance competitions - jazz; [oth. writ.] "My Dog Tixie," Anthology of Poetry by Young Americans, 1993 ed., "Dreams," Arcadia Poetry Anthology, Winter 1994, "You'll Find A Good Realtor When..." published several times in local real estate guide.; [pers.] Live life to its max, don't give up. You can make of life what you want.; [a.] Pullman, WA

CANFIELD, CHERYL
[b.] December 7, 1947, New Jersey; [p.] Kenneth and Lillian Cope; [m.] Harry (Deceased), March 13, 1967; [ch.] Michael, Jeffrey, Laurie, Tami; [ed.] Netcong High School, Several Banking Courses; [occ.] Supervisor in Banking; [pers.] I have written many poems for family and friends, both as tributes and for gifts. I love to write and would like to pursue a career in the field if possible.; [a.] Stanhope, NJ

CAO, NGOC THI
[pen.] Ngoc Thi Cao; [b.] October 27, 1979, Tra-Vinh, Vietnam; [p.] Ngoc-Le Thi Tram, Tu Thien Cao; [ed.] High School Senior of West Liberty Community High School; [occ.] Student; [memb.] Library Club, FHA, Upward Bound, Culture Diversity Club; [hon.] National Honor Society, Youth Saluted Program, Who's Who Among American Students, All American Scholar, United States Achievement Academy, Girl State Nominee; [oth. writ.] One of my poems has been approved for publication.; [pers.] The romantic poets greatly influenced my writing, and I think that romanticism is a vivid mirror that reflects only the beauty of human kind through nature. Thus, we are celestial as nature itself.; [a.] West Liberty, IA

CARAVELLO, KELLY ANN
[b.] April 19, 1975, Brooklyn, NY; [p.] Vincent Caravello, Jane Caravello; [ed.] Sheepshead Bay High School, John Jay College of Criminal Justice; [occ.] Accountant; [hon.] Dean's List 95-96, National Dean's List 94-95, National Dean's List 95-96; [oth. writ.] On display at John Jay; [pers.] It doesn't matter where you come from in life, but what you make of your life.; [a.] Brooklyn, NY

CARAYANNIS, DR. GEORGE
[pen.] George Carayannis; [b.] November 8, 1936, Athens, Greece; [m.] Carol Carayannis, February 18, 1995; [ch.] George, Nicole; [ed.] PH.D. Marine Sciences, Univ.

of Delaware, M.S. Oceanography, Univ. of Hawaii, M.S. Chemistry, Roosevelt Univ. Chicago, B.S. Chemistry and Mathematics; [occ.] Retired; [memb.] National Society of Arts and Letters (NSAL), Co-founder officer and member, "Tsunami Society," International Society for National Hazards Mitigation, Society of Ex; [hon.] Numerous awards for international contributions and scientific leadership in Disaster Mitigation; [oth. writ.] Over 150 publications, articles reports, short stories, monoplams, several published poems. A book of poems in preparation. Internet address http://www.peocitves.com/Athens/Acropolis/ 4870; [pers.] To me poetry has been the expression of pain, pleasure, love, agony, truth and wonder. So, with an occasional and mere lyrical inspiration, but always with a genuine philosophical curiosity, persistence and sincerity I tried to give meter, music and some tolerance to my search for personal identity and for me spiritual and sensual values of life as I saw them subjectively during my continuous metamorphosis over the years.; [a.] Honolulu, HI

CARLIN, MADELINE
[b.] July 30, 1925, Smithfield, WV; [p.] Robert and Ethnel Shreve; [m.] William J. Carlin, December 24, 1946; [ch.] Sue, Jan, Joe, Melanie and Amy; [ed.] A.B. and (almost) Masters Degree in Elementary Education (I lack 6 hours - Masters); [occ.] Retired; [hon.] Have had a book of poetry published; [pers.] Many individuals have an impulsive spirit, I say follow the most intriguing and spontaneous example to meet day to day goals.; [a.] Smithfield, WV

CARNEY, PATRICK
[pen.] Patrick Carney; [b.] August 24, 1949, Phoenix, AZ; [p.] Thomas and Leonara Carney; [m.] Omega Carney, September 14, 1973; [ch.] Thomas, Andrew, Andrea; [ed.] NAU - Business; [occ.] Bakery Manager; [oth. writ.] Co written - "In my Arms" - "Sounds of Leaving"; [pers.] To write assures ones immortality.; [a.] Mayer, AZ

CARON, VERITY K.
[b.] May 31, 1982, Long Island, NY; [p.] John and Pat Caron; [ed.] Chesapeake public schools, now in ninth grade; [hon.] I've won a few school contests, and one cash prize of 10 dollars; [oth. writ.] Over 20 unpublished novels, several poems, and two award-winning short stories.; [pers.] This poem started as something on a Mother's Day card. Then I gave it to others, because all mothers deserve to be thanked.; [a.] Chesapeake, VA

CARRICK, WILLIAM PATRICK
[b.] December 27, 1950, Coffeyville, KS; [p.] Wilma Carrick, (My Father is dead); [m.] Lois Carrick, May 22, 1992; [ch.] I have a step son named Buddy; [ed.] Graduated from High School in Topeka, Kansas. I have some college and night classes in Art. Went to Kaw Area Vocational School. Technical Drafting.; [occ.] I am a member of the Y.M.C.A. and later became a lifeguard for about 5 years.; [oth. writ.] I am also a singer song writer. I play the guitar. I have a little over 80 songs. A third of them are Christian songs. I have played for the church I used to attend. And shared poems as well.; [pers.] My poems and songs reflect on who I am and how I feel and what God has done in my life. I hope I can reflect to my fellow man on how good God is and life itself.; [a.] Topeka, KS

CARSON, EMILIE R.
[b.] March 2, 1979, Wheeling, WV; [p.] John and Joann Carson; [ed.] High School (Oak Glen High School); [occ.] Student; [memb.] American Diabetes Association; [hon.] Excellent Ratings at Voice Competition, 1st place

for 2 years at Steubenville Mall Voice Contests Sang at Capitol Music Hall - 1996; [oth. writ.] "The World Through A Black Man's Eyes", "Oh, Sweet Love", "The Forbidden", many others published in school magazine.; [pers.] I write about feelings, dreams, and the problems of the world. My greatest influence to write, was my 11th grade English teacher, Rebecca Vukas.; [a.] New Cumberland, WV

CARUCCI, CATHERINE GIBLIN
[b.] January 21, 1937, Teaneck, NJ; [p.] Catherine and Thomas Giblin; [m.] Richard S. Carucci Sr., October 19, 1957; [ch.] King Michael, Laura, Richard, L. Sharon; [memb.] Notary Public; [oth. writ.] Hundreds of poems 4 books, 6 court reportedly educate books; [pers.] Read a child a story to awaken their imagination teach them to read to awaken their universe to them.; [a.] Hackensack, NJ

CARVER, MARY KAY FIFE
[pen.] Kay; [b.] July 21, 1956, Reform, AL; [p.] Comer Fife, Marie F. Fife; [m.] Terry W. Carver, October 30, 1974; [ch.] Eric Paul, Adam Fife; [ed.] Gordo High School, Gordo, AL; [occ.] Business Assistant, Dr. C. Daniel Propst DMD, PC; [memb.] Temple Baptist Church Baptist Women's Mission Group; [oth. writ.] Several other poems, some published in school newspapers, one poem has been written as a song.; [pers.] I strive to touch other lives daily, not only through my poetry, but with a positive outlook on life, hoping to make someone smile and be happy. I have recently been inspired to write more by a dear friend and co-worker, Mary Jo Miller.; [a.] Northport, AL

CARY JR., MICHAEL T.
[b.] October 23, 1981, Newport News, VA; [p.] Lynn Diane Cary and Michael Cary Sr.; [ed.] Warwick High School 9th grade; [hon.] Certificate of Merit for Young Authors Program. Certificate for participation in the Virginia Young Readers Program, A poem published in the Anthology of Poetry by Young Americans in Asheboro, NC called "Spring"; [a.] Newport News, VA

CASE, KELLI A.
[b.] April 11, 1968, Cincinnati, OH; [m.] Christopher Case, September 20, 1994; [ch.] Cullen Case; [ed.] CDA, RDA; [occ.] Housewife/Mother; [memb.] Cerebral Palsey Foundation, National Association Board of Certified Dental Asst. NADA; [hon.] Clermont College Best of show (Art Award) top 10% of class for state board exams.; [pers.] I'd like to dedicate this poem to J.C. and Edna Kuhlman, for without them I would not be. I love you grandma and grandpa. My heart and dreams are with you.; [a.] Cincinnati, OH

CASTELLANO, SHARON
[pen.] Sharon Castellano; [b.] August 29, 1959, Athens, TX; [p.] Willie Brewer, Mavis Brewer; [m.] Dominic Castellano, May 28, 1996; [ch.] Angelia Marie, Christi Lynn; [ed.] Kaufman High National Institute of Technology College; [occ.] Computer Programmer; [hon.] Dean's List in college; [oth. writ.] Poem published in local newspaper.; [pers.] I express my feelings through my poems. Writing helps me to get my message across without offending anyone.; [a.] Lindale, TX

CASTLEBERRY, CHRISTINA E.
[b.] January 13, 1979, Fort Worth, TX; [p.] Mr. and Mrs. Walter E. Castleberry; [ed.] P.L. Dunbar H.S.E.P. (High School), Austin College, Candidate for B.S. May 2000; [occ.] Full Time College Student majoring in Sociology/ Pre-Medical Stud.; [memb.] Austin College Pre-Medical Society, Austin College Community Service Station,

Cook Children's Medical Center Volunteer; [hon.] Golden Rule Award for Community Service, President Scholar at Austin College, Piper Scholar in Texas, Advanced Placement Scholar, Dean's List at Austin College; [oth. writ.] Anthology of Poetry, Scientific Research, and Essays for school projects and scholarship contest.; [a.] Fort Worth, TX

CASTOR, CAROL
[b.] February 3, 1944, Bend, OR; [p.] Keith and Lena Morrison; [m.] William H. Castor (Divorced), August 28, 1965; [ch.] William F. Castor; [ed.] Ponca City High School, (OK), Univ. of Okla, BFA 1967, Art Students League of New York; [occ.] Artist; [memb.] American Society of Portrait Artists, P.E.O. Sisterhood; [hon.] Community Serv. award '84, Vinita Hall of Fame award '93, AAUW Woman of Achievement award '85, Who's Who in the South and Southwest, Who's Who in American Women; [pers.] Art and poetry afford vehicles for contemplating beauty and meaning in the human condition.; [a.] Vinita, OK

CASTRO, JACQUELINE MONIQUE
[pen.] Jackie; [b.] March 21, 1983, Miami, FL; [p.] Anibal F. and Maria C. Castro; [ed.] I am attending St. Brendan Elementary, 8th grade, next year I will be attending St. Brendan High School, and then I am planning to attend Florida State University.; [occ.] Student; [memb.] I belong to a softball team and a basketball team.; [oth. writ.] I have written other poems, such as "Love," "Dove," "Halloween Night," and "I Am,"; [pers.] I have a natural art inside of me. All my love has been put down on paper. And I just let my mind go when I'm writing.; [a.] Miami, FL

CATO, EVANGELIST SANDRA McMILLAN
[pen.] Lady Bug; [b.] March 8, 1948, San Francisco, CA; [p.] Roger W. McMillan, Levator McMillan; [m.] Evangelist Terry L. Cato, November 20, 1985; [ch.] Michael Grimes, Cassandra Fomby, Sgt. Stacey Houston; [ed.] College degrees, Galileo High School, S.F. City College, Laney Jr. College, S.F. Skills Center, Vision Christian University; [occ.] Licensed Pastoral Counselor, Writer, Evangelist; [memb.] Better Life Fellowship ever Prayer Ministry; [hon.] Ordained Minister 1992, Master's Degree in Christian Counseling; [oth. writ.] Writing published in local newspaper, several Booklets written and greeting cards.; [pers.] I know with God that all things are possible and we've been fearfully and wonderfully made in his image. I strive to touch the life's of those hurting...; [a.] Federal Way, WA

CAUDLE, IRIS LUCELLE
[pen.] John Smith; [b.] April 30, 1948, Shawnee, OK; [p.] Woodrow Caudle and Thelma; [m.] Was T. N. Bohannon, September 19, 1964; [ch.] Ken and Tom Bohannon; [ed.] Del City High, Oklahoma Christian College, North Texas State University; [occ.] Professional Cook; [memb.] Church of Christ; [hon.] National Honor Society, Alpha Lambda Delta; [oth. writ.] Attempting to write my own autobiography title may change when finished. Work is only half completed. "Princess Unveiled."; [pers.] I love to write about love and life and duty. My favorite writer is Solomon and King David of the Holy Bible.; [a.] Denton, TX

CERVANTES, TIFFANY
[b.] January 6, 1978, Bluffton, OH; [p.] Janet and Joe Cervantes; [m.] John Kinnamon (Boyfriend); [ed.] Ottawa - Glandorf High School; [occ.] Labor; [hon.] Highest Grade Point Average; [oth. writ.] One other poem published in a local newspaper in memory of my uncle for his birthday on Christmas Eve.; [pers.] I would like

at this time to say thank you to my mom, my dad, my family and my boyfriend. Also to say I love you all!!!; [a.] Ottawa, OH

CHAHLA, SAYDI
[pen.] Saydi Chahla; [b.] September 17, 1986, Ramsey College; [p.] Ella and Rita Chahla; [ed.] IHM - St. Luke's School Ms. Burns, Mrs. Grillo, Ms. O'Neill, O'Leavy, Mrs. McHale, Ms. Reardon, Mrs. Ricciardi, Sister Pauline.; [memb.] YMCA; [hon.] National Physical Fitness Award; [oth. writ.] I have entered Once Upon a Story, and Dare.; [pers.] I want to thank Elia, Rita, Elise, Rose and Danny Chahla. My editer Nancy Moser. With out them this would never had happened; [a.] Saint Paul, MN

CHANCE, VICTORIA J.
[b.] February 9, 1954, Gardner, KS; [p.] Orville and Iolene Karstetter; [m.] James E. Chance, December 27, 1980; [ed.] Park College, Parkville, MO, B.A. degree anticipated 12/97; [occ.] Full-time student; [hon.] Presidential scholar, Dean's List Park College, Parkville, MO, sustained superior performance award, IRS, 1989 and 1980.; [pers.] Reading (especially poetry) opens doors to other worlds. It feeds your soul.; [a.] Kansas City, MO

CHAPMAN, ERIC L.
[pen.] Gangsta, Slim II; [b.] August 16, 1973, Jackson, TN; [p.] Virginia A. Chapman, Roy M. Blalark Jr.; [m.] Quintella Y. (Hardin) Chapman, December 20, 1997; [ed.] Washington Douglas Elementary, Tigrett Junior High School, Jackson Central Merry High School, Class of 1991; [occ.] 1. Retired Factory Worker, 2. Real Estate Agent, 3. Up and Coming Black Entrepreneur; [memb.] Lifetime Member NAACP; [hon.] Outstanding Boy Chorus, Student of the Year 87-88; [oth. writ.] "As I Hold Your Hands", "My Love", "Thinking of U", "My Best Friend", "Long Road We've Traveled", "It Takes Two", "Against All Odds, One In A Million", "Every Man For Himself", "The 1st Love Of My Life", "African Violet", "A Heart As Large As Mine", "Depressed And Stressed Out", "Right Kinda Love"; [pers.] "The hardest part of being hard is to be real", Mr. Mike. "Never give up and never give out stop and catch your breathe and start back at it again" Sarah Ma. Chapman.; [a.] Jackson, TN

CHARETTE, BROOKE L.
[b.] August 22, 1971, Nashua, NH; [p.] Carol Charette, Cookie Charette; [ed.] Alvirne High, currently seeking clinical psychology degree; [occ.] Nanny; [memb.] PADI Scuba divers, Red Cross, International Nanny Association; [hon.] Dean's List; [oth. writ.] Honored short story on drug abuse, poetry in High School literary magazine, article Boston Parents paper; [pers.] Life's lessons are often disguised in many masks: Disappointment, painful regrets, and even happiness. The challenge is to uncover the trickery of the masquerade and grow from the hidden lessons - Brooke L. Charette; [a.] Reading, MA

CHARLES, SANDRA L.
[b.] March 5, 1961, Cincinnati, OH; [p.] Joseph Dettone and Florence Cox; [m.] John D. Charles, March 21, 1992; [ch.] Felicia Claxton, Sean Claxton, Megan Charles; [ed.] Hughes High; [occ.] Postal Clerk, Harte-Hanks Direct Mktg. Cincinnati, Ohio; [pers.] This poem was inspired by my children and I dedicate it to them.; [a.] Cincinnati, OH

CHARPIED, BRANDON TAYLOR
[pen.] B.T.; [b.] April 13, 1987, East Meadow, NY; [p.] Donna and Frank Charpied; [ed.] Presently a Freshman in Farmingdale High School; [oth. writ.] Christmas Cheer published in 1993.; [a.] Farmingdale, NY

CHASE, MICHELLE L.
[b.] January 14, 1983, Erie, PA; [p.] Don and Barbara Chase; [ed.] Riviera Elementary School, Stone Junior High; [occ.] Babysitting, Gardening; [memb.] National Junior Honor Society; [hon.] I'm an Honor Roll student in school, meaning I get mostly all A's. I also won an award for Design An Ad for the Florida Today Newspaper.; [oth. writ.] Several poems written in school that have gone on to other levels.; [pers.] When you feel terrific, notify your face. Don't worry be happy! Smile. A Quitter Never Wins and A Winner Never Quits, Smile, God Loves You!; [a.] Palm Bay, FL

CHENAULT, PAUL
[pen.] Paulie Chimes; [b.] October 29, 1977; [p.] Paula and Chuck Chenault; [ch.] Kristopher Chenault (Theory); [ed.] Disciple of life; [occ.] Representative of AT&T at Edward Blank Assoc.; [memb.] Lifelong member of the Brotherhood of the Eternal Sleep; [hon.] After all I've been through I'm honored to still be alive, to have gone through it all, and come out better than I went in.; [oth. writ.] Nothing else published, but plenty of songs and poems completed, with a lot more in the works.; [pers.] I'd like to thank everyone who made this possible, you know who you are. I write from my soul, and that will never change. It's who I am. Hi, Susan!!; [a.] Crowley, TX

CHENEY, ADAM J.
[b.] October 27, 1974, Ogden, UT; [p.] Dr. Merlih and Dr. Donna Cheney; [m.] Olivia Henderson; [ed.] Ogden High School, Weber State University, Cambridge University, England; [occ.] Undergrad student, Chief Editor, Metaphor (WSU Publication); [memb.] National Honor Society, Honours Programme, WSU; [hon.] 1st place WSU Tech writing contest, 1st place Writing Center Fiction Contest, Guest Reader, Honours Programme Showcase, Honorable mention WSU Poetry Contest; [oth. writ.] Numerous poems published locally, short stories published locally.; [pers.] Literature should refine our minds and quicken our sense of life.; [a.] Ogden, UT

CHERRY, FRANCES
[b.] November 1, 1926, Trinity, TX; [p.] William Thomas and Ida Johns; [m.] "The Late" Roy Wilson Cherry, June 7, 1947; [ch.] Three boys: Ronald Wilson Cherry, John Thomas Cherry, Robert Lee Cherry, 5 grandchildren: Tressa, Jason, Ashley, Nichols and Matthew; [ed.] I only made it through High School, graduated in Trinity, TX but my boys got their College Education and post graduate, one his Doctor of Theology; [occ.] In New Orleans my husband was a College Graduate. I am a retired home maker and widowed of the year; [hon.] I have never tried to get an honor or award for writings that I have done. I only do it for my pleasure. Poem submitted, "Old Glory."; [oth. writ.] I have written several poems of special occasion but never sent them away to be published. I just find peace and joy in sitting with pen in hand and counting my blessings that God has sent my way.; [pers.] Our flag should be held with dignity and respect, and carried by the men who have risked their lives in battle for our sake.; [a.] Colmesneil, TX

CHEZUM, TIFFANY
[b.] September 18, 1988, Rock Island, IL; [p.] Michael Chezum, Alice Chezum; [ed.] I am eight years old and in the fifth grade; [occ.] Student; [hon.] Honor Roll, Scholastic Awards; [oth. writ.] I love writing stories and poems but I have not had them published.; [pers.] I like writing mainly about nature. I want to write poems that people can picture in their minds. I like the challenge and the excitement of creative writing.; [a.] Viola, IL

CHIASSON, LAUREN
[m.] John Zawadski; [ch.] Leah Isabell; [occ.] Writer, Entertainer; [memb.] Currently - Member of Planet Earth; [pers.] I am a multi-level artist, writing, (poetry-story lyrics), performance-art, dance, comedy. As we grow and change so does the 'muse' - our source of inspiration. Like a spring I am always finding fresh inspiration surfacing. Being a mother (Leah, 3 1/2) has made me more appreciative of the moments that are creatively mine exclusively. I am an MC at The River Gallery, a folk cafe in Northville, Michigan. I perform my work interwoven with stories and humor weekly. There is nothing - (besides motherhood, which is a gift), that gives me greater pleasure than to create a pathos with an audience of joy, humor and echoes of the soul.

CISNEROS, DANNY E.
[pen.] Daniel "Ox" Cisneros; [b.] January 11, 1980, Harlingen, TX; [p.] JoAnn Baker, Arnold Cisneros; [ed.] S.H.S., T.V.H.S., Sanger High School, Sanger, TX; [occ.] Temecula Valley High School; [memb.] Temecula, CA; [oth. writ.] Several other poems and short stories.; [pers.] I wrote this for the one I loved. She taught me that "With God All Things Are Possible" and this is proof. Thank You Kelli.; [a.] Temecula, CA

CLAMPIT JR., ROBERT E.
[b.] March 14, 1962, Oakland, CA; [m.] Jill E.; [occ.] Electronic Film Assembler; [memb.] Walkegan Lodge #78 A.F.&A.M.; [pers.] I hope one day we will all look inside ourselves and discover our common link, and if my poems help one person do that then it will have been all worth it.; [a.] Burlington, WI

CLAPP, DONALD R.
[b.] August 15, 1931, Northampton, MA; [p.] Elmer and Maxine Clapp; [m.] Betty J. Foskett Clapp, June 30, 1956; [ch.] David and Donna; [ed.] Northampton High, Oberlin College, Boston U. School of Fine and Applied Arts; [occ.] Retired; [memb.] Green Valley Poetry Society, New England Historical and Genealogical Soc., Church Choir; [pers.] Although my Education was that of a musician and teacher, I have enjoyed a variety of endeavors. Painting, Sculpting Clay, Poetry lapidary work, silver smiting, and electronic technology.; [a.] Green Valley, AZ

CLARK, DAVID G. W.
[b.] March 10, 1975, Keflavik; [p.] Leonard and Shirley Clark; [ed.] High School Diploma, Adrian High School; [occ.] College Student; [hon.] Eagle Scout; [pers.] Love is a feeling that joins two people together in a mysterious way, for on this earth there are two people who are soul mates, which we all are in search of, to make us whole, as one not two individuals.; [a.] Adrian, MI

CLARK, DEBORAH H.
[b.] August 24, 1964, Elmira, NY; [p.] Ernest Hartman and Carol Hartman; [ch.] Elisha Raye; [ed.] Bloomfield High School; [occ.] Assistant Director, CIGNA Health Care; [pers.] My writing is a personal journey of discovery and understanding which enhances my life and my loves.; [a.] Bloomfield, CT

CLARK, DONNA P.
[b.] May 21, 1959, Miami, FL; [p.] Marion P. and Helen L. Parker; [m.] Ricky L. Clark, October 1, 1978; [ch.] Bronson Christopher, Chelsea Lynn; [ed.] William Byrd H.S., Vinton, Va.; [occ.] Home-maker, Home-schooling Children; [pers.] I feel my poetry is a gift from the Lord and I give Him all the glory for it.; [a.] Kernersville, NC

CLARK, MARGOT F.
[pen.] MFC; [b.] March 7, 1921, Knoxville, TN; [p.] John and Anita Fridge; [m.] David B. Clark, November 26, 1977; [ch.] Elizabeth (17), Veronica (16); [ed.] Sulphur High School, McNeese State University; [occ.] Disabled - 14 yrs.; [memb.] Heritage Presbyterian Church, Elder, past Girl Scout Leader 6 yrs.; [hon.] "Quill and Scroll," award H.S., McNeese Student Union Board and Student Government Association, Numerous Band Medals in Jr. High and H.S., Elder Presbyterian Church, Articles written up in Sulphur H.S. paper and home newspaper; [oth. writ.] I have a collection of my own poems (not published) called, "Experience of Life."; [pers.] I would like my poetry to allow those who read it to feel an emotion and to think about experiences in their lives.; [a.] Houston, TX

CLARKE, DAWN M.
[b.] November 16, 1957, Hyannis, MA; [p.] Earle and Josephine Clarke; [ch.] Ryan John, Kevin Douglas; [ed.] Dennis Yormouth High, Cape Cod Community College, A.S. Criminal Justice; [occ.] Paramedic, Cape Cod, MA; [memb.] American Heart Association; [pers.] To quote a romantic poet of whom I truly admire, R. Sexton "I will leave this earth knowing that I did not do all I had to do. But hope that whatever I leave behind will say I cared".; [a.] Sandwich, MA

CLAUSEN, NATASHA H.
[b.] April 11, 1980, Vista, CA; [p.] Gordon Clausen, Hope Clausen; [pers.] Poetry is a reflection, a revelation, and a hope. Without it, lessons would be forgotten, and dreams would be lost.; [a.] Liberty, SC

CLAYTON, KATHY J.
[b.] March 6, 1959, Tell City, IN; [p.] Daisy James, Cletus James; [m.] Hugh Ross Clayton Jr., April 1, 1978; [ch.] Timothy Ross, Russell Alan, James Gregory; [ed.] Perry Central High School, Leopold, IN Vincennes University Jasper Center, Jasper, IN; [occ.] Patient Accounting, Perry County Memorial Hospital, Tell City, IN; [memb.] First United Methodist Church Youth Coordinator, Southern Indiana walk to Emaus Community; [hon.] Tell City United Methodist 1996 Volunteer of the year, Dean's List, Hoosier Scholar; [a.] Tell City, IN

COATS, PHYLLIS
[b.] July 23, 1959, Anniston, AL; [p.] Dianne and Joes H. White; [m.] Robert Coats, November 1, 1979; [ch.] One daughter and one son; [occ.] Home school man and wife; [memb.] Hopeful Baptist Church, Feed The children, The Artist Guild; [pers.] This poem was my way of dealing with the death of my Granny, Della LeCroy. In my soul, heart and mind, this very loving, unselfish lady will be forever with me.; [a.] Lake City, FL

COBB, NANCY U.
[b.] August 30, 1977, Raleigh, NC; [ed.] Hollins College Class of 2000; [a.] Roanoke, VA

COFFMAN, RUBY PEARL
[pen.] Ruby Pearl Coffman; [b.] November 30, 1902, Indian Territory, OK; [p.] W. H. and Fannie Corum Coffman; [ed.] Graduate of Madill, Okla. Hi School, B.A. Degree - Southeastern State College, Durant, Okla. (Primary Teacher 40 yrs.), all in Okla. but 4 yrs. in Portales N.M., last 24 years in Ardmore-Franklin Grade School; [occ.] Retired since 1964; [memb.] Carter County Teacher's Assn., Lifetime member of Okla. Edu. Assn. (O.E.A.), Ardmore Church of Christ, Our Civic Chorus for 10 yrs., Kappa, Kappa, Iota (K.K.I.); [hon.] Have read some of my poems at Teacher's Meetings and at Church fellowships. Have always loved poetry - some

favorite poets - most early poets and - Christina Rosetti, Stevenson, De La Mare - a few; [oth. writ.] I have a collection of 20 poems - written, mainly, in the 60's and 70's. In the 80's and 90's - mainly verses for "new babies, marriages, graduates, or birthdays. (I enjoy reading my poems.); [pers.] I have tried to portray, with words, in an attractive way, the natural beauty of God's Creation - "The Outdoors" the beautiful color changes - the noises and activity of the "Outside".; [a.] Ardmore, OK

COGGINS, DEBBIE
[b.] March 20, 1959, Fullerton, CA; [m.] John Coggins, September 8, 1989; [ch.] Paula Riordan, Carrie Rosebeary and Sara Adams; [ed.] Westark Community College, Arkansas Tech. University; [occ.] Registered Nurse, Director of Nursing Services; [memb.] American Nurses Association; [hon.] Phi Beta Kappa Dean's List; [oth. writ.] Book of poetry compiled, pending publication, not yet completed.; [pers.] My poetry reflects life experiences and my feelings. I love all types of poetry.; [a.] Fifty Six, AR

COGNAT, MARY J.
[pen.] Mary J.; [b.] April 28, 1976; [p.] Glenn Cognat, Kathleen Moon; [ed.] Copiague Senior H.S., Coastal Carolina University, Suffolk Community College, Life; [occ.] Waitress at a Catering Hall; [oth. writ.] A private collection of my own.; [pers.] Every player in this game of life has something to say. I quietly do it with a pen, and the world keeps turning.; [a.] Copiague, NY

COHEN, GEORGE JOSEPH
[b.] March 16, 1961, Nyack, NY; [p.] Ira and Ethel; [ed.] Ramapo College of New Jersey, B.S. June 1983; [occ.] Insurance Benefits Administrator; [memb.] Coach, Bear Mt. Hockey Club, Ramapo College Alumni Assoc. United Way, Big Birds, Big Sis, Rockland Co.; [oth. writ.] Short stories, essays.; [a.] Stony Point, NY

COKUSLU, LYNDA M.
[b.] June 11, 1956, Atlanta, GA; [m.] Fethi Cokuslu, 1980's from Istanbul, Turkey; [ch.] Sasha, Sedef and Samantha; [memb.] International Society of Poets and Poets Guild, Learning Disabilities Assn., Travelers Protective Assn.; [hon.] Editor's Choice Award for, "Horseman's Last Song."; [oth. writ.] Horseman's Last Song in Library of Poetry's The Colors of Thought. "Francis Ann," in Poet's Guild Anthology. "Living Under Glass," in Sparrowgrass Anthology. Poem in a Treasury of Verse.; [a.] Hapeville, GA

COLCHADO, BARBARA
[b.] July 16, 1945, Richmond, VA; [p.] William A. Gatke, Elizabeth Gatke; [m.] Cruz Colchado, February 12, 1983; [ch.] Leonard W. Monnier; [ed.] Sarasota High, Somer's Business College; [occ.] Co-owner and operator of very small vegetable farm; [oth. writ.] This was the eighth poem I wrote. The first one entered in a contest. Have now written about 27.; [pers.] All my poems are Holy Spirit inspired and I praise our Lord daily, for the gift He has given me. My goal is to spread His words and to always give Him all the glory.; [a.] West Columbia, SC

COLE, DARLA L.
[pen.] Dennis Harper Jr.; [b.] March 14, 1970, Elkton, MD; [p.] Dave and Gladys Jarrell; [m.] Jerry Cole, April 29, 1994; [ch.] Corey and Kayla Reynolds; [ed.] H.S. Grad. - Mullens High - Mullens WV, Hairstylist Academy Statesville, NC; [occ.] Mgr. Twin State Corporation Beckley, WC 25801; [hon.] Academic All - American Honor Roll; [pers.] In hour of my Uncle Dennis Harper Jr., who died in Vietnam, who I never knew and also for my mother, who I love Dearly.; [a.] Beckley, WV

COLEMAN, BRENDA A.
[b.] September 24, 1960, San Francisco, CA; [p.] Mr. and Mrs. Eddie Coleman; [ed.] Deep Creek High School - 1977 Graduate, Old Dominion Univ. - Non Graduate; [occ.] Entertainer (Guitarist, Vocalist, Composer, Keyboards); [hon.] Psychology Award Who's Who...High School American Students; [oth. writ.] Many; [pers.] Live... from the heart.; [a.] Pensacola, FL

COLLETT, JULIA DIXON
[b.] September 3, 1923, Saint Louis, MO; [p.] Irene Rives and Forney Dixon; [m.] Leslie, July 17, 1944; [ch.] Juleta, Stephen, Douglas, Melissa and Rosanne; [ed.] 1941 Normandy High Grad., Wash. U. Psychology Classes; [occ.] Retired Exec. Sec. and Administrative Asst.; [memb.] Assembly of God, St. Louis Genealogical Society, Distinguished Member International Society of Poets; [hon.] Diamond Homer Recipient Famous Poets Society Hollywood, CA for 'True Codependent', September, 1996, 10 Editor's Choice Awards, National Library of Poetry, 6th place in Mtn. View Contest 1996; [oth. writ.] Eulogy on Groundhog Day, published: Julias Country Kitchen, Valentine Thoughts, Hershey Hugs, Codependency Release, Country Typewriter, Ozark Cookin', True Codependent, Potato Salad Recipe, Since You Went Away, Recycled Gifts, Lady Blue, Pine Bluff 1930, My Valentine; [pers.] Director, Laureates of Missouri Writers Group in St. Ann, MO, Author of Codependency In Verse and My Way Out.; [a.] Saint Ann, MO

COLOMB, ROSS
[pen.] Vex; [b.] November 5, 1979, New Orleans; [p.] Charlotte and Dennis Colomb; [pers.] In order to express ourselves we must first know ourselves. We must come to accept who we are and what we stand for.; [a.] Roswell, GA

COLON, MILTON
[b.] April 26, 1963, Brooklyn, NY; [p.] Milton Colon, Luz Colon; [ed.] St. Johns High School, Suffolk Community College; [pers.] I believe life depends upon the way truth is sought.; [a.] Brentwood, NY

CONKLE, OLIVIA
[b.] July 13, 1977, Bellflower, CA; [p.] Victor and Karen Conkle; [ed.] CVCS; [occ.] Office Manager and Freelance Writer; [oth. writ.] Kastel Shoes Catalog and Hang-Tags, inspiration: Dustin Deardorff; [pers.] Follow your heart and everything else will fall into place. Thank you to all who have inspired me.; [a.] Dana Point, CA

CONNELY, W. JEAN
[b.] August 17, 1955, McCook, NE; [p.] William H. and Delores E. (Dewey) Davis; [m.] Douglas J. Connely, June 11, 1983; [ch.] Justin R. Koetter, Megan M. Connely; [ed.] Trenton High School, Trenton, Nebraska; [occ.] New Accounts Representative - Poudre Valley REA Ft. Collins, Colorado; [memb.] Faith United Church, Windsor, CO; [oth. writ.] Several other poems, a few eulogies and memorials, prayers. None published.; [pers.] Most of my writings have been for family and friends for events in their lives and in mine. I enjoy writing poems and memorials for those I care for because it comes from my heart, therefore I can personalize it for them. It is a way I can easily express my feelings.; [a.] Windsor, CO

CONOVER, ASHLEY AMANDA
[pen.] Ashley Amanda Conover; [b.] February 18, 1984, Salt Lake City, UT; [p.] Jim and Marianne Conover; [ed.] Presently attending Westridge Middle School in the 7th grade; [memb.] MESA; [hon.] 1995 1st place Literature - Reflections, 1994 1st place Literature - Reflec-

tions, 1996 2nd place Literature - Reflections; [pers.] I spend every spare minute of my time creating poems and writing stories. Writing is a wonderful way of expressing yourself!; [a.] Price, UT

CONRAD, CHARLES J.
[pen.] Charles J. Conrad; [b.] December 15, 1969, Roaring Spring, PA; [p.] Charles E. Conrad, Roseanne G. Conrad; [ed.] Blair County Christian High School, Liberty University; [occ.] Neon Production, Blair Sign Company; [hon.] Keystone Christian Education, Association State and Regional Essay Awards; [oth. writ.] Sports reporter for college newspaper at Liberty University.; [pers.] Through writing, my desire is to express how God's love provides hope during life's most formidable circumstances.; [a.] Claysburg, PA

COOK, BRITTANY
[b.] December 13, 1981, Naples, FL; [p.] Richard Cook, Mary Ann Cook; [ed.] Freshman at The Academy High School; [occ.] Volunteer at Southwest Reginal Hospital; [hon.] Placed in the 1995 Lee County Writing Contest; [oth. writ.] Personal stories or journals. Never been published.; [pers.] I do what I love, and I love writing.; [a.] Bonita Springs, FL

COOK, NORMAN D.
[b.] April 16, 1946, Kona, KY; [p.] Can and Dee Cook; [m.] Connie, July 5, 1997; [ed.] Purdue Univ., Capital Univ.; [occ.] Sporting Products Developer and Distributor; [memb.] Masonic Lodge, Scottish, Rite, Shriner; [hon.] Numerous sales, Leadership and public contributions; [oth. writ.] Many romantic at this time kept private.; [pers.] "Have no fear that life might end, only that it may never have begun."; [a.] Savannah, GA

COOPER, IDA
[pen.] T. Bug; [b.] September 28, 1968, Tuscaloosa; [p.] Annie Cooper, John Cooper; [m.] Ivan, March 23, 1996; [ch.] Yolanda Cooper, Jennifer Cooper, Denorris Cooper; [ed.] Holt High; [occ.] Cook; [memb.] Mt. Zion Baptist Church P.T.A.; [pers.] I want to thank God. And I hope my poem will help someone.; [a.] Tuscaloosa, AL

COOPER, SHELLEY
[pen.] Annabella Wine; [b.] July 23, 1948, Tulsa, OK; [p.] Gayle Lucas, Polly Lucas; [m.] Stephan C. Cooper Sr., May 5, 1973; [ch.] Stephan C. Cooper Jr. (Clay); [ed.] Claremore High School, Okla. Military Academy; [occ.] Secretary, S.T.E.P.S. Alternative School, Chapel Hill ISD, Tyler, Texas; [memb.] Sylvania Baptist Church, Tyler, Tx., Chapel Hill Educational Secretaries and Aides Association; [oth. writ.] Haiku published in a Methodist publication.; [pers.] This poem was inspired by a friend whose mother had passed away. She shared with me that she and her husband at the same moment, unbeknownst to one another, saw formed in the clouds her mother lying in her casket.; [a.] Tyler, TX

COOPER, VICTORIA
[pen.] Tori Kat; [b.] December 29, 1982, Claremore, OK; [p.] John Cooper, Trudy Cooper; [ed.] Student of Bixby Public Schools; [memb.] Bixby Schools Gifted and Talented Organization (GTO); [oth. writ.] Writes monthly poetry corner in Junior High School Newspaper; [pers.] I'm only in a depression when I'm pushed into it, and I'm extremely hard to push; [a.] Bixby, OK

CORBITT, MILLIE B.
[b.] August 30, 1912, Shirley, AR; [p.] Joshua Bonner, Eva Bonner; [m.] Walter R. Corbitt, October 12, 1930; [ch.] Walter L., Wesley R., James A., Rita B., Vera R., Helen A.; [ed.] 8th Grade; [occ.] Homemaker; [hon.]

Who's Who in Poetry for Outstanding Achievement in Poetry, Won "Golden Poet Award for 1989" for poem "Turn Backward Time", Honorable Mention for Poem "Progress" 1990, World of Poetry!; [oth. writ.] I have a book of poems (never published) that I have written over the years. As one can see I have a good many years. I am now 84 years old. Still writing and love it.; [pers.] I can't remember when I wrote my first poem. My father wrote poetry, my grandfather wrote. My sister and brother both write. I guess it runs in the family.; [a.] Texarkana, AR

CORN, JESSICA
[pen.] The Black Enchantress and Duchess; [b.] June 2, 1981, Henderson County; [p.] Keith and Lisa Corn; [ed.] Still a student at East Henderson High School, 10th grade; [oth. writ.] (Current) short story and apx. 120 other poems.; [pers.] I have been greatly influenced and inspired by Edgar Allan Poe and William Shakespeare and also through personal experience.; [a.] Lirconia, NC

CORRERO, MICHAEL D.
[pen.] A. Gardner; [b.] November 9, 1959, Atlanta, GA; [p.] Sam P. Correro, Barbara J. Correro; [ed.] Delta Academy, High School, Mississippi Delta Junior College (M.D.J.C.) Assoc. Degree, Computer Science; [occ.] Systems Analysis, National Data Corp. (NDC), Atlanta, GA; [pers.] With the coming of the information age and new technologies, I hope mankind doesn't lose sight of the significance of a good book. I can't live without books.; [a.] Atlanta, GA

COTE, KAREN A.
[b.] August 6, 1966, Connecticut; [p.] George and Patricia Tripp; [m.] Gary D. Cote Sr., May 17, 1986; [ch.] Gary Jr. and Travis J. (Deceased); [occ.] Mother, Housewife, Student; [oth. writ.] Currently writing a book for children about death. I also write poems for my family and friends.; [pers.] The poem written in this book was written in memory of my son Travis who died at the age of two as a result of a car accident on November 17, 1995. The truest gift that you can share with others is a piece of yourself, a piece of your heart.; [a.] Ellington, CT

COTTERMAN, MICHAEL R.
[pen.] Michael R. Cotterman; [b.] November 16, 1954, Zanesville; [p.] Douglas and Donna Cotterman; [ed.] Bachelor of Arts in Studio Art, Oral Roberts University; [occ.] Newspaper printer; [oth. writ.] Poems: "The Blacksmith's Prayer," "The Unicorn's Shoe."; [pers.] Jesus is the source of the creative spark.; [a.] Worthington, OH

COTTOM, DAWN
[pen.] Dawn Molchan, Dawn Nickels; [b.] March 18, 1963, Toledo, OH; [p.] George W. and Reva E. Truax; [m.] James C. Cottom, November 23, 1995; [ch.] Angie, Jessie, Carl and Bradley and Angel; [ed.] Graduated from Woodward H.S. and have 2 yrs. college; [occ.] Cook at Will Rogers Elementary, Ama, TX; [oth. writ.] "Moving On," published in Treasured Poems of America, Fall 96, "The Crimes of Being Old," and "Loneliness of Death," published in Masterpieces of Modern Verse, 1985.; [pers.] This poem is dedicated to my husband, Jimmy, with all my love.

COTTRELL, SHIRLEY HUGHES
[b.] August 19, 1947, Richwood, WV; [p.] Nyle B. Hughes, Pauline Hughes; [m.] John L. Cottrell, July 9, 1966; [ch.] April Dawn, Candice Lee; [ed.] East Bank High School; [occ.] Owner-self employed, Shirley Seal Inc.; [memb.] Christ United Methodist Church, Sincerity Chapter #295 O.E.S., Past President Glendale PTA, Bridger Jr. High PTSA, Past Secretary, Independence Council of PTA's, President Independence Girls Softball

Association; [hon.] D.A.R. Citizenship Awards East Bank High School, Pop Warner Volunteer Coach of the year, "Proud Grandmother to Brooke"; [oth. writ.] No other poems. This poem was written for my Daddy for showing me pride and love throughout my days with him. My Dad had brain cancer and died December, 1985. I gave this poem to him June, 1985.; [pers.] This poem was written for my Daddy for Father's Day, 1985. My Dad was very ill and I wanted to give him something very special this year to show him a little of how I felt about him. He died December, 1985.; [a.] Independence, MO

COURI, CRISTINA
[b.] March 17, 1986, Holy Name Hospital, Teaneck, NJ; [p.] Maria and Ronald Couri; [ed.] Presently in 5th Grade at Luther Lee Emerson School in Demarest, New Jersey; [occ.] Student in 5th Grade I'm striving to work up to my goal, becoming a famous writer. I've been greatly influenced by my wonderful Fifth Grade teachers Mrs. A. Ross and Mrs. D. Ross; [pers.] What you are becoming is more important than what you are accomplishing.; [a.] Demarest, NJ

COUTURIER, DEBRA J.
[pen.] Debra J. Couturier; [b.] March 3, 1958, Goshen, IN; [p.] Marcile and Henry Cripe; [m.] Alain J. Couturier, July 14, 1990; [ch.] Nicholas Henry and Alexander Alan; [ed.] Goshen High Indiana University; [occ.] Registered Nurse; [memb.] Goshen City Church of the Brethren; [hon.] Sigma Theta Tau; [oth. writ.] "To My Love," published in The Isle of View; [pers.] My writings strive to elicit those emotions which allow us to be kinder, more loving people; [a.] Middlebury, IN

COX, J. LEANNE
[pen.] J. Cox, Leanne Cox; [b.] April 9, 1975, Georgia; [p.] Debora and Robert Garner; [m.] Christopher Janis; [occ.] International Customs Broker; [oth. writ.] Poem published in National Library of Poetry's Anthology "Songs On The Wind".; [pers.] If even one person can relate to my poetry and I have made them feel, I have accomplished something wonderful.; [a.] Arlington Heights, IL

CRAIG, DAVID
[b.] July 5, 1938; [p.] Robert and Constance Craig; [m.] Lois Craig, April 22, 1961; [ed.] 12 years Academic and Technical 2 1/2 yrs. and a lifelong self-educational pursuit/goal to read all the great classics of poetry, prose, history, philosophy, religion, biography, and much non-fiction.; [occ.] Out of work Telecommunications Analyst (voice and lowspeed data). And seeking new directions. I love to write and love the written word.; [memb.] Biblical Archaeological Society, Historic Preservation Trust, GOP; [hon.] Not applicable. No Pulitzers or Nobels or other coveted mantle-piece metallics. I am not without a normal supply of ego and pride, but the pursuit of awards, medals, honors, etc. has never in itself been of interest to me. Of course, I recognize and honor those who achieve them as a bi-product of sheer talent, merit, and hardwork and imagination when doing the things they love to do best.; [oth. writ.] Only that I am an impulsive writer. Letters primarily to editors, all relatives and acquaintances and many famous historical personages covering an eclectic array of topics. In high school I used to enjoy making up poems in the style and meter of famous bards (Sandburg, Poe, etc.). As a young Marine I was one of those GIs who ala Cyrano used to write other guys proxy-love-letters and miscellaneous hate-mail to creditors.; [pers.] If I were to describe myself, I would have to say I consider myself a modern version of a Renaissance Man. A man who is steady in adversity, loyal in friendship, true to his word.

A man who knows and loves his God, his family and his country. An eternal optimist but grounded in realism. One who is well aware of mankind's fallen nature but believes in his ability to rise above it and achieve great things.; [a.] Matawan, NJ

CRAIG, PENNY
[pen.] Penny Lane, Penny Morgan; [b.] January 31, 1972, Mount Vernon, IL; [m.] Kevin R. Craig, December 12, 1995; [occ.] Restaurant Management, Old Wives' Tales Restaurant, Portland OR; [a.] Portland, OR

CRAWFORD-MCFIELD, LORRIE
[pen.] Princess; [b.] January 28, 1960, Crystal Springs, MS; [p.] Mr. and Mrs. Calbin W. Crawford; [m.] Eddie McField Sr.; [ch.] Eddie McField Jr.; [ed.] Utica High, Utica Community College, Jackson State University; [occ.] Residence Education Activities Assistant at Miss. School for the deaf; [memb.] Faith Christian Center (Church) MAACP member, Courtesy Committee; [hon.] Who's Who Among American Junior Colleges (1979) Miss Thespian, Best Actress of Drama Guild; [oth. writ.] Monologue: "Show Me The Way" a variety of poems, both of spiritual and secular tones, a few lyrics one in recording with family (immediate family) "I'm on the Lord's side".; [pers.] Love your soul enough to let it live abundantly yet wisely refuse to be shortchanged by the compass of ignorance.; [a.] Jackson, MS

CRONK, SEADRA
[pen.] Seadra Miller-Thiessen; [b.] July 9, 1980, Arcadia, CA; [p.] Bernita Cronk; [ed.] I am currently a junior at Gabrielino High School in San Gabriel, CA; [memb.] Pep (song leader); [hon.] I've sent two different poems to three different anthologies. You, Sparrow Grass Poetry Forum, and the National Anthology of Poetry. So far I'm a semifinalist in your contest and Sparrowgrass. The other has yet to contact me.; [oth. writ.] "The Walkers," there are many other writings, however they wouldn't fit, and "The Walkers," is the only other poem I've entered in a contest, and made to semi-finals with.; [pers.] Never underestimate the power of a pencil. And always remember that sometimes a piece of paper is your best friend.; [a.] San Gabriel, CA

CROSON, RANDOLPH
[b.] April 21, 1957, Baltimore, MD; [p.] Ralph Croson; [m.] Evelyn Croson; [ch.] Randolph Jr., Jonathan Everett, Zuri Cete, Atira; [a.] Cincinnati, OH

CROWELL, TERESA JONES
[b.] October 7, 1955, Harbor City, CA; [p.] Verne and Jean Jones; [m.] Rick Crowell, September 6, 1995; [ch.] Michal Davis, Rachall Shaw, David Yoder, John Yoder, Jim Shaw, Jill Crowell; [ed.] Photography Diploma; [occ.] Photographer, poetry writer, wood carver, furniture maker; [hon.] (Certificate of Award) on Hand Carved Grand Grizzly Bear Clock; [pers.] I write poetry for the way I feel and the beautiful things around me, and the most important people in my life. I have grandchildren: Jimmy G. Shaw, Natsha Davis, James Davis, Alex Shaw, Angel Davis; [a.] Moyie Springs, ID

CROWLEY, ROBERT EDWARD
[b.] June 25, 1983, Charleston, SC; [p.] Jerald and Elma Crowley; [occ.] Student - Berkeley Middle School, Moncks Corner, SC; [memb.] Hopewell Baptist Church; [hon.] National Jr-Beta Club, ACE Program, Aspiring Artist of Berkeley County; [a.] Moncks Corner, SC

CULAFIC, PETER M.
[b.] March 8, 1961, Chicago, IL; [p.] Miladin N. Culafic and Katarina Z. Culafic; [m.] Laura M. Culafic, May

27, 1989; [ch.] Nicholas M. Culafic; [ed.] Morton West High School, Morton College; [occ.] Police Officer for the Village of North Riverside, Illinois; [memb.] Fraternal Order of Police, Illinois Police Association, Police Benevolent Association; [hon.] Current President of the North Riverside Fraternal Order of Police Lodge #110. Current treasurer and unit reporter for the North Riverside Police Benevolent Association Unit #73. And current trustee for the North Riverside Police Pension Board.; [oth. writ.] Reporter for the North Riverside Police Benevolent Association #73, writing unit news articles quarterly for the last several years.; [pers.] I am truly proud and grateful to be a police officer as reflected in my poetry.; [a.] North Riverside, IL

CUMMINS, MARJORIE
[pen.] Gypsy Holtze, Trela Andrews; [b.] August 7, 1980, Grand Rapids; [p.] Leo Cummins, Pauline Cummins; [ed.] South Haven High School (Class of 1998); [occ.] Student, Writer; [memb.] First Congregational Church Mission Board and High School Youth Group, South Haven High School Symphony Orchestra, South Haven High School "Critic" Staff; [hon.] South Haven High School, Symphony Orchestra, Most Improved Musician 1996; [oth. writ.] Several poems and articles in my school paper (The Critic).; [pers.] Respect your loved ones, but don't let them tell you who you are. Follow your heart and your dreams...; [a.] South Haven, MI

CUNNINGHAM, SHARON SUE
[b.] March 12, 1950, Adrian, WV; [p.] Francis Tenney and Emma Cobb; [m.] Rondall Lee Cunningham Sr., August 23, 1967; [ch.] Kelly Sue, Randall Lee, Angela Lee, Mary Jo, and Rebecca Lynn; [ed.] Riverside High School, Painesville, Ohio; [occ.] Rehabilitation worker and Housewife (taking care of my handicapped daughter); [memb.] Worldwide Church of God; [hon.] The National Library of Poetry selected my poem, "Stair Steps," as a semi-finalist for the final competition held in summer of 1997. This poem will also be published in the anthology called "Through the Looking Glass."; [oth. writ.] I am continuously creating my own original poems from memories of the past, special events and special people, and whatever seems to inspire me to make one up at the moment. I currently have over 60 original poems.; [pers.] The majority or my poems are written about my family and special events. This one is titled, "Stair Steps." This poem is very special to me because it brings back memories of my five children. My children are very close in age and while they were growing up they reminded me of stair steps.; [a.] Four States, WV

CURLEY, CAROLINE
[b.] August 14, 1915, Omaha, NE.; [p.] Henry J. Dilgard, Carrie Davis Dilgard; [m.] Marvin Taves, December 25, 1942, Divorced -1976, Robert Curley, April 15, 1985 - Divorced -1990; [ch.] John Taves, Peter Taves; [ed.] White Bear H. S. Bethel Jr. College, Hamline U., U of MN. Grad School, The Johns U., Catholic U.; [occ.] Retired; [memb.] AARP, NRTA, Presbyterian, Democrat, Women's Auxiliary to the Oregon Symphony, Eastmoreland Branch; [hon.] DAR Award for Excellence in History, Alpha Kappa Delta, Kappa Delta Epsilon, Pi Gamma Mu. Listed in Personalities of the South, 1969, World Who's Who of Women, 1973, Who's Who in the East, 1979 through 1990; [pers.] "A word fitly spoken is like apples of gold in pictures of silver." Prov. 25:11. "A Merry Heart doeth good like a medicine." Prov. 17:22. "Pray without ceasing" 1st. Th. 5:17. "In everything give thanks." 1st. Th. 5:18. (King James Version, Holy Bible, 1937.; [a.] Portland, OR

CURREY, DAVID
[b.] February 27, 1971, El Paso, TX; [p.] Martha and Jim Currey (Richard Bussell, Father); [m.] Kimberly Currey, September 10, 1994; [ed.] Coronado High School, University of Texas, El Paso; [occ.] Vice President at Currey, Adkins, Cook and Co., El Paso, TX; [memb.] Rotary International; [pers.] The world we know is merely an insignificant part of something bigger which we know very little about.; [a.] El Paso, TX

CUTHAIR, DELBERT D.
[b.] September 21, 1972, Durango, CO; [p.] Veronica Silva; [ch.] Brittny Leann Cuthair; [occ.] Oilfield Technician; [memb.] Member of Southern Ute Indian Tribe (Ignacio Co); [a.] Durango, CO

DAGGETT, CATHERENE E.
[pen.] Owl; [b.] October 3, 1919, Baltimore, MD; [p.] Charles and Catherine Dietz; [m.] Edward Daggett, June 9, 1946; [ch.] Three; [ed.] High School, Jr. College; [occ.] Retired; [memb.] American Legion Aux., Past District President, Charter President of above, Foster Parents, Sec. Chamber of Commerce; [hon.] Sunday School Teacher; [oth. writ.] Local Papers, Bermuda Paper; [a.] Betterton, MD

DANCHEVA, ROUMIANA
[pen.] Demeter Hadji Vasilev; [b.] January 21, 1946, Telish, Bulgaria, Europe; [p.] Stoian Dancev, Manka Dancev; [m.] May '74 - Divorced October '76; [ch.] Nickolina Guergeva; [ed.] 32 Tech. High School, University of Architecture and Civil Engineering, Sofia Bulgaria Europe, EDV-Munchen, Germany, Glendale College, Ca, Postgrad, Bulgaria, Sofia; [occ.] Child-care, Self-improvement; [memb.] A.I.P. (American Inst. of Physics), The Smitsonian Institution, Air and Space, International Relationships; [hon.] Master's degree in civil engineering recognized in USA, advanced technologies self-educ-reading books from ancient times and life time, Bulgarian, Russian, German, English languages; [oth. writ.] Professional not-published, now how technology projects etc., new technologies and scientific projects.; [pers.] "Explore the world for future generations," "Get the step to 21st century shorter way than you ever expect."; [a.] Corona-Elmhurst, NY

DANIEL, GERALDINE P.
[pen.] J. P. Daniel; [b.] January 23, 1947, Tallassee, AL; [p.] Erma L. Kennebrew and James L. Kennebrew; [m.] Robert L. Daniel; [ch.] Kim, Debra, Gerard, Tracy and Micheal Potts; [ed.] Early childhood degree from Alabama State University; [occ.] Pre-school Teacher at Head Start; [memb.] American Heart Association; [oth. writ.] Someone To Talk To, Happy Birthday Son, My Grandmother; [pers.] I write from the heart my about inner feelings.; [a.] Tallassee, AL

DANIEL, PATRICIA A.
[b.] June 27, 1957, Fort Dix, NJ; [p.] Frank and Nelcie Williams; [m.] John H. Daniel Jr., September 24, 1988; [ch.] Jordyn Rene, Justin Scott, Jeremy Tate; [ed.] Edison High, Rutgers College, Rutgers University, New Brunswick, NJ; [occ.] Manger, AT&T, Piscataway, NJ; [memb.] Project Management Institute, (PMI), Workshop Leader for Creative Living Women's Conference (CLWC), Founder of Women with a Message Fellowship Ministry; [hon.] Corporate Circle of Excellence Award, Team Awards; [oth. writ.] Winner and Honorable Mention of New York Magazine contests.; [pers.] Nothing brings me more joy than to share my treasures of expression that God alone has placed within me and by grace alone has allowed me to give away.; [a.] Edison, NJ

DANNI, TODD
[b.] April 18, 1975, Williamsville, NY; [p.] Patricia A. Gavin and F. Robert Danni; [ed.] 4-year Bachelor degree in Criminal Justice and Economic Management from Buffalo State College; [occ.] Fitness Equipment Specialist; [memb.] U.S. Junior Hockey Assn.; [oth. writ.] Other poems published in local school papers; [pers.] I am only going to be young once, and trying to be young forever!; [a.] Amherst, NY

DARNELL, WILLIAM
[pen.] William Darnell; [b.] December 11, 1926, Hollywood, CA; [p.] B. B. Darnell; [m.] Verna M. Darnell; [ch.] Girls: Delores, Gail, JoAnn, Denise, Boy: Don; [ed.] Elementary: MGM Little Red School House, Culver City, Ca., University of California Berkeley 1950; [occ.] Chess Coach, Instructor, Washoe County School District, Reno, Nevada; [memb.] St. Therese Church of the Little Flower Catholic Church, Foster Grandparent Program, Reno. Veterans of Foreign Wars, American Legion, Disabled American Veterans; [hon.] Distinguished Flying Cross, Air-Medal (W.W.II) U.S. Navy, (Former Aviation Pilot (Lt.) U.S. Navy; [oth. writ.] Many articles, and some poetry published in local newspapers and National (slick) magazines. Also: Forever And A Day, 1996, The National Library of Poetry, 1 Poetry Plaza, Owings Mills, MD 21117-6282.; [pers.] "My poetry is dedicated to The Wordsmith, Jo Belmont, who has given so many hours to administration of Young Masters Chess Club, Inc. and Project Chess, a Non-Profit, Tax deductible Organization." "When your memory goes—forget it!"; [a.] Reno, NV

DASH, PRATIK A.
[b.] June 11, 1988, Fort Worth, TX; [p.] Prabir Dash, Prajesh Dash; [ed.] Moore Elementary 3rd Grade student; [pers.] To my family who gave me the inspiration to write poetry.; [a.] Lewisburg, TN

DAVE, REENA
[b.] November 26, 1996, Punjab, India; [m.] Peresh Dave, May 11, 1992; [ed.] Elmont Memorial H.S. St. John's University; [occ.] Admin. Assist.; [memb.] Brahmin Society of NY; [oth. writ.] Poem "God Makes The Laugh" published in Images Magazine; [pers.] To me, writing is not a form of art but more like a get - away into paradise, my personal paradise.; [a.] Flushing, NY

DAVENPORT, JANINA
[pen.] Janina Davenport; [b.] May 13, 1914, Holyoke, MA; [p.] Joseph Smiertka, Bertha Sredniawa; [ch.] Kent Davenport, Jane Oates; [ed.] Greenfield High, Pratt Institute, Univ. of Mass. at Amherst in Soviet and Eastern European Studies, Arizona State Univ. at Tempe, B.S. in Science; [occ.] Retired Reg. Nurse, served 5 years in Navy Nurse Corps.; [memb.] Deerfield Art Assoc. Polish Genealogical Society of MA, Polish Genealogical Society of CT and Eastern New England, Navy Nurse Corp. Association, Am bi-lingual, have tutored Polish immigrants, also Japanese wives in English language in Amherst whose husbands are here for a few years at Univ. of Mass.; [hon.] One Man Art Show in Placerville Calif. Navy Commendation for work done while on duty when Ammunition Dump explosion occurred at Belleveu, MD 1943; [oth. writ.] Discovering lost relatives in Zakopane, Poland through one of my prof while studying Arts and Crafts in Poland. Poems have appeared in local newspaper. Also my 5 summer sessions spent at various universities in Poland, appeared in local newspaper from 1971-79 under communism. "How we became Unitarians in 1927."; [pers.] Widen your horizons by knowing people in other cultures...for life is very short.; [a.] Amherst, MA

DAVENPORT, JOSHUA
[b.] November 7, 1979, Warren County; [p.] David and Patricia Davenport; [occ.] High School Student; [oth. writ.] Too many to name them all; [a.] McMinnville, TN

DAVID, EVA-MARIE
[b.] August 22, 1982, Bryan, TX; [p.] Richard A. and Jeanne M. David; [ed.] Mercy High School, Class of 2000, Farmington Hills, MI; [memb.] Girl Scouts of America, U.S. Swimming, Model United Nations; [hon.] Girl Scouts Silver Award, Honor Roll; [oth. writ.] "Harmless", Anthology of Poetry by Young Americans, 1996 ed.; [a.] Farmington Hills, MI

DAVIDSON, YASMIN
[pen.] Yasmin Davidson; [b.] March 7, 1978, New York; [p.] Vindell Mason and Sydney Davidson; [ed.] Currently attending Bethun-Cookman College. I am a freshman, majoring in Nursing but hope to switch to Pre-med next semester; [occ.] Student; [memb.] Mount Sinai Seventh Day Adventist Church; [hon.] Dean List, Bethune, Cookman High School student Certificate of Excellence, Who's Who Among America's, Certificate of merit, limited Methodist Center of Teacher Certificate of Academic Excellence, United Federation Merit Award, Bethune-Cookman College, Honorary Certificate, Alpha Kappa Alpha; [oth. writ.] Poems, some published in my church magazine and high school paper; [pers.] I try to be the best I can be hoping to make a difference along the way.; [a.] Queens Village, NY

DAVILA-RONDA, DALYIA
[pen.] Dalyia Davila-Ronda; [b.] April 5, 1974, Bronx, NY; [p.] Jose F. and Vilma F. Davila; [m.] Joseph Ronda, November 10, 1994; [ed.] I didn't finish High School because of family problems. I'm working on getting my G.E.D. My high school was Grace H. Dodge; [occ.] Housewife, Cadet Officer; [memb.] Star of the Sea, Sea Cadet Corps; [hon.] Athletic Awards (Swimming Track), Architecture, Art, Community Service, Fund Raising, Math, Social Studies; [oth. writ.] I have more poems that I have written.; [pers.] I like to express my feelings by writing. I hope to help other girls in the future.; [a.] Bronx, NY

DAVIS, HANNAH L.
[pen.] Hannah L. Davis; [b.] July 21, 1983, Baltimore, MD; [p.] Linda Pohlhaus; [ed.] Went to the Country School from K-6. Currently an 8th grader at St. Michaels High School where I was a 7th grader too.; [occ.] Student; [hon.] Outstanding Art Award, Principles Honor Roll for the past 2 years, all 4 terms; [oth. writ.] No other published works. I write a lot on my own though.; [pers.] There was always this little creative spark inside of me. I hope one day it'll become a fire.; [a.] McDaniel, MD

DAVIS, IDA
[b.] June 13, 1928, Salem, OH; [p.] William Fish, Mary Fish; [m.] Boyce W. Davis, January 20, 1947; [ch.] Frances, Wayne, Dale, Cindy; [ed.] High School, by Dayton G.E.D. Center 348 West First Street, Dayton, Ohio, 11-5-1980; [occ.] Housewife; [hon.] World History, February 3, 1969, World History April 7, 1969, American History July 9, 1969, Science January 15, 1970; [oth. writ.] I write small story letters and poems, "My Little One," is the only one I have ever sent in; [pers.] I strive to understand how and when the whole universal was formed and by whom.

DAVIS, JIM
[b.] June 10, 1923, Chicago, IL; [p.] Hazel Davis, Hollis Finch (Step Father); [m.] Doris Davis, October 27, 1943; [ch.] Lisa, Stephen; [ed.] Bachelor of Science, Upper Iowa University, Fayette, Iowa; [occ.] Artist-Cartoonist,

Columnist; [memb.] American Legion, Lions Club, United Methodist Ch.; [hon.] Who's Who in American Colleges and Universities 1947-1948; [oth. writ.] Weekly Column in Northern Wyoming Daily News, Worland, Wyoming; [pers.] I determine each day not to take myself too seriously - and pray that I never lose my sense of humor.; [a.] Worland, WY

DAVIS, LEXIE
[b.] August 31, 1958, San Diego, CA; [m.] Regina Davis, January 24, 1986; [ch.] Joshua, age 3½; [ed.] Oceanside High School, Mira Costa College; [occ.] Self-employed, Business and Management Consultant; [memb.] Portland Victory Fellowship; [oth. writ.] Many poems and songs; [pers.] A poem is a creation, and has a creator. Having worked at the Air National Guard Base (guarding F-4 fighting jets) in Reno, NV, I was impressed with the design of the F-4 jets. If I flew over a volcano, and then dropped into it all the raw materials needed to create an F-4 jet, how long would I have to wait before an F-4 jet came flying out of the volcano? The human body and its intricate design makes the fighter jet look like a child's toy. I can't believe mankind evolved on its own, any more than someone reading my poem could believe it wrote itself.; [a.] Portland, OR

DAVIS, SHEILA L.
[pen.] Nefertiti Ra-Temu; [b.] September 14, 1934, New York City, NY; [p.] Judge Davis Sr., and Cora Lee Wilson Davis; [ed.] City College of NY: BA in Foreign Language (Germany and Spanish), Minor in Secondary Education, Bank Street College of Education - NYC: Graduate courses in Elementary Education, The American College - Bryn Mawr Pennsylvania: Professional Degrees: CLU and ChFC; [occ.] Financial Planner, Income Tax Specialist (Self-Employed), Factoring Broker; [memb.] AARP, Central Harlem Senior Citizen - Kennedy Branch; [hon.] Certificates for Voluntary Work as a USO Hostess and Entertainer, Hostess and Entertainer at Montrose Veterans Hospital, Treasurer and Newsletter Editor/Publisher/Writer for the CCVY Black Alumni Society and the CCVY Onyx Society, Treasurer and Volunteer for the twelve good deeds.; [oth. writ.] Non-Published Poems, Essays, Prose, Articles, Movie Script, Published Newsletters; [pers.] I wish to express the positive aspects of the human condition and experience in order to instill hope and elevate the spirit. Sometimes I need to express my pain, in the hope that those feeling the same pain will be catharticized.; [a.] New York, NY

DAVIS, SYLVIA
[b.] September 1, 1911, Chicago, IL; [p.] William D. Davis, June 6, 1937; [ch.] Kenneth Davis, MD, Russel Davis, JDD, Darlyne Engelman; [ed.] De Paul University High School, De Paul University, De Paul University Law School, Truman College Dean's List, The Art Institute of Chicago, BAE, Illinois Institute of Technology, MSAE; [occ.] Artist, High School Art Teacher (Waller High School), English Teacher; [memb.] Municipal Art League, S.A.I.C. Alumni, I.T.T. Alumni, Rho Sigma Delta Sorority; [hon.] Numerous exhibits and awards - De Paul University, Municipal Arts League - publications in "Arts and Activities" magazine, two books published, won first prize - US. First Class postage stamp to be issued, Edgewater Art Guild; [pers.] My ultimate goal has always been to have mankind appreciate and enjoy all art in every form.; [a.] Chicago, IL

DAVIS, TERRI H.
[pen.] thDavis; [b.] November 20, 1970, Chicago, IL; [ed.] Oak Grove High School, Oral Roberts University;

[hon.] National Dean's List, Provost's List; [oth. writ.] Several unpublished poems and short stories.; [pers.] My writing always represents feelings and questions common to all mankind. Inspiration, therefore, often comes from the subject of the writing itself.; [a.] Tulsa, OK

DAVIS, WILLIAM R.
[b.] April 13, 1926, San Bernardino, CA; [m.] Maria Davis, July 24, 1965; [ch.] Robert, Peter, John, Christina, Elizabeth; [ed.] Univ. of Oregon; [occ.] Sales Manager; [memb.] Knights of Columbus; [oth. writ.] Many poems.; [pers.] Poems reflect my thoughts.; [a.] Petaluma, CA

DAVIS JR, CLARICE
[pen.] Dobbie; [b.] December 21, 1964, Galveston, TX; [p.] Bessie Simmons, Clarice Davis Sr.; [ch.] Blake Gregory Davis, Precious Rollins; [ed.] La Marque High; [occ.] Artist; [hon.] Many various Navy Achievement Awards; [oth. writ.] Several poems published for The Observer newspaper; [pers.] In my writings, I'm always attempting to expose personal hidden truths to the reader. Emotional trauma acts as a catalyst for my inspiration.; [a.] Galveston, TX

DAVISON, EILEEN M.
[b.] August 28, 1978, New York; [p.] Colleen and Robert Davison; [ed.] Saint Mary Central High School; [hon.] Excellence in Leadership, Excellence in Academics; [a.] Neenah, WI

DAYE, YVONNE
[ed.] Merl Grove High; [occ.] Homemaker Technician; [oth. writ.] Several poems, unpublished, several children's stories, unpublished. A novel, unpublished, an article that was published in the local newspaper. Currently working on non-fiction book.; [pers.] We can achieve world peace if we first have inner peace. You cannot be at peace with anyone if you're not at peace with yourself.; [a.] Hartford, CT

DE LAUDER, LILY
[m.] Edward, 1952; [ch.] Michael, Stephen and Paul; [ed.] Catholic Schools in England, Valley College, Van Nuys, CA; [occ.] Homemaker; [memb.] Ham-radio Operator; [hon.] Award for service in Valley Presbyterian Hospital Emergency Room ten years volunteer; [oth. writ.] "Sleep Softly My Son," story of Paul, my son who was killed, several poems, short stories, essays.; [pers.] Writing helped me through grief after my son's death. I also write to make my granddaughter laugh - I love animal stories.; [a.] North Hollywood, CA

DEAN, JULES
[b.] July 25, 1956, Sumter, SC; [p.] Joan and Julian Beard; [ch.] Andee Dean; [ed.] Booker T. Washington High, Stella Adler Academy of Acting; [occ.] Screenwriter/Actress; [memb.] Screen Actors Guild and American Federation of Television and Radio Artists (AFTRA); [hon.] National Honor Society and Who's Who In America; [oth. writ.] Screenplays "The Companion" and "League of Honor", 1st poem published at age 12 in school.; [pers.] Music extremely inspires me along with the passion of works such as Dante and Shakespeare.; [a.] North Hollywood, CA

DEATON, HOWARD A.
[pen.] Howard A. Deaton; [b.] January 2, 1917, El Paso, TX; [p.] E. S. and Alice Deaton; [m.] Shelby Minor Deaton, October 5, 1943; [ch.] Durelle Steffens, Howard Deaton II; [ed.] High School; [occ.] Retired; [memb.] T.C.W., Church of Christ; [hon.] Hon. Discharge CCC, Hon. Discharge USAF; [oth. writ.] Various poems, 1 short story.; [pers.] Treat all like you want to be treated.; [a.] Saint Louis, MO

DEBRITA, DANIELLE C.
[b.] April 3, 1984, Pensacola, FL; [p.] Linda D. DeBrita; [ed.] I am completing 7th grade at a Montessori Middle School. I was home schooled until I started Montessori in 6th grade.; [occ.] Student (7th grade); [pers.] Like soft thoughts of prose flowing; [a.] Pensacola, FL

DECKER, BRETT MICHAEL
[b.] November 5, 1970, Sandusky, OH; [p.] John Erie Decker, Sharon Decker; [ed.] Brother Rice High School, Albion College, Johns Hopkins University, National Journalism Center; [occ.] National Political Reporter, Television Producer Evans and Novak, Washington, DC; [memb.] Detroit Athletic Club, National Press Club, United Autoworkers of America, Sigma Chi Fraternity, Federalist Society, Old St. Mary's Roman Catholic Church of Chinatown; [pers.] "All roads lead to Rome eventually".; [a.] Alexandria, VA

DECKER, HARVEY E.
[b.] March 6, 1973, Joliet, IL; [p.] Edward and Athalean Decker; [ed.] A Senior at Western Kentucky University; [occ.] Student; [memb.] History Book Club and American Tae Kwando and Haikido Academy; [hon.] Dean's list; [pers.] The course of history is an ongoing event in which each of us hopes to leave our mark.; [a.] Leitchfield, KY

DEFIBAUGH, LILY M.
[pen.] Lily M. Defibaugh; [b.] April 15, 1916, Everett, PA; [p.] George and Blanche McGraw; [m.] Walter Defibaugh (Deceased), June 25, 1938; [ch.] Lee Defibaugh; [ed.] High School; [occ.] Retired; [memb.] United Methodist Church; [hon.] Several published in local paper and church paper; [oth. writ.] Just poems for friends and loved ones for special occasions and many for my own pleasure.; [pers.] I write simply to bring joy to others and many to bring honor and glory to God.; [a.] Bedford, PA

DEIKE, MARIA
[pen.] Locaweda; [b.] October 21, 1980, Waterloo, IA; [p.] Kenn and Mary Deike; [ed.] Attended Plainfield Elementary, and am now in Nashua-Plainfield High School; [occ.] I help my parents on their hog operation and corn and soybean crops.; [memb.] Sunday School teacher, Active member in FFA. I am also am in chorus, future problem solvers, and a member of the First United Church of Christ; [hon.] Received the "Hoby" award for leadership. Holding a reporters office for the local FFA; [oth. writ.] I have put many school articles in the paper, but currently I have been just writing for enjoyment, and for future generations to see.; [pers.] In this beautiful and mysterious world a walk down an old curvy dirt road can bring memories to a person, and thoughts can seem real. The small things in life give us the opportunities to look ahead of our paths with possibilities and to look back with the memories.; [a.] Plainfield, IA

DEL CAMPO, EVA MARTHA
[pen.] Ave (for my paintings); [b.] March 27, 1934, Havana, Cuba; [p.] Miguel Llaneras and Eva Rodriguez; [m.] Dr. Enrique Julio Del Campo, May 5, 1954, (December 14, 1975, Divorced); [ch.] Two sons, one daughter; [ed.] Accountant - (Business School Havana) Fine Arts School (Havana) Ballet, Languages Institute (Havana) Piano, Investigative Training and Work; [occ.] Disable Coronary Disease, (Cardiac Arr.); [memb.] AARP in the Past - The Rifle Ass.; [hon.] "I Am Alive", 62 yrs. old, "The United States of America Citizenship"; [oth. writ.] I write in English, Spanish-French, Italian, Sicilian and Doodle in German. For the past 12 years I have been studying Japanese. I write a lot of Haiku's (Working on books).; [pers.] "We are just a spec of dust in the Universe".; [a.] Miami Beach, FL

DELORME, JOEL WILLIAM
[pen.] Joedy Smith; [b.] March 22, 1960, Chilton, WI; [p.] Joel N. and Joanne C. DeLorme; [m.] Kimberlee DeLorme, January 11, 1992; [ch.] Jeshua Michael, Josiah Fox; [ed.] Parkview High, UW, White Water College (BSE), UW, Madison (MSE); [occ.] High School Teacher; [oth. writ.] Working on my first novel, The Front Porch.; [pers.] We are escorted to heaven on the shoulders of those whom we have helped.; [a.] Footville, WI

DEMATTIES, EULAH GRACE
[b.] January 19, 1911, Oneonta, NY; [p.] Irving Harvey and Florence (Spencer) Harvey; [m.] Joseph F. DeMatties, August 31, 1933; [ch.] Joseph, Ernest, Irving, Albert, Allison, Murray, Darlynn, and Margaret; [ed.] High School GED, School for Practical Nurses, Albany, NY, February 1961; [occ.] Nurse 20 years: Glens Falls, NY Hospital, Retired March 1981, Private Duty Nurse 1981-1988; [hon.] Published in the American Poetry Anthology, Volume X, No. I: "The Stars Tell The Story"; [oth. writ.] "To a Kindergarten Graduate" June 1984, "Our Hands" September 1983, "Childhood in the Adirondacks" May 1989, "The Imaginary Winky Worm" - All in Warrensburg, NY News; [pers.] I like to write of special people we should remember, children and their wonderful ways, and things of special beauty. Some very special people: Our town doctor, the parish priest, an inventor and my dad and mom.; [a.] Warrensburg, NY

DEMPSEY, MARK
[b.] April 25, 1963, Morristown, NJ; [p.] Margaret and Bill Dempsey; [m.] Barbara Glennon Dempsey, June 11, 1988; [ch.] Sean and Erin; [ed.] Morristown High, Morris County College; [occ.] Driver for Morris County M.V.A.; [pers.] I would like to help people realize their inner self, so they can help other people; [a.] Morristownship, NJ

DESIATO, DANIELLE
[b.] July 7, 1980, Abington, PA; [p.] Perry and Maria DeSiato; [ed.] Council Rock High School; [occ.] Student; [memb.] Key Club (Community Service Program), Marching Band, Spanish Club; [hon.] Spanish National Honors Society; [oth. writ.] Several poems published in Sensations.; [pers.] The greatest accomplishment is to have experienced living for oneself.; [a.] Richboro, PA

DEWEES, KEITH D.
[pen.] Paula Salem; [b.] May 17, 1958, Smyrna, TN; [p.] Sarah Deluca, Harry Dewees; [ed.] Hancock Elementary, Avon Park Jr. High School, Plymouth-Whitemarsh Senior High, Allegheny Community; [occ.] Unemployed, however I continue to fill the post of Librarian for a therapy house; [memb.] Bible Baptist Church; [hon.] Volleyball and other sports achievement certificates, Church Scouts travel school, nurse's aide and first place Blue Ribbon in a craft show; [oth. writ.] Short stories in primary school, poetry in High School and College, poetry and books since then. Several books are works in progress.; [pers.] God has been my mainstay, my example. My other influences have been Sci-Fi/Fantasy and romances. I stand against the victimization of violence by creating strong, Christ-centered characters and upbeat conclusions.; [a.] Wescosville, PA

DEYOUNG, DONALD W.
[pen.] Wayne Young; [b.] March 10, 1957, Muskegon, MI; [p.] John and Corina DeYoung; [ch.] Don Jr., Courtney and Katie; [ed.] Assoc. Decree from Muskegon Commu-

nity College; [occ.] Project Engineer; [memb.] Fellowship Reformed Church; [hon.] Has a poem published in High school The "Unknown Land," in Young Americans around 1973; [oth. writ.] Unknown Land, What Is Love?, No Ties, Dealing With Me Pain, Dreams; [pers.] I continue to thank the Lord daily for the life I live and all the blessings He has given me.; [a.] Muskegon, MI

DIAMOND, HARVEY
[b.] February 2, 1945, New York; [ch.] One son - Beau, 19 yrs old; [occ.] Author; [oth. writ.] Fit for Life, Fit for Life II, Your Heart - Your Planet, You Can Prevent Breast Cancer!; [pers.] With unconditional love, if you will see God at the center of every person, every object and every situation, then everything in your life will be God smiling back at you.; [a.] Sarasota, FL

DIAZ, ISMAEL C.
[pen.] Diaz; [b.] July 15, 1967, Douglas, AZ; [pers.] "Life is short and sour. Only we can make it long and sweet."; [a.] Douglas, AZ

DICARLO, DONNA ANN
[pen.] Donna Ann DiCarlo; [b.] February 23, 1964, Queens, NY; [p.] Marilynn and Joseph DiCarlo; [m.] Thomas Charles Cooper, November 6, 1991; [ed.] Comsewouge High School, Suffolk County Community College; [occ.] Home Maker/Home Health Care Aide; [memb.] American Red Cross, Adult CPR, Central Florida Chapter; [hon.] Won one second place award for singing, "When Love Is Kind," solo., won second place for a duet with girl friend Doreen Defina in high school; [oth. writ.] My sign is Pisces, Fathers, Winter, Spring, Summer and Fall, Pandas.; [pers.] The poem "Ever Lasting Love," is a tribute to my late Mother Marilynn Loretta Marcello DiCarlo. I wish she could be here with me to share my joy.; [a.] Orlando, FL

DICKERSON, DARCIE
[b.] January 18, 1979, Winfield, KS; [p.] Robert and Vesper Dickerson; [ed.] Winfield High School - Senior; [occ.] Dietary Aide at Cumbernaid Village (Retirement Home); [memb.] American Legion Auxiliary for 14 yrs.; [hon.] Cellist in High School Orchestra and Winfield Regional Symphony; [oth. writ.] "A Hard Good-Bye," published and printed by the National Library of Poetry in The Isle of View anthology.; [pers.] I enjoy learning through experience and that is why I try to share my own personal experiences through my writing.; [a.] Winfield, KS

DIETZ, JAMES
[b.] August 5, 1947, Brooklyn, NY; [p.] George and Margaret Dietz; [ed.] Adelphi University, Garden City, NY; [occ.] General Manager, Tetra Dynamics Transportation Division; [memb.] 5 years Detroit Tigers Pitcher (1966-1973) - 2 years Armed Forces; [pers.] Special thanks to Mary Beth Scarola; [a.] Levittown, NY

DIGNAZIO, CHARLES E.
[b.] February 17, 1958, Oakland, CA; [p.] Ronald V. Dignazio, Peggy E. Mace; [ed.] Board of Education, Baltimore MD, some college; [occ.] Food and Beverage Accounting Clerk for the Mohegan Sun Casino; [memb.] NAVI Open Water I Scuba Diver; [hon.] Arrow of Light, Life Scout, 50 Miler a Foot/A Float Historic Trails Award, Paul Bunyon Axe Award, Ondes, Member of Order of The Arrow, Pokaroket District Tomahawk Award, 25 years Veteran of BSA; [pers.] I believe in letting people find their own trouble and the answers they are looking for, whatever may happen.; [a.] Westerley, RI

DILLINGHAM III, JAMES L.
[b.] November 30, 1970, York, SC; [m.] Staley M. (Williams) Dillingham, October 25, 1995; [ch.] Kaila Marissa Dillingham; [ed.] Augustus R. Johnson Health Science, and Engineering High School, 1989; [occ.] Mattress Maker, Serta Mattress Co.; [pers.] All things are possible, through Jesus!; [a.] Augusta, GA

DILLON, KATHERINE
[b.] September 3, 1960, Detroit, MI; [p.] Dorothy Dillon - Bob and Bev Dillon; [ch.] Danny Wyrembelski; [ed.] Adlai Stevenson High, Macomb College; [occ.] Gruhn Guitars; [memb.] Goodlettsville Elementary PTO; [hon.] Dean's List, 'The Greatest Mommy Award'; [oth. writ.] More to come; [pers.] My writing is influenced by my life experiences and my hopes and dreams for a better world for all, especially the children...; [a.] Goodlettsville, TN

DINGER, CHRIS
[b.] May 4, 1978, Princeton, WV; [p.] Michael Dinger and Anita Coeburn; [ed.] Bluefield High School, Bluefield State College; [occ.] Student; [oth. writ.] "The Drifter" published in "Into the Unknown" several other unpublished poems.; [a.] Bluefield, WV

DIPPLE, TAMMY
[b.] November 29, 1978, Davenport, IA; [p.] Dale and Rosemary Dipple; [ed.] Muscatine High School, plan to attend Community College in Fall of '97; [hon.] Perfect in Attendance in High School, on the Honor Roll all through school.; [oth. writ.] Several poems have been published in school and local newspapers also in Iowa Spinoff.; [pers.] I strive to create writing that will not be judged by only the content but enjoyed by all people!; [a.] Montpelier, IA

DOBELMANN, STEVEN
[b.] August 8, 1983, Saint Charles; [p.] Mark and Kathy Dobelmann; [ed.] 7th grade; [occ.] Student; [hon.] First place in children's division of the Mississippi Madness right writers group; [oth. writ.] Cowboy Prayer, Blow Up In My Face, Things Better Change, Looking Through The Bible, Too Smart for Him, The Dream, Path of the Lord, Marvin, Alarm Clock, I don't know.; [a.] Louisiana, MO

DOLHANCYK, DIANA
[b.] December 13, Cleveland OH; [p.] Peter Dolhancyk and Diana Dribus Dolhancyk; [m.] Leonard Pamin; [ch.] Diana Anne, Louis Peter; [ed.] West Tech High, Titus College of Cosmetology (licensed); [occ.] Writer, [memb.] International Society of Poets (a distinguished lifetime member, 1995), Member of the Poets' Guild, International Society of Authors and Artists (1996), Arthritis Foundation, sponsor of a young girl in India for the past 16 years; [hon.] Awards for outstanding achievement in poetry from the National Library of Poetry for the following: "The Parting," in Journey of the Mind, 1994; "The Parting," in East of the Sunrise, 1995; "Stormy," in Songs on the Wind, 1994; "Stormy," in Beyond the Stars, 1995; "Shadow Side," in At Water's Edge, 1995; "Eclipse," in A Delicate Balance, 1995; "Burnt By Love," in Windows of the Soul, 1995; "Web of Guilt," in Where Dawn Lingers, 1996; "The View," in A Muse to Follow, 1996; "The View," in Portraits of Life, 1996; "Photographer," in Fields of Gold, 1997; "Love No More," in Best Poems of 1996, "The Happening," in Best Poems of the '90s; chosen for both Best Poems anthologies (an honor). From the International Society of Poets: Nominee for Poet of the Year, 1995, received an "International Poet of Merit Award," a nominee for "Best Poets of 1996," received a "Bronze Medal Award." From Creative Arts and Science Enterprises: received the "Accomplishment of Merit Award for Literary Achievement," "CAT" won two awards (award certificate, plus Editor's Preference Award of Excellence), "Accomplishment of Merit Award" for the outstanding literary achievement entitled "Shadow Side."; [oth. writ.] "Little Boy" published in Poet's Corner Magazine, Fall

1996; Published in the National Library of Poetry anthologies listed above, as well as in Creative Arts and Science Enterprise publications: Journey to Our Dreams, 1996, Promises to Keep, 1996, Starburst, The Journal of the International Society of Authors and Artists, and Between the Quotes. Published by Sparrowgrass Poetry: "The View," in Treasured Poems of America, Summer 1996, Honorable Mention; "But Isn't the Flower Lovely?" in Poetic Voices of America, Summer 1996; "The Photographer," in Poetic Voices of America, Fall 1996; "The Happening" and "The Parting," in Treasured Poems of America, Summer 1997. Published by Poet's Guild: "Snowscape," "Rain," "Letters," "Love No More," and "Happiness," in Best New Poems, Winter 1996. Published by Quill Books: "Snowscape," in Treasure the Moment, Fall 1996. The poem, "The Parting," in Sun Star Newspaper, along with a picture and write-up on the front page, 1995. I was asked to appear on "Poetry Today," New York Radio, NY City, WRTN 93.5 FM with renowned star, actress and singer, Florence Henderson. A personal interview and professional reading of my poem, "Shadow Side" (1997).; [pers.] Always give someone a smile, you never know whose heart you might lighten. Love is the most important thing we can give or receive.; [a.] North Royalton, OH

DONALDSON, CAPT. HUNTER BANNERMAN
[pen.] Capt. Hunter; [b.] April 23, 1948, Tallahassee, FL; [m.] Andrea C. Donaldson, 1991; [ch.] Capt. Hunter III; [ed.] University of Tennessee, U.S. Coast Guard Master, P.A.D.I. (Professional Association of Dive Instructors); [occ.] Charter Boat Captain, Dive Instructor, Owner, Lode Key Boat Rentals and, Genuine Draft Charters.; [memb.] Director, Lower Keys Chamber of Commerce, Reef Association, member, P.A.D.I.; [hon.] V.I.P. Al and Tipper Gore's personal dive instructor. Secret service approved. Won 2 days on "Wheel of Fortune" in 1995! How many can say all the above?; [oth. writ.] "Perfect Partners", "Touch The Sea Collection", "The Forgiving Queen", "You, Too", "No Judge, No Jury", "Ocean's Creature, Nature's Teacher" Outdoor Editor, "Lower Keys Barometer," weekly newspaper; [pers.] Behind Family as #1, comes top love and appreciation for our living coral reef ecosystem. Next comes priority of sharing it with others, as the relationships beneath the sea are amazingly similar to our own.; [a.] Big Pine Key, FL

DONALDSON, JANIE C.
[b.] February 7, 1936, Davie Cty., NC; [p.] J. C. and Ina Mae Collette; [m.] Ellis T. Donaldson, August 31, 1957; [ch.] Alan James and Denise Collette; [ed.] A.B. Degree, Catawba College, Salisbury, NC; [occ.] Retired Teacher, English, French, R.J. Reynolds High School Winston Salem, NC; [memb.] Academic Scholarship to Catawba, 2 R.J. Reynolds Teacher's Scholarships to Europe.; [pers.] I try to do my best so that I'm proud of yesterday, and I look forward to tomorrow.; [a.] Winston Salem, NC

DONEGAN, FRANCES
[pen.] Frances Edna Donegan; [b.] January 1, 1968, El Paso, TX; [p.] Judy and Danny Rawinsky; [m.] John Searfoss, May 24, 1997; [ch.] Jessica and Jennifer Carter; [ed.] College, Grayson; [occ.] Student of Social Work; [oth. writ.] Hopeful, Dead Earth, Truly Free, For This Day, Rag Doll, all unpublished Hair of Gold; [pers.] I have always loved to write, my children are my inspiration. Both being survivors of childhood diseases.; [a.] Denison, TX

DONOVAN, LINDA
[pen.] Linda Donovan; [b.] February 11, 1948, Buffalo; [p.] Gordon & Eileen Donovan; [ch.] Kelly, Jeffrey, Patrick and Carleen; [ed.] South Park High School, The Sawyer School of Nursing and Business; [occ.] I'm in nursing; [hon.] Nursing Certificate of Completion

Achievement and Accomplishment in Attendance; [oth. writ.] The Tree House, The Winter Winds, The Summers Night, The Cat, The Shadow In The Window, The Night Stranger, The Shock in the Night, and the The Twinkling Dawn.; [pers.] I would like to have all my work printed. I enjoy writing. I like swimming, reading, and ice skating.; [a.] Buffalo, NY

DONOVAN, PATRICIA A.
[b.] November 15, 1960; [p.] John and Gayle Keen; [m.] Frank Donovan, June 2, 1984; [ch.] Kathleen; [ed.] University of Maryland, College Park; [occ.] Owner of Pacific Paralegal Services; [pers.] Good poetry is like a kiss for the mind.; [a.] Lancaster, CA

DORN, GARY
[b.] June 7, 1953, San Diego, CA; [p.] Margaret Fountain and Floyd Dorn; [m.] Roberta Dorn, August 30, 1996; [ch.] Marlon W. Dorn and Mahogany L. Dorn, step-children Nareka, Nyishi, and Nija; [ed.] Abraham Lincoln High School, Kelsey-Jenny College, San Diego, CA; [occ.] Accounting/Information Systems, Gateways Hospital, Los Angeles CA [oth. writ.] "As We Look the Other Way," "Without Friendship," "Open Up Your Heart," "I'm a Proud Man," plus others.; [pers.] Wisdom can only be called wisdom when it is applied, otherwise it is ignorance.; [a.] Los Angeles, CA

DOUGLAS, RUSSELL E.
[b.] October 11, 1954, Riverside, CA; [p.] Kenneth Douglas, Donna Douglas; [m.] Kathy Douglas, May 5, 1985; [ch.] Matthew Edward, Christopher Ryan; [ed.] Fontana High School, University of Redlands, CA; [occ.] Information Systems, Taco Bell, Riverside CA [a.] Rialto, CA

DOWDELL, ELIZABETH A.
[b.] August 14, 1961, Buffalo, NY; [m.] Willie F. Dowdell, April 16, 1982; [ch.] Angel and Dionysius; [ed.] High School Grad.; [occ.] Housewife, Veteran from the US Army; [hon.] Good Conduct Medal AAM with 3 gold Cluster, Army Service Medal, Overseas Ribbon; [oth. writ.] This poem is dedicated to my family.; [pers.] I'm glad that God gave me the strength and the knowledge to write down my words of hope.; [a.] Tampa, FL

DRAGE, SHIRLEY
[b.] January 22, 1950, Wausau, WI; [p.] Maynard and Alice Wiemann; [m.] Dick Drage, February 16, 1974; [ed.] Wausau Sr. High School, University of Wisconsin Marathon Campus; [occ.] Senior Assistant Underwriter, Commercial Casualty Insurance Co.; [memb.] International Society of Poets, International Poetry Hall of Fame; [hon.] International Poet of Merit Award, 3 Editor's Choice Awards, Interview on Radio show Poetry Today; [oth. writ.] Several poems published in anthologies by the National Library of Poetry and Sparrowgrass Poetry Forum.; [pers.] Being shy, poetry allows my thoughts and feelings to be expressed in away I never thought possible.; [a.] Lewisville, TX

DRAYTON, NYLA
[pen.] Shor-De; [b.] August 4, 1978, Gary; [p.] Joyce and James Drayton; [ed.] High School Graduate; [memb.] Triumph the Kingdom and God and Christ Church; [hon.] Only this one; [oth. writ.] The Pain Within, My Heart, Time's Has Changed, How Much Can U Handle, Dreamy Man and Home; [pers.] I am honored and I dedicate this to "Chops" and his family.; [a.] Gary, IN

DRINNON, JANIS BOLTON
[b.] July 28, 1922, Pineville, KY; [p.] Clyde Herman and Violet Hendrickson Bolton; [m.] Kenneth C. Drinnon, June 13, 1948, First Baptist Church, Middlesboro, KY; [ch.] Dena Drinnon Foulk, M. David E. Foulk, grandchildren: Bethany Erah Foulk, Jonathan David Foulk, Julia Elizabeth Foulk; [ed.] Middlesboro, KY High School, journalism classes at Lincoln Memorial University, Harrogate, TN, 1947-1948, commercial art certificate from Art Instruction School, 1968, correspondence courses with Newspaper Institute of America, drama instruction and singing lessons with private teachers.; [occ.] Homemaker; [memb.] New Hopewell Baptist Church, Knoxville, TN, distinguished member of International Society of Poets.; [hon.] Editors Choice Awards by The National Library of Poetry for six poems - "When Our Purpose Here Is Done" published in The Dark Side Of The Moon in 1994, "Blessings" published in The Best Poems Of 1995, "My Daily Best" published in Windows Of The Soul in 1995, "Going Home" published in The Best Poems Of 1996, "On Call" published in Through The Hourglass in 1996, "He Is Real" published in Best Poems of The 90's. Nominated for Poet Of The Year for 1995 and 1996 by The International Society of Poets. Selected for the Silver 25th Edition of Marquis Who's Who in the South and Southwest and 52nd Edition of Marquis Who's Who in America. Elected to The International Poetry Hall of Fame.; [oth. writ.] While attending college, wrote articles for local newspaper. Recently had poems published in anthologies.; [pers.] I have always enjoyed the finer things of life and nature, especially those that are spiritually uplifting and bring beauty to the soul. My family has always come first in my life. I have never been much for organizations, preferring to be a doer rather than a participant.; [a.] Knoxville, TN

DRUMMER, MICHAEL K.
[b.] May 3, 1970, Chicago, IL; [p.] Fred and Catherine Drummer; [ed.] Northern Virginia Community College and Virginia Commonwealth University, Major: Criminal Justice, Minor: Psychology; [occ.] Strategic Support Representative (Telecommunications); [memb.] Delta Chi Fraternity Inc.; [a.] Sterling, VA

DU BOIS, BRIAN
[b.] January 28, 1975, Lodi, CA; [p.] David and Claudia Cuthbert, Richard Dubois; [ed.] Bear Creek High School, Delta College, Sacramento State University; [occ.] Bekins/Pacific Storage Company; [memb.] Active in Bear Creek High School Baseball Program as a Freshmen Baseball Coach; [oth. writ.] No other professional works published at this time. I am currently working on a fiction novel and various poetry works.; [pers.] I am in the search for the perfect poem that jerks at your heart until the last line when it all comes together and makes sense.; [a.] Stockton, CA

DUARDO, JOHN
[b.] October 23, 1970, Somerset, JN; [p.] The Late Rocco Duardo, Marie Duardo; [ed.] Bound Brook High School, Berkeley College of Business; [hon.] Deans and Presidents List; [oth. writ.] Several poems that have not been published.; [pers.] I write about people and places when I feel there is a need to do so. This poem is dedicated to my late father Rocco and to my family and friends for their closeness and comfort during this emotional and traumatic time.; [a.] Bound Brook, NJ

DUBROC, LINDA
[b.] August 19, 1943, Echo, LA; [p.] Virgie Guillot, Curtis Guillot (Deceased); [m.] Divorced; [ch.] Gary, Dwain, Pennie Dubroc, Angel Harre II; [ed.] 12 grade graduate; [hon.] I have had honors and awards for athletics and coaching sports. None ever for writing poems; [oth. writ.] I have written other poems but never sent them anywhere, only for my own reading; [pers.] I love to write and make up poems. I am engaged at this time to be married on September 13 this year. This is both our second marriage, we are 53 years young.; [a.] Pineville, LA

DUBRUL, LARRY
[b.] September 19, 1941, Michigan; [p.] Louis and Gladys Dubrul; [m.] Mary, July 23, 1966; [ch.] Scott and Chad; [occ.] Electrician; [pers.] Above all - be flexible; [a.] Santa Margarita, CA

DUFFY, TIMOTHY
[pen.] Sean O'Ryan; [b.] February 24, 1950, Teaneck, NJ; [p.] Robert Duffy and Lenora Dugan; [ch.] Sean R. and Ryan T.; [ed.] Several Universities Esp. William Paterson: Poli. Sci. B.A. Rutgers: Inter'l Relat. MA. American Grad. Schl. of Int'l Mgt. (Thunderbird); [occ.] Writer/Poet, Int'l Mgt. MA; [memb.] Distinguished Member of International Society of Poets, National Authors Registry, Vagabond Poets, Christian Writers Guild; [hon.] International Poetry Hall of Fame, Editors Choice (Several Times), President's Award for Literary Excellence, Honorable Mention, several of many awards; [oth. writ.] Magazine articles, Newspaper, poems, 2 poetry books, entitled Several Sittings on a Park Bench, poetic praise: Jesus Christ is Lord.; [pers.] Of poetry: it is a peephole into infinity. To poets: write on!; [a.] Monmouth Beach, NJ

DUPONT, THOMAS M.
[b.] December 31, 1967, Norwich, CT; [p.] Walter and Yvonne DuPont; [ed.] 12th Grade Education, graduated from Rogers High School 1987; [occ.] Piece Worker, Lott Industry's Telegraph; [memb.] E.A.A.C. Employee Advocacy Advisory Counsel, St. Clements Catholic Church; [hon.] Employee of the Year Award 1995; [pers.] I am disabled and in a wheelchair. Writing poetry is my way of sharing my thoughts and feelings with others.; [a.] Toledo, OH

DURGIN, DODI ANN
[pen.] Dodi Ann Durgin; [b.] June 10, 1971, Evanston, IL; [p.] Terry and Julie; [ed.] Round Lake Sr. High School, College of Lake County, Loyola University of Chicago, Arizona State University; [occ.] Professional Student, various P/T jobs; [memb.] Emerging Leaders Program, National Honor Society, Health Occupations students of America; [hon.] Phi Theta Kappa Hnr Soc., Dean's List Loyola University Chicago State Champion Medical Terminology; [oth. writ.] Published letter in American Health Magazine, Student, Long Ridge Writer's Group; [pers.] I write in reflection of my personal struggle to seek God's eternal salvation; [a.] Wauconda, IL

DURO, JOHN S.
[pen.] Jon-Michael Duro; [b.] August 3, 1956, Alliance, OH; [p.] Anne-Margaret Adams Duro and Hayon Duro; [ch.] Michael Scott; [ed.] Four years plus College, Major, Marketing no degree (as yet) pursuing, Akron University, Alliance High School; [occ.] Self-employed, Merchandising and Service Company; [memb.] World Hunger Program at Brown University, Stand for Children Participant; [hon.] National Honor Society, Dean's List; [oth. writ.] Several poems published in poetry collections, as well as song lyrics.; [pers.] My writings are strongly influenced by the caring and love that my parents endlessly gave to me, and influenced by the hope and unconditional love of all children.; [a.] Carrollton, OH

DUVALL, HENRY
[pen.] Henry Ellis Duvall; [b.] August 16, 1967, Dapdennell, AR; [p.] Thomas and Nettie Duvall; [m.] Teresa (Diane) Behr, April 18, 1987; [ch.] Kristina (5 yrs), Kendell (4 yrs); [ed.] Atkin's Public School 1985; [occ.] Disabled since 1995; [memb.] Moreland Freewill Baptist Church; [oth. writ.] I have wrote two novels to face the truth of a friend lost, that I am in the

process of trying to get published.; [pers.] I feel that there is as much responsibility as there is honor with writing, because you can take down or expand someone's dreams through writing.; [a.] Pelsor, AR

DWYER, ODIN L.
[b.] December 26, 1974, Anchorage, AL; [p.] Phyllis Ministero, Ivan Rockwell; [ed.] Orono High Drexel University; [oth. writ.] Currently working on my first book of poems.; [pers.] The future is unknown, don't let your soul be the same. Explore your mind, and the world around it.; [a.] Glenburn, ME

DYKES, SANDI
[pen.] Dykes, Sandi; [b.] November 13, 1978; [p.] Judy Allen, David Dykes; [ed.] I am a senior at Wilcox County High School; [occ.] Student; [hon.] The greatest awards I have received are the love and support of family and friends.; [oth. writ.] I have no other poems published but plan to in the near future.; [pers.] I want to dedicate this poem to T.J. Cole. I have loved you a long time and will continue to love you always.; [a.] Rochelle, GA

EARL, IOLA W.
[pen.] Winnie Strick; [b.] November 8, 1936, Queens, NY; [p.] Chester Strickland, Alice Bergen Strickland; [m.] James John Earl, March 3, 1956; [ch.] James L. John, Doris, Donald, Evelyn, and Gerald; [ed.] John Adams High School, B.A. Early Childhood Education, Queens College, CUNY, Queens, NY; [occ.] Homemaker, Grandmother of 12; [memb.] Wyckoff Association in America, American Topical Assn. (Stamp Collecting), Women's Republican Club/Queens Cty. L.I. Federation of Women's Clubs, Queensboro Federation of Parents Clubs, Past-President's Assn.; [hon.] Generoso Pope Scholarship Award, Brotherhood Award Church Activities, Church School, VBS Teacher, Choir; [oth. writ.] Children's book in process, often write poems for family and friends as gifts for special occasions and for church convention themes. Some poems printed in church papers.; [pers.] God gives the inspiration and I write it down! To God be the glory!; [a.] Kew Gardens, NY

EARLY, DOROTHY
[pen.] Dottie Griffith; [b.] December 22, 1952, Miami, FL; [p.] Edy Seufert and Lloyd Griffith; [m.] Terry Early, January 27, 1994; [ch.] Andrew Michael, Danielle Lynn; [ed.] Miami Springs High, Polk Community College; [occ.] Housewife; [oth. writ.] Jr. High Newspaper collection at home.; [pers.] I write spontaneously and from my heart. I am especially influenced by nature and my surroundings!; [a.] Sugar Land, TX

EASLEY, CHRISTINE SUE
[pen.] Christine S. Easley; [b.] November 29, 1961, Ravenna, OH; [p.] Lawrence and Janet Goray; [m.] William Robert Easley, March 17, 1986; [ch.] Samantha Colleen Easley and William Lawrence Easley (In Memory); [ed.] Streetsboro High School, Maplewood Area Joint Vocational School, Kent State University; [occ.] Housewife; [memb.] I currently belong to the Girl Scouts where I volunteer as a leader with the Daisy Girl Scout troop in Shalersville, Ohio; [hon.] I've made it to Semi-Finalist round in the National Library of Poetry contest. Having a poem published.; [a.] Mantua, OH

EASTER, SHIRLEY
[b.] March 25, 1949, Bono, AR; [p.] Mr. and Mrs. Alvey Sidney Easter; [m.] Widow, July 7, 1964; [ch.] Two; [occ.] Artist; [hon.] Ribbons for Artist Work Oil; [pers.] My heart overflows with beautiful thoughts I am daring to share to all.; [a.] Desert Hot Springs, CA

ECK, KENNETH FRANK
[b.] February 4, 1917, Alma, KS; [p.] Clarence J. and Rosa B. Eck; [m.] Ouida Landon, July 2, 1938, (Died, September 18, 1968), Lorraine Rubotom, April 14, 1989; [ch.] Alan Grantland Eck, Mark Warren Eck, Dana Landon Eck (3 sons); [ed.] Healdton High School, Southwestern Okla. State Univ., BS Pharmacy, Summa Cum Laude; [occ.] Semi Retired Pharmacist, Relief Work for Eck Drug, Healdton, OK, Eck Drug - Waurika, OK; [memb.] V.F.W., American Legion, Okla. Pharmacist Assoc., American Pharm. Assoc., National Assoc. of Community Pharmacists, Oilpatch Seniors, Church of Christ, Lions Club, Chamber of Commerce AARP, OK, Pharmacy Heritage Found, Okla. Historical Society, Area Agency on Aging Adv Board, S.W. Okla. State Univ., Alumna Assoc., Healdton Alumni Assoc.; [hon.] 1961 Healdton Citizen of the Year, 1988 Pharmacy Bowl of Hygeia, 93-94 Who's Who in South and Southwest, 94-95 Who's Who in Science and Engineering, 95-96 Who's Who in Medicine and Health Care, 97-98 Who's who In The World, 88 Healdton Alumnus of the Year, Outstanding Alumnus, S.W. Ok. State U., 96 Pharmacy Heritage Hall of Fame; [oth. writ.] Weekly Column in Healdton Herald Newspaper "Oilpatch Mania"; [pers.] I have a short story I hope to publish, I am joining a group of writers, I hope to write historical novels and non-fiction. I plan to use my years of experience to help others, in my writings.; [a.] Healdton, OK

EDENS, MARGARET
[b.] October 31, 1960, Cleve, OH; [p.] George and Margaret Hensley; [m.] Russell Issac Edens, October 13, 1981 - August 24, 1987; [ed.] Cleveland Central Catholic and Normandy High School; [occ.] Housekeeper; [hon.] 1st and 2nd place awards in track and field; [oth. writ.] I usually give my poems to friends on Birthdays and Christmas.; [pers.] I am a lover not a fighter. I have been influenced by friends and early English and American Poets; [a.] Cleveland, OH

EDWARDS, F. KATHERINE
[pen.] F. Katherine Edwards; [b.] September 21, 1948, Illinois; [p.] Orville and Shirley Nutter; [ch.] Thad, Thomas, Trevor; [ed.] College of St. Theresa and College of Dudage, Adn.; [occ.] RN, Volunteer Teacher at Treehaven Institute on the Pine Ridge Reservation, SD., Summertime; [hon.] National Honor Society; [oth. writ.] Have served as a Public Information Representative for the Bahais, locally and at the Bahai World Congress in 1992 in N.Y.C., NY; [pers.] Being a member of the Bahai faith, I believe strongly in the unity of mankind, of the unity of all religions, and that there is one God. We are all part of this one world, and now is a critical time.; [a.] Round Lake Park, IL

EDWARDS, YEVONNE
[pen.] Vonn Vonnie, Western Artist: Hickie; [b.] May 23, 1927, Colorado; [p.] J. B. White and F. O. Clasby; [m.] Richard R. Edwards (Deceased), 1948; [ch.] David R. Edwards (Deceased), Marcy Edward Adler, Attorney; [ed.] High School, College Classes Colorado and Oregon, Art Schools, Cartoonist School, Jones Real Estate College Colorado; [occ.] Retired, Grandmother, Artist, Writer, Freelance; [memb.] Church, Boston, Mass., Colorado Real Estate, Oregon Senior Citizens, Aspen Poppers Riders Colorado; [hon.] Beta Sigma Phi, Rider's Awards, Art Awards Al Grandmother, writer's by line; [oth. writ.] Freelance Articles, City Editor Colorado Mountain town weekly newspaper, "Wooland Parkview," cartoons published helping others.; [pers.] I believe in a wonderful spiritual outlook and understanding of life. Staying young at heart and in mind.; [a.] Lake Oswego, OR

ELDER, ROBERT
[pen.] Rob. E.; [b.] June 23, 1973, El Paso, TX; [p.] John and JoAnn Elder; [ed.] Coronado High, U.T. El Paso, Attending Texas Tech. Univ.; [occ.] Student; [memb.] Art student at Texas Tech. University with an emphasis in painting, English Minor plan on attending graduate school; [pers.] I have an opinion and a feeling about everything. I am also very emotional. Writing and painting allow me to release my thoughts and worries.; [a.] Sierra Blanca, TX

ELKINS, JERRI LEA
[pen.] Mousie; [b.] April 21, 1978, Charleston, WV; [p.] George and Kathy Elkins; [oth. writ.] Short stories come so natural and I enjoy writing them along with poetry.; [pers.] In the stream of life I will win and I will loose, but I will never forget what means the most.; [a.] Lake Worth, TX

ELLES, VIOLA
[b.] June 26, 1976, Velbert, Germany; [p.] Magdalena Elles, Siegfried Elles; [ed.] Palm Springs High School, College of the Desert; [occ.] Receptionist; [pers.] I strive to reflect the beauty in all that life holds in my writing and to retain a child like fascination with the details of life.; [a.] Desert Hot Springs, CA

ELLIOTT, BARBARA
[b.] October 30, 1953, Kansas City, MO; [p.] B. W. and Thelma Biggerstaff; [m.] Charles; [ed.] Associate Degree Applied Science; [occ.] Registered Nurse; [pers.] Nearing completion of a book about my mother—her life, her illness, her death, and her gifts to me. Title: Mama: For The Many Gifts You've Given Me—This One's For You!! A daughter's reflections of living and dying with Alzheimer's Disease, and the insights my Mother gives me during her life, death, and after life. Her final gift: through her death, she gave life to my spirit. A step by step journey through the course of this terrible disease, I share my feelings of denial, fear, hopelessness, helplessness, anger, guilt, grief, and frustrations associated with taking care of a terminally ill family member. Alzheimer's disease, robs a person of many things—but with faith, patience, courage and love, you can get through it, get past it, and hear from your loved one from the "other side." Occasionally, something good comes out of something bad. In this case, a spiritual awareness, born out of grief and pain, that grows each day.; [a.] Kansas City, MO

ELLIOTT V, HENRY FRANKLIN
[b.] March 18, 1977, Buffalo, NY; [p.] Dorothea Saterfiel, David Ciminelli; [ed.] Northport High School, NY, Story Brook University, NY; [occ.] Student, United States World Artistic Roller Skater; [memb.] United States Amateur Confederation of Roller Skating, Sigma-Alpha-Mu Fraternity; [hon.] State, Regional, National Artistic Roller Skating Champion, World Team Member - Artistic roller Skating. Advanced Placement Art Award - Art and Music Festival Winner - Honors Writing Award - Varsity Football Most Valuable Player; [oth. writ.] (Unpublished favorites) Time, Place, and space - essay My Addiction, My Thoughts - Poem Gateway - Poem, The Gift? - Poem, To The Fritecre Artist: Rebirth Reflections: The Moon - series.; [pers.] Time, place, and space gives us the knowledge to understand. Perspective lets us be abstract.; [a.] Parma, OH

ELLIS, FRANCES H.
[pen.] Huguenin Ellis; [b.] August 11, 1926, Macon, GA; [p.] Martha and Marshall J. Ellis; [ed.] B.A. Duke University, M.A. Columbia University, Graduate Stud-

ies at NYU, Washington University, St. Louis Cambridge University S.; [occ.] Retired Professor of English; [oth. writ.] 'Til now, I had never written a poem - only Jingles and Limericks! But now, at my advanced age and stage, I have fallen deeply, madly in love for the first time in my life - the muse has spoken!; [pers.] Who knows what other wondrous things might happen!; [a.] Columbus, GA

EMBRY, JEAN L.
[pen.] Jeano (Sometimes); [b.] Montclaire, NJ; [ed.] B.A., Art and Music, Masters in Psychology and Counselling and Guidance Univ. of North Colorado, Greeley, CO; [occ.] (Recently retired from Dept. of Army, 1995), Teacher, Psychology and preparing for success at GA Military College, Fort Gordon, GA, also poet and story teller.; [memb.] Amer. Asso. of University Women, Delta Sigma Theta Sorority, Inc., Toastmasters International, Federally Employed Women, Amer. Society for Training and Development, Savannah River Sierra Club, Augustin Opera Sponsor, Member of Cronies, Inc.; [hon.] Dept. of Army Commendation for CTM, ATM and ATM-Bronze accomplishments, Toastmasters Award for Youth Leadership Progr., ASTD Award for Outstanding Service, Director's Award for Outstanding Service and Dedication to Nursing Students at Eisenhower Army Medical Center and many other awards and honors; [oth. writ.] I have written a voluminous amount of poetry and short stories. Plan to publish (or have published) a book of Poetry in the near future. (Have been writing poetry since I was 6 years old - and my business is called "Pieces of the Puzzle", because of the many things I do.; [pers.] I always endeavor to reflect my adoration of my creator, my experiences, memories and sensitivities, as well as my pleasures and sense of humor in my poetry and story telling. I love life and I try to live it to the fullest!; [a.] Augusta, GA

ENGLANDER, RICHARD M.
[b.] January 6, 1935, Kingston, NY; [p.] Helen M. and Irving Englander; [m.] Dorothy G. Englander, October 19, 1957; [ch.] Mimi, Scott, Daniel; [ed.] The Manlius School 1953, Siena College, B.A. English 1957, Completed Major at Oxford Univ. England 1956; [occ.] President, Archiplets Hardware and Specialty Co., Inc.; [hon.] Distinguished Military Graduate, Siena College 1957, Awarded Regular Army Commission; [pers.] I hope my compassion for those less fortunate is evident in anything I write.; [a.] Albany, NY

ENSLEY, JIM
[pen.] Jim Ensley; [b.] August 23, 1961, Calhoun, GA; [p.] Ray Bradley Ensley and Ruth Ensley Anderson; [m.] Carrie Lynn Ensley, April 21, 1994; [ch.] Jimmy Lynn and Billy Randall Ensley; [ed.] Calhoun High School; [occ.] Entertainment Manager, Actor and Screenwriter, Poet; [memb.] Eligible for Screen Actors Guild, Olympics TAE Kwon Do Academy (Hollywood, Ca); [hon.] Bronze Halo Award Southern California Motion Picture (1983); [oth. writ.] Several articles published in Hometown New Paper (Calhoun Times) entitled "Hollywood Highlights", 3 screenplays "West Bound 18 Wheeler", (Comedy) "The Idol" (Horror) "Kung-Fu (Martial Arts Comedy) and several Country and Western songs and poems; [pers.] It is my hope that my literary works will encourage others to always follow and pursue their dreams regardless of what their dreams may be, as Elvis Presley once recorded "Follow That Dream".; [a.] Hollywood, CA

ESTES, GYL
[b.] April 23, 1960, Tupelo, MS; [p.] Mr. and Mrs. Bobby Estes; [ed.] Nettleton High School, Itawamba Junior College School of Nursing; [occ.] RN (Registered Nurse)

and Self owned business, "Rags for men and the East Room"; [hon.] Valedictorian, Star Student, Math and English award, Girls State, Laberta Dillard Nursing Scholarship; [oth. writ.] Numerous poems, non published; [pers.] During a personal prayer time, I was inspired to write this poem in memory of my brother, Timothy Michael Estes, who died suddenly from an automobile accident August 6, 1991.; [a.] Tupelo, MS

EVANS, MARSHA RENEE
[pen.] "Gods Freeman 1 Corinth 7:22"; [b.] October 10, Philadelphia, PA; [p.] Late Great Evangelist Ruth L. Thomas, Late Brother Dover Vernon Thomas; [m.] Alonzo Evans Jr., December 11, 1984; [ch.] Kyle Damion, Sophia Christina, Francois Pierce, Natalie Olivia; [occ.] Public Relations Specialist, Phila, Penna; [oth. writ.] "Get Here If You Can", "Just Passing Through", "And They Said It Was A House", "We People", "I Have Chosen God"; [pers.] This poem gives honor and glory to my saviour, the Lord Jesus Christ, for the publishing of this writing is a Landmark in my life. To the Father, Son and Holy Ghost, Amen.

EVANS, SHIRLEY ANN
[b.] July 5, 1936, Spirit Lake, IA; [p.] Amil Jensen and Ruth Lucas; [m.] Donald O. Evans, July 14, 1957; [ch.] Donald D. Doyle and Timothy Wayne; [ed.] Truman High School (MN) Bookkeeper, Wallaces Dept. Store, Fairmont, MN, Secretary, Childs Insurance Co., Fairmont, MN; [occ.] Retired; [memb.] Horicon Church of Christ, Truman, MN, Treas./Sec'y Horicon Cemetery, Martin County Historical Society, St. David's Society of Minnesota; [a.] Granada, MN

EVANS JR., ROBERT A.
[pen.] 360 degrees; [b.] February 26, 1971, Dover, DE; [p.] Robert Evans, Louise Evans; [m.] Theresa Acree; [ch.] Chlesea Rae, Katianna Angelique; [ed.] Newark High School Ohio State University and Columbus State University; [occ.] Promoter and Public Relations expert; [hon.] President of Student Council Sports and Athletic Awards; [oth. writ.] Published in "Poetic Voices Of America."; [pers.] Our experiences give us our own individual we must realize our experiences!!; [a.] Columbus, OH

EVEN, JEAN
[b.] October 9, 1951, Lynchburg, VA; [p.] James and Laura Catherine Fortune; [m.] Paul F. Even, March 29, 1975; [ch.] Joshua W. Even and Rebecca L. Even; [ed.] High School Diploma from North Kingston High School, AA degree Business Administration from Coastal Carolina Community College, current student with Long Ridge Writers Group, instructor J. Anne Helgren; [oth. writ.] Prayer Warrior's Quest, in progress Prayer Request in progress; [pers.] Be careful for nothing, but in everything by prayer and supplication with thanksgiving let your requests be made known unto God. - Philippians 4:6.; [a.] Twentynine Palms, CA

EVERHART JR., NUMA LEE
[pen.] Numa; [b.] March 19, 1926, Davidson Co.; [p.] Numa and Esther Everhart, SN; [m.] Violet B. Everhart, December 23, 1945; [ch.] Six; [ed.] High School - 2 years of college, I.C.S. Diploma (Business); [occ.] Retired (AT&T Mgt.); [memb.] Abbotts Creek Baptist Ch., Davidson Water Inc. Board of Dir., R.N.C., former PTA Pres. two schools, Lions Club President, etc., etc, former Justice of Peace; [hon.] World War II Vet., Bronze Star, Purple Heart; [oth. writ.] Many letters to Editor of High Point Enterprize Newspaper. 50 to 75 poems (not published). Starting to publish a book entitled "Short, Sunday, School, Sermonettes.; [pers.] Thinking of and writ-

ing poetry keeps my mind fresh and anew. I love America, and our faith in God who created us all.; [a.] High Point, NC

FABBRI, MARILYN AND MARK
[b.] August 1935, March 1952, Cleve, OH, New Kensington, PA; [p.] Catherine and Ben Meder, Louis and Sophie Fabbri; [m.] Mark, Marilyn, August 18, 1975; [ed.] Grammar School/High School Music and The Arts, Ohio, PA and FL; [occ.] Musicians and coaching others in the music and writing field; [hon.] Have won many awards for original music and performance and are still making headlines in our local paper in AZ; [oth. writ.] We have various other writings that date back to the mid 70's that have been published. "Space Mountain," "Day Without the Sun", "Sky Queen" to name a few.; [pers.] If most of humanity only realized how short the moment of our lives - we, in earnest, try with each passing day to focus into the minds, heart and feelings of others and truly appreciate with gratitude, a small fraction of the reason for being.; [a.] Golden Valley, AZ

FAHRNE, LYNNE E.
[pen.] Lindy; [b.] June 5, 1955, Allegan, MI; [p.] Richard and Shirley Boss Sr.; [m.] Richard Fahrne Sr., May 6, 1978; [ch.] Richard Jr. and Ryan Fahrne; [ed.] Plainwell High School, Allegan Country Leadership League; [occ.] Homemaker, and volunteer for Allegan County Health Department; [memb.] Shelbyville Methodist Church, Ch.A.D.D. (children with attention deceit disorder); [hon.] This is my first award. I am so excited!! It is also very rewarding raising my two sons, who have mental illness problems (A.D.D. and depression). Every person I have ever prayed for, or helped, making them smile and giving them a better day was my reward; [oth. writ.] Pete (poetry), Prayer (poetry) (sent to another contest, I didn't hear back from these folks) also some other short stories and poems, just for my own amusement.; [pers.] To try to always find the goodness in people instead of looking for the bad in people. Better to have tried and failed than to have never tried at all.; [a.] Shelbyville, MI

FAIR, MIKE
[b.] January 10, 1947, Carlisle, PA; [p.] Kenneth Fair and Doris (Staley) Fair; [m.] (2nd) Vicki (Murphy) Fair, December 29, 1990 and (1st) Judi (Lucero) Fair (Deceased), August 21, 1971; [ch.] (2nd) Eileen and (1st) Karen, David, Amy and Brian; [ed.] BS US Air Force Academy (70), MA Univ Northern Colorado (78), MBA Western New England College (81); [occ.] Lt Colonel, USAF (Ret); [a.] Lexington, MA

FAULKNER, CYNTHIA
[pen.] "Cindy"; [b.] January 26, 1957, Kansas City, MS; [p.] Avies and Eudora Greenwood; [m.] Clark Faulkner, November 30, 1976; [ch.] Chonte', Cody, Chidon, Capoketti, Chanda, Grandchildren: Aireona, Marquez, Martez, Son-in-law: Michael; [ed.] Associate in Applied Science from Avery Institute of Technology, Diploma in Computer Programming from Computer Learning Center; [occ.] Computer Operator at a bank, "Financial Federal Trust and Savings"; [memb.] Golden Neo-life Diamite International; [hon.] Award for Brain Storming a new product in 1995, called "Elementary Saving Accounts" for children in school, grades 1st - 12th. Opening accounts with $1.00 at my job. I won "Grand Prize," a 1996 Toyota Corolla Car through Golden Neo-life Diamite Sweepstake, I'm a part-time distributor for this nutritionist company; [oth. writ.] A song called, "Guide Me By My Hand, Lord." Also a children's book, named, "Going on Vacation in a Car with my Family." It hasn't

been published yet.; [pers.] We make a living by what we get, we make a life by what we give. Life is what we make it, and all thanks due to God.; [a.] Hazel Crest, IL

FAULL, BRENNA
[b.] May 28, 1982, Eads, Co.; [p.] James F. and April Faull; [ed.] Lamar High School, Lamar, CO; [occ.] Student, 9th grade; [a.] Lamar, CO

FEDER, STEVEN
[b.] April 3, 1958, New York; [p.] Myra Feder, Martin Feder; [m.] Tracey Feder, May 28, 1990; [ch.] Cara Paige Feder; [ed.] Some college and a lot of life; [occ.] Writer - Director; [memb.] American Film Institute, Independent Film Producers West, New York Friars Club, Screen Actors Guild; [hon.] Audience Award Hamptons Film Festival, Gold Special Jury Award Worldfest Charleston, Bronze Award Dramatic Feature Worldfest Charleston, Gold Special Jury Award Worldfest Houston; [oth. writ.] "The Big Gig," credit - writer, producer, short subject film, "The Cottonwood," feature motion picture credit: Writer/director/producer, "It Had To Be You," feature film script credit - writer, director, producer.; [pers.] "The road not taken," by Frost says it all.; [a.] Los Angeles, CA

FEGTER, LUCY
[pen.] Pollyanna; [b.] September 13, 1945, Kearney, NE; [ch.] Lucinda, Susan, Richard; [occ.] Dietary Aid Community, Care of America at Grand Island and Community Living Assistant Mid-Nebraska; [oth. writ.] In process of putting together poems and writings on my life as a survivor of sexual, and verbal and emotional abuse. Wrote poems for Crisis Center and C.C.A. newsletter.; [pers.] I hope what I have gone through and have put it on paper, will someday help someone else. Give them the courage to speak out.; [a.] Grand Island, NE

FENNELL, JOSHUA
[pen.] Paprika; [b.] May 25, 1968, Newark, NJ; [p.] Joshua Fennell, Elizabeth Fennell; [ch.] God Children Markus and Malcolm; [ed.] St. Benedicts Prep. Essex County College.; [occ.] Retail Assistant Store Manager; [memb.] Bally's Fitness; [hon.] Several Customer Service Awards, The Award Of Life.; [oth. writ.] Many not seen yet; [pers.] I believe in 3 words. Live love and die. Live till you love, love till you die I want people to realize that, if you don't learn to love and live then when you die, your soul will never rest.; [a.] Newark, NJ

FERRER, TRACY
[b.] January 11, 1972, San Juan, PR; [p.] Charles Ferrer and Alicia Perez; [ed.] Georgetown University Saint John's School, PR; [occ.] Sales Professional at Mayor's Jeweler's, Inc.; [hon.] Dean's List; [oth. writ.] Various Elementary poems published in High School Journals, writings of myself and to myself

FETHEROLF, RUSSELL JOHN
[occ.] Songwriter, Musician, Computer Technician; [memb.] A.S.C.A.P., American Society of Composers, Authors and Publishers; [oth. writ.] Published songwriter, numerous musical compositions have been performed in Motion Pictures and Television; [a.] Newbury Park, CA

FIALA-HAUGH, GLORIA M.
[b.] May 28, 1938, Dayton, OH; [p.] Ralph and Bea Fiala; [m.] Richard Haugh Fostoria (Divorced now), January 9, 1960; [ch.] Sharon, Ted, Dot and Brenda; [ed.] Bellevue High Mercy Hosp., Teffin Toledo Sandusty School of Msg. grad. and Fisher Titus Grad., Findlay Winebrenner Grad.; [occ.] Nurse and Student, Factory Worker; [memb.] Who's Who Women of World,

American Heart Assn., St. Patrick's Church and Nat'l. Right To Life Son (26 yrs.); [hon.] Who's Who Women of World 1995, 1996 and 1997, "Quilt and Serol Soc. Prince Kevin of Australia Award on Service To Humanity 1996, Nat'l. Library of Poetry 2 years; [oth. writ.] "Have A Joyful Christmas Day", and "Someday", p. Ralph Fiala, Bea Fiala, Bellevue High, Sandusty School of Msg. Winebrenner, Findlay and Mercy Hospital Tiffin.; [pers.] I live today and earn tomorrow.; [a.] Tiffin, OH

FIELDS, SHELLEY E.
[b.] Yonkers, NY; [occ.] Registered Nurse; [oth. writ.] Fifty-four (54) unpublished poems.; [pers.] I try to live peacefully. I also try to remember that whenever something bad happens only good can follow, and look for the wisdom.; [a.] Philadelphia, PA

FISHER, HELEN T.
[pen.] Helen Fisher; [b.] December 12, 1914, Peoria, IA; [p.] Rev. Harry and Dena Bultema (Deceased); [m.] Martin Timmer (Deceased), Jose Fisher, January 2, 1967; [ch.] Charles M. Timmer, Marcia T., Dale T., Louise T., Mary T., Janice T.; [ed.] High School; [occ.] Homemaker; [memb.] Berean Church (my father started), also Calvary Bible Church, Boca Raton Community Church, Florida; [hon.] Six Happily married children, 5 Happily married stepchildren, 21 grandchildren, 5 great grandchildren, 17 step grandchildren, 6 step great grandchildren; [oth. writ.] I am not a poet, oh, how will I know it, during a long, long night, it is just fun to write since I have 6 wonderful children, I'm bound to have many grandchildren and they all like to receive pictures and letters then I'm the recipient of many great letters which is so much better.; [pers.] I am happy to be a mother, grandmother, great grandmother, children are a blessing, the Bible says and they certainly are.; [a.] Grand Haven, MI

FITZGERALD, MASON HOUSTON
[pen.] Mason H. Fitzgerald; [b.] December 11, 1912, Rio Viata, TX; [p.] John Houston Fitzgerald and Eula Carter Fitzgerald; [m.] Martha Moreland Fitzgerald, June 28, 1937; [ch.] Marvin Houston Fitzgerald and Michael Mason Fitzgerald (Deceased); [ed.] High School Graduate; [occ.] Locomotive Engineer - Retired; [memb.] Church of Jesus Christ of Latter Day Saints, Free and Accepted Masons, Yorkrite, Order of Eastern Star, Benevolent and Protective Order of Elks, Brotherhood of Locomotive Engineers; [oth. writ.] Poetry: One In A Million, Sunrise, Happiness, My Home; [pers.] I feel that each one of us is here in earth, for a purpose. We are to be fair, trustworthy, honest and make life as pleasant for others as we possibly can! I believe that the Lord does guide and direct our actions, day by day, as long as we are worthy. But when we cease to ask for guidance, He is not apt to give us the feeling of doing right from wrong. I feel that Shakespeare expressed it very well, when he said, "to thine own self be true, and it follows, as the night follows the day, thou cans't not be false to any man."; [a.] Globe, AZ

FLANIGAN, TAMMY
[b.] November 19, 1971, Ingleside, TX; [p.] Buster and Linda Flanigan; [ed.] From first grade to the 9th grade; [hon.] Editors Choice Award for Outstanding Achievement in Poetry; [oth. writ.] This poem will be 7 poems that has been published in 7 different books.; [pers.] This poem is about people thinking that they are better than everyone else, but we are all equal in God's eyes.; [a.] Ingleside, TX

FLASINSKA, ALINKA
[b.] February 17, 1987, Poland; [p.] Stan Flasinska, Urszula Flasinska; [ed.] Plainview Elementary School; [occ.] 4th Grade Student; [memb.] Ardmore Area

Aquatic Assoc., 4-H Club; [hon.] Superintendent's Honor Roll, Grand Award Winner, Carter County Science Fair; [a.] Ardmore, OK

FLEMING, KENNETH WAYNE
[b.] October 21, 1957, Waco, TX; [p.] Estel and Earline Fleming; [m.] Anita June Fleming, April 17, 1988; [ch.] Alicia Beth Covington; [ed.] Benton High School, Benton, LA; [occ.] Power Plant Boiler Operator; [pers.] Sometimes there are feelings deep down inside of us that we don't even realize until we express ourselves on paper!; [a.] Buckner, AR

FLEMING, RHONDA K.
[b.] September 13, 1962, Windsor, MO; [p.] Larry and Mary Fleming; [ed.] A.A. from Tarrant County Junior College, BSN from University of Texas-Arlington; [occ.] Nurse; [memb.] Association of Operating Room Nurses; [oth. writ.] Poems published in "Amidst the Splendor", "Essence of a Dream", and one to be published in "Best Poems of 1997." Several other poems published in magazines and school publications.; [pers.] "Faith like light, should always be simple and unbending, while love, like warmth, should beam forth on every side, and bend to every necessity of our brother.; [a.] Irving, TX

FLETCHER, MARY C.
[pen.] Little Moma; [b.] December 18, 1935, HSU, AL; [p.] Robert and Pauline Tibbs; [m.] Eugene Fletcher, February 19, 1955; [ch.] Debra, Tina, Eugene Jr., Mavian Angela; [ed.] 12th grade; [occ.] Human Service Asst., 20 years with State of AL; [pers.] I would love for the world to know Jesus.; [a.] Huntsville, AL

FLOOD, JESSICA
[pen.] Jessi; [b.] April 18, 1986, Up State, NY; [p.] Scott Flood; [ch.] (My dog) Stud Muffin; [ed.] 5th grade, Teacher Tom Iveson; [occ.] Student; [memb.] Laguna Elementary School, Volleyball, Basketball, Desert Taekwondo Southwest; [hon.] Math Masters and Blue Honor Roll 1996; [oth. writ.] Songs and other poems.; [pers.] I'd like to thank my friends Danille, Savannah, Ronie, Jenny, and Teia for being, and also my father Scott Flood.; [a.] Tucson, AZ

FLUTY, WARREN
[b.] June 7, 1937, Wayne County, WV; [p.] James Fluty Sr., Dixie Fluty (Both Deceased); [m.] Ethel Sartin Fluty, December 30, 1990; [ed.] Two years College, Southern West VA, Community College, Williamson WV; [occ.] Retired; [memb.] Life Membership, VFW Post #1064 Huntington, WV, Life Member DAV. Post 52, Kenova WV Member of The American Legion, Post #16 Huntington, WV; [hon.] VFW Commander and (1994) Chief Award, VFW Gold (1993) Award, VFW National Veterans Service Fund Award 1995-1996, National Defense Service Medal, Vietnam Campaign Medal, Vietnam Service Medal with one bronze star, Meritorious Unit Commendation Medal; [pers.] I believe in God, the creator of mankind. I'm thankful to be an American. Each morning and each night I ask God for guidance and His blessings.; [a.] Huntington, WV

FOON, ROBERT M.
[b.] April 23, 1955, Detroit, MI; [p.] Regina Foon and Dr. Herman Foon; [ed.] Lahser High School, Bloomfield Hills, MI, graduated June, 1973, received high school diploma; [occ.] Optical dispenser; [oth. writ.] I have written 13 other poems that have never been published. I also wrote a song (A soft, peaceful piece of music, without words) in 1985 entitled, "The Love Goes On", for which I received a copyright on March 12, 1986, from Register of Copyrights, Library of Congress, Washing-

ton, DC.; [pers.] Every poem I have written flowed out from my heart and took approximately 20 minutes to write. No words were ever changed while writing those poems. They were about people, feelings, and life. At the time of those writings, I didn't know God, but I know Him now because I have received Jesus Christ as my personal God and Savior. May the Lord Jesus Christ be glorified through all my writings because He gave me this talent.; [a.] Hazel Park, MI

FORNARO, ROSALIE
[pen.] Rosie; [b.] November 10, 1946, Brooklyn, NY; [p.] Ann and Frank Mancuso; [m.] Alberto Fornaro, January 9, 1965; [ch.] Al, Frank, Anthony; [ed.] Graduated at top of my class from Jamaica Vocational High School, Secretarial Course.; [occ.] Sales lady at Toys R Us, Artist and writer; [hon.] Regents award and Orchaster award and Typing award; [oth. writ.] Several poems of life and love.; [pers.] Never go to bed mad. Look around, the world is a very beautiful place. Never take life for granted - it can be taken away from you at any time. Love your children.; [a.] Apache Junction, AZ

FORSYTHE, THELMA
[pen.] Thelma Forsythe; [b.] May 6, 1911, Mount Vernon, IN; [p.] James F. Dye, Ida Rose Dye; [m.] John W. Forsythe, March 20, 1982; [ch.] Two sons; [ed.] High School; [occ.] Retired; [memb.] Supreme Council of the Royal Arcanum; [pers.] All of my life I have been an avid lover of poetry. It is my favorite form of reading material!; [a.] Saint Louis, MO

FORTSON, SANDY LEE
[b.] February 6, 1962, Statesville NC; [p.] John W. Fortson, Joye W. Fortson; [ed.] West Iredell High School, Mitchell Community College, Gardner-Webb University; [hon.] Phi Theta Kappa, Dean's List, Most Outstanding Business Student Award; [oth. writ.] Story accepted for publication in Foothills Piedmont Tales. (Goes to press in spring 1997.); [pers.] My hope is that my writing will somehow inspire and motivate others in realizing their own dreams by looking beyond their own surroundings and circumstances.; [a.] Statesville, NC

FOUCAULL, MARY FRANCIS FAITH
[b.] March 23, 1951, Everett; [p.] Deceased; [ch.] Chas 21; [ed.] High School; [memb.] Registered lifetime member of Songwriters Club of America, Member of Humane Society of the United States; [hon.] Hollywood song jubilee, Jeff Roberts Record Company, NCA Records and National Library of Poetry; [oth. writ.] Been published in several issues of My Legacy, The Pet Gazette, Poetry of the People, Poetry Break, The Acorn, The Advocate, Night Roses, Peckerwood, plus more.; [pers.] I have been writing poems for around seventeen years. The first one I ever wrote was about my daughter. I've come a long way since then in my poems.; [a.] Seattle, WA

FOWLER, JAMIE NICOLE
[b.] June 26, 1980, Calhoun, GA; [p.] Lamar Fowler and Ellney Beem; [ed.] Junior in High School, Dalton High; [occ.] Student; [memb.] American Legion Auxiliary; [hon.] Nominated for the Who's Who Award; [oth. writ.] I have written other poems, never sent them to anyone or let people read them.; [pers.] I am very honored that my poem has met your standards to become a finalist.; [a.] Spokane, WA

FOX, PAT
[ed.] B.S., University of Central Florida, currently pursuing Ph.D., California Institute of Integral Studies; [occ.] College Instructor; [memb.] Institute of Noetic Sciences, National Writers' Union; [hon.] Teacher of the Year

1995, Semifinalist in Annual Screenplay and Fiction contest (The Writer's Network) 1995; [oth. writ.] Editorials, Opinion Editor of local newspaper, screenplays, magazine articles, samples available at: http?:// home.earthlink.net/patfox; [pers.] We have the good fortune of living in a time when the mechanistic determinism that has shaped our existence is giving way to a new paradism of holism. It feels right to speak of the marriage of the observer and the observed. Like going home.; [a.] Winter Park, FL

FOX, RACHELLE
[pen.] Rachel Fox; [b.] June 23, 1904, Sallisaw, OK; [m.] Lincoln Fox, October 9; [ed.] ASU, Independent Studies Europe, Mid East; [occ.] Co-owner Art Studio Gallery; [oth. writ.] Articles SW Art Magazine, "Mood, Media and Idea," 1980, Photography Cover Photo, Sculpture Review Magazine, 1988, Video Photography, "Global Family Tree Of Life," 1977.; [pers.] "I'd like to write storm surviving words, not just granulated sentences that melt away."; [a.] Paonia, CO

FRANCO, NINA
[pen.] Nina Franco; [b.] January 16, 1953, Queens, NY; [p.] Frank and Theresa Braile; [m.] Charles Franco, June 3, 1978; [ch.] Marco and Flavia Franco; [ed.] Commack High School North; [occ.] Full Time Mother and Homemaker; [memb.] Girl Scout Leader, and Religion Teacher; [oth. writ.] "It's dark now" published in Brook Spring '93.; [pers.] Poetry has been one art form, an avenue in which to express my inability and capabilities, with intent to find peace, with myself, my world, and my God.; [a.] East Setauket, NY

FRANKLIN, PAULA
[b.] June 20, 1959, Chicago, IL; [p.] George and Joanne Franklin; [ed.] At present I'm attending Governors State University, I'm seeking a Bachelors degree in Psychology; [occ.] CFO, Chief Financial Officer at auto repair shop (family Business); [hon.] Awards for volunteering for different organizations in the health field; [oth. writ.] I have many other poems. None published. I've written a book on auto repair but as of yet not published it.; [pers.] The poem I sent in came as I was sitting in nature. It brings my spiritual side into words.; [a.] Glenwood, IL

FRATICELLI, BRIAN
[b.] December 31, 1971, Delaware; [ed.] Associates of Arts and Sciences Degree in Criminal Justice from Delaware Technical and Community College; [oth. writ.] As of this publication, I had written a total of 105 poems and 2 songs.; [a.] New Castle, DE

FRAZIER, RHONDA L.
[b.] November 14, 1955, Nashville, TN; [p.] Willie Claude Herring, Barbara Jean Herring; [m.] Larry K. Frazier, August 12, 1978; [ch.] Anjaleigh Renee Herring; [ed.] East Nashville High, Tennessee State University; [occ.] Homemaker; [oth. writ.] I began writing poems in 1993. I have just begun to submit these poems for critical review beginning in 1996.; [pers.] I strive to write honestly. My writings are based solely upon my own individual feelings and life experiences.; [a.] Maryville, TN

FREEMAN, ESTHER L.
[b.] May 19, 1923, Kansas City, KS; [p.] Mr. and Mrs. Homer LeRoy Lynn (Thelma); [m.] Harold F. Freeman, July 14, 1940; [ch.] Harold Philip; [ed.] High School, Midwest Bible and Missionary Institute (1951), now Calvary Bible College, Kansas City, MO; [occ.] Homemaker; [memb.] Church, Vallejo Bible Church; [oth. writ.] "Calling All Juniors," Voice Magazine, periodi-

cal of Independent Fundamental Churches of America, bi-monthly page (for Jr. age children), other poems, several music compositions, Sunday school materials.; [pers.] My abilities of composing poems and music have been given me by the Lord Jesus Christ - and I acknowledge this with humble gratitude.; [a.] Vallejo, CA

FRENCH, DANNIELLE
[pen.] Ellie, Coco; [b.] November 14, 1982, Cover'd Alene; [p.] Kathleen A. Blake; [ed.] I'm in 8th grade; [memb.] Memberships are BMG music, and I think thats' all; [hon.] I have won two bowling trophies and a D.A.R.E. Medal; [oth. writ.] One of my favorite poems I've written is called "You".; [pers.] If you have a dream go for it. Don't let anyone tell you that you can't reach your dream, because you can.; [a.] Chewelah, WA

FROCK, KATHY LYNN
[b.] August 2, 1958, Wichita, KS; [p.] Norma Jeanne King and Chester R. Frock; [ch.] Brianna, Joshua, Miranda, Amanda; [ed.] High School Graduate; [occ.] Patience Escort, Sterile Tech, Housekeeper; [oth. writ.] I have written approximately 170 poems, but this is the first one to be published.; [pers.] People and events inspire my poetry. I draw deep within myself to bring forth the true feelings in my heart.; [a.] Halstead, KS

FUGATE, MARTHA T.
[b.] September 23, 1920, Clark County, ID; [p.] Dr. R. D. Tucker and Sarah M. McDonald; [m.] Ralph G. Fugate Dec'd, March 8, 1945; [ch.] Sarah, Becky, R.D.; [ed.] Midway H.S., Jefferson Co. Idaho, Brigham Young Univ. Provo, UT. Taught English, Taught Bombing in W.W. II Helped with Fam. Bus.; [occ.] Retired except for writing; [memb.] D.A.R., Daughters of Utah Pioneers, Utah State Poetry Soc., L.D.S. Church; [hon.] 1st Place Sonnet, 1996 U.S.P.S. (20 other Sonnets Placed) 1st Place poem at B.Y.U. (Published) Poems in "Utah Sings" 1996 Edition by U.S.P.S.; [oth. writ.] An Historical, Biographical Novel, "Your Move, Dr. Tucker" self-published. (Made back expenses!); [pers.] My poems "Prayer for talent" pretty much says it: Do the best you can in every way you can!; [a.] Midway, UT

FULTON SR., RALPH E.
[b.] November 21, 1950, Los Angeles, CA; [p.] E.J. Fulton and Rosa Lee Via; [m.] Melvora E. Moore-Fulton, February 14, 1996, 2nd marriage; [ch.] 6 natural 1 son, 5 adopted children; [ed.] Freemont and Washington High, L.A. Southwest College, Elcamino College, Los Angeles Trade Tech College, Grace Bible Institute, Long Beth, Bus. Admin. Major, AA Degree in Fashion Design and Pextiles (L.A. Trade Tech.); [occ.] Field Service Representative for Southern Calif. Gar Co.; [memb.] L.E.A.P. Foundation Member (Linking Education and Progress), Faithful Central Baptist Church Member Men's Fellowship Group, Project M.I.S.T.E.R. Member, (Men in Schools to Establish Relationships) Mentor Teach and Train Youths of single parent moms and volunteer with D.A.R.E. Program, on parents advisory council with city of English; [hon.] Assistant on Junior Drill Team-Duvet Bch., Deans Honor UST, Southwest Southwest College; [oth. writ.] On file but (Not yet published) "The Timeless Corner", "Are You Really Giving?", "The Lost Shadow", "The Great Brainwash". Published Newsletters for various family pic-nic and Family Reunions, publish newsletters for Moore Christian Academy, Assist with Slogans and sayings in Publications Thru Church Donate Time Writing Poems for co-workers.; [pers.] The self extinction of America's Youths today contributes to the Glorificat of Drugs, Guns, and Gangs, Raising the Conscious of Society to the problem is my purpose through the use of poetry while offering solutions through the use of humor and entertainment during the education.

FUNARI, ANTHONY
[pen.] Anthony Funari; [b.] August 18, 1973, Trenton, NJ; [p.] Lorraine and Reynolds Funari; [ed.] McCorristin High, Mercer County Col., and Stockton College. Major is History, for secondary education.; [occ.] Black Jack Dealer in Atlantic City's Tropicana.; [pers.] An ignorant man thinks he holds all the answers, but a wise man is willing to learn.; [a.] Smithville, NJ

FUNK, RACHEL B.
[b.] August 1, 1986, Boston, MA; [p.] Edward A. and Ellen M. Funk; [ed.] 5th grade, Brophy Elementary School, Framingham, Mass.; [occ.] Student; [hon.] Honor Student, Young author; [pers.] A personal hobby is writing poems and short stories for other young people; [a.] Framingham, MA

FURGUSON, STEPHANIE
[pen.] Stephanie J. Mitchell; [b.] August 9, 1977, Franklin, IN; [p.] Phillip and Jacquline Mitchell; [m.] Shannon D. Furguson, October 22, 1994; [ch.] Alexis Emery Furguson; [ed.] Wilmington Senior High School, currently at Southern State Community College earning an Associates in fine arts and chemistry; [occ.] Domestic Engineer/Student; [memb.] Art Club, Industrial Arts Club, Choices Club, SADD, Forensics Club; [hon.] 1991-1992 AHA, IFS English Award, 1991-1992 World History Certificate, Honorable mention art award; [pers.] God's most divine gift to mankind was emotions and for one person to extend into the depths of another persons soul and jumble up the emotions from within bewilders my mind. Thanks, God.; [a.] New Vienna, OH

GADPAILLE, DORIS
[m.] Ivanhoe, August 27, 1949; [ch.] Three; [ed.] High School PMA; [memb.] St. Francis Clown Ministry; [pers.] "My child you are growing and you will learn."; [a.] Hollis, NY

GAFFNEY, ZOOK
[pen.] Zook Gaffney; [b.] February 19, 1948, Brooklyn, NY; [p.] Charles J. and Terry Gaffney; [ed.] Seton Hall Univ., Germaine School U.S. Navy; [occ.] Disabled Vietnam Veteran; [memb.] Vietnam Veterans, VFW, American Legion; [hon.] U.S. Navy Good Conduct Medal, Honorable Medical Discharge, Seton Hall Univ. Dean's List; [oth. writ.] "Eating Little Dogs During The Revolution", 10 Year Poetry Anthology, Self Published 1978; [pers.] I got turned on by Allen Ginsberg, Charles Bukowski, Walt Whitman, Kurt Vonnegut, Ernest Hemmingway, Jack Kerouac and William Burroughs whose works all played a major influence in my writing. Everybody should try writing poetry.; [a.] Frenchtown, NJ

GAILEY, RENE MARIE
[pen.] Rene Gailey; [b.] May 1, 1962, Sandusky, OH; [p.] Col. David and Rosemarie Frutchey, Mr. and Mrs. Jerry Ashton; [m.] Billy Dean Gailey, September 3, 1989; [ch.] Aleshia Dawn Broomfield (daughter) and Joshua Dean Gailey (step-son); [ed.] Graduated 12th grade - Waukesha, North High School - Waukesha, WI, Vernon Regional Jr. College, Cosmetology Vernon, TX; [occ.] Licensed Cosmetologist; [memb.] United Methodist Church, Wagoner Oklahoma, OK Board of Cosmetology, American Cancer Society; [hon.] Top Student Honors - Vernon Regional Jr. College - Cosmetology; [oth. writ.] Personal enjoyment and satisfaction of expressing true feelings.; [pers.] I express myself and life in writing. I am influenced by true happenings and other people's thoughts. We are who we are and life is really what it is.; [a.] Wagoner, OK

GALLEGOS, ANNETT M.
[pen.] Lili Gal; [b.] February 26, 1969, Oklahoma City, OK; [p.] Rose Blair and Anna Crosby; [m.] John A. Gallegos, November 19, 1988; [ch.] Jordan Johnny and Ashlee Hunter; [ed.] South East High - Lincoln, NE, Denver West High - Center for International Studies, Denver, CO, Platte College - Aurora, CO; [occ.] Bilingual Wire Transfer Representative; [hon.] FBLA President - 1986-1987, International Studies - Exchange - Scholarship, Editor's Choice Award - 1996, The National Library of Poetry; [oth. writ.] Poem published in Anthology "Portraits Of Life" -1996, Poem published in a Denver Public Schools Publication - "Blueberry, Ltd" - in 1982 at age 13; [pers.] Become acquainted with your inner self and learn what is "Your" reality. It is only then that your senses come alive and you are able to teach others that there are no limitations, no boundaries when it comes to the imagination.; [a.] Denver, CO

GALLO, PATRICIA
[b.] December 16, 1964, Los Angeles; [p.] Sigfrido and Ofelia Martinez-Dela Torre; [m.] Ronald F. Gallo Jr., April 18, 1992; [ch.] Sahara Louise Gallo; [pers.] To my daughter Sahara, you are you are my greatest moment in my life, love mom.; [a.] Baldwin Park, CA

GAMEL, FRED
[pen.] Fred Gamel; [b.] June 4, 1944, Rockmart, GA; [p.] Charles and Sylvia Gamel; [m.] Beth, April 26, 1980; [ch.] Peter, Matthew, Mark; [ed.] Kennesaw State University, Campbell High School, Smyrna, GA; [occ.] Manager Telecommunications Turner Broadcasting; [memb.] VVA (Vietnam Veterans of America); [hon.] American Theater Critics, Best New Play to originate outside NYC for 83-84 (Wasted); [oth. writ.] Wasted, Play The Prophets, Poetry Novel; [pers.] To Randall Jarrell, a poet first, critic by trade and a poor judge of traffic...I miss your presence.; [a.] Kennesaw, GA

GARNEAU, EDNA
[b.] February 25, 1910, Hoxie, KS; [p.] Clarice E. (Hales) Sitterly and Erwin F. Sitterly; [m.] Arthur J. Garneau, September 4, 1928; [ch.] MayBelle E. Tipton, Nancy S. Dartford, Sandra J. Paine; [ed.] Elementary School and High School - Salina, KS, University of Connecticut, 1984 (Bachelor of General Science Degree); [occ.] Retired; [memb.] Connecticut State Music Teachers' Association, Institute of Metaphysics (as an ordained minister); [pers.] Had a stroke in 1988, currently a nursing home resident.; [a.] Brooklyn CT

GARR, WANDA F.
[b.] May 7, 1950, Jamestown, KY; [p.] Willie Mae and Clarence Garr; [ed.] BS, Eastern Kentucky Univ., MA, University of Kentucky, MPA, Kentucky State Univ., Doctoral Candidate, Univ. of Kentucky; [occ.] Business Teacher, Secondary level; [memb.] National Education Assoc., Kentucky Education Assoc., Fayette County Education Assoc., Kentucky Association of Gifted Education, Pilgrim Baptist Church; [hon.] Editor's Choice Award, 1996, The National Library of Poetry, Commonwealth Incentive Award, Univ. of Kentucky, Who's Who in American Education; [oth. writ.] Poems published by The National Library of Poetry: "Time", "Dear, Dear MLK (A Birthday Tribute)", "Peace", "One Brave Soldier".; [pers.] Writing poetry is a creative way of expressing thoughts and feelings. Sharing poetry is a way to grow by making new and dear friendships.; [a.] Lexington, KY

GARRETSON, JOHANNA A.
[b.] January 14, 1917, Java Island, Indonesia; [p.] Jan and Phien Van Haastert (Dutch); [m.] John D. Garretson (American), May 4, 1954 in the Hague; [ch.] 2 Sons (Adopted) in Java; [ed.] (Dutch) Junior College, assistant librarian, after W.W.II followed Business Courses in The Hague. (Holland); [occ.] Retired; [memb.] Volunteered for 15 yrs. in Hospital in Escondido (CA) Since '93 member of Sen. Cit. in Glendora (Ca); [hon.] One pin for volunteering 7.500 hrs. in Hospital in Escondido Ca. Helping patients, no other rewards.; [oth. writ.] Some essays in Dutch before W.W.II in Java (lost in war). Started in S. Dimas in 1994. Entired the NLP contest; [pers.] Love nature or God's creations.; [a.] San Dimas, CA

GARRETT, HANNAH E.
[b.] August 28, 1985, Greensboro, NC; [p.] Randall and Theresa Garrett; [ed.] Stoneville Elementary School, Western Rockingham Middle School; [occ.] Sixth grade student; [memb.] Student Council, Band, News Team, Providence Baptist Church; [hon.] Honor Roll, Presidential Honors Math Award; [oth. writ.] Book - "My Famous Dog"; [a.] Stoneville, NC

GASINK, WARREN A.
[b.] September 1, 1927, Sioux City, IA; [p.] John Alfred Gasink and Mary Haas Gasink; [m.] Verna Jean Clausen, 1950, (Divorced, 1960), Margaret Nobis, 1962, (Divorced, 1973), Christina Catalano, 1979, (Divorced, 1980); [ch.] Roxanne Lynell Gasink, Cope, Reyna B., John Alfred Gasink B.; [ed.] B.A. Morningside College 1953, M.A. University of Southern California, 1995, UCLA, 1958-1959; [memb.] National Forensic League, Pi Kappa Delta, Speech Association of America, Eastern Speech Association, American Forensic Association, Eastern Forensic Association, Phi Rho Pi, Tau Kappa Epsilon, American Legion, Veterans of Foreign Wars, Association of Pennsylvania State College and University Faculty; [hon.] Nominated for George Orwell Award, 1991. Degree of Special Distinction, Pi Kappa Delta, in Oratory, Debate, and Instruction. Outstanding Leadership Award, National Multiple Sclerosis Society. Boy Scouts of America, Eagle Rank. Many forensics awards as both student and faculty member. Numerous awards for poetry.; [oth. writ.] Who's Who In America, 1995, 1996, 1997, Who's Who In American Education, Who's Who In the East, Who's Who In The World, Who's Who In Media and Communications.; [pers.] The fine arts - music, poetry, painting, sculpture,, etcetera develop in each of us an inner,r all - pervading sense of beauty, worth, and humanness. When we find the rhythms and melodies in nature, in love, in life, we discover the only unfading values. Each of us can be taught to sense the beauty in viewing, hearing, and creating notes and rhythms, colors, the interrelationships of line and space in architecture, the caressing movement of sculpture, or the music and melody inherent in all language. Only when we let ourselves react to these subtle but oh-so-real joys, do we become complete and whole.; [a.] Stroudsburg, PA

GATES, TINA
[b.] July 3, 1966, Bellevue, WA; [p.] Kyle and Linda Foreman; [m.] Mark Gates, July 27, 1991; [ed.] Issaquah High School; [occ.] Unique Printing Bindery and Fulfillment Dept.; [oth. writ.] Nothing published - just given copies of poems to family.; [pers.] I do not sit down purposely to write my poems, they come to me through inspiration from the Lord either in my sleep or during times of great emotion. Psalms 32-8, "I will instruct you and teach you in the way you should go, I will counsel you with my eye upon you."; [a.] Hayden, ID

GAUTNEY, JONI
[b.] October 2, 1968, S. Lake Tahoe, CA; [oth. writ.] "Wisdom's Teachings", "Rising of the Storm", "Passion Persevered", and "An Angel Visited Me" published by

write magazine.; [pers.] My love for poetry started when I was in the fourth grade, where I used to write about Mr. Magoo and his potions. Since then, my poetry has been inspired by happenings in my life and those around me. It has, in all senses, become my favorite form of creativity and expression, providing a path to a higher learning of myself.; [a.] Davis, CA

GAYLORD, SHARON DENISE
[b.] September 5, 1964, Jacksonville, FL; [p.] Jimmy Kelly and Verlene Wallace; [m.] John R. Gaylord Jr., July 28, 1990; [ch.] Clifton J. and Erin Elizabeth; [ed.] Currently in Dental School in pursuit of a DMD degree; [occ.] Full/time student UMD NJ; [memb.] ASDA (American Student Dental Association); [pers.] This poem is dedicated to my grandmother, Ivera Kelly Crews. It is a token of my love and respect for her, as well as other strong maternal figures who have passed on to a better place. She's dearly missed.; [a.] Roselle, NJ

GEIST, MARLENE Y.
[pen.] Marlene Y. Geist; [b.] November 12, 1972, Nebraska; [p.] Enrique Elizondo, Cristina Elizondo; [m.] Darrell J. Geist, June 20, 1992; [ch.] Charise Ellen, Bonita Marlene, and Marcella Cristina and a baby on it's way; [ed.] West High, Institute of Children's Literature; [occ.] Homemaker; [pers.] "Life's tasks maybe hard at times, try not to give up. Tomorrow maybe better". Think positive when all else fails.; [a.] Denver, CO

GEORGE, LAUREN
[b.] July 26, 1953, New York; [ed.] Background in Ballet, Studied at Carnegie Hall, Acting, performed off-Broadway with the 'Everyman Company', studied HB Studio; [occ.] Career Developed in TV and film Production, and now Public Relations and publishing; [memb.] Give readings throughout NYC, including "Poet to Poet" group; [oth. writ.] Currently working on a collection of my poetry, book soon to be published.; [pers.] Belief is causal. So, dig deep to discover what you truly believe, seek guidance through love into light, and then make magic real. Give thanks and spread a little happiness everyday.; [a.] New York, NY

GERSTENSCHLAGER, SHERRY A.
[b.] December 29, 1954, Peterborough, Ontario, Canada; [p.] Earl and Helen Belsey; [m.] Jeff G. Gracey (Fiance); [ch.] Pammy Lampereur, Kelly Laplataey, David Gerstenschlager; [occ.] Artist and Writer; [pers.] Thank you to Jeff who is my critic and listening ear.; [a.] Clifton, CO

GEYMAN, ANGELA K.
[b.] March 31, 1979, Indianapolis, IN; [p.] Carol Holzer, Chris Geyman; [ed.] Graduate South Ripley High School May 1997, Plan to attend Ball State University in the fall of 1997; [occ.] Student; [memb.] South Ripley Show Choir, Math Club, FCA, SAE, Student Council; [hon.] Quill and Scroll; [oth. writ.] Feature Writer for "Raider's Riot," school newspaper.; [a.] Versailles, IN

GIBSON, PATRICIA M.
[pen.] Patty Gibson; [b.] March 6, 1984, Florence, SC; [p.] Aileen and Marty Gibson; [ed.] I am in the 7th grade and I go to Andrew Jackson Middle School, Kershaw, SC; [occ.] Student; [memb.] Junior Optimist Club and Andrew Jackson Softball team; [hon.] Many school awards and swimming awards.; [oth. writ.] "Sometimes the wind is..." was published in a kids magazine called "Boodle". Many others unpublished.; [pers.] I write for special occasions or special people, sometimes for a gift to someone I care about.; [a.] Heath Springs, SC

GIEG, LUCILE
[b.] February 26, 1929, Marshall, IL; [p.] Forest and Gladys Irwin; [ch.] Norma Lynn Sinclair, Kenneth W. Gieg II; [ed.] Masters of Art in Urban Affairs, St. Louis University (1986); [occ.] Fiscal Manager for the Kathy J. Weinman Shelter for Battered Women and Their Children; [hon.] Who's Who in American Colleges and Universities 1981-1982, Award of Honor-Recognition of Achievement in Human Services (St. Louis Com. College 1978-1979); [pers.] I believe we each have the responsibility to do all that is within our power to help those who are less fortunate.; [a.] Saint Louis, MO

GILBERTSON, LANCE
[pen.] Lance Gilbertson; [b.] April 21, 1975, Fairbanks, AK; [p.] Lawrence Gilbertson, Linda Crawford; [m.] Danette Gilbertson, December 27, 1994; [ch.] Julian A. Gilbertson; [ed.] High School Graduate (12th grade); [occ.] Unemployed; [hon.] 4 Army Achievement Medals, State Champion Wrestler at 189 lbs.; [pers.] Was strongly influenced by Edgar Poe. I think he's the greatest writer of all time. Do unto others before they do unto you.; [a.] Delta Junction, AK

GINNANE, MARA
[b.] March 21, 1982, San Francisco; [p.] Joan Sangree; [ed.] Currently a Freshman in High School; [occ.] Student, Grand County High School; [memb.] National Honor Society; [hon.] Full Scholarship to, "Desert Writer's Workshop," 4.0 student; [a.] Castle Valley, UT

GIORDANO, RON J.
[pen.] Giordano; [b.] June 7, 1940, Chicago, IL; [p.] Nick and Florence; [m.] Darla M., September 23, 1967; [ch.] Ron C. and Courtney N.; [ed.] Ron C - Criminal Justice Courtney attending Un. of Iowa; [occ.] President, H.S. Cricker, Printer food and pharmaceutical labels and cartons; [memb.] Columbian Club Fl. Chgo.; [hon.] Inst. of Pkg. Professionals certified - outstanding achievement corp. Contribution, Society of Pkg. Professionals, Packaging Technology (BD of DIR) Joint Civic Committee; [oth. writ.] Primarily unpublished poems, never released.; [pers.] My poems are influenced by what we have been given on this earth to enjoy, most of which is the purist beauty of nature, love and those things in life which are free.; [a.] Woodstock, IL

GIPSON, D. TEX
[b.] June 20, 1954, Tyler, TX; [p.] Hoot Gipson, Mary Gipson; [ch.] Roy, Amanda, Heather, Johnathan, McKenna; [occ.] Plumber; [hon.] Offered Diamond Homer Trophy and public presentation of my poetry at Famous Poets Society Convention in Anaheim, CA was not able to attend.; [oth. writ.] Published in Tucson newspaper published in "Famous Poems of the Twentieth Century" anthology; [pers.] I strive to express, through my poetry, the fears, hopes, and questions of the common man.; [a.] Flint, TX

GIRTON, MELISSA E.
[b.] August 27, 1981, Fort Worth, TX; [p.] Keith E. Girton and Pamela M. Girton; [ed.] Freshman at Lock Haven High School; [occ.] Student; [memb.] Lock Haven High Sch. Drama Club and Lock Haven High School Track Team, Immaculate Conception Church; [hon.] 1st place in Fire Prevention Essay Contest, Honor Student, 1st place in Lock Haven Science Fair '94; [a.] Woolrich, PA

GLENN, SHELIA
[b.] April 9, 1959, Detroit, MI; [p.] Grover and Emogene Wofford; [m.] Eric Glenn, June 27, 1981; [ch.] La Trina, Erika and Marcus; [ed.] Spring Arbor College, Redford

High School; [occ.] Senior Trainer w/ a major health care organization (BCBS); [memb.] Family Victory Fellowship Church, Director of Victory Kids Club; [hon.] This will be my first; [oth. writ.] Currently, personal memoirs.; [pers.] To pursue every God given talent and ability within me while living, laughing and growing old gracefully. My peace is to express my innermost thoughts and feelings.; [a.] Southfield, MI

GODBEE, MS. ADRIAN LEE
[pen.] Ms. Adrian Lee Godbee; [b.] September 8, 1978, Douglas, GA; [p.] Ricky O. and Barbara J. Godbee; [ed.] Savannah High School, Armstrong Atlantic State University; [occ.] Customer Service Rep. at Custom Computer Centers, Inc.; [memb.] Future Business Leaders of America, Church of Jesus Christ of Latter-day Saints; [hon.] Honor Graduate in 1996, Honor Roll, Sun Trust Poetry Contest, Numerous awards with FBLA and Georgia Mock Trial Competitions throughout High School years. Awards through participating in church programs and auxiliaries.; [oth. writ.] Personal book of poetry and songs not yet published. Also, speeches, essays, and reports.; [pers.] I speak from within. I ask questions. I listen, I learn...and then I write.; [a.] Bloomingdale, GA

GODI, JACOB RAJU
[pen.] J. R. Godi; [b.] June 22, 1959, Matyapuri, A.P., India; [p.] Late Rev. Christian Godi (F), Mrs. Sundar-Amma Godi (M); [ed.] Masters in English Literature, Masters in Education; [occ.] Lecturer in English, A.P.S.W.R. College, India 533406; [oth. writ.] "Andamyna Nakshatram" an anthology of poems in telugu language.; [pers.] My pen shall be my weapon forever in the war to concur peace and love amongst the mankind.; [a.] Bensalem, PA

GOFORTH, ETHELINE
[pen.] 'Tot'; [b.] March 8, 1932, West Virginia; [p.] Troy and Clara Lusk; [m.] Clyde (Deceased), November 27, 1951; [ch.] Dorothy, Clyde (Joe) Kim; [ed.] McComas High, W. Va. Bluefield State College; [occ.] Self employed; [pers.] I love writing and hope to do more the next year, as I have plans to retire; [a.] Lorain, OH

GOINS, DOLORES
[pen.] Lois; [b.] September 18, 1956, Baltimore, MD; [p.] Willie and Mamie Goins; [ch.] Alaya Dyson; [ed.] BA in English, BS in Elementary Education; [occ.] English Teacher, Baltimore City Public Schools; [oth. writ.] I have written plays, short stories, and other poems. I am currently working on becoming published.; [pers.] Writing is a medium through which a person can pour out his soul. It is like music not sung. It is therapeutic and cleansing.; [a.] Baltimore, MD

GOLDEN, SEAN
[b.] July 7, 1982; [p.] Virginia Golden, Lawrence Golden; [ed.] Attend school '71, 8th Grade, Buffalo, New York; [occ.] Student; [pers.] It is difficult to adequately express my gratitude to my great grandmother born 1892 in Alabama for making the choice she made.; [a.] Buffalo, NY

GOLDMAN, RICHARD
[b.] August 15, 1980, New York; [p.] Alan and Sandy; [ed.] Bethpage High School - Junior Year; [occ.] Student - Junior in High School; [memb.] B'nai B'rth Youth Organization; [oth. writ.] The Irony Of My Life, You're The One; [pers.] The conquest of your desires forms a road to your dynasty, which can only be corrupted by regrets about chances missed and people lost.; [a.] Plainview, NY

GONDA, CLIFF
[b.] November 13, 1937, Ann Arbor, MI; [p.] Joseph and Ruth Gonda; [m.] Deanna D., August 26, 1961; [ch.] Sharon Elizabeth, Kenneth Allen; [ed.] H.S. Grad., Brown City, MI; [occ.] Assembler, Medtronics; [hon.] Selected three times to display artwork in Grand Rapids Art Museum; [oth. writ.] Editor of Ship's Newspaper, U.S. Navy 1958 Editorials in local newspapers.; [pers.] Rest not, rust not.; [a.] Wyoming, MI

GONZALES, RUTH S.
[pen.] Rocel Goles; [b.] July 9, 1980, Philippines; [p.] Alfredo G. Gonzales and Estelita S. Gonzales; [ed.] Thomas Starr King Middle School, John Marshall High School; [occ.] 10th grade student; [memb.] Golden West Christian Church Youth Group; [hon.] Jeweled Crown awarded by Thomas Starr King Middle School; [pers.] I express my thoughts and feelings in the poems I write whenever I'm in the mood and greatly inspired.; [a.] Los Angeles, CA

GOODING, WALTER F.
[b.] September 25, 1910, Philadelphia, PA; [p.] Harry E. Gooding and Ada Dawson; [m.] Ruth (61 years), Leah (5 years); [ch.] Walter Jr., Richard and 12 great grandchildren; [ed.] Fifth Grade School; [occ.] Minister/Retired; [oth. writ.] Much Ministry in my life.; [pers.] I have had and still do a very exciting full life in the Ministry - in my work, in my home life. Have loved every minute of it.; [a.] New Port Richey, FL

GORDON, BRIAN THOMAS
[b.] June 28, 1979, Winston-Salem, NC; [p.] David and Victoria Gordon; [ed.] South Stokes High School, Appalachian State University (Fall of 1997); [occ.] Employed at Lowes Foods; [hon.] A-Honor Roll, perfect attendance, all-district symphonic Band, Piano Classes. NCMFA Honors Orchestra; [oth. writ.] Poems in High School newspaper; [pers.] I like to write to express what I feel. Most of my poems are for children. They show me what this world has to look forward to.; [a.] Pinnacle, NC

GORDON, MARY CATHERINE
[b.] March 28, 1957; [ch.] Gina Gordon; [pers.] I want people to come to know Jesus as their personal saviour. I am deeply moved by the Bible and especially the Psalms are my favorite, and I believe it.; [a.] Wheeling, WV

GOSMAN, ANGELA G.
[b.] May 20, 1964, Montgomery Co.; [p.] Robert and Geraldine Stonestreet; [m.] Timothy A. Gosman, July 29, 1984; [ch.] Three: Trevor, Kristin, and Jason; [ed.] Wheaton High School 12 graduate, FCC - Job Training Agency, non-credit course; [occ.] Bus Operator MCPS; [memb.] Thespian Society #85; [hon.] Automotive Award presented by Ida Mae Garrett 1982, Lifetime member International Thespian Society 1983, Presidential Physical Fitness Award, JTA Certificate of Completion FCC; [oth. writ.] I have many other writings, none published. I write poems for friends and family. I enjoy making people happy through my writings.; [pers.] I feel writing brings out one's most inner personal feelings. Often when confronted I'm lost for words, but give me a piece of paper and the words are easily found deep within the heart.; [a.] Frederick, MD

GOTTBREHT, JOYCE M.
[b.] April 8, 1937, England; [p.] Deceased, both English; [m.] Donald Leo, July 23, 1981; [ch.] Three Sons (2 in England), 1 stepson and 3 stepdaughters in USA; [occ.] Retired, Home Occupation, Crafts Laminating, Exotic Birds; [memb.] Jefferson County Planning Commissioner (Oregon), Economic Development Committee for Jefferson County, I am very interested in my community and its future development; [oth. writ.] None published, a file of unpublished.; [pers.] I enjoy poetry. My family likes my cards, as I always have a special poem for the occasion. I didn't start writing poems until I came to the USA in 1981, I still surprise myself when I read past work, that I really wrote it!!; [a.] Culver, OR

GOUGEON, CHRISTINE
[pen.] Christine Gougeon; [b.] September 19, 1966, Trenton, MI; [p.] Joan and Bernard Gougeon; [ch.] Virginia Faith Gougeon; [ed.] Bachelor of Social Work; [occ.] Social Worker; [pers.] In God we find everything.; [a.] River Rouge, MI

GOVIL, VISHAL
[b.] December 4, 1982, New York; [p.] Arun and Vandana Govil; [ed.] Buckley Country Day School N.Y. Tampa Prep. School FL.; [occ.] Student; [hon.] Head Masters Award, Honors Gold Medal, Several Articles and poems published in local newspapers; [pers.] I try to reflect the observations of our daily life in my poems.; [a.] Lutz, FL

GOZDERA, WLADYSLAWA
[pen.] Vladis; [b.] February 20, 1940, Poland; [p.] G. W. Kasperek; [m.] Mieczyslaw, September 19, 1958; [ch.] Mariola; [ed.] Master Education, Poland; [occ.] Matron; [memb.] Catholic Club; [hon.] Artex Publishing Honor Diploma 1996, V tome Anthology Emigrant, Poems in Polish Language; [oth. writ.] Several poems published in newspapers - Polish Daily Ethnic News.; [pers.] I'm originally from Austria-Vienna. I came to the USA to pursue my education and writing.; [a.] Brooklyn, NY

GRANIERO, RONALD
[b.] September 6, 1937, Long Branch, NJ; [p.] Louis and Anne Graniero; [m.] Erica Marmora Graniero, October 23, 1965; [ch.] Andrea, Stephanie and Steven; [ed.] Long Branch High School, Rutgers University B.A., School of St. Philip Neri, Immaculate Conception Seminary; [occ.] Owner of Cruise Travel Agency; [memb.] Society of St. Vincent De Paul; [oth. writ.] Short stories published in The Anthologist, Rutgers University literary magazine.; [pers.] I believe our good deeds precede us into the eye of the needle and smooth the passage through. Thanks to Robert Frost for the inspiration, "...promises to keep and miles to go before I sleep."; [a.] Oceanport, NJ

GRANT, JAMAL K.
[b.] September 16, 1963, Trinidad, WI; [p.] Desmond Grant and Cecelia Julien; [ch.] Kevin, Devin, Ebonique; [ed.] Prospect Heights H.S.; [memb.] St. Ann, St. Catherine Spiritual Baptist Church; [oth. writ.] Several unpublished poems.; [pers.] I hope my writing will help the unity of all mankind, and give a spiritual upliftment.; [a.] Brooklyn, NY

GRAVES, ANITA
[b.] December 7, 1957, McNairy, TN; [p.] Clarence Hooper and Rachel Boyd Hooper; [m.] Rickie Hugh Graves, December 23, 1985; [ch.] Randal Hugh Graves; [ed.] McNairy Central High, Union University (B.A.), Memphis State Masters and 45 plus (educ.); [occ.] Reading and Math Teacher, Bethel Springs Elem.; [memb.] Mt. Zion Baptist Church; [hon.] 1st Place Ink Drawing 1993, 1st Place Ink Drawing 1994, 2nd Place Ink Drawing 1995 in the Shiloh Art Contest, Feathers, Fur and Fins Contest: 1st Mixed Media, 2nd Oil Pastel; [oth. writ.] Articles published in local newspaper.; [pers.] Make time for your family so you can grow together, not separately.; [a.] Bethel Springs, TN

GRAVES, DIANE ELIZABETH
[b.] November 27, 1977, Redlands, CA; [p.] Janet Shelburne, Peter Graves; [ed.] Redlands High School, finished freshman year at McGill University (Montreal, Quebec); [occ.] Administrative Assistant, Tektronix, OR, Factory, Tektronix, OR; [oth. writ.] Several poems posted on internet web sites, bilingual Spanish-English poetry.; [a.] Portland, OR

GRAY, THOMAS M.
[b.] March 28, 1952, Sterling, IL; [p.] Leroy and Mabel Gray; [ed.] A.A.S. Degree in H.V.A.C. from Sauk Valley College in Dixon, IL; [occ.] Quality Analysis for Motorola; [hon.] Several times on President's List and Dean's List while attending Sauk Valley College; [oth. writ.] Many other poems have I written, although I have never attempted to have them published.; [pers.] There is good and bad within all people. We should strive to forgive the bad in others and to bring out their good, and our own, as well.; [a.] Williams Bay, WI

GREEN, ALLEN M.
[pen.] Allen Michael Green; [b.] September 26, 1946, Michigan; [p.] Dona Mitchell; [m.] Mary Ann Green, Vanessa Jessica, August 8, 1992; [ch.] Two daughters; [ed.] B.S. (with honors) 1974, Eastern Michigan University, M.A. (with honors) 1975, Eastern Michigan University; [occ.] President/Owner A. Green Financial Group; [memb.] Ypsilanti Historical Society; [hon.] Registered Investment Advisor, Registered Representative, Numerous Production Awards; [oth. writ.] Novel, "Modern Divorce Wars", various financial articles in local newspapers, collection of poems from 1969 to present.; [a.] Ypsilanti, MI

GREEN, DEBBIE
[b.] January 2, 1949, Fort Worth, TX; [p.] David Green and Kathryn Bates; [ch.] Paul and Mae Simpson; [ed.] BA - Baylor University, Waco TX Med University of Wisconsin - Stout Menomonie WI; [occ.] Writer; [hon.] Who's Who in American Colleges and Universities, 1971, Human Worth Award, 1968; [oth. writ.] "How to Support A Friend Through Divorce," numerous song lyrics - folk, R&B, CW, Essays: "On Becoming A Rebel," "Teaching About Chippewa Treaty Rights." Study Guide: "Building a Foundation for Conflict Resolution." I am working on a book entitled, "The Demise of the Suffering Servant," inspired by my suicide attempt and subsequent divorce.; [pers.] Wordsworth said, "Poetry is the spontaneous overflow of powerful feelings reflected in tranquility," so powerful for me that I have mostly settled for corny song lyrics. To tackle true poetry is for me a challenge that I approach with deep reverence.; [a.] Menomonie, WI

GREEN, DERWINN
[b.] December 22, 1976, Beaufort, SC; [p.] Ralph Green, Joanna Green; [ed.] Eleanor Christensen Montessori, Beaufort High School, Howard University; [occ.] Student, Journalist (Staff writer for the Community News); [memb.] Society of Professional Journalists (SPJ), Palmetto Project, Mentor Program and Volunteer Service/Charity, National Honor Society; [hon.] Cited Who's Who Among America's High School Students, Howard University Trustee Scholarship, Alpha Phi Alpha Achievement Award, Academic Varsity Letter, 1993 Junior Scholar, graduated top 10% of Senior Class with honors; [oth. writ.] Several poems published in academic literary magazines, articles for the Community News, Beaufort Gazette.; [pers.] Listen to your heart, hope and dream. Believe in yourself even if no one else does and express yourself in the way 'you' see fit.; [a.] Washington, DC

GREEN, MARVIN L.
[b.] January 1, 1948, Seattle, WA; [p.] David and Etheline Green; [m.] Evelyn L. Green, June 20, 1987; [ch.] Dion White, C. Monique Green; [ed.] Franklin High 1962-65, Washington Jr. High 1959-62, Colman Elementary 1953-59; [occ.] Administrative Specialist; [memb.] DAs (Exclusive); [hon.] Class Comedian 1965; [oth. writ.] "Upon Request"; [pers.] Patience is handled differently by everyone - waiting too long is a benefit to no one...; [a.] Seattle, WA

GREEN, SHELIA D.
[m.] William R. Green; [ch.] Tracie D. Green; [ed.] Pascagoula High School, Mississippi Gulf Coast Community College; [occ.] Administrative Services, Chevron Products Co.; [memb.] First United Methodist Church of Goutier MS; [a.] Goutier, MS

GREENE, YOLANDA C.
[b.] September 28, 1975, Philadelphia; [p.] Norman and Debra Greene; [ed.] Junior at University of Pittsburgh at Greensburg, but currently taken classes at the Community College of Philadelphia; [occ.] Assistant Treasurer at Bright Hope Federal Credit Union; [memb.] O.B.A. - Organization of Black Awareness; [oth. writ.] My True Feelings, Fear of the One I love, Doubt, Misunderstood, Being Strong, ?????????, and The Only Way Out; [pers.] Never dwell on the past just think about the future because you cannot change what has happened.; [a.] Philadelphia, PA

GREGG, KATHERINE
[pen.] F/K/A/ Marie Gawronski Johnson; [b.] June 1947, Chicago, IL; [ed.] Morton West H.S. '65, Loyola University (Dean's List) National College of Education-Human Services; [occ.] Spiritual Counseling, (private practice); [memb.] Cuyamungue Institute, Todo Institute, Oasis Center Life Member; [oth. writ.] Several poems published in Oasis Center's "Here and Now," newsletter, created and edited newsletter for several organizations.; [a.] Skokie, IL

GRIBBLE, DORIS LEE
[b.] April 27, 1934, Valley Bend, WV; [p.] John McElwee, Greta McElwee; [m.] James Gribble, Deceased, November 7, 1952; [ch.] Deborah Lynn, David Lee, Jeffrey Wayne; [ed.] Tygart Valley High School graduate; [occ.] Retired Administrative Secretary; [memb.] The Church of Christ; [oth. writ.] "My Heart's Treasure Chest," and "Life's Web," previously published in the National Library of Poetry; [pers.] My aspiration is to share encouragement of hope through poetic expression that there is joy beyond this life of trials to all who seek God's promise.; [a.] Chesapeake, VA

GRICE, MARIA C.
[pen.] M. C. Quinones (REE); [b.] December 19, 1972, Puerto Rico; [p.] Carmen M. Morales and A. Quinones; [m.] Jeffery L. Grice, February 27, 1993; [ch.] Jordan and Sharrieff Grice; [ed.] Warren Harding High School, Housatonic Comm College; [occ.] Social Security Adm.; [pers.] Always believed in me.; [a.] Bridgeport, CT

GRIESBACH, JEFFREY R.
[b.] November 22, 1966, Wisconsin; [a.] Wisconsin

GRIFFING, STEVEN L.
[b.] September 27, 1956, Canberra, ACT, Australia; [p.] Penelope Griffing; [ed.] Oberlin College (B.A.), California State U. L.A. (Teacher Credential); [occ.] Newspaper Delivery person Columbia Dispatch; [memb.] Columbus Outdoor Pursuits; [pers.] God is beautiful. God is bright. God is big. Everyone is beautiful. Everyone is bright. Everyone can speed.; [a.] Columbus, OH

GRUNDY JR., THOMAS A.
[b.] September 10, 1933, California; [m.] Bertha L., December 7, 1963; [ch.] Thomas and Robert; [occ.] Retired; [pers.] My thoughts are from this wondrous world around me, and my love for family.; [a.] Grand Junction, CO

GRUPENHOF, ALOYSIUS LEO
[pen.] A.L.G.; [b.] December 4, 1909, Cincinnati, OH; [p.] Frank and Pauline; [m.] Marie Nee Geiman, December 31, 1934; [ch.] Jacquline, Angeline, Lois, Virginia, Mary Jo, Joan; [ed.] Elementary 4th Grade, Carpenter Trade School 3 yrs.; [occ.] Retired Union Carpenter, Local 698 Covington, KY; [memb.] Ft. Thomas Retired Mens Club, Catholic Foresters, 55 Club; [hon.] Music Manuscripts are in the Library of NKU. Life story told on Cable T.V. All books are in Thomas Moore College, KY; [oth. writ.] Self-Instruction Music, All Instrument Taughts, Composer of 321 Versatile Music Manuscripts, Children's Chicken Talk Book, 167 page Poetry Book, 23 1/2 degree Life Book.; [pers.] Self taught musician, play all music instruments played football 12 yrs. self educated, Jack of all trades.; [a.] Fort Thomas, KY

GUARINO, ANN
[b.] September 6, 1940, Buffalo, NY; [p.] John Carlino, Ann Carlino; [ch.] Vincent Joseph, Michael John; [ed.] Batavia High School, Genesee Community College, Continental School of Beauty Culture and Hair Design, Alfred College on going education, Hair, Skin Care and Business Mgmnt.; [occ.] Hair Stylist; [memb.] Look Better, Feel Better Program, National Association of Hairdressers, Toastmasters, St. Anthony's Roman Catholic, Church Altar and Rosary Society; [hon.] Continental Student Contest Master Award for Creative Hair Design; [pers.] I desire to enlighten the hearts and souls of the universe with great love, wisdom, and illumination. My influence has been from my own personal trials and tribulations which comes through in my poems.; [a.] Batavia, NY

GUILD, RHEA C.
[pen.] Rhea C. Guild; [b.] May 19, 1907, Midway, UT; [p.] Henry and Emily Coleman; [m.] Lawrence Winfield Guild, December 31, 1930; [ch.] Cynthia, Lawrence II, Marcia; [ed.] Brigham Young University, School Teacher, Utah State University, Russell School of Expression, Curry School of Expression; [occ.] Retired but busy, involved; [memb.] N.H.F.W.C. Laconia W.C. Am. Mothers - A.A.R.P., D.A.R., Daughters of Utah pioneers Historical Society. C.W.A., L.D.S., Mormon church; [hon.] 1967 NH Mother of year pres. N.H. E.F.W.C. Women's Club Grand Marshall of Gilford, N.H. debating, dramatic, oratorical girl scout, civic leader, golden circle award, corrective surgery wrath Laconia State Mental Mental School; [oth. writ.] One year old, The Power of Purity, April Rain, November, Queen Anne's Lace, Two Grand mothers remembered; [pers.] I love poetry, I love dream dramatics, I love people, I love nature, I love my family; [a.] Laconia, NH

GUILLORY, FRANCINE
[b.] November 30, 1943, Oberlin, LA; [p.] Mr. and Mrs. C. Guillory; [ed.] B.A., English, M.A., Theology, M.A., Holistic Health/Wellness; [occ.] Psychotherapist; [memb.] Acadiana Friends of Jung, Louisiana Counseling Asso., Nature Conservancy; [pers.] Writing poetry is an important way for me to connect with my soul and hopefully to inspire others to do the same.; [a.] Breaux Bridge, LA

GUILLORY, HAZEL E.
[pen.] Hazel McGowan Guillory; [b.] August 12, 1944, Houston, TX; [p.] Theodore Seals, Elizabeth Felder; [ch.] Velsen, Wilbert, and Christopher; [ed.] Jack Yates High, University of Houston, Houston Community College; [occ.] Substitute Teacher for Houston Independent School District; [memb.] P.T.A., Mading Elementary, Jack Yates Alumni, University of Houston Alumni; [oth. writ.] Poetry Collection, "Dreams of a Woman Child." Published feature writer, Houston Forward Times Newspaper, 1978-1981.; [pers.] Poetry is the personification of the soul. Great writers are born, not made.; [a.] Houston, TX

GUILLOT, ANGELA KNIGHT
[b.] February 28, 1961, Raceland, LA; [p.] Bert and Leafy Knight; [m.] Mark J. Guillot, July 31, 1982; [ch.] Paul Joseph and Matthew Jacob; [ed.] High School Graduate, Central Lafourche High School, College, Nicholls State University, A.S. Nursing; [occ.] Registered Nurse; [memb.] American Legion Auxiliary, Tau Beta Sigma Sorority; [hon.] Junior Auxilliare of the Year, Outstanding Pledge for Tau Beta Sigma Scholarships, Merit Scholarship, T.H. Harris Scholarship, All star Marching Band, Outstanding Nursing Student Flag Corps Captain; [oth. writ.] Published poems in (3) other Anthologies, on audio cassette for Sounds of Poetry, wrote article for technical School publication.; [pers.] Writing is an escape from reality. My busy life gets hectic sometimes, and when I write, it is my own mini vacation. I enjoy writing for my family and friends.; [a.] Baton Rouge, LA

GUM, ROBIN M.
[p.] Mary L. Baird, Robert P. Baird; [ch.] James W., Heather M., Tonya R.; [pers.] I write poems as I feel them, through my experiences in life. They are all very personal and not often shared outside of family and friends.; [a.] Belton, MO

GUNNING JR., FREDERICK
[pen.] Adonis, Kreep; [b.] November 1, 1974, Roaring Springs, PA; [p.] Frederick, Lavinia Gunning Sr.; [m.] Adaliz Gunning Jr., July 10, 1993; [ch.] Kaylani, Talisa Gunning Jr.; [ed.] ELI Whitney R.V.T.S., G.C.T.C. College; [occ.] Electrician, student at G.C.T.C. College; [oth. writ.] Several other writings not yet published, but looking to get published.; [pers.] My writings are inspired by events that have happened or thoughts I have had. The poem "Love Through My Eyes," is dedicated to my late Grandma, Shirley Gunning.; [a.] East Haven, CT

GUTHRIE, MEGAN
[b.] May 11, 1982, Minot, ND; [p.] Edward Guthrie, Dawn Guthrie; [ed.] Gosnell High School; [occ.] Student; [memb.] Beta Club, Future Leaders of America; [hon.] Student of the Year; [pers.] I enjoy writing because it gives me a chance to express my thoughts, feelings, and emotions.; [a.] Gosnell, AR

GUTIERREZ, ELIZABETH
[b.] September 30, 1976, Pharr, TX; [p.] George and Gloria Gutierrez; [ed.] A current student at South Texas Community College, studying to be a Computer Specialist; [memb.] Heavenly Splendor Worship Temple; [pers.] I have to say that the one and only inspiration came from Jesus Christ through the Holy Spirit.; [a.] San Juan, TX

HACKNEY, TRACY
[b.] October 13, 1980, ARH; [p.] Shelia Bowmon and Larry Hackney; [ed.] Runyon Elementary Grade School, Sophomore at Belfry High School; [memb.] FBLA, DECA; [hon.] Reading Award and other not so amazing recognition.; [oth. writ.] Majority Rules, Absent, Kindred, Black Skies, Creep, Scits a frontic, Boredom, Resecretion, Three White Horses, Truth Denied, Free, Why, and Dark Eyes; [pers.] From my pain comes words which will guide and inspire, boring in my soul setting my mind on fire.; [a.] McAndrews, KY

HAILEY, GERALD A.
[b.] May 28, 1955, Huntsville, MO; [p.] Marlin and Martha Hailey; [ed.] Grade school unit 5 and 6 Glendale Union High School, Glendale Community College; [occ.] Systems Wiring; [hon.] Two safety awards, employee of the week and of the month; [a.] Glendale, AZ

HALEY, LISA DIANNE
[b.] May 17, 1967, Ashland, OH; [p.] Ross and Barb Oehling, Vicky Enderby; [m.] Ronald W. Haley, June 29, 1985; [ch.] Christina Marie, Michael Wayne; [ed.] High School Education, North-Western - Two years Vocational School; [occ.] Household Engineer; [memb.] Ashland Church or The Nazarene Committee Member of Christian Womens Club; [hon.] Received an award for Poetry by Carlton Press; [oth. writ.] I have over one hundred poems that would some day like published in book form; [pers.] I am a Christian and know God has given me the gift of poetry. I write to help myself through trials of life and to help others through theirs. I give God the glory.; [a.] West Salem, OH

HALL, DEBRA K.
[b.] July 8, 1948, Anderson, IN; [ed.] Markleville High, Beauty School, Master Cosmetologist, 2 Computer Training, 2 Robotics Training, 2 Semesters Business at Anderson University; [occ.] Retired, (Total permanent Disability) General Motors; [oth. writ.] Several poems, mostly about family members.; [pers.] Always had a "knack" for writing - next is a book (a goal for years), now I have time to write it.; [a.] Anderson, IN

HALL, KIMBERLY ANNE
[pen.] Kim Hall; [b.] May 7, 1966, Grand Rapids, MI; [p.] William and Sally Hall; [ed.] Graduated from Wayland Union (May 1984); [occ.] Clean Rooms International Inc., General Labor; [memb.] Tennessee Songwriters Association International; [oth. writ.] Two cassette tapes - Hollywood Gold, "Dreaming and Misunderstood," Together We Stand, "How could it Happen and Hang 'Em."; [a.] Dorr, MI

HALL, LESLIE
[b.] March 22, 1961, Kansas City, MO; [p.] Fred and Kelly Hall; [ch.] Shawn Phillip; [ed.] High School Grad., Long Ridge Writers Group (in process); [occ.] Transportation Broker; [memb.] Academy of American Poets, Poetry Society of America, United States Golf Association; [oth. writ.] Interview with President of Karo Blue Society published Radio Waves, Poetry published in Potpourri.; [pers.] Speak and write from your heart - stay open and read, read, read...; [a.] Holden, MO

HALL, VALERIE L.
[pen.] Val Hay; [b.] March 14, 1953, Bremerton, WA; [p.] Hazel and Lee James; [m.] Susan L. Hay, January 1, 1993; [ch.] Laura D. Hall, MD; [ed.] College of Lake County, Brevard Community College, University of Central Florida; [occ.] Registered Nurse, Hospice of St. Frances; [memb.] Phi Theta Kappa, Dean's List, Art Study award - Nancy Dillen; [hon.] Local Art shows, Editor and Chief of Mark Ozz Publishing; [oth. writ.] Finishing a children's book called, "An Angel Under My Bed."; [pers.] I have learned to celebrate diversity through the love of Susan and Laura, Aunt Donnie and my mother.; [a.] Titusville, FL

HALL, VERA
[pen.] "V" "VH"; [b.] November 7, 1950, Yazoo City, MS; [p.] Melvin Hall, Katherine Hall; [ch.] Garvin R. Austin, Todd Hall; [ed.] McNair High, Coahoma Jr. College and Mississippi Valley State College; [occ.] Housemother; [memb.] Belzoni First SDA Church;

[hon.] Honorable throughout High School and College. Crisco Trophy in home economics at McNair High.; [oth. writ.] Several articles published in local newspapers, Belzoni Banner and The Clarion-Ledger; [pers.] It is my desire to reach the inner spirit of man in my writing. My home-economic's teacher was an inspirational role model to me. Her adoration of God's creation has encouraged me to write. My goal is to write of the beauty of the earth and how to maintain it.; [a.] Belzoni, MS

HALL JR., JAMES C.
[pen.] Jimmie Hall; [b.] September 5, 1946, Quincy, FL; [p.] Berniece Virginia and James C. Hall, Sr.; [m.] Diana Arnita, May 6, 1972; [ch.] James C. III and Jaela C.; [ed.] Chester High School, Chester, PA, Marriott Management School, Bethesda, MD, Palmers' Writers School, Brockton, MS, Electronic Data Processing Institute, Philadelphia, PA; [occ.] Oil Refinery, Process "B" Operator; [memb.] American Pool Players Assoc., Arbor Day Foundation, National Rifle Assoc., National Chess Club, Computer Associates of America; [hon.] "Delaware County Black Hall of Fame", (Football - Wide Receiver Dallas Cowboys), Employee of the Year (Mariott Corp.), Employee of the Year (Hilton Corp.), Employee of the Year (Associated Air Frt.); [oth. writ.] Epitaph To A Leader (Dr. Martin Luther King, Jr.), "Come Meet Arnold" (short story), "My Mother's Hands" (Poem), "Soul Rebirth" (Poem), "We Come To Go" (Poem), Where Crystal Streams Through Endless Years, Flow O'er The "Golden Sand", and Where The Old Grow Young Again, I'll Hold "My Mother's Hand!"; [a.] Wilmington, DE

HALLSTROM, JOYCE D.
[b.] August 13, 1965, North Bend, WA; [oth. writ.] "Charlie's Path," published in the anthology The Isle of View.; [pers.] This poem is dedicated to my mother Shirley, sisters Kathy and Wendy and my good friend Melissa, all of whom are exceptional mothers.; [a.] Redmond, WA

HAMILTON, MICHELLE LEE
[b.] March 24, 1978; [p.] Rose and Leo Hamilton; [ed.] Home School and High School Education. Also Christian Elementary; [occ.] Childcare; [memb.] FFA, 4-H Youth Leader, Assembly of God Youth and children leader/sponsor.; [oth. writ.] I have written several other poems but have not yet made any of them public.; [oth. writ.] I have written several other poems but have not yet made any public.; [pers.] I strive to write the truth in my writing whether it be from my heart or from the world. I have been greatly influenced by Jesus Christ my Lord and Savior and the Word of God my Father.; [a.] Waukesha, WI

HAMM, MICHAEL
[pen.] Weldon Like; [b.] April 20, 1948, Fort Worth, TX; [p.] Allen and Marie Hamm; [m.] Elizabeth S. Hamm, February 14, 1985; [ch.] Courtney Elizabeth; [ed.] Graduate, Diablo Valley College, Communication and Creative Writing Major; [occ.] Optician, Precision Optics, Anderson, CA; [pers.] I wrote the poem "no answers," along with many others in 1968. I strive to maintain a completely original style in my writings of today as I did then.; [a.] Cottonwood, CA

HANKINS, JO
[b.] November 13, 1945, Covina, CA; [p.] George E. Dithridge, Barbara L. Dithridge; [ch.] Mark H. Winters; [ed.] Bella Vista High, College of Notre Dame, Pacific School of Religion; [occ.] Bookkeeper; [a.] Tualatin, OR

HANNAH, JOHN THOMAS
[pen.] John T. Hannah; [b.] August 1, 1929, Munising, MI; [p.] John W. Hannah, Cleo Hannah; [m.] Mary Louise Hannah (Deceased, 1992), June 7, 1952; [ch.] Michelle, Kathleen, Charles, John (Tim); [ed.] Ord High, NE, Newspaper Apprenticeship, Leadership School, Ft. Benning, GA; [occ.] Retired from Newspaper Industry former small business owner, retired; [memb.] Former Member of Optimist Club, Eagles Lodge, Elks Lodge, present Member of Moose Lodge in Concord, CA; [hon.] (Honor) Ft. Benning, GA, (Honor) Mich. Nat'l. Guard, (Medals) Mich. Nat'l. Guard, (Monetary) In House Newspaper Article, not published, (Plaque) Coaching in Little League; [hon.] Short story, not pub., article about our flag, not pub., novel, not finished. Article on affordable housing, published in newspaper. Condensed 50 yrs. Autobiography, since 1947, not pub.; [pers.] Have always enjoyed writing when time has permitted.; [a.] Bay Point, CA

HANNAWELL, ERICA JO
[pen.] E. J. Hannawell; [b.] May 17, 1979, Beloit, WI; [p.] George and Vickie Hannawell; [ed.] Evansville High School, Blackhawk, Tech.; [occ.] Housekeeping, Baker Manufacturing; [memb.] Rock Valley YFC (Youth for Christ); [pers.] One of the best rewards when writing poetry is when someone reads it and it reminds them of something in their life.; [a.] Evansville, WI

HANSEN, JESSICA DANIELLE
[b.] March 12, 1983, Sacramento, CA; [p.] Randy and Chris Hansen; [ed.] I am attending Foothill Farms Jr. High, will be in high school (9th) in the 1997-1998 school year; [occ.] Student; [hon.] MVP Volleyball trophy, Honor band (French horn); [oth. writ.] "Dear Grandpa", "Are You Scared", "About God", "Sisters"; [pers.] I never expected to have my poem published, this is my first time. I usually only write to make myself feel better when I'm down.; [a.] North Highland, CA

HANSON, ASHLI
[b.] March 8, 1983, Danville, IL; [p.] Peter E. and Jeri A. Hanson; [ed.] Covington Elementary and Covington Middle School; [occ.] Student; [memb.] 4-H Girl Scouts, Calvary Baptist Church, Danville, IL Sport Leagues; [hon.] Science Fair Awards, Resevered Champion - 4-H drawing, 2nd place in the Oratorical Contest; [pers.] I believe poetry is the eye of the writer's heart.; [a.] Covington, IN

HARPER, KATHLEEN ANN ROBINSON
[pen.] Robin Taney; [b.] December 20, 1946, Norfolk, VA; [p.] Margaret and Erskine Robinson; [ch.] Deborah Gail and William David Jr.; [ed.] Riverside School of Practical Nursing, Thomas Nelson Community College; [occ.] L.P.N.; [oth. writ.] Done as a hobby; [pers.] I love to read and my writing is done just for fun.; [a.] Hampton, VA

HARRIS, CARLA LYNETTE
[b.] July 28, 1987, Greensboro; [p.] Duree Ann Lowe; [m.] Carl Louis Lowe Jr., July 14, 1991; [ch.] Shanta Rena Harris, Tina Marie Harris; [ed.] High School; [occ.] She goes to school 4th Grade - Bethany; [a.] Reidsville, NC

HARRIS, TERRY
[ed.] B.S. Degree in Social Science from a Mississippi University; [occ.] Bio Medical Researcher and Educator; [memb.] ASQC, Association of Quality Control; [hon.] Inventor and Author of the Shadow Math Formula and Cell Theory of a National Science Student's Creed; [oth. writ.] Several poems published, a National Nurses Creed.; [pers.] Jesus is the reason why I sing.; [a.] Columbus, MS

HARRISON, CATHY A.
[pen.] Cathy A. Franco, Gould Harrison; [b.] May 23, 1963, Stockton, CA; [m.] Richard B. Harrison, June 21, 1986; [ch.] Todd, Jennica; [ed.] Lincoln High, San Joaquin Delta College, C.S.U. Stanislaus; [occ.] Reading Teacher, Sutherland School, Stockton, CA; [memb.] Muscular Dystrophy Association; [oth. writ.] Todd's Challenge, a children's book and Transcending Illusions, a biography. (To be published).; [pers.] My journey in this life is exploring and expressing emotions in connection with physical health challenges.; [a.] Stockton, CA

HART JR., ROY V.
[b.] December 11, 1929, Sioux City, IA; [p.] Mr. Roy V. Hart Sr., Pearl M. Hart; [m.] Bertha D. Hart, March 13, 1983; [ed.] Macksville High School, Macksville, Kansas; [occ.] Retired Jig and fixture Builder; [memb.] V.F.W.; [hon.] MHS, Kinsley, Kansas Music Festival, 1948, Vocal, Song Bells Of The Sea, rating: Highly Superior, Pratt, Kansas Festival Bells of the sea Rating, Superior; [oth. writ.] Several songs and poems unpublished.; [pers.] I become a Christian, 1982, since then, I strive to express my, Lord Jesus Christ in the songs I sing, in nursing homes, Church and Senior Citizen Recreation Center.; [a.] Tulsa, OK

HARTMAN, RUTH G.
[pen.] Sometimes go by Rudi; [b.] April 17, 1948, San Francisco, CA; [p.] William J. Nixon and Doris J. Nixon; [m.] Marcus M. Hartman, December 14, 1968; [ch.] William M. Hartman, Alicia M. Hartman; [ed.] Sunnyvale High, Ponce College of Beauty Shasta JC; [occ.] Dude Rancher, Coffee Creek Ranch, Coffee Creek, CA; [memb.] Dude Ranchers Assoc., Trinity Chamber of Commerce, US Chamber of Commerce, Shasta Cascade Wonderland Assoc., Calif., Hotel and Motel Assn. (bd. dirs. 1992 - present, mem. educational committee, mem. governmental affairs com.) International Platform Assn.; [hon.] Marquis Who's Who in America 1997, Who's Who in American Women 1993-1997, Who's Who in Finance and Industry 1997, The World Who's Who of Women 1996, Who's Who in the West 1996 Nominated for Woman of the Year 1996 (American Biographical Institute, Inc); [oth. writ.] Several poems unpublished and an unfinished novel about my family.; [pers.] I try to capture each moment in time as it reflects on me. A thank you to all my teachers who taught that a story must form a picture with words.; [a.] Coffee Creek, CA

HASKIN, KATHERINE KING
[b.] August 15, 1946, Troy, NY; [m.] Robert Haskin, November 25, 1967; [ch.] Matthew and Rachel; [oth. writ.] I have many poems but they have not been published; [pers.] I write what is in my heart and of life around me. I have loved poetry all my life.; [a.] Waterford, NY

HATHAWAY, JIM
[b.] May 31, 1919, Chicago, IL; [p.] George and Maude Hathaway; [m.] (Present) Hylda Hathaway, June 16, 1973; [ch.] Four by previous marriage; [ed.] High school graduate, some college, some correspondence school; [occ.] Semi-retired. Own small business; [oth. writ.] In the past have written articles in the field of radio and electronics, published in technical magazines. I am now just beginning to write general interest material.; [pers.] Often I am moved to write with expressions of empathy for fellow humans who have, in various ways, suffered innocently from life's inexplicable vicissitudes. I have very deep concerns over the problems of alcohol abuse and drugs.; [a.] Lexington, NE

HAWKINS, SANDRA
[pen.] Louise Jay; [b.] November 18, 1950, LaGrande, OR; [p.] Betty and William Pistorius; [ch.] William, Jennifer; [ed.] High School, some College, Institute of Children's Literature, still attending Writers Digest school; [occ.] Directory Assistance Operator; [memb.] International Society of Poets (Internet and Museum), Communication Workers of America, Telephone Pioneers of America; [hon.] Summit Club, National Library of Poetry, West Jordan Department of Public Safety, JRW Publishers; [oth. writ.] Best Poems 1996 (Mother) Best Poems 1997 (Listen) Where Dawn Lingers (A Place Closer to Home) Through the Looking Glass (Angel Tree) A Treasury of Verse (Angel Tree) Silence of Yesterday (Slow Love).

HAYES, MRS. BEN
[pen.] Granny Hayes; [b.] November 8, 1894, Indian Terr. Tahlequah, OK; [p.] George and Elizabeth Rogers; [m.] Benjamin F. Hayes, July 11, 1913; [ch.] Six, 3 girls, 3 boys; [ed.] Attended Northeastern State College; [occ.] Retired; [oth. writ.] None published; [pers.] Granny Hayes, Born 1894 Lillie Ann Rogers, in Indian Territory North Eastern Oklahoma, Admitted to Cherokee Tribal Roll at age six, Attended School Northeastern State College, (now NSU), in 1913 married Benjamin Franklin Hayes, a young business man of Tahlequah, distant cousin of Rutherford B. Hayes, the 19th President of the United States, Vows administered in the rain under the shelter of a large oak tree on Northeastern State College Campus, Honeymooned on Illinois river camping in a tent. Hobbies include gardening, needle work, cooking and caring for others.; [a.] Arlington, TX

HEATON, ARLENE
[b.] February 23, 1947, Henderson County, NC; [p.] Z. W. and Essie Garren Warren; [m.] John E. Heaton, December 28, 1985; [ch.] Jim Kesterson II, Kimberly K. Garren, Geoffrey Heaton, Stephanie H. King; [ed.] Graduated High School 1965; [occ.] Disabled in a wheelchair, a victim of multiple sclerosis; [hon.] 1964 was awarded "Distinguished Citizen Award," for representing N.C. at at New York World's Fair. (Gov. Terry Sanford 1968 Awarded "Ambassador" to Hendersonville for going to Mexico City Olympics; [pers.] I love people, and there are some characters out there. I love old houses with a personality, that don't look like others and modernized. You can learn a lot about a person, just by watching.; [a.] Hendersonville, NC

HEIKEN, JANIE R.
[b.] October 11, 1946, Starke, FL; [p.] Ancil and Geraldine Griffis; [ch.] Ray III, Kenneth, Virgil III, Brice, Joel, Lucas, Brandon and Angel; [ed.] Bradford Graduate 1964; [oth. writ.] "Death Walks", "Angels", "Time", "John", "Dreams", many others.; [pers.] My children are now and have always been my inspiration to life. They are my gift of sunlight from "God" above.; [a.] Dozier, AL

HENDERSON, JEREMY P.
[pen.] Dark Rose; [b.] March 14, 1980, Opp, AL; [p.] Earl and Deborah Henderson; [ed.] K-11, Opp High School, Opp, AL.; [occ.] Student; [memb.] AJAS, FFA, FHA, and FBLA; [oth. writ.] Lover's Hatred, Time, Earth Painting, Today, Scorned Woman, Games I Play, Lover-Friend, and many more; [pers.] "How red can a rose be which has never known the love of me." J.P. Henderson.; [a.] Opp, AL

HENDRICKS, JAN
[b.] Royal Oak, MI; [m.] J. Mark Hendricks, June 17, 1978; [ch.] Jason Mark, Jordan Lee; [ed.] B.A. Spring

Arbor College (Magna Cum Laude), M.S.W. University of Michigan; [occ.] Poet, Author, International Speaker; [memb.] Certified Social Worker, State of Michigan; [hon.] Alpha Kappa Sigma, Dean's List; [oth. writ.] Anthology of personal poetry, "Jan's Song....One Verse at a Time." Currently writing a book about affirmation.; [pers.] As a Christian, my poetry is an expression of my faith journey.; [a.] Plymouth, MI

HENNEMANN II, RICHARD
[b.] November 27, 1976, Fitchburg, MA; [p.] Richard and Brenda Hennemann; [ed.] Gardner High, MWCC; [occ.] Aspiring golfer, starving artist; [hon.] Dean's List; [oth. writ.] Various other poems, songs and stories. I am currently working on my first album with hopes of its completion in late 1997 or early 1998.; [pers.] I would like to thank all those who have helped and inspired me along the way, friends and family. To my Mom, Dad, Colleen and Jessica, I am grateful for all that each of you have given me and I love you all very much. My poetic and spiritual influences include Roger Waters, William Corgan and John C. Stone. 'A broken heart is still a heart, a broken man is still a man.'; [a.] Gardner, MA

HENRY, STEPHANIE
[pen.] S.L.H.; [b.] October 24, 1978, Caldwell, ID; [p.] Martha Shippy, Gene Henry; [ed.] Attending Skyview High School as a 12th Grader; [occ.] Clerk at Wonder Bread; [oth. writ.] I have written several other poems that have not been published.; [pers.] I hope to reach others through my poetry. I'm greatly inspired by my favorite poet, Robert Lee Frost.; [a.] Nampa, ID

HENSLEY, MARY HELEN
[b.] February 23, 1969, Roanoke, VA; [p.] Dick and Helen Hensley; [ed.] Carlisle School (HS) 1987, Coker College BA Communications/Graphic Design 1991, Sherman College of Straight Chiropractic; [occ.] Chiropractic Student; [memb.] Currently President of the Student Body at Sherman College of Straight Chiropractic; [a.] Inman, SC

HERBERT, CESARINA MARIA
[pen.] Cesarina Maria Rossetti; [b.] August 23, 1911, Casto, Italy; [p.] Julio Rosseti, Angela Frassa Rossetti; [m.] Divorced; [ch.] Mariae Tumelty, Rossett Herbert, and Claren Herbert; [ed.] Burlingame High Interstate College of Personology, Delores Premiere School of Cosmetology; [occ.] Owner and Manager of own Properties.; [memb.] Girl Scout Leader, Boy scout Den Mother, American Red Cross, Swimming Instructor, Earthquake Safety Program; [oth. writ.] Poems published in, At Water's Edge, Best Poems of 1996, Spirit of the Age, A Muse to Follow, Where Dawn Lingers, Across the Universe, Best Poems of the '90, Through the Hourglass, Sunshine and Daydreams, Amidst the Splendor, Frost at Midnight, Of Moonlight and Wishes, Essence of a Dream; [pers.] In my writing, my goal is to express and project the basic reality of all life, as life is presented to me.; [a.] Hillsborough, CA

HICKMAN, NIMMIE S.
[b.] April 28, 1964; [p.] Joseph Harris and Emma Johnson; [m.] Donald M. Hickman Sr., September 20, 1986; [ch.] Donald Jr., (DJ) and Derek; [ed.] J. Sargeant Reynolds L.S. Business Administration; [occ.] Energy Acquisition Specialist; [oth. writ.] Many poems have been written and kept in a private diary for future publications. Others have been forwarded to friends as token of friendship.; [pers.] My poetry reflects my inner spiritual awareness. Whatever I find difficult to convey in words is written and expressed in my writings.; [a.] Fredericksburg, VA

HICKS, AMANDA K.
[pen.] Amanda K. Hicks; [b.] June 18, 1970, Camden, TN; [p.] Carol and Jeff Jones and Jimmy Allen; [m.] Raymond Hicks, July 13, 1996; [ch.] Stephen and Jayson Rushing; [ed.] Graduate of West Tenn. Business College; [occ.] Secretary for The Carl Perkins Center; [pers.] To thine oneself be true.; [a.] Jackson, TN

HIDVEGI, ERICA I.
[pen.] Rickie; [b.] July 25, 1966, Queens, NY; [p.] Ernest Hidvegi and Tamara Cesek; [ed.] Shaker Hts High, Boheckers Business College and Presently Ursuline College, Major: Psychology Minor: Journalism, Undergrad Status: Mid-Soph; [occ.] Medical Asst/Office Mngr. Meridia Southe Pointe Hospital Cleveland Ohio; [hon.] Honorable Mention or Poetry submission 1989 to World of Poetry titled Reality of Love.; [oth. writ.] Several unpublished poems, research papers for college classes, three-five psychological case studies, thesis and one recognized poem sent to world of Poetry 1989, see honors.; [pers.] The expectations I have to shift the current negative attitudes of the world will be reflected in my writings. These shall inspire the spirit of souls to whom life has been a negative blur, as poets Robert frost and John Dunne have inspired me."; [a.] Chagrin Falls, OH

HIGGINBOTHAM, JENNY
[b.] December 19, 1997, Hollywood, FL; [p.] Wanda Higginbotham; [ed.] Currently attending Walter C. Young Middle School, 8th Grade; [pers.] This poem is written and dedicated to my father, Gary Higgenbotham, who died in April of 1990. He will always be loved and remembered.; [a.] Pembroke Pines, FL

HILL, ALICE LORRAINE
[pen.] "The Oklahoma Poet"; [b.] January 15, 1935, Moore, OK; [p.] Robert E. and Alma Alice Hill; [m.] James H. Shiver (divorced 1967), 1959; [ch.] Debra Hrboka, Pamela Spangler, Eric H. H. Shiver, Lorraine Smith; [ed.] Double BS, Four Masters Equivalences Assocs. Gen Ed., BS, Accounting/Business Lifetime Equivalences from state of CA in Bus., Accounting, Real Estate, and Computers: Honorary ordained minister of Gospel Ministries, 1981; [occ.] Educator, Researcher, Writer; [memb.] National Assocs. Female Exec., American Assoc of University Women, National Teachers Assoc., Ventura Co. Prof. Women's Networking, Ventura County Writers Assocs., American Biographical Assoc., Intrn'l Biographical Centre, English Fellows, Intn'l Poetry Society; [hon.] Life Time Achievement, and Gold Record Award. Listed in many Who's Who Books all over the world, Intn'l Women of Year, 1994/1995: Title, "Most Admired Woman of Decade, 1994, International Cultural Diploma of Honor, 1995, Dist Poet Merit of Award; [oth. writ.] Congressional Record Poem, 1975, "America, We Love You", Many poems published in many different places. Lyrics set to music by musicians. Various Articles and editorials, book, Morning's Twilight, 1971, and many legal documentaries, 1996: Congressional Record Poem of 1975, made an International song by world renown composer, Dr. Boyco Stovonov from Japan. He changed the America to "The Land of Lands"; [pers.] There is so much suffering we can change by just becoming more aware of the needs of others. I try to illicit more understanding and caring for others and to poetry ways we can help each other as well as people less fortunate than we are.; [a.] Oxnard, CA

HILL, NOLA
[b.] October 26, 1981, Princeton, WV; [p.] Bill and Judy Hill; [ed.] K-8th grade Oakvale, Elementary and Middle School, Oakvale, WV, now attending Pikeview High

School, Princeton, WV; [occ.] 9th grade student; [memb.] JROTC, Pikeview Panthers 9th grade Basketball Team, New Zion Baptist Church; [oth. writ.] Poems and stories for school and for my own enjoyment.; [pers.] I love people and I have a lot of friends. I write to express my feelings.; [a.] Princeton, WV

HILLHOUSE, EDWARD F.
[b.] January 31, 1952, Anderson, SC; [p.] Mr. and Mrs. E. F. Hillhouse; [m.] Judy K. Hillhouse, June 25, 1977; [ch.] Amanda, Rachel; [ed.] BS Electrical Engineering, Clemson University, Clemson, SC 1975; [occ.] Mercer Engineering Research Center, Director of Computer and Electronics Engineering; [pers.] My love of poetry was kindled in junior high school by an extraordinary writing teacher, Mrs. Joan Allen. Now, thirty years later, I shall begin to apply many lessons learned.; [a.] Warner Robins, GA

HILLOL, RAY
[pen.] Hillol Ray, Hee Ray (means Diamond); [b.] Near Calcutta, India; [p.] Nibaran Chandra and Angur Lata Ray; [m.] Mrs. Manjusree Ray, December 7, 1981; [ch.] Brian, Ryand; [ed.] M.S., Environmental Engg., North Dakota State Univ., B.S., Civil Engg., Univ. of Calcutta, India; [occ.] Environmental Engineer, U.S. EPA, Dallas, TX; [memb.] American Assn. for the Advancement of Science, American Chemical Society, American Industrial Hygiene Assn., American Meteorological Society, American Nuclear Society, American Society of Civil Engineers, American Water Works Assn. Instrument Society of America, Institution of Diagnostic Engineers, Great Britain (Fellow), Royal Society of Health, Great Britain (Fellow); [hon.] Poet Laureate, "Who's Who in APAC (Asian Pacific American Community)", "Earth Day" Poet-recognized by U.S. President Bill Clinton, Vice President Al Gore Jr., and current Indian Ambassador to USA, poems published in NLP anthologies: Edge of Twilight, Best Poems of 1995, A Delicate Balance, Of Sunshine and Daydreams, Best Poems of the '90s, Essence of a Dream, The Best Poems of 1997, received rave reviews in national newspapers and invitations for own poetry recital; [oth. writ.] "Deshantoereer Itikotha" (in Bengali) i.e. Amusing History of Immigrant, "Hashir Khorak" (Book of Limerick poems in Bengali), poems (in English) regularly published in EPA and APAC newsletters, technical articles in professional journals in USA, England and India, short stories, songs, limericks and several hundred Bengali poems published in renowned journals and magazines in Asia, Europe, Canada, and U.S.A., Award Winning Crossword Puzzle Writer (awarded by Allied Chemical Corporation, NJ and Council of Scientific and Industrial Research (C.S.I.R.), New Delhi, India.; [pers.] Lust for material things lasts forever, but joy of freedom will end never.; [a.] Garland, TX

HINDS, JOSEPH T.
[b.] March 19, 1960, Trinidad, WI; [p.] Elgart and Carol Hinds; [m.] Stephanie Boseman Hinds; [ch.] Laurence, Joshua, Joey and Terrance; [ed.] Attended: P.S. DuPont High, Wilm. Del., Graduated from Glasgow High, Newark, Del., attended Columbus College of Art and Design, Graduated in 1985, Illustration Design Major; [occ.] Senior Stylist, Lettering Designer at Paramount Cards, RI; [hon.] Award in art from Omega Psi Phi Fraternity, State of Delaware Award for Bicentennial Poster Contest, Project Business Junior Achievement Award, Winner of Prose, in short story contest "A Lonely Christmas," at American Greeting Cards '87; [oth. writ.] The short story, "A Lonely Christmas," published locally in Cleveland Ohio at American Greeting Cards, I also have other written work but, they are like everything I write,

through ??? of emotional situations.; [pers.] I feel very blessed and honored - thank you - "I get great joy in making others happy." I extend special thanks to my sister JoAnne, my best friend Wayne C., and both my brothers, love to you all.; [a.] Cranston, RI

HINSON, MICHAELA KIRKHAM
[b.] September 17, 1966, Houston, TX; [p.] Don Kirkham, Jean Smith Kirkham; [m.] Buddy J. Hinson, August 4, 1990; [ed.] Sam Houston State University, Willis High School; [occ.] English Teacher; [hon.] Dean's List, President's List, Who's Who Among American High School Students; [pers.] Commit your works to the Lord, and your thoughts will be established. (Proverbs 16:3); [a.] Huntsville, TX

HIRTER, EILEEN
[b.] June 4, 1919, Saint Paul, MN; [p.] Henry and Agnes King; [m.] Arthur Hirter, January 22, 1940; [ch.] Three; [ed.] High School; [occ.] House wife, homemaker; [a.] Portland, OR

HIXENBAUGH, ROBERT
[pen.] Robbie; [b.] January 21, 1985, Fairmont, WV; [p.] Robert Hixenbaugh, Debrah Hixenbaugh; [ed.] 5th grade; [hon.] Author of a great book; [oth. writ.] The Man That Disappeared; [a.] Burton, WV

HIXON, MAXINE SPYRES
[pen.] Maxine Spyres Hixon; [b.] January 29, 1926, Stilwell, OK; [p.] Dewey Spyres and Bonnie Spyres; [m.] Carl W. Hixon (Minister), October, 1945; [ch.] Tena, Pamela and Ronald; [ed.] Sallisaw High School, North Eastern State Teachers College; [occ.] Retired Real Estate Broker, Minister's Wife; [memb.] Missionary Baptist Church; [oth. writ.] Several poems published in National Church papers and in local newspapers.; [pers.] I try to set forth Christian Values, based in God's word, the Bible.; [a.] Conway, AR

HOEMANN, JAMES
[b.] September 13, 1973, Saint Louis, MO; [p.] Daniel Hoemann, Kathleen Hoemann; [ed.] Wentzville High, Ranken College; [occ.] Student of History at Lindenwood College, St. Charles, MO; [memb.] The Boy Scouts of America; [hon.] Dean's List, Alpha Lambda Delta; [pers.] My father has been my biggest influence. He paints passionate pictures of life that can be felt but seen only through his eyes.; [a.] O'Fallon, MO

HOFFMAN JR., DAVID L.
[b.] April 8, 1969; [ed.] B.S. The Citadel, 1991, J.D. University of Florida College of Law, 1997, University of Montpellier, France, Estudio International Sampere, Madrid, Spain; [occ.] Attorney in Charleston, S.C.; [memb.] Society of Distinguished Citadel Men, Plantegenet Society, Barons of the Magna Charta, Royal Order of the Crown, Sons of the Confederacy, Sons of the American Revolution, Phi Kappa Phi; [hon.] Citadel Scholar Scholarship, Hibernian Scholarship, Richard M. Schmidt Scholarship, Rufus Sprott Scholarship, First Honor Graduate, South Carolina Criminal Justice Academy, "Magna Cum Laude," The Citadel, Dean's List, UF College of Law; [oth. writ.] Numerous, unrepresented works, for example: A series of Children's books, a fictional novel, an anthology of poems; [pers.] Imagination is the name of the friend that will never leave my side. I visit my friend every day and now I share this friend with you.; [a.] Mount Pleasant, SC

HOFSTAD, PAUL J.
[pen.] Hoff; [b.] December 18, 1964, Florala, AL; [p.] Swede and Jean Hofstad; [m.] Heidi Marie Hofstad,

December 21, 1991; [ch.] Holly, Spencer; [ed.] 12th Grade, Graduate of Fort Walton Reach High, Ft. Walton Beach, FL; [occ.] U.S. Navy Ams' (Aw); [pers.] I write about events in my life, tragic or good. But it usually takes something in nature to put a picture in my mind of how I want to write my poetry; [a.] Virginia Beach, VA

HOGG, GARY NEIL
[b.] January 12, 1966, Milledgeville, GA; [p.] Tommy and Linda Hogg; [m.] Polly Hogg, January 27, 1988; [ch.] Crissy, J. T., and Brandon; [ed.] Griffin High School; [occ.] Kaolin Miner; [memb.] Freedom Church, Union local 50237 (United Paperworkers Int.); [oth. writ.] Several poems and short stories all non-published.; [pers.] All of God's creation's are poetry in motion.; [a.] Milledgeville, GA

HOLLEMAN IV, WILLIAM J.
[b.] January 9, 1955, Borger, TX; [p.] Paul and Mamie Holleman; [m.] Janice Elaine Holleman, November 26, 1994; [ch.] Ami Lora Felker Holleman; [occ.] Rancher/Cowboy; [hon.] Honorable Discharge U.S. Navy; [pers.] Poetry is the music of the heart.; [a.] Laytonville, CA

HOLLOWAY, BRETT A.
[b.] May 6, 1966, Okc., OK; [p.] William R., Barbara M. Holloway; [ed.] GED, US Coast Guard currently attending University of Biblical Studies and Seminary; [occ.] Free lance Writer Poet, and Minister; [memb.] Oklahoma Poetry Society Oklahoma Writers Federation; [oth. writ.] Poetry published in local publication.; [pers.] I am indebted to my Lord and Saviour Jesus Christ and the continuing discovery of the beauty and joy of life.; [a.] Oklahoma City, OK

HOLTRY, JESSICA
[pen.] Jessica Holtry; [b.] April 25, 1987, Carlisle, PA; [p.] Randy and Tamra Holtry; [ed.] Currently in the 4th grade at James Burd Elementary School, Shippensburg, PA; [oth. writ.] Has a poetry corner in a monthly newspaper of The First Wesleyan Church in Shippensburg, PA.; [pers.] I write poetry in the hopes that my readers will become closer to God.; [a.] Newburg, PA

HOOKS, CAMMIE LOISE PEEPLES
[pen.] Doonie Peeples; [b.] October 27, 1907, Winona, MS; [p.] Lindsay and Cora Farley Peeples; [m.] Deceased; [ch.] Virginia, Imogene and Diana; [ed.] Educated in a number of different schools; [occ.] Retired teacher; [memb.] First Baptist Church of Oxford; [oth. writ.] Poems published in magazines and papers. Story published in Montgomery County History Book. Working on my memoires; [pers.] My goal in life is to try to obtain the wisdom, understanding and strength I need to do whatever the Lord my God would have me do. I make mistakes because I am human. I try to learn from those mistakes and use them as stepping stones instead of stumbling blocks.; [a.] Oxford, FL

HOPSON, JOEL EDWARD
[b.] October 31, 1972, Kenmore, NY; [p.] N. Edward and Patricia S. Hopson; [ed.] Currently student at Miami Univ. (Ohio), Geology and Spanish Majors; [occ.] Student; [pers.] El que no se aventura no cruza la mar.; [a.] Oxford, OH

HORN JR., HENDRIK
[b.] August 10, 1971, Benoni, South Africa; [p.] Hendrick and Sue Horn; [ed.] Electronic Engineer, N.Dip-Durban, SA Computer Engineering Technology, AS, Fort Lauderdale, FL, USA; [occ.] Service and Installation Mgr, Amway Distributor; [memb.] Sports Car Club of America, Abundant Life Christian Centre,

Margate Florida; [hon.] 1995 ITGT SCCA Regional Racing Champion, Orator of the year 1985, Top Elec. Student 1991, Graduate Broward Community College with High Honors; [oth. writ.] "A Word From The Heart," poems that reach deep into the soul of man, daily devotional.; [pers.] Mankind was designed to have fellowship with their loving creator, without His touch on my life I'll just be an empty tingling brass vessel - God is all I want and need.; [a.] Coconut Creek, FL

HORNE, GENE MICHEL
[b.] October 21, 1956, Chaumont, FR; [p.] Michelle Andre Jeanne Horne and Jerry Gene Horne; [m.] Widowed, October 27, 1984; [ch.] Casey McClelland; [ed.] B.S. Agricultural Mechanization, University of Arkansas 1993; [occ.] Agricultural Credit Officer; [memb.] Society of Agricultural Engineers; [hon.] Only thru work.; [oth. writ.] Personal only.; [a.] Morrilton, AR

HORNE, ROBERT M.
[b.] January 31, 1960, Shamokin, PA; [p.] Marlin and Ruth Horne; [m.] Alison, August 31, 1996; [ed.] B.S. Degree from Lancaster Bible College, High School, Susquehanna Valley Christian Academy; [occ.] Pastor, First Baptist Church of Trevorton PA; [oth. writ.] This is my first writing.; [pers.] This is my first attempt at writing poetry. I feel very blessed and thank the Lord for this opportunity to glorify Him. I also hope people will never forget the POW issue and will one day bring them home.; [a.] Trevorton, PA

HOTALING, LINDA M.
[pen.] Linda Button; [b.] September 18, 1953, Corning, NY; [p.] Elsie A. Naylor, George W. Button (Deceased); [m.] Divorced; [ch.] Stacy, Alina, Skipper, Gina; [ed.] High School Diploma (GED), most of my ongoing education surrounds my job; [occ.] 22 yrs Govt. Inspection, Dresser Rand, Painted Post, NY Local 313; [memb.] Executive Board Shop Steward, District 3 Rep.; [oth. writ.] I have written solely for myself and friends, family. This would be my first publication. I write as a way to express my feelings about many things.; [pers.] This poem reflects the feelings I have towards my grandchildren and my daughter's impending divorce.; [a.] Painted Post, NY

HOTCHKISS, DIANNA D.
[b.] December 17, 1934, Kewanee, IL; [p.] Jonn K. Cantrell Sr. and Dorothea F. Matson; [m.] Charles Jr. Hotchkiss, March 9, 1982; [ch.] 11 boys, 4 girls (previous marriage); [ed.] 11th grade and G.E.D.; [occ.] MHP - ATP Mental Health Professional - Adolescent Treatment Professional Children's Home For Abused Children; [oth. writ.] First time.; [pers.] I've lost 3, two sons and now my oldest daughter due to domestic violence. 1 week after her death I sat at work and wrote this poem, my statement is in my poem, from my heart.; [a.] Sheffield, IL

HOUSHOLDER, AARON J.
[b.] August 8, 1973, Anderson, IN; [p.] Donald and Glenda Housholder; [occ.] Graduate student, Ball State University; [oth. writ.] "The Kiss," "Unworthy," "It Rained Today."; [a.] Anderson, IN

HUBBARD, IRIS L.
[b.] September 30, 1952, Indep, MO; [p.] Shirley and Joe Shepherd - Estel Parshall; [m.] Gary E. Hubbard, April 24, 1970; [ch.] Beau-Jesse, Coleman-Neal, Amy-Sue, Shane-Lightfoot, Hubbard and two girls that are special like my own, Susan-Rene, Amy-Marie [ed.] Blue Springs RIV; [occ.] Housewife and mother; [pers.] My love and faith of God has always been my staff to lean on in all things; [a.] Independence, MO

HUBBARD, PHYLLIS
[pen.] Phyl; [b.] December 30, 1954, Alabama; [p.] Leonte' Karyann Moore Hubbard; [ch.] LaGena Fox and Nakia Dean; [ed.] American Business Institute, Brooklyn, New York, Executive Secretary Degree; [occ.] Executive Secretary; [memb.] Oriental Grand Chapter Eastern Star, The Jim Couch Foundation, Inc.; [hon.] The One Hundred Year Civil Service Award; [pers.] This poem is dedicated to my Momma. Momma, we love you. From your daughters and sons.; [a.] Englewood, NJ

HUDSON, ROOSEVELT
[pen.] Ric Velle; [b.] Mississippi; [p.] Roosevelt and James Ella; [ch.] Christine, Kiechea, Patrice and Pierre; [ed.] Graduated from Westinghouse H.S. 1976. Associate Degree from Kennedy King College, May 13, 1996; [occ.] Operations Tech.; [hon.] Editor's Choice Award for Poems, "A Secret Kept, And When As A Child"; [oth. writ.] "A Secret Kept" published 1996 best poems of the 90s. "When As A Child", copyright 1995, in Windows Of The Soul, "The National Library, of Poetry.; [oth. writ.] In this world no one is perfect, we work to perfect, in deed and in thought.; [a.] Chicago, IL

HUEGEL, VALENTINE J.
[pen.] Val from Brooklyn; [b.] August 9, 1942, Bronx, NY; [p.] Valentine P. Huegel, Myndert Huegel; [m.] Theresa Huegel, June 28, 1971; [ch.] Joseph, Jennifer, Jeffrey, Jonathan; [ed.] B.A. St. Francis College, addt'l work St. Johns U., Grad. work NYU, College New Rochelle; [occ.] Assistant Director Police Athletic League (PAL) Summer Reading Program; [memb.] Knights of Columbus; [hon.] St. Francis College Scholarship, Member of First St. Francis College Red and Blue Club, Board of Directors Athletic Alumni, Windsor Terrace Neighborhood Honoree; [oth. writ.] Grants and Funding Proposals for Senior Citizens, Block Assn'n., Computer Grants for Schools, New School Charters, PAL Funding; [pers.] Formerly Development Industrial Chemist for 15 years, H.S. Chemistry Teacher for 12 1/2 years, Coach of Local Teams over years, track, football, baseball, regular caller Wfan Sports Radio.; [a.] Brooklyn, NY

HUFF, LAUREN
[b.] November 20, 1984, Milledgeville, GA; [p.] Rosy and Steve Huff; [ed.] 6th grade at Baldwin Middle School, our principal is Sammy Hall; [memb.] Beta Club, D.A.R.E. Member, Academic Games Member, Drill Team Member in Elem. School; [hon.] Many awards at school, honor roll, academic achievement award, highest ITBS score; [oth. writ.] Many other writings, it is my hobby!

HUGGETT, ALLYSON
[b.] December 24, 1968, California; [m.] Keith Huggett, April 22, 1994; [ed.] BA, English Literature, Cal. State Univ., Dominguez Hills; [occ.] Substitute Teacher; [a.] Vacaville, CA

HUGHES, JESSIE LYNNE
[b.] October 19, 1984, Belleville, KS; [p.] Bill and Jolene Hughes; [ed.] Home School; [memb.] Lawton City Ballet; [oth. writ.] Mothers, Raking The Leaves, My Dad's Truck, God's Taste, Books, Quilts; [a.] Duncan, OK

HUGHES, KELLIE D.
[pen.] K. Denyse; [b.] December 8, 1971, San Gabriel, CA; [p.] Morris W. Hughes and Joann T. Hughes; [ch.] Etana Sarai Hughes; [ed.] Pasadena High, Mt. San Antonio College, Pasadena City College; [occ.] Full-time mother and child care provider; [memb.] Confirmed Word Faith Center Sanctuary Choir and Soloist Bureau; [oth. writ.] Several unpublished poems and short stories.;

[pers.] Poetry is the heart's song. It stems from life's very essence of experience and guides us to look deeper and change. I adore the works of Langston Hughes and maya Angelou.; [a.] Duarte, CA

HUNSINGER, CARLOS L.
[b.] May 21, 1909, Hooker, OK; [p.] Leonard and Lena Hunsinger; [m.] Rosetta, June 16, 1973; [ch.] Nancy, Lynn, Wayne, Ronald, Gaylord; [ed.] BA, University of Colorado, Boulder, Co. LLB, University of Maryland, Baltimore, Md.; [occ.] Retired; [oth. writ.] The Art of Argument, My Life Among the Wallabies, Pioneer Vistas.; [a.] Eureka, CA

HUNTER, BRENDA K.
[b.] April 10, 1952, Bennetsville, SC; [p.] Teal and Gladys Brooks; [m.] John D. Hunter Sr., June 9, 1979; [ch.] Five boys; [ed.] High School - A. L. Brown Kann N.C., Rowan Cabarrus Comm. College - Salis., NC; [occ.] Hospice Nurse LPN; [memb.] National Hospice Nurses Organization, Member of Central Bap. Church Kannapolis, NC; [hon.] Poem displayed at National Hospice Art Exhibit in Arizona '96.; [oth. writ.] Several poems written about or patients in Hospice service.; [pers.] I strive to find the good in all things, that God may receive honor and glory.; [a.] Salisbury, NC

HUNTER, JUANITA
[b.] December 26, 1936, Comfort, TX; [p.] Juan and Theresa Frausto; [m.] Orville M. Hunter, 1966; [ch.] One; [ed.] 5th; [occ.] Laundry worker retire now; [pers.] I had never wrote anything before; [a.] Kerrville, TX

HUNTER, ROSETTA
[b.] December 5, 1978, RAF Lakenheath, Branden, Suffolk; [p.] Theodis Hunter, Leila Hunter; [ed.] Central High School; [memb.] UAMS, FBLA, Christian Fellowship, Youth Council, Gospel Lighthouse Pentecostal Church; [hon.] Mix and Triple Choir, Academic Award, Southwest Jr. High Raceres Student of the Mouth, Academic Achievement Award in Recognition of Outstanding Scholarship Choir III; [pers.] I'm a person who is privilege to do anything that is new. And this is one of them. I try to speak the truth in my writing and letting feel what I've felt.; [a.] Little Rock, AR

HURTE, CHERYL
[b.] January 15, 1944, Hayward, CA; [p.] LaVerne and Joseph Cissell; [m.] Stanley Hurte, April 24, 1965; [ch.] Tamara Alexander, Richard, Byron, Joseph and Heather Hurte; [ed.] Washington Union High; [occ.] Secretary; [memb.] Foothill Blvd. Church of Christ; [oth. writ.] Several poems to be published in "Poetic Voices of America," by Sparrowgrass Poetry, June 1997, several poems to be published in, "Treasured Poems of America," by Sparrowgrass Poetry, Fall of 1997.; [pers.] I hope my writings will inspire others to recognize that, although our world is rapidly changing, they can feel secure in the fact that some things never change. We should always strive to become wiser, so that we may recognize, and hold onto, that which is forever valuable.; [a.] Oroville, CA

HUSKISSON, JANET
[b.] May 22, 1956, Hammond, IN; [p.] Emil and Lila Thompson; [m.] George Huskisson, January 1, 1977; [ch.] Jesse and Danny; [ed.] High School - T.F. North, Graduated '75, 1 yr. college - Hammond Business College; [occ.] Supervisor at Calumet College - Tami-Lou's Cleaning Services; [oth. writ.] Other original poems not submitted.; [pers.] I like to write poems which express my feelings, such as the loss of my father in 1993.; [a.] Lake Station, IN

HUTTON, KATHLEEN R.
[b.] March 27, 1988, Torrance, CA; [p.] William P. Hutton and Susan A. Fitch-Hutton; [ed.] St. Catherine Laboure School; [occ.] Student; [memb.] Girl Scouts of America, North Torrance Little League - Rangers (Minor Division); [hon.] Student of the Month, September, 1996, St. Catherine Laboure School, Torrance, CA; [pers.] Education is the most important thing in my life. It is an opportunity everyone should have.; [a.] Torrance, CA

HYATT, MARC
[b.] November 13, 1970, Easley, SC; [p.] Mark and Brenda Hyatt; [ed.] BS - Double Majored in Marketing and Management, presently pursuing a psychology masters at Appalachian State University; [occ.] Community College Instructor, Musician, Ocean Lifeguard, Student; [memb.] American Marketing Association, United States Lifesaving Association; [oth. writ.] Compact disc recording with my band, Yellow Phive Conspiracy (Y5C), titled Bad Karma Diet. I did the songwriting, vocals and guitar of the CD.; [pers.] Life is one big learning experience. Everything is connected and happens for a reason. I try to capture these moments, good and bad in my work.; [a.] Marion, NC

IHA, RHIANNON
[b.] October 29, 1977, Lakewood, WA; [p.] Paul and Elaine Iha; [ed.] Gig Harbor High School, The University of Puget Sound; [occ.] Student; [hon.] Dean's List, National Merit Finalist; [a.] Gig Harbor, WA

IHDE, LAUREL K.
[b.] December 27, 1972, Aurora, IL; [p.] Lyle and Linda Ihde; [ed.] West Aurora High School, 1991, currently enrolled at William Tyndale College, BA in History Dec. 1998; [occ.] Student; [memb.] Member of Praise Band at Rockpointe Community Church in Sterling Heights MI, member of Student Executive Board at William Tyndale College; [hon.] Won essay portion of the "Miss St. Clair Shores Pageant," in 1994, and won 1st runner-up for 1993 and 1994 (same pageant).; [oth. writ.] Just personal writings and poetry, currently working on a Devotional Book published in College Newspaper.; [pers.] My inspiration for my life and writing is my Lord and savior Jesus Christ. Through Him all things are possible.; [a.] Saint Clair Shores, MI

ILEGIEUNO, FATIYA
[b.] February 18, 1983, Mercer Medical Center; [p.] Robert and Cynthia Ilegieuno; [hon.] Dean's list for outstanding achievement in project S.M.I.L.E. at Mercer County Community College, won Black History Month essay contest, and received academic honors during my school years up to the present time.; [oth. writ.] One of my poems called, "Success," was published in the Nubian News Newspaper, in Trenton, New Jersey.; [pers.] My writing is reflected on how my inner spirit feels but also it enhances my potential which is to be a lawyer in the future. I have been greatly influenced by my parents.; [a.] Trenton, NJ

IMPERATO, ARNOLD
[b.] September 2, 1954, Bronx, NY; [p.] Neil and May Imperato; [ed.] St. Harvabas Elementary, Bronx NY, 1960-68, Iowa Prep., New Rochelle NY, 1968-72, Iowa College 1972-73, Institute of Medical Technology, Mt. Vernon 1993, Westchester Community College 1988; [occ.] Musician, Composer, Poet; [hon.] 1974 Winner of WRVR for Best New Jazz-Rock Group "Orion". Performance at Lincoln Center NYC. 1974-81 Studied with "Jazz Great" Art Davis A Basis who has recorded and performed with Dizzy Gillespie John Coltrane Max Roach NYS Certified E.K.G. Technician; [oth. writ.] So

Near So Far/Rare Trees 1993, Portrait of Lady Day 1991, One More Chance 1996, No Long Goodbyes 1996, I Journey Alone 1996; [pers.] Through the trials of life and a search for spiritual happiness I have been fortunate to be able to communicate my feelings into words I have been greatly influenced by the music of Miles Davis and John Colttane as well as the poetry and writing of Edgar Allen Poe.; [a.] Yonkers, NY

ININ, MENIELI MELI
[b.] January 2, 1953, Georgetown, SC; [p.] John H. Simmons and Evelyn E. Simmons; [ch.] Lillie and Men Men; [ed.] Minister of Science of Life and Death Hell and Heaven; [occ.] Minister of Heaven and Hell; [memb.] Gate keepings, I'll keep the gate of hell and heaven.; [hon.] Musical contracts for writers of lyrics and compositions in majestic records.; [oth. writ.] I write to my ministers, and minister and take notes and verses from the Bible.; [pers.] I keep in contact, with my God on my creator by, communication.; [a.] New York, NY

INTHAPANGNA, DAN
[b.] April 21, 1978, Laos; [p.] Ming B. Inthapangna; [ed.] Bullitt Central High School; [pers.] "I think it's better to find someone to live and love, than to find no one to live and never love. Remember, time the present is here now, we all hold the future in our hands. But how?" I love to thank my older sister Vongmany for giving her time to strive, and influence me in my life. Thank you very much to remind me to stop and just think.; [a.] Shepherdsville, KY

IRONS, CHARLOTTE ALEXIS
[b.] October 12, 1983, Lubbock, TX; [p.] Donna and Tom Irons; [ch.] Currently 7th Grade; [hon.] Academic Excellence 1996 TAAS - English and score 100; [oth. writ.] The Mixed Up Player, To Be Beautiful, Hard To Believe, Friends, Together As Friends, Love, Christmas, Hate, Selena, Dumped, Time, Ugly... Dirty, Crazy Cristina, Sounds, Do You Remember?, Life And Death, Getting Away, Searching, Flowers, Love That's Black And Blue; [pers.] When I was 11 years old my mother passed away, so I moved to live with my Dad. My poem "Not The Same" is dedicated to that wonderful woman.; [a.] Corinth, TX

ISENHOUR, CRYSTAL RUTH
[pen.] Chris Everheart; [b.] January 8, 1982, Hickory, NC; [p.] John Isenhour, Angela Isenhour; [ed.] Currently attending Newton-Conover High School as a freshman; [occ.] Teen-ager; [pers.] My poetry reflects my most innermost thoughts and feelings.; [a.] Conover, NC

ISON, SUETTA L.
[b.] August 10, 1972, Ashland, KY; [p.] Larry W. and Nancy S. Ison; [ed.] Majoring in English Education at The University of Kentucky; [occ.] Full-time student; [memb.] American Association of University Women, Future Teachers of America, Women in Communication; [hon.] Dean's List, English Merit Award, National Merit Scholar, Phi Beta Kappa; [oth. writ.] Poems including: "This is Who I Am" and "Extinguished Luminosity"; [pers.] A constant never won a race watching from the sidelines or wishing for the victory. The only way one can lose is to never try!; [a.] Ashland, KY

JACINTO, DIANA
[b.] September 22, 1958, Inglewood, CA; [p.] James Render, June Render; [m.] Leonard Jacinto, August 3, 1984; [ch.] Thomas, Daniel, Ashley; [ed.] Wilcox High School; [occ.] Homemaker; [oth. writ.] Several other unpublished poems.; [pers.] This poem was written for my mom on Mother's Day 1995.; [a.] Santa Clara, CA

JACKSON, BARBARA BENICE MILES
[pen.] B. Miles Jackson; [b.] June 24, 1948, Fort Worth; [p.] C. B. Miles and Maybelle Dugan Miles; [m.] Divorced; [ch.] One child, Tracy Jackson and grandchild, Amber Jackson; [ed.] I.M. Terrell Class of '66; [occ.] Work at home/Poet; [memb.] Carter Metropolitan, CME Church; [hon.] State Employee of the Year 1990, Usher of the Year for Usher's of Carter Metropolitan Church; [oth. writ.] Poetry - Atmospheric Conditions, Go Your Way, Acient of Day, Silent Voices, A Sign, Void of Times, Be Sure, Answer, Keep Times, Changing Times, Christmas Stills, Loving Intention, What Did You See, Look Up And I Know Turn; [pers.] I'm great times of sorrow and sadness - look up and know.; [a.] Arlington, TX

JACKSON, DIANA
[b.] August 30, 1954, Cincinnati; [p.] Jack and Shirley Stahl; [m.] Ray Jackson, May 24, 1976; [ed.] MI Notre Dame High School; [occ.] Receptionist for a Printing Company; [oth. writ.] None published many many written I started writing when I was 10 years old finally got the courage to enter.; [pers.] My husband is a musician. We often write together and share ideas. I believe in the beauty and power of nature. I write every day.; [a.] Cincinnati, OH

JACKSON, DOROTHY
[b.] November 9, 1927, Arlington, KY; [p.] Will and Beulah West Russell; [m.] Darrel Jackson, January 23, 1988; [ch.] Kathy Pulley Lee; [ed.] Central High, Clinton, KY; [occ.] Home maker; [memb.] Order of the Eastern Star, Mt. Olive United Methodist Church; [pers.] Fill your heart with hope and fill your life with laughter.; [a.] Mayfield, KY

JACKSON JR., MRS. POLK
[pen.] Rose Marie Jackson; [b.] July 10, 1957, Atlantic, TX; [p.] Virgil, Johnson Moesia; [m.] Polk Jackson Jr., January 18, 1977; [ch.] Junior Polk, Ruby Marie, and Larue Polk Jackson; [occ.] Unemployed, Widow; [memb.] San Francisco School Volunteers; [oth. writ.] My lonely heart resurrected our father one love mourn I'm not afraid.; [a.] San Francisco, CA

JACOBS, JOHN I.
[b.] March 6, 1923, Canton, OH; [p.] Thomas Jacobs, Edna Jacobs; [m.] Jean H. Jacobs, October 16, 1948; [ch.] John Jr., Thomas; [ed.] Clarke College, Mississippi College, Golden Gate Seminary, Luther Rice Seminary; [occ.] Retired; [memb.] Friends of the Library; [hon.] "Scroll of Honor," for 16 years service with F.M.B. of S.B.C.; [oth. writ.] Song published: "What He Did One Day," other songs unpublished (Lyrics only), several poems. One awaiting publication: "The Bank Window Lady."; [a.] Booneville, MS

JANISSE, TASHA N.
[b.] September 18, 1982, Portland, OR; [p.] Robert Janisse, Pamela Kingsley; [ed.] Valley Catholic Middle School, OR, Saint Mary's College High School, CA; [occ.] Student; [memb.] United Black Student Unions of California; [pers.] My primary motivation, my brother's death, is also a release for me. Hopefully, I can bring others to see they aren't alone on the journey of grief. Parents and close friends: Thanks for support, my dream is reality. R.I.P. Bobby Janisse Jr.; [a.] Hayward, CA

JARDY JR., GORDON V.
[b.] May 15, 1954, Cleveland, OH; [ed.] Gordon and Dolores Jardy; [ed.] Holy Name High School, Cleveland State University, Regent College, Fuller Theological Seminary; [occ.] Lutheran Campus Minister of Greater Cleveland; [memb.] Rock and Roll Hall of Fame

and Museum, Cleveland Indians Season Ticket Holder; [oth. writ.] Article on prayer in "World Christian" Magazine; [pers.] To be someone who actively seeks first the kingdom of God.; [a.] Cleveland, OH

JAROSLAWSKI, ANDREW
[pen.] Yendreck Yarowavski; [b.] March 20, 1965, Konin, Poland; [p.] Alina Jaroslawski, Grzegorz Jaroslawski; [m.] Divorced; [ch.] Matthew Andrew Maria, Caroline Andrea Dominica, Paul-Bernard Grzegorz; [ed.] The Catholic University in Lublin, Poland, master's degree in sociology; [occ.] Factory worker at Motorola; [memb.] The Friends of the Catholic University on Lublin; [oth. writ.] This is my first poem to be published.; [pers.] Surrounded by an aura of futility, I'm striving for creative independence. I feel inspired by life experiences of C. K. Norwid and J. Lechon. Writing poetry is both intellectual and linguistic exercise.; [a.] Des Plaines, IL

JAY, MARANDA LYNNE
[pen.] Mandy J.; [b.] August 26, 1985, Boise, ID; [ed.] Pioneer Elementary Meridian Middle School; [occ.] Student; [hon.] 1996 President's Academic Achievement Award; [pers.] I enjoy writing as a release of my inner feelings.; [a.] Meridian, ID

JAYASURIYA, LUKE
[b.] February 20, 1929, Colombo, Sri Lanka; [p.] M. A. F. Jayasuriya; [m.] M. Elizabeth Perera; [ch.] M. B. Fernando, M. Beatrice Fernando, M. Trixie Fernando, M. Viola Perera, Rev. Clyde Jayasuriya, M. C. F. Jayasuriya, M. Ivan F. Jayasuriya; [ed.] B.A. in Philosophy, M.A. in Education, Ph.D. in Philosophy of Religion at the Papal Athenaeum, Kandy, Sri Lanka, The Fordham University, Bronx, NY; [occ.] Priest retired from active service; [hon.] Several awards presented by The National Library of Poetry; [oth. writ.] Several poems in The National Library of Poetry Publications. Book published in Vernacular: I. Pem Mihira, II. Life of St. Maria Goretti, III. Life of St. Ignatius of Loyola; [pers.] I am interested in mystical theology - East and West.; [a.] Haverhill, MA

JEFFERSON, TEKAKWITHA
[pen.] Puggie, T.J.; [b.] April 30, 1962, New Orleans, LA; [p.] Rosemary Landry, Whitney Barconey; [m.] Keith Jefferson, February 26, 1983; [ch.] Winona Tekakwitha Jefferson, Keith Jerome Jefferson, Jr.; [ed.] DuVal Senior High School graduated of 1980", Lanham, MD; [oth. writ.] Several poems published with a local news weekly.; [pers.] Congratulations to my mother, Catherine Copeland and Darrell Landry for being my inspiration believing that I was God gifted with a talent, struggling with me to continue on striving with my writing, never giving up hope that one day it shall be known. They once said, "Believe in yourself as I believe in you."; [a.] New Orleans, LA

JENSEN, ERIC
[pen.] Eric Jensen; [b.] September 22, 1962, San Francisco, CA; [p.] Eugene and Phyllis Jensen; [ed.] Chenango Valley High School; [memb.] First United Methodist Church; [oth. writ.] I have written several other unpublished poems. Had a poem published in the church Bulletin.; [pers.] I try to show my faith and trust in God. Hoping others will be touched and inspired by the words.; [a.] Sayre, PA

JENSEN, JOYCE M.
[b.] July 26, 1940, Iron River, WI; [p.] Harold and Frances Ferguson; [m.] Elwood L. Jensen, September 21, 1957; [ch.] 6, grandchildren, 12; [ed.] High School, Wild Rose WI; [occ.] Welfare worker, state of Wiscon-

sin, Waushara County; [memb.] Wisconsin Social Services Association; [oth. writ.] Numerous unpublished articles and poems pending; [pers.] I write from my heart about personal experiences; [a.] Pine River, WI

JENSEN, SANDRA
[b.] November 11, 1963, Medford, MA; [p.] Charles W. Crilley, Jane R. Crilley (Mitchell); [m.] Steven Paul Jensen, February 14, 1987; [ch.] Ashley Jordan, Amanda Corinne, Mitchell Paul, Dylan Paul; [ed.] Our Lady of Nazareth Academy, Wakefield, MA; [occ.] Homemaker; [hon.] National Library of Poetry "Editor's Choice Award"; [oth. writ.] Several poems based on the many aspects of childhood.; [pers.] My inspiration in writing is greatly influenced by the wonder and innocence of childhood, my own as well as my children's. Blessed are those who view the world through the eyes of a child.; [a.] Reading, MA

JESSOP, RHODA
[b.] July 11, 1964, Utah; [ch.] Sharon, Maureen, Rachel, Robert; [ed.] College, currently studying in Speech and Hearing Sciences; [occ.] Student; [memb.] NSSLHA Theatrical Society Choir; [hon.] Dean's List; [oth. writ.] Poetry and prose for family and friends and special causes; [pers.] I use words to frame emotion into something tangible.; [a.] Draper, UT

JOHANNING, LINDA
[b.] October 5, 1954, Canton, OH; [p.] George and Louise Barrett; [m.] Mark Johanning, October 2, 1976; [ch.] Benjamin; [ed.] Lincoln High School; [occ.] Word Processor, Southeastern Academy; [hon.] National Honor Society; [oth. writ.] Article for Heartland Magazine, two essays for local newspaper.; [a.] Kissimmee, FL

JOHNSON, AMBER L.
[pen.] A. L. Johnson; [b.] December 14, 1982, Conway, AR; [p.] Margaret L. Johnson; [ed.] Current Student at Conway Jr. High School, 8th grade; [occ.] Student; [memb.] Mt. Calvary Free Will Baptist Church, Band Member; [hon.] School Honor Roll; [oth. writ.] "Play On," published in the book Anthology of Poetry by Young Americans.; [pers.] All of us have our own "Darkened Room," and there is always hope to be found inside it.; [a.] Conway, AR

JOHNSON, ANTHONY GABRIEL
[b.] December 12, 1930, Colorado Springs, CO; [p.] Gabriel and Alvina Johnson; [m.] L. Aleta Johnson, March 7, 1954; [ed.] B.A. Colorado College, Psychology, M.A. Colorado College, Educational Psychology; [occ.] Retired Educator; [memb.] Many organizations relating to education and science across professional career; [hon.] Distinguished Teacher, White House Commission on Presidential Scholars, 1994, Washington, DC, Citation by Mayor and City Council of City of Colorado Springs, Colorado, as a Distinguished Scholar, 1994; [oth. writ.] Legacy of a Santa Fe Trail Teamster (book). Poems: Spanish Peaks, Sastrugi, Russian Olives, Grimm Gantnor, Carbide, Quicksilver, Emovere, Stetson, Wind Lace, Bureaucrats, The Glass Eye, Burrs, Seeing, Reality, Release, etc. Eagle Tree, Bones, Decimal Point, The Drop, Popcorn, Morning Ice, The Raider, Desert Rock IV, The Past.; [pers.] The greatest virtue and strength of the human species is that we are all unique - a portion of the universe that can reflect upon its own condition.; [a.] Colorado Springs, CO

JOHNSON, BERNADETTE L.
[b.] June 13, 1942, North Adams, MA; [p.] Mary Louise and Louis Boudreau; [m.] James F. Johnson, September 18, 1971; [ch.] Kevin James, Derron Paul; [ed.] BA Anna

Maria College, Paxton, MA, MBA, Western New England College, Springfield, MA; [occ.] Student Services Representative, Baystate Medical Center School of Nursing in Springfield, MA; [memb.] New Valley Singers, Christ Church Cathedral (Episcopal) Choir, Steering Committee, Star Island Conference on the Arts, Sierra Club; [hon.] Outstanding Graduate Student—MBA Western New England College; [oth. writ.] Chapbook, "Balloons Don't Fly in this Weather," (Plowman Ministries, Ontario, Canada), Several poems published in various journals, academic and commercial (US), poem accepted for publication in United Kingdom.; [pers.] I enjoy traditional poetry as well as free verse and modern that is intriguing and artistic but not obscure.; [a.] Southwick, MA

JOHNSON, BREANNA V.
[b.] May 31, 1986, Oregon, Salem; [p.] Wayland and Virginia Johnson; [occ.] 5th grader; [memb.] Honors Choir, Salem School Performing Arts, School Band School Choir, Clarinet, Piano; [hon.] Elementary School President; [pers.] I enjoy writing and someday I wish to be an actress, a writer or a teacher.; [a.] Salem, OR

JOHNSON, GREGORY E.
[pen.] Eric John; [b.] July 30, 1957, Falconer, NY; [p.] Bennie and Veronica Johnson; [m.] Kim Johnson (Separated, February 22, 1996), September 9, 1978; [ch.] Sarah born May 29, 1979, Krista born July 19, 1985; [ed.] Graduated from Washingtonville H.S. Washingtonville, NY; [occ.] Motor Equipment Operator for town of Goshen, NY Hwy. Dept.; [hon.] Editors choice award from The National Library of Poetry Lyrical Heritage edition Re: "In The Blink of an Eye," 1996; [oth. writ.] Many various types of relationship and inspirational poems.; [pers.] When hearts have been shattered, writing mends the soul, and if love has an ending so must eternity.; [a.] Chester, NY

JOHNSON, JAMES W.
[b.] September 22, 1949, Chillicothe, MO; [p.] Leo and Norma Johnson; [ed.] One year College, Low Country Technical College, Beaufort, SC; [occ.] 100% Disabled Vet; [memb.] VFW, DAV; [oth. writ.] Soldiers Memory, Old Glory, The Silent Men, Natures Grace, Independence Day.; [a.] Frenchburg, KY

JOHNSON, JANA
[b.] May 28, 1979, Osceola; [p.] Gary and Jan Johnson; [ed.] Student at Mississippi County Christian Academy; [occ.] 12th grade Student; [memb.] I am a member of the French Club 2 years at M.C.C.A. and the Varsity Basketball team. I have been a member of math and science club for the past 3 years at M.C.C.A.; [hon.] In basketball: All conference and all tournament in 11th grade. All conference in 12th grade. Rebound award in 11th grade. "All Wendy's Classic," Also in 11th grade.; [oth. writ.] "Angel Descending"; [pers.] In my poetry, I tend to write about personal experiences or my friends' experiences. Sometimes I sit down and just begin writing a poem, then revise it later.; [a.] Osceola, AR

JOHNSON, LINDA
[b.] September 29, 1952, Houston, TX; [p.] Mrs. Cora B. Johnson; [ed.] Texas Southern University Texas School of Business Medical Assistant; [occ.] Kinda and learning Centre Houston, TX; [hon.] Honorable Mention in another Poetry Contest in 1990. I also received a golden poet award in 1991 for the Butterfly.; [pers.] I try to express my inner feelings through my poetry. And I hope that in some way, I can touch people with my writing.; [a.] Houston, TX

JOHNSON, LORNA MARIE
[b.] January 27, 1958, San Francisco, CA; [p.] Connie Johnson; [ed.] Oceana High; [occ.] Pacifica, CA, Partner and Manager to Magician, Magic Jeanne, and Credit Manager for Briggs and Riley in Half Moon Bay, CA; [memb.] Magicals International; [oth. writ.] Several brochures for small companies. Script for magic shows. Corporate Policies and Procedures.; [pers.] One day at a time, through the art of meditation one's dreams can come true.; [a.] Pacifica, CA

JOHNSON, MICHELE
[b.] May 29, 1953, Missouri; [p.] Bernice Grant and Dorsey Grant; [ch.] Arniece, Shanika, Brendan and Diamond; [occ.] Home maker; [hon.] My honors and awards are being a good mother and making them happy and proud of me.; [oth. writ.] It's in the Air Because; [pers.] I love writing poems from my heart and soul because they make me happy when I write and make me feel good inside.; [a.] Saint Louise, MO

JOHNSON, WILLIAM
[b.] January 7, 1950, Kansas City; [p.] Raymond and Margaret Johnson; [ed.] Rockhurst College; [pers.] I intend to stress the power of the mind, good and bad, in the physical world.; [a.] Kansas City, MO

JOHNSON-WHITED, SHELLY
[b.] February 5, 1963, Marion, IN; [p.] Bernie and Sally Johnson; [m.] Scott Whited, August 5, 1989; [ch.] Taylor, Marie, Christopher, Justin, Jason; [ed.] Marion High School - 1981, Ball State University (BS) - 1986, Ball State University (MA) -1987; [occ.] Special Ed. teacher (EH, LD) Hamilton Southeastern Middle School Fishers, IN 46038; [memb.] National Honor Society- International Behaviorology Assoc. (TIBA), CEC; [hon.] Stephen Bufton Memorial Award, Dean's List (BSU); [oth. writ.] Several articles for local newspapers, developed the Add Connection, a newsletter for parents of Add children.; [pers.] My written work often reflects a positive attitude and outlook on various subjects. This piece is dedicated to one of the great teachers in my childhood, Mrs. Betty Fletcher.; [a.] Noblesville, IN

JOHNSTON, RUTH VICTORIA
[b.] October 30, 1946, Midland, MI; [p.] A. D. and Coral Ordway; [m.] Jerome W. Johnston, August 28, 1967; [ch.] Michael Waine (Deceased), Matthew Jereome and Marti Rae; [ed.] Midland High School, Delta Community College; [memb.] St Agnes Catholic Church - Sanford, MI; [hon.] Dean's List, graduated with honors, Libran Arts Degree; [pers.] I was inspired to write this poem in memory of my mother who passed away in December, 1992 the angels and mansion were described to us during her dying process.; [a.] Midland, MI

JONES, ANTHONY W.
[b.] January 30, 1986, Ridgewood, NJ; [p.] William and Marilyn Jones; [ed.] Currently 5th Grade, Franklin School Saddle Brook, New Jersey; [hon.] Numerous awards in baseball, football and wrestling; [pers.] Being published at my age helps me to want to further my goals in writing.; [a.] Saddle Brook, NJ

JONES, E. BARBARA
[b.] January 23, Wilkes-Barre, PA; [p.] Edith and Alex Gutkoski; [m.] Paul E. Jones Jr., January 23; [ed.] Laceyville High, PA, Brooklyn College, NY, Barbizon School of Modeling NY; [occ.] Home Maker; [hon.] Art Exhibits, Miss Life of Georgia, Editors Choice Awards from N.L.P.; [oth. writ.] Poems published by N.L.P. in two anthologies, "The Voice Within," and "The Best Poems of the 90's."; [pers.] When others enjoy my artistry, it makes me very happy.; [a.] Fairburn, GA

JONES, ESTES I.
[pen.] Lucky Jones; [b.] May 28, 1923, Gromore, WA; [p.] Isaac and Jewell Jones; [m.] Jorina Elizabeth (Pentler) Jones, October 16, 1947; [ch.] One, Michael Douglas Jones; [ed.] High School 4 years, College 2 years, Biography: Dollar a Day Cowboy, Meat Cutter, Heavy equipment operator, 30 years US Navy, Retired, 1968, Business operator, Policeman, Deputy Sheriff, Firefighting Contractor; [occ.] Retired United States Navy (Catholic); [memb.] Masonic Lodge, Twisp, Wash. Shrine, El Katif Temple, Spokane, Wa. VWF American Legion, Scottish Rite, Grand Lodge of Washington Masons, Past Master Masonic Lodge, Past Commander VFW Post, Past Commander American Legion, Member El Katif Shrine Temple, Spokane, Wa.; [hon.] Numerous awards and citations from Naval Service; [oth. writ.] Several un-published poems.; [pers.] "Never became a has-been until after you have reached retirement age."; [a.] Winthrop, WA

JONES, GENE M.
[b.] August 28, 1951, Grenada, W.I.; [p.] Louise Jones and George Garvey; [m.] Shirley C. Jones, March 19, 1974; [ch.] Three, Paulina, Paul, Pamela; [ed.] St. Andrews Anglican Senior School and St. Andrews Anglican Secondary School, Grenada, W.I., Medger Evers College, Bkly., NY; [occ.] Management Staff of Service Master; [memb.] West Bank United Seventh Day Adventist Church; [hon.] Dean's List; [a.] Marrero, LA

JONES, VICTORIA
[b.] August 7, 1975, Salisbury, MD; [p.] Linda and Ralph Jones; [ed.] West Virginia Wesleyan College, 1 year, then transferred to Bowie State University, currently a senior, graduation date Dec. 1997; [memb.] Marketing Association, Financial Chair Person, Investment Club, Member St. Charles Church; [hon.] Dean's List 1993, 1995, 1996, Certificate of Achievement 1995-96; [pers.] The woman who I wrote about in my poem truly influenced my life, and I am just glad that she could see me blossom into the beautiful flower that I've become.; [a.] Chance, MD

JORDAN, J. TODD
[m.] Ruth Thompson, April 16, 1994; [ed.] University of Alabama; [occ.] Free-lance writer; [memb.] World Wildlife Federation, Environmental Defense Fund; [pers.] "Do... or do not. There is no try." - Yoda; [a.] Niles, OH

JORDAN, RUEHAME L.
[pen.] R. Louise Milligan; [b.] August 13, 1942, Coshocton, OH; [p.] John and Catherine Milligan; [m.] Jerry Jordan, June 18, 1961; [ch.] Michael Jordan, Michael Sallee; [ed.] BA Education, Masters of Religious Education; [occ.] Elementary Teacher; [a.] Orlando, FL

JORGE, JEWEL ATHENA
[b.] March 27, 1961, New York; [p.] Sara and Nathan George; [ch.] One daughter Makeba Adella Jorge; [ed.] Two yrs. at John Jay College - Full-time two yrs. at College New Rochelle - part time; [occ.] Secretary at the General Board of Global Ministries 3 1/2 yrs.; [hon.] Scholarship to Dance Theatre of Harlem - Ballet. Valedictorian Graduate from Royal Business School type 80 wpm 110 cpm Shorthand - Gregg; [oth. writ.] My first poem written at the age of 15 was "Constiquous Between Man and Woman", second poem called "Woman Who Wants To Be Claimed" third poem "I'm Back In The Groove" Fourth poem "A Special Private Friend".; [pers.] What you expect others to be, you be first!!! Peace, Love, and Understanding.; [a.] New York, NY

JOSHUA, MR. SATTY O.
[pen.] Josh; [b.] Nigeria; [p.] Joshua Amopho, Mary Joshua-Amopho; [m.] Rita Benjamin-Joshua; [ch.] Abigail, Kitoye, Atarah, Kebin and Eella; [ed.] Morrisville College - NY City College of New York, Pace University - NY; [occ.] Network Engineer - Lucent Technologies; [memb.] IEEE, ISP, International Poetry Hall of Fame, Norsed; [hon.] Editor's Choice Award 1995 and 1996, International Poetry Hall of Fame, Copyright Award from the Library of Congress; [oth. writ.] Published several poems with World of Poetry Press, National Library of Poetry, and a completed manuscript "Friendship, Love and Pain" with Vantage Press.; [pers.] In a world filled with evil, let your light remain shining, for light is needed most where darkness is prevalent.; [a.] Montclair, NJ

JOYNER, CHERYL OSLEBER
[b.] March 9, 1950, Chicago, IL; [p.] Helen and Charles Osleber; [m.] William R. Joyner II, June 1990; [ch.] Joseph Charles and Jeffrey Michael; [ed.] Western Illinois University; [occ.] Photographer Image Maker (owner); [memb.] International Freelance Photographers Assoc. and Palm Beach County Cultural Council Artist; [hon.] Professional Dance Teacher Award Photographs Displayed: Chamber of Commerce, Jupiter - Tequesta, FL Hutchinson Island - House of Refuge, Martin Cty. Wildlife Refuge; [oth. writ.] Currently involved in photographic essay on Key West, Fl., also published in Quill Books, "Treasure The Moments."; [pers.] Attempting to articulate the visual images evoked by my photographs.; [a.] Jupiter, FL

JULIA, GOMBERG
[b.] July 25, 1978, Moscow, Russia; [p.] Toya Gomberg, Vladimir Gomberg; [ed.] Be'er Hagolah Institutes, Pace University; [hon.] Pace Honors Program; [oth. writ.] A few poems and short stories in a private collection (not published); [pers.] Yesterday's the past, tomorrow is future, but to day is a gift. That's why H's called "The Present."; [a.] Brooklyn, NY

JUSTICE, JOSHUA C.
[b.] July 9, 1982, Toronto, Ontario; [p.] Jim Justice, Vivian Justice; [ed.] The Westminster Schools; [occ.] Student, Programmer; [memb.] Mensa, Atlanta Macintosh users' Group, Macromedia Developer; [hon.] President's Education Awards Program, Outstanding Academic Male, Lifetime Achievement Award, National Honor Roll, American Junior High School Mathematics Examination; [oth. writ.] Other poems have received the Mosiac Writing Award (Gold, 1996).; [pers.] "Nil Sine Labore." And never doubt that freedom of speech is at least a important as itself. Winston was alive, but at what cost?; [a.] Norcross, GA

JUTRAS, LINDA C.
[pen.] Linds; [b.] January 6, 1954, Providence, RI; [m.] Divorced; [ch.] Anthony Michael; [ed.] H.S. Bishop Keough; [occ.] Clerk Prov. Post Office; [pers.] Troubled by the equal value humanistic system, I wish to be liberated. To become again - without a battle - without shock - harmony - one day at a time.; [a.] Pawtucket, RI

KALINOWSKI, JUDITH A.
[b.] Thief River Falls, MN; [p.] Thomas and Margaret Kalinowski; [ed.] Alumnus of Marquette University in Milwaukee, Wisconsin; [occ.] Educator - I am a Science teacher in Milwaukee, Wisconsin; [memb.] Member of the South Milwaukee Yacht Club; [hon.] 1989 - Teacher of the Year Award in Milwaukee, WI; [oth. writ.] Nothing has been published. Most of what has been written

was done for pleasure and personal gratification.; [pers.] Accepting the role of educator, with a capacity to influence the future, is an awesome responsibility. Few powers on Earth are greater.; [a.] South Milwaukee, WI

KANE, FRANK
[b.] August 20, 1978, Philadelphia; [p.] Gerald Kane, Josie Kane; [ed.] Northeast Catholic High School, The Art Institute of Philadelphia; [occ.] Student; [hon.] Awards in Creativity, and the arrow of light; [oth. writ.] One poem published in a local high paper titled "Echoings" 2 unpublished books titled "Orange" vols 1 and 2.; [pers.] Writing is a release in which your emotions can flow directly out of your soul on to paper.; [a.] Philadelphia, PA

KAUTZ, LORINE ALICE
[pen.] Dutch; [b.] October 28, 1915, Downs, KS; [p.] Albert and Alice Laura Ray; [m.] Leo K. Kautz (Deceased - Vet. War II), October 19, 1932; [ch.] Nine children, 6 living; [ed.] 3 years of High School; [occ.] Retired Senior Citizen; [oth. writ.] I have other poems that I write. I do this just to pass the time away others are longer.; [a.] Independence, MO

KEARNS, ELIZABETH
[pen.] Liz; [b.] July 11, 1922, Grand Rapids, MI; [m.] Lewis G. Kearns, June 22, 1992; [ch.] Bruce Haque, Lee Haque, Cynthia Hulinger; [ed.] Univ. Washington (Seattle) Northwestern Univ.; [occ.] Retired Former Owner/Mgr. Adv. Agency; [memb.] Women's Athletic Club of Chicago, Congregational, UCC Church, El Conquistador Country Club; [oth. writ.] Extensive technical writing in advertising and public relations; [pers.] Never harbor a negative thought.; [a.] Bradenton, FL

KELS, JOANNA GRANT
[b.] December 3, 1981, Farmington, CT; [p.] Barry and Jane Kels; [ed.] The Renbrook School 1986-1996, Miss Porter's School 1996-2000; [occ.] Student; [memb.] Theater Club, Student Council, 1st Flute, Squash Team; [hon.] Honor Roll Student; [oth. writ.] School Newspapers; [pers.] To Mom and Dad: Your love for me, guides my way. You have taught me to be a good person and you have taught me how to love and be loved. I respect you as my parents, care for you as my friends, and learn from you as my teachers. I love you both!; [a.] Avon, CT

KENTNER, RAY GARDNER
[b.] April 26, 1899, Louisville, NY; [p.] Almeda Hunter; [m.] Darwin Kentner, September 11, 1924; [ch.] Clifford, Almeda, George, Alice; [ed.] Quit school to help work on family farm.; [occ.] Retired from raising a family, farming and selling farm equip.; [memb.] Masons 70 plus yrs., Grange; [oth. writ.] Many short poems and writings to my friends and family.; [pers.] To Corrie: Thanks for the life we shared. Being married 70 plus years is hard work and we cherished them dearly.; [a.] Waddington, NY

KERNAN, SARAH J.
[b.] November 8, 1982, Annapolis, MD; [p.] John and Catherine Kernan; [ed.] Grade School, 8th grade Westwood Middle School; [occ.] Student; [pers.] Be happy and believe in yourself.; [a.] Gainesville, FL

KERRIGAN, BETTE BEASLER
[b.] September 1, 1936, Wisconsin; [p.] Tony and Betsy Hanson Beasler; [ch.] Ol-Son - Jason R. Kerrigan, Ol-Foster Son - Ernest Fletcher; [ed.] Winona Senior High, Winona, MN Peninsula Community College, Port Angeles, WA, Antioch University, Seattle, WA (BA, MA) Psychology with focus in Geriatrics.; [occ.]

Psychogeriatrician, Doctorate in Clinical Hypnosis California Own, Operate Senior Residence Private Practice working in the field of Metaphysics. Counseling, Death and dying; [memb.] I belong to and am an officer in several organizations Past President, Hospice ot Clallam Co., PP Son's of Norway, PP Daughter's of Norway, Parents Without Partners.; [oth. writ.] This is my first writing to be shared with the public. On a passing thought I impulsively submitted my poem. Actually I don't claim ownership, my guides gave this and other beautiful, meaningful sonnets to share with everyone. My writings are more spiritual than cerebreal.; [pers.] My purpose, I've discovered, in this lifetime, is to serve mankind with love and kindness. I hope to compile my writings into a book. We live in a world of grace, what we do with it effects the outcome. It is our responsibility to handle this gift with care, to cherish it, to love it, to nurture it. God's goodness shines in each living being. Man has tarnished this glow by his actions. God pleads with us not to fail our mission.; [a.] Port Angeles, WA

KEY, SUSAN HODGSON
[b.] January 2, 1965, Pennsylvania; [p.] Charles and Jennifer Hodgson; [ed.] B.S. May 1987 (Major, Personnel Management) Currently in MBA program at Eastern Ill. Univ., Charleston IL; [occ.] Human Resource Admin., GSI, Paris IL; [memb.] SHRM (Professional Human Resource), Kiwanis; [pers.] Quite that I believe in: "Hold the vision of your completed dream in your mind, see your heart's desire, feel the thrill of accomplishment, offer grateful thanks in advance. Don't ask how it will come to pass, just know that it will."; [a.] Arcola, IL

KHALESSI, MOHAMMAD
[b.] January 29, 1956, Shiraz, Iran; [p.] Abbas Khalessi, Fatemeh Kazemi; [m.] Monica Gomez, March 21; [ed.] Diploma in Natural Science, Shiraz-Iran, BA, Liberal Studies, California State University of Los Angeles; [occ.] Teacher, ESL (English as a second language); [hon.] Certificate of Appreciation for outstanding service to students in June 1993 from United Education Institute; [pers.] Be myself, be humorous, be positive and help others. Have an appreciation for art, literature and nature, love animals. Be honest with myself and others. I was influenced by Omar Khayam, Persian Poet, 1048 AD; [a.] Burbank, CA

KIDD, JENNI
[b.] January 10, 1983, Decatur, TX; [p.] Sam and Kathy Kidd; [ed.] 8th Grade at Paradise Jr. High; [occ.] Student; [memb.] Trinity Word Church Youth Group; [hon.] National Honor Roll Society; [oth. writ.] Several unpublished poems and songs.; [pers.] I try to show that you can be anything if you just keep striving for your dream.; [a.] Paradise, TX

KIMBROUGH, EUNICE LORRINE
[pen.] Lorrine Kimbrough; [b.] August 24, 1936, Jefferson Co., AL; [p.] Paul L. Gurley (Deceased, July 27, 1929), Margaret C. Bolack; [m.] Vernon L. Kimbrough (Deceased, July 19, 1996), April 4, 1955; [ch.] Three boys, Paul, Greg, Tim Kimbrough; [ed.] '56 Tarrant High School Graduate, Tarrant, Alabama (1956); [occ.] Senior Citizen; [memb.] Mt. View Miss. Baptist Church, Cullman, Alabama; [oth. writ.] Scribblings; [pers.] The only way to see life clearly is to focus on Christ.; [a.] Cullman, AL

KING, MICHAEL ANTHONY
[b.] February 7, 1973, San Diego, CA; [p.] Stephen King, Kathy King; [ed.] Serra High, CA, Southcast

Community College, NE; [occ.] Gas Station Boy; [pers.] Margrett King, my Grandmother, I thank you very much.; [a.] Lincoln, NE

KIRKPATRICK, BLAIR
[b.] October 11, 1965, Ainsworth, NE; [p.] Jim and Ellie Kirkpatrick; [ed.] Ainsworth Public High School, Kearney State College, Boston University School of Theology; [occ.] Pastor, First Cong. United Church of Christ, Burwell; [memb.] Sigma Tau Delta (English Honorary); [oth. writ.] Columns and poetry for school newspapers.; [pers.] I view poetry as a vehicle for discovery, both for the author and the reader. Its veiled nature teaches to push beyond the surface for our truths.; [a.] Burwell, NE

KLINE, AMY C.
[b.] March 22, 1974, Connecticut; [ed.] Brevard Community College, University of Connecticut, University of Central Florida. Pursuing a degree in elementary education.; [memb.] SCEC, Apple Corps volunteer; [oth. writ.] I wrote for a high school magazine for two years and I also wrote for a daily newspaper in Connecticut.; [a.] Cape Canaveral, FL

KLINE, MS. SAMANTHA
[b.] June 1, 1979, WPAFB, Dayton, OH; [p.] Kevin and Kay Kline; [ed.] Curwensville Area School Kalst grade, homeschooled to graduation, diploma through PAHSA program; [occ.] Student, prospective landscaper; [memb.] Pioneers 4-H Club, Bible Truth Church, Susquehanna Valley Writer's Club; [hon.] Numerous ribbons and awards from fairs for craft related articles; [oth. writ.] Various poems and several short stories published in home school newsletters.; [pers.] I thank the Lord for giving me the abilities that he has.; [a.] Paxinos, PA

KNAUFT, MARGUERITE VIRGINIA
[pen.] Marguerite Virginia Knauft; [b.] March 6, 1917, Plaza, WA; [p.] Mr. W. G. Dodge, Daisy Dodge - died in 1920; [m.] Emil H. Knauft (Pastor), June 11, 1939; [ch.] Richard, Daniel and Joan; [ed.] Completed High School at Fairfield, WA 1935, attended Walla Walla College 2 years, graduated from Prt Horon MI Jr. College in 1960 with degree in Nursing - RW (National); [occ.] I am a retired R.N., worked 27 years; [memb.] I am a member of the Seventh Day Adventist Church and Pastor's Wife for 57 years, a member for 62 years. We served in Rehab after WW II in Austria.; [oth. writ.] Have had a couple of articles published in "Women's Ministry," (S.D.A.) 1993-94 poem published in high school paper.; [pers.] Religious poetry is my favorite and nature.; [a.] Mead, WA

KNERR, THEODORE
[b.] July 25, 1931, Phila, PA; [occ.] Artist (Abstract Painter); [pers.] I am a messenger rather than a conscious creator of this poem. I had no preconceptions. I simply let each word slowly well up and wrote it down without trying to understand it in context or make any choice about it. Reading it came as a shock to me. Upon its arrival in 1994, I began a head-on encounter with personal problems which has produced forgiveness for myself and others, and real transformation - "Green Awakenings."; [a.] New York, NY

KNIGHT, WILLIAM E.
[b.] February 1, 1922, Tarrytown, NY; [p.] Arthur O. and Mabel J. Knight; [m.] Ruth L. Knight, August 14, 1946; [ch.] Jeffrey William and Peter Edwards; [ed.] Yale: BA and MA, USAAF Pilot training (B-24s), Industrial College of the Armed Forces, State Department's Senior, Seminar in Foreign Policy; [occ.] Author; [memb.] American Foreign Service Assn., Diplomatic

and Consular Officers, Retired Army Navy Country Club, Washington Independent Writers, Randolph Mountain Club; [oth. writ.] The Tiger Game, 1986, The Bamboo Game, 1993, Footprints in the Sand (Light Verse), 1995, Contributions to journals; [a.] Bethesda, MD

KOCH, BARBARA A.
[pen.] BBK; [b.] April 1, 1959, Queens, NY; [ed.] Patchogue - Medford High School; [occ.] Author; [oth. writ.] Fist Novel, "a murder of crows," currently published on the world wide web, by Biblio Bytes, Inc. access code: HTTP://WWW.BB.COM; [pers.] I think, therefore I am.; [a.] Yaphank, NY

KOONTZ JR., PAUL
[pen.] Francois de Marbois; [b.] February 17, 1953, Paterson, NJ; [p.] Alma (Whritenour) and Paul Koontz Sr.; [m.] Theresa Freeland, August 16, 1975; [ch.] Paul III, Rachel; [ed.] B.A. William Paterson College, Wayne N.J. 1975; [occ.] Self Employed Builder, and Income Tax Preparer; [memb.] Knights of Columbus, The National Writer's Association, Jefferson Youth Soccer; [oth. writ.] "Pathways to the Truth," (1996), "President Clinton challenged America to design a better tax plan and a common American responds," (1993); [a.] Jefferson Township, NJ

KOSSEY, KATHLEEN M.
[b.] March 2, 1980, Adrian, MI; [p.] Michael E. and Mary H. Kossey; [ed.] Elementary, Middle School, Bishop D.J. O'Connell High School, Tecumseh High School; [occ.] Student (High School Junior); [memb.] Tecumseh Area Soccer Club (TASC), Tecumseh High Band, Boy Scouts of America Veterinary Explorer, 4-H; [hon.] Michigan Summer Institute (seeks sustaining the environment through education, knowledge, and skill), Junior Varsity Athletic Award; [pers.] I am the second oldest of nine children.; [a.] Tecumseh, MI

KOULAKANI, AHMAD M. S.
[pen.] A-Koulakani; [b.] September 13, 1952, Tehran, Iran; [p.] Ozra and Hasan; [m.] Maryam, November 14, 1991; [ch.] Gazelle Koulakani; [ed.] M.A. Communication; [occ.] Manager, Teacher; [oth. writ.] Automatic Dolls Mr. Obedient. Number of films criticism. All published in Farsi language in Iran in Ferdousi magazine.; [pers.] My current poetry is highly influenced by contemporary Persian poets as well as 5th or 6th century, like Omar Khayam, Hafez, Romi and Molana.; [a.] Aliso Viejo, CA

KOUPO, KATE
[pen.] Kate Koupo; [b.] January 30, 1917, Collinsville, IL; [p.] Joseph and Mary Savant; [m.] William Koupo, April 6, 1935; [ch.] Two; [ed.] Grade School and High School; [occ.] Retired; [hon.] Coloring as a child, spelling in grade school, owner of 3 businesses. Supervisor for 15 years in a hospital. Grades A and B all my years in grade school; [oth. writ.] I worked by myself in my business. Husband had a job and helped after hours. I have good common sense.; [pers.] Father was a coal miner. Never asked for any help. We lived in an Era that never will be again.

KOWAL, DANA CHRISTINE
[b.] January 12, 1970, Butler, PA; [ed.] B.S. Elementary Education/early childhood from slippery Rock University of PA; [occ.] Employed with Sylvan Learning Center, Butler PA; [memb.] PA Science Teacher Association (PSTA), Association for Supervision and Curriculum Development (ASCD); [oth. writ.] Poems: "The Student," and "Sir Christopher," published by Sparrowgrass Poetry Forum, Sisterville, WV. They will appear in the June 1997 Anthology Poetic Voices of

America.; [pers.] Poetic themes are inspired by everyday life events. My most admired author is Robert Fulghum, author of, All I Really Need to Know I Learned in Kindergarten." He makes one think of the meaning and depth of our lives through the use of reflection and humor.; [a.] Butler, PA

KOZAK, MARGE
[b.] January 19, 1928, PA; [p.] Grace and Steve Burns; [m.] May 29, 1948; [ch.] Four; [ed.] 12th Grade; [occ.] Disabled; [a.] Berea, OH

KOZENKO, MATT
[pen.] Mattew, Kozy; [b.] July 6, 1976, Geneva, OH; [p.] Bill and Claudine Kozenko; [ed.] Ledgemont High, U.S. Naval Schools; [occ.] Self Employed Electrician; [hon.] Letter of Accommodation from an Admiral of U.S. Navy; [oth. writ.] All of my other poems are awaiting a chance to be heard.; [a.] Thompson, OH

KOZIN, JOHN
[b.] September 30, 1939, Ukraine; [p.] Stefan and Alexandra; [ch.] Dawn and Lisa (Daughters); [ed.] Chadsey High School, Wayne State University, Detroit, Michigan; [occ.] Work for an electronic distributor; [oth. writ.] Poems and observations on man's place in the universe.; [pers.] Fascinated by the paradox of the human condition, prolific reader of classic and eastern philosophies, mythology and good science fiction.; [a.] Covina, CA

KRAMP, LOUIS C.
[b.] July 11, 1928, Ohio; [p.] Lours Kramp Sr. and Caroline Kramp; [m.] Inez Lofthus, March 25, 1951; [ch.] Kathleen, Jonathan Carolyn and Robyn; [ed.] Moody Bible Institute, Gordon College, Southern Illinois University; [occ.] Business Consultant; [memb.] Fourth Presbyterian Church, Board: Democracy In Action, Board: Impact Group; [hon.] Young Man of the Year, Billings, Montana 1960, State of Montana 1960; [oth. writ.] Essays on "Community".; [pers.] Eagerly anticipating the day that all things shall once again be made whole.; [a.] Oakton, VA

KRASS, ROBERT J.
[b.] August 21, 1951, Ashland, MA; [ch.] 2 children, 3 dogs; [ed.] 1969 Triadelphia HS, Wheeling WV, 1992 University of New York, Regents College, BS, Sociology; [occ.] Merchant Marines 1969, US Navy 1971-1992; [pers.] Rose to CPO (E-7) in 8 years, Selected as Chief Warrant Officer and eventually Limited Duty Officer attaining the rank of Navy Lieutenant in 1989. Lived in several interesting locations including: Athens Greece, Jacksonville FL, Pensacola FL, Norfolk VA and Philadelphia PA. Started writing poetry early in life (although mostly to woo the ladies, especially my wife). I have composed several poems to mark special family occasions and a series of poems dedicated to newly commissioned US Navy ships that I have worked with since my military retirement.

KUERNER, KARL J.
[pen.] Karl J. Kuerner; [b.] January 12, 1957, Chadds Ford, PA; [p.] Margaret, Karl; [m.] Louise Kline Kuerner, September 22, 1984; [ed.] Attended Art Institute of Phila. 1975-76, Studied painting under Carolyn Wyeth from 1970-1977 (NC Wyeth Daughter); [occ.] Artist Teacher at Darlington Fine Arts Center, Wawa, PA, since 1979; [memb.] Brandywine River Museum Chadds Ford, Pa., Represented by Newman Galleries Phila. Pa.; [hon.] Paintings in collections of Brandywine River Museum, Christian C. Sanderson Museum, and many private collections

throughout U.S.; [pers.] I was always taught...love what you paint,...paint what you love. I feel that also can be expressed in my writing.; [a.] Chadds Ford, PA

KUPSY, NICK
[b.] December 8, 1977, Upper Darby, PA; [p.] William S. Kupsy; [ed.] Upper Darby Senior High School Class of 1996, 19082 Delaware County Community College; [occ.] Prep Cook, T-Bonz Bart Grille, Havertown PA; [pers.] "Dark clouds may hang over me something but I'll work it out." Depend on yourself, not chemicals, to find the answers to your problems.; [a.] Upper Darby, PA

KUZNICKI JR., BEN
[b.] October 8, 1962, Alpena; [p.] Ben and Judy Kuznicki; [ch.] Ben Kuznicki III; [ed.] A.A.S. Degree in Machine Tool and a B.S. Degree in Production Management; [occ.] Manage Process Engineering for Mfg. Firm; [oth. writ.] I have written many other poems but they have remained private and unpublished.; [pers.] Only faith in the Lord, and trust in time, will remove the pain, from this heart of mine.; [a.] Presque Isle, MI

LAGASSE, JAMIE LYNN KNIGHT
[pen.] Jamie Lagasse; [b.] May 5, 1977, Richfield, UT; [p.] Jon and Linda Burt, Paul Knight; [m.] Matthew Lagasse, April 22, 1994; [ch.] Zachary Kaden Knight; [ed.] Richfield High; [occ.] Housewife, Crossing Guard; [hon.] Have some awards for my poetry form Grade School, and County Fair; [pers.] My influence comes from things or people and everyday life around me and I put it in my poems.; [a.] Richfield, UT

LAGUD, RYAN J.
[b.] May 24, 1980, Rochester, PA; [p.] Jim and Dawnette Lagud; [ed.] Currently a Junior at Center High School; [pers.] I have a collection of poems I've written over the past few months in hopes of someday publishing my own Anthology.; [a.] Monaca, PA

LAHOOD, JULIE ANN
[b.] May 31, Martins Ferry, OH; [p.] Thelma and Joseph LaHood; [ed.] St. Mary Academy, Monroe, Mich., Loyola U., Chicago, Ill., Ray College of Design, Chicago, Ill.; [occ.] Owner Historic Properties, Monroe, Mich. (Boyhood Home of Gen. Custer); [memb.] Nat'l. Tourist for Historic Preservation, Monroe Country Historical Soc., Monroe, Mich., Chicago Historical Society, Chicago, Ill.; [hon.] Modeling School, Ray College of Design, Staged my own style show, Vocal and Piano Awards as a child in Martins Ferry, Ohio; [oth. writ.] "Winter Days," Editor's choice award, Of Sunshine and Daydreams, Nat'l. Library of Poetry, 1996.; [pers.] I am registered in the state of Illinois, and State of Michigan to sell Cherokee Indian Moccasins. I enjoy reading about the Indian Territory, and our Western History.; [a.] Saint Charles, IL

LAIDLEY, ALVIN
[b.] April 14, 1908, Carmichaels, PA; [p.] L. T. and Katherine Laidley; [m.] Jeanne Silvain Laidley, March 19, 1947; [ch.] Joseph T. Laidley; [ed.] B.A. (Biology), B.Mus. (Piano), Waynesburg College and Conservatory of Music, Waynesburg, PA, graduate work at the Eastman School and Georgetown Univ.; [occ.] Retired Chief, Staff Training Division, UNESCO, Paris, France; [hon.] Distinguished Alumnus and Presidential Medal, Waynesburg College, Citizen of the Year (1996), Carmichaels Grange; [oth. writ.] "An Introduction to Fifty Representative Novels," published by Waynesburg College (1983), and several learned articles in "The Lamp," W.C. periodical.; [pers.] I believe, like Socrates, that the purpose of life is the acquisition of knowledge in order to attain wisdom and ultimately an understanding of the nature of God.; [a.] Carmichaels, PA

LAIRD, DAVID A.
[b.] February 12, 1985, Warren, OH; [p.] Robert M. (Sr.) and Irma Valerio Laird; [ed.] Presently in Sixth Grade Garfield Elementary School Warren, Ohio; [occ.] Honor Student; [memb.] Student Council - Garfield Elementary St. Piusx Church (Altar Boy - 4 yrs.) (where I am a member or the School Band) was in Warren City Schools Creative and Perform my Arts Program; [hon.] Honor student - past 3 yrs. Received 'Superior' ratings past two yrs. (96-97) National Federation Junior Festivals - Piano Solo poem published in 1996 Edition - of the 'Anthology of Poetry' by Young Americans; [oth. writ.] 'Tentacles of Terror' in Anthology of Poetry - 1996 Edition; [a.] Warren, OH

LAIRD, JAMES
[b.] March 1, 1975, Saint Louis, MO; [p.] Mary L. and John M. Laird Jr.; [ed.] Hazelwood Central Senior High, Northeast Missouri State University, Saint Louis University, Currently attending University of Missouri, St. Louis; [occ.] Student - Biology/Chemistry/Biochem/Pre-Med Major; [memb.] John Knox Presbyterian Church, University of Missouri, St. Louis Chemistry Club, Gateway Miata Club; [hon.] Dean's List (NMSU), High Achievement in History (SLU), High Achievement in Philosophy (UMSL), Research Internship with professor at Mallinkrodt Medical Inc. (Spring 97'); [pers.] I wish to relate to people in my writing, to remind them that they are not alone in their feelings.; [a.] Florissant, MO

LAMB, EUGENIA
[b.] Norfolk, VA; [p.] James Lamb, Eugenia Lamb; [ed.] Washington High Virginia College (Various Courses) in the process of furthering my college degree; [occ.] Data Clerk; [memb.] Red Cross Asc. America Heart Asc., First Baptist Church; [hon.] Proformance Awards (work), Conventions (plaques); [oth. writ.] Poems and essays written for Anniversaries, Conventions, and plays.; [pers.] I want my poems to reflected, the faith in mankind and hoping to see the excellencies in him. Give one to another by helping one to help himself, to be self reliant then he's able to contribute back in various ways.; [a.] Norfolk, VA

LANE, EVA
[b.] February 18, 1970, Greeneville, TN; [p.] Dennis and Joyce Lane; [ch.] Two boys, Calynn, Kevin; [ed.] South Greene and North Greene High, Laughlin Hospital CNA, Training Program; [occ.] Certified Nursing Aide; [oth. writ.] A Fight With Death, Medicine Of God, Scared Mind, Capture Rose, Forever Roses, Wishful Thinking, Light Of God and many more, but all non-published.; [pers.] This poem "A Child of Abuse" is based on my childhood and others like me. I hope when one reads this poem it will open their eyes and hearts to the problem with abuse.; [a.] Greeneville, TN

LANGFORD, BETTY
[pen.] Cherri Hallum; [b.] August 19, 1975, Calhoun County, MS; [p.] David and Betsy Hallum; [ed.] Delta State University, NWCC, hoping to enter Radiology School; [occ.] Student; [a.] Vardaman, MS

LANT, GREG
[b.] May 11, 1977, Nebraska City, NE; [p.] Rodger and Cathy Lant; [ed.] Nebr City Sr High, 1995 Univ. of Nebr, at Kearney - 1 year; [occ.] Retail Grocery Movement Specialist; [memb.] National Forensics League; [hon.] Honor Roll, Speech and Drama Awards, Letterman; [oth. writ.] Personal volumes and songs/lyrics.; [pers.] To ease pain, heal and to allow "the music be my master".; [a.] Nebraska City, NE

LAUDETT, JANET
[b.] October 3, 1965, Fredonia, KS; [p.] Jim and Leah Carter, Harry and Carolyn Tyler; [m.] Terry Laudett, September 18, 1993; [ed.] Fairland High School, Fairland, OK, NEO A and M College, Miami, OK Missouri Southern State College, Joplin, MO; [occ.] Homemaker; [memb.] Jenks Church of Christ, Jenks, OK, Active in singing group in the Church; [oth. writ.] I've written all my life, but this is my first time to be published.; [pers.] Through all the seasons of our lives, whether rain or shine, even when we can't feel or see Him, God is there, loving us and caring for us.; [a.] Glenpool, OK

LAVALLEY, DAVID EUGENE
[b.] August 13, 1967, NAMC; [p.] William Alfred and Pauline; [ed.] Graduated Harrison High School, attended North Arkansas Community College; [occ.] Novelist; [memb.] International Society of Poets; [oth. writ.] Two poems already published.; [pers.] I hope to someday realize an income with which I can do others good. I also hope to provide entertainment for readers.; [a.] Western Grove, AR

LAVAN, CHRISTOPHER E.
[pen.] Christ "B. C." Lavan; [b.] January 31, 1984, Lake Charles, LA; [p.] Michael Lavan Sr. and Betty J. Sims; [ed.] Episcopal Day School 7th grade; [occ.] Middle School Student; [memb.] Mt. Olive Bapt. Church, A.A.U. Basketball League; [hon.] State Science Fair - 4th place - 1996 Honor Roll Student grades 1-7 Piano Recital Award; [pers.] "I can do al things through Christ who strengthens me."; [a.] Lake Charles, LA

LAVOIE, ANNETTE N.
[b.] December 16, 1935, Springfield, MA; [p.] George J. Lavoie and Edna M. (Cote) Lavoie; [m.] Happily Divorced!; [ch.] R. Mark Proulx; [ed.] High School of Commerce; [occ.] Semi-Retired Legal Secretary, Agawam, MA; [pers.] "The Direction of The Wind," is my first and only poem and the inspiration for this poem came from the lesson I learned through my own personal experience.; [a.] West Springfield, MA

LEACH, WILLIAM H.
[pen.] W. Henry Lanesworth; [b.] June 22, 1929, Saint Louis, MO; [p.] Romie and Clara Leach; [m.] Barbara Ann, December 17, 1950; [ch.] Ronda, Rita, Robin, Rodney, Renee; [ed.] Salisbury High, Junior College KC, MO; [occ.] Owner - The Mission Press, Merriam, KS; [oth. writ.] Several unpublished poems and stories.; [pers.] Time is merely an interval between the beginning and the end and the beginning has just begun.; [a.] Bucyrus, KS

LEE, MILLIE M.
[b.] February 24, 1935, Balto County; [p.] Richard L. and Florence E. Leaf; [m.] Richard E. Lee; [ch.] Judy M. and Regina L.; [ed.] Franklin High, Reisterstown, MD; [occ.] Vice Pres. and Partner in Husband's Co., R.E. Lee Bldg Contractor; [pers.] Always loved writings of substance. Influenced by 10th and 11th grade teacher, Ethel Parsons (Deceased).; [a.] Reisterstown, MD

LEE-ROLLINS, BRENDA
[pen.] Brenda J. Mosley; [b.] January 13, 1951, Memphis, TN; [p.] Lee and Louise Mosley (Deceased); [m.] Sanders Rollins Jr., November 14, 1988; [ch.] Two: Preston Lee and Stacey Smith; [ed.] Klonike School, TN, Northview Jr. High - Duarte, CA, Duarte High School, Duarte, CA, Citrus Jr. College, Azusa Hollywood Business, College, CA; [occ.] Disabled - Discoig Lupus; [memb.] Southern California Lupus Foundation, United Women's Guild, (Monrovia), So District Ushers Foun-

dation, Los Angeles, California; [hon.] Teacher Training Vacation Bible School, School of Ushering, Xerox - Art Contest, Service Corp Int'l - Salesmanship, Most Dedicated Usher - Monrovia, CA, send to Hawaii - all expenses paid, Certificates: 1.) Introduction to Basics - Cobol, Xerox - Pasadena, CA, 2.) Reading and Evaluating Financial Reports, 3.) Job Developer - Women in Non-Traditional Trade Jobs - sent to Atlanta, GA, all expenses paid, Los Angels Urban League; [oth. writ.] Poetry at my church: Second Baptist, Bishop Dr. Wm. L. Dillard, Pastor; [pers.] I love to bring out the best in the worst of people - "Greater is He that is in me, than He that is in the world." I John 4:4; [a.] Monrovia, CA

LEHTO, SUE
[b.] April 24, 1947, Weed, CA; [p.] Art and Ruth Stanley; [m.] Rod Lehto, April 22, 1985; [ch.] 1 Cocker Spaniel-Toby; [ed.] Retired from Pacific Bell; [occ.] Pacific Bell Pioneers; [pers.] This was my first poem that my husband inspired. It was written on the back of a brown paper bag while we were deer hunting.; [a.] Chico, CA

LEMIEUX, ALEXANDRA
[b.] January 21, 1980, Norwich, CT; [p.] David and Linda Lemieux; [ed.] Will graduate St. Bernard High School in 1998; [hon.] Various awards for academics and dance, National Honor Roll; [oth. writ.] Publication in local magazine, writing for the school newsletter, The Shield.; [a.] Uncasville, CT

LEONARD JR., ROBERT TIRRELL
[pen.] R. T. Leonard, Robert Leonard Jr.; [b.] January 18, 1971, Winchester Hospital; [p.] Joan M. Perry and Robert Tirrell Leonard; [ed.] Middlesex Community College, Boston Bartenders School of America, Connecticut School of Broadcasting; [occ.] Host, Part Time Bartender, Boston Burlington Marriot; [memb.] The International Society of Poets, United Amateur Press Association of America; [hon.] Editor's Choice Award 1996 - National Library of Poetry; [oth. writ.] "Release," Memories of Tomorrow 1996, "Shadow Walker," Isle of View 1997. "The Dark Divide," (a self published page of poetry, with 70 circulated monthly, by U.A.P.A.A. "Instant Coffee," Marriot News, Burlington MA.; [pers.] Favorite authors: H. P. Lovecraft, Edgar Allen Poe, "I search for truth, reality, and the dark lore of emotions." "I have often wondered if the majority of mankind ever pause to reflect upon the occasionally titanic significance of dreams, and of the obscure world to which they belong." H. P. Lovecraft.; [a.] Woburn, MA

LEOPARDI, DANIEL J.
[b.] December 6, 1975, Carlisle, PA; [p.] Daniel R. Leopardi, Barbara Leopardi; [m.] Jody May Serris (to be), October 11, 1997; [ed.] Graduate of Cumberland Valley High School and Cumberland Perry Vocational School; [occ.] Forklift Driver at Exert Logistics, Mechanicsburg, PA; [oth. writ.] I have been working on a book for about 5 years. It is a book of poetry and it will be called, "Green Mind."; [pers.] I like to write about ideas, moods, people, everyday life and how I perceive things. I would like to be discovered and get my book published.; [a.] Boiling Springs, PA

LEPKOWSKI, TINA
[b.] October 26, 1967, Chicago, IL; [p.] Mitchell Lepkowski, Sharon Lepkowski; [ch.] Kenneth Franklin; [occ.] Mold Technician; [pers.] Dedicated to my loving mother, in memory of her beloved brothers, Martin and Howard Berger.

LESLIE, CYNTHIA
[b.] September 16, 1962, Warren, AR; [p.] C. E. and

JoAnn Williams; [m.] James D. Leslie, December 31, 1994; [ch.] L. J. Leslie; [ed.] BA in English earned from University of Arkansas at Monticello; [occ.] Computer Specialist at Millcreek of Arkansas at Fordyce; [memb.] St. Mary's Episcopal Church, Monticello, AR, Monticello Area Computer User's Group (MACUG); [hon.] MACUG Newsletter, editor; [pers.] Humanity expresses itself through words, for this reason we should write and speak deliberately and with purpose.; [a.] Monticello, AR

LEWIS, CHARLES A.
[pen.] Chick Lewis, Snoopy; [b.] March 21, 1918, Saint John, NB, Canada; [p.] William (Cook) Lewis, Thomas R. Lewis; [m.] Ruth (Basto) Lewis, September 25, 1945; [ch.] Five - 3 girls, 2 boys; [ed.] Commercial Course, Shead Memorial High School, Eastport, Grad. June 1936, Univ. Md. Off. Campus - 8 credits Business Adm. Economics; [occ.] Retired U.S. Army CWO, Joined Oct. 20, 1939, Retired Jan. 31, 1960; [memb.] Veterans of Foreign Wars of US, The American Legion, Knights of Pythias; [hon.] Army Commendation, Asiatic-Pacific Campaign Medal, German, Army of Occupation Medal, "The Golden Spur," Knights of Pythias; [oth. writ.] Several poems published in "Army Times," some in local and statewide newspapers, e.g. "Maine Times," "The Quoddy Tides," "Eastport Sentinel," "The Colors Advertiser."; [pers.] Always enjoyed the poems of Robert Service and Ogden Nash among many others.; [a.] Eastport, ME

LEWIS, HORACIO D.
[b.] January 17, 1944, Rep. of Panama; [p.] Clarence E. and Daisy Bell Lewis; [m.] Susan, June 18, 1983; [ch.] Sheena, Sonrisa, Benjamin; [ed.] Columbia Pacific University (Ph.D.), Northeastern Ill. Univ. (M.A.), Harvard Univ. (Cert.) Morningside College (B.Sc.), Canal Zone College (A.A.), Universidad Nacional De Panama (Cert.) Colegio Abel Bravo (Bachillerato En Ciencias); [occ.] Director of Diversity Programs and National Consultant/Speaker; [memb.] National Assc. for Multicultural Education, Research Board of Advisors (American Biographical Institute, Inc.); [hon.] NCCJ "Community Builder" Award, listed in several "Who's Who" publications, the Council of College Presidents Award, The Mayor of the City of Wilmington (DE) award, Panama's President Rernon Cantera Gold Medal of Achievement; [oth. writ.] Books: Quadrangulated Inequality my life in verse, I might as well move to the moon, guidelines for Infusing Multicultural Education into school curricular and co-curricular programs, 100 poems and other impressions and moves of articles/book chapters.; [pers.] If you are waiting for am afterlife, you may already be dead.; [a.] Newark, DE

LEWIS, SHELDON J.
[b.] March 2, 1924, Vernal, UT; [p.] James Donald and Genevra Lewis; [m.] Rae R. Lewis, April 29, 1996; [ch.] Linda, Larry, Sherry, Vicki; [ed.] High School and some college; [occ.] Retired; [oth. writ.] Poems I have submitted to the National Library of Poetry that have been published in The Rainbow End and Best Poems of 1997.; [pers.] I decided to put some of my thoughts on life into poems. When I heard of what you might think about my writing, you say you like my poems so I like sending then to you.; [a.] Hayton, UT

LIBMAN, GRIGORIY
[b.] September 3, 1934, City Gomel, Byelorussia; [p.] Iosif Ligman (father), Golda Ligman (mother); [ch.] Yelena Vasilevitsky (daughter), Igoz Ligman (son); [ed.] Moscow High, Forest Technical College, 1968; [occ.] Constructor-Engineer; [memb.] U.A.E.E.J. and Associa-

tion of Immigrants from CIS in New York; [hon.] 1) Certificate of Appreciation, the Jewish Heritage Festival in 1994, 2) Certificate of honorary member, the club beer-lover JCH of Bensonhurst, December 16, 1994; [oth. writ.] My several poems published in local newspapers, in magazines "Start," in "Almanac Poetry," which was issued in San Jose, 1994 by Innovative Graphics, in February '97 was published my article by newspaper the "Jewish World" The publishing "House Driver Kier" will publish my book in May '97.; [pers.] I was a president of the New American Culture Club "Haticvah" in 1995. I came out with my poems in concerts and meetings in Jewish community centre.; [a.] Brooklyn, NY

LIGHTSEY, ANNIE MAE FAULK
[pen.] Annie Mae F. Lightsey; [b.] January 2, 1900; [p.] Sidney J. Faulk, Ida Mae Faulk; [m.] John Edward Lightsey, September 24, 1919; [ch.] Six; [ed.] Maryville College, Maryville, Tennessee; [memb.] Southern Methodist Church, U.D.C.; [oth. writ.] "Along The Way With Annie Mae", and many poems.; [pers.] Mother died February 4, 1995. She was a member of Southern Methodist Church - and a life long member of UDC and attended Maryville College in Maryville, Tenn.; [a.] Centreville, AL

LINDSTROM, LISA M.
[pen.] Leo; [b.] August 8, 1961, Minneapolis, MN; [p.] Wane and Carol Engebrit; [m.] Jeff, July 25, 1992; [ed.] Charles A. Lindbergh Sr. H.S., German U of Minnesota, 1 year literature; [occ.] Poet, Publisher, Office Manager, Insurance Consultant, Housewife; [memb.] Charles Member, All American Eagle Racers, Distinguished Member, International Society of Poets, Member, North American Book Exchange; [hon.] 2 Poet of Merit Awards, I.S.P., Several Editor's Choice Awards, National Library of Poetry; [oth. writ.] 1st Book, "Adequate Justice - Beginning Healing Through Poetry," 2nd Book in publishing process, "Observing and Feeling While I am Healing," 3rd book being written now, "Slamming the Ancient Door Forevermore To A Distant Shore."; [pers.] Write from the heart. It's very therapeutic and frees pent up emotions. It allows room for more positive influences.; [a.] Yorba Linda, CA

LINGERFELT, JODY
[b.] April 8, 1959, Rockford, IL; [m.] Michael; [ch.] Destinie, Vanessa, Michelle and Charles; [pers.] The written word is like a best friend to me and in my opinion the fine art of communication.; [a.] Siloam Springs, AR

LINK, DAWN E. LAUTH
[b.] August 6, 1974; [p.] Mr. and Mrs. Gordon Lauth; [m.] Jayson L. Link, August 5, 1995; [ed.] Chalker High School, Kent State University; [memb.] Leavittsburg Church of God; [hon.] Dean's List; [oth. writ.] "Above It All," published in ICON-Kent State University Trumbull Campus literary magazine; [pers.] "Let us take comfort in knowing that in heaven all things become new."; [a.] Warren, OH

LINK, THOMAS W.
[pen.] Tom Link; [b.] March 23, 1969, St. Ann's Hospital, Columbus, OH; [p.] Charles Link and Shelby J. Link; [ed.] Madison Plains High School, I then furthered my education at Ohio University studying Aviation, Anthropology, and Creative Writing Courses.; [occ.] Acct. Exec. in electronics and some free lance writing; [memb.] Southwestern Schools, Library Association; [hon.] Arion Music Award, other Music and Drama Awards, The Spirit of America Marching Band: Representing the U.S.A. in the 1986 World's Fair in Vancouver, Canada; [oth. writ.]

Other poems: Plateau of Breezes, Silhouettes, Lion Eyes, and a biography called Sonny's Ride; [pers.] Everyone is given the hand that is dealt them, but that doesn't mean that you can't trade two of your own for another pair. Life courses can change if you let them.; [a.] Columbus, OH

LINN, ANN
[b.] December 31, 1945, Wadena, MN; [p.] Elvera Crandall; [m.] Richard Linn, February 24, 1979; [ch.] Terri, David, Michael, Diane; [occ.] Secretary/Treasurer, Linn, Inc., Minnetonka, MN; [pers.] I believe that every person should strive to reach their fullest potential.; [a.] Minnetonka, MN

LINO, DEVIN
[b.] October 29, 1981, Milton, FL; [p.] Patricia and Steve Adensam; [ed.] Ingleside High School, De Portola Middle School; [hon.] I was awarded 200 dollars for an invention submitted in the Invent America Contest, also I was awarded 20 dollars for first place in an essay contest; [pers.] Strive to do your best and you can accomplish anything.; [a.] Aransas Pass, TX

LISTER, YAMONTE KEE
[pen.] Yummie; [b.] March 20, 1977, Houston, TX; [p.] Brenda J. Lister; [ed.] Graduated from Klein Forest High School; [occ.] Student at Prairie View A&M University; [memb.] Houston Northwest Community Baptist Church, Health Occupations Students of America - HOSA - American Heart Association; [hon.] President/Vice Pres. and Parliamentarian of HOSA (Health Occupations Students of America); [oth. writ.] Many unpublished poems in my Book of Imaginations! (All my poems); [pers.] In my writings, I hope to release all of my readers into the realm of poetry, and all that lives within true poets and poetry!; [a.] Houston, TX

LISTHROP, ENGRED
[b.] March 12, 1948, Trinidad, W.I.; [p.] Albert and Elvira Listhrop; [ch.] Anastasia, Joel Listhrop; [ed.] Elementary Education in Trinidad, W.I., B.S. degree Business Management, Medgar Evers College, Bklyn., U.S.A.; [occ.] Teacher; [oth. writ.] Unpublished; [pers.] I am a sunbeam for Jesus sparkling fires for others to find him.; [a.] Brooklyn, NY

LLOYD, CAROL
[pen.] Carol Lloyd; [b.] June 7, 1943, Philadelphia, PA; [p.] George and Irene Grieff; [m.] John, October 12, 1963; [ch.] John, Dawn, Crista; [ed.] John Bartram High School; [occ.] Environmental Service Worker; [memb.] International Society of Poets; [hon.] Editor's Choice Award 1995 and 1996; [oth. writ.] Winter Showers, A Day In Your Life, Three Faces, Colors of Day, Touch Me, and many others.; [pers.] I draw my writings from personal experience and life around me as I see it.; [a.] Glenolden, PA

LOCKMILLER, EARL
[b.] June 6, 1925, Chattanooga, TN; [p.] Evelyn and M. B. Lockmiller; [m.] Inez Malone Lockmiller, September 20, 1947; [ch.] Sondra Lockmiller Humphreys; [ed.] Tenn. Wesleyan College, U.S. Command and Gen. Staff College, Industrial Coll. of the Armed Forces; [occ.] Retired Col. US Army; [memb.] Veterans Organizations; [oth. writ.] Several songs and poems unpublished.; [pers.] I try to portray a central thought or theme with widely accepted interest, focused to attract reader attention to a desired segment of the theme.; [a.] Athens, TN

LOCKWOOD, NATALIE
[b.] August 9, 1977, Rochester, NY; [p.] Beverly and Albert Lockwood; [ed.] I went to School of the Arts high school in Rochester. I am now attending S.U.N.Y. Geneseo in Geneseo N.Y.; [occ.] Student, Sociology Major; [pers.] Living honestly with yourself under all circumstances is a major key in true happiness. And fate is the exactitude of unintentions.; [a.] Rochester, NY

LODATO, RODNEY
[b.] December 12, 1962, Rochester, NY; [p.] Michael Lodato, Irene Lodato; [m.] Christine Lodato, February 21, 1987; [ch.] Randall Michael, Bethany Anne; [ed.] East High School Roch. NY; [occ.] Bakery Supervisor; [pers.] Hold on to your dreams.; [a.] Rochester, NY

LONG, ROBERT J.
[pen.] Bob Long; [b.] October 9, 1934, Dayton, OH; [p.] William and Alice Lou Long; [m.] Joy Long, October 20, 1955; [ch.] Jim, Douglas, Jeff, Lynn; [ed.] Attended - Wittedberg University and U. South Fla. in Psychology attended many seminars and courses in Mental Health Field; [occ.] Retired; [memb.] Retired from Sarasota Memorial Hospital as "Mr. Music of Sarasota" also Excel Employee of 1993 also Retired from International Harvester Co - Spfld Ohio; [hon.] US Navy Hospital Corps for 22 years I was honored with entertaining with music sing a long and activities at Lakeside Pavilion Sarasota Memorial Hosp. and did many groups there and nursing homes; [oth. writ.] Working on writing several songs and also a book on "Letting Go" of stress.; [pers.] I like to express myself in both music and poems and try to reach others - Writing makes me feel closer to God; [a.] Venus, FL

LONG JR., HENRY A.
[pen.] Hank; [b.] November 4, 1948, Columbia, PA; [p.] Henry Long and Francis Fritz; [m.] Debra L. Long, June 21, 1996; [ch.] Stepson, Nate Evans; [ed.] Columbia High, Franklin and Marshall College; [occ.] Maintenance Supervisor; [oth. writ.] Most of my writings are tucked away in a personal folder and seldom read by anyone else.; [pers.] My family: wife - Deb, stepson - Nate, brother Jeff and sisters Deb, Francine and Annette are the most common thoughts of my pen!; [a.] Manheim, PA

LOPEZ, JOSEPH D.
[b.] September 13, 1960, Brooklyn, NY; [p.] Mr. and Mrs. Jose R. Lopez; [m.] Stephanie Lopez, May 10, 1983; [ed.] High School, went into the army, 3 years; [occ.] Electrical Supplies. I worked as undertaker; [oth. writ.] My brother Ramon within this walls. to my dear Father; [pers.] I like to write poems, I play guitar, I play baseball in a local team. I love all kind of sports. In my writings I like to reflect the general daily life.; [a.] Brooklyn, NY

LOPEZ, TED
[pen.] L. Lolo; [b.] July 4, 1968, Vaja Cal., Mexico; [p.] Jesus and Josefina Lopez; [ed.] Hartnell College; [occ.] Correctional Officer for the State of California S.V.S.P.; [memb.] C.C.P.O.A; [pers.] We as a society must learn to be spiritual again.; [a.] Salinas, CA

LOUDIN, TRAVIS LEE
[b.] November 16, 1985, Alliance, OH; [p.] Melinda Loudin; [ed.] Sunset Park Elem.; [occ.] Student; [hon.] 3 yrs. Honor Roll; [pers.] I am academically gifted and a good student in school.; [a.] Wilmington, NC

LOWE, ELLA
[pen.] Alyce; [b.] March 30, 1966, Itta Bena, MS; [p.] Mary Lowe and Roosevelt Lowe (Deceased); [ed.] c/o 1985-Hitchcock High School, c/o 1994-College of The Mainland; [occ.] Maintenance - Elementary School Teacher; [hon.] 3 College Poetry Winners 2 Honorable Mentioned Houston Poetry Society Club 1996 Semi-Finalist The National Library of Poetry; [oth. writ.] I have written two Poetry Book, but they both are unpublished, I am working on my third book now.; [pers.] I would like to thank God for my talent. I would not have gotten this for without my best friend bill spillar, who always believed in me and supported my work and Terry Holmberg Who taught me how to write with my heart and soul.; [a.] La Marque, TX

LOWE, MICHELLE MARIE
[b.] June 11, 1969, Brooklyn, NY; [p.] Edward and Gloria Lowe; [ed.] New Utrecht High School; [occ.] New York City Police Officer; [pers.] All of my writing is for my very own muse. You know who you are and I love you.; [a.] Brooklyn, NY

LUCAS, GRACIE
[pen.] Gracie Lucas; [b.] February 17, 1942, Nashville, TN; [p.] Jesse and Mildred Gunn; [ed.] High School, Speech classes, public speaking; [occ.] Hospital Jacks General ER Family Representative; [hon.] Horse show Award Hospital Quality Plus award, Hospital Guest awards, Honor of having my poem "Gentry's Bluff" published in book Through the Looking Glass; [oth. writ.] Several other poems "unpublished"; [pers.] I credit my love for poetry writing to my love for God and His creations. Also for my fellow man.; [a.] Jackson, TN

LUCAS, VALERIE RUTH
[pen.] Valerie R. Prytula; [b.] October 15, 1953, Detroit; [p.] Carl Prytula, Agnes L. Prytula; [m.] Norris Edward Lucas, October 15, 1993; [ch.] Meredith Rose, Carl Alexander; [ed.] Lake Shores High School 1973, Macomb Community College 1990, A.S. in Graphic Design; [occ.] Freelance Artist; [pers.] We artists are never poor or empty, because we have so much inside, our drive to create is the overflow.; [a.] Mount Clemens, MI

LUDEMAN, RITA MARIE
[pen.] Rita Wright; [b.] June 18, 1957, Mount Clemens, MI; [p.] Alois Ludeman, Rita Ludeman; [ed.] St. Lawrence, Utica High, Oakland Community College; [occ.] Property Manager, University Club Apartments, Detroit, MI; [pers.] Inspiration came to me after the untimely demise of my beloved fiance. A kind and loving man which I will hold in my heart and cherish his memory forever. He has greatly influenced and enriched my life.; [a.] Northville, MI

LUDWIKOWSKI, WILLIAM J.
[pen.] Mr. L.; [b.] June 27, 1932, Exeter Township, PA; [p.] John and Estella (nee Zajdawicz) Ludwikowski; [ch.] William J. Ludwikowski II (Deceased); [ed.] HS, numerous Military Schools, AA (SAC), BS (Ed), (SWTSU); [occ.] Military, Business, Education (Retired); [memb.] NCOA, SWISU Alumni, Princeton Alumni Assn., (Honorary), CCHS Alumni Assn., TX Historical Society (DRT), Salesman Missions, Oblate Missions, AAU, Natl. SS House Sr.: Statue of Liberty Foundation, Sacred Heart League, PTA, Hypnosis Society of America; [hon.] Numerous Military Awards and Decorations, Who's Who in American Teachers, DRT-History Teacher of Texas, SSAISD Teacher and Citizen's Award, Nom. TX Swim Hall of Fame, Presidential Teachers Award Nom., TX AAU Swim Coach of Year, Numerous Teacher Awards, TX Special Olympics Coach Award, Cum Laude Graduate, Honorary Life Member PTA; [oth. writ.] Education Articles - Philosophical Short Saying (School and State); [pers.] I write to share with others to help find their true self and a high regard to live life with feeling. My influence comes from mental, physical, and spiritual happenings throughout my years, especially from knowing my son, Bill, and his zest to do his best in life with faith unwavering.; [a.] San Antonio, TX

LUPA, BIANA
[b.] July 18, 1984, Odessa, Ukraine; [p.] Marina Lupa, Grigory Lupa; [ed.] Intermediate School; [hon.] Elementary School Scholarship Award, Honor Roll Student Award; [oth. writ.] Several other poems; [pers.] Never give up hope even if others do. Believe in yourself it's all for you; [a.] Brooklyn, NY

LUTON-SEGREST, CHERYL
[pen.] Cheri Segrest; [b.] November 5, 1958, Baltimore, MD; [p.] Gilbert G. and Norma J. Luton; [m.] Victor W. Segrest, July 28, 1979; [ch.] Victor Winston, Jason Luton, Scott Gilbert; [ed.] West Granada Hills High, L.A. Valley College; [occ.] Homemaker, Amateur Writer, Poet; [pers.] Writing has always been a comfort to the soul. This is my first publication. Poetry is the romance of the soul.; [a.] Palmdale, CA

LUTZ, RACHELLE T.
[b.] April 5, 1985, Miami, FL; [p.] Gayle Lutz, George Lutz; [ed.] Am currently a Student of Calais, ME Educational System; [memb.] Girl Scouts of America; [hon.] Numerous Girl Scout Badges; [a.] Calais, ME

LUZIER, ANN MARGARET
[b.] December 7, 1981, Clearfield, PA; [p.] Arthur (Buck) and Mary (Ann) Luzier; [ed.] Philipsburg Osceola High School; [occ.] Student; [pers.] My Dad always has been and always will be my greatest inspiration.; [a.] West Decatur, PA

LYNN, RICHARD ALAN
[b.] December 16, 1972, Lewistown, PA; [p.] Gary Lynn and Karlene Partchey; [ed.] I've always looked at what this world has to offer and teach us as meaningless. To find wisdom one must search God's word recurrently and not lose sight of past experiences.; [occ.] PA Army National Guard; [memb.] I'm a member of Calvary Bible Church and Trinity United Methodist Church where I sometimes speak on Thursday Nights; [hon.] 5 of my other poems are being published by Sparrowgrass poetry forum in this years edition of poetic voices of America.; [oth. writ.] I've written a few devotionals and have recently considered writing a years worth and having them published. I've written letters to several churches last year.; [pers.] All the honor this servant may obtain, belongs to the holy one and Jesus is His name. Christ is the reason for everything I do in this life because He's the one who promises eternal life.; [a.] Lewistown, PA

LYON, CARA
[b.] April 17, 1980, Auburn, CA; [ed.] Currently Completing High School (11th grade); [occ.] Student; [oth. writ.] Just my personal collection of my own poems.; [a.] Newcastle, CA

MACMASTER, DAVID
[b.] March 18, 1976, Townsend, MA; [p.] Robert and Marcia MacMaster; [ed.] North Middlesex Regional High School, Fitchburg State College; [occ.] Student; [memb.] American Marketing Assoc.; [pers.] I try to reflect the simple elements of the world. I have been greatly influenced by authors like James Joyce.; [a.] Townsend, MA

MAGEE, KENYA MCFARLAND
[b.] Austin, TX; [m.] Robert Magee Jr., June, 1972; [ch.] Christine Magee, Robby Magee; [ed.] B.S. Elem Ed. from Univ. of Houston, Alvin High School; [occ.] Church Secretary Light Christian Center, Alvin, TX; [a.] Alvin, TX

MAIR, BARBARA Y.
[b.] January 29, 1954, Jamaica, WI; [p.] Albert Mair, Hyacinth Cunningham; [ed.] Excelsior High, Eugene Bible College, Oral Roberts University; [occ.] Counselor; [memb.] Christian Association for Psychological Studies, American Association for Marriage and Family Therapy; [hon.] Honors Oral Roberts Univ. National Dean's Lost. Listed in 18th Edition of Who's Who of American Women. Graduate Studies Award for Excellence Dean's List Eugene Bible College; [pers.] I consider life to be a journey and therefore strive to learn and grow daily on that journey.; [a.] New York, NY

MALIK, INSIA
[b.] February 9, 1988, New York, NY; [occ.] Student; [a.] Englewood Cliffs, NJ

MANIS JR., JAMES ELLIS
[b.] October 7, 1950, Knoxville, TN; [p.] James E. Manis, Nancy Jones; [m.] Darlene Marie Manis, December 25, 1992; [ch.] Tiffany, Destany, James, Joseph; [ed.] Completed 12th grade Murray Wright High, Detroit MI 1969; [occ.] Machine Technician, Powertrain Div. of General Motors; [memb.] United Auto Workers Local 163; [oth. writ.] Published in Edge of Twilight, poem "Rear View Mirror."; [pers.] How high is up, how low is down? On whose brown should we place a crown?; [a.] Detroit, MI

MANN, CHARLES CHRISTOPHER
[b.] November 8, 1975, Mexico City; [p.] Charles and Andrea Mann; [ed.] Undergraduate, California State U. at Northridge CA, majoring in Political Science, minoring in English and Japanese; [occ.] Pre-Law program, currently Tutor in the Japanese Dept.; [memb.] International Club - officer, ESOL Program St. UCLA - preparing to teach English in Japan; [hon.] Dean's List, selected by Foothill College as U.S. representative to Co-op Tokyo Corporation, summer of 1996.; [oth. writ.] Short stories, poems, playlets - unpublished.; [pers.] Particularly fond of Shakespeare.; [a.] West Hills, CA

MANSFIELD, KATHY WILLIAMS
[b.] April 15, 1959, North Carolina; [p.] Mary and Mack Williams; [ch.] Anthony and Kendra Mansfield; [ed.] High School graduate 2 yrs. Nursing, 2 yrs. Psychology; [occ.] Community Focus Health Nurse and House Manager for New Partners Inc.; [memb.] First Assembly Church of God and Bible Club, YMCA American Heart Association, MADD Mothers Against Drunk Drivers, Institute of Children's Literature; [hon.] Voted most talented in College I won three short story writing contest. DECA Treasure in High School, school store manager; [oth. writ.] I have written several more poems 7 country songs 8 gospel songs and several children's songs and am working on a children's book. I have won several writing short story contest.; [pers.] I strive to make a difference in the lives of others, by spreading Peace, Love and Kindness, and giving all glory to my Heavenly Father.; [a.] Reidsville, NC

MANSURI, MAHEVISH A.
[pen.] Rossy; [b.] February 14, 1980, India; [p.] Abdulkabar (father), Badrunisha (mother); [ed.] 11th grade at South Brunswick MS; [occ.] Student; [memb.] GRASP, Reality Theater; [oth. writ.] In my diary, which I write at night before going to bed.; [pers.] When people are in love, they don't think of the future or they don't care about anything. But when his or her heart breaks, then they say you came into my life like the flowers blooming and you were gone like the wind.; [a.] Dayton, NJ

MARBEN, BEVERLY
[pen.] Beverly Marben; [b.] July 27, 1946, Minneapolis, MN; [p.] Fred Koch, Theresa Koch; [m.] Ronald Marben, June 29, 1968; [ch.] Brenda Bruestle, Sandra Ledford; [occ.] Homemaker; [pers.] Poetry is my greatest blessing and responsibility, for I can analyze a thought or resolve a question through the discipline of poetry and help others with the same thoughts and questions who cannot.; [a.] Farmington, MN

MARCHION JR., FRANK J.
[b.] April 15, 1948, Hartford, CT; [m.] Angie, November 26, 1971; [ch.] Three: Andrea, Frank III, Amy; [ed.] South Catholic High, Hartford Ct, Hartford Community College; [occ.] Automobile Sales Manager; [memb.] Greater Hartford Automobile Dealer Association, St. Patrick Church, Collinsville, Ct.; [hon.] Ford Professional Sales Manager Award 1991, Served U.S. Navy 1969-1971, Vietnam Service Medal, Good Conduct Medal; [oth. writ.] "The Lake," published in, "Songs of Youth," while in High School; [pers.] The inspiration for my writing comes from life experiences and observations, and my love of my creator and love of family.; [a.] Collinsville, CT

MARCIN, KATHLEEN M.
[b.] August 28, 1959, Winchester, MA; [p.] Mary T. McGough, William Marcin; [ch.] Kathleen Nora; [ed.] Chelmsford Schools, Northern Essex CC; [occ.] Provider Specialist, Lahey Hitchcock Clinic; [oth. writ.] Currently working on compilation of poetry and state play.; [pers.] I believe my mother was right, "There are no insurmountable obstacles."; [a.] Methuen, MA

MARES, KASSANDRA
[pen.] Kassy; [b.] September 11, 1982, Temple, TX; [p.] Roger and Sheila Meyers; [ed.] Moody High School; [occ.] Student (Freshmen); [pers.] I like writing poetry because it helps me with my feelings.; [a.] Moody, TX

MARINE, DENISE K.
[b.] October 8, 1973, Milwaukee, WI; [p.] Robert and Sandra Marine; [ed.] A.A. in Accounting, currently working on a B.A. in Writing and English; [occ.] Circulation Assistant in my College's Library; [oth. writ.] Four poems published in various anthologies, including A New Found Light, Lonely Hearts Meet, The Raging Wind and Grandma's Peace Lily.; [pers.] My writing is my power of expression. The words I speak are passive and weak. The words I write are vivid and dramatic. Now, please hear what I am not saying.; [a.] Milwaukee, WI

MARK, ELIZA
[b.] March 28, 1976, Bethel, AK; [p.] Carl Mark; [ed.] High School, Nightmute High School; [occ.] Baby sitting; [hon.] N.Y.O.; [oth. writ.] Other poems.; [pers.] I was so depressed when I wrote, "If I Have Died." After being with my friends. They got me so depressed and I made that poem.; [a.] Bethel, AK

MARKEN, MARISE
[b.] March 6, 1947, Colombo, Ceylon; [p.] Trevor and Eileen Bilsborough; [m.] Bennie Edwin Marken, August 28, 1976; [ed.] Ladies College, Colombo, St. Bridget's Convent, Colombo (Arts Major, Graduate), Amarasekera School of Art (12 yrs); [occ.] I "Temp" as a secretary/Data entry opr/Word processor; [hon.] At 16 years old, I won an art competition (first prize) and had two of my pen and ink drawings displayed in Colombo Art Gallery for one year.; [oth. writ.] I have written several stories for children, articles, poems and a young adult book titled, "The Office Cat," but none are published as yet!; [pers.] "Simple Pleasures," are hearts treasures that steady us through the storms of life. True happiness lies within us and cannot be bought!; [a.] Ramona, CA

MARKO, TAMMY L.
[pen.] Peace Maker; [b.] October 31, 1962, Passaic, NJ; [p.] Margaret I. Marko and Paul Marko; [ed.] I learned

tremendously from my parents and sisters, but more so from myself, life is education. The world is my school; [occ.] Crafts women; [pers.] There is a light, a spirit in each of us. All of us want to live in peace - stop waiting for someone else to start it. Begin the kindness, peace, love and helpfulness today. Whatever it is, you won't know unless you try!; [a.] Edison, NJ

MAROOFI, MUSA
[b.] May 5, 1943, Kabul, Afghanis; [p.] Mohamad Osman Pashtun, Tahira; [m.] Fazila R. Maroofi, July 3, 1971; [ch.] Miss Romance N. Maroofi; [ed.] B.A. (Law and Pol. Sc.) Kabul University, D.S.S. (Pol. Sc.) Oxford University, G.B., M.A. (Int. Relations) Queens College, N.Y., M.L.C. (Law) G.W.U. Washington, D.C.; [occ.] President of Law and Citizenship, Inc., Director of Middle Easters Studies Taf.; [hon.] Awards of cash at high school, Columbo Plan Scholarship to Oxford UN., Fulbright Scholarship, Legal Training Scholarship, One year honorary membership of American Political Science Association; [oth. writ.] History of Political thought, translation from French K.U. 67 Administrative Law K.U. 68 Afghan Politics in the process of modernization Political quarterly Queens College 1972 Hundreds of academic essays, short stories for radio and T.V. in English, Persian and Pashtu.; [pers.] God is both beautiful and perfect. He created beauty in order to help mankind achieve perfection. Appreciating beauty is a process on the way to achieving perfection. Peace is one of the elements that create beauty. Any commission of violence upsets the rules of beauty as well as perfection. To abide by the rules of beauty is to worship its creator.; [a.] Vienna, VA

MARRERO JR., LOUIS A.
[b.] July 29, 1956, Chicago, IL; [p.] Jorge Gonzalez, Maria V. Gonzalez; [ch.] Louis Marrero III, Desiree N. Smith; [ed.] St. Mary's Cathedral, Jr. High #4 (Philippines), Air Force Community College; [occ.] Administrative Specialist and Portrait Artist; [memb.] American Veterans Association, Big Brothers Association; [hon.] Citizens award in Great Falls, MT. Air Force Commendation Medal and other military awards; [oth. writ.] "Timid Night," and several other unpublished poetry along with poetry published in a NJ Journal; [pers.] The vastness and glory of the miracle we live on, must be cherished and humanity has been given permission to the challenges of the soundrous earth. Let's protect her...; [a.] Trenton, NJ

MARSH, PAUL
[b.] November 9, 1964, Newton, MA; [p.] Phillip Marsh, Lucille Marsh; [m.] Nancy Roth, July 28, 1996; [ed.] Bentley College (B.S.), Boston College (MBA); [occ.] Systems Analyst, Fresenius Medical Care, Lexington, MA; [memb.] The Progressive Chavurah, The Milton Players; [oth. writ.] Several pieces published in various Judaic publications.; [pers.] My writing style incorporates my Jewish spirituality into impressions of people and events that are close to me.; [a.] Waltham, MA

MARSHALL, VIRGINIA MOORE
[b.] May 21, 1923, Woodbury, KY; [p.] Eugene Moore, Lucy Moore; [m.] Joe Marshall, April 17, 1960; [ch.] Joseph Timothy, Virginia Dawnelle; [ed.] BA, WKU, Bowling Green, KY, MA Columbia Univ., N.Y. City; [occ.] Retired Teacher, Fort Knox High, Art Hist and Bowling Green, KY Art Educ. English current, writing and watercolor painting, Summer classes art for children, poetry - art print; [memb.] KY Art Educ. Assoc., American Heart Assoc., Feed The Children, Eastwood Baptist Church Leader of G.A.S., Kentucky Colonel; [hon.] Alpha Delta Kappa, Dean's List (cum laude), Archival Resources in KY, Reflections of the Past, Publication mate-

rial for Mental Health, Optimist Club for our Newspaper Articles of Community Projects - Health, Elder Hostel, Heart, Education; [oth. writ.] Arts and crafts lessons in weekly news, poetry publication this fall of my many poems, short story in "Ladies Home Found"; [pers.] Alone there is often little we can do together. There is little at which we need fail. These are many roads to peace, but only one direction. Keep faith.; [a.] Bowling Green, KY

MARTIN, AMANDA MARIE
[b.] October 14, 1981, Bridgeport, CO; [p.] Angelina Alix and Charles Martin; [ed.] Sophomore in High School - Fashion Technology Bpt. Conn.; [occ.] Student; [memb.] Editorial Staff for the School year book.; [hon.] Young Authors Award a variety of in School Awards. A Special Poetry Award was designed just for me.; [oth. writ.] "Untitled" in River Edge, in '95 - published. A collection of writings by Amanda Martin - published by Young Authors - Assoc.; [pers.] I write for the enjoyment of others.; [a.] Bridgeport, CT

MARTIN, DANIEL
[b.] July 21, 1985, Livingston, NJ; [p.] Michael and Edith Martin; [ed.] 6th Grade - Roosevelt Middle School, West Orange, NJ; [occ.] Student; [memb.] YABA - Young American Bowling Alliance; [hon.] Consistent Honor Roll, Student of the Month: Roosevelt Middle School, President's Award for Educational Excellence, 1st place - NJ Math League for 5th G$raders, Emmett Laduke Leadership Award, Student Congress President: Pleasantdale Elementary School; [pers.] "The two hardest things to handle in life are failure and success" - Unknown.; [a.] West Orange, NJ

MARTINDALE, TRACY
[pen.] Tracy Martindale; [b.] October 9, 1963, San Diego, CA; [p.] William and Zella Glynn; [m.] Bruce Martindale, November 13, 1989; [ch.] Amber; [ed.] 12 yrs.; [occ.] Medical Records Coordinator; [memb.] Moose Lodge of America; [oth. writ.] Several poems not published at this time.; [pers.] I like to touch and stir the emotions of other people through my poetry.; [a.] Middleburg, FL

MARTINEZ, BOB G.
[b.] June 1949, New Mexico; [p.] Mrs. Mary Jane Martinez; [m.] Annette Elizabeth, February 10, 1973; [ch.] Lita (20 years) in college; [ed.] High School in Denver from 1964 to 1968; [occ.] Security Guard at the Denver Merchandise Mart; [memb.] Distinguished Member of NLP-ISP, Columbine Poets of Colorado, and Mile High Poetry Society; [hon.] Many Editor's Choice Awards (NCP-ISP); [oth. writ.] My Time to Rhyme, My Journey in Life from 1949 to 1994 (Unbroken Poem) 302 pages long... and side tracks, a compilation of 45 of my poems; [pers.] Reading poetry, you observe one's heart where true ministry delights to impart.; [a.] Denver, CO

MARTINEZ, CYNTHIA A.
[pen.] Cindy; [b.] January 28, 1954, Marrinette, WI; [p.] Gloria Sievert and Curtis Sievert; [m.] Juan A. Martinez, October 21, 1976; [ch.] Jessica Tito Celia Martinez; [ed.] I went all the way through school, I graduated from 12th grade; [occ.] Instructional Aide, I go to school at College of the Desert Palm Desert CA; [hon.] I've had some printed in magazines and newspapers before when I was in High School in Green Bay Wis.; [oth. writ.] Yes I have a lot of writings that I have done, I've written. I wrote one once before when I was 12 years old and it was called, "Lonely Girl."; [pers.] I am deeply pleased with my writing. I love to write, I have always I wanted to write, since I was 12 years old.; [a.] Desert Hot Spring, CA

MASHBURN, DONALD RAY
[b.] February 11, 1935, Oklahoma City, OK; [p.] Mr. and Mrs. E. B. Mashburn; [ch.] Anita Renee, Leann Michele; [ed.] Capitol Hill Sr. High; [occ.] Service Tech.; [memb.] VFW; [pers.] I strive to write the best and most interesting poems to read.; [a.] Oklahoma City, OK

MASSEY, MICHELLE MONIQUE
[pen.] M3; [b.] June 16, 1979, Louisiana; [p.] Carmen Massey; [ed.] Plan to attend Holy Cross College, Notre Dame in the fall of 1997 as an entering freshman; [hon.] National Honor Society, All-American Scholar, Who's Who Among American H.S. Students, first girl in the state of LA to play on a high school boy's football team (in the first 100 in the U.S. of A.); [oth. writ.] Several poems published in school magazines, wrote the graduating class of '97' poem for our school year book published in "Reflections," and "Treasured Poems of America," both in 1997.; [pers.] "The best poems come from a sudden burst of feeling, they never take too long to write, and there are usually no scratch-outs" M3.; [a.] West Monroe, LA

MAYO, DANIEL
[b.] December 3, 1975, Cold Spring, NY; [p.] Richard Mayo, Marilyn Mayo; [ed.] James I. O'Neill H.S., University of Hartford; [memb.] Theta Chi Fraternity; [oth. writ.] An extensive catalogue of songs that has yet to be published; [pers.] My writing is greatly influenced by what I feel inside. Each line is a reflection of my heart, mind and soul.; [a.] Garrison, NY

MCCAIN, QUEENIE E.
[b.] April 15, 1949, Roxboro, NC; [p.] Mr. and Mrs. Dock Roberts; [m.] James Lantry McCain, March 1, 1969; [ch.] Tony McCain, Tammy and Tara; [ed.] Elem., High School and 2 yr. of College Ass. degree; [occ.] None I'm on lay off; [memb.] None ex. Time books Income Opp. Books; [hon.] I made Dean's List while in college I was pres. of Sgr. at College; [oth. writ.] Only in my spare time I write to ease my mind, and to see what if part of my life that I could have done.; [pers.] Words to the wise. Enhance, extend, expand your minds, its for a life time. Thank you for your time that you invested in my poem, this was and is my great fortitude that I can new.; [a.] Danville, VA

MCCANN, JOSHUA AKRUN
[b.] May 1, 1978, Chicago, IL; [p.] Carolyn Adams and Minnie McCann, Leroy McCann (Grandparents); [ed.] I attended First Lutheran in Blue Island, IL, Later, I attended De La Salle High School. Now I am currently enrolled student at Northern Illinois Univ. in DeKalb, IL; [occ.] I am currently in the Northern Illinois University Black Choir; [memb.] National Honors Society, Lambda Sigma Sophomore Honors Society; [oth. writ.] I currently have two unpublished poetry books called "Poetic Harmonies" and "Black Ambitions". I am also working on two novels Vengeance Has No Sorrow and I Was Born Too Fat.; [pers.] The day that Minnie dropped her panties on State Street.; [a.] Chicago, IL

MCCLUNE, KRISTIN ELIZABETH
[b.] January 2, 1985, Long Beach, CA; [p.] Michael M. and Elizabeth A. McClune; [occ.] Student in Elementary School (Westwood Basics Plus in Irvine, CA); [memb.] United States Tennis Association (1995-Present); [hon.] Irvine Unified School District Science Fair Award (1995 and 1997), Honor Roll (1990-Present); [pers.] I strive to do my best at all times, and I wish for peace and happiness for all mankind.; [a.] Irvine, CA

MCCLUSKEY, STEPHEN
[b.] June 30, 1966, Manhattan, NY; [p.] Francis

McCluskey, Barbara McCluskey; [m.] Eileen McCluskey, December 13, 1987; [ch.] Sean Edwards, Shannon Marie; [ed.] Holy Trinity H.S. Nassau Comm College, Hofstra University Nyack College; [occ.] Insurance Broker Sales; [oth. writ.] Songwriting and Collaboration credit, Independent label musical recordings.; [pers.] The poem included in this volume is dedicated to the memory of Barbara McCluskey, whose life and example serves as a constant inspiration.; [a.] Wantagh, NY

MCCOLLEY, PAULINE K.
[b.] September 12, 1952, Prairie City, IA; [p.] Wilbur and Luella Van Ryswyk; [m.] Mark S. McColley, June 10, 1995; [ch.] Ryan Paul Carrington, Rochelle Diane Carrington; [ed.] Prairie City High School; [occ.] Corporate Secretary, Blue Cross Blue Shield of Iowa, Des Moines, IA; [memb.] Urban Heights Evangelical Covenant Church, Urbandale, IA; [hon.] 176th fastest typist in the world (122 net wpm), international competition 1991; [oth. writ.] I have written hundreds of pieces. This is the first time I have entered my work in competition and the first time I've submitted my work for possible publication.; [pers.] My poems are an outpouring of my soul's search for God.; [a.] Urbandale, IA

MCCONNELL, JOHN
[b.] March 22, 1915, Davis City, IA; [p.] Evangelist J. S. and Hattie McConnell; [m.] Anna Marie Zacharias McConnell, December 25, 1967; [ch.] Connie, Cary, Christa; [ed.] One year of High School, One Semester Pepperdine Univ., Employment in Library when I was 15 made me an avid reader; [occ.] Founder, the Earth Day Web Site (WWW. Earth site org.) to promote my ideas of earth day - earth trustees; [memb.] St. Johns Lutheran Church, Chairman Emeritus, Earth Society Foundation, (NGO United Nations); [hon.] Chosen to Inaugurate and ring the new peace bell at UN center in Vienn March 20, 1996, Earth Genius Award, World Genius Convention, Awards from Rotary, Lions, UN Society of Writers; [oth. writ.] 1970 earth day proclamation 34 signatures added in support included UN S/G U Thant, Margaret Mead, Buzz Aldrin, Arafat, Y. Menuhin, 1969 Declaration of Planetary Rights, 1985 77 Theses On The Care Of Earth, 1980 Earth Charter, 1990 Earth Magna Charta.; [pers.] Global commitment by individuals and institutions to think and act as responsible trustees of Earth is the key to earth rejuvenation. The more Earth trustees, the more people can trust each other, and the more we can trust the future.", [a.] Ridgewood, NY

MCFARLIN, SUSAN
[b.] July 25, 1956, Watertown, SD; [p.] William, Mildred Kones; [m.] Glen McFarlin, February 17, 1995; [ch.] Christina, David, Richard; [ed.] Watertown Senior High School, one Sem. at Mt. Marty College; [occ.] House wife; [hon.] Honorable Mention in Ducks Unlimited Stamp Contest when I was a teenager; [pers.] I strive to put into words, my feeling and passion for life, nature existing in harmony as one.; [a.] Gillette, WY

MCKEEVER, BRANT D.
[b.] April 25, 1934, Shamokin, PA; [p.] Richard McKeever, Mildred McKeever; [m.] Ethelda Owens McKeever, June 1, 1956; [ch.] Candy, Janice, Melody, Penny; [ed.] Shamokin High School USMC - Memphis NAS Aircraft Engine School; [occ.] Retired from E. I. duPont and Co. 37 years chemical plant maintenance; [memb.] 1st Baptist Church, Gold Wing Road Riders Association, Christian Motorcyclist Association, Good Sam Camping Club; [hon.] Sgt. in USMC; [oth. writ.] Poems for Motorcycle newsletters re safety, trips, rallies and funny happenings. About and for our camping

group, related to spiritual things for Sunday lessons, about family, my past history, our children growing up (love notes to my wife) - valentines, birthdays, etc.; [pers.] My writings cover a wide and vast variety of subjects, humor, serious, myself, friends, situations, trips, safety, relatives, feelings, etc. Have been asked by others to write poems to fit some of their situations.; [a.] Millington, TN

MCLAIN, FLOYD M.
[b.] November 12, 1932, Haines City, FL; [p.] Riley and Gertrude (Elkins) McLain; [m.] Miyoko, 1953; [ch.] Kathleen, John, Gwendolyn, Quila; [ed.] US Navy Enlisted Ref.; [occ.] Ret.; [memb.] International Society of Poets; [hon.] National Library of Poetry; [oth. writ.] "Ode to Leviathan," poem.; [pers.] My life is like the flower, blooming in the yard, for more I give no regard. "For now we see through a glass, darkly,..."; [a.] Tampa, FL

MCLAUGHLIN, CLARA FLOWERS
[pen.] Clara Flowers McLaughlin; [b.] February 10, 1940, Wollaston, MA; [p.] Pansy and Mark Flowers; [m.] Chaplain Terry McLaughlin, August 25, 1967; [ch.] Adopted: Todd and Nicole; [ed.] Masters in Gifted Education, K-12, B.S. in Elem Ed., 29 yrs. of Teaching; [occ.] Teacher: 8th grade US Hist.; [memb.] NEA, SCEA, Shandon Baptist Church, Hopkins Middle School Faculty; [hon.] To be a minister's wife for 24 years. To be a chaplain's wife for 9 years. To mother 2 wonderful adopted children. To teach/influence 2,000 young lives over the 29 years in education.; [oth. writ.] Just a few articles in local newspapers and 1,000's of notes to parents over the years. I've written essays/poems for friends, birthdays and anniversaries.; [pers.] I have learned to write about my feelings and emotions, freely. By sharing myself with words, I have opened my world to others. Others, then, have brought harmony to my life. Harmony brings peace.; [a.] Columbia, SC

MCLAURIN, TERESA
[b.] November 19, 1984, New York, NY; [p.] James and Lydia McLaurin; [ed.] Richard L. Rice Elementary, Marlton Middle (Junior High); [hon.] Art displayed at Perkins Institute of Art. Poem was displayed at Borders Book Store. Made the Honor Roll 2 semesters in a row. Award for excellence in art.; [pers.] Poetry has always been something I was just born with like my gift of art. I always try my best at everything and never give up.; [a.] Marlton, NJ

MCMAHON, MEGHAN
[b.] June 10, 1982, Lake Forest, IL; [p.] Edward McMahon and Christine McMahon; [ed.] Freshman at Joel Barlow High School; [occ.] Student (Freshman in High School); [hon.] National Junior Honor Society and High Honor Roll; [pers.] It is a great accomplishment to be able to put true feeling onto paper. Having to constantly battle my chronic illness, Cystic Fibrosis, I feel blessed that I am one of those who feels they can express emotions to others that way and who deeply enjoys it. Emotions are the keys to our souls and I am honored to share them with others.; [a.] Easton, CT

MCMILLAN, LEE
[pen.] Lee McMillan; [b.] July 28, 1919, Oregon; [p.] Leland and Stanford Hanford - Ethel Hanford; [m.] W. M. McMillan, November 2, 1991; [ch.] 2 of my own plus 5 step children; [ed.] B of A, public health, Microbiology; [occ.] Retired; [memb.] Retired from my writers club, belong to History club of Los Gatos, Calif, and also 3 square dancing clubs.; [oth. writ.] Years ago some children's stories; [pers.] Every morning dawns with new

hopes and aspirations... a chance to start again. Every evening lends its peace and inspirations. Sunset blesses us with thoughts of what has been. And we sleep in loving peacefulness.; [a.] Saratoga, CA

MCNABB, JENNYKATE
[pen.] JennyKate; [b.] September 12, 1986, Rhode Island; [p.] Jan Roberge McNabb; [ed.] 5th grade (completing in June '97) Ann Antolini School, New Hartford, CT. (public Sch.); [occ.] Student (and avid reader of Braille!); [memb.] Warner Theatre Center for the Arts and the JMS Dance Center (4 yr. veteran actress in an original musical play, "Through a Child's Eyes," by Val Vitalo); [hon.] Winner of the Coalition for Peace and Justice, "Piece of Peace" contest (2/97), "Character Counts," presenter, Hartford, CT. '96 rally, guest presenter on Children's Rights with Judge Charles Gill at various rallies and public speaking engagements throughout CT.; [oth. writ.] "Children of Peace," (award winner 2/97), "The Sound of Love," (unpub.), "Rain," and numerous others yet unpublished. "Sugar Plum," pub '92 Who's Who of Animals (Edited by Breen), published at age 5. Numerous newspaper publications of poetry, "All About Me," has been published in the American Pediatric Association newsletter, the international very special arts publication, a newsletter of character courts and promotion which has recently reproduced old masters paintings tactically for the blind!; [pers.] "As a blind child, I don't see things as others do. I don't see their color, their clothing, etc. I have greater vision because I see them for who they are... inside."; [a.] New Hartford, CT

MCNAMARA, DAWN
[b.] February 16, 1978; [ed.] Point Pleasant Beach High School, Monmouth University; [occ.] College Student Majoring in Theater Production; [oth. writ.] This is my first publication. I have written many poems, for my own personal reasons.; [a.] Point Pleasant Beach, NJ

MCPHILLIPS, SHAUN
[b.] October 15, 1924, Philadelphia; [p.] Violet and Joseph McPhillips; [ed.] Presently in my 3rd year of college at Phila Community College. I am a political Science Major; [occ.] Sales Representative for Nabisco Corporation; [memb.] Member of Tau Kappa Epsilon International Fraternity; [a.] Philadelphia, PA

MCVICKER, MILDRED E.
[b.] November 6, 1937; [ed.] Spencer High School, Elyria Business College, Norwalk Bible Institution; [occ.] Retired Children's Librarian; [oth. writ.] First one of my poems ever submitted to be published.; [a.] Murfreesboro, TN

MEAD, DIXIE LAWSON
[pen.] Dixie Lawson-Mead; [b.] August 11, 1939, Logan, OH; [p.] Florence and Clarence Lawson; [m.] William H. Mead, March 24, 1961; [ch.] Three; [ed.] High School Grad., and have been studying for over a decade with a retired professor in humanities; [occ.] Professional dog groomer; [hon.] Only bowling trophies; [oth. writ.] Poetry and travel journals which I have not tried to publish yet; [pers.] To recognize and appreciate the beauty of all creation is to acknowledge the wonder and significance of life.; [a.] San Jose, CA

MEADE, VIVIAN
[b.] May 29, 1925, Renville, MN; [m.] Harry Bonnema (Deceased), Jeff Meade; [ch.] (Bonnema) Kenneth Wayne, Kelvin Kerry, Doreen Kaye and Lynnette Marie; [occ.] Founder and Sec/Treas. of H.I.S. Prison Outreach (an organization able to issue receipts for tax exempt donations); [oth. writ.] Several children's Sunday school

stories, games, puzzles, and poems.; [pers.] I believe if inmates accept Christ while in prison they will remain while in Society when released as productive law abiding citizens.; [a.] Raymond, MN

MEADOWS, TERESA
[b.] April 26, 1962, Pauls Valley, OK; [p.] James and Beulah Whitefield; [m.] Quincy Meadows, June 30, 1988; [ch.] Amber; [ed.] Grad. High School, Mid-Am Vo-Tech; [occ.] Housewife, mother; [hon.] 10 yrs. Ser. for State, Nat. Library of Poetry, Int. Soc. of Poets; [oth. writ.] God's Gift to Women, My Father, My Mother, My Nephew and num. others; [pers.] This poem was written for a family member who will always very dear to me. I would do everything in my power to always help him and be there for him.; [a.] Pauls Valley, OK

MEHTA, JELAM
[b.] December 8, 1971, Orange, NJ; [p.] Uday and Ellen Mehta; [ed.] Bloomfield College, NJ, presently a student, major Sociology; [occ.] Student; [memb.] Alpha Phi Sorority; [hon.] Dean's List; [oth. writ.] I've written other poems but they have not been published yet.; [pers.] To live a good life is to live one with love and without wanting to hurt others.; [a.] Newton, NJ

MEINK, ANGELA M.
[b.] April 1, 1983, Illinois; [p.] Dane and Tine Meink; [ed.] Highland Schools, Highland Junior High; [memb.] Member of Highland Bullpops, Pom Pom Dance Team; [hon.] Maintain 4.33 grade point average and increasing it steadily.; [oth. writ.] Poetry - True Love, Friendships Come and Friendships Go, First Love, and many others. I've written some stories, and got many compliments on the one about my dog, Budweiser's, death.; [pers.] I'm 13 years old, and writing poetry is a way for me to express my thoughts and feelings. I write my best work when something big happens, good or bad.; [a.] Alhambra, IL

MELLO, MARY JANE
[b.] July 22, 1959, Garden City, MI; [p.] Henry Carmack, Mildred Carmack; [m.] Thomas Mello, May 5, 1984; [ch.] Thomas Colt, Alan Emerson; [ed.] East Detroit High School, Pontiac Business Institute; [occ.] Home maker; [pers.] We all have much to learn. If we take the time to listen to each other, we can put the puzzle of life together, and with God's love we'll laminate it.; [a.] Warren, MI

MERO, JAMES H.
[pen.] James H. Mero; [b.] August 14, 1918, Escanaba, MI; [p.] Joseph and Myrtle (Patterson) Mero; [m.] Leona (Harris) Mero, January 29, 1943; [ch.] Debra Sue; [ed.] Escanaba High School, Cloverland Commercial College, Houghton N.Y.A. School; [occ.] Retired U.S. Civil Service and U.S. Army; [memb.] Reserve Officers Assn., The Retired Officers Assn., Warrant Officers Assn., four genealogical societies, AF and AM, Virginia Air and Space Museum, founding member American Air Museum in Great Britain.; [hon.] Honorary Member Masonic Fraternity, Honorary Faculty Member, QM School US Army Outstanding Meritorious Civilian Svc. Commendation, 30 yr government Svc. Award. Military Awards: Four medals WW II, Armed Forces Reserve Medal, Meritorious Svc. Unit Insignia; [oth. writ.] Books published: Two Research Guides, Family History Book, editor of two books and chief editor and compiler of a Church Centennial History.; [pers.] Hobbies: Oil portrait painting and pencil and pastel sketching, genealogy, writing poetry, researching, writing and compiling history and genealogy books.; [a.] Hampton, VA

METZGER, ZELPHA
[b.] November 19, 1980, Meade, KS; [p.] Agnes Chockmickler and Randy Metzger; [ed.] 1 year at Apache Junction High School getting GED; [occ.] Bus Boy for Los Vasqueros, "The Cowboys"; [hon.] 3rd grade, given award from governor for reading the most books, 6th grade, Lion's Club published essay, 7th gr. Hands Across the Border, 8th gr. honor society, Cheerleading; [oth. writ.] I started writing poetry at the age of 14 and now I have over 200 poems. I also like to write essays but mainly poems; [pers.] Writing poetry has helped me to deal with emotional problems and I believe it can help others.; [a.] Apache Junction, AZ

MEYER, GAIL J.
[b.] August 28, 1968, Covington, KY; [p.] Geraldine and George Meyer; [ed.] St. Johns Elementary, Holmes High School; [pers.] This poem was possible with some inspiration from my father.; [a.] Covington, KY

MEYER VON STADELHOFEN, COUNT
[pen.] Henri; [b.] December 18, 1916, Geneva, Switzerland; [p.] Marcel and Anne-Louise Meyer De Stadelhofen; [m.] Madeleine Meyer De Stadelhofen, May 5, 1944; [ch.] Eric Jacques Michel; [ed.] University Law - Classical Studies; [occ.] Ecrivain - Journalite; [memb.] Count - Master in Law; [hon.] Laureate of Litteroture, Prix St. Vincent (Italy), Prix St. Exupery (France); [oth. writ.] Numerous books and articles - last book - an important study: "Napoleon and Americo"; [pers.] Director in Switzerland, Europa 1 - Director Teli-Monte-Carlo.; [a.] Cocoa Beach, FL

MEZA, JUAN CARLOS
[pen.] Juan Carlos Meza; [b.] October 9, 1972, Valencia, Venezuela; [p.] Martha De Osorio and Juan Meza; [ed.] Elementary - Middle School, High School at (Francisco Javier) in Venezuela, South America; [occ.] Mail Room "Herald Record" Middletown; [memb.] Martha De Osorio - Club's; [oth. writ.] "Poems to Melitza" (Poesy), "Melancholias" (Poesy), "Wind's Love (Novel), none published.; [pers.] I thank the Lord for my life, for letting me write romantic poetry and for letting me reflect on my letter, my end less love for Melitza Jimenez.; [a.] Middletown, NY

MEZZANOTTE, GENEVIEVE D.
[pen.] Genevieve D. Mezzanotte; [b.] January 20, 1921, Timber Lake, SD; [p.] Judge Raymond and Cecelia Dillman; [m.] Matthew N. Mezzanotte, February 11, 1958; [ed.] No degrees, various Fine Arts Schools; [occ.] Business Executive, Own Companies Investing in Real Estate; [memb.] Friend and Reader Folger Shakespeare Library, Various Charitable Organizations; [hon.] Delta Sigma Theta, Nat'l President's Award 1996; [oth. writ.] Personal short stories and poetry unpublished.; [pers.] I write and paint to record my voice and vision in its unique finger-print image for better or for worse.; [a.] Washington, DC

MICHALOSKY, BETH
[b.] December 23, 1972, Ohio; [p.] Judith Wolf and Paul Michalosky; [ch.] David Gerald Scott Michalosky; [ed.] Graduated Gateway Technical School of Elkhorn, WI; [occ.] Furniture Refinisher for Furniture Classics of Powder Springs, GA; [memb.] P.T.A.; [hon.] State Competitions of Wisconsin in Choir, Swing Choir and Flute. I received 2 gold awards in flute, 1 silver and 1 bronze in choir; [oth. writ.] My writings have been primarily personal, although I have written plays in High School.; [pers.] I enjoy writing poetry about people, and relevant in life. Poetry shows each of us our reflective vulner-

ability. When you search and find each poets meaning you find part of yourself.; [a.] Powder Springs, GA

MICKLE, CYNTHIA W.
[b.] January 21, 1957, Winston Salem, NC; [p.] James W. Williamson, Ethel Ray; [m.] Moultrie L. Mickle, September 17, 1977; [ch.] Samuel David, Rachel Michelle; [ed.] East Forsyth High School, attended Forsyth Tech. Community College; [occ.] Homemaker; [pers.] I give credit for my written work to God. For it is through Him that I found peace, hope, faith and joy out of what others would call tragedy.; [a.] Winston Salem, NC

MIDDLETON, PATRICIA
[b.] January 2, 1963, Philadelphia; [ch.] Gregory and Angella Middleton; [ed.] Germantown High, Temple University; [occ.] Consultant, Bell Atlantic, Philadelphia, PA, 15 years; [memb.] Church of Our Lord Jesus Christ, Inc., Sunday School Dept, Greater Refuge Church Young People's Union and Missionary Dept.; [hon.] First and Second place winner in local and state Oratorical contests, Founder and Editor of "The Companion", a quart-te.ly newsletter for women featuring inspirational poetry.; [oth. writ.] Several poems have been published and many recited at weddings, funerals, banquets, and various church services.; [a.] Philadelphia, PA

MILGROVE, APRIL M.
[b.] January 29, 1983, Portland, OR; [p.] Kent D. Milgrove and Rhonda Benson; [ed.] I am in 8th grade at Hood River Middle School in Hood River, Oregon; [occ.] Student; [hon.] 1) Award of merit for "Artistic Contribution" in Artscrawl 1990 in Vancouver, WA, 2) 1st place May 1994 in "PetPourri" Photo Contest in Vancouver, WA, 3) November 1995 Certificate of Honor for Outstanding Academic Achievements at Hood River Middle School, Hood River, OR, 4) April 1996 Certificate of Special Recognition for Choir at Hood River Middle School, Hood River OR; [pers.] I just try and treat people the way I want to be treated.; [a.] Hood River, OR

MILLER, ALICIA DANIELLE
[b.] October 19, 1983, St. Joseph, MI; [p.] Ernest Sr. and Darlene Miller; [ed.] McCord Renaissance Center, 8th Grade; [occ.] Student; [memb.] Inter-City Sail Club; [hon.] Honor Roll, Principal's List, Citizenship, Perfect Attendance, the Principal Pal Award; [oth. writ.] The Bee (book) - 1st grade, many reports, My Book of Poetry - 6th grade; [pers.] I began writing at a young age and was greatly influenced by my mother. Never settle for less and always do your best.; [a.] Benton Harbor MI

MILLER, FLORENCE JULIA
[pen.] Florence O'Neil; [b.] August 27, 1974, Jefferson Co., MO; [p.] Richard G. and Lelia A. Donnelly; [m.] Robert N. Miller Jr., June 3, 1996; [ch.] Heather Marie, Samantha Lynn; [pers.] I enjoy writing about my strong feelings and personal persuations. I am influenced by great works of literature such as the Bible, plays written by Shakespeare, and modern author Robert James Waller.; [a.] Thomasboro, IL

MILLER, KEN
[b.] July 30, 1949, Morgantown, WV; [p.] Bill Miller (Deceased), Louise Wright; [m.] Sheryl L. Miller, February 12, 1972; [ch.] Kristin L. Miller; [ed.] DuVal High, Prince George's Community College, The American University; [occ.] Grocery Store Dairy Stocker/Checker, Safeway, Dunkirk, MD; [memb.] U.S. Congressional Staff Member (1970-1992), Distinguished Member of The International Society of Poets, Member of The Calvert County Poetry Club; [hon.] Two NLP's Editor's

Choice Awards, Elected into The International Poetry Hall of Fame, four of my poems selected for the NLP's "Sound of Poetry" series; [oth. writ.] A poem, "Alone", in the NLP's anthology, Where Dawn Lingers. A poem, "Pressing Thoughts", in the NLP's anthology, Through The Hourglass. A poem, "In Between", in the NLP's special edition, The Best Poems of the 90's. A poem, "Epitaph", in the NLP's forthcoming anthology, In Dappled Sunlight. A poem, "Overdose of Memories", in the NLP's forthcoming anthology, The Best Poems of 1997; [pers.] "A Loser Wins Beauty", which appears in this anthology, I had thought about using for the Poet's Corner's Niche Craft Contest dealing with "Beauty". I had second thoughts, however, and submitted it with one of the monthly stamps instead. This poem is more positive than most of my work. I think it shows that I have a hopeful side.; [a.] Owings, MD

MILLER, KENNETH A.
[b.] May 16, 1953, Washington, DC; [p.] Opal R. and Robert C. Miller; [m.] Jung S. (Kim) Miller; [ch.] One, William K. Miller (17 yrs); [ed.] Univ. of MD (Far East Div.), Grad of the Army Management Staff College (AMSC) Class of 96-1; [occ.] U.S. Army Criminal Investigation Command, Public Affairs Specialist; [memb.] AMSC Allumni Assoc.; [hon.] U.S. Army Broadcast Award, Commanders Award for Civilian Service; [oth. writ.] Several news articles and stories published in Army newspapers and publications.; [pers.] Life's experience is the best teacher. I try to share those experiences when putting pen to paper.; [a.] Burke, VA

MILLER, MARLENE HOPE
[pen.] R.M.M.; [b.] October 14, 1952, Statesville, NC; [p.] William G. and Mary Leigh Hope; [m.] Dennie L. Miller, June 30, 1974; [ch.] Kevin Gill Hope, Kristina Nicole Miller, Kory Lee Miller, Jamie Bryce Sheets; [ed.] North Iredell High, Olin, NC; [occ.] Hair Stylist, disabled; [memb.] Rocky Hill Baptist Ch; [oth. writ.] "Let Me Down Easy," first poems published or received recognition.; [pers.] I truly believe in living one day at a time to its fullest. Quote: The two greatest thieves in life are the regrets of the past and the fear of the future.; [a.] Statesville, NC

MILLER, SCOTT LEE
[b.] August 10, 1987; [p.] Shannon Miller; [ed.] Jim Allen Elementary, PATS Center for Gifed Children; [occ.] 4th grade Student; [memb.] United States Taekwon Do Alliance; [hon.] Certificate of Dedication, Decided First Degree Black Belt, Award of Merit Mathematics Superstar, 1992 Molino Ruritan Coloring Contest 1st place, 1996 P.A.T. Literature Contest, "Just Open Your Eyes"; [oth. writ.] Space Invaders; [pers.] I'm only 9 years old and in the 4th grade. I strive very hard to keep up my straight "A" average in my school work.; [a.] Cantonment, FL

MILLER JR., THOMAS J.
[b.] June 29, 1947, Granite City, IL; [p.] Thomas Miller, Olga Miller; [m.] Bonita (Holland) Miller, June 11, 1969; [ch.] Tim, Jeff, Keith, Sandy; [ed.] Madison High School, Southern Illinois U. Edwardsville; [occ.] English Teacher, High School and Belleville Area College; [memb.] Knights of Columbus, Holy Family School Athletic Committee; [a.] Granite, IL

MILLON, AMBER
[b.] October 1, 1985, San Diego, CA; [p.] Andy and Sheri Millon; [ed.] Elementary School; [occ.] 5th grade student, Highland Ranch Elementary School; [oth. writ.] Various short poems and stories as part of school projects; [a.] San Diego, CA

MILLS, REE
[b.] March 17, 1916, Marble, AR; [p.] Samuel and Martha Qualls; [m.] Claude Williams Mills, April 4, 1940; [ch.] Billy Paul, Claude Allen, Jimmy Lynn; [ed.] High School North West Arkansas School of Cosmetology; [occ.] Retired; [oth. writ.] Poem (Mary) Madison Co. Record, Poem and 3 drawings published in Reflections, Conway, AR. Short story (Oak Grove) Ark. History collections.; [pers.] No matter how dark the storm, look for the rainbows following the storms.; [a.] Springdale, AR

MIRES, JUANITA
[pen.] Juanita Poole Mires; [b.] December 28, 1941; [p.] Ardell McNair Poole and Walter Poole; [m.] Clark Douglas Mires, Ph.D., November 27, 1996; [ch.] Madison D. LaFever, Leslie E. Gregory III and Perria Leigh Burnett; [ed.] 1-10 grades, G.E.D. 1982 in Dalhart, Texas, 1-10 Grades in Helena Arkansas; [occ.] Housewife; [oth. writ.] "Come Walk With me", "Miss You", "My Friend", "I Wish A Tomorrow", "I Fly Free", "Halloween Sights"; [pers.] "With faith and belief one's dreams will come true."; [a.] Amarillo, TX

MIRSAIDI, GABRIELLE
[b.] August 22, 1983, San Luis Obispo; [p.] Ovsanna Basmajian, Jwad Mirsaidi; [ed.] Head Start, Pucheco Elementary, Laguna Jr. High; [occ.] Student; [hon.] Honor Roll (4th-6th), Principals Pride Award, Sportmanship Award, Most Improved Award, Elk National Shootout 1st, Elk National Shootout 2nd; [oth. writ.] Alone (unpublished), Dreams (unpublished), Shoes (unpublished).; [pers.] I've always said I'll show them, well I have. And to Mrs. Yost (my English teacher) giving me a "C" on my poetry pocket, you should be ashamed.; [a.] San Louis Obispo, CA

MISENHIMER, ANN R.
[pen.] Ann Mise; [b.] December 30, 1934, Troy, NY; [p.] Joseph Rosenholtz, Blanche Rosenholtz; [m.] Jay B. Misenhimer, June 6, 1993; [ch.] Wendy Ellen, Brian Lee (Segel); [ed.] Troy High, LaSalle Jr. College; [occ.] Administrative Assistant, Free-lance Interior Designer; [memb.] Literacy Volunteer; [oth. writ.] Children's Book: The Adventures of Meishi-Soo, The Mop Dog, many poems.; [pers.] As music may fill the air with sweetness, poetry cleanses the soul. Writing has freed me of many emotions-happy and sad.; [a.] Cohoes, NY

MISKIEWICZ, LEONARD A.
[b.] October 20, 1927, Pittsburgh, PA; [p.] Alexander Miskiewicz, Mary Tepsich; [ed.] U.S. Navy 12 1/2 yrs. as Air Controller; [occ.] Disability Retired Letter Carrier; [memb.] A.M. Legion; [hon.] Given Honorable: By smallest country in world. Hutt River Providence in area Perth, Australia Citizen of Year - 1994 - 1990 for my water saver went into Who's Who Of American Inventors; [pers.] Let us all examine our minds and correct our mistakes of past. Give Jesus, true God our lives.; [a.] Pittsburgh, PA

MISRA, SIDHARTHA
[b.] September 23, 1969, Meerut, India; [p.] Darshan Misra, Jagdish P. Misra; [ed.] Ingraham Institute English School, Masters in Computer Applications, Institute of Management Technology GZO, India; [occ.] Sr. Software Consultant, HCL America Inc.; [memb.] Metropolitan Museum of Art; [hon.] Scholarship Recipient in the Master's Program, Appreciation letter for a project in Bombay; [pers.] I have been greatly influenced by Shakespeare - Richard II, Nehru, Wordsworth.; [a.] Irvine, CA

MOLLAN, VIVIAN
[b.] November 24, 1925, West Allis, WI; [p.] Karl Gloff, Clara Ramm; [m.] Frank Andrew Mollan, May 26, 1951; [ch.] Mark, Michael, Robert - Deceased; [ed.] To 12th Grade in Albion Mich. Returned to Milwaukee in 1943, attended Milwaukee Adult high school 1967; [occ.] Retired; [pers.] Poem was written as I sat next to my dying son Robert in December, 1996. He was so special in life that I had to keep his memory alive. He said, "I want to be a good memory."; [a.] Milwaukee, WI

MONSCHEIN, ANNEMARIE
[b.] May 5, 1967, Austria; [p.] Alois Fessler, Maria Fessler; [m.] Wagner Alberto Pinargote; [ch.] Cat: Maxie; [ed.] Ph.D. Candidate in International Relations; [occ.] Researcher for a hedge fund Castlerock Management; [memb.] National Association for Female Executives; [hon.] B.A. Magna Cum Laude; [oth. writ.] A few not yet published love poems.; [pers.] Poems are a joyful moment, in which to view the world upon a different angle.; [a.] Brooklyn, NY

MONTANARI, JASON T.
[b.] March 3, 1978, Baltimore, MD; [p.] Robert and Connie Montanari; [ed.] 1st Year College Student; [occ.] Student; [memb.] Friends of the National Park at Gettysburg; [hon.] Still to come!; [oth. writ.] Just getting into the area more actively; [pers.] Two for today because tomorrow may never come.; [a.] Baltimore, MD

MONTGOMERY, BARRY
[b.] February 9, 1959, Oakland, CA; [m.] Michele; [ch.] J. D. and Jarrod; [oth. writ.] Nothing published, but I keep my own book of my poems.; [a.] Livermore, CA

MONTGOMERY II, ODELL
[pen.] Mariba; [b.] September 22, 1948, Asbury Park, NJ; [p.] Mr. O. V. Montgomery, Mrs. Lucille Montgomery; [ch.] Mr. Micheal Eugene Montgomery; [ed.] Attended Colleges and Universities in Wis, Wash. D.C., Mass, and New York. Booker T. Washington High, Tulsa, Okla.; [occ.] Freelance Waiter; [oth. writ.] Poems published in Encore Magazine, and local papers in Cambridge and Boston, Mess, also Beloit, Wis, and Chicago, IL; [pers.] Poetry is the harmony produced in the mist of mankind's chaos.; [a.] Rochester, NY

MONTON, SUSISA
[b.] December 7, 1921, Philippines; [p.] Fernando and Eduvigis Josol; [m.] F. Y. Monton (Deceased), October 3, 1953; [ch.] One, Sharon Monton Robinson; [ed.] High School Salutatorian, Misamis Occidental High School, Oroquieta, Mis. Occ. Philippines, Elementary Teacher's Certificate P.N.S., Graduate Nurse, St. Luke's Hospital School of Nursing, Registered Nurse, CA; [occ.] R.N. - now retired; [memb.] 1. American Legion Auxiliary of the Manuel Roxas Post #798, Stockton, CA, 2. Legionarios del Trabajo, Inc. of Stockton, CA, 3. Filipino Women's Club of Stockton and Vicinity; [hon.] Salutatorian, High School Member, Honor Roll, College, Nursing Service Award from the San Joaquin County Board of Supervisors, CA; [oth. writ.] Poems and short stories in The Bisaya, a weekly magazine in the Philippines (years ago), poems and quips published in The Immigrants, a Stockton Magazine and Newspaper in Stockton, CA.; [pers.] I had been encouraged to write by a favorite teacher of mine in high school. She was my role model and inspiration.; [a.] Lathrop, CA

MONTOYA, CAROLYN S.
[b.] August 30, 1962, Vian, Oklahoma; [p.] William and Carolyn Miller; [m.] Arthur Montoya, August 7,

1989; [ch.] Kevin, Cassandra Lynn, and Yvonne Montoya; [ed.] Northeastern State University in Tahlequah, Oklahoma; [occ.] Educator - 6th grade teacher, Peter Pendleton Elementary School, Coachella, CA; [pers.] Although our dreams may change or fade throughout the years we must endure these times with open minds and hearts.; [a.] Palm Desert, CA

MOORE, DEBBIE S.
[b.] December 19, 1958, Topeka, KS; [p.] John and Dorothy Holt; [m.] Vernon Moore, April 16, 1987; [ch.] Trish and Megan Rainey; [ed.] High School Grad., Cosmetology/Electrology School, University of Maryland (Europe), U.S. Army, U.S. Army Instructor, Electrical, and Writer's Course; [occ.] Electrical/Electronics Quality Control Test Technician for a shipyard, writer; [memb.] Isle of Hope Volunteer Fire Dept, Tybee Island First Response/Rescue, Disabled American Veterans, American Heart Association, Emergency Medical Team (state and national); [hon.] Letters of Commendation for Saving Lives, Army Service Ribbon, Overseas Service Ribbon, NGOPLDG Ribbon, Soldier of the Cycle Award/ Promotion, Distinguished Honor Graduate, Army Good Conduct Medal, Army Achievement Medal, Army Commendation Medals; [oth. writ.] Poetry: Heartstrings, On Bended Knee, The Haunting Song, She Sits Alone Children's Book: Peneplope, the Peculiar Purple Porpoise; [a.] Savannah, GA

MOORE, JOHN F.
[pen.] DelBert The Spring Poet; [b.] March 29, 1907, White Co., IN; [p.] John F. and Heltie M. Moore; [m.] Mary M. Mitchell, June 6, 1931; [ch.] Clarissa Ann and Ralph M.; [ed.] High School; [occ.] Retired; [memb.] 100F 50 yrs.; [oth. writ.] Several poems published in local newspaper; [pers.] I try to tell things as they are.; [a.] Remington, IN

MOORE, KENNETH J.
[b.] March 29, 1940, Enid, OK; [p.] Joseph D. and Theda B. Moore; [m.] Wilma L. Greenfield; [ch.] Sara, Scott, Tim, Andy and Kali; [ed.] B.S. Business, M.B.S. Psychology, Ph.D. Social Welfare; [occ.] Chair and President, Sodner Federal Mortgage Co. and Adjunct Professor, Florida Atlantic University; [memb.] National Association of Social Workers, Economic on Social Work Education; [oth. writ.] (A) Professional Journal Articles: (3) (B) Chapter, Monograph, University of California, Berkeley, (C) Novel, in process (D) Training Modules for Department of Human Services, Florida, First and only poem submission; [pers.] To begin to understand another person one must consider their biological, psychological and sociological economic history. If that doesn't work, read their horoscope; [a.] Boca Raton, FL

MOORE, MARILYN S.
[b.] July 26, 1939, Somerset, PA; [p.] G. Harold and Jeannette Sheffer; [ch.] Garin, Patricia, Bill and Cheryl; [ed.] Graduate - Camp Hill H.S. Camp Hill, PA; [occ.] Housekeeper; [memb.] P.M. Middletown Chapter O.E.S., P.P. Order of Amaranth, White Shrine, Loyal Order of Moose and Shell's Lutheran Church; [hon.] Past Matron O.E.S., Past Patron Order of Amaranth, Past Mother Advisor of International Order of Rainbow for Girls; [pers.] As a good christian I strive to live each day to devote myself to help others in any way I can be of service. I write from my heart for God's love.; [a.] Harrisburg, PA

MORAUD, GEORGETTE
[b.] Saint Junien, France; [p.] Marcel and May Moraud; [m.] Gene Murphy; [ch.] Maureen, Kathleen, Eugene III, Georgette, John; [ed.] Primary, Secondary - France Undergrad., Grad. USA; [occ.] Retired Mod. Lang. Prof.;

[memb.] AATF, AAUP, MLA, elected: Societf Des Profs. Franc. En Amerique, Ecoles Des Hts. Etudes, Setours Internationaux Linguistiques and Cultures, Pi Delta Phi, Nat. French Honor Society, Phi Sigma Iota, Nat. Romance Language; [hon.] Honor Society, Recipient of 5 Awards for Excellence in Teaching; [a.] Geneva, NY

MORCH, DEREK A.
[b.] July 18, 1976, Chicago, IL; [p.] Anton and Vivian Morch; [ed.] Attended Maine South High School in Park Ridge, IL and currently attending Truman State University in Kirksville, MO; [occ.] Student; [memb.] Psychology Club 1996; [hon.] Member of National Dean's List, Dean's List in Fall of 95, President Combined Ability Scholar, MTA (Maine Teacher's Association) Scholarship Winner; [oth. writ.] Have been published in school newspaper and the literary magazine of Truman State University, "Windfall."; [a.] Wildwood, MO

MOREAU, KATHY
[pen.] Kathy Potts Moreau; [b.] October 25, 1952, Meadville, PA; [p.] Anthony and Stella Potts; [m.] Marcel (Frenchie) Moreau, June 15, 1996; [ch.] Samuel Potts, Jen and Trevor Moreau; [ed.] Cambridge Springs High, Cambridge Springs, PA; [occ.] Housewife/Homemaker; [oth. writ.] Several unpublished poems and short stories; [pers.] My poems are dedicated in memory of my mother, Stella Potts 1913-1990. Special thank you to my husband, son, sisters and brothers. They are my inspiration.; [a.] Columbus, PA

MORENO, JESSICA
[b.] August 12, 1982, Houston, TX; [p.] Bertha Meding; [ed.] 8th Grade; [occ.] Student; [memb.] YMCA; [oth. writ.] I wrote a book at the age of 13 "Angel Kill Montygon".; [pers.] I enjoy poetry because it makes me feel relaxed.; [a.] C.B., IA

MORGAN, LOIS M.
[b.] December 7, 1907, Dee, OR; [p.] Joseph B. Dimmick and Lucy C. Lenz; [m.] Rolla D. Griffith and Wilbert P. Morgan, January 20, 1929 and April 2, 1961; [ch.] Maxine McCormic, Mary Lou Griffith, and Marlene Loisdotter; [ed.] Mt. Hood Grade School, Parkdale High School, Oregon State Tuberculosis Hospital Nurses Training - The Dalles; [occ.] Telephone Operator, Homemaker, and Practical Nurse; [memb.] Mt. Hood Dramatic Club, VFW Auxiliary, St. Mary's Altar Society, Maryknoll Missions, Practical Nurses Assn., Societies of the Little Flower, St. Francis and many more that contribute to poor and needy individuals. She always shared what she had, even when it was only a widow's mite.; [hon.] Winner in Kenai (Alaska) Peninsula College Poetry Contest, 1995. Publication of "The Wind and I," in Driftwood, 1995. A very humble person, she "kept her light under a bushel."; [oth. writ.] 280 poems, not published in local newspapers (1962-1996). Unpublished diaries, one published song, one book, Echoing Reflections: The Poetry of Lois M. Morgan, 1993; [pers.] Mom's quiet yet infections appreciation of beauty and grandeur of nature, and of the goodness and greatness of humans, resonates throughout her poetry. She never took them for granted, but met each morning with her senses awake to a glorious reality atop the everyday world of work and worry. Despite the paralysis of MS, humor activated her mind, and care of others, her spirit. (Written by her daughters.); [a.] Hood River, OR

MORIZZO, MICHAEL V.
[b.] October 20, 1958, Corona, NY; [p.] Michael D. Morizzo, Carmela Morizzo; [ch.] Deborah Michelle; [ed.] Newfield H.S.; [occ.] U.S.P.S.; [a.] Port Jefferson Station, NY

MORLEY, LYNN
[pen.] "Babes In Toyland"; [b.] November 26, 1955, Minneapolis, MN; [p.] Bob and June Morley; [ch.] Nicholas - 16, Jennifer - 15, Angela - 13 and Samantha - 6; [ed.] St. Louis Park High, Cambridge Comm. College; [occ.] Lic in-home Daycare Provider; [memb.] Christ of King Church; [hon.] Although I haven't been honored with any awards, I feel my best accomplishment in life is being a super parent to my four children.; [oth. writ.] Several poems written to family members, lovers and friends.; [pers.] Been greatly influenced by my journey through life. Best time to write my poetry art in the early AM with coffee!; [a.] Cambridge, MN

MORONEY, ALAN
[b.] November 29, 1966, Westminster, England; [p.] Brian Moroney (Deceased), Catherine Richards Moroney; [ed.] Brighton, Hove and Sussex VITH Form College; [occ.] Writer/Journalist; [memb.] Amnesty International, T.A.S.K., Brunswick Village Cricket Club; [hon.] Diplomas in Swedish and Davish Languages; [oth. writ.] Screenplays (not published yet), Journalistic pieces in local magazines and in cyberspace. Poems converted to songs by band (Deep South).; [a.] Webster, TX

MOSKOWITZ, CHARLOTTE ROYAL
[b.] November 3, Galveston, TX; [p.] George and Bess Moskowitz; [ed.] Ball High School with honors, I attended Texas University and SMU; [occ.] Song Writer, Poet and Comedian; [memb.] As George Burns said "I would not belong to any club that would have me as a member."; [oth. writ.] I had been writing since I was a little child, but I had to get someone to read it to me since I couldn't read. I had three books published, the first two were blurred, the third was a coloring book for the Dan Quail Vice-Presidential Library. I always seemed to have just missed coming up with a good title. I wrote "From Here To A Very Very Far Place", "Big Women", "The Rise And Fall Of The Roman Candle", "I'm O.K. You Ain't", and a story about the shoe business "Alice In Bunyon Land", and the training of a chef titled "Through The Cooking Class". My one play called "Julius Grab Her" had a very happy ending, everyone was glad it was over.; [pers.] My favorite philosopher was Will Rogers who said "I never met a man I didn't like", or was that Elizabeth Taylor? I have a friend who has a grandfather who is a philosopher, in fact, he is a prophet (and his grandmother is a total loss) nevertheless, he asked me one day do you know the difference between love and herpes? "Herpes last forever". My favorite saying is abstinence is not bad if practiced in moderation. On a personal note, I do hope one day to attain the highest of all Jewish Honors..."Mench-Hood".

MOSS, KISHA
[b.] June 8, 1981, Frankfurt, Germany; [p.] Willie T. Moore; [ed.] Butler High; [memb.] Foreign Language Honor Society, Student Council; [oth. writ.] "The Book of Thoughts," not published.; [a.] Hephzibah, GA

MOSTELLER, NIKI
[pen.] N. LaJean M.; [b.] July 21, 1960, Tulare, CA; [p.] Lowell and Naomi Mosteller; [ed.] AA Degree from "The College of the Sequoias," in Visalia, California; [occ.] Artist; [memb.] Art Club, FHA; [hon.] "Bank of America Award," and "Art Club Scholarship award," I was on the Presidents List, I won awards for my art work; [oth. writ.] My art work shown in art galleries; [pers.] Tell Phil my dreams of becoming a writer are coming true, so don't give up your dreams.; [a.] Corcoran, CA

MOWERY, DR. SANDRA ANN
[pen.] "Sunshine"; [b.] May 24, 1948, Greensburg, PA;

[p.] Guy and Wanda Paluzzi; [ch.] One daughter Layla, seventeen; [ed.] Elementary Jr and Sr. High School Community College Palmer Chiropractic College; [occ.] Chiropractic Physician Emergency Chiropractic Px., Az.; [memb.] Business and Professional; [hon.] Mostly Professional and Academic and Clinical; [oth. writ.] Unpublished writings: Inspirational, Informative, Investigative, Conscious Upliftment; [pers.] "The common thread that unites us, is the life that we have within us."; [a.] Phoenix, AZ

MULLINGS, EMILY
[pen.] Sunshine; [b.] August 26, 1947, Winter Haven, FL; [m.] Roger Mullings, January 28, 1967; [ch.] Glenn, Michael, Scott; [ed.] H.V. Cooper High School, Southern Business College; [occ.] Teach Handicapped Children, No. Marion Middle School, Citra, FL; [memb.] United Daughters of the Confederacy; [oth. writ.] Poem and article published in a local periodical; [pers.] Good health is something we all hope to enjoy for as long as we can. Massage therapy helped me regain my health and for this reason I chose to write a poem about it.; [a.] Ocala, FL

MUMM, PAT
[b.] March 5, 1939, Yuma, CO; [p.] Bud and Jesta Wall; [m.] Darrell Mumm, May 4, 1958; [ch.] Kyle, Todd, Shona; [ed.] High School Grad. E.M.T., C.P.R. teacher; [occ.] Rancher - Housewife; [pers.] If one of my poems brings a smile to someone I am happy. I usually include a poem in every Christmas card, get well card or birthday card.; [a.] Wray, CO

MUNOZ, DAGOBERTO
[pen.] Dake Munoz; [b.] July 3, 1938, El Salv., CA; [p.] Maria T. Ortiz and Miguel A. Munoz; [ed.] Computer Scientist, Comm. Data Chief; [occ.] Merch Material Handler; [memb.] Management Club; [oth. writ.] Mirror Of The Past, Let's Time Decide, To The Brave Soldiers; [pers.] Dedicated to Vicky my inspiration, and only love on her birthday.; [a.] La Puente, CA

MURRY, JEREMY WADE
[b.] July 26, 1981, Montgomery, AL; [p.] Samuel E. Murry (Deceased) and Jimmie R. Murry; [ed.] 8th grade at Electric Elmore Co. High; [memb.] Calvary Baptist Church Choir, Tallassee, Modmon Woodmen Jr. Club; [oth. writ.] Poems; [a.] Tallassee, AL

MYERS, GISELA
[b.] April 11, 1928, Germany; [p.] Margaretha and Wilhelm Strauch; [m.] Elbert Myers (Deceased); [ch.] Ralf, Dan and Steven Myers; [ed.] BS in French and German from MSU; [occ.] Retired; [oth. writ.] Unpublished poetry; [pers.] I enjoy writing poetry "From the Heart"; [a.] Warner Robins, GA

NAIL, GEARY LYNN
[pen.] Choctaw Nail; [b.] September 5, Shawnee, OK; [p.] A. C. and Pearl Nail; [ed.] Grad High School Shawnee High School, Shawnee Opla 12 grade; [pers.] God has given me the talent to write about things upon this earth and hope and blessing and peace within ourselves. I cannot do this alone; [a.] Shawnee, OK

NASH, KATHY M. MATHER
[b.] December 15, 1964, Flint, MI; [p.] Leland and Edna Mather; [m.] Gregory M. Nash, June 1, 1996; [ch.] Sama and Niki; [ed.] Kearsley High School, Ross Medical; [hon.] American Medical Technologists, Registered Medical Assistant; [oth. writ.] Several poems written for family and friends; [pers.] I thank Jesus for giving me the talent to write. And I thank my mother and my husband for urging me to write and to publish my poems.; [a.] Flint, MI

NCUBE, TRYPHINE S.
[pen.] Tryphine S. Ncube; [b.] May 8, 1970; [p.] Elizabeth Ncube; [occ.] Freelance Writer; [memb.] ABBWA (American Black Book Writers Association), Gotham Writer's Workshop; [oth. writ.] Published newspaper articles, currently working on my first novel entitled 'when I have reached the point of suffocation'.; [pers.] For each day that I am able to rise and write a page I say a dozen thank yous. I draw my inspiration from the power above and from legends such as Toni Morrison and Zora Neal Houston before her.; [a.] West Babylon, NY

NEILSON, HOLLY
[b.] February 3, 1973, Nantucket, MA; [p.] Carol Inch; [m.] Phillip Neilson, February 14, 1991; [ch.] Christopher Patrick, Sara Ashlee; [pers.] To my mother, the strongest woman I've ever known, a single mother at fifteen, in good times and in bad, we made it together.; [a.] Sandy, UT

NEISS, WYNNE M.
[b.] New York City; [m.] Joseph R. Neiss; [ch.] Kenneth J. Neiss, Thomas R. Neiss; [ed.] Julia Richman H.S., Spenser Bus. School; [occ.] Retired; [memb.] Order of the Easter Star, Clowns of America, Penn. Ohio and New York (P.O.N.Y.) Clown Ass'n., Long Island Klown Enthusiasts (L.I.K.E.); [hon.] Past Grand Officer, O.E.S.; [oth. writ.] Some poems published in newspapers and local publications.; [pers.] I am a clown and my clown name is "Doodles." As a clown I hope to make you smile.; [a.] Earlton, NY

NELSEN, NORMAN R.
[b.] December 12, 1936, Staten Island, NY; [p.] Bernhard and Glady's Nelsen; [m.] Divorced; [ch.] Ronald Keith Nelsen (Deceased), Katherine Elizabeth Nelsen; [ed.] Princeton University, AB 1958, Woodrow Wilson School of Public and International Affairs; [occ.] Retired; [memb.] The Presbyterian Church, Basking Ridge, NJ, The Historical Society of the Somerset Hills, NJ (Trustee); [hon.] Phi Beta Kappa, National Library of Poetry Editor's Choice Awards '95, '96, '97; [oth. writ.] "Revival," in Sea of Treasure, "Critters Who Aren't Quitters," in Spirit of the Age, "On Castle Rock Road," in Where Dawn Lingers, "A Risky Mission," in Across the Universe, "Loonacy," in Best Poems of the 90's, "The Tree Tao," in Portraits of Life, "Mass Murder in a Cathedral Town," in Daybreak on the Land, "Water and Wind: The Word and the Spirit," in The Colors of Thought, "Poetic Justice," in Of Moonlight and Wishes; [pers.] "At Appomattox Court House," in Into the Unknown, "A Bellyful of Wisdom," in Silence of Yesterday, "The Circle to Salvation," in Etches in Time, "Provident in Paradise," in the Isle of View, all published by the National Library of Poetry; [a.] Basking Ridge, NJ

NELSON, DANIEL
[b.] March 20, 1983, Mission Hills, CA; [p.] Cynthia and Bruce Nelson; [ed.] Currently attending eight grade at Sierra Vista Jr. High will be at Canyon High School in Fall 1997; [occ.] Student at Sierra Vista Jr. High, Canyon Country, CA; [memb.] A.Y.S.O. (American Youth Soccer Organization), CJSF (California Junior Scholarship Federation); [hon.] Student of the Month, Science Proficiency Award, English Proficiency Award, History Proficiency Award; [oth. writ.] Poem published in "The Anthology of Poetry by Young Americans" The Game (1996). Reporter/Layout Editor for "Vista View" newspaper (At Sierra Vista Junior High).; [pers.] "My future goal is to become a professional journalist for a major newspaper."; [a.] Canyon Country, CA

NELSON, STACEY-ANN VEONIE
[pen.] Michelle; [b.] November 24, 1974, Jamaica; [p.] Melva Vassell; [ed.] Preparatory, High School, College; [pers.] The ability to write poetry does not start from the calendar of age, but from the honesty and purity of the heart. This is my original thought.

NEMEC, MORGAN LAMAR
[b.] February 24, 1984, Austin, TX; [p.] Sandra and Ted Nemec Jr.; [ed.] Saint Cyril and Methodious Catholic School, Georgetown Jr. High School; [memb.] YAC (Young Authors Club); [oth. writ.] Two other poems.; [pers.] Poetry lets me express my innermost feelings. I was inspired by my recently deceased grandfather and cousin.; [a.] Jarrell, TX

NERNESS, CYNTHIA M.
[b.] August 2, 1965, Windom, MN; [p.] Michael and Eileen Pankonin; [m.] Mr. Stacey G. Nerness, October 10, 1992; [ch.] Joshua Emmanuel Nerness; [ed.] 1983 graduate of Windom Area High School, Windom, Minnesota, 1994 Graduate of Southwestern Technical College, Jackson, Minnesota, of the Medical Secretary Course; [occ.] Medical Transcriptionist, Mankato, Minnesota; [memb.] The 700 Club; [hon.] President's Honor List; [oth. writ.] Several unpublished poems and children's books in process.; [pers.] The Lord heard my cry and blessed us with a son. My desire is to touch the soul and offer hope through spiritually - inspired expressions.; [a.] Mapleton, MN

NEWTON, SARAH NELL
[pen.] Saint; [b.] April 21, 1945, Hart County; [p.] Katie Mae and James E. Newton; [ed.] 12th Grade (Didn't finished, studying nurses aide, through the newspaper at home). Amateur songwriter; [occ.] No college, grades wasn't good enough. Graduated. Did Housework in New York; [memb.] Mental Health, Group FL. Night Time Group Member, prayer meetings. Jacksonville, FL. Trinity Church In Jacksonville, FL; [hon.] Jacksonville, FL. Keepsafe Day Time Adult Program, peer leader; [oth. writ.] I wrote two songs, that was sent back to me, not made public.; [pers.] I graduated from High School, May 23, 1963. I went to N.Y.C. a week later, outs of a newspaper under employment. I lived in a nice home as a maid.; [a.] Hartwell, GA

NICHOLSON JR., WESLEY
[pen.] WNJ; [b.] June 19, 1949, Cleveland, OH; [ed.] B.S. Tele-Communication, Kent State University 1977; [occ.] Meter Reader; [hon.] 1985-86 Karamu House recipient of "The Gilpin Award."; [oth. writ.] "Thinking," and "Lovers," published by Quail Books.; [pers.] I wish the whole world could be free and at peace.; [a.] Cleveland, OH

NICKSON, TERRY
[pen.] Opera; [b.] May 22, 1965, New Jersey; [p.] Lille Mae Nickson and Charles Clark; [ch.] Kamisha A. Nickson; [ed.] High School Graduate, working on associates degree in computer science; [occ.] Home-business in Arts and crafts, taking care of my child; [hon.] One poem published in West Virginia, one courters Pendent from singing in high school choir three years in a row.; [oth. writ.] Lyrics written and ready for composers, (to set to music); [pers.] I strive to be a better person, and to reach my most ultimate Goal, to sing professionally and get that recording contract. A to someday write a book.; [a.] Neptune, NJ

NORTON, HARRY C.
[b.] September 27, 1920, Lexington, ME; [p.] Leroy and

Edith Norton (Deceased); [m.] Jennie Quimby Norton, December 28, 1943; [ch.] Six: 2 boys/4 girls; [ed.] High School, Central High 1939, New Portland ME; [occ.] Retired Municipal Officer (Town of Norridgewock ME); [memb.] Grange, 100F 39 yrs., Baptist Church; [oth. writ.] None previously published - Recipe for Rest, Hold Firm Arcturus, Samly on Ship, Agreverance for Riches, Spiritual, Our First Baby Girl, Family, many others.; [pers.] I write on whatever subject that enthralls me: the beauty of nature, family devotions, religious, complementary poems, comedy, and sometimes song poems. I just get satisfaction expressing my feelins in this manner. I hav e my own collection. I am anxious to read Through th eLooking Glass to enjoy others' talents. ; [a.] Norridgewock, ME

O'BRIAN, KAYLA
[b.] October 14, 1991, Eau-Claire, WI; [p.] Rich and Shiela O'Brian; [ed.] Preschool; [memb.] Eleva Lutheran Church; [pers.] Accept who you are, because that's how God made you!; [a.] Eleva, WI

O'BRIEN, SHANNON ELIZABETH MARIE
[b.] January 30, 1981, North Tarrytown, NY; [p.] Linda (O'Brien) Herso, Dennis O'Brien; [ed.] 10th grade student at Ossining High School; [occ.] Student/Babysitter; [hon.] Distinguished honor student; [oth. writ.] Many, however they were never entered for publication.; [pers.] "There are many hills in life you must walk up before you get on level ground."; [a.] Ossining, NY

O'NEILL, MATTHEW J.
[b.] August 24, 1960, Council Bluffs, IA; [p.] Maurice and Marie O'Neill; [m.] Michelle, June 16, 1990; [ch.] Kylie and Kellen O'Neill; [ed.] St. Albert H.S., I.W.C.C., San Francisco College of Mortway Science; [occ.] Funeral Director, Belm - Belford Funeral Home; [memb.] St. Peters Church, Sertoma Club, Knights of Columbus, St. Albert Alumni Assoc.; [a.] Council Bluffs, IA

O'ROURKE, LAURIE LASHOMB
[b.] April 16, 1965, Ogdensburg, NY; [p.] Robert and Cynthia Lashomb; [m.] Patrick O'Rourke, September 21, 1996; [ed.] B.S.B.A. - LeMoyne College (Syracuse, NY), J.D. - University of Richmond's, T.C. Williams School of Law, (Richmond, VA); [occ.] Attorney; [memb.] The Florida Bar, Appellate Practice and Advocacy Section; [hon.] Dean's List, American Bar Association/Law Student Division Achievement Awards; [oth. writ.] Various poems written for pleasure (not published), various articles written and published in law school newspaper.; [pers.] My poetry is usually inspired by events occurring in my life at the time of the writing.; [a.] Cocoa, FL

O'TOOLE JR., ALBERT
[b.] June 3, 1936, Paulsboro, NJ; [p.] Albert O'Toole, Charlotte O'Toole; [m.] Karen S. O'Toole, May 23, 1981; [ch.] Kelly and Billy O'Toole, Patricia Hampton, Robert Simcox, Sonya Bisceglie; [ed.] Haddon Heights High, NJ; [occ.] Custodian, Roy Moore Elementary Custodian, Colorado Mt. College, Rancher; [memb.] Garfield Youth Services - Pals United Way Fund, Distribution Committee; [hon.] Longest Matched Pal in Garfield Youth Service in County; [oth. writ.] Nothing published; [pers.] I find beauty and inspiration in people, places, nature and things all around us. I just love life.; [a.] Rifle, CO

OBI-RAPU, CHRIS
[b.] July 8, 1950, Nigeria; [p.] Josiah Okolo and Monica Onyisi; [m.] Victoria Chukwudi, November 28, 1981; [ch.] Nkem Elfrida and Chichi Belinda; [ed.] Diploma Mass Communication, University of Lagos, Nigeria; [occ.] Freelance Producer, Director, Writer (Film Video); [memb.] Member Nigeria Guild of Television Producers Directors; [hon.] Award winning Producer Director in Nigeria before I immigrated to U.S.A. in 1995.; [oth. writ.] Several television drama and comedy scripts shown on network service of Nigeria Television Authority.; [pers.] "Do unto others as you would like them do unto you" - This Biblical saying is my guide in all my dealings with others.; [a.] Brooklyn Park, MN

ODELL, EMILY
[b.] March 23, 1979, Charlotte, NC; [p.] Mary Howell, Alice Odell, David Odell; [ed.] Dutch Fork High School, Irmo, SC; [memb.] Spanish Club, Beta Club, Junior Classical League; [hon.] Certificate of Award for Language Arts, Reading Achievement Award, Legacy Staff Award; [oth. writ.] Several unpublished books; [pers.] I have been greatly influenced by the Harlem Renaissance poets.; [a.] Columbia, SC

ODOM, JAMES
[pen.] J. C. Odom; [b.] December 13, 1978, Natchez, MS; [p.] Norma and Gary Odom; [ed.] I am a senior at Block High School in Jonesville, LA. I plan to attend LA Tech University in Ruston, LA; [memb.] FBLA (Future Business Leaders of America), Fellowship of Christian Students, First Baptist Church, Block High Football team; [hon.] I received 2nd-team all-District in football, I am an honor roll student at Block High School. I completed the Red Cross Life saver course and was awarded my lifeguard and C.P.R. license in '95.; [oth. writ.] I have written over 50 poems and four short stories; [pers.] I believe that poetry is a way for people to express their feelings. Also, I believe that in all we do, we should thank our gracious God above.; [a.] Jonesville, LA

ODUDU, JOSEPHINE
[pen.] Chizoba; [b.] March 26, 1964, Nigeria; [p.] Florence Umekwe and Wilson Umekwe; [m.] Gabriel Odudu, March 25, 1990; [ch.] Gabriella and Christopher Odudu; [ed.] Columbia and Snyder High Schools in NJ. Jersey City State College, Long Beach City College - California; [occ.] Program Director with Social Vocational Services, California; [memb.] Formerly with American Cancer Society and currently with American Dietary Association; [hon.] Was (chosen as) class author in high school, made honor roll several times in high school, made the Dean's List several times in college. Received an academic achievement award in college from the Dean.; [oth. writ.] Some published poetry in the local paper, my work was published regularly in my school's literary magazine known as, "word". I've established a quarterly newsletter in my job where my poetry is appreciated by many readers.; [pers.] "I write because I have to, the Lord sent me to the world, granted me with the gift of the word in which to use in giving hope to the hopeless, smiles to the saddened, strength to the weak and to use words to bring out the positive in everything.; [a.] Bellflower, CA

OLBINSKI, LUCAS
[pen.] Lucas Olbinski; [b.] January 19, 1974, Warsaw, Poland; [p.] Malgorzata and Rafal; [ed.] Grade School and High School in Warsaw, Poland. Two years College of Economy in Suendborg, Denmark. Attending Second year at University of Odense in Denmark; [occ.] Student of Medicine; [hon.] Various Honours and Awards throughout my schooling years for excellence. And good standing; [oth. writ.] Numerous poems never published.; [pers.] Poetry has become an expression of my inner most emotions, thoughts and reflections. Poetry has helped me focus on the state of my soul.; [a.] Forest Hills, NY

OLSEN, RONALD P.
[b.] March 16, 1960, Philadelphia, PA; [p.] Martin and Iris; [m.] Karen, May 15, 1982; [ch.] Aubrie Lynn; [ed.] N.E. High School, Phila., PA; [occ.] Manager (Store); [oth. writ.] Several poems about love, life and personal experiences.; [pers.] I did not start writing poetry till I was 30 yrs. old, the birth of my daughter inspired me to write my 1st poem called "Tears of Joy" and since then, poetry has come to me naturally.; [a.] Sicklerville, NJ

OMANDAM-BYRNE, EASTER
[pen.] TerDam; [b.] April 22, 1962, Cebu City, Philippines; [p.] Tony Omandam, Fely Paras; [m.] Desmond Edward Byrne, September 11, 1993; [ed.] Bachelor's Degree in Commerce, major in Accounting; [occ.] Payroll Manager, LifeStream Behavioral Center, Leesburg, FL, Owner/Manager, Knowledge, Inc., Eustis, FL; [memb.] Ministry to the Sick and Shut-Ins, St. Mary's Catholic Church, Eustis, FL, Lay Carmelite Order, Orlando, FL, Treasurer, VisMinda Association, (Filipino-American Association of FL); [hon.] Rotary Group Study Exchange Team to Australia, 1990, Plaque of Appreciations: 1) Association of Barangay Councils, Cagayan de oro City, Philippines, 1991, 2) Carmen Valley Lodge No. 250, F. and A.M. Masonic District 17, Philippines, 1989, 3) University of the Philippines Law Center, Institute of Judicial Admn., Cagayan de Oro City, Philippines, 1992, Outstanding Teacher, College of Commerce - Cagayan Capitol Colleges Philippines, 1990, Founder, Philippine Association of Secretaries, Cagayan de Oro Chapter, 1986; [pers.] Do not fight for success too much. Fight for a way that you can make use of your talent and abilities. What are honors for? Honor and glory are for the Almighty!; [a.] Eustis, FL

ORTEGA, JENNIFER
[b.] April 19, 1985, El Monte, CA; [p.] David and Anna Ortega; [ed.] William Northrup Elementary and Middle School; [hon.] Outstanding Student, Drill Team, Cheerleading, Music, Creative Writing, Art and Dare Awards; [oth. writ.] A thank you poem and an I am poem.; [pers.] I enjoy all music and love to write and read. I attend Northrup School and am age 11. I play the violin and clarinet and hope to get all my writings published.; [a.] Alhambra, CA

ORTIZ, BETTY
[b.] August 5, 1968, Chicago; [p.] Betty and Miguel A. Ortiz; [m.] JoAnn DiSalvo, June 20, 1995; [ed.] Lane Tech H.S. 1986, Malcolm X College, St. Francis Paramedic Program; [occ.] Paramedic, Medtrans of Illinois; [memb.] Women's Softball, Windy City Sports; [hon.] Editor's Choice Award in past anthology; [oth. writ.] Several poems published in prior anthologies. Many others written for friends and loved ones.; [pers.] I hope that my poems help others as they help me. They help me acccept the death of my mother and help me express my love for her. That because of her I am today.; [a.] Chicago, IL

OSBORN, LESLEY
[b.] April 26, 1951, Commack, NY; [p.] Dr. and Mrs. George M. Rosen; [ch.] Joseph, Harris; [ed.] Commack H.S., Skidmore College; [hon.] National Honor Society, B.A. Biology; [oth. writ.] Monthly column in national dog publication, several children's books, other poetry; [pers.] I write through my emotions - whatever they may be.; [a.] Plantation, FL

OSTA, GERARD J.
[b.] May 1, 1960, Schenectady, NY; [p.] William Osta, Laura Lazzari-Osta; [ed.] Mohonasen High School, Hudson Valley Community College, Siena College, and Franklin Pierce Law Center; [occ.] Law Clerk; [memb.] The Roman Catholic Church; [oth. writ.] Several unpublished poems, thoughts, observations, and stories.;

[pers.] My mission is to seek out and express creation's profundity which is so often hidden by banal or vain pursuits.; [a.] Schenectady, NY

OWENS, RAVEN
[b.] March 29, 1968, Rocky Mount, NC; [p.] Wendell R. Owens Sr., Ellen Watson Owens; [ed.] Northern Nash Senior High School Rocky Mount, NC; [occ.] Self-employed; [pers.] This poem was my first and written out of love for one beautiful sweet girl. Love can bring out the best in all of us!; [a.] Rocky Mount, NC

PACKER, CONNIE B.
[b.] November 6, 1943, Afton, WY; [p.] Elmo John and Melba Beyeler; [m.] (Widow) Jerry E. Packer, April 14, 1962; [ch.] Raymond, Robyn and Carol; [ed.] Some college at Utah State Univ. Ogden High, Cokeville Wyo. Elementary; [occ.] Airbag Assembly; [memb.] Cowboy Poets of Idaho Assoc.; [oth. writ.] 2 books of poetry (self-pub.) Cowboy Boots and Pony Tails I and II; [pers.] If you can't find something to laugh about everyday, life isn't worth living.; [a.] Brigham City, UT

PAGANO, MICHAEL T.
[b.] October 15, 1961; [occ.] Town of Hempstead; [oth. writ.] Many poems never released or shown to anyone.; [pers.] There is nothing I nor you can't do.; [a.] Long Beach, NY

PAGUNTALAN, EDNA N.
[pen.] Maria Eden Rose Doloroso; [b.] November 2, 1963, Miag-Ao, Iloilo, Philippines; [p.] Mr. and Mrs. Faustino and Rita Paguntalan; [ed.] B.S.E. (2nd year irregular), B.S. Psychology (Inclination to Human Relationships) doing self-evaluation, I.C.S. Journalism, Short Story; [occ.] Childcare/Learning Center, Cashier/U.S.O. Naval Station Ingleside, Texas; [memb.] Student Catholic Action Legion of Mary and any other Marian Devotions Catechetical Teachings; [hon.] "Best Reader" 1976-77; [oth. writ.] The above courses, I took the basics in those areas of studies. (and self-know-how), no any item has been publish, yet, I've plans of sharing some of my writings. I'm trying to finish up a project, needs further studies.; [pers.] Failures are the lessons of life, a conflict to know that there's a reason to strive for... to be rediscover and to learn to resolve. Finding for facts, justify criticisms and seek for the truth.; [a.] South San Francisco, CA

PALAZZO, L. SCOTT
[b.] November 22, 1957, Philadelphia, PA; [p.] John and Antoinette Palazzo; [m.] Cathlene Clare, March 29, 1980; [ed.] World Travel; [occ.] Producer/Director; [hon.] 1996 Grammy Award Nominee, "Best Director", Long Form Music Video Category; [pers.] "Carpe Diem", The time to live is now! For there are no promises about tomorrow. Read a book, buy a meal for a homeless person and eat with them, listen to more Dylan.; [a.] Studio City, CA

PALMER, KRISTINE M.
[b.] December 23, 1969, Kankakee, IL; [p.] Donald and Delourese Kanaouse; [m.] John F. Palmer, June 22, 1991; [ed.] BS General Engineering From Univ. of IL Champaign, EIT Exam; [occ.] Design Engineer (Mechanical and Structural); [memb.] Sigma Zeta Eureka College Gamma Epsilon U of I Honor Societies Also Alpha-Chi National Honor Society; [hon.] Dean's List, National Dean's List, US Achievement Academy and Scholarship, Presidential Scholar Eureka College, Randolph P. Hoelscher Award for Outstanding Junior in General Engineering U of I; [oth. writ.] A few poem published in college pamphlets.; [pers.] I believe a person will continue to grow if he/she can reflect of life's experiences and learn

from them as he/she locks for new horizons. Limits are set by man and broken by his ideals.

PANELLA, PATRICK
[pen.] Patrick Panella; [b.] August 28, 1966, Newark, NJ; [p.] Gerald and Donna Panella; [m.] Lucia Panella, May 24, 1992; [ch.] Gabriella Alexandra; [ed.] High School Graduate; [occ.] Monmouth County Corrections Officer; [memb.] United States Marine Corps., 1984-1988; [pers.] In this world of give and take, There are only a few who give, what it takes, is the best quote I ever heard.; [a.] Jackson, NY

PAPAVLO, ATHENA
[b.] September 17, 1977; [p.] James and Eugenia; [ed.] Graduate of the P.A.S.S. program, Manchester School of Technology '95.; [occ.] Music Specialist at Circuit City; [memb.] Member of WERC - Wolf Education Research Center; [hon.] Music Specialist of the month at work; [pers.] The majority of my writing has to do with my own personal situations.; [a.] Manchester, NH

PAPE, TAMMY
[b.] July 21, 1978, Appling, GA; [p.] Dorothy and Paul Pape; [ed.] Harlem High, Harlem, GA., Augusta Beauty College, Augusta, GA; [occ.] Currently in sales; [memb.] Lewis Memorial Methodist Church, Evans, GA, Trinity Iwana Club; [hon.] Future Homemakers of America (FHA) Achievement Award, Peer Counseling Award at School; [oth. writ.] Have written about 30 more poems, unpublished. Have written a Romance-Horror book but not published as yet.; [pers.] I write from the heart and mostly from my inner feelings; [a.] Appling, GA

PAPPAS, RICHARD
[pen.] Richard Pappas; [b.] February 15, 1942, Pittsburgh, PA; [p.] Mary Galla, Anthony Pappas; [ed.] Carnegie High, Technician Training School; [occ.] Janitor; [pers.] Fooling around writing poetry sure beats cleaning toilets, with a little luck I might make a buck.; [a.] Carnegie, PA

PARKER, MARTHA SUE
[pen.] Sue Crabtree; [b.] March 24, 1941, Kentucky; [p.] Hermon and Margaret Crabtree; [m.] Dennis E. Parker, November 6, 1993; [ch.] Peggy Sue, Darlene, Sherry, James, I have five grandchildren and 1 great-grandchild. My family has five generations already (me) and my daughter "Peggy"; [ed.] Grass Lake High, Accomplished Artist (Oils), Seamstress Evening Gowns, Weddings, Craft of all kinds; [occ.] Domestic engineer and Mary Kay Beauty Consultant; [memb.] O.E.S. Order of the Eastern Star, A the Daughter of the Nile (Shrine's), North Lights School of Arts, Bob Ross Artist Club; [oth. writ.] Several Poems; [pers.] I would like to say that Jesus Christ, is my inspiration and I owe all I am to Him. Sorry this typewriter is old.; [a.] Tekonsha, MI

PARKS, SILKY
[b.] September 19, 1970, Albany, GA; [p.] Arrie Tift and Jerry Tift; [ch.] Austin Holes; [ed.] Westover High School, Darton College, Albany Technical Institute; [oth. writ.] Have written 125 poems, 2 articles, and am currently writing a novel titled, "Momma Use To Say."; [pers.] "I can't save the world, but I can make a difference."; [a.] Marietta, GA

PARRISH, JENNIFER
[b.] October 31, 1966, Columbus, OH; [p.] Jack and Mary Parrish; [ed.] Ohio University, BS Communications; [occ.] Court Investigator, Franklin County Probate Court; [memb.] Executive Secretary Lawyers, Christian Fellowship, Chairperson Ohio Court Investigators

Committee; [pers.] We were, are, and will be saved through Grace rising through constant revelations steadily transforming our wills to the will of the Father.; [a.] Washington, OH

PARSONS, KRYSTAL L.
[b.] April 24, 1978, Kansas City, MO; [p.] Randy Parsons and Dena Boswell; [m.] Robert Scott Rushing; [ch.] Tyler Scott Rushing; [a.] Camden Point, MO

PATEL, HIMMAL M.
[pen.] "Shivam Sunderam"; [b.] March 22, 1918, Ahmedabad, India; [p.] Maganlal Patel (Father) and Reraben (Mother); [m.] Shankaben; [ch.] Pinesh, Veena, Deepika and Vipul; [ed.] Science Graduate B.Sc., (Bombay University, India), Principal subject: Chemistry; [occ.] Writing the folk-roles of every country in my language for children and writing poetry into English; [hon.] Some of my books publications are awarded prizes by Indian Government, while some of my books have been awarded by State Government (Gujarat State of India); [oth. writ.] I have written in Gujarat language (a major language of India - mother tongue of "Gandhi" some 30 books for children's - Folk tales of Asia, Europe, Australia, Africa and America (some books are awarded prizes by Indian Govt.; [a.] Charlotte, NC

PATTERSON, ANN
[b.] August 5, 1938, Pauls Valley, OK; [p.] Wilburn and Mildren Gross; [m.] Ken Patterson (Divorced), June 18, 1960 to January 31, 1976; [ch.] Tracey Dean, Nancy Ann, Beverly Jeanne; [ed.] Modesto High School, Modesto California, Modesto Junior College, Modesto (AA Degree), CA, Fresno State University, Fresno, CA (BA Degree), College of Idaho, Caldwell, Idaho (Masters in Counselling); [occ.] Fund Development Consultant, to Charitable and Educational Organizations; [memb.] National Society of Fund Raising Executives (NSFRE), Idaho Development Network, Boise, ID, Association for Healthcare in Philanthrophy, President: Non-profit Solutions, Inc.; [hon.] Distinguished Citizen by the Idaho Statesman, Boise, ID, (Sept. 1986), Accredited Membership in NAHD (now AHIP) Nat'l. Assoc. Hosp. Devel.; [oth. writ.] Published poems in periodicals, articles in professional Journal of National Association for Hospitals in Philanthrophy (AHIP).; [pers.] I have always loved the written word, reading and sharing poetry and prose as a child, as a parent and now as a grandmother. God blesses me through both the simple and the profound.; [a.] Homedale, ID

PATTERSON, GEORGE ROBERT
[b.] March 12, 1955, Columbia, SC; [p.] Paul and Ethel Patterson; [m.] Debra Ann Kerr Patterson, May 8, 1994; [ch.] Dodi, Angela, Melissa; [oth. writ.] I have a collection of Poetry and Lyrics, short stories and novels. Debra and I have written one novel together. Most of these works are yet unpublished.; [pers.] I write about the depths of human experience, the good, the bad, the mysterious and the unknown. I have lived the tragedies and rejoiced in the victories. Through it all I have become convinced that Jesus Christ is the only solution to the dilemma of mankind. Anything else is counterfeit and therefore not even a viable option.; [a.] Milledgeville, GA

PATTON, PATRICK R.
[b.] March 8, 1978, Fontana, CA; [p.] Richard and Laurie Patton; [ed.] San Clemente High School, Saddleback Community College; [oth. writ.] Various other poems and short stories.; [pers.] Poetry and all writings are not meant to be interpreted with only one answer. All scripture is meant to allow every reader to

open themselves to their own thoughts and emotions kept hidden by societal complexities.; [a.] San Clemente, CA

PAUL, DAVID A.
[b.] February 21, 1982, Whidbey Island, WA; [p.] Loraine Swift and David Paul; [ed.] Currently 9th Grade, attending Flour Bluff High School; [occ.] Student; [oth. writ.] Adolescence, The Test, The Real World, Missed Shot, Nirvana, The Tree, Battlefield, Last Poem; [a.] Corpus Christi, TX

PAYNE, NORMA DOTSON
[b.] January 22, 1918, Forest, IL; [p.] Mr. and Mrs. E. L. Dotson; [m.] Jess Willard Payne, March 3, 1948; [ch.] Teri Ann Payne Nunnally; [ed.] Millirin University, B.S., Northwestern University, U of Chicago, M.S., U of Illinois; [occ.] Retired from 33 years of Teaching; [memb.] AXSL, Ami Legion Auxiliary, Winona Study Club, Van Buren Golf Club; [hon.] Who's Who in World of Women for distinguished achievement, Who's Who in Missouri Education, Personalities of the Mid-West 1977-1978, Who's Who in Child Development 1986, For service in the Red Cross during World War II, a certificate from President Truman, and Induction into the International Poetry Hall of Fame; [oth. writ.] Several poems interred in the National Library of Poetry; [pers.] Sharing my poems with others is like being rewarded with a bouquet of roses; [a.] Van Buren, MO

PEAKE, JOSEPH
[b.] March 19, 1923, Houston, TX; [p.] Charlotte Peake (Sturm); [m.] Mabel B. Peake, April 20, 1943; [ch.] Joseph Jr. and Pamela Post; [ed.] Two yrs. College; [occ.] Retired Federal Examiner; [memb.] National Association of Retired Federal Employees, Palomar Unitarian Universalist Fellowship; [oth. writ.] Written letters to the local newspaper editor about drugs, income tax, English only, and other subjects. A poem was printed in the Azusa, Ca local paper, "If it is to be."; [pers.] Served in the army during WW II and Korea. Retired a Lt. Col. I have 6 grandchildren and 3 great grandchildren.; [a.] Carlsbad, CA

PEDERSON, RANDALL JAMES
[b.] September 16, Everett, WA; [p.] Gary and Rosamary Pederson

PEIRSON, ALESIA
[b.] December 10, 1980, Stuart, FL; [a.] Stuart, FL

PELIS, SUSAN E.
[pen.] Dawn Light; [b.] April 28, 1951, Frankfort, IN; [p.] Carl and Christine Zich; [m.] Divorced; [ch.] David Matthew, Dawn Marie; [ed.] North Side High School - Fort Wayne IN, Ill. and Taylor Univ. (both in Ft. Wayne), Columbus State Community College (Columbus, Ohio); [occ.] Food Service - Bob Evans (Columbus, Ohio); [memb.] First Apostolic Church of Dublin, OH; [hon.] Honor Roll at Columbus State - GPA 3.22, won School Spelling Bee in 6th grade; [oth. writ.] Poems published in Church Bulletin, Devotional Essays published in Church Devotional Booklets. Guideposts.; [pers.] My writing talent is a gift from God. I seek to glorify God in my writing and to encourage others.; [a.] Columbus, OH

PENDERGRAFT, MICHAEL
[b.] August 23, 1954, San Antonio, TX; [p.] Roy and Carylene Pendergraft; [m.] Christine, March 31, 1997; [ed.] San Antonio College; [occ.] Bus Driver; [pers.] Don't be afraid to get out of your comfort zone; [a.] Pittsburgh, CA

PEREZ, MARCIA
[pen.] The Traveller; [b.] January 8, 1979, RAF

Lakenheath, England; [p.] Luis Perez, Debra Perez; [ed.] Home schooled, current freshman at Southern Nazarene University; [pers.] My poetry is a mirror which reflects the struggling souls of my generation and beckons to travellers as a place to escape the disillusionment of reality.; [a.] Oklahoma City, OK

PERKINS, SHARROD
[pen.] Sharrod Perkins, Red Prince (on occasions); [b.] December 25, 1972, Statesboro, GA; [p.] William Perkins, Billie V. Byrd; [ch.] Tevahn Perkins, Courtney Reese; [ed.] Statesboro High School; [occ.] Machine Operators, Cooper Wiss Tool Factory; [memb.] Tao Kudo Kwan Martial Arts Association.; [hon.] Black Belt in Martial Arts, 1989 Karate Champion, Graduate of Basic Modeling School.; [pers.] I write about how I feel about life, and its situations. My two biggest influences and inspirations are belief in God, and singer, song writer and producer Kenneth "Babyface" Edmonds; [a.] Statesboro, GA

PERKINS-PELTO, ANNA M.
[pen.] A. M. Perkins and Samantha Cain; [b.] October 30, 1958, Oakland, CA; [p.] Wyatt Perkins Sr., Joyce Perkins; [m.] Gene Pelto, December 27, 1986; [ch.] Isaac Ward, Gene Michael, Terry Ray and Carrie Michele; [ed.] Stayton Union High School Academy of Hair Design, Chemeketa Community College, International Correspondence Schools; [occ.] Hairdresser, Inventor, Business Woman (I own the Jean Pocket Purse Co.), writer.; [memb.] Contributor to North Shore Animal League, National Cancer Research Center, Paralyzed Veterans of America, Children's Cancer Society; [hon.] 2nd place Oregon Amateur Hair stylist Competition, SUHS Honor Roll; [oth. writ.] A poem published in the 3rd Annual Literary Magazine printed by SUHS in May of 1975 titled, "Seeds."; [pers.] I believe that with God all things are not only possible but probable. That humankind can and must overcome our weakness to achieve peace.; [a.] Enid, OK

PERKINSON, MANDEE
[pen.] Wolf McGuiness; [b.] February 8, 1979, Atlanta, GA; [p.] Dennis Perkinson, Jo-Anne Perkinson; [ed.] Attending West Chester East High School; [hon.] First place in Chester County Festival of Arts in 1994 (Charcoal drawing); [oth. writ.] Short stories and poems published in school anthologies, working on a novel.; [pers.] Some feelings cannot be expressed to others by direct statement. They must be shown and be able to be seen and felt through writing or other arts.; [a.] West Chester, PA

PERL, DON
[b.] February 9, 1943, Binghamton, NY; [p.] Julia Sall and Jerome Perl; [m.] Mimi Marshall (Partner); [ch.] One son: Jonah, Two stepchildren: Rashaun and Justin; [ed.] B.A. University of Rochester 1964, J.D. Syracuse University College of Law 1967, Teaching License Metropolitan State College, August 1981; [occ.] Language Arts Teacher; [memb.] Colorado Education Association and Greeley Educational Association; [oth. writ.] A novel, The Law of Bedlam.; [pers.] Writing can shed light on life's haunting mysteries.; [a.] Greeley, CO

PERLICH, RAMONA
[b.] November 29, 1951, Marinette, WI; [p.] Delores and Francis Raygo; [m.] Karl Perlich, April 22, 1988; [ed.] Marinette High School, Madison Area Technical College, Portland Community College; [occ.] Assistant Relationship Manager, U.S. Bank of Oregon; [hon.] Honor Scholarship from Marinette High School; [oth. writ.] Poetry, Newsletters for Clubs, Newsletter for Condo Assoc.; [a.] Vancouver, WA

PERODEAU, JONATHAN
[b.] May 12, 1986, Hartford, CT; [p.] Michael Perodeau Sr.; [ed.] Presently 5th Grade, West Hill School, Rocky Hill, CT; [occ.] Student; [a.] Rocky Hill, CT

PERRY, CARLITA
[b.] May 18, 1968, Alexandria, LA; [p.] Rev. and Mrs. Robert R. Perry Sr.; [ed.] Bachelor of Science, Electrical Engineering, Minor, Mathematics; [occ.] Electrical Engineer for South Carolina Public Service Authority; [memb.] Delta Sigma Theta Sorority, Institute of Electrical and Electronics Engineers (IEEE); [hon.] Dean's List; [oth. writ.] "My book of poetry," contains eleven poems.; [pers.] I'm a firm believer that with God all things are possible. Hard work and perseverance do pay off.; [a.] Myrtle Beach, SC

PETERS, LYNNE
[pen.] Cynthia Escovar; [b.] July 20, 1956, Virginia; [p.] Mr. and Mrs. Richard L. Wagner; [ed.] 12 yrs. of school - grad. '75, Northwestern Leigh H.S., 1 1/2 yrs. Lehigh Com. Col, Business Admin.; [occ.] Songwriter, Poet, Singer; [memb.] Cancer Society; [hon.] Art Religion; [oth. writ.] A lot, however, first of many to get into contest.; [pers.] I try to reflect love has no boundaries by state lines or borders. I have many life experiences to give others heart felt poems to relate to their own experiences.; [a.] Allentown, PA

PETERSON, JANELLE
[pen.] Nell; [b.] January 29, 1979, Baraboo; [p.] Wayne, Karen Peterson; [ed.] I am now in my Senior year of high school. I am planning on going to school for Architecture design in the fall.; [occ.] Waitress; [pers.] I have always enjoyed writing. I have many journals and other poems.; [a.] Westfield, WI

PETTIT, CRYSTAL
[b.] June 11, 1982, Oak Lawn, IL; [p.] Eddie and Laura Pettit; [ed.] Freshman at Bolingbrook High School in the Honors Program; [oth. writ.] "Victory" published in the Anthology of Poetry by Young Americans 1996 Edition.; [pers.] In my poetry, I try to reflect Christ and His wonderful sacrifice. God has influenced me the most and I give Him all the glory for my talent.; [a.] Bolingbrook, IL

PHILLIPS, ROBIN LYNN
[pen.] Reneah Roberts; [b.] January 20, 1967, Lebanon, PA; [p.] Diane Schater; [ed.] Indiana University Northwest; [occ.] Artist/Painter; [memb.] Unity Church, Humane Society; [oth. writ.] Submitted poetry book in the works.; [pers.] I am inspired by all writers and poets, above all I am inspired by love.; [a.] Griffin, IN

PICKARD, JAMES EUGENE
[pen.] Erick Ostrom; [b.] January 19, 1942, Salina, KS; [p.] Mr. and Mrs. R. J. Pickard; [ed.] Eleventh Grade, Salina Senior High, Salina, Kansas; [occ.] Semi-retired worked for Jefferson Co. Schools 23 1/2 yrs; [memb.] I do attend Mile High Church of Religious Science, Denver, Colorado; [hon.] Honorable discharge from Kansas Nat'l. Guard 1969, was a 1st cook in our unit for six years till released from service; [oth. writ.] I'm just testing the waters, so to speak, beginning to write. I've always liked to write.; [pers.] I try to keep an upbeat attitude about my personal life and optimistic projection to others and in my writing of poetry.; [a.] Denver, CO

PICKENS, ALBERT
[b.] May 11, 1983, Albany, NY; [p.] Albert William and Sandra Doris Pickens; [ed.] I'm in 8th grades at Sand Creek Middle School in Colonie NY; [occ.] School Student; [memb.] Sand Freek Jazz band and 8th grade band;

[hon.] I've won awards in Cub Scouts and in karate; [oth. writ.] Many poems such as, "The Destiny Of A Boy," and "Branch of Man kind." I also write and play songs on the piano and guitar.; [pers.] Find it wrong to judge others even if they have judged.; [a.] Albany, NY

PITTMAN, WYONA
[pen.] Wyona Pittman; [b.] September 8, 1933, Point Pleasant, WV; [p.] Irene and Arthur Cheesebrew; [ch.] One daughter; [ed.] High School grad; [occ.] Home health Aide; [oth. writ.] The Window - last year's submission to your contest; [pers.] I always write poems from life's experiences about things I either feel or see. Please include the dedication of this poem to my sister-in-law, B.J.C.; [a.] Columbus, OH

PITTS, TARA L.
[pen.] Tara Louise Pitts; [b.] May 6, 1971, Wheat Ridge, CO; [p.] A. Douglas Pitts, Renee L. Pitts; [ed.] BA Political Science, Minor in Psychology, University of Utah 94, graduate of Alcohol and Drug Abuse Counselor Education, Alpha Omega Academy 96'; [occ.] Behavior Specialist and Parental Counselor, Tucson Indian Center; [memb.] Delta Delta Delta 93', Alpha Omega Honorary Society 92-93, Univ. of Utah ASW board member for Programs and Activities 92-93; [hon.] National Delta Delta Delta Scholarship list, awarded internship for lobbying firm for city rights, Washington D.C.; [pers.] My creative expression springs forth from an intense curiosity in the intricacies and beauty of human nature.; [a.] Tucson, AZ

PLUNKETT, PABLO BOINS
[b.] January 25, 1948, Camaguey, Cuba; [p.] Eustace Boins and Felicia Plunkett; [ed.] High School in Camaguey, Cuba; [occ.] Security Coordinator at a homeless shelter; [hon.] National Humanitarian Award issued to Phoenix Group Inc. of which I was a part. Awarded by newsweek magazine, in Washington DC, May 1995.; [oth. writ.] Unpublished; [pers.] I wish every president - leader - ruler and dictator in the world would recognize when they're wrong, so we'd have a better world.; [a.] Minneapolis, MN

PLYLER, MARCIE LYNN
[b.] June 24, 1988, Brookville, PA; [p.] Randon and Carol Plyler; [ed.] 3rd Grade Student in The Brookville Area School District; [memb.] 3rd year Brownie in the Keystone tall tree girl scouts; [pers.] I developed a love for writing from my second grade teacher Mrs. Barnes who encouraged us to keep a journal in class which I wrote in every day at school.; [a.] Summerville, PA

POHUSKI, HEATHER MANON
[pen.] Manon Poe; [b.] August 12, 1978, Rochester, PA; [p.] Patricia and Rodney Pohuski; [ed.] Beaver Falls High School, Beaver County Area Vocational Technical School, Beaver Falls Beauty Academy; [occ.] Printing Press Operator, Beaver Falls Printing Company; [hon.] Beaver Falls Wolves Club Outstanding Vocational Technical Student Award, Servistar Outstanding Vocational Technical Student Scholarship Award; [pers.] Poetry is my way of releasing my feelings of pain and anger. My greatest influences have been Kurt Cobain, Courtney Love, and Jim Morrison.; [a.] New Galilee, PA

POLIKOFF, DANIEL JOSEPH
[b.] May 7, 1957, Chicago, IL; [p.] Alexander Polikoff and Barbara Garland Polikoff; [ed.] B.A. Cornell University 1979 - Summa Cum Laude, Ph.D. Cornell University, Dept. of Comparative Literature 1996; [occ.] Writer - Teacher Councillor; [memb.] National Coalition Against The Death Penalty; [hon.] German Aca-

demic Teaching Service Fellow; [oth. writ.] Translations of Rilkes Smack to Orphans, Christian Review, a book in Riller (Rue Riller) in progress.; [pers.] Blend the art and wisdom of the tradition with the imperstive to "make of new".; [a.] San Francisco, CA

POLISE, JOHN
[b.] March 5, 1959, New York; [p.] Vincent Polise, Roseanne Polise; [m.] Susan, July 15, 1984; [ed.] 1-12 grade school, no college; [occ.] Dept. of Environmental Protection (Laborer) water supply; [oth. writ.] None published; [pers.] I feel in time all is foreign as all is loved, and a light will shine around us... forever. Thank you for considering my work.; [a.] New York, NY

POLLACK, JACKIE ANN
[b.] September 26, 1973, Minneapolis, MN; [ch.] Anntonette King; [occ.] Mother; [oth. writ.] The lady in my life (Dedicated to Zona Jensen) Love is Like, Life in a Bottle, Every Dog Has His Day.; [pers.] I am living proof that however many hard times life has brought you, you can find a way to survive. I'm no longer a victim, I'm a survivor.; [a.] Anaheim, CA

POLLARD JR., LEWIS
[b.] September 1, 1926, Sedring; [p.] Lewis and Mellie Pollard; [m.] Irene (McKinnie) Pollard, September 3, 1948; [ch.] Vaden and Velda; [ed.] High School; [occ.] Foreman over Shell Pit; [pers.] I have written many poems but I have never published any of them.; [a.] Lake Placid, FL

PORTILLO, JOHANNA C.
[pen.] Bucky; [b.] June 16, 1978, Chicago, IL; [p.] Lupe and Christina Portillo; [ed.] Curie High School, De Paul University College; [occ.] I donate my time to my foster brothers and sister.; [memb.] Who's Who Among American High School Students, The Lion's Club, American Cancer Association, Esperanza Community Services Working with Handicap Kids; [hon.] Awards: Who's Who Among American High School Students, Literature Award, Solo Competition Award for Drums, Honors: English Honor Society, National Honor Society; [oth. writ.] Won writing award for Best Teacher and it was published in the Brighton Park Newspaper. Articles also published in the Curiosity Newspaper, Curie High School.; [pers.] I strive to follow my Dad's footsteps and become a great police officer in the town of Cicero. I have been influenced by the poet Edgar Allan Poe for many years.; [a.] Chicago, IL

POTTS, DWAYNE
[b.] July 29, 1969, Dayton, OH; [p.] Donald R. and Dorothy S. Potts; [ed.] Milton - Union High, University of Dayton, Baldwin-Wallace College; [occ.] Mechanical Engineer; [pers.] My parents have been living examples to me concerning what is most important in life. For this I am eternally grateful.; [a.] Cuyahoga Falls, OH

POWELL, CALVIN LEWIS
[b.] July 22, 1972, Miami, FL; [p.] Lucy Powell, Eddie Powell (Mother Deceased); [ed.] Miami Central Senior High, Florida Memorial College; [occ.] Financial Associate; [memb.] National Association of Black Accountants, National Dean's List; [hon.] All American Scholars Award, National Collegiate Business Merit Award; [oth. writ.] "I Thank You Mother", fields of Gold (The National Library of Poetry) Several unpublished poems of which I am in the process of trying to get exposure and get them published.; [pers.] The greatest Love of all is the Love passed on to me by my beloved Mother (deceased) before she passed away. Therefore, it is Love that lead me to the "Art of Poetry".; [a.] West Palm Beach, FL

POWER, MARK
[b.] August 14, 1960, Havana, IL; [p.] James W. Power, Laura Power; [m.] Reta Power, May 17, 1980; [ch.] Johnny Dale, Jacquelyn, Jaymi Erin; [ed.] Sangamon State University, Lincoln College; [occ.] Self-employed; [memb.] International Society of Poets, International Poetry Hall of Fame, http://www.poets.com/Mark Power.html, Phi Theta Kappa National Honor Society; [hon.] Undergraduate Program Marshall, Literature (SSU), Board of Regents Scholar (SSU), President's List (LC), The National Dean's List (LO), Florence Molen award for English (LC), Marcia Stuart Brooks award for Creative Writing (LC); [oth. writ.] Published poem "Adrift," in A Moment To Reflect, "Adrift," also appears on audio tape, "The Sound of Poetry," published poem "Twilight," in The Best Poems of 1997.; [pers.] The rhythmic voice of poetry speaks to all of us. Whether we read it or whether we write it, we cannot escape its song.; [a.] Easton, FL

PREVOST, CHRISTINA
[b.] March 2, 1971, Somerville, MA; [p.] Linda and Richard Meloni; [ed.] Medford Vocational Tech. High; [occ.] Install Co-ordinator for Home Depot; [oth. writ.] Unpublished as of now.; [pers.] Think of your regrets as a learning experience and that is turn can only make you stronger. To my parents I will never forget you.; [a.] Medford, MA

PROCTOR, PATRICIA M.
[pen.] Petra; [b.] April 21, 1954, Wausau, WI; [p.] Felix Petroski and Margaret (Publ) Petroski; [m.] Michael V. Proctor, May 5, 1973; [ch.] Michael V. Proctor II, Brandon Lee Proctor and Tanya Lee Proctor; [ed.] Wausau West High, Wausau, WI; [hon.] Honored with a framed certificate plaque and a diamond homer award at an award winning ceremony held at the Hyatt Regency Alicante, in Anaheim, California on September 27, 1996; [oth. writ.] Four poems published in the "Famous Poems of the Twentieth Century" additional poems published in "Famous Poems of 1996" by the famous poets society of Hollywood, California; [pers.] My poetry comes from deep within my soul, God's green earth and my sincerest faith for a better tomorrow!; [a.] Wausau, WI

PROUDFOOT, CHARMAINE L.
[pen.] Charie; [b.] October 16, 1966, Georgia; [p.] Pastor Georgia Hill; [ed.] Oakridge High School; [occ.] Pizza Hut; [oth. writ.] Journals; [pers.] Thank you Library of Poetry for encouraging me in my talent of writing poetry.; [a.] Orlando, FL

PROVOST, MELISSA
[b.] January 25, 1980, Ellsworth, A.F.B.S.D; [p.] Ronald Provost, Debra Provost; [ed.] High School Student; [occ.] Student; [pers.] I write my poems based on my feelings. I'm influenced by all mankind, and their way of life.; [a.] Moosup, CT

PRUDEN, SCOTT L.
[pen.] Scrap; [b.] April 28, 1951, Salem, IL; [p.] Charles H. and Zella L. Pruden; [ch.] Todd C. Pruden; [ed.] One year Junior College, Emergency Medical Technician (E.M.T.), Instructor, C.P.R. American Heart Assn.; [occ.] T.S.P. Drywall Hanging; [memb.] North American Hunting Club, International Freelance Photographers Organization, C.M.A./A.S.A.C.; [hon.] Survival, Evasion, Escape Volunteer, Twin Willows N.C. (2); [oth. writ.] "Bloody Hand", "Just for Me", "For Yellow Eyes", "Reward Offered", "Onion Soup", "A Small Thing".; [pers.] We must endure the time we have, however long, to the best of our ability, with some measure of honor and dignity.; [a.] Salem, IL

PRUSH, KENNETH
[b.] April 4, 1975, Long Island, NY; [pers.] Like most poetry, this piece was written to impress a girl. It wasn't until later that it occurred to me. It might also be construed as referring to the moon.; [a.] Redondo Beach, CA

PUKALO, LINDA A.
[b.] September 12, 1951, Detroit, MI; [p.] Rudolph P. Sdao, Jessie M. Sdao; [m.] James G. Pukalo, June 29, 1984; [ch.] Jason Gregory, Anthony James (Deceased); [ed.] Southfield Senior High, Oakland Community College; [occ.] A Mom, CEO "Rainbow Originals," Part Time Bank Teller; [memb.] The Make-A-Wish Foundation of Eastern NC; [oth. writ.] Poems for special events.; [pers.] After our son died from a congenital heart defect, I used stained glass to create a unique "Rainbow Window" for the children at Duke Hospital in his memory. I create "Memory Crystals," to fund my dream of putting "Rainbow Windows" in all children's hospitals. I started writing as a way to express the insight our son's life has brought to me, with the hope of helping someone on a similar journey to carry on.; [a.] Raleigh, NC

QUALLS, KEVIN
[b.] September 8, 1972, Dallas, TX; [ed.] The Criswell College, B.A., currently enrolled in the Master of Divinity Program at Southwestern Baptist Theological Seminary; [a.] Mesquite, TX

QUAM, ZACHARY ADAM
[b.] December 18, 1987, Redmond, OR; [p.] Mother: Stephanie D. Wilson and Mark J. Wilson, Father: Eric A. Quam; [ed.] Third Grader at Englewood Elementary School, Salem, OR; [occ.] Student; [memb.] Boys and Girls Club, Youth Basketball and Soccer; [hon.] Talented and Gifted Program; [a.] Salem, OR

QUEZADA, ERICA
[b.] May 14, 1981, Gilroy, CA; [p.] Rafael, Debra Quezada; [ed.] 9th grade; [memb.] Parkside Gym; [hon.] Music-Saxophone Bronze and Silver medal; [pers.] I love reading religious books as well as poetry and drama. I'm infatuated with my dreams, and wish Adam and Eve never ate the apple.; [a.] Gilroy, CA

QUINN, BILL
[pen.] Vernon B. Kinney III; [b.] July 28, 1959, Hamilton, OH; [p.] Hugh and Beverly; [m.] Carri, April 23, 1994; [ch.] Madyson (1); [ed.] English Major, Ohio U., Occupational Therapy Senior, U. of Findlay; [occ.] Occupational Therapy Asst.; [memb.] American Occupational Therapy Assoc., Ohio Occupational Therapy Assoc.; [hon.] Evans Scholar Dean's List Fall, Winter, Spring, Summer '95-96', Fall 96-97; [oth. writ.] Shooting star (novel) articles in various publications.; [pers.] Life is a gift and should be treated with respect. I try to be original and creative when writing.; [a.] Columbus, OH

QUINN, JAN
[pen.] Jan Quinn; [b.] January 2, 1965, Pullman, WA; [p.] Jack and Lorraine Quinn; [ed.] Studying Secondary Literature Education at Eastern Washington University; [occ.] Assistant Customer Service Supervisor; [pers.] That imagination is the future don't be afraid to use it.; [a.] Spokane, WA

QUINN, TARYN
[pen.] Taryn Quinn; [b.] July 29, Hamilton, OH; [p.] Beverly and High Quinn; [m.] Michael Cannistraci, December 31, 1990; [ed.] CCHS High, Wittenburg University, The Ohashi Institute, The Gotham Writer's Workshop; [occ.] Actress/Director and Writer, Administration and Production Assistant; [memb.] Actor's Eq-

uity Association, Screen Actors Guild, American Federation of Radio and T.V. Artists, Friends of the Amazon Forest, and essential Peace Making Workshops; [hon.] Theatre World Listing - '91, '92, '93, '94; [oth. writ.] Currently in process - an original screenplay based on true events - "Chasing Light."; [pers.] I have an incurable curiosity in the heart's wisdom, the power of the human mind and finding joy in life's struggles.; [a.] New York, NY

QUINT, LORI A.
[b.] October 9, 1962, Waterbury, CT; [p.] Joseph Strileckis, Dale Strileckis; [m.] Mark Quint Sr., August 7, 1992; [ch.] Leanne Marie, Shari Alaina, Mark Wayne, Joshua Alexander, Rebekah No'elle; [ed.] Watertown High, Computer Processing Institute; [occ.] School Bus Driver, Ryder Student Transportation Service; [pers.] My writing comes directly from the heart, using real feelings.; [a.] Torrington, CT

QUIRK, HEATHER MARIE
[b.] December 6, 1982, Lake Charles, LA; [p.] Kenneth Quirk, Teresa Wall (Divorced); [ed.] Episcopal Day School; [occ.] Student; [memb.] Southwest Cheerleading Association; [hon.] Published poem in Anthology of Poetry for Young Americans; [oth. writ.] "Color"; [a.] Lake Charles, LA

RACE, CHERYL G.
[b.] July 1, 1960, Spokane, WA; [p.] George and Betty Krist; [m.] Ronald R. Race, July 9, 1983; [pers.] I wish to give the Lord Jesus Christ all the glory for giving me this poem. I feel this is more proof of His powerful ways...; [a.] Olympia, WA

RAFI, SAMEERA
[b.] July 7, 1980, Karachi, Pakistan; [p.] Shaista Rafi and Rafi Rehman; [ed.] Student at Kerr High School, I am planning to take Medical School in future; [occ.] Student; [hon.] I am honored to have one of my poems selected by National LIbrary of Poetry, I have gotten a few awards, past years, in English, Math, and Art; [oth. writ.] I prefer writing journals and poems, but nothing had been published yet.; [pers.] I started writing poems for my English class. Ms. Dean made me write three different kinds of poems for grade and that's when I found out that I could write a poem myself.; [a.] Houston, TX

RAGAZINCKY, SHEILA RAE
[b.] July 12, 1966, Sycamore, IL; [p.] Rose Biba; [m.] David Louis Ragazincky, February 19, 1990; [ch.] Candie and James Keeling, Bobby-Jo and Samantha Ragazincky; [hon.] Silver Poet, Golden Poet, Honorable mention for my version of "Now I Lay Me Down To Sleep."; [pers.] I don't write poetry to be somebody, but only to possibly touch somebody else's life with my words.

RAGUSE, SHELLEY
[b.] June 22, 1980, Aurora, IL; [p.] Nancy and Dave Raguse; [ed.] Boulder Hill Elementary School, Thompson Jr. High School, Oswego High School (Junior); [occ.] Student; [hon.] Athletic Awards, Honor Roll in Jr. High and High School; [oth. writ.] Curiosity, Too Young To Die; [pers.] Always appreciate what life hands you. Never take things for granted, especially your family.; [a.] Montgomery, IL

RAINEY, STACEY
[b.] September 22, 1969, Wilkes-Barre, PA; [p.] John Gill (Bishop), Martha Gill; [m.] Divorced; [ch.] Cynthia Mae, Kayla Margae; [ed.] Clearfield High, DuBois Business College; [occ.] Seamstress; [hon.] Associate Business Degree, Legal Secretarial; [oth. writ.] I have many other writings in a variety of topics at home, but none

have been published. "God, Make Me Your Soldier," is the first one I've sent in.; [pers.] If I can touch one person's heart through the poems and songs I've written, then I've accomplished my goal by using the talent that God gave me. With God, all things are possible.; [a.] Clearfield, PA

RAMAGE, DONNA L.
[pers.] Poems come from a safe guarded place in my being - when life experiences challenge my normal response - my safe guarded place cries to be heard.; [a.] Missouri City, TX

RAMIREZ, KENNIA
[b.] April 14, 1970, New York City, NY; [p.] Miguel and Ann Ramirez; [ed.] Four years of High School and two years of College; [occ.] Work at J.P Morgon; [memb.] Member at Empire Supporters Club, RMLAC also cien por cien to Enrique Iglesias Fan Club; [oth. writ.] Some of my favorite authors are Isabel Allende, Gabriel Garcia Marquez and Tennessee Williams.; [pers.] Got inspired to express myself and to heal my heart through my writing. Usually death inspires me to write. But other emotions are also expressed. Music is vital to one's life.; [a.] New York, NY

RAMIREZ, ROSIE M.
[b.] May 8, 1973, Davis, CA; [p.] Jose and Maria Ramirez; [ch.] Rosemarie Ramirez; [ed.] Madison High School, Yuba College; [occ.] Supervisor Security Guard, Mother, Student; [hon.] "Student of the Month" award, "Employee of the month" award, 1991 - Valedictorian; [a.] Winters, CA

RANDLE, TIARA DA'NETTE
[b.] May 6, 1981, Houston, TX; [p.] Rosa Randle, Clifford Parks; [ed.] Sam Houston High School, Houston, TX; [occ.] Student; [memb.] ROTC, Student Government, Teen help line; [hon.] Purple Heart (ROTC), Physical Fitness; [oth. writ.] None published; [pers.] All of my poetry comes from personal experiences. If I don't have any inspiration I have a writer's block.; [a.] Houston, TX

RAPPOLD, JENNIFER
[pen.] Jen Woods Rappold; [b.] December 16, 1950, Northampton, MA; [p.] Charles Woods, Geraldine Woods; [m.] Wayne Rappold, November 14, 1970; [ch.] Wayne Harold, David Charles, Mark Daniel; [ed.] B.F.A. - University of Wisconsin in Madison, Cardinal Stritch College in Milwaukee; [occ.] Artist; [memb.] Chicago Artist's Coalition, WI, Women in the Arts, Cedarburg Artists Guild; [hon.] Purchase Award - Wausau Festival of the Arts, Ozaukee Art Center Artist Award; [oth. writ.] A collection of traditional and non-traditional forms of haiku exhibited in conjunction with my abstract oil paintings.; [pers.] Historically, artists have used other areas of creativity in combination with or as inspiration for their paintings, I use written verse as my starting point.; [a.] Fredonia, WI

RASCHKE, MARY ANN S.
[b.] September 22, 1949, Glendale, CA; [p.] Albert M. Sherer, Eugenia E. Sherer; [ed.] Sylmar High School, Linn-Benton Community College; [occ.] School Bus Driver; [memb.] First Baptist Church, Wapiti Archery Club; [pers.] I believe God can turn every situation and heartache into something good and beautiful and I try to reflect that in my writing.; [a.] Lebanon, OR

RASKA, SUSIE
[pen.] Susie; [b.] July 28, 1950, Redwing, MN; [p.] Gilbert - Dorothy Rightman; [m.] Marvin J. Raska, June 28, 1986; [ch.] Troy Kralewski; [occ.] Assistant Manager at Conoco Auto Stop; [oth. writ.] "Togetherness"

RAY, SARAH BROOKS
[b.] September 17, 1952, Carlisle, PA; [p.] Walter Kyle Brooks, Hattie Watts Brooks Blake; [m.] Ronald J. Ray, November 24, 1973; [ch.] Hannah Ray Goss, Joshuas Ray, Josnah M. Ray, Meraiah S. Ray; [ed.] (Dean's List) American Paramedical Academy, Atlanta, GA, (Honor Graduate) Beaufort High School, Beaufort, SC; [occ.] Admissions Director at Long Term Nursing Facility; [hon.] Honor's Diploma, Dean's List; [oth. writ.] Poetry written for family and friends - none previously submitted for publication.; [pers.] The Love in a good family never dies, even when its members do.; [a.] Conyers, GA

RAZO, MODESTO
[pen.] M.A.R., M.R.; [b.] July 3, 1979, Pacoima, CA; [p.] Maximina Alcala De Razo; [ed.] Pacoima Elementary, Pacoima Jr. High, San Fernando High School; [occ.] High School Student at San Fernando High School; [memb.] M.E.C.H.A., La Razo Unida; [hon.] Community Service Award, Perfect Attendance for 1995-1996 School Year; [oth. writ.] Several poems though none published.; [pers.] I thank God and my mother and last but not least the rest of my family and Rosario Ramos for telling me never to give up. If wishes were dollars we'd all be wealthy.; [a.] Pacoima, CA

REED, ADRIANA
[b.] July 5, 1954, Naples, Italy; [p.] Vincenzo Esposito, Iolanda Esposito; [m.] Ronald E. Reed, June 13, 1981; [ch.] Alberto Vicenzo; [ed.] High School in Naples, Italy, Michelangelo Buonaroti High School, Buckeye Business Management, LaFayette Academy; [occ.] General Manager, Henri's Cloud Nine, Minerva, Ohio; [memb.] East Sparta Methodist Church, Carrollton Jaycee Women (Past), East Sparta Methodist Church, Outreach and Care Committee; [hon.] Jaycee Woman of the Year 1981, Slim Dimension Instructor of the Year 1987; [oth. writ.] I have written over 100 poems, and kept them in a book for several years. "We Are" is one of my favorites.; [pers.] In this life there are many hurting people. My hope is that somehow I can reach out to someone with a comforting word, a healing hand, and an open heart.; [a.] Magnolia, OH

REED, STELLA
[pen.] Starr; [b.] Niagara Falls, NY; [m.] Norman W. Reed; [ch.] Two; [ed.] High School, 2 years of College; [occ.] Domestic Engineer; [memb.] Lewiston Council of Arts; [hon.] Dean's List; [oth. writ.] None, this is my first. Idle hours, no space in my life; [pers.] "Be it friend or stranger, leave everyone with a smile." My first poem dedicated to my visually handicapable daughter working on her Masters Degree in Social Services.; [a.] Lewiston, NY

REED JR., ROBERT
[b.] November 26, 1970, Chicago, IL; [p.] Robert and Lorraine Reed; [ed.] University of Wisconsin, Barron County, WITC Rice Lake; [occ.] Grocery Management; [oth. writ.] Writing articles for the UW-BC campus newspaper; [pers.] The theme of my writing is man vs. his environment and his ongoing struggle with the forces surrounding him.; [a.] Cameron, WI

REEVES, JERRY D.
[b.] October 19, 1934, Duncan, OK; [p.] Minnie and Claude Reeves; [m.] Margaret L. (Sanders) Reeves, January 4, 1963; [ch.] Christopher D. Reeves; [ed.] Master of Science in Engineering, Ariz. State University, Bachelor of Science, Mechanical Engineering, ASU, MBA, Defense System Mgt. College; [occ.] Retired USAF Officer (Major) Retired Corp. (Director) and retired Aerospace consultant; [memb.] Tall Beta Pi (Hon), the re-

tired Officer's Association (Military); [hon.] Three Air Force Commendations and Meritorious Conduct Medals, Dean's List, Distinguished Graduate Defense Systems Management College, Distinguished Grad-officer Training Program, "with distinction" from Ariz. State University.; [oth. writ.] Various articles for technical and management publications (professional journals), numerous letters to the editors published in state papers.; [pers.] I believe great poems originate within the deeper depths of the soul, exposing it for all to see, saying thanks for sharing this time with me.; [a.] Tempe, AZ

REGAN, KATHLEEN M.
[b.] October 30, 1948, Milwaukee, WI; [p.] Dorothy and Daniel Regan; [m.] John Patrick Noonan; [ch.] Lauran Stephenie Elshoff; [ed.] Continuing Education at The School of Spiritual Psychology, Milwaukee, WI; [occ.] Certified Reiki Master/Teacher, Certified Rebirther and Aromatherapist; [memb.] International Breathwork Foundation, School of Spiritual Psychology Graduate Association Standing Committee Member, Design Committee Member and Business Development Committee, Chairperson of "Women Writing," (A Biannual Poetry Publication), Associate Member of Institute of Noetic Sciences; [oth. writ.] Several poems published in the Biannual Poetry Publication "Women Writing," article for the Autism Society of S.E. Wisconsin, Lectures on Healing Energy and Aromatherary.; [pers.] My writing reflects my personal, spiritual journey called life, supported by the love of a like-minded community and my faith in universal guidance and healing.; [a.] Shorewood, WI

REID, MICHAEL L.
[b.] February 8, 1950, Hickory, NC; [p.] Fred W. Sr. and Verna P. Reid; [m.] August 29, 1973; [ch.] April Nichole Reid; [ed.] Not much formal education as I left school in the 9th grade. I attended Granite Falls Elem. and Jr. High Schools; [occ.] I work in the Shipping Dept. of Sherrill Furn in Hickory, NC; [hon.] I have no honors or awards, as I don't feel that I have done anything to deserve any. If I have done anything it was not I but God through me so He should get any honors or awards not I.; [oth. writ.] I have written other poems but I have never had one published. I have written other things but they have only been read by a few. I do not feel these things to be good enough to be read by all.; [pers.] Love, honor, and respect God, your parents, your country, and each other. All things are beautiful in God's eyes. I have a dream that all will learn to love one another and live in peace, God and each other are all we have in this world.; [a.] Granite Falls, NC

REITMEYER, RACHEL A.
[pen.] Rachel A. Reitmeyer; [b.] September 29, 1975, Houston, TX; [p.] Rev. Ralph and Ruth Reitmeyer; [ed.] High School - 1994 Texas City High School, Texas Lutheran University 1998; [occ.] Student; [memb.] Delta Zeta Sorority, Delta Alpha Delta, Memorial Lutheran Church, Students Make A Difference (SMAD); [hon.] Lutheran Brotherhood Scholarship, Moody Foundation Scholarship, Dean's List, David Schaper Memorial Scholarship, Academic Excellence Award; [oth. writ.] Articles for the Lone Star Lutheran and Ethos Magazine of Texas Lutheran University.; [pers.] Throughout my education I have gained a love for British Literature and Poets such as Blake and Wordsworth. For me, writing has become a passion and a strong form of expression.; [a.] Texas City, TX

REMY, HILTER
[pen.] The Poet; [b.] November 10, 1949, Port-Au-Prince, Haiti; [p.] Omelia Julien, Herleus Remy; [m.]

Michaelle Remy, May 5, 1987; [ch.] Mike, Vivaldi, Barbara, Marvin and Jeff; [ed.] High School tolissaint Louverture (Hait.) High School Student ICS High School; [occ.] Officer (Security) or Security Officer; [memb.] Member of International Society of Poets; [hon.] Semi-finalist of 1996 Contest of portraits of life Editor's Choice Award 1996. NY State Security Officer Training Certificate. Lab Medical Institute Siloe, Port-Ay-Prince, Hait, Graduated; [oth. writ.] Poems' Book Titled Reflexions. To publish on this summer 97 (French - English and Creol); [pers.] My philosophical statement is the Realism and God is nothing else just love.; [a.] Brooklyn, NY

RESENDIZ, NANETTE MONICA
[b.] May 27, 1962, Tyler, TX; [p.] James H. Smart and Nancy S. Daniels; [m.] Jose Pedro Resendiz, August 20, 1981; [ch.] Juanita, Anita, Benito, Rosita; [memb.] St. Mark the Evangelist Catholic Church, Plano, Texas; [pers.] Spiritual gifts comfort our hearts.; [a.] Wylie, TX

REYNOLDS, MARY A.
[b.] June 20, 1922, Killingly, CT; [p.] John Lacey and Jane Dowling; [m.] Charles B. Reynolds, November 26, 1942; [ch.] Five; [ed.] Eight yrs. Grammar and 3 yrs. High Sch.; [occ.] Retired; [hon.] 1st Prize on "what Christmas means," (you have it) in 1946, 2 "My Puppy," 1st prize in 8th grade in 1936; [oth. writ.] Just the ones I sent you. All were published by you except one. Title, "A Child's Prayer."; [pers.] I just write poetry part time. With 5 children and a job you don't have the time. I also won first prize on 2 of the poems you have.; [a.] Danielson, CT

RHINE, JERROD
[b.] May 12, 1980, Toronto, OH; [p.] John and Sonja Rhine; [ed.] Currently attending Edison High School; [occ.] Student; [memb.] Member of Bell Chapel United Methodist Church, Boy Scouts of America, Member of High School Cross-Country and Track teams; [oth. writ.] Have written for years, but nothing has ever been published.; [pers.] I wish to stress peace among people so that one day there will be no differences between people.; [a.] Toronto, OH

RICH, BARBARA
[b.] July 23, 1964, Louisville, KY; [p.] Carol and Floyd Thurman; [m.] James Rich, May 4, 1987; [ch.] Talia Ann, Trenton Wayne; [a.] Fairdale, KY

RICHARDS, DENISE
[b.] December 31, 1944, Marshalltown, IA; [p.] Roy F. Barker, Doris Barker; [m.] Dale Richards, January 29, 1988; [ed.] Graduated Western High, Anaheim, CA June 1963, 2 years College, last attended Cypress College, Cypress, CA, 1 year Paralegal at Anchorage JC, Anchorage, AK; [occ.] Retired Secretary, now a housewife; [memb.] American Diabetes Assoc., Phi Beta Gamma, Thespian Society Musician's Union; [hon.] Dean's List, AJC; [oth. writ.] "These Are the Things I Love About You," pub. by Blue Mountain Arts, "I'm Hurting Inside Again," and "1991 Christmas Thoughts," pub. by The Radical, Anchorage Alaska, "Rose Of A Day," "Someone," et al pub. by local papers.; [pers.] I have been writing poetry since my 11th grade English teacher taught our class to love it by introducing us to works of many poets, from which my favorite came to be Robert Frost; [a.] Cleveland, OH

RIDGE II, JACK H.
[pen.] One Eyed Jack; [b.] May 28, 1951, Richmond, CA; [p.] Paulene and Jack H. Ridge; [m.] Marcella Joyce

Ridge, August 19, 1972; [ch.] Rebecca, Desray, Jack III; [ed.] Home School Alaska Territory, Belfair Elementary, North Mason High School, Olympic College, PSNS Apprentice and the school of Hard Knocks; [occ.] Ridge Rental and Properties Manager, and TRF Shipfitter; [memb.] National Geographic, Boy Scouts, Girl Scouts, L.D.S. Church, United States Citizen; [hon.] I am honored to be alive, I am honored to be healthy, I am awarded with a loving wife and life mate and three loving children.; [oth. writ.] There are 80 poems so far. My favorite are I Want To Be, The Chimest, Bear, Specimen, Gram, A Soldier, and Trash.; [pers.] I write about my personal life, about my dreams past and present. Some are funny, some are sad, and some get you mad. They all have a meaning in the first letter of each line.; [a.] Belfair, WA

RIDLON, CYNTHIA
[b.] April 10, 1956, Woodbury, NJ; [p.] Joyce and Bill Doe; [m.] Tim Ridlon, July 1, 1978; [ch.] Benjamin, Jessica; [ed.] Damascus High School, B.S. Biology, Shepherd College, M.S. Biomedical Sciences, Hood College; [occ.] Raising my children; [memb.] Friends of Perrysburg Civic Organization; [hon.] Dean's list, 4.0, graduated Cum Laude from College; [oth. writ.] Two articles in the Journal of Liquid Chromatography.; [pers.] Working in cancer research, my writing dealt with the emotion of discovery. In writing poems I am inspired by the discovery of emotions.; [a.] Perrysburg, OH

RIECK, ALLISON C.
[pen.] My Choice; [b.] February 2, 1980, Rochester, NY; [p.] Lorraine and Charles H. Rieck III; [ed.] Gananda Central High School; [oth. writ.] Many short stories published in school literary magazines. One short story published in Ripples, a magazine for creative expression.; [a.] Walworth, NY

RIEDMATTER, REGINA A.
[b.] June 28, Cleveland, OH; [p.] Wilma and Frank Riedmatter; [ed.] Mt. St. Joseph College Cum Laude, Major: Latin, Xavier University, Major: Spanish Masters Degree, International Univ. of Mexico, 3.9 average; [occ.] Retired Spanish and Latin Teacher; [hon.] Dean's List, Auxilium Latinum Trophy; [oth. writ.] Several articles published in St. Anthony messenger magazine.; [pers.] When you die no one will remember whether you wore a cloth coat or a full length mink, whether you drove a cadallac or a chery. What they will remember are things you gave them. Do your giving while you're living, then you're knowing where its going.; [a.] Cincinnati, OH

RIETH, SUSANNE BARBARA HINES
[b.] November 28, 1980, Brooklyn, NY; [p.] Susan Hines and Michael Rieth; [ed.] Fontbonne Hall Academy, Brooklyn, NY; [occ.] Student; [memb.] National Honor Society, Irish History Society, Great Books, St. Thomas More Choir; [hon.] Woman in Science Award, Criminal Justice Award, Outstanding Achievement, Chemistry Seg. Math I and II, Gold English Medal, NEDT 2 yrs. Outstanding Achievement Major Art, History; [oth. writ.] "She Other Side"; [a.] Breesport, NY

RIHA, KATE GAYNOR
[pen.] K. G. Riha; [b.] October 2, 1951, Detroit, MI; [p.] Robert Michael and Jayne Gaynor; [m.] Patrick; [ch.] Jennifer Ann; [occ.] Entertainment and Trade Show Production; [a.] Kansas City, MO

RINEWALT, KENT
[pen.] Norman Kent; [b.] May 31, 1952, Lamesa, TX; [p.] Edwin (Deceased) and Hazel; [m.] Heidi, March 22, 1980; [ch.] Daniel 15, Lee 11, Betsy 9; [ed.] Klondike

High, South Plains College, Texas Tech; [occ.] Cotton Producer; [hon.] International Literary Awards "Honorable Mention"; [oth. writ.] Published in seek 1990; [pers.] Writing has a magical way of giving immortality to deceased people and pets who were and are very special.; [a.] La Mesa, TX

RINN, ROSEMARIE ANN
[pen.] Rose Rinn; [b.] December 19, 1982; [p.] Anna Troia, Peter Rinn; [ed.] Presently in 7th grade; [occ.] Student; [memb.] National Junior Honor Society, YMCA, Dance Squad, Drill Team, John Muir Middle School; [hon.] National Junior Honor Society, 3rd place for competition for dance; [oth. writ.] I have a packet of unpublished poems.; [pers.] "Your Dreams Are Your Reality."; [a.] Burbank, CA

RIPPY, JACQUALINE
[pen.] Jaye Snowden; [b.] October 22, 1957, Tullahoma, TN; [p.] Chester Williams, Mickie Cooper Williams; [ch.] Dameon LeTon Rippy; [ed.] Tullahoma High School, TTC-Shelbyville, Motlow State Community College; [occ.] Fiscal Technician, MSCC, Tullahoma, TN (Job Training Division); [memb.] TN State Employees Association, MSCC Support Staff Committee (92-94), MSCC Fund Raising Committee (93-94), Annual Report Committee (91-96); [hon.] Chairperson WEEA Grant Writing Committee (received $307,261.00 Federal Grant) Treasurer MSCC Photography Club (89-91), Hostess BPA Competition (91-92), Brother's United Scholarship, Who's Who of American High School (75), Participant in Tullahoma Literacy Video and MSCC Campus Video; [oth. writ.] Poetry published in Motlow State Community College monthly newsletter "Inklings", and several articles in local newspapers.; [pers.] My sole existence is to simplify life's complexities through poetry, short stories and songs. Greatly influenced by early poets and authors. Elizabeth Barrett Browning, Poe, Sandburg and Twain.; [a.] Tullahoma, TN

RISNER, SANDRA
[pen.] S. R. Lee; [b.] October 14, 1947, Lawrence, MA; [p.] Rosemary Gilmartin Bohne; [ch.] Kellie and Julie; [ed.] Two years college, Northern Essex, 1 year Andover Jr. College; [occ.] Office Mgr.; [memb.] Mt. Vernon Neighborhood Assoc., Lay Associate of Presentation of Mary Academy, Sacred Heart Charismatic Prayer Community; [oth. writ.] Aired on WCCM Radio/Lawrence, MA. Songs: "Let Freedom Ring Out", "I've Seen the Light", "Marriage Trinity", aired on Nat'l Radio (The American Christian count down) "Freedom Bells".; [pers.] I strive to reflect the inner person. To reach into the depths of the soul and then share what I find with my brothers and sisters.; [a.] Lawrence, MA

RITZ, KIM EILEEN
[b.] April 24, 1958, Riverside, CA; [p.] Donavon Dale and Marlene Margaret Ritz; [ch.] Krystal Marie, Kayla Marlene, Kurt Donavon; [ed.] Bloomington High School, Medical Services Training; [occ.] Office Manager, Fair Price Carpets, Riverside, CA; [memb.] Harvest Christian Fellowship Church; [pers.] I believe there is a message in my poems that can be found helpful in one's travels through the path of life. If I have accomplished this much, I feel I will have achieved something good, that it was meant that I should.; [a.] Grand Terrace, CA

RIVERA, DALE
[pen.] Puma; [b.] June 31, 1959, Bronx, NY; [p.] Mrs. Joyce Rivera, Mr. Robert Taylor; [ed.] G.E.D. and attended Bronx Community College; [occ.] Unemployed (Schooling); [memb.] Merchant Marines, Seamen's

Union; [hon.] 1.) Honorable Mentions from World of Poetry's, Mrs. Eddy Lou Cole, (2 times), Title: "Yes-today's Gone", 2.) Song: I've written songs to contract stars for an album - "American Music", 9/7/88 Title: "Treat Thee Ole Self Nice" (and other songs I wrote), Producer of Country Ceations Music Company: Mr. Phillip A. Wright (Nashville, TN); [oth. writ.] Poems: 1.) The Decent Man, 2.) "Yes-Today's Gone", 3.) "The Eyes - A Very Important Asset, 4.) The Poem Songs: 1.) "Treat Thee Ole Self Nice", 2.) "I Don't Need No Mistakes," "When You Leave," 3.) Crown Music Production, Treat Myself Right; [pers.] I want to thank my mother for saying that my poetry was good, "Winter Wonderful" that I've written in my elementary years, just for my school's interest in my works of art.; [a.] Long Island City, NY

RIVERA, MARILYN
[b.] February 23, 1980, Chicago, IL; [p.] Louise and Benjamin Rivera; [ed.] Sophomore in High School; [hon.] Young Authors, 6th Grade; [oth. writ.] Journaling, stories, poems; [pers.] I'd like to be someone in the future, but not very sure what I want to be. My writing comes from the heart and I write when things go bad for me. I love to write a lot.; [a.] Bridgeport, CT

RIVERS, ROSETTA C.
[b.] September 22, 1942, Farmville, VA; [p.] Harry S. and Rosetta B. Hall; [ch.] Katrina, Julius, Adrienne, Judith, St. Julian, Undretta, Angela; [ed.] R.R. Moton High, Kittrell High, Kittrell Jr. College, Institute of Business and Technology; [occ.] Secretary/Bookkeeper; [memb.] American Legion Aux #336, Greater Fellowship Miss. Baptist Church, Mayor's Commission on Literacy; [pers.] My poem is an expression of my most personal feelings. I like all of the works by Maya Angelou.; [a.] Philadelphia, PA

ROBERTS, DONNA M.
[pen.] D. M. Roberts; [b.] September 8, 1956, Calumet, MI; [p.] Peter Balma, La Vern Balma; [ch.] Andrew David, Jennifer Lynn; [ed.] Maine North Township H.S., University of Wisconsin; [occ.] Administration Mgr., Schumberg, IL; [memb.] Echanbow, Religion of the Light and Sound of God; [oth. writ.] Collection of poems (yet to be published); [pers.] My goal in writing is to reflect truth that can be expressed in a simple, loving way, with the ability to expand the consciousness and heart of the reader; [a.] Mundelein, IL

ROBERTS, LORETTA
[b.] May 4, 1944, New Goshen; [p.] Nellie Wardle and Gean Wardle; [m.] Timothy Roberts Sr., January 3, 1969; [ch.] Timothy Jr, Eric, Janet, and Angela; [ed.] Gerstmeyer Tech. High; [a.] West Terre Haute, IN

ROBERTSON, CYNTHIA
[pers.] Cynthia Robertson lives and writes in Las Cruces, New Mexico.; [a.] Las Cruces, NM

ROBERTSON, SANDRA ROBERTS
[pen.] Sandy Robertson; [b.] July 17, 1954; [p.] August and Cora Roberts; [m.] Thomas W. Robertson Jr., January 11, 1975; [ch.] Justin Thomas Robertson, Dane August Robertson; [ed.] Madison-Mayodan High School, Rockingham Community College; [occ.] Work as substitute teacher in Rockingham County; [memb.] Ellisboro Baptist Church, Women on Missions, American Business Women's Association; [pers.] I am the youngest of 13 children and in April, 1996, our Dad of 86 years was put into a nursing home. When we visited there, I looked around and this is how I think some felt.; [a.] Madison, NC

ROBINSON, JANICE K.
[b.] March 18, 1941, Indianapolis, IN; [p.] Deceased; [m.] Irvin H. Robinson, July 14, 1958; [ch.] Three and 5 grandchildren; [ed.] High School; [occ.] Housewife; [memb.] American Life League, Inc., TBN, Ch. of God Prophecy, Life Outreach International; [hon.] Newspapers, Reading of Poem in Funeral Homes, Memorial Services, Church's, poem listed in, "Tomorrow's Dream", poem listed in, "Of Sunshine and Day Dreams", poem listed in, "Best Poem's of the 90's, poem will be coming out in a book called, "Through the Looking Glass", all of these books are by The National Library of Poetry; [oth. writ.] I have written several other poems and two songs. Also two short stories, in which are not published.; [pers.] From the depth of my inter being, I am moved on to write poetry. My desire is to bless all mankind that comes in contact with my writing. I have been greatly influenced by God Almighty.; [a.] Bloomington, IN

ROBINSON, MARK TREVOR
[b.] October 1, 1969, Muscatine, IA; [p.] Carol Sue Robinson and Carroll Wesley Robinson; [ed.] Pine Ridge Job Corps. Chadron, Neb. Obtained High School Diploma - B.A.M. Certification. Attended from November 2, 1993 to April 13, 1995; [occ.] JRs Janitorial Service. Office Cleaning/Floor Maintenance; [memb.] Currently none. I was a center leader while at Pine Ridge, I was also the President of the Student Government Association for a Term of 7 months; [hon.] I was awarded the residential student of the month spoke to community organizations about Job corps and its purpose and intentions; [oth. writ.] Solace Winter, Of A Rose and Thorns, The Embrace, Innocence Misled, Sweet Voxes, Century's Cry, Under A Tear's Shelter. Currently, I have no works of mine published. This would be my first. I have many more I intend to enter in other contests.; [pers.] There has been only one to influence me to write, and that person would be myself. Of course, there was/is encouragement by others. I get a certain esteem when writing, most of which are about life-death, nature and the way the world is today.; [a.] Conesville, IA

ROBLES-PIMENTEL, ELSA
[b.] February 19, 1924, Puerto Rico; [p.] Jose and Carmen Robles; [m.] Alberto Pimentel, May 1948; [ch.] Alberto Jr., Roberto, and Gilberto; [ed.] Sociology - Community Relations Advocate; [occ.] Retired; [memb.] National Puerto Rican Professional Women's Club; [hon.] Image 1980, Montgomery County Hispanic Coalition 1981, National Puerto Rican Women's Club 1982, National Urban League 1984, Maryland Working Women 1996; [oth. writ.] Children's Stories, "Not in my Family," (a drug prevention play), poems, "I Invite You To Live," "What Is Christmas", "Forget Me Not," "Like Roses," "De Que Color Es Lu Alma," and other poems in Spanish.; [pers.] I was born totally blind in my right eye. Philosophy: Limitation is a state of mind. Overcome obstacles and reach your goals and dreams, regardless of inconveniences.; [a.] Silver Spring, MD

RODRIGUES JR., JOSEPH
[b.] July 27, 1943, Honolulu, HI; [p.] Joseph and Sarah Rodrigues Sr.; [m.] Carol Berini Rodrigues, September 16, 1968; [ed.] Graduate of Balboa High School, San Francisco, in the year 1961, 2 years college of Marine, Kentfield, CA Studied Art Appreciation 1972-1974; [occ.] U.S. Army Retired, Investor and Collector of Comic Book Art; [memb.] PVA and disabled Veterans of America, International Society of Poets, Distinguished Member since 1996; [hon.] Several "Editors Choice awards" for outstanding achievement in poetry; [oth. writ.] My work has been published in seven poetry anthologies titled: "No Bugles in the Morning", "Battle-Zone", "Af-

ter The Fall", "Gunship", "Terror Is The Night", "Greenwood Cove", and "Whirlwinds of Light"; [pers.] The words I write are feelings expressed through my personal life experiences in reflecting nature, the goodness of mankind and the horrors of war.; [a.] Belvedere, CA

RODRIGUEZ, MILLIE
[b.] March 5, 1960, San Juan, PR; [p.] Pedro and Lourdes Rodriguez; [ed.] Twin Lakes High, Palm Beach Junior College, A.A. Degree in Journalism; [occ.] Collections Manager, First Collect, Inc., Dallas, TX; [memb.] American Collectors Association; [hon.] Certified Collector Designation, Assistant Vice President, Lomas Mortgage USA, Military Letter of Commendation, USAR 1978; [oth. writ.] Editor of "The Collector," company publication, Lomas Mortgage USA, free lance writer for the Miami Herald weekend section 1982, currently working on a novela; [pers.] The purpose of life is to develop the soul, and through writing I discover that truth.; [a.] Dallas, TX

RODRIGUEZ, SHAWN D.
[b.] July 8, 1980, New York, NY; [p.] Francine Rodriguez, Amilcar Rodriguez; [ed.] Edward R. Murrow High School Student; [occ.] High School Student; [pers.] If you shoot for the moon and miss, you will always be among the stars, play to win.; [a.] Brooklyn, NY

ROGERS, CANDIDA
[pen.] Candi Rogers; [b.] May 23, 1981, Hanford, CA; [p.] Ronald and Cherel Rogers; [ed.] Attending High School as a sophomore at Corcoran High; [memb.] The Church of Jesus Christ of Latter day Saints, Soccer Team, Track Team, Band, Church Youth Group, Corcoran Free Style Wrestling Club; [hon.] Young woman in excellence, gospel in action, 3rd place regional wrestling; [oth. writ.] Many different poems in which I hope to be published later.; [pers.] I'm grateful for this talent God has given me. I'm also very grateful for my parents who believe in me. Thanks to my friends for always reading my poetry no matter how dumb it was.; [a.] Corcoran, CA

ROGERS, JOHN
[b.] February 4, 1924, Denver, CO; [p.] Ruth and Harry Hammerich; [m.] Sadie Ione, June 3, 1967; [ch.] David Randolph; [ed.] High School, two years college; [occ.] Retired - 33 1/2 years from Communication Industry; [memb.] Ahmes, Temple of the Mystic Shrine; [hon.] U.S. Navy, Honorable Discharge WW II, also U.S.N.R. Honorable Discharge Korea; [pers.] I changed my name in WW II because of the war in the European Theatre!; [a.] Sacramento, CA

ROGERS, ROSEANNA
[b.] March 28, 1951, Detroit, MI; [p.] Edward and Helen Rogers; [ed.] Taylor Center High School, Graduated in 1969, Wayne State Univ., Graduated in 1974, Bach. of Science Degree; [occ.] Client Serv. Rep., Quest Diagnostics, Inc., Auburn Hills, MI; [memb.] St. Constance Catholic Church, Taylor, MI, I teach 2nd grade religious education at St. Constance; [pers.] I am very close to my family. I love children. I enjoy spending time with my nieces and nephews, and with my students in religious Ed.; [a.] Pontiac, MI

ROLIN, SUMMER
[b.] January 29, 1982; [occ.] Student - Livingston High School - Livingston, Texas; [a.] Onalaska, TX

ROMANO, ANNETTE M.
[b.] May 5, 1983, San Antonio, TX; [p.] Joe and Karen Romano; [ed.] 8th grade, Strath Haven Middle School, Wallingford, PA 19086; [occ.] Student; [pers.] One must understand the origins of one's culture, then and only

then, will one begin to understand one's potential impact on the world.; [a.] Wallingford, PA

ROSS, DEMOND
[b.] Seattle, WA; [ed.] Palmdale High School, Palmdale, CA; [pers.] Personal experiences, the ups and downs of society, and a vivid imagination, I feel are essentials, for me, in being able to express myself fully in creative writing.; [a.] Renton, WA

ROSS, LARRY
[b.] December 8, 1950, Greensboro, NC; [p.] Maggie Shaw Young; [m.] Aminata A. Ross, August 17, 1994; [ed.] G.E.D. from Guilford Tech. Community College. 2 years College A and T State University; [occ.] 100% Disabled veteran; [hon.] Highest Score PCPT U.S. Military (Army); [pers.] Law is another way of saying, first come first served. It is but a tool of checks and balances. The problem is, the checks are balanced on the backs of the everyday Joe.; [a.] Greensboro, NC

ROSSOW, RANDAL R.
[pen.] Randal R. Rossow; [b.] September 10, 1959, Reno, NV; [p.] Leo J. and Jacquelyn M. Rossow; [m.] Linda K. Rossow, [ch.] Glorianna L. Rossow; [oth. writ.] "Learning," National Library of Poetry. "Inspiration," The National Library of Poetry.; [a.] Reno, NV

ROTHENBERG, PAULETTE C.
[b.] November 18, 1943, Washington, DC; [p.] Rae Kaufman, Sam Rothenberg (Both Deceased); [ch.] Ben Rothenberg; [ed.] Mt. Sinai School of Nursing, Hunter College BSH; [occ.] Visiting Nurse Service of N.Y., Staff Nurse; [memb.] Sierra Club (Life member), NRDC; [oth. writ.] Occasional articles for a community newspaper, Passionate responses to various events in my life stimulating writing. Belongs, below. I especially feel this way about my poetry.; [pers.] I like to read a lot. I love modern dance. Dance is poetry to me. Sorrowfully I am merely a watcher, so I put it into them inadequacy of words.; [a.] New York, NY

ROY, EVA M.
[b.] October 31, 1932, Owosso, MI; [p.] Frank Austin and Viola (Sanders) Austin; [m.] Gordon D. Roy, June 27, 1959; [ch.] Brian and Lisa; [ed.] Ovid High Graduate; [occ.] Retired; [memb.] International Society of Poets, Famous Poets Society, National Library of Poetry, Lakeview Baptist Church; [hon.] Distinguished poet award, nine golden poet awards, three ISP merit plaques, 50 award of merit awards, Poet's Hall of Fame; [oth. writ.] Poems in newspapers, poems in school newsletters, reading poems for children and adults.; [pers.] Writing for my family and friends is an inspiration from God almighty.; [a.] Lakeview, MI

RUBIO, JEFFREY JOE
[b.] May 19, 1964, Los Angeles, CA; [p.] Joe L. Rubio and Arminda M. Baker; [m.] Nancy E. Rubio, June 28, 1996; [ch.] Diana M. Ogaz; [ed.] Santa Fe Springs High School, Cerritos College and Clark College; [occ.] Coder at the Vancouver Clinic, Vancouver, Washington; [oth. writ.] I have a lot of poems that I've written over the past years. But none ever published.; [pers.] Most of what I've written comes from what I see and feel through life's experiences. I've come to enjoy the fullness that God has given me in everything.; [a.] Vancouver, WA

RUD, SHERRI
[pen.] Sherri Rud; [b.] November 11, 1968, Grand Ford, ND; [p.] Ernie Rud, Nancy Hofland; [ch.] Jessica and Brianna Rud; [ed.] Graduated from East Grand Forks Sr. High; [occ.] I work for service master, housekeep-

ing; [pers.] What inspired me to write this poem, was going through treatment and being away from my girls and having to turn all my problems over to my higher power, God; [a.] Thompson, ND

RUIZ, JENNIFER
[b.] January 3, 1981, Pleasanton, TX; [p.] Elvia Ruiz; [ed.] Pleasanton High, Sophomore; [occ.] Student; [memb.] Future Homemakers of America, Saint Andrews Church; [hon.] Several U.I.L. Awards from trophies to medals.; [pers.] I appreciate all the help and encouragement you gave me Ms. Bailey. And to those who didn't believe in me I hope that your careers are as promising.; [a.] Pleasanton, TX

RUMP, JENNA
[b.] July 11, 1984, Cincinnati, OH; [p.] Douglas E. Rump and Linda Lee Rump; [ed.] Completed Elementary Education. Currently a seventh grade student at South Ripley Jr., Sr. High School; [occ.] Student; [memb.] Girl Scouts of America, 4-H, Volleyball, Band, Choir, Confirmation Class at St. Paul Lutheran Church.; [hon.] 1st place in D.A.R. essay contest, President's Education award for academics, South Ripley Raider Award, God and Country award, 1st, 2nd, and Best of Category in local Media Fair; [pers.] What is right is not always popular, what is popular is not always right!; [a.] Versailles, IN

RUSHING, DANA
[pen.] Dana Rushing; [b.] November 16, 1949, Borger, TX; [p.] James and Pat Wright; [ch.] Marcy Rushing; [ed.] B.S. Rehabilitation Science, M.Ed. Administration and Counseling, Course work for Ph.D. Psychology; [occ.] Director of Operations for Care Link, Inc. (a health care management and consulting company); [memb.] Metro Rotary Club (Grand Prairie), Foundation Board of DFW Medical Center, Commission on the Disabled; [hon.] Journalism Scholarship: 1970, Grand Prairie Chamber of Commerce Volunteer Award for 1996 Bicycle Ride; [oth. writ.] Book of Poetry, 1991, various poems and short stories published in local newsletters and one National Corporate newsletter.; [pers.] For years I have struggled with the "meaning of life". I have now come to the realization that the meaning of life is what I make it. It is, for me, being the very best that I can be and giving to others.; [a.] Grand Prairie, TX

RUSSELL, EVANGELINE DENISE
[pen.] Evangelist E. D. Russell; [b.] January 14, 1960, Hickman, KY; [p.] Charles L. Shields and Bertha M. Shields; [m.] Divorced, December 8, 1979; [ch.] Ebony - 18, Valencia - 11, Jaulleh - 10, Sarina - 3 and Peter - 15; [ed.] Attended Northwestern H.S. - Grad. 78, Attended Mott Comm College - 79-81, 85, Major: Gen. Bus. Bus. Admn.; [occ.] Homework/Missionary; [memb.] Deliverance C.O.G.I.C.; [oth. writ.] A Mystical Voyage; [pers.] He increases as I decrease.; [a.] Flint, MI

RUSSELL, JACQUELINE
[b.] October 18, 1949, Oklahoma; [m.] Clifford Russell Sr.; [ch.] Six children, 1 with our Lord and ten grandchildren; [occ.] Independent Para-Legal and Contract Driver Service; [pers.] Expressionistic by nature, I strive for dramatic closures that alone sum my total feelings.; [a.] Guthrie, OK

RUST, KAREN ELIZABETH MILLER
[pen.] Mommy; [b.] June 24, 1950, Clarksville, TX; [p.] George Davis, Earline Davis; [m.] Joe Dee Rust, December 29, 1970; [ch.] Robert J. Miller Jr. and Brian Ashley Miller; [ed.] Clarksville High School, Clarksville TX; [occ.] Store Clerk; [pers.] I wrote this poem for only one reason. It was to put my love for my sons in writing,

because it has outgrown my heart. In this poem they will always know how much I love them.; [a.] Avery, TX

RYAN, TRACY L.
[b.] July 31, 1968, Creve Ceour, MO; [p.] Richard Flechsig, Juanita Flechsig; [m.] Christopher Ryan, March 2, 1996; [ch.] Pending; [ed.] N. Clayton Sr., High Clayton State College; [occ.] Receptionist, Augusta Iron and Steel Works, Inc., Augusta GA 30904; [hon.] Who's Who Among American High School Students 1995 and 1996; [pers.] All poems are for children. We need to enrich their lives as well as their minds.; [a.] Augusta, GA

SABBAR, SHANNON
[b.] March 1, 1977, Hammond, IN; [p.] David Sabbar, Marsha Sabbar; [occ.] Pre-Medical Student at the University of Pittsburgh; [memb.] Alpha Epsilon Delta, Lambda Sigma; [pers.] Through introspection, the humanity of man can persevere.; [a.] Yardley, PA

SAGENDORF, STEVEN MARK
[pen.] Steven Sagendorf; [b.] September 14, 1966, Summit, NJ; [p.] Dorothy J. Sagendorf, Leonard Sagendorf; [m.] Divorced; [ch.] Lauren R. Sagendorf, Ryan S. Sagendorf; [ed.] New Providence High School, Fairleigh Dickinson University, Madison, NJ; [occ.] Associate Editor, Martindale Hubbell Law Directories; [memb.] Writers Connection, San Jose, California; [hon.] United States Navy Letter of Appreciation for superior performance of duty during May 8, 1989 - June 23, 1989 San Diego, California. United States Navy Reserves from December 1, 1988 - September 22, 1993, Honorable Discharge (Navy Cook) (Stationed California, Connecticut, New Jersey); [oth. writ.] Feature Film Scripts titled, "Happy Father's Day," drama, "I did, I don't, I do!" romantic comedy. Several poems; [pers.] "True artistic ability is like a tightrope, it's a fine line between genius and madness." I have been greatly influenced by the writings of Tennessee Williams and Ernest Hemingway.; [a.] New Providence, NJ

SALAMA, JEANNE
[b.] July 9, 1957, Saint Louis, MO; [p.] Joan and Charles Colson; [ch.] Misty, Dana, Tony, Michael and Joey; [ed.] Normandy High School, St. Louis, Missouri; [occ.] Mother; [pers.] Always love and respect your children, they are the most precious gifts you can ever receive.; [a.] Cartersville, GA

SALDANA, AMELIA
[b.] July 19, 1983, Houston, TX; [p.] Emilia and Bernardino Saldana; [ed.] R.P. Harris Elementary, Tice Elementary, Harvard Elementary, Purple Sage Elementary, Cunningham Middle School; [oth. writ.] For Harvard Elementary's "Favorite Creations," "Creative Choices," and Cunningham Middle School's "Creative Cats," books.; [pers.] I want to thank God, my creative writing teacher, Ms. Massey, and my family for their support and influencing me to get a step further toward my goals.; [a.] Houston, TX

SALINAS, JOSEPH G.
[pen.] Joseph G. Salinas; [b.] December 11, 1969, Karnes City, TX; [p.] Jesse and Yolanda Salinas; [occ.] Home Disabled; [oth. writ.] No where to turn, if they could see me now, and feelings.; [pers.] I was born with Cerebral Palsy, and I am confined to a wheelchair, cannot talk nor have control of hands. I use a computer with a special device to do my writings.; [a.] Kenedy, TX

SALTERS JR., LEONARD A.
[b.] September 10, 1951, Wilkes-Barre, PA; [p.] Leonard Salters Sr., Elizabeth Salters; [ed.] Robert E. Peary High School, Montgomery College; [occ.] Technical Shift

Supervisor, Aspen System Corporation, Rookville, MD; [hon.] Dean's List; [oth. writ.] Articles for sports-type newsletter; [pers.] Imagery has always been my main focal point. I strive to paint pictures with words.; [a.] Gaithersburg, MD

SAMPSON, MARTHA
[b.] Greenville, TX; [p.] M/M E. W. Hathorne; [m.] Rev. H. L. Sampson, March 25, 1933; [ch.] Don, Dan; [ed.] College, Seminary; [oth. writ.] The Broken Dolly, a novel of fiction; [pers.] At eighty-two years of age I'm still working to excel in at least one thing. In my younger days, to be a good minister's wife and a good mother. Now in widowhood, a good artist and author.

SARGE, BRIAN ANDREW
[b.] January 31, 1977, Elk Grove Village, IL; [p.] Nick and Mary Sarge; [ed.] Roswell High School; [occ.] Soldier (U.S. Army); [oth. writ.] None available to public at this time.; [pers.] Influenced by the darker side of humanity, I attempt to reflect the music I listen to, such as: Nine Inch Nails, Smashing Pumpkins, Pink Floyd, The Doors, David Bowie. I also play drums, life just North of Atlanta.; [a.] Roswell, GA

SASSANO, GEORGE A.
[b.] September 18, 1954, Houston, TX; [p.] Johnny Sassano and Louise McMurry; [m.] Susan Sassano, May 21, 1976; [ch.] Nathan Wayne, Jennifer Nicole; [ed.] Pasadena (TX) High Community College of the Air Force, Assoc Science; [occ.] Electronic Technician - on the Global Positioning System, Kwajalein Island; [memb.] National Taxpayer's Union American Legion, American Veterans, Air Force Sergeants Association, Christian Coalition; [pers.] I believe we all should strive for a higher sense of morality by children God first in our lives, raising our children in the way He would have them go, honoring our spouses, obeying our parents, and respecting the rights of each individual.; [a.] Powell, WY

SCANLON, HEATHER A.
[b.] June 3, 1973, Holyoke, MA; [p.] Joyce and Terence Scanlon; [ed.] Westfield High School, 1992, Manhattanville College, 1996 (BA), presently in Pace Law School, White Plains, NY; [occ.] Student; [oth. writ.] Poems published in local newspapers.; [a.] Westfield, MA

SCHAEFER, ROBIN
[b.] February 13, 1980, Cincinnati; [p.] Donna and Jack Schaefer; [ed.] Home Schooling; [occ.] Lab Rat at the Museum of Natural History and Science; [oth. writ.] Writings in other Anthologiess.; [pers.] Write what you feel.; [a.] Cincinnati, OH

SCHARBOR, DEBBIE
[pen.] Debbie Sckarbor; [b.] December 31, 1959, Pittsburgh, PA; [p.] Andrew and Marion Yanosick; [m.] Divorced; [ch.] Jessica, Joshua; [ed.] Graduated 1977 North Ridgeville High School Associates Degree in Child Care; [occ.] Owner and Director, Cuddle Care Day and Pre-School; [memb.] Cavanaugh Missionary Baptist Church, Salvation Army Volunteer; [hon.] Outstanding Child Care Giver - 1993; [oth. writ.] "Little One Please Sleep," published by the Missionary Baptist Association; [pers.] I believe before you find love with anyone else you must first find the love within yourself. My poetry is a reflection of my heart and I thank the Lord for the ability to express it.; [a.] Fort Smith, AR

SCHLANG, ARLENE
[b.] April 21, Brooklyn, NY; [p.] Nelson and Mae Roth; [m.] David Schlang, May 9, 1948; [ed.] PS 139, Erasmus High School, Hunter College NY, Former Soloist New

Opera Co.; [occ.] Housewife; [memb.] The Metropolitan Club NY City, Nautilus, Beach and Country Club, Atlantic Beach L.I., N.Y. Life Member of the Actor's Fund; [oth. writ.] Novel to be published, lyrics and music; [pers.] I feel great inspiration in the reading and writing of poetry, and in the singing of opera.; [a.] New York, NY

SCHMITT, RONALD R.
[b.] May 21, 1952, Wauwatosa, WI; [p.] James and Phyllis Weber; [m.] Sandra L. Schmitt, August 29, 1980; [ch.] Christopher, Ron Jr., Cynthia, Ronda, Jason; [ed.] Graduate Pulaski High School, Milwaukee, WI; [pers.] My poetry is based on personal experiences in my life and true heart feelings. My wife is a big influence on poems I have written.; [a.] Mayville, WI

SCHOFIELD, GARY
[pen.] Wayne; [b.] January 16, 1959, Pensacola, FL; [p.] Bobby and Betty Schofield; [ed.] Pensacola High School; [occ.] Disabled; [oth. writ.] Some; [pers.] I love to draw and to write poems for fun.; [a.] Milton, FL

SCHOLL, MOLLY
[b.] January 11, 1989; [pers.] Molly was introduced to poetry by Mrs. Margaret Bruen in first grade at St. Dennis/St. Columbia School. Molly was 7 years old when she wrote this poem.

SCHOTT, KENDRA
[b.] September 26, 1982, Alliance, NE; [p.] Ken and Jean; [ed.] Alliance High School, Freshman; [pers.] I encourage all people with goals and dreams to strive for success. Believe in yourself.; [a.] Alliance, NE

SCHRAMER, DIANA K.
[b.] September 19, 1961, Sandwich, IL; [p.] Lerman De Spain, Georgia De Spain; [m.] John L. Schramer, October 21, 1983; [ch.] Matthew John; [ed.] Sandwich Community H.S., Waubonsee Community College; [occ.] Homemaker; [memb.] Our Savior's Lutheran Church; [oth. writ.] Articles in Church, monthly newsletter, "Lightshine," Short story published in newspaper, "The Somonauk Reporter."; [a.] Sandwich, IL

SCHREINER, BETH L.
[b.] May 25, 1971, Newark, NJ; [p.] Robert and Beverly Schreiner; [ed.] Country College of Morris; [occ.] Administrative Assistant, Oncology Research, Novartis; [memb.] Phi Theta Kappa (Honor Society); [oth. writ.] Many poems and short stories which have not been published yet.; [pers.] I have always tried to follow my mother's advice: Do what you love or you've just wasting your life.; [a.] Bloomfiled, NJ

SCHUCHTER, SUSAN W.
[b.] January 5, 1966, Kingsport, TN; [p.] Walter Willis, Alice Willis; [m.] David C. Schuchter, April 17, 1993; [ed.] Hancock County High, Sneedville, TN, East Tennessee State Univ., Johnson City, TN; [occ.] Controller, Vifan USA Inc., Morristown, TN; [memb.] First Methodist Church, Morristown, TN, Institute of Management Accountants; [hon.] High School Valedictorian, College Dean's List, Outstanding Student, AS degree Summa Cum Laude, BBA degree Magna Cum Laude; [pers.] I want to thank my husband, family and friends for believing in me and encouraging me to pursue my writing.; [a.] Morristown, TN

SCHULTZ, CARL D.
[b.] August 23, 1963, Beaufort, SC; [ed.] A graduate of Meridian High School, Meridian, Mississippi in 1981 and Mississippi State University in 1986, Bachelor Degree in Political Science; [occ.] Infantry Officer; [pers.]

The true challenge begins when trying to make many understand, that he's not retarded or impotent. Thus Dingo Transcends idol, Idiom, or Idea; [a.] Meridian, MS

SCHUMACHER, BRADFORD
[b.] January 12, 1976, Neillsville, WI; [p.] David Schumacher, Paula Schumacher; [ed.] Ambassador's Christian High School; [pers.] I give God all the glory, for He is the one who inspires me. "But thou O Lord art a shield for me, my glory and the lifter up of my head" Psalms 3:3; [a.] Marshfield, WI

SCHWARTZ, ERIC
[pen.] Eric DelShaman; [b.] September 15, 1928, New York City; [ed.] Rockland Community College; [occ.] I deliver pizza (and wings) for Domino's; [memb.] Columbia House Music Club; [hon.] "Class Writer," in High School, English Honor Society, Winner of Ann Arlys Bowler National Poetry Contest; [oth. writ.] I am hoping to publish a book, many of my poems have been published in collections.; [pers.] Stop complaining, apathy is death's supermarket.; [a.] New City, NY

SCHWIETERMAN, JUNE BREWSTER
[b.] December 6, 1965, Willoughby, OH; [p.] Thomas and Beryl Brewster; [m.] Larry Thomas Dixon (Fiance); [ch.] Noah Isaac, Joshua Thomas, Danielle Nicole, Larry Thomas; [ed.] South Sumter High, night course for Bookkeeping, South Sumter High; [occ.] Homemaker and mother of four; [hon.] Silver Poet Award by World of Poetry; [pers.] I would like to give a special thanks to Duane Johnson, for encouraging me to allow others to read my writings. To all troubled teens, someone does care! Me.; [a.] Panama City, FL

SCIFRES, ZACH M.
[b.] Little York, IN; [m.] Anna Elizabeth Hahn; [ch.] Catherine and Robert; [ed.] Degree in engineering from Purdue and in medicine from University of Indiana; [oth. writ.] Short stories, essays, newspaper articles.

SCOBY, ROBERT
[b.] August 12, 1981, Chicago, IL; [p.] Mrs. Beverly Scoby; [ed.] Grammar School - Park Manor - Chicago High School 2 years Maryvale Phoenix; [occ.] A student at Maryvale High School; [memb.] JROTC - Color guard-drill team-rifle team gymnastics for the school cheer leading squad; [hon.] Honor Roll - Super intendent's Honor Roll - 2nd place states science Fair-Chicago IL; [pers.] I dedicate the poem to my mom my sister, grandma and uncle Wally.; [a.] Phoenix, AZ

SCOTT, VERONICA
[pen.] V; [b.] March 16, 1959, Baltimore, MD; [p.] Marie McGinnis, William G. McGinnis Sr.; [m.] Marcus V. Scott, January 14, 1989; [ch.] Karl King, Rakela, Nickolas; [ed.] Attended Univ of MD, Heidelberg, Germany 1977 -1980, attended Coppin State University, Balto, MD 1983, Professional Career Development Institute graduated August 1996 Interior Decorat, International Correspondence School 1997 Graduate (Photography); [occ.] Owner and Director, Riverdale Performing Arts Center (to open Spring 1998) Owner and Designer, V's of Riverdale (Decorator); [memb.] National Association of Female Executives, Handyman Club of America; [hon.] Listed in 1995 National Who's Who, Owner of Historical Property, Nationally recognized by the Department of Natural Resources; [oth. writ.] Unpublished "Women for Sale"; [pers.] My poetry reflects my life experience the good, the not so good and the happier moments. Keeping It Real!; [a.] Jonesboro, GA

SCOTT WAYLAND, SUSANNE M.
[pen.] Susanne Scott; [b.] May 6, 1948, Philadelphia, PA; [p.] John A. Scott and Margaret M. Essig-Scott; [m.] Luther R. Wayland, April 10, 1985; [ch.] Travis Scott; [ed.] Friends Central School, Moore College of Art, Philadelphia College of Art, Tulsa University (Anthropology-Archeology Dept.); [occ.] Rancher - Farmer raise cattle, horses and Border Collies; [memb.] C.A.S.A. (Court Appointed Special Advocate) for children, Habitat for Humanity, National Cattleman's Beef Association, American Paint Horse Assoc, American Quarter Horse Assoc, American Border Collie Assoc., Philbrook Art Museum; [oth. writ.] Op. Ed pieces or local newspapers - articles for local newspapers - one fiction novel and one true crime novel in progress on going nature diary.; [pers.] My writing is influenced by my natural observations, as a rancher - farmer, my Quaker schooling and beliefs, as well as personal experience and convictions.; [a.] Morris, OK

SEARLE, CERENA LYNN
[b.] January 25, 1981, La Grande, OR; [p.] Deborah Anne Welker; [ed.] Current Sophomore at Craig High School, Craig, AK; [occ.] Student; [hon.] Honor Roll, Teen-Peer Helper, 97 Alaska Youth Congress on Alcohol and Teen Drug Abuse, Ambassador; [pers.] I believe poetry is the key to one's own imagination.; [a.] Craig, AK

SEARS, KENNETH B.
[pen.] Ken Sears; [b.] January 12, 1911, Middlefield, OH; [p.] Edith Stoll, Edward Sears; [m.] Harriet Sloan, October 1, 1935; [ch.] Three girls, 5 boys; [ed.] 4 yrs. High School, several courses at Lake-Sumter Community College; [occ.] Retired Postmaster; [memb.] Tavares Lodee #234 7&am Orland, FL, Scottish Right, Eustis, FL, York Right, Past President, Florida Chapter N.C.T.; [hon.] 33 Degrees Scottish Rite Mason Convent General, Estis, York Rite Life Member Kiwanis Honorary Memerr Umatilla, FL, Masonic Lodge; [oth. writ.] Articles and poems, Golden Lifestyle of Fla.; [pers.] I love pencils. When I hold their smooth polished surface in my fingers words seem to flow from them.; [a.] Tavares, FL

SEAVY, ANDREW
[b.] February 24, 1983, Everett, WA; [p.] Kim Seavy, Jody Seavy; [ed.] Continuing; [occ.] Student; [memb.] Aqhya, Boy Scouts; [hon.] Silver Pass Award; [oth. writ.] Alien's Holiday, On Induction Night; [pers.] Take some, leave some, have same.; [a.] Everett, WA

SEILS, NATASHA M.
[b.] March 25, 1970, Edgerton, WI; [p.] Robert and Gena Peterson; [m.] Daniel P. Seils, February 14, 1992; [ch.] One son, Kyle Joseph and 1 on the way due September 16, 1997; [ed.] Graduated Edgerton Senior High; [occ.] Dietary Cook for Alternative Living Service, Wynfield; [pers.] I got started writing poems when I was a teenager. My very best friend and I wrote in our study classes. I wrote to express my emotions that I was feeling at the time. Or sometimes something else comes along that sounds good like my poem, 'A Better Place!'; [a.] Madison, WI

SELMAN, LISA
[b.] February 22, 1981, Star County Knox, IN; [p.] Rhonda and Ted Selman; [ed.] I am a Sophomore and I attend night school at Memorial High School in Elkhart, Indiana; [occ.] I am a cashier at a Citgo Gas Station; [oth. writ.] I enjoy horseback riding, listening to music, I love dancing, and going out with friends.; [pers.] Those who arise from rough spots and lonely times will achieve their happiness.; [a.] Elkhart, IN

SELVAGE, JOHN VERNON
[pen.] John Vernon Selvage; [b.] August 30, 1925, Rocky Ford, CO; [p.] Harvey Albert Selvage and Verna King Selvage; [m.] MaryLoue Farris Selvage, 1954; [ch.] Diana, Creg, Gordon, Yvonne; [ed.] Although I attended public school and attended college briefly in Pueblo, CO., I'm basically educated through a life time of travel (from New Zealand to Florance, Italy) and work (from extensive restaurant ownership to construction) I served I will and am former marine.; [occ.] Disabled/retired; [memb.] Carpenters District Union of America, Colorado Share Program, Y.M.C.A. and AARP, Automobile Association of America, Assoc., Friends of the Lakewood Library; [hon.] Former Golden Gloves/amateur Program Honorary poet Laureate/Santa Fe, NM Leadership Denver Associate; [oth. writ.] Poems and short stories (unpublished); [pers.] My early influences in literature were Damon Runyon and Jack London. As my life nears being 3/4 full, I think often of another of my favorite writer's words, "My candle burns at both ends..." Indeed it is with this alacrity that life seems to be moving!; [a.] Wheat Ridge, CO

SEMPLE, VIRGINIA L.
[pen.] Virginia Semple; [b.] August 17, 1923, Kalamazoo, MI; [p.] Walter P. Fuller, Helen M. Fuller; [m.] James C. Semple (Deceased), December 24, 1950; [ch.] Wanda Leigh Hawkins; [ed.] Pasadena Jr. College, Calif., Music, Sports Class of '42, Palomar College, Calif., Art Student; [occ.] Art Student, Poet; [memb.] AMVET, VFW, PVA, USCO, (As a navy wife - WW II) Organized; [hon.] Two Gold Cups, Bowling Blue Ribbons, Track and Field, Swimming and Driving 1941 Pasadena, CA; [oth. writ.] I have written poems for a monthly "Calendar" put out by the Gateway Retirement Community, where I have lived for three years. "Get Well" cards also. Make my own cards.; [pers.] As an athlete, I made team work and fair play a priority. I've done a lot of exploring and inventing. To see and learn something new every minute is fascinating to me. My love and respect for nature, lets me draw and write from my heart.; [a.] Poway, CA

SERRITELLA, ELIZABETH
[b.] March 20, 1961, Chicago, IL; [p.] Anthony J. and Caroline R. Serritella; [ed.] Schaumburg High; [occ.] Inspection Quality Motorola Inc.; [memb.] Saint Marcelline Catholic Parish; [hon.] Confirmed Christian; [oth. writ.] Personal poems to personal friends and loved ones.; [pers.] Inspired by nature, music, romantic piano, church, fond of spiritual, religious items. Astronomy and astrology. Meditation, reflection, relaxation are favorite treasures of mine.; [a.] Schaumburg, IL

SHAEFFER, RANDY J.
[pen.] Randy Shaeffer; [b.] November 25, 1966, Maryland; [p.] Don and Pat Shaeffer; [m.] Kelly Shaeffer, May 4, 1996; [ed.] High School, some college courses; [occ.] Machinist, Lyricist, Vocalist; [memb.] N.H.R.A., D.R.A.W.; [oth. writ.] A prose for D.R.A.W. Drag Racing Association of Women; [pers.] Don't live in fear of tomorrow, live for the day.; [a.] Hanover, PA

SHAMBAUGH, IDA
[b.] January 19, 1941, Dallas, TX; [p.] Mr. and Mrs. Leslie Owens Sr.; [m.] George H. Shambaugh, October 15, 1959; [ch.] George Jr. (Deceased) and Paul (Police officer); [ed.] Toulon Elem. and High School (Toulon, Illinois), CCCC Jacksonville, NC (Council on Aging) Nursing; [occ.] Retired (nurse); [memb.] NCO Club (SJAFB, NC) (Goldsboro, NC) active in SIDS Research, NC Baptist Women Women's Bowling Congress, many charitable organizations, Dr. Mom Assoc.; [hon.] Awards in past years involving "Little League," employee of the

month (work), Cub Scouts, school fund raising (as parents and grandparents), AF Achievement (spouse) "Member of the Most loved wife in the world quote "spouse" Lifetime membership; [oth. writ.] "Special Delivery," "Grandpa," "That Special Knock," The Policeman's Son," "Color Coded," many, many others; [pers.] Family is my inspiration - my "guardian angel" is my guiding force and my philosophy is "the complexity of simplicity."; [a.] Four Oaks, NC

SHARPE, LOIS
[b.] September 29, 1944, Chester, PA; [p.] Helen and Joseph Mercadante; [m.] C.L. "Doc" Sharpe, October 19, 1963; [ch.] Richard Jeffrey, Kristin Renee; [ed.] Penncrest High School, Mary Washington College; [occ.] Homemaker; [memb.] Chapel in University Park Choir, Firestone Band Parents, (Akron, OH), Mobberly Baptist Church Sunday School, Christian Women's Club; [hon.] National Honor Society, French Award, President of Junior Board of Akron City Hospital; [pers.] Since I belong to the Lord, and He is the giver of gifts, I seek to honor Him with the written word, and in all else.; [a.] Longview, TX

SHELDEN, MARGE
[b.] August 2, 1925, Marlette, MI; [p.] Merle and Norman Landon; [m.] Deceased; [ch.] Katherine, Elizabeth and Frances; [ed.] Marlette High School (MI); [occ.] Retired, Consultant, Community Volunteer; [memb.] Ganges United Methodist Church, Lake Michigan Shore Assn. Bd. of Directors, Saugatuck-Douglas Historical Society, Pier Cove Ravine Trust Assn.; [hon.] V.P. National Assn. of Women Exec., Director National ATHENA Award Foundation (national recognition program for women), Lansing Regional Chamber of Commerce, 25 yrs., Award Mulliken Village Council (MI), Civic Award, Mulliken Dist. Library, President's Award 1993 ATHENA Award Recipient presented by ATHENA Owner/Operator, Shelden Insurance Agency; [oth. writ.] Poems published in Lansing State Journal (MI) and in various professional/business newsletters. Family poem book of 150 poems.; [pers.] I have two personal mottos: "Confront the Issue," and "You must do the things you think you cannot do." I have mentored and encouraged many young women in business to believe in themselves and their ideas.; [a.] Fennville, MI

SHELDON-JOHNSON, PATRICIA
[pen.] Patricia Sheldon - Johnson; [b.] March 14, 1952, Cromwell, CT; [p.] Willard Sheldon and Virginia Waters Sheldon; [m.] Skip Johnson, February 24, 1995; [ch.] Linda, Darren, Iris, Matthew and Timmy and 1 grandson Christopher; [ed.] Monument Mountain Regional H.S.; [occ.] Certified Home Health Aide; [memb.] United Church of Christ; [pers.] I try to personalize all my poetry for situation and persons. I'm writing them for. I use my gift of words as personal gifts from me and God. Love is a gift that's free.; [a.] Elizaville, NY

SHELTON, VICKI J.
[pen.] Victoria Shelton; [b.] Mineral Wells, TX; [p.] Clyde E. Poe and Bonnie L. Poe; [m.] Roger D. Shelton; [ch.] Jason L. and Anita J. Seagroves; [oth. writ.] This is my first publication. Several poems and songs are in the process of copyrights and hopeful for future publications.; [pers.] To enlighten a heart, bring a smile or touch a soul is an act of love. Without it we are nothing. The love of God and the love from and for my family is my inspiration for writing and for living.; [a.] Santo, TX

SHETTER, NINA M.
[b.] July 28, 1922, Dale Co, AL; [p.] Richard Baker and Dora K. McGill Baker; [m.] Lonzo C. Shetter, Feb-

ruary 9, 1983; [ch.] Nina Gail Starkey Long and Sherea Botsford; [ed.] Draughns - Massy Business College Montgomery, AL, 1 year college; [occ.] Retired; [memb.] River Oaks Baptist Church, Moose Lodge, Local Chapter AARP - President; [hon.] I was honored to be a minister wife for 18 yrs.; [oth. writ.] None published.; [pers.] I just write for my own hobby - Christianity influenced me.; [a.] Fort Worth, TX

SHIELDS, JOE
[b.] April 20, 1973, Fort Benning, GA; [p.] Terry and Joe Shields; [ed.] The Hun School of Princetown (NJ), Roanoke College (VA); [occ.] Examiner of Credentials, State Dept of Education, NJ; [memb.] Sigma Chi, Silly Wash; [hon.] Andrew Murphy Award For Fiction (Roanoke); [oth. writ.] Several Stories published in Roanoke College's On Concept's Edge; [pers.] A great deal can be learned about humanity through the works of Irish writers and poets.; [a.] Bordentown, NJ

SHIELDS, JULIA
[pen.] Julia Averitt; [b.] July 29, 1959, San Antonio, TX; [p.] Mary Bass and Philip Bass; [m.] X-husband John Averitt, May 23, 1992; [ch.] William Averitt, Christina and Stephanie Shields; [ed.] Southwest Paramedical in San Antonio Medical Assistant - San Antonio College EM.T. - OJT - Nurses Aide; [occ.] Full Time Student Welding Vocational/College Basic Counselling; [hon.] Only Honor Student of my class in 1984 - Medical Assistant Class; [oth. writ.] I had a poem published in a newsletter for the Animal Defense League (I worked for in 1995), and it went out to 6,500 people in San Antonio TX. I saved a few copies have them at home. I'm from San Antonio, TX; [pers.] I'm a recovering alcoholic and addict, I turned myself in when I relapsed - so I wouldn't die out there. I'm going to school now and doing good in welding, I write a lot of poems, and I can't wait to go home to, my 3 children, Christina, Stephanie of William, 17, 16 and 4 years.; [a.] Gatesville, TX

SHIFFLETT, APRIL DAWN
[b.] July 13, 1980; [p.] Mary and Bobby Shifflett; [ed.] I am a junior at Spotswood High School in Penn Laird, VA; [memb.] The SADD Club, Choral Group, Mountain Melodies, 3 yrs. on the Volleyball team at Spotswood, 2 yrs. Junior Olympics Volleyball; [hon.] I have received awards for Recreational Basketball and Volleyball.; [oth. writ.] I've had another poem published in the newspaper and another poem published in Anthology of Poetry by Young Americans in 1994.; [a.] Elkton, VA

SHINELDECKER, CHARLE R.
[pen.] Gary Austin; [b.] October 29, 1940, Muskegon, MI; [p.] Leon and Dorothy Shineldecker; [m.] Divorced, December 27, 1960; [ch.] Jackie and Lorie; [ed.] High School; [occ.] Factory Worker; [oth. writ.] Have written numerous songs, (Country and Gospel). Recorded two of my songs in Dallas, TX., in 1988 now that babies gone - precious memories of you; [a.] Spring Lake, MI

SHONTZ, NICHOLAS
[b.] April 17, 1984, Sidney, MT; [p.] John and Anita Shontz; [ed.] 7th Grade, Helena Middle School, Honor Roll; [memb.] Boy Scouts, Arsenal Soccer Team; [hon.] 1st Place, Literature, Reflections Contest; [pers.] My poems reflect my inner feelings. I am outgrowing asthma and to climb Mount Helena, 5,468 feet, was a major accomplishment!; [a.] Helena, MT

SHORES, JUDY ANN DENISE
[b.] August 23, 1967, Mobile, AL; [p.] Barbara Chessor (Carmichael); [m.] John C. Shores, May 2, 1993; [ch.] Nikia, Alaina, Adriana and Bahtia; [ed.] I graduated from

St. Paul Central High School in June 1985 at the top 25% of my class. I have completed two years of college, Alpena Community College in Michigan and American River College in Sacramento, CA. I've also attended two technical schools in the United States Air Force.; [occ.] I am a full-time wife/mother; [memb.] Member of New Venture Christian Fellowship Voices of Praise Gospel Choir; [hon.] Who's Who Among American High School Students 1984, U-Pop Student of the Year 1982-83, Honor Roll 1982-85, Top 25% graduating, Honor Graduate in Administrative Specialist Technical School - 1985, several awards in U.S. Air Force - 1985-1991; [oth. writ.] Other poems never before published. My goal is a book of poems as well as three novels of which I have started on two.; [pers.] The poem "Oh Woman" was truly inspired by the Lord Jesus Christ. I desire to live for Him and in every thing I do I want to give God the glory.; [a.] Oceanside, CA

SHORT, CORI
[b.] January 26, 1968, Seattle, WA; [p.] Robert Sawyer, Christine Floren; [m.] Nathan Short, August 11, 1990; [ch.] Landan and Keatan Short, my children are the inspiration for the breath in my days.; [ed.] High School; [occ.] Homemaker, part time model; [oth. writ.] Many non published poems I hold close to my heart.; [pers.] Writing is a form of self expression for me. It helps me greatly cope with many different situations in my life. It would be a dream of mine to touch people with my poetry.; [a.] Auburn, WA

SHORTER, VERONICA
[b.] August 25, 1972, Greenville, MS; [p.] Flora Shorter, Tommy Shorter; [ch.] Marnika Shorter, Sharkara Chew; [ed.] Riverside High School, Mississippi Delta Community College; [occ.] Sales Associate, Bookland Store in the Greenville Mall, Greenville, MS; [memb.] Future Business Leaders of America, Old Evening Star Baptist Church; [oth. writ.] Several poems I have wrote, but never attempted to send them off to any contest.; [pers.] I'm greatly inspired and influenced by Maya Angelou. But my desires to write comes from my most inner thoughts and feelings.; [a.] Greenville, MS

SIBLEY, JASON SANFORD
[b.] November 28, 1971, Saint Simons Island, GA; [p.] John A. Sibley III and Nancy Baxter; [ed.] BA University of North Carolina at Chapel Hill; [occ.] Marine Ecologist; [pers.] This poem was written for my grandfather Harry S. Baxter on his seventy-sixth birthday. It was written at Amelia Island, Florida; [a.] San Diego, CA

SIGALA, JOHN J.
[b.] April 20, 1949, Salinas, CA; [p.] John and Francis Sigala (Deceased); [ch.] Alexander, Nichole; [ed.] Two years J.C. College; [occ.] "Retired" Viet Nam aror U.S.M.C., Veteran; [memb.] "Retired" I was an "March 11" infantry in Kha Sahn, Viet Nam, there I was wounded, and forced to retire the corp.; [hon.] Purple Heart, Viet Nam Certificates Awards from Veterans Administration Volunteer Work. "Recognition for "Volunteer Coordinator" for "Vet, Vol. Companion Program"; [oth. writ.] I entered a poem I wrote about and for the Golden Gate Bridge's 50th anniversary, but never received any response, so I guess I didn't win that contest.; [pers.] "Never give your mate "All your love and all your money". If you have extra, give if away, If someone offers you their extra except it, so you won't offend one.; [a.] Oakland, CA

SIGMAN, CHARLES
[b.] November 16, 1925, Bradenton, FL; [p.] Chester C. and Jessie M. Sigman; [m.] Louise W. Sigman, May 4,

1958; [ch.] Caroline Jane Sigman; [ed.] Ocala High School, Jones Business College; [occ.] Retired Rural Carrier, 33 years with U.S. Postal Service; [memb.] First United Methodist Church, American Legion (50 yrs.) Veterans of Foreign Wars, Chapter President of Nat'l. Assn. of Retired Federal Employees; [hon.] Certificates From Retired Seniors Volunteer Programs: Meals-on-Wheels driver, Transporting Patients to University and VA Hospitals. Award plaques from Central Florida Blood Bank: 40 yrs./13 gals.; [pers.] I try not to take myself seriously, and that's easy when I observe how ridiculously funny serious can be. Makes sense to me!; [a.] Ocala, FL

SIGMON, IAN
[b.] March 1, 1978, Hamilton, OH; [p.] Camille Sigman, Michael Sigmon; [ed.] Hamilton High School; [occ.] University student; [hon.] Winner — Bib Blue Poetry Contest; [oth. writ.] Poems published in "Manuscripts" literary magazine; [pers.] My goal is to amalgamate many systems of thought, exoteric and esoteric, into a consummate philosophy that will help to enhance human consciousness.; [a.] Hamilton, OH

SILVA, BRET DAVID
[b.] December 29, 1969, Brighton, MA; [p.] Helen Marie Maroun; [ed.] Methuen High School, Peabody High School, Hillside Private School - Marlboro, MA (for boys); [occ.] Deliver newspapers; [memb.] Saint Anthony Church Lawrence, MA; [hon.] I was in the senior chorus in private school and I received an award for being a great student in that class. I received an award for winning a race in Middle School! (Running); [oth. writ.] I am unhappy to say this is my first poem. To be published and put in a contest.; [pers.] I try to write things to help other people or to help a situation that needs help. If it will help people I like to write about what I care about.; [a.] Lawrence, MA

SILVEIRA, JARED
[b.] September 24, 1970, Hackensack, NJ; [p.] Jorge Silveira, Ertha Silveira; [ed.] Park Hill High School; [occ.] Package Sorter Ups in Lenexa, Kansas; [memb.] New Covenant Baptist Church - Outreach Committee, Visitation, Youth Steering Comm.; [oth. writ.] The Undersea published in "Reflections" Junior High Poetry Magazine in June '84 and Sandcastles published in "Embers" Fall '91 plus countless of other unpublished poems.; [pers.] In my poems I try to display a piece of me, I try to say things that has never been said and ask questions that has never been asked.; [a.] Parkville, MO

SILVER, LAUREN REBECCA
[b.] June 3, 1980, Newark, NJ; [p.] Ronald Silver, Susan Silver; [ed.] South Orange Middle School, South Orange, The Milton School, Milburn, Whippany Park High School, Whippany; [occ.] Student; [oth. writ.] As per request too many to list.; [pers.] It is my hope that our minds are expanded through the literary work of others.; [a.] Florham Park, NJ

SIMONE, DONNA LEE
[pen.] S. A. above; [b.] June 23, 1948, Tracy, CT; [p.] Donald and Lilian; [m.] Philip, August 29, 1969; [ch.] Four; [ed.] High School; [occ.] House wife and Rest. Manager Prior to her death from cancer; [memb.] D.A.R., W.I.B.C.; [hon.] Honor guard captain for drum and bugle cor.; [oth. writ.] Not yet published.; [pers.] Treat everyone as you would like to be treated.; [a.] Durham, CT

SIMONELLI, ANNA
[b.] March 2, 1929, Providence, RI; [p.] Laura and Raymond Marenaro; [m.] Joseph P. Simonelli, July 4, 1951; [ed.] Hope High School; [occ.] Retired;

[memb.] St. Ann's Church, Prov. AARP, Davinci Center; [hon.] Editors Awards from Nat'l Library of Poetry, RI Honor Society, High School; [oth. writ.] Have been submitting poems monthly for nursing home newsletters, have written poems since the 60's. I write from my heart, find it relaxing and a therapy.; [pers.] Depending on my mood will result the kind of poem written whether sad, humorous, realistic or imaginative. This is the third poem I've had published and feel deeply honored.; [a.] Providence, RI

SIMS, RUTH
[pen.] Ruth Sims; [b.] December 18, 1946, Wadsworth, OH; [p.] Fred and Evelyn Hilbert; [m.] Marty Sims (Deceased, July 31, 1996), January 9, 1989; [ch.] One, Beverly Long; [ed.] High School graduate courses in Horse Training, Wayne County School Career Center, Computers, Accounting Business Courses; [occ.] Horse farmer and work in a finishing department at profile in Sharon center; [memb.] Involved in 4-H program with daughter, National Home Gardening Club; [hon.] Won Ribbons in Spelling contest when in Elementary School; [oth. writ.] In process of working on short stories for children and other poetry.; [pers.] My husband Marty told me to write about my own experiences and my life here on our farm. Write what you know about. Write from the heart.; [a.] Rittman, OH

SKAMEL III, JOSEPH PATRICK
[b.] October 4, 1968, Minot, ND; [p.] Joe and Martha Skamel; [ch.] Emily Anna Skamel Haggard; [ed.] Rantoul Twn. High, Rantoul, IL; [occ.] Computer Production Coordinator Cargill, Inc., Wayzata, MN; [oth. writ.] "Carousal Ride" in "A Sea of Treasures".; [a.] Robbinsdale, MN

SKINNER, LINDA
[pen.] Lynn; [b.] October 28, 1952, Warrenton, VA; [p.] Lewis and Louise Frazier; [m.] Robert M. Skinner, October 20, 1990; [ch.] Robert Lewis Skinner; [ed.] Culpeper Co. High School, Art Instruction School, Thomas Nelson Common. College; [occ.] Home maker/mother; [hon.] I am a notary, it's a great honor in itself just being a mother of such a wonderful and loving son, Robert Lewis; [oth. writ.] I wrote this for my son, "Joey The Flying Squirrel," unfortunately, I haven't had much luck in getting it published at this time. (But, I'm not giving up!); [pers.] I have always gotten immense pleasure and satisfaction of putting my ideas and thoughts, feelings down on paper, hoping it gives other people happiness as much as it does for me.; [a.] Woodford, VA

SKINNER JR., JAMES A.
[pen.] James A. Skinner Jr.; [b.] August 15, 1964, Pittsburgh, PA; [p.] James Skinner Sr., Ruth Skinner; [m.] Deanna Skinner, January 16, 1988; [ed.] Avonworth High School; [occ.] Logistics Planner, U.S. Air Force Reserve; [oth. writ.] Various poems; [a.] Oakdale, PA

SLASTEN, GUENNADI N.
[pen.] Gene Nicholas Slaston, Slagen; [b.] May 4, 1957, Kegichevka, Ukraine; [p.] Nikolai Slaston, Vera Boiko-Slaston; [ch.] Marina Slasten; [ed.] Schwerin Russian Secondary School (Germany), B.A./M.A. in Philology, Education, Translation at Kishinev State University (Moldavia), Moscow Institute of Information (Russia); [occ.] Construction Worker, Songwriter; [memb.] The International Society of Poets Distinguished Member, Human Rights Watch; [hon.] Several "Editor's Choice Awards" 1995, 1996, election to the International Poetry Hall of Fame by the National Library of Poetry. Nominations as Poet of the Year in 1995 and 1996, The International Poet of Merit Award, The International Society of Poets, 1995; [oth. writ.] Over a dozen poems and nearly

two dozen songs in Russian and in English, some poems and song lyrics published by the National Library of Poetry, Poets' Guild, JMW Publishing Co.; [pers.] My beloved readers, now a days we have real means for creating a common auxiliary language to be spoken by all and every one. Interlinguistics can help people to create such a universal language of love, peace, and cooperation for the whole of mankind.; [a.] Brooklyn, NY

SLINKARD, KATIE
[b.] September 23, 1978, Garnett, KS; [p.] Ron and Thelma Slinkard; [ed.] Graduating Senior from Haven High School in May 1997. Attending college in Oklahoma in August 1997; [memb.] High School Band and Flag Corp, Student Council, and Yearbook Staff; [hon.] Honor Roll (4 years), Regional Soloists and Ensemble; [oth. writ.] Articles in School Newspaer and Yearbook.; [pers.] I wrote this poem about my mentor. After my Dad I look up to Troy Aikman because of his accomplishments and his aspirations.; [a.] Burrton, KS

SMIGLEY, MELISSA
[b.] April 3, 1967, Eugene, OR; [p.] John and Myrtle Smigley; [ed.] BS University of Oregon, studied Theatre and Political Science; [occ.] Media Relations with a Major newspaper; [memb.] Screen Actors Guild; [hon.] John F. Kennedy Center, Irene Ryan Acting Semi-finalist; [pers.] With love to my mother and father and great appreciation for their love and support.; [a.] Washington, DC

SMITH, ASHLEY NICOLE
[pen.] Divine Addiction; [b.] September 1, 1981, Scottsboro, AL; [p.] Darrell Smith, Raven Smith; [ed.] 9th Grade Section High School, Section, AL; [occ.] Student; [pers.] Life is only till the end but death is forever and if you've lived your life afraid of death you've lived your life dead.; [a.] Section, AL

SMITH, BECKY HOLLAND
[b.] November 4, 1955, Fort Pierce, FL; [oth. writ.] Several songs and short stories. But nothing published.; [a.] Dixie, GA

SMITH, CERDAN ADRIAN
[b.] August 21, 1952, Columbia Hospital, Washington, DC; [p.] Naomi Smith, Leroy Smith; [ch.] Cerdan Vayda Smith Jr.; [ed.] McKinley High Sch. grad, 72" Maryland Sch. of Art/Design 1 yr.; [occ.] Designer Actor Model poet/inventor-Disable/retired; [memb.] Y.M.C.A.; [hon.] Cocoran sch. of Art/Smithsonian sch. of Art of Washington D.C. Models Guild of Hollywood Calif., Romantic time National Inter/Model Contestant finalist FT with Texas 95" Hubert Humphrey award 1968; [oth. writ.] The Human Factor "96", "The Connoisseur of Life", "Ducks in the `Olpond".; [pers.] The true secrets of true success is the "Humble", appreciation" of positive Lessons taught in the Discovery of Adversity" my own original statement - by Cerdan Adrian Smith.; [a.] Bellflower, CA

SMITH, COLLINS A.
[b.] January 17, 1960, Racine, WI; [p.] Calvin F. Smith Sr., (June A. Smith, Deceased); [ch.] One son, Joshua Campeau; [ed.] I have a GED; [occ.] Assistant Manager for International Service System Inc.; [memb.] I am an enrolled member of The Minnesota Chippewa Tribe, Mississippi Band, Leech Lake Reservation; [hon.] I was an honor graduate in the Army National Guard graduating in the top 10 of my battalion.; [oth. writ.] A brothers plea. The nosy neighbor.; [pers.] After living 20 years of my life in a blur. I intend to live the rest of my life clean and sober.; [a.] Racine, WI

SMITH, CONSTANCE
[b.] June 19, 1949, Pasadena, TX; [p.] Stan and Lois Stanowski; [m.] Joseph D. Smith, March 12, 1977; [ch.] Lisanne, Leah, Laura; [ed.] Schreiner College, B.A. English; [occ.] Tutor, Schreiner College, Freelance Writer, Homemaker; [memb.] Christian Coalition, Concerned Women of America, Vol. Fire Dept. Ladies Auxiliary, Literary Volunteers of America; [hon.] Phi Kappa Phi, Scholar with Distinction, President's List - 2 years, Panhellenic Council of Excellence in Scholarship; [oth. writ.] Several poems published in local newspapers and church programs, column in eight local newspapers 5 years.; [pers.] It is my hope that whatever I write inspires someone else to fulfil God's plan for his or her life.; [a.] Mountain Home, TX

SMITH, COREY
[b.] February 26, 1959, Oak Park, IL; [p.] Silvernail Smith and Anne Geddes; [ch.] Emily, Jordan and Corey (twins); [ed.] Oak Park River Forest High School; [occ.] Meat Cutter; [pers.] I dedicate this poem to my girl friend Debbie who I love so dearly and my cousin Ernest Hemingway who I never met.; [a.] Tinley Park, IL

SMITH, DEENA ANN
[b.] November 25, 1952, Brookville, PA; [p.] Marilyn Jean Swartz Fager, Paul V. Felton; [m.] Steven Paul Smith, April 21, 1973; [ch.] Tiffany Anna Smith; [occ.] Artist; [hon.] Photography; [pers.] When the spirit is held captive by life's influence, past or present, release and acceptance is often found by putting pen to page, and allowing the ink, forming the words that lead to understanding.; [a.] Brookville, PA

SMITH, ELIZABETH ANN
[pen.] Lizz Smyth; [b.] July 9, 1962, Bronx, NY; [p.] Lawrence Smith, Margarite Smith; [ed.] Valley Central High Life!; [occ.] Freelance Artist; [memb.] Board Member, Middletown Art Group, Board Member, Art for AIDS Inc., Orange County Arts Council, Warwick Art League; [hon.] 32 Ribbons from 1st place to honorable mention Fine Arts, Ceramics, photography.; [oth. writ.] My paintings, photographs have been shown in local papers. I have had a secret passion for poetry and creative writing for as long as I can remember. Articles and photos published in a local paper, The Unlimited News.; [pers.] Passion, pain love, heartbreak, truth - a few of the reasons I write - Life, death and everything in between.; [a.] Middletown, NY

SMITH, GERALD W.
[b.] December 25, 1935, Wyandotte, MI; [m.] Margaret Amross, December 28, 1957; [ed.] B.A., MSU, East Lansing, M.D.I.V. Colgate Rochester, D.Min. GTF, Doctoral Dissertation: "Curriculum in Death and Dying Education," Graduate Theological Foundation, Notre Dame Indiana; [occ.] Ordained Episcopal Priest and State Police Chaplain, St. Augustine's Episcopal Church, Mason, MI, Past Employment: Retired Airline Pilot (10 yrs), Retired Teacher (22 yrs.), FAA/Air Traffic Controller (1 yr.); [hon.] Biography in Who's Who in Aviation as youngest airline captain in U.S.A. at 23 years old 1959, and president of Michigan Aerospace Education Association 1975; [oth. writ.] "Death and Dying Education for Young People,", Article published in fellows yearbook: Graduate Theological Foundation, Wyadham Hall Press, Donaldson, Indiana 1988.; [pers.] "May the human spirit never give up with the difficulties of faith and reason to find meaning in life.".; [a.] Mason, MI

SMITH, JAMES F.
[b.] March 5, 1959, Magnolia, AR; [p.] William and Louise Smith; [m.] N. Kathy Smith, April 4, 1992; [ch.]

Janae' and Justin Smith; [ed.] M.S. in Animal Nutrition and B.S. in Animal Science from University of Arkansas; [occ.] Admission Counsellor for Job Corbs; [memb.] Gamma Sigma Delta; [hon.] Friend of 4-H Award; [pers.] Hard steps aren't always stairs.; [a.] Russellville, AR

SMITH, JAMES MATHEW
[pen.] Jamie; [b.] August 10, 1976, Portland, OR; [p.] Howard and Vicky Smith; [ed.] Musician, Songwriter; [occ.] Musician, Songwriter; [oth. writ.] I have had poems read over the local radio and one published in, "The Isle of View."; [pers.] Lingering on a beach admiring the wind, then a giant scorpion burrows its way through the sand. As I turn to run, I am confronted by three doors, each door is labled: anger, fear, and despair. "You're only a victim by choice," said a silent voice. If God speaks in a whisper, does the Devil shout?; [a.] Vancouver, WA

SMITH, JOSIE
[b.] September 17, 1912, Bernie, MO; [p.] Joseph Grayum, Ethel Grayum; [m.] Charles F. Smith, March 25, 1933; [ch.] Gaylon, Nancy, Shirley, Charles, Kay, David; [ed.] 8th Grade; [occ.] Retired Painter and Wall Paper Hanger; [memb.] General Baptist Treasurer and Missionary Ladies; [oth. writ.] Several poems published in newspapers.; [pers.] My poems reflect the way I have lived and hopefully encourage people to live a better life in Christ.; [a.] Bernie, MO

SMITH, LONNY A.
[b.] February 22, 1961, Sandusky, OH; [p.] Jackie Lee Smith, Alma Lucille Bailey; [m.] Diane L. Wright-Smith, December 14, 1991; [ch.] Kari Nicole, Kristi Marie, Ashton Lee, Chandler Austin; [ed.] Magoffin County High School; [occ.] Supervisor of Communications and Signals, Norfolk Southern Corporation; [oth. writ.] All unpublished: Forgive Me, I Am, The Touch, Look, Dear Brother, Imagine, Hope, My Wife, Thoughts, A Dream, The Gift, The Garden, That Winter's Night, Life's Mystery, The Quilt, A Child's Voice, My Family, A Place, A Time, and many more yet unpublished; [pers.] I smile at the world in hopes that it will smile back; [a.] Huntington, WV

SMITH, MISTY
[b.] September 5, 1980, Numberg, Germany; [p.] Jim Smith, Sheila Smith; [ed.] Harrison High School; [occ.] Student; [memb.] Cross Country, Track, Journalism, Church Youth Group, and French Club; [hon.] Honorable mention in fiction writing for Showcase Southwest; [oth. writ.] I write for the school newspaper, I have submitted stories and poetry into local contests.; [a.] Cleves, OH

SMITH, NEIL BENTLEY
[b.] September 16, Frimley, England; [p.] Patricia Smith, Peter Reginald Bentley Smith; [m.] Elena Rose Marie Smith (Nee Gleman), December 1, 1990; [ed.] Coventry University; [occ.] Editor; [hon.] BA (Honors) Economics; [oth. writ.] Glasgow Gazette; [pers.] Two cats - Peaches and Tybalt.; [a.] Dove Canyon, CA

SMITH, NORMA
[b.] San Francisco, CA; [p.] Deceased; [m.] Divorced; [ed.] Attended Univ. of Calif.; [occ.] Retired; [memb.] MENSA; [oth. writ.] Published, with former husband, a "Little Magazine" we called "Contour." Wrote some stories and poetry for that magazine and other mags.; [a.] Oakdale, CA

SMITH, PAULETTE BALLREE
[b.] November 21, 1960, Wayne County; [p.] Emmette and Shirley Ballree; [m.] Cecil Smith, February 16,

1979; [ch.] Chad, Joshua, Phillip, Skyler; [occ.] House-wife; [oth. writ.] I have a lot written but have not sub-mitted any others.; [pers.] I have been writing poems all my life I have only put them in the local paper until now or wrote just for my own pleasure (this poem in memory of my mother); [a.] Mount Olive, NC

SMITH, RICHARD
[b.] July 26, 1978, Missoula, MT; [p.] Richard C. Smith, Nancy L. Smith; [ed.] Rosamond High, Class of 1997; [memb.] Order of the Arrow, Boy Scouts of America; [hon.] Eagle Scout; [oth. writ.] Over sixty unpublished poems; [pers.] I follow no pattern, the words just flow to the page.; [a.] Rosamond, CA

SNOW, ELIZABETH HOPE
[b.] August 28, 1966, Logensport, IN; [p.] Howard and Lucille McGee; [m.] Matthew Loren Snow, June 7, 1990; [ch.] Ashley, Dakota and Noah; [ed.] Neosho High School; [pers.] "All things work together for good to those who love God." Thank you Jesus for my talent. I give all the glory to you.; [a.] Arlington, TX

SOBALA, RON
[b.] July 30, 1960, Waco, TX; [ch.] Chase; [ed.] BBA Marketing, Baylor University Waco, TX; [occ.] Com-mercial Sales, Cable/Telecommunications; [hon.] Mu Alpha Theta Math; [oth. writ.] You Take My Breath Away; [pers.] "If we don't look inside ourselves we'll never see what God has blessed us with."; [a.] Houston, TX

SOFFER, RACHEL
[pen.] Jenni; [b.] New York City; [p.] Lissa and Mark Soffer; [ed.] South Valley Elementary School, Moorestown, NJ, Moorestown Middle School, Moorestown Friends School, Moorestown, NJ; [occ.] Student; [memb.] Young Life, American Horse Show Association, Honor Roll; [hon.] Honor Roll, Sophomore Poetry Award second place in local contest; [oth. writ.] About 150 poems and short stories, which I wish to pub-lish in the future; [pers.] I love words, and have a great passion for them, because if you must be anything in life, be passionate.; [a.] Moorestown, NJ

SOLUNAC, MIKE
[b.] December 25, 1940, Lapovo-Yugo; [p.] Sveta, Bosa; [m.] Dusica, November 1, 1970; [ch.] Alex Peter and Vesna; [ed.] Leney College, Oakland CA; [occ.] Teach-ing Trades; [memb.] Sports Club; [hon.] Many Athlet-ics Awards; [oth. writ.] I have many poems in three lan-guages. would you like some more?; [pers.] I am very proud when I get a chance to teach young people and what they learn helps them in their life so they never forget me.; [a.] Clinton Twp., MI

SORENSON, LEONARD
[pen.] Len Sorenson; [b.] April 30, 1913, Todd County, NV; [p.] Mr. and Mrs. Gilbert Sorenson; [m.] Viola Wallin, November 25, 1939; [ch.] Sharon Stangler, Col-leen Hanson; [ed.] 3 yrs. High School, Spokane, Wash-ington, 2 yrs. at Lewis and Clark, and 1 yr. at North Central High School; [occ.] Retired; [memb.] National Committee to Preserve Social Security and Medicare; [hon.] Numerous Bowling Awards 2 poems in the Na-tional Library of Poetry; [a.] Benson, MN

SOUTHERLAND, JANICE
[b.] November 23, 1960, Akron, OH; [ch.] Shannon Colleen, Marie Renee; [ed.] University of Akron; [hon.] Editor's Choice Award, 1994; [pers.] In all my writings, I try to recall and reflect on emotions and experiences that I have had. I feel that many emotions and experi-ences are the same for many, what is different is how we

deal with them.; [a.] Ravenna, OH

SOVEREIGN, FELECIA
[pen.] Felecia Sovereign; [b.] September 8, 1962, San Francisco, CA; [m.] August 9, 1986; [ch.] Three; [ed.] High School Graduate Menlo Atherton High School; [occ.] Mother, manages family business from home; [oth. writ.] Personal poems for family and friends.; [pers.] I grew up knowing very little about God. He led me to Jesus. Jesus led me to the 12 steps. Writing is one way I express my love to God and people.; [a.] Sacramento, CA

SPALDING, ALAN
[b.] February 27, 1980, La Cross, WI; [p.] Randy and Pauline Spalding; [ed.] Winona Senior High School; [a.] Dakota, MN

SPANO, NICOLE
[b.] June 16, 1982, Cobleskill, NY; [p.] Diane Spano; [ed.] I'm in 8th grade at Cobleskill-Richmondville School; [occ.] Student at Cobleskill, Richmondville; [memb.] School Clubs Gymnastics, Track and Soccer; [hon.] Gold Card for responsibility, MVP softball player; [oth. writ.] I write a lot of poems: How Come and Why, the Love Song, My Love, Hate of Father, Love of Mother and lots more.; [pers.] I write my po-ems because of my hard time dealing with my parents' divorce and the way of being loved and hated at all the same time.; [a.] Cobleskill, NY

SPARKS, BRUCE G.
[pen.] Bruce G. Sparks; [b.] March 1, 1939, Sioux City, IA; [p.] Allen R. and Clara H. Sparks; [ed.] Morningside College, Sioux City, Iowa, Kansas State Univ., Manhat-tan, Kansas; [occ.] Retired; [hon.] First place for poem, "America, I Love You," from local radio station contest; [oth. writ.] Poetry, approx. 100 other poems published. One short story.; [pers.] Be creative in all things. Love, peace and joy.; [a.] Sioux City, IA

SPARKS, SONDRA
[pen.] Rriel Cichoke; [b.] October 10, 1954, Dimmitt, TX; [m.] Widow; [ch.] Jennifer, Michael Jeramie and Josh Alaina; [ed.] College at Central Texas College of Killeen, TX, Photojournalist in Military; [occ.] Aspir-ing Writer; [memb.] Nominated as a member of Interna-tional Society of Poets; [hon.] Elected into International Poetry Hall of Fame; [oth. writ.] "Raven's Forever More".; [pers.] In my words I try to paint the pictures I see in the souls of myself and others. In doing this help even one person to accept and acknowledge their feel-ings.; [a.] Columbia, SC

SPENCER, MELISSA ANN
[pen.] Missy; [p.] Rick Spencer, Wendy Spencer; [ch.] April L. Spencer, Melissa A. Spencer; [ed.] 5th Grade; [occ.] Student; [a.] Littleton, WV

SPENCER, REBECCA A.
[b.] April 2, 1981, Hazard, KY; [p.] Bill and Virginia Spencer; [pers.] My poetry expresses my own personal experiences and trials in which God helps me see the errors of my ways and how to benefit from them.; [a.] Hazard, KY

SPENCER, STEPHANIE DENISE
[b.] April 9, 1977, Mount Sterling, KY; [p.] Johnie and Debbie Spencer; [ed.] Graduate of Menifee Co. High School; [pers.] Hard work can make dreams come true.; [a.] Mariba, KY

SPROUSE, JAMES R.
[pen.] Graham Richardson; [b.] September 26, 1957,

Gallatin, TN; [p.] James M. and Betty D. Sprouse; [m.] Patti G. Sprouse, June 7, 1981; [ch.] Paul R. and Erica E. Sprouse; [ed.] Gallatin High School, Tennessee Temple University, University of Mississippi, University of Tennessee; [occ.] English professor, Pensacola Chris-tian Culture; [memb.] South Atlantic Modern Language Association; [oth. writ.] Various academic articles and book reviews published in the South Atlantic Review, Studies in the Age of Chaucer, Manuscripts and the Secol Review.; [pers.] I hold doctoral degree in medieval stud-ies. My poem reflects my interest in both early Christian church history and medieval culture.; [a.] Pensacola, FL

ST. CLAIR, KATHY
[pen.] "Katrina"; [b.] October 10, 1948, Akron, OH; [p.] William Motz, Jean Motz; [m.] Ron St. Clair, December 22, 1967; [ch.] Amy Rene, Jeannine Marie, Andrea Dawne; [ed.] Garfield High, Idabelle Firestone School of Nursing; [occ.] Registered Nurse, Childrens Services Board Clinic, Akron, Ohio; [memb.] Ohio Nurses Asso-ciation, Arlington Memorial Baptist Church; [hon.] Only this one; [oth. writ.] Poems published in local newspapers and newsletters.; [pers.] "Love makes the world go round." I enjoy writing about love and the beauty of nature. Ev-eryone needs love in this world.; [a.] Akron, OH

STACEY, NICOLA J.
[pen.] Nicola J. M. Stacey; [b.] October 5, 1907, Belfast, Northern Ireland; [oth. writ.] In books, Silence of Yes-terday and Best poems of 1997; [pers.] Poetry can ex-press thoughts and feelings which can otherwise be diffi-cult to share; [a.] Woodruff, UT

STAGGS, WILLODEAN
[b.] December 18, 1919, Wabash, IN; [p.] Richard Rhoads, Lena; [m.] Dan Staggs (Deceased), February 1, 1957; [ch.] Ted, Janelle, Dan Ruth; [ed.] Wabash High; [oth. writ.] Two poems and some articles for church pa-pers.; [pers.] I am seventy-seven but I can't remember a time after I learned to read that I didn't love poetry. It speaks a language all its own.; [a.] Vero Beach, FL

STALEY, JERRY DEAN
[pen.] Jerry Staley; [b.] April 3, 1942, Randolph, CO; [p.] C. W. and Viola Staley; [m.] Doretha Polson Staley, October 23, 1978; [ch.] Jerry, Angela, Kimbrely, and Melody; [ed.] 4 yrs. Trade School, 2 yrs. Electronics, Electrical, Electrician and Electronics Tech.; [occ.] Maint. Electrician and Electronic Tech., P. Lorillard To-bacco Co.; [pers.] Poetry is the expressway to a persons integral being.; [a.] Greensboro, NC

STANLEY, ABRA LAYNE
[b.] July 4, 1974, Evanston, IL; [p.] Joy Stanley, Patti Stanley; [ed.] Bellevue High, University of Oregon, Cornish, Central, Washington University, University of London; [occ.] Student, (working to get MFA) Actor/ Theatre Management; [memb.] Kappa Alpha Theta, Sanguine Players (founding member), Children's Activ-ity Museum; [hon.] "Newcomer of the year 1996," Na-tional Dean's List '96-'97, Performer/Instructor for Pa-cific Northwest Children's Touring Show (2 years), BBC exchange student, VFW Auxiliary scholarship; [oth. writ.] Poems published in Andred, several press releases for "The Daily Record."; [pers.] Writing often helps me understand how I'm feeling. The images can also transport me to other magical places. It heals the soul.; [a.] Medina, WA

STAPLES, DEBRA
[pen.] Kateri Lane; [b.] July 29, 1956, Plymouth, MA; [p.] Eben Staples, Elaine Staples; [ch.] Chandra Lee Pina; [ed.] Plymouth Carver High Springfield Technical Com-

munity College; [occ.] Homemaker; [memb.] Our Lady of Mount Carmel Church; [pers.] This poem was written for Debra lane Whittaker who inspired a true and tender meaning of love in my heart, and in my life.; [a.] Springfield, MA

STAPLES, HEATHER
[pen.] Heather Staples; [b.] May 1, 1972, Somers Point, NJ; [p.] James and Kathi Haughey; [ch.] Brandon Edward and Justin Casey; [ed.] Lyndon State College; [occ.] President Counselor and AIDS Educator; [memb.] Catamont Arts Center, Community AIDS Project and Wildearth; [oth. writ.] Other poems; [pers.] I believe that if we take care of the Earth and nurture our souls, we can go to greater lengths of understanding the Earth and our places in it.; [a.] Saint Johnsbury, VT

STARNER, ROBBY
[b.] September 26, 1982, Rogers, AR; [p.] Tim and Carol; [a.] Rogers, AR

STECH, CATHY
[b.] December 12, 1965, Burlington, VT; [p.] Albert Belval, Norma Belval; [m.] Shawn Stech, April 27, 1991; [ch.] Ellie Jane, Joshia Michael; [ed.] Colchester High School; [occ.] Daycare Owner, St. Albans Vermont; [hon.] Presidential classroom scholarship; [pers.] My writing comes from my heart, hoping to touch other hearts.; [a.] Saint Albans, VT

STEELE, MISTY
[pen.] Crystal Litz; [b.] May 7, 1978, Columbus, OH; [p.] Sally Steele; [m.] April 1, 1977; [ch.] Four; [ed.] 12th grade; [occ.] LPN V, Medical Center; [oth. writ.] When A Man Love A Women. Poem. "Time Flies, Then and Now, I am Like. Dreams Go On, I Know Why and What, No Sense, all poems of mine.; [pers.] "You'll never know how great it is unless you let someone read it." So all ways give it a try before you give up!:; [a.] Huntington, WV

STEEVES, LAUREN
[b.] March 27, 1986, Stoneham, MA; [p.] Kenneth Steeves, Brenda Steeves; [ed.] Grade 5, John F. Kennedy School; [hon.] Honor Student; [oth. writ.] "He Will Be Here Soon," School poetry contest, "Celebration of Young Poets."; [pers.] My 4th grade teacher "Mrs. Beaudette" inspired me into poetry.; [a.] Billerica, MA

STEGER, HEIDI
[b.] March 4, 1968, Fort Hood, TX; [p.] William and Joy Steger; [ed.] Gannon University, Mercyhurst Preparatory High School; [occ.] Title Abstractor, self-employed; [pers.] "Failure is the condiment that gives success its flavor." -Truman Capote.; [a.] Erie, PA

STEINBRECHER, CHRISTINA
[pen.] Neysed; [b.] May 3, 1983, Syracuse, NY; [p.] Mr. and Mrs. Charles Steinbrecher; [ed.] Currently an 8th Grade, Regents Student, Attending North Syracuse Junior High School; [occ.] Student at North Syracuse Junior High School; [memb.] A member of Aspects, Group involving students or peers struggling with parental loses.; [hon.] Honored at North Syracuse Junior High School as December '96, Student of the Month and selected as an Honor Roll Student; [oth. writ.] Several poems kept in a journal and expressed in English Literature from selective school activities.; [pers.] I enjoy writing for the enjoyment of life. I always try selecting pieces of positive information into my writings.; [a.] North Syracuse, NY

STELLATO, MICHAEL
[pen.] Mike; [b.] November 16, 1983, Hackensack, NJ; [p.] Elizabeth Stellato; [ed.] 7th grade at Corpus Christi

School Hasbrouck Heights NJ; [occ.] Student; [memb.] Lodi Girl's and Boy's Club and Babe Ruth Baseball League; [hon.] Christian Conduct Award, many baseball trophies and homerun balls from Little League. Many basketball awards.

STELLMAN, PHYLLIS
[b.] August 13, 1947, Bronx, NY; [p.] Morris and Tillie Kleiman; [m.] Jack Stellman, March 25, 1989; [ch.] Tracey Rose, Elaine Hofheimer, Grandchildren: Jamie Rose, Sammy Rose, Shannen Hofheimer, Derrick Hofheimer, salutatorian Mark Tadin Jr.; [ed.] Lincoln High School (top 2 of class), Kinesboro College, IBM certified in Business advice and Construction Solution Pak Software, Editor of School Paper; [occ.] Controller for all American Homes, Inc.; [memb.] NAFE, Marco Island Jewish Center, Naples Chamber of Commerce; [hon.] Winner of Columbia University Journalism Scholarship in grade school, Regents Scholarship, National Merit Honoree, IBM Software Training Certification, Editor of "Student Voices," school newspaper, numerous Medals and Trophies for Ballroom Dancing; [oth. writ.] Poems and short stories, and articles for "Student Voices." Have been writing an autobiography about my trials and tribulations, called "Reborn."; [pers.] I write to express feelings and emotions too strong to allow to pass silently.; [a.] Marco Island, FL

STEPP, MARILYN
[b.] June 15, 1957, Amarillo, TX; [p.] John and Rosemary Swartz; [m.] Rusty Stepp, June 21, 1975; [ch.] Christopher James Stepp; [ed.] Associate Degree in Interior Design; [occ.] Artist in Design; [oth. writ.] "The World Can See", "When The Wind Blows"; [pers.] I am influenced by the love I have for the people I write about. "Heartstrings Tied With Love" is my third poem to write.; [a.] Amarillo, TX

STERN, HARRIET
[b.] April 18, NYC; [p.] Ray and Julie Kaifetz; [m.] Mike, December 14, 1983; [ch.] Two; [ed.] High School; [occ.] Retired; [memb.] Doris Day Humane Soc., Deborah Hosp., City of Hope, Wildlife Fund; [oth. writ.] Children's story; [pers.] Enjoy poetry because it expresses many feelings and sentiments one is sometimes afraid to express out loud; [a.] Tamarac, FL

STETAR, KANDICE
[b.] April 3, 1982; [p.] Shonee Stetar (mom); [ed.] Currently Freshman at Peters Township High School; [pers.] I find an ironic truth within Alfred Adler, and Charles Dickens' quotes and writings. I try to reflect my writings towards these.; [a.] McMurray, PA

STEWART, CHAKITA
[b.] February 23, 1980, Detroit; [p.] Ann Ewing and Leon Stewart; [ed.] 11th grade; [hon.] "Love is a Passion," was also published in Murray Wright's Book of Poems which was my old High School; [oth. writ.] So Many Ways and Thinking Of You.; [pers.] I love to write. My poems are based on my feelings above love, romance, sex, and relationships.; [a.] Detroit, MI

STEWART, DWIGHT
[pen.] Stewie; [b.] October 27, 1972, Jamaica; [p.] Aaron and Dorothy Stewart; [oth. writ.] I have written other poems which I have given to my church. My work reflects my faith in Christ and how that faith has made me worthy to become the son of God.; [pers.] I believe everyone is longing to be whole and complete. And I also believe that a relationship with Jesus Christ is the only way to achieve that. My writings reflect this!; [a.] Houston, TX

STIFFLER, TILLIE
[b.] March 20, 1982, El Dorado, AR; [p.] Debbie Sumers and Gary Stiffler; [ed.] 9th grade; [occ.] Student; [memb.] Monticello High School Band, The Rushing Memorial United Methodist Church; [pers.] I believe that to be a good writer you should always write about yourself, what you believe in, but mostly how you truly feel inside.; [a.] Monticello, AR

STODOLA, ADAM W.
[b.] February 2, 1983, Rice Lake, WI; [p.] Nancy S. Stodola; [ed.] 8th Grade; [occ.] Student; [memb.] Drama Club; [hon.] Volley Ball; [pers.] I would like to dedicate this poem to Nancy Stodola (my mother), Krystal Thayer who pushed me to do what I believe in. Jessica Stodola, and grandparents and all of my friends. Take life as it comes.; [a.] Rice Lake, WI

STOKELY, KATHY BURRELL
[pen.] Kabrel Stokely; [b.] May 20, 1957, Haywood County; [p.] Raymond L. and Ethel T. Burrell; [m.] Frederick Royal Stokely, August 7, 1976; [ch.] Frederick II, Meggan Leigh; [ed.] Pisgah Senior High; [occ.] Housewife, Mother, Aspiring Author, Volunteer; [memb.] International Fellowship of Christians and Jews; [oth. writ.] "Without Your Love Tonight," Coltrain Records, Nashville, TN, "A World of Love In Poetry," numerous poems, novels, editorials for local paper; [pers.] Voluntarism is the greatest expression of love for humanity.; [a.] Clyde, NC

STOREY, LAWRENCE R.
[b.] February 1, 1921, Rochester, NY; [p.] William H. Storey, Angeline Elizabeth Hacker; [m.] Shirley Jean Van Stean Storey, April 1, 1954; [ch.] William Henry Storey, Alberta Marie Brabitz, Tammy Lynn Antoine; [ed.] 10 yrs. High, Madison High, Rochester, N.Y., some education in NACCCA; [occ.] Retired; [memb.] NACCCA - CCC scouts, National Assoc. of Civian Conservation Corp., American Legion Post 134, Irondequoir N.Y., Veterans of the Battle of the Bulge Inc., Charter Member of Redman's Past Sachem, American Diabetes Assoc.; [hon.] Past Sachem - Redmans, Fire Brigade, Stromburg Carlson, Captain; [pers.] Dedicate poem to father-in-law Peter C. Vanstean if possible.; [a.] West Melbourne, FL

STOUT, LINDA S.
[b.] March 19, 1951, Illinois; [p.] Robert E. and Vera Lu Jeffers; [m.] Daniel L. Stout, June 1, 1980; [ch.] Sheri S. Duhe, Brandon L. Jeffers; [ed.] Shelbyville High School, Macon Co., Memorial Hosp., Phoenix School of Welding, Louisiana State University, Hammond Tech. Inst., River Parish Tech. Inst.; [occ.] Retired; [memb.] Reserve Christian Fellowship; [hon.] Lamb's Book of Life; [oth. writ.] None published, all in personal library.; [pers.] All that I do with all that has been done - will be in the end...to glorify the Lord, I love so much. This poem was a reflection of a love put in my life that will influence the remainder of my life-forever.; [a.] Reserve, LA

STRADLING, RYAN J.
[b.] February 6, 1974, Sewickley, PA; [ed.] Riverside High, Clemson University; [occ.] Computer Programmer; [pers.] To live in fear, you haven't lived at all, to live without it, you won't live long.; [a.] Huntsville, AL

STRAND, CINDY
[pen.] Mrs. C. Lee White; [b.] May 12, 1953, Salt Lake City, UT; [p.] Mr. and Mrs. Albert E. Strand; [m.] Richard Michael White, October 13, 1973, (Divorced); [ed.] Sky Line High, University of Utah, SLC Utah., Bellevue Community College, Bellevue, WA; [occ.] Computer

Information Systems; [memb.] Phi Theta Kappa Honors Fraternity, International Society of Poets, Kappa Alpha Theta Sorority, National Trust for Historic Preservation; [hon.] "Editor's Choice Award" from National Library of Poetry, Presidential Honor Roll and Dean's Honor Roll at Bellevue Community College; [oth. writ.] "One Last Goodbye", "If I Were A Tree", "Spirit of American Freedom", "American Indian: Cool Is Your Nurtured Forest", "Little Tom Tom", "Enchanted Love", "Embrace of Nite"; [pers.] To the reader, good poetry is a fountain of the spirit.; [a.] Seattle, WA

STRAUS, LJUBICA
[pen.] Ljuba; [b.] May 27, 1939, Sarajevo, YU; [p.] Jovo Savic, Jospava Savic; [m.] Arthur Straus, September 4, 1975; [ch.] Olivia de Alderete; [ed.] College of Sarajevo, University of Belgrade; [occ.] Executive Vice President, Rue Talma Trading, New York, NY; [memb.] Enroller for the National Association for the Self-Employed; [oth. writ.] Triangle of Life, a collection of true stories in a book of poetry inspired by the voice of God; [pers.] I believe the numerous people that I have met all over the world have given me positive energy which is reflected in my poetry.; [a.] Brooklyn, NY

STREET, RUTH A.
[b.] September 24, 1967, Beech Grove, IN; [p.] Judith Fraizer, Ralph E. Long Sr.; [m.] Robert W. Street Jr., October 25, 1985; [ch.] Jonathan W. Street; [ed.] Danville High School, South Eastern Illinois College; [occ.] House wife; [pers.] I finally found a way to express myself of my childhood hurts. It comes from deep within. A place where I thought I could never express I give a special thanks to the one who has inspired me - Mary L. Summers.; [a.] Eldorado, IL

STRONG, PHYLLIS A.
[pen.] Phyllis Baty; [b.] February 8, 1941, Marshall, IN; [p.] Don Baty (Deceased), Beatrice Parker Baty; [m.] Divorce, 1977; [ch.] Six: Debra McCall, Dianna Wilkison, Wesley Strong, Donna Barcia, Terry Davis Strong, Tonia Dierksen; [ed.] Elementary, Crawfordsville, Ind., High School, Sanford High, Sanford, Fla.; [occ.] Public Relations; [memb.] Press Sec'ty, Sumner County Songwriters, Assoc., C.M.A. (Country Music Assoc.), Faith is the Victory Church, Habitat for Humanity; [hon.] Semi-Finalist, North American Open Poetry Contest, Poem published in Through the Looking-Glass; [ed.] Editorials for Sumner County Songwriters, Assoc., Jingles for W.P.B. Radio Broadcasting, Lyrics, country songs.; [pers.] I strive to relate to total humanity, to touch people with love and hope for prosperity and world peace, also prayers that the world unites in God!; [a.] Nashville, TN

STUDY, MARY L.
[b.] September 26, 1928, Boston, IN; [p.] Howard and Ruby Thomas; [ch.] Sandra, Paula, William, Craig plus 10 GC + 5 GG children; [ed.] GED graduate at age 60; [occ.] Retired Homemaker; [memb.] 1st Assembly of God Church, Richmond, IN; [pers.] The love of Jesus inspired this poem. He is my life.; [a.] Tacoma, WA

STURDIVANT, KIMBERLY
[b.] August 22, 1958, Huntsville, AL; [p.] George and Minnie Sturdivant; [ed.] Ph.D. Counseling, University of Alabama, M.A. Rehabilitation Counseling, University of Alabama, B.S. Psychology, University of Alabama; [occ.] Advocate, Alabama Dept. of Mental Health/Mental Retardation; [memb.] Certified Rehabilitation Counselor; [pers.] "I attempt to create images through my selection of words."; [a.] Tuscaloosa, AL

SUAZO, CHARMAINE
[pen.] Sunshine Maxy Million; [b.] August 3, 1969, Central America; [p.] Thomas and Margaret Suazo; [ch.] Raphael and Christian Cole; [occ.] Receptionist; [memb.] Church of the Harvest and Harvest House (Food and clothing for the less fortunate and a little love); [hon.] My honor and award comes when I experience a frown turned upside down, a smile is like sunshine. And of course the mere recognition of the National Library of Poetry is absolutely divine.; [pers.] Life is a journey and during my quest for revelation, there lies within my soul a purpose to raise society's dominant consciousness. To connect with one's innermost being is the essence of truly living.; [a.] North Hollywood, CA

SULLIVAN, BARBARA R.
[pen.] Aliyah; [b.] August 24, 1953, Cleveland, OH; [p.] Anthony and Ruth De Nardis; [m.] Robert M. Sullivan, December 20, 1994; [ch.] Celeste, Jason, Kristina; [memb.] Graphics Artist; [hon.] C.A.R.T.A.; [pers.] I feel that poetry is the expression of Divine Revelation.; [a.] Cleveland, OH

SULLIVAN, FLORENCE
[pen.] Florence Sullivan; [b.] March 4, 1951, Salisbury, MD; [p.] Margaret R. Conner, Irving Dallas Ruark; [m.] Carl Glen Sullivan, June 30, 1990; [ch.] Bill Strouth Jr. and Angela Jarvis; [ed.] Diploma, Travel School, Woodridge Business Institute, Licensed Insurance Agent; [occ.] Receptionist/CSR; [memb.] First Baptist Church of Fruitland, Md., Save the Children Foundation, Feed the Children Foundation; [oth. writ.] Many religious poems, various poems written and read at funerals, various poems of other subject matter.; [pers.] I would just like to give all the praise and glory to God for whatever talent I have, possible only because of Him!; [a.] Salisbury, MD

SULLIVAN, LILLIAN
[b.] February 8, 1934, El Paso, TX; [p.] Minnie L. and Joe D. Jarvis; [m.] Delmer L. Sullivan, September 10, 1949; [ch.] Charlotte, Lynette, Sue, Gary; [ed.] GED - Alamogordo, NM Community College; [occ.] Retired Homemaker, Office Manager; [memb.] Republican Women's Club, Relief Society of the Church of Jesus Christ of Latter Day Saints, 1st Counselor Young Women's Mutual Improvement Association; [hon.] District Delegate to Republican Convention, Foster Mother, Founding Member New Mexico School for Handicapped, Founding Member Tularosa Teen Center, Board of Directors Teen Center; [oth. writ.] Several other poems.; [pers.] I've always loved the romantic poets.; [a.] Kennewick, WA

SULLIVAN, MERIAM K.
[b.] March 2, 1925, Rockford, IL; [p.] Mr. and Mrs. Roger Keister; [m.] William T. Sullivan, May 11, 1946; [ch.] (5) 3 girls, 2 boys; [ed.] Lake County (Illinois) College in Art and Psychology; [occ.] Retired; [a.] Hudson, FL

SULLIVAN, SHARON V.
[b.] December 2, 1945, Waterbury, CT; [p.] Francis and Eleanor Volovski; [m.] Thomas D. Sullivan, July 7, 1973; [ch.] Sean and Daniel; [ed.] BA, Fairleigh Dickinson University, Rutherford, NJ, also attended Trinity College, Wash, DC; [occ.] Office manager, Dennis Studio Photographers; [memb.] St. John the Evangelist Church Choir, singer and musician; [hon.] National French Honor Society, College Dean's List, Scholarship to study in France Graduation Magna Cum Laude; [oth. writ.] Several other poems, some of which have been published by a loyal YMCA group.; [pers.] My writing is

dedicated to all the special people who have supported me on life's journey and to God, who is spirit and inspiration. I want to share a love for life!; [a.] Bergenfield, NJ

SUMMERFORD, E. DANNER
[pen.] Danner; [b.] February 19, 1986, Birmingham, AL; [p.] Dr. John P. Summerford; [m.] Leigh Ann Summerford; [ed.] Verner Elementary; [occ.] Elementary Student; [pers.] I enjoy writing. I love playing with my cats. This poem was a Christmas gift in 1995 for my family.; [a.] Tuscaloosa, AL

SWAINE, MARCIA
[b.] August 12, 1941, Ventura, CA; [p.] Mike and Ada Condelos; [m.] Robert Swaine, July 12, 1963; [ch.] Scott; [ed.] Santa Barbara City College, AA in Psych.; [occ.] Accountant; [oth. writ.] Faerie Queen Mystic; [pers.] Fantasy and romance influence my writing.; [a.] Goleta, CA

SWANGER, DEBRA
[pen.] Darnell Appling; [b.] January 3, 1961, Tarpon Springs, FL; [p.] Joseph Swanger, Hazel Swanger; [ch.] Michael Anthony; [ed.] Palmetto High, Andon College; [occ.] Marketing Representative; [memb.] Human Rights Campaign; [pers.] Melissa: Without a doubt, my very best friend, Michael: My greatest joy, Shae: Through our indifferentism, this poem was possible, my life: "A True Phenomenon".; [a.] Acampo, CA

SWINDELL, PATRICIA LYNN
[b.] November 6, 1947, Houston, TX; [p.] Harold and Laverne Stowe; [m.] Harold Wayne Swindell, November 4, 1989; [ch.] Sean Stephen and Sherry Lynn (not Swindell - Prev. Marriage); [ed.] High School Graduate; [occ.] Homemaker; [pers.] Quote I wrote with poem: "May we all be rainbow people." "May We All Help and Heal The World."; [a.] Channelview, TX

SYKES, SHARON
[b.] January 14, 1968, New York; [p.] Viola Mosley; [ed.] Kingsborough Community College; [occ.] Senior Clerk; [memb.] Ophelia De' Vore Modeling School; [hon.] Best Dress; [oth. writ.] Brothers and Sisters; [pers.] I am only human. Not without sin. Not without fault. Please try to accept "me". Simply as "me". For all of us to simply "be".; [a.] Brooklyn, NY

SYM, NICK
[b.] June 13, 1951, Holland; [p.] Peter and Corrie Sym; [m.] Divorced; [ch.] Jason Sym; [ed.] Grade 12, Extended to Computer Upgrade; [occ.] Student for CNE Computer Networking Exe.; [oth. writ.] Too many to list.; [pers.] I would like to dedicate this poem to Peggy Roberts for the inspiration and push.; [a.] Brompton, Ontario, Canada

SZVERCSAK, ANGELA W.
[b.] January 24, 1983, Arad, Romania; [p.] Lou and Mona Szvercsak; [ed.] Elementary and Middle School; [occ.] Student 8th grade; [oth. writ.] Lots but mostly homework.; [a.] West Bloomfield, MI

TAFT, HEATHER M.
[b.] May 18, 1971, Burlington, VT; [p.] Marilee C. Jeff; [ed.] Essex High School, University of Vermont; [occ.] English teacher (currently on leave); [hon.] North Atlantic Conference Scholar I Athlete; [a.] Long Key, FL

TAKACS, LISA
[b.] July 27, 1982, Evergreen Park, IL; [p.] Dale and Debra Takacs; [ed.] St. Columba Elementary School, Freshman at Morgan Park High School (recently); [occ.] Busgirl at Graddini's Restaurant; [a.] Chicago, IL

TANNER, VIVIAN GAINES
[b.] August 23, 1925, Newport, RI; [p.] George and Mary Gaines; [m.] John T. Paxton, July 27, 1995; [occ.] Artist, poet; [memb.] Board of Directors of Hyde Park Chamber of Commerce; [hon.] Black Achievers, Special Constituency Award from Dutchess County Arts Council, 1996 Salute to Woman KWCA, numerous art awards, community activist; [oth. writ.] A book of poetry, "Gems of Wisdom," covers and illustrations for Hudson Valley echoes beauty hints column for Mid-Hudson Herald; [pers.] I thank the Divine, the source of all creation, without it we are nothing.; [a.] Poughkeepsie, NY

TAYLOR, DONALD
[b.] October 10, 1976; [p.] Cathy and Allen Taylor; [ed.] Second Year Student at South Seattle CC; [pers.] Jesus is the greatest lover. Just ask Him in your life and He will fill your heart. Read Matthew 13:45-46.; [a.] Seattle, WA

TAYLOR, JASON ANDREW
[b.] May 24, 1972, Arizona; [p.] Virgina and Dennis Lee; [pers.] A great man, who in manhood, retains the heart of a child. We must be great men.; [a.] Phoenix, AZ

TAYLOR, PATRICIA LYNNE
[pen.] P. Lyn Taylor; [b.] September 6, 1967, Oahu, HI; [p.] Charles and Joan Taylor; [ed.] Brandon High School, Brenau Women's College, Georgia Southern University, Hillsborough Community College; [occ.] Student, Paralegal; [memb.] Chi Omega, Brenau College; [hon.] National High School Award for, "I Have A Dream," essay. President of Junior Jayceettes in High School Honors English, GSU; [oth. writ.] Poetry since age 16, novel (fiction) unpublished, 2 short stories, unpublished, "I Have A Dream," published in High School Literary magazine, "Arie."; [pers.] My poems came from deep within the soul of all my combined experiences. My life is in my poetry. I admire William Blake's work.; [a.] Brandon, FL

TAYLOR, SCOTT A.
[b.] June 19, 1969, Stuttgart, Germany; [p.] Linda Taylor, Reece Taylor; [ed.] Richard High School, Johnson and Wales Culinary College, Tarrant County Junior College; [occ.] PBX Supervisor at Hyatt Regency D/7W; [memb.] National Gay and Lesbian Task Force, Human Rights Campaign, and Dallas Gay and Lesbian Alliance; [hon.] Johnson and Wales H.E.C.E. Scholarship; [pers.] I love to bring out the beauty in things that are regarded as "Dark".; [a.] Azle, TX

TEAGUE, LANCE
[b.] May 12, 1964, Wilkes County, NC; [p.] Gladys Gore and Everett Teague; [m.] Rebecca Reagen-Teague, February 18, 1987; [ed.] Master Degree in Nutrition; [occ.] Owner of Applied Herbal Science and Combat Martial Arts School; [memb.] YMCA Board of Directors; [hon.] US Navy Seal for 11 years - Seal Instructor for 5 years. Served in 5 Theatres of combat; [oth. writ.] Boys to men and high stakes novels in progress about U.S. Navy Seal Commando units.; [pers.] Success comes at the risk of failure. I can do anything through Christ who strengthens me.; [a.] Wilkesboro, NC

TEMPLE JR., DONALD M.
[b.] May 28, 1951, Newton, MA; [occ.] Welder, Mechanic; [pers.] Thank you! For finding my poem, "The Rose," worthy of publication. Though I have never sought to have my poetry published before, it has been shared with many friends across the U.S., Canada, and more recently, Ireland. I'm sort of a poetic Johnny Appleseed. It is the magic of life that inspires words to flow, and in my own way I try to make the world a magi-

cal place for everyone. That is why it is such an honor to be a part of your anthology. So many more will have the chance to share the magic. Mr. Ely, if it is at all possible I'd like to have the following poem inserted in my biographical data section. For what better way to describe a poet than with a poem?; [a.] Shrewsbury, MA

TERRY, ADRIAN G.
[pen.] Ada Kohn; [p.] Edgar and Margaret Thomason; [m.] William Terry, 1933; [ch.] Four; [ed.] 4th year; [occ.] Retired; [memb.] Member of Baptist Church

TERRY, JEANNELLA
[b.] April 2, 1968, Indiana; [m.] Lonnie Terry, July 13, 1991; [ch.] Jeffrey Dile, Destiny Dile, Lonnie Terry II; [ed.] Arlington High School, Owen Valley High; [occ.] Housewife, Mother, and Roofer; [oth. writ.] I've written several poems, but none have ever been published. I write them for my own personal pleasure.; [pers.] I am influenced in my writing poems, by every day happenings and for the love of my family and friends.; [a.] Cloverdale, IN

TESTERMAN, J. D.
[b.] March 27, 1963, Tulsa, OK; [p.] Dr. Jack D. Testerman and Lula Mae Donaghe; [m.] Melanie Ledbetter Testerman, May 28, 1988; [ch.] Scott, Elise and Alec; [ed.] High School - Springfield, MO, Univ. of S.W. LA - Lafayette, LA; [pers.] I would like to thank my wife, Melanie, without whom none of this would be possible. You will always be my Juliet.; [a.] Burneyville, OK

THACKER, DEBRA
[b.] October 19, 1979, West Virginia; [p.] Robin and James Thacker; [ch.] One, James Edward Litton; [ed.] G.E.D.; [occ.] S.T.N.A.; [oth. writ.] My father holds all of my poems. I have been writing since I was ten.; [pers.] My poems reflect on good things coming out of something bad. Too many people dwell on their past. When really they need to look forward to a bright future.; [a.] Lodi, OH

THAGGARD, CAROLYN JOAN
[pen.] CJ; [b.] September 12, 1988, Jacksonville, FL; [p.] Maura A. Sullivan, Craig W. Thaggard; [ed.] Evans School; [occ.] Student; [oth. writ.] A Hero; [a.] Saugus, MA

THIESSE, BILLIEJEAN
[b.] July 7, 1974, Fairview, OH; [p.] Jerry C. Thiesse, Reba L. Thiesse; [ed.] Ohio State University; [occ.] Student; [hon.] United States Army Veteran; [pers.] Dedicated to my mother and father. Thank you for believing in me. I love you both more than words can ever say.; [a.] Sullivan, OH

THOMAS JR., JOSEPH
[b.] June 8, 1926, New Eagle, PA; [p.] Catherine Thomas, Joseph Thomas Sr.; [m.] Carol M. Thomas, March 6, 1948; [ch.] Wendy Jo, Janice Carol, Joseph Denver; [ed.] High School, Wellsburg, WV., Miami, FL. University, Football Scholarship, Drafted into U.S. Army World War II, served two years in Germany with 310th infantry, 78th Div.; [occ.] Football Consultant, Coach, Player Personnel Director. United States American Football All Star Team; [memb.] Kiwanis International, V.F.W., American Legion, B.O.P.E., Dapper Dan, National Football League Alumni, National Football League Players Assoc. Retired Members and Philadelphia Eagles Chapter.; [hon.] Kiwanis International, WV District Distinguished President-Wellsburg Club 1982-83. Distinguished Lt. Governor WV. Division One 1983-84. Outstanding Secretary WV Division One, Secretary of the year WV District 1986-87. Dapper Dan McKelvey Award 1988. Recognized by Bethany WV College 1979

and WV Northern College 1987 for working with the youth of Brooke County, WV. Played and coached football on all levels of the game. Inducted into minor league PRO hall of fame class of 1994; [oth. writ.] "Reading, Writing, Arithmetic and Youth Football," copyright 1985, Library of Congress catalog card number 85-51983. Unpublished song lyrics for each of my three children, seven grand children, and several for my wife. Two unpublished poems. "A Friend," and "Trees."; [pers.] My song lyrics came easy from the love in my heart, my poems from the love of God, and my book from the love of the youngsters participating and their safety while playing contact football.; [a.] Wellsburg, WV

THOMAS-McCALL, DOROTHY
[b.] August 9, 1966, Mississippi; [p.] Lillie Marie Thomas; [m.] Marcus H. McCall, September 4, 1992; [ch.] Nyobee McCall, Marcus McCall II; [ed.] Simmons High School, Tougaloo College; [occ.] Child Care Worker; [pers.] We must always strive for our best because we will know always when we did and when we did not.; [a.] Lauderhill, FL

THOMPSON, MICHAEL KEITH
[b.] April 7, 1985, Reading, PA; [p.] Kevin and Lucia Thompson; [ed.] Currently (Feb. '97) in Sixth Grade at Cabrini Academy, Reading, PA; [occ.] Student; [memb.] Cabrini Academy Student Council; [hon.] Good Citizenship Award (6-96), 1st place, 6th Grade Natural Science, Cabrini Academy Science Fair (1-97); [pers.] "You can't steal second base and keep one foot on first".; [a.] Shillington, PA

THOMPSON, RICHARD
[b.] February 16, 1964, Brooklyn, NY; [p.] Charles Lene Leonora Thompson; [m.] Arlene Thompson, September 16, 1995; [ed.] John Dewey H.S. Brooklyn, NY Academic Diploma, Borough of Manhattan Community College New York, NY - Business Administration Degree; [occ.] Administrative Assistant; [oth. writ.] Nothing serious. Just wrote small poems (love poems) to my wife, family and friends.; [pers.] Life is a path to follow. Along the way, everyone obtains knowledge to various degrees. Whether you learn from a baby to the most noted scholar, you must take it and pass the information along. That is love.; [a.] Roswell, GA

THORNTON, LORI
[b.] January 30, 1971, Cortland, NY; [p.] Douglas and Virginia Rindge; [m.] William C. Thornton, September 18, 1993; [ed.] Northern Lehigh High School, St. Lukes Hospital School of Nursing, Penn State University; [occ.] Registered Nurse, Hemodialysis Clinic, Palmerton PA; [memb.] Pet Sitters International; [hon.] National Choral Award 1989, John Phillip Sousa Jazz award 1989; [pers.] The best of writings are those which are seen everyday but viewed differently by all of mankind.; [a.] Orefield, PA

THORSEN, RENA CRANE
[pen.] "Shugah"; [b.] October 19, 1918, Fennville, MI; [p.] U. S. Crane, Lena Crane; [m.] Frederick H. Thorsen, (Deceased, 1960), January 6, 1940; [ch.] Christie Ann, Jon C., Sally Caroline and Steven F.; [ed.] Fennville High, Davenport/Parsons Business College, Mars Hill College (courses), ICS (courses); [occ.] Retired from Western Michigan University, Kalamazoo, Michigan; [memb.] Alpine First Baptist Church, in (Tioga) Pineville, La., Joy Club and Joy Chorale, Alpine Home Missionary Assoc., Fennville H.S. Alumni Assoc., TREA Senior Citizens League, National Assoc. to protect H.S. Sec. and Medicare; [hon.] Volunteer Service Award (Rapides Parish Library and Friends of the Library), Alexandria,

Louisiana; [oth. writ.] "My Mountaintop in N.C.," (submitted to the National Library of Poetry - 1996) and "Joys in the North Carolina Mountains," (submitted 1997.); [pers.] My whole life and self are devoted to serving Jesus Christ, who is so wonderful, awesome, forgiving, and so loving, a great and glorious Master and Lord! I hope His light shines through me to help all the children wherever I am, and through my poetry.; [a.] Pineville, LA

THURLWELL, EVA
[pen.] Autumn; [b.] March 1, 1959, Ottawa, Ontario, Canada; [ed.] Two years in College; [occ.] Teacher; [oth. writ.] Revolving Doors, Healing Dwells Here, Weaving of Love, The Challenge Within (song), The Kingdom of God (song), One in Three; [pers.] I believe God is everywhere.

THURMAN, DAPHNE
[b.] November 2, 1967, Hollandale, MS; [p.] Minnie Morris, Sylvester Morris; [m.] Eugene Thurman, March 27, 1989; [ch.] Alishia, Jenene, Sierra Rigene; [ed.] Simons High, Alcorn State UNV; [occ.] Housewife; [pers.] Self confidence is an important part of success.; [a.] Aberdeen Proving Ground, MD

TIENKEN, JENNIFER R.
[pen.] Jennifer R. Tienken; [b.] October 9, 1974, Smithfield, NC; [p.] James E. and Diane Reardon; [m.] Louis R. Tienken, June 6, 1992; [ed.] South Johnston Jr. High; [occ.] Housewife/Homemaker; [memb.] Member Barbourtown Church of God, Rhema Bible Reading Corresp. Course; [hon.] Certificate of Completion from Worldwide Bible Study Correspondence Course, Certificate of Recognition from my church - young adult secretary, certificate of completion Emmaus Bible Correspondence School; [oth. writ.] Have other writings not published; [pers.] My love for writing began as a young child. My desire is that all hearts will turn to our everlasting and merciful Father.; [a.] Smithfield, NC

TO, BETTINA
[pen.] Betti, Elizabeth; [b.] August 9, 1985, Indianapolis, IN; [p.] Loc To, Lethu Duong; [ed.] I'm in the fifth grade in Oaklandon Elementary. I also attended La Petite Academy; [occ.] My current occupation is a student.; [hon.] I'm an honor roll student. I won first place in third grade spelling bee.; [oth. writ.] I also wrote poems like "Lie," "I love...", "If The World Were...", "The Orphan." I'm proud of my writings.; [pers.] I'm interested in poets because of the interesting things that flow through my mind.; [a.] Indianapolis, IN

TODD, BERYL
[b.] April 13, 1913, Enid, OK; [p.] Bessie and Z. B. Bird; [m.] Stanford D. Todd (Deceased 1985), 1952; [ed.] Enid High - 1933 1 yr. Phillips U. in Enid, Studied Harp with Macel 3 yrs Granjany in N.Y., My University Degree Pan Ames. 1965 and Tax. University; [occ.] Retired Teacher past I taught Reading in Jr. High and English 17 yrs.; [memb.] Zonta Club at Phillips U. Methodist Church, Harp Organization, Poetry Club; [hon.] Some Awards over the years, Harpist extensively in both Okla. and Texas; [oth. writ.] A Child's Story Poetry. Have had many poems published - local newspapers and Church Bulletin etc. (A sermon on one of my poems).; [pers.] I love nature, having hunted or years and I study Human nature, people. Love is important in all living things.; [a.] Donna, TX

TOLSON, FRANCES
[b.] September 15, 1913, Licking Co., OH; [p.] H. H. and Mary Hoover; [m.] Melvin L. Tolson (Deceased, January 18, 1994), November 8, 1953; [ch.] 1 Step-

daughter (Deceased), 4 grandchildren, 4 great grandchildren; [ed.] Bachelors, Ohio State Univ., Master's, Art Education, Kent State University; [occ.] Retired Art Teacher; [memb.] State retired Teachers Assoc., Carroll Retired Teachers Assoc., Carroll County Commission for Advancement of the Arts; [hon.] Who's Who in American Education, Who's Who in the Arts 1971-1972; [oth. writ.] Christian Life Letters, The Lookout, Free Press Standard, World of Poetry, Christian Evangelist; [pers.] I try to put emotions into words that paint pictures.; [a.] Carrollton, OH

TOOTHMAN, BARBARA
[b.] June 1939, Clarksburg, WV; [p.] Glenn and Goldia Keith; [m.] David A. Toothman, December 1957; [ch.] Casondra and Brian Toothman; [ed.] Victory HIgh School: W.V. Business College, Vocational Technical Center; [occ.] Certified C.N.A./H.H.A.and Hostess at Ritz-Carlton Hotel; [memb.] First Baptish Church of Naples, 700 Club, Flying Hospital.; [hon.] Golden Poet Award 1987 from the World of Poetry.; [oth. writ.] Have had several poems published in Vista magazine, poem published in "New American Poetry Anthology 1988." Also have had articles published in local newspaper and in my hotel Newsletter.; [pers.] My poetry is written to search our souls for eternal peace.; [a.] Naples, FL

TOPPAN, JENNIFER
[b.] June 17, 1981, Exeter, NH; [p.] Sandra Hall, Peter Toppan; [ed.] Ryan High (10th grade); [occ.] Student; [memb.] Swarovski Collectors Society, and Ryan High Industrial Technology; [pers.] This poem was inspired by a great friend, who I wish could be more.; [a.] Denton, TX

TOTH, CHARLES J.
[b.] August 30, 1953, New Brunswick, NJ; [p.] Joseph and Lucy Toth (Deceased); [m.] Divorced; [ch.] Melissa Toth, Holly Toth; [ed.] B.A. Rutgers College 1975, Spanish; [occ.] Child Support Specialist Investigator, Middlesex County, NJ; [memb.] Sumerser Bible Baptist Church, Dean's List; [hon.] Phi Delta Kappa; [pers.] I write poems to encourage others. As a Born-Again Christian, I am greatly influenced by Jesus.; [a.] Franklin Park, NJ

TRAVIS, ANNA MARY
[pen.] Anna M. Travis or Country Music Lady; [b.] November 2, 1928, Kingsport, TN; [p.] Garvie and Ida Cassel Nunley; [m.] Norman C. Travis, December 23, 1988; [ch.] Two: Larry and Edgar Pullium; [ed.] Blountville High School and Peorie School of Nursing, Dixon School of Music, Wilson School of Music and a course from Stamps Piano and Organ from Paul Bessler, MA; [occ.] Retired Director of Nursing and Country Gospel Singer; [memb.] Musicians Local 26, Rebekah Lodge, Freewill Baptist Church also Elgible for Membership in Daughters of American Revolution; [hon.] Several Bible School Awards, Reading Award, Kingsley Grade School, Kingsport, Tenn., Book Award, Blountville High School, Tenn., Money Award for singing, Kingsley school, Tenn., several awards from Salvation Army for my Country and Blue Grass Connection Band. 4H and Blue Ribbon Awards from Starmaker Promotions, Award from coalition of disabled, Perin, IL, award for comedy, Peoria Mama's Band, Peoria, IL; [oth. writ.] I write country and Gospel songs. I wrote a song poem about Thanksgiving that Bartonville News published (a local paper, Bartonville, IL.) I also wrote a song, "What Christmas Means To Me," that Caterpillar Tractor Co. published in their news, East Peoria, IL.; [pers.] I strive to write about what I feel in my heart. To reach out and touch someone with a thought that might be their dreams for a brighter tomorrow.; [a.] Saint Petersburg, FL

TRIMMELL, JERRY L.
[b.] January 11, 1974, Frankfurt, Germany; [ed.] Courtesy of William Faulkner, Franz Kafka, Gertrude Stein, and the Marquis de Sade; [occ.] The ladder, I think; [memb.] International Center of Photography, Local Chapter #597 Cake and Sodomy Bridge Club, Melvins Army; [oth. writ.] "The Wife's Handkerchief Inside The Ghost Of Hamlet", "Were It Just, It Would Surely Fail To Give Us An erection", "Roped And Pumped" others.; [pers.] As the great Oscar Wilde one said, "A really well-made buttonhole is the only link between Art and Nature".; [a.] Wichita, KS

TSENG, SHARON
[b.] December 10, 1979, Baltimore, MD; [p.] Leeying Tseng and Dr. Jeenan Tseng; [ed.] International Baccalaureate Program, Richard Montgomery High School; [occ.] Student; [a.] Rockville, MD

TUCKER, MICHAEL L.
[b.] November 15, 1977, Philadelphia; [p.] James and Josephine; [ed.] Northeast Catholic High School for Boys, Penn State University; [occ.] College Student (Psych. Major), Poet, Songwriter; [memb.] Vice President of A.P.T.T. (A place to talk) A Peer Counseling Organization for Penn State Students; [hon.] Who's Who Among American High School Students 1992-1994; [pers.] My reality is Jello, but my dreams are fragile; [a.] Philadelphia, PA

TUCKER, OSCAR D.
[b.] July 31, 1929, Tuscaloosa, AL; [p.] Willie and Virginia Tucker; [m.] Martha N., February 10, 1954; [ch.] Georgia, Ann, Shirley, Terry, Wylie, Victor Bolicia; [ed.] Industrial High, AL A and M Univ., Tuskegee Univ., Univ. of AL; [occ.] Retired Educator (Teacher, Principal, Supt.); [memb.] Retired Senior Volunteer Program (RSVP), AARP, Board of Trustees, AL A and M Univ., Executive Committee, AL Sr. Citizens Hall of Fame (1992).; [hon.] Elected to Alabama Senior Citizen Hall of Fame, High School Chemistry Teacher Award 1971, Presented by Alabama Section American Chemical Society, Alabama Gerontological Society President's Award (1991).; [oth. writ.] None worth mentioning.; [pers.] I have no penchant for words, there was simply a burst of inspiration on a given day, at a given hour while walking on a beautiful beach by a great body of life giving water. Lady luck, at one time or another, smiles upon us all.; [a.] Tuscaloosa, AL

TURLEY, ROBERT L.
[b.] October 29, 1966, Garland, TX; [p.] Judith D. Miller, David L. Miller, Leslie B. Turley; [m.] Kelly M. Malacara-Turley, July 11, 1992; [ed.] Garland High School, University of Texas at Arlington, B.A., Exercise and Sport Studies; [occ.] English Teacher and Athletic Coordinator at Schackelford Junior High; [memb.] Texas High School Coaches' Association, United Educators Association; [hon.] 1996-97 "Teacher of the Year," Shackelford Junior High in Arlington, Texas; [pers.] I try to reflect on my feelings at any given moment in my life. I believe that we succeed in life by overcoming obstacles, therefore, obstacles are not what keeps us down. Our lack of self-discipline does.; [a.] Arlington, TX

TUTTY, DOUGLAS E.
[pen.] Tut; [b.] December 19, 1952, Newark, NJ; [p.] John Tutty, Phyllis Tutty; [m.] Divorced; [ch.] Jesse James, Brandon John; [ed.] Alton Boxborough Regional H.S., BSBA Chapman University, Orange, CA; [occ.] Purchasing/Merchandising Manager; [pers.] Nature's voices speak the truths of the universe, man must stop and listen, God reveals himself.; [a.] Mesa, AZ

TYLER, BECKY
[b.] September 5, 1966, Medina, OH; [p.] Roy J. Eacott Jr., Judy Eacott; [m.] Ronald Tyler, October 25, 1986; [ch.] Daniel, Matthew and Andrew; [ed.] John F. Kennedy High School, North American Correspondence School - Medical/Dental Assistance; [occ.] Pharmacy Technician, Discount Drug Mart, Cleveland, OH; [memb.] Calvary Chapel Assembly of God, Columbia Station, Ohio; [oth. writ.] This is my first poem written for my mother on Mother's Day 1982; [pers.] This poem is dedicated in memory to my mother, Judy, thank you for guiding me, loving me, and being my best friend. You will always be in my heart.; [a.] Cleveland, OH

UMEMOTO, JASON
[b.] September 20, 1967; [p.] Gordon and Ann Umemoto; [m.] Nancy Cassandro; [ch.] Gian; [ed.] Fountain Valley High School, California Polytechnic University, San Luis Obispo, University of California, Irvine; [occ.] Landscape Architecture; [memb.] American Society of Landscape Architects, Clarb, Sierra Club; [oth. writ.] Journey's of a Wide-Eyed Traveler (self published); [pers.] I strive to interpret and express the many variations of the human experience through my writings.

UPTON, DAVID LEE
[pen.] Frog; [b.] January 11, 1953, Huntsville, AL; [p.] James R. and Mary A. Upton; [m.] Cynthia, November 30, 1972; [ch.] Jennifer, James, Crystal; [ed.] High School, Tect. College; [occ.] Dispatcher, Ingalls Ship Building; [hon.] Had poem published in last year's "Endless Harmony"; [oth. writ.] As of today over 200 poems written.; [pers.] Love to write on personal experiences.; [a.] Pascagoula, MS

UTICK, ANDREA
[b.] August 20, 1983, Helena, MT; [ed.] Hawthorne Elementary, C.R. Anderson Middle School; [occ.] I'm in school - receiving my education and stuff like that; [memb.] C.R. Anderson Student Council, Children International donation society, and Olympia Sales Club; [hon.] Best Poetry Notebook, Most Graceful, Second Place winner in 1991-1992 Hawthorne Elementary School Worlds Finest Chocolate selling contest; [oth. writ.] Book: A Rainbow of Poetry, Poems: Love, Winter, Tulip, A Loose Lark, Dream, Those Eyes (published) The Paper, Lips, Those Intimidating Slopes, Water to Blood, Fairy, Glow, Newt, Hair, Wings, You; [pers.] The personal goal I set with my poetry is to move someone, whether it be by laughing, crying, or whatever. I want people to remember my poetry by the way it made them feel.; [a.] Helena, MT

VALNOHA, OTTO R.
[b.] February 7, 1926, Czechoslovakia; [m.] Sophia - American, October 8, 1961; [ch.] Tom, Debbie, Mike; [ed.] I am not an educated man, and yet I respect those who are that I can learn from them.; [occ.] Retired; [hon.] Those who excel award of recognition 1991-92 from the Illinois State of Education.; [oth. writ.] Wrote personal life story of my life dedicated to my wife and children. Memory with tears. "At The Time" of German occupation, and Communist overthrow.; [pers.] I become citizen 1967 and I am proud to be American that give me the freedom I lost when I was young.; [a.] Round Lake, IL

VAN GIESSENBURG, RUDOLF CAREL D'ABLAING
[pen.] Micha-el; [b.] July 19, 1923, Bandung, West Java, Indonesia; [p.] Rudolf Carel d'Ablaing Van Giessenburg and Carnelia Ottille Elisabeth d'Ablaing Van Giessenburg (Nee Korinth); [m.] Henriette Juliana d'Ablaing Van Giessenburg (Nee. Smelt), September 18, 1956; [ch.] Madeleine Elisabeth and Tania Erica; [ed.] Dutch College - B (Mathematical): Electronics Engineering School, California Real Estate, Organization and Management, Water Utility Sciences, Environmental Sciences; [occ.] Retired Electronics Reliability Engineer (Hughes Aircraft); [hon.] Dean's List Santa Ana College (4.0 GPA), "Dorlogs Herinnerings Kruis". (WW 2 Medal), "Eereteken Voor Orde and Vrede", (Medal for Order and Peace Restoring Action); [oth. writ.] "A Little Flame of God's Love" (Poem) "A Vision"; [pers.] "A heart that knows to suffer in silence - knows also to love - in silence: My love for people is my asset - not theirs, their love in return is their asset - not mine, their lack of love is their liability - not mine. I love them just the same!; [a.] Santa Ana, CA

VAN VALKENBURG, LELAND
[pen.] LeeTall; [b.] May 27, 1977, Albion, NY; [p.] Lloyd and Pat VanValkenburg; [ed.] Naples Central School, Finger Lakes Community College, Finger Lakes Area Vocation Center; [occ.] Student at Finger Lakes Community College; [memb.] Writer's Digest Magazines; [pers.] I would like to give some understanding of what goes on in the world.; [a.] Naples, NY

VANDERLICK, LINDA L.
[b.] January 8, 1965, Doylestown, PA; [p.] Ronald Barlow; [m.] Luc F. Vanderlick, July 14, 1986; [ch.] Mytye and Amber; [a.] Jamison, PA

VAUGHAN, DORIS
[b.] August 21, 1930, Lawrenceville, VA; [p.] Warner and Otelia Walker (Deceased); [m.] Clyde Vaughan Sr. (Deceased), November 6, 1954; [ch.] Sharon Hoskins, Clyde Vaughan Jr., Gregory Vaughan; [ed.] St. Paul's High, St. Paul's Poly. Institute, B.S., University of Michigan, A.M.L.S., Institute of Children's Literature (pres.); [occ.] Retired; [memb.] Holy Trinity A.M.E. Church Missionary president, member of Alpha Kappa Alpha Sorority, Member of Literacy Volunteers of America, AARP, AAUP, American Library Association; [hon.] Was granted a fellowship to attend the University of Michigan Library School, Monetary Award and Certificate from Letterkenny Army Depot for work performance, English Award (1952) I am presently enrolled in a writing course.; [oth. writ.] Poem published in local newsletter; [pers.] Despite the problems we face in our lives today, I like to focus on the beauty and serenity of God's world.; [a.] Xenia, OH

VELINO, JOHN
[b.] August 1, 1969, South Kingston, RI; [p.] John and Kathy Velino; [ed.] Belleville East, Southern Illinois at Carbondale; [memb.] Big Brother/Big Sister; [oth. writ.] Memories Of Tomorrow, The Best Poems of 1997; [pers.] Only motivation required is a blank piece of paper and a pen.; [a.] Belleville, IL

VERRETTE, JULIE A.
[b.] March 19, 1941, Michigan; [p.] Mr. and Mrs. L. C. Verrette; [ch.] Elizabeth, Tim, Mike; [ed.] B.A. Psychology, Univ. of Miami, M.A. Counseling, Michigan State Univ.; [occ.] Summer Place Kennel, Sled Dog Musher, 22 Alaskan Huskies; [memb.] WI Trailblazers Sled Dog Assoc.; [oth. writ.] I imagine my future sled dog gate (article). poem, room in the Inn riding the rides. U.P. (MI) Writers Assoc., Int'l. Sled Dog Assoc.; [pers.] In my fifties, I drastically altered my life to allow me, alone, to live, away from the corporate world, in the wilderness, raising, breeding and running dogs in partnership - in health.; [a.] Florence, WI

VICKERY, AS SAYRDAH SADDAM HUSSEIN ROBERT
[pen.] Norma Morgan Vickery; [b.] September 2, 1931, Florida, U.S.; [p.] Lacy Austin Flowers and Margaret H. Flowers; [m.] Saddam Hussein Robert Vickery, December 18, 1985; [ed.] Pinellae County Florida Public Schools Graduate North Word Elem 1943, Clearwater Junior High 1946, Clearwater Senior High 1949; [occ.] Hotel Model Housekeeping Ramada; [memb.] Past memberships many community service organizations, Nu Phi Mu, Beta Sigma Phi (President Nu Phi Mu), "C-30" officer, Woman's Club - Civilian Women; [hon.] None - Recently; [oth. writ.] Numerous honorable mentions, "Golden Poet," other poetry contests.; [pers.] Andeem a Khelee f'a U.S. Navy Wa Zoupee f'a Maines A baka taba min a bahuf aaax ba'hassel f'fenes.; [a.] Jacksonville, FL

VIDDEN, VERNON
[b.] October 14, 1930, Fertile, MN; [p.] Herman and Christine Vidden (Deceased); [m.] Bernice Erna Vidden, June 8, 1958; [ed.] High School graduate (1945, Fertile MN) and two years trade school (newspapers since graduations); [occ.] Retired Grand Forks Herald (ND), nearly 26 years; [memb.] American Legion Post No. 157, East Grand Forks, MN, 35 years member; [hon.] High School Journalism Award, Column entitled "Kidden With Vidden" (1948-1949); Retirement Plaque, Grand Forks (ND) Herald (1969-1995); [pers.] The poetic and profound beauty of earth and sky has been beautifully portrayed through thoughtful and inquisitive minds. I believe as we learn more we gain greater knowledge for our benefit.; [a.] East Grand Forks, MN

VISLAR, DIANE JEANNETTE
[b.] August 7, 1970, El Paso, TX; [p.] Josefina V. McCollum, Robert L. Moore; [m.] Ivan L. Carter (Fiance); [ch.] Kiana LaShay, Ivan Lydell Jr.; [ed.] Andress High, El Paso Texas; [occ.] Customer Service Rep., Mail Boxes Etc., Cartersville, GA; [a.] Cartersville, GA

VODA, OFELIA ALARID
[pen.] Ofelia Alarid Voda; [b.] March 13, 1945, Ensenada, Mexico; [p.] Jose Alarid, Fan Alarid; [m.] Allen; [ed.] Hermiston High, Mount St. Mary's College; [occ.] Real Estate; [memb.] Assistance League of Las Vegas, Long Beach, Los Angeles Sailing Assoc., Greater L.V. Board of Realtors; [a.] Las Vegas, NV

VOGT JR., CARL
[b.] May 24, 1932, San Diego, CA; [p.] Carl and Norma W. Vogt; [m.] Donna Mae Vogt, June 4, 1983; [ed.] AA Degree, English, 1956, San Diego Junior College, San Diego, CA; [occ.] Retired; [memb.] American Ex-prisoners of War, Disabled American Veterans; [hon.] Combat Infantryman's Badge, Bronze Star, Purple Heart, P.O.W. Medals; [oth. writ.] Various poems, all unpublished; [pers.] The basis for most of my poems were done when I was a prisoner of war. My mind was the only weapon I could use. I hope that no person will ever have to experience the horrors of war!; [a.] Snohomish, WA

VOYTKO, BESSIE J.
[b.] September 23, 1919, Cambridge, OH; [p.] Stephan and Marina Jurkovich; [m.] Peter S. Voytko Sr., August 30, 1942; [ch.] Lydia Jean, Marjorie, Paula Mae, Betsy Lou, Peter Stephen II; [ed.] Unlimited; [memb.] Lakewood Historical Society, Right to Life Society, Charter Founder and Member of Ronald Reagan Republican Center, Concerned Women for America, Pentecost Lutheran Altar Guild; [hon.] Good neighbor AM 850 WRMR, was honored to be invited to the White House for spring and fall briefings during Reagan-Bush Era; [oth. writ.] "As Darkness Falls," a biography of my father's life, emphasizing his faith. Articles for Cleveland, P.D. Cleveland Press, Lakewood Sun Post, Lutheran Messen-

ger; [pers.] "Be honorable in all you do or else one will suffer the consequences."; [a.] Lakewood, OH

VUYANCIH, BRIAN
[b.] December 31, 1978, Cleveland; [p.] Peter Vuyancih and Sharon Vuyancih; [ed.] Euclid High School; [occ.] Student; [pers.] Contradiction is the opening of the mind.; [a.] Euclid, OH

WAGNER, EDMUND G.
[b.] June 10, 1913, Watertown, SD; [p.] Edmund B. and Gladys L. Wagner; [m.] Wlacyra M. Wagner, March 23, 1970; [ch.] Philip F. Wagner; [ed.] University of Minnesota, BSCE (Bachelor of Civil Engineering), MPH (Mast. of Public Health), Ph.D. (in progress); [occ.] Sanitary Engineer, Semi-Retired; [memb.] American Waterworks Association (Refemember), Inter American Assoc. of Sanitary Engineering, American Assoc. of Retired Persons; [hon.] Medalha de Guerra (Brazil), Army Commendation (High Performance), South American Theater Ribbon, Hempshire award; [oth. writ.] Water Supply for Small Communities, Waste Disposal for Small Communities, Upgrading Water Treatment Plants (All published by World Health Organization).; [pers.] Echoing down through the canyons of time, the voices of my heritage call to me. Search and you will find. Write and you will achieve.; [a.] Orlando, FL

WALKER, ELISABETH
[b.] June 21, 1986, Norwich, CT; [p.] Ann Jillson and Fred Walker; [occ.] Student; [a.] Preston, CT

WALKER, ILIANA A.
[b.] October 6, 1964, Bronx, NY; [p.] Victor Santiago, Evelyn Santiago; [m.] Frank J. Walker Jr., December 3, 1994; [ch.] Anthony, Iliana Jr., Christopher, Michelle; [ed.] Sachem H.S. North Campus, Wilfred Academy of Beauty; [occ.] Homemaker; [pers.] My greatest inspiration is the love that my husband and I share.; [a.] Johnstown, PA

WALKER, MARGARET
[pen.] Margo; [b.] May 25, 1952, Coosada, AL; [p.] Ed and Arlenia Walker; [ch.] Alicia Henderson; [ed.] Compton High School, Compton Jr. College, Chaffey College; [occ.] Unemployed/Special Education Aide; [memb.] Congregation of Jehovah's Witnesses; [hon.] I took acting class in College and received a standing oration for 2 minute scene from, "Sorry Wrong Number."; [oth. writ.] Thoughts and poems written in my diary.; [pers.] I love creating. I've works of all kind. I'm just beginning to connect with the creative person inside of me.; [a.] Fontana, CA

WALLACE, THOMAS S.
[pen.] Thomas S. Wallace; [b.] July 30, 1952, Johnstown, PA; [p.] John F. and Janet Wallace; [m.] Linda Laslo-Wallace, September 20, 1997; [ed.] Greater Johnstown High, Mount Aloysius College; [occ.] Steelworker/Cardiovascular Tech.; [pers.] This poem was inspired by and dedicated to my future mother-in-law Margaret Laslo.; [a.] Johnstown, PA

WALLACE, WILLIAM W.
[pen.] William (Bill) Wallace; [b.] December 7, 1923, East Point, GA; [p.] William J. and Callie Mae Wallace; [m.] Warrene E. Wallace, March 22, 1943; [ch.] Sandra, Andrea, Terry and Yvonne; [ed.] High School - Southwest DeKalb High School, attended many literature classes in Adult Training, at Jr. Colleges such as Daytona Bch. Jr. Community College; [occ.] Retired Southern Bell Tel. Gd. 30 yrs.; [memb.] Member ASCAP, NSAI Casements Songwriters Work Shop, Play Acoustic Guitar, can play

tune on most any string instrument and Bugle (National Gard) Bugle calls on Trumpet; [hon.] I guess I wasn't or aren't good enough or talented enough. I did win a Yellow Ribbon in a Minor Sou. Bell Contest in 1965 for Poem "A Poor Boy Woke Up"; [oth. writ.] Newspaper editorials etc., like yours, no income from writing. Recorded two records "Words of Happiness", "Big Black Dog", in the 60's and 70's produced a record in 70's by Disc. Jockey Dave Brockman "My Angel's Gone To Hell".; [pers.] I've been making verse and rhyme naturally since 4th Grade. And loving it. To bad someone in the business can't recognize raw talent. "Phi. Statement" On the way to the cemetery I'll have something ready to swing by and drop off at a publisher's house.; [a.] New Smyrna Beach, FL

WALLACE SR., TERRY W.
[pen.] Weetie; [b.] September 30, 1950, Dyess, AR; [p.] Sam and Faye Wallace; [m.] Debbi M. Wallace, September 20, 1992; [ch.] Terry W. (Booey) Wallace II; [ed.] Wilson High School, Wilson, AR, Florida Bible College, Hollywood, FL, Charleston College of Biblical Studies, Charleston, SC; [occ.] Pastor and Quality Auditor for Colson Caster Corp.; [memb.] March of Dimes Steering Committee, VFW; [hon.] Former Presidential Guard for Richard Nixon; [oth. writ.] Several poems published in newspapers, study guides for Biblical Training, songs and short stories.; [pers.] In 1991 a personal tragedy gave birth to an unknown hidden talent - poetry.; [a.] Walnut Ridge, AR

WALTON, JOE
[b.] Oklahoma; [p.] Tom C. and Anna Wilborn Walton; [m.] Shaaron Lee Pruett Walton, September 5, 1959; [ch.] Tom (Thomas) Allen Walton, Linda Crystal Burchett; [ed.] Monterey High, Pasadena College, Nazarene Theological Seminary; [occ.] Minister - Congregational Church, Del Rey Oaks, CA; [oth. writ.] Tommy and the Rainmaker; [a.] Salinas, CA

WARREN, BELVA
[b.] July 5, 1930, Pittsburgh, PA; [p.] Deceased; [m.] Deceased, October 11, 1952; [ch.] 4 grandchildren - Melissa, Bill, Jonathan, Hannah, 3 daughters, Jan, Julie and Jacey; [ed.] BA - Chatham College, Pgh., PA. several courses at Butter University, University of Indianapolis, and Liberty University; [occ.] Teachers - 5th grade - Kingsway Christian School (27 years); [memb.] Kingsway Christian Church; [oth. writ.] I've "dabbled" in writing all my life. I've never had anything published before. (This is so exciting!); [pers.] You're never too old to learn! I'm 66 and still enjoying new horizons. As a teacher, I try to impart this philosophy to my students.; [a.] Brownsburg, IN

WARREN, LENOR M.
[pen.] Lee; [b.] October 31, 1919, Chicago, IL; [p.] John and Nicole Pandell; [m.] Charles Warren, July 1, 1949; [ch.] Son and daughter, Henry G. and Charlyene J.; [occ.] Retired; [memb.] Moose Lodge #747 Women's Amvets Auxiliary 66, Phillip Carpenter Amvets Auxiliary 66 of Wheeling, Ill., 60090; [hon.] Poppy Citations, Children's Memorial Hospital - Chgo. Ill, Auz State Award; [a.] Wheeling, IL

WARREN-COOPER, MRS. ELLA
[pen.] Angel, Disciple; [b.] January 4, 1953, Smith County, Tyler, TX; [p.] Virgil and Lula M. Warren; [m.] Arther L. Cooper, August 25, 1983; [ch.] Melvin Jr., and two stepsons Phil and Cleve Cooper; [ed.] Emmett Scott High, John Tyler High, Barrow Cosmetology School, Tyler Junior College, O.I.C. - Opportunity Career School; [occ.] Americorp Vista (Community Worker), Business Management, Volunteer Service;

[memb.] Berry's Temple C.O.G.I.C. Church, NAACP, Member of Inaugural Class of Americorp Vista; [hon.] Someone Special Volunteer Award, Tyler Community Store Front, City of Tyler, Volunteer Award Boy Scouts of America Troop #149, The Leadership Foundation, Editor's Choice Award, for Outstanding Achievement, in Poetry, presented by The National Library of Poetry; [oth. writ.] Biography titled "Too Young To Cope", Newspaper Events, Tyler Various Poetry, "No Peace Maker", "Memories of M. L. King", "Thank You Martin", etc., articles written in Smith Country Herld News, "Ebony Journal"; [pers.] I always remember, the scripture, I will lift up mine eyes unto the hills for whence cometh my help...cometh from the Lord: Psalm 121 and a from a Dear Friend, Mr. Curtis Humphrey, 88 yr. old, photographer. "If you think you can you will."; [a.] Tyler, TX

WATSON, DAN
[pen.] Dan Shirley; [b.] August 16, 1946, Brookland, AR; [p.] Leonard and Hazel Watson; [m.] Shirley Ann (Brumit) Watson, April 30, 1966; [ch.] James Daniel Jr. and Stacy Glen; [ed.] Nettleton High Sch. (Grad. 1964), Combat Const. Machine Opers. Course, Ft. Leonard Wood, MO; [occ.] County Emp., Craighead Cty. Highway Dept.; [memb.] Cache River Pentecostal Church, American Handy Man Assoc., American Assoc. Retired Persons; [hon.] Semi-Finalist North American Open Poetry Contest; [oth. writ.] Several Poems (unpub.), Few Gospel songs (pub. soon hopefully).; [pers.] I want to look for and see the good in any person. My first love is gospel, but I also like country, folk, western polka, and easy listening music. Hobbies - gardening, fishing, hunting, playing keyboard.; [a.] Jonesboro, AR

WATSON, SHIRLEY D.
[b.] April 11, 1923, Scranton, PA; [p.] W. D. Davis and Carolyn Miller Davis; [m.] William E. Watson, December 30, 1944; [ch.] Two, both artists; [ed.] A. A. Journalism, 10 yrs. Music-Soprano, 4 yrs. Painting; [occ.] Homemaker; [memb.] Colonial Dames XVII Century; [hon.] 2 Best of Shows Painting - Watercolor and Oils; [oth. writ.] Poems. All poems are original with me. You have my permission to publish the poem chosen for semi-finals.; [pers.] "No star was ever lost we once have seen. We always may be what we might have been."; [a.] Naples, FL

WATSON, VIRGINIA L.
[b.] June 2, 1961, Bethesda, MD; [p.] William T. and Alise B. Burriss; [m.] Darrell V. Watson, June 20, 1981; [ch.] Shawnte Holiday, Darrell Jr., Kimberly Annalise; [ed.] Gaithersburg High School, G'burg, MD, U.S. Army Veteran; [hon.] Motherhood; [oth. writ.] Autobiography written at St. Joseph College, Rensseler, in "A", Father Denny, English "Core".; [pers.] "If I could change the world", Eric Clampton.; [a.] Dayton, OH

WEAVER, SAM P.
[pen.] Polk; [b.] July 17, 1941, Shreveport, LA; [p.] Sam and Den A. Weaver; [m.] Albert (Deceased), June 25, 1988; [ed.] A.C. Steer, attended North Western of Louisiana (University, TV), Byrd High School; [occ.] Poet-Song-Writers Prison Ministry, Land Overseer; [hon.] Being a member of the body of Christ; [oth. writ.] Angels Defined, Two Birthday Wishes, The Night is Far Spent, (Think Beyond) - (Peace of Mind), Spiritually Correct, Gentle Prompting, God's Spirit Winds, You Can Belong, Gods Spirit Connection; [pers.] As a Christian writer I try to relate messages to the reader that will make him or her mindful of the truth, goodness and meaning of God's love.; [a.] Shreveport, LA

WEEKS, MICHAEL D.
[b.] June 17, 1968, Columbus, OH; [p.] Mary Lou

Weeks, David Weeks; [m.] Diane Christine Weeks, April 2, 1995; [ch.] Jacob Michael Weeks; [ed.] 1 year of college - fusball, ping pong; [oth. writ.] Many poems, children's book in progress; [pers.] I dedicate my poem to my wife, the love of my life, who is a wonderful mother to our newborn son. Being the best husband and father I can be are my passions "If all else fails,...".; [a.] Independence, KY

WEINSTEIN, DRUCILLA
[b.] September 11, 1982, Wlfd./Merd., CT; [p.] Terri and Barry Weinstein; [ed.] Presently a freshman at Pennridge High School; [occ.] Paper Carrier; [memb.] St. Stephen's U.C.C. choir and Clowns for Christ, Students Against Destructive Decisions (S.A.D.D.), Pennridge Rams Marching Band; [hon.] Citizenship Award (1996); [pers.] I write to escape the pressures of my life as a teenager. It has become my way of indirectly expressing myself.; [a.] Perkasie, PA

WEISS, ERIC
[b.] February 5, 1979, Framingham, MA; [p.] Suzanne and David Weiss; [ed.] Nashoba H.S., Worcester Academy; [occ.] Student; [pers.] "Poetry is a spontaneous over flow of powerful emotion recollected in tranquility." W. Wordsworth to Danielle, her vision warms my soul and guides my hand.; [a.] Bolton, MA

WELBY, RICHARD E.
[b.] February 19, 1925, De Moinesta; [p.] Delia Welby (Mother); [m.] Janet E. Welby, April 22, 1973; [ch.] Nancy and Constance; [ed.] 3 years College - no degree; [occ.] Private Detective; [memb.] VFW American Legion AOPA - Patrol Craft Sailors Assc. National Association of Legal Investigators (Nali); [hon.] Grade Champion, Detroit News Spelling Bee 1935. WW II Campaign Ribbon; [oth. writ.] Other poems and news articles, short story about shipmate lost at sea in storm. Turner published it.; [pers.] Making money is easy! The mark of true success, is how many elections have you taken part in thru life?!; [a.] Lancaster, CA

WELCH, JILL C.
[b.] March 20, 1974, Davenport, IA; [p.] Jim and Jan Welch; [ed.] Alleman High School, Iowa State University - 2 years, St. Ambrose University - 2 years, Biology Degree; [occ.] Waitress (Possible Peace Corps Volunteer soon though); [memb.] Alpha Zeta, College of Agriculture Honorary Fraternity, Iowa State University; [hon.] St. Ambrose Woman's Basketball Scholarship 2 years, Iowa State University, College of Agriculture Honorary Fraternity, Alpha Zeta Member, [pers.] All I have to do is lift my wings and fly, but I'll never know if I don't try. If I don't get my feet up off the ground, who's to stop me from going another round?; [a.] Bettendorf, IA

WELCH, LAWRENCE A.
[b.] November 2, 1931, Barre, VT; [p.] Leslie Welch, Ruby Colby; [ed.] High School, 12 years, 4th honors from Bradford Academy Bradford, VT; [occ.] Retired; [hon.] University of Vermont Scholarship; [oth. writ.] Numerous poems about the seasons and family, etc.; [a.] Northfield, VT

WELLER, KENNETH L.
[pen.] Ken; [b.] August 24, 1951, Allentown, PA; [p.] Ralph and Joyce Hains; [ed.] GED - US Army; [occ.] Crane Oper.; [a.] Kutztown, PA

WELLS, MARY E.
[b.] Dott., WV; [p.] Ellie S. Crigger, Doll Crigger; [m.] Abraham L. Wells (Deceased), 1956; [ch.] William D. Wells, Ravenna Wells, Abraham A. Wells, Ambie L.

Wells, Mary L. Wells; [occ.] Homemaker; [hon.] I have been told by a lot of people that I have been gifted as Ministry in songs to help others and (English Teacher told me I was a good lyrics composer songwriter which I've never had any published as yet; [oth. writ.] Love to write poems, songs, too many to mention in my comps books.; [pers.] I have been enjoying writing songs plus poems from my heart. Since 1962 the reading of God's word places in my heart to write songs and poems to lift up others.; [a.] Bluefield, WV

WEST, MARY ELLEN
[pen.] Randie Kay Sanders; [b.] January 26, 1952, Jackson, MI; [p.] Adoptive: Mr. and Mrs. Allan Penn, Real: Mr. and Mrs. Bill Sanders; [m.] Clyde West, April 29, 1978; [ch.] Bob and Bruce Daniels, Rob, Mike and Heidi West; [ed.] Hanover-Horton H.S. Horton, MI; [occ.] Student studying to be counselor, Church Secretary; [memb.] Unity Church of Jackson, Domestic Harmony; [hon.] Graduated sixth, various honorable mentions or girl Friday stuff in previous jobs.; [oth. writ.] In several poems have published Poetry Corner of local newspaper, poems written and given as gifts, poems have appeared in past work places' newsletters also.; [pers.] Believe in your dreams, mine came true after 42 years. Everyone has a special gift if they would just let God express it through them even if it is simply a smile. My poetry comes to me sometimes in the middle of the night, as this one did.; [a.] Jonesville, MI

WEST, MICKIE T.
[pen.] Miriam Cervonka; [b.] June 10, 1944, Philadelphia, PA; [p.] Miriam Schwoyer and William Cervonka; [m.] Divorced; [ch.] David Allen West; [ed.] Central Bucks High, University of San Diego, Graduate Program; [occ.] Legal Assistant; [oth. writ.] Unpublished poems; [pers.] The greatest influences in my life have been the ancient philosophers such as Plato and Socrates, as well as my ongoing studies of the Eastern religions, Spirituality and Metaphysics. I believe in spiritual growth through personal introspection.; [a.] Philadelphia, PA

WHEELER JR., JOHN A.
[b.] August 8, 1917, Marion, SC; [p.] Col. J. A. Wheeler and Lucia Oakman Talley; [m.] Dorothy Louise Starke, February 16, 1940; [ch.] Jeannine Louise, John Stuart, Dorothy Elise, Robert Douglas; [ed.] School of Foreign Service, Geotestown University Class of 1942, OCS WWII Infantry School Grad., Convenient 2nd lit.; [occ.] Retired, U.S. Gorset Executive Retired July 1, 1972; [memb.] Veterans of Foreign Wars, D.A.V., Long time member of Greencastle CC and Brooks Manor CC. Both clubs now no longer exist, (over 25 years) member Mended Heart Associates; [hon.] Ordinary order of Croix de Guerre (Free French) WWII, Rupple Heart U.S. Army WWII Victory Medal (W 3 batte stuss) WWII; [oth. writ.] Several short poems, two short stories, one novel, unfinished.; [a.] Wheaton, MD

WHITE, DAVID
[pen.] David White; [b.] April 30, 1963, Santa Rosa, CA; [p.] Mr. Warren M., Gloria Ann White; [m.] Lisa Kay White, October 10, 1992; [ch.] Kyle Lee White; [ed.] Completed 12th grade, G.E.D. United State Army, Fort Leanwood, MO; [occ.] Food Service; [memb.] North American Hunting Club; [hon.] Army Achievement Award, State Service Ribbon, Honorable Discharge Army, Honorable Discharge Army National Guard, Editor's Choice Award 1996, and Editor's Choice Award 1997. Plus other Editor's Choice Award, Best Poem of '97; [oth. writ.] Too Babby Heart, Heart to Heart, Hand Me A Dream in Bottle, Stormy Dream's, Shallow Heart, As We Part, Child Play, Essence Mind's of Writer, A

Heart to Behold, Tunnel of Funnel, many more unpublish, but soon be.; [pers.] I have a dream to see my poetry know, the thoughts of love, I hold for special people close too my heart. Which inspired and believe there a dream. I strive to share my thought's with others.; [a.] Grand Island, NE

WHITE, KATE
[b.] May 24, 1987, Marietta, GA; [p.] Ferne and William White; [ed.] Currently in 4th Grade of The Walker School, Marietta, GA; [memb.] Girl Scouts of America, Junior Jazz Company, Dancers Workshop, Saturday School for Scholars and Leaders at GA State Univ.; [pers.] Kate is 10 years old. She wants to be a writer when she grows up. Kate enjoys dancing, music. She also loves to read and play chess.

WIGGINS, CYNTHIA
[b.] June 13, 1926, Cuba, KY; [p.] Brown and Pearl McPherson; [m.] Harold Wiggins, August 16, 1941; [ch.] James Richard and Gary Paul Wiggins; [ed.] High School and some college courses; [occ.] Writer, producer of my songs; [memb.] Nashville, Gospel Association, and Country Christian Music, member of Church of Christ, member of The International Poetry Hall of Fame; [hon.] Hearing my songs played and sung on various radio and T.V. programs and seeing my poetry and other writings in printed publications; [oth. writ.] In four different newspapers and two magazines at various times, also I have written for different poetry publications.; [pers.] To use any talent I have been blessed with to promote better understanding in any language and to leave a special message of hope to others.; [a.] Mayfield, KY

WILCOX, KRISTIN
[pen.] Kris; [b.] October 27, 1982, Hudson; [p.] Marc and Deena Suddreth; [ed.] South Caldwell 9th Grade; [memb.] Michael Jackson Fan Club, Beta Club; [hon.] 4 Awards of National Fitness, 6 President Physical Fitness Awards and 3rd Place in Science Fair in 1995 and 1st Place in Science Fair for 1997.; [oth. writ.] Alone which was published in a Voyage to Remember and an untitled one which was published in Lyrical Heritage.; [a.] Lenoir, NC

WILDMAN, TAMMY
[b.] November 18, 1968, Indiana; [p.] Arnold and Mary Houser (Deceased); [m.] Andrew Wildman, November 21, 1987; [ch.] Adam, Alan, Amber; [ed.] 11th grade 1/2 yr., received GED June '96; [occ.] Housewife/Mother; [pers.] I'd like to thank my father and husband for believing in me. And also my children for thinking "Mommy can do anything".; [a.] Montezuma, IN

WILKERSON, LEWIS VILL
[pen.] LVW; [b.] April 19, 1967, Houston, TX; [p.] Billie Wilkerson, Hazel Barlow; [ch.] Tabatha Yvonne, Latasha Nicole; [ed.] Jack Yates High; [occ.] Operations Specialist on board U.S.S. Antietam (CG-54); [memb.] American Legion, Mount Erie Baptist Church; [hon.] 2nd award "Navy Achievement Medals," 3rd award "Good Conduct Medals," "Navy Humanitarian Medal," "National Defense Medal," "Coast Guard Expedition Medal," "Battle of Efficiency Ribbon/Silver "E" (3rd award), "Meritorious Unit Commendation Ribbon; [oth. writ.] A large amount of poems/songs ranging from spiritual to day or night thoughts traveling thru an open mind.; [pers.] Subjects which I write about, are meant to help someone find the way out of whatever they may be in.; [a.] San Diego, CA

WILKERSON, MARIE LEE
[b.] September 14, 1983, Pomona, CA; [p.] Randy and Dolores Wilkerson; [ed.] Attends Dixie Middle School,

St. George, Utah 8th grade 13 years old, Honor Roll student; [occ.] Student; [hon.] Good Citizenship Award Math Award, Honor Roll student Little Miss Phelan 1992 in Calif. Miss American Starlet of Utah 1995; [a.] Saint George, UT

WILLIAMS, ETHEL
[b.] September 7, 1938, Fairfield, NC; [p.] Herbert and Isabell Harris; [m.] Leon Williams, November 23, 1956; [ch.] 6 girls, 7 boys; [ed.] High School and Bible College Graduate; [occ.] Co-Pastor of Evangelist with Refuge Temple Ministries; [memb.] Refuge Temple Ministries Women's Aglow International; [oth. writ.] Book - God's Amazing Grace; [pers.] Writing is a God given gift to me. I write, hoping to inspire.; [a.] Seaford, DE

WILLIAMS, MARY
[b.] July 21, 1940, Sweetwater, TX; [p.] Lyle and Rene Deffebach; [m.] Tommy Williams, May 25, 1963; [ch.] Julie Brown, Blair Williams; [ed.] BS in Elem. Ed., U of TX, Austin, M.Ed. in Elem. Ed., Texas Tech University, other courses, Sul Ross University, McMurry University; [occ.] Teacher of Literacy I-II at Price Daniel Unit TDCJ; [memb.] NEA, Texas State Teachers Assn., Delta Kappa Gamma (honorary female teacher's society), Methodist Church, Emmaus; [hon.] Female Member of the Year, First United Methodist Church, fourth of July Valuable Church Member, High School Poetry Honors, Who's Who in American Teachers; [oth. writ.] Couple of other poems.; [pers.] My grandmother who lived with us was a prolife poetess. I received my love of poetry from her.; [a.] Snyder, TX

WILLIAMS, MONT DAVID
[pen.] Sleep Payne; [b.] June 26, 1963, Rocky Ford, CO; [ed.] Self; [occ.] Artist; [hon.] Illustrations and Cover Design for Dangerous Passage, Illustrations for Cheyennes at Dark Water Creek (both books by William Y. Chalfant and published by University of Oklahoma Press, Norman and London - I considered it an honor to illustrate both of these books); [oth. writ.] Sleep and Movement, My Marijuana, The Lands, Gobs Of Lines Crawling, Gumbo With Momo; [pers.] Truth - scream it.; [a.] Westminster, CO

WILLOUGHBY, MEGHAN
[b.] June 17, 1982, Owensboro, KY; [p.] Gary and Leneisa Willoughby; [ed.] 9th grade in private school; [occ.] Student; [pers.] I reach down into the depths of my soul to create poetry that the world can relate to.; [a.] Beaver Dam, KY

WILSON, GARY G. H.
[pen.] GGH Wilson; [b.] December 13, 1967, Jamaica, WI; [p.] George and Norma Wilson; [ed.] St. Catherine High and Excel Community College, Jamaica, West Indies; [occ.] Financial Advisor/Prudential Securities; [oth. writ.] A book entitled "For The Wise And Not Too Wise, Philosophies of life."; [pers.] Time spent for knowledge is worthy attainment of wisdom.; [a.] East Elmhurst, NY

WILSON, KELLI D.
[b.] June 17, 1983, North Kansas City; [p.] Paul D. and Melody A. Wilson; [ed.] Currently in the Eight Grade, will be a freshman August '97', (Renick Junior High (8th) (Moberly Senior High (9th)); [occ.] Student; [pers.] I enjoy poetry and writing it, I did not think I could do poetry until I write that one. ("It Didn't Hurt To Try").; [a.] Moberly, MO

WILSON, LADONNA MAE
[pen.] LaDonna DeBarkley; [b.] February 16, 1943, Sapulpa, OK; [p.] Thomas Jefferson and Retha

Baldwin Barkley; [m.] Eddie Joe Wilson, June 23, 1961; [ch.] Elizabeth Ann, Rebeca and Mary Catherine; [ed.] Central High, Tulsa, OK. Rogers State College, Rhema Bible College; [occ.] Wife, Companion, Mother, Grand Mother, Nanny and Friend; [memb.] Rhema Bible Church, National Geographic Society, Smithonian Institute Member, Tulsa Zoo Friends; [oth. writ.] I have written many poems which I have not made known to man, as yet. Ephesians 3:3, that by revelation as I wrote before in brief.; [pers.] I try to reflect "The Bible", which is "The Inspired Word of God", I feel the Family Unit, as a whole, is the backbone of America! 1 John 4:4 Greater is he, that is in me, than he that is in the world.; [a.] Inola, OK

WILSON, MARGARET JO
[pen.] M. J. Wilson; [b.] October 20, 1917, Virginia; [p.] Robin Florence Jenkins; [m.] Felix B. Wilson, May 17, 1945; [ch.] 4 daughters; [ed.] High School, 1 year Mitchell College; [occ.] Retired (Secretary); [oth. writ.] Poems in an issue several years ago; [a.] Pfafftown, NC

WILSON, STEVEN
[pen.] Easy Money; [b.] October 17, 1966, Chicago; [p.] Walter, Alice Wilson; [m.] Valerie (Fiancee); [ch.] Steven Jr., Monique, Ashley, Jeremian; [ed.] Chicago Vocational High School; [occ.] Shipping Clerk; [hon.] Perfect Attendance; [pers.] I strive to let people know that no matter how bad this world gets, Jehovah God is capable of making all dreams come true.; [a.] Chicago, IL

WILSON, TAMARA
[b.] September 19, 1983, Philadelphia; [p.] Rylanda and Lewis Wilson; [ed.] Restoration Nursery School, Henry H. Houston School (Elementary), Holy Cross Elementary School; [occ.] 8th grade student; [hon.] Author of "Gifts," published in A Celebration of Pennsylvania Young Poets, 1995, Creative Communication, Forest Grove, Oregon publisher.; [a.] Philadelphia, PA

WILSON JR., JOHNNY L.
[pen.] Logan Wilson; [b.] August 25, 1977, Fort Thomas, KY; [p.] John and Anne Wilson; [occ.] Work for Conair Airlines "Ground Crew"; [memb.] United States Airforce Auxiliary; [pers.] I was influenced by poetry by my H.S. teacher when she taught a quarter of poetry.; [a.] Fort Wright, KY

WINCENTSEN, ERIC
[b.] February 17, 1972, Phoenix, AZ; [ed.] College Student Longoing Arizona State University; [memb.] Myama Corporation; [oth. writ.] "Shattered," short story, published in the Traveler Magazine, 1991. Several newspaper articles. "The 7 Never Dims," recorded by local musician Eric Paul Johnson.; [pers.] Writing is a release. All tears and hopes are momentarily cleared from the soul. Briefly, all life's goals are achieved, and happiness, though fleeting, is found.; [a.] Scottsdale, AZ

WITCHGER, THERESA MARIE
[b.] September 2, 1979; [p.] William and Kathleen Witchger; [ed.] I went to St. Pius X Grade School from Grades K through 8th. I am presently attending Brebeuf Jesuit Preparatory High School.; [oth. writ.] I have had several poems published in Seasons, a literary magazine.; [pers.] "He who laughs, lasts."; [a.] Indianapolis, IN

WITTEN, DAVID W.
[b.] February 18, 1974, Wichita, KS; [p.] Janice and Raymond Witten; [occ.] Sous Chef; [a.] Wichita, KS

WOMACK, DOROTHY E.
[b.] October 6, 1952, Dallas, TX; [p.] Vivian H. Hanby;

[m.] Riley Womack, June 6, 1970; [ed.] CPS Business Degree: MTSU, Murfreesboro, TN; [occ.] Housewife; [oth. writ.] Poems (230), Songs: (46), Self help articles: (575), Books: (2) My book "Passage Into Paradise," is about my mother's 4 yrs. of suffering before she died and things I learned. All of these are, as yet, unpublished works. I have help articles published by Christ Church, Nashville, TN - about 10 yrs. ago. Reason for poem: I wrote, "Paint me a Picture," based on expriences my own mother had as she was actually dying. She described these specifics to me and I compiled them into a poem. My mother was a self-taught artist at 68 yrs. old and painted for nearly 10 yrs.; [pers.] I am inspired by spiritual insights, experiences, and truths. I view everything with an eye towards God's viewpoint, and all my poems, songs, self help articles and books reflect my profound belief in a life hereafter.; [a.] Tullahoma, TN

WOOD, ANDREE R.
[b.] February 10, 1929, Chicago, IL; [p.] Alice Fortier, Andre Robitaille; [m.] Richard L. Wood, January 14, 1956; [ch.] Mary, Matthew, Melissa, Elizabeth and John; [ed.] B.A. Northern Ill. University, M.A. Northern Ill. Univ.; [occ.] Archaeologist - Field Research Assistant, Ancient Blood Residues; [memb.] Archaeological Institute of America; [hon.] Included in Who's Who of American Women - 1997-1998; [oth. writ.] Blood Residue Analysis on Ancient Tools. Research Paper Pub. in Journal of Field Archaeology, Article Pub. in LA Research on Ancient Turkish Funeral Rites. Several poems published in News and Notes, Oriental Institute, U. of Chicago.; [a.] Barrington Hills, IL

WOOD MULLER, DONNA S.
[pen.] Donna S. Wood; [b.] May 3, 1976, Saint Joseph Hospital; [p.] Margo and Douglas Wood; [m.] Stephen J. Muller, May 24, 1997; [ch.] Sarah Elisabeth Wood; [ed.] Shawnee Mission West, Graduate of 1995; [occ.] Cashier for two companies; [pers.] Hearts and minds can't be read so in hopes of bringing a better and brighter future for yourself and those around you share your dreams and ideas.; [a.] Overland Park, KS

WOODCOCK, MARY A.
[pen.] Marie Alena; [b.] September 7, 1945, Ione, WA; [p.] Leonard and Merle Scott; [m.] James Robert Woodcock, June 27, 1964; [ch.] Two, Christy, James; [ed.] High School - 1 year Law Enforcement - 4 years Drawing and other Art - Misc. College Courses - EMT Training and Cert.; [occ.] Self employed; [memb.] National Rifle Assoc., National Home Gardening Club; [oth. writ.] Have been writing poems - songs - and short stories since I was a kid. This was my 1st attempt to have anything published.; [pers.] While living in Alaska had the great opportunity to take college. Art courses from internationally known artist Ray Troll and also discovered I had abilities in the art field never imagined. I have intentions of printing some of my art in the near future. Possibly including some of my poems along with my art work. Literature, art, and photography have always been a great interest to me. I also have a great love for gardening (esp. organic) and preserving our natural resources. My favorite saying is: If you see someone without a smile - give him one of yours!; [a.] Helena, MT

WOODMAN, J. RUSSELL
[b.] December 5, 1969, Laconia, NH; [p.] Edward Woodman, Annika Woodman; [m.] Cheryl D. Woodman, May 27, 1994; [ed.] Winnacunnet High School, University of New Hampshire at Durham, University of Maine at Fort Kent; [occ.] Computer Systems Administrator; [memb.] Aroostook Amateur Radio Association,

American Radio Relay League, HTML Writer's Guild; [hon.] Honor Roll, Dean's List; [oth. writ.] Several unpublished short stories and numerous poems and articles for work and school publications.; [pers.] Poetry by my hand reflects my love of nature and of the life contained within it, and is influenced by the talents of Walt Whitman and e.e. cummings.; [a.] Caribou, ME

WOODRUFF, JEANNE
[b.] November 24, 1956, Grand Island, NE; [p.] Mary Hitchler (Deceased March 28, 1997), Paul Hitchler, (Father Deceased); [ch.] Jeff and Michael; [ed.] Grand Island Senior High (1975), Central Community College, Grand Island, NE (1995); [occ.] Preschool Teacher, Grow, Learn and Play Child Care Center, Grand Island; [memb.] NAEYC National Association for the Education of Young Children; [hon.] Central Community College Honor Graduate; [pers.] My writing is most inspired by the beauty of nature, and by the love, pride and gratitude I have for my children.; [a.] Grand Island, NE

WOODS, BILL C.
[pen.] Bill C. Woods; [b.] March 7, 1939, Lewisburg, TN; [p.] Tom and Marie Woods; [m.] Betty Haynes, February 18, 1989; [ch.] Jim and Wendy; [ed.] B.S. Degree, Middle Tennessee State University; [occ.] Purchasing Manager; [memb.] APICS West Church of Christ; [hon.] Dean's List, Certified in Production and Inventory Control, CPIM Designation; [oth. writ.] Poems about friends and my personal life, none published; [pers.] Write poetry to relieve stress from work.; [a.] Lewisburg, TN

WOYDA, ANITA VICTORIA
[b.] September 26, 1941, Germany; [p.] Franz and Maria Woyda; [m.] Divorced; [ch.] Mark Raisis, Maria Dawson; [ed.] Educated in Germany, High School equivalent, self taught in English culture and language; [memb.] Kryon Quarterly, Wildlife Federation, Friends of Library of Palm; [oth. writ.] 5 minutes to midnight - video meditation tapes - Audio article in Palm Beach Post; [pers.] As a longtime student and teacher of New Age Philosophy, I passionately believe in the appropriateness of life on Planet Earth; [a.] Palm Springs, FL

WRIGHT, LINNIE MAXINE TIMMS
[b.] August 26, 1926, Kilgore, TX; [p.] Leonard Timms, Carrie Bowie Timms (Deceased both parents); [m.] Malcolm Nathaniel Wright, September 16, 1945; [ch.] Ten, two sets of twins; [ed.] Danville Elementary, North Chapel High, Kilgore High, College, Jarvis Christian College, Prairie View A&M University, Hempstead, Texas and E.T. State, Commerce Texas; [occ.] Housewife - Retired School Teacher - Special Education for 26 years; [memb.] Heroines of Jericho, AARP, Associate Mem. Sheriffs Association, Church Choir Mem., Secretary Cypress District Sunday School and N.B.C. of Christian Education; [hon.] Vacation Bible School director for 24 years - Appreciation award in 1993 for musician St. Mark Bapt. Church, and Pleasant Hill Baptist Church, Sulphur Springs Texas; [oth. writ.] Prose selections about workers in Cypress clinic - poetry "From The Old To The New" moving "From The Old School Building to the New building at North Hopkins ISD Poems about Fannindel ISD and its People It's Praise"; [pers.] I have been listening to speakers and reading poems and essays that inspired me to try my thoughts on paper about God's things that surround me and praising His creation in all things.; [a.] Sulphur Springs, TX

WRIGHT, SHARON SUE
[b.] February 24, 1944, Williamstown, WV; [p.] Everett

Kimble, Maud Kimble; [m.] Clifton H. Wright, March 11, 1967; [ch.] Terence Ray, Sonia Sue; [ed.] Howard City High School, Howard City, MI; [occ.] Folder Operator, Amway Corp. Ada, MI; [pers.] "My First Love," was an inspiration of accepting our Lord as personal savior. I pray these words might inspire others to do the same and fall in love for the very first time.; [a.] Rockford, MI

WRIGHT, SHAWN
[pen.] Shawn Wright; [b.] January 26, 1978, Bentonville, AR; [p.] Elizabeth Shipman, Buddy Wright; [ed.] High School graduate, Rogers High School, class of 1996; [occ.] Parts Dept., Bob Moleney Ford, Rogers, AR; [hon.] Editors award - NLP; [oth. writ.] "A Shining Light to See," published in Memories of Tomorrow. Many others unpublished.; [pers.] Writing has done so much for me. Writing is a very personal release for my feelings. Poetry is my way of bringing out my feelings and emotions. Everyone's are special.; [a.] Rogers, AR

WYNN, GEORGE H.
[b.] March 31, 1911, Buchanan, MI; [p.] Paul and Elizabeth; [m.] Anne, June 1, 1963; [ch.] Judith and Richard; [ed.] BA 1933 Western Mich. U., MD 1938 Univ. of Mich.; [occ.] Retired - January 1, 1980; [memb.] Life member of Michigan State Medical Society, Lenawee Country Club Adrian, MI, (Honorary Member), Innisbrook, Hilton CC Tarpon Springs, FL; [hon.] I was honored for having served as chief of staff of the Bixley Hospital, Adrian, Mich. for 14 years. Read a citation from the City Commission. Also a citation from Western Mich Univ. for being a football player and an "A" student.; [oth. writ.] Theme - "Abraham Lincoln" - Senior English Class. (Won medal) ("Big Deal!").; [pers.] My wife tells me not to mention I was a doctor, thinking it might influence any award. I called myself a "country doctor" - and am proud of it.; [a.] Palm Harbor, FL

YALE, LINDA ANN
[pen.] L. A. Yale; [b.] June 24, 1950, Lynwood, CA; [p.] Earl and Ada Moore; [m.] Eugene P. Yale, September 12, 1980; [ch.] Suzanne 14, James 12; [ed.] El Cajon Valley High School, Eng. Lit. and Physical Geography A.B.s from San Diego State University; [occ.] Household Manager and Mom, Volunteer; [oth. writ.] Children's stories, Natural History Essays; [pers.] I feel a strong connection to the natural world, and must be a part of it regularly. My writing often stems from a desire to awaken this need in others.; [a.] El Cajon, CA

YANNOTTA, JERILYN
[b.] July 18, 1971, New Jersey; [p.] Annette Capiello, Angelo Yannotta; [occ.] Assistant, WBC Industries Westfield, New Jersey; [oth. writ.] Poems, short stories, novels, only 1 other poem was published.; [pers.] I believe in Eastern Philosophy, when you think of doing something, not wasting any time doing it, or it could alter the rest of your day, or even life.; [a.] Berkeley Heights, NJ

YOKELEY, REBECCA
[b.] June 12, 1981, Boonville, MO; [p.] Bob and Violet Yokeley; [ed.] Sophomore in High School; [occ.] Student; [pers.] This poem is dedicated in memory of my Grandmother Rhoda Mullins.; [a.] Forsyth, MO

YORK, GARY LEE
[pen.] Neon Knight; [b.] August 3, 1959, Georgetown, OH; [p.] Dorothy Carter; [ed.] High School diploma and 2 years at Southern Hill JVS; [occ.] Disabled - was Carpenter; [memb.] No memberships at this time; [hon.] High Skills Award in Carpentry at Southern Hills JVS in 1977; [oth. writ.] Heaven's Call, Prayer, Memories,

My Lady, Drinking and Driving, Winter Wind, Christmas, The Bible and The Cross, In The Eyes of The Lion Lady Heater; [pers.] My poems are all inspired. I always feel better after I have put my words on paper. Hopefully the reader will too.; [a.] Hamersville, OH

YOSHINO, LAURIE FAY
[b.] February 27, 1968, Los Angeles, CA; [ed.] A.A. East Los Angeles College, Currently at Cal State, Los Angeles, Majoring in Social Work; [occ.] Student; [pers.] "I know if I can challenge myself to do anything, the outcome is a great achievement for a disabled Asian woman."; [a.] Alhambra, CA

YOST, CHARLES EDWARD
[p.] Dalores G. Yost; [ch.] Brad and Colleen Yost; [ed.] Fergus Co. HI, U of Montana, U of WA, Seattle U; [occ.] Sec/Treas Television Assoc. of Republic WA; [memb.] Trinity Lutheran Ch. Republic Kiwanis Club, Republic Chamber Commerce, ATO Frat (Alpha Tau Omega); [oth. writ.] Unpublished personal poems.; [pers.] To reflect in poetry that the Lord's Grace is sufficient for all mankind.; [a.] Republic, WA

YOUNG, ANGHARAD BRANSFORD
[pen.] Ann Young; [b.] January 25, 1943, Ardmore, OK; [p.] Frankie and Byron Bransford; [m.] Dr. Lyle O. Young, January 30, 1965; [ch.] Alison and Stephanie; [ed.] B.A. University of North Texas, M.A. Northeastern State University, Ed. D. University of Tulsa; [occ.] Licensed Professional Counselor and Licensed Marital and Family Therapist; [memb.] American Counselors Association National Employment Counselors, Delta kappa Gamma, Phi Delta Kappa, Kappa Delta Phi, Assistance League PEO, Delta Gamma Alum.; [hon.] Who's Who in American Colleges and Universities Kappa Kappa Iota Scholar Award, National Distinguished Service Registry for Counseling and Development; [oth. writ.] Chapter on Stress in The Whole Book Of Health Co author on How To Get The Job You Want Poems and articles in other publications - newspapers, small magazines, curricula.; [pers.] God gave mankind life and choice. I believe both are to be used positively for self and others.; [a.] Tulsa, OK

YOUNG, FRAN
[b.] April 18, 1940, High Rolls, NM; [p.] Earl and Bessie Hudman; [m.] Leland Young, September 14, 1986; [ch.] Lee Wallace; [ed.] Alamogordo High, Alamogordo, NM; [occ.] Disabled; [oth. writ.] My first poem is to be printed by the National Library of Poetry in "Tracing Shadows" summer 1997. It is also to be on tape "The Sound of Poetry" this year.; [pers.] Most of my poetry is narrative version from personal experience or for special people in my life. I have liked poetry from a very early age, especially Edgar Allen Poe.; [a.] Lubbock, TX

ZARGARIAN, AMARAS
[b.] January 6, 1987, Tehran, Iran; [p.] Vigen and Mared; [ed.] Elementary 4th Grade Balboa School, Glendale in Tehran, Iran; [occ.] Student; [memb.] Girl Scouts of America; [oth. Writ.] Poems: My Dream, The Wicked Old Witch, Christmas Eve, Trick-or-Treating; [pers.] When I grow up, I want to be a reporter and writer. I came to U.S. June 1995. I only knew Armenian and Persian.; [a.] Glendale, CA

ZIEMANN, MARVIN J.
[pen.] Marvin J. Ziemann; [b.] January 8, 1945, Lodi, CA; [p.] Emil and Bertha Ziemann; [m.] Kim, December 17, 1980; [ch.] Keri Raenne, Kandi Sheranne; [ed.] Lodi, High School, Delta College; [occ.] Outside Route Salesman, Lodi, CA; [memb.] Emanuel Lutheran Church,

Local 439 Teamsters; [hon.] Plaques for Outstanding Sales in my occupation; [oth. writ.] Some commended letters to local newspapers editors.; [pers.] I rely mainly on keeping an open mind. Like writing down good words and ideas when they first enter.; [a.] Lodi, CA

ZINDLER, J. D.
[b.] September 2, 1956, Bozeman, MT; [p.] Daniel and Christine Zindler; [m.] Lizbeth (Polly) Zindler, November 14, 1980; [ch.] Cody Daniel, Ry Cameron; [ed.] Bozeman Senior High, Montana State University, University of Montana; [occ.] Tele-Communications; [memb.] Bridger Creek Golf Association, Rocky Mountain Elk Foundation, Bozeman Little League Association; [oth. writ.] Numerous poems and song lyrics; [pers.] Favorite poets, W.S. Merwin, Peter Everwine, William Stafford, Robert Frost, and Richard Hugo whom I studied under at the University of Montana. Richard Hugo was both friend and mentor and all who knew him are richer. For having had the opportunity.; [a.] Bozeman, MT

INDEX
OF POETS

Index

Hall, Vera 391
Halliday, Mary Ann 104
Hallstrom, Joyce D. 55
Hambleton, Kyle 157
Hamilton, Allexandra 367
Hamilton, Michelle L. 342
Hamilton, Nichol 128
Hammer, Megan 33
Hampton, C. Sterling 187
Handley, Margaret K. 338
Haney, Carol 363
Hanik, Ronald Jr. 435
Hanisko, Terry 132
Hankee, Daniel 355
Hankins, Jo 99
Hanna, Crystal 230
Hanna, Dale 314
Hannah, John T. 113
Hannawell, Erica J. 189
Hansen, Deanna Lynn 462
Hansen, Jessica 432
Hanson, Ashli 254
Hanson, Jane Huelster 108
Hanson, S. L. 43
Harbour, Nathaniel W. 308
Hardesty, Nick 66
Hardin, Michelle 145
Harley, Yvonne H. 22
Harmon, Colleen 89, 193
Harp, Gladys Spencer 36
Harp, Matthew 61
Harper, Dennis Jr. 211
Harper, Kathleen 308
Harris, Billy E. 93
Harris, Brandon 416
Harris, Carla Lynette 465
Harris, Chris 222
Harris, Colleen 360
Harris, John 293
Harris, Leslie Faith 371
Harris, Minnie P. 60
Harris, Terry 329
Harrison, Cathy A. Franco 76
Harrison, Donald M. 27
Harrison, Melissa 321
Harrison, Mose E. 309
Hart, Alice C. 26
Hart, Lucinda 232
Hart, Roy V. Jr. 176
Hart, Tracy Beth 72
Hartman, Ruth G. 328
Harvey, Betty 99
Harvey, Michael 204
Hasenmiller, Scott D. 66
Haskin, Katherine M. 175
Haskins, Christine D. 202
Haspels, John 427
Hatcher, Christina 334
Hathaway, Jim 215
Haugh, Gloria M. Fiala 107
Havemeier, Jason 491
Hawkins, Jeff 192
Hawkins, Sandra 20
Hawkins, Willie 53
Hawks, Brett 89
Hayden, Cathrine C. 389
Hayden, Eric 471
Hayes, Dave 327
Hayes, Granny 205
Hayes, Jean E. 320
Haynes, Jacky L. 413

Hazen, Cara M. 120
Heath, Paula J. 12
Heatherington, Joyce 190
Heaton, Arlene 86
Hebert, Chrissy 350
Hebert, Frances L. 365
Hebert, Joel 443
Heckenstaller, Terese 32
Heffelfinger, Daniel 333
Hefflin, Cassandra 234
Heiberg, Elvin Ragnvald 352
Heiken, Janie 264
Heine, M. Jean 322
Hejma, Sarah Bailey 455
Heljenek, Brian T. 426
Heller, Dean 182
Heller, Heinz A. 101
Hellums, Greta C. 487
Helmick, Patricia L. 166
Helphingstine, Amber 284
Helwig, Lois M. 340
Henderson, Charles E. 197
Henderson, Jeremy 178
Henderson, Nicole R. 309
Hendricks, Jan 208
Hendricks, Matthew 78
Hendricks, Nikole 442
Henley, Justin Scott 332
Henley, Kayse Lauren 420
Hennemann, Richard M. II 99
Henning, Allen 352
Henry, Donna M. 198
Henry, Stephanie Leann 427
Hensley, Lisa D. 115
Hensley, Mary Helen 291
Hepp, Kellie A. 470
Herman, Justin 198
Herren, Stephanie D. 41
Herring, Dorothy 156
Herring, Linda F. 248
Herrmann, Vicki 482
Hert, Chad 444
Heskett, Jack W. 188
Hess, Kent DeMar 112
Hess, Madeline C. 98
Hess, Trevor Tyler 211
Heyd, Linda M. 73
Hickman, Nimmie S. 401
Hicks, Amanda 215
Hicks, Amie 434
Hicks, Brian 35
Hicks Lee, Betty J. 305
Hicks, Robert Allen 172
Hidvegi, Erica I. 309
Hieronymus, Margaret E. 30, 31
Higginbotham, Jenny 492
Higgins, E. Chipman 38
Higgins, Sarah J. 489
Higgs, Gale L. 271
Hightower, Kelli 240
Hill, Alice Lorraine 8
Hill, Alonzo 369
Hill, Crystal 149
Hill, Mandy 208
Hill, Nola 228
Hill, Victor 248
Hill, Virginia 479
Hillhouse, Edward F. 384
Hindel, Erika R. 310
Hinds, Joseph 247
Hines, Tamara L. 349

Hinkel, Stephanie 54
Hinson, Michaela Kirkham 65
Hirten, Eileen F. 146
Hixenbaugh, Robbie 324
Hixon, Maxine Spyres 106
Hocko, Jennifer M. 197
Hoemann, James E. 437
Hoffman, David L. Jr. 276
Hoffman, Pete 137
Hoffman-Stern, Harriet 406
Hoffmann, Cathy L. 36
Hofstod, Paul J. 273
Hogan, Betty 346
Hogg, Gary N. 452
Hoilien, Catherine E. 7
Holland, Billie 426
Holle, Freda 367
Holleman, William J. 111
Holliday, Virge 209
Holliger, E. H. 227
Hollingsead, Linda 307
Hollingsworth, Lisa R. 86
Holloway, Brett A. 320
Holmes, Bernice 13
Holmes, Priscilla 312
Holmes, Sandra Merrill 341
Holmes, Susan A. 4
Holtry, Jessica L. 203
Hood, Jennefer 106
Hood, Sarah 416
Hooper, William 437
Hoose, Keith D. 400
Hoosier, Dorothy Elois 142
Hoover, Allison Christy 11
Hopkins, Ruth P. 217
Hopperstad, Haley 419
Hopson, Joel Edward 422
Horahan, Katie 254
Horan, Mary 320
Horn, Hendrik Jr. 379
Hornaday, Estella 279
Horne, Gene M. 435
Horne, Robert 235
Horney, Leslie 259
Horton, Joyce J. 3
Hotaling, Linda M. 104
Hotchkiss, Dianna 383
Houchens, Janel I. 164
Hougesen, Becky Sue 487
Houghton, Ed 351
Houle, Josee 487
Housholder, Aaron J. 100
Howard, Annette K. 208
Howard, Deborah G. 312
Howard, Jessica 201
Howell, Evelyn M. 195
Howell, William E. 139
Hower, Nathan S. 42
Hubbard, Iris L. 313
Hubbard, James William 110
Hubbard, Phyliss 290
Huber, Lura 363
Hubler, David E. 416
Hudgens, Sue Graham 415
Hudson, Kellie 216
Hudson, Nikki L. 418
Hudson, Rebecca S. 104
Hudson, Roosevelt 6
Huebner, T. H. 173
Huegel, Valentine 329
Huff, Lauren 188

Huffman, Mark H. 215
Hufnagle, Tyler 196
Huggett, Allyson 144
Hughes, Barbara 153
Hughes, Jessie Lynne 17
Hughes, Kellie D. 60
Hughes, Shanna 419
Hughes, Stephanie 295
Hughey, Michelle Denise 492
Huls, Therese 213
Hunsinger, Carlos L. 169
Hunt, Arlie L. II 5
Hunt, Mathew L. 448
Hunt, Melanie Anne 447
Hunt, Phyllis L. 3
Hunter, Consuela 176
Hunter, Juanita 168
Hunter, Kaye 400
Hunter, Marian T. 35
Hunter, Roseta 470
Huq, Samihah 383
Hurlebaus, Sara 434
Hurte, Cheryl 56
Huskey, Roy Wayne 336
Huskisson, Janet 228
Hutchins, Brandy 469
Hutchinson, Rose Emma 275
Hutton, Carol 48
Hutton, Kathleen 105
Hyatt, Marc 482

I

Ibarra, Ida 122
Ibele, Margaret R. 428
Ide, Calina 195
Igbonegun, Jennifer 470
Iha, Rhiannon 246
Ihde, Laurel K. 118
Ilegieuno, Fatiya Anima 265
Imoto, Jaime 309
Imperato, Arnold 96
Ingram-Mack, Sybil 364
Inin, Menieli Meli 320
Inman-Sievers, Marcella G. 93
Inthapangna, Dan 373
Irons, Alexis 115
Irvin, Tiffany 307
Irvine, Teri A. 95
Isban, Adam 106
Isenhour, Crystal R. 375
Ison, Suetta L. 70
Ives, Timothy J. 436
Ivey, Marjorie M. 425
Ivie, Christi G. 46
Izzarone, Janis 388
Izzo, Thomas 101

J

Jabradally, Jean C. 44
Jacinto, Diana 464
Jackman, Cheryl 234
Jackson, Barbara Miles 68
Jackson, Diana 430
Jackson, Dorothy 258
Jackson, Julie 116
Jackson, Lawrence 343
Jackson, Mamie L. 357
Jackson, Rose Marie 92
Jackson, Trudy L. 73
Jacobs, Frances J. 141